226.5

Exposition of the Gospel of JOHN

Three Volumes Complete and Unabridged in One

Arthur W. Pink

VOLUME ONE—*John 1 to 7*

Ministry Resources Library

Zondervan Publishing House • Grand Rapids, MI

Exposition of the Gospel of John

Ministry Resources Library is an imprint of Zondervan
Publishing House, 1415 Lake Drive, S.E.,
Grand Rapids, Michigan 49506

ISBN 0-310-31180-2

Printed in the United States of America

85 86 87 88 89 90 / 24 23 22 21 20 19

FOREWORD

The Gospel of John is probably the best known of the four gospels, and contains many insights into the life of Christ lacking in the other three gospels. John presents Christ as the Son of God, the Shepherd of His sheep.

Arthur W. Pink devoted more than fifteen years to this commentary on John. He taught the book on five separate occasions during his many pastorates, besides lecturing on it during Bible conferences and other gatherings. He developed this series around two major theses: ascertain from God the meaning of the text, and apply its lessons most effectively to those who hear and read these words.

Pink's complete exposition includes three volumes, herein contained in one cover. Because it avoids the technical and aims at the practical, it is not a dry commentary or a ponderous exposition suited only to seminarians. Rather, it is designed for laymen and students who are looking to God for spiritual sustenance.

At the close of each chapter is a list of questions which bear on the passage to be expounded in the succeeding chapter. Readers who give these careful and prayerful study before turning to the text will find these questions helpful in understanding God's Word, and encouraging the personal study of it by others.

This exposition is complete and exhaustive, taking up the Gospel of John verse by verse, devoting extra attention to the difficult passages and encouraging independent study on the part of God's people today.

THE PUBLISHERS

December, 1975

CONTENTS

	Foreword	7
1.	Introduction	9
2.	Christ, the Eternal Word: 1:1-13	17
3.	Christ, the Word Incarnate: 1:14-18	32
4.	Christ's Forerunner: 1:19-34	49
5.	Christ and His First Disciples: 1:35-51	62
6.	Christ's First Miracle: 2:1-11	77
7.	Christ Cleansing the Temple: 2:12-25	90
8.	Christ and Nicodemus: 3:1-8	103
9.	Christ and Nicodemus (Concluded): 3:9-21	120
10.	Christ Magnified by His Forerunner: 3:22-36	140
11.	Christ at Sychar's Well: 4:1-6	154
12.	Christ at Sychar's Well (Continued): 4:7-10	171
13.	Christ at Sychar's Well (Continued): 4:11-19	188
14.	Christ at Sychar's Well (Concluded): 4:20-30	200
15.	Christ in Samaria: 4:31-42	215
16.	Christ in Galilee: 4:43-54	226
17.	Christ at the Pool of Bethesda: 5:1-15	240
18.	The Deity of Christ: Sevenfold Proof: 5:16-30	254
19.	The Deity of Christ: Threefold Witness to It: 5:31-47	272
20.	Christ Feeding the Multitude: 6:1-13	285
21.	Christ Walking on the Sea: 6:14-27	304
22.	Christ the Bread of Life: 6:28-40	316
23.	Christ in the Capernaum Synagogue: 6:41-59	333
24.	Christ and His Disciples: 6:60-71	351
25.	Christ and the Feast of Tabernacles: 7:1-13	367
26.	Christ Teaching in the Temple: 7:14-31	381
27.	Christ in the Temple (Concluded): 7:32-53	396
28.	Christ and the Adulterous Woman: 8:1-11	415

29.	Christ the Light of the World: 8:12-32	430
30.	Christ the Light of the World (Concluded): 8:33-59	448
31.	Christ and the Blind Beggar: 9:1-7	467
32.	Christ and the Blind Beggar (Continued): 9:8-23	480
33.	Christ and the Blind Beggar (Concluded): 9:24-41	494
34.	Christ the Door: 10:1-10	509
35.	Christ the Good Shepherd: 10:11-21	526
36.	Christ One with the Father: 10:22-42	542
37.	Christ Raising Lazarus: 11:1-10	560
38.	Christ Raising Lazarus (Continued): 11:11-27	578
39.	Christ Raising Lazarus (Concluded): 11:28-44	599
40.	Christ Feared by the Sanhedrin: 11:45-57	619
41.	Christ Anointed at Bethany: 12:1-11	635
42.	Christ's Entry into Jerusalem: 12:12-20	653
43.	Christ Sought by Gentiles: 12:20-36	670
44.	Christ's Ministry Reviewed: 12:37-50	685
45.	Christ Washing His Disciple's Feet: 13:1-11	699
46.	Christ's Example for Us: 13:12-20	715
47.	Christ's Warnings: 13:21-38	733
48.	Christ Comforting His Disciples: 14:1-11	752
49.	Christ Comforting His Disciples (Continued): 14:12-20	768
50.	Christ Comforting His Disciples (Concluded): 14:21-31	783
51.	Christ the True Vine: 15:1-6	800
52.	Christ the True Vine (Concluded): 15:7-16	821
53.	Christ Fortifying His Disciples: 15:17-27	839
54.	Christ Vindicated by the Spirit: 16:1-11	853
55.	Christ Glorified by the Spirit: 16:12-22	869
56.	Christ's Concluding Consolations: 16:23-33	887
57.	Christ Interceding: 17:1-5	903
58.	Christ Interceding (Continued): 17:6-12	920
59.	Christ Interceding (Continued): 17:13-19	937
60.	Christ Interceding (Concluded): 17:20-26	953
61.	Christ in the Garden: 18:1-11	968
62.	Christ Before Annas: 18:12-27	986
63.	Christ Before Pilate: 18:28-40	1003
64.	Christ Before Pilate (Concluded): 19:1-11	1019
65.	Christ Condemned to Death: 19:12-24	1034

66. Christ Laying Down His Life: 19:25-42 1049
67. Christ Risen from the Dead: 20:1-10 1067
68. Christ Appearing to His Own: 20:11-23 1082
69. Christ and Thomas: 20:24-31 1104
70. Christ by the Sea of Tiberius: 21:1-14 1118
71. Christ and Peter: 21:15-25 1132
72. Conclusion 1148

CHAPTER ONE

Introduction

It is our purpose to give (D. V.) a verse by verse exposition of the fourth Gospel in the course of this series of studies, but before turning to the opening verses of chapter I it will be necessary to consider John's Gospel as a whole, with the endeavor of discovering its scope, its central theme, and its relation to the other three Gospels. We shall not waste the reader's time by entering into a discussion as to who wrote this fourth Gospel, as to where John was when he wrote it, nor as to the probable date when it was written. These may be points of academical interest, but they provide no food for the soul, nor do they afford any help to an understanding of this section of the Bible, and *these* are the two chief things we desire to accomplish. Our aim is to open up the Scriptures in such a way that the reader will be able to enter into the meaning of what God has recorded for our learning in this part of His Holy Word, and to edify those who are members of the Household of Faith.

The four Gospels deal with the earthly life of the Saviour, but each one presents Him in an entirely different character. Matthew portrays the Lord Jesus as the Son of David, the Heir of Israel's throne, the King of the Jews; and everything in his Gospel contributes to this central theme. In Mark, Christ is seen as the Servant of Jehovah, the perfect Workman of God; and everything in this second Gospel brings out the characteristics of His service and the manner in which He served. Luke treats of the humanity of the Saviour, and presents Him as the perfect Man, contrasting Him from the sinful sons of men. The fourth Gospel views Him as the Heavenly One come down to earth, the eternal Son of the Father made flesh and tabernacling among men, and from start to finish this is the one dominant truth which is steadily held in view.

As we turn to the fourth Gospel we come to entirely different ground from that which is traversed in the other three. It is true, the period of time covered by it is the same as in Matthew, Mark, and Luke, some of the incidents treated of by the "Synoptics" come before us here, and He who has occupied the central position in the narratives of the first three Evangelists is the same One that is made pre-eminent by John; but otherwise, everything is entirely new. The viewpoint of this fourth Gospel is more elevated than that of the others; its contents bring into view spiritual relationships rather than human ties; and, higher glories are revealed as touching the peerless Person of the Saviour. In each of the first three Gospels Christ is viewed in *human* relationships, but not so in John. The purpose of this fourth Gospel is to show that the One who was born in a manger and afterward died on the Cross had higher glories than those of King, that He who humbled Himself to take the Servant place was, previously, "equal with God," that the One who became the Son of Man was none other than, and ever remains, the Only Begotten of the Father.

Each book of the Bible has a prominent and dominant theme which is peculiar to itself. Just as each member in the human body has its own particular function, so every book in the Bible has its own special purpose and mission. The theme of John's Gospel is *the Deity of the Saviour*. Here, as nowhere else in Scripture so fully, the Godhood of Christ is presented to our view. That which is outstanding in this fourth Gospel is the Divine Sonship of the Lord Jesus. In this Book we are shown that the One who was heralded by the angels to the Bethlehem shepherds, who walked this earth for thirty-three years, who was crucified at Calvary who rose in triumph from the grave, and who forty days later departed from these scenes, was none other than the Lord of Glory. The evidence for this is overwhelming, the proofs almost without number, and the effect of contemplating them must be to bow our hearts in worship before "the great God and our Saviour Jesus Christ" (Titus 2:13).

Here is a theme worthy of our most prayerful attention. If the Holy Spirit took such marked care to guard the perfections of our Lord's humanity—seen for example, in the words of the angel to Mary "that *Holy Thing* which shall be born of thee," "made in *the likeness* of sin's flesh," etc. — equally so has the Inspirer of the Scriptures seen to it that there is no uncertainty touching the Divine Sonship of our Saviour. Just as the Old Testament prophets made known that the Coming One should be a Man, a perfect Man, so did Messianic prediction give plain intimation that He should be *more* than a man. Through Isaiah God foretold, "For unto us a Child is born, unto us a Son is given: and the government shall be upon His shoulder: and His name shall be called Wonderful, Counseller, *The Mighty God,* The Everlasting Father, The Prince of Peace." Through Micah He declared, "But thou, Bethlehem Ephratah, though thou be little among the thousands of Judah yet out of thee shall he come forth unto me that is to be Ruler in Israel; Whose goings forth have been *from the days of eternity.*" Through Zechariah He said, "Awake, O Sword, against my Shepherd, and against *the man that is my Fellow,* saith the Lord of Hosts: smite the Shepherd, and the sheep shall be scattered." Through the Psalmist He announced, "The Lord said *unto my Lord,* Sit thou at my right hand, until I make thine enemies thy footstool." And again, when looking forward to the second advent, "Thou art *my Son;* this day have I begotten thee (or, 'brought thee forth')." In these days of wide-spread departure from the faith, it cannot be insisted upon too strongly or too frequently that the Lord Jesus is none other than the Second Person of the blessed Trinity, co-eternal and co-equal with the Father and the Holy Spirit.

In keeping with the special theme of this fourth Gospel, it is here we have the full unveiling of Christ's Divine glories. It is here that we behold Him dwelling with God before time began and before ever the creature was formed (see 1:1, 2). It is here that He is denominated "The only begotten of the Father, full of grace and truth" (1:14). It is here we read of John the Baptist bearing record "that this is the Son of God" (1:34). It is here that we read "This beginning of miracles did Jesus in Cana of Galilee, and *manifested forth his glory*" (2:11). It is here we are told that the Saviour said "Destroy this temple, and in three days I will raise it up" (2:19). It is here we learn that "The Father loveth the Son, and hath given all things into his hand" (3:35). It is in this Gospel we hear Christ saying, "For as the Father raiseth up the dead, and quickeneth them; even so the Son quickeneth whom he will. For the Father judgeth no man, but hath committed all judgment unto the Son: that all should honor the Son, even as they honor the Father" (5:21-23). It is here we find Him declaring, "Before Abraham was, I am" (8:58). It is here He affirmed "I and my Father are One" (10:30). It is here He testifies "He that hath seen me hath seen the Father" (14:9).

Before we take up John's Gospel in detail, a few words should also be said concerning the scope of the fourth Gospel. It must be evident at once that this is quite different from the other three. There, Christ is seen in human relationships, and as connected with an earthly people; but here He is viewed in a Divine relationship, and as connected with a heavenly people. It is true the mystery of the "Body" is not unfolded here—that is found only in what the Apostle Paul wrote as he was moved by the Holy Spirit—rather is it the Family relationship which is here in view: the Son of God together with the sons of God. It is also true that the "heavenly calling," as such, is not fully unfolded here, yet are there plain intimations of it, as a careful study of it makes apparent. In the first three Gospels Christ is seen connected with the Jews, proclaiming the Messianic kingdom, a proclamation which ceased, however, as soon as it became evident that the nation had rejected Him. But here in John's Gospel His rejection is anticipated from the beginning, for in the very first chapter we are told, "He came unto his own, *and his own received him not*." The limitations which obtain in connection with much which is found in the first three Gospels does not, therefore, obtain in John's. Again, in John's Gospel the Saviour is displayed as the Son of God, and as such He can be known only by believers. On this plane, then, the Jew has no priority. The Jew's claim upon Christ was purely a *fleshly* one (arising from the fact that He was "the Son of David"), whereas believers are related to the Son of God by *spiritual* union.

As there may be some of our readers who have been influenced by *ultra*-dispensational teaching we deem it well to here call attention to other points which help to fix the true dispensational bearings and scope of this fourth Gospel. There are those who make no distinction between John's Gospel and the Synoptics, and who insist that this fourth Gospel is entirely Jewish, and has nothing but a remote application to believers of the present dispensation. But this, we are assured, is a serious mistake. John's Gospel, like his Epistles, concerns *the family of God.* In proof of this we request the reader to weigh carefully the following points:

First, in 1:11-13 we read, "He came unto his own, and his own received him not. But as many as received him, to them gave he power to become the sons of God, even to them that believe on his name; which were born, not of blood, nor of the will of the flesh, nor of the will of man, but of God." From these verses we may notice three things: first, the Jews as a nation rejected the Sent One of the Father, they "received him not;" second, a company did "receive him," even those that "believed on his name"; third, this company are here designated "the sons of God," who were "born . . . of God." There is nothing which in any wise resembles this in the other Gospels. Here only, in the four Gospels, is the truth of the new birth brought before us. And it is by new birth we enter the family of God. As, then, the family of God reaches out beyond Jewish believers, and takes in all Gentile believers too, we submit that John's Gospel cannot be restricted to the twelve-tribed people.

Second, after stating that the Word became flesh and tabernacled among us, "and *we* beheld his glory, the glory as of the only begotten of the Father (which is a glory that none but believers behold!), full of grace and truth," and after summarizing John the Baptist's witness to the Person of Christ, the Holy Spirit through the Evangelist goes on to say, "and of his fulness have all *we* received, and grace for grace." Surely this verse alone establishes the point of *who* it is that is here being addressed. The Jewish nation never received "of his fulness"—*that* can be predicated of believers only. The "all we" of verse 16 is the "*as many as*" received Him, to them gave He power to become "*the sons of God*" of verse 12.

Third, in the tenth chapter of John, we read that the Saviour said, "I am the good shepherd, and know my sheep, and am known of mine. As the Father knoweth me, even so know I the Father: and I lay down my life for the sheep" (vv. 14, 15). Immediately following this He went on to say, "And *other sheep* I have, which are not of this fold; them also I must bring, and they shall hear my voice, and there shall be one fold, and one shepherd" (v. 16). Who were these "other sheep?" Before we can answer this, we must ascertain who were the "sheep" referred to by Christ in the first fifteen verses of this chapter. As to who *they* were there can be only one answer: they were not the nation of Israel as such, for they had "received him not"; no, they were the little company who *had* "received him," who *had* "believed on his name." But Christ goes on to speak of a future company of believers, "*other* sheep I *have* (speaking as God who calleth those things which be not as though they were: Rom. 4:17), them also I must bring." Clearly, the "*other* sheep" which had not been brought into the fold at the time the Saviour then spake, were believers from among the Gentiles, and these, together with the Jewish believers, should be "one fold" (or, better "one flock"), which is the equivalent of one family, the family of God.

Fourth, in John 11:49-52 we read, "and one of them, named Caiaphas, being the high priest that same year, said unto them, Ye know nothing at all, nor consider that it is expedient for us, that one man should die for the people, and that the whole nation perish not. And this spake he not of himself: but being high priest that year, he prophesied that Jesus should die for that nation, and not for that nation only, but that also he should *gather together in one* the children of God that were scattered abroad." This was a remarkable prophecy, and contained far more in it than Caiaphas was aware. It made known the Divine purpose in the death of the Saviour and revealed what was to be the outcome of the great Sacrifice. It looked out far beyond the bounds of Judaism, including within its range believing sinners from the Gentiles. The "children of God that were scattered abroad" were the elect found among all nations. That they were here termed "children of God" while viewed as still "scattered abroad," gives us the *Divine* viewpoint, being parallel with "other sheep I *have*." But what we desire to call special attention to is the declaration that these believers from among the Gentiles were to be "gathered together in one," not into one "body" (for as previously said, the body does not fall within the scope of John's writings), but one family, the family of God.

Fifth, in John 14:2 and 3 we read that Christ said to His disciples, "In My Father's house are many mansions: if it were not so, I would have told you. I go to prepare a place for you. And if I go and prepare a place for you, I will come again and receive you unto myself that where I am, there ye may be also." How entirely different this is from anything that is to be found in the first three Gospels scarcely needs to be pointed out. In them, reference is invariably made to the coming of "the Son of man," but here it is the rapture of the saints to heaven, and the taking of them to be where Christ now is that is expressly mentioned. And manifestly this can in no wise be limited to Jewish believers.

Sixth, without attempting to develop this point at any length it should be noticed that the relation which the Holy Spirit sustains to believers in this Gospel is entirely different from what is before us in the first three. Here only do we read of being "born of the Spirit" (3:5). Here only is He denominated their "Comforter" or Advocate (see 14:16); and here only do we read of Him "abiding forever" with believers (see 14:16).

Seventh, the High Priestly prayer of the Saviour which is recorded in John 17, and found nowhere else in the Gospels, shows plainly that more than Jewish believers are here contemplated, and evidences the wider scope of this fourth Gospel. Here we find the Saviour saying, "Father, the hour is come; glorify thy Son, that thy Son also may glorify thee: as thou hast given him power over *all flesh,* that he should give eternal life to as many as thou hast given him." The "as many as thou hast given him" takes in the whole family of God. Again, in verse 20 the Lord Jesus says, "Neither pray I for these alone, but for *them also which shall believe* on me through their word:" the "these" evidently refers to Jewish believers, while the "them also" looked forward to Gentile believers. Finally, His words in verse 22, "and the glory which thou gavest me I have given them; *that they may be one,* even as we are one" shows, once more, that the whole family of God was here before Him.

In bringing this chapter to a close we want to prepare the reader for the second of the series. In the next chapter we shall (D.V.) take up the first section of the opening chapter, and it is our earnest desire that many of our readers will make these verses the subject of prayerful study and meditation. The Bible teacher who becomes a substitute for diligent study on the part of those who hear him is a hindrance and not a help. The business of the teacher is to turn people to the searching of the Scriptures for themselves, stimulating their interest in the Sacred Word, and instructing them *how* to go about it. With this end in view, it will be our aim to prepare a series of questions at the close of each chapter bearing on the passage to be expounded in the succeeding one, so that the reader may study it for himself. Below are seven questions on the passage for the portion we shall take up in the next lesson, and we earnestly urge our readers to *study* the first thirteen verses of John 1, and to concentrate upon the points raised by our questions.

1. What "beginning" is referred to in John 1:1?
2. How may I obtain a better, deeper, fuller knowledge of God Himself? By studying nature? By prayer? By studying Scripture? Or—how?
3. *Why* is the Lord Jesus here termed "The Word?" What is the exact force and significance of this title?
4. What is the meaning of John 1:4—"The *Life* was the *Light* of men?"
5. The fact that the Saviour is termed "the Light" in 1:7, teaches us *what?*
6. What does John 1:12 teach concerning what a sinner must do to be saved?
7. What is the exact meaning of each clause in 1:13?

Pray over and *meditate* much upon each of these questions, and above all "Search the Scriptures" to find God's answers. Answers to these questions will be found in the next chapter, in the course of our exposition of John 1:1-13.

CHAPTER TWO

Christ, the Eternal Word

John 1:1-13

In the last chapter we stated, "Each book of the Bible has a prominent and dominant theme which is peculiar to itself. Just as each member in the human body has its own particular function, so, every book in the Bible has its own special purpose and mission. The theme of John's Gospel *is the Deity of the Saviour.* Here, as nowhere else in Scripture so fully, the Godhood of Christ is presented to our view. That which is outstanding in this fourth Gospel is the Divine Sonship of the Lord Jesus. In this book we are shown that the One who was heralded by the angels to the Bethlehem shepherds, who walked this earth for thirty-three years, who was crucified at Calvary, who rose in triumph from the grave, and who forty days later departed from these scenes, was none other than the Lord of glory. The evidence for this is overwhelming, the proofs almost without number, and the effect of contemplating them must be to bow our hearts in worship before 'the great God and our Saviour Jesus Christ' (Titus 2:13)."

That John's Gospel *does* present the Deity of the Saviour is at once apparent from the opening words of the first chapter. The Holy Spirit has, as it were, placed the key right over the entrance, for the introductory verses of this fourth Gospel present the Lord Jesus Christ in Divine relationships and unveil His essential glories. Before we attempt an exposition of this profound passage we shall first submit an analysis of its contents. In these first thirteen verses of John 1 we have set forth: —

1. The Relation of Christ to Time — "In the beginning," therefore, Eternal: 1:1.
2. The Relation of Christ to the Godhead — "With God," therefore, One of the Holy Trinity: 1:1.

3. The Relation of Christ to the Holy Trinity—"God was the Word"—the Revealer: 1:1.
4. The Relation of Christ to the Universe—"All things were made by him"—the Creator: 1:3.
5. The Relation of Christ to Men—Their "Light": 1:4, 5.
6. The Relation of John the Baptist to Christ—"Witness" of His Deity: 1:6-9.
7. The Reception which Christ met here: 1:10-13.
   (a) "The world knew him not": 1:10.
   (b) "His own (Israel) received him not": 1:11.
   (c) A company born of God "received him": 1:12, 13.

"In the beginning was the word, and the word was with God, and the word was God. The same was in the beginning with God. All things were made by him; and without him was not anything made that was made" (John 1:1-3). How entirely different is this from the opening verses of the other Gospels! John opens by immediately presenting Christ not as the Son of David, nor as the Son of man, but as the Son of God. John takes us back to the beginning, and shows that the Lord Jesus had no beginning. John goes behind creation and shows that the Saviour was Himself the Creator. Every clause in these verses calls for our most careful and prayerful attention.

"In the beginning was the word, and the word was with God, and the word was God." Here we enter a realm which transcends the finite mind, and where speculation is profane. "In the *beginning*" is something we are unable to comprehend: it is one of those matchless sweeps of inspiration which rises above the level of human thought. "In the beginning *was the word,*" and we are equally unable to grasp the final meaning of this. A "word" is an expression: by words we articulate our speech. The *Word* of God, then, is Deity expressing itself in audible terms. And yet, when we have said this, how much there is that we leave unsaid! "And the word was *with God,*" and this intimates His separate personality, and shows His relation to the other Persons of the blessed Trinity. But how sadly incapacitated are we for meditating upon the relations which exist between the different Persons of the Godhead. "And *God was the word.*" Not only was Christ the Revealer of God, but He always was, and ever remains, none other than God Himself. Not only was our Saviour the One through whom, and by whom, the Deity expressed itself in audible terms, but He was Himself co-equal with the Father and the Spirit. Let us now approach the Throne of grace and there seek the mercy and grace we so sorely need to help us as we turn now to take a closer look at these verses.

"Our God and Father, in the name of Thy dear Son, we pray Thee that Thy Holy Spirit may now take of the things of Christ and show them unto us: to the praise of the glory of Thy grace. Amen."

"In THE BEGINNING," or, more literally, "in beginning," for there is no article in the Greek. In what "beginning?" There are various "beginnings" referred to in the New Testament. There is the "beginning" of "the world" (Matt. 24:21); of "the gospel of Jesus Christ" (Mark 1:1); of "sorrows" (Mark 13:8); of "miracles" (or "signs"), (John 2:11), etc. But the "beginning" mentioned in John 1:1 clearly antedates all these "beginnings." The "beginning" of John 1:1 *precedes* the making of the "all things" of 1:3. It is then, *the beginning of creation, the beginning of time.* This earth of ours is old, how old we do not know, possibly millions of years. But "the word" was before all things. He was not only *from* the beginning, but He was *"in* the beginning."

"In beginning:" the absence of the definite article is designed to carry us back to the most remote point that can be imagined. If then, He was before all creation, and He *was,* for *"all* things were made *by him;"* if He was "in the beginning," then He was Himself *without beginning,* which is only the negative way of saying He was *eternal.* In perfect accord with this we find, that in His prayer recorded in John 17, He said, "And now, O Father, glorify thou me with thine own self with the glory which I had with thee *before the world was."* As, then, the Word was "in the beginning," and if in the beginning, *eternal,* and as none but God Himself is eternal, the absolute Deity of the Lord Jesus is conclusively established.

"WAS the word." There are two separate words in the Greek which, in this passage, are both rendered "was": the one means

to exist, the other *to come into being.* The latter word (egeneto) is used in 1:3 which, literally rendered, reads, "all things through him *came into being,* and without him *came into being* not even one (thing) which has *come into being;*" and again we have this word "egeneto" in 1:6 where we read, "there *was* (became to be) a man sent from God, whose name was John;" and again in 1:14, "And the word *was made* (became) flesh." But here in 1:1 and 1:2 it is "the word (*ito*) with God." As the Word He did not come into being, or begin *to be,* but He *was* "with God" from all eternity. It is noteworthy that the Holy Spirit uses this word *"ito,"* which signifies that the Son *personally subsisted,* no less than four times in the first two verses of John 1. Unlike John the Baptist who *"became* (egeneto) a man," the "word" *was* (*ito*), *that is, existed* with God before time began.

"Was THE WORD." The reference here is to the Second Person in the Holy Trinity, the Son of God. But *why* is the Lord Jesus Christ designated "the word?" What is the exact force and significance of this title? The first passage which occurs to our minds as throwing light on this question is the opening statement in the Epistle to the Hebrews: "God who at sundry times and in divers manners spake in time past unto the fathers by the prophets, hath in these last days spoken unto us by his Son." Here we learn that Christ is the final *spokesman* of God. Closely connected with this is the Saviour's title found in Revelation 1:8—"I am Alpha and Omega," which intimates that He is *God's alphabet,* the One who spells out Deity, the One who utters all God has to say. Even clearer, perhaps, is the testimony of John 1:18: "No man hath seen God at any time; the only begotten Son, which is in the bosom of the Father, he hath *declared him.*" The word "declared" means *tell out,* cf. Acts 15:14, and 21:19; it is translated "told" in Luke 24:35. Putting together these three passages we learn that Christ is the One who is the Spokesman of God, and One who spelled out the Deity, the One who has declared or told forth the Father.

Christ, then, is the One who has made the incomprehensible God intelligible. The force of this title of His found in John 1:1, may be discovered by comparing it with that name which is given to the Holy Scriptures—"the Word of God." What are the Scriptures? They are the *Word* of God. And what does that mean? This: the Scriptures reveal God's mind, express His will, make known His perfections, and lay bare His heart. This is precisely what the Lord Jesus has done for the Father. But let us enter a little more into detail:—

(a) A "word" is a *medium of manifestation.* I have in my mind a thought, but others know not its nature. But the moment I clothe that thought in words it becomes cognizable. Words, then, make objective unseen thoughts. This is precisely what the Lord Jesus has done. As the Word, Christ has made manifest the invisible God.

(b) A "word" is a *means of communication.* By means of words I transmit information to others. By words I express myself, make known my will, and impart knowledge. So Christ, as the Word, is the Divine Transmitter, communicating to us the life and love of God.

(c) A "word" is a *method of revelation.* By his words a speaker exhibits both his intellectual caliber and his moral character. By our words we shall be justified, and by our words we shall be condemned. And Christ, as the Word, reveals the attributes and perfections of God. How *fully* has Christ revealed God! He displayed His power, He manifested His wisdom, He exhibited His holiness, He made known His grace, He unveiled His heart. In Christ, and nowhere else, is God fully and finally told out.

"And the word was WITH GOD." This preposition "with" seems to suggest two thoughts. First, the Word was in *the presence* of God. As we read, "Enoch walked *with* God," that is, he lived in fellowship with God. There is a beautiful verse in Proverbs 8 which throws its light on the meaning of "with" in John 1:1, and reveals the blessed relation which obtained from all eternity between the Word and God. The passage begins at 8:22 where "wisdom" is personified. It tells us of the happy fellowship which existed between the Word and God before ever the world was. In 8:30 we read, "Then I was *by him,* as one brought up with him: and I was daily his delight, rejoicing always before him." In addition to the two thoughts just sug-

gested, we may add that the Greek preposition "pros" here translated "with" is sometimes rendered "toward," but most frequently "unto." The Word was toward or unto God. One has significantly said, "The word rendered *with* denotes a perpetual tendency, as it were, of the Son to the Father, in unity of essence."

That it is here said "the word was with God" tells of His *separate personality*: He was not "in" God, but "with" God. Now, mark here the marvelous accuracy of Scripture. It is not said, "the word was with the Father" as we might have expected, but "the word was with *God*." The name "God" is common to the three Persons of the Holy Trinity, whereas "the Father" is the special title of the first Person only. Had it said "the word was with the Father," the Holy Spirit had been excluded; but "with God" takes in the Word dwelling in eternal fellowship with both the Father and the Spirit. Observe, too, it does not say, "And God was with God," for while there is plurality of Persons in the Godhead, there is but "one God," therefore the minute accuracy of "the WORD was with God."

"And the word WAS GOD," or, more literally, "and God was the word." Lest the figurative expression "the word" should convey to us an inadequate conception of the Divine glories of Christ, the Holy Spirit goes on to say, "and the word was *with God*," which denoted His separate personality, and intimated His essential relation to the Godhead. And, as though that were not strong enough, the Holy Spirit expressly adds, "and *God was* the word." Who could express God save Him who is God! The Word was not an emanation of God, but God Himself made manifest. Not only the revealer of God, but God Himself revealed. A more emphatic and unequivocal affirmation of the absolute Deity of the Lord Jesus Christ it is impossible to conceive.

"The same was in the beginning with God." The "same," that is, the Word; "was," that is, subsisted, not began to be; "in the beginning," that is, before time commenced; "with God," that is, as a distinct Personality. That it is here repeated Christ was "*with* God," seems to be intended as a repudiation of the early Gnostic heresy that Christ was only an *idea* or *ideal IN* the mind

of God from eternity, duly made manifest in time—a horrible heresy which is being re-echoed in our own day. It is not said that the Word was in God; He was, eternally, "*with* God."

Before we pass on to the next verse, let us seek to make practical application of what has been before us, and at the same time answer the third of the seven questions asked at the close of the previous chapter; "How may I obtain a better, deeper, fuller knowledge of God Himself? By studying nature? By prayer? By studying Scripture? Or—how?" A more important question we cannot consider. What conception have you formed, dear reader, of the Being, Personality, and Character, of God? Before the Lord Jesus came to this earth, the world was without the knowledge of the true and living God. To say that God is revealed in nature is true, yet it is a statement which needs qualifying. Nature reveals the existence of God, but how little it tells of His character. Nature manifests His *natural* attributes—His power, His widsom, His immutability, etc.; but what does nature say to us of His *moral* attributes—His justice, His holiness, His grace, His love? Nature, as such knows no mercy and shows no pity. If a blind saint unwittingly steps over the edge of a precipice he meets with the same fate as if a vile murderer had been hurled over it. If I break nature's laws, no matter how sincere may be my subsequent repentance, there is no escaping the penalty. Nature conceals as well as reveals God. The ancients had "nature" before them, and what did they learn of God? Let that altar, which the Apostle Paul beheld in one of the chief centers of ancient learning and culture make answer—"to the UNKNOWN GOD" is what he found inscribed thereon!

It is only in Christ that God is fully told out. Nature is no longer as it left the Creator's hands: it is under the Curse, and how could that which is imperfect be a perfect medium for revealing God? But the Lord Jesus Christ is the Holy One. He was God, the Son, manifest in flesh. And so fully and so perfectly did He reveal God, He could say, "He that hath seen me hath seen the Father" (John 14:9). Here, then, is the answer to our question, and here is the practical value of what is before us in these opening verses of John's Gospel. If the believer would enter into a better, deeper, fuller knowledge of God, he must prayerfully study *the person and work of the Lord Jesus Christ as revealed in the Scriptures!* Let this be made our chief business, our great delight, to reverently scrutinize and meditate upon the excellencies of our Divine Saviour as they are displayed upon the pages of Holy Writ, then, and only then, shall we "increase in the knowledge of God" (Col. 1:10). The "light of the knowledge of the glory of God" is seen *only* "in the face of Jesus Christ" (II Cor. 4:6).

"All things were made by him; and without him was not anything made that was made" (1:3). How this brings out, again, the absolute deity of Christ! Here creation is ascribed to Him, and none but *God* can create. Man, with all his boasting, is unable to bring into existence a single blade of grass. Observe, that the *whole* of creation is here ascribed to the Word—"*all* things were made by him." This would not be true if He were Himself a creature, even though the first and the highest creature. But nothing is excepted—"*all* things were made by *him*." Just as He was before all things, and therefore, *eternal*; so was He the Originator of all things, and therefore, *omnipotent*.

"In him was life; and the life was the light of men" (1:4). This follows logically from what has been said in the previous verse. If Christ created all things He must be the Fountain of *life*. He is the Life-Giver. We understand "life" to be used here in its widest sense. Creature life is found in God, for "in him we live and move and have our being"; spiritual life or eternal life, and resurrection life, are also found "in Him." If it be objected that the Greek word for "life" here is "zoe," and that zoe has exclusive reference to *spiritual* life, we answer, Not always: see Luke 12:15; 16:25 (translated "life-time"), Acts 17:25, etc., where, in each case, "zoe" has reference to human (natural) life, as such. Thus, "zoe" includes within its scope *all* "life."

"*And the Life was THE LIGHT of men.*" What are we to understand by this? Notice two things: this statement in verse 4 follows immediately after the declaration that "all things were made" by Christ, so that it is *creatures*, as such, which are here in view; second, it is "men," as men, not only believers, which are here referred to. The "life" here is one of the Divine titles of the Lord Jesus, hence, it is equivalent to saying, "*God* was the *light* of men." It speaks of the relation which Christ sustains to men, all men – He is their "light." This is confirmed by what we read in verse 9, "That was the true light, which *lighteth every man* that cometh into the world." In what sense, then, is Christ as "the life" the "*light* of men?" We answer, In that which renders men accountable creatures. Every rational man is morally enlightened. All rational men "show the *work* of the law written in their hearts, their conscience also bearing witness" (Rom. 2:15). It is this "light," which lightens every man that cometh into the world, that constitutes them responsible human beings. The Greek word for "light" in John 1:4 is "phos," and that it is not restricted to spiritual illumination is plainly evident from its usage in Matthew 6:23, "If therefore the light that is in thee be darkness, how great is that darkness," and also see Luke 11:35; Acts 16:29, etc.

Let no reader infer from what has been said that we are among the number who believe the unscriptural theory that there is in every man a spark of Divine life, which needs only to be fanned, to become a flame. No, we expressly repudiate any such satanic lie. By nature, spiritually, he is "dead in trespasses and sins." Yet, notwithstanding, the natural man is a responsible being before God, to Whom he shall give an account of himself; responsible, because the work of God's law is written in his heart, his conscience also bearing witness, and this, we take it, is the "light" which is referred to in John 1:4, and the "lighteneth" in John 1:9.

"And the light shineth in darkness; and the darkness comprehended it not" (1:5). This gives us still another of the Divine titles of Christ. In verse 1 He is spoken of as "the word." In verse 3 as the Maker of all things. In verse 4 as "the life." Now, in verse 5 as "the light." With this should be compared I John 1:5 where we read "*God is light.*" The conclusion, then, is irresistible, the proof complete and final, that the Lord Jesus is none other than God, the second Person in the Holy Trinity.

The "Englishman's Greek New Testament" renders the last clause of 1:5 as follows – "and the light in the darkness appears, and the darkness it apprehended not." This tells us of the effects of the Fall. Every man that comes into this world is lightened by his Creator, but the natural man disregards this light, he repels it, and in consequence, is plunged into darkness. Instead of the natural man "living up to the light he has" (which none ever did) he "loves darkness rather than light" (John 3:19). The unregenerate man, then, is like one that is blind —he is in the dark. Proof of this appears in the fact that "the Light in the darkness appears, and the darkness apprehended it not." All other darkness yields to and fades away before light, but here *"the darkness"* is so impenetrable and hopeless, it neither apprehends nor comprehends. What a fearful and solemn indictment of fallen human nature! And how evident it is that nothing short of a miracle of saving grace can ever bring one "out of darkness into God's marvelous light."

"There was a man sent from God, whose name was John" (1:6). The change of subject here is most abrupt. From "the Word" who was God, the Holy Spirit now turns to speak of the forerunner of Christ. He is referred to as *"a man,"* to show us, by way of contrast, that the One to Whom he bore witness was *more* than Man. This man was "sent from God," so is every man who bears faithful witness to the Person of Christ. The name of this man was "John" which, as etymologists tell us, signifies "the gift of God."

"The same came for a witness, to bear witness of the light, that all through him might believe" (1:7). John came to bear witness of "the light." Weigh well these words: they are solemn, pathetic, tragic. Perhaps their force will be the more evident if we ask a question: When the sun is shining in all its beauty, who are the ones that are unconscious of the fact? Who need to be *told* it is shining? The blind! How tragic, then, when we read that God sent John to "bear witness of the light" How pathetic that there should be any need for this! How solemn the statement that men have to be told "the light" is now in their midst. What a revelation of man's fallen condition. The Light shone in the darkness, but the darkness comprehended it not. Therefore, did God send John to bear witness of the Light. God would not allow His beloved Son to come here unrecognized and unheralded. As soon as He was born into this world, He sent the angels to the Bethlehem shepherds to proclaim Him, and just before His public ministry began, John appeared bidding Israel to receive Him.

"The same came *for a witness.*" This defines the character of the preacher's office. He is a "witness," and a witness is one who knows what he says and says what he knows. He deals not with speculations, he speaks not of his own opinions, but he testifies to what he knows to be the truth.

"To bear witness *of the light.*" This should ever be the aim of the preacher: to get his hearers to look away from himself to Another. He is not to testify of himself, nor about himself, but he is to "preach Christ" (I Cor. 1:23). This is the message the Spirit of God will own, for Christ has said of Him, "He shall glorify *me*" (John 16:14).

"That all through him might believe." "That" means "in order that." "To bear witness" defines the character of the preacher's *office*: to "bear witness of the light" makes known the preacher's *theme;* that "all through him might believe" speaks of the *design* of his ministry. Men become believers through receiving the testimony of God's witness. The "all" is the same as in 6:45.

"He was not that light, but was sent to bear witness of that light" (1:8). No, John himself was not "that light," for "light" like "life" is to be found only in God. Apart from God all is darkness, profound and unrelieved. Even the believer has no light *in himself*. What saith the Scriptures? "For ye were sometimes darkness, but now are ye the light *in the Lord*" (Eph. 5:8). There is a statement found in John 5:35 which, as it stands in the A.V., conflicts with what is said here in 1:8. In 5:35 when speaking of John, Christ said, "He was a burning and shining *light*," but the Greek word used here is entirely different from that translated "light" in 1:8, and in the R.V. it is correctly translated "He was *the lamp* that burneth and shineth." This word used of John, correctly translated "lamp," points a striking contrast between the forerunner and Christ as "the light." A lamp has no inherent light of its own – it has to be supplied! A "lamp" has to be carried by another! A "lamp" soon burns out: in a few hours it ceases to shine.

"That was the true light, which lighteth every man which cometh into the world" (1:9). Bishop Ryle in his most excellent notes on John's Gospel, has suggested that the adjective "true" has here at least a fourfold reference. First, Christ, is the "*true* light" as the Undeceiving Light. Satan himself, we read, "is transformed into an angel of light" (II Cor. 11:14), but he appears as such only to *deceive.* But Christ is the *true* Light in contrast from all the false lights which are in the world. Second, as the "*true* light," Christ is the *Real* Light. The *real* light in contrast from the dim and shaded light which was conveyed through the types and shadows of the Old Testament ritual. Third, as the "*true* light" Christ is the Underived Light: there are lesser lights which are borrowed and reflected, as the moon from the sun, but Christ's "light" is His own essential and underived glory. Fourth, as the "*true light,*" Christ is the Super-eminent Light, in contrast from all that is ordinary and common. There is one glory of the sun, and another glory of the moon, and another of the stars; but all other lights pale before Him who is "the light." The latter part of this ninth verse need not detain us now, having already received our consideration under the exposition of verse four. The light which "every man" has by nature is the light and reason and conscience.

"He was in the world, and the world was made by him, and the world knew him not" (1:10). "He was in the world" refers, we believe, to His incarnation and the thirty-three years during which He tabernacled among men. Then it is said "and the world was made by him." This is to magnify the Divine glory of the One who had become incarnate, and to emphasize the tragedy of what follows, "and the world knew him not."

"He was in the world." *Who* was? None other than the One who had made it. And how was He received? The great Creator was about to appear: will not a thrill of glad expectancy run around the world? He is coming not to judge, but to save. He is to appear not as a haughty Despot, but as a Man "holy, harmless, undefiled;" not to be ministered unto, but to minister. Will not such an One receive a hearty welcome? Alas, "the world knew him not." Full of their own schemes and pursuits, they thought nothing of Him. Unspeakably tragic is this, yet something even more pathetic follows.

"He came unto his own, and his own received him not" (1:11). How appropriate are the terms here used: note the nice distinction: "He was in the world" and, therefore, within the reach of inquiry. But to the seed of Abraham He "came," knocking as it were, at their door for admission; but "they *received him not*." The world is charged with ignorance, but Israel with unbelief, yea, with a positive refusal of Him. Instead of welcoming the Heavenly Visitant, they drove Him from their door, and even banished Him from the earth. Who would have supposed that a people whose believing ancestors had been eagerly awaiting the appearance of the Messiah for long ages past, would have rejected Him when He came among them! Yet so it was: and should any ask, How could these things be? we answer, This very thing was expressly foretold by their own prophet, that He *should* possess neither form nor comeliness in their eyes, and when they should see Him there would be no beauty that they should desire Him. Ah! would it have been any wonder if He had turned away from such ingrates in disgust! What blessed subjection to the Father's will, and what wondrous love for sinners, that He remained on earth in order that He might later die the death of the Cross!

But if the world "knew him not," and Israel "received him not," was the purpose of God defeated? No, indeed, for that *could not be*. The counsel of the Lord "shall stand" (Prov. 19:21). The marvelous condescension of the Son could not be in vain. So, we read, "but as many as received him, to them gave he power to become the sons of God, even to them that believe on his name" (vs. 12). This tells us of the human side of salvation, what is required of sinners. Salvation comes to the sinner through "receiving" Christ, that is, by "believing on his name." There is a slight distinction between these two things, though in substance they are one. Believing, respects Christ as He is exhibited by the Gospel testimony: it is the personal acceptance as truth of what God has said concerning His Son. Receiving, views Christ as presented to us as God's Gift, presented to us for our acceptance. And "as many as," no matter whether they be

Jews or Gentiles, rich or poor, illiterate or learned, receive Christ as their own personal Saviour, to them is given the power or right to become the sons (better "children") of God.

But *who* receive Him thus? Not all by any means. Only a few. And is this left to chance? Far from it. As the following verse goes on to state, "which were born, not of blood, nor of the will of the flesh, nor of the will of man, but of God" (1:13). This explains to us *why* the few "receive" Christ. It is because they are born of God. Just as verse 12 gives us the human side, so verse 13 gives us the Divine. The Divine side is the new birth: and the taking place of the new birth is "not of blood," that is to say, it is not a matter of heredity, for regeneration does not run in the veins; "nor of the will of the flesh," the will of the natural man is opposed to God, and he has *no will* God-ward until he has been born again; "nor of the will of man," that is to say, the new birth is not brought about by the well-meant efforts of friends, nor by the persuasive powers of the preacher; "but of God." The new birth is a Divine work. It is accomplished by the Holy Spirit applying the Word in living power to the heart. The reception Christ met during the days of His earthly ministry is the same still: the world "knows him not;" Israel "receives him not;" but a little company *do* receive him, and who these are Acts 13:48 tells us—"as many as were ordained to eternal life believed." And here we must stop.

Preparatory to our next chapter, we are anxious that the reader should study the following questions:

1. In John 1:14 the word "dwelt" signifies "tabernacled." The Word tabernacled among men. It points us back to the Tabernacle of Israel in the wilderness. In *what* respects did the Tabernacle of old typify and foreshadow Christ?
2. "We beheld his glory" (1:14): what is meant by this? *what* "glory?" At least a threefold "glory."
3. In what sense was Christ "before" John the Baptist (see 1:15)?
4. What is the meaning of 1:16?

5. Why are we told that the law was *given* by Moses, but that grace and truth *came* by Jesus Christ (*see* 1:17)?
6. Was there any "grace and truth" *before* Jesus Christ came? If so, what is meant by them *coming* by Jesus Christ?
7. How many contrasts can you draw between Law and Grace?

CHAPTER THREE

Christ, the Word Incarnate

John 1:14-18

We first submit a brief Analysis of the passage which is to be before us—John 1:14-18. We have here:—

1. Christ's Incarnation—"The word became flesh": 1:14.
2. Christ's Earthly sojourn—"And tabernacled among us:" 1:14.
3. Christ's Essential Glory—"As of the only Begotten:" 1:14.
4. Christ's Supreme excellency—"Preferred before:" 1:15.
5. Christ's Divine sufficiency—"His fulness:" 1:16.
6. Christ's Moral perfections—"Grace and truth:" 1:17.
7. Christ's Wondrous revelation—Made known "the Father:" 1:18.

"And the word was made (became) flesh, and dwelt among us" (1:14). The Infinite became finite. The Invisible became tangible. The Transcendent became imminent. That which was far off drew nigh. That which was beyond the reach of the human mind became that which could be beholden within the realm of human life. Here we are permitted to see through a veil that, which unveiled, would have blinded us. "The word became flesh:" He became what He was not previously. He did not cease to be God, but He became Man.

"And the word became flesh." The plain meaning of these words is, that our Divine Saviour took upon Him human nature. He became a real Man, yet a sinless, perfect Man. As Man He was "holy, harmless, undefiled, separate from sinners" (Heb. 7:26). This union of the two natures in the Person of Christ is one of the mysteries of our faith—"Without controversy *great is the mystery* of godliness: God was manifest in the flesh" (I Tim. 3:16). It needs to be carefully stated. "The word" was His Divine title; "became flesh" speaks of His holy humanity. He was, and is, the God-man, yet the Divine and human in Him were never confounded. His Deity, though veiled, was never laid aside; His humanity, though sinless, was a real humanity; for as incarnate, He "*increased* in wisdom and stature, and in favor with God and man" (Luke 2:52). As "the word" then, He is the Son of God; as "flesh," the Son of man.

This union of the two natures in the Person of Christ was necessary in order to fit Him for the office of Mediator. Three great ends were accomplished by God becoming incarnate, by the Word being made flesh. First, it was now possible for Him *to die*. Second, He can now be touched with the feeling of *our* infirmities. Third, He has left us an *example*, that we should follow *His* steps.

This duality of nature was plainly intimated in Old Testament prediction. Prophecy sometimes represented the coming Messiah as human, sometimes as Divine. He was to be the woman's "seed" (Gen. 3:15); a "prophet" like unto Moses (see Deut. 18:18); a lineal descendant of David (see II Sam. 7:12); Jehovah's "Servant" (Isa. 42:1); a "Man of sorrows" (Isa. 53:3). Yet, on the other hand, He was to be "the Branch *of the Lord*, beautiful and glorious" (Isa. 4:2); He was "the wonderful Counsellor, the Mighty God, the Father of the ages, the Prince of peace" (Isa. 9:6). As Jehovah He was to come suddenly to His temple (see Mal. 3:1). The One who was to be born in Bethlehem and be Ruler in Israel, was the One "whose goings forth had been from the days of eternity" (Mic. 5:2). How were those two different sets of prophecy to be harmonized? John 1:14 is the answer. The One born at Bethlehem was the Divine and eternal Word. The Incarnation does not mean that God dwelt in a man, but that God became Man. He became what He was not previously, though He never ceased to be all that He was before. The Babe of Bethlehem was Immanuel – God with us.

"And *the word* became flesh." It is the design of John's Gospel to bring this out in a special way. The *miracles* recorded therein illustrate and demonstrate this in a peculiar manner. For example: He turns the water into wine – but how? He, Himself, did nothing but *speak the word*. He gave His command to the servants and the transformation was wrought. Again; the nobleman's son was sick. The father came to the Lord Jesus and besought Him to journey to his home and heal his boy. What was our Lord's response? "Jesus *said unto him,* Go thy way, thy son liveth" (John 4:50), and the miracle was performed. Again; an impotent man was lying by the porch of Bethesda. He desired some one to put him into the pool, but while he was waiting another stepped in before him, and was healed. Then the Lord Jesus passed that way and saw him. What happened? "Jesus *saith unto him,* Rise," etc. The word of power went forth, and the sufferer was made whole. Once more: consider the case of Lazarus, recorded only by John. In the raising of the daughter of Jairus, Christ took the damsel by the hand; when He restored to life the widow's son of Nain, He touched the bier. But in bringing Lazarus from the dead He did nothing except speak the word, "Lazarus, come forth." In all of these miracles we *see the Word at work.* The One who had become flesh and tabernacled among men was eternal and omnipotent—"the great God (the Word) and our Saviour (became flesh) Jesus Christ." (Titus 2:13).

"And dwelt (*tabernacled*) among us." He pitched His tent on earth for thirty-three years. There is here a latent reference to the tabernacle of Israel in the wilderness. That tabernacle had a typical significance: it forshadowed God the Son incarnate. Almost everything about the tabernacle adumbrated the Word made flesh. Many and varied are the correspondences between the type and the Anti-type. We notice a few of the more conspicuous.

1. The "tabernacle" was a *temporary appointment.* In this it differed from the temple of Solomon, which was a permanent structure. The tabernacle was merely a tent, a temporary convenience, something that was suited to be moved about from place to place during the journeyings of the children of Israel. So it was when our blessed Lord tabernacled here among men. His stay was but a brief one—less than forty years; and, like the type, He abode not long in any one place, but was constantly on the move—unwearied in the activity of His love.

2. The "tabernacle" was *for use in the wilderness.* After Israel

settled in Canaan, the tabernacle was superseded by the temple. But during the time of their pilgrimage from Egypt to the promised land, the tabernacle was God's appointed provision for them. The *wilderness* strikingly foreshadowed the conditions amid which the eternal Word tabernacled among men at His first advent. The wilderness home of the tabernacle unmistakably foreshadowed the manger-cradle, the Nazarite-carpenter's bench, the "nowhere" for the Son of man to lay His head, the borrowed tomb for His sepulchre. A careful study of the chronology of the Pentateuch seems to indicate that Israel used the tabernacle in the wilderness rather less than thirty-five years!

3. *Outwardly the "tabernacle" was mean, humble, and unattractive in appearance.* Altogether unlike the costly and magnificent temple of Solomon, there was nothing in the externals of the tabernacle to please the carnal eye. Nothing but plain boards and skins. So it was at the Incarnation. The Divine majesty of our Lord was hidden beneath a veil of flesh. He came, unattended by any imposing retinue of angels. To the unbelieving gaze of Israel He had no form nor comeliness; and when they beheld Him, their unanointed eyes saw in Him no beauty that they should desire Him.

4. The "tabernacle" was *God's dwelling place.* It was there, in the midst of Israel's camp, He took up His abode. There, between the cherubim upon the mercy-seat He made His throne. In the holy of holies He manifested His presence by means of the Shekinah glory. And during the thirty-three years that the Word tabernacled among men, God had His dwelling place in Palestine. The holy of holies received its anti-typical fulfillment in the Person of the Holy One of God. Just as the Shekinah dwelt between the two cherubim, so on the mount of transfiguration the glory of the God-man flashed forth from between two men—Moses and Elijah. "We beheld his *glory*" *is the language* of the tabernacle type.

5. The "tabernacle" was, therefore, *the place where God met with men.* It was termed "the tent of meeting." If an Israelite desired to draw near unto Jehovah He had to come to the door of the tabernacle. When giving instructions to Moses concerning the making of the tabernacle and its furniture, God said, "And

thou shalt put the mercy seat above upon the ark; and in the ark thou shalt put the testimony that I shall give thee. And *there* I will meet with thee, and I will commune with thee" (Exod. 25: 21, 22). How perfect is this lovely type! Christ is the *meeting-place* between God and men. No man cometh unto the Father but by Him (see John 14:16). There is but one Mediator between God and men—the Man Christ Jesus (see I Tim. 2:5). He is the One who spans the gulf between deity and humanity, because He is Himself both God and Man.

6. The "tabernacle" was *the center of Israel's camp.* In the immediate vicinity of the tabernacle dwelt the Levites, the priestly tribe: "But thou shalt appoint the Levites over the tabernacle of testimony, and over all the vessels thereof, and over all things that belong to it: and they shall minister unto it, and shall *encamp round about* the tabernacle" (Num. 1:50), and around the Levites were grouped the twelve tribes, three on either side—see Numbers 2. Again; we read, that when Israel's camp was to be moved from one place to another, "Then the tabernacle of the congregation shall set forward with the camp of the Levites *in the midst of the camp*" (Num. 2:17). And, once more, "And Moses went out, and told the people the words of the Lord, and gathered the seventy men of the elders of the people, and set them *round about the tabernacle.* And the Lord came down in a cloud and spake unto him" (Num. 11:24, 25). How striking is this! The tabernacle was the great *gathering center.* As such it was a beautiful foreshadowing of the Lord Jesus. He is our great *gathering-center.* And His precious promise is, that "where two or three are gathered together in my name, there am I *in the midst of them*" (Matt. 18:20).

7. The "tabernacle" was *the place where the Law was preserved.* The first two tables of stone, on which Jehovah had inscribed the ten commandments were broken (see Exod. 32:19); but the second set were deposited in the ark in the tabernacle for safe keeping (see Deut. 10:2-5). It was only there, within the holy of holies, the tablets of the Law were preserved intact. How this, again, speaks to us of Christ! He it was that said, "Lo, I come: in the volume of the book it is written of me; I delight to do thy will, O my God; yea, thy *law is within* my heart" (Psa.

40:7, 8). Throughout His perfect life He preserved in thought, word and deed, the Divine Decalogue, honoring and magnifying God's Law.

8. The "tabernacle" was the *place where sacrifice was made.* In its outer court stood the brazen altar, to which the animals were brought, and on which they were slain. There it was that blood was shed and atonement was made for sin. So it was with the Lord Jesus. He fulfilled in His own Person the typical significance of the brazen altar, as of every piece of the tabernacle furniture. The body in which He tabernacled on earth was nailed to the cruel Tree. The Cross was the altar upon which God's Lamb was slain, where His precious blood was shed, and where complete atonement was made for sin.

9. The "tabernacle" was *the place where the priestly family was fed.* "And the remainder thereof shall Aaron and his sons eat: with unleavened bread shall it be eaten *in the holy place;* in the court of the tabernacle of the congregation they shall eat it . . . The priest that offereth it for sin shall eat it: *in the holy place* shall it be eaten" (Lev. 6:16, 26). How deeply significant are these scriptures in their typical import! And how they speak to us of Christ as the Food of God's priestly family today, that is, all believers (see I Peter 2:5). He is the Bread of Life. He is the One upon whom our souls delight to feed.

10. The "tabernacle" was *the place of worship.* To it the pious Israelite brought his offerings. To it he turned when he desired to worship Jehovah. From its door the Voice of the Lord was heard. Within its courts the priests ministered in their sacred service. And so it was with the Anti-type. It is "*by him*" we are to offer unto God a sacrifice of praise (see Heb. 13:15). It is in Him, and by Him, *alone,* that we can worship the Father. It is through Him we have access to the throne of grace.

Thus we see how fully and how perfectly the tabernacle of old foreshadowed the Person of our blessed Lord, and why the Holy Spirit, when announcing the Incarnation, said, "And the word became flesh, and *tabernacled* among us." Before passing on to the next clause of John 1:14, it should be pointed out that there is a series of striking contrasts between the wilderness tabernacle and Solomon's temple in their respective foreshadowings of Christ.

(1) The tabernacle foreshadowed Christ in His first advent; the temple looks forward to Christ at His second advent.

(2) The tabernacle was first, historically; the temple was not built until long afterwards.

(3) The tabernacle was but a temporary erection; the temple was a permanent structure.

(4) The tabernacle was erected by Moses the *prophet* (which was the office Christ filled during His first advent); the temple was built by Solomon the king (which is the office Christ will fill at His second advent).

(5) The tabernacle was used in the wilderness – speaking of Christ's humiliation; the temple was built *in Jerusalem*, the "city of the great King" (Matt. 5:35) – speaking of Christ's future glorification.

(6) The numeral which figured most prominently in the tabernacle was five, which speaks of *grace*, and grace was what characterized the earthly ministry of Christ at His first advent; but the leading numeral in the temple was twelve which speaks of *government*, for Christ shall rule and reign as *King* of kings and *Lord* of lords.

(7) The tabernacle was unattractive in its externals – so when Christ was here before He was as "a root out of a dry ground;" but the temple was renowned for its outward magnificence – so Christ when He returns shall come in power and great glory.

"*And we beheld his glory.*" "We beheld" refers, directly, to the first disciples, yet it is the blessed experience of all believers today. "But we all . . . *beholding*, as in a glass (mirror) *the glory of the Lord*" (II Cor. 3:18). The term used in both of these verses seems to point a contrast. In John 12:41 we read, "These things said Isaiah, when he *saw* his glory, and spake of him," the reference being to Isaiah 6. The Old Testament celebrities only had occasional and passing glimpses of God's glory. But, in contrast from these who only "saw," we – believers of this dispensation—"*behold* his glory." But more particularly, there is a contrast here between the beholding and the non-beholding of God's glory: the Shekinah glory abode in the holy of holies, and therefore, was *hidden*. But we, now, "behold" the Divine glory.

"We beheld his glory." What is meant *by this*? Ah! who is competent to answer. Eternity itself will be too short to exhaustively explore this theme. The glories of our Lord are infinite, for in Him dwelleth all the fulness of the Godhead bodily. No subject ought to be dearer to the heart of a believer. Briefly defined, "We beheld his glory" signifies His supreme excellency, His personal perfections. For the purpose of general classification we may say the "glories" of our Saviour are fourfold, each of which is capable of being subdivided indefinitely. First, there are His *essential* "glories," as the Son of God; these are His Divine perfections, as for example, His Omnipotence. Second, there are His *moral* "glories," and these are His human perfections, as for example, His meekness. Third, there are His *official* "glories," and these are His mediatorial perfections, as for example, His priesthood. Fourth, there are His *acquired* "glories," and these are the reward for what He has done. Probably the first three of these are spoken of in our text.

First, "We beheld his glory" refers to His *essential* "glory," or Divine perfections. This is clear from the words which follow: "The glory as of the only begotten of the Father." From the beginning to the end of His earthly life and ministry the Deity of the Lord Jesus was plainly evidenced. His supernatural birth, His personal excellencies, His matchless teaching, His wondrous miracles, His death and resurrection, all proclaimed Him as the Son of God. But it is to be noted that these words, "we beheld his *glory*," follow immediately after the words "tabernacled" among men. We cannot but believe there is here a further reference to the tabernacle. In the tabernacle, in the holy of holies, Jehovah made His throne upon the mercy seat, and the evidence of His presence there was the *Shekinah glory*, frequently termed "the cloud." When the tabernacle had been completed, and Jehovah took possession of it, we read, "then a *cloud* covered the tent of the congregation, and *the glory* of the Lord filled the tabernacle" (Exod. 40:34). It was the same at the completion of Solomon's temple: "The *cloud* filled the house of the Lord, so that the priests could not stand to minister because of the cloud, *for the glory* of the Lord had filled the house of the Lord" (I Kings 8:10, 11). Here "the cloud" and "the glory" are clearly identified. The Shekinah glory, then, was the standing sign of God's presence in the midst of Israel. Hence, after Israel's apostasy, and when the Lord was turning away from them, we are told, "And *the glory* of the Lord went up from the midst of the city" (Ezek. 11:23). Therefore, when we read, "The Word . . . tabernacled among men, and we beheld his *glory*" it was the proof that none other than Jehovah was again in Israel's midst. And it is a remarkable fact, to which we have never seen attention called, that at either extremity of the Word's tabernacling among men the *Shekinah glory was evidenced.* Immediately following His birth we are told, "And there were in the same country shepherds abiding in the field, keeping watch over their flock by night. And, lo, the angel of the Lord came upon them, *and the glory of the Lord shone round about them*: and they were sore afraid" (Luke 2:8, 9). And, at His departure from this world, we read "And when he had spoken these things, while they beheld, he was taken up; and *a cloud* received him out of their sight" (Acts 1:9)—not "clouds," but "a cloud!" "We beheld his glory," then, refers, first, to His Divine glory.

Second, there also seems to be a reference here to His *official* "glory," which was exhibited upon the Holy Mount. In II Peter 1:16 we read, "For we have not followed cunningly devised fables, when we made known unto you the power and coming of our Lord Jesus Christ, but were eyewitnesses of his *majesty.*" The reference is to the Transfiguration, for the next verse goes on to say, "For he received from God the Father honor and *glory,* when there came such a voice to him from the excellent glory, This is my beloved Son, in whom I am well pleased." It is the use of the word "glory" here which seems to link the transfiguration-scene with John 1:14. This is confirmed by the fact that on the Mount, "while he yet spake, behold, a *bright cloud* overshadowed them" (Matt. 17:5).

Third, there is also a clear reference in John 1:14 to the

moral "glory" or perfections of the God-Man, for after saying "we beheld his glory," John immediately adds (omitting the parenthesis) *"full of grace and truth."* What marvelous grace we behold in that wondrous descent from heaven's throne to Bethlehem's manger! It had been an act of infinite condescension if the One who was the Object of angelic worship had deigned to come down to this earth and reign over it as King; but that He should appear in weakness, that He should voluntarily choose poverty, that He should become a helpless Babe—such grace is altogether beyond our ken; such matchless love passeth knowledge. O that we may never lose our sense of wonderment at the infinite condescension of God's Son.

In His marvelous stoop we behold *His glory*. Greatness is never so glorious as when it takes the place of lowliness. Power is never so attractive as when it is placed at the disposal of others. Might is never so triumphant as when it sets aside its own prerogatives. Sovereignty is never so winsome as when it is seen in the place of service. And, may we not say it reverently, Deity had never appeared so glorious as when It hung upon a maiden's breast! Yes, we behold His glory—the glory of an infinite condescension, the glory of a matchless grace, the glory of a fathomless love.

Concerning the *acquired* "glories" of our Lord we cannot now treat at length. These include the various rewards bestowed upon Him by the Father after the successful completion of the work which had been committed into His hands. It is of these acquired glories Isaiah speaks, when, after treating of the voluntary humiliation and death of the Saviour, he gives us to hear the Father saying of Christ, "Therefore will I divide him a portion with the great, and he shall divide the spoil with the strong; *because* he hath poured out his soul unto death" (Isa. 53:12). It is of these acquired glories the Holy Spirit speaks in Philippians 2, where after telling of our Lord's obedience even unto the death of the Cross, He declares, *"Wherefore* God also hath highly exalted him, and given him a name which is above every name" (Phil. 2:9). And so we might continue. But how unspeakably blessed to know, that at the close of our great High Priest's prayer, recorded in John 17, we find Him saying,

"Father, I will that they also, whom thou hast given me, be with me where I am; that they may behold *my glory*, which thou hast given me" (v. 24)!

Before we pass on to the next verse we would point out that there is an intimate connection between the one which has just been before us (see v. 14) and the opening verse of the chapter. Verse 14 is really an explanation and amplification of verse 1. There are three statements in each which exactly correspond, and the latter throw light on the former. First, "in the beginning was the word," and that is something that transcends our comprehension; but "and the word became flesh" brings Him within reach of our sense. Second "and the word was with God," and again we are unable to understand; but the Word "tabernacled among us," and we may draw near and behold. Third, "and the word was God," and again we are in the realm of the Infinite; but "full of grace and truth," and here are two essential facts concerning God which come within the range of our vision. Thus by coupling together verses 1 and 14 (reading the verses in between as a parenthesis) we have a statement which is, probably, the most comprehensive in its sweep, the profoundest in its depths, and yet the simplest in its terms to be found between the covers of the Bible. Put these verses side by side:—

(1) "*In the beginning* was the word:"

  (a) "And the word became flesh" tells of *the beginning* of His human life.

(2) "And the word was *with God*"

  (b) "And tabernacled among us" shows Him *with men*.

(3) "And the word *was God*"

  (c) "Full of grace and truth," and this tells *what God is*.

"John bare witness of him, and cried, saying, This was he of whom I spake, He that cometh after me is preferred before me: for he was before me" (1:15). Concerning the ministry and testimony of John the Baptist we shall have more to say in our next chapter, D.V., so upon this verse we offer only two very brief remarks. First, we find that here the Lord's forerunner bears witness to Christ's supreme excellency: "He that cometh after me is *preferred* before me," he declares, which, in the Greek, signifies Christ had His *being* "before" John. Second,

"For he *was* before me." But, historically, John the Baptist was born into this world six months before the Saviour was. When, then, the Baptist says Christ "was *before*" him, he is referring to His eternal existence, and, therefore, bears witness to His deity.

"And of his fulness have all we received, and grace for grace" (1:16). The word "fulness" is still another term in this important passage which brings out the absolute Deity of the Saviour. It is the same word which is found in Col. 1:19 and 2:9—"For it pleased the Father that in him should all fulness dwell;" "For in him dwelleth all the fulness of the Godhead bodily." The Greek preposition "ek" signifies "out of." Out of the Divine fulness have all we (believers) "received." *What* is it we have "received" from Christ? Ah, what is it *we have not* "received!" It is out of His inexhaustible "*fulness*" we have "received." From Him we have "received" life (see John 10:28); peace (see 14:27); joy (see 15:11); God's own Word (see 17:14); the Holy Spirit (see 20:22). There is laid up in Christ, as in a great storehouse, *all* that the believer needs both for time and for eternity.

"And grace for grace." Bishop Ryle tells us the Greek preposition here may be translated two different ways, and suggests the following thoughts. First, we have received "grace *upon* grace," that is, God's favors heaped up, one upon another. Second, "grace *for* grace," that is, new grace to supply old grace; grace sufficient to meet every recurring need.

"For the law was given by Moses, but grace and truth came by Jesus Christ" (1:17). A contrast is drawn between what was "given" by Moses, and what "came" by Jesus Christ; for "grace and truth" were not merely "given," they "*came* by Jesus Christ," came in all their fulness, came in their glorious perfections. The Law was "given" to Moses, for it was not his own; but "grace and truth" were not "given" to Christ, for *these* were His own *essential* perfections. On looking into this contrast we must bear in mind that the great point here is the *manifestation of God*: God as He was manifested through the Law, and God as He was made known by the Only Begotten Son.

Was not the Law "truth?" Yes, so far as it went. It announced what God righteously demanded of men, and therefore, what men ought to be according to God's mind. It has often been said, the Law is a transcript of God's mind. But how inadequate such a statement is! Did the Law reveal what God *is*? Did it display all His attributes? If it did, there would be nothing more to learn of God than what the Law made known.

Did the Law tell out the *grace* of God? No; indeed. The Law was holy, and the commandment holy, just, and good. It demanded obedience; it required the strictest doing and continuance of *all* things written in it. And the only alternative was death. Inflexible in its claims, it remitted no part of its penalty. He that despised it "died *without mercy*," and, "every transgression and disobedience received a just recompense of reward" (Heb. 10:28; see Heb. 2:2). Such a Law could never justify a *sinner*. For this it was never given.

The inevitable effect of the Law when received by the unsaved is just that which was produced at Sinai, to whom it first came: "And they said unto Moses, Speak *thou* with us, and we will hear: but let not *God* speak with us, lest we die" (Exod. 20:19). "Now therefore why should we die? for this great fire will consume us: if we hear the voice of the Lord our God any more, then we shall die" (Deut. 5:25). Why such terror? Because "they could not endure that which was commanded" (Heb. 12:20). This terror was the testimony which the Law extorts from every sinner, to whom it is brought home *as God's* Law; it is "the ministration of condemnation, and of death" (II Cor. 3:7, 9). It has a "glory," indeed, but it is the glory of thunder and lightning, of fire, of blackness, and of darkness, and the sound of the trumpet, and of the voice of words, which only bring terror to the guilty conscience. But, blessed be God, there is "a glory that excelleth" (II Cor. 3:10).

"*Grace and truth* came by Jesus Christ." The "glory that excelleth" is the glory of "the word that became flesh, the glory as of the only begotten of the Father full of grace and truth." The Law revealed God's justice, but it did not make known His mercy; it testified to His righteousness, but it did not exhibit His grace.

It *was* God's "truth," but not the full truth about God Himself. "By the law is the knowledge of sin;" we never read "by the law is the knowledge of God." No; the "law entered that the offense might abound," "sin by the commandment became exceeding sinful." It made known the heinousness of sin; it condemned the sinner, but it did not fully reveal God. It exhibited His righteous hatred of sin and His holy determination to punish it: it exposed the guilt and corruption of the sinner, but for ought it could tell him, it left him to his doom. "For what the law could not do, in that it was weak through the flesh, God sending his own Son in the likeness of sinful flesh, and for sin, condemned sin in the flesh: That the righteousness of the law might be fulfilled in us, who walk not after the flesh, but after the Spirit" (Rom. 8:3, 4).

"Grace *and* truth." These are fitly and inseparably joined together. We cannot have the one without having the other. There are many who do not like salvation by *grace,* and there are those who would tolerate grace if they could have it without the *truth.* The Nazarenes could "wonder" at the *gracious* words which proceeded out of His mouth, but as soon as Christ pressed the *truth* upon them, they "were filled with wrath," and sought to "cast him down headlong from the brow of the hill whereon their city was built" (Luke 4:29). Such, too, was the condition of those who sought Him for "the meat that perisheth." They were willing to profit from His *grace,* but when He told them the *truth* some "murmured" at Him, others were "offended," and "many of his disciples went back and walked no more with him" (John 6:66). And in our own day, there are many who admire the grace which came by Jesus Christ, and would consent to be saved by it, provided this could be without the intrusion of the truth. But this cannot be. Those who reject the truth, reject grace.

There is, in Romans 5:21, another sentence which is closely parallel, and really, an amplification of these words "grace and truth" – "Grace reigns *through righteousness,* unto eternal life by Jesus Christ our Lord." The grace which saves sinners is no mere moral weakness such as is often to be found in human government. Nor is "the righteousness of God," through which grace reigns, some mere *semblance* of justice. No; on the Cross Christ was "set forth a *propitiation* (a perfect satisfaction to the broken Law) through faith in his blood, to declare his (God's) *righteousness* for the remission of sins" (Rom. 3:25). Grace does not ignore the Law, or set aside its requirements; nay verily, "it *establishes* the law" (Rom. 3:31): establishes it because inseparably linked with "truth;" establishes it because it reigns "through righteousness," not at the expense of it; establishes it because grace tells of a Substitute who kept the Law for and endured the death penalty on behalf of all who receive Him as their Lord and Saviour; and establishes it by bringing the redeemed to "delight" in the Law.

But was there *no* "grace and truth" before Jesus Christ came? Assuredly there was. God dealt according to "grace and truth" with our first parents immediately after their transgression—it was grace that sought them, and provided them with a covering; as it was truth that pronounced sentence upon them, and expelled them from the garden. God dealt according to "grace and truth" with Israel on the passover night in Egypt: it was grace that provided shelter for them beneath the blood; it was truth that righteously demanded the death of an innocent substitute in their stead. But "grace and truth" were never *fully* revealed till the Saviour Himself appeared. By Him they "came:" in Him they were personified, magnified, glorified.

And now let us notice a few contrasts between Law and Grace:

1. Law addresses men as members of the old creation; Grace makes men members of a new creation.
2. Law manifested what was in Man—sin; Grace manifests what is in God—Love.
3. Law demanded righteousness from men; Grace brings righteousness to men.
4. Law sentences a living man to death; Grace brings a dead man to life.
5. Law speaks of what men must do for God; Grace tells of what Christ has done for men.
6. Law gives a knowledge of sin; Grace puts away sin.
7. Law brought God out to men; Grace brings men in to God.

"No man hath seen God at any time; the only begotten Son, which is in the bosom of the Father, he hath declared him" (John 1:18). This verse terminates the Introduction to John's Gospel, and *summarizes* the whole of the first eighteen verses of John 1. Christ has "declared"—told out, revealed, unveiled, displayed the Father; and the One who has done this is "the only begotten Son, which *is* in the bosom of the Father." The "bosom of the Father" speaks of proximity to, personal intimacy with, and the enjoyment of the Father's love. And, in becoming flesh, the Son did not leave this place of inseparable union. It is not the "Son which *was*," but "which *is* in the bosom of the Father." He retained the same intimacy with the Father, entirely unimpaired by the Incarnation. Nothing in the slightest degree detracted from His own personal glory, or from the nearness and oneness to the Father which He had enjoyed with Him from all eternity. How we ought, then, to honor, reverence, and worship the Lord Jesus!

But a further word on this verse is called for. A remarkable contrast is pointed. In the past, God, in the fulness of His glory, was unmanifested—"No man" had seen Him; but now, God is fully revealed—the Son has "declared" Him. Perhaps this contrast may be made clearer to our readers if we refer to two passages in the Old Testament and compare them with two passages in the New Testament.

In I Kings 8:12 we read, "Then spake Solomon, The Lord said that he would dwell *in the thick darkness*." Again, "*Clouds and darkness* are round about him" (Psa. 97:2). These verses tell not what God is in Himself, but declare that under the Law He was not revealed. What could be known of a person who dwelt in "thick darkness!" But now turn to I Peter 2:9, "But ye are a chosen generation, a royal priesthood, an holy nation, a peculiar people; that ye should show forth the praises of him who hath called you *out of darkness* into his marvelous *light*." Ah, how blessed this is. Again, we read in I John 1:5, 7, "God is light, and in him is no darkness at all . . . but if we walk *in the light*, as he is in the light, we have fellowship one with another." And this, because the Father has been fully "declared" by our adorable Saviour.

Once more: turn to Exodus 33:18—"And he said, I beseech thee, show me thy glory." This was the earnest request of Moses. But was it granted? Read on, "And the Lord said, Behold, there is a place by me, and thou shalt stand upon a rock: and it shall come to pass, while my glory passeth by, that I will put thee in a cleft of a rock, and will cover thee with my hand while I pass by: And I will take away mine hind, and thou shalt see my back parts: *but my face shall not be seen.*" Character is not declared in a person's "*back* parts" but in his face! That Moses saw not the face, but only the back parts of Jehovah, was in perfect accord with the dispensation of Law in which he lived. How profoundly thankful should we be that the dispensation of Law has passed, and that we live in the full light of the dispensation of Grace! How deeply grateful should we be, that we look not on the back parts of Jehovah "for God, who commanded the light to shine out of darkness, hath shined in *our* hearts, to give the light of the knowledge of the glory of God in the face of Jesus Christ" (II Cor. 4:6). May grace be given us to magnify and adorn that superlative grace which has brought us out of darkness into marvelous light, because the God whom no man hath seen at any time has been fully "declared" by the Son.

We conclude, once more, by drawing up a number of questions on the passage which will be before us in the next chapter (John 1:19-34), so that the interested reader, who desires to "Search the Scriptures" may give them careful study in the interval.

1. Why did the Jews ask John if he were Elijah, 1:21?
2. What "prophet" did they refer to in 1:21?
3. What are the thoughts suggested by "voice" in 1:23?
4. Why did John cry "in the wilderness" rather than in the temple, 1:23?
5. "Whom ye know not," 1:26—What did this prove?
6. What are the thoughts suggested by the Saviour's title "The Lamb of God," 1:29?
7. Why did the Holy Spirit descend on Christ as a "dove," 1:32?

CHAPTER FOUR

Christ's Forerunner

John 1:19-34

Following our usual custom, we begin by submitting an Analysis of the passage which is to be before us. In it we have:—

1. The Jews' inquiry of John, and his answers, 1:19-26,
   (1) "Who art thou?" Not the Christ: 19, 20.
   (2) "Art thou Elijah?" No: 21.
   (3) "Art thou that prophet?" No: 21.
   (4) "What sayest thou of thyself?" A "voice:" 22, 23.
   (5) "Why baptizeth thou?" To prepare the way for Christ: 24-26.
2. John's witness concerning Christ: 1:27.
3. Location of the Conference, 1:28.
4. John proclaims Christ as God's "Lamb," 1:29.
5. The purpose of John's baptism, 1:30-31.
6. John tells of the Spirit descending on Christ at His baptism, and foretells that Christ shall baptize with the Spirit, 1:32, 33.
7. John owns Christ's Deity, 1:34.

Even a hurried reading of these verses will make it evident that the personage which stands out most conspicuously in them is John the Baptist. Moreover, we do not have to study this passage very closely to discover that, the person and the witness of the Lord's forerunner are brought before us here in a manner entirely different from what we find in the first three Gospels. No hint is given that his raiment was "of camel's hair," that he had "a leathern girdle about his loins," or that "his meat was locusts and wild honey." Nothing is recorded of his stern Call to Repentance, nor is anything said of his announcement that "the kingdom of heaven is at hand." These things were foreign to the design of the Holy Spirit in this fourth Gospel. Again; instead of referring to the Lord Jesus as the One "whose fan is in his hand," and of the One who "will thoroughly purge his floor, and gather his wheat into his garner, but he will burn up the chaff with unquenchable fire" (Matt. 3:12), he points to Him as "the Lamb of God which taketh away the sin of the world." And this is most significant and blessed to those who have been divinely taught to rightly divide the Word of Truth.

Without doubt John the Baptist is, in several respects, one of the most remarkable characters that is brought before us in the Bible. He was the subject of Old Testament prophecy (Isa. 40); his birth was due to the direct and miraculous intervention of God (Luke 1:7, 13); he was "filled with the Holy Spirit even from his mother's womb" (Luke 1:15); he was a man "sent from God" (John 1:6); he was sent to prepare the way of the Lord (Matt. 3:3). Of him the Lord said, "Among them that are born of women there has not risen a greater than John the Baptist" (Matt. 11:11); the reference being to his *positional* "greatness," as the forerunner of the Messiah: to him was accorded the high honor of baptizing the Lord Jesus. That Christ *was* referring to the *positional* "greatness" of John is clear from His next words, "notwithstanding he that is least *in* the kingdom of heaven is greater than he." To have a place in the kingdom of heaven will be a more exalted position than to be heralding the King outside of it, as John was. This, we take it is the key to that word in John 14:28, where we find the Lord Jesus saying, "My Father is *greater* than I"—greater not in His person, but in His position; for, at the time the Saviour uttered those words He was in the place of subjection, as God's "Servant."

Our passage opens by telling of a deputation of priests and Levites being sent from Jerusalem to enquire of John as to who he was: "And this is the record of John, when the Jews sent priests and Levites from Jerusalem to ask him, Who art thou?" (1:19). Nothing like this is found in the other Gospels, but it is in striking accord with the character and scope of the fourth Gospel, which deals with spiritual rather than dispensational relationships. The incident before us brings out *the spiritual ignorance* of the religious leaders among the Jews. In fulfillment of Isaiah's prophecy, the Lord's forerunner had appeared in the wilderness, but, lacking in spiritual discernment, the leaders in Jerusalem knew not who he was. Accordingly, their messengers came and enquired of John, "Who art thou?" Multitudes of people were flocking to this strange preacher in the wilderness, and many had been baptized by him. A great stir had been made, so much so that "men mused in their hearts of John, whether he were Christ, or not" (Luke 3:15), and the religious leaders in Jerusalem were compelled to take note of it; therefore, did they send a deputation to wait upon John, to find out who he really was, and to enquire into his credentials.

"And he confessed, and denied not; but confessed, I am not the Christ" (1:20). These words give plain intimation of the Spirit in which the priests and Levites must have approached John, as also of the design of "the Jews" who had sent them. To them the Baptist was an interloper. He was outside the religious systems of that day. He had not been trained in the schools of the Rabbins, he had held no position of honor in the temple ministrations, and he was not identified with either the Pharisees, the Sadducees, or the Herodians. From whence then had he received his authority? Who had commissioned *him* to go forth bidding men to "Repent." By what right did *he* baptize people? One can imagine the tone in which they said to John, "Who art *thou?*" No doubt they expected to intimidate him. This seems clear from the fact that we are here told, "and he confessed, and *denied not.*" He boldly stood his ground. Neither the dignity of those who had sent this embassy to John, nor their threatening frowns, moved him at all. "He confessed, and denied not." May like courage be found in us when we are challenged with an "Who art thou?"

"But confessed, I am not the Christ." Having taken the firm stand he had, did Satan now tempt him to go to the other extreme? Failing to intimidate him, did the enemy now seek to make him boastfully exaggerate? Christ had not then been openly manifested: John was the one before the public eye, as we read in Mark 1:5, "And there went out unto him all the land of Judea, and they of Jerusalem, and were all baptized of him in the river of Jordan" (Mark 1:5). Now that the multitudes were flocking to him, and many had become his disciples (cf. John 1:35), why not announce that he was the Messiah himself! But he instantly banished such wicked and presumptuous thoughts, if such were presented by Satan to his mind, as most likely they were, or, why tell us that he "confessed I am not the Christ?" May God deliver us from the evil spirit of boasting, and keep us from ever claiming to be anything more than what we really are—sinners saved by grace.

"And they asked him, What then? Art thou Elijah? And he saith, I am not" (1:21). *Why* should they have asked John if he were Elijah? The answer is, Because there was a general expectation among the Jews at that time that Elijah would again appear on earth. That this was so, is clear from a number of passages in the Gospels. For instance, when the Lord asked His disciples, "Whom do men say that I the Son of man am?" they answered, "Some say that thou art John the Baptist (who had been slain in the interval), some *Elijah,* and others Jeremiah, or one of the prophets" (Matt. 16:13, 14). Again; as the Lord Jesus and His disciples came down from the Mount of Transfiguration, He said unto them, "Tell the vision to no man until the Son of man be raised from the dead." Then, we read, "His disciples asked him, saying, Why then say the scribes that *Elijah must first come?"* (Matt. 17:9, 10). The expectation of the Jews had a scriptural foundation, for the last verses of the Old Testament say, "Behold, I will send you *Elijah the prophet* before the coming of the great and dreadful day of the Lord: And he shall turn the heart of the fathers to the children, and the heart of the children to their fathers, lest I come and smite the earth with a curse" (Malachi 4:5, 6). This prophecy has reference to the return to earth of Elijah, to perform a ministry just before the second advent of Christ, similar in character to that of John the Baptist before the first public appearing of Christ.

When asked, "Art thou Elijah?" John replied, emphatically, "I am not." John had much in common with the Tishbite, and his work was very similar in character to the yet future work of Elijah; nevertheless, he was not Elijah himself. He went before

Christ "in the spirit and power of Elijah" (Luke 1:17), because he came "to make ready a people prepared for the Lord."

Next, John's interrogators asked him, "Art thou that prophet?" (1:21). *What* "prophet?" we may well enquire. And the answer is, The "prophet" predicted through Moses. The prediction is recorded in Deut. 18:15, 18: "The Lord thy God will raise up unto thee a prophet from the midst of thee, of thy brethren, like unto me; unto him ye shall hearken . . . I will raise them up a prophet from among their brethren, like unto thee, and will put my words in his mouth; and he shall speak unto them all that I shall command him." This was one of the many Messianic prophecies given in the Old Testament times, which received its fulfillment in the person of the Lord Jesus Christ. "Art thou that prophet?" John was asked; and, again, he answered, "No."

"Then said they unto him, Who art thou? that we may give an answer to them that sent us. What sayest thou of thyself?" (1:22). Searching questions were these—"*Who* art thou?"; "what sayest thou of *thyself?*" John might have answered, and answered truthfully, "I am the son of Zacharias the priest. I am one who has been filled with the Holy Spirit from my birth." Or, he might have replied, "I am the most remarkable character ever raised up by God and sent unto Israel." "What sayest thou of thyself?" Ah! that was indeed a searching question, and both writer and reader may well learn a lesson from John's reply, and seek grace to emulate his lovely modesty—a lesson much needed in these days of Laodicean boasting.

"He said, I am the voice of one crying in the wilderness, Make straight the way of the Lord, as said the prophet Isaiah" (1:23). Here was John's answer. "What sayest thou of thyself?" "I am the *voice* of one crying in the wilderness," he said. Becoming humility was this. Humility is of great price in the sight of God, and has had a prominent place in the men whom He has used. Paul, the greatest of the apostles, confessed himself "less than the least of all saints" (Eph. 3:8). And John here confesses much the same thing, when he referred to himself as "the voice of one crying in the wilderness." Reader, what reply would *you* make to such a query—"What sayest thou of *thyself?*" Surely you would not answer, "I am an eminent saint of God: I am living on a very exalted plane of spirituality: I am one who has been much used of God." Such self-exaltation would show you had learned little from Him who was "meek and lowly in heart," and would evidence a spirit far from that which should cause us to own that, after all, we are only "unprofitable servants" (Luke 17:10).

When John referred to himself as "the voice," he employed the very term which the Holy Spirit had used of him seven hundred years previously, when speaking through Isaiah the prophet – "The voice of him that crieth in the wilderness, Prepare ye the way of the Lord, make straight in the desert a highway for our God" (Isa. 40:3). And we cannot but believe this appellation was selected with Divine discrimination. In a former chapter, when commenting upon the titles of the Lord Jesus, found in John 1:7 – "The light" – we called attention to the fact that Christ referred to His forerunner (in evident contrast from Himself as "the light") as "the *lamp* that burneth and shineth" (John 5:35, R.V.). And so here, we are satisfied that another contrast is pointed. Christ is "the Word;" John was but "the voice." What, then, are the thoughts suggested by this figurative title?

In the first place, the word exists (in the mind) *before* the voice articulates it. Such was the relation between Christ and His forerunner. It is true that John was the first to appear before the public eye; yet, as the "Word," Christ had existed from all eternity. Second, the voice is simply the vehicle or medium *by which* the word is expressed or *made known.* Such was John. The object of his mission and the purpose of his ministry was to bear witness to "the Word." Again, the voice is simply heard but not seen. John was not seeking to display himself. His work was to get men to listen to his God-given message in order that they might *behold* "the Lamb." May the Lord today make more of His servants John-like; just "voices," *heard but not seen!* Finally, we may add, that the word endures *after* the voice is *silent.* The voice of John has long since been stilled by death, but "the Word" abideth forever. Appropriately, then, was the one who introduced the Messiah to Israel, termed the "voice." What wonderful depths there are in the Scriptures! How much is contained in a single word! And how this calls for prolonged *meditation* and humble prayer!

"The voice of one crying *in the wilderness.*" What a position for the Messiah's forerunner to occupy! Surely his place was in Jerusalem. Why then did not John cry in the temple? Why, because Jehovah was no more there in the temple. Judaism was but a hollow shell: outward form there was, but no life within. It was to a nation of legalists, Pharisee ridden, who neither manifested Abraham's faith nor produced his works, that John came. God would not own the self-righteous formalism of the Jews. Therefore, the one "sent of God" appeared *outside* the religious systems and circles of that day. But why did John preach "*in the wilderness?*" Because the "wilderness" symbolized the spiritual *barrenness* of the Jewish nation. John could only mourn over that which was not of God, and everything about him was in keeping with this: his food was that which he found in the wilderness, and his *prophet's* garment testified to the failure that was evident on every hand.

"And they which were sent were of the Pharisees. And they asked him, and said unto him, Why baptizest thou then, if thou be not that Christ, nor Elias, neither that prophet?" (1:24, 25). This final question put to John by the embassy from Jerusalem confirms what we have said upon v. 20. The religious leaders among the Jews were disputing John's right to preach, and challenging his authority to baptize. He had received no commission from the Sanhedrin, hence "why baptizest *thou?*" John does not appear to have answered the last question directly, instead, he turns to them and speaks of Christ.

"John answered them, saying, I baptize with water: but there standeth one among you, whom ye know not" (1:26). John continued to stand his ground: he would not deny that he baptized with water, or more correctly, *in* water, but he sought to get them occupied with something of greater importance than a symbolical rite. There is much to be learned from John's answer here. These men were raising questions about baptism, while as yet they were utter strangers to Christ Himself—how like many today! Of what use was it to discuss with these Pharisee-commissioned "priests and Levites" the "*why*" of baptism, when they were yet in their sins? Well would it be for the Lord's servants and those engaged in personal work for Christ, to carefully heed what is before us here. People are willing to argue about side issues, while the vital and central Issue remains undecided! And only too often the Christian worker follows them into "By-path meadow." What is needed is for us to ignore all irrelevant quibbles, and press upon the lost the claims of *Christ* and their *need* of accepting Him as their Lord and Saviour.

"There standeth one among you, whom ye *know not*." How this exposed Israel's* condition! How this revealed their spiritual ignorance! And how tragically true, in principle, is this today. Even in this so-called Christian land, while many have heard about Christ, yet in how many circles, yes, and in religious circles too, we may say, "there standeth one among you, whom ye know not!" O the spiritual blindness of the natural man. Christ, by His Spirit, stands in the midst of many a congregation, unseen and unknown.

"He it is, who coming after me is preferred before me, whose shoe's latchet I am not worthy to unloose" (1:27). What a noble testimony was this! How these words of John bring out the Divine glory of the One he heralded! Remember *who* he was. No ordinary man was John the Baptist. The subject of Old Testament prophecy, the son of a priest, born as the result of the direct intervention of God's power, filled with the Holy Spirit from his mother's womb, engaged in a ministry which drew great multitudes unto him, and yet he looked up to Christ as standing on a plane infinitely higher than the one he occupied, as a Being from another world, as One before whom he was not worthy to stoop down and unloose His shoes. He could find no expression strong enough to define the difference which separated him from the One who was "preferred before" him. Again we

* "We must not, however, limit this picture to Israel, for it is equally applicable and pertinent to sinners of the Gentiles too. Israel in the flesh was only a sample of fallen man as such. What we have here is a pointed and solemn delineation of human depravity . . . its normal application is to the whole of Adam's fallen race. Let every reader see here a portrait of what he or she is by nature. The picture is not a flattering one we know. No, it is drawn by one who searches the innermost recesses of the human heart, and is presented here to humble us." (A.W.P.). And so all through.

say, How these words of John bring out the Divine glory of the One he heralded!

"These things were done in Bethabara beyond Jordan, where John was baptizing" (1:28). There is, of course, some good reason *why* the Holy Spirit has been pleased to tell us *where* this conference took place, whether we are able to discover it or not. Doubtless, the key to its significance is found in the meaning of the proper nouns here recorded. Unfortunately, there is some variation in the spelling of "Bethabara" in the Greek manuscripts; but with Gesenius, the renowned Hebrew scholar, we are firmly inclined to believe this place is identical with "Bethbarah" mentioned in Judges 7:24, and which signifies "House of Passage," which was so named to memorialize the crossing of the Jordan in the days of Joshua. It was here, then, (apparently) at a place whose name signified "house of *passage,*" beyond Jordan, the symbol of *death,* that John was baptizing as the forerunner of Christ. The meaning of this should not be hard to find. The significance of these names correspond closely with the religious position that John himself occupied, and with the character of his mission. *Separated* as he was from Judaism, those who responded to his call to repent, and were baptized of him "confessing their sins," *passed out* of the apostate Jewish system, and took their place with the little remnant who were "prepared for the Lord" (Luke 1:17). Well, then, was the place where John was baptizing named "Bethbarah"—House of Passage.

"The next day John seeth Jesus coming unto him, and saith, Behold, the lamb of God, which taketh away the sin of the world" (1:29). "Behold the lamb of God:" the *connection* in which these words are found should be carefully noted. It was the day following the meeting between John and the Jerusalem delegation, a meeting which evidently occurred in the presence of others also, for John continues "this is he of whom *I said,* after me cometh a man which is preferred before me," which is a word for word reference to what he had said to those who had interrogated him on the previous day—see v. 27; when he had also declared to those priests and Levites "which were sent of the Pharisees" (v. 24), "there standeth one among you, whom ye know not."

"Behold the lamb of God." The force of this Call was deeply significant when viewed in the light of its setting. The Pharisees were looking for a "prophet," and they desired a "king" who should deliver them from the Roman yoke, but they had no yearnings for a *Saviour-priest*. The questions asked of John betrayed the hearts of those who put them. They appeared to be in doubt as to whether or not the Baptist was the long promised Messiah, so they asked him, "Art thou *Elijah*? Art thou *that prophet*?" But, be it noted, no enquiry was made as to whether he was the one who should deliver them "from the wrath to come!" One would have naturally expected these *priests* and *Levites* to have asked about the *sacrifice,* but no; apparently they had no *sense of sin!* It was under *these* circumstances that the forerunner of Christ announced Him as "the *lamb* of God," not as "the *word* of God," not as "the *Christ* of God," but as *THE LAMB*. It was the Spirit of God presenting the Lord Jesus to Israel in the very office and character in which they stood in deepest need of Him. They would have welcomed Him on the *throne,* but they must first accept Him on the *altar*. And is it any different today? Christ as an Elijah—a Social-Reformer—will be tolerated; and Christ as a Prophet, as a Teacher of ethics, will receive respect. But what the world needs first and foremost is the Christ of the Cross, where the Lamb of God offered Himself as a sacrifice for sin.

"Behold *the lamb* of God." There before John stood the One whom all the sacrifices of Old Testament times had foreshadowed. It is exceedingly striking to observe the progressive order followed by God in the teaching of Scripture concerning "the lamb." First, in Gen. 4, we have the Lamb *typified* in the firstlings of the flock slain by Abel in sacrifice. Second, we have the Lamb prophesied in Gen. 22:8 where Abraham said to Isaac, "God will provide himself a lamb." Third, in Ex. 12, we have the Lamb slain and its blood *applied*. Fourth, in Isa. 53:7, we have the Lamb *personified*: here for the first time we learn that the Lamb would be a Man. Fifth, in John 1:29, we have the Lamb *identified,* learning *who* He was. Sixth, in Rev. 5, we have the Lamb *magnified* by the hosts of heaven. Seventh, in the last chapter of the Bible we have the Lamb *glorified,* seated upon the eternal throne of God, Rev. 22:1. Once more; mark the orderly development in the *scope* of the sacrifices. In Gen. 4 sacrifice is offered for the *individual*—Abel. In Ex. 12 the sacrifice avails for the whole *household.* In Lev. 16, on the annual Day of Atonement, the sacrifice was efficacious for the entire *nation.* But here in John 1:29 it is "Behold the lamb of God which taketh away the sin *of the world*"—Gentiles are embraced as well as Jews!

"Behold *the lamb of God.*" What are the thoughts suggested by this title? It points to His moral perfections, His *sinlessness,* for He was the "lamb without blemish and without spot" (I Peter 1:19). It tells of His gentleness, His voluntary offering Himself to God on our behalf—He was "led" (not driven) as "a lamb to the slaughter" (Acts 8:32, R.V.). But, more especially, and particularly, this title of our Lord speaks of *sacrifice*—He was "the lamb of God which *taketh away the sin* of the world," and this could only be through death, for "without shedding of blood is no remission." There was only one way by which sin could be taken away, and that was by death. "Sin" here signifies *guilt* (condemnation) as in Heb. 9:26; and "the world" refers to the world of *believers,* for it is only those who are in Christ for whom there is now "no condemnation" (Rom. 8:1); it is the world of believers, as contrasted from "the world of the ungodly" (II Pet. 2:5).

"This is he of whom I said, After me cometh a man which is preferred before me, for he was before me. And I knew him not: but that he should be made manifest to Israel, therefore am I come baptizing with water" (1:30, 31). Here for the third time John declares that Christ was "preferred before him"—(see vss. 15, 27, 30). It affirmed His pre-existence: it was a witness to His eternality. Then John tells of the purpose of his baptism. It was to make Christ "manifest" to Israel. It was to prepare a people for Him. This people was prepared by them taking the place of sinners before God (Mark 1:5), and that is why John baptized in Jordan, the river of death; for, being baptized in Jordan, they acknowledged that *death was their due.* In this, John's baptism differs from Christian baptism. In Christian baptism the believer does not confess that death is his due, but he shows forth the fact that he *has already* died, died to sin, died *with Christ* (Rom. 6:3, 4).

"And John bare record, saying, I saw the Spirit descending from heaven like a dove, and it abode upon him" (1:32). This has reference, of course, to the occasion when Christ Himself was baptized of John in the Jordan, when the Father testified to His pleasure in the Son, and when the Spirit descended upon Him as a dove. It manifested the *character* of the One on whom He came. The "dove" is the bird of love and sorrow: apt symbol, then, of Christ. The love expressed the sorrow, and the sorrow told out the depths of His love. Thus did the heavenly Dove bear witness to Christ. When the Holy Spirit came upon the disciples on the Day of Pentecost, we read "there appeared unto them cloven tongues like as *of fire*, and it sat upon each of them" (Acts 2:3). "Fire," uniformly signifies Divine *judgment*. There was that in the disciples which needed to be judged—the evil nature still remained within them. But, there was nothing in the Holy One of God that needed judging; hence, did the Holy Spirit descend upon *Him* like a dove!

"And I knew him not: but he that sent me to baptize with water, the same said unto me, Upon whom thou shalt see the Spirit descending and remaining on him, the same is he which baptizeth with the Holy Spirit" (1:33). The word "remaining" is rendered "abiding" in the R.V., and this is one of the characteristic words of the fourth Gospel. The other three Gospels all make mention of the Lord Jesus being anointed by the Holy Spirit, but John is the only one that says the Spirit "abode" upon Him. The Holy Spirit did not come upon Him, and then leave again, as with the prophets of old—He "abode" on Christ. This term has to do with the *Divine* side of things, and speaks of fellowship. We have the same word again in John 14:10, "Believest thou not that I am in the Father, and the Father in me? The words that I say unto you, I speak not from myself, but the Father *abiding* in me doeth his works" (R.V.). So, in John 15, where the Lord Jesus speaks of the fundamental requirement in spiritual fruit-bearing—*fellowship* with Himself—He says, "He that *abideth* in me, and I in him, the same beareth much fruit"

(John 15:5 R.V.). That Christ shall "baptize with (or 'in') the Holy Spirit" was another proof of His Godhood.

"And I saw, and bare record that this is the Son of God" (1:34). Here the witness of John the Baptist to the person of Christ terminates. It is to be noted that the forerunner bore a seven-fold witness to the excellency of the One he heralded. First, he testified to His *pre-existence*—"He *was* before me," v. 15. Second, He testified to His *Lordship,* v. 23. Third, he testified to His *immeasurable superiority*—"I am not worthy to unloose" His "shoe's latchet," v. 27. Fourth, he testified to His *sacrificial work*—"Behold the lamb," v. 29. Fifth, he testified to His *moral perfections*—"I saw the Spirit descending from heaven like a *dove,* and it *abode* upon him," v. 32. Sixth, he testified to His *Divine right* to baptize with the Holy Spirit, v. 33. Seventh, he testified to His *Divine Sonship,* v. 34.

The questions below concern the passage which we shall expound in the next chapter, namely, John 1:35-51, and to prepare our readers for it we ask them to give these questions their prayerful and careful study:—

1. Why did Christ ask the two disciples of John, "What seek ye?" 1:38.
2. What is signified by their reply, "Where dwellest thou?" 1:38.
3. What important practical truth is incorporated in 1:40, 41?
4. What blessed truth is illustrated by "findeth" in 1:43?
5. What is meant by, "in whom is no guile?" 1:47.
6. What attribute of Christ does 1:48 demonstrate?
7. To what does Christ refer in 1:51?

CHAPTER FIVE

Christ and His First Disciples

John 1:35-51

We first submit a brief Analysis of the passage which is to be before us. We would divide it as follows:—

1. John points to Christ as God's Lamb, 1:35, 36.
2. The effect of this on two of his disciples, 1:37.
3. Christ's searching question, the disciples' reply and communion with Christ, 1:38, 39.
4. The effect of this on Andrew, 1:40-42.
5. Christ finds and calls on Philip to follow Him, 1:43, 44.
6. The effect of this on Philip, 1:45, 46.
7. The meeting between Christ and Nathanael, 1:47-51.

The central truth of the passage we are about to study is, How the first of Christ's disciples were brought into saving contact with Him. It may be that some of our readers have experienced a difficulty when studying these closing verses of John 1 as they have compared their contents with what is found in Mark 1:16-20: "Now as he walked by the sea of Galilee, he saw Simon and Andrew his brother casting a net into the sea: for they were fishers. And Jesus said unto them, Come ye after me, and I will make you to become fishers of men. And straightway they forsook their nets, and followed him. And when he had gone a little farther thence, he saw James the son of Zebedee, and John his brother, who also were in the ship mending their nets. And straightway he called them: and they left their father Zebedee in the ship with the hired servants, and went after him" (cf. Matt. 4:18-22; Luke 5:1-11). Many have wondered how to harmonize John 1:35-42 with Mark 1:16-20. But there is nothing *to* harmonize, because there is *no* contradiction between them. The truth is, that Mark and John are not writing on the same subject. Mark treats of something which happened at a later date than that of which John writes. John tells us of the *conversion* of these disciples, whereas Mark (as also Matthew and Luke) deals with their *call to service*—a service which concerned the lost sheep of the house of Israel. That John omits the call to service (which each of the other three evangelists record) brings out, again, the special character of his Gospel, for he treats not of dispensational but of *spiritual* relationships, and therefore was it reserved for him to describe *the conversion* of these first disciples of Christ.

It is deeply interesting and instructive to mark attentively the manner in which these first disciples found the Saviour. They did not all come to Him in the same way, for God does not confine Himself to any particular method—He is *sovereign* in this, as in everything. It had been well if this had been kept in mind, for then had many a doubt been dispelled and many an heartache removed. How many there are who have listened to the testimony of some striking conversion, and have reproached themselves and made themselves miserable because *their* experience was a different one. How many churches there are which have their annual two weeks "protracted" meetings, and then conduct themselves as though there were no other souls that needed salvation during the remaining fifty weeks of the year! How many there are who imagine no sinner can be saved except at a "mourner's bench!" But all of these are so many ways of *limiting* God, that is, holding limited conceptions of God.

Of the four cases of conversion described in our passage (we say *four,* for the two mentioned in verse 35 are linked together) *no two were alike!* The first two heard a preacher proclaiming Christ as "the lamb of God," and, in consequence, promptly sought out the Saviour for themselves. Simon Peter, the next one, was "brought" to Christ by his brother, who had followed and found the Saviour on the previous day. Philip, the third one, seemed to have no believer to help him, perhaps no fellow creature who cared for his soul; and of him we read, "Jesus would go forth into Galilee, and *findeth* Philip, and saith unto him, Follow me" (1:43). While the last, Nathanael, was sought out by his now converted brother Philip, and was warmly invited to come and see Christ for himself; and while making for

Him, the Saviour, apparently, advanced toward and met the seeking one. Putting the four together we may observe that the first found Christ as the result of a *preacher's message.* The second and fourth found Christ as the result of *the personal work* of a believer. In the case of the third there was *no human instrument* employed by God. The fact that the first came to Christ as the result of the ministry of John the Baptist, seems to show that God puts the *preaching* of the Word as of first importance in the saving of sinners. The fact that God honored the personal efforts of two of these early converts, shows He is pleased to give a prominent place to *personal work* in His means of saving souls. The fact that Philip was saved apart from all human instrumentality, should teach us that God has not reached the end of His resources even though preachers should prove unfaithful to their calling, and even though individual believers are too apathetic to go forth bidding sinners to come to Christ.

It is also to be noted that not only did these first converts find the Saviour in a variety of ways, but also that Christ Himself *dealt* differently with each one. For the two mentioned in v. 35 there was a searching question to test their motives in following Christ—"What seek ye?" For Simon Peter there was a striking declaration to convince him that Christ knew all about him, followed by a gracious promise to reassure his heart. For Philip there was nothing but a peremptory command—"Follow me." While for Nathanael there was a gracious word to disarm him of all prejudice and to assure his heart that the Saviour stood ready to receive him. Thus did the Great Physician deal with each man according to his individual peculiarities and needs.

Finally, observe how this passage brings out the *suitability* of Christ for all kinds of men. It is blessed to behold here, how the Saviour drew to Himself men of such widely different types and temperaments. There are some superficial sceptics who sneeringly declare that Christianity only attracts those or a particular type—the effeminate, the emotional, and the intellectually feeble. But such an objection is easily refuted by the facts of common observation. Christ has been worshipped and served by men and women of every variety of temperament and calling. Those who have delighted to own His name as The Name "which is above every name" have been drawn from every walk of life, as well as from every nation and tribe under the sun. Kings and queens, statesmen and soldiers, scientists and philosophers, poets and musicians, lawyers and physicians, farmers and fishermen have been among the number who have cried, "Worthy is the lamb." And in the cases of these early converts we find this principle strikingly illustrated.

The unnamed disciple of v. 35 is, by common consent, regarded as John, the writer of this fourth Gospel. John was the disciple who leaned on the Master's bosom, devoted and affectionate. He was "the disciple whom Jesus loved:" he was, apparently, the only one of the twelve who stood by the Cross as the Saviour was dying. Andrew seems to have been a man with a calculating mind, what would be termed today, of a practical turn: no sooner had he come to Christ, than he goes at once and finds his brother Simon, tells him the good news that they had found the Messiah, and brought him to Jesus; and, *he* was the one to observe the lad with the five barley loaves and two small fishes, when the hungry multitude was to be fed (John 6:8, 9). Simon Peter was hot-headed, impulsive, full of zeal. Philip was sceptical and materialistic: he was the one to whom our Lord put the test question, "Whence shall we buy bread, that these may eat?" to which Philip replied, "Two hundred pennyworth of bread is not sufficient for them, that every one of them may take *a little*" (John 6:5, 7); and again, Philip was the one who said to Christ, "Lord, *show us* the Father, and it sufficeth us" (John 14:8). Nathanael, of whom least is known, was, evidently of a meditative and retiring disposition, whose life was lived in the back-ground, but of an open and frank nature, one "in who was no guile." How radically different, then, were these men in type and temperament, yet each of them found in Christ that which met his need and satisfied his heart! We regard these first converts as representative and illustrative cases, so that it behooves us to study each separately and in detail.

"Again the next day after John stood, and two of his disciples" (1:35). This is the place to ask the question, *What* was the fruitage of John's mission? What results accrued from his ministry? They were very similar to what may be expected to attend the labors of a servant of God, who is used of His Master, today. John had borne faithful witness to Christ: how had his ministry been received? In the first place, the religious leaders of his day *rejected* the testimony of God (Luke 7:30). In the second place, great crowds were attracted, and men of all sorts attended upon his ministry (Luke 3:7-15). In the third place, only a few were *really* affected by his message, and stood ready to receive the Messiah when He appeared. It has been much the same all through the ages. When God sends forth a man to take an active and prominent part in His service, the religious leaders look upon him with suspicion, and hold aloof in their fancied superiority. On the other hand, the vulgar, curious crowds, ever hungering for the novel and sensational, are attracted; but comparatively few are really touched in their consciences and hearts.

"Again the next day after John stood, and two of his disciples; and looking upon Jesus as he walked, he saith, Behold the lamb of God" (1:35, 36). Once more the Lord's forerunner heralds Him as "the lamb of God" (cf. v. 29). This teaches us that there are times when the servant of God needs to *repeat* the same message. It also informs us that the central and vital truth which God's messenger must press, unceasingly, is the *sacrificial* work of Christ. Never forget, brother preacher, that your chief concern is to present your Master as "the *lamb* of God!" Notice, also, we are told, "John *stood,* and two of his disciples; and *looking* upon Jesus as he walked, he saith, *Behold* the lamb of God." The words we have placed in italics call attention to a most important moral principle: if we would "look upon Jesus," if we would "Behold the lamb," we must *stand still;* that is, all fleshly activity must cease; we must come to the end of ourselves. This was the first truth which God taught Israel after they had been delivered from Egypt: as they were being pursued by the Egyptians, and came to the Red Sea, God's servant cried, "Fear ye not, *stand still,* and see the salvation of the Lord" (Ex. 14:13).

"And the two disciples heard him speak" (1:37). These two men were John and Andrew. By calling they were fishermen. They had already attached themselves to John, and had not only been baptized but were eagerly awaiting the promised Messiah and Saviour. At last the day arrived when their teacher, whom they trusted as God's prophet, suddenly checked them in their walk, and no doubt with almost breathless interest, laid his hand upon them, and pointing to a passing Figure, cried, "Behold the lamb of God!" There, in actual bodily form, was the One for whom the ages had waited. There, within reach of their own eyes, was the Son of God, who was to offer Himself as a sacrifice for sin. There, right before them, was He of whom one of these very two men later wrote, "That which was from the beginning, which we have heard, which we have seen with our eyes, which we have looked upon, and our hands have handled, of the word of Life" (I John 1:1).

How often this experience has been duplicated—duplicated *in principle,* we mean. How many of us used to hear Christ spoken of while as yet we had no personal knowledge of Him! We sat under a preacher who magnified His excellencies, we heard men and women singing "Thou O Christ art all I want, more than all in Thee I find," and we were impressed by the testimonies of God's saints as they bore witness to that Friend who sticketh closer than a brother. As we listened, our hearts yearned for a similar experience, but as yet we had no personal acquaintance with Him. When one day, perhaps we were waiting on the ministry of one of God's servants, or maybe we were alone in our room reading a portion of the Scriptures, or perhaps down on our knees crying to God to reveal His Son to us, or possibly, we were attending to the daily round of duty, when suddenly He who until then had been only a name, was revealed to us by God as a *living reality*. Then we could say with one of old, "I *have* heard of thee by the hearing of the ear: but *now* mine eye seeth thee" (Job 42:5).

And what is the consequence of such an experience? Ah! now the soul has been awakened, it feels some action is demanded of it. Such an one can no longer sit and *listen* to descriptions of Christ—he must rise and seek Him on his own account. Individual acquaintance with this unique and Divine Person is now desired above everything. The one thus awakened now seeks the

Lord with all his heart. Thus it was with these two disciples of John. As they heard their master say "Behold the lamb of God," we read, "they *followed* Jesus" (v. 37).

"Then Jesus turned and saw them following, and saith unto them, What seek ye?" (1:38). No sincere soul seeks or follows after Christ in vain. "Seek and ye shall find" is His own blessed promise. Accordingly, we find the Saviour turning to and addressing these enquiring souls. "What seek ye?" He says to them. At first sight this question strikes us as strange. Some, perhaps, have regarded it as almost a rebuff; yet it cannot be that. Personally, we look upon these words of our Lord as designed to test the *motive* of these two men, and to help them understand their own *purpose.* There are a great variety of motives and influences which make people become the outward and professed followers of Christ. In the days of which our passage treats, many soon "followed" Christ because the crowd streamed after Him and carried them along with it. Many "followed" Him for what they could get — the loaves and fishes, or the curing of their ailments and the healing of their loved ones. For a time many "followed" Him, doubtless, because it was the popular and respectable thing to do. But a few "followed" because they felt their deep need of Him, and were attracted by the perfections of His Person.

So it was then, and so it is now. Christ desired to be followed intelligently or not at all — that is, He will not accept formal or superstitious worship. What He wants is the heart — the heart that seeks Him for Himself! Hence the heart-searching question was put to these two men, "What seek ye?" What, dear reader, would be *your* answer to such a question? What seekest thou? The true answer to this question reveals your spiritual state. Let no one suppose he is not seeking anything. Such were an impossibility. Every heart has its object. If your heart is not set upon Christ Himself, it is set upon something which is not Christ. "*What* seek ye?" Is it gold, fame, ease and comfort, pleasure, or — what? On what is your *heart set?* Is it an increased knowledge of Christ, a more intimate acquaintance with Him, a closer walk with Him? Can you say, in measure at least, "As the heart panteth after the water brooks, so panteth my soul after thee, O God" (Psa. 42:1)!

It is beautiful to notice the reply made by these two earnest souls. "Master," they said, "Where dwellest thou?" (1:38). It seems strange that their answer to the Lord's query has puzzled so many who have pondered it. Most of the commentators have quite missed the point of these words and failed to see any direct connection between the question put by the Saviour and the reply He received. "Where dwellest thou?" Let us emphasize each word separately.

"*Where* dwellest thou?" How pathetic and tragic! What a question to ask the Son of God! How it brought out His humiliation! There was no need to ask where Caiaphas or Pilate dwelt, for everybody knew. But who among men cared to know, or could have told these two men if asked, where *Christ* dwelt?

"Where *dwellest* thou?" This was no question of mere idle curiosity. It showed that they longed to be *with Him.* What they desired was *fellowship,* as would have been made more evident if the translators had rendered it "Where *abidest* thou?" for "abiding" ever has reference to communion.

"Where dwellest *thou?*" they asked, in answer to "*What* seek ye?" It was not a "what" but a "whom" that their hearts were set upon. It was not a blessing, but the Blesser Himself that their spirits sought.

Unspeakably blessed it is to listen to the Saviour's response to the request made by these two inquiring souls: "He saith unto them, Come and see" (1:39). Ah, He knew their desires. He had read their hearts. He discerned that they sought His presence, His person, His fellowship. And He never disappoints *such* longings. "Come" is His gracious invitation. "Come" was a word which assured them of His welcome. "Come" is what He still says to all who labor and are heavy laden.

"And see" or "look:" this was, we believe, a further word to *test* them. When Christ conducted these two men to His dwelling place, would a brief visit suffice them? No, indeed. Mark the remainder of the verse, "they came and saw where he dwelt, and abode with him that day: for it was about the tenth hour." So fully had He won their confidence, so completely had He attracted their hearts to Himself, that though this was the first day of meeting with the Saviour, they *abode* with Him. Yes, they "abode" with *Him*. This is the word which uniformly speaks of *spiritual fellowship*. They abode with Him that day; for it was about the tenth hour; that is 4 P.M. We doubt not they remained with Him that night, but this is not expressly stated, and why? Ah, the Holy Spirit would not say they abode with *Him* "that night," for there *is no night* in His presence! Notice, too, the name of the place where He dwelt is not given. They "abode with him," where this is we are not told: He was but a *stranger* here, and those who follow Him must be strangers too. "They abode *with* him." How blessed! His abiding place was *theirs* too. And so shall it be for all believers throughout eternity. Has He not said, "I will come again, and receive you unto myself; that where I am, *there* ye may be also" (John 14:3)?

"One of the two which heard John speak, and followed him, was Andrew, Simon Peter's brother. He first findeth his own brother Simon, and saith unto him, We have found the Messiah, which is, being interpreted, the Christ" (1:40, 41). How this tells of the *satisfaction* which these two disciples had found in Christ! They wished to share with others their newborn joy! Andrew now sought out his brother Simon, and said to him, "We have found the Christ." That it is here said "*He* first findeth his own brother," implies that John (who ever seeks to hide himself, never once mentioning himself by name) did the same with *his* brother, James, a little later. This is the happy privilege of every young believer—to tell others of the Saviour he has found. For this no college training is required, and no authority from any church need be sought. Not that we despise either of these, but *all* that is needed to tell a perishing sinner of the Saviour is a heart acquaintance with Him yourself. It was not that Andrew went forth as a preacher, for *that* work he needed training, training by Christ Himself. But he set out to bear simple yet earnest witness of the Saviour he had found. The one whom he sought was his own brother, and this illustrates the fact that our personal responsibility *begins* with those nearest to us. Witness should first be borne in our own family circle.

"And he brought him to Jesus. And when Jesus beheld him, He said, Thou art Simon the son of Jona (or, perhaps better, 'the son of John'): thou shalt be called Cephas, which is by interpretation, A stone" (1:42). Here we find the Lord giving Simon a blessed promise, the force of which must be sought in what he was by nature. By natural temperament Simon was fiery and impetuous, rash and unstable. What would *such* a man's thoughts be, when he first heard Andrew? When he learned that Christ was here, and received invitation to go to Him, when he knew that the Master was seeking loyal and devoted servants, would he not say, That is all right for steady, reliable Andrew, but not for such as me? Would he not say, Why, I would be a stumbling-block to the cause of Christ: my impetuous temper and hasty tongue will only hinder, not help? If such thoughts passed through his mind, as we think most likely, then how these words of Christ which now fell on his ears must have reassured his heart: "When Jesus *beheld* him, he said, Thou art Simon the son of John." Thus the Lord showed that He was already thoroughly acquainted with Simon. But, He adds, "Thou shalt be called, A stone." "Cephas" was Aramaic, and signifies "a rock." "Petros" is the Greek and signifies "a stone." Peter is the English form of both Cephas and Petros. How blessed, then, was this promise of our Lord! "Thou art Simon" (his natural name), vacillating and unstable. Yes, I *know* all about you, "But thou shalt be called Cephas" (his new name), "a rock," fixed and stable. Christ, thus, promised to undertake for him. What a blessed fulfillment did this promise receive after the Saviour's resurrection!

We believe, though, there is a deeper meaning in this verse, and one which has a wider application, an application to all believers. In these verses which treat of the third "day," we have that which belongs, strictly, to the Christian dispensation. Peter must be viewed as a *representative* character. Thus viewed, everything turns upon *the meaning* of the proper nouns here. Simon means "hearing." Son of Jona is, correctly rendered we believe, in the R.V. "son of John," and John signifies "God's gift." We become Christians by hearing God's Word (Rom. 10:17), and this spiritual hearing is *God's gift,* and every believer becomes a *stone;* comp. "Ye also, as living stones, are built up a spiritual house" (I Pet. 2:5).

"The day following Jesus would go forth into Galilee, and findeth Philip, and saith unto him, Follow me" (1:43). How precious is this! What a lovely illustration of His own declaration "The Son of man is come *to seek* and to save that which was lost" (Luke 19:10). How it shows us the Good Shepherd going after this lone sheep of His! What we read of here is equally true of every case of genuine conversion. Whether the Lord uses a human instrument or not, it is Christ Himself who seeks out and finds each one who, subsequently, becomes His follower. Our seeking of Him is only the reflex action of His first seeking us, just as we love Him because He *first* loved us.

"Now Philip was of Bethsaida, the city of Andrew and Peter. Philip findeth Nathanael, and saith unto him, We have found him, of whom Moses in the law, and the prophets, did write, Jesus of Nazareth, the son of Joseph" (1:44, 45). Here, again, we see the effect that Christ's revelation of Himself has upon the newly born soul. The young believer partakes of the spirit of the One in whom he has believed. The compassion of the Saviour for the lost now fills his heart. There is a going out of his affections toward the perishing. He cannot remain silent or indifferent. He must tell others of the Saviour he has found, or rather, of the Saviour who has found him.

"And Nathanael said unto him, Can there any good thing come out of Nazareth?" (1:46). The one who seeks to win souls must expect to be met with objections. Many a sinner is hiding behind queries and quibbles. How then shall we meet them? Learn from Philip. All that he said to Nathanael in reply to his question, was, "Come and see." He invited his brother to come and *put Christ to the test* for himself. This is the wise way: do not be turned aside by the objections of the one to whom you are speaking, but continue to press upon him *the claims of Christ,* and then trust God to bless His own Word, in His own good time.

"Jesus saw Nathanael coming to him, and saith of him, Behold an Israelite indeed in whom is no guile" (1:47). Nathanael was honest and open. His question to Philip was no mere evasion, or hypocritical quibble; rather was it the voicing of a genuine difficulty. This must not be forgotten in our dealings with different souls. We must not conclude that *all* questions put to us are asked in a carping spirit. There are some people, many perhaps, who have *real* difficulties. What they need is light, and in order to obtain this they need to come to Christ. So in every case we cannot err if we present Christ and His claims upon each soul we meet. Nathanael was an "Israelite, indeed, in whom was no guile." We take it, he illustrates in his person one of the qualifications for becoming a good-ground hearer of the Word, namely, to receive that Word into "an honest and good heart."

"Nathanael saith unto him, Whence knowest thou me? Jesus answered and said unto him, Before that Philip called thee, when thou wast under the fig tree, I saw thee" (1:48). How this incident evidences the Deity of Christ! It displayed His *omniscience.* Christ saw Nathanael, and read his heart, *before* he came to Him. And, dear reader, He sees and reads each of us, too. Nothing can be hid from His all-seeing eye. No guise of hypocrisy can deceive Him.

"Nathanael answered and saith unto him, Rabbi, thou art the Son of God; thou art the king of Israel" (1:49). This was sure evidence that a Divine work had been wrought in Nathanael's soul. The eyes of his understanding were opened to behold the Divine glory of the Saviour. And promptly does he confess Him as "the Son of God." It is significant that in this fourth Gospel we find there are just *seven* who bear witness to Christ's Deity. First, John the Baptist (1:34); second, Nathanael (1:49); third, Peter (6:69); fourth, the Lord Himself (10:36); fifth, Martha (11:27); sixth, Thomas (20:28); seventh, the writer of this Gospel (20:31).

"Jesus answered and said unto him, Because I said unto thee I saw thee under the fig tree, believest thou? thou shalt see greater things than these. And he saith unto him, Verily, verily, I say unto you, Hereafter ye shall see the heaven open, and the angels of God ascending and descending upon the Son of man" (1:50, 51). Nathanael had been deeply impressed by what he had just witnessed, namely, this manifestation of Christ's omniscience. But, says the Lord, he should yet see greater things. Yea, the time should come when he should behold an open heaven, and the earth directly connected with it. He should see that to which in the far past, the dream and vision of Jacob had pointed: that which should be the antitype of the ladder which linked earth to heaven, was Christ Himself, and Nathanael with all believers, will see "the angels of God ascending and descending upon the Son of man."

It only remains for us to point out that here in the last half of John 1 we have three very remarkable *typical pictures*, treating of three distinct Dispensations. The first is found in 1:19-28. The second begins at 1:29 – "The next day" – and ends at 1:34. The third begins at 1:35 – "Again the next day" – and ends at 1:42.

I. In John 1:19-28 we have a typical picture of *the Old Testament Dispensation.*

1. Note the mention of the "priests and Levites" (v. 19), as representing the whole Levitical economy.
2. Note that "Jerusalem" is referred to here in this section (v. 19), but in none of the others.
3. Note how Israel's spiritual state during Old Testament times is here pictured by the ignorance and lack of discernment of the Jews (v. 19).
4. Note the reference here to "Elijah," and "that Prophet" who was to be like unto *Moses* (v. 21).
5. Note that John is here seen in the *wilderness* (v.23), symbolical of Israel's spiritual barrenness up to the time of Christ's appearing.
6. Note how accurately John's words, "there standeth one among you, whom ye know not" (v. 26), depicted Israel's blindness to the presence of Jehovah in their midst all through the Old Testament era.
7. Note that John bears witness to One who was to come "*after*" him (v. 27): such was the witness borne to Christ during Old Testament times.

II. In John 1:29-34 we have a typical picture of *the Messianic Dispensation* (embracing the period of Christ's public ministry on earth) intimated here by the words "The *next* day" (v. 29).

1. Note "John seeth Jesus coming unto him" (v. 29): this gives the historic beginning of *that* dispensation, for "the law and the prophets were until John" (Luke 16:16).
2. John proclaims Christ as "the lamb of God" (v. 29): it was to offer Himself in sacrifice that He had come here.
3. "After me" (v. 30); that is, after John the Baptist, who represented in his own person the terminal of the Old Testament dispensation.
4. "And I knew him not" (v. 31): this represents the ignorance of the Jews when Christ appeared.
5. "He shall be made manifest *to Israel*" (v. 31): cf. Matt. 15: 24, "I am not sent but unto the lost sheep of the house of Israel."
6. "The Spirit . . . abode upon *him*" (v. 32), and upon no others during that dispensation.
7. "This is the Son of God" (v. 34): it was as such Israel rejected Him.

III. In John 1:35-43 we have a typical picture of the *Christian* Dispensation, intimated by "Again the *next* day" (v. 35);

1. "The next day after, John *stood*" (v. 35): the end of John's *activities* were now reached: cf. v. 39 "the tenth hour"—the full measure of Israel's responsibility (cf, the ten commandments) was now reached.
2. There is here a turning away from Judaism, represented by John, and a following of the Lord Jesus (vv. 35-37): note Jesus "walked"—this was in contrast from John "stood."
3. It is as "the Lamb of God" Christians first know Christ (v. 36).
4. "They followed Jesus" (v. 37): this is what the Christian walk is,—"He has left us an example that we should follow his steps" (I Pet. 2:21).
5. Believers now *abide* with Christ (v. 39): that is, they enjoy *communion* with Him, meanwhile hidden from the world.
6. Christianity is to be propagated by the personal efforts of individual believers (vv. 40, 41).

7. Unto Simon Christ said, "Thou shalt be called a *stone*" (v. 42): it is as "living stones" that believers of *this* dispensation are "built up a spiritual house" (I Pet. 2:5), which is "a habitation of God through the Spirit" (Eph. 2:22).

The following questions are given to be studied so as to prepare the reader for our next chapter on John 2:1-11:—

1. "And the third day" (2:1)—after what? And *why* mention *which* "day?"
2. Why is a marriage scene introduced at this point?
3. Why is the "mother" of Jesus so prominent?
4. What is signified by the two statements made by the Lord to His mother in 2:4?
5. What is the typical significance of the "*six* waterpots of *stone*" (2:6)?
6. Of what is "wine" (2:10), the emblem?
7. What are the central lessons to be learned from this first miracle of Christ?

CHAPTER SIX

Christ's First Miracle

John 2:1-11

First of all we will give a brief and simple Analysis of the passage before us: —

1. The Occasion of the Miracle: a marriage in Cana, v. 1.
2. The Presence there of the Mother of Jesus, v. 1.
3. The Saviour and His Disciples Invited, v. 2.
4. Mary's Interference and Christ's Rebuke, vv. 3, 4.
5. Mary's Submission, v. 5.
6. The Miracle Itself, vv. 6-8.
7. The Effects of the Miracle, vv. 9-11.

We propose to expound the passage before us from a threefold viewpoint: first, its *typical* significance, second, its *prophetic* application, third, its *practical* teaching. It is as though the Holy Spirit had here combined three pictures into one. We might illustrate it by the method used in printing a picture in colors. There is first the picture itself in its black-edged outline; then, on top of this, is filled in the first coloring — red, or yellow, as the case may be; finally, the last color — blue or brown — may be added to the others, and the composite and variegated picture is complete. To use the terms of the illustration, it is our purpose to examine, separately, the different tints and shadings in the Divine picture which is presented to our view in the first half of John 2.

I. The typical Significance.

It is to be carefully noted that this second chapter of John opens with the word "and," which indicates that its contents are closely connected with what has gone before. One of the things that is made prominent in John 1 (following the Introduction, which runs to the end of v. 18) is the *failure of Judaism*, and the turning away from it to Christ. The failure of Judaism (seen in the ignorance of the Sanhedrin) is made plain by the sending of priests and Levites from Jerusalem to enquire of John who he was (1:19). This is made still more evident by the pathetic statement of the Baptist, "There standeth one among you, whom ye know not" (1:26). All this is but an amplication of that tragic word found in 1:11—"He came unto his own, and his own received him not." So blind were the religious leaders of Israel, that they neither knew the Christ of God stood in their midst, nor recognized His forerunner to whom the Old Testament Scriptures bore explicit witness.

Judaism was but a dead husk, the heart and life of it were gone. Only one thing remained, and that was the setting of it aside, and the bringing in "of a better hope." Accordingly, we read in Gal. 4:4, "But when the fulness of time was come, God sent forth his Son." Yes, the fulness of God's time *had* come. The hour was ripe for Christ to be manifested. The need of Him had been fully demonstrated. Judaism must be set aside. A typical picture of this was before us in John 1. The Baptist wound up the Old Testament system ("The law and the prophets were *until John*"—Luke 16:16), and in John 1:35-37 we are shown two (the number of competent testimony) of His disciples leaving John, and following the Lord Jesus.

The same principle is illustrated again in the chapter now before us. A marriage-feast is presented to our view, and the central thing about it is that *the wine had given out*. The figure *is* not difficult to interpret: "Wine" in Scripture is the emblem of *joy*, as the following passage will show: "And wine that *maketh glad* the heart of man" (Psa. 104:15); "And the vine said unto them, Should I leave my wine, *which cheereth God and man?*" (Judges 9:13). How striking, then, is what we have here in John 2! How accurate the picture. Judaism still existed as a religious system, but it ministered no comfort to the heart. It had degenerated into a cold, mechanical routine, utterly destitute of joy in God. Israel had lost the joy of their espousals.

"And there were set there six waterpots of stone, after the manner of the purifying of the Jews" (v. 6). What a portrayal of Judaism was this! Six is the number of *man*, for it was on the sixth day man was made, and of the Superman it is written, "Let him that hath understanding count the number of the beast: for it is the number of a man; and his number is six hundred threescore six" (Rev. 13:18). Yes, there were *six* waterpots standing there, not seven, the perfect number. All that was left of Judaism was of the flesh; God was not in it. As we read later on in this Gospel, the "feasts of the Lord" (*Lev.* 23:2) were now only "the feast of *the Jews*" (2:13, etc.).

Observe, too, that these six waterpots were of "stone," not silver which speaks of redemption, nor of gold which tells of Divine glory. As we read in Isa. 1:22, "Thy silver is become dross," and again in Lam. 4:1, "How is the gold become dim?" Profoundly significant, then, were these waterpots of *"stone."* And what is the more noticeable, *they were empty*. Again, we say, what a vivid portrayal have we here of Israel's condition at that time! No wonder the wine had given out! To supply *that* Christ was needed. Therefore, our chapter at once directs attention to Him as the One who alone can provide that which speaks of joy in God. Thus does John 2 give us another representation of the failure of Judaism, and the turning away from it to the Saviour. Hence, it opens with the word "and," as denoting the continuation of the same subject which had been brought out in the previous chapter.

In striking accord with what we have just suggested above, is the further fact, that in this scene of the Cana-marriage feast, the mother of Jesus occupies such a prominent position. It is to be noted that she is not here called by her personal name—as she is in Acts 1:14—but is referred to as "the mother of Jesus." (2:1). She is, therefore, to be viewed as a *representative* character. In this chapter Mary occupies the same position as the Baptist did in John 1. She stands for the *nation of Israel*. Inasmuch as through her the long promised "seed" had come, Mary is to be regarded here as gathering up into her person the entire Abrahamic stock.

What, then, does the Holy Spirit record here of Mary? Were her actions on this occasion in keeping with the representative character she filled? They certainly were. The record is exceedingly brief, but what is said is enough to confirm our line of interpretation. The mother of Jesus exhibited a woeful lack of spiritual discernment. It seems as if she presumed so far as to *dictate* to the Lord. Apparently she ventured to order the Saviour, and tell Him what to do. No otherwise can we account for the reply that He made to her on this occasion—"Woman, what have I to do with thee?" It was a pointed rebuke, and as such His words admonished her for her failure to render Him the respect and reverence which, as the Lord of Glory, were His due.

We believe that this unwonted interference of Mary was prompted by the same carnal motive as actuated His unbelieving "brethren" (i.e. other sons of Mary and Joseph) on a later occasion. In John 7:2-5 we read, "Now the Jew's feast of tabernacles was at hand. His brethren therefore said unto him, Depart hence, and go into Judea, that thy disciples also may see the works that thou doest. For there is no man that doeth anything in secret, and he himself seeketh to be known openly. If thou do these things, show thyself to the world. For neither did his brethren believe in him."

Mary wanted the Saviour to openly display His power and glory, and, accordingly, she was a true representative of the Jewish nation. Israel had no thought and had no heart for a suffering Messiah; what they desired was One who would immediately set up His kingdom here on earth. Thus, in Mary's ignorance (at that time) of the real character of Christ's mission, in her untimely longing for Him to openly display His power and glory, and in Christ's word of rebuke to her, "What have I to do with thee?" we have added evidence of the typical significance of this scene at the Cana marriage-feast—*the setting aside of Israel after the flesh.*

II. THE PROPHETIC APPLICATION.

What is recorded here in the first part of John 2 looks beyond the conditions that obtained in Israel at that time. The miracle which Christ performed at Cana possessed a *prophetic* significance. Like so much that is found in Scripture, the passage before us needs to be studied from a twofold viewpoint: its *immediate* and its *remote* applications. Above, we have sought to bring out what we believe to be the direct significance of this incident, in its typical and representative suggestiveness. Now we would turn for a moment to contemplate its more distant and prophetic application.

"And the third day:" so our chapter opens. The Holy Spirit presents to our view a *third day scene.* The third day is the day of *resurrection.* It was on the third day that the earth emerged from its watery grave, as it was on the third day the barren earth was clothed with vegetable life (Gen. 1:9, 11). There is an important scripture in Hosea 6:2 which should be placed side by side with John 2:1: "*After two days* will he revive us: *in the third day* he will raise us up, and we shall live in his sight." For almost two thousand years (two Days with God—see II Pet. 3:8) Israel has been without a king, without a priest, without a home. But the second "Day" is almost ended, and when the third dawns, their renaissance shall come.

This second chapter of John presents us with a prophetic foreshadowing of the future. It gives us a typical picture of Christ—the Third Day, following the two days (the two thousand years) of Israel's dispersion. Then will Israel *invite* Jesus to come to them: for, not until they say "Blessed is he that cometh in the name of the Lord" will He return to the earth. Then will the Lord be *married* to the new Israel, see Isa. 54; Hosea 2, etc. Then will Christ turn the water into wine—fill Israel's hearts with joy. Then will Israel say to the Gentiles (their servants), "Whatsoever he saith unto you, do." Then will Israel render unqualified obedience to Jehovah, for He will write His law in their hearts (Jer. 31:33). Then will Christ "manifest His glory" (John 2:11)—cf. Matt. 25:31; and thus will the best wine be reserved for Israel until the last.

Having touched, somewhat briefly, upon the typical and prophetic significance of this miracle, we turn now to consider,

III. THE PRACTICAL TEACHING.

"And the third day there was a marriage in Cana of Galilee; and the mother of Jesus was there: And both Jesus was called, and his disciples, to the marriage" (vv. 1, 2). Christ here sanctifies the marriage relationship. Marriage was ordained by God in Eden and in our lesson, the Saviour, for all time, set His stamp of approval upon it. To be present at this marriage was almost Christ's first public appearance after His ministry commenced. By gracing this festive gathering, our Lord distinguished and glorified this sacred institution. Observe that Christ was *invited* to be there. Christ's presence is essential to a happy marriage. The marriage where there is no place for our Lord and Saviour cannot be blest of God: "*Whatsoever* ye do . . . do *all* to the glory of God" (I Cor. 10:31).

"And when they wanted wine, the mother of Jesus saith unto him, They have no wine" (2:3). Mary's words seem to indicate two things: first, she ignored His Deity. Was she not aware that He was more than man? Did she not know that He was God manifest in the flesh? and, therefore, omniscient. *He* knew that they had no wine. Second, it appears as though Mary was seeking to exert her parental authority, by suggesting to Him what He ought to do under the circumstances.

"Jesus saith unto her, Woman, what have I to do with thee?" (2:4). This is an elliptical expression, and in the Greek literally read, "What to Me and thee?" We take it that the force of this question of our Lord's was, What is there common to Me and thee – cf Matt. 8:29 for a similar grammatical construction. It was not that the Saviour resented Mary's inviting His aid, but a plain intimation that she must allow Him to act in His own way. Christ here showed that His season of subjection to Mary and Joseph (*Luke* 2:51) was over, His public ministry had now commenced and she must not presume to dictate to Him.

Many of our readers, no doubt, have wondered why Christ here addressed His mother as "Woman." Scholars tell us that at the time our Lord used this word it would not sound harsh or rough. It was a designation commonly used for addressing females of all classes and relationships, and was sometimes employed with great reverence and affection. Proof of this is seen in the fact that while on the Cross itself Christ addressed Mary as "Woman," saying, "Behold thy son" (John 19:26 and see also 20:13, 15).

But we believe our Lord chose this word with Divine discrimination, and for at least two reasons. First, because He was here calling attention to the fact that He was more than man, that He was none less than the Son of God. To have addressed her as "mother" would have called attention to *human* relationships; but calling her "woman" showed that *God* was speaking to her. We may add that it is significant that the two times Christ addressed His mother as "woman" are both recorded in the Gospel of *John* which sets forth His Deity.

Again, the employment of this term "woman" denotes Christ's omniscience. With prophetic foresight He anticipated the horrible idolatry which was to ascribe Divine honors to her. He knew that in the centuries which were to follow, men would entitle her the Queen of angels and the Mother of God. Hence, He refused to use a term which would in any wise countenance the monstrous system of Mariolatry. Christ would here teach us that Mary was only a *woman*—"Blessed *among* women" (Luke 1:28) but not "blessed *above* women."

"Mine hour is not yet come" (2:4) became the most solemn watchword of His life, marking the stages by which He drew nigh to His death. *Seven* references are made in this Gospel to that awful "hour." The first is in our present passage in John 2:4. The second is found in 7:30—"Then they sought to take him: but no man laid hands on him, because *his hour* was not yet come." The third time is found in 8:20—"And no man laid hands on him; for *his hour* was not yet come." The fourth is in 12:23—"And Jesus answered them, saying, *The hour* is come, that the Son of man should be glorified." The fifth is in 12:27—"Now is my soul troubled; and what shall I say? Father, save me from *this hour*: but for this cause came I unto *this hour*." The sixth is in 16:32—"Behold, *the hour* cometh, yea, is now come, that ye shall be scattered, every man to his own, and shall leave me alone: and yet I am not alone, because the Father is with me." The seventh is in 17:1— "These words spake Jesus, and lifted up his eyes to heaven, and said, Father, *the hour* is come; glorify thy son, that thy son also may glorify thee." This "hour" was the hour of His *humiliation*. It was the "hour" of His suffering. But *why* should Christ refer to this "hour" when Mary was seeking to dictate to Him? Ah, surely the answer is not far to seek. That awful "hour" to which he looked forward, was the time when He *would be subject* to *man's* will, for then

He would be delivered up into the hands of sinners. But until then, He was not to be ordered by man; instead, He was about His *Father's* business, seeking only to do *His* will.

"His mother saith unto the servants, Whatsoever he saith unto you, do" (2:5). This is very beautiful. Mary meekly accepted the Lord's rebuke, recognized His rights to act as He pleased, and left the matter entirely in His hands. There is an important and much neglected lesson here for each of us. How prone *we* are to dictate to God! How often we are disposed to tell Him *what* to do! This is only another evidence of that detestable self-will which still operates in the believer, unless Divine grace subdues it. Our plain duty is to commit our way unto the Lord and then leave Him to supply our need in His own good time and manner.

We turn now to consider the miracle which Christ performed here at Cana. And first, a few words upon the *occasion* of it. The Lord Jesus recognized in this request of Mary's a call from His Father. He discerned in this simple act of furnishing the wedding-guests with wine a very different thing from what His mother saw. The performing of this miracle marked an important crisis in the Saviour's career. His act of turning the water into wine would alter the whole course of His life. Hitherto He had lived in quiet seclusion in Nazareth, but from this time on He would become a public and marked character. From henceforth He would scarcely have leisure to eat, and His opportunity for retired communion with the Father would be only when others slept. If He performed this miracle, and manifested forth His glory, He would become the gazing stock of every eye, and the common talk of every tongue. He would be followed about from place to place, thronged and jostled by vulgar crowds. This would provoke the jealousy of religious leaders, and He would be spied upon and regarded as a public menace. Later, this would eventuate in His being seized as a notorious criminal, falsely accused, and sentenced to be crucified. All of this stood out before Him as He was requested to supply the needed wine. But He did not shrink. He had come to do the will of God, no matter what the cost. May we not say it reverently, that as He stood there by Mary's side and listened to her words, that *the Cross* challenged Him. Certainly it was here anticipated, and hence His solemn reference to His "hour" yet to come.

In the second place, the *manner* in which the miracle was performed is deserving of our closest attention. "And there were set there six waterpots of stone, after the manner of the purifying of the Jews, containing two or three firkins apiece. Jesus saith unto them, Fill the waterpots with water. And they filled them up to the brim. And he saith unto them, Draw out now, and bear unto the governor of the feast. And they bare" (2:6-8). Christ was the One to work the miracle, yet the "servants" were the ones who seemed to do everything. *They* filled the waterpots, *they* drew off the wine, *they* bore it to the governor of the feast. There was no visible exhibition of putting forth of Divine power. Christ pronounced no magical formula: He did not even command the water to become wine. What was witnessed by the spectators was men at work, not God creating out of nothing. And all this speaks loudly to us. It was a parable in action. The means used were human, the result was seen to be Divine.

This was Christ's first miracle, and in it He shows us that God is pleased to use human instrumentality in performing the wonders of His grace. The miracle consisted in the supplying of wine and, as previously pointed out, wine symbolizes joy in God. Learn then, that the Lord is pleased to employ human agents in bringing joy to the hearts of men. And *what* was the element Christ used on this occasion in producing the wine? It was *water*. Now "water" is one of the symbols of the written Word (see Eph. 5:26). And how may we His servants, today, bring the wine of joy unto human hearts? By ministering the Word (see Eph. 5:26). And how may we His servants, today, "servants" Christ's command to fill those six empty waterpots of stone with water, might have seemed meaningless, if not foolish; but their obedience made them fellow-workers in the miracle! And to the wise of this world, who put their trust in legislation, and social amelioration, it seems useless to go forth unto the wicked with nothing more in our hands than a Book written almost two thousand years ago. Nevertheless, it has pleased God "by the foolishness of preaching to save them that believe" —foolish, that is, in the estimate of the worldly wise. Here then is blessed instruction for the servants of God today. Let us go forth with the Water of life, implicitly obeying the commands of our Lord, and He will use us to bring the wine of Divine joy to many a sad heart.

In the third place, consider the *teaching* of this miracle. In it we have a striking picture of *the regeneration of a sinner*. First, we see the condition of the natural man before he is born again: he is like an empty waterpot of stone—cold, lifeless, useless. Second, we see the worthlessness of man's religion to help the sinner. Those waterpots were set apart "after the manner of the purifying of the Jews"—they were designed for ceremonial purgation; but their valuelessness was shown by their emptiness. Third, at the command of Christ they were filled with water, and water is one of the emblems of the written Word: it is the Word which God uses in quickening dead souls into newness of life. Observe, too, these waterpots were filled "up to the brim"—God always gives good measure; with no niggardly hand does He minister. Fourth, the water produced wine, "good wine" (v. 10): symbol of the Divine joy which fills the soul of the one who has been "born of water." Fifth, we read "*This* beginning of miracles did Jesus." That is precisely what the new birth is—a "miracle." And not only so, it is always the "beginning of miracles" for the one newly born: regeneration is ever the *initial* work of grace. Sixth, observe "this beginning of miracles did Jesus in Cana of Galilee, and *manifested forth His glory.*" It is thus, in the regeneration of dead sinners, that the "glory" of our Saviour and Lord is "manifested." Seventh, observe, "And His disciples *believed* on him." A dead man cannot believe. But the first movement of the newly born soul is to turn to Christ. Not that we argue an interval of time between the two, but as cause stands to effect so the work of regeneration precedes the act of believing in Christ—cf. II Thess. 2:13: first, "sanctification of the Spirit," which is the new birth, *then* "belief of the truth."

But is there not even a deeper meaning to this beginning of Christ's miracles? Is it not profoundly significant that in this first miracle which our Saviour performed, the "wine," which is the symbol of *His shed blood,* should be so prominent! The marriage-feast was the occasion of joy and merriment; and does not God give us here something more than a hint that in order for His people to be joyous, the precious blood of His Son must be first poured forth! Ah, that is the foundation of every blessing we enjoy, the ground of all our happiness. Hence did Christ *begin* His supernatural works of mercy by producing that which spoke of His sacrificial death.

"When the ruler of the feast had tasted the water that was made wine, and *knew not* whence it was: (but the *servants* which drew the water *knew;*) the governor of the feast called the bridegroom" (2:9). This parenthetical statement is most blessed. It illustrates an important principle. It was the *servants* — not the "disciples," nor yet Mary — who were *nearest* to the Lord on this occasion, and who possessed the knowledge of His mind. What puzzled the "ruler of the feast" was no secret to these "servants." How different are God's ways from ours! The Lord of glory was here as "Servant." In marvelous grace He came "not to be ministered unto, but to minister:" therefore, are those who are humble in service, and those engaged in the humblest service, *nearest to Him.* This is their reward for turning their backs upon the honors and emoluments of the world. As we read in Amos 3:7 — "Surely the Lord God will do nothing, but he revealeth his secret unto (Ah, unto whom?) *his servants* the prophets." It is like what we read in Psa. 103:7 — "He *made known* his ways unto Moses;" and who was Moses? Let Scripture answer: "Now the man Moses was *very* meek *above all* the men which were upon the face of the earth" (Num. 12:3)! Yes, "the *meek* will he guide in judgment: and the *meek* will he teach his way" (Psa. 25:9).

Those who determine to occupy the position of authority (as *Mary* did here) are not taken into the Lord's secrets. Those who wish to be in a place like the "*ruler* of the feast," know not His thoughts. But those who humble themselves to take the *servant* position, who place themselves at Christ's disposal, are the ones who share His counsels. And in the day to come, when He will provide the true wine of the kingdom, those who have served Him during the time of His absence, shall then be under Him the dispensers of joy. Has he not promised, "If any man *serve me*, him will my Father *honor?*"

"And saith unto him, Every man at the beginning doth set forth good wine; and when men have well drunk, then that which is worse: but thou hast kept the good wine until now" (2:10). This illustrates the ways of men and the ways of God. The world (and Satan also) gives its best first, and keeps the worst for the last. First the *pleasures* of sin – for a season – and then the *wages* of sin. But with God it is the very opposite. He brings His people into the wilderness before He brings them into the promised inheritance. First the Cross then the crown. Fellow believer, for us, the best wine is yet to be: "The path of the just is as the shining light, that shineth *more and more* unto the perfect day" (Prov. 4:18).

One more observation on this passage and we must close. What a message is there here for the unsaved! The natural man has a "wine" of his own. There is a carnal happiness enjoyed which is produced by "the pleasures of sin" – the merriment which this world affords. But how fleeting this is! How unsatisfying! Sooner or later this "wine," which is pressed from "the vine *of the* earth" (Rev. 14:18), gives out. The poor sinner may be surrounded by gay companions, he may be comfortably circumstanced financially and socially, yet the time comes when he discovers he has "no wine." Happy the one who is conscious of this. The discovery of our own wretchedness is often the turning point. It prepares us to look to that One who is ready "to give unto them beauty for ashes, the oil of *joy* for mourning, the garment of praise for the spirit of heaviness" (Isa. 61:3). Unbelieving friend, there is only One who can furnish the true "wine," the "good" wine, and that is the Lord Jesus Christ. *He* can satisfy the longing of the soul. *He* can quench the thirst of the heart. *He* can put a song into thy mouth which not even the angels can sing, even the song of Redemption. What then must *you* do? What price must you pay? Ah, dear friend, listen to the glad tidings of grace: "Repent ye, and believe the Gospel" (Mark 1:15).

And now, we give a number of questions to prepare the interested student for the lesson to follow. Study, then, and prayerfully meditate on the following questions:—

1. *Why* is the cleansing of the temple referred to just here? —Note its place in the other Gospels.
2. Why did not Christ *drive out* "the doves?" v. 16.
3. What was indicated by the Jews' demand for a "sign?" v. 18.
4. Why did Christ point them forward to His *resurrection?* vv. 18-21.
5. Did the Lord's own disciples believe in the promise of His resurrection? If not, why? v. 22.
6. What solemn warning does v. 23 point?
7. What does v. 25 prove concerning Christ?

CHAPTER SEVEN

Christ Cleansing the Temple

John 2:12-25

"After this he went down to Capernaum, he, and his mother, and his brethren, and his disciples: and they continued there not many days" (John 2:12). This verse comes in as a parenthesis between the two incidents of the Cana marriage-feast and the cleansing the temple. Like everything else in this chapter, it may be studied from a twofold viewpoint, namely, its immediate application and its remote. In both of these applications the reference to *Capernaum* is the key, and Capernaum stands for two things—Divine favor and Divine judgment; see Matt. 11:23.

Taking the immediate application first, this verse tells us that for a short season Israel occupied the position of being in God's peculiar favor. The mother of Jesus (as we saw in our last chapter) stands for the nation of Israel, and particularly for Israel's *privileges*—for she was the one most honored among women. "His brethren" represents the nation of Israel in *unbelief;* proof of this is found in John 7:5. "His disciples" were the little remnant in Israel who *did* believe in Him, see 2:11. With these, the Lord Jesus went down to Capernaum; but they "continued there not many days." Not for long was Israel to enjoy these special favors of God. Soon Christ would leave them.

But this twelfth verse also has a prophetic significance. Its double application being suggested by the twofold meaning of Capernaum. Capernaum, which was exalted to heaven, was to be brought down to hell. Hence the force of "He went *down* to Capernaum." So it was with the nation of Israel. They had been marvelously favored of God, and they should be as severely punished. They should go *down* into the place of punishment—for this is what Capernaum speaks of. And this is exactly where the Jews have been all though this Christian dispensation. And how blessed to note that as the mother, brethren, and disciples of Christ (who represented, respectively, the nation of Israel privileged, but unbelieving, and the little remnant who did believe) went *down* to Capernaum—the place of Divine judgment—that the Lord Jesus went *with them.* So it has been throughout this Christian dispensation. The Jews have suffered severely, under the chastisements of God, but the Lord had been *with them* in their dispersion— otherwise they had been utterly consumed long, long ago. The statement "they continued there *not many days*" is also in perfect keeping with its prophetic significance and application. Only *two* "days" shall Israel abide in that place of which Capernaum speaks; on the third "day" they shall be delivered—see Hosea 6:2.

Let us now give a brief and simple Analysis of the passage which is to be before us: the Cleansing of the Temple:—

1. The Time of the Cleansing, v. 13.
2. The Need of the Cleansing, v. 14.
3. The Method of Cleansing, vv. 15, 16.
4. The Cause of the Cleansing, v. 17.
5. The Jews' demand for a Sign and Christ's reply, vv. 18-22.
6. Christ's miracles in Jerusalem and the unsatisfactory result, vv. 23, 24.
7. Christ's knowledge of the human heart, v. 25.

We shall study this passage in a manner similar to that followed in our exposition of the first half of John 2, considering first, the *typical* meaning of the cleansing of the Temple; and, second, its *practical* suggestions.

I. THE TYPICAL MEANING.

The first of the questions which we placed at the end of the last chapter, and which we asked our readers to meditate on in preparation for this, was, "*Why* is the cleansing of the temple referred to just here?" The careful student will have noticed that in each of the other Gospels, the cleansing of the temple is placed right at the close of our Lord's public ministry, as one of the last things He did before His apprehension. But here, the Holy Spirit has placed Christ's cleansing of the temple almost at the beginning of His public ministry. This has led the majority of the commentators to conclude that these were two totally different occasions and incidents, separated by a space of three years. In support of this conclusion some plausible arguments are advanced, but we are not at all sure of their validity. Personally, we are strongly inclined to believe that what is recorded in Matt. 21:12, 13 is the same incident as is before us here in John 2, and that the Holy Spirit has ignored the chronological order (as is so often the case in the Gospels) for His own good reasons. What these reasons may be we shall suggest below. Before advancing them, let us first state why we regard the cleansing of the temple here in John 2 as being identical with that which is described in Matt. 21:12, 13, and the parallel passages in Mark and Luke.

The points of likeness between the two are so striking that unless there is irrefutable evidence that they are separate incidents, it seems to us the most natural and the most obvious thing to regard them as one and the same. We call attention to seven points of resemblance.

First, Matthew places the cleansing of the temple at the beginning of the *Passover* week, and John tells us that "the Jews" *Passover* was at hand (2:12).

Second, Matthew mentions those that "*sold* and bought" being in the temple (21:12); John says the Lord found in the temple "those that *sold* oxen," etc. (2:14).

Third, Matthew refers to the presence of those that "sold *doves*" (21:12); John also speaks of the "*doves*" (2:16).

Fourth, Matthew tells us that Christ "*overthrew* the tables of the money-changers" (21:12); John also tells us that Christ "*overthrew* the tables" (2:15).

Fifth, Matthew mentions that Christ "*cast out all them* that sold and bought in the temple" (21:12); John declares He "*drove them all out* of the temple" (2:15). Note, in the Greek it is the *same* word here translated "drove" as is rendered "cast out" in Matthew!

Sixth, Matthew declares Christ said, "My house shall be called a house of prayer; but ye have made it a den of thieves" (21:13); John records that the Lord said, "Make not my Father's house a house of merchandise" (2:16). We have no doubt that the Lord made *both* of these statements in the same connection, but John records the one which expressly affirmed His Divine Sonship. In each case Christ declared the temple was God's.

Seventh, Matthew records how Christ spent the night in Bethany, and next morning He returned to Jerusalem, and was in the temple teaching, when the chief priests and elders of the people came to Him and said, "By what authority *doest thou these things?*" (21:23). John also records that after Christ had cleansed the temple, the Jews said to Him, "What sign showest thou unto us, seeing that *thou doest these things?*" (2:18).

If, then, our conclusion be correct, that this cleansing of the Temple occurred at the close of our Lord's ministry, the question returns upon us, *Why* has the Holy Spirit taken this incident out of its chronological setting and placed it by the side of our Lord's miracle where He changed the water into wine? We believe the answer to this question is not far to seek. We suggest that there was a double reason for placing this incident in juxtaposition with the Cana marriage-feast scene. First, it furnished added proof of the abject failure of Judaism; second, it completed the prophetic picture of Christ in the Millenium which John 2 supplies. We shall enlarge upon each of these points below.

In the previous chapters we have pointed out how that in the opening portion of John's Gospel two things are noticed repeatedly—the setting aside of Judaism, and the turning away from it to Christ. This was emphasized at some length in our last chapter, where we showed that the giving out of the wine at the Cana marriage-feast, and the presence of the six waterpots of stone standing there empty, symbolized the spiritual condition of Israel at that time—they had lost the joy of their espousals and were devoid of spiritual life.

In the passage which is now before us, an even darker picture still is presented to view. Here all figures and symbols are dropped, and the miserable state of Judaism is made known in pointed and plain terms. Up to this stage, Israel's miserable condition spiritually, had been expressed by *negatives;* the Messiah was there in their midst, but, said His forerunner to the Jerusalem embassy, Him "ye know *not*" (1:26); so, again, in the first part of chapter 2, "They have *no* wine" (2:3). But here, in the second half of John 2, the *positive* evil which existed is fully exposed—the temple was profaned.

"And the Jews' passover was at hand, and Jesus went up to Jerusalem" (2:13). Here is the first key to that which follows. The "*Lord's* passover" (Ex. 12:11) had degenerated into "the passover of *the Jews.*" But this is not the particular point upon which we would now dwell. What we would call attention to, particularly, is the time-mark given here. Two things are linked together; the passover and the cleansing of the temple. Now the reader will recall at once, that one of the express requirements of God in connection with the observance of the passover was, that all leaven must be rigidly excluded from the houses of His people. The passover was a busy time for every Jewish family: each home was subject to a rigorous examination, lest ceremonial defilement, in the form of leaven, should be found therein. "No leaven in your houses" was the requirement of the Law.

Now the center of Israel's ceremonial purity was the temple, the Father's House. Israel gloried in the temple, for it was one of the chief things which marked them off from all other nations, as the favored people of God. What other race of people could speak of Jehovah dwelling in their midst? And now Jehovah Himself was there, incarnate. And what a sight met His eye! The House of prayer had become a house of merchandise; the holy place of worship was now "a den of thieves." Behold here the light shining in the darkness and exposing the real nature of things. No doubt the custodians of the temple would have stood ready to excuse this reproach upon God's honor. They would have argued that these money changers and cattle dealers, in the temple courts, were there as a convenience to those who came to the temple to worship. But

Christ lays bare their real motive. "Den of thieves" tells us that the love of money, *covetousness*, lay at the bottom of it all.

And what is "covetousness?" What is the Divine symbol for it? Let us turn the light of Scripture on these questions. Notice carefully what is said in I Cor. 5:6-8. Writing to the Corinthian believers, the Holy Spirit through the apostle Paul says, "Your glorying is not good. Know ye not that a little leaven leaveneth the whole lump? Purge out therefore the old leaven, that ye may be a new lump, as ye are unleavened. For even Christ our passover is sacrificed for us: Therefore let us keep the feast, not with old leaven, neither with the leaven of malice and wickedness; but with the unleavened bread of sincerity and truth." To what was he referring here under the figure of "leaven?" Mark what follows: "I wrote unto you in an epistle not to company with fornicators: yet not altogether with the fornicators of this world, or with the covetous, or extortioners, or with idolators" (vv. 9, 10). *Leaven,* then, here refers (among other things) to *covetousness, extortion and idolatry*. Now go back again to John 2. The feast of the passover was at hand, when all leaven must be removed from Israel's dwellings. And there in the temple, were the cattle dealers and moneychangers, actuated by *covetousness* and *practicing* extortion. What horrible desecration was this! Leaven in the temple of God!

But let us turn on the light of one more passage. In Col. 3:5 we read, "covetousness, which is *idolatry*." Ah, does not this reveal the emptiness of Israel's boast! The nation prided itself upon its monotheism—they worshipped not the many gods of the heathen. The Jews boasted that they were free from idolatry. Yet *idolatry*—"covetousness"—*was* the very thing the Son of God found in His Father's House. Note again, the force of I Cor. 5:10, covetousness, extortion, and idolatry are the three things there mentioned under the symbol of "leaven." Here, then, is the first reason why the Holy Spirit has placed this incident just where He has in this Gospel. It furnishes a striking climax to what has gone before. Put together these three things, and see what a glaring picture they give us of Judaism: first, a *blinded priesthood* (John 1:19-26); second, a *joyless nation* (no "wine," John 2:3); third, a *desecrated temple*. (John 2:16).

We turn now to consider

II. THE PRACTICAL LESSONS.

1. We see here the holy zeal of Christ for the Father's house. "Worshippers coming from remote parts of the Holy Land, found it a convenience to be able to purchase on the spot the animals used in sacrifice. Traders were not slow to supply this demand, and vying with one another they crept nearer and nearer to the sacred precincts, until some, under pretense of driving in an animal for sacrifice, made a sale within the outer court. This court had an area of about 14 acres, and was separated from the inner court by a wall breast high, and bearing intimations which forbade the encroachment of Gentiles on pain of death. Round this outer court ran marble colonnades, richly ornamented and supported by four rows of pillars, and roofed with cedar, affording ample shade to the traders.

"There were not only cattle-dealers and sellers of doves, but also money-changers; for every Jew had to pay to the Temple treasury an annual tax of half a shekel, and this tax could be paid only in sacred currency. No foreign coin, with its emblem of submission to an alien king, was allowed to pollute the Temple. Thus there came to be need of money-changers, not only for the Jew who had come up to the feast from a remote part of the empire, but even for the inhabitants of Palestine, as the Roman coinage had displaced the shekel in ordinary use.

"Cattle-dealers and money-changers have always been notorious for making more than their own out of their bargains, and facts enough are on record to justify our Lord calling this particular market 'a den of thieves.' The poor were shamefully cheated, and the worship of God was hindered and impoverished instead of being facilitated and enriched. The worshipper who came to the temple seeking quiet and fellowship with God had to push his way through the touts of the dealers, and have his devotional temper dissipated by the wrangling and shouting of a cattlemarket. Yet although many must have lamented this, no one had been bold enough to rebuke and abolish the glaring profanation" (*Dr. Dods*). But the Lord Jesus Christ could not suffer His Father's house to be reproached thus. Zeal for God consumes Him and without hesitation He cleanses the temple of those who defiled it.

2. "And when he had made a scourge of small cords, he drove them all out of the temple, and the sheep, and the oxen; and poured out the changers' money, and overthrew the tables" (2:15). How this brings out the *Deity* of Christ! First, He identifies Himself with the temple, terming it "My Father's house," and thus affirming His Divine Sonship. This was something which none other had dreamed of doing. Neither Moses, Solomon nor Ezra, ever termed the tabernacle or the temple *his* "Father's house." Christ alone could do this. Again; mark the result of His interference. One man, single handed, takes a whip and the whole crowd flees in fear before Him. Ah, this was no mere man. It was the terror of *God* that had fallen upon them.

3. This incident brings before us a side of Christ's character which is almost universally ignored today. We think of the Lord Jesus as the gentle and compassionate One. And such He was, and still is. But this is not all He is. God is *Light* as well as Love. God is *inflexibly righteous* as well as infinitely gracious. God is *holy* as well as merciful. And we do well to remind ourselves of this. Scripture declares "it is a fearful thing to fall into the hands of the living God," as all who defy Him will yet discover. Scripture speaks of "the *wrath* of the lamb," and our lesson furnishes us with a solemn illustration of this. The unresisting money-changers and cattle-dealers, fleeing in terror before His flashing eye and upraised hand, give warning of what shall happen when the wicked stand before the throne of His judgment.

4. This incident rebukes the present-day desecration of the house of prayer. If the holy anger of the Lord Jesus was stirred when He beheld the profanation of that House which was to be a "house of prayer," if the idolatrous commercialization of it caused Him to cleanse it in such a drastic manner, how must He now regard many of the edifices which have been consecrated to His name! How tragically does history repeat itself. The things which are now done in so many church-houses – the ice cream suppers, the bazaars, the moving picture shows and other forms

of entertainment—what are these but idolatrous commercialization of these "houses of prayer." No wonder that such places are devoid of spirituality and strangers to the power of God. The Lord will not tolerate an unholy mixture of worldly things with spiritual.

5. One of the questions we drew up at the close of the last chapter was, "Why did not Christ *drive out* the 'doves'?" The answer to this is found in Isa. 52:13, where God through His prophet, declared of the Messiah then to come, "Behold, my servant shall deal prudently." The "prudence" of Christ was strikingly evidenced by His mode of procedure on this occasion of the cleansing of the temple. The attentive reader will observe that He distinguished, carefully, between the different objects of His displeasure. The oxen and sheep He *drove out*, and these were in no danger of being lost by this treatment. The money of the changers He *threw on the ground*, and this could be easily picked up again and carried away. The doves He simply ordered to be *taken away*: had He done more with them, they might have flown away, and been lost to their owners. Thus, the perfect One combined wisdom with zeal. How differently would Moses or Elijah have acted under similar circumstances. But even in His anger Christ deals in *prudence*. Christ *rebuked* all, yet none were really injured, and nothing was lost. O that we may learn of Him Who has left us such a perfect example.

6. "Then answered the Jews and said unto him, What sign showest thou unto us seeing that thou doest these things?" (2:18). This demand for a "sign" evidenced their blindness, and gave proof of what the Baptist had said—"There standeth one among you whom ye know not" (1:26). To have given *them* a sign, would only have been to confirm them in their unbelief. Men who could desecrate God's house as they had, men who were utterly devoid of any sense of what was due Jehovah, were judicially blinded, and Christ treats them accordingly: "Jesus answered and said unto them, Destroy this temple, and in three days I will raise it up" (v. 19). He spoke in language which was quite unintelligible to them. "Then said the Jews, Fortv and six years was this temple in building,

and wilt thou rear it up in three days? But He spake of the temple of his body" (2:20, 21). But why should the Lord express Himself in such ambiguous terms? Because, as He Himself said on another occasion, "Therefore speak I to them in parables: because seeing they see not; and hearing they hear not, neither do they understand" (Matt. 13:13). Yet, in reality, our Lords' reply to these Jews was much to the point. In raising Himself from the dead He would furnish the final proof that He was God manifest in flesh, and if God, then the One Who possessed the unequivocal right to cleanse the defiled temple which bore His name. It is very significant to compare these words of Christ here with what we find in Matt. 21:24-27, spoken, we doubt not, on the same occasion. When challenged as to His authority, Matthew tells us He appealed to the witness of His *forerunner,* which was primarily designed for the Jews after the flesh. But John mentions our Lord's appeal to His own *resurrection,* because this demonstrated His Deity, and has an evidential value for the whole household of faith.

7. Another of the questions asked at the close of the previous chapter was "Did the Lord's own disciples believe in the promise of His resurrection?" The answer is, No, they did not. The evidence for this is conclusive. The death of the Saviour shattered their hopes. Instead of remaining in Jerusalem till the third day, eagerly awaiting His resurrection they retired to their homes. When Mary Magdalene went to tell His disciples that she had seen the risen Christ, they "believed not" (Mark 16:11). When the two disciples returned from Emmaus and reported unto the others how the Saviour had appeared unto them and had walked with them, we are told, "neither believed they them" (Mark 16:13). The testimony of these eyewitnesses seemed to them as idle tales (Luke 24:11). But how is this to be explained? How can we account for the persistent unbelief of these disciples? Ah, is not the answer to be found in the Lord's teaching in the Parable of the Sower? Does He not there warn us, that the great Enemy of souls comes and *catches away* the "seed" sown! And this is what had taken place with these disciples. They had heard the Saviour say He *would* raise up the temple of His body in three days, but instead of treasuring up this precious promise in their hearts, and being comforted by it, they had, through their unbe-

lief, allowed the Devil to snatch it away. Their unbelief, we say, for in verse 22 we are told, "When therefore he was risen from the dead, his disciples remembered he had said this unto them; and they believed the Scriptures, and the word which Jesus had said." It was not until *after* He had risen that they "remembered" and "believed" the word which Jesus had said. And what was it that enabled them to "remember" it then? Ah, do we not recall what Christ had said to them on the eve of His crucifixion, "But the Comforter, the Holy Spirit, whom the Father will send in my name, he shall teach you all things, *and bring all things to your remembrance,* whatsoever I have *said* unto you" (John 14:26). What a striking and beautiful illustration of this is given us here in John 2:22!

8. "Now when he was in Jerusalem at the passover, in the feast, many believed in his name, when they saw the miracles which he did. *But Jesus did not commit himself unto them,* because he knew all" (2:23, 24). What a word is this! How it evidences human depravity! Fallen man is a creature that God will not trust. In Eden Adam showed that man after the flesh is not to be trusted. The Law had proved him still unworthy of the confidence of God. And now this same character is stamped upon him by the Lord Jesus Himself. As another has said, "Man's affections may be stirred, man's intelligence informed, man's conscience convicted; but still God cannot trust him." (J. E. B.). Man in the flesh is condemned. Only a new creation avails before God. Man must be "born again."

9. "Jesus did not *commit himself* unto them" (v. 24). The Lord's example here is a warning for us. We do well to remember that all is not gold that glitters. It is not wise to trust in appearances of friendliness on short acquaintance. The discreet man will be kind to all, but intimate with few. The late Bishop Ryle has some practical counsels to offer on this point. Among other things he said, "Learn not to place yourself rashly in the power of others. Study to develop a wise and a happy moderation between universal suspiciousness and that of making yourself the sport and prey of every pretender and hypocrite."

10. "Jesus did not commit himself unto them, because he knew all, and needed not that any should testify of man: *for he*

knew what was in man" (2:24, 25). Here we are shown the Saviour's perfect knowledge of the human heart. These men could not impose upon the Son of God. He knew that they were only "stony ground" hearers, and therefore, not to be depended upon. They were only intellectually convinced. Our Lord clearly discerned this. He knew that their profession was not from the heart. And reading thus their hearts He manifested His *omniscience.* The force of what is said in these closing words of John 2 will be made more evident if we compare them with I Kings 8:39: "Hear thou in heaven thy dwelling-place, and forgive—whose heart thou knowest; (for thou, *even thou only,* knowest the hearts of all the children of all men.)"

It only remains for us to point out how that there is a series *of most* striking contrasts between the two incidents recorded in the first and second parts of this chapter—the making of water into wine at the Cana marriage-feast, and the cleansing of the Temple. 1. In the one we have a *festive* gathering; in the other a scene of Divine *judgment.* 2. To the former the Lord Jesus was *invited;* in the later He took the initiative *Himself.* 3. In the former case He employed *human instruments;* in the latter He acted all *alone.* 4. In the former He *supplied* the wine; in the latter He *emptied* the temple. 5. In the former, His fact of making the wine was *commended;* in the cleansing of the temple, He was *challenged.* 6. In the former Christ pointed forward to His *death* (see 2:4); in the latter He pointed forward to His resurrection (see 2:19, 21). 7. In ie former He "manifested forth his *glory*" (2:11); in the latter He manifested His "zeal" for His Father's House (2:17).

Let the student prayerfully study and meditate upon the following questions in preparation for the next lesson, when we shall give an exposition of the first portion of John 3.

1. Why is Nicodemus referred to in this connection? v. 1.
2. Why are we told he came to Jesus "by night?" v. 2.
3. Was Nicodemus' conclusion justifiable? v. 2.
4. *Why* cannot a man "see" the kingdom of God except he be "born again?" v. 3.

5. What did Nicodemus' ignorance demonstrate? v. 4.
6. What does "born of water" mean? v. 5.
7. In what other ways is the blowing of the Wind analogous with the activities of the Holy Spirit in regeneration? v. 8.

CHAPTER EIGHT

Christ and Nicodemus

John 3:1-8

We begin with the usual Analysis of the passage that is to be before us:—

1. The Person of Nicodemus, v. 1.
2. The official Position of Nicodemus, v. 1.
3. The Timidity of Nicodemus, v. 2.
4. The Reasoning of Nicodemus, v. 2.
5. What did Nicodemus' ignorance demonstrate? v. 4.
6. The Stupidity of Nicodemus, v. 4.
7. The Instructing of Nicodemus, vv. 5-8.

"There was a man of the Pharisees, named Nicodemus, a ruler of the Jews: The same came to Jesus by night, and said unto him, Rabbi, we know that thou art a teacher come from God: for no man can do these miracles that thou doest, except God be with him" (3:1, 2). Nicodemus was a "ruler of the Jews," which means, most probably, that he was a member of the Sanhedrin. As such, he is to be viewed here as a representative character. He gives us another phase of the spiritual condition of Judaism. First, he came to Jesus "by night" (v. 2); second, he was altogether lacking in spiritual discernment (vv. 4, 10); third, he was dead in trespasses and sin, and therefore, needing to be "born again" (v. 7). As such, he was a true representative of the Sanhedrin—Israel's highest ecclesiastical court. What a picture, then, does this give us again of Judaism! For the Sanhedrin it was *nighttime,* they were in the dark. And like Nicodemus, their representative, the Sanhedrin were devoid of all spiritual discernment, and had no understanding in the things of God. So, too, like Nicodemus, his fellow-members were destitute of spiritual apprehension. Again we say, What light does this cast upon

Judaism at that time! So far, we have seen a *blinded* priesthood (1:21, 26); second, a joyless nation (2:3); third, a *desecrated* Temple (2:16); and now we have a *spiritually* dead Sanhedrin.

"The same came to Jesus by night." And *why* did Nicodemus come to the Lord Jesus by night? Was it because he was ashamed to be seen coming to Him? Did he approach Christ secretly, under cover of the darkness? This is the view generally held, and we believe it to be the correct one. Why else should we be told that he came "by night?" What seems to confirm the popular idea is that each time Nicodemus is referred to in the Gospel afterwards, it is *repeated* that he came to Jesus "by night." In John 7:50, 51 we read, "Nicodemus saith unto them, (he that came to Jesus by night, being one of them,) Doth our law judge any man, before it hear him, and know what he doeth?" And again in John 19:39 we are told, "And there came also Nicodemus, which at the first came to Jesus by night, and brought a mixture of myrrh and aloes, about a hundred pound weight." What is the more noticeable is that something *courageous* is recorded of Nicodemus: his boldness in reprimanding the Sanhedrin, and his intrepidity in accompanying Joseph of Arimathea at a time when all the apostles had fled. It seems as though the Holy Spirit had emphasized these bold acts of Nicodemus by reminding us that at first he acted timidly. One other thing which appears to confirm our conclusion is his use of the personal pronoun when Nicodemus first addressed the Saviour: "Rabbi," he said, "*we* know that thou art a teacher come from God." Why speak in the plural number unless he hesitated to commit himself by expressing *his own* opinion? and so preferred to shelter behind the conclusion drawn by others, hence the "we."

"The same came to Jesus by night, and said unto him, Rabbi, we know that thou art a teacher come from God: for no man can do these miracles that thou doest, except God be with him" (3:2). This was true, for the miracles of Christ differed radically from those performed by others before or since. But this very fact warns us that we need to examine carefully the credentials of other miracle-workers. Is the fact that a man works miracles a sure proof that he comes from God, and that God is with him?

To some the question may appear well-nigh superfluous. There are many who would promptly answer in the affirmative. How could any man perform miracles "except God be with him?" It is because this superficial reasoning prevails so widely that we feel it incumbent upon us to dwell upon *this* point. And it is because there are men and women today that work miracles, who (we are fully persuaded) *are not* "sent of God," that a further word on the subject is much needed.

In these times men and women can stand up and teach the most erroneous doctrines, and yet if they proffer as their credentials the power to perform miracles of healing, they are widely received and hailed as the servants of God. But it is generally overlooked that Satan has the power to work miracles, too, and frequently the great Deceiver of souls bestows this power on his emissaries in order to beguile the unstable and confirm them in error. Let us not forget that the magicians of Egypt were able, up to a certain point, to duplicate the miracles of Moses, and whence obtained they this power unless from that old Serpent, the Devil! Let us not forget the warning of the Holy Spirit in II Cor. 11:13, 14, "For such are false apostles, deceitful workers, transforming themselves into the apostles of Christ. And no marvel; for Satan himself is transformed into an angel of light." And, finally, let us not forget it is recorded in Scripture that of the Antichrist it is written, "Even him, whose coming is after the working of Satan with all power and signs and lying wonders" (II Thess. 2:9). Yes, Satan *is* able to work miracles, and also to deliver this power to others. So, then, the mere fact that a certain teacher works miracles is no proof that he is "come from God."

It is because we are in danger of being beguiled by these "deceitful workers" of Satan, who "transform themselves into the apostles of Christ," that we are exhorted to "believe not every spirit, but try the spirits whether they are of God: because many false prophets are gone out into the world" (I John 4:1). And it should not be forgotten that the church at Ephesus was commended by Christ because they had heeded this exhortation, and in consequence had "tried them which say they are apostles, and are not, and hast found them liars" (Rev. 2:2). "But," it will be asked, "*how* are we to test those who come unto us in the name of Christ?" A most important and timely question. We answer, *Not* by the personal *character* of those who claim to come from God, for as II Cor. 11:14, 15 tells us, "Satan himself is transformed into an angel of light. Therefore it is no great thing if his ministers also be transformed as *the ministers of righteousness*." And *not* by their power to work miracles. How then? Here is the Divinely inspired answer, "To the law and to the testimony: if they speak not according to *this word*, it is because there is no light in them" (Isa. 8:20). They must be tested by the written Word of God. Does the professed servant of God teach that which is in accord with the Holy Scriptures? Does he furnish a "Thus saith the Lord" for every assertion he makes? If he does not, no matter how winsome may be his personality, nor how pleasing his ways, no matter how marvelous may be the "results" he "gets," God's command is, "If there come any unto you, and bring not *this doctrine* (this teaching), receive him not into your house, neither bid him Godspeed" (II John 10). Let us emulate the Bereans, of whom it is recorded in Acts 17:11, "they received the word with all readiness of mind, and searched the scriptures daily, whether those things were so."

And how did the Lord receive Nicodemus? Notice, He did not refuse him an audience. It was night-time, and no doubt the Saviour had put in a full day, yet He did not seek to be excused. Blessed be His name, there is no unacceptable time for a sinner to seek the Saviour. Night-time it was, but Christ readily received Nicodemus. One of the things which impresses the writer as he reads the Gospels, is the blessed *accessibility* of the Lord Jesus. He did not surround Himself with a bodyguard of attendants, whose duty it was to insure his privacy and protect Him from those who could be a nuisance. No; He was easily reached, and blessedly approachable—quite unlike some "great" preachers we know of.

And what was Christ's response to Nicodemus' address? This "ruler of the Jews" hailed Him as "a teacher come from God," and such is the only conception of the Christ of God. But it is not as a Teacher the sinner must first approach Christ. What the sinner needs is to be "born again," and in order to do this he must have a *Saviour*. And it is of these very things our Lord speaks to Nicodemus—see verses 3 and 14. Of what value is teaching to one who is "*dead* in trespasses and sins," and who is even now, under the condemnation of a holy God! A saved person is a fit subject for teaching, but what the unsaved need is preaching, preaching which will expose their depravity, exhibit their deep need of a Saviour, and then (and not till then) reveal the One who is mighty to save.

Christ ignored Nicodemus' address, and with startling abruptness said, "Verily, verily, I say unto thee, Except a man be born again, he cannot see the kingdom of God." This brings us to the central truth of the passage before us—the teaching of our Lord upon the new birth. Here we find that He speaks of first, the supreme Importance of the new birth (v. 3); second, the Instrument of the new birth—"water" (v. 5); third, the Producer of the new birth—"the Spirit" (v. 5); fourth, the imperative Necessity of the new birth—a new nature, "spirit" (v. 6); sixth, the obvious Imperativeness of the new birth (v. 7); seventh, the Process of the new birth (v. 8). Let us consider each of these points separately.

1. The supreme *Importance* of the new birth. This is exhibited here in a number of ways. To begin with, it is profoundly significant that the new birth formed the first subject of the Saviour's teaching in this Gospel. In the first two chapters we learn of a number of things He *did*, but here in John 3 is the first discourse of Christ recorded by this apostle. It is not *how* man should live that we are first instructed by Christ in this Gospel, but how men are *made alive* spiritually. A man cannot live before he is born; nor can a dead man regulate his life. No man can live Godwards until he has been born again. The importance of the new birth, then, is shown here, in that the Saviour's instruction upon it is placed at the *beginning* of His teaching in this Gospel. Thus we are taught it is of basic, fundamental importance.

In the second place, the *importance* of the new birth is declared by the solemn terms in which Christ spoke of it, and particularly in the manner in which He prefaced His teaching upon it. The Lord began by saying, "Verily, verily," which means "Of a truth, of a truth." This expression is employed by Christ only when He was about to mention something of a momentous nature. The double "verily" denoted that what He was about to say was of solemn and weighty significance. Let the reader learn to pay special attention to what follows these "Verily, verily's" of the Saviour, found only in John.

In the third place, Christ here plainly intimated the supreme *importance* of the new birth by affirming that "Except a man be born again, he *cannot* see the kingdom of God" (v. 3). If then the kingdom of God cannot be seen until a man is born again, the new birth is shown to be a matter of vital moment for every descendant of Adam.

"Except a man be born again, he cannot see the kingdom of God" (3:3). There is some doubt in our mind as to exactly what is referred to here by "the kingdom of God." In the first place, this expression occurs nowhere else in this Gospel but here in John 3:3, 5. In the second place, this fourth Gospel treats of spiritual things. For this reason we think "the kingdom of God" in this passage has a moral force. It seems to us that Romans 14:17 helps us to understand the significance of the term we are here studying. "For the kingdom of God is not meat and drink; but righteousness, and peace, and joy in the Holy Spirit." In the third place, the kingdom of God could not be "seen" by Nicodemus except by the new birth. We take it, then, that the "kingdom of God" in John 3 refers to the *things* of God, spiritual things, which are discerned and enjoyed by the regenerate here upon earth (cf. I Cor. 2:10, 14). The word for "see" in the Greek is "eidon," which means "to know or become acquainted with." The full force, then, of this first word of Christ to Nicodemus appears to be this: "Except a man be born again he cannot come to know the things of God." Such being the case, the new birth is seen to be a thing of profound importance.

"Nicodemus saith unto him, How can a man be born when he is old? can he enter the second time into his mother's womb, and be born?" (3:4). What a verification was this of what the Lord had just told Nicodemus. Here was proof positive that this ruler of the Jews was altogether lacking in spiritual discernment, and quite unable to know the things of God. The Saviour had expressed Himself in simple terms, and yet this master of Israel altogether missed His meaning. How true it is that "the natural man receiveth not the things of the Spirit of God; for they are foolishness unto him: neither can he know them, because they are spiritually discerned" (I Cor. 2:14), and in order to have spiritual discernment a man must be born again. Till then he is blind, unable to *see* the things of God.

2. The *Instrument* of the new birth. "Jesus answered, Verily, verily, I say unto thee, Except a man be born of water and of the Spirit, he cannot enter into the kingdom of God" (v. 5). Regeneration is a being born "of water." This expression has been the occasion of wide difference of opinion among theologians. Ritualists have seized upon it as affording proof of their doctrine of baptismal regeneration, but this only evidences the weakness of their case when they are obliged to appeal to such for a proof text. However, it may be just as well if we pause here and give the scriptural refutation of this widely held heresy.

That baptism is in no wise essential to salvation, that it does not form one of the conditions which God requires the sinner to meet, is clear from many considerations. First, if baptism be necessary to salvation then no one was saved before the days of John the Baptist, for the Old Testament will be searched from beginning to end without finding a single mention of "baptism." God, who changes not, has had but one way of salvation since Adam and Eve became sinners in Eden, and if baptism is an indispensable prerequisite to the forgiveness of sins, then all who died from Abel to the time of Christ are eternally lost. But this is absurd. The Old Testament Scriptures plainly teach otherwise.

In the second place, if baptism be necessary to salvation, then every professing believer who has died during this present dispensation is eternally lost, if he died without being baptized. And this would shut heaven's door upon the repentant thief, as well as all the Quakers and members of the Salvation Army, the vast majority of whom have never been baptized. But this is equally unthinkable.

In the third place, if baptism be necessary to salvation, then we must utterly ignore every passage in God's Word which teaches that salvation is by grace and not of works, that it is a free gift and not bought by anything the sinner does. If baptism be essential to salvation, it is passing strange that Christ Himself never baptized any one (see John 4:2), for He came to "save his people from their sins." If baptism be essential to salvation, it is passing strange that the apostle Paul when asked point blank by the Philippian jailer, "What must I do to be saved?" answered by saying, "Believe on the Lord Jesus Christ, and thou shalt be saved." Finally, if baptism be essential to salvation, it is passing strange the apostle Paul should have written to the Corinthians, "I thank God I baptized none of you, but Crispus and Gaius" (I Cor. 1:14).

If then the words of Christ "born of water" have no reference to the waters of baptism, what do they signify? Before replying directly to this question, we must observe how the word "water" is used in other passages in this Gospel. To the woman at the well Christ said, "Whosoever drinketh of the *water* that I shall give him shall never thirst; but the *water* that I shall give him shall be in him a well of *water* springing up into everlasting life" (John 4:14). Was this literal "water?" One has but to ask the question to answer it. Clearly, "water" is here used *emblematically*. Again, in John 7:37, 38 we are told, "In the last day, that great day of the feast, Jesus stood and cried, saying, If any man thirst, let him come unto me, and drink. He that believeth on me, as the scripture hath said, out of his belly shall flow rivers of living *water*." Here, too, the word "water" is *not* to be understood literally, but emblematically. These passages in John's Gospel are sufficient to warrant us in giving the word "water" in John 3:5 a figurative meaning.

If then the Lord Jesus used the word "water" emblematically in John 3:5, to *what* was He referring? We answer, The *Word* of God. *This* is ever the instrument used by God in regeneration. In every other passage where the *instrument* of the new birth is described, it is *always* the Word of God that is mentioned. In Psa. 119:50 we read, "For Thy *word* hath *quickened* me." Again, in I Cor. 4:15 we find the apostle saying, "I have *begotten* you *through the gospel.*" Again, we are told "Of his own will *begat* he us with (what? – baptism? no but with) the *word* of truth" (James 1:18). Peter declares, "Being *born again*, not of corruptible seed, but of incorruptible, by the *word of God*, which liveth and abideth for ever" (I Peter 1:23).

The new birth, then, is by the Word of God, and one of the *emblems* of the Word is "*water.*" God employs quite a number of emblems to describe the various characteristics and qualities of His Word. It is likened to a "lamp" (Psa. 119:105) because it illumines. It is likened unto a "hammer" (Jer. 23:29) because it breaks up the hard heart. It is likened unto "water" because it *cleanses*: see Psa. 119:9; John 15:3; Eph. 5:26: "Born of water" means born of the cleansing and purifying Word of God.

3. The *Producer* of the new birth. "Born of water, and *of the Spirit*" (John 3:5). The Holy Spirit of God is the Begetter, the Word is the "seed" (I John 3:9) He uses. "That which is born of the flesh is flesh: and that which is *born of the Spirit* is spirit" (John 3:6). And again, "It is *the Spirit that quickeneth;* the flesh profiteth nothing" (John 6:63). Nothing could be plainer. No sinner is quickened apart from the Word.

The order which is followed by God in the new creation is the same He observed in the restoring of the old creation. A beautiful illustration of this is found in Gen. 1. The opening verse refers to the original creation of God. The second verse describes its subsequent condition, after it had been ruined. Between the first two verses of Gen. 1 some terrible calamity intervened – most probably the fall of Satan – and the fair handiwork of God was blasted. The Hebrew of Gen. 1:2 literally reads, "And the earth *became* a desolate waste." But six days before the creation of Adam, God began the work of restoration, and it is indeed striking to observe the order He followed. First, darkness abode upon "the face of the deep" (Gen. 1:2); second, "And the Spirit of God moved upon (Hebrew 'brooded over') the face of the waters"; third, "And God said, Let there be light" (Gen. 1:3); fourth, "And there was light." The order is exactly the same in the new creation. First, the unregenerate sinner is in darkness, the darkness of spiritual death. Second, the Holy Spirit moves upon, broods over, the conscience and heart of the one He is about to quicken. Third, *the Word* of God goes forth in power. Fourth, the result is "light" — the sinner is brought out of darkness into God's marvelous light. The Holy Spirit, then, is the One who produces the new birth.

4. The imperative *Necessity* of the new birth. "*Except* a man be born of water and of the Spirit, *he cannot enter into the kingdom of God*" (3:5). By his first birth man enters this world a sinful creature, and because of this he is estranged from the thrice Holy One. Of the unregenerate it is said, "Having the understanding darkened, being *alienated from the life of God* through the ignorance that is in them, because of the blindness of their heart." Unspeakably solemn is this. When Adam and Eve fell they were banished from the Paradise, and each of their children were born outside of Eden. That sin shuts man out from the holy presence of God, was impressively taught to Israel. When Jehovah came down on Sinai to give the Law unto Moses (the mediator), the people were fenced off at the base of the Mount, and were not suffered to pass on pain of death. When Jehovah took up His abode in the midst of the chosen people, He made His dwelling place inside the holy of holies, which was curtained off, and none was allowed to pass through the veil save the high priest, and he but once a year as he entered with the blood of atonement. Man then is *away from God*. He is, in his natural condition, where the prodigal son was — in the far country, away from the father's house — and except he be born again he cannot enter the kingdom of God.

"Except a man be born of water and of the Spirit, he *cannot* enter into the kingdom of God." This is not an arbitrary decree, but the enunciation of an abiding principle. Heaven is a prepared place for a prepared people. And this is the very nature of the case. An unregenerate man who has no relish at all for spiritual things, who is bored by the conversation of believers, who finds the Bible dull and dry, who is a stranger to the throne of grace, would be *wretched* in heaven. Such a man could not spend eternity in the presence of God. Suppose a fish were taken out of the water, and laid upon a salver of gold; suppose further that the sweetest of flowers surrounded it, and that the air was filled with their fragrance; suppose, too, that the strains of most melodious music fell upon its ears, would that fish be happy and contented? Of course not. And why not? Because it would be out of harmony with its environment; because it would be lacking in capacity to appreciate its surroundings. *Thus* would it be with an unregenerate soul in heaven.

Once more. The new birth is an imperative necessity because the natural man is altogether devoid of spiritual life. It is not that he is ignorant and needs instruction: it is not that he is feeble and needs invigorating: it is not that he is sickly and needs doctoring. His case is far, far worse. He is *dead* in trespasses and sins. This is no poetical figure of speech; it is a solemn reality, little as it is perceived by the majority of people. The sinner is spiritually lifeless and needs quickening. He is a spiritual corpse, and needs bringing from death unto life. He is a member of the old creation, which is under the curse of God, and unless he is made a new creation in Christ, he will lie under that curse to all eternity. What the natural man needs above everything else is life, Divine life; and as birth is the gateway to life, he *must* be born again, and except he be born again, he *cannot* enter the kingdom of God. This is final.

5. The *Character* of the new birth. But what is the new birth? Precisely what is it that differentiates a man who is dead in sins from one who has passed from death unto life? Upon this point there is much confusion and ignorance. Tell the average person that he must be born again and he thinks you mean that he must reform, mend his manner of life, turn over a new leaf. But reformation concerns only the outer life. And the trouble with man is within. Suppose the mainspring of my watch were broken, what good would it do if I put in a new crystal and polished the case until I could see my face in it? None at all, for the seat of the trouble is inside the watch. So it is with the sinner. Suppose that his deportment was irreproachable, that his moral character was stainless, that he had such control of his tongue that he never sinned with his lips, what would all this avail while he still had (as God says he has) a *heart* that is "deceitful above all things, and desperately wicked?" The new birth, then, is something more than reformation.

Others suppose, and there are thousands who do so, that

being born again means *becoming religious.* Tell the average church-goer that "Except a man be born again he cannot see the kingdom of God," and these solemn words afford him no qualms. *He* is quite at ease, for he fondly imagines that he *has been* born again. He will tell you that he has *always* been a Christian: that from early childhood he has believed in Christianity, has attended church regularly, nay, that he is a church-member, and contributes regularly toward the support of the Gospel. He is very religious. Periodically he has happy feelings; he says his prayers regularly, and on Sundays he reads his Bible. What more can be required of him! And thus many are lulled to sleep by Satan. If such an one should read these lines, let him pause and seriously weigh the fact that it was man eminently *religious* that the Saviour was addressing when He declared, "Except a man be born of water and of the Spirit, he cannot enter into the kingdom of God." Nicodemus was not only a religious man, he was a *preacher,* and yet it was to him Christ said, "Marvel not that I said unto thee, *Ye* must be born again."

There are still others who believe that the new birth is *a change of heart,* and it is exceedingly difficult to convince them to the contrary. They have heard so many preachers, orthodox preachers, speak of a change of heart, that they have never thought of challenging the scripturalness of this expression, yet it *is* unscriptural. The Bible may be searched from Genesis to Revelation, and nowhere does this expression "change of heart" occur upon its pages. The sad thing is that "change of heart" is not only *un*scriptural, but is it *anti*scriptural, untrue, and therefore, utterly misleading. In the one who has been born again there is no change of heart though *there is* a change of life, both inward and outward. The one who is born again now loves the things he once hated, and he hates now the things he once loved; and, in consequence, his whole line of conduct is radically affected. But, nevertheless, it remains true that his old heart (which is "deceitful above all things and desperately wicked") remains in him, *unchanged,* to the end.

What, then, is the new birth? We answer, It is not the removal of anything from the sinner, nor the changing of anything within the sinner; instead, it is the communication of something to the sinner. The new birth is the impartation of the new nature. When I was born the first time I received from my parents *their* nature: so, when I was born again, I received from God *His* nature. The Spirit of God begets within us a spiritual nature: as we read in II Peter. 1:4, "Whereby are given unto us exceeding great and precious promises: that by these ye might be *partakers of the divine nature.*"

It is a fundamental law which inheres in the very nature of things that like can only produce like. This unchanging principle is enunciated again and again in the first chapter of Genesis. There we read, "And the earth brought forth grass, and herb yielding seed *after his kind,* and the tree yielding fruit, whose seed was in itself, *after his kind*" (1:12). And again, "And God created great whales, and every living creature that moveth, which the waters brought forth abundantly, *after their kind,* and every winged fowl *after his kind*" (1:21). It is only the blindness and animus of infidelistic evolutionists who affirm that one order of creatures can beget another order radically different from themselves. No; that which is born of the vegetable is vegetable; that which is born of the animal is animal. And that which is born of sinful man is a sinful child. A corrupt tree cannot bring forth good fruit. Hence, "That which is born of the flesh *is flesh.*" It cannot be anything else. Educate and cultivate it all you please, it remains flesh. Water cannot rise above its own level, neither can a bitter fountain send forth sweet waters. That which is born of flesh is flesh; it may be refined flesh, it may be beautiful flesh, it may be religious flesh. But it is still "flesh." On the other hand, "That which is born of the Spirit is *spirit.*" The child always partakes of the nature of his parents. That which is born of man is human; that which is born of God is Divine. That which is born of man is sinful, that which is born of God is spiritual.

Here, then, is the character or nature of the new birth. It is not the reformation of the outward man, it is not the education of the natural man, it is not the purification of the old man, but it is the creation of a new man. It is a Divine begetting (James 1:18). It is a birth of the Spirit (John 3:6). It is a being made a new creation (II Cor. 5:17). It is becoming a partaker of the Divine nature (II Pet. 1:4). It is a being born into God's family. Every born again person has, therefore, *two* natures within him: one which is carnal, the other which is spiritual. These two natures are contrary the one to the other (Gal. 5:17), and in consequence, there is an unceasing warfare going on within the Christian. It is only the grace of God which can subdue the old nature; and it is only the Word of God which can feed the new nature.

6. The *obvious Imperativeness* of the new birth. "Marvel not that I said unto thee, Ye must be born again" (3:7). Without doubt, Nicodemus was startled. The emphatic statements of Christ staggered him. The vital importance and imperative necessity of the new birth were points which had never exercised his conscience or engaged his serious attention. He was amazed at the Saviour's searching declarations. Yet he ought not to have been. Really, there was no cause for him to stand there in open-mouthed wonderment. "Marvel not," said Christ. It was as though the Lord had said, "Nicodemus, what I have said to you should be obvious. If a man is a sinner, if because of sin he is blind to the things of God, if no amount of religious cultivation can change the essential nature of man, then it is *patent* that his deepest need is to be born again. Marvel not: it is a self-evident truth."

That entrance into the kingdom of God is only made possible by the new birth, that is, by the reception of the Divine nature, follows a basic law that obtains in every other kingdom. The realm of music is entered by birth. Suppose I have a daughter, and I am anxious she should become an accomplished musician. I place her under the tuition of the ablest instructor obtainable. She studies diligently the science of harmony, and she practices assiduously hours every day. In the end, will my desire be realized? Will she become an accomplished musician? That depends upon one thing – was she *born* with a musical nature? Musicians are born, not manufactured. Again; suppose I have a son whom I desire should be an artist. I place him under the instruction of an efficient teacher. He is given lessons in drawing; he studies the laws of color-blending; he is taken to the art galleries and observes the productions of the great masters.

And what is the result? Does he blossom out into a talented artist? And again it depends solely on one thing—was he *born* with the nature and temperament of an artist? Artists are born, not manufactured. Let these examples suffice for illustrating this fundamental principle. A man *must* have a musical nature if he is to enter the kingdom of music. A man *must* have an artistic nature if he is really to enter the realm of art. A man must have a mathematical mind if he is to be a mathematician. There is nothing to "marvel" at in this: it is self-evident; it is axiomatic. So, in like manner, a man *must* have a spiritual nature before he can enter the spiritual world: a man *must* have God's own nature before he can enter God's kingdom. Therefore "Marvel not . . . ye *must* be born again."

7. The *Process* of the new birth. "The wind bloweth where it listeth, and thou hearest the sound thereof, but canst not tell whence it cometh, and whither it goeth: so is every one that is born of the Spirit" (3:8). A comparison is here drawn between the wind and the Spirit. The comparison is a *double* one. First, both are *sovereign in their activities;* and second, both are *mysterious in their operations.* The comparison is pointed out in the word "so." The first point of analogy is found in the word "where it listeth" or "pleaseth"; the second is found in the words "canst not tell."

"The wind *bloweth* where it pleaseth . . . *so* is every one that is born of the Spirit." The wind is *irresponsible*: that is to say, it is sovereign in its action. The wind is an element altogether beyond man's control. The wind neither consults man's pleasure, nor can it be regulated by his devices. So it is with the Spirit. The wind blows where it pleases, when it pleases, as it pleases. So it is with the Spirit.

Again; the wind is *irresistible.* When the wind blows in the fulness of its power it sweeps everything before it. Those who have looked upon the effects of a tornado just after it has passed, know something of the mighty force of the wind. It is so with the Spirit. When He comes in the fulness of His power, He breaks down man's prejudices, subdues his rebellious will, overcomes all opposition.

Again; the wind is *irregular*. Sometimes the wind moves so softly it scarcely rustles a leaf, at other times it blows so loudly that its roar can be heard miles away. So it is in the matter of the new birth. With some the Holy Spirit works so gently His work is imperceptible to onlookers; with others His action is so powerful, so radical, revolutionary, His operations are patent to many. Sometimes the wind is only local in its reach, at other times it is widespread in its scope. So it is with the Spirit. Today He acts on one or two souls, tomorrow, He may—as at Pentecost—"prick in the heart" a whole multitude. But whether He works on few or many He consults not man; He acts as *He* pleases.

Again; the wind is *invisible*. It is one of the very few things in nature that is invisible. We can *see* the rain, the snow, the lightning's flash; but not so the wind. The analogy holds good with the Spirit. His Person is unseen.

Again; the wind is *inscrutable*. There is something about the wind which defies all effort of human explanation. Its origin, its nature, its activities, are beyond man's ken. Man cannot tell whence it cometh or whither it goeth. It is so with the activities of the Holy Spirit. His operations are conducted secretly; His workings are profoundly mysterious.

Again; the wind is *indispensable*. If a dead calm were to continue indefinitely all vegetation would die. How quickly *we* wilt when there is no wind at all. Even more so is it with the Spirit. Without Him there could be no spiritual life at all.

Finally, the wind is *invigorating*. The life-giving properties of the wind are illustrated every time a physician orders his sick patient to retire to the mountains or to the seaside. It is so, again, with the Spirit. He is the One who strengthens with might in the inner man. He is the One who energizes, revives, empowers.

How marvelously full was the figure employed by Christ on this occasion. How much is suggested by this single word "wind." Let the above serve as an example of the great importance and value of prolonged meditation upon every word of Holy Writ.

God has thrown an impenetrable veil over the beginnings and processes of life. That we live we know, but *how* we live we cannot tell. Life is evident to the consciousness and manifest to the senses, but it is profoundly mysterious in its operations. It is so with the new life born of the Spirit. To sum up the teaching of this verse: "The wind bloweth" – there is the fact. "And thou hearest the sound thereof" – there is evidence of the fact. "But knowest not whence" – there is the mystery behind the fact. The one born again knows that he has a new life, and enjoys the evidences of it, but *how* the Holy Spirit operates upon the soul, subdues the will, creates the new life within us, belongs to the deep things of God.

Below will be found a number of questions bearing on the passage which is to be before us in the next chapter. In the meantime let each reader who desires to become a "workman that needeth not to be ashamed" diligently study the whole passage (John 3:9-21) for himself, paying particular attention to the points raised by our questions:–

1. What does v. 9 go to prove?
2. What solemn warning does v. 10 point?
3. What is the force of the contrast between earthly things and heavenly things in v. 12?
4. How are we to understand v. 13 in view of Enoch's and Elijah's experiences?
5. What Divine attribute of Christ is affirmed in v. 13?
6. What is the connection between v. 14 and the context?
7. Why was a "serpent" selected by God to typify Christ on the Cross? v. 14. Study carefully the first nine verses of Numbers 21.

(No doubt the reader will be glad to know that the Author has published a booklet containing the substance of the above entitled **The New Birth**, which the Lord has been pleased to own in blessing to many. Price 15 cents per copy. Order from the Bible Truth Depot, Swengel, Pa. — I. C. H.).

CHAPTER NINE

Christ and Nicodemus (Concluded)

John 3:9-21

We begin with an Analysis of the passage which is before us:—

1. The Dullness of Nicodemus, vv. 9, 10.
2. The Unbelief of Nicodemus, vv. 11, 12.
3. The Omnipresence of Christ, v. 13.
4. The Necessity of Christ's Death, vv. 14, 15.
5. The Unspeakable Gift of God, v. 16.
6. The Purpose of God in sending Christ, v. 17.
7. Grounds of Condemnation, vv. 18-21.

In our last chapter we dealt at length with Nicodemus' interview with Christ, and sought to bring out the meaning of our Lord's words on that occasion. We saw how the Saviour insisted that the new birth was an imperative *necessity;* that, even though Nicodemus were a Pharisee, a member of the Sanhedrin, nevertheless, unless he was born again he could not see the kingdom of God, i.e. come to know the things of God. We also saw how the Lord explained the *character* of the new birth as a being "born of water (the Word) and of the Spirit"; that regeneration was not a process of reformation or the improving of the old man, but the creating of an altogether new man. That which is born of flesh is flesh, and no artifices of men can ever make it anything else. If a sinner is to enter the kingdom of God he *must* be born again. Finally, we saw how the Saviour likened the operations of the Spirit in bringing about the new birth to the sovereign but mysterious action of the wind. The Saviour had used great plainness of speech, and one had thought it impossible for an intelligent man to miss His meaning. But observe the next verse.

"Nicodemus answered and said unto him, How can these things be?" (3:9). How this reveals the natural man! It is true that Nicodemus was an educated man and, doubtless, one of exemplary moral character; but something more than education and morality are needed to understand the things of God. God has spoken plainly, and in simple terms, yet notwithstanding, the natural man, unaided, has no capacity to receive what God has recorded in His Holy Word. Even though God became incarnate and spoke in human language, men understood Him not. This is demonstrated again and again in this Gospel. Christ spoke of raising the temple of His body, and they thought He referred to the temple standing in Jerusalem. He spoke to the Samaritan woman of the "living water," and she supposed Him to be referring to the water of Jacob's well. He told the disciples He had meat to eat they knew not of, and they thought only of material food (4:32). He spoke of Himself as the Living Bread come down from heaven which, said He, "is my flesh, which I will give for the life of the world," and the Jews answered, "How can this man give us his flesh to eat?" (6:51, 52). He declared, "Yet a little while am I with you, and then I go unto Him that sent me. Ye shall seek me, and shall not find me; and where I am, thither ye cannot come," and His auditors said, "Whither will he go, that we shall not find him? Will he go unto the dispersed among the Gentiles?" (7:33-35). Again, He said, "I go my way, and ye shall seek me, and shall die in your sins: whither I go, ye cannot come"; and the Jews replied, "Will he kill himself? because he saith, Whither I go, ye cannot come" (8:21, 22). He declared, "If ye continue in my word, then are ye my disciples indeed; And ye shall know the truth, and the truth shall make you free," and they answered, "We be Abraham's seed, and were never in bondage to any man: how sayest thou, Ye shall be made free?" (8:31-33). And so we might continue through this Gospel. What a commentary upon human intelligence; what a proof of man's stupidity and blindness!

And Nicodemus was no exception. Master in Israel he might be, yet he was ignorant of the ABC of spiritual things. And why? What is the cause of the natural man's stupidity? Is it because he is in the dark: "The way of the wicked is as darkness: they know not at what they stumble" (Prov. 4:19).

The testimony of the New Testament is equally explicit: "Having the understanding darkened, being alienated from the life of God through the ignorance that is in them, because of the blindness of their heart" (Eph. 4:18). How humbling all this is. How it exposes the folly of the proud boasting of men upon their fancied wisdom and learning! The natural man is in the dark because he is blind. Yet how rarely is this stressed in the modern pulpit. How very rarely do most of the Bible teachers of the day emphasize and press the blindness of natural man, and his deep need of Divine illumination! These things are not palatable we know, and a faithful exposition of them will not make for the popularity of those who preach them: yet are they sorely needed in these days of Laodicean complacency. Let any one who desires to follow the example which our Saviour has left us, read through the four Gospels at a sitting, with the one purpose of discovering how large a place *He* gave in His preaching to the depravity of man, and most probably the reader will be greatly surprised.

"How can these things be?" Nicodemus was at least honest. He was not ashamed to own his ignorance, and ask questions. Well for many another if they would do likewise. Too many are kept in ignorance by a foolish pride which scorns to take the place of one seeking light. Yet this is one of the prime requirements in any who desire to learn. It applies as much to the believer as to the unbeliever. If the Christian refuses to humble himself, if he disdains the attitude of "What I see not, teach thou me" (Job 34:32); if he is unwilling to receive instruction from those taught of God, and above all, if he fails to cry daily to God "Open thou mine eyes, that I may behold wondrous things out of thy law" (Psa. 119:18), he will not, and cannot, grow in the knowledge of the truth.

"Jesus answered and said unto him, Art thou a master of Israel, and knowest not these things?" (3:10). It is to be noted that our Lord here employed the same term in interrogating Nicodemus as this ruler of the Jews used at the beginning when addressing Christ, for in the Greek the word for "teacher" in v. 2 is the same as the one rendered "master" in v. 10. It is exceedingly striking to observe that in the brief record of this interview we find the Lord employing just seven times the very expression used by Nicodemus himself. We tabulate them thus:

1. Nicodemus declared, "*We know,*" vs. 2.
   Christ said, "That which *we know* we speak" (Gk.), v. 11.
2. Nicodemus said, "*Thou art a teacher,*" v. 2.
   Christ said, "*Art thou a teacher?*" v. 10.
3. Nicodemus said, "*Except* God *be* with him," v. 2.
   Christ said, "*Except* a man *be,*" v. 3.
4. Nicodemus asked, "How can a *man be born?*" v. 4.
   Christ answered, "Except *a man be born,*" v. 5.
5. Nicodemus asked, "*Can he enter?*" v. 4.
   Christ answered, "*He cannot enter,*" v. 5.
6. Nicodemus asked, "*How* can?" v. 9.
   Christ asked, "*How* shall?" v. 12.
7. Nicodemus asked, "How can *these things* be?" v. 9.
   Christ asked, "knowest not *these things?*" v. 10.

It is really startling to behold this remarkable correspondency between the language of Nicodemus and the words of the Saviour, and surely there is some important lesson to be learned from it. What are we to gather from this employment by Christ of the terms first used by Nicodemus? Does it not illustrate a principle and teach a lesson for all Christian workers? Let us state it this way: Christ met this man on his own ground, and made his own language the channel of approach to his heart. How simple, yet how important. Have we not often been puzzled to know how to approach some person in whose soul we were interested? We wondered just where was the place to begin. Well, here is light on the problem. Make *his own utterances* the starting point of your address. Turn his own words around against him, and whenever possible, invest them with a deeper meaning and a higher application.

"Jesus answered and said unto him, Art thou a master of Israel, and knowest not these things?" What a rebuke this was! It was as though the Lord had said, "You a teacher, and yet untaught yourself? You a lightholder, and yet in the dark! You a master of Israel, and yet ignorant of the most elementary spiritual truths!" How searching, and how solemn! To what extent is this true of the writer and the reader? Ah, must we not all of us hang our heads in shame? How little we know of what we ought to know. How blind we are! So blind that we need to be *guided* into the truth (John 16:13)! Is not our sorest need that of going to the great Physician and seeking from Him that spiritual "eyesalve," so that He may anoint our eyes that we can see (Rev. 3:18)? God forbid that the haughtiness of Laodiceanism should prevent us.

Ere passing on to the next verse let us point out one more lesson from that now before us – v. 10. Even a religious teacher may be ignorant of Divine truth. What a solemn warning is this for us to put no confidence in any man. Here was a member of the Sanhedrin, trained in the highest theological school of his day, and yet having no discernment of spiritual things. Unfortunately he has had many successors. The fact that a preacher has graduated with honors from some theological center is no proof that he is a man taught of the Holy Spirit. No dependence can be placed on human learning. The only safe course is to emulate the Bereans, and bring everything we hear from the platform and pulpit, yes, and everything we read in religious magazines, to the test of the Word of God, rejecting everything which is not clearly taught in the Holy Oracles.

"Verily, verily, I say unto thee, We speak that we do know, and testify that we have seen; and ye receive not our witness" (3:11). As pointed out above, this was Christ's reply to what Nicodemus had said in his opening statement. "We know that thou art a teacher come from God" declared this representative of the Sanhedrin. In response, our Lord now says, "We speak that *we do know,* and testify that we have seen." At a later stage in the conversation, Nicodemus had asked, "How can these things be?" (v. 9). What Christ had said concerning the new birth had struck this ruler of the Jews as being incredible. Hence this solemn and emphatic declaration – "We speak that we do know, and testify that we have seen." Christ was not dealing with metaphysical speculations or theological hypotheses, such as the Jewish doctors delighted in. Instead, He was affirming that which He knew to be a Divine reality, and testifying to that which had an actual existence and could be seen and observed.

What an example does our Lord set before all His servants! The teacher of God's Word must not attempt to expound what is not already clear to himself, still less must he speculate upon Divine things, or speak of that of which he has no experimental acquaintance. Rather must he speak of that which he knows and testify to that which he has seen.

"And ye receive not our witness." There is an obvious connection between this statement and what is recorded in the previous verse. There we find Christ chiding Nicodemus for his ignorance of Divine truth; here He reveals the *cause* of such ignorance. The reason a man does not *know* the things of God, is because he *receives not* God's witness concerning them. It is vitally important to observe this order. First receiving, then knowledge: first believing what God has said, and then an understanding of it. This principle is illustrated in Heb. 11:3—"Through faith we understand." This is the *first* thing predicated of faith in that wonderful faith chapter. Faith is the root of perception. As we believe God's Word, He honors our faith by giving us a knowledge of what we have believed. And, if we believe not His Word we shall have no understanding whatever of Divine things.

"If I have told you earthly things and ye believe not, how shall ye believe, if I tell you heavenly things?" (3:12). This is closely connected with the previous verse. There, the Lord Jesus lays bare the cause of man's ignorance in the things of God; here He reveals the condition of *growth* in knowledge. God's law in the spiritual realm corresponds with that which operates in the natural world: there is first the blade, then the ear, and last the full corn in the ear. God will not reveal to us a higher truth until we have thoroughly apprehended the simpler ones first. This, we take it, is the moral principle that Christ here enunciated. "Earthly things" are evident and in measure comprehensible, but "heavenly things" are invisible and altogether beyond our grasp until Divinely revealed to us. As to the local or immediate reference, we understand by the "earthly things" the new birth which takes place here upon earth, and the Lord's reference to the "wind" as an illustration of the Spirit's operations in bringing about the new birth. These were things that Nicodemus ought to have known about from Ezek. 36:25-27. If, then, Nicodemus believed not God's Word concerning these earthly things, of what avail would it be for Christ to speak to him of "heavenly things?" We pause to apply this searching principle to ourselves.

Why is it that our progress is so slow in the things of God? What is it that retards our growth in the knowledge of the truth? Is not the answer to these and all similar questions stated above: "If I have told you earthly things, and ye believe not, how shall ye believe, if I tell you heavenly things?" The earthly things are things pertaining to the earthly realm. They are the things which have to do with our present life here upon earth. They are the commands of God which are for the regulation of our daily walk down here. If we believe not *these,* that is, if we do not appropriate them and submit ourselves to them, if we do not receive and heed them, then will God reveal to us the higher mysteries—the "heavenly things?" No, indeed, for that would be setting a premium on our unbelief, and casting pearls before swine.

Why is it that we have so little light on many of the prophetical portions of Scripture? Why is it that we know so little of the conditions of those who are now "present with the Lord?" Why is it that we are so ignorant of what will form our occupation in the eternal state? Is it because the prophecies are obscure? Is it because God has revealed so little about the intermediate and eternal states? Surely not. It is because we are in no condition to receive illumination upon these things. Because we have paid so little earnest heed to the "earthly things" (the things pertaining to our earthly life, the precepts of God for the regulation of our earthly walk) God withholds from us a better knowledge of "heavenly things," things pertaining to the heavenly realm. Let writer and reader bow before God in humble and contrite confession for our miserable failures, and seek from Him that needed grace that our ways may be more pleasing in His sight. Let our first desire be, not a clearer apprehension of the Divine mysteries, but a more implicit obedience to the Divine requirements. As we turn to God's Word, let our dominant motive be that we may learn God's mind *for us* in order that we may do it, and not that we may become wise in recondite problems. Let us remember that "strong meat belongeth to them that are of full age, even those *who by* reason of *use* have their senses (spiritual senses) *exercised* to discern both good and evil" (Heb. 5:14).

"And no man hath ascended up to heaven, but he that came down from heaven, even the Son of man which is in heaven" (3:13). The connection between this verse and the preceding one seems to be as follows. The "heavenly things" to which the Lord had referred had not till then been clearly revealed to men. To ascend to heaven, and penetrate the hidden counsels of God, was an utter impossibility to fallen man. Only the Son, whose native residence was heaven, was *qualified* to reveal heavenly things.

But what did the Lord mean when He said, "*No man* hath ascended up to heaven?" This verse is a favorite one with many of those who believe in "Soul Sleep" and "Annihilation." There are those who contend that between death and resurrection man ceases to be. They appeal to this verse and declare it teaches *no* man, not even Abel or David, has yet gone to heaven. But it is to be noted that Christ did not say, "no man hath *entered* heaven," but, "no man hath *ascended* up to heaven." This is an entirely different thing. "Ascended" no man had, or ever will. What is before us now is only one of ten thousand examples of the minute and marvelous accuracy of Scripture, lost, alas, on the great majority who read it so carelessly and hurriedly. Of Enoch it is recorded that he "was *translated* that he should not see death" (Heb. 11:5). Of Elijah it is said that he "*went up* by a whirlwind into heaven" (II Kings 2:11). Of the saints who shall be raptured to heaven at the return of Christ, it is said that they shall be "*caught up*" (I Thess. 4:17). Of Christ alone is it said that He "*ascended.*" This at once marks His uniqueness, and demonstrates that in *all* things He *has* "the pre-eminence" (Col. 1:18).

But observe further that the Lord said, "even the Son of man *which is* in heaven." In heaven, even while speaking to Nicodemus on earth. This is another evidence of His Deity. It affirmed His Omnipresence. It is remarkable to see that every essential attribute of Deity is predicated of Christ in this Gospel, the special object of which is to unveil His Divine perfections. His *eternality* is argued in 1:1. His Divine *glory* is mentioned in 1:14. His *omniscience* is seen in 1:48 and again in 2:24, 25. His matchless *wisdom* is borne witness to in 7:46. His unchanging love is affirmed in 13:1. And so we might go on indefinitely.

"And as Moses lifted up the serpent in the wilderness, even so must the Son of man be lifted up" (3:14). Christ had been speaking to Nicodemus about the imperative necessity of the new birth. By nature man is dead in trespasses and sins, and in order to obtain life he must be born again. The new birth is the impartation of Divine life, *eternal life*, but for this to be bestowed on men, the Son of man *must* be lifted up. Life could come only out of death. The sacrificial work of Christ is the basis of the Spirit's operations and the ground of God's gift of eternal life. Observe that Christ here speaks of the lifting up of the Son of *man*, for atonement could be made only by One in the nature of him who sinned, and only as *Man* was God's Son capable of taking upon Him the penalty resting on the sinner. No doubt there was a specific reason why Christ should here refer to His sacrificial death as a "lifting up." The Jews were looking for a Messiah who should be lifted up, but elevated in a manner altogether different from what the Lord here mentions. They expected Him to be elevated to the throne of David, but before this He must be lifted up upon the Cross of shame, enduring the judgment of God upon His people's sin.

To illustrate the character, the meaning, and the purpose of His death, the Lord here refers to the well-known incident in Israel's wilderness wanderings which is recorded in Numbers 21. Israel was murmuring against the Lord, and He sent fiery serpents among the people, which bit them so that some of the people died and many others were sorely wounded from their poisonous bites. In consequence, they confessed they had sinned, and cried unto Moses for relief. He, in turn, cried unto God, and the Lord bade him make a serpent of brass, fix it on a pole, and tell the bitten Israelites to look to it in faith and they should be healed. All of this was a striking foreshadowing of Christ being lifted up on the Cross in order that He might save, through the look of faith, those who were dying from sin. The type is a remarkable one and worthy of our closest study.

A "serpent" was a most appropriate figure of that deadly and destructive power, the origin of which the Scriptures teach us to trace to *the* Serpent, whose "seed" sinners are declared to be. The poison of the serpent's bite, which vitiates the entire system of its victim, and from the fatal effects of which there was no deliverance, save that which God provided, strikingly exhibited the awful nature and consequences of *sin*. The *remedy* which God provided was the exhibition of the *destroyer destroyed*. Why was not one of the actual serpents spiked by Moses to the pole? Ah, *that* would have marred the type: that would have pictured judgment executed on the sinner himself; and, worse still, would have misrepresented our sinless Substitute. In the type chosen there was the likeness of a serpent, not an actual serpent, but a piece of brass *made* like one. So, the One who is the sinner's Saviour was sent "in the likeness of sin's flesh" (Rom. 8:3, Gk.), and God "made him to be sin for us, who knew no sin; that we might be made the righteousness of God in him" (II Cor. 5:21).

But how could a *serpent* fitly typify the Holy One of God? This is the very last thing of all we had supposed could, with any propriety, be a figure of Him. True, the "serpent" did not, could not, typify Him in His essential character, and perfect life. The brazen serpent only foreshadowed Christ as He was "lifted up." The lifting up manifestly pointed to the Cross. What was the "serpent?" It was the reminder and emblem of *the curse*. It was through the agency of that old Serpent, the Devil, that our first parents were seduced, and brought under the curse of a Holy God. And on the cross, dear reader, the holy One of God, incarnate, was made a curse for us. We would not dare make such an assertion, did not Scripture itself expressly affirm it. In Gal. 3:13 we are told, "Christ hath redeemed us from the curse of the law, being made a curse for us." There was no flaw, then, in the type. The foreshadowing was perfect. A "serpent" was the only thing in all nature which could accurately prefigure the crucified Saviour made a curse for us.

But *why* a "serpent" of brass? That only brings out once more the perfect accuracy of the type. "Brass" speaks of two things. In the symbolism of Scripture brass is the emblem of *Divine judgment*. The *brazen* altar illustrates this truth, for on it the sacrificial animals were slain, and upon it descended the consuming fire from heaven. Again; in Deut. 28, the Lord declared unto Israel, that if they would not hearken unto His voice and do His commandments (v. 15), that His curse should come upon them (v.16), and as a part of the Divine judgment with which they should be visited, He warned them, "Thy heaven that is above thy head shall be *brass*" (v. 23). Once more, in Rev. 1, where Christ is seen as *Judge*, inspecting the seven churches we are told, "His feet were like fine *brass*" (v. 15). The "serpent," then, spoke of the *curse* which sin entailed; the "brass" told of God's *judgment* falling on the One made sin for us. But there is another thought suggested by the brass. Brass is harder than iron, or silver or gold. It told, then, of Christ's mighty strength, which was able to *endure* the awful judgment which fell upon Him—a mere creature, though sinless, would have been utterly consumed.

From what has been said, it will be evident that when God told Moses to make a serpent of brass, fix it upon a pole, and bid the bitten Israelites look on it and they should live, that He was preaching to them the Gospel of His grace. We would now point out seven things which these Israelites were *not bidden* to do.

1. They were not told to *manufacture some ointment* as the means of healing their wounds. Doubtless, that would have seemed much more reasonable to them. But it would have destroyed the type. The religious doctors of the day are busy inventing spiritual lotions, but they effect no cures. Those who seek spiritual relief by such means are like the poor woman mentioned in the Gospel: she "suffered many things of many physicians, and had spent all that she had, and was nothing bettered, but rather grew worse" (Mark 5:26).

2. They were not told to *minister to others* who were wounded, in order to get relief for themselves. This, too, would have appealed to their sentiments as being more practical and more desirable than gazing at a pole, yet in fact it had been most impracticable. Of what use would it be for one to jump into deep water to rescue a drowning man if he could not swim a stroke himself! How then can one who is dying and unable to deliver himself, help others in a similar state. And yet there are many today engaged in works of charity with the vain expectation that giving relief to others will counteract the deadly virus of sin which is at work in their own souls.

3. They were not told to *fight the serpents.* If some of our moderns had been present that day they would have urged Moses to organize a Society for the Extermination of Serpents! But of what use had that been to those who were *already* bitten and dying? Had each stricken one killed a thousand serpents they would still have died. And what does all this fighting sin amount to! True, it affords an outlet for the energy of the flesh; but all these crusades against intemperance, profanity and vice, have not improved society any, nor have they brought a single sinner one step nearer to Christ.

4. They were not told to make an *offering to the serpent* on the pole. God did not ask any payment from them in return for their healing. No, indeed. Grace ceases to be grace if any price is paid for what it brings. But how frequently is the Gospel perverted at this very point! Not long ago the writer preached on human depravity, addressing himself exclusively to the unsaved. He sought by God's help to show the unbeliever the terribleness of his state and how desperate was his need of a Saviour to deliver him from the wrath to come. As we took our seat, the pastor of the church rose and announced an irrelevant hymn and then urged everybody present to "re-consecrate themselves to God." Poor man! That was the best he knew. But what pitiful blindness! Other preachers are asking their hearers to "Give their hearts to Jesus"—another miserable perversion. God does not ask the sinner to *give* anything, but to *receive* HIS CHRIST.

5. They were not told to *pray* to the serpent. Many evangelists urge their hearers to go to the "mourner's bench" or "peni-

tent form" and there plead with God for pardoning mercy, and if they are dead in earnest they are led to believe that God has heard them for their much speaking. If these "seekers after a better life" believe what the preacher has told them, namely, that they have "prayed through" and have now "got forgiveness," they feel happy, and for a while continue treading the clean side of the Broad Road with a light heart; but the almost invariable consequence is that their last state is worse than the first. O dear reader, do not make the fatal mistake of substituting prayer for faith in Christ.

6. They were told not to *look at Moses.* They *had* been looking to Moses, and urging him to cry to God on their behalf; and when God responded, He took their eyes from off Moses, and commanded them to look at the brazen serpent. Moses was the Law-giver, and how many today are looking to him for salvation. They are trusting in their own imperfect obedience to God's commandments to take them to heaven. In other words, they are depending on their own works. But Scripture says emphatically, "Not by works of righteousness which we have done, but according to his mercy he saved us" (Titus 3:5). The Law was given by Moses, but *grace and truth* came by Jesus Christ, and Christ alone can save.

7. They were not told to look at *their wounds.* Some think they need to be more occupied with the work of examining their own wicked hearts in order to promote that degree of repentance which they deem a necessary qualification for salvation. But as well attempt to produce heat by looking at the snow, or light by peering into the darkness, as seek salvation by looking to self for it. To be occupied with myself is only to be taken up with that which God has condemned, and which already has the sentence of death written upon it. But, it may be asked, "Ought I not to have that godly sorrow which worketh repentance *before* I trust in Christ?" Certainly not. You cannot have a godly sorrow till you are a godly person, and you cannot be a godly person until you have submitted yourself to God and obeyed Him by believing in Christ. *Faith* is the beginning of all godliness.

We have developed the seven points above with the purpose of exposing some of the wiles by which the Enemy is deceiving a multitude of souls. It is greatly to be feared that there are many in our churches today who sincerely think they are Christians, but who are sincerely mistaken. Believing that I am a millionaire will not make me one; and believing that I am saved, when I am not, will not save me. The Devil is well pleased if he can get the awakened sinner to look at anything rather than Christ — good works, repentance, feelings, resolutions, baptism, anything so long as it is not Christ Himself.

Turning now from the negative to the positive side, let us consider, though it must be briefly, one or two points in the type itself. First, Moses was commanded by God to make a serpent of brass — it was of *the Lord's providing* — and the spiritual significance of this we have already looked at. Second, Moses was commanded to fix this brazen serpent upon a pole. Thus was the Divine remedy *publicly* exhibited so that all Israel might look on it and be healed. Third, the Lord's promise was that "it shall come to pass, that every one that is bitten, when he looketh upon it, shall live" (Num. 21:8). Thus, not only did God here give a foreshadowing of the *means* by which salvation was to be brought out for sinners, but also the *manner* in which the sinner obtains an interest in that salvation, namely, *by looking away from himself to the Divinely appointed object of faith,* even to the Lord Jesus Christ. How blessed this was: the brazen serpent was "lifted up" so that those who were too weak to crawl up to the pole itself, and perhaps too far gone to even raise their voices in supplication could, nevertheless, lift up their eyes in simple faith in God's promise and be healed.

Just as the bitten Israelites were healed by a look of faith, so the sinner may be saved by looking to Christ by faith. Saving faith is not some difficult and meritorious work which man must perform so as to give him a claim upon God for the blessing of salvation. It is not on account of our faith that God saves us, but it is through the means of our faith. It is in believing we *are* saved. It is like saying to a starving man, He that eats of this food shall be relieved from the pangs of hunger, and be refreshed and strengthened. Eating is no meritorious performance, but, from the nature of things, eating is the indispensable *means* of relieving hunger. To say that when a man believes he shall be saved, is just to say that the guiltiest of the guilty, and the vilest of the vile, is *welcome* to salvation, if he will but receive it in the only way in which, from the nature of the case, it can be received, namely, by personal faith in the Lord Jesus Christ, which means believing what God has recorded concerning His Son in the Holy Scriptures. The moment a sinner does that he *is saved,* just as God said to Moses, "It *shall* come to pass, that every one that is bitten, *when* he looketh upon it, *shall live.*"

"*Every one* that is bitten." No matter how many times he may have been bitten; no matter how far the poison had advanced in its progress toward a fatal issue, if he but *looked* he should "live." Such is the Gospel declaration: "*whosoever believeth* in him should not perish, but have everlasting life." There is no exception. The vilest wretch on the face of the earth, the most degraded and despised, the most miserable and wretched of all human kind, who believes in Christ shall be saved by Him with an everlasting salvation. Not sin but unbelief can bar the sinner's way to the Saviour. It is possible that some of the Israelites who heard of the Divinely appointed remedy made light of it; it may be that some of them cherished wicked doubts as to the possibility of them obtaining any relief by looking at a brazen serpent; some may have hoped for recovery by the use of ordinary means; no matter, if these things were true of them, and later they found the disease gaining on them, and then they lifted up a believing eye to the Divinely erected standard, *they too* were healed. And should these lines be read by one who has long procrastinated, who has continued for many long years in a course of stout-hearted unbelief and impenitence, nevertheless, the marvelous grace of our God declares to you, that "*whosoever believeth* in him should not perish, but have everlasting life." It is still the "accepted time"; it is still "the day of salvation." Believe now, and *thou* shalt be saved.

Man became a lost sinner by a *look,* for the first thing recorded of Eve in connection with the fall of our first parents is that "The woman *saw* that the tree was good for food" (Gen. 3:6).

In like manner, the lost sinner is saved by a look. The Christian life *begins* by looking: "*Look* unto me, and be ye saved, all the ends of the earth: for I am God, and there is none else" (Isa. 45:22). The Christian life *continues* by looking: "let us run with patience the race which is set before us, *looking* unto Jesus the author and finisher of faith" (Heb. 12:2). And at the *end* of the Christian life we are still to be looking for Christ: "For our conversation (citizenship) is in heaven; from whence also we *look* for the Saviour, the Lord Jesus Christ" (Phil. 3:20). From first to last, the one thing required is *looking* at God's Son.

But perhaps right here the troubled and trembling sinner will voice his last difficulty—"Sir, I do not know that I am looking in the correct way." Dear friend, God does not ask you to look *at your look,* but at CHRIST. In that great crowd of bitten Israelites of old there were some with young eyes and some with old eyes that looked at the serpent; there were some with clear vision and some with dim vision; there were some who had a full view of the serpent by reason of their nearness to the uplifted type of Christ; and there were, most probably, others who could scarcely see it because of their great distance from the pole, but the Divine record is "It shall come to pass, that *every one* that is bitten, when he *looketh* upon it, shall live." And so it is today. The Lord Jesus says, "Come unto me, all ye that labor and are heavy laden, and I will give you rest." He does not define the *method* or the *manner* of coming, and even if the poor sinner comes groping, stumbling, falling, yet if only he *will* "come" there is a warm welcome for him. So it is in our text: it is "whosoever believeth"—nothing is said about the *strength* or the *intelligence* of the belief, for it is not the character or degree of faith that saves, but Christ Himself. Faith is simply the eye of the soul that looks off unto the Lord Jesus, Do not rest, then, on your faith, but on the Saviour Himself.

"For God so loved the world, that he gave his only begotten Son, that whosoever believeth in him should not perish, but have everlasting life" (3:16). Christ had just made mention of His death, and had affirmed that the Cross was an imperative necessity; it was not "the Son of man *shall* be lifted up," but "the Son of man *must* be lifted up." There was no other alternative. If the claims of God's throne were to be met, if the demands of justice were to be satisfied, if the sin was to be put away, it could only be by some sinless One being punished in the stead of those who should be saved. The righteousness of God required this: the Son of man *must* be lifted up.

But there is more in the Cross of Christ than an exhibition of the righteousness of God; there is also a display of His wondrous *love*. V. 16 explains v. 14, as its opening word indicates. V. 16 takes us back to the very foundation of everything. The great Sacrifice was provided by Love. Christ was God's love-gift. This at once refutes an error that once obtained in certain quarters, namely, that Christ died in order that God might be induced to pity and save men. The very opposite is the truth. Christ died because God *did* love men, and *was* determined to save them that believe. The death of Christ was the supreme demonstration of God's love. It was impossible that there should be any discord among the Persons of the Godhead in reference to the salvation of men. The will of the Godhead is, and necessarily must be, one. The Atonement was not the cause, but the effect, of God's love: "In this was manifested the love of God towards us, because that God sent his only begotten Son into the world, that we might live through him. Herein is love, not that we loved God, but that he loved us, and sent his Son to be the propitiation for our sins" (I John 4:9, 10). From what other source *could* have proceeded the giving of Christ to save men but from *LOVE*—pure sovereign benignity!

The Love of God! How blessed is this to the hearts of believers, for only believers can appreciate it, and they but very imperfectly. It is to be noted that here in John 3:16 there are seven things told us about God's love: first, the *tense* of His love—"God so *loved*." It is not God *loves*, but He "loved." That He loves us now that we are His children, we can, in measure, understand; but that He should have loved us *before* we became His children passes knowledge. But He did. "God commendeth his love toward us, in that, *while we were yet sinners* Christ died for us" (Rom. 5:8). And again: "Yea, I have loved thee with *an everlasting love*: therefore with lovingkindness have I drawn thee" (Jer. 31:3). Second, the *magnitude* of His love—"God *so* loved." None can define or measure that little word "so." There are dimensions to the breadth, and length, and depth, and height of His wondrous love, that none can measure. Third, the *scope* of God's love – "God so loved *the world*." It was not limited to the narrow bounds of Palestine, but it flowed out to sinners of the Gentiles, too. Fourth, the *nature* of God's love – "God so loved the world that *he gave*." Love, real love, ever seeks the highest interest of others. Love is unselfish; it gives. Fifth, the *sacrificial character* of God's love – "he gave *his only begotten Son*." God spared not His BEST. He freely delivered up Christ, even to the death of the Cross, Sixth, the *design* of His love – "That whosoever believeth on him *should not perish*." Many died in the wilderness from the bites of the serpents: and many of Adam's race will suffer eternal death in the lake of fire. But God purposed to have a people who "should not perish." Who this people are is made manifest by their "believing" on God's Son. Seventh, the *beneficence* of God's love – "But have *everlasting life*." This is what God imparts to every one of His own. Ah, must we not exclaim with the apostle, "Behold, *what manner of love* the Father hath bestowed upon us"! (I John 3:1). O dear Christian reader, if ever you are tempted to *doubt* God's love go back to the Cross, and see there how He gave up to that cruel death His "only begotten Son."

"For God sent not his Son into the world to condemn the world; but that the world through him might be saved" (3:17). This verse enlarges upon the beneficient nature and purpose of God's love. Unselfish in its character – for *love* "seeketh not her own" – it ever desires the good of those unto whom it flows forth. When God sent His Son here it was not to "condemn the world," as we might have expected. There was every reason why the world should have been condemned. The heathen were in an even worse condition than the Jews. Outside the little land of Palestine, the knowledge of the true and living God had well nigh completely vanished from the earth. And where God is not known and loved, there is no love among men for their neighbors. In every Gentile nation idolatry and immorality were rampant. One has only to read the second half of Rom. 1 to be made to marvel that God did not then sweep the earth with the besom of destruction. But no; He had other designs, gracious designs. God sent His Son into the world that the world through Him "might be saved." It is to be remarked that the word "might" here does not express any uncertainty. Instead it declares the *purpose* of God in the sending of His Son. In common speech the word "might" signifies a contingency. It is only another case of the vital importance of ignoring man's dictionaries and the way he employs words, and turning to a concordance to see how the Holy Spirit uses each word in the Scriptures themselves. The word "might"—as a part of the verb—expresses *design*. When we are told that God sent His Son into the world that through Him "the world might be saved," it signifies that "through him the world *should* be saved," and this is how it is rendered in the R. V. For other instances we refer the reader to I Pet. 3:18—"might bring us to God" implies no uncertainty whatever, but tells of the object to be accomplished. For further examples see Gal. 4:5; Titus 2:14; II Pet. 1:4, etc., etc.

"He that believeth on him is not condemned: but he that believeth not is condemned already, because he has not believed in the name of the only begotten Son of God" (3:18). For the believer there is "no condemnation" (Rom. 8:1), because Christ was condemned in his stead—the "chastisement of our peace" was upon Him. But the unbeliever is "condemned already." By nature he is a "child of *wrath*" (Eph. 2:3), not corruption merely. He enters this world with the curse of a sin-hating God upon him. If he hears the Gospel and receives not Christ he incurs a new and increased condemnation through his unbelief. How emphatically this proves that the sinner is *responsible* for his unbelief!

"And this is the condemnation, that light is come into the world, and men loved darkness rather than light, because their deeds were evil" (3:19). Here is the *cause* of man's unbelief: he loves the darkness, and therefore hates the light. What a proof of his depravity! It is not only that men are *in* the dark, but they *love* the darkness—they prefer ignorance, error, superstition, to the light of truth. And the reason why they love the darkness and hate the light is because their deeds are evil.

"For every one that doeth evil hateth the light, neither cometh to the light, lest his deeds should be reproved. But he that doeth truth cometh to the light, that his deeds may be made manifest, that they are wrought in God" (3:20, 21). Here is the final test. "*Every one that* doeth (practices) evil hateth the light, neither cometh to the light," and why? – "lest his deeds should be reproved." *That* is why men refuse to read the Scriptures. God's Word would condemn them. On the other hand, "he that doeth truth," which describes what is characteristic of every believer, "cometh to the light" – note the perfect tense – he comes *again and again* to the light of God's Word. And for what purpose? To learn God's mind, that he may cease doing the things which are displeasing to Him, and be occupied with that which is acceptable in His sight. Was not this the final word of Christ to Nicodemus, addressed to his *conscience?* This ruler of the Jews had come to Jesus "by night," as though his deeds would not bear the light!

For the benefit of those who would prepare for the next lesson we submit the following questions:

1. What does the "much water" teach? v. 23.
2. What was the real purpose of the Jews in coming to John and saying what is recorded in v. 26?
3. What is the meaning of v. 27?
4. What vitally important lesson for the Christian is taught in v. 29?
5. What is the meaning of v. 33?
6. What is meant by the last half of v. 34?
7. How does v. 35 bring out the Deity of Christ?

CHAPTER TEN

Christ Magnified by His Forerunner

John 3:22-36

We give first a brief Analysis of the passage which is to occupy our attention. Here we see:

1. The Lord Jesus and His Disciples in Judea, v. 22.
2. John baptizing in Aenon, vv. 23, 24.
3. The attempt to provoke John's jealousy, vv. 25, 26.
4. The humility of John, vv. 27, 28.
5. The joy of John, v. 29.
6. The preeminence of Christ, vv. 30-35.
7. The inevitable alternative, v. 36.

Another typical picture is presented in the passage before us, though its lines are not so easily discernible as in some of the others which we have already looked at.

The spiritual state of Judaism as it existed at the time of our Lord's sojourn on earth is revealed in three pathetic statements; first, the Jews were occupied with the externals of religion (v. 25); second, they were envious of the results attending the ministry of Christ (v. 26); third, they rejected the testimony of the Saviour (v. 32). How pointedly did these things expose the condition of Israel as a nation! With no heart for the Christ of God, and ignorant, too, of the position occupied by His forerunner (v. 28), they were concerned only with matters of ceremonialism. Religious they were, but for a Saviour they felt no need. They preferred to wrangle over questions of "purification," rather than go to the Lord Jesus for the Water of life. But this was not all. They were *jealous* of the outward success that attended the ministry of the Lord Jesus in its early stages. How this revealed their hearts! Plainer still is what we read of them in v. 32 – the testimony of Christ they "received not." The Saviour was not only "despised" by them, He was "rejected," too. Once more, then, is the awful condition of Judaism made manifest before our eyes.

"After these things came Jesus and his disciples into the land of Judea; and there he tarried with them, and baptized" (3:22). This must be read in the light of John 4:2. By linking these two verses together an important principle is established: what is done by the servants of Christ *by His authority* is as though it had been done by Christ immediately. It is the same as what we read of in II Cor. 5:20: "Now then we are ambassadors for Christ, as though God did beseech you by us: *we* pray you *in Christ's stead*, be ye reconciled to God." It is the same in prayer. When we really pray to the Father in the name of Jesus Christ, it is as though Christ Himself were the suppliant.

"And John also was baptizing in Aenon near to Salim, because there was much water there: and they came, and were baptized" (3:23). The meaning of the names of these places—like all others in Scriptures—are deeply significant. Aenon signifies "place of springs," Salim means "peace." What a blessed place for John to be in! These names point a striking contrast from "the wilderness of Judea" and "the region round about Jordan" (cf. Matt. 3:1, 5), which speak of drought and death. Surely there is a most important lesson taught us here, and a most precious one too. The place of drought and death was where God had called the forerunner of Christ to labor, and as he there bore faithful witness to the Lord Jesus it became *to him* a place of "springs" (refreshment) and "peace!" Such is ever the experience of the obedient servant of God.

"John *also* was baptizing." There is a word of great practical importance here for many a servant of God. The Lord Jesus was there in Judea in person, and His disciples were with Him, baptizing. The crowds which at first attended the preaching of John had now deserted him, and were thronging to Christ (v. 26). What then does the Lord's forerunner do? Does he decide that his work is now finished, and that God no longer has need of him? Does he become discouraged because his congregations were so small? Does he quit his work and go on a long vacation? Far, far from it. He faithfully persevered: "John *also* was baptizing." Has this no message for us? Perhaps these lines may be read by some who used to minister to big crowds. But these are no more. Another preacher has appeared, and the crowds flock after him. What then? Must you then conclude that God has set you aside? Are you suffering this experience to discourage you? Or, worse still, are you *envious* of the great success attending the labors of another! Ah, fellow-servants of Christ, take to heart this word—"John *also* was baptizing." His season of popularity might be over: *his* light might be eclipsed by that of a greater: the crowds might have become thin; but, nevertheless, he plodded on and faithfully persevered in the work God had given him to do! "And *let us* not be weary in well doing: for in due season we shall reap, *if we faint not*" (Gal. 6:9). John performed his duty and fulfilled his course.

"John also was baptizing in Aenon near to Salim, *because* there was *much water* there." This is one of the many verses in the New Testament which plainly intimates the *mode* of baptism. If baptism were by sprinkling or by pouring, "*much* water" would not be required. The fact that John baptized in Aenon "*because* there was much water there" strongly implies that the scriptural form of baptism is immersion. But the one who desires to know and carry out God's mind is not left to mere inferences, forceful though they may be. The very word "baptized" (both in the Greek and in English) signifies "to dip or immerse." The Greek words for "sprinkling and pouring" are entirely different from the one for baptize. Again; the example of our blessed Lord Himself ought to settle all controversy. No unprejudiced mind can read Matt. 3:16 without seeing that the Lord Jesus was immersed. Finally, the testimony of Rom. 6 is unequivocal and conclusive. There we read, "We are *buried* with Him *by baptism* into death" (v. 3).

"Then there arose a question between some of John's disciples and the Jews about purifying" (3:25). The "Jews" mentioned here are the same as those we read of in 1:19, who sent a delegation unto the Baptist to inquire who he was. There is a slight difference between the ancient Greek MSS, and following a variation of reading the R.V. says, "There arose therefore a questioning on the part of John's disciples with *a Jew* about purifying." But we are thoroughly satisfied that here, as in the great majority of instances, the A.V. is preferable to the R.V. Clearly it is "the Jews" of 1:19 who are before us again in 3:25. This is seen from what we read in v. 28: "Ye yourselves bear me witness, *that I said,* I am not the Christ, but that I am sent before him." The Baptist reminds them of the testimony he bore before their representatives on the previous occasion, for John 3:28 corresponds exactly with John 1:20 and 23.

"And they came unto John, and said unto him, Rabbi, he that was with thee beyond Jordan, to whom thou bearest witness, behold, the same baptizeth, and all men come to him" (3:26). What was the object of these Jews? Was not their motive a malicious one? Were they not seeking to make John envious? It would certainly appear so. Why tell him of the outward success of Christ's ministry if it were not to provoke the jealousy of His harbinger? And cannot we detect the Enemy of souls behind this! This is ever a favorite device with him, to make one servant of the Lord envious at the greater success enjoyed by another. And alas! how frequently does he gain his wicked ends thus. It is only those who seek not honor of men, but desire only the glory of their Lord, that are proof against such attacks.

A striking example of the above principle is found in connection with Moses, who "was very meek, above all the men which were upon the face of the earth" (Num. 12:3). In Num. 11:26, 27 we read, "But there remained two of the men in the camp, the name of the one was Eldad, and the name of the other Medad: and the spirit rested upon them; and they were of them that were written, but went not out unto the tabernacle: and they prophesied in the camp. And there ran a young man, and told Moses, and said, Eldad and Medad do prophesy in the camp." Now notice what follows—"And Joshua the son of Nun, the servant of Moses, one of his young men, answered and said, My lord Moses, forbid them." Even Joshua was jealous for his master's sake. But how blessedly did Moses rebuke him: "And Moses said unto him, Enviest thou for my sake? would God that *all* the Lord's people were prophets and that the Lord would put his spirit upon them!"

The same unselfish spirit is seen in that one who referred to himself as "less than the least of all saints" (Eph. 3:8). While the beloved apostle was a prisoner in Rome, many of the brethren waxed confident, and were bold to speak the word without fear. True, some preached Christ of envy and strife, and some also of good will. How then did the apostle feel? Did he think these others were seeking to take advantage of his absence? Was he jealous of *their* labors? Not so: he said: "Notwithstanding . . . I therein *do rejoice,* yea, and will rejoice" (Phil. 1:14-18). So, again, he learns of the ministry of Philemon in refreshing the saints, and to him he writes, "we have *great joy* and consolation *in thy* love, because the bowels of the saints are refreshed *by thee,* brother" (Philemon 7). May more of this spirit be found in us and in other of the Lord's servants as we learn of how God is using them.

"John answered and said, A man can receive nothing, except it be given him from heaven" (3:27). It is beautiful to see how John conducted himself on this occasion. His reply was most becoming. First, he bows to God's sovereign will (v. 27). Second, he reminds his tempters of his previous disclaimer of any other place being his save that of one "sent before" the Lord (1:28). Third, he declared that Israel belonged to Christ, not to himself (v. 29). Fourth, he affirms that his own joy was fulfilled in seeing men turning to the Lord Jesus (v. 29). Finally, he insists that while Christ must "increase," he must "decrease" (v. 30). Blessed self-abnegation was this.

"John answered and said, A man can receive nothing, except it be given him from heaven." John was not at all surprised at the lack of spiritual perception in these Jews. The things of God cannot be discerned by the natural man. Before a man can even "receive" spiritual things they must first be "given him from heaven." And in the bestowment of His gifts God is sovereign. We are fully satisfied that the contents of this twenty-seventh verse contains the key to much that is puzzling. There are some brethren, beloved of the Lord, who do not see the truth of believer's baptism; there are others who stumble over the subject of predestination. What may be as clear as sunlight to us, is dark to them. But let us not be puffed up by our superior knowledge.

Let us remember the admonition of the apostle Paul, "For who maketh thee to differ from another? and what hast thou that thou didst not receive? now if thou didst *receive* it, why dost thou glory (boast), as if thou hadst not received it?" (I Cor. 4:7).

But on the other hand, there is no excuse for ignorance in the things of God. Far from it. God has plainly made known His mind. His blessed Word is here in our hands. The Holy Spirit has been given to us to guide us into *all* truth. And it is our responsibility to believe and understand all that is recorded for our learning: "And if any man think that he knoweth anything, he knoweth nothing yet as he *ought* to know" (I Cor. 8:2). Nevertheless, there is the Divine side, too; and *this* is what is before us here in John 3:27. What did the Lord Jesus say in response to the unbelief of the cities wherein His mightiest works were done? "Jesus answered and said, I thank thee, O Father, Lord of heaven and earth, because thou hast hid these things from the wise and prudent, and *hast revealed* them unto babes. Even so, Father: for so it seemed good in thy sight" (Matt. 11:25, 26). What did He say to Peter, when that apostle bore such blessed testimony to His Messiahship and Deity? "Jesus answered and said unto him, Blessed art thou, Simon Bar-Jona: for flesh and blood hath not *revealed it* unto thee, but *my Father* which is in heaven" (Matt. 16:17). And what is recorded of Lydia? "And a certain woman named Lydia, a seller of purple, of the city of Thyatira, which worshipped God, heard us: *whose heart the Lord opened,* THAT (in order that) she attended unto the things which were spoken of Paul" (Acts 16:14).

And yet God is not capricious. If it is not "given" to us the fault is all our own. We "have not" because we "ask not" (James 4:2). Or, we "find" not, because we are too lazy to "search" diligently for the precious things of God. Here is His sure promise, provided we meet the conditions annexed to it: "My son, if thou wilt *receive* my words, and hide my commandments with thee; So that thou incline thine ear unto wisdom, and apply thine heart to understanding; Yea, if thou criest after knowledge, and liftest up thy voice for understanding; If thou *seekest* her as silver, and *searchest* for her as for hid treasures; Then shalt thou understand the fear of the Lord, and *find the knowledge of God*" (Prov. 2:1-5).

"Ye yourselves bear me witness, that I said, I am not the Christ, but that I am sent before him" (3:28). John now announces what he was not, and what he was. He was but the messenger before the face of Christ, His forerunner. A subordinate place, therefore, was *his*. How blessed was this. These Jews were seeking to stir up the pride of John. But the Lord's servant takes his proper place before them. He reminds them that he was only one "sent before" Christ.

"He that hath the bride is the Bridegroom: but the friend of the Bridegroom, which standeth and heareth him, rejoiceth greatly because of the Bridegroom's voice: this my joy therefore is fulfilled" (3:29). The first thing which claims our attention here is the opening sentence of this verse. Who is meant by the "bride" which the Lord Jesus even then was said to "*have?*" In seeking the answer to this question, particular attention should be paid to the *connection* in which this statement is found, the *circumstances* under which it was made, and also to the *person* who uttered it. The *connection* in which this occurs is discovered by going back to John 3:22, 23. The disciples of Jesus, as well as John himself, were "baptizing." This was not Christian baptism, for that was not instituted until after the death and resurrection of the Saviour. This baptism, therefore, was *kingdom* baptism, and was one of the conditions of entrance into it (cf. Matt. 3). The *circumstances* under which this statement was made is seen in that John 3:29 formed part of the Baptist's reply to those who were seeking to arouse his envy over the fact that the crowds were now flocking to Christ. The *person* who uttered it was not Paul the apostle to the Gentiles, but John the Baptist, whose ministry was *confined* to Israel, and who here styles himself "the friend of the Bridegroom."

When the Baptist said "He that hath the bride, is the bridegroom," he was not referring to the Church, the Body of Christ, for of that he knew nothing whatever, nor did any one else save the Triune God. At that time Christ was not forming a church, but as "the minister of the circumcision" He was presenting

Himself to Israel. A repenting and believing few gathered around Him. That the twelve apostles *are* connected with Christ in an *earthly* relationship (though also, of course, members of the household of faith, and of the family of God) is clear from the words of the Saviour: "Jesus said unto them, Verily I say unto you, That ye which have followed me, in the regeneration, when the Son of man shall sit in the throne of his glory, *ye* also shall sit upon twelve thrones, judging the twelve tribes *of Israel*" (Matt. 19:28). This is something which the apostle Paul—the apostle of the Gentiles, the one through whom God made known the truth of one Body—will never do.

"He that *hath* the bride" was the language of faith. The company who will form the "bride" was then far from being complete; only a nucleus was there, but *faith* viewed the purpose of God concerning Israel as *already accomplished*. But "he that *hath* the bride" rules out the one body, for *that* did not begin to be formed until several years later. If further proof of the correctness of what we have written be asked for, it is at once forthcoming in the very next sentence: "But the *friend of the bridegroom,* which standeth and heareth him, rejoiceth greatly because of the bridegroom's voice: this *my* joy therefore is fulfilled." Without a doubt this refers to John the Baptist himself. But in no possible sense was *he* associated with heralding the truth of the Church which is the Body of Christ. His own language, as recorded in John 1:31 is final: "But that he should be made manifest *to Israel,* therefore, *am I come* baptizing with water."

Let it be clearly understood that in this chapter we are neither denying nor affirming that the Body of Christ will be His *heavenly* bride. *That* does not fall within the compass of the present passage. What we have attempted to do is to give a faithful exposition of John 3:29, and the "bride" there plainly refers to a company of regenerated Israelites, a company not yet completed. The work of gathering out *that* company has been *interrupted* by the rejection of Christ by the Jewish nation as a whole, and this has been followed by the present *period*. But after the Body of Christ has come "in the unity of the faith, and the knowledge of the Son of God, unto a perfect *man,* unto the measure of the stature of the fulness of Christ" (Eph. 4:13) God will *resume* His work with Israel and *complete* that company which is to be gathered out from them.

"But the friend of the bridegroom, which standeth and heareth him, rejoiceth greatly because of the bridegroom's voice" (v. 29). This is very blessed. Notice first, how we have repeated here what we called attention to when considering John 1:35-37: the two disciples of John "stood" before they heard their master "speak" and say "Behold the lamb of God." The order is the same in the verse now before us—"Which standeth *and* heareth him." Standing signifies the cessation of activity: it denotes an act of concentrated attention. The principle illustrated is a deeply important one. It is one which needs to be pressed in this day of hustling and bustling about, which is only the product of the *energy of the flesh.* We must "stand" before we can "hear *Him.*"

"This my joy therefore is fulfilled" (v. 29). How precious is this! Joy of heart is the fruit of being *"occupied with Christ!"* It is standing and hearing *His voice* which delights the soul. But again we say that the all-important prerequisite for this is a cessation of the activities of the flesh. *His* voice cannot be heard if we are rushing hither and thither in fellowship with the fearful bedlam all around us. The "better part" is not to be like Martha—"cumbered about *much serving*"—but is to "sit" at the feet of the Lord Jesus like Mary did, *hearing* His word (see Luke 10:38-42). Notice, too, the tense of the verbs in John 3:29: "stand*eth* and hear*eth.*" The perfect tense expresses *continuous* action: again and again, daily, this must be done, if our joy is to be filled full. Is not our failure at this very point the explanation of our joyless lives?

"He must increase, but I must decrease" (3:30). Blessed climax was this to the lovely modesty of John, and well calculated to crush all party feeling and nip in the bud any jealousy there might be in the hearts of his own disciples. In principle this is inseparably connected with what he had just said before in the previous verse. The more I "decrease" the more I delight in standing and hearing the voice of that blessed One who is Altogether Lovely. And so conversely. The more I stand and hear

His voice, the more will He "increase" before me, and the more shall I "decrease." I cannot be occupied with two objects at one and the same time. To "decrease" is, we take it, to be less and less occupied with ourselves. The more I am occupied with Christ, the less shall I be occupied with myself. Humility is not the product of direct cultivation, rather it is a *by-product*. The more I try to be humble, the less shall I attain unto humility. But if I am truly occupied with that One who was "meek and lowly in heart," if I am constantly beholding *His* glory in the mirror of God's Word, then shall I be "changed into *the same image from* glory to glory, even as by the Spirit of the Lord" (II Cor. 3:18).

The passage now before us contains the final testimony of the Baptist to the Lord Jesus Christ. In it the Saviour and His servant are sharply contrasted. In witnessing to the manifold glories of his Master, John the Baptist draws a seven-fold contrast. First, John was one who could receive *nothing*, except it were given him from heaven (v. 27); where as Christ was the One to whom the Father "hath given *all things*" (v. 35). Second, Jesus was the Christ, whereas John was only one "sent before Him" (v. 28). Third, Christ was the "bridegroom," whereas John was but the "friend" of the Bridegroom (v. 29). Fourth, Christ must "increase," whereas John himself must "decrease" (v. 30). Fifth, John was "of the earth," whereas the Lord Jesus had come "from above," and "is above all" (v. 31). Sixth, John had only a measure of the Spirit, but of Christ it is witnessed, "God giveth not the Spirit by measure unto him" (v. 34). Seventh, John was but a servant, whereas the Saviour was none less than the Son of the Father (v. 35). What a blessed and complete testimony was this to the immeasurable superiority of the Lord of Glory!

"He that cometh from above is above all: he that is of the earth is earthly, and speaketh of the earth: he that cometh from heaven is above all" (3:31). John now witnesses to the person, the glory, and the testimony of Christ. It seems to us that John is here giving point to one of the seven contrasts contained in this testimony which he here drew between Christ and himself. "Earth and earthly" must not be understood to signify "world and worldly." John was of the earth, and spoke of things which pertain to the earth. But the Lord was from heaven, and is above all. All other messengers that God has sent had much earthiness about them, as those of us who are His servants now have much of it. We are limited by our finite grasp. The bodies of death in which we dwell are a severe handicap. Our vision is largely confined to the things of earth. But there were no limitations to the Lord Jesus: He was the Son of God from heaven, pure, perfect, omniscient.

"And what he hath seen and heard, that he testifieth" (3:32). The testimony which Christ bore was a perfect one. The prophets received their message from the Holy Spirit, and they spoke of things which they *had not* "seen" – see Matt. 13:17. There are things which the angels desire to look into, but they were too mysterious for them to fathom – see I Pet. 1:12. But our Lord Jesus Christ knows "heavenly things" by His own perfect knowledge, for He hath ever dwelt in the bosom of the Father. *He* knew the mind of God for He is God.

"And no man receiveth his testimony" (3:32). How radically different was this word of John from that of the Jews who declared "all men come to him," v. 26! One lesson we may draw from this is the unreliability of statistics which seek to tabulate spiritual results. Those Jews were looking at the outward appearance only, and from that point of view the cause of Christ seemed to be prospering in an extraordinary way. But the Lord's forerunner looked beneath the surface, at the true spiritual results, and his verdict was "no man receiveth his testimony." Beware then of statistics, they depend largely on the one who compiles them. Some who are sanguine, will say everything that is pleasing and encouraging; others, who are more serious and severe in their judgment, will say much that is depressing.

"No man receiveth his testimony." This is not to be understood without qualification, for the very next words declare "he that *hath* received his testimony hath set to his seal that God is true." It is evident that what John meant was that *comparatively* none received the testimony of Christ. Compared with the crowds which came to Him, compared with the nation of Israel as a whole, those who "received" Christ's testimony were so few, that they were as though none at all received it. And is it not the same today? In this favored land Christ is preached to multitudes, and many there are who hear about Him; but, alas! how few give evidence of having really received His testimony into their hearts!

And *why* is it that men receive not the testimony of this One who "cometh from heaven" (v. 31), who testifies of what He has seen and heard (v. 32), and who has the Spirit without measure (v. 34), yea, who is none other than the Son beloved of the Father (v. 35)? It is because they are *earthly*. The message is too heavenly for them. They have no relish for it. They have hearts only for things below. Others are too learned to believe anything so simple: it is still to the Jews a stumblingblock, and to the Greeks foolishness. They will not believe God; and *how can they* while "they receive honor from men!" With others it is *pride* that hinders. They think themselves good enough already. They are pharisaical. They are too high-born to see their need of being born again. They are too haughty to take the place of empty-handed beggars and receive God's *gift*. But the root reason for rejecting the testimony of Christ is that, "men loved darkness rather than light, because their deeds were evil" (3:19). Men are so depraved their hearts are hardened and their understandings are darkened, and therefore, do they prefer the darkness to the light.

"He that hath received his testimony hath set to his seal that God is true" (3:33). To "set to his seal" means to certify and ratify. By faith in the Lord Jesus the believer has come to know God as a reality. Hitherto he heard of and talked about an unknown God, but now he knows God for himself, and declares his faith in His fidelity. God says, "He that believeth on the Son hath everlasting life," and the believer finds that God is true, for he lives now in newness of life. The Lord says, "He that believeth on him is not condemned," and the believer *knows* it is so, for the burden of guilt is gone from his conscience. Those who receive Christ's testimony as true, take it unto themselves. They rest their souls upon it. They make it their own. They allow nothing to make them doubt what He has said. No matter whether they can thoroughly understand it or no; no matter whether it seems reasonable or unreasonable, they implicitly believe it. Whether their feelings respond or not, makes no difference—the Son of God has spoken, and that is enough.

"For he whom God hath sent speaketh the words of God: for God giveth not the Spirit by measure unto him" (3:34). The Lord Jesus Christ was sent here by God, and He spoke only the words of God. Testimony to this fact was borne to Him by the Father on the Mount of Transfiguration: "This is My beloved Son, in whom I am well-pleased: hear ye him" (Matt. 17:5). And Christ differed from every other messenger sent from God —in *all* things *He* has "the pre-eminence." Others *had* the Spirit "by measure." They knew but fragments of the truth of God. To them the Spirit came and then went again. Moreover, their gifts varied: one had a certain gift from the Spirit, another an entirely different gift. But God gave not the Spirit "by measure" unto Christ. The Lord Jesus knew the full truth of God, for He Himself is the Truth. On Him the Spirit did not come and go; instead, we read, He "*abode* upon him" (John 1:32). And further: Christ was endowed with every Divine gift. In contrast from the fragmentary communications of God through the prophets (see Heb. 1:1), Christ fully and finally received the mind of God. We believe that the full meaning of these words that Christ had the Spirit "without measure" is a statement that is strictly parallel with what we read in Col. 2:9, "For in Him dwelleth *all the fulness* of the Godhead bodily."

"The Father loveth the Son, and hath given all things into his hand" (3:35). What a glorious testimony was this! Christ was more than a messenger or witness for God, He was the "Son" beloved of the Father. Not only so, He was the One into whose hand the Father had "given all things." How this brings out, again, the absolute Deity of Christ! To none but to One absolutely equal with Himself could the Father give *"all things."*

"He that believeth on the Son hath everlasting life: and he that believeth not the Son shall not see life; but the wrath of God abideth on him" (3:36). Here is the inevitable alternative. Salvation comes through believing, believing on the Son. How Divinely simple! Those who believe on the Son have "everlasting life" as a present possession, though the full enjoyment as well as the full manifestation of it are yet future. But those who believe not the Son "shall not see life," neither enter into it nor enjoy it; instead, the wrath of a sin-hating God "abideth" on them. It is upon them even now, and if they believe not, it shall abide on them for ever and ever. How unspeakably solemn! How it behooves every reader to seriously and honestly face the question – To which class do I belong? – to those who believe on the Son, or to those who believe not on the Son?

The following questions concern the next lesson:

1. What are we to learn from the statement that "Jesus himself baptized not"? 4:2.
2. Why did the Lord "leave Judea" when He knew the Pharisees were jealous? 4:3.
3. What prophetic foreshadowing do we have in John 4:3, 4?
4. Why was it that Christ "must needs" go through Samaria? 4:4.
5. What are we to learn from the fact that the meeting between Christ and the Samaritan woman occurred at a "well?" 4:6.
6. Why are we told that it was "Jacob's well"? 4:6.
7. What is suggested by the "sixth hour"? 4:6.

CHAPTER ELEVEN

Christ at Sychar's Well

John 4:1-6

We begin with the usual Analysis of the passage that is to be before us. In it we see:—

1. The Lord's knowledge of the Pharisees' jealousy, v. 1.
2. The disciples of the Lord baptizing, v. 2.
3. The Lord leaving Judea and departing into Galilee, v. 3.
4. The constraint of Divine grace, v. 4.
5. The Journey to Sychar, v. 5.
6. The Saviour's weariness, v. 6.
7. The Saviour resting, v. 6.

Like the first three chapters of John, this fourth also furnishes us with another aspect of the deplorable spiritual state that Israel was in at the time the Lord was here upon earth. It is remarkable how complete is the picture supplied us. Each separate scene gives some distinctive feature. Thus far we have seen, first, a blinded Priesthood (1:19, 26); second, a joyless Nation (2:3); third, a desecrated Temple (2:14); fourth, a spiritually-dead Sanhedrin (3:7); fifth, the person of Christ despised (3:26) and His testimony rejected (3:32). Now we are shown the heartless indifference of Israel toward their semi-heathen neighbors.

Israel had been highly privileged of God, and not the least of their blessings was a written revelation from Him. But though favored with much light themselves, they were selfishly indifferent toward those who were in darkness. Right within the bounds of their own land (for Samaria was a part of it), dwelt those who were semi-heathen, yet had the Jews no love for their souls and no concern for their spiritual welfare. Listen to the tragic plaint of one of their number: "The Jews have no dealings with the Samaritans" (John 4:9). The heartless indifference of the favored people of God toward the Samaritans is intimated further in the surprise shown by the disciples when they returned and found the Saviour talking with this Samaritan woman (see 4:27). It was, no doubt, in order to rebuke them that the Saviour said, "Say not ye, There are yet four months, and then cometh harvest? Behold, I say unto you. Lift up *your* eyes, and look on the fields; for they are white already to harvest" (4:35). Thus, this heartless neglect of the Samaritans gives us another glimpse of Israel's state at that time.

But not only does John 4 give us another picture of the miserable condition the Jews were in, but, once more, it contains a prophetic foreshadowing of the future. In the closing verses of the previous chapter we are shown the person of Christ despised (3:26) and His testimony rejected (3:32). This but anticipated the final rejection of Christ by the Nation as a whole. Now in marvelous consonance with this, the very next thing we see is Christ *turning to the Gentiles!* The order here, as everywhere, is perfect. As we all know, this is exactly what happened in God's dispensational dealings with the earth. No sooner did the old dispensation end, end with Israel's rejection of Christ, than God in mercy turned to the Gentiles (Rom. 11, etc.). This is intimated in our lesson, first, by the statement made in v. 3: the Lord Jesus "*left Judea,* and departed again into *Galilee*"—cf. Matt. 4:15—"Galilee of the *Gentiles!*" Second, in the fact that here the Lord Jesus is seen occupied not with the Jews but with the Samaritans. And third, by what we read of in v. 40—"and He abode *there* two days." How exceedingly striking is this! "He abode there *two days.*" Remember that word in II Pet. 3:8, which declares "One day is with the Lord as a thousand years, and a thousand years as one day." Two "days," then or 2,000 years is the length of time that Christ was to be away from the Jews in Judea. How perfect and accurate is this picture!

At the close of the seventh chapter we called attention to the importance of noticing the relation of one passage to another. This is a principle which has been sadly neglected by Bible students. Not only should we be diligent to examine each verse in the light of its context, but also each passage as a whole should be studied *in its relation* to the complete passage which precedes and follows it. By attending to this it will often be found that the Holy Spirit has placed in juxtaposition two incidents—miracles, parables, conversations, as the case may be—in order to point a contrast, or series of contrasts between them. Such we saw was plainly the case with what we have in the first and second halves of John 2, where a sevenfold contrast is to be noted. Another striking example is before us here. There is a manifest antithesis between what we have in the first half of John 3 and the first half of John 4.

As we study John 3 and 4 together, we discover *a series of striking contrasts*. Let us look at them. First, in John 3 we have "a *man* of the Pharisees *named* Nicodemus:" in John 4 it is an *un*named *woman* that is before us. Second, the former was a man of rank, a "Master of Israel:" the latter was a woman of the lower ranks, for she came "to draw water." Third, the one was a favored Jew: the other was a despised Samaritan. Fourth, Nicodemus was a man of high reputation, a member of the Sanhedrin: the one with whom Christ dealt in John 4 was a woman of dissolute habits. Fifth, Nicodemus sought out Christ: here Christ seeks out the woman. Sixth, Nicodemus came to Christ "by night:" Christ speaks to the woman at mid-day. Seventh, to the self-righteous Pharisee Christ said, "Ye must be born again:" to this sinner of the Gentiles He tells of "the gift of God." How much we miss by failing to compare and contrast what the Holy Spirit has placed side by side in this wondrous revelation from God! May the Lord stir up all of us to more diligent *study* of His Word.

"When therefore the Lord knew how the Pharisees had heard that Jesus made and baptized more disciples than John, (Though Jesus himself baptized not, but his disciples,) He left Judea, and departed again into Galilee" (4:1-3). Even at that early date in Christ's public ministry the Pharisees had begun to manifest their opposition against Him. But this is not difficult to understand, for the teaching of the Lord Jesus openly condemned their hypocritical practices. Morever, their jealousy was aroused at this new movement, of which He was regarded as the head. The Baptist was the son of a priest that ministered in the Temple, and this would entitle him to some consideration. But here was a man that was regarded as being no more than the son of a carpenter, and who was He to form a following! And, too, He was of Nazareth, now working in Judea! And "out of Nazareth," they taught, "could arise no prophet" (John 7:52). A spirit of rivalry was at work, and the report was being circulated that "Jesus was making and baptizing more diciples than John." Every one knew what crowds had flocked to the preaching and baptizing of that Elijah-like prophet, crying in the wilderness. Was it to be suffered then, that this One of poor parentage should eclipse the Baptist in fame? Surely not: that could not be allowed at any cost.

"When therefore the Lord knew . . . he left Judea." What a word is this! There is no hint of any one having informed Him. That was not necessary. The One who had humbled Himself to the infinite stoop of taking upon Him the form of a servant, was none other than "the *Lord*." This One whom the Pharisees contemptuously regarded as the Nazarene-carpenter, was none other than the Christ of God, in whom "dwelt all the fulness of the God-head bodily." "The Lord *knew*," at once displays His omniscience. Nothing could be, and nothing can be, hidden from Him.

"The Pharisees had heard that Jesus made and baptized more disciples than John" (1:1). It is important to observe the order of the two verbs here for they tell us who, alone, are eligible for baptism. When two verbs are linked together thus, the first denotes the action, and the second *how* the action was performed. For example; suppose I said, "He poured oil on him and anointed him." You could not say, "He anointed him and poured oil on him," unless the anointing and the pouring were two different acts. Therefore, the fact that "baptizing" here comes after, and not before, the verb "made," proves that they were *disciples* first, and were "baptized" subsequently. It is one of many passages in the New Testament which, uniformly, teaches that only one who is already a believer in Christ is qualified for baptism.

"Though Jesus himself baptized not, but his disciples" (1:2). This is but a parenthetical statement, nevertheless, it is of considerable importance. It has been well said by the late Bishop

Ryle, "This verse intimates that baptism is neither the first nor the chief thing about Christianity. We frequently read of Christ preaching and praying, once of His administering the Lord's Supper, but 'baptize' He did not – as though to show us that baptism has nothing to do with salvation."

"He left Judea, and departed again into Galilee " (1:3). This is exceedingly solemn. To cherish the spirit of jealousy and rivalry is to drive away the Lord. When the Saviour sent forth the twelve on their mission to the cities of Israel, He bade them "And whosoever will not receive you, when ye go out of that city, shake off the very dust from your feet for a testimony against them" (Luke 9:5). And again, when sending forth the seventy, He said to them, "But into whatsoever city ye enter, and they receive you not, *go your ways* out into the streets of the same, and say, Even the very dust of your city, which cleaveth on us, we do wipe off against you" (Luke 10:10, 11). But before He did this, He first set them an example. If "no man" would receive His testimony in Judea (3:3), then He would *leave* for other parts. He would not stay to cast pearls before swine.

No doubt the preaching of the Lord Jesus in Judea, and especcially the circumstance of baptizing many of the people (through the instrumentality of His disciples) had greatly angered the Jewish rulers, and probably they had already taken steps to prevent the progress of this One whose teaching so evidently conflicted with theirs, and whose growing influence over the minds of the people threatened to weaken their authority. Our Lord knew this, and because His hour was not yet come, and much was to be done by Him before He finished the work the Father had given Him to do, instead of waiting until He should be driven out of Judea, He left that district of His own accord, and retired into Galilee, which, being remote from Jerusalem, and under the governorship of Herod, was more or less outside of their jurisdiction and less subject to the power of the Sanhedrin.

"In going from Judea into Galilee, our Lord's most direct route lay through Samaria, which was a district of Palestine, bounded on the south by Judea, and on the north by Galilee, on the west by the Mediterranean Sea, and on the east by the river Jordan. It was possible to go from Judea into Galilee by crossing the Jordan, and passing through Perea; but this was a very circuitous route, though some of the stricter Jews seemed to have been in the habit of taking it, to avoid intercourse with the Samaritans. The direct route lay through Samaria" (Dr. J. Brown).

Samaria was a province allotted to Ephraim and the half tribe of Manasseh in the days of Joshua (see Josh. 16 and 17, and particularly 17:7). After the revolt of the ten tribes, the inhabitants of this district had generally ceased to worship at the Temple in Jerusalem, and following first the wicked idolatry introduced by Jeroboam the son of Nebat (see I Kings 12:25-33, and note "Shechem" in v. 25), they fell an easy prey to the Gentile corruptions introduced by his successors. After the great body of the ten tribes had been carried away captives, and their district left almost without inhabitant, the king of Assyria planted in their province a colony of various nations (II King 17:24) who, mingling with the few original inhabitants of the land, formed unto themselves a strange medley of a religion, by combining the principles and rights of Judaism with those of oriental idolaters. As the inspired historian tells us, they "feared the Lord, and made unto themselves of the lowest of them priests of the high places, which sacrificed for them in the houses of the high places. They feared the Lord, and served their own gods, after the manner of the nations who carried them away from thence . . . So these nations feared the Lord, and served their graven images, both their children, and their children's children: as did their fathers, so do they unto this day" (II Kings 17:32, 33, 41). Thus, the original dwellers in Samaria were, to a great extent, heathenized.

At the time of the return of the remnant of Israel from the Babylonian captivity, the Samaritans offered to enter into an alliance with the Jews (Ezra 4:1, 2), and on being refused (Ezra 4:3) they became the bitter enemies of the Jews and their most active opposers in the rebuilding of their Temple and capital (see Neh. 4 and 6). According to Josephus (see his "Antiquities" XI:7, 2; XIII:9), at a later date Manasseh, the son of Jaddua the high priest, contrary to the law, married the daughter of Sanballat, the chief of the Samaritans, and when the Jews insisted that he should either repudiate his wife, or renounce his sacred office, he fled to his father-in-law, who gave him an honorable reception, and by the permission of Alexander the Great built a temple to Jehovah on Mount Gerizim, in which Manasseh and his posterity officiated as high priests, in rivalry to the Divinely instituted ritual at Jerusalem—see also I Macc. 3:10.

The Samaritans received as Divine the five books of Moses, and probably, also, some at least of the prophetic oracles; but they did not acknowledge the authenticity of the historical books written by the Jews, who they regarded as their worst enemies. The natural consequence of all these circumstances was, that the Jews and Samaritans regarded each other with much more rancorous dislike than either of them did the idolatrous nations by which they were surrounded. Hence when his enemies said unto Christ, "Say we not well that thou art a Samaritan?" (John 8:48), we can understand better the venom behind the insult. Hence, too, it makes us bow our hearts in wonderment to find the Lord Jesus representing Himself as "a certain Samaritan" (Luke 10:33) as we learn of the depths of ignominy into which He had descended and how He became the despised and hated One in order to secure our salvation.

"And he must needs go through Samaria" (4:4). The needs-be was a moral and not a geographical one. There were two routes from Judea to Galilee. The more direct was through Samaria. The other, though more circuitous, led through Perea and Decapolis to the southern shores of Gennesaret. The former was the regular route. But the reason why the Lord "must" go through Samaria, was because of a Divine *needs-be*. From all eternity it had been ordained that *He should* go through Samaria. Some of God's elect were there, and these *must* be sought and found—cf. the Lord's own words in John 10:16, "And other sheep I have, which are not of this fold: them also I *must* bring." We shall never appreciate the Gospel until we go back to the basic truth of *predestination,* which puts God first, which makes the choice His before it is ours, and which, in due time, brings His grace to bear upon us with invincible power.

Election is of *persons*—predestination is of *things*. All the great movements of the universe are regulated by God's will,—

But if the great movements, then the small movements for the great depend upon the small. It was predestinated that our Saviour should go through Samaria, because there was a chosen sinner there. And she *was* a chosen sinner, for if not she never would have chosen God, or known Jesus Christ. The whole machinery of grace was therefore set in motion in the direction of one poor lost sinner, that she might be restored to her Saviour and to her God. That is what we wish to see in our own experience—to look back of ante-mundane ages, and date our eternal life from the covenant. To say:

Father 'twas Thy love that knew us
Earth's foundation long before
That same love to Jesus drew us
By its sweet constraining power,
And will keep us
Safely now and ever more
(*Dr. G. S. Bishop*).

It is not difficult to understand *why* the Lord must *needs* go through Samaria. There were those in Samaria whom the Father had given Him from all eternity, and these He "must" save. And, dear reader, if you are one of God's elect there is a *needs be* put on the Lord Jesus Christ to save *you.* If you are yet in your sins, you will not always be. For years you may have been fleeing from Christ; but when His time comes He will overtake you. However you may kick against the pricks and contend against Him; however deeply you may sin, as the woman in our passage, He will most surely overtake and conquer you. Yea, even now He is on the way!

"Then cometh he to a city of Samaria, which is called Sychar, near to the parcel of ground that Jacob gave to his son Joseph. Now Jacob's well was there. Jesus therefore, being wearied with his journey, sat thus on the well: and it was about the sixth hour" (4:5, 6). How truly human was the Lord Jesus! He would in all points be like unto His brethren, so He did not exempt Himself from fatigue. How fully then can He sympathize with the laborer today who is worn out with toil! To the Saviour, a long walk brought weariness, and weariness needed rest, and to rest He "sat thus" on the well. He was, apparently, more worn than the disciples, for *they* continued on into the village to buy food. But He was under a greater mental strain than they. He had a weariness they knew nothing about.

"Of the Son of man being in heaven, whilst upon earth, we have learnt in the previous chapter (3:13). Now, though Divine, and therefore in heaven, He was truly a man upon earth. This mystery of His person none of us can fathom (Matt. 11:27). Nor are we asked to. We have to believe it. 'Perfect God, and perfect Man: of a reasonable soul and human flesh subsisting'—such has been the language of confession of the western part of Christendom for many an age. Now there are some conditions incident to humanity. There are others, in addition, connected with *fallen* humanity, such as liability to sickness, to disease, and even to death. To these last, of course, the holy Son of God *was not,* though a man, subject; yet, as being a man He was able to die, and willingly gave up His life for His people. But to sickness and bodily decay, as the Holy One, in whom was no sin, He was not, and *could not have been, subject*. On the other hand, from conditions incident to humanity, as hunger, thirst and weariness, He was not exempt. In the wilderness He was hungry. On the Cross He was thirsty. Here at the well He was weary. Into what circumstances, then, did He voluntarily come, and that in obedience and love to His Father, and in love to His own sheep! He, by whom the worlds were made, was sitting a weary man by Jacob's well, and there at first alone. One word from the throne, and the whole angelic host would have flown to minister to Him. But that word was not spoken. For God's purpose of grace to souls in Samaria was to be worked out at Sychar" (*C. E. Stuart*).

"Jesus therefore being *wearied*." This brings out the *reality* of Christ's humanity. He was just as really and truly Man as He was God. In stressing His absolute Deity, we are in danger of overlooking the reality of His humanity. The Lord Jesus was perfect Man: He ate and drank, labored and slept, prayed and wept. And what a precious thought is there here for Christian workers: the Saviour knew what it was to be "weary"—not weary *of* well doing, but weary *in* well doing. But it is blessed to see how the Holy Spirit has guarded the glory of Christ's person here. Side by side with this word upon His humanity, we are shown His Divine omniscience—revealed in His perfect knowledge of the history of the woman with whom He dealt at the well. This principle meets us at every turn in the Gospels. At His birth we behold His humiliation—lying in a *manger*—but we discover His Divine glory, too, for the angels were sent to announce the One born as "Christ the Lord." See Him *asleep* in the boat, exhausted from the toil of a heavy day's work: but mark the sequel, as He rises and stills the storm. Behold Him by the grave of Lazarus, groaning in spirit and weeping: and then bow before Him in worship as He, by a word from His mouth, brings the dead to life. So it is here: "wearied with his journey," and yet displaying His Deity by reading the secrets of this woman's heart.

"Jesus therefore being wearied with his journey, sat thus *on the well*" (4:6). This illustrates another important principle, the application of which is often a great aid to the understanding of a passage, namely, noticing *the place* where a particular incident occurred. There is a profound significance to *everything* in Scripture, even the seemingly unimportant details. The character of the place frequently supplies the key to the *meaning* of what is recorded as occurring there. For instance: the children of Israel were *in Egypt* when the Lord delivered them. Egypt, then, symbolizes the place where we were when God apprehended *us,* namely, *the world* in which we groaned under the merciless taskmasters that dominated us. John the Baptist preached *in the wilderness,* for it symbolized the spiritual barrenness and desolation of Israel at that time. When the Lord Jesus enunciated the laws of His kingdom, He went up into *a mountain*—a place of elevation, symbolic of *His throne* of authority from which He delivered His manifesto. When He gave the parables He "sat by the *sea side*" (cf. Isa. 17:12, 13; Ezek. 26:3; Dan. 7:2; Rev. 17:5, for the "sea" in its symbolic significance). The first four parables of Matt. 13 pertain to the *public* profession of Christianity, hence these were given in the hearing of the "great multitudes;" but the next two concerned only the Lord's own people, so we read "Then Jesus sent the multitude away, and *went into the house*: and his disciples came unto him" (Matt. 13:36). When the Lord portrayed the poor sinner as the one to whom He came to minister (under the figure of the good "Samaritan") He represented him as a certain man who "went *down* from Jerusalem [foundation of peace] to Jericho [the city of the curse]." So, again, in Luke 15 the prodigal son is seen in "the *far country*" (away from the father), and there feeding on the husks which the swine did eat—another picture giving us *the* place where the sinner is morally.

The above examples, selected almost at random, illustrate the importance of observing *the place* where each event happened, and *the position* occupied by the chief actors. This same principle receives striking exemplification in the passage before us. The meeting between the Saviour and this Samaritan adulteress occurred at Sychar which means "purchased"—so was the "gift of God" that He proffered to her. And, as He revealed to her her soul's deep need He sat "on the well." The "well" was a *figure of Himself*, and its water was the emblem of *the salvation* that is to be found in Him. One authority for these statements is Isa. 12:3, "Therefore with joy shall ye draw water out of *the wells* (Heb. 'the well') of *salvation*." What a remarkable statement is this! It is the key to the typical significance of many an Old Testament passage. The "well" of the Old Testament Scriptures foreshadowed Christ and what is to be found in Him. We shall now turn to some of the Old Testament passages where the "well" is mentioned, and discover how remarkably and blessedly they foreshadowed this One who gave the water of life to the woman of Samaria.

1. The first time the "well" is mentioned in Scripture, is in Gen. 16:6, 7, 13, 14. "But Abram said unto Sarai, Behold, thy maid is in thy hand; do to her as it pleaseth thee. And when Sarai dealt hardly with her, she fled from her face. And the angel of the Lord found her by a fountain of water in the wilderness . . . And she called the name of the Lord which spake unto her, Thou God seest me . . . for she said, Have I also here looked after Him that seeth me? Wherefore the well was called, The well of him that liveth and seeth me." Note the following points: First, the "well" (the "fountain of water" of v. 7 is termed the "well" in v. 14) was the place where the angel of the Lord *found* this poor outcast. So *Christ* is where God meets the sinner, for "no man cometh unto the Father" but by Him.

Second, this well was located in the wilderness – fit symbol of *this world*. The "wilderness" well depicts the state of heart we were in when we first met Christ! Third, the "well" was the place where *God* was *revealed*. Hagar, therefore, termed it, "the well of him that liveth and seeth me." So, again, Christ is *the Revealer* of God – "He that hath seen me, hath seen the Father."

2. In Gen. 21:14-19 we read, "And Abraham rose up early in the morning, and took bread, and a bottle of water, and gave it unto Hagar, putting it on her shoulder, and the child, and sent her away: and she departed, and wandered in the wilderness of Beersheba. And the water was *spent* in the bottle, and she cast the child under one of the shrubs. And she went, and sat her down over against him a good way off, as it were a bow shot: for she said, Let me not see the death of the child. And she sat over against him, and lift up her voice, and wept. And God heard the voice of the lad; and the angel of God called to Hagar out of heaven, and said unto her, What aileth thee, Hagar? fear not; for God hath heard the voice of the lad where he is . . . and God *opened* her eyes, and she saw *a well of water*." How inexpressibly blessed is this in its typical suggestiveness! Notice the following points: First, we have before us again an outcast, and one whose water was spent, for she had but "a bottle:" like the prodigal son, she "began to be in want." Second, she had cast away her child to die, and there she sat *weeping*. What a picture of the poor, desolate, despairing sinner! Third, *God* "opened her eyes," and what for? In order that she might *see* the "well" that had been there all the time! Ah, was it not so with thee, dear Christian reader? It was not thine own mental acumen which discovered that One of whom the "well" here speaks. It was God who *opened* thine eyes to *see* Him as the One who alone could meet thy desperate and deep need. What do we read in Prov. 20:12 – "The hearing ear, and *the seeing eye*, the Lord hath made even both of them." And again in John 5:20 we are told, "And we know that the Son of God is come, and hath *given us an understanding*, that (in order that) we may know Him that is true."

3. In this same chapter the "well" is mentioned again in another connection: "And Abraham took sheep and oxen, and gave them unto Abimelech; and both of them made *a covenant*. And Abraham set seven ewe lambs of the flock by themselves. And Abimelech said unto Abraham, What mean these seven ewe lambs which thou hast set by themselves? And he said, For these seven ewe lambs shalt thou take of my hand, that they may be a witness unto me, that I have digged this well. Wherefore he called that place *the well of the oath;* because there they sware both of them" (Gen. 21:27-31). Here we find the "well" was the place of the "covenant" (v. 27), which was ratified by an "oath" (v. 31). And what do we read in Heb. 7:20-22?—"And inasmuch as not without *an oath* he was made priest: (For those priests were made without an oath; but this with an oath by him that said unto him, The Lord sware and will not repent, Thou art a priest forever after the order of Melchisedec:) By so much was Jesus made a surety of a better testament [*covenant*]."

4. In Gen. 24:10-12 we read, "And the servant took ten camels of the camels of his master, and departed; for all the goods of his master were in his hand: and he arose, and went to Mesopotamia, unto the city of Nahor. And he made his camels to kneel down without the city by *a well* of water at the time of the evening, even the time that women go out to draw water. And he said, O Lord God of my master Abraham, I pray thee, send me good speed this day." Not only is each typical picture perfect, but the order in which they are found evidences Divine design. In the first scriptures we have glanced at, that which is connected with the "well" suggested the meeting between the Saviour and the *sinner*. And in the last passage, the covenant and the oath speak of that which tells of the sure ground upon which our eternal preservation rests. And from that point, every reference to the "well" has that connected with it which is appropriate of *believers* only. In the last quoted passage, the "well" is the place of *prayer:* so, the believer asks the Father in the name of Christ, of whom the "well" speaks.

5. In Gen. 29:1-3 we read, "Then Jacob went on his journey, and came into the land of the people of the east. And he looked,

and behold a *well* in the field, and, lo, there were three flocks of sheep lying by it; for out of that well they watered the flocks." This is very beautiful. How striking is the contrast between this typical scene and the first that we looked at in Gen. 16. There, where it is a *sinner* and Christ which is in view, the "well" is located in the *wilderness*—figure of the barrenness and desolation of the sinner. But here, where the sheep are in view, the "well" is found in the *field*—suggesting the "green pastures" into which the good Shepherd leads His own. Notice there were "three flocks of sheep" that were lying by this "well," their position denoting *rest*, that rest which Christ gives His own. Here in the *field* were the three flocks lying *"by* it"—the well. It is only *in Christ* that we find rest.

6. In Ex. 2:15-17 we are told, "Now when Pharaoh heard this thing, he sought to slay Moses. But Moses fled from the face of Pharaoh, and dwelt in the land of Midian; and he sat down by a *well.* Now the priest of Midian had seven daughters: and they came and drew water, and filled the troughs to water their father's flock. And the shepherds came and drove them away: but Moses stood up and helped them, and watered their flock." How marvelous is this type. First, Pharaoh the king of Egypt prefigures Satan as the god of this world, attacking and seeking to destroy the believer. From him Moses "fled." How often the great Enemy frightens us and gets us on the run. But how blessed to note the next statement here: fleeing from Pharaoh to Midian, where he now dwells, the first thing that we read of Moses is, "he sat down by a well." Thank God there is One to whom we can flee for refuge—the Lord Jesus Christ to whom the "well" pointed. To this well the daughters of Jethro also came, for water. But the shepherds came and *drove them away.* How many of the "under-shepherds" today are, by their infidelistic teaching, driving many away from Christ. Nevertheless, God still has a Moses here and there, who will *"stand up and help"* those who really desire the Water of Life. But be it noted, before we can "help" others we must first be resting on the well for ourselves, as Moses was.

7. "And from thence they went to Beer: that is the *well* whereof the Lord spake unto Moses, Gather the people together,

and I will give them water. Then Israel sang this song, Spring up, O well; *sing ye unto it*" (Num. 21:16, 17). What a word is this! The well is personified. It is made the object of song. It evokes praise. No interpreter is needed here. Beloved reader, are you "singing" unto *the* "Well?"

8. "Now Jonathan and Ahimaaz stayed by En-rogel; for they might not be seen to come into the city: and a wench went and told them; and they went and told king David. Nevertheless a lad saw them, and told Absalom: but they went both of them away quickly, and came to a man's house in Bahurim, which had a *well* in his court: *whither they went down.* And the woman took and spread a covering over the well's mouth, and spread ground corn thereon; and *the thing was not known*" (II Sam. 17:17-19). Here we find the "well" providing *shelter* and *protection* for God's people. Notice there was a "covering" over its mouth, so that Jonathan and Ahimaaz were *hidden* in the well. So it is with the believer—"your life is *hid with Christ* in God" (Col. 3:3). How striking is the last sentence quoted above, "And the thing was not known!" The world is in complete ignorance of the believer's place and portion in Christ!

9. "And David longed, and said, O that one would give me drink of the water of the *well* of Bethlehem, which is by the gate!" (II Sam. 23:15). Nothing but water from the well of *Bethlehem* would satisfy David.

10. "Drink waters out of thine own cistern, and running waters out of *thine own well*" (Prov. 5:15). What a blessed climax is this. The "well" is *our own,* and from its "running waters" we are invited to "drink."

We sincerely pity any who may regard all of this as fanciful. Surely such need to betake themselves to Christ for "eyesalve," that their eyes may be enabled to behold "wondrous things" out of God's Law. To us this study has been unspeakably blessed. And what meaning it all gives to John 4:6—"Jesus, therefore, being wearied with His journey sat thus on *the well.*"

But there is one other word here that we must not overlook, a word that gives added force to the typical character of the picture before us, for it speaks of the *character* of that Salvation which is found *in* Christ. "Now *Jacob's* well was there" (John 4:6). There are three things in connection with this particular "well" that we need to consider. First, this well was *purchased* by Jacob, or more accurately speaking, the "field" in which the well was located was purchased by him. "And Jacob came to Shalem, a city of *Shechem,* which is in the land of Canaan, when he came from Padan-Aram; and pitched his tent before the city. And he *bought* a parcel of a field, where he had spread his tent, at the hand of the children of Hamor, Shechem's father, for an hundred pieces of money" (Gen. 33:18, 19). The word "Sychar" in John 4:6 signifies *purchased.* What a well-chosen and suited place for Christ to speak to that woman of the "*gift* of God!" But let it never be forgotten that this "gift" costs *us* nothing, because it cost *Him* everything.

Second, the "parcel of ground" in which was this well, was afterwards taken by Joseph with "*sword* and bow;" "And Israel said unto Joseph, Behold, I die: but God shall be with you, and bring you again unto the land of your fathers. Moreover I have *given* to thee one portion above thy brethren, which I took out of the hand of the Amorite with *my sword* and with my bow" (Gen. 48:21, 22)—that this is the *same* "parcel of ground" referred to in Gen. 33 is clear from John 4:5. The reference in Gen. 48 must be to a later date than what is in view in Gen. 33. The Amorites were seeking to rob Jacob of his well, and therefore an appeal to arms was necessary. This, we believe, foreshadowed the present interval, during which the Holy Spirit (while Satan is yet the "Prince of this world" and ever seeks to oppose and keep God's Jacobs away from the "well") is bringing salvation to souls by means of the "sword" (Heb. 4:12).

Third, this portion purchased by Jacob, and later secured by means of the "sword and bow," was *given to Joseph* (see Gen. 48:21, 22). This became a part of Joseph's "birthright," for said Jacob "I have given to thee one portion *above* thy brethren." This ought to have been given to Reuben, Jacob's "firstborn," but through his fall into grievous sin it was transferred to Joseph (see I Chron. 5:1). How marvelously accurate the type! Christ the second Man takes the inheritance which the first man forfeited and lost through sin! Putting these three together, we have: the "well" purchased, the "well" possessed, the "well" enjoyed.

And here we must stop. In the next chapter we shall, D.V., consider carefully each sentence in vv. 7-11. Let the student ponder prayerfully:—

1. What are we to learn from the fact that the Saviour was the first to speak? v. 7.
2. Why did He begin by asking her for a drink? v. 7.
3. Was it merely a drink of water He had in mind! If not, what was it?
4. What is the force and significance of the parenthetical statement of v. 8?
5. What does the woman's answer (v. 9) go to prove?
6. What is the "gift of God?" v. 10
7. Why does Christ liken salvation to "living water?" Enumerate the different thoughts suggested by this figure.

CHAPTER TWELVE

CHRIST AT SYCHAR'S WELL (Continued)

John 4:7-10

First, a brief Analysis of the passage which is to be before us:—

1. The Woman of Samaria, v. 7.
2. The Saviour's request, v. 7.
3. The Saviour's solitariness, v. 8.
4. The Woman's surprise, v. 9.
5. The Woman's prejudice, v. 9.
6. The Saviour's rebuke, v. 10.
7. The Saviour's appeal, v. 10.

In the last chapter we pointed out the deep significance underlying the words of John 4:4—"He *must needs* go through Samaria." It was the constraint of sovereign grace. From all eternity it had been foreordained that the Saviour should go through Samaria. The performing of God's eternal decree required it. The Son, incarnate, had come there to do the Father's will—"Lo, I come to do *thy* will, O God." And God's will was that these hated Samaritans should hear the Gospel of His grace from the lips of His own dear Son. Hence, "He must *needs* go through Samaria." There were elect souls there, which had been given to Him by the Father, and these also He "*must* bring" (see John 10:16).

"Now Jacob's well was there. Jesus therefore, being wearied with his journey, sat thus on the well" (4:6). Observe, particularly, that the Lord Jesus was beforehand with this woman. *He* was at the well first! "I am found of them that sought me not" (Isa. 65:1) is the language of the Messiah in the prophetic word centuries before He made His appearance among men, and this oracle has been frequently verified. His salvation is not only altogether *unmerited* by those to whom it comes, but at first, it is always *unsought* (see Rom. 3:11), and of every one who is numbered among His peculiar people it may be as truly said, as of the apostles, "Ye have not chosen me, but I have chosen you" (John 15:16). When we were pursuing our mad course of sin, when we were utterly indifferent to the claims and superlative excellency of the Saviour, when we had no serious thought at all about our souls, He—to use the apostle's peculiarly appropriate word—"apprehended" us (Phil. 3:12). *He* "laid hold of" us, aroused our attention, illumined our darkened understanding, that we might receive the truth and be saved by it. A beautiful illustration of this is before us here in John 4.

Yes, the Lord was beforehand with this woman. He was found of one who sought Him not. It was so with the idolatrous Abraham (Josh. 24) in the land of Chaldea: the Lord of glory appeared to him while he was yet in Mesopotamia (Acts 7:2). It was so with the worm Jacob, as he fled to escape from his brother's anger (Gen. 28:10, 13). It was so with Moses, as he went about his shepherd duties (Ex. 3:1, 2). In each instance the Lord was found by those who sought Him not. It was so with Zacchaeus, hidden away amid the boughs of the trees—"Zacchaeus, make haste, and come down," was the peremptory command, for, saith the Lord, "to day, I *must* abide at thy house" (Luke 19:5). It was so with Saul of Tarsus, as he went on his way to persecute the followers of the Lamb. It was so with Lydia, "whose heart *the Lord opened*, that she attended unto the things which were spoken of Paul" (Acts 16:14). And, let us add, to the praise of the glory of God's grace, but to our own unutterable shame, it was so with the writer, when Christ "apprehended" him; apprehended him when he was altogether unconscious of his deep need, and had no desire whatever for a Saviour. Ah, blessed be His name, "*We love* him, *because* he *first* loved us!"

But let not the false conclusion be drawn that the sinner is, therefore, irresponsible. Not so. God has placed within man a moral faculty, which discerns between right and wrong. Men *know* that they are sinners, and if so they need a Saviour. God now commands *all* men everywhere to "repent," and woe be to the one who disobeys. And again we read, "And this is *his commandment*, That we should believe on the name of his Son

Jesus Christ" (I John 3:23), and if men refuse to "believe" their blood is on their own heads. Christ receives *all* who come to Him. The Gospel announces eternal life to "whosoever believeth." The door of mercy stands wide open. But, notwithstanding, it remains that men love darkness rather than light, and so strong is their love for the darkness and so deep-rooted is their antipathy against the light, that, as the Lord declared, "No man can come to me, except the Father which hath sent me draw him" (John 6:44). Here, again, is the Divine side, and it is this we are now pressing.

"And it was about the *sixth* hour. There cometh a woman of Samaria to draw water" (4:6, 7). This means it was the sixth hour after sunrise, and would be, therefore, midday. It was at the time the sun was at its greatest height and heat. Under the glare of the oriental sun, at the time when those exposed to its strong rays were most weary and thirsty, came this woman to draw water. The hour corresponded with her spiritual condition —weary and parched in her soul. "The *sixth* hour." What a significant line is this in the picture! Six invariably speaks of man in the flesh.

"*There cometh* a woman of Samaria to draw water" (v.7). This was no accident. She chose this hour because she expected the well would be deserted. But, in fact, she went to the well that day, at that time, because *God's* hour had struck when she was to meet the Saviour. Ah, our least movements are directed and over-ruled by Divine providence. It was no accident that the Midianites were passing by when Joseph's brethren had made up their minds to slay him (Gen. 37:28), nor was it merely a coincidence that these Midianites were journeying to Egypt. It was no accident that Pharaoh's daughter went down to the river to bathe, nor that she "saw" the ark, which contained the infant Moses, "among the flags" (Ex. 2:5). It was no accident that at the very time Mordecai and the Jews were in imminent danger of being killed, that Ahasuerus could not sleep, and that he occupied himself with reading the court records, which told of how, aforetime, Mordecai had befriended the king; and which led to the deliverance of God's people. No; there are no accidents in the world that is presided over by a living, reigning God!

"There cometh a woman of Samaria *to draw water.*" To "draw water" was her object. She had no thought of anything else, save that she should not be seen. She stole forth at this hour of the midday sun because a woman of her character—shunned by other women—did not care to meet any one. The woman was unacquainted with the Saviour. She had no expectation of meeting *Him*. She had no idea she would be converted that day—that was the last thing *she* would expect. Probably she said to herself, as she set forth, "No one will be at the well at this hour." Poor desolate soul. But there *was* One there! One who was *waiting* for her—"sitting *thus* on the well." He knew all about her. He knew her deep need, and He was there to minister to it. He was there to overcome her prejudices, there to subdue her rebellious will, there to *invite Himself* into her heart.

"Jesus saith unto her, Give me to drink" (4:7). Link together these two statements: "Jesus, therefore, being *wearied* with his journey . . . Jesus *saith* unto her, Give me to drink." There was everything to make Him "weary." Here was the One who had been the center of Heaven's glory, now dwelling in a world of sin and suffering. Here was the One in whom the Father delighted, now enduring the contradiction of sinners against Himself. He had, in matchless grace, come "unto his own," but with base indifference they "received him not." He was not wanted here. The ingratitude and rebellion He met with, the jealousy and opposition of the Pharisees, the spiritual dullness of His own disciples—yes, there was everything to make Him "weary." But, all praise to His peerless name, He never wearied in His ministry of grace. There was never any love of ease with Him: never the slightest selfishness: instead, nothing but one unbroken ministry of love. Fatigued in body He might be, sick at heart He must have been, but not too weary to seek out and save this sin-sick soul.

"Jesus said unto *her*." How striking is the contrast between what we have here and what is found in the previous chapter! There we are shown Nicodemus coming to Christ "by night," under cover of the darkness, so that he might guard *his reputation.* Here we behold the Lord Jesus speaking to this harlot in the full light of day—it was midday. Verily, *He* "made himself of *no reputation!*"

"Jesus said unto her, Give me to drink." The picture presented is unspeakably lovely. Christ seated on the well, and what do we find Him doing? Sitting alone with this poor outcast, to settle with her the great question of eternity. He shows her *herself,* and reveals *Himself!* This is exactly what He does with every soul that He calls to Himself. He takes us apart from the maddening world, exposes to us our desperate condition, and then makes known to us in whose Presence we are, leading us to ask from Him that precious "gift" which He alone can impart. Thus did He deal here with this Samaritan adulteress. And how this incident makes manifest the wondrous grace and infinite patience of the Saviour in His dealings with sinners! Tenderly and patiently He led this woman, step by step, touching her heart, searching her conscience, awakening her soul to a consciousness of her deep need. And how this incident also brings out the depravity of the sinner—his spiritual blindness and obstinacy; his lack of capacity to understand and respond to the Saviour's advance; yea, his slowness of heart to believe!

"Jesus saith unto her, Give me to drink." The first thing the Saviour did (note that He took the initiative) was to ask this woman for a drink of cold water—considered the very cheapest gift which this world contains. How the Son of God humbled Himself! Among the Jews it was considered the depth of degradation even to hold converse with the Samaritans; to be beholden to them for a favor would not be tolerated at all. But here we find the Lord of glory asking for a drink of water from one of the worst in this city of Samaritans! Such was His condescension that the woman herself was made to marvel.

"Give me to drink." Here was the starting point for the Divine work of grace which was to be wrought in her. Every word in this brief sentence is profoundly significant. Here was no "ye must be." The very *first* word the Saviour uttered to this poor soul, was "*give.*" It was to *grace* He would direct her thoughts. "Give me," He said. He immediately calls the attention of the sinner to Himself—"Give *me.*" But what was meant by "Give me *to drink?*" To what did the Saviour refer? Surely there can be no doubt that His mind was on something other than literal water, though, doubtless, the first and local significance of His words had reference to literal water. Just as the "weariness" of the previous verse has a deeper meaning than physical fatigue, so this "Give me to drink" signifies more than slaking His thirst. This world was a dry and thirsty land to the Saviour, and the only refreshment He found here was in ministering His grace to poor needy sinners, and receiving from them their faith and gratitude in return. This is fully borne out in the sequel, for when the disciples returned and begged Him to eat, He said unto them, "I have meat to eat that ye know not of" (v. 32). When, then, the Saviour said to this woman, "Give me to drink," it was refreshment of spirit He sought.

"Give me to drink." But how could she, a poor, despised and blinded sinner, "give" to *Him?* Ah, she could not. She must first ask of Him. She had to receive herself before she could give. In her natural state she had nothing. Spiritually she was poverty-stricken; a bankrupt. And this it was that the Saviour would press upon her, in order that she might be led to *ask* of Him. When, then, the Saviour said, "Give me to drink," He was making a demand of her with which, at this time, she was *unable* to comply. In other words, He was bringing her face to face with her *helplessness.* We are often told that God never commands us to do what we have no ability to perform, but He does, and that for two very good reasons: first, to awaken us to a sense of our impotency; second, that we might seek from Him the grace and strength we need to do that which is pleasing in His sight. What was the Law—that Law that was "holy, just and good"—given for? Its summarized requirements were, "Thou shalt love the Lord thy God with all thy heart . . . and thy neighbor as thyself." But what man ever did this? What man *could* do it? Only one—the God-man. Why, then, was the Law given? On purpose to reveal man's *impotency.* And why was that? To bring man to cast himself at the foot of God's omnipotency: "The things which are *impossible* with men *are* possible with God" (Luke 18:27). This is the first lesson in the school of God. This is what Christ would first teach this needy woman, v. 10 establishes that beyond a doubt—"Jesus answered and said unto her, If thou knewest the gift of God, and who it is that saith to thee, Give me to drink; thou wouldest have *asked* of him." But it was the moral impossibility which Christ put before this woman that aroused her curiosity and interest.

"For his disciples were gone away unto the city to buy meat" (4:8). This was no mere coincidence, but graciously ordered by the providence of God. Christ desired this poor soul to be *alone* with Himself! This Gospel of John presents Christ in the very highest aspect in which we can contemplate Him, namely, as God manifest in the flesh, as the eternal Word, as Creator of all things, as the Revealer of the Father. And yet there is none of the four Gospels in which this glorious Person is so frequently seen alone with sinners as here in John. Surely there is Divine design in this. We see Him alone with Nicodemus; alone with this Samaritan woman; alone with the convicted adulteress in John 8; alone with the man whose eyes He had opened, and who was afterwards put out of the synagogue (John 9:35). Alone with God is where the sinner needs to get—with none between and none around him. This is one reason why the writer, during the course of four pastorates, never made use of an "inquiry room," or "penitent form." Another reason was, because he could find nothing resembling them in the Word of God. They are human inventions. No priest, no intermediary, is necessary. Bid the sinner retire by himself, and get alone with God and His Word.

"For his disciples were gone away unto the city to *buy* meat." The word "buy" here points a contrast. Occurring just where it does it brings into relief the "gift" of God to which the Saviour referred, see vv. 10 and 14. Another has suggested to the writer that the action of the disciples here furnishes a striking illustration of III John 7: "taking nothing of the Gentiles." These disciples of Christ did not beg, they bought.

"Then saith the woman of Samaria unto him, How is it that thou, being a Jew, asketh drink of me, which am a woman of

Samaria? for the Jews have no dealings with the Samaritans" (4:9). The Saviour's request struck this woman with surprise. She knew the extreme dislike which Jews cherished towards Samaritans. It was accounted a sin for them to have any friendly intercourse with that people. The general tendency of this antipathy may be judged from the following extracts from the Jewish rabbins by Bishop Lightfoot:—"It is prohibited to eat the bread, and to drink the wine of the Samaritan." "If any one receives a Samaritan into his house, and ministers to him, he will cause his children to be carried into captivity." "He who eats the bread of a Samaritan, is as if he ate swine's flesh."

Aware of this extreme antipathy, the Samaritan woman expresses her amazement that a person, whom, from His dress and dialect, she perceived to be a Jew, should deign to ask, much less receive a favor from a Samaritan—"How is it that thou, being a Jew, asketh drink of me, which am a woman of Samaria?" Ah, "little did she think," to borrow the words of one of the Puritans, "of the glories of Him who sat there before her. He who sat on the well owned a Throne that was placed high above the head of the cherubim; in His arms, who then rested Himself, was the sanctuary of peace, where weary souls could lay their heads and dispose their cares, and then turn them to joys, and to guild their thorns with glory; and from that holy tongue, which was parched with heat, should stream forth rivulets of heavenly doctrine, which were to water all the world, and turn deserts into a paradise" (*Jeremy Taylor*).

"Then saith the woman of Samaria unto him, How is it that thou, being a Jew, asketh drink of me?" In a previous chapter we have pointed out the sevenfold contrast which exists between the cases of Nicodemus and this Samaritan woman. Here we call attention to a striking analogy. The very first word uttered by Nicodemus in response to the Saviour's initial statements was "How?" (3:4); and the very first word of this woman in reply to Christ's request was "How?" Both of them met the advances of the Saviour with a sceptical "How:" there were many points of dissimilarity between them, but in this particular they concurred. In His dealings with Nicodemus Christ manifests Himself as the "truth;" here in John 4 we behold the "grace" that came by Jesus Christ. "Truth" to break down the religious prejudices of a proud Pharisee; "grace" to meet the deep need of this Samaritan adulteress.

"We are full of 'how's.' The truth of God, in all its majesty and authority, is put before us; we meet it with a *how!* The grace of God, in all its sweetness and tenderness, is unfolded to our view; we reply with a *how?* It may be a theological 'how,' or a rationalistic 'how,' it matters not, the poor heart will reason instead of believing the truth, and receiving the grace of God. The *will* is active, and hence, although the conscience may be ill at ease, and the heart be dissatisfied with itself, and all around, still the unbelieving 'how' breaks forth in one form or another. Nicodemus says, 'How can a man be born when he is old?' The Samaritan says, 'How canst thou ask drink of me?'" (C. H. M., from whom we have taken several helpful thoughts).

Thus it is ever. When the Word of God declares to us the utter worthlessness of nature, the heart, instead of bowing to the holy record, sends up its unholy reasonings. When the same truth sets forth the boundless grace of God, and the free salvation which is in Christ Jesus, the heart, instead of receiving the grace, and rejoicing in the salvation, begins to reason as to *how* it can be. The fact is, the human heart is *closed* against God—against the truth of His Word, and against the grace of His heart. The Devil may speak and the heart will give its ready credence. Man may speak and the heart will greedily swallow what he says. Lies from Satan and nonsense from men all meet with a ready reception by the foolish sinner; but the moment *God* speaks, whether it be in the authoritative language of *truth,* or in the winsome accents of *grace,* all the return the heart will make is an unbelieving, rationalistic, infidelistic "*How?*" Anything and everything for the natural heart save the truth and grace of God. How deeply humbling all this is! How it ought to make us hide our faces with shame! How it should make us heed that solemn word in Ezek. 16:62, 63,

"And thou shalt know that I am the Lord: That thou mayest remember, and be confounded . . . Because of thy shame. when I am pacified toward thee for all that thou hast done, saith the Lord God."

"Then saith the woman of Samaria unto him, How is it that thou, being a Jew, asketh drink of me, which am a woman of Samaria?" How completely this manifested the *blindness* of the natural heart—"*thou* being a *Jew.*" She failed to discern the excellency of the One talking to her. She knew not that it was the Lord of glory. She saw in Him nothing but a "Jew." She was altogether ignorant of the fact that He who had humbled Himself to take upon Him the form of a servant, was none other than the Christ of God. And Christian readers, it was thus with each of us before the Holy Spirit quickened us. Until we were brought out of darkness into God's marvelous light, we "saw in him no beauty that we should desire him." All that this poor woman could think of was the *old prejudice*—"thou a Jew . . . me a woman of Samaria." So it was with you and me. When the sinner first comes into the presence of God the latent enmity of the carnal mind is stirred up, and, until Divine grace has subdued us, all we could do was to prevaricate and raise objections.

"Jesus answered and said unto her, If thou knewest the gift of God, and who it is that saith to thee, Give me to drink; thou wouldest have asked of him, and he would have given thee living water" (4:10). Our Lord was not to be put off with her "how?" He had answered the "how" of Nicodemus, and He would now answer the "how" of this woman of Sychar. He replies to Nicodemus, eventually, by pointing to Himself as the great antitype of the brazen serpent, and by telling him of the love of God in sending His Son into the world. He replies to the woman, likewise, by telling her of "the *gift* of God." It is beautiful to observe the spirit in which the Saviour answered this poor outcast. He did not enter into an argument with her about the prejudices of the Samaritans, nor did He seek to defend the Jews for their heartless treatment of them. Nor did He deal roughly with her and reproach her for her woeful ignorance and stupidity. No; He was seeking her salvation, and with infinite patience He bore with her slowness of heart to believe.

"Jesus answered and said unto her, If thou knewest the *gift* of God and *who* it is that saith to thee, Give me to drink."

There is where the root of the trouble lay. Man neither knows his need, nor the One who can minister to it. This woman was ignorant of "the *gift* of God." The language of *grace* was an unknown tongue. Like every other sinner in his natural state, this Samaritan thought *she* was the one who must do the giving. But salvation does not come to us in return for *our* giving. God is the Giver; all we have to do is receive. "If thou knewest the gift of God." What is this? It is salvation: it is eternal life: it is the "living water" spoken of by Christ at the end of the verse.

"If thou knewest the gift of God, and *who it is* that saith to thee, Give me to drink." But this woman did not know Who it was that spoke to her, nor of the marvelous condescension of this One who had asked her for a "drink." Had she done so, she, in turn, would have "asked of Him." He was ready to give, if she would but take the place of a receiver, and thus make *Him* the Giver; instead of her wanting to take the place of a giver and make Him the Receiver.

"Thou wouldest have asked of him." It is blessedly true that the only thing between the sinner and eternal life is an "ask." But asking proceeds from knowing. "If thou *knewest* . . . thou wouldest have *asked*." But O how reluctant the sinner is to take this place. God has to do much for him and in him before he is ready to really "ask." The sinner has to be brought to a realization of his awful condition and terrible danger: he must see himself as lost, undone, and bound for the lake of fire. He has to be made to see his desperate need of a Saviour. Again, God has to show him the utter vanity and worthlessness of everything of this world, so that he experiences an acute "thirst" for the Water of Life. He has to be driven to despair, until he is made to wonder whether God can possibly save such a wretch as he. He has to be stript of the filthy rags of his own self-righteousness, and be made willing to come to God just as he is, as an empty-handed beggar ready to receive Divine charity. He has to really come into the presence of Christ and have personal dealings with Him. He has to make definite request for himself. This, in part, is what is involved, before the sinner will "ask." Before we *ask*, God has to deal with the conscience, enlighten the understanding, subdue the rebellious will, and open the heart, the door of which is fast closed against Himself. All of this is what Christ did with this woman of our lesson. We are not saved because of our seeking; we have to be sought. "And who it is that saith to thee:" notice, particularly, this "*who* it is," not "*what* it is"—it is not doctrine any more than doing. It is personal dealings with Christ that is needed; with Him who is the Source and Giver of "life."

Attention has often been called to the striking contrast in the manner of our Lord's speech with Nicodemus and His method of dealing with this poor Samaritan adulteress. The Lord did not deal with souls in any mechanical, stereotyped way, as it is to be feared many Christian-workers do today. No; He dealt with each according to the condition of heart they were in. Christ did not begin with the Gospel when dealing with Nicodemus. Instead, He said, "Marvel not that I said unto thee, Ye must be born again." There is no good news in a "ye must be." If a man must be born again, what is *he* going to do in order that he *may be?* What does all his past life amount to?—no matter how full of deeds of benevolence, acts of kindness, and religious performances. Just nothing: *a new* beginning has to be made. But not only is an entirely different order of life imperative, but man has to be "born from above." What, then, can the poor sinner do in the matter? Nothing, absolutely nothing. To tell a man he "must be born again" is simply a shut door in the face of all fleshly pretentions; and that is precisely what Christ intended with Nicodemus.

But *why* shut the door before Nicodemus? It was because he belonged to the Pharisees. He was a member of that class, one of whom Christ portrayed as standing in the Temple and saying to God, "I thank thee, that I am not as other men are, extortioners, unjust, adulterers," etc. (Luke 18:11). Nicodemus was not only a highly respectable and moral man, but he was deeply religious. And what he most needed was just what he heard, for the Lord Jesus never made any mistakes. Nicodemus prided himself upon his respectability and religious standing: evidence of this is seen in his coming to Jesus "by night"—he was conscious of how much he risked by this coming; he feared he was endangering his reputation among the people by visiting this Nazarene. Therefore his self-righteousness must be smashed up; his religious pride must be broken down. The force, then, of what our Lord said to this ruler of the Jews was, "Nicodemus, with all your education and reformation, morality and religion, you have not begun to live that life which is pleasing to God, *for that* you must be born again." And this was simply to prepare the way *for* the Gospel; to prepare a self-righteous man to receive it.

How entirely different was our Lord's speech with this woman at the well! To her He never so much as mentions the need for the new birth; instead, He tells her at once of the "gift of God." In the case of this woman there was no legalistic and religious pattern to be swept away. Her moral character and religious standing were already gone. But it was far otherwise with Nicodemus. It is very evident that he felt he *had* something to stand upon and glory in. What he needed to know was that all of this in which he prided himself was worthless before God. Even though a master of Israel, he was utterly *unfit* to enter God's *kingdom,* and nothing could show him this quicker than for the Lord to say unto him "Ye must be born again."

Do what you will with nature, educate, cultivate, sublimate it as much as you please; raise it to the loftiest pinnacle of the temple of science and philosophy; summon to your aid all the ornaments and ordinances of the legal system, and all the appliances of man's religion; make vows and resolutions of moral reform; weary yourself out with the monotonous round of religious duties; betake yourself to vigils, fastings, prayers, and alms, and the entire range of "*dead* works," and after all, yonder Samaritan adulteress is as near to the kingdom of God as you, seeing that you as well as she "*must* be born again." Neither you nor she has one jot or tittle to present to God, either in the way of title to the kingdom, or of capacity to enjoy it. It is, and must be, *all of grace,* from beginning to end.

What, then, is the remedy? That to which Christ, at the close, pointed out to Nicodemus: "As Moses lifted up the serpent in the wilderness, even so must the Son of man be lifted up: That whosoever believeth in him should not perish, but have eternal life" (3:14, 15). But for whom was this brazen serpent intended? Why, for any bitten creature, just because he *was* bitten. The wound was the title. The title to what? To look at the serpent. And what then? He that looked, *lived.* Blessed Gospel, "look and live." True for Nicodemus: true for the woman of Sychar: true for every sinbitten son and daughter of Adam. There is no limit, no restriction. The Son of Man has been lifted up, that *whosoever looks to Him,* in simple faith, might have what Adam in innocency never possessed, and what the law of Moses never proposed, even "everlasting life."

The Gospel meets men on a common platform. Nicodemus had moral character, social standing, religious reputation; the woman at the well had nothing. Nicodemus was at the top of the social ladder; she was at the bottom. You could hardly get anything higher than a "Master of Israel," and you could scarcely get anything lower than a Samaritan adulteress; yet so far as standing before God, fitness for His holy presence, title to heaven was concerned, they were both on one common level. But how few understand this! So far as standing before God was concerned there was "no difference" between this learned and religious Nicodemus and the wretched woman of Sychar. To Nicodemus Christ said, "Ye must be born again;" this brief statement completely swept away the foundation from under his feet. Nothing less than a new nature was required from him; and nothing more was needed for her. Uncleanness could not enter heaven, nor could Phariseeism. Each must be born again. True, there was a great difference morally and socially between Nicodemus and this woman—that goes without saying. No sensible person needs to be told that morality is better than vice, that sobriety is preferable to drunkenness, that it is better to be an honorable man than a thief. But none of these will save, or contribute anything toward the salvation of a sinner. None of these will secure admittance into the kingdom of God. Both Nicodemus and the Samaritan adulteress were dead; there was no more spiritual life in the one than in the other.

"Jesus answered and said unto her, If thou knewest the gift of God, and who it is that saith to thee, Give me to drink; thou wouldest have asked of him, and he would have given thee living water." There are some who regard the "living water" here as the Holy Spirit, and there is something to be said in favor of this view; but personally, while not dissenting from it, we think that more is included within the scope of our Lord's words. We believe the "living water" has reference to *salvation,* salvation in its widest sense, with all that it embraces. The figure of "water" is most suggestive, and like all others which are found in Scripture calls for prayerful and prolonged meditation in order to discover its fulness and beauty. At least seven lines of thought appear to be suggested by "water"—living water—as a figure of the salvation which Christ gives.

1. Water is *a gift from God.* It is something which man, despite all his boasted wisdom, is quite unable to create. For water we are absolutely dependent upon God. It is equally so with His salvation, of which water is here a figure. 2. Water is something which is *indispensable to man.* It is not a luxury, but a vital necessity. It is that without which man cannot live. It is equally so with God's salvation—apart from it men are eternally lost. 3. Water is that which meets a *universal need;* it is not merely a local requirement, but a general one. All are in need of water. It is so with God's salvation. It is not merely some particular class of people, who are more wicked than their fellows, for all who are outside of Christ are lost. 4. Water is that which first *descends from the heavens.* It is not a product of the earth, but comes down from above. So is it with salvation: it is "of the Lord." 5. Water is a *blessed boon*: it cools the fevered brow, slakes the thirst, refreshes and satisfies. And so does the salvation which is to be found in Christ. 6. Water is something of which *we never tire.* Other things satiate us, but not so with water. It is equally true of God's salvation to the heart of every one who has really received it. 7. Water is *strangely and unevenly distributed by God.* In some places there is an abundance; in others very little; in others none at all. It is so with God's salvation. In some nations there are many who have been visited by the Dayspring from on high; in others there are few who have passed from death unto life; while in others there seem to be none at all.

"He would have given thee living water." How blessed this is! The living water is without money and without price: it is a "gift." This gift can be obtained from Christ alone. This gift can be procured from Christ only by asking Him for it. How blessed the gift! How wondrous the Giver! How simple the terms! Here, then, was the Christ of God preaching to this poor fallen woman the Gospel of His grace. Here was the Messiah in Israel winning to Himself a despised Samaritan. This is hardly what *we* would have looked for. And how the *unexpected* meets us again and again in these Gospels! How vastly different were things from what we had imagined them! Here was the Son of God, incarnate, born into this world; and where would we expect to find His cradle? Why, surely in Jerusalem, the "city of the great king." Instead, He was born in Bethlehem, which was "little among the thousands in Judah." Yes, born in Bethlehem, and cradled in a *manger*—the very last place we had looked for Him! And for what purpose has He visited this earth? To offer Himself as a sacrifice for sins. To whom shall we go to learn more about this? Surely, to the priests and Levites. Ah, and what do we learn about them in this Gospel? Why, *they* were the very ones who knew not the One who stood in their midst (John 1:26). No, if we would learn about Him who had come to be the great sacrifice, we must turn away from the priests and Levites, and go yonder into the "wilderness"—the last place, again, we would think of—and listen to that strange character clad in raiment of camel's hair, with a leathern girdle about his loins; and *he* would tell us about the Lamb of God which taketh away the sin of the world. Once more: suppose it had been *worship* we had desired to learn about, whither had we betaken ourselves? Why, surely, to the Temple—*that,* of all places, must be where the Lord God is worshipped in the truest form. But again would our quest have been in vain, for the Father's house was now but "a house of merchandise." Whom had we sought out if instruction in the things of God had been our desire? Why, surely, one of those best qualified to teach us would be Nicodemus, "a Master of Israel." But again would we have met with disappointment.

Now if *we* would have gone to Nicodemus to learn of the things of God, who among us would have imagined these very truths being revealed by a weary Traveller by one of Samaria's wells, to an audience of one! Who were the Samaritans to be privileged thus? Should we not expect to find this much-favored woman, and a people so highly honored, as being the descendants of some race of age-long seekers after God? Would we not conclude they must be the offspring of men who for long centuries had lived in one continued and supreme endeavor to purge their thoughts and ceremonies from every false and impure admixture? But read again II Kings 17 for the inspired account of the unlovely origin of the Samaritans. *They* were two-thirds heathen! Ah! after reading this chapter would *we* not have expected to find *worship* in Jerusalem and *idolatry* in Samaria! Instead of which, we find idolatry in Jerusalem, and (before we are through with John 4) the true worship in Samaria. And what does all this go to prove? It shows that the wisdom of this world is foolishness with God. It demonstrates how utterly incompetent we are for drawing conclusions and reasoning about *spiritual* things. It exemplifies what was said long ago through Isaiah: "For my thoughts are not your thoughts, neither are my ways your ways, saith the Lord" (55:8). How foolish are man's reasonings; how wise God's "foolishness!"

And here we must stop. In the next lesson we shall continue our study of this wondrous and blessed chapter. In the meantime, let the students prayerfully ponder the following questions:—

1. What particular trait of the sinner's heart is manifested by the woman in the next statement? v. 11.—we do not mean her blindness or stupidity.
2. What spiritual truth did she unconsciously voice when she said, "the well is deep"? v. 11.
3. What God-dishonoring principle was enunciated by her in v. 12?
4. To what was Christ referring when He said, "this water"? v. 13.
5. How does v. 14 bring out the eternal security of the believer?
6. What did the woman mean by her words in v. 15?
7. Why did Christ say to her, "Go, call thy husband?" v. 16.

CHAPTER THIRTEEN

Christ at Sychar's Well (Continued)

John 4:11-19

In viewing the Saviour's conversation with this Samaritan woman as a sample case of God's gracious dealings with a sinner, we have seen, thus far: First, that the Lord took the initiative, being the first to speak. Second, that His first word to her was "Give" – directing her thoughts at once to *grace;* and that His next was "me" leading her to be occupied with *Himself.* Third, that He brings her face to face with her helplessness by asking her for a "drink," which in its deeper meaning, signified that He was seeking her faith and confidence to refresh His spirit. Fourth, this was met by an exhibition of the woman's prejudice, which, in principle, illustrated the enmity of the carnal mind against God. Fifth, Christ then affirmed that she was ignorant of the way of salvation and of His own Divine glory. Sixth, He referred to eternal life under the expressive figure of "living water." Seventh, He assured her that this living water was offered to her as a "gift," on the condition that she was to "ask" for it, and thus take the place of a receiver. This brief summary brings us to the end of verse 10, and from that point we will now proceed, first presenting an Analysis of the verses which immediately follow:–

1. The Woman's Ignorance, v. 11.
2. The Woman's Insolence, v. 12.
3. The Saviour's Gracious Promise, vv. 13, 14.
4. The Woman's Prejudice Overcome, v. 15.
5. The Saviour's Arrow for the Conscience, v. 16.
6. The Saviour's Omniscience Displayed, vv. 17, 18.
7. The Woman's Dawning Perception, v. 19.

As we read the first section of this blessed narrative we were struck with the amazing condescension of the Lord of Glory, who so humbled Himself as to converse with this fallen woman of Samaria. Now, as we turn to consider the section which follows, we cannot fail to be impressed with the wondrous patience of the Saviour. He had invited this wretched creature to ask from Him, and He promised to give her living water; but instead of promptly closing with His gracious offer, the woman continued to raise objections. But Christ did not turn away in disgust, and leave her to suffer the merited results of her waywardness and stubbornness; He bore with her stupidity, and with Divine long-sufferance wore down her opposition, and won her to Himself.

"The woman saith unto him, Sir, thou hast nothing to draw with, and the well is deep: from whence then hast thou that living water?" (4:11). Four things are brought out by this statement. First, her continued blindness to the glory of Him who addressed her. Second, her occupation with material things. Third, her concentration on the means rather than the end. Fourth, her ignorance of the Source of the "living water." Let us briefly consider each of these separately.

In v. 9 we find that this woman referred to Christ as "a Jew." In replying, the Saviour reproached her for her ignorance by saying, "If thou knewest the gift of God, and *who* it is that saith to thee, Give me to drink; thou wouldest have asked of him" (v. 10). It is true she had never before met the Lord Jesus, but this did not excuse her. It was because she was blind that she saw in Him no beauty that she should *desire* Him. And it is only unbelief which prevents the sinner today from recognizing in that One who died upon the cross the Son of God, and the only One who could save him from his sins. And unbelief is not a thing to be pitied, but blamed. But now that Christ had revealed Himself as the One who dispensed the "gift" of God, the Samaritan woman only answered, "Sir, *Thou hast* nothing to draw with!" Poor woman, how little she knew as yet the Divine dignity of that One who had come to seek and to save that which was lost. How complete was her blindness. And how accurately does she picture *our* state by nature. Exactly the same was our condition when God, in infinite mercy, began His dealings with us—our eyes were closed to the perfections of His beloved Son, and "we hid as it were our faces from him."

"Sir, thou hast nothing *to draw with*." How this shows the trend of her thoughts. Her mind was centered upon wells and buckets! And this, again, illustrates a principle of general application. This woman is still to be viewed as a representative character. Behold in her an accurate portrayal of the sinner, as we see her mind concentrated upon *material things*. Her mind was occupied with the world—its duties and employments—and hence she could not rise to any higher thoughts: she could not discern *who* it was that addressed her, nor *what* He was offering. And thus it is with all who are of the world: they are kept away from the things of Christ by the things of time and sense. The Devil uses just such things to keep the soul from the Saviour. "Let it be what it may, let it be only a waterpot, he cares not, so long as it occupies the mind to the exclusion of the knowledge of Christ. He cares not for the instrument, so long as he gains his own ends, to draw the mind away from the apprehension of spiritual things. It may be pleasure, it may be amusement, gain, reputation, family duties, lawful employments, so that it keeps the soul from fixing on Christ. This is all he wants. A waterpot will serve his purpose, just as well as a palace, so that he can blind them, '*lest* the light of the glorious Gospel of Christ, who is the image of God, should shine unto them'" (J. N. Darby, from whom we have extracted other thoughts, embodied in our exposition above and below).

Ah! dear friend, Is there anything which has thus been keeping you away from Christ—from seeking His great salvation, and obtaining from Him the "living water?" That thing may be quite innocent and harmless, yea, it may be something praiseworthy in itself. Even lawful employments, family duties, may keep a soul from the Saviour, and hinder you from receiving His priceless gift. Satan is very subtle in the means he employs to blind the mind. Did you ever notice that in the Parable of the Sower the Lord tells us that the things which "choke the Word" are "the cares of this world, and the deceitfulness of riches" (Matt. 13:22)?

Should an unsaved soul read these lines we ask you to *see yourself* in the case of this woman, as far as we have yet considered it. Her thoughts were on the purpose which had brought her to the well—a lawful and necessary purpose, no doubt, but one which occupied her mind to the exclusion of the things of Christ! She could think of nothing but wells and buckets—she was, therefore, unable to discern the love, the grace, the winsomeness of that blessed One who sought her salvation. And how many a man there is today so busily occupied with making a living for his family, and how many a woman so concerned with the duties of the home—lawful and necessary things—that Christ and His salvation are *crowded out!* So it was with this Samaritan woman. She thought only of her *bodily* need: her mind was centered on the common round of daily tasks. And thus it is with many another now. They are too busy to take time to study the things of God. They are too much occupied with *their* "waterpots" to listen to the still small voice of God.

"Sir, thou hast nothing to draw with." These words illustrate another principle which, in its outworkings, stands between many a sinner and salvation. The woman's mind was centered on *means,* rather than the end. She was occupied with something to "draw with," rather than with Christ. And how many today are concerned far more with their own efforts and doings than with the Saviour Himself. And even where their eyes are not upon their own works, they are frequently turned to the evangelist, or to the 'inquiry room,' or 'the mourner's bench.' And where this is not the case, the Devil will get them occupied with their own repentance and faith. Anything, so long as he can keep the poor sinner from looking to *Christ alone.*

And, too, we may observe how this woman was *limiting* Christ to the use of means. She supposed He could not provide the "living water" unless He had something to "draw with." And how many imagine they cannot be saved except in some 'Revival Meetings,' or at least in a church-house. But when it pleases God to do so, He acts independently of all means (the Word excepted). When He desires to create a world, He speaks and it is done! He rains manna from heaven; furnishes water out of the rock, and supplies honey from the carcass of the lion!

"The woman saith unto him, Sir, thou hast nothing to draw with and the well is deep: from whence then hast thou that living water?" She continues to raise objections, and press her questions. No sooner had the Lord answered one than she brings forward another. The Lord had replied to her "How?" by telling of the "gift" of God, the "living water." Now she asks "Whence?" this was to be obtained. She knew not the Source from whence this "living water" proceeded. All she knew was that the well was deep.

"The well is deep." And there is a deep meaning in these words. The well *is* deep—far deeper than our hands can reach down to. From whence then shall man obtain the "living water?" *How* shall he procure "eternal life?" By keeping the Law? Nay, verily, for "by the deeds of the law there shall no flesh be justified" (Rom. 3:20). Is it by cultivating the best that is within us by nature? No, for "in my flesh dwelleth no good thing" (Rom. 7:18). Is it by living up to the light we have, and doing the best we know how? No, for we are "without strength" (Rom. 5:6). What then? Ah! dear reader, listen: This "living water" is not a wage to be earned, a prize to be sought, a crown to be won. No; it is a gift, God's free gift in Christ: "The gift of God is eternal life through Jesus Christ our Lord" (Rom. 6:23); yes; the well *is* deep. Into awful depths of suffering had the Saviour to descend before the life-giving Water could be furnished to sinners.

"Art thou greater than our father Jacob, which gave us the well, and drank thereof himself, and his children, and his cattle?" (4:12). As another has said, "How little she knew, as yet, of the One she was addressing. The well might be deep, but there is something deeper still, even her soul's deep need; and something deeper than that again, even the grace that had brought Him down from heaven to meet her need. But so little did she know of Him, that she could ask, 'Art thou greater than our father Jacob, which gave us the well?' She knew not that she was speaking to Jacob's God—to the One who had formed Jacob and given him all that he ever possessed. She knew nothing of this. Her eyes were yet closed, and this was the true secret of her '*How?*' and '*Whence?*'"

How much this explains! When we find people asking questions, unbelieving questions, concerning the things of God, it is a sure sign that they need to have their eyes opened. The rationalist, the critic, and the infidel are blind. It is their very blindness that causes them to ask questions, raise difficulties, and create doubts, They deem themselves very clever, but they do only exhibit their folly. However, in the case of this Samaritan woman her questions proceeded not from a bold infidelity, but from nature's blindness and ignorance, and therefore the Lord dealt patiently with her. He knew how to silence a rationalist, and ofttimes He dismissed a carping critic in a summary manner. But there were also occasions when, in marvelous condescension and gracious patience, He waited on an ignorant inquirer for the purpose of resolving his difficulties and removing his fears. And thus it was at the well at Sychar. He was not to be put off with her quibbling, nor could He be wearied by her dullness. He bore with her (as He did with each of us) in marvelous longsufferance, and left her not until He had fully met the deep need of her soul by the revelation of Himself.

"Art thou greater than our father Jacob, which gave us the well, and drank thereof himself?" Once again we may discover here a deeper significance than what appears on the surface. Attention is called to the *antiquity* of the well from which Jacob and his children drank. Beautiful is the underlying spiritual lesson. The "well" is as old as man the sinner. The salvation of which the "water" of this "well" speaks, had refreshed the hearts of Abel and Enoch, Noah and Abraham, and all the Old Testament saints. God has had but one way of salvation since sin entered the world. Salvation has always been by grace, through faith, altogether apart from human works. The Gospel is no novelty: it was "preached before unto Abraham" (Gal. 3:8). Yea, it was preached to Adam and Eve in the Garden of Eden, when, clothing our fallen first parents with coats of skins (Gen. 3:21), God made known the fact "without shedding of blood is no remission," and that through *the* death of an innocent substitute a covering was provided which fitted the guilty and the defiled to stand unabashed in the presence of the thrice holy One, because "accepted in the Beloved."

"Jesus answered and said unto her, Whosoever drinketh of this water shall thirst again" (4:13). The Lord Jesus was not to be put off. He was determined to reveal Himself to this sin-sick soul. "Whosoever drinketh of this water shall thirst again." The seat of the "thirst" within man lies too deep for the waters of this earth to quench. The "thirst" of man's soul is a spiritual one, and that is why material things are unable to slake it. Earth's deepest well may be fathomed and drained, and the needy soul remain thirsty after all. Men and women may take their fill of pleasure, yet will it fail to satisfy. They may surround themselves with every comfort and luxury that wealth can provide, and the heart still be empty. They may court the honors of the world, and climb to the highest pinnacle of human fame, but the plaudits of men will leave an aching void behind them. They may explore the whole realm of philosophy and science, until they become as wise as Solomon, but like Israel's king of old, they will discover that all under the sun is only "vanity and vexation of spirit." Over all the wells of this world's providing must be written, "Whosoever drinketh of this water shall thirst again."

This is true not only of the material, the mental, and the social realms, but of the religious, too. Man may awaken within us certain desires, but he cannot satisfy them. Man may exhort and persuade, and we may make resolutions, amend our lives, become very religious, and yet "thirst again." The religious systems of human manufacture hold not the Water of Life. They do but disappoint. Nothing but the "living water" can quench our thirst and satisfy our hearts, and only *Christ* can give this.

"Whosoever drinketh of this water shall *thirst again*." What an awful illustration of this is furnished in Luke 16. There the Saviour sets before us a man clothed in purple and fine linen, who fared sumptuously every day. He drank deeply of the wells of this passing world; but he thirsted again. O see him, as the Son of God lifts the veil which hides the unseen; see him lifting up his eyes in hell-torments, craving, but craving in vain, a single drop of water to cool his parched tongue. There is not as much as a drop of water in hell! There he thirsts, and the unspeakably dreadful thing is that he will thirst *forever and ever*. Fearfully solemn is this for all; but perfectly appalling for the children of ease and luxury, and they who spend their time going from well to well of this world, and giving no serious thought to an eternity of burning in the lake of fire. O that it may please God to cause some such to give these lines a thoughtful consideration, and arrest their attention, and lead them to the Lord Jesus Christ, the Giver of that living water of which whosoever drinketh shall never thirst.

"But whosoever drinketh of the water that I shall give him shall never thirst" (4:14). Here is satisfaction to the soul. The one who has *asked* and *received* is now satisfied. The Lord goes on to say, "but the water that I shall give him shall be in him a well of water springing up into everlasting life." The believer now has a well of living water within, ever fresh, ever flowing, ever springing up toward its native source, for water always seeks its own level. But let us weigh each expression. "Whosoever *drinketh.*" What is drinking? It is ministering to a felt need. It is a personal act of appropriation. It is a taking into myself that which was, previously, without me. "Of the water that I shall *give* him." This "water" is "eternal life," and this is not bought or won, but is received as a "gift," for the "gift of God is eternal life through Jesus Christ our Lord." "Shall never thirst:" here the Lord speaks according to the *fulness* of the gift bestowed: as to our *enjoyment* of it, that is conditioned upon the way in which faith maintains us in fellowship with the Giver. "Never thirst" denotes a satisfying portion. "Never thirst" argues the eternal security of the recipient. Were it possible for a believer to forfeit salvation through unworthiness, this verse would not be true, for every lost soul will "thirst," thirst forever in hell. "Shall be in him a well of water springing up into everlasting life": this "gift," this "living water," is a present possession, imparted by grace, and is something within the believer.

"But whosoever drinketh of the water that I shall give him shall never thirst." To borrow again the language of the eloquent Puritan: "Here we labour, but receive no benefit; we sow many times, and reap not; we reap, and we do not gather in; or gather in, and do not possess; or possess and do not enjoy; or if we enjoy, we are still unsatisfied: it is with anguish of spirit and circumstances of vexation. A great heap of riches makes neither our clothes more warm, our meat more nutritive, nor our beverage more palatable. It feeds the eye but never fills it. Like drink to a person suffering from dropsy, it increases the thirst and promotes the torment. But the grace of God fills the furrows of the heart; and, as the capacity increases, it grows itself in equal degrees, and never suffers any emptiness or dissatisfaction, but carries contentment and fulness all the way; and the degrees of augmentation are not steps and near approaches to satisfaction, but increasings of the capacity. The soul is satisfied all the way, and receives more, not because it wanted any, but that it can now hold the more, being become more receptive of felicity; and in every minute of sanctification, there is so excellent a condition of joy that the very calamities, afflictions, and persecutions of the world, are turned into felicities by the activity of the prevailing ingredient: like a drop of water falling into a tun of wine, it is ascribed into a new form, losing its own nature by a conversion in one more noble. These were the waters which were given us to drink, when, with the rod of God, the Rock, Christ Jesus, was smitten. The Spirit of God moves forever upon these waters; and, when the angel of the covenant had stirred the pool, whosoever descends hither shall find health and peace, joys spiritual, and the satisfaction of eternity" (*Jeremy Taylor*).

"The woman saith unto Him, Sir, give me this water, that I thirst not, neither come hither to draw" (4:15). She is still more or less in the dark. The natural mind is occupied with natural things, and it contemplates everything through that medium; it is confined to its own little circle of feelings and ideas; and can neither see nor feel anything beyond it; it lives in its own cramped realm, finds there its own enjoyment and employment, and if left to itself, will live and die there. Poor woman! The Saviour of sinners was before her, but she knew Him not. He was speaking words of grace to her, but as yet, she did not fully comprehend. He had asked for a drink, and she had replied with a "*How?*" He had told her of God's gift, and she had replied with a "*Whence?*" He had spoken of an everlasting well, and she seeks only to be spared the trouble of coming hither to draw.

And yet while all that we have just said above is no doubt true, nevertheless, as we take a closer look at this last statement of the woman, we may detect signs more hopeful. Her words afford evidence that the patient dealing of Christ with her was not in vain, yea, that light was beginning to illumine her darkened understanding. Note, she now appropriates His word, and says, "Sir, *give* me to drink." Relief from daily toil was, no doubt, the thought uppermost in her mind; yet, and mark it well, she was now *willing* to be indebted to a "Jew" for that! There was still much ignorance; but her prejudice was being overcome; her heart was being won. What, then, is the next step? Why, her *conscience* must be reached. A sense of need must be created. And how is this accomplished? By a conviction of sin. The first thought in connection with salvation, the prime meaning of the word itself, is that of deliverance from something. Salvation implies danger, and the sinner will not flee to Christ as a Refuge from the wrath to come until a due sense (not merely of wretchedness, but) of guilt is upon him. There can be no blessing till there is conviction and confession of sin. It is not until we discover our case to be truly *desperate* that we betake ourselves to Christ—until then, we attempt to prescribe for ourselves. Herein lies the force of the Saviour's next word.

"Jesus said unto her, Go, call thy husband, and come hither" (4:16). It is strange that so many have missed the point of this. A little meditation will surely discern not only the solemnity, but the blessedness, of this word from the Saviour, to the woman whose heart was slowly opening to receive Him. It is mainly a matter of finding the proper emphasis. Two things the Lord bade her do: the first was solemn and searching; the second gracious and precious. "*Go*," He said, "call thy husband"—that was a word addressed to her conscience. "And *come hither*"—that was a word for her heart. The force of what He said was this: If you really want this living water of which I have been telling you, you can obtain it only as a poor, convicted, contrite sinner. But not only did He say "Go," but He added "Come." She was not only to go and call her husband, but she was to come back to Christ *in her true character*. It was a marvelous mingling of "grace" and "truth." Truth for her conscience; grace for her heart. Truth which required her to come out into the light of her proper character, as a self-confessed sinner; grace which invited her to return to the Saviour's side. Well may we admire the wonderful ways of Him "in whom are hid all the treasures of wisdom and knowledge" (Col. 2:3).

"The woman answered and said, I have no husband. Jesus saith unto her, Thou hast well said I have no husband: For thou hast had five husbands: and he whom thou now hast is not thy husband: in that saidst thou truly" (4:17, 18). How this exhibits the Deity of Christ! He revealed His omniscience. He knew all about this woman—her heart, her life, her very thoughts; nothing could be hid from Him. She might be a complete stranger to Him in the flesh, yet was He thoroughly acquainted with her. It was the same with Peter: the Saviour knew him thoroughly the first time they met, see 1:42 and our comments thereon. So, too, He saw Nathanael under the fig tree before he came to Him. And so, dear reader, He knows all about *you*. Nothing can be concealed from His all-seeing eye. But this will not trouble you if everything has been brought out into the light, and confessed before Him.

"The woman saith unto Him, Sir, I perceive that thou art a prophet" (4:19). A "prophet" is God's spokesman. This poor soul now recognized the voice of *God*. He had spoken more deeply than any man to her soul. The Divine arrow of conviction had pierced her conscience, and the effect is striking: "I *perceive*." Her eyes were beginning to open: she sees something. She discovers herself to be in the presence of some mysterious personage whom she owns as God's spokesman. It was through her conscience the light began to enter! And it is ever thus. O dear reader, have you experienced this for yourself? Has *your* conscience been in the presence of that Light which makes all things manifest? Have you seen yourself as guilty, undone, lost, Christless, hell-deserving? Has the arrow ever entered your conscience? Christ has various arrows in His quiver. He had an arrow for Nicodemus, and He had an arrow for this adulteress. They were different arrows, but they did their work. "He that doeth truth cometh to the light, that his deeds may be made manifest" (3:21) was the arrow for the master in Israel. "Go, call thy husband" was His arrow for this Samaritan woman. The question of sin and righteousness must be settled in the presence of God. Has, then, this vital and all-important matter been settled between *your soul* and God? If so, you will be able to appreciate the sequel—the remainder of this wonderful and blessed narrative.

There is a principle here of great importance to the believer. An exercised conscience precedes intelligence in the things of God. Spiritual illumination comes through the heart more than through the mind. They who are most anxious to have a better understanding of the Holy Oracles need to pray earnestly for God to put His fear upon them, that they may be more careful in avoiding the things that displease Him. One of our deepest needs is a more sensitive conscience. In Heb. 5:11-13 we read of those who were "dull of hearing" and incapacitated to receive the deeper things of God. "Dullness of hearing" does not mean they were suffering from a stupefied mind, but rather from a calloused conscience. The last verse of Heb. 5 speaks of those who were qualified to receive the deeper truths: "But strong meat belongeth to them that are of full age, even those who by reason of use *have their senses exercised* to discern both good and evil." Thus it was for our learning that we are shown that perception of spiritual things came to the Samaritan woman through, and as the result of, a conscience active in the presence of God.

As preparation for the next lesson we ask the interested reader to ponder the following questions:—

1. What is signified by "salvation is of the Jews"? v. 22.
2. What is meant by worshipping "in spirit and in truth"? v. 24.
3. Make a careful study of passages both in the Old and New Testaments which speak of "worship."
4. What is implied by the woman's words in v. 25?
5. What constrained the disciples to remain silent? v. 27.
6. What is the force of the "then" in v. 28?
7. What principle is illustrated by the woman leaving her waterpot?

CHAPTER FOURTEEN

Christ at Sychar's Well (Concluded)

John 4:20-30

In the last chapter we continued our exposition of John 4 down to the end of v. 19. It is of surpassing interest to follow the course of the Saviour's dealings with the poor Samaritan adulteress — the Divine patience, the infinite grace and tenderness, the faithful application of the truth to her heart and conscience. We have been struck, too, with the expose of human depravity which this instance furnishes: not simply with the dissolute life of the woman, but with her prejudice, her stupidity, her occupation with material things, her procrastination — all so many exhibitions of what is in us by nature: "As in water face answereth to face, so the heart of man to man" (Prov. 27:19.) In the attitude of this sinner toward Christ we see an accurate portrayal of our own past history. Let us now resume at the point where we left off in our last.

We append an Analysis of the passage which is to be before us:—

1. The place of worship, vv. 20, 21.
2. Worshippers sought by the Father, vv. 22, 23.
3. The character of acceptable worship, v. 24.
4. The woman's desire for Christ, v. 25.
5. Christ fully reveals Himself, v. 26.
6. The disciples' surprise and silence, v. 27.
7. The gratitude and zeal of a saved soul, vv. 28-30.

"Our fathers worshipped in this mountain; and ye say, that in Jerusalem is the place where men ought to worship" (4:20). This woman was not regenerated, though she was on the very eve of being so. She was at that point where it is always very difficult (if not impossible) for us to determine on which side of the line a person stands. Regeneration is an instantaneous act and experience, but preceding it there is a process, sometimes brief, usually more or less protracted. During this process or transitional stage there is a continual conflict between the light and the darkness, and nothing is very clearly defined. There is that which is the fruit of the Spirit's operations, and there is that which springs from the activities of the flesh. We may detect both of these at this point in John 4.

In the previous verse the woman had said, "Sir, I perceive that thou art a prophet." This evidenced the fact that light was beginning to illumine her understanding: there was the dawning of spiritual intelligence. But immediately following this we discover the workings of the flesh—"*Our* fathers worshipped in this mountain; and *ye* say, that in Jerusalem is the place where men ought to worship." Here was the enmity of the carnal mind showing itself again. It was a return to the old prejudice, which was voiced at the commencement of conversation—see v. 9. The subject of *where* to worship was one of the leading points of contention between the Jews and the Samaritans. The Lord had introduced a very disquieting theme. He had spoken directly to her conscience; He had been convicting of Sin. And when a sinner's conscience is disturbed, instinctively he seeks to throw it off. He endeavors to turn aside the sharp point of the accusing shaft, by occupying his mind with other things.

There is little doubt that this woman raised the subject of worship at this stage for the purpose of diverting a theme of conversation which was far from agreeable or creditable to her. "Sir, I perceive that thou art a prophet," she had said, and so, glad of an opportunity to shift the discourse from a subject so painful, she introduces the great point of controversy between the Jews and the Samaritans, that she might hear His opinion respecting it. And, too, this woman was really interested in the friendly advances of this mysterious Stranger who had spoken to her so graciously and yet so searchingly: and doubtless she was anxious to know how *He* would decide the age-long dispute. It is no uncommon thing for persons living in sin, not merely to pretend, but really to *have* an interest in, and a zeal for, what they term 'religion.' Speculation about points in theology is frequently found in unnatural union with habitual neglect of moral duty. Ofttimes a sinner seeks protection from shafts of conviction which follow the plain violation of the law of God, by discussions respecting orthodoxy and heterodoxy. Ah! "who can understand the errors" of that deceitful and desperately wicked thing, the human heart!

In this question of the woman we may discover an underlying principle of general application. Her conscience had been exercised over sin, in the presence of God, and the effect upon her, as upon most quickened souls, was to be concerned with the matter of "worship" — *where* to worship is the question which now engages the attention. Really, it is only *self* again in one of its ten thousand forms. First the sinner is conscious of his prejudice; then he is occupied with his sins; then he turns to his own repentance and faith; and then where to worship — anything but Christ Himself! So it was with this woman here. The Lord had pointed out what it was that kept her from asking for the "gift of God," namely, *ignorance*. True, she was clear on some points. She was versed in the contention between the Jews and the Samaritans; she had been instructed in the difference between Jerusalem and Gerizim; she knew all about "father Jacob." But there were two things she did not know: "The *gift* of God" and "*who* it was that was speaking to her." As yet she knew not Christ as the all-sufficient Saviour for lost sinners. Her mind was engaged with the problem of where to worship.

Was it not thus with most of us? Following our first awakening, were we not considerably exercised over the conflicting claims of the churches and denominations? Where ought I to worship? Which denomination shall I join? In which church shall I seek membership? Which is the most scriptural of the different sects? These are questions which the majority of us faced, and probably many sought the solution of these problems long before they had found rest in the finished work of Christ. After all it was only another 'refuge' in which we sought shelter from the accusing voice which was convicting us of our lost condition.

"Our fathers worshipped in *this* mountain; and ye say, that *in Jerusalem* is the place where men ought to worship" — some worship here; some worship there; where *ought* we to worship? Important as this question is, it is not one to be discussed by a convicted sinner. The all-important thing for him is to find himself in the presence of the revealed Saviour. Let this be deeply pondered, clearly understood, and carefully borne in mind. "A convicted sinner can never become a devoted saint, until he finds his happy place at the feet of a revealed Saviour" (C. H. M.). Irreparable damage has been done to souls by occupying them with churches and denominations, instead of with a Saviour-God. If the sinner joins a church before he has received Christ he is in greater danger than he was previously. The church can neither save nor help to save. Many regard the church as a stepping stone *to* Christ, and frequently they find it but a stumbling-stone away *from* Christ. No stepping stones to Christ are needed. He has come all the way from heaven to earth, and is so near to us that no stepping stones are required. Mark how strikingly this is illustrated in one of the Old Testament types:

"An altar of earth thou shalt make unto me, and shalt sacrifice thereon thy burnt offerings, and thy peace offerings, thy sheep, and thine oxen: in all places where I record my name I will come unto thee, and I will bless thee. And if thou wilt make me an altar of stone, thou shalt not build it of hewn stone; for if thou lift up thy tool upon it, thou hast polluted it. Neither shalt thou go up by steps unto mine altar, that thy nakedness be not discovered thereon" (Ex. 20:24-26). It is to be noted that these instructions concerning "the altar" follow immediately on the giving of the Law, for it foreshadowed that which was to succeed the Legal dispensation, namely, the Cross of Christ, on which the great Sacrifice was offered. Note also it was expressly prohibited that the altar of stone should not be built from *hewn* stones. The stones must have no human tools lifted up upon them; no human labor should enter into their preparation. Neither were there to be any steps up to God's altar. Any attempt to climb up to God will only expose our shame. Indeed, steps *up* are not necessary for us, for the Lord Jesus took all the steps *down* to where we lay in our guilt and helplessness.

What stepping-stone did this woman of Samaria require? None at all, for Christ was there by her side, though she knew

Him not. He was patiently dislodging her from every refuge in which she sought to take shelter. He was seeking to bring her to the realization that she was a great sinner, and He a great Saviour, come down here in marvelous grace to save her, not only from the guilt and penalty of sin, but also from its dominion and power. What could "this mountain," or that "Jerusalem" do for her? Was it not obvious that a prior question, of paramount importance, claimed her serious attention, namely, What she was to do with her sins?—how she was to be saved? What relief could places of worship afford her burdened heart and guilty conscience? Could she find salvation in Gerizim? Could she procure peace in Jerusalem's temple? Could she worship the Father in spirit and in truth in either the one or the other? Was it not plain that she needed salvation before she could worship anywhere?

"Jesus saith unto her, Woman, believe me, the hour cometh, when ye shall neither in this mountain, nor yet at Jerusalem, worship the Father" (4:21). The Lord turned her attention to a subject of infinitely greater importance than the place of worship, even the nature of acceptable worship; assuring her that the time was at hand when controversies respecting the place of worship would be obsolete. "The hour cometh, when ye shall neither in this mountain, nor yet at Jerusalem, worship the Father." The meaning of this evidently is that "The time is just at hand when the public worship of God the Father should not be confined to any one place, and when the controversy as to whether Jerusalem or Gerizim had the better claim to that honor would be superceded."

"Ye worship ye know not what: we know what we worship: for salvation is of the Jews" (4:22). Here we see 'truth' mingling with 'grace.' Christ not only dealt in faithfulness. He was, and is, "the faithful and true witness." The Lord, in a very brief word, settled the disputed point—the Samaritans were wrong, the Jews right; the former were ignorant, the latter well instructed. Christ then added a reason to what He had just said—"*for* salvation is of the Jews." We take it that "salvation" here is equivalent to "the Saviour," that is, the Messiah. In this way was the word used by Simeon—"Lord, now lettest thou thy servant depart in peace, according to thy word: For mine eyes have seen thy *salvation*" (Luke 2:29, 30). So, too, the word was used by John the Baptist, "And all flesh shall see the *salvation* of God" (Luke 3:6). The force then of Christ's declaration was this: The Saviour, the Messiah, is to arise from among the Jews, and therefore the true worship of Jehovah is to be found among them.

It may be inquired, Why should the Lord Jesus refer to Himself under the impersonal word "salvation"? A moment's reflection will show the propriety of it. Christ was continuing to press upon this woman the fact that she was a sinner, and therefore it was useless to occupy her mind with questions about places of worship. What she needed was salvation, and this salvation could only be had through the knowledge of God revealed as Father, in the face of Jesus Christ. Such is the ground, and the only ground, of true spiritual worship. In order to worship the Father we must know Him; and to know Him is salvation, and salvation is eternal life.

What a lesson is there here for every Christian worker respecting the manner to deal with anxious souls. When we are speaking to such, let us not occupy them with questions about sects and parties, churches and denominations, creeds and confessions. It is positively cruel to do so. What they need is salvation – to know God, to believe on the Lord Jesus Christ. Let us shut them up to this one thing, and refuse to discuss anything else with them until they have received the Saviour. Questions about church-membership, the ordinances, etc., have their place and interest; but manifestly they are not for convicted sinners. Too many are so foolishly anxious to swell the ranks of *their* party, that they are in grave danger of thinking more about getting people to join *them* than they are about leading anxious souls simply and fully to Christ. Let us study diligently the example of the perfect Teacher in His dealings with the woman of Sychar.

"But the hour cometh, and now is, when the true worshippers shall worship the Father in spirit and in truth: for the Father seeketh such to worship him" (4:23). Here is the point which the Lord now presses upon this anxious soul. A new order of things was about to be established, and under it God would be manifested not as Jehovah (the covenant-keeping God) but as "the Father," and then the great question would not be *where* to worship, but how. Then the worshipper at Jerusalem will not be accounted the true worshipper because he worships there, nor the worshipper at Gerizim the false worshipper because he worships there; the one who worships in spirit and in truth, no matter where he may worship, he and he alone is the genuine worshipper.

To "worship in *spirit,*" is to worship spiritually; to "worship in *truth,*" is to worship truly. They are not two different kinds of worship, but two aspects of the same worship. To worship spiritually is the opposite of mere external rites which pertained to the flesh; instead, it is to give to God the homage of an enlightened mind and an affectionate heart. To worship Him truly is to worship Him according to the Truth, in a manner suited to the revelation He has made of Himself; and, no doubt, it also carries with it the force of worshipping truly, not in pretense, but sincerely. Such, and such alone, are the acceptable worshippers.

"God is a Spirit: and they that worship him must worship him in spirit and in truth" (4:24). This is a most important verse and treats of a most important but sadly misunderstood subject, namely, that of worship. Much of that which is termed "worship" today is fleshly rather than spiritual, and is external and spectacular, rather than internal and reverential. What are all the ornate decorations in our church-houses for? the stained glass windows, the costly hangings and fittings, the expensive organs! But people at once reply, 'But God's house must be beautiful, and He surely loves to have it so.' But why will not such objectors be honest, and say, '*We* love to have it so, and therefore, God should too'? Here, as everywhere else, God's thoughts are entirely different from man's. Look at the tabernacle which was made according to the pattern which Jehovah Himself showed to Moses in the mount! 'Yes,' people reply, 'but look at Solomon's temple!' Ah, *Solomon's,* truly. But look at it, and what do we see? Not one stone left upon another! Ah, dear reader, have you ever stopped to think what the future holds for this world and all its imposing structures? The world, and all that is therein, will be burned up! Not only the saloons and the picture shows, but also its magnificent cathedrals and stately churches, erected at enormous expense, while half of the human race was hastening to the Lake of Fire without any knowledge of Christ! Does this burning up of them look as though God esteemed them very highly? And if His people pondered this, would they be so ready to put so much of their money into them? After all, is it not the lust of the flesh, and the lust of the eye—denominational pride—which lies behind it all?

"God is a Spirit: and they that worship him must worship him in spirit and in truth." Note how emphatic this is—MUST. There is no alternative, no choice in the matter. This "must" is final. There are three "musts" in this Gospel, equally important and unequivocal. In John 3:7 we read, "Ye *must* be born again." In John 3:14, "The Son of man *must* be lifted up." In John 4:24, "God *must* be worshipped in spirit and in truth." It is indeed striking to observe that the first of these has reference to the work of God the Spirit, for He is the One who effects the new birth. The second "must" has reference to God the Son, for He was the One who had to die in order for atonement to be made. The third "must" respects God the Father, for He is the object of worship, the One who "seeketh" worshippers. And this order cannot be changed. It is only they who have been regenerated by God the Spirit, and justified by the Atonement of God the Son, who can worship God the Father. "The sacrifice of the wicked is an abomination to the Lord" (Prov. 15:8).

What is worship? We answer: First, it is the *action of the new nature* seeking, as the sparks fly upward, to return to the Divine and heavenly source from which it came. Worship is one of the three great marks which evidences the presence of the new nature—"We are the circumcision, which worship God in the spirit, and rejoice in Christ Jesus, and have no confidence in the flesh" (Phil. 3:3)—in the Greek there is no article before "spirit" or "flesh;" the spirit refers to the new nature, which is born of the Spirit.

In the second place, worship is the *activity of a redeemed people*. Israel did not worship Jehovah in Egypt; there they could only "sigh," and "cry," and "groan" (see Ex. 2:23, 24). It was not until Israel had passed through the Red Sea that we are told "Then sang Moses and the children of Israel this song unto the Lord, and spake, saying, *I will sing unto the Lord*" (Ex. 15:1); and note, this was the Song of Redemption – the words "redeemed" and "redemption" are not found in Scripture until this chapter is reached: see v. 13.

In the third place, worship *proceeds from the heart.* "This people draweth nigh unto me with their mouth, and honoreth me with their lips; but their *heart* is far from me. But *in vain do they worship me*" (Matt. 15:8, 9). Worship is a redeemed heart *occupied with God,* expressing itself in adoration and thanksgiving. Read through the Redemption Song, expression of Israel's worship, in Ex. 15, and notice the frequent repetition of "Thou," "Thee," and "He." Worship, then, is the occupation of the heart with a *known God;* and everything which *attracts* the flesh and its senses, *detracts* from real worship.

"God is a spirit: and they that worship him must worship him in spirit and in truth." There is no choice in the matter. This emphatic "must" bars out everything which is of the flesh. Worship is not by the eyes or the ears, but "in spirit," that is, from the *new nature.* The more spiritual is our worship the less formal and the less attractive to the flesh will it be. O how far astray we have gone! Modern "worship" (?) is chiefly designed to render it pleasing to the flesh: a 'bright and attractive service', with beautiful surroundings, sensuous music, and entertaining talks. What a mockery and a blasphemy! O that we all would heed that pointed word in Psa. 89:7; "God is greatly to be feared in the assembly of the saints, and to be had in reverence of all them that are about him" – how different things would then be.

Is a choir needed to 'lead' worship? What choir was needed to aid the Saviour and His apostles as they sung that hymn in the upper room, ere going forth into the Garden? (Matt. 26:30). What choir was needed to assist the apostles, as with bleeding backs they sang praises to God in the Philippian dungeon? Singing to be acceptable to God *must* come from the heart. And *to whom* do the choirs sing – to God, or to the people? The attractiveness of singing has been substituted for "the foolishness of preaching." The place which music now holds in many of our public services is a solemn "sign of the times" to those who have eyes to see. But is music wrong? Has not God Himself bestowed the gift? Surely, but what we are now complaining about is church-singing that is professional and spectacular, that which is of the flesh, and rendered to please the ear of man. The *only* music which ever passes beyond the roof of the church in which it is rendered is that which issues from born again people, who "sing with grace in their hearts *unto the Lord*."

"God is a spirit: and they that worship him must worship him in spirit and in truth." We must worship "in spirit," and not merely with the physical senses. We cannot worship by admiring grand architecture, by listening to the peals of a costly organ or the anthems of a highly trained choir. We cannot worship by gazing at pictures, smelling of incense, counting of beads. We cannot worship with our eyes or ears, noses or hands, for they are all "flesh," and *not* "spirit." Moreover, spiritual worship must be distinguished sharply from *soulical* worship, though there are few today who discriminate between them. Much, very much, of our modern so-called worship is soulical, that is, emotional. Music which makes one "feel good," touching anecdotes which draw tears, the magic oratory of a speaker which thrills his hearers, the clever showmanship of professional evangelists and singers who aim to 'produce an atmosphere' for worship (?) and which are designed to move the varied emotions of those in attendance, are so many examples of what is soulical and not spiritual at all. True worship, spiritual worship, is decorous, quiet, reverential, occupying the worshipper with God Himself; and the effect is to leave him not with a nervous headache (the inevitable reaction from the high tension produced by soulical activities) but with a peaceful heart and a rejoicing spirit.

"The woman saith unto him, I know that Messias cometh, which is called Christ: when he is come, he will tell us all things" (4:25). Here is the Saviour's reward for His gracious patience in dealing with this woman. Slowly but surely the

Word had done its work. At last this poor soul has been driven from every false refuge, and now she is ready for a revealed Saviour. She is through with her prevarication and procrastinations. She had asked *"How?"*, and Christ had graciously answered her. She had inquired *"Whence?"*, and had received a kindly reply. She had said, *"Where?"*, and this difficulty had been disposed of too. And now her questions ceased. She speaks with greater confidence and assurance—"I know that Messias cometh." This was tantamount to saying, "I want *Christ.*"

"Jesus saith unto her, I that speak unto thee am he" (4:26). For the seventh and last time (in this interview) the Lord addressed this soul whose salvation He sought and won. The moment the Samaritan woman expressed her desire for Christ, He answers, "You have Him; He is now speaking to you." Nothing more was needed. The Saviour of sinners stood revealed. That was enough. All was settled now. "It was not a mount nor a temple; Samaria nor Jerusalem. She had found Jesus—a Saviour-God. A detected sinner and a revealed Saviour have met face to face, and all is settled, once and forever. She discovered the wonderful fact that the One who had asked her for a drink, knew all about her—could tell her all that ever she did, and yet He talked to her of salvation. What more did she want? Nothing" (C. H. M.).

"And upon this came his disciples, and marvelled that he talked with the woman: yet no man said, What seekest thou? or, Why talkest thou with her?" (4:27). Once again we may discern the providential dealings of God, regulating and directing the slightest movements of His creatures. These disciples of Christ left the Saviour seated on the well, while they went into the city to buy meat (v. 8). Had they remained they would only have been in the way. The Lord desired to have this woman alone with Himself. His purpose in this had now been accomplished. Grace had achieved a glorious victory. Another brand had been plucked from the burning. The poor Samaritan adulteress had now been brought out of sin's darkness into God's marvelous light. The woman had plainly expressed her desire for the Christ to appear, and the Lord had revealed Himself to her. "And *upon this came* His disciples." Though they had not been permitted to hear what had been said between Christ and this woman, they returned in time to witness the happy finale. They needed to be taught a lesson. They must learn that the saving grace of God was not limited to Israel, that it was reaching out to sinners of the Gentiles, too. They "marvelled" as they beheld their Master talking to this despised Samaritan, but they held their peace. A Divine constraint arrested them. None of them dared to ask Him a question at that moment.

"The woman then left her waterpot, and went her way into the city" (4:28). Here is the blessed climax. The patient work of the condescending Saviour was now rewarded. The darkness was dissipated: "The light of the knowledge of the glory of God in the face of Jesus Christ" (II Cor. 4:6) now shone into the heart of this believing sinner. Four times had this woman referred directly to herself, and it is striking to note the contents and order of her respective statements. First, she *acknowledged her thirst*—"Give me this water *that* (in order that) *I thirst not*" (v. 15). Second, she *confessed her sin*—"I have no husband" (v. 17). Third, she evidenced *a dawning intelligence*—"I perceive" (v. 19). Fourth, she *avowed her faith*—"I know that Messias cometh" (v. 25). Finally, she leaves her waterpot and goes forth to testify of Christ.

"The woman then left her waterpot and went her way into the city." Notice carefully the word "then," which is parallel with the "upon this" of the previous verse. Both look back to what is recorded in v. 26—"Jesus saith unto her, I that speak unto thee am." It will be noted that the final word of this verse is in italics, which signifies there is no corresponding word in the Greek. Omitting the word "he" the verse as it reads in the A.V. is unintelligible. We are satisfied that the correct reading would give "Jesus saith unto her, I *am* that speaketh unto thee." It was the enunciation of the sacred "I am" title of Jehovah (see Ex. 3:14); it was the solemn affirmation that God was addressing her soul. It is a parallel utterance to John 8:58. The pronunciation of this ineffable Name was attended with awe-inspiring effects (cf. John 18:6). This explains, here, the silence of the disciples who marvelled when they found their Master talking with the woman, but asked Him no question. It accounts for that Divine constraint resting upon them. Moreover, it gives added force and significance to what we read of in v. 28 – "The woman *then* left her waterpot." The weary Traveller by the well stood revealed as God manifest in flesh.

"The woman then left her waterpot." Ah, was not that a lovely sequel! She "left her waterpot" because she had now found a well of "living water." She had come to the well for literal water; *that* was what she had desired, and on what her mind was set. But now that she had obtained salvation, she thought no more of her "waterpot." It is ever thus. Once there is a clear *perception* of Christ to the soul, once He is *known* and received as a personal Saviour, there will be a turning away from that on which before the carnal mind was centered. Her mind was now stayed upon Christ, and she had no thought of well, water, or waterpot. The Messias' glory was now her end and aim. Henceforth, "for me to live *is Christ*" was her object and goal. She knew the Messiah now, not from hearsay, but from the personal revelation of Himself, and immediately she began to proclaim Him to others.

"And went her way into the city, and saith to the men, Come, see a man, which told me all things that ever I did: is not this the Christ?" (4:28, 29). How beautiful! Transformed from a convicted sinner into a devoted saint. The work had been thorough – nothing could be put to it, nor anything taken from it: because God had done it (Ecc. 3:14). There was no placing this woman on probation. There was no telling her she must hold out faithful to the end if she would be saved – wretched perversion of men! No; she *was* saved; saved for all eternity. Saved by grace through faith, apart from any works of her own. And now that she is saved, she wants to tell others of the Saviour she had found. The love of Christ constrained her. She now had His nature within her, and therefore has she a heart of compassion of the lost.

"Christian reader, be this our work, henceforth. May our grand object be to invite sinners to come to Jesus. This woman began at once. No sooner had she found Christ for herself, than she forthwith entered upon the blessed work of leading others to His feet. Let us go and do likewise. Let us by word and deed—'by all means,' as the apostle says—seek to gather as many as possible around the Person of the Son of God. Some of us have to judge ourselves for lukewarmness in this blessed work. We see souls rushing along the broad and well-trodden highway that leadeth to eternal perdition, and yet, how little are we moved by the sight! How slow are we to sound in their ears, that true, that proper Gospel note, 'Come!' O, for more zeal, more energy, more fervor! May the Lord grant us such a deep sense of the value of immortal souls, the preciousness of Christ, and the awful solemnity of eternity, as shall constrain us to more urgent and faithful dealing with the souls of men" (C. H. M.).

"And saith to the men, Come, see a man, which told me all things that ever I did: is not this the Christ?" "*Come*" was the word of invitation that this newly-born soul extended to those men. It was a word she had learned from Christ's own lips (v. 16). It is the great word of the Gospel. It is the word which has resulted in peace to countless hearts. The last recorded words of this woman show her now as an active servant for Christ. It is remarkable to find that this final word of the woman was her seventh—the *perfect* number. Seven times, no more and no less, had Christ spoken to her—telling of the perfectness of His work in dealing with her. Six times she spoke to Him (the number of man in the flesh) before she was fully saved; and then to this is added the last recorded word when she went forth to tell others of the One who had saved her; making seven in all—this last one, the *seventh,* evidencing the *perfect work* which Christ had wrought in her!

Our next lesson will be devoted to John 4:31-42. Let the interested reader study the following questions:—

1. What is the central theme of verses 31-42?
2. What does verse 31 reveal to us about the disciples?
3. What did Christ mean when He said that doing the will of God provided Him with "meat to eat"? vv. 32, 34.

4. What "work" of the Father did Christ "finish"? v. 34.
5. In applying what is said in v. 38 to ourselves what should be the true effect upon us?
6. What does "the Saviour of the world" signify? v. 42.

CHAPTER FIFTEEN

Christ in Samaria

John 4:31-42

We begin with the usual Analysis of the passage which is to be before us. In it we see:—

1. The Disciples' Solicitude, v. 31.
2. The Disciples' Ignorance, v. 32.
3. The Disciples Instructed, vv. 34-38.
4. The Samaritan Converts, v. 39.
5. The Samaritan's Request, v. 40.
6. The Samaritan Converts added unto, v. 41.
7. The Samaritan's Confession, v. 42.

Verses 31-38 form a parenthesis and tell us something of what transpired during the interval that followed the woman's leaving the well and the Samaritans coming to Christ because of her testimony to Him. They record a conversation which took place between the Lord and His disciples. The disciples, it will be remembered, had "gone away unto the city to buy meat," and had returned from their quest, to find their Master engaged in conversation with a woman of Samaria. They had marvelled at this, but none had interrogated Him on the matter. As they had heard the Saviour pronounce the ineffable "I am" title (v. 26), a Divine restraint had fallen upon them. But now the interview between the Lord Jesus and the Samaritan harlot was over. Grace had won a glorious victory. A sinner had been brought out of darkness into God's marvelous light, and in consequence, had gone forth to tell others the good news which meant so much to her own heart.

Once more the Saviour was left alone with His disciples. They had returned in time to hear His closing words with the woman, and had seen the summary effect they had on her. They had witnessed that which should have corrected and enlarged their cramped vision. They had been shown that whatever justification there might have been in the past for the Jews to have "no dealings with the Samaritans," this no longer held good. The Son of God had come to earth, "full of grace and truth," and the glad tidings concerning Him must be proclaimed to all people. This was a hard lesson for these Jewish disciples, but with infinite patience the Lord bore with their spiritual dullness. In what follows we have a passage of great practical importance, which contains some weighty truths upon service.

"In the meanwhile His disciples prayed him, saying, Master, eat" (4:31). A little earlier in the day the disciples had left their Master sitting on the well, wearied from the long journey. Accordingly, they had procured some food, and had returned to Him with it. But He evidenced no desire for it. Instead of finding Christ weary and faint, they discovered Him to be full of renewed energy. He had received refreshment which they knew not of. This they could not understand, and so they begged Him to eat of that which they had brought Him. Their request was a kindly one. Their appeal to Him was well meant. But it was merely the amiability of the flesh. The 'milk of human kindness' must not be mistaken for the fruit of the Spirit. Sentimentality is not spirituality.

"But he said unto them, I have meat to eat that ye know not of" (4:32). This was scarcely a rebuke: it was more a word of instruction for their enlightenment. Their minds were upon material things; the Lord speaks of that which is spiritual. "Meat" was used as a figurative expression for that which satisfied. Christ's heart had been fed. His spirit had been invigorated. What it was that had refreshed Him we learn from His next utterance. It was something the disciples "knew not of." Not yet had they discovered that the one who gives out of the things of God is also a receiver. In dispensing spiritual blessing to others, one is blest himself. Peace and joy are a part of the reward which comes to him who does the will of God. The obedient servant has "meat to eat" that those not engaged in service know nothing about. These, and other principles of service, were what the Lord would now press upon His disciples.

"Therefore said the disciples one to another, Hath any man brought him ought to eat?" (4:33). This confirmed what Christ had just said: disciples of His they might be, but as yet they were very ignorant about spiritual things. Their minds evidently dwelt more upon material things, than the things of God. They knew very little about the relation of Christ to the Father: their thoughts turned at once to the question as to whether or not any *man* had "brought him ought to eat." Even good men are sometimes very ignorant; yea, the best of men are, until taught of God. "How dull and thick brain'd are the best, 'till God rend the veil, and enlighten both the organ and the object" (John Trapp, 1650, A.D.). But let us not smile at the dullness of those disciples; instead, see in them an exhibition of our own spiritual stupidity, and need of being taught of God.

"Jesus saith unto them, My meat is to do the will of him that sent me, and to finish his work" (4:34). What did Christ mean? In what sense is doing the will of God "meat" to one who performs it? What is the *Father's* "work?" And how was Christ "finishing" it? The answer to those questions must be sought in the setting of our verse, noting its connection with what has gone before and what follows. We must first ascertain the leading subject of the passage of which this verse forms a part.

As we proceed with our examination of the passage it will become more and more evident that its leading subject is *service*. The Lord was giving needed instruction to His disciples, and preparing them for their future work. He sets before them a concise yet remarkably complete outline of the fundamental principles which underlie all acceptable service for God. The all-important and basic principle is that of absolute obedience to the will of God. The servant must do the will of his master. This the perfect Servant Himself exemplified. Note how He refers to God. He does not say here, "My meat is to do the will of the Father," but "the will of *Him that sent me.*" That shows it is service which is in view.

Now what was "the will" of the One who had sent Christ into the world? Was it not to deliver certain captives from the hands of the Devil and bring them from death unto life? If there is any doubt at all on the point John 6:38 and 39 at once removes it—"For I came down from heaven, not to do mine own will, but the will of him that sent me. And *this is* the Father's will which hath sent me, that of all which he hath given me I should lose nothing, but should raise it up again at the last day." This at once helps us to define *the Father's* "work"—"and finish his work," which must not be confounded with the work that was peculiarly the Son's: though closely related, they were quite distinct. The "will" of the Father was that all those He had "given" to the Son should be saved; His "work" had been in *appointing* them unto salvation—"For God hath not appointed us to wrath, but to obtain salvation by our Lord Jesus Christ" (I Thess. 5:9). Appointment unto salvation (see also II Thess. 2:13) is peculiarly the work of the Father; the actual saving of those appointed is the work of the Son, and in the saving of God's elect the Son *finishes* the "work" of the Father. An individual example of this had just been furnished in the case of the Samaritan woman, and others were about to follow in the "many" who should believe on Him because of her testimony (v. 39), and the "many more" who would believe because of His own word (v. 41).

How all this casts its own clear light on v. 4 of this fourth chapter, and explains to us the force of the "must" here. The Lord had not journeyed to Samaria to gratify His own desire, for "he pleased not himself." In infinite grace the Son of God had condescended to lay aside (temporarily) His glory and stooped to the place of a Servant; and in service, as in everything else, He is our great Exemplar. He shows us *how* to serve, and the first great principle which comes out here is that joy of heart, satisfaction of soul, sustenance of spirit—"meat"—is to be found in doing the will, performing the pleasure, of the One who sends forth. Here, then, the perfect Servant tells us what *true* service is—the simple and faithful performance of that which has been marked out for us by God. Our "meat"—the sustenance of the laborer's heart, the joy of his soul—is not to be sought in results (the "increase") but in doing the will of Him that sent us forth. That was Christ's meat, and it must be ours, too. This was the first lesson the Lord here teaches His disciples about Service. And it is the first thing which each of us who are His servants now, need to take to heart.

"Say not ye, There are yet four months, and then cometh harvest? behold, I say unto you, Lift up your eyes, and look on the fields; for they are white already to harvest" (4:35). It is very evident that it is the subject of Service which is still before us, and the principle enunciated in this verse is easily perceived. However, let us first endeavor to arrive at the local force of these words, and their particular significance to the disciples, before we reduce them to a principle of application to ourselves.

"Say not ye, There are yet four months, and then cometh harvest? behold, I say unto you, Lift up your eyes, and look on the fields, for they are white already to harvest." There is no need to conclude that the disciples had been discussing among themselves the condition of the fields through which they had walked on their way to the city to buy meat; though they may have done so. Rather does it seem to us that the Lord continued to instruct His disciples in figurative language. There seems no doubt that the Saviour had in mind the spiritual state of the Samaritans and the estimate formed of them by His disciples. Possibly the Samaritans who had listened to the striking testimony of the woman now saved were on their way toward the well, though yet some considerable distance away, and pointing to them the Saviour said to the disciples, "Lift up your eyes" and behold their state.

"Lift up your eyes, and look on the fields; for they are white already to harvest." This was plainly a rebuke. The disciples regarded Samaria as a most unlikely field to work in; at best much sowing would be required, and then a long wait, before any ripened grain could be expected. They never dreamed of telling them that the Messiah was just outside their gates! Must they not have hung their heads in shame when they discovered how much more faithful and zealous had been this woman than they? Here, then, is a further reason why Christ "must needs go through Samaria"—to teach His disciples a much needed *missionary* lesson.

What, now, is the application to us of the principle contained in this verse? Surely it is this: we must not judge by appearances. Ofttimes we regard certain ones as hopeless cases, and are tempted to think it would be useless to speak to *them* about

Christ. Yet we never know what seeds of Truth may have been lodged in their hearts by the labors of other sowers. We never know what influences may be working: ofttimes those who seem to us the most unlikely cases, when put to the test are the most ready to hear of the Saviour. We cannot tell how many months there are to harvest!

"And he that reapeth receiveth wages, and gathereth fruit unto life eternal: that both he that soweth and he that reapeth may rejoice together" (4:36). If the previous verse contained a rebuke, here was a word to encourage. "He that reapeth receiveth wages" seems to mean, This is a work in which it is indeed a privilege to be engaged, for the laborer receives a glorious reward, inasmuch as he "gathereth fruit unto life eternal." The reward is an eternal one, for not only do those saved through the labors of the reaper receive eternal life, but because of this the joy of both will be eternal too. "That both he that soweth and he that reapeth may rejoice together." The sower may have labored hard toward the salvation of souls, and yet never be permitted to witness in this life the success which God gave to his efforts. The reaper, however, does witness the ingathering; nevertheless, both sower and reaper shall rejoice together in the everlasting salvation of those garnered through their joint efforts.

"And herein is that saying true, One soweth, and another reapeth" (4:37). There is a timely warning here. To "reap" is not everything, blessed as the experience is: to "sow" is equally important. The bountiful crop garnered at Sychar was, under God, the result of the labors of earlier sowers. These Samaritans were already informed about the appearing of the Messiah, and for this knowledge they were indebted to the faithful ministry of earlier servants of God. That one sows and another reaps had been exemplified in the case of the converted adulteress. Christ had met the need which the testimony of the prophets had awakened within her.

How gracious of the Lord to recognize and own the labors of those earlier sowers! Apparently their work had counted for little. They had sown the seed, yet seemingly the ground on which it had fallen was very unpromising. But now, under the beneficent influence of the Sun of righteousness came the harvest, and the Lord is not slack to remind His disciples of their indebtedness to the labors of those who had gone before. Doubtless, Philip would recall these words of Christ in a coming day (see Acts 8). And what comfort is there here for the sower today! His labors may seem to go for nothing, but if he is diligent in sowing the proper "seed," let him know that sooner or later all faithful service is rewarded. *He* may not "reap," but "another" *will*—"Therefore, my beloved brethren, be ye stedfast, unmoveable, always abounding in the work of the Lord, forasmuch as ye know that your labor *is not in vain* in the Lord" (I Cor. 15:58).

"I sent you to reap that whereon ye bestowed no labour: other men laboured, and ye are entered into their labours" (4:38). There is no doubt a historical reference here which points us back to what is recorded in Matt. 10, from which we learn that the Lord had sent forth the twelve apostles to "preach," and to "heal the sick" (vv. 7, 8.). This was in Judea, and the success of their labors is indicated in John 4:1, 2—they had made and baptized many disciples. One can imagine the elation of the disciples over their success, and it was to repress their vanity that Christ here says to them, "I sent you to reap that whereon ye bestowed no labour: other men laboured, and ye are entered into their labours." He reminds them that they had prospered because others had laboured before them. It was a word encouraging to the sower, sobering to the reaper. We may observe, in passing, that when *the Lord sends us* forth to *"reap,"* He directs us to fields which have already been sown. It should also be noted that the toil of the sower is more arduous than that of the reaper: when Christ says, "Other men *laboured,* and ye (the reapers) are entered into their (the sowers') labours" He used a word which signified "to toil to the point of exhaustion," indeed it is the same word which is used of the Saviour at the beginning of this chapter, when we read, "Jesus therefore, being *wearied* with His journey." Luther was wont to say, "The ministry is not an idle man's occupation." Alas that so often it degenerates into such.

Sowing and reaping are two distinct departments of Gospel ministry, and spiritual discernment (wisdom from God) is requisite to see which is the more needed in a given place. "To have commenced sowing at Sychar would have indicated a want of discernment as to the condition of souls in that city. To have concluded from their success at Sychar, that all Samaria was ready to receive the Lord, would have been manifestly erroneous, as the treatment He met with in one of the villages of Samaria at a later period in His life clearly demonstrates. This, surely, can speak to us, where sowing and reaping may go on almost side by side. The work in one place is no criterion of what that in another place should be; nor does it follow, that the laborer, highly blessed in one locality, has only to move to another, to find that field also quite ready for his reaping-hook" (C. E. Stuart).

"And many of the Samaritans of that city believed on him for the saying of the woman, which testified, He told me all that ever I did" (4:39). At first glance it looks as though this verse introduces a change of subject, yet really it is not so. This verse, as also the two following, enunciates and illustrates other principles of *service*. In the first place, we are shown how that God is pleased to use feeble messengers to accomplish mighty ends. Frequently He employs weak instruments to make manifest His own mighty power. In this, as in everything else, the Lord's thoughts and ways are very different from ours. He employed a shepherd lad to vanquish the mighty Goliath. He endowed a Hebrew slave with more wisdom than all the magicians of Babylon possessed. He made the words of Naaman's servants to have greater effect upon their august master than did those of the renowned Elisha. In making selection for the mother of the Saviour, He chose not a princess, but a peasant woman. In appointing the heralds of the Cross, fishermen were the ones called. And so a mighty work of grace was started there in Sychar by a converted harlot. "How unsearchable are his judgments, and his ways past finding out!"

"And many of the Samaritans of that city believed on him for the saying of the woman, which testified, He told me all that ever I did." The full force of this can only be appreciated as we go back to what is told us in verses 28 and 29. She did not say. 'Of what use can I be for Christ? —I who have lost character with men, and have sunken into the lowest depths of degradation!' No; she did not stop to reason, but with a conscience that had been searched in the presence of the Light and its burden of guilt removed, with a heart full of wonderment and gratitude to the One who had saved her, she immediately went forth to serve and glorify Him. She told what she knew; she testified of what she had found, but in connection with a *Person.* It was *of Him* she spoke; it was *to Him* she pointed. "*He* told me," she declared, thus directing others to that One who had dealt so blessedly with her. But she did not stop there. She did not rest satisfied with simply telling her fellow-townsmen of what she had heard, nor Whom she had met. She desired others to meet with Him for themselves. "*Come*" she said; Come *to Him* for yourselves. And God honored those simple and earnest words: "Many of the Samaritans of that city believed on him for (because of) the saying of the woman." Thus are we shown the great *aim* in service, namely, to bring souls into the presence of Christ Himself.

"So when the Samaritans came unto him, they besought him to abide with them; and he abode there two days. And many more believed because of his Word; and they said to the woman, Now we believe, not because of thy speaking: for we have heard for ourselves, and know that this is indeed the Saviour of the world" (4:40-42, A. R. V.). We have quoted from the A. R. V. because we believe it is the more correct here. The A. V. makes these Samaritans say, "For we have heard him ourselves, and know that this is indeed the Christ, the Saviour of the world." The majority of the Greek MSS. do not contain the words "the Christ" in v. 42. These Samaritans had learned from the lips of the woman *who* He was, "the Christ;" now they had discovered for themselves *what* He was—the One who met their deepest need, "The Saviour."

The above scripture places Samaria in striking contrast from the unbelief and rejection of the Judeans and those dwelling in Jerusalem, where so many of His mighty works had been done, and where it might be expected multitudes would have received

Him. Here in Samaria was a people who seemed most unpromising; no record is given of Christ performing a single miracle there; and yet many of these despised Samaritans received Him. And is it not much the same today? Those whom we would think were most disposed to be interested in the things of God are usually the most indifferent; while those whom we are apt to regard as outside, if not beyond, the reach of God's grace, are the very ones that are brought to recognize their deep need, and become, ultimately, the most devoted among the followers of the Lamb.

Let us now seek to gather up into a terse summary the leading lessons of the verses which have been before us. The whole passage has to do with *service*, and the fundamental principles of service are here enunciated and illustrated. First, we learn the *essential requirement* of service, as illustrated in the example of the Samaritan woman – a personal acquaintance with the Saviour, and a heart overflowing for Him. Second, we are taught the *spirit* in which all service should be carried on – the faithful performance of the task allotted us; finding our satisfaction not in results, but in the knowledge that the will of God has been done by us. Third, we are shown the *urgency* of service – the fields already white unto harvest. Fourth, we have *encouragement* for service – the fact that we are gathering "fruit unto life eternal." Fifth, we learn about the *interdependence* of the servants – "one soweth and another reapeth:" there is mutual dependence one on the other: a holy partnership between those who work in the different departments of spiritual agriculture. Sixth, we have a *warning* for servants: they who are used to doing the reaping must not be puffed up by their success, but must remember that they are entering into the labors of those who have gone before. Finally; we are taught here the *aim* ever to be kept in view, and that is to bring souls into the presence of Christ, that they may become independent of us, having learned to draw directly from Him.

We would call attention to the following points brought out in these verses. First, the worldwide missionary need signified in the Lord's words in v. 35. Second, to the *distinctive characteristic* of this Age as seen in *the absence* of any public miracles. There is no hint of Christ performing any miracles here in Samaria: nor is He doing so publicly in the world today. Third, to the *means employed* as indicated in vv. 39 and 41, where we are told that it was the woman's testimony, and the Word which caused many of the Samaritans to "believe." Thus it is throughout this Age. It is the personal testimony of believers and the preaching of the Word, which are the Divinely appointed means for the propagation of Christianity. Fourth, we may note the *striking prominence of the Gentiles* in this typical picture: "Many of the *Samaritans* . . . *believed on Him.*" While there is a remnant of Israel "according to the election of grace" (typified in the few disciples who were with Christ), nevertheless, it is the Gentile element which predominates in the saved of this Age. Fifth, mark that Christ is owned here not as "The Son of man," nor as "The Son of David," but as "The Saviour *of the world.*" This title does not mean that Christ is the Saviour of the human race, but is a general term, used in contradistinction from Israel, including all believing Gentiles scattered throughout the earth.

Thus, once more, we discover that with marvelous skill the Holy Spirit has caused this historical narrative which traces the actions of the Saviour in Samaria, and which records the instructions He there gave to His disciples, to embody a perfect outline which sets forth the leading features of this present Era of Grace, during which God is taking out of the Gentiles a people for His name. This should cause us to search more diligently for the hidden beauties and harmonies of Scripture.

Below are the questions for the next lesson: —

1. How does v. 43 bring out the perfections of Christ?
2. How does "the Galileans received Him" (v. 45) confirm, "no honor in His own country" (Galilee) of v. 44?
3. Why are we told Christ was in Cana when He healed the nobleman's son? v. 46.
4. Why are we told the nobleman belonged to Capernaum? v. 46.
5. In what way does v. 48 apply to us today?
6. What does the word "yesterday" in v. 52 tell us about the nobleman?

CHAPTER SIXTEEN

Christ in Galilee

John 4:43-54

What has been before us from v. 4 to the end of v. 42 in this chapter is in the nature of a parenthesis, inasmuch as these verses record what occurred in Samaria, which was outside the sphere of Christ's regular ministry in Judea and Galilee. Here in the last twelve verses of the chapter we are brought onto familiar ground again. It would seem then, that we may expect to find a continuation of what was before us in the first three chapters of John's Gospel, namely, historical events and practical teaching in both of which the Divine and moral glories of the Lord Jesus are displayed, and beneath the narrative of which we may discern hidden yet definitely defined typical and prophetical pictures.

We saw in our earlier studies that two things are made very prominent in the opening chapters of this Gospel. First, the failure of Judaism, the deplorable condition of Israel. Some solemn portrayals of this have already been before us. In the second place, we have seen the Holy Spirit drawing our attention away from Israel to Christ; and then at the beginning of chapter four a third principle has been illustrated, namely, a turning from Judaism to the Gentiles. Furthermore, we have observed that not only do we have depicted in these opening sections of our Gospel the sad spiritual state of Israel at the time our Lord was here upon earth, but the narrative also furnishes us with a series of striking foreshadowings of the future. Such is the case in the concluding section of John 4.

Here, once more, we are reminded of the pitiable condition of Judaism during the days of Christ's public ministry. This is brought out in a number of particulars, which will become more evident as we study them in detail. First, we have the express testimony of the Lord Himself that He had no honor "in his own country." This was in vivid contrast from His experiences in Samaria. Second, while we are told that "the Galileans received him," it was not because they recognized the glory of His person, or the authority and life-giving value of His words, but because they had been impressed by what they had seen Him do at Jerusalem. Third, there is the declaration made by Christ to the nobleman — intended, no doubt, for the Galileans also — "except ye see signs and wonders, ye will not believe." All of this serves to emphasize the condition of the Jews — their inability to recognize the Lord Jesus the Christ of God, and their failure to set to their seal that what He spake was the truth.

It is the practical lessons taught by this passage which are to occupy our attention in the body of this chapter. Before pondering these we submit an Analysis of this closing section of John 4:—

1. Christ goes into Galilee, v. 43.
2. Christ's tragic plaint, v. 44.
3. Christ received by the Galileans, v. 45.
4. The nobleman's request of Christ, vv. 46, 47.
5. Christ's reply, vv. 48-50.
6. The nobleman's journey home, vv. 50-53.
7. This miracle Christ's second in Galilee, v. 54.

"Now after two days he departed thence, and went into Galilee" (4:43). Different indeed are God's ways from ours. During those days spent in Samaria many had believed on Christ to the saving of their souls. And now the Saviour leaves that happy scene and departed into a country where He had received no honour. How evident it is that He pleased not Himself! He had come here to do the will of the Father, and now we see Him following the path marked out for Him. Surely there is an important lesson here for every servant of God today: no matter how successful and popular we may be in a place, we must move on when God has work for us elsewhere. The will of the One who has commissioned us must determine all our actions. Failure must not make us lag behind, nor success urge us to run before.

Neither must failure make us fretful and feverish to seek another field, nor success cause us to remain stationary when God bids us move on. The one, perhaps, is as great a temptation as the other; but if we are following on to know the Lord, then shall we know when to remain and when to depart.

"Now after two days he departed thence, and went into Galilee." This resumes and completes what is said in vv. 3 and 4. The Lord, accompanied by His disciples, left Judea because of the jealousy and enmity of the Pharisees. He "departed again into Galilee" (v. 3). But before He goes there, "he must needs go through Samaria" (v. 4). We have learned something of the meaning of that "must needs." But the need had now been met, so the Lord Jesus departed from Samaria and arrives at Galilee. The religious leaders in Jerusalem regarded Galilee with contempt (see 7:41, 52). It was there that "the poor of the flock" were to be found. The first three Gospels record at length the Galilean-ministry of the Redeemer, but John's gives only a brief notice of it in the passage now before us.

"For Jesus himself testified, that a prophet hath no honour in his own country" (4:44). The reference is to what is recorded in Luke 4. At Nazareth, "where he had been brought up," He entered the synagogue and read from Isaiah 60, declaring "This day is this scripture fulfilled in your ears." Those who heard Him "wondered," and said, "Is not this Joseph's son?" They were totally blind to His Divine glory. The Lord replied by saying, "Ye will surely say unto me this proverb, Physician, heal thyself: whatsoever we have heard done in Capernaum, do also here in thy country. And he said, Verily I say unto you, No prophet is accepted in his own country" (Luke 4:23, 24). Proof of this was furnished immediately after, for when Christ referred to God's sovereign dealings of old in connection with Elijah and Elisha, we are told, "And all they in the synagogue, when they heard these things, were filled with wrath, And rose up, and thrust him out of the city, and led him to the brow of the hill whereon their city was built, that they might cast him down headlong" (vv. 28, 29). Thus was He dishonoured and insulted by those among whom His preministerial life had been lived.

He was without honour in "his own country," that is, Galilee; and yet we now find Him returning there. Why, then, should He return thither? The answer to this question is found in Matt. 4: "Now when Jesus had heard that John was cast into prison, he departed *into Galilee;* And leaving Nazareth, he came and dwelt in Capernaum which is upon the sea coast, in the borders of Zabulon and Napthalim: *That it might be fulfilled* which was spoken by Esaias the prophet, saying, The land of Zabulon, and the land of Naphthalim, by the way of the sea, beyond Jordan, *Galilee of the Gentiles;* The people which sat in darkness saw great light; and to them which sat in the region and shadow of death light is sprung up" (vv. 12-16). This furnishes us with another instance of the obedience of the perfect Servant. In the volume of the Book it was written of Him. Prophecy is not only an intimation of what will be, but a declaration of what shall be. Prophecy makes known the decrees of God. As, then, Christ had come here to do the will of God, and God's will (revealed in the prophetic word) had declared that the people in Galilee who walked in darkness, should see a great light, etc. (Isa. 9:1, 2) the Lord Jesus Christ goes there.

"For Jesus himself testified, that a prophet hath no honour in his own country." How this reveals to us the heart of the Saviour! He was no stoic, passing through these scenes, unmoved by what He encountered: He was not insensible to the treatment He met with, He "*endured* such contradiction of sinners against himself" (Heb. 12:3). The indifference, the unbelief, the opposition of Israel, told upon Him, and caused His visage to be "marred more than any man" (Isa. 52:14). Hear Him, as by the spirit of prophecy, He exclaims, "I have labored in vain, I have spent my strength for nought, and in vain: yet surely my judgment is with the Lord, and my reward with my God" (Isa. 49:4). So here, when we hear Him testifying, "A prophet hath no honour in his own country," we can almost catch the sob in His voice. For two days He had experienced the joys of harvest. His spirit had been refreshed. The "meat" which had been ministered to His soul consisted not only of the consciousness that He had done the will of the One who had sent Him, but also in the faith and gratitude of the woman who had believed on Him. This had been followed by the Samaritans beseeching Him to tarry with them, and the consequent believing of many of them because of His word. But such joyful harvesting was only for a very brief season. Two days only did He abide in Samaria. Now, He turns once more to Galilee, and He goes with sad foreboding.

"For Jesus himself testified, that a prophet hath no honour in his own country." His use of the word "prophet" here is very suggestive. It was the word that the woman had used when her perceptive faculties began to be illumined (v. 19). There, in Samaria, He *had been* honored. The Samaritans believed His bare word, for no miracles were performed before them. But now in Galilee He meets with a faith of a very inferior order. The Galileans received Him *because* they *had seen* "all the things that he did at Jerusalem at the feast" (v. 45). So, too, the nobleman's house (v. 53) did not believe until a miracle had been performed before their eyes. Thus a solemn contrast is pointed. In Galilee He is not honoured for His person's and word's sake; in Samaria He was. As prophet He was not honoured in Galilee; as a miracle-worker He was "received." This principle is frequently exemplified today. There is many a servant of God who is thought more highly of abroad than he is at home. It is a true saying that "familiarity breeds contempt." Ofttimes a preacher is more respected and appreciated when visiting a distant field than he is by his own flock.

"Then when he was come into Galilee, the Galileans received him, having seen all the things that he did at Jerusalem at the feast: for they also went unto the feast" (4:45). How this brings out the fickleness and the shallowness of human nature. For upwards of twenty years the man Christ Jesus had lived in Galilee. Little or nothing is told us about those years which preceded His public work. But we know that He did all things well. His manner of life, His ways, His deportment, His every act, must have stood out in vivid contrast from all around Him. Had His fellow-townsmen possessed any spiritual discernment at all they must have seen at once that Jesus of Nazareth was indeed the Holy One of God. But they were blind to His glory. The perfect life He had lived quietly among them was not appreciated. As the Son of God incarnate He was unknown and unrecognized.

But now things were changed. The humble Carpenter had left them for a season. He had commenced His public ministry. He had been to Jerusalem. There He had sternly corrected the Temple abuses. There He had performed such miracles that "many believed on his name" (2:23). Many of the Galileans who were in attendance at the Feast had also witnessed His wonderful works, and they were duly impressed. On their return home they would doubtless tell others of what they had witnessed. And now that the Lord Jesus returns to Galilee, He is at once "received." Now that His fame had spread abroad the people flocked around Him. Such is human nature. Let a man who lived in comparative obscurity leave his native place, become famous in some state or country, and then return to his home town, and it is astonishing how many will claim friendship, if not kinship, with him. Human nature is very fickle and very superficial, and the moral of all this is to warn us not to place confidence in any man, but to value all the more highly (because of the contrast) the faithfulness of Him who changes not.

"So Jesus came again into Cana of Galilee, where he made the water wine. And there was a certain nobleman, whose son was sick at Capernaum" (4:46). *Why* should we be told *where* the Lord was when He performed the miracle of healing the nobleman's son? Why, after mentioning Cana, is it added, "Where he made the water wine"? And why tell us in the last verse of the chapter, "This is again the second miracle that Jesus did, when he was come out of Judea into Galilee?" Surely it is apparent at once that we are to place the two miracles that were wrought at Cana side by side. The Holy Spirit indicates there is some connection between them, something which they have in common. Following this hint, a close study of the record of these two miracles reveals the fact that there is a series of striking comparisons between them, apparently seven in number.

In the first place, both were *third day* scenes: in 2:1 we read, "And the third day there was a marriage in Cana of Galilee;" and in 4:43 we are told, "Now after two days he departed thence, and went into Galilee." Second, when Mary came to Christ and told Him they had no wine, He *rebuked her* (2:4), so when the nobleman asked Christ to come down and heal his sick child the Lord *rebuked* him (4:48). Third, in each case we see the *obedient response* made by those whom the Lord commanded (2:7 and 4:50). Fourth, in both miracles we see *the Word at work*: in each miracle the Lord did nothing but speak. Fifth, in both narratives mention is made of the *servant's* knowledge (2:9 and 4:51). Sixth, the sequel in each case was that they who witnessed the miracle *believed*: in the one we read, "And his disciples believed on him" (2:11); in the other we are told, "And himself believed, and his whole house" (4:53). Seventh, there is a designed similarity in the way in which *each narrative concludes*: in 2:11 we are told, "This beginning of miracles did Jesus in Cana of Galilee," and in 4:54, "This is again the second miracle which Jesus did, when he was come out of Judea into Galilee." Here is another example of the importance of comparing two incidents which are placed side by side in Scripture (sometimes for the purpose of comparison, at others in order to point a series of contrast); here we have an example of comparison between two miracles which, though separated in time and in the narrative, both occurred at the same place, and are the only miracles recorded in the New Testament as being wrought in Cana.

"And there was a certain nobleman, whose son was sick at Capernaum." The word "nobleman" signifies a royal officer: probably he belonged to Herod's court; that he was a man of station and means is evident from the fact that he had servants (v. 51). But neither rank nor riches exempt their possessor from the common sorrows of human kind. Naaman was a great man, but he was a leper (II Kings 5:1). So here was a nobleman, yet his son lay at the point of death. The rich have their troubles as well as the poor. Dwellers in palaces are little better off than those who live in cottages. Let Christians beware of setting their hearts on worldly riches: as Bishop Ryle well says, "They are uncertain comforts, but certain cares." No doubt this nobleman had tried every remedy which money could produce. But money is not almighty. Many invest it with an imaginary value that it is far from possessing. Money can not purchase happiness, nor can it ensure health. There is just as much sickness among the aristocracy as there is among the common artisans.

"When he heard that Jesus was come out of Judea into Galilee, he went unto him" (4:47). This domestic trial was a blessing in disguise, for it caused the anxious father to seek out Christ, and this resulted in him believing, and ultimately his whole house believed. God uses many different agents in predisposing men to receive and believe His Word. No doubt these lines will be read by more than one who dates his first awakening to the time when some loved one lay at death's door – it was then he was made to think seriously and saw the need for preparing to meet God. It is well when trouble leads a man *to* God, instead of away from God. Affliction is one of God's medicines; then let us beware of murmuring in time of trouble.

"And besought him that he would come down, and heal his son: for he was at the point of death" (4:47). This nobleman evidently had a measure of faith in the ability of the great Physician, otherwise he had not sought Him at all. But the measure of his faith was small. He had probably learned of the miracles which the Lord had performed at Jerusalem, and hearing that He was now in Galilee – only a few miles distant – he goes to Him. The weakness of his faith is indicated in the request that the Lord should "come down" with him to Capernaum. He believed that Christ could heal close by, but not far away; at short range, but not at a distance. How many there were who thus limited Him. Jairus comes to Christ and says, "My little daughter lieth at the point of death: I pray thee, *come and lay thy hands on her,* that she may be healed; and she shall live" (Mark 5:23). The woman with the issue of blood said, "If I may *touch* but his clothes, I shall be whole" (Mark 5:28). So, too, Martha exclaimed, "Lord, if thou hadst *been here,* my brother had not died" (John 11:21). But let us not censure them, rather let us condemn our own unbelief.

But different far from this "nobleman" was the faith of the centurion that sought the Lord on behalf of his sick servant, and who said, "Lord, I am not worthy that thou shouldst come under my roof: but speak the word only, and my servant shall be healed" (Matt. 8:8). It seems to us this is the reason (or one reason, at least) why we are told here in John 4 that the nobleman came from Capernaum, so that we should link the two together and note the comparisons and contrasts between them. Both resided at Capernaum: both were Gentiles: both were men of position: both came to Christ on behalf of a sick member of his household. But in Matt. 8 the centurion simply spread his need before Christ and refrained from dictating to Him; whereas the nobleman bids the Saviour "come down" to Capernaum. In Matt. 8 we find that the Lord offered to accompany the centurion—"Jesus saith unto him, I will come and heal him" (v. 7). He does the very opposite here in John 4. In Matt. 8 the centurion declines the Lord's offer and says, "Speak the word only;" where as the nobleman meets Christ's rebuke by repeating his original request—"Sir, come down ere my child die" (v. 49). Thus we see again the value of observing the law of Comparison and Contrast.

"Then said Jesus unto him, Except ye see signs and wonders, ye will not believe" (4:48). This was a rebuke. Not only was the faith of this nobleman weak, but he so far forgot himself as to dictate to the Lord Jesus, and tell Him what to do. The force of Christ's reply seems to be this: 'You are demanding signs of Me *before* you will *fully* trust your boy's case into My hands.' This is a serious mistake which is made by many seeking souls. We must not be so wickedly presumptuous as to tell God *how* to act and *what* to do. We must state no terms to the Lord Most High. He must be left to work in His own way. "Except ye see signs and wonders ye will not believe." How this brings out the *omniscience* of Christ! He knew this man's heart. A measure of faith he had, but he was afraid to fully commit himself. The Lord knew this, and so addressed Himself to the suppliant accordingly.

"Except ye see signs and wonders ye will not believe." How searching this is! Is it not a word that many of us need? Is it not at this very point we most often fail? We ask God for a certain thing, and we have a measure of faith that it will be given us; but in the interval of waiting the bare word of God is not sufficient for us—we crave a "sign." Or again; we are engaged in some service for the Lord, and we are not without faith that our labors will result in some fruitage for Him, but ere the fruit appears we become impatient, and we long for a "sign." Is it not so? Is it true of *you,* dear reader, that "except ye see signs and wonders, *ye* will not believe?" Ah! have we not all of us cause to cry, "Lord, I believe; help thou mine unbelief" (Mark 9:24)? Fellow-worker, God has declared that His Word *shall not* return unto Him void (Isa. 55:11). Is not that sufficient? Why ask for "signs"? Fellow-Christian, God has declared that if we ask anything according to His will, He heareth us (I John 5:15). Is not His promise enough? Why, then, crave for "signs"?

"The nobleman saith unto him, Sir, come down ere my child die" (4:49). While it is evident that the nobleman was still slow of heart to commit himself, unreservedly, into the hands of Christ; nevertheless, it is good to see the spirit in which he received the Lord's rebuke. Though he was a nobleman he did not become angry when corrected; instead, he "suffered the word of exhortation," and with commendable importunity continued to plead his suit.

"The nobleman saith unto him, Sir, come down ere my child die." Bishop Ryle has a helpful word on this: "There is here a salutary lesson for the young. Sickness and death come to the young as well as the old. But the young are slow to learn this lesson. Parents and children are apt to shut their eyes to plain facts, and act as if the young never die young. The gravestones in our cemeteries show how many there are who never reached to man's estate at all. The first grave ever dug on earth was for a young man! The first one who ever died was not a father, but a son! He, then, who is wise will never reckon confidently on long life. It is the part of wisdom to be prepared."

We trust these words will come home to the hearts of Christian parents who read this chapter. In the action of this father who came to Christ on behalf of his child there is an example which you will do well to emulate. If you are not deeply concerned about the soul's welfare of your children, who is likely to be? It is *your* bounden duty to teach them the Word of God it is your holy privilege to bring them in prayer to God. Do not turn over to a Sunday School teacher what is incumbent upon you. Teach your little ones the Scriptures from their earliest infancy. Train them to memorize such verses as Psa. 9:17; Jer. 17:9; Rom. 6:23, etc., and God has promised to honor them that honor Him. Be not discouraged if you are unable to detect any response, but rest on the promise, "Cast thy bread upon the waters, and thou shalt find it again after many days."

"The nobleman saith unto him, Sir, come down ere my child die." How the response of Christ to this request brought out the perfections of Jehovah's Servant! This "nobleman," remember, occupied a high social position; most likely he was a member of Herod's court. To any man governed by fleshly considerations and principles, this would have been a tempting opportunity to make a favorable impression in society; it offered a chance to gain a footing in high places, which a man of the world would have quickly seized. But the Lord Jesus never courted popularity, nor did He ever toady to people of influence and affluence. He ever refused to use the ways of the world. *He* "condescended to men of low estate," and was the Friend not of princes and nobles, but of "publicans and sinners." Well may each servant of God take this to heart.

"Jesus saith unto him, Go thy way; thy son liveth" (4:50). The Lord never turns away a soul that truly seeks Him. There may be much ignorance (as indeed there is in all of us), there may be much of the flesh mixed in with our appeals, but if the heart is really set on Him, He always responds. And not only so, invariably He does far more for us than we ask or think. It was so here. He not only healed the son of this nobleman, but He did so immediately, by the word of His power.

"Jesus saith unto him, Go thy way; thy son liveth." This nobleman was a Gentile, for there were no "nobles" among the Jews; and in harmony with each similar case, the Lord healed his son from a distance. There are three, possibly four, different cases recorded in the Gospels, where Christ healed a Gentile, and in each instance He healed from a distance. There was a reason for this. The Jews were in covenant relationship with God, and as such "nigh" to Him. But the Gentiles, being "aliens from the commonwealth of Israel, and strangers from the covenants of promise" were "far off" (Eph. 2:12, 13), and this fact was duly recognized by the Saviour.

"And the man believed the word that Jesus had spoken unto him" (4:50). Here once more, we are shown the Word (John 1:1, 14) at work. This comes out prominently in the miracles described in this Gospel. The Lord does not go down to Capernaum and take the sick boy by the hand. Instead, He speaks the word of power and he is healed instantly. The "words" *He* spake were "spirit and life" (John 6:63). And this imparting of life at a distance by means of the word has a message *for us* today. If Christ could heal this dying boy, who was at least ten miles away, by the word of His mouth, He can give eternal life today by His word even though He is away in heaven. *Distance is no barrier to Him.*

"And the man believed the word that Jesus had spoken unto him, and he went his way." This is very blessed. It shows us the power of the spoken word not only on the boy that was healed, but on his father, too—"Faith cometh by hearing, and hearing by the word of God" (Rom. 10:17). The nobleman had heard the word of God from the lips of the Son of God, and real faith, saving faith, was now begotten within him. He raises no objections, asks no questions, makes no demurs; but with implicit confidence in which he had heard, he believed, and went his way. No "signs" were needed, no feelings required to impart assurance. "He believed, and went his way." This is how salvation comes to the sinner. It is simply a matter of taking God at His word, and setting to our seal that He is true. The very fact that it is God's word guarantees its truthfulness. This, we believe, is the only instance recorded in the New Testament where a "nobleman" believed in Christ—"not many noble are called" (I Cor. 1:26).

"And as he was now going down, his servants met him, and told him, saying, Thy son liveth. Then enquired he of them the hour when he began to amend. And they said unto him, Yesterday at the seventh hour the fever left him" (4:51, 52). The word "yesterday" brings out a striking point. Cana and Capernaum were only a comparatively short distance apart: the journey could be made in about four hours. It was only one hour after midday when the Saviour pronounced the sick boy healed. Such implicit confidence had the nobleman in Christ's word, he did not return home *that* day at all!

I can picture the father on his way back home, going along happy and rejoicing. If some one had enquired as to the occasion of his joy, he would have been told it was because his child, at the point of death, had been restored. Had the enquirer asked *how* the father *knew* his child was now well, his answer would have been, 'Because I have the word of Christ for it—what more do I need!' And, dear reader, we too, shall be full of peace and joy if we rest on the sure Word of God (Rom. 15:13). The father's enquiry of his servants was not because of unbelief, but because he delighted to hear a recountal of what God had wrought. As John Wesley remarked on this verse, "The more exactly the works of God are considered, the more faith is increased."

"So the father knew that it was at the same hour, in the which Jesus said unto him, Thy son liveth: and himself believed, and his whole house" (4:53). The nobleman's faith here is not to be regarded as any different from what is attributed to him in v. 50: it is simply a repetition, brought in here in connection with his house believing, too. It is a very rare thing to find a believing wife and believing children where the father, the head of the house, is himself an unbeliever. What an example does this incident furnish us of the mysterious workings of God! —a boy brought to the point of *death* that a whole house might have *eternal life.*

Let the reader study carefully the following questions in preparation for the next lesson:—

1. What is the meaning of "Bethesda," and what is the significance of the "five porches"? v. 2.
2. Why are we told the impotent man had suffered thirty-eight years? v. 5.

3. Why did Christ ask the impotent man such a question as is recorded in v. 6?
4. What does the man's answer denote? v. 7.
5. What important principle is illustrated in v. 11?
6. What moral perfection of Christ is seen in v. 13?

CHAPTER SEVENTEEN

Christ at the Pool of Bethesda

John 5:1-15

We begin with the usual Analysis: —

1. Jesus in Jerusalem at the feast, v. 1.
2. The pool of Bethesda and the sick congregated about it, vv. 2-4.
3. The impotent man and Christ's healing of him, vv. 5-9.
4. The healed man and his critics, vv. 10-12.
5. The man's ignorance, v. 13.
6. Christ's final word with him, v. 14.
7. The man confesses Jesus, v. 15.

The scene introduced to us in this passage is indeed a pathetic one. The background is the pool of Bethesda, around which lay a great multitude of impotent folk. The great Physician approaches this crowd of sufferers, who were not only sick but helpless. But there was no more stir among them than in the quiet waters of the pool. *He* was neither wanted nor recognized. Addressing one of the most helpless of the sufferers, the Lord asked him if he is desirous of being made whole. Instead of responding to the sympathetic Inquirer with a prompt request that He would have mercy upon him, the poor fellow thought only of the pool and of some man to help him into it. In sovereign grace the Saviour spoke the life-giving word, and the man was immediately and perfectly healed. Yet even then he was still ignorant of the Divine glory of his Benefactor. The healing took place on the Sabbath day, and this evoked the criticism of the Jews; and when they learned that it was Jesus who had performed the miracle "they sought to slay him." All of this speaks loudly of the condition of Judaism, and tells of the rejection of the Christ of God.

"After this there was a feast of the Jews" (5:1). "After this" or, as it should be. "After these things," is an expression which is characteristic of John's Gospel as "Then" is of Matthew, "Immediately" of Mark, and "It came to pass" of Luke. It occurs seven times in this Gospel (3:22; 5:1; 5:14; 6:1; 7:1, 11:11; 21:1) and nine times in the Apocalypse. "It gives one the thought of Jesus acting according to a plan and times marked out 'in the volume of the Book' (Psa. 40:7) and of which He renders an account in John 17" (M. Taylor).

"After this there was a feast of the Jews; and Jesus went up to Jerusalem" (5:1). There is nothing to indicate which of the Feasts this was. Some think it was the Passover, but this we believe is most unlikely, for when *that* feast is referred to in John it is expressly mentioned by name: see 2:13; 6:4; 11:55. Others think it was the feast of Purim, but as that was a human invention and not of Divine institution we can hardly imagine the Lord Jesus going up to Jerusalem to observe it. Personally we think it much more likely that the view of almost all the older writers is the correct one, and that it was the feast of Pentecost that is here in view. Pentecost occurred fifty days after the Passover, and the feast mentioned in John 4:1 follows the Passover mentioned in 2:13. Pentecost is one of the three great annual Feasts which the law required every male Israelite to observe in Jerusalem (Deut. 16), and here we see the Lord Jesus honoring the Divine Law by going up to Jerusalem at the season of its celebration. Doubtless there was a typical reason why the name of this feast should not be given here, for that to which the feast of Pentecost pointed received no fulfillment in the days of our Lord's early ministry—contrast Acts 2:1.

"Now there is at Jerusalem by the sheep market a pool, which is called in the Hebrew tongue Bethesda, having five porches" (5:2). We believe the reference here is to the sheep "gate" of Neh. 3:1. At first glance Neh. 3 does not seem to be very interesting reading, and yet there is much in it that is precious. It describes the rebuilding of the walls of Jerusalem in the days when a remnant of Israel returned from the Babylonian captivity. Various portions in the work of reconstruction were allotted to different individuals and companies. These portions or sections were from gate to gate. Ten gates are mentioned in the chapter. The first is the sheep gate (v.1) and the last is "The gate Miphkad" which means "judgment," and speaks, perhaps, of the judgment-seat of Christ; and then the chapter concludes by saying, "And between the going up of the corner *unto the sheep gate* repaired the goldsmiths and the merchants." Thus the circle is completed, and at the close we are brought back to the point from which we started—"The sheep gate." This is the gate through which the sacrificial animals were brought to the temple—the "lamb" predominating, hence its name. The sheep gate, then, points us at once to Christ, and tells of His Cross.

Now in the light of what we have just said, how exceedingly significant and blessed to note that we are here told the pool which was called Bethesda, meaning mercy, was by the "sheep" (gate). It is only in Christ that the poor sinner can find mercy, and it is only through His sacrifice on the Cross that this mercy is now obtainable for us in Him. What an instance is this of the great importance of noting carefully every little word in Scripture! There is nothing trivial in the Word of God. The smallest detail has a meaning and value; every name, every geographical and topographical reference, a message. As a further example of this, notice the last words of the verse—"having five porches." The number of the porches here is also significant. In Scripture the numerals are used with Divine design and precision. Five stands for *grace* or *favor*. When Joseph desired to show special favor to his brother Benjamin we read, "And he took and sent messes unto them from before him: but Benjamin's mess was *five* times so much as any of theirs" (Gen. 43:34); and again we are told, "To all of them he gave each man changes of raiment; but to Benjamin he gave three hundred pieces of silver, and *five* changes of raiment" (Gen. 45:22). *Five* and its multiples are stamped on every part of the tabernacle. It was with *five* loaves the Lord Jesus fed the hungry multitude. The fifth clause in the Lord's prayer is, "*Give* us this day our daily bread." The *fifth* Commandment was the only one with a *promise* attached to it; and so we might go on. Thus we see the perfect propriety of *five* porches (colonnades) around the pool of *Mercy*, situated "by the *sheep* (gate)"!

"In these lay a great multitude of impotent folk, of blind, halt, withered, waiting for the moving of the water" (5:3). What a picture of the Jewish nation at that time! How accurately does the condition of that multitude of sufferers describe the spiritual state of Judaism as it then existed! God had dealt with their father in sovereign mercy and marvelous grace, but the Nation as such appreciated it not. A few here and there took the place of lost sinners, and were saved, but the "great multitude" remained in their wretchedness. Israel as a people were *impotent*. They had the Law, made their boast in it, but were unable to keep it. Not only were they impotent, but "blind"—blind to their own impotency, blind to their wretchedness, blind to their desperate need, and so blind to the Divine and moral glories of the One who now stood in their midst "they *saw* in him *no* beauty that they should desire him." A third word describing their condition is added, "halt:" the term signifies one who is lame, crippled. Israel had the Law but they were unable to walk in the way of God's commandments. A blind man is able to grope his way about: but a cripple cannot walk at all. Again; we are told this "great multitude" were "withered." This, no doubt, refers to those whose hands were paralyzed (cf. Matt. 12:10; Luke 6:6), and as a description of Israel it tells us that they were totally incapacitated to work for God. What a pitiable picture! First, a general summing up of their state—"impotent." Second, a detailed diagnosis under three descriptive terms—"blind" (in their understandings and hearts), "halt" (crippled in their feet, so that they were unable to walk), "withered" (in their hands so that they were unable to work). Third, a word that speaks of their response to the prophetic word—"*waiting*"; waiting for the promised Messiah, and all the time ignorant of the fact that He was there in their midst! Who but the Spirit of God could have drawn so marvelously accurate a picture in such few and short lines!

We must not, however, limit this picture to Israel, for it is equally applicable and pertinent to sinners of the Gentiles too. Israel in the flesh was only a sample of fallen man as such. What we have here is a pointed and solemn delineation of human depravity, described in physical terms; its moral application is to the whole of Adam's fallen race. Let every reader see here a portrait of what he or she is by nature. The picture is not flattering we know. No; it is drawn by One who searcheth the innermost recesses of the human heart, and is presented here to humble us. The natural man is *impotent*—"without strength" (Rom. 5:6). This sums up in a single word his condition before God: altogether helpless, unable to do a single thing for himself. Then follows an amplification of this impotency, given in three (the number of full manifestation) descriptive terms. First, he is *blind.* This explains the lethargic indifference of the great multitude today—sporting on the very brink of the Pit, because *unable to see* the frightful peril that menaces them; making merry as they hasten down the Broad Road, because incompetent to discern the eternal destruction which awaits them at the bottom of it. Yes, blind indeed is the natural man: "The way of the wicked is as darkness: they knew not at what they stumble" (Prov. 4:19).

"Halt": lame, crippled, unable to walk. How inevitably this follows the other! How can one who is spiritually blind walk the Narrow Way that leadeth unto life? "Mine eye affecteth mine heart" (Lam. 3:51), and out of the heart are the issues of life (Prov. 4:23); if then the eye be evil, the body also is full of darkness (Luke 11:34). Halt—lame—a cripple—if, then, such an one is ever to come to Christ he *must* indeed be "drawn" (John 6:44).

"Withered"—blind eyes, crippled feet, paralyzed hands: unable to see, unable to walk, unable to work. How striking is the order here! Consider them inversely: a man cannot perform good works unless he is walking with God; and he will not begin to walk with God until the eyes of his heart have been opened to see his need of Christ. This is the Divine order, and it never varies. First the eyes must be opened, and then an illumined understanding prepares us to walk worthy of the vocation wherewith we are called; and that, in turn, equips us for acceptable service for God. But so long as the eyes are "blind" the feet will be "halt" and the hands "withered."

"Waiting for the moving of the water." Surely this is not hard to interpret. This pool was the object in which the great multitude placed all their hopes. They were waiting for its waters to be "troubled" so that its curative property might heal them. But they waited in vain. The one invalid who is singled out from the crowd had been there "a long time," and little had it availed him. Is it not thus with the *ordinances* of the religious world? How many there are—"a great multitude" indeed—which place their faith in the waters of baptism, or in the 'mass' and 'extreme unction'! And *a long time* all such will have to wait before the deep need of their *souls* will be met.

"For an angel went down at a certain season into the pool, and troubled the water: whosoever then first after the troubling of the waters stepped in was made whole of whatsoever disease he had" (5:4). We return now to the Jewish application of our passage. The waters of this pool reflect the Sinaitic law, which was "given by the disposition of angels"; that law which promised "life" to him who did all that it enjoined. But whoever kept the law? Whoever obtained life by meeting its demands? None of Adam's fallen race. The law was "weak through the flesh." A perfect man could keep it, but a sinner could not. Why, then, was the law given? That the offense might abound; that sin might be shown to be exceeding sinful; that the sinner might discover his sinfulness. His very efforts to keep the law, and his repeated failures to do so, would but make manifest his utter helplessness. In like manner, when the angel troubled the water of Bethesda so that the first to step into it might be made whole, this only magnified the sufferings of those who lay around it. How could those who were "impotent" *step in!* Ah! they could not. Was, then, God mocking man in his misery? Nay, verily. He was but preparing the way for that which was "better" (Heb. 11:40). And this is what is brought before us in what follows.

"And a certain man was there, which had an infirmity thirty and eight years" (5:5). How this serves to confirm our interpretation of the previous verse, and what an illustration it furnishes us again of the deep significance of every word of Scripture. Why should the Holy Spirit have been careful to tell us the exact length of time this particular sufferer had been afflicted?

What is the meaning and message of this "thirty and eight years"? Are we left to guess at the answer? No, indeed. Scripture is its own interpreter if we will but take the trouble to patiently and diligently search its pages and compare spiritual things with spiritual (I Cor. 2:13). Thirty-eight years was exactly the length of time that Israel spent in the wilderness after they came under law at Sinai (see Deut. 2:14). There it was, in the Wilderness of Sin, that of old Israel manifested their "impotency" – blind, halt, withered – under law.

"When Jesus saw him lie, and knew that he had now been a long time in that case, he saith unto him, Wilt thou be made whole?" (5:6). Here is Light shining in the darkness, but the darkness comprehended it not. The very shining of the Light only served to reveal how great was the darkness. There was a great multitude of sick ones lying around that disappointing pool, and here was the great Physician Himself abroad in the land. Bethesda thickly surrounded, and Christ Himself passing by unheeded! Truly the "darkness comprehended not." And is it any different today? Here is human religion with all its cumbersome machinery and disappointing ordinances *waited on,* and the grace of God slighted. Go yonder to India with its myriad temples and sacred Ganges; visit Thibet, the land of praying-wheels; turn and consider the devotees of Mohammed and their holy pilgrimages; come nearer home, and look upon the millions of deluded Papists with their vigils and fasts, their beads and holy water; and then turn in to the religious performances in many of the Protestant churches, and see if there are any differences in the underlying principles which actuate them. They one and all fail, utterly fail, to meet the deep need of the soul. One and all they are unable to put away sin. And, yet, sad to say, they one and all supplant the Christ of God – *He* is not wanted; *He* passes by unnoticed.

Such is fallen human nature. The whole world lieth in the wicked one (I John 5:19), and were it not for sovereign grace every member of Adam's race would perish eternally. Grace is the sinner's only hope. Desert he has none. Spirituality he has none. Strength he has none. If salvation is to come to him, it *must* be by grace, and grace is unmerited favor shown toward the hell-deserving. And just because grace is this, God exercises His sovereign prerogative in bestowing His favors on whom He pleases—"For he saith to Moses, I will have compassion on whom I will have compassion" (Rom. 9:16). And let none murmur against this and suppose that any one is wronged thereby. Men prate about God being unjust, but if justice, real justice, bare justice, be insisted on, hope is entirely cut off for all of us. Justice requires that each should receive his exact due; and what, dear reader, is your due, my due, but judgment! Eternal life is a gift, and if a gift it can neither be earned nor claimed. If salvation is God's gift, who shall presume to tell Him the ones on whom He ought to bestow it? Was salvation provided for the angels that fell? If God has left them to reap the due reward of their iniquities, why should He be charged with injustice if He abandons to themselves those of mankind who love darkness rather than light? It is not that God *refuses* salvation to any who truly seek it. Not so; there is a Saviour for every sinner who will repent and believe. But if out of the great multitude of the impenitent and unbelieving God determines to exercise His sovereign grace by singling out a few to be the objects of His irresistible power and distinguishing favors, who is wronged thereby? Has not God the right to dispense His charity as seemeth best to Himself (Matt. 20:15)? Certainly He has.

The sovereignty of God is strikingly illustrated in the passage now before us. There lay a "great multitude" of impotent folk: all were equally needy, all equally powerless to help themselves. And here was the great Physician, God Himself incarnate, infinite in power, with inexhaustible resources at His command. It had been just as easy for Him to have healed the entire company as to make a single individual whole. *But He did not.* For some reason not revealed to us, He passed by the "great multitude" of sufferers and singled out one man and healed him. There is nothing whatever in the narrative to indicate that this "certain man" was any different from the others. We are not told that *he* turned to the Saviour and cried "Have mercy on *me.*" He was just as blind as were the others to the Divine glory of the One who stood before him. Even when asked "Wilt thou be made whole?" he evidenced no faith whatever; and after he had been healed "He wist not who it was" that had healed him. It is impossible to find *any* ground in the man himself as a reason for Christ singling him out for special favor. The *only* explanation is the mere sovereign pleasure of Christ Himself. This is proven beyond the shadow of doubt by His own declaration immediately afterwards—"For as the Father raiseth up the dead, and quickeneth them; even so the Son quickeneth *whom he will*" (v. 21).

This miracle of healing was a parable in action. It sets before us a vivid illustration of God's work of grace in the spiritual realm. Just as the condition of that impotent multitude depicts the depravity of Adam's fallen race, so Christ singling out this individual and healing him, portrays the sovereign grace of Him who singles out and saves His own elect. Every detail in the incident bears this out.

"When Jesus saw him lie, and knew that he had been now a long time in that case." Note the individuality of this. We are not told that he saw *them*—the "great multitude"—but *him*. The eyes of the Saviour were fixed on that one who, out of all the crowd, had been given to Him by the Father before the foundation of the world. Not only are we told that Christ "saw him," but it is added, "and knew that he had been now a long time in that case." Yes, He knew all about him; had known him from all eternity—"I am the good shepherd, and *know* my sheep" (John 10:11). And then we read, "And *saith* unto him." It was not the man who spoke first, but Christ. The Lord always takes the initiative, and invites Himself. And it was thus with you, Christian reader, when sovereign grace sought you out. You, too, were lying amid the "great multitude of impotent folk," for by nature you were a child of wrath, "even as others" (Eph. 2:3). Yes, you were lying in all the abject misery of a *fallen* creature—blind, halt, withered—unable to do a thing for yourself. Such was your awful state when the Lord, in sovereign grace, drew near to you. O thank Him now that He did not pass you by, and leave you to the doom you so richly deserved. Praise Him with a loud voice for His distinguishing grace that singled *you* out to be an object of His sovereign mercy. But we must now consider the force of the Saviour's question here.

"He saith unto him, Wilt thou be made whole?" (5:6). Does it seem strange that such a question should be put to that sufferer? Would not being made whole be the one thing desired above all others by a man who had suffered for thirty-eight years? Was not the very fact that he was lying there by the pool an indication of what he wished? Why, then, ask him "Wilt thou be made whole?" Ah! the question is not so meaningless as some might suppose. Not always are the wretched willing to be relieved. Invalids sometimes trade on the sympathy and indulgence of their friends. Others sink so low that they become despondent and give up all hope, and long for death to come and relieve them. But there is something much deeper here than this.

Did not the Saviour ask the question to impress upon this man the utter helplessness of his condition! Man must be brought to recognize and realize his impotency. Whilever we console ourselves we will do better next time, that is a sure sign we have not come to the end of ourselves. The one who promises himself that he will amend his ways and turn over a new leaf has not learned that he is "without strength." It is not till we discover we are helpless that we shall abandon our miserable efforts to weave a robe of righteousness for ourselves. It is not till we learn we are impotent that we shall look *outside* of ourselves to Another.

No doubt one reason why Christ selected so many incurable cases on which to show forth His power, was in order to have suitable objects to portray to us the irreparable ruin which sin has wrought and the utter helplessness of man's natural estate. The Saviour, then, was pressing upon the man the need of being made whole. But more: when the Saviour said, "Wilt thou be *made* whole?" it was tantamount to asking, 'Are you willing to put yourself, just as you are, into My hands? Are you ready for Me to do for you what you are unable to do for yourself? Are you willing to be my debtor?'

"The impotent man answered, Sir, I have no man, when the water is troubled, to put me into the pool: but while I am coming, another steppeth down before me" (5:7). How sadly true to life. When the great Physician said, "Wilt thou be made whole?" the poor sufferer did not promptly answer, 'Yea Lord; undertake for me.' And not thus does the sinner act when first brought face to face with Christ. The impotent man failed to realize that Christ could cure him by a word. He supposed he must get into the pool. There are several lines of thought suggested here, but it is needless to follow them out. The poor man had more faith in means than he had in the Lord. And, too, his eye was fixed on "man," not God: he was looking to human kind for help. Again we would exclaim, How true to life! Moreover, he thought that he had to do something—"While I *am* coming." How this uncovers the heart of the natural man! How pathetic are the closing words of this verse! What a heartless world we live in. Human nature is full of selfishness. Christ is the only unfailing Friend of the friendless.

"Jesus saith unto him, Rise, take up thy bed, and walk" (5:8). If the Saviour waited until there was in the sinner a due appreciation of His person, none would ever be saved. The sufferer had made no cry for mercy, and when Christ inquired if he were willing to be made whole there was no faith evidenced. But in sovereign grace the Son of God pronounced the life-giving word, yet it was a word that addressed the human responsibility of the subject. A careful analysis of the command of Christ reveals three things. First, there must be *implicit confidence in His word.* "Rise" was the peremptory command. There must be a hearty recognition of His authority, and immediate response to His orders. "Believe on the Lord Jesus Christ, and thou shalt be saved" is something more than a gracious invitation; it is a command (I John 3:23). Second, "Take up thy bed"—a cotton pallet, easily rolled up. There was to be no thought of failure, and no provision made for a relapse. How many there are who take a few feeble steps, and then return to their beds! The last state of such is worse than the first. If there is faith in the person of Christ, if there is a submission to His authority, then the new life within will find an outlet without: and we shall no longer be a burden to others, but able to shoulder our own burdens. Third, "And walk." I like that word coming here. It is as though the Saviour said, 'You were unable to walk *into* the water: you could not walk *in* order to be cured, but now that you are made whole, "walk!"' There are duties to be faced of which we have had no previous experience, and we must proceed to discharge them in faith; and in that faith in which He bids us do them will be found the strength needed for their performance.

"And immediately the man was made whole, and took up his bed, and walked: and on the same day was the sabbath" (5:9). How blessed! The cure was both instantaneous and complete. Christ does not put the believing sinner into a salvable state. He *saves,* saves us with a perfect and eternal salvation the moment we believe: "I know that, whatsoever God doeth, it shall be forever: nothing can be put to it, nor anything taken from it" (Ecc. 3:14). We need hardly say that we are here shown, once more, the Word at work. The Saviour did nothing but speak, and the miracle was accomplished. It is thus the Son of God is revealed to us again and again in this fourth Gospel.

"The Jews therefore said unto him that was cured, It is the sabbath day: it is not lawful for thee to carry thy bed" (5:10). How true to life again! The one who surrenders to his Lord must expect to encounter criticism. The one who regulates his life by the Word of God will be met by the opposition of man. And it is the *religious* world that will oppose most fiercely. Unless we subscribe to *their* creed and observe *their* rules of conduct, persecution and ostracism will be our lot. Unless we are prepared to be brought into bondage by the traditions of the elders we must be ready for their frowns. Christ was not ignorant of the current teaching about the Sabbath, and He knew full well what would be the consequences should this healed man carry his bed on the sabbath day. But he had come here to set His people free from the shackles which religious zealots had forged. Never did He toady to the public opinion in His day; nor should we. There are thousands of His people who need to be reminded of Gal. 5:1: "Stand fast therefore in the liberty wherewith Christ hath made us free, and be not entangled again with the yoke of bondage." If the child of God is regulated by the Scriptures and knows that he is pleasing his Lord, it matters little or nothing what his fellowmen (or his fellow-Christians either) may think or say about him. Better far to displease them than to be entangled again in the yoke of bondage, and thus "*frustrate* the grace of God" (Gal. 2:21).

"He answered them, He that made me whole, the same said unto me, Take up thy bed, and walk" (5:11). This sets a fine example for us. How simply he met his critics. He did not enter into an argument about their perverted view of the Sabbath: he did not charge them with want of sympathy for those who were sufferers, though he might have done both. Instead, he hid behind Christ. He fell back upon the Word of God. Well for us when we have a "Thus saith the Lord" to meet our critics.

"Then asked they him, What man is that which said unto thee, Take up thy bed and walk? And he that was healed wist not who it was" (5:12, 13). This illustrates the fact that there is much ignorance even in believers. We ought not to expect too much from babes in Christ. This man had been healed, and he had obeyed the command of his Benefactor; but not yet did he perceive His Divine glories. Intelligence concerning the person of Christ follows (and not precedes) an experimental acquaintance with the virtues of His work.

"For Jesus had conveyed himself away, a multitude being in that place" (5:13). This brings out the moral perfections of the Saviour. It evidences the meekness of the Divine Servant: He ministered without ostentation. He never sought to be the popular idol of the hour, or the center of an admiring crowd. Instead of courting popularity, He shunned it. Instead of advertising Himself, He "received not honor from men." This lovely excellency of Christ appears most conspicuously in Mark's Gospel: see 1:37, 38, 44; 7:17, 36; 8:26, etc.

"Afterward Jesus findeth him in the temple, and said unto him, Behold, thou art made whole: sin no more, lest a worse thing come upon thee" (4:14). The Lord had withdrawn from the man. Christ had retired in order that he might be tested. New strength had been given him; opportunity was then afforded for him to use it. The restored sufferer did not falter. The One who had saved him was obeyed as Lord. The Jewish critics had not intimidated him. That a work of grace had been wrought in his soul as well as in his body is evidenced by the fact that he had gone to the House of Prayer and Praise. And there, we are told, the Lord Jesus found him. This is most blessed. Christ was not to be met with in the throng, but He was to be found in the temple!

Having dealt in "grace" with the poor helpless sufferer Christ now applied the "truth." "Sin no more" is a word for his conscience. Grace does not ignore the requirements of God's holiness: "Awake to righteousness, and sin not" (I Cor. 15:34) is still the standard set before us. "Lest a worse thing come unto thee" reminds us that the believer is still subject to the government of God. "Whatsoever a man soweth, that shall he also reap" (Gal. 6:7). is addressed to believers, not unbelievers. If we sin we shall suffer chastisement. Bishop Ryle has pointed out that there is here an important message for those who have been raised from a bed of sickness. "Sin no more": renewed health ought to send us back into the world with a greater hatred of sin, a more thorough watchfulness over our ways, a greater determination to live for God's glory.

"The man departed, and told the Jews that it was Jesus, that had made him whole" (5:15). This gives beautiful completeness to the whole incident. Here we see him who had been healed confessing with his lips the One who had saved him. It would seem that as soon as the Lord Jesus had revealed Himself to this newly-born soul, that he had sought out the very ones who had previouly interrogated and criticized him, and told them it was Jesus who had made him whole.

Study the following questions on the next lesson, 5:16-31:

1. What is the force of Christ's answer in v. 17?
2. What is the meaning of Christ's words in v. 19?
3. How does v. 20 bring out the Deity of Christ?
4. What does v. 23 go to prove about Christ?
5. How does v. 24 establish the eternal security of the believer?
6. Why should the "Son of man" be the Judge? v. 28.
7. Does v. 30 speak of Christ's humanity or Deity?

CHAPTER EIGHTEEN

THE DEITY OF CHRIST: SEVENFOLD PROOF

John 5:16-30

We present our customary Analysis of the passage which is to be before us. It sets forth the *absolute equality* of the Son with the Father: –

1. In Service, vv. 16-18.
2. In Will, v. 19.
3. In Intelligence, v. 20.
4. In Sovereign Rights, v. 21.
5. In Divine Honors, vv. 22-23.
6. In Imparting Life, vv. 24-26.
7. In Judicial Power and Authority, vv. 27-30.

There is an intimate connection between the passage before us and the first fifteen verses of the chapter: the former provides the occasion for the discourse which follows. The chapter naturally divides itself into two parts: in the former we have recorded the sovereign grace and power of the Lord Jesus in healing the impotent man on the Sabbath day, and the criticism and opposition of the Jews; in the latter we have the Lord's vindication of Himself. The second half of John 5 is one of the profoundest passages in this fourth Gospel. It sets forth the Divine glories of the incarnate Son of God. It gives us the Lord's own teaching concerning His Divine Sonship. It also divides into two parts: in the former is contained the Lord's sevenfold declaration of His Deity; in the latter, beginning at v. 41, He cites the different witnesses to His Deity. We shall confine ourselves now to the former section. May the Spirit of Truth whose blessed work it is to "glorify" the One who is now absent from these scenes illumine our understandings and enable us to rightly divide this passage of God's inspired Word.

The miracle of the healing of the impotent man, which engaged our attention in the last chapter, has several outstanding and peculiar features in it. The abject misery and utter helplessness of the sufferer, the sovereign action of the Great Physician in singling him out from the multitude which lay around the Pool of Bethesda, the total absence of any indication of him making any appeal to Christ or exercising any faith in Him previous to his healing, the startling suddenness and spontaneity of the miracle, the Lord's command that he should "take up his bed" on the Sabbath day, are all so many items that at once arrest the attention. The turning of the healed man's steps toward the Temple, evidenced that a work of grace had been wrought in his soul as well as in his body. The grace of the Lord is seeking him out in the Temple and the faithful words there addressed to his conscience, give beautiful completeness to the whole scene. All of this but serves to emphasize the enormity of what follows:

As soon as the healed man had learned Who it was that had made him whole, he went and "told the Jews that it was Jesus" (v. 15). What, then, was their response? Did they immediately seek this Blessed One who must be none other than their long-promised Messiah? Did they, like the prophetess Anna, give thanks unto the Lord, and speak "of him to all them that looked for redemption in Jerusalem" (Luke 2:38)? Alas, it was far otherwise. Instead of being filled with praise, they were full of hatred. Instead of worshipping the Sent One of God, they persecuted Him. Instead of coming to Him that they might have life, they sought to put Him to death. Terrible climax was this to all that had gone before. In chapter one we see "the Jews" ignorant as to the identity of the Lord's forerunner (1:19), and blind to the Divine Presence in their midst (1:26). In chapter two we see "the Jews" demanding a sign from Him who had vindicated the honor of His Father's House (2:18). In chapter three we are shown "a ruler of the Jews" dead in trespasses and sins, needing to be born again (3:7). Next we see "the Jews" quibbling or quarreling with John's disciples about purifying (3:25). In chapter four we learn of their callous indifference toward the Gentile neighbors—"the Jews have no dealings with the Samaritans" (4:9). Then, in the beginning of chapter five, we read of "a feast of the Jews," but its hollow mockery is exposed in the scene described immediately afterwards—a "feast," and then "a great multitude of impotent folk, of blind, halt, withered!" Now the terrible climax is reached when we are told, "And therefore did the Jews persecute Jesus, and sought to slay him, because he had done these things on the sabbath day" (5:16). Beyond this they could not go, save, when God's time had come, for the carrying out of their diabolical desires.

"And therefore did the Jews persecute Jesus, and sought to slay him, because he had done these things on the sabbath day" (5:16). Unspeakably solemn is this, for it makes manifest, in all its hideousness, that carnal mind which is enmity against God. Here was a man who had been afflicted for thirty and eight years. For a long time he had lain helplessly by the pool of Bethesda, unable to step into it. Now, of a sudden, he had risen up in response to the quickening word of the Son of God. Not only so, he carried his bed, and walked. The cure was patent. That a wondrous miracle had been wrought could not be gainsaid. Unable to refute it, the Jews now vented their malice by persecuting the Divine Healer, and seeking to put Him to death. They sought to kill Him because He had healed on the Sabbath day. What a situation! They dared to put themselves against the Lord of the Sabbath. The One who had performed the miracle of healing was none other than the Son of God. In criticising Him, they were murmuring against God Himself. Therefore, we say we have here an out and out exposure of that carnal mind which is enmity *against God*: that carnal mind which, my reader, is by nature, in each of us. How this reveals the awful depravity of the fallen creature. How it demonstrates our deep need of a Saviour! How it makes manifest that wondrous grace of God which provided a Saviour for such incorrigible rebels.

"But Jesus answered them, My Father worketh hitherto, and I work" (5:17). This was not the only occasion when the Lord Jesus was criticised for healing the sick on the Sabbath day, and it is most instructive to observe (as others before us have pointed out) the various replies He made to His opponents as these are recorded by the different Evangelists. Each of them narrates the particular incident (and the Lord's words in connection with it) that most appropriately accorded with the distinctive design of His Gospel. In Matt. 12:2, 3 we find that Christ appealed to the example of David and the teaching of the Law, which was well suited for record in this Gospel. In Mark 2:24, 27 we read that He said, "The sabbath was made for man," that is, it was designed to serve man's best interests—this in the Gospel which treats most fully of service. In Luke 13:15 we find the Lord Jesus asking, "Doth not each one of you on the sabbath loose his ox or his ass from the stall, and lead him away to watering?": here, in the Gospel of Christ's humanity, we find Him appealing to human sympathies. But in John 5 Christ takes altogether higher ground and makes answer suited to His Divine glory.

"But Jesus answered them, My Father worketh hitherto, and I work." Here is the first of the seven proofs which Christ now gives of His absolute Deity. Instead of pointing to the example of David or appealing to human sympathies, Christ identifies Himself directly with "the Father." In saying "*My Father* worketh hitherto *and I* work" He affirms His absolute equality with the Father. It would be nothing short of blasphemy for a mere creature—no matter how exalted his rank or how great his antiquity—to couple himself with the Father thus. When He speaks of "My Father . . . and I" there is no misunderstanding the claim that He made. But let us ponder first the *pertinency* of this affirmation.

"My Father worketh hitherto." It is true that on the seventh day God rested from all His creative works. As we read in Gen. 2:3, "And God blessed the seventh day, and sanctified it: because that in it He had rested from all His work which God created and made." That seventh day of rest was not needed by Him to recuperate from the toil of the six days' labor, for "the everlasting God, the Lord, the Creator of the ends of the earth, fainteth not, neither is weary" (Isa. 40:28). No; but it is otherwise with the creature. Work tires us, and rest is a physical and moral necessity, and woe be to the man or woman who ignores the merciful provision "made for man." If we refuse to rest throughout one day each week, God will compel us to spend at least the equivalent of it upon our backs on a bed of sickness—"Be not deceived; God is not mocked." God, at the beginning, set before His creatures a Divine example, and pronounced the Day of Rest a "blessed" one, and blessing has always attended those who have observed and preserved its rest. Contrariwise, a curse has descended, and still descends, on those who rest not one day in seven. God not only blessed the seventh day, but He "hallowed" it and the word "hallow" means to set apart for sacred use.

While it is true that God rested on that first seventh day from all His creative work, He has never rested from His governmental work, His providential work, supplying the needs of His creatures. The sun rises and sets, the tides ebb and flow, the rain falls, the wind blows, the grass grows on the weekly Rest Day as well as on any other. What we may term works of necessity and works of mercy—that is upholding and sustaining the whole realm of creation and the daily recurring needs of His creatures—God never rests from.

Now says Christ, "My Father worketh hitherto, and I work." All through the centuries has the Father been working. Nor had His working been restricted to the material realm. In illuminating the understandings of men, in convicting their consciences, in moving their wills, had He also "worked hitherto." If, then, it was meet that God the Father worked with unremitting patience and mercy, if the Father ministered to the wants of His needy creatures on the Sabbath day, then by parity of reason it must also be right for God the Son, the Lord of the Sabbath, to engage in works of necessity and mercy on the weekly Rest Day. Thus the Lord Jesus unequivocally claims absolute equality with the Father in service.

"Therefore the Jews sought the more to kill him, because he not only had broken the Sabbath, but said also that God was his Father, making himself equal with God" (5:18). There was no mistaking the force of Christ's declaration. By saying "My Father . . . and I" He had done what, without the greatest impropriety, was impossible to any mere creature. He had done what Abraham, Moses, David, Daniel, never dreamed of doing. He had placed Himself on the same level with the Father. His traducers were quick to recognize that He had "made himself equal with God," and they were right. No other inference could fairly be drawn from His words. And mark it attentively, the Lord Jesus did not charge them with wresting His language and misrepresenting His meaning. He did not protest against their construction of His words. Instead of that He continued to press upon them His Divine claims, stating the truth with regard to His unique personality and presenting the evidence on which His claim rested. And thus did He vindicate Himself not only from the charge of Sabbath-violation in having healed by His Divine word a poor helpless sufferer on that day, but also of blasphemy, in making an assertion in which by obvious implication, was a claim to equality with God.

Christ's claim to absolute equality with God only fanned the horrid flame of the enmity in those Jewish zealots—they "sought the more to kill him." A similar scene is presented to us at the close of John 8. Immediately after being told that the Lord Jesus said "Before Abraham was I am" (another formal avowal of His absolute Deity) we read, "*Then* took they up stones to cast at him" (vv. 58, 59). So again in the tenth chapter we find that as soon as He had declared "I and Father are one" "*Then* the Jews took up stones again to stone him" (vv. 30, 31). Thus did the carnal mind of man continue to display its inveterate enmity against *God.*

"Then answered Jesus and said unto them, Verily, Verily, I say unto you, The Son can do nothing of himself, but what he seeth the Father do: for what things soever he doeth, these also doeth the Son likewise" (5:19). This is a verse which has been a sore puzzle to many of the commentators, and one used frequently by the enemies of Christ who deny His Deity. Even some of those who have been regarded as the champions of orthodoxy have faltered badly. To them the words "The Son can do nothing of himself" seem to point to a blemish in His person. They affirm a limitation, and when misunderstood appear to call for a half apology. The only solution which seems to have occurred to these men who thus dishonor both the written and the incarnate Word, is that this statement must have reference to the humanity of Christ. But a moment's reflection should show that such a conclusion is wide of the mark. The second half of this nineteenth verse must be studied and interpreted in the light of the first half.

It is to be noted that the verse opens by saying "Then *answered* Jesus and said unto them, Verily, Verily, I say unto you, the Son can do nothing of himself, but what he seeth the Father do." *What* was it that He was replying to? *Who* was it that He was here "answering"? The previous verse quickly decides. He was replying to those who sought to kill Him; He was answering His enemies who were enraged because He had "made himself equal with God." In what follows, then, we have the Lord's response to their implied charge of blasphemy. In v. 19 we have the second part of the vindication of His claim that He and the Father were one. Thus it will be seen that the words "The Son can do nothing of himself" respect His Deity and not His humanity, separately considered. Or, more accurately speaking, they concern the Divine glory of the Son of God incarnate.

"The Son can do nothing of himself but what he seeth the Father do." Does this mean that His ability was limited? or that His power was restricted? Do His words signify that when He "made himself of no reputation (R. V. emptied himself) and took upon him the form of a servant" (Phil. 2:7) that He was reduced to all the limitations of human nature? To all these questions we return an emphatic and dogmatic No. Instead of pointing to an imperfection, either in His person or power, they, rightly understood, only serve to bring out His peerless excellency. But here as everywhere else, Scripture must be interpreted by Scripture, and once we heed this rule, difficulties disappear like the mists before the sun.

It will be seen that in v. 30 we have a strictly parallel statement, and by noting what is added there the one in v. 19 is more easily understood. "The Son can do nothing of himself" of v. 19 is repeated in the "I can do nothing of myself" in v. 30, and then in the closing words of v. 30 we find that the Lord explains His meaning by giving as a reason — "Because I seek not mine own will, but the will of the Father which hath sent me."

The limitation is not because of any defect in His person (brought about by the incarnation) nor because of any limitation in His power (voluntary or imposed); it was solely a matter of *will.* "The Son can do *nothing of himself,*" literally, "nothing *out of* himself," that is, "nothing" as proceeding from or originating with Himself. In other words, the force of what He said was this: 'I cannot act independently of the Father.' But was that a limitation which amounted to a defect? Indeed no; the very reverse. .Do the words "*God* that *cannot* lie" (Titus 1:2) and "God cannot be tempted with evil" (James 1:13) point to a blemish in the Divine nature or character? Nay, verily, they affirm Divine perfections. It was so here in the words of Christ.

But may it not be that Christ is here speaking in view of His mediatorial position, as the servant of the Father? We do not think so, and that for three reasons. In the first place, John's Gospel is not the one which emphasizes His servant-character; that is unfolded in Mark's. In this Gospel it is His Deity, His Divine glory, which is prominent throughout. Therefore, some explanation for this verse must be found consonant with that fact. In the second place, our Lord was not here defending His mediatorship, His Divinely-*appointed* works; instead, He was replying to those who deemed Him guilty of blasphemy, because He had made Himself equal with God. Our third reason will be developed below.

"The Son can do nothing of himself." This we have attempted to show means, "the Son cannot act independently of the Father." And why could He not? Because *in will* He was absolutely *one* with the Father. If He were *God* the Son then His will must be in perfect unison with that of *God* the Father, otherwise, there would be two absolute but conflicting wills, which means that there would be two Gods, the one opposing the other; which in plainer language still, would be affirming that there were two *Supreme* Beings which is, of course, a flat contradiction of terms. It was just because the Lord Jesus was the Son of *God,* that His will was in fullest harmony with the will of the Father. Man can will independently of God, alienated from Him as he is. Even the angels which kept not their first estate, yea, one above them in rank, the "anointed cherub" himself could, and did say, "I will" (see Isa. 14:13 and 14, five times repeated). But the Son of God could not, for He was not only very Man of very man but also very God of very God.

It was this in the God-man which distinguished Him from all other men. He never acted independently of the Father. He was always in perfect subjection to the Father's will. There was no will in Him which had to be broken. From start to finish He was in most manifest agreement with the One who sent Him. His first recorded utterance struck the keynote to His earthly life—"Wist ye not that I must be about *my Father's* business?" In the temptation when assailed by the Devil, He stedfastly refused to act independently of God. "My meat is to do the will of him that sent me" ever characterized His lovely service. And, as He nears the end, we have the same blessed excellency displayed, as we behold Him on His face in the Garden, covered with bloody sweat, as He confronts the thrice awful Cup, yet does He say, "Not my will, but thine be done."

"The Son can do nothing of himself, but what he seeth the Father do." The word for "seeth" (blepo) signifies to contemplate, to perceive, to know. It is used in Rom. 7:23; 11:8; I Cor. 13:12; Heb. 10:25, etc. When, then, the Son exerts His Divine power, it is always in the conscious knowledge that it is the will of the Father it *should be* so exerted.

"The Son can do nothing of himself, but what he seeth the Father do: for what things soever he doeth, these also doeth the Son likewise." Here is an assertion which none but a Divine person (in the most absolute sense of the term) could truthfully make. Because the Son can do nothing but what the Father does, so, on the other hand, "What things soever the Father doeth, these also doeth the Son likewise." Note well this word "likewise." Not only does He do *what* the Father does, but He does it *as* He does it, that is, in a manner comporting with the absolute perfections of their common Divine nature. But what is ever more striking is the all-inclusive "whatsoever." Not only does He perform His works with the same Divine power and excellency as the Father does His, but the Son also does *all* "whatsoever he (the Father) doeth." This is proof positive that

He is speaking here not in His mediatorial capacity, as the servant, but in His essential character as one absolutely equal with God.

We cannot refrain from quoting here part of the most excellent comments of the late Dr. John Brown on this verse: —"All is *of* the Father—all is *by* the Son. Did the Father create the universe? So did the Son. Does the Father uphold the universe? So does the Son. Does the Father govern the universe? So does the Son. Is the Father the Saviour of the world? So is the Son. Surely the Jews did not err when they concluded that our Lord made Himself 'equal with God.' Surely He who is so intimately connected with God that He does what God does, does all God does, does all in the same manner in which God does it; surely such a person cannot but be equal with God." To this we would add but one word: Scripture also reveals that in the future, too, the will of the Father and of the Son will act in perfect unison, for, in the last chapter of the Bible we read that the throne of Deity on the new earth will be "the throne of God *and of the lamb*" (Rev. 22:1). But before passing on to the next verse let us pause for a brief moment to make application to ourselves. "The Son can do nothing of himself." How this rebukes the selfwill in all of us! Who is there among the saints who can truthfully say, I can do nothing at my own instance; my life is entirely at God's disposal?

"For the Father loveth the Son, and showeth him all things that himself doeth: and he will show him greater works than these, that ye may marvel" (5:20). Here again the carnal mind is puzzled. If Christ be the Son of God why does He need to be "*shown*." When we "show" a child something it is because it is ignorant. When we "show" the traveller the right road, it is because he does not know it. Refuge is sought again in the mediatorship of Christ. But this destroys the beauty of the verse and mars the unity of the passage. What seems to point to an imperfection or limitation in Christ's knowledge only brings out once more His matchless excellency.

"For the Father loveth the Son and showeth him all things that himself doeth." The opening word "For" intimates there is a close connection between this and the verse immediately preceding, as well as with the whole context. It intimates that oui Lord is still submitting the proof that He *was* "equal with God." The argument of this verse in a word is this: The Father has no secrets from the Son. Because He is the Son of God, the Father loveth Him; that is to say, because they are in common possession of the same infinite perfections, there is an ineffable affection of the Father to the Son, and this love is *manifested* by the Father "showing the Son all things." There is no restraint and no constraint between them: there is the most perfect intimacy because of their co-equality. Let me try to reduce this profound truth to a simple level. If an entire stranger were to visit your home, there are many things you would not think of "showing" him – the family portrait-album for example. But with an intimate friend or a loved relative there would be no such reluctance. The illustration falls far short we know, but perhaps it may help some to grasp better the line of thought we are seeking to present.

But not only do the words "the Father loveth the Son" make manifest the perfect intimacy there is between them, but the additional words "showeth him *all things* that himself doeth" evidences another of the Divine glories of Christ, namely, the absolute *equality of intelligence* that there is between the Father and the Son. Let us again bring the thought down to a human level. What would be the use of discussing with an illiterate person the mathematics of the fourth dimension? What's the value of taking a child in the first grade and "showing" *him* the solution of a problem in algebra? Who, then, is capable of understanding all the ways and workings of God? No mere creature. Fallen man is incapable of knowing God. The believer learns but gradually and slowly, and only then as he is taught by the Holy Spirit. Even the unfallen angels know God's mind but in part – there are things they desire "to look into" (I Pet. 1:12). To whom then could God show the full counsel of His mind? And again we answer, To no mere creature, for the creature however high in rank has no capacity to grasp it. The finite cannot comprehend the infinite. Is it not self-evident, then, that if the Father showeth the Son "*all things* that himself doeth"

He *must be* of the *same* mind as the Father? that they are one, absolutely equal in intelligence! Christ *has* the capacity to apprehend and comprehend "all things that the Father doeth," therefore, He must be "equal with God," for none but God could measure the *Father's* mind perfectly.

"The idea seems to be this, that the love of the Father, and of the Son, their perfect complacency in each other, is manifest in the perfect knowledge which the Son has of the period *at* which, the purpose *for* which, and the manner *in* which, the Divine power equally possessed by them is to be put forth. It is in consequence of this knowledge, as if our Lord had said – 'That in this case (the healing of the impotent man) I have exercised Divine power while My Father was exercising it'

"And He adds, 'Still further – still more extraordinary manifestations of this community of knowledge, will, and operation of the Father, and of the Son, will be made.' 'He will show him greater works than these, that ye may marvel,' or 'that ye shall marvel'; that is, we apprehend, 'the Son, in consequence of His perfect knowledge of the mind, and will, and operations of His Divine Father, will yet make still more remarkable displays of that Divine power which is equally His Father's and His *own*' – such displays as will fill with amazement all who witness them. What these displays were to be, appears from what follows: He had healed the impotent man, but He was soon to raise to life some who had been dead; nay, at a future period He was to raise to life all the dead and act as the Governor and Judge of all mankind" (Dr. John Brown).

"For as the Father raiseth up the dead, and quickeneth them; even so the Son quickeneth whom he will" (5:21). This verse presents the fourth proof of Christ's Deity. Here He affirms His absolute equality with the Father *in sovereign rights*. This affords further evidence that the Lord Jesus was not here speaking as the dependent Servant, but as the Son of God. He lays claim to Divine sovereignty. The healing of the impotent man was an object-lesson: it not only demonstrated His power, but it illustrated His absolute sovereignty. He had not healed the entire company of impotent folk who lay around the pool; instead, He had singled out just one, and had made him whole. So He works and so He acts in the spiritual realm. He does not quicken (spiritually) all men, but those "whom He will." He does not quicken the worthy, for there are none. He does not quicken those who seek quickening, for being dead in sin, none begin to seek until they are quickened. The Son quickeneth whom He will: He says so, that ends the matter. It is not to be reasoned about, but believed. To quicken is to impart life, and to impart life is a Divine prerogative. How this confirms our interpretation of the previous verses! It is the *Divine rights* of Christ which are here affirmed.

"For as the Father raiseth up the dead, and quickeneth them; even so the Son quickeneth whom he will." The verse opens with the word "for," showing it is advancing a reason or furnishing a proof in connection with what had been said previously. In our judgment it looks back first to v. 19 and gives an illustration of "what things soever he (the Father) doeth, these also doeth the Son likewise"—the Father quickens, so does the Son. But there is also a direct connection with the verse immediately preceding. There he had referred to "greater works" than healing the impotent man. Here, then, is a specimen—quickening the dead: making alive spiritually those who are dead in sins. This is a further demonstration of His absolute equality with the Father.

"For the Father judgeth no man, but hath committed all judgment unto the Son: That all men should honour the Son, even as they honour the Father. He that honoureth not the Son honoureth not the Father which hath sent him" (5:22, 23). This declaration that the Father judgeth no man—better "no one"—is especially noteworthy. The Father is the One whom we might most naturally expect to be the Judge. He is the first who was wronged. It is His rights (though not His exclusively) which have been denied. His governmental claims have been set at naught. He was the One who sent here the Lord Jesus who has been despised and rejected. But instead of the Father being the Judge, He hath "committed all judgment unto the Son," and the reason for this is "that all should honour the Son, even as they honour the Father." There is then, or more correctly, there will be, absolute equality between the Father and the Son *in Divine honors.*

"Verily, verily, I say unto you, He that heareth my word, and believeth on him that sent me, hath everlasting life, and shall not come into condemnation; but is passed from death unto life" (5:24). Once more we find the Lord, as in v. 17, linking Himself in closest union with the Father: "heareth *my* Word, and believeth *him that sent* me." But as we have already dwelt at such length on the dominant thought running all through our passage, we turn now to consider other subordinate though most blessed truths. This verse has been a great favorite with the Lord's people. It has been used of God to bring peace and assurance to many a troubled soul. It speaks of eternal life as a present possession—"*hath* everlasting life," not shall have when we die, or when the resurrection morning comes. Two things are here mentioned which are evidences and results of having everlasting life, though they are usually regarded as two conditions. The hearing ear and the believing heart are the consequences of having eternal life and not the qualifications for obtaining it. Then it is added, "and shall not come into condemnation": this guarantees the future—"There is therefore now no condemnation to them which are in Christ Jesus" (Rom. 8:1). No condemnation for the believer because it fell upon his Substitute. Another reason why the believer shall not come into condemnation is because he has "passed from death," which is the realm of condemnation, "into life."

"Verily, verily, I say unto you, The hour is coming, and now is, when the dead shall hear the voice of the Son of God: and they that hear shall live" (5:25). This continues the same thought as in the previous verse, though adding further details. "The dead shall hear:" what a paradox to the carnal mind! Yet all becomes luminous when we remember that it is the voice of the Son of God they hear. *His* voice alone can penetrate into the place of death, and because His voice is a life-giving voice, the dead hear it and live. The capacity to hear accompanies the power of the Voice that speaks, and it is just because that Voice is a life-giving one that the *dead* hear it at all, and hearing, live. Here then is the sixth proof presented for the Deity of Christ:

the Son claims absolute equality with the Father *in the power to give life.*

"For as the Father has life in himself; so hath he given to the Son to have life in himself" (5:26). This confirms what we have just said above, while bringing in one further amplification. The Father hath "life in himself." "It belongs to His nature; He has received it from no one; it is an essential attribute of His necessarily existing nature: He so has life that He can impart, withdraw, and restore it to whomsoever He pleases. He is the fountain of all life. All in heaven and in earth who have life, have received it from Him. They have not life in themselves" (Dr. John Brown). Now in like manner the life of Christ is not a derived life. "In him *was* life" (John 1:4). He is able to communicate life to others because the Father hath "given to the Son to have life in himself." The word "given" must be understood figuratively and not literally, in the sense of appointed, not imparted: see its usage in Isaiah 42:6; 49:8; 55:4. So also the word "given him to *have,*" signifies to hold or administer. Thus, inasmuch as all creatures live and move and have their being in God, but in contrast from them Christ has "life *in himself,*" He cannot be a mere creature but must be "equal with God."

"And hath given him authority to execute judgment also, because he is the Son of man. Marvel not at this: for the hour is coming, in the which all that are in the graves shall hear his voice, And shall come forth; they that have done good, unto the resurrection of life; and they that have done evil, unto the resurrection of damnation" (5:27-29). This brings us to the seventh proof for the absolute Deity of Christ: He is co-equal with the Father *in judicial authority and power.*

"And hath given him authority to execute judgment also, because he is the Son of man." The "also" seems to point back to v. 22, where we are told, "The Father judgeth no man, but hath committed all judgment unto the Son." Judgment has been committed to the Son in order that all should honor Him even as they honor the Father. But here in v. 27 Christ gives an additional reason: the Father has also appointed the Lord Jesus to execute judgment "because he is the Son of man." It was because the Son of God had become clothed with flesh and walked this earth as Man, that He was despised and rejected and His Divine glories disowned. This supplies a further reason why it is meet that the Son of man should be Judge in the last great day. The despised One shall be in the place of supreme honor and authority. All will be compelled to bow the knee before Him; and thus will He be glorified before them and His outraged rights vindicated.

Next follows a reference to the resurrection of all that are in the graves. These are divided into two classes. First, they that have done good unto the resurrection of life. This refers to the resurrection of the saints. They that have "done good" is a characteristic description of them. It has reference to their walk which manifests the new nature within them. In the previous verses (24, 25) we have had life, eternal life, imparted to the spiritually dead by the sovereign power of the Son of God. This is His own life which is communicated to them. The Christ-life within is seen by Christ-like acts without. This is forcibly and beautifully brought out in the language which the Lord Jesus here uses when referring to His people. Just as in Acts 10:38 the apostle sums up the earthly life of Christ by saying He "went about *doing good,*" so here the Lord Jesus speaks of His own as "they that have *done good,*" that is, have manifested His own life. These will come forth at the time of His appearing (I Cor. 15:23; I Thess. 4:16); come forth "unto a resurrection of life" for then they shall enter fully and perfectly into the unhindered activities and joys of that life which is life indeed.

"And they that have done evil" describes the great company of the unsaved. These, too, shall "come forth." All the ungodly dead will hear His voice, and obey it. They refused to hearken to Him while He spoke words of grace and truth, but then they shall be compelled to hear Him as He utters the dread summons for them to appear before the great white throne. They would not believe on Him *as the Saviour of sinners,* but they will have to own Him as "Lord of the dead" (Rom. 14:9). Unspeakably solemn is this. Not a vestige of hope is held out for them. It is not a resurrection of probation as some modern perverters of God's truth are now teaching, but it is the resurrection "unto damnation." Nothing awaits them but impartial judgment, the formal and public pronouncement of their sentence of doom, and after that nothing but an eternity of torment spent in the lake which burneth with fire and brimstone. As they had sinned in physical bodies so shall they suffer in physical bodies. Instead of having glorified bodies, they shall be raised in bodies marred by sin and made hideous by evil—"shame and everlasting contempt" (Dan. 12:2) describes them. Though capable of enduring "tribulation and anguish" (Rom. 2:9) they shall not be annihilated by the flames (any more than were the physical bodies of the three Hebrews in Babylon's fiery furnace) but continue forever—"salted with fire" (Mark 9:49): the "salt" speaks of a *preservative* element which prevents decay.

"I can of mine own self do nothing: as I hear, I judge: and my judgment is just; because I seek not mine own will, but the will of the Father which hath sent me" (5:30). The first part of the verse need not detain us, for it has already received consideration under our exposition of v. 19. The second half of the verse adds a further word concerning the judgment. "My judgment is just:" this is profoundly solemn. Christ will deal not in grace, but in inflexible righteousness. He will administer *justice,* not mercy. This, once more, excludes every ray of hope for all who are raised "unto damnation."

Two additional thoughts in connection with the Deity of Christ come out in these last verses. First, the fact that "all that are in the graves shall hear" the voice of Christ and shall "come forth," proves that He is far more than the most exalted creature. Who but *God* is able to regather all the scattered elements which have gone to corruption! Second, who but *God* is capable of acting as Judge in the Great Assize! None but He can read the heart, and none but He possesses the necessary wisdom for such a stupendous task as determining the sentence due to each one of that vast assemblage which will stand before the great white throne. Thus we see that from start to finish this wonderful passage sets forth the Godhood of the Saviour. Let us then honor Him even as we honor the Father, and prostrate ourselves before Him in adoring worship.

Let the interested reader study carefully the following questions preparatory to our next lesson on John 5:31-47: —

1. How many witnesses are there here to the Deity of Christ?
2. What is the meaning of v. 31?
3. What is the significance of the first half of v. 34, after Christ had already referred to "John"?
4. What warning is there in the second half of v. 35?
5. What is the force of "ye think" in v. 39?
6. Who is referred to in the second half of v. 43?
7. What is the moral connection between receiving honor of men and not believing in Christ? v. 44.

CHAPTER NINETEEN

THE DEITY OF CHRIST: THREEFOLD WITNESS TO IT

John 5:31-47

We begin with our usual Analysis of the passage which is to be before us: —

1. Christ's Witness not independent of the Father: vv. 31, 32.
2. The Witness of John: vv. 33, 34.
3. Christ's Witness to John: v. 35.
4. The Witness of Christ's Works: v. 36.
5. The Witness of the Father: vv. 37, 38.
6. The Witness of the Scriptures: v. 39.
7. Christ's Witness against the Jews: vv. 40-47.

As we pass from chapter to chapter it is ever needful to keep in mind the character and scope of this fourth Gospel. Its chief design is to present the Divine glories of Christ. It was written, no doubt, in its first and local application to refute the heresies concerning the person of the Lord Jesus which flourished toward the end of the first century. Less than fifty years after the Lord departed from these scenes and returned to His Father in heaven, the horrible system of Gnosticism, which denied the essential Deity of the Saviour, was spread widely throughout those lands where the Gospel had been preached. Whilst it was generally allowed that Christ was a unique personage, yet, that He was "equal with God" was denied by many. Nor is that very surprising when we stop to think how much there was which would prove a stumbling block to the natural man.

Outwardly, to human eyes, Christ appeared to be an ordinary man. Born into a peasant family; cradled amid the most humble surroundings; carried away into Egypt to escape the cruel edict of Herod, and returning later, only to grow to manhood's estate in obscurity; working for years, most probably, at the carpenter's bench—what was there to denote that He was the Lord of Glory? Then, as He began His public ministry, appearing not as the great of this world are accustomed to appear, with much pomp and ostentation; but, instead, as the meek and lowly One. Attended not by an imposing retinue of angels, but by a few poor and unlettered fishermen. His claims rejected by the religious leaders of that day; the tide of popular opinion turning against Him; the very ones who first hailed Him with their glad Hosannas, ending by crying, "Away with him: crucify him." Finally, nailed in shame to the cruel tree; silent to the challenge to descend from it; and there breathing out His spirit—that, *that* was the last the world saw of Him.

And now by the year A. D. 90 almost all of His original disciples would be dead. Of the twelve apostles who had accompanied Him during His public ministry, only John remained. On every side were teachers denying the Deity of Christ. There was thus a real need for an inspired, authoritative, systematic presentation of the manifold glories of His divine person. The Holy Spirit therefore moved John—the one who of all the early disciples knew Christ best, the one whose spiritual discernment was the keenest, the one who had enjoyed the inestimable privilege of leaning on the Master's bosom—to write this fourth Gospel. In it abundant evidence is furnished to satisfy the most credulous of the Deity of the Lord Jesus. It is to the written Word God now refers all who desire to know the truth concerning His beloved Son, and in it are presented the "many infallible proofs" for the Godhood of our blessed Redeemer. Chiefest of these are to be found in John's Gospel.

In the chapter we are now studying we find record of a remarkable miracle performed by the Lord Jesus which signally displayed His Divine power. He had singled out a most hopeless case and by a word had made whole, instantly, one that had suffered with an infirmity for thirty and eight years. Because this miracle had been performed on the Sabbath day, the Jews persecuted the Lord Jesus. In gracious condescension the Lord replied to their criticism by giving them a sevenfold declaration of His equality with the Father. This we examined at some length in maintaining it, so immeasurable is the blessing when received, so tremendous is the stake involved in its loss, God has vouchsafed us the amplest, clearest, fullest evidence.

"If I bear witness of myself, my witness is not true" (5:31). Every commentator we have consulted expounds this verse as follows: The witness which I have just borne to Myself would not be valid unless it is supported by that of others. The law of God requires two or three witnesses for the truth to be established. Therefore if I bear witness of Myself, says Christ, and there is none to confirm it, it is "not true," i.e., it is not convincing to others. But we most humbly dissent from any such interpretation. The word of a mere man *does* need confirmation: but not so that of God the Son. To affirm or suggest that *His* witness must be ratified by the testimony of others so as to establish its validity, is deeply dishonoring to Him. And we are both amazed and saddened that such a view should be put forth by many excellent men.

"If I bear witness of myself, my witness is not true." The key to this verse lies in what has gone before. Divorce it from its context, and we must expect to find it difficult; but examine it in our last chapter; now, in the passage before us, we find that He closed by bringing in the evidence of various unimpeachable witnesses who testified to the veracity of His claims. In view, then, of what is to be found here, there can be no excuse whatever for ignorance, still less for unbelief, upon this all-important subject. So bright was Christ's glory, so concerned was the Father in the light of its setting, and all becomes clear. This verse simply reiterates in another form what we find the Saviour saying at the beginning of the previous verse. "I can of mine own self do nothing" means, I cannot act independently of the Father: I am so absolutely one with Him that His will is My will; mine, His. So, now, He declares, "If I bear witness of myself, my witness is not true." He speaks hypothetically – "if." "I bear witness of myself" means, If I bear witness *independently* of the Father. In such a case, "my witness is not true." And why? Because such would be insubordination. The Son can no more bear witness of Himself independently of the Father, than He can of Himself work independently of the Father.

"There is another that beareth witness of me; and I know that the witness which he witnesseth of me is true" (5:32). This explains the previous verse and confirms our interpretation of it. The "other" who is here referred to as "bearing witness" of Him, is not John the Baptist, as some have strangely supposed, but the Father Himself. Reference, *not appeal*, is made to John in vv. 33, 34. Observe now that our Lord did not here say, "There is *One* that beareth witness of me" and *His* witness is true, but "there is *another* that beareth witness of me." He would no more dissever the Father and His witness from Himself, than He would bear witness to Himself independently of the Father. This is strikingly confirmed by what we read in John 8: "The Pharisees therefore said unto him, Thou bearest record of thyself; thy record is not true. Jesus answered and said unto them, Though I bear record of myself, yet my record is true . . . Ye judge after the flesh; I judge no man. And yet if I judge, my judgment is true: *for I am not alone, but I and the Father* that sent me" (vv. 13-16).

"Ye sent unto John, and he bare witness unto the truth" (5:33). Here our Lord reminds "the Jews" (v. 16) how, when they had sent an embassy unto His forerunner (see 1:19), that he "bear witness unto the truth." Notice the abstract form in which this is put. Christ did not say, "He bear witness unto *me*," but "unto the truth." This witness is recorded in John 1:20-27. First, John confessed that he was not the Christ, but simply "the voice of one crying in the wilderness, Make straight the way of the Lord." Then, he testified to the presence of One in their midst whom they knew not, One of whom he said, "He it is, who coming after me, is preferred before me, whose shoes latchet I am not worthy to unloose." Such was the Baptist's witness to the delegates of these same Jews.

"But I receive not testimony from man: but these things I say, that ye might be saved" (5:34). The Son of God continues to occupy the same high ground from which He had spoken throughout this interview. "I receive not testimony from man" shows that He had *not appealed* to the witness of John in confirmation of His own declarations. His purpose was quite otherwise: "These things I say, that ye might be saved." The witness which John had borne to "the truth" was fitted to have a salutary effect on those who heard him. John's testimony was a merciful concession which God had made to the need of Israel. Christ Himself did not stand in need of it; but *they* did. God sent His messenger before His Son to prepare the way for Him. His ministry was designed to arouse men's attention and to produce in them a sense of their deep need of the One who was about to be manifested.

"But I receive not testimony from man." This word "receive" is explained to us in v. 44 where it is interchanged with "seek." It means to lay hold of, or grasp at. Christ would not bemean Himself by subpoening human witnesses. His claim to be equal with God rested on surer ground than the testimony of a man. But He had *reminded* these Jews of what John had said to their representatives on an earlier occasion, and this that they "might be saved," for salvation comes by believing God's "witness unto the truth."

"He was a burning and a shining light: and ye were willing for a season to rejoice in his light" (5:35). This was most gracious of Christ. John had given faithful witness to the One who was to come after him; and now the Son of God bears witness to *him*. A beautiful illustration is this of the promise that if we confess Christ before men, so He will yet confess us before God. "A burning and shining light" – more correctly, "lamp," see R.V. – the Lord calls him. Burning inwardly, shining outwardly. John's light had not been hid under a bushel, but it had shone "before men." Ah! dear reader, will the Saviour be able to say of *you,* in a coming day, "He was a burning and shining lamp"? Is the light that is within thee "burning" or is it just *flickering?* Is your lamp "trimmed," and so "shining," or is it shedding but a *feeble* and *sickly* glow? Great is the need for burning and shining "lamps" in the world today. The shadows are fast lengthening, the darkness increases, and the "midnight" hour draws on apace. "And that, knowing the time, that now it is high time to awake out of sleep: for now is our salvation nearer than when we believed. The night is far spent, the day is at hand: let us therefore cast off the works of darkness, and let us put on the armour of light" (Rom. 13:11, 12).

"And ye were willing for a season to rejoice in his light" (5:35). This provides us with an illustration of the stony-ground hearers of the parable of the Sower. Concerning this class Christ says, "But he that received the seed into stony places, the same is he that heareth the word, and anon *with joy receiveth it;* Yet hath he not root in himself, but dureth for a while" (Matt. 13: 20, 21). Such were these Jews: "for a season" they rejoiced in John's light. But the difference between real believers and mere professors is not in how they begin but how they end. "He that endureth to the end shall be saved": enduring to the end is not a condition of salvation, but an evidence of it. So, again, when Christ says, "If ye continue in my word, then are ye my disciples indeed:" continuing in Christ's word is a proof that we are His disciples. We take it that which caused these Jews to "rejoice" for a season in John's light, was the testimony which he bore to the Messiah, then about to appear. This was good news indeed, for to them this meant deliverance from the Roman yoke and the destruction of all their enemies. But when the Messiah was actually manifested He instead announced that He had come to save the lost, and when He demanded repentance and faith, their joy soon faded away.

"But I have greater witness than that of John: for the works which the Father hath given me to finish, the same works that I do, bear witness of me, that the Father hath sent me" (5:36). Here is the first witness to which Christ appeals in proof of His Deity. His "works" bore unmistakable witness to Him. He gave hearing to the deaf, speech to the dumb, sight to the blind, cleansing to the leper, deliverance to the captives of the Devil, life to the dead. He walked the waves, stilled the wind, calmed the sea, He turned water into wine, cleansed the Temple single-handed, and fed a great multitude with a few loaves and fishes. And these miracles were performed by His own inherent power. To these works He now directs attention as furnishing proof of His Deity. Quite frequently did He appeal to His "works" as affording Divine testimony: see John 10:25, 38; 14:11; 15:24.

The late Bishop Ryle called attention to five things in connection with our Lord's miracles. "First, their *number*: they were not a few only, but very many. Second, their *greatness*: they were not little, but mighty interferences with the ordinary course of nature. Third, their *publicity*: they were not done in a corner, but generally in open day, and before many witnesses, and often before enemies. Fourth, their *character*: they were almost always works of love, mercy and compassion, helpful and beneficient to man, and not merely barren exhibitions of power. Fifth, their *direct appeal to man's senses*: they were visible, and would bear any examination. The difference between them and the boasted miracles of Rome, on all these points, is striking and conclusive." To these we might add two other features: Sixth, their *artlessness*. They were not staged mechanically: they happened in the natural course of our Lord's ministry. There was nothing pre-arranged about them. Seventh, their *efficacy*. There was as much difference between the miracles of healing performed by Christ and those of His miserable imitators which are being so widely heralded in our day, as there is between *His teaching* and that given out by these pretenders who claim to heal in His name. Christ's cures were instantaneous, not gradual; complete and perfect, not faulty and disappointing.

"The same works that I do, bear witness of me." Ere passing on to the next verse, we pause to apply these words to ourselves. *Our* works, too, bear witness of us. If ours are "dead works," wood, hay, and stubble which shall be burned up in the coming Day, that proves we are carnal, walking after the flesh; and such a witness will dishonor and grieve Him whose name we bear. But if we abound in "good works," this will show that we are walking after the spirit, and men (our fellow-believers) seeing our good works will glorify our Father which is in heaven. What, then, my reader, is the "witness" which *your* "works" are bearing? What the writer's? Let us "be careful to *maintain* good works? (Titus 3:8).

"And the Father himself, which hath sent me, hath borne witness of me. Ye have neither heard his voice at any time, nor seen his shape" (5:37). The miracles performed by our Lord were not the only nor the most direct evidence which proved His Deity. The Father Himself had borne witness. The majority of the commentators refer this to the baptism of Christ, when the Father's voice declared, "This is my beloved Son, in whom I am well pleased." But we scarcely think this is correct. Immediately following, our Lord went on to say, "Ye have neither heard his voice at any time, nor seen his shape." What, then, would be the force of Christ here appealing to the Father's witness at the Jordan if these detractors of His had not heard that Voice? Personally, we think that Christ refers, rather, to the witness which the Father had borne to His Son through the prophets during Old Testament times. This seems to give more meaning to what follows – the Old Testament economy was characterized by an *invisible* God, neither His voice being heard, nor His shape seen.

"And ye have not his word abiding in you: for whom he hath sent, him ye believe not" (5:38). Here our Lord begins to make solemn application of what He had said to the consciences and hearts of these Jews. Note the awful charges which He brings against them: "ye *have not* his word abiding in you" (v. 38); "Ye *will not* come to me" (v. 40); "*ye have not* the love of God in you" (v. 42); "*ye receive me not*" (v. 43); "*ye seek not* the honor that cometh from God only" (v. 44); "*ye believe not*" (v. 47). But notice carefully the basic charge: "ye have not his word abiding in you." *This* explained all the others. This was the cause of which the others were but the inevitable effects. If God's Word has no place in man's hearts they will not come to Christ, they will not receive Him, they will not love God, and they will not seek the honor that cometh from God only. It is only as the Word is hidden in our hearts that we are preserved from sinning against God.

"Search the scriptures; for in them ye think ye have eternal life: and they are they which testify of me" (5:39). This is the last witness which our Lord cites, and, for us, it is the most important. John has long since passed away; the "words" of Christ are no longer before men's eyes; the voice of the Father is no more heard; but the testimony of the Scriptures abides. The Scriptures testified of Christ, and affirmed His Deity. Their witness was the climax. The Holy Writings, given by inspiration of God, were the final court of appeal. What importance and authority does He attach to them! Beyond them there was no appeal: above them no higher authority: after them no further witness. It is blessed to note the *order* in which Christ placed the three witnesses to which He appealed in proof of His equality with God. First, there was the witness of His own Divine works. Second, there was the witness which the Father had borne to Him through the prophets. Third, there was the testimony of the Holy Scriptures, written by men moved by the Holy Spirit. Thus in these three witnesses there is a remarkable reference made to each of the three Persons in the Holy Trinity.

"Search the Scriptures" was both an appeal and a command. It is to be read, as in our A.V., in the imperative mood. The proof for this is as follows: First, the *usage* of the word. The Bible is its own interpreter. If scripture be compared with scripture its meaning will be plain. In John 7:52 we find the only other occurrence of the Greek word (ereunao) in John's Gospel, here translated "search"; "They answered and said unto him, Art thou also of Galilee? *Search,* and look: for out of Galilee ariseth no prophet." When the Pharisees said to Nicodemus "Search and look," they were *bidding* him search the Scriptures. Thus, in both instances, the word has the imperative and not the indicative force. Again; to give the verb here the indicative force in John 5:39 is to make the first half of the verse pointless; but to render it in the imperative gives it a meaning in full accord with what precedes and what follows. "For in them ye think ye have eternal life." The pronoun "ye" is emphatic. The word "think" does not imply it was a doubtful point, or merely a matter of human opinion. It is rather as though Christ said unto them, 'This is one of the articles of *your* faith: ye think (are persuaded), and rightly so; then act on it. Search the Scriptures (in which you are assured there is eternal life) and you will find that they, too, testify of Me.' The word "think" does not imply a doubt, but affirms an assurance. (Cf. Matt. 22:42, etc.).

"Search the Scriptures." Here is a command from the Lord. The authority of His Godhood is behind it. "Search," He says; not merely "read." The Greek word is one that was used in connection with hunting. It referred to the hunter stalking game. When he discovered the tracks of an animal, he concentrated all his attention on the ground before him, diligently searching for other marks which would lead him to his quarry. In a similar way, *we* are to study God's Word, minutely examining each expression, tracing every occurrence of it, and ascertaining its meaning from its usage. The grand motive for such earnest study is, that the Scriptures "testify" *of Christ.* May writer and reader give daily heed to this Divine admonition, to "*Search*" the Scriptures.

"And ye will not come to me, that ye might have life" (5:40). It was not lack of evidence but perversity of will which kept these Jews from coming to Christ. And it is so still. The Lord Jesus stands ready to receive all who come to Him; but by nature men are unwilling, unwilling to come to Him that they "might have life." But why is this? It is because they fail to realize their awful peril: did they but know that they are standing on the brink of the Pit, they would flee from the wrath to come. Why is it? It is because they have no sense of their deep and desperate need: did they but apprehend their awful condition —their wickedness, their blindness, their hardheartedness, their depravity—they would hasten to the great Physician to be healed by Him. Why is it? It is because the carnal mind is enmity *against* God, and Christ is God.

"I receive not honor from men" (5:41). Here again the Lord maintains His dignity and insists upon His Divine self-sufficiency. I "receive not" signifies, as in vv. 34 and 44, "I seek not" honor from men. "When I state My claims, and complain that you disregard them, it is not because I wish to ingratiate Myself with you; not because I covet your approbation or that of any man, or set of men. He did not need their sanction: He could receive no honor from their applause. His object was to secure the approbation of His Divine Father, by faithfully executing the commission with which He was entrusted; and so far as they were concerned, His desire was not that He should be applauded by them, but that they should be saved by Him. If He regretted, and He did most deeply regret their obstinate unbelief and impenitence, it was for their own sakes, and not for His own. Such was the unearthly, unambitious spirit of our Lord, and such should be the spirit of all His ministers" (Dr. John Brown).

"But I know you, that ye have not the love of God in you" (5:42). How this makes manifest the *omniscience* of Christ! He who searcheth the heart knew the state of these Jews. They posed as worshippers of the true and living God. They appeared to be very jealous of His honor. They claimed to be most punctilious in the observance of His Sabbath. But Christ was not deceived. He knew they had not the love of God in them, and this was why they refused to come to Him for life. It is so now. The reason why men despise the claims of Christ is not because of any want of evidence on the side of those claims, but because of a sinful indisposition on their part to attend to those claims. They have not the love of God in them; if they had, they would receive and worship His Son.

"I am come in my Father's name, and ye receive me not: if another shall come in his own name, him ye will receive" (5:43). Unspeakably solemn is this. Israel's rejection of Christ has only prepared the way for them to accept the Antichrist, for it is to him our Lord referred in the second part of this verse. Just as Eve's rejection of the truth of God laid her open to accept the Devil's lie, so Israel's rejection of the true Messiah has thoroughly prepared them, morally, to receive the false Messiah; who will come in his own name, doing his own pleasure, and seeking glory from men. Thus will he thoroughly expose the corrupt heart of the natural man. How this exhibits what is in the fallen creature and demonstrates his depravity!

"How can ye believe, which receive honour one of another, and seek not the honour that cometh from God only" (5:44). "Honour" signifies approbation or praise. While these Jews were making it their chief aim to win the good opinion of each other, and remained more or less indifferent to the approval and approbation of God, they would not come to Christ for life. To come to Christ they must humble themselves in the dust, by taking the place of lost sinners before Him. And to receive Him as their Lord and Saviour, to live henceforth for the glory of that One who was despised and rejected of men, would at once separate them from the world, and would bring down upon them contempt and persecution. But there is no middle ground: "the friendship of the world is enmity with God." If we are determined to be honored and smiled upon by our fellowmen, we shall remain alienated from God.

"Men are deceived today by the thought of building up man, the improvement of the race, the forming of character, holding on to themselves as though all that man needed was change of direction. Man is himself evil, a sinner by nature, utterly alienated from the life of God. He needs life, a new one. For what else did Christ come but that He might give it? He is not to be received with honors such as men pay to high officials, for they are like the men who pay the honor, but He is from above and above all, and has eternal life to give. He needs emptiness for His fulness, sinfulness for His holiness, sinners for His salvation, death for His life; and he who can make out his case of being lost and helpless gets all. It is not that men should do their best by leaving off vices and reforming, and pay devout respect to the name of Jesus and to religious rites, adding this to their goodness for God's acceptance. It is that they should be as the poor man in the beginning of this chapter, indebted to Christ for everything: they must be receivers instead of givers. Receiving honor from one another vitiates the whole idea in regard to God and His Christ. We honor Him only when we are saved by Him; then, as saved, worshipping and rejoicing in Christ Jesus the Lord" (Malachi Taylor).

"Do not think that I will accuse you to the Father: there is one that accuseth you, even Moses, in whom ye trust. For had ye believed Moses, ye would have believed me: for he wrote of me" (5:45, 46). Our Lord concludes by intimating to these Jews that they would yet have to give an account of their rejection of Him before the tribunal of God, and there they would see as their accuser the great legislator of whom they boasted, but whose testimony they rejected. Here, then, was the final reason why they would not come to Him for life—they believed not the written Word of God.

"There is one that accuseth you, even Moses, in whom ye trust. For had ye believed Moses, ye would have believed me: for he wrote of me." How solemn and searching is this! If there is one thing those Jews *thought* they believed, it was Moses and his writings. They contended earnestly for the law: they venerated the name of Moses above almost all of their national heroes. They would have been ready to die for what Moses taught. And yet here is the Son of God solemnly declaring that these Jews *did not believe* Moses, and furnishing proof by showing that if they had really believed Moses' writings they had believed in Christ, of whom Moses wrote. How terribly deceptive is the human heart! "There is a way *that seemeth right unto a man,* but the end thereof are the ways of death" (Prov. 14:12). O, dear reader, make certain that *you* believe, *really,* savingly believe on the Son of God.

"But if ye believe not his writings, how shall ye believe my words?" (5:47). How this exposes the "Higher Critics!" If they believe not the writings of Moses, no matter what their ecclesiastical connections or religious professions, it is sure proof that they are unsaved men—men who have not believed in Christ. The Old Testament Scriptures are of equal authority with the teaching of Christ: they are equally the Word of God.

Let the following questions be studied for the next lesson:—

1. What do the opening words of v. 1 denote?
2. In what respects is v. 2 repeated today?
3. What is the significance of v. 4 coming just before the feeding of the multitude?
4. How may we apply to ourselves Christ's questions in v. 5?
5. Wherein do Philip and Andrew represent us? vv. 7-9.
6. What are the spiritual lessons suggested by v. 11?

CHAPTER TWENTY

Christ Feeding the Multitude

John 6:1-13

Of all the miracles performed by the Lord Jesus the feeding of the five thousand is the only one recorded by each of the four Evangelists. This at once intimates that there must be something about it of unusual importance, and therefore it calls for our most diligent study. The Holy Spirit has – if we may reverently employ such language – described this miracle in the most matter-of-fact terms. No effort is made to emphasize the marvel of it. There is an entire absence of such language as an uninspired pen would naturally have employed to heighten the effect on the reader. And yet, notwithstanding the simplicity and exceeding brevity of the narrative, it is at once evident that this incident of the feeding of the hungry multitude was a signal example of Christ's almighty power. As Bishop Ryle has noted, of all the wonderful works which our Saviour did none was quite so public as this, and none other was performed before so many witnesses. Our Lord is here seen supplying the bodily needs of a great crowd by means of five loaves and two small fishes. Food was called into existence which did not exist before. To borrow another thought from Bishop Ryle: In healing the sick and in raising the dead, something was amended or restored which *already* existed; but here was an absolute creation. Only one other miracle in any wise resembles it – His first, when He made wine out of the water. These two miracles belong to a class by themselves, and it is surely significant, yea most suggestive, that the one reminds us of His precious blood, while the other points to His holy body, broken for us. And here is, we believe, the chief reason why this miracle is mentioned by all of the four Evangelists: it shadowed forth *the gift of Christ Himself.* His other miracles exhibited His power and illustrated His work, but this one in a peculiar way sets forth the *person* of Christ, the Bread of Life.

Why, then, was this particular miracle singled out for special prominence? Above, three answers have been suggested, which may be summarized thus: First, because there was an *evidential value* to this miracle which excelled that of all others. Some of our Lord's miracles were wrought in private, or in the presence of only a small company; others were of a nature that made it difficult, in some cases impossible, for sceptics to examine them. But here was a miracle, performed in the open, before a crowd of witnesses which were to be numbered by the thousand. Second, because of the *intrinsic nature* of the miracle. It was a creation of food: the calling into existence of what before had no existence. Third, because of *the typical import* of the miracle. It spoke directly of the *person* of Christ. To these may be added a fourth answer: The fact that this miracle of the feeding of the hungry multitude is recorded by all the Evangelists intimates that it has a *universal application*. Matthew's mention of it suggests to us that it forshadows Christ, in a coming day, feeding Israel's poor—cf. Psa. 132:15. Mark's mention of it teaches us what is the chief duty of God's servants—to break the Bread of Life to the starving. Luke's mention of it announces the sufficiency of Christ to meet the needs of all men. John's mention of it tells us that Christ is the Food of God's people.

Before we consider the miracle itself we must note its setting—the manner in which it is here introduced to us. And ere doing this we will follow our usual custom and present an Analysis of the passage which is to be before us:—

1. Christ followed into Galilee by a great multitude, vv. 1, 2.
2. Christ retires to a mountain with His disciples, v. 3.
3. Time: just before the Passover, v. 4.
4. The testing of Philip, vv. 5-7.
5. The unbelief of Andrew, vv. 8, 9.
6. The feeding of the multitude, vv. 10, 11.
7. The gathering up of the fragments, vv. 12, 13.

"After these things Jesus went over the sea of Galilee, which is the sea of Tiberias" (6:1). "After these things": the reference is to what is recorded in the previous chapter—the healing of the impotent man, the persecution by the Jews because this had been done on the Sabbath day, their determination to kill Him because He had made Himself equal with God, the lengthy reply made by our Lord. After these things, the Lord left Jerusalem and Judea and "went over the sea of Galilee." It is similar to what was before us in John 4:1-3. The Son of God would not remain and cast precious pearls before swine. He departed from those who despised and rejected Him. Very solemn is this, and a warning to every unbeliever who may read these lines.

"And a great multitude followed him, because they saw his miracles which he did on them that were diseased" (6:2). How completely these people failed in their discernment and appreciation of the person of Christ! They saw in Him only a wonderful Magician who could work miracles, a clever Physician that could heal the sick. They failed to perceive that He was the Saviour of sinners and the Messiah of Israel. They were blind to His Divine glory. And is it any otherwise with the great multitude today? Alas, few of them see in Christ anything more than a wonderful Teacher and a beautiful Example.

"And a great multitude followed him, because they saw his miracles which he did on them that were diseased." How sadly true to life. It is still idle curiosity and the love of excitement which commonly gathers crowds together. And how what we read of here is being repeated before our eyes in many quarters today. When some professional evangelist is advertised as a 'Faith-healer' what crowds of sick folk will flock to the meetings! How anxious they are for physical relief, and yet, what little real concern they seem to have for their *soul's* healing!

"And Jesus went up into a mountain, and there he sat with his disciples" (6:3). This may be regarded as the sequel to what we read of in v. 2, or it may be connected with v. 1, and then v. 2 would be considered as a parenthesis. Probably both are equally permissible. If we take v. 2 as giving the cause *why* our Lord retired to the mountain with His disciples, the thought would be that of Christ withdrawing from the unbelieving world. The miracles drew many *after* Him, but only a few *to* Him. He knew why this great multitude "followed him," and it is solemn to see Him withdrawing to the mountain with His disciples. He will not company with the unbelieving world: His place is among His own. If v. 3 be read right on after v. 1, then we view the Saviour departing from Judea, weary (cf. Mark 6:31) with the unbelief and self-sufficiency of those in Jerusalem. "He went up into a mountain into another atmosphere, setting forth the elevation with the Father to which He retired for refreshment of spirit" (Malachi Taylor). Compare John 6:15 and 7:53 to 8:2 for other examples in John's Gospel.

"And the Passover, a feast of the Jews, was nigh" (6:4). This seems introduced here in order to point again to the empty condition to Judaism at this time. The Passover was nigh, but the Lamb of God who was in their midst was not wanted by the formal religionists. Yea, it was because they were determined to "kill him" (5:18), that He had withdrawn into Galilee. Well, then, may the Holy Spirit remind us once more that the Passover had degenerated into "a feast *of the Jews*." How significant is this as an introductory word to what follows! The Passover looks back to the night when the children of Israel feasted on the lamb; but here we see their descendants hungering! Their physical state was the outward sign of their emptiness of soul. Later, we shall see how this verse supplies us with one of the keys to the dispensational significance of our passage.

"When Jesus then lifted up his eyes, and saw a great company come unto him, he saith unto Philip, Whence shall we buy bread, that these may eat?" (6:5). While the multitude did not know Christ, His heart went out in tender pity to them. Even though an unworthy motive had drawn this crowd after Christ, He was not indifferent to their need. Matthew, in his account, tells us "And Jesus went forth, and saw a great multitude, and was *moved with compassion* toward them" (14:14). So also Mark (6:34). The absence of this sentence here in John is one of the innumerable evidences of the Divine authorship of Scripture. Not only is every word inspired, but every word is in its suited place. The "compassion" of Christ, though noted frequently by the other Evangelists, is *never* referred to by John, who dwells upon the dignity and glory of His Divine person. Compassion is more than pity. Com-passion signifies to suffer with, along side of, another. Thus the mention of Christ's compassion by Matthew tells us how near the Messiah had come to His people; while the reference to it in Mark shows how intimately the Servant of Jehovah entered into the sufferings of those to whom He ministered. The absence of this word in John, indicates His elevation above men. Thus we see how everything is most suitably and beautifully placed. And how much we lose by our ungodly haste and carelessness as we fail to mark and appreciate these lovely little touches of the Divine Artist! May Divine grace constrain both writer and reader to handle the Holy Book more reverently, and take more pains to acquaint ourselves with its exhaustless riches. It would be a delight to tarry here, and notice other little details mentioned by the different evangelists which are omitted from John's account —such as the fact that Matthew tells us (*before* the miracle was performed) that "it was evening," and that the disciples bade their Master "send the multitude away"—but perhaps more will be accomplished if we leave the reader to search them out for himself.

"When Jesus then lifted up his eyes, and saw a great multitude come unto him, he saith unto Philip, Whence shall we buy bread, that these may eat? And this he said to prove him: for he himself knew what he would do" (6:5, 6). In reading the Scriptures we fail to derive from them the blessings most needed unless we apply them to our own hearts and lives. Unlike all others, the Bible is a *living* book: It is far more than a history of the past. Stript of their local and incidental details, the sacred narratives depict characters living and incidents transpiring *today*. God changes not, nor do the motives and principles of His actions. Human nature also is the same in this twentieth century as it was in the first. The world is the same, the Devil is the same, the trials of faith are the same. Let, then, each Christian reader view Philip here as representing himself. Philip was confronted with a trying situation. It was *the Lord* who caused him to be so circumstanced. The Lord's design in this was to "prove" or test him. Let us now apply this to ourselves.

What happened to Philip is, in principle and essence, happening daily in *our* lives. A trying, if not a difficult, situation confronts us; and we meet with them constantly. They come not by accident or by chance; instead, they are each arranged by the hand of the Lord. They are God's testings of our faith. They are sent to "prove" *us*. Let us be very simple and practical. A bill comes unexpectedly; how are we to meet it? The morning's mail brings us tidings which plunge us into an unlooked-for perplexity; how are we to get out of it? A cog slips in the household's machinery, which threatens to wreck the daily routine; what shall we do? An unanticipated demand is suddenly made upon us; how shall we meet it? Now, dear friends, *how* do such experiences find us? Do we, like Philip and Andrew did, look at our resources? Do we rack our minds to find some solution? or do our first thoughts turn to the Lord Jesus, who has so often helped us in the past? *Here,* right here, is the test of our faith.

O, dear reader, have we learned to spread each difficulty, as it comes along, before God? Have we formed the habit of instinctively turning to Him? What is your feebleness in comparison with His power! What is your emptiness in comparison with His ocean fulness? Nothing! Then look daily to Him in simple faith, resting on His sure promise, "My God *shall* supply *all* your *need*" (Phil. 4:19). Ah! you may answer, It is easy to offer such advice, but it is far from easy to *act* on it. True. Yea, of yourself it is impossible. Your need, and my need, is to *ask* for faith, to *plead* for grace, to *cry* unto God for such a sense of helplessness that we shall lean on Christ, and on Him alone. Thus, ask and *wait,* and you shall find Him as good as His word. "Why art thou cast down, O my soul? and why art thou disquieted within me? hope thou in God: for I shall yet praise him, who is the health of my countenance, and my God" (Psa. 43:5).

The birds without barn,
  Or storehouse are fed;
From them let us learn
  To trust for our bread.
His saints what is fitting
  Shall ne'er be denied,
So long as, 'tis written
  "The Lord will provide."

When Satan appears,
To stop up our path,
And fills us with fears,
We triumph by faith:
He cannot take from us,
Though oft he has tried,
The heart-cheering promise,
"The Lord will provide."

"Philip answered him, Two hundred pennyworth of bread is not sufficient for them, that every one of them may take a little" (6:7). Let us see in Philip, once more, a portrait of ourselves. First, what does this answer of Philip reveal? It shows he was occupied with circumstances. He was looking on the things which are seen—the size of the multitude—and such a look is always a barrier in the way of faith. He made a rapid calculation of how much money it would require to provide even a frugal meal for such a crowd; but he calculated without Christ! His answer was the language of unbelief—"Two hundred pennyworth of bread is not sufficient for them, that every one of them may *take a little.*" Fancy talking of "a little" in the presence of Infinite Power and Infinite Grace! His unbelief was also betrayed by the very amount he specified—two hundred pennyworth.

Nowhere in Scripture are numbers used haphazardly. Two hundred is a multiple of twenty, and in Scripture twenty signifies *a vain expectancy*, a coming short of God's appointed time or deliverance. For example, in Gen. 31:41 we learn how that Jacob waited *twenty* years to gain possession of his wives and property; but it was not until the twenty-first that God's appointed deliverance came. From Judges 4:3 we learn how that Israel waited *twenty* years for emancipation from Jabin's oppression; but it was not until the twenty-first that God's appointed deliverance came. So in I Sam. 7:2 we learn how that the ark abode in Kirjath-Jearim for *twenty* years, but it was in the twenty-first that God delivered it. As, then, twenty speaks of *insufficiency*, a coming short of God's appointed deliverance, so two hundred conveys the same idea in an *intensified* form. Two hundred is always found in Scripture in an *evil* connection. Let the reader consult (be sure to look them up) Josh. 7:21; Jud. 17:4; I Sam. 30:10; II Sam. 14:26; Rev. 9:16. So the number here in John 6:7 suitably expressed Philip's *unbelief*.

How surprising was this failure in the faith of Philip. One would have supposed that after all the disciples had witnessed of the Lord's wonder-working power they had learned by this time that all fulness dwelt in Him. We should have supposed their faith was strong and their hearts calm and confident. Ah—*should* we? Would not our own God-dishonoring unbelief check such expectations? Have we not discovered how weak *our* faith is! How obtuse our understanding! How earthly our minds and hearts! In vain does the Lord look within us sometimes for even a ray of that faith which glorifies Him. Instead of counting on the Lord, we, like Philip, are occupied with nature's resources. Beware, then, of condemning the unbelief of Philip, lest you be found condemning yourself too.

How often has the writer thought, after some gracious manifestation of the Lord's hand on his behalf, that he *could* trust Him for the future; that the remembrance of His past goodness and mercy would keep him calm and confident when the next cloud should drapen his landscape. Alas! When it came how sadly he failed. Little did we know our treacherous heart. And little do we *know* it even now. O dear reader, each of us need the upholding hand of the Lord *every* step of our journey through this world that lieth in the Wicked one; and, should that hand be for a single moment withdrawn, we should sink like lead in the mighty waters. Ah! nothing but *grace* rescued us; nothing but *grace* can sustain us; nothing but *grace* can carry us safely through. Nothing, *nothing* but the distinguishing and almighty grace of a sovereign God!

"One of his disciples, Andrew, Simon Peter's brother, saith unto him, There is a lad here, which hath five barley loaves, and two small fishes: but what are they among so many?" (6:8, 9). Unbelief is *infectious*. Like Philip before him, Andrew, too, seemed blind to the glory of Christ. "What are they among so many?" was the utterance of the same old evil heart of unbelief which long ago had asked, "Can God furnish a table in the wilderness?" (Psa. 78:10). And how the helplessness of unbelief comes out here! "That every one may take *a little*," said Philip; "*What are these* among so many?" asked Andrew. What mattered the "many" when the Son of God was there! Like Philip,

Andrew calculated without Christ, and, therefore he saw only a hopeless situation. How often we look at God through our difficulties; or, rather, we *try* to, for the difficulties *hide* Him. Keep the eye on Him, and the difficulties will not be seen. But alas! what self-centered, skeptical, sinful creatures we are at best! God may lavish upon us the riches of His grace – He may have opened for us many a dry path through the waters of difficult circumstances – He may have delivered us with His outstretched arm in six troubles, yet, when the *seventh* comes along, instead of resting on Job 5:19, we are distrustful, full of doubts and fears, just as if we had never known Him. Such frail and depraved creatures are we that the faith we have this hour may yield to the most dishonoring distrust in the next. This instance of the disciples' unbelief is recorded for our "learning" – for our humbling and watchfulness. The same unbelief was evidenced by Israel in the wilderness, for the human heart is the same in all ages. All of God's wonders in Egypt and at the Red Sea were as nothing, when the trials of the wilderness came upon them. Their testings in "the wilderness *of sin*" (Ex. 16:1) only brought out of their hearts just what this testing brought out of Philip's and Andrew's, and just what similar testing brings out of ours – blindness and unbelief. The human heart, when proved, can yield nothing else, for nothing else is there. O with what fervency should we daily pray to our Father, "Lead us not into temptation [trial]"!

"And Jesus said, Make the men sit down" (6:10). How thankful we should be that God's blessings are dispensed according to the riches of His grace, and not according to the poverty of our faith. What would have happened to that multitude if Christ had acted according to the faith of His disciples? Why, the multitude would have gone away unfed! Ah! dear reader, God's blessings *do* come, despite all our undeserving. Christ never fails, though there is nothing but failure in us. His arm is never withdrawn for a moment, nor is His love chilled by our skepticism and ingratitude. To hear or read of this may encourage one who is merely a professing Christian to *continue* in his careless and God-dishonoring course; but far otherwise will it be with a *real* child of God. The realization of the Lord's unchanging goodness,

His unfailing mercies—despite our backslidings—will melt him to tears in godly sorrow.

"And Jesus said, Make the men sit down." How patient was the Lord with His disciples. There was no harsh rebuke for either Philip or Andrew. The Lord knoweth our frame and remembers that we are dust. "Make the men sit down" was a further test; this time of their *obedience*. And a searching test it was. What was the use of making a hungry multitude sit down when there was nothing to feed them with? Ah! but *God* had spoken; *Christ* had given the command, and that was enough. When He commands it is for us to obey, not to reason and argue. Why must not Adam and Eve eat of the tree of knowledge? Simply because God had forbidden them to. Why should Noah, in the absence of any sign of an approaching flood, go to all the trouble of building the ark? Simply because God had commanded him to. So, today. Why should the Christian be baptized? Why should the women keep silence in the churches? Simply because God has *commanded* these things—Acts 10:48; I Cor. 14:34.

It is indeed blessed to note the response of the disciples to this command of their Master. Their faith had failed, but their obedience did not. Where both fail, there is grave reason to doubt if there is spiritual life dwelling in such a soul. Their obedience evidenced the genuineness of their Christianity. "If faith is weak, obedience is the best way in which it may be strengthened. 'Then shall *ye know*,' says the prophet, 'if ye *follow on* to know the Lord.' If you have not much light, walk up to the standard of what you have, and you are sure to have more. This will prove that you are a genuine servant of God. Well, this is what the disciples seemed to do here. The light of their faith was low, but they heard the word of Jesus, 'Make the men sit down.' They can act if they cannot see. They can obey His word if they cannot see that all fulness dwells in Him to meet every difficulty. So they obey His command. The men sit down, and Jesus begins to dispense His blessings. And thus by their act of obedience, their faith becomes enlightened, and every want is supplied. This is always the result of walking up to the light we have got. 'To him that hath shall more be given.'

That light may be feeble, it may be only a single ray irradiating the darkness of the mind; nevertheless, it is what God has given you. Despise it not. Hide it not. Walk up to it, and more shall be added.

"And we may notice here how all blessings come down to us through the channel of obedience. The supply for every want had been determined beforehand in the Saviour's mind, for 'he himself knew what he would do' (v. 6). Yet though this were so, it was to flow through this medium—so intimately and inseparably is the carrying out of all God's purposes of grace toward us connected with obedience to His commands. This is the prominent feature in all God's people. '*Obedient children*' is the term by which they are distinguished from those who are of the world. 'He became obedient' was the distinguishing feature in the character of the divine Master, and it is the mark that the Holy Spirit sets upon all His servants. Obedience and blessing are inseparably connected in God's Word. 'If any man will *do* his will, he shall know of the doctrine whether it be of God.' 'He that hath my commandments and *keepeth* them, he it is that loveth me; and he that loveth me shall be loved by my Father, and *I will love him and will manifest myself to him*'" (Dr. F. Whitfield)

"And Jesus said, Make the men to sit down." But why "sit down"? Two answers may be returned. First, because God is a God of order. Any one who has studied the works of God knows that. So, too, with His Word. When His people left Egypt, they did not come forth like a disorderly mob; but in ranks of fives—see Ex. 13:18 margin. It was the same when they crossed the Jordan and entered Canaan—see Josh. 1:14 margin. It was so here. Mark says, "They sat down in ranks, by hundreds, and by fifties" (6:40). It is so still: "Let all things be done decently and in order" (I Cor. 14:40). Whenever there is confusion in a religious meeting—two or more praying at the same time, etc.—it is a sure sign that the Holy Spirit is not in control of it. "God *is not* the author of confusion" (I Cor. 14:33).

"Make the men sit down." Why? Secondly, may we not also see in this word the illustration of an important principle pertaining to the spiritual life, namely, that we must sit down if we would be fed—true alike for sinner and saint. The activities of the flesh must come to an end if the Bread of life is to be received by us. How much all of us need to ask God to teach us to be quiet and sit still. Turn to and ponder Psa. 107:30; Isa. 30:15; I Thess. 4:11; I Pet. 3:4. In this crazy age, when almost everybody is rushing hither and thither, when the standard of excellency is not how well a thing is done, but how quickly, when the Lord's people are thoroughly infected by the same spirit of haste, this is indeed a timely word. And let not the reader imagine that he has power of himself to comply. We have to be "*made*" to "sit down"—frequently by sickness. Note the same word in Psa. 23:2—"He *maketh me* to lie down in green pastures."

"Now there was much grass in the place" (6:10). How gracious of the Holy Spirit to record this. Nothing, however trifling or insignificant, is unknown to God or beneath His notice. The "much cattle" in Nineveh (Jonah 4:11) had not been forgotten by Him. And how minutely has the Word of God recorded the house, the situation of it, and the name and occupation of one of the Lord's disciples (Acts 10:5, 6)! Everything is before Him in the registry of heaven. God's eye is upon every circumstance connected with our life. There is nothing too little for Him if it concerns His beloved child. God ordered nature to provide cushions for this hungry multitude to sit upon! Mark adds that the grass was "green" (6:39), which reminds us that we must rest in the "green pastures" of His Word if our souls are to be fed.

"So the men sat down, in number about five thousand" (6:10). This is another beautiful line in the picture (cf. the *five* loaves in v. 9), for five is ever the number which speaks of *grace*, that is why it was the dominant numeral in the Tabernacle where God manifested His grace in the midst of Israel. Five is four (the number of the creature) plus one—God. It is God adding His blessing and grace to the works of His hand.

"And Jesus took the loaves" (6:11). He did not scorn the loaves because they were few in number, nor the fish either because they were "small." How this tells us that God is pleased to use small and weak things! He used the tear of a babe to move the heart of Pharaoh's daughter. He used the shepherd-rod of Moses to work mighty miracles in Egypt. He used David's sling and stone to overthrow the Philistine giant. He used a "little maid" to bring the "mighty" Naaman to Elisha. He used a widow with a handful of meal to sustain His prophet. He used a "little child" to teach His disciples a much needed lesson in humility. So here, He used the five loaves and two small fishes to feed this great multitude. And, dear reader, perhaps He is ready to use you – weak, insignificant, and ignorant though you be – and make you "mighty through God, to the pulling down of strongholds" (II Cor. 10:4). But mark it carefully, it was only as these loaves and fishes were placed in the *hands of Christ* that they were made efficient and sufficient!

"And Jesus took the loaves." He did not despise them and work independently of them. He did not rain manna from heaven, but used the means which were to hand. And surely this is another lesson that many of His people need to take to heart today. It is true that God is not limited to means, but frequently He employs them. When healing the bitter waters of Marah God used a tree (Ex. 15:23-25). In healing Hezekiah of his boil He employed a lump of figs (II Kings 20:4-7). Timothy was exhorted to use a "little wine for his stomach's sake and his often infirmities" (I Tim. 5:23). In view of such scriptures let us, then, beware of going to the fanatical lengths of some who scorn all use of drugs and herbs when sick.

"And when he had given thanks" (6:11). In all things Christ has left us a perfect example. He here teaches us to acknowledge God as the Giver of every good gift, and to own Him as the One who provides for the wants of all His creatures. This is the least that we can do. To fail at this point is the basest ingratitude.

"He distributed to the disciples, and the disciples to them that were set down" (6:11). Here we are taught, again, the same lesson as the first miracle supplied, namely, that God is pleased to use human instruments in accomplishing the counsels of His grace, and thus give us the inestimable honor and privilege of being "laborers together with God" (I Cor. 3:9). Christ fed the hungry multitude *through His disciples*. It was their work as truly as it was His. His was the increase, but theirs was the distribution. God acts according to the same principle today. Between the unsearchable riches of Christ and the hungry multitudes there is room for consecrated service and ministry. Nor should this be regarded as exclusively the work of pastors and evangelists. It is the happy duty of every child of God to pass on to others that which the Lord in His grace has first given to them. Yea, this is one of the *conditions* of receiving more for ourselves. This is one of the things that Paul reminded the Hebrews of. He declared he had many things to say unto them, and they were hard to be interpreted because they had become dull (*slothful* is the meaning of the word) of hearing, and unskilled in using the Word. Consequently, instead of teaching others—as they ought—they needed to be taught again themselves (Heb. 5:11-13). The same truth comes out in that enigmatical utterance of our Lord recorded in Luke 8:18: "for whosoever hath, to him shall be given; and whosoever hath not, from him shall be taken even that which he seemeth to have." The one who "hath" is the believer who makes *good use* of what he has received, and in consequence more is given him; the one who "seemeth to have" is the man who hides his light under a bushel, who makes not good use of what he received, and from him this is "taken away." Be warned then, dear reader. If we do not use to God's glory what He has given us, He may withhold further blessings from us, and take away that which we fail to make good use of.

"He distributed to the disciples, and the disciples to them that were set down." One can well imagine the mingled feelings of doubt and skepticism as the twelve left the Saviour's side for the hungry multitude, with the little store in their baskets. How doubt must have given place to amazement, and awe to adoration, as they distributed, returned to their Master for a fresh supply, and continued distributing, giving a portion of bread and fish to each till all were satisfied, and more remaining at the close than at the beginning! Let us remember that Jesus Christ is "the same yesterday and today and for ever," and that all fulness dwells in Him. By comparing Mark 6:41 it will be found that there the Holy Spirit has described the *modus operandi* of the miracle: "He looked up to heaven, and blessed, and *brake* the loaves, and *gave* to his disciples." The word "brake" is in the aorist tense, intimating an instantaneous act; whereas "gave" is in the imperfect tense, denoting the continuous action of giving. "This shows that the miraculous power was in the hands of Christ, between the breaking and the giving" (Companion Bible).

"He distributed to the disciples, and the disciples to them that were set down." What a lesson is there here for the Christian servant. The apostles first received the bread from the hands of their Master, and then "distributed" to the multitude. It was not *their* hands which made the loaves increase, but *His!* He provided the abundant supply, and their business was to humbly receive and faithfully distribute. In like manner, it is not the business of the preacher to make men value or receive the Bread of life. *He* can not make it soul-saving to any one. This is not his work; for this he is not responsible. It is *God* who giveth the "increase"! Nor is it the work of the preacher to *create* something new and novel. His duty is to *seek* "bread" at the hands of his Lord, and then *set it* before the people. What *they* do with the Bread is *their responsibility!* But, remember, that we cannot give out to others, except we have first received ourselves. It is only the full vessel that overflows!

"And likewise of the fishes as much as they would" (6:11). "Precious, precious words! The supply stopped only with the demand. So, when Abraham went up to intercede with God on behalf of the righteous in Sodom, the Lord never ceased granting till Abraham had ceased asking. Thus also in the case of Elisha's oil; so long as there were empty vessels to be found in the land, it ceased not its abundant supply (II Kings 4:6). Likewise also here, so long as there was a single one to supply, that supply came forth from the treasuries of the Lord Jesus. The stream flowed on in rich abundance till all were filled. This is grace. This is what Jesus does to all His people. He comes to the poor bankrupt believer, and, placing in His hand a draft on the resources of heaven, says to him, 'Write on it what thou wilt.' Such is our precious Lord still. If we are straitened, it is not in

Him, but in ourselves. If we are poor and weak, or tried and tempted, it is not that we cannot help ourselves – it is because we do not ('All things *are* yours', in Christ, I Cor. 3:22 A.W.P.). We have so little faith in things unseen and eternal. We draw so little on the resources of Christ. We come not to Him with our spiritual wants – our empty vessels – and draw from the ocean fulness of His grace.

"'As much as they would'. Precious, precious words. Remember them, doubting, hesitating one, in all thy petitions for faith at the throne of grace. 'As much as they would.' Remember them, tried and tempted one, in all thy pleadings for strength to support thee on thy wilderness way. 'As much as they would'. Remember them, bereaved and desolate one, whose eyes are red with weeping, bending over the green sod, beneath which all thy earthly hopes are lying, and with a rent in thine heart that shall never be healed till the morning of resurrection – remember these words as thy wounded and desolate spirit breaks forth in mournful accents on a Saviour's ear for help and strength. And, guilty one, bowed down with a lifetime's load of sin, traversing the crooked bypaths of the broad road to ruin; a wilful wanderer from thy God; as the arrow of conviction penetrates thy soul, and as thine agonizing voice is heard crying for mercy – remember these precious, precious words, 'as much as they would'. 'Him that cometh unto Me I will in no wise cast out'" (Dr. F. Whitfield).

"When they were filled" (6:12). God gives with no niggardly hand. "When they were *filled*" – what a contrast is this from the words of Philip, "That every one of them may take *a little*"! The one was the outpouring of Divine grace, the other the limitation of unbelief. Christ had fed them from His own inexhaustible resources, and when *He* feeds His people He leaves no want behind. Christ, and He alone, *satisfies*. His promise is, "He that cometh to me shall never hunger; and he that believeth on me shall never thirst" (John 6:35). Do you know, dear reader, what it is to be "filled" from His blessed hand – filled with peace, filled with joy, filled with the Holy Spirit!

"Gather up the fragments that remain, that nothing be lost" (6:12). All were filled and yet abundance remained! How wonderful and how blessed this is. All fulness dwells in Christ, and that fulness is exhaustless. Countless sinners have been saved and their souls satisfied, and yet the riches of grace are as undiminished as ever. Then, too, this verse may be considered from another angle. "Gather up the fragments." There was abundance for all, but the Lord would have no waste. How this rebukes the wicked extravagance that we now behold on every hand! Here, too, the Holy One has left us a perfect example. "Gather up the fragments" is a word that comes to us all. The "fragments" we need to watch most are the fragments of our time. How often these are wasted! "Let *nothing* be lost"! "Gather them up"—your mis-spent moments, your tardy services, your sluggish energies, your cold affections, your neglected duties. Gather them up and use them for His glory.

"Therefore they gathered them together, and filled twelve baskets with the fragments of the five barley loaves, which remained over and above unto them that had eaten" (6:13). How this confirms what we have said about giving out to others. The loaves were augmented by division and multiplied by subtraction! We are never impoverished, but always enriched by giving to others. It is the *liberal* soul that is made fat (Prov. 11:25). We need never be anxious that there will not be enough left for our own needs. God never allows a generous giver to be the loser. It is miserliness which impoverishes. The disciples had more left at the finish than they had at the beginning! They "filled twelve baskets," thus the twelve apostles were also provided with an ample supply for their own use too! *They* were the ones who were enriched by ministering to the hungry multitude! What a blessed encouragement to God's servants today!

In closing, let us call attention to another of the wonderful typical and dispensational pictures which abound in this Gospel. The passage which has been before us supplies a lovely view of the activities of God during this dispensation. It should be carefully noted that John 6 opens with the words, "After these things." This expression always points to the beginning of a *new* series—cf. 5:1; 7:1; 21:1; Rev. 4:1, etc. In John 4 we have two typical chapters which respect *the Gentiles*—see the closing portions of chapters 15 and 16. Hence John 5 *begins* with "After this." John 5 supplies us with a typical picture of *Israel*—see chapter 17. Now as John 6 opens with "After these things," we are led to expect that the dispensational view it first supplies will respect *the Gentiles* again and not the Jews. This is confirmed by the fact that the remainder of the verse intimates that Christ had now left Judea and had once more entered Galilee of the Gentiles. Further corroboration is found in that Philip and Andrew figure so prominently in the incident which follows—cf. John 12:20-22 which specially links *them* with the *Gentiles*. In the remainder of the passage we have a beautiful view of Christ and His people during the present dispensation. Note the following lines in the picture:—

First, we behold the Lord *on high* and His people "seated" *with Him* (v. 3). This, of course, typifies our *standing;* what follows contemplates our *state*. Second, we are shown the *basis* of our blessings: "And the passover, a feast of the Jews, was nigh" (v. 4). The Passover speaks of "Christ our passover sacrificed for us" (I Cor. 5:7). But note, it is not only "the passover" which is mentioned here, but also "the passover, a *feast*" (note the absence of this in John 2:13!), which beautifully accords with what follows—typically, believers *feeding* on Christ! But we are also told here that this "passover" was "a feast of *the Jews*." This is parallel with John 4:22—"Salvation is *of* the Jews." It is a word to humble us, showing our indebtedness to Israel, cf. Rom. 11:18: "Thou bearest not the root, but the root thee." Third, the people of God, those who in this dispensation are fed, are they who "come unto Him" (v. 5)—Christ. Fourth, Christ's desire (v. 5) and purpose (v. 6) to feed His own. Fifth, His saints are a people of little faith (cf. Matt. 8:26), who fail in the hour of testing (vv. 5-9). Sixth, His people must "sit down" in order to be "fed." Seventh, Christ ministers to His people in sovereign *grace* ("five loaves" and "five" thousand men, vv. 10, 11) and gives them a satisfying portion—"They were *filled*" (v. 12).

It is beautiful to observe that *after* the great multitude had been fed, there "remained" *twelve* full baskets, which tells of the abundance of grace reserved for *Israel*. This also gives meaning to, "A feast of the Jews *was nigh*" (v. 4).

Let the following questions be studied with a view to the next chapter: —

1. Why did Christ "depart"? v. 15.
2. Why were the disciples "afraid"? v. 19.
3. What spiritual lessons may be drawn from vv. 17 to 21?
4. How harmonize the first half of v. 27 with Eph. 2:8, 9?
5. What is meant by Christ being "sealed"? v. 27.

CHAPTER TWENTY-ONE

Christ Walking on the Sea

John 6:14-27

We begin with our customary Analysis of the passage which is to be before us:

1. The Response of the people to the miracle of the loaves: vv. 14, 15.
2. The Retirement of Christ to the mount: v. 15.
3. The Disciples in the storm: vv. 16-19.
4. The Coming of Christ to them: vv. 20, 21.
5. The people follow Christ to Capernaum: vv. 22-25.
6. Christ exposes their motive: v. 26.
7. Christ presses their spiritual need upon them: v. 27.

The opening verses of the passage before us contain the sequel to what is described in the first thirteen verses of John 6. There we read of the Lord ministering, in wondrous grace, to a great multitude of hungry people. They had no real appreciation of His blessed person, but had been attracted by idle curiosity and the love of the sensational—"because they saw his miracles which he did on them that were diseased" (v. 2). Nevertheless, the Son of God, in tenderest pity, had supplied their need by means of the loaves and the fishes. What effects, then, did this have upon them?

Christ had manifested His Divine power. There was no gainsaying that. The crowd were impressed, for we are told, "Then those men, when they had seen the miracle which Jesus did, said, This is of a truth that prophet which should come into the world" (6:14). The title "that prophet" has already been before us in 1:21. The reference is to Deut. 18:15, where we read that, through Moses God declared, "The Lord thy God will raise up unto thee a prophet from the midst of thee, of thy brethren, like unto me; unto him ye shall hearken." These men, then, seemed ready to receive the Lord as their Messiah. And yet how little they realized and recognized what was due Him as "that prophet" – the Son of God incarnate. Instead of falling down before Him as undone sinners, crying for mercy; instead of prostrating themselves at His feet, in reverent worship; instead of owning Him as the Blessed One, worthy of their hearts' adoration, they would "take him by force to make him a king" (6:15); and this, no doubt, for *their own ends*, thinking that He would lead them in a successful revolt against the hated Romans. How empty, then, were their words! How little were their consciences searched or their hearts exercised! How blind they still were to the Light! Had their hearts been opened, the light had shone in, revealing their wretchedness; and then, they would have taken their place as lost and needy sinners. It is the same today.

Many there are who regard our Lord as a Prophet (a wonderful Teacher), who have never seen their need of Him as a Refuge from the wrath to come – a doom they so thoroughly deserve. Let us not be misled, then, by this seeming honoring of Christ by those who eulogize His precepts, but who despise His Cross. It is no more a proof that they are saved who, today, own Christ as a greater than Buddha or Mohammed, than this declaration by these men of old – "This is of a truth that prophet which should come into the world," evidenced that they had "passed from death unto life."

"When Jesus therefore perceived that they would come and take him by force" (6:15). This is very solemn. Christ was not deceived by their fair speech. Their words sounded very commendable and laudatory, no doubt, but the Christ of God was, and is, the Reader of hearts. He knew what lay behind their words. He discerned the spirit that prompted them. "Jesus therefore *perceived*" is parallel with John 2:24, 25: "But Jesus did not commit himself unto them, *because he knew* all, and needed not that any should testify of man: for he *knew* what was in man." "Jesus therefore perceived" is a word that brings before us His Deity. The remainder of v. 15 is profoundly significant and suggestive.

"When Jesus therefore perceived that they would come and take him by force, to make him a king, he departed again into a mountain himself alone" (6:15). These Jews had owned Him (with their lips) as *Prophet,* and they were ready to crown Him as their *King,* but there is another office that comes in between these. Christ could not be their King until He had first officiated as *Priest,* offering Himself as a Sacrifice for sin! Hence the doctrinal significance of "He departed again into a mountain himself *alone,*" for in His priestly work He is unattended—cf. Lev. 16:17!

But there was also a moral and dispensational reason why Christ "departed" when these Jews would use force to make Him a King. He needed not to be *made* "a king," for He was *born* such (Matt. 2:2); nor would He receive the kingdom at *their* hand. This has been brought out beautifully by Mr. J. B. Bellet in his notes on John's Gospel:—"The Lord would not take the kingdom from zeal like this. This could not be the source of the kingdom of the Son of Man. The 'beasts' may take their kingdoms from the winds striving upon the great sea, but Jesus cannot (Dan. 7:2, 25). This was not, in His ear, the shouting of the people bringing in the headstone of the corner (Zech. 4:7); nor the symbol of His people made willing in the day of His power (Psa. 110:3). This would have been an appointment to the throne of Israel on scarcely better principles than those on which Saul had been appointed of old. His kingdom would have been the fruit of their revolted heart. But that could not be. And besides this, ere the Lord could take His seat on Mount Zion, He must ascend the solitary mount; and ere the people could enter the kingdom, they must go down to the stormy sea. And these things we see reflected here as in a glass."

It should be noted that Matthew tells us how Christ "went up into a mountain apart *to pray*" (14:23); so, too, Mark (6:46). The absence of this word in John is in beautiful accord with the character and theme of this fourth Gospel, and supplies us with another of those countless proofs for the Divine and verbal inspiration of the Scriptures. In this Gospel we never see Christ *praying* (John 17 is *intercession,* giving us a sample of His priestly ministry on our behalf in heaven: note particularly vv.

4 and 5, which indicate that the intercession recorded in the verses that follow was *anticipatory* of Christ's return to the Father!), for John's special design is to exhibit the *Divine* glories of the Saviour.

"And when even was now come, his disciples went down unto the sea, And entered into a ship" (6:16, 17). Matthew explains the reason for this: "And straightway Jesus constrained his disciples to get into a ship, and to go before him unto the other side, while he sent the multitudes away" (14:22). The Lord desired to be alone, so He caused the disciples to go on ahead of Him. It would seem, too, that He purposed to teach them another lesson on faith. This will appear in the sequel.

"And entered into a ship, and went over the sea toward Capernaum. And it was now dark, and Jesus was not come to them" (6:17). What we have here, and in the verses that follow, speaks unmistakably *to us*. It describes the conditions through which we must pass as we journey to our Home above. Though not of the world, we are necessarily in it: *that* world made up of the wicked, who are like "the troubled sea." The world in which we live, dear reader, is the world that rejected and still rejects the Christ of God. It is the world which "lieth in the wicked one" (I John 5:19), the friendship of which is enmity with God (James 4:4). It is a world devoid of spiritual light; a world over which hangs the shadow of death. Peter declares the world is "a dark place" (II Pet. 1:19). It is dark because "the light of the world" is absent.

"It was now dark, and Jesus was not come to them." Sometimes Christ withholds the light of His countenance even from His own. Job cried, "when I waited for light, there came darkness" (30:26). But, thank God, it is recorded, "Unto the upright there ariseth light *in* the darkness" (Psa. 112:4). Let us remember that the darkness is not created by Satan, but by God (Isa. 45:7). And He has a wise and good reason for it. Sometimes He withholds the light from His people that they may discover "the *treasures* of darkness" (Isa. 45:3).

"Jesus was not come to them. And the sea arose by reason of the great wind that blew" (6:17, 18). This tested the faith and patience of the disciples. The longer they waited the worse things became. It *looked* as though Christ was neglectful of them. It *seemed* as though He had forgotten to be gracious. Perhaps they were saying, If the Master had been here, this storm would not have come up. Had He been with them, even though asleep on a pillow, His presence would have cheered them. But He was not there; and the darkness was about them, and the angry waves all around them—fit emblems of the opposition of the world against the believer's course. It was a real test of their faith and patience.

And similarly does God often test us today. Frequently our circumstances are dark, and conditions are all against us. We cry to the Lord, but He "does not come." But let us remind ourselves, that God is never in a hurry. However much the petulance of unbelief may seek to hasten His hand, He waits His own good time. *Omnipotence* can afford to wait, for it is always sure of success. And because omnipotence is combined with infinite wisdom and love, we may be certain that God not only does everything in the right way, but also at the best time: "And therefore will the Lord *wait,* that he may be gracious unto you, and therefore will he be exalted, that he may have mercy upon you: for the Lord is a God of judgment: blessed are all they that *wait* for him" (Isa. 30:18).

Sometimes the Lord "waits" until it is eventide before He appears in His delivering grace and power. The darkness becomes more gloomy, and still He *waits.* Yes, but He *waits* "to be gracious." But why? Could He not be gracious without this waiting, and the painful suspense such waiting usually brings to us? Surely; but one reason for the delay is, that *His* hand may be the more evident; and another reason is, that *His* hand may be the more appreciated, when He does intervene. Sometimes the darkness becomes even more gloomy, well-nigh unbearable; and still He *waits.* And again, we wonder, Why? Ah! is it not that all *our* hopes may be disappointed; that *our* plans may be frustrated, till we reach our wit's *end* (Psa. 107:27)! And, then, just as we had given up hope, He breaks forth unexpectedly, and we are startled, as were these disciples on the stormlashed sea.

"So when they had rowed about five and twenty or thirty furlongs, they see Jesus walking on the sea" (6:19). These lines will, doubtless, be read by more than one saint who is in a tight place. For you, too, the night is fearfully dark, and the breakers of adverse circumstances look as though they would completely swamp you. O tried and troubled one, read the blessed sequel of John 6:17, 18. It contains a word of cheer for *you,* if your *faith* lays hold of it. Notice that the disciples did not give up in despair — they continued "rowing" (v. 19)! And ultimately the Lord came to their side and delivered them from the angry tempest. So, dear saint, whatever may be the path appointed by the Lord, however difficult and distasteful, *continue therein,* and in His own good time the Lord *will* deliver you. Again we say, Notice that the disciples continued their "rowing." It was all they could do, and it was all that was required of them. In a little while the Lord appeared, and they were at the land. Oh may God grant both writer and reader perseverance in the path of duty. Tempted and discouraged one, remember Isa. 30:18 (look it up and memorize it) and *continue rowing!*

There is another thing, a blessed truth, which is well calculated to sustain us in the interval *before* the deliverance comes; and it *will* if the heart appropriates its blessedness. While the storm-tossed disciples were pulling at the oars and making little or no progress, the Lord was on high — not below, but above them — master of the situation. And, as Matthew tells us, He was "praying." And on high He is now *thus* engaged on *our* behalf. Remember this, O troubled one, your great High Priest who is "touched with the feeling of your infirmities" is above, ever living to intercede. *His* prayers undergird you, so that you cannot sink. Mark adds a word that is even more precious — "And he saw them toiling in rowing" (6:48). Christ was not indifferent to their peril. His eye was upon them. And even though it was "dark" (John 6:17) He *saw them.* No darkness could hide those disciples from Him. And this, too, speaks to *us.* We may be "*toiling* in rowing" (the Greek word means "fatigued"), weary of the buffeting from the unfriendly winds and waves, but there is One above who is not unconcerned, who sees and knows our painful lot, and who, even now, is preparing to come to our side. Turn your eyes away from your frail barque, away from the surrounding tempest, and "look off unto Jesus, the author and finisher of faith " (Heb. 12:1).

"So when they had rowed about five and twenty or thirty furlongs, they see Jesus walking on the sea, and drawing nigh unto the ship: and they were afraid" (6:19). This shows how little faith was in exercise. Matthew tells us, "And when the disciples saw him walking on the sea, they were troubled" (14:26). Think of it, "troubled" and "afraid" of Jesus! Does some one say, That was because the night was dark and the waves boisterous, consequently it was easy to mistake the Saviour for an apparition? Moreover, the sight they beheld was altogether unprecedented: never before had they seen one walking on the water! But if we turn to Mark's record we shall find that it was not dimness of physical sight which caused the disciples to mistake their Master for a spectre, but dullness of spiritual vision: "They considered not the miracle of the loaves: for *their heart was hardened.*" Their fears had mastered them. They were not expecting deliverance. They had already forgotten that exercise of Divine grace and power which they had witnessed only a few short hours before. And how accurately (and tragically) do they portray us—so quickly do we forget the Lord's mercies and deliverances in the past, so little do we really expect Him to answer our prayers of the present.

"But he saith unto them, "It is I; be not afraid" (6:20). This is parallel in thought with what we had before us in v. 10. The scepticism of Philip and the unbelief of Andrew did not prevent the outflow of Divine mercy. So here, even the hardness of heart of these disciples did not quench their Lord's love for them. O how deeply thankful we ought to be that "He hath not dealt with us after our sins; nor rewarded us according to our iniquities" (Psa. 103:10). From beginning to end He deals with us in wondrous, fathomless, sovereign grace. "It is I," He says. He first directs their gaze to Himself. "Be not afraid," was a word to calm their hearts. And this is His unchanging order. Our fears can only be dispelled by looking in faith to and having our hearts occupied with Him. Look around, and we shall be disheartened. Look within, and we shall be discouraged. But look unto Him, and our fears will vanish.

"Then they willingly received him into the ship: and immediately the ship was at the land whither they went" (6:21). Now that He had revealed Himself to them; now that He had graciously uttered the heart-calming "Be not afraid"; now that He had (as Matthew and Mark tell us) spoken that well-known word "Be of good cheer": they "willingly received him into the ship." Christ does not force Himself upon us: He waits to be "received." It is the welcome of our hearts that He desires. And is it not just because this is so often withheld, that He is so slow in coming to our relief – i.e. "manifesting himself" to us (John 14:21)! How blessed to note that as soon as *He* entered the ship, the end of the voyage was reached for them. In applying to ourselves the second half of this twenty-first verse, we must not understand it to signify that when Christ has "manifested" Himself unto us that the winds will cease to blow or that the adverse "sea" will now befriend us; far from it. But it means that the *heart* will now have found a Haven of rest: our fears will be quieted; we shall be occupied not with the tempest, but with the Master of it. Such are some of the precious spiritual lessons which we may take to ourselves from this passage.

"The day following, when the people which stood on the other side of the sea saw that there was none other boat there, save that one whereinto his disciples were entered, and that Jesus went not with his disciples into the boat, but that his disciples were gone away alone; (Howbeit there came other boats from Tiberias nigh unto the place where they did eat bread, after that the Lord had given thanks:) When the people therefore saw that Jesus was not there, neither his disciples, they also took shipping, and came to Capernaum, seeking for Jesus" (6:22-24). The multitude, whose hearts were set on making the Miracle-worker their "king," apparently collected early in the morning to carry their purpose into effect. But on seeking for Jesus, He was nowhere to be found. This must have perplexed them. They knew that on the previous evening there was only one boat on their side of the sea, and they had seen the disciples depart in this, alone. Where, then, was the Master? Evidently,

He who had miraculously multiplied five loaves and two fishes so as to constitute an abundant meal for more than five thousand people, must also in some miraculous manner have transported Himself across the sea. So, availing themselves of the boats which had just arrived from Tiberias, they crossed over to Capernaum, in the hope of finding the Lord Jesus there; for they knew that this city had, for some time, been His chief place of residence. Nor was their expectation disappointed.

"And when they had found him on the other side of the sea, they said unto him, Rabbi, when camest thou hither? Jesus answered them and said, Verily, verily, I say unto you, Ye seek me, not because ye saw the miracles but because ye did eat of the loaves, and were filled" (6:25, 26). There was, perhaps, nothing wrong in their question, "Rabbi, when camest thou hither?" But to have answered it would not have profited them, and that was what the Lord sought. He, therefore, at once showed them that He was acquainted with their motives, and knew full well what had brought them thither. Outwardly at least, these people appeared ready to honor Him. They had followed Him across the sea of Galilee, and sought Him out again. But He read their hearts. He knew the inward springs of their conduct, and was not to be deceived. It was the Son of God evidencing His Deity again. He knew it was temporal, not spiritual blessing, that they sought. When He tells them, "Ye seek me, not because ye *saw* the miracles (or "signs") but because ye did eat of the loaves," His evident meaning is that they realized not the spiritual significance of those "signs." Had they done so, they would have prostrated themselves before Him in worship. And let us remember that "Jesus Christ is the same yesterday, and today, and forever." Christ still reads the human heart. No secrets can be withheld from Him. He knows why different ones put on religious garments when it suits their purpose—why, at times, some are so loud in their religious pretensions—why thy profess to be Christians. Hypocrisy is very sinful, but its folly and uselessness are equally great.

"Labour not for the meat which perisheth, but for that meat which endureth unto everlasting life, which the Son of man shall give unto you" (6:27). The expression used here by Christ is a relative and comparative one: His meaning is, Labour for the latter rather than for the former. The word "labour" is very expressive. It signifies that men should be in deadly earnest over spiritual things; that they should spare no pains to obtain that which their souls so imperatively need. It is used *figuratively*, and signifies making salvation the object of intense desire. O that men would give the same diligence to secure that which is imperative, as they put forth to gain the things of time and sense. That to which Christ bids men direct their thoughts and energies is "meat which endureth"—*abideth* would be better: it is one of the characteristic words of this Gospel.

When our Lord says, "*Labour* . . . for that meat (satisfying portion) which endureth unto everlasting life," He was not inculcating salvation by works. This is very clear from His next words—"which the Son of man shall *give* unto you." But He was affirming that which needs to be pressed on the half-hearted and those who are occupied with material things. It is difficult to preserve the balance of truth. On the one hand, we are so anxious to insist that salvation is by grace alone, that we are in danger of failing to uphold the sinner's responsibility to *seek* the Lord with all his heart. Again; in pressing the total depravity of the natural man, his *deadness* in trespasses and sins, we are apt to neglect our duty of calling on him to repent and believe the Gospel. This word of Christ's, "Labour . . . for the meat which endureth" is parallel (in substance) with "*Strive* to enter in at the strait gate" (Luke 13:24), and "every one *presseth into* the kingdom of God" (Luke 16:16). "For him hath God the Father sealed" (6:27). What is meant by Christ being "sealed" by God the Father? First, notice it is as "Son *of man*" that He is here said to be "sealed." That is, it was as the Son of God, but *incarnate*. There are two prime thoughts connected with "*sealing*:" identification, and attestation or ratification. In Rev. 7 we read of God's angel "sealing" twelve thousand from each of the tribes of Israel. The sealing there consists of placing a mark on their foreheads, and it is for the purpose of identification: to distinguish and separate them from the mass of apostate Israel. Again, in Esther 8:8 we read, "Write ye also for the Jews, as it liketh you, in the king's name, and seal it with the king's ring: for the writing which is written in the king's name, and *sealed* with the king's ring, *may no man reverse.*" Here the thought is entirely different. The *king's* "seal" there speaks of authority. His seal was added for the purpose of confirmation and ratification. These, we doubt not, are the principle thoughts we are to associate with the "sealing" of Christ.

The historical reference is to the time when Christ was baptized—Acts 10:38. When the Lord Jesus, in marvellous condescension, had identified Himself with the believing remnant in Israel, taking His place in that which spoke of death, the Father there singled Him out by "anointing" or "sealing" Him with the Holy Spirit. This was accompanied by His audible voice, saying, "This is my beloved Son, in whom I am well pleased." Thus was the Christ, now about to enter upon His mediatorial work, publicly *identified and accredited* by God. The Father *testified to* the perfections of His incarnate Son, and communicated official authority, by "sealing" Him with the Holy Spirit. This declaration of Christ here in v. 27 anticipated the question or challenge which we find in v. 52, "How can *this man* give us his flesh to eat?" The sufficient answer, already given, was "*for* him hath God the Father sealed." So, too, it anticipated and answered the question of v. 30: "What sign showest *thou* then, that we may see, and believe thee?" Just as princes of the realm are often authorized by the king to act in governmental and diplomatic affairs on his behalf, and carry credentials that bear the king's seal to confirm their authority before those to whom they are sent, so Christ gave proof of His heavenly authority by His miracles: "God anointed Jesus of Nazareth with the Holy Ghost *and with power*" (Acts 10:38).

It is blessed to know that we, too, have been "sealed": Eph. 1:13. Believers are "sealed" as those who are *approved* of God. But observe, carefully, that it is *in Christ* we are thus distinguished. "*In whom* also after that ye believed, ye were *sealed* with that Holy Spirit of promise." Christ was "sealed" because of His own intrinsic perfections; we, because of our identification and union with Him! "Accepted *in the beloved*" (Eph. 1:6) gives us the same thought. Mark, though, it is not said (as commonly misunderstood) that the Holy Spirit *seals us,* but that the Holy Spirit Himself *is* God's "Seal" upon us—the distinguishing sign of identification, for sinners do not have the Holy Spirit (Jude 19).

Let the student ponder the following questions, preparatory to our next chapter:—

1. What does the question in v. 28 intimate?
2. What is the meaning of v. 29?
3. What do verses 30 and 31 demonstrate in connection with those people?
4. In how many different respects is "bread" a suited emblem of Christ?
5. What is the meaning of v. 35—Does a believer ever "hunger" or "thirst"?
6. *Who* have been given to Christ by the Father? v. 37.
7. What comforting truth is found in v. 39?

CHAPTER TWENTY-TWO

CHRIST, THE BREAD OF LIFE

John 6:28-40

Below we give an Analysis of the passage which is to be before us: —

1. The Inquiry of the legalistic heart: v. 28.
2. The Divine answer thereto: v. 29.
3. The Scepticism of the natural heart: vv. 30, 31.
4. Christ the true Bread: vv. 32-34.
5. Christ the Satisfier of man's heart: v. 35.
6. The Unbelief of those who had seen: v. 36.
7. Christ's Submission to the Father's will: vv. 37-40.

It is both important and instructive to observe the connection between John 5 and John 6: the latter is, doctrinally, the sequel to the former. There is both a comparison and a contrast in the way Christ is presented to us in these two chapters. In both we see Him as the Source of life, Divine life, spiritual life, eternal life. But, speaking of what is characteristic in John 5, we have life *communicated* by Christ, whereas in John 6 we have salvation *received* by us. Let us amplify this a little.

John 5 opens with a typical illustration of Christ imparting life to an impotent soul: a man, helpless through an infirmity which he had had for thirty-eight years, is made whole. This miracle Christ makes the basis of a discourse in which He presented His Divine glories. In v. 21 we read, "As the Father raiseth up the dead, and quickeneth them: even so the Son *quickeneth whom he will.*" The same line of thought continues through to the end of v. 26. Thus, Christ there presents Himself in full Godhead title, as the Source and Dispenser of life, sovereignly imparted to whom He pleases. The one upon whom this Divine life is bestowed, as illustrated by the case of the impotent man, is regarded as entirely *passive;* he is called into life by the all-mighty, creating voice of the Son of God (v. 25). There is nothing in the sinner's case but the powerlessness of death until the deep silence is broken by the word of the Divine Quickener. *His* voice makes itself heard in the soul, hitherto dead, but no longer dead as it hears His voice. But nothing is said of any searchings of heart, any exercises of conscience, any sense of need, any felt desire after Christ. It is simply Christ, in Divine sufficiency, speaking to spiritually dead souls, empowering them (by sovereign "quickening") to hear.

In John 6 Christ is presented in quite another character, and in keeping with this, so is the sinner too. Here our Lord is viewed not in His essential glories, but as the Son incarnate. Here He is contemplated as "the Son of man" (vv. 27, 53), and therefore, as in the place of humiliation, "come down from heaven" (vv. 33, 38, 51, etc.). As such, Christ is made known as the Object of desire, and as the One who can meet the sinner's need. In John 5 it was Christ who *sought out* the "great multitude" of impotent folk (vv. 3, 6), and when Christ presented Himself to the man who had an infirmity thirty and eight years, *he* evidenced no desire for the Saviour. He acted as one who had no heart whatever for the Son of God. As such he accurately portrayed the dead soul when it is first quickened by Christ. But in John 6 the contrast is very noticeable. Here the "great multitude" *followed him* (vv. 2, 24, 25), with an evident desire for Him—we speak not now of the unworthy motive that prompted that desire, but the desire itself as *illustrative* of a truth. It is this contrast which indicates the importance of noting the relation of John 5 and 6. As said in our opening sentences, the latter is the sequel to the former. We mean that *the order* in the contents of the two chapters, so far as their contents are typical and illustrative, set forth the *doctrinal order* of truth. They give us the *two* sides: the Divine and the human; and here, as ever, the Divine comes first. In John 5 we have the *quickening* power of Christ, as exercised according to His sovereign prerogative; in John 6 we have illustrated the *effects* of this in a soul already quickened. In the one, Christ approaches the dead soul; in the other, the dead soul, now quickened, *seeks* Christ!

In developing this illustration of the truth in John 6, the Holy Spirit has followed the same order as in John 5. Here, too, Christ works a miracle, on those who typically portray the doctrinal characters which are in view. These are sinners already "quickened," but not yet saved; for, unlike quickening, there is a *human* side to salvation, as well as a Divine. The prominent thing brought before us in the first section of John 6 is *a hungry multitude.* And how forcibly and how accurately they illustrate the condition of a soul just quickened, is obvious. As soon as the Divine life has been imparted, there is a stirring within; there is a sense of need awakened. It is the life turning toward its Source, just as water ever seeks its own level. The illustration is Divinely apt, for there are few things of which we are more *conscious* than when we are assailed by the pangs of hunger. But not so with a *dead* man, for he is unconscious; or with a *paralyzed* man, for he is incapable of feeling. So it is spiritually. The one who is dead in trespasses and sins, and paralyzed by depravity, has no hunger for God. But how different with one who has been Divinely "quickened"! The first effect of quickening is that the one quickened awakes to consciousness: the Divine life within gives capacity to discern his sinfulness and his need of Christ.

Mark, too, what follows in the second section of John 6. The same line of truth is pursued further. Here we see the disciples in darkness, in the midst of a storm, rowing towards the Place of Consolation. What a vivid illustration does this supply of the experiences of the newly quickened and so *awakened* soul! It tells of the painful experiences through which he passes ere the Haven of Rest is reached. Not yet is he really saved; not yet does he understand the workings of Divine grace within him. All he is conscious of is his sense of deep need. And it is then that Satan's fiendish onslaughts are usually the fiercest. Into what a storm is he now plunged! But the Devil is not permitted to completely overwhelm the soul, any more than he was the disciples in the illustration. When God's appointed time arrives, Christ draws nigh and says, "I am: be not afraid." *He* stands revealed before the one who was seeking Him, and *then* is He "*willingly* received into the ship"—He is gladly embraced by faith, and received into the heart! *Then* the storm is over, the desired haven is reached, for the next thing we see is Christ and the disciples *at* "Capernaum" (place of consolation). Thus, in the feeding of the *hungry* multitude, and in the delivering of the disciples from *the storm-tossed sea,* we have a most blessed and wonderful illustration of Christ meeting and satisfying the conscious need of the soul previously quickened.

It will thus be seen that all of this is but introductory to the great theme unfolded in the middle section of John 6. Just as the healing of the impotent man at the beginning of John 5 introduced and prepared the way for the discourse that followed, so it is in John 6. Here the prominent truth is Christ in the place of humiliation, which He had voluntarily entered as man, "come down from heaven"; and thus as "the bread of life" presenting Himself as the Object who alone can supply the need of which the quickened and awakened soul is so conscious*.

"Then said they unto him, What shall we do, that we might work the works of God?" (6:28). This question appears to be the language of men temporarily impressed and aroused, but still in the dark concerning the way to Heaven. They felt, perhaps, that they were on the wrong road, that something was required of them, but what that something was they knew not. They supposed they had to *do* some work; but *what* works they were ignorant. It was the old self-righteousness of the natural man, who is ever occupied with his own doings. The carnal mind is flattered when it is consciously *doing* something for God. For his doings man deems himself entitled to reward. He imagines that salvation is due him, because he has *earned* it. Thus does he reckon the reward "not of grace, but of debt." Man seeks to bring God into the humbling position of debtor *to him.* How unbelief and pride degrade the Almighty! How they rob Him of His glory!

"What shall we do that we might work the works of God?" It seems almost incredible that these men should have asked such

* We do not think the time would be wasted if the above paragraphs were re-read before proceeding farther.

a question. Only a moment before, Christ had said to them "Labour not for the meat which perisheth, but for that meat which endureth unto everlasting life, which the Son of man shall *give* unto you" (v. 27). But the carnal mind, which is enmity against God, is unable to rise to the thought of a gift. Or, rather, the carnal heart is unwilling to *come down* to the place of a beggar and a pauper, and receive everything for nothing. The sinner wants to do something to earn it. It was thus with the woman at the well: until Divine grace completed its work within her, she knew not the "gift of God" (John 4:10). It was the same with the rich young ruler: "Good Master, what shall I *do* to inherit eternal life?" (Luke 18:18). It was the same with the stricken Jews on the day of Pentecost: "Men and brethren, what shall we *do*?" (Acts 2:37). It was the same with the Philippian jailer: "Sirs, what must I *do* to be saved?" (Acts 16:30). So it was with the prodigal son—"Make me as one of thy *hired servants*" (one who *works* for what he receives) was his thought (Luke 15:19). Ah! dear friends, God and man are ever the same wherever you find them!

"Jesus answered and said unto them, This is the work of God, that ye believe on him whom he hath sent" (6:29). In what lovely patient grace did the Lord make reply! In blessed simplicity of language, He stated that the one thing that God requires of sinners is that they *believe* on the One whom He has sent into the world to meet their deepest need. "This is the work of God" means, this is what God requires. It is not the works of the law, nor the bringing of an offering to His temple altar; but faith in Christ. Christ is the Saviour appointed by God, and *faith in Him* is that which God approves, and without which nothing else can be acceptable in His sight. Paul answered the question of the Philippian jailer as the Lord before him had done—"What must I *do* to be saved?": "*Believe* on the Lord Jesus Christ and thou shalt be saved" was the reply (Acts 16:31). But again we say, Man had rather *do* than "believe." And why is this? Because it panders to his pride: because it repudiates his utter ruin, inasmuch as it is a denial that he is "without strength" (Rom. 5:6): because it provides for him a platform on which he can boast and glory. Nevertheless, the one and only "work" which God will accept is faith in His Son.

But, perhaps some one will raise the question, Is it possible that I can ever enter heaven without good works? Answer: No; you cannot enter heaven without a good character. But those good works and that character of yours must be *without a flaw*. They must be as holy as God, or you can never enter *His* presence. But how may I secure such a character as that? Surely that is utterly impossible! No, it is not. But how then? By a series of *strivings* after holiness? No; that is *doing* again. Do nothing. Only believe. Accept the Work already done—the finished work of the Lord Jesus on our behalf. This is what God asks of you—give up your own doings and receive that of My beloved Son. But are you ready to do this? Are you willing to abandon your own doings, your own righteousness, and to accept His? You will not till you are thoroughly convinced that *all* your doings are faulty, that all *your* efforts fall far short of God's demands, that all your own righteousness is tarnished with sin, yea, is as "filthy rags." What man will renounce his own work in order to trust to that of another, unless he be first convinced that his own is worthless? What man will repose for safety in another till he be convinced that there is no safety in trusting to himself? It is impossible. Man cannot do this of himself: it takes "the work of God." It is the convicting power of the Holy Spirit, and that alone, which brings the sinner to *renounce* his own works and *lay hold* on the Lord Jesus for salvation.

O dear reader, we would solemnly press this upon you. Is the finished work of Christ the *only* rock on which your soul is resting for eternal life, or are you still secretly trusting to your own doings for salvation? If so, you will be eternally lost, for the mouth of the Lord hath spoken it—"He that believeth not shall be damned." Your own doings, even if they were such as you wish them to be, could never save you. Your prayers, your tears, your sorrowings for sin, your alms-givings, your church-goings, your efforts at holiness of life—what are they all but *doings* of your own, and if they were all perfect they could not save you. Why? Because it is written, "By the deeds of the law there shall no flesh be justified in his sight." Salvation is not a thing to be *earned* by a religious life, but is a free gift received by faith – Rom. 6:23.

"They said therefore unto him, What sign showest thou then, that we may see, and believe thee? What dost thou work?" (6:30). How this exhibits the works of unbelief! How difficult it is, yea impossible, for the natural man, of himself, to accept Christ and His finished work by "simple" faith! Truly, nothing but the Spirit of God can enable a man to do it. The Lord had said, "Believe." They replied, "Show us *a sign*." Give us something we can *see* along with it. Man must either see or feel *before* he will believe. "We do not mean to say that salvation is not by believing on Christ, but we want some *evidence* first. We will believe if we can have some evidence on which to believe. Oh, perfect picture of the natural heart! I come to a man – one who has probably for years been making a profession of religion – and I say to him, 'Have you got eternal life dwelling in you? Do you know that you are a saved man, that you have passed from death unto life?' The reply is, 'No, I am not sure of it.' Then you do not believe on the Lord Jesus. You have not accepted the finished work of Christ as yours. He replies, 'Yes, I do believe on Christ.' Then remember what He has said, 'He that believeth *hath* everlasting life.' He does not *hope* to have it. He is not *uncertain* about it. 'He *hath* it,' says the Son of God. The man answers, 'Well, I would believe this if I could only feel better. If I could only see in myself some *evidences* of a change, then I could believe it, and be as certain of it as you are.' So said these people to the Lord – give us some evidence that we may see and believe. Do you not see that you are thus making salvation depend on the evidences of the Spirit's work *within* you, instead of the finished work of the Lord Jesus *for* you? You say, I would believe if I could only *feel* better – if I could only *see* a change. God says, Believe *first*, then you shall feel – then you shall see. God reverses your order, and you must reverse it too, if you would ever have peace with God. Believe, and you will then have in your heart a *motive* for a holy life, and not only so, you will walk in liberty, and peace, and joy" (Dr. F. Whitfield).

"They said therefore unto him, What sign showest thou then, that we may see, and believe thee? What dost thou work?" The force of that is this: You have asked us to receive you as the One sent of God. What sign, then do you show; where are your credentials to authorize your mission? And this was asked, be it remembered, on the morning following the feeding of the five thousand! It seems unthinkable. Only a few hours before they had witnessed a miracle, which in some respects, was the most remarkable our Lord had performed, and from which they had themselves benefitted. And yet, does not our own sad history testify that this is true to life? Men are surrounded by innumerable evidences for the existence of God: they carry a hundred demonstrations of it in their own persons, and yet how often do they ask, What *proof* have we that there *is* a God? So, too, with believers. We enjoy countless tokens of His love and faithfulness; we have witnessed His delivering hand again and again, and yet when some fresh trial comes upon us—something which completely upsets *our* plans, the removal, perchance, of some earthly object around which we had entwined our heart's affections—we ask, Does God really care? And, maybe, we are sufficiently callous to ask for another "sign" in proof that He does!

"Our fathers did eat manna in the desert; as it is written, He gave them bread from heaven to eat" (6:31). Here they drew a disparaging contrast between Christ and Moses. It was the further workings of their unbelief. The force of their objection was this: What proof have we that Thou art greater than Moses? They sought to deprecate the miracle they had witnessed on the previous day by comparing Moses and the manna. It was as though they had said, 'If you would have us believe on you as the Sent One of God, you must show us greater works. You have fed five thousand *but once,* whereas in Moses' day, our fathers at bread for forty years!' It is striking to note how they harped back to their "fathers." The woman at the well did the same thing (see 4:12). And is it not so now? The experiences of "the fathers", what *they* believed and taught, is still with many the final court of appeal.

"Our fathers did eat manna in the desert; as it is written, He gave them bread from heaven to eat." Their speech betrayed them, as is evident from their use of the word "manna." The late Malachi Taylor pointed out how this was "a name always used by their father, of wilfulness, persistently ignoring Jehovah's word 'bread', and now uttered by them, because it was so written. It is notable that they of old never called it anything at all but 'manna' (meaning 'What is this?'), except when they dispised it (Num. 21:5); and then they called it 'light bread.' And Jehovah named it 'manna' in Num. 11:7 when the mixed multitude fell a lusting for the flesh-pots of Egypt. What lessons for us as to our thoughts of Christ, the Bread of God! In Psa. 78:24, where God is recounting the *evil ways* of Israel through the wilderness, He calls it 'manna'; but in Psa. 105:40, where all *His mercies* pass in review, calling for praise, it is called 'bread'. Again we say, What lessons for us!"

"Then Jesus said unto them, Verily, verily, I say unto you, Moses gave you not the bread from heaven; but my Father giveth you the true bread from heaven" (6:32). With good reason might our blessed Lord have turned away from His insulting challengers. Well might He have left them to themselves. But as another has said, "Grace in Him was active. Their souls' interests He had at heart" (C.E.S.). And so, in wondrous condescension, He speaks to them of the Father's "Gift", who alone could meet their deep need, and satisfy their souls. And has He not often dealt thus with thee, dear reader? Cannot you say with the Psalmist, "He hath not dealt with us after our sins; nor rewarded us according to our iniquities" (Psa. 103:10)? Instead of turning away in disgust at our ingratitude and unbelief, He has continued to care for us and minister to us. O how thankful ought we to be for that precious promise, and the daily fulfillment of it in our lives, "I will *never* leave thee, nor forsake thee."

"Then Jesus said unto them, Verily, verily, I say unto you, Moses gave you not that bread from heaven; but my Father giveth you the true bread from heaven." The error of the Jews here should be a warning to us. They thought Moses gave them the manna. But it was God and not Moses. He was only the humble instrument. They ought to have looked through the instrument to God. But the eye rested, where it is ever so prone to rest—on the human medium. The Lord here leads them to look beyond the human instrument to God—"Moses gave you not that bread . . . but my Father," etc. O what creatures of sense we are. We live so much in the outward and visible, as almost to forget there is anything beyond. All that we gaze upon here is but the avenue to what eye hath not seen, nor ear heard. All the temporal gifts and blessings we receive are but the finger of the Father beckoning us within the inner shrine. He is saying to us, 'If My works be so beautiful, if My gifts be so precious, if My footprints be so glorious, what must *I* be?' Thus should we ever look through nature, to nature's God. Thus shall we enjoy God's gifts, when they lead us up to Him; and then shall we not make idols of them, and so run the risk of their removal. Everything in nature and in providence is but the "Moses" between us and God. Let us not be like the Jews of old, so taken up with Moses as to forget the "greater than Moses," whence they all proceed.

"For the bread of God is he which cometh down from heaven, and giveth life unto the world" (6:33). The Father's provision for a dying world was to send from heaven His only begotten Son. There is another suggestive contrast here, yea, a double one. The manna had no power to ward off death—the generation of Israel that ate it in the wilderness died! How, then, could *it* be the "true bread"? No; *Christ* is the "true bread," for He bestows "life." But again: the manna was only for Israel. No other people in the desert (the Amorites, for instance) partook of the manna; for it fell only in Israel's camp. But the true Bread "giveth life unto the world." The "world" here does not include the whole human race, for Christ does not *bestow* "life" on every descendant of Adam. It is not here said that the true Bread *offereth* "life unto the world," but He "*giveth* life." It is the "world" of believers who are here in view. The Lord, then, designedly employs a word that reached beyond the limits of Israel, and took in elect Gentiles too!

"For the bread of God is he which cometh down from heaven, and giveth life unto the world." Three different expressions are used by our Lord in this passage, each having a slightly varied meaning; the three together, serving to bring out the fulness and blessedness of this title. In v. 32 He speaks of Himself as the "true bread from heaven": "true" speaks of that which is real, genuine, satisfying; "from heaven" tells of its celestial and spiritual character. In v. 33 He speaks of Himself as "the bread of God," which denotes that He is Divine, eternal. Then, in v. 35 He says, "I am the bread of life": the One who imparts, nourishes and sustains life.

"Then said they unto him, Lord, evermore give us this bread" (6:34). This was but the outcome of a fleeting impression which had been made by His words. It reminds us very much of the language of the woman at the well, "Sir, give me this water, that I thirst not, neither come hither to draw" (4:15), and those who recall our comments on that verse will remember the motive that prompted her. The words of these men but served to make their rejection of Him more manifest and decisive when they fully grasped His meaning: v. 36 proves this conclusively—"But I said unto you, That ye also have seen me, and believe not."

"And Jesus said unto them, I am the bread of life" (6:35). The Lord places Himself before us under the figure of bread. The emblem is beautifully significant, and like all others used in Scripture calls for prolonged and careful meditation. First, bread is a *necessary* food. Unlike many other articles of diet which are more or less luxuries, this is essential to our very existence. Bread is the food we cannot dispense with. There are other things placed upon our tables that we can do without, but not so with bread. Let us learn the lesson well. Without Christ we shall perish. There is no spiritual life or health apart from the Bread of God.

Second, bread is a food that is *suited to all.* There are some people who cannot eat sweets; others are unable to digest meats. But *all* eat bread. The physical body may retain its life for a time without bread, but it will be sickly, and soon sink into the grave. Bread, then is adapted to all. It is the food of both king and artisan. So it is with Christ. It meets the need of all alike; He is able to satisfy every class of sinners—rich or poor, cultured or illiterate.

Third, bread is a *daily* food. There are some articles of food which we eat but occasionally; others only when they are in season. But bread is something we need every day of our lives. It is so spiritually. If the Christian fails to feed on Christ daily, if he substitutes the husks of religious forms and ceremonies, religious books, religious excitement, the glare and glitter of modern Christianity, he will be weak and sickly. It is failure at this very point which is mainly responsible for the feebleness of so many of the Lord's people.

Fourth, bread is a *satisfying* food. We quickly tire of other articles of diet, but not so with this. Bread is a staple and standard article, which we must use all our lives. And does not the analogy hold good again spiritually? How often have we turned aside to other things, only to find them but husks! None but the Bread of life can satisfy.

Fifth, let us note *the process* through which bread passes before it becomes food. It springs up—the blade, the ear, the full corn in the ear. Then it is *cut down,* winnowed, and *ground* into flour, and finally subjected to the *fiery* process of the oven. Thus, and only thus, did it become fit to sustain life. Believer in Christ, such was the experiences of the Bread of God. He was "*bruised* for our iniquities." He was subjected to the fierce fires of God's holy wrath, as He took our place in judgment. O how wonderful—God forbid that we should ever lose our sense of wonderment over it. The Holy One of God, was "made a curse for us." "It pleased the Lord to bruise him." And this in order that He might be the *Bread* of life to us! Let us then feed upon Him. Let us draw from His infinite fullness. Let us ever press forward unto a more intimate fellowship with Him.

"And Jesus said unto them, I am the bread of life: he that cometh to me shall never hunger; and he that believeth on me shall never thirst" (6:35). In v. 33 Christ had spoken of giving life to "the world"—the world of believers, the sum total of the saved. Now He speaks of the individual—"*he* that cometh to me . . . *he* that believeth." A similar order is to be observed in v. 37—note the "all" is followed by "him." There is, no doubt, a shade of difference between "believing on" Christ, and "coming to" Him. To "believe on" Christ is to receive God's testimony concerning His Son, and to rest on Him alone for salvation. To "come to" Him—which is really the effect of the former—is for the heart to go out to Him in loving confidence. The two acts are carefully distinguished in Heb. 11:6: "without faith it is impossible to please him: for he that cometh to God must believe that he is: and that he is the rewarder of them that diligently seek him." I must know who the physician is, and believe in his ability, before I shall go to him to be cured.

But what are we to understand by "shall never hunger" and "shall never thirst"? Does the Christian *never* "hunger" or "thirst"? Surely; then, how are we to harmonize his experience with this positive declaration of the Saviour? Ah! He speaks here according to the fulness and satisfaction there is *in Himself*, and not according to our imperfect apprehension and appreciation of Him. If we are straitened it is in ourselves, not in Him. If we *do* "hunger" and "thirst," it is not because He is unable, and not because He is unwilling, to satisfy our hunger and quench our thirst, but because we are of "little faith" and fail to draw daily from His fulness.

"But I said unto you, That ye also have seen me, and believe not" (6:36). Even the sight of Christ in the flesh, and the beholding of His wondrous miracles, did not bring men to believe on Him. O the depravity of the human heart! "Ye also have seen me, and believe not." This shows how valueless was their request: "Lord, evermore give us this bread" (v. 34). It is unspeakably solemn. They trusted in Moses (9:28), they had rejoiced for a season in John the Baptist's light (5:35); they could quote the Scriptures (6:31), and yet they believed not on Christ! It is difficult to say how far a man may go, and yet come short of the one thing needful. These men were not worse than many others, but their unbelief was manifested and declared; consequently, Christ addresses them accordingly. This, indeed, would be the result in every case, were we left to our own thoughts of Christ. Be warned then, dear reader, and make sure that *yours* is a *saving* faith.

"But I said unto you, that ye also have seen me, and believe not." Was, then, the incarnation a failure? Was His mission fruitless? That could not be. There can be no failure with God, though there is much failure in all of us to understand His purpose. Christ was not in anywise discouraged or disheartened at the apparent failure of His mission. His next word shows that very conclusively, and to it we turn.

"All that the Father giveth me shall come to me" (6:37). Here the Lord speaks of a definite company which have been given to Him by the Father. Nor is this the only place where He makes mention of this people. In John 17 He refers to them seven times over. In v. 2 He says, "As thou hast given him power over all flesh, that he should give eternal life to *as many as thou hast given him.*" So again in v. 6 He says, "I have manifested thy name unto the men *which thou gavest me* out of the world: Thine they were, and thou gavest them me." And again in v. 9 He declares, "I pray not for the world, but *for them which thou hast given me;* for they are thine." See also verses 11, 12, 24. Whom those are that the Father gave to Christ we are told in Eph. 1:4—"According as he hath *chosen* us in him before the foundation of the world." Those given to Christ were God's *elect,* singled out for this marvellous honor before the foundation of the world: "God hath from the beginning chosen you to salvation" (II Thess. 2:13). But let us notice the exact connection in our passage wherein Christ refers to the elect.

In v. 36 we find our Lord saying to those who had no heart for Him, "ye also have seen me, and believe not." Was He, then, disheartened? Far from it. And why not? Ah! mark how the Son of God, here the lowly Servant of Jehovah, *encourages* Himself. He immediately adds, "All that the Father giveth me *shall* come to me." What a lesson is this for every under shepherd. Here is the true haven of rest for the heart of every Christ worker. Your message may be slighted by the crowd, and as you see how many there are who "believe not" it may appear that your labor is in vain. Nevertheless "the foundation of God *standeth sure,* having this seal, the Lord knoweth *them that are his*" (II Tim. 2:19). The eternal purpose of the Almighty cannot fail; the sovereign will of the Lord Most High cannot be frustrated. *All,* every one, that the Father gave to the Son before the foundation of the world *"shall* come to him." The Devil himself cannot keep one *of them* away. So take heart fellow-worker. You may seem to be sowing the Seed at random, but God will see to it that part of it falls onto ground which He has prepared. The realization of the invincibility of the eternal counsels of God will give you a calmness, a poise, a courage, a perseverance which nothing else can. "Therefore, my beloved brethren, be ye steadfast, unmoveable, always abounding in the work of the Lord, forasmuch as *ye know* that your labor is *not in vain* in the Lord" (I Cor. 15:58).

"All that the Father giveth me shall come to me." But while this is very blessed, it is solemnly tragic and deeply humbling. How humiliating for us, that in the presence of incarnate life and love in the person of the Lord of glory, no one would have come to Him, *none* would have benefitted by His mission, had there not been those who were given to Him by the Father, and on whose coming He could, therefore, reckon. Man's depravity is so entire, his enmity so great, that in *every* instance, his will would have resisted and rejected Christ, had not the Father determined that His Son *should have* some as the trophies of His victory and the reward of His coming down from heaven. Alas that our deadness to such love should have called forth such sighs as seem to breathe in these very words of Christ!

"And him that cometh to me I will in no wise cast out" (6:37). Let us not miss (as is so commonly done) the connection between this clause and the one which precedes it. "Him that cometh to me" is explained by "all that the Father giveth me." *None* would come to Him unless the Father had first predestinated that they should, for it is only *"as many as* were ordained to eternal life" that believe (Acts 13:48). Each one that the Father had given to Christ in eternity past, "cometh" to Him in time—comes as a lost sinner to be saved; comes having nothing, that he may receive everything.

The last clause "I will in no wise cast out" assures the eternal preservation of everyone that truly cometh to Christ. These words of the Saviour do not signify (as generally supposed) that

He promises to *reject none* who really come to Him, *though that is true;* but they declare that under no imaginable circumstances will He ever expel any one that *has* come. Peter came to Him and was saved. Later, he *denied* his Master with an oath. But did Christ "cast him out"? Nay, verily. And can we find a more extreme case? If Peter *was not* "cast out," *no* Christian ever was, or ever will be. Praise the Lord!

"For I came down from heaven, not to do mine own will, but the will of him that sent me" (6:38). This is most instructive. The force of it is this: Those whom the Father had given the Son—*all* of them—*would* come to Him. It was no longer the Son in His essential glory, quickening whom *He* would, as in 5:21, but the Son incarnate, the "Son of man" (6:27), *receiving* those the Father "drew" to Him (6:44)! "Therefore be it who it might, He would in no wise cast him out: enemy, scoffer, Jew or Gentile, they would not come if the Father had not sent them" (J.N.D.). Christ was here to do *the Father's* will. Thus does Christ assure His own that He will save to the end *all* whom the Father had given Him.

"For I came down from heaven not to do mine own will, but the will of him that sent me." How greatly does this enhance the value of the precious words at the close of the preceding verse, when we see that our *coming to Christ* is not attributed to man's fickle will, but as the effect of the Father's drawing to the Saviour each one given to Him in the counsels of that Father's love before the foundation of the world! So, too, the *reception* of them is not merely because of Christ's compassion for the lost, but as the obedient Servant of the Father's will, He welcomes each one brought to Him—brought by the unseen drawings of the Father's love. Thus our security rests *not upon anything in us or from us,* but upon the Father's choice and the Son's obedient love!

"And this is the Father's will which hath sent me, that of all which he hath given me I should lose nothing, but should raise it up again at the last day" (6:39). How blessedly this, too, explains the closing words of v. 37! *Eternal predestination guarantees eternal preservation.* The "last day" is, of course, the last day of the Christian dispensation. *Then* it shall *appear* that He *hath not* lost a single one whom the Father gave to Him. Then shall He say, "Behold I and the children which God hath given me" (Heb. 2:13).

"And this is the will of him that sent me, that every one which seeth the Son, and believeth on him, may have everlasting life: and I will raise him up at the last day" (6:40). Christ had just spoken of the Father's counsels. He had disclosed the fact that the success of His ministry depended not on man's will—for that was known to be, in every case, so perverse as to *reject* the Saviour—but on the drawing power of the Father. But here He leaves, as it were, the door wide open to any one any where who is disposed to enter: "that *every one* which seeth the Son, and believeth on him, may have everlasting life." Yet it is instructive to note the order of the two verbs here: "believing" on Christ is the result of "seeing" Him. He must first be *revealed* by the Spirit *before* He will be received by the sinner. Thus did our Lord disclose to these men that a far deeper and infinitely more important work had been entrusted to Him than that of satisfying Israel's poor with material bread—not less a change than that of raising up at the last day all that had been given to Him by the Father, without losing so much as one.

The following questions are submitted to help the student for the next chapter on John 6:41-59:—

1. Wherein does v. 44 rebuke their "murmuring"?
2. What ought to have been their response to v. 44?
3. Who are the "all" that are "taught of God"? v.45.
4. What is meant by "not die"? v. 50.
5. What are the various thoughts suggested by "eat"? v. 51.
6. What is the difference in thought between vv. 53 and 56?
7. What is meant by "I live by the Father"? v. 57.

CHAPTER TWENTY-THREE

Christ in the Capernaum Synagogue

John 6:41-59

The following is submitted as an Analysis of the passage which is to be before us:

1. The murmuring of the Jews: vv. 41, 42.
2. Christ's rebuke: vv. 43-45.
3. The glory of Christ: v. 46.
4. Christ, the Life-giver: vv. 47-51.
5. The criticism of the Jews: v. 52.
6. Christ's solemn reply: v. 53.
7. The results of feeding on Christ: vv. 54-59.

The first thirteen verses of John 6 describe the feeding of the multitude, and in vv. 14 and 15 we are shown what effect that miracle had upon the crowd. From v. 16 to the end of v. 21 we have the well-known incident of the disciples in the storm, and the Lord walking on the sea and coming to their deliverance. In vv. 22 to 25 we see the people following Christ to Capernaum, and in vv. 26 to 40 we learn of the conversation which took place between them and our Lord—most probably in the open air. At v. 41 there is a break in the chapter, and a new company is introduced, namely, "the Jews"; and from v. 59 it is clear that *they* were in the synagogue. In this Gospel "the Jews" are ever viewed as antagonistic to the Saviour—see our notes on 5:15. Here they are represented as "murmuring" because the Lord had said, "I am the bread which came down from heaven." This does not prove that *they* had heard His words which are recorded in v. 33. Note it does not say in v. 41 that the Lord had said *this* "unto them": contrast vv. 29, 32, 35! Most probably, the words He had spoken to "the people" of v. 24—words which are recorded in the verses which follow, to the end of v. 40—had been *reported* to "the Jews." Hence, vv. 41 to 59 describe the conversation between Christ and the Jews in the Capernaum synagogue, as the preceding verses narrate what passed between the Saviour and the Galileans. The Holy Spirit has placed the two conversations side by side, because of the similarity of their themes.

"The Jews then murmured at him, because he said, I am the bread which came down from heaven" (6:41). "In John 'the Jews' are always distinguished from the multitude. They are the inhabitants of Jerusalem and Judea. It would, perhaps, be easier to understand this Gospel, if the words were rendered 'those of Judea', which is the true sense" (J.N.D.). These Jews were "murmuring," and it is a significant thing that the same word is used here as in the Septuagint (the first Gentile translation of the Hebrew Old Testament) of Israel murmuring in the wilderness. In few things does the depravity of the human heart reveal itself so plainly and so frequently as in *murmuring* against God. It is a sin which few, if any, are preserved from.

The Jews were murmuring against Christ. They were murmuring against Him because He had said, "I am the bread which came down from heaven." This was a saying that offended them. And why should *that* cause them to murmur? They were, of course, completely blind to Christ's Divine glory, and so were ignorant that this very One whom some of them had seen grow up before their eyes in the humble home of Joseph and Mary in Nazareth, and the One that some of them, perhaps, had seen working at the carpenter's bench, should make a claim which they quickly perceived avowed His Deity. It was the pride of the human heart disdaining to be indebted to One who had lain aside His glory, and had taken upon Him the form of a servant. They refused to be beholden to One so lowly. Moreover, they were far too self-satisfied and self-righteous to see any need for One to come down from heaven *to them,* much less for that One to die upon the Cross to meet their need and thus become their Saviour. *Their* case, as they thought, was by no means so desperate as that. The truth is, they had *no hunger* for "the bread which came down from heaven." What light this casts on the state of the world today! How it serves to explain the common treatment which the Lord of glory still receives at the hands of men! Pride, the wicked pride of the self-righteous heart, is responsible for unbelief. Men despise and reject the Saviour because they feel not their deep need of Him. Feeding upon the husks which are fit food only for swine, they have no appetite for the true Bread. And when the claims of Christ are really pressed upon them they still "murmur"!

"And they said, Is not this Jesus, the son of Joseph, whose father and mother we know? how is it then that he saith, I came down from heaven?" (6:42). This shows that these Jews understood Christ's words "I am the bread which came down from heaven" as signifying that He was of Divine origin; and in this they were quite right. None but He could truthfully make the claim. This declaration of Christ meant that He had personally existed in heaven before He appeared among men, and, as His forerunner testified, "He that cometh from above is above all" (John 3:31): above all, because the first man and all his family are of the earth, earthy; but "the second man is the Lord from heaven" (I Cor. 15:47). And for the Lord to become Man required the miracle of the virgin birth: a supernatural Being could only enter this world in a supernatural manner. But these Jews were in total ignorance of Christ's superhuman origin. They supposed Him to be the natural son of Joseph and Mary. His "father and mother," said they, "we *know*." But they did not. His Father, they knew not of, nor could they, unless the Father revealed Himself unto them. And it is so still. It is one thing to receive, intellectually, as a religious dogma, that Jesus Christ is the Son of God; it is altogether another to *know* Him as such for myself. Flesh and blood cannot reveal this to me (Matt. 16:17).

"Jesus therefore answered and said unto them, Murmur not among yourselves. No man can come to me, except the Father which hath sent me draw him: and I will raise him up at the last day" (6:43, 44). This word is very solemn coming just at this point, and it is necessary to note carefully its exact connection. It was a word which at once exposed the moral condition and explained the cause of the "murmuring" of these Jews. Great care must be taken to observe what Christ did not say, and precisely what He did say. He did not say, "No man can come to me, except the Father hath given him to me," true as that certainly is. But He spoke here so as to address their human responsibility. It was not designed as a word to repel, but to humble. It was not closing the door in their face, but showed how alone that door could be entered. It was not intended as an intimation that there was no possible hope for them, rather was it a pointing out the direction in which hope lay. Had Saul of Tarsus then been among the number who heard these searching words of Christ, they would have applied in full force in his own case and condition; and yet it became manifest, subsequently, that *he* was a vessel of mercy, given to the Son by the Father before the foundation of the world. And it is quite possible that some of these very Jews, then murmuring, were among the number who, at Pentecost, were drawn by the Father to believe on the Son. The Lord's language was carefully chosen, and left room for that. John 7:5 tells us that the Lord's own brethren (according to the flesh) did not believe on Him at first, and yet, later, they ranked among His disciples, as is clear from Acts 1:14. Let us be careful, then, not to read *into* this 44th verse what is not there.

"No man can come to me, except the Father which hath sent me draw him" (6:44). These words of Christ make manifest the depths of human depravity. They expose the inveterate stubbornness of the human will. They explain the "murmuring" of these Jews. In answering them thus, the obvious meaning of the Saviour's words was this: By your murmuring you make it evident that *you* have not come to Me, that you are not disposed to come to Me; and with your present self-righteousness, you never will come to Me. Before you come to Me you must be converted and become as little children. And before that can take place, you must be the subjects of Divine operation. One has only to reflect on the condition of the natural man in order to see the indubitable truth of this. Salvation is most exactly suited to the sinner's needs, but it is not at all suited to his natural inclinations. The Gospel is too spiritual for his carnal mind: too humbling for his pride: too exacting for his rebellious will: too lofty for his darkened understanding: too holy for his earth-bound desires.

"No man can come to me, except the Father which hath sent me draw him." How can one who has a high conceit of himself and his religious performances admit that all his righteousnesses are as filthy rags? How can one who prides himself on his morality and his religiousness, own himself as lost, undone, and justly condemned? How can one who sees so little amiss in himself, who is *blind* to the fact that from the crown of his head to the sole of his foot there is no soundness in him (Isa. 1:6), earnestly seek the great Physician? No man with an *un*changed heart and mind will ever embrace God's salvation. The inability here, then, is a moral one. Just as when Christ also said, "*how can ye,* being evil, speak good things?" (Matt. 12:34). And again, "*How can ye believe,* which receive honour one of another?" (John 5:44). And again, "Even the Spirit of truth; whom the world *cannot* receive" (John 14:17). Water will not flow uphill, nor will the natural man act contrary to his corrupt nature. An evil tree cannot bring forth good fruit, and equally impossible is it for a heart that loves the darkness to also love the light.

The depravity of man is, from the human side, the only thing which will explain the general rejection of the Gospel. The only satisfactory answer to the questions, Why is not Christ cordially received by all to whom He is presented? Why do the majority of men despise and reject Him? is—man is a fallen creature, a depraved being who loves sin and hates holiness. So, too, the only satisfactory answer which can be given to the questions, Why is the Gospel cordially received by any man? Why is it not obstinately rejected by all? is, In the case of those who believe, God has, by His supernatural influence, counteracted against the human depravity; in other words, the Father has "drawn" to the Son.

The condition of the natural man is altogether beyond human repair. To talk about exerting the will is to ignore the state of the man behind the will. Man's will has not escaped the general wreckage of his nature. When man fell, *every* part of his being was affected. Just as truly as the sinner's heart is estranged from God and his understanding darkened, so is his will enslaved by sin. To predicate the freedom of the will is to *deny* that man is totally depraved. To say that man *has* the power within himself to either reject or accept Christ, is to *repudiate* the fact that he is the captive of the Devil. It is to say *there is* at least one good thing in the flesh. It is to flatly contradict this word of the Son of God—"No man *can* come to me, *except* the Father which hath sent me draw him."

Man's only hope lies *outside* of himself, in Divine help. And this is what we meant above when we said that this word of Christ was not intended to close the door of hope, but pointed out the direction in which hope lay. If it be true that I cannot get away from myself; if it be true that my whole being is depraved, and therefore at enmity with God; if it be true that I am powerless to reverse the tendency of my nature, what then can I do? Why, *acknowledge* my helplessness, and *cry* for help. What should a man do who falls down and breaks his hip? He cannot rise: should he, then, lie there in his misery and perish? Not if he has *any desire for relief*. He will lift up his voice and summon assistance. And if these murmuring Jews had *believed* what Christ told them about their helplessness, this is what *they* had done. And if the unsaved today would only believe God when He says that the sinner is *lost,* he, too, would call for a Deliverer. If I cannot come to Christ except the Father "draws" me, then my responsibility is to *beg* the Father *to* "draw" me.

In what, we may inquire, does this "drawing" consist? It certainly has reference to something more than the invitation of the Gospel. The word used is a strong one, signifiying, the putting forth of power and *obliging* the object seized to respond. The same word is found in John 18:10; 21:6, 11. If the reader consults these passages he will find that it means far more than "to attract." *Impel* would give the true force of it here in John 6:44.

As said above, the unregenerate sinner is so depraved that with an unchanged heart and mind he will never come to Christ. And the change which is absolutely essential is one which God alone can produce. It is, therefore, by Divine "drawing" that any one comes to Christ. *What* is this "drawing"? We answer, It is the power of the Holy Spirit overcoming the self-righteousness of the sinner, and convicting him of his lost condition. It is the Holy Spirit awakening within him a sense of need. It is the power of the Holy Spirit overcoming the pride of the natural man, so that he is ready to come to Christ as an empty-handed beggar. It is the Holy Spirit creating within him an *hunger* for the bread of life.

"It is written in the prophets, And they shall be all taught of God" (6:45). Our Lord confirms what He had just said by an appeal to the Scriptures. The reference is to Isa. 54:13: "And all thy children shall be taught of the Lord." This serves to explain, in part at least, the meaning of "draw." Those drawn are they who are "taught of God." And who are these, so highly favored? The quotation from Isa. 54 tells us: they are God's "children"; His own, His elect. Notice carefully *how* our Lord quoted Isa. 54:13. He simply said, "And they shall be *all* taught of God." This helps us to define the "all" in other passages, like John 12:32: "I, if I be lifted up from the earth, will draw *all* unto Me." The "all" *does not mean* all of humanity, but all of God's children, all His elect.

"Every man therefore that hath heard, and hath learned of the Father, cometh unto me" (6:45). This also throws light on the "drawing" of the previous verse. Those drawn are they who have "heard" and "learned of the Father." That is to say, God has given them an ear to hear and a heart to perceive. It is parallel with what we get in I Cor. 1:23, 24: "But we preach Christ crucified, unto the Jews a stumblingblock, and unto the Greeks foolishness: But unto them which are *called,* both Jews and Greeks, Christ the power of God, and the wisdom of God." "Called" here refers to the effectual and irresistible call of God. It is a call which is heard with the inward ear. It is a call which is instinct with Divine power, drawing its object to Christ Himself.

"Not that any man hath seen the Father, save he which is of God, he hath seen the Father" (6:46). This is very important. It guards against a false inference. It was spoken to prevent His hearers (and us today) from supposing that some *direct* communication from the Father is necessary before a sinner can be saved. Christ had just affirmed that only those come to Him who had heard and learned of the Father. But this does not mean that such characters hear His *audible* voice or are *directly* spoken to by Him. Only the Saviour was [and is] in *immediate* communication with the Father. We hear and learn from the Father *only* through His written Word! So much then for the primary significance of this verse according to its local application. But there is far more in it than what we have just sought to bring out.

"Not that any man hath seen the Father, save he which is of God, he hath seen the Father." How this displays the *glory* of Christ, bringing out, as it does, the infinite distance there is between the incarnate Son and all men on earth. No man had seen the Father; but the One speaking *had*, and *He* had because He is "of (not "the Father" but) God." *He* is a member of the Godhead, Himself very God of very God. And because He had "seen the Father," He was fully qualified to speak of Him, to reveal Him—see John 1:18. And who else *could* "declare" the Father? How else could the light of the Father's love and grace have shined into our hearts, but through and by Christ, His Son?

"Verily, verily, I say unto you, He that believeth on me hath everlasting life" (6:47). Christ still pursues the line of truth begun in v. 44. This forty-seventh verse is not an invitation to sinners, but a doctrinal declaration concerning saints. In v. 44 He had stated what was essential from the Divine side if a sinner come to Christ: he must be "drawn" by the Father. In v. 45 He defined, in part, what this "drawing" consists of: it is hearing and learning of the Father. Then, having guarded against a false inference from His words in v. 45, the Saviour now says, "He that believeth on me hath everlasting life." Believing *is not* the cause of a sinner obtaining Divine life, rather is it the *effect* of it. The fact that a man believes, is the evidence that he *already* has Divine life within him. True, the sinner *ought* to believe. Such is his bounden duty. And in addressing sinners from the standpoint of human responsibility, it is perfectly proper to say 'Whosoever believeth in Christ shall not perish *but have* eternal life.' Nevertheless, the fact remains that *no* unregenerate sinner ever did or ever will believe. The unregenerate sinner ought to *love* God, and love Him with all his heart. He is commanded to. But he *does not,* and *will not,* until

Divine grace gives him a new heart. So he ought to believe, but he will not till he has been quickened into newness of life. Therefore, we say that when any man *does* believe, is found believing, it is proof positive that he is *already* in possession of eternal life. "He that believeth on me *hath* (already has) eternal life": cf. John 3:36; 5:24; I John 5:1, etc.

"I am that bread of life" (6:48). This is the first of the seven "I am" titles of Christ found in this Gospel, and found nowhere else. The others are, "I am the light of the world" (8:12); "I am the door" (10:9); "I am the good shepherd" (10:11); "I am the resurrection and the life" (11:25); "I am the way, the truth, and the life" (14:6); "I am the true vine" (15:1). They all look back to that memorable occasion when God appeared to Moses at the burning bush, and bade him go down into Egypt, communicate with His people, interview Pharaoh, and command him to let the children of God go forth into the wilderness to worship Jehovah. And when Moses asked, Who shall I say hath sent me?, the answer was, "Thus shalt thou say unto the children of Israel, I AM hath sent me unto you" (Ex. 3:14). Here in John, we have a *sevenfold* filling out of the "I am"—I am the bread of life, etc. Christ's employment of these titles at once identifies Him with the Jehovah of the Old Testament, and unequivocally demonstrates His absolute Deity.

"I am that bread of life." Blessed, precious words are these. 'I am that which every sinner needs, and without which he will surely perish. I am that which alone can satisfy the soul and fill the aching void in the unregenerate heart. I am that because, just as wheat is ground into flour and then subjected to the action of fire to fit it for human use, so I, too, have come down all the way from heaven to earth, have passed through the sufferings of death, and am now presented in the Gospel to all that hunger for life.'

"Your fathers did eat manna in the wilderness, and are dead. This is the bread which cometh down from heaven, that a man may eat thereof, and not die" (6:49, 50). This is an amplification of v. 48. There He had said, "I am that bread of life"; here He describes one of the characteristic qualities of this "life." The Lord draws a contrast between Himself as the Bread of life and the manna which Israel ate in the wilderness; and also between *the effects* on those who ate the one and those who should eat the other. The fathers did eat manna in the wilderness, but they died. The manna simply ministered to a temporal need. It fed their bodies, but was not able to immortalize them. But those who eat the true bread, shall not die. Those who appropriate Christ to themselves, those who satisfy their hearts by feeding on Him, shall live forever. Not, of course, on earth, but with Him in heaven.

"This is the bread which cometh down from heaven, that a man may eat thereof, and not die" (6:50). It is obvious that Christ gives the word "die" a different meaning here from what it bears in the previous verse. There He had said that they, who of old ate manna in the wilderness, "are dead": natural death, physical dissolution being in view. But here He says that a man may eat of the bread which cometh down from heaven, and "not die": that is, not die spiritually and eternally, not suffer the "second death." Should any object to this interpretation which gives a different meaning to the word "death" as it occurs in two consecutive verses, we would remind him that in a single verse the word is found twice, but with a different meaning: "Let the dead bury their dead" (Luke 9:60).

This is one of the many, many verses of Scripture which affirms the eternal security of the believer. The life which God imparts in sovereign grace to the poor sinner, is not a life that may be forfeited; for, "the gifts and calling of God are without repentance" (Rom. 11:29. It is not a life which is perishable, for it is "hid with Christ in God" (Col. 3:3.) It is not a life which ends when our earthly pilgrimage is over, for it is "eternal life." Ah! what has the world to offer in comparison with this? Do the worldling's fondest dreams of happiness embrace the element of unending continuity? No, indeed; *that* is the one thing lacking, the want of which spoils all the rest!

"I am the living bread which came down from heaven" (6:51). How evident it is then that Christ is here addressing these Jews on the ground, not of God's secret counsels, but, of their human responsibility. It is true that none will come to Him save as they are "drawn" by the Father; but this does not mean that the Father refuses to "draw" any poor sinner that really *desires* Christ. Yea, that very desire *for* Christ is the proof the Father has commenced to "draw." And how Divinely simple is the way in which Christ is received—"If any man [no matter who he be] *eat* of this bread he shall live forever." The figure of "eating" is very suggestive, and one deserving of careful meditation.

In the first place, eating is *a necessary act* if I am to derive that advantage from bread which it is intended to convey, namely, bodily nourishment. I may look at bread and admire it; I may philosophize about bread and analyze it; I may talk about bread and eulogize its quality; I may handle bread and be assured of its excellency—but unless I *eat* it, I shall not be nourished by it. All of this is equally true with the spiritual bread, Christ. Knowing the truth, speculating about it, talking about it, contending for it, will do me no good. I must *receive* it into my heart.

In the second place, eating is *responding to a felt need.* That need is hunger, unmistakably evident, acutely felt. And when one is *really* hungry he asks no questions, he makes no demurs, he raises no quibbles, but gladly and promptly partakes of that which is set before him. So it is, again, spiritually. Once a sinner is awakened to his lost condition; once he is truly conscious of his deep, deep need, once he becomes aware of the fact that without Christ he will perish eternally; then, whatever intellectual difficulties may have previously troubled him, however much he may have procrastinated in the past, *now* he will need no urging, but promptly and gladly will he receive Christ as his own.

In the third place, eating implies *an act of appropriation.* The table may be spread, and loaded down with delicacies, and a liberal portion may have been placed on my plate, but not until I commence to *eat* do I make that food my own. Then, that food which previously was without me, is taken inside, assimilated, and becomes a part of me, supplying health and strength. So it is spiritually. Christ may be presented to me in all His attractiveness, I may respect His wonderful personality, I may admire His perfect life, I may be touched by His unselfishness and tenderness, I may be moved to tears at the sight of Him dying on the cruel Tree; but, not until I *appropriate* Him, not until I *receive* Him as mine, shall I be saved. Then, He who before was outside, will indwell me. Now, in very truth, shall I know Him as the bread of life, ministering daily to my spiritual health and strength.

In the fourth place, eating is an intensely *personal act*: it is something which no one else can do for me. There is no such thing as eating by proxy. If I am to be nourished, I must, myself, eat. Standing by and watching others eat will not supply *my* needs. So, dear reader, no one can believe in Christ for you. The preacher cannot; your loved ones cannot. And you may have witnessed others receiving Christ as theirs; you may later hear their ringing testimonies; you may be struck by the unmistakable change wrought in their lives; but, unless *you* have "eaten" the Bread of life, unless you have personally received Christ as yours, it has all availed you nothing. "If any man eat of this bread, he shall live forever." Divinely simple and yet wonderfully full is this figure of eating.

"And the bread that I will give is my flesh" (6:51). Exceedingly solemn and exceedingly precious is this. To "give" His "flesh" was to offer Himself as a sacrifice, it was to voluntarily lay down His life. Here, then, Christ presents Himself, not only as One who came down from heaven, but as One who had come here to die. And not unto we reach this point do we come to the heart of the Gospel. As an awakened sinner beholds the person of Christ, as he reads the record of His perfect life down here, he will exclaim, "Woe is me; I am undone." Every line in the lovely picture which the Holy Spirit has given us in the four Gospels only condemns me, for it shows me how *unlike* I am to the Holy One of God. I admire His ways: I marvel at His perfections. I wish that I could be like Him. But, alas, I am altogether *unlike* Him. If Christ be the One that the Father delights in, then verily, He can never delight in me; for His ways and mine are as far apart as the east is from the west. O what is to become of me, wretched man that I am! Ah! dear reader, what had become of every one of us if Christ had *only* glorified the Father by a brief sojourn here as the perfect Son of man?

What hope had there been if, with garments white and glistening, and face radiant with a glory surpassing that of the midday sun, He had ascended from the Mount of Transfiguration, leaving this earth forever? There is only one answer: the door of hope had been fast closed against every member of Adam's fallen and guilty race. But blessed be His name, wonderful as was His descent from heaven, wonderful as was that humble birth in Bethlehem's lowly manger, wonderful as was the flawless life that He lived here for thirty-three years as He tabernacled among men; yet, that was not all, that was not the most wonderful. Read this fifty-first verse of John 6 again: "I am the living bread which came down from heaven: if any man eat of this bread, he shall live for ever: and the bread that I will give is my flesh, which I will give for the life of the world." Ah! it is only in a *slain* Christ that poor sinners can find that which meets their dire and solemn need. And His "flesh" He gave in voluntary and vicarious sacrifice "for the life of the world": not merely for the Jews, but for elect sinners of the Gentiles too. His meritorious life was substituted for our forfeited life. Surely this will move our hearts to fervent praise. Surely this will cause us to bow before Him in adoring worship.

"The Jews therefore strove among themselves, saying, How can this man give us his flesh to eat?" (6:52). "It is difficult, or rather impossible, to say what was the precise state of mind which this question indicated on the part of those who proposed it. It is not unlikely that it expressed different sentiments in different individuals. With some it probably was a contemptuous expression of utter incredulity, grounded on the alleged obvious absurdity of the statement made: *q.d.*, 'The man is mad; can any absurdity exceed this? We are to live for ever by eating the flesh of a living man!' With others, who thought that neither our Lord's words nor works were like those of a madman, the question probably was equivalent to a statement—'These words must have a meaning different from their literal signification, but what can that meaning be?'

"These 'strivings' of the Jews about the meaning of our Lord's words were 'among themselves'. None of them seemed to have stated their sentiments to our Lord, but He was perfectly aware of what was going on among them. He does not, however, proceed to explain His former statements. They were not ready for such an explication. It would have been worse than lost on them. Instead of illustrating His statement, He reiterated it. He in no degree explains away what had seemed strange, absurd, incredible, or unintelligible. On the contrary, He becomes, if possible, more paradoxical and enigmatical than ever, in order that His statement might be more firmly rooted in their memory, and that they might the more earnestly inquire, 'What can these mysterious words mean?' He tells them that, strange and unintelligible, and incredible, and absurd, as His statements might appear, He had said nothing but what was indubitably true, and incalculably important" (Dr. John Brown).

"Then Jesus said unto them, Verily, verily I say unto you, Except ye eat the flesh of the Son of man, and drink his blood, ye have no life in you" (6:53). This verse and the two that follow contain an amplification of what He had said in v. 51. He was shortly to offer Himself as a substitutionary victim, an expiatory sacrifice, in the room of and in order to secure the salvation, of both Jews and Gentiles. And this sacrificial death must be appropriated, received into the heart by faith, if men are to be saved thereby. Except men "eat the flesh" and "drink" the blood of Christ, they have "no life" in them. For a man to have "no life" in him means that he continues in spiritual death: in that state of condemnation, moral pollution, and hopeless wretchedness into which sin has brought him.

Observe that it is as Son of man He here speaks of Himself. How could He have suffered death if He had not become incarnate? And the incarnation was in order to His death. How this links together the mysteries of Bethlehem and Calvary; the incarnation and the Cross! And, as we have said, the one was in order to the other. He came from heaven to earth in order to die: "but now once in the end of the world hath he appeared to put away sin by the sacrifice of himself" (Heb. 9:26). "But we see Jesus, who was made a little lower than the angels *for* the suffering of death " (Heb. 2:9).

"Except ye eat the flesh of the Son of man, and drink his blood, ye have no life in you." Difficult as this language first appears, it is really blessedly simple. It is not a dead Christ which the sinner is to feed upon, but on the *death of* One who is now alive forever more. His *death* is mine, when appropriated by faith; and thus appropriated, it becomes *life* in me. The figure of "eating" looks back, perhaps, to Gen. 3. Man *died* (spiritually) by "eating" (of the forbidden fruit) and he is *made alive* (spiritually) by an act of eating!

"Whoso eateth my flesh, and drinketh my blood, hath eternal life; and I will raise him up at the last day" (6:54). Notice the change in the tense of the verb. In the previous verse it is, "Except ye *eat*"; here it is "whoso *eateth*." In the former, the verb is in the aorist tense, implying a single act, an act done once for all. In the latter, the verb is in the perfect tense, denoting that which is continuous and characteristic. V. 53 defines the difference between one who is lost and one who is saved. In order to be saved, I must "eat" the flesh and "drink" the blood of the Son of man; that is, I must appropriate Him, make Him mine by an act of faith. This act of receiving Christ is done once for all. I cannot *receive* Him a second time, for He never leaves me! But, having received Him to the saving of my soul, I now feed on Him constantly, daily, as the Food of my soul. Ex. 12 supplies us with an illustration. First, the Israelite was to apply the shed blood of the slain lamb. Then, as protected by that blood, he was to *feed* on the lamb itself.

"Whoso eateth my flesh, and drinketh my blood, hath eternal life; and I will raise him up at the last day." This confirms our interpretation of the previous verse. If we compare it with v. 47 it will be seen at once the "eating" is equivalent to "believing." Note, too, that the tense of the verbs is the same: v. 47 "believeth," v. 54 "eateth." And observe how each of these are *evidences* of eternal life, already in possession of the one thus engaged: "He that believeth on me *hath* eternal life"; "Whoso eateth my flesh, and drinketh my blood, *hath* eternal life."

This passage in John 6 is a favorite one with Ritualists, who understand it to refer to the Lord's Supper. But this is certainly a mistake, and that for the following reasons. First, the Lord's Supper had not been instituted when Christ delivered this discourse. Second, Christ was here addressing Himself to unbelievers, and the Lord's Supper is for saints, not unregenerate sinners. Third, the eating and drinking here spoken of are in order to salvation; but eating and drinking at the Lord's table are for those who have been saved.

"For my flesh is meat indeed, and my blood is drink indeed" (6:55). The connection between this and the previous verse is obvious. It is brought in, no doubt, to prevent a false inference being drawn from the preceding words. Christ had thrown the emphasis on the "eating." Except a man ate His flesh, he had no life in him. But now our Lord brings out the truth that there is nothing *meritorious* in the act of eating; that is to say, there is no mystical power in faith iself. The nourishing power is in the *food* eaten; and the potency of faith lies in its *Object.*

"For my flesh is meat indeed, and my blood is drink indeed." Here Christ throws the emphasis on *what it is* which must be "eaten." It is true in the natural realm. It is not the mere eating of anything which will nourish us. If a man eat a poisonous substance he will be killed; if he eat that which is innutritious he will starve. Equally so is it spiritually. "There are many strong believers in hell, and on the road to hell; but they are those who believed a lie, and not the truth as it is in Christ Jesus" (Dr. J. Brown). It is Christ who alone can save: Christ as crucified, but now alive for evermore.

"He that eateth my flesh, and drinketh my blood, dwelleth in me, and I in him" (6:56). In this, and the following verse, Christ proceeds to state some of the blessed *effects* of eating. The first effect is that the saved sinner is brought into vital union with Christ, and enjoys the most intimate *fellowship* with Him. The word "dwelleth" is commonly translated "abideth." It always has reference to *communion.* But mark the tense of the verb: it is only the one who "eateth" and "drinketh" constantly that abides in unbroken fellowship with Christ.

"He that eateth my flesh, and drinketh my blood, dwelleth in me, and I in him." This language clearly implies, though it does not specifically mention the fact, that Christ would rise from the dead, for only as risen could He dwell in the believer, and the believer in Him. It is, then, with Christ risen, that they who feed on Him as slain, are identified—so marvelously identified, that Scripture here, for the first time, speaks of *union* with our blessed Lord.

"As the living Father hath sent me, and I live by the Father: so he that eateth me, even he shall live by me" (6:57). How evident it is, again, that Christ is here speaking of Himself as the Mediator, and not according to His essential Being: it is Christ not in Godhead glory, but as the Son incarnate, come down from heaven. "I live by the Father" means He lived His life in *dependence* upon the Father. This is what He stressed in replying to Satan's first assault in the temptation. When the Devil said, "If thou be the Son of God, command," etc., he was not (as commonly supposed) casting doubt on the Deity of Christ, but asking Him to make a wrong use of it. "If" must be understood as "since," same as in John 14:2; Col. 3:1, etc. The force of what the Tempter said is this: Since you *are* the Son of God, *exercise* your Divine prerogatives, *use* your Divine power and supply your bodily need. But this ignored the fact that the Son had taken upon Him the "form of a servant" and had entered (voluntarily) the place of subjection. Therefore, it is of *this* the Saviour reminds him in His reply—"*Man* shall not *live* by bread alone, but by every word that proceedeth out of the mouth of *God*." How beautifully this illustrates what Christ says here, "I live by the Father"! Let us then seek grace to heed its closing sentence: "so he that eateth me, even he shall live by me." Just as the incarnate Son, when on earth, lived in humble dependence on the Father, so now the believer is to live his daily life in humble *dependence* on Christ.

"This is that bread which came down from heaven: not as your fathers did eat manna, and are dead: he that eateth of this bread shall live forever" (6:58). There is an important point in this verse which is lost to the English reader. Two different words for eating are here employed by Christ. "Your fathers did *eat* (ephazon) manna"; "he that *eateth* (trogon) of this bread shall live forever." The verb "phago" means "to eat, consume, eat up." "Trogo" signifies "to feed upon," rather than the mere act of eating. The first, Christ used when referring to

Israel eating the manna in the wilderness: the second, was employed when referring to believers feeding on Himself. The one is a carnal eating, the other a spiritual; the one ends in death, the other ministers life. The Israelites in the wilderness saw nothing more than an objective article of food. And they were like many today, who see nothing more in Christianity than the objective side, and know nothing of the spiritual and experiential! How many there be who are occupied with the externals of religion – outward performances, etc. How few really *feed* upon Christ. They admire Him objectively, but receive Him not into their hearts.

"These things said he in the synagogue, as he taught in Capernaum" (6:59). What effect this discourse of Christ had on those who heard Him will be considered in our next chapter. Meanwhile, let the interested reader meditate upon the following questions: –

1. At what, in particular, were the disciples "offended": vv. 60, 61?
2. What is the meaning of v. 63?
3. What is the force of the "therefore" in v. 65?
4. What does the "going back" of those disciples prove: v. 66?
5. Why did Christ challenge the twelve: v. 67?
6. What was the assurance of Peter based on: v. 68?
7. Why was there a Judas in the apostolate: v. 71? How many reasons can you give?

CHAPTER TWENTY-FOUR

Christ and His Disciples

John 6:60-71

The following is submitted as an Analysis of the passage which is to be before us:

1. Many disciples offended at Christ's discourse: v. 60.
2. Christ's admonition: vv. 61-65.
3. Many disciples leave Christ: v. 66.
4. Christ's challenge to the Twelve: v. 67.
5. Simon Peter's confession: vv. 68, 69.
6. Christ corrects Peter: v. 70.
7. The betrayer: v. 71.

The passage before us is one that is full of pathos. It brings us to the conclusion of our Lord's ministry in Galilee. It shows us the outcome of His ministry there. Here, He had performed some wonderful miracles, and had given out some gracious teachings. It was here, that He had turned the water into wine; here, He had healed the nobleman's son, without so much as seeing him; here, He had fed the hungry multitude. Each of these miracles plainly accredited His Divine mission, and evidenced His Deity. None other ever performed such works as these. Before such evidence unbelief was excuseless. Moreover, He had presented Himself, both to the crowd outside and to the Jews inside the synagogue, as the Bread of life. He had freely offered eternal life to them, and had solemnly warned that, "except ye eat the flesh of the Son of man, and drink his blood, ye have no life in you" (v. 53). What, then, was their response to all of this?

It is indeed pathetic to find that here in Galilee Christ met with no better reception than had been His in Judea, and it is striking to see how closely the one resembled that of the other. He had begun His ministry in Judea, and, for a season, His success there, judged by human standards, seemed all that could be desired. Crowds followed Him, and many seemed anxious to be His disciples. But all is not gold that glitters. It soon became evident that the crowds were actuated by motives of an earthly and carnal character. Few gave evidence of any sense of *spiritual* need. Few, if any, seemed to discern the real purpose of His mission. A spirit of partisanship was rife, so we read, "When therefore the Lord knew how the Pharisees had heard that Jesus made and baptized more disciples than John, he left Judea, and departed again into Galilee" (John 4:1, 3).

How was it, then, in Galilee? It was simply a repetition of what had happened in Judea. Human nature is the same wherever it is found: that is why history so constantly repeats itself. Here in Galilee, the crowds, had followed Him. For a brief season, He was their popular idol. And yet, few of them manifested any signs that their consciences were stirred or their hearts exercised. Fewer still understood the real purport of His mission. And now that He had declared it, now that He had pressed upon them their spiritual need, they were offended: many who had posed as His disciples, turned back, and walked no more with Him.

How many of the Lord's servants have had a similar experience. They entered some field of service, and for a time the crowd thronged their ministry. For a season they were popular with those among whom they labored. But, then, if the servant was faithful to his Master, if he pressed the claims of Christ, if he shunned not to declare *all* the counsel of God, —then, how noticeable the change! Then, arose a "murmuring" (6:41); there was a "striving" among those who heard him (6:52); there was a querulous "This is a *hard* saying" (v. 61); there was a "many" of "the disciples" going back, and walking "no more with him" (v. 66). But sufficient for the servant to be as his Master. Let him thank God that there *is* a little company left who recognize and appreciate "the words of eternal life" (v. 68), for *they* are of far greater price in the sight of God than "the many" who "went back." Ah! dear reader, this is indeed a *living* Word, mirroring the fickle and wicked heart as faithfully today as it did two thousand years ago!

"Many therefore of his disciples, when they heard this, said, This is an hard saying; who can hear it?" (6:60). The wonderful discourse in the synagogue, following the one given to the people on the outside, was now over. We are here shown the effect of it on the disciples. A "disciple" means one who is a learner. These "disciples" are carefully distinguished from "the twelve." They were made up of a class of people who were, in measure, attracted by the person of Christ and who were, more especially, impressed by His miracles. But how *real* this attraction was, and how *deep* the impression made, we are now given to see. When Christ had presented Himself not as the Wonder-worker, but as the Bread of God; when He had spoken of giving His flesh for the life of the world, and of men drinking His blood, which signified that He would die, and die a death of violence; when He insisted that except they ate His flesh and drank His blood "they had no life" in them; and, above all, when He announced that man is so depraved and so alienated from God, that except the Father draw him, he would never come to Christ for salvation: they were all offended. It will be seen, then, that we take the words, "This is an hard saying; who can hear it?" as referring to the whole of the discourse which Christ had just delivered in the Capernaum synagogue.

"Many therefore of his disciples, when they had heard this, said, This is an hard saying; who can hear it?" The simple meaning of this is, that these disciples were offended. It was not that they found the language of Christ so obscure as to be unintelligible, but what they had heard was so irreconcilable with *their own* views that they would not receive it. What their own views were, comes out plainly in John 12. When Christ signified what death He should die, "The people answered him, We have heard out of the law that Christ *abideth for ever*: and how sayest thou, The Son of man must be lifted up?" (v. 34).

In applying the above verse to ourselves, two things should be noted. First, that when today professing Christians criticize a servant of God who is really giving out Divine truth, and complain that his teaching is "An hard saying," it is always to be traced back to the same cause as operated here. Many disciples will still reject the Word of God when it is ministered in the power of the Spirit, and they will do so because it *conflicts* with their own views and contravenes the traditions of their fathers! In the second place, note that these men complained among themselves. This is evident from the next verse: "When Jesus *knew in himself* that his disciples murmured at it." They did not come directly to Christ and openly state their difficulties. They did not ask Him to explain His meaning. And why? Because they were not really anxious *for light*. Had they been so, they would have sought it from Him. Again we say, How like human nature today! When the Lord's messenger delivers a word that is distasteful to his hearers, they are not manly enough to come *to him* and tell him their grievance, far less will they approach him seeking help. No, like the miserable cowards they are, they will skulk in the background, seeking to sow the seeds of dissension by criticizing what they have heard. And such people the servant of God will have no difficulty in placing: they may wear the badge of disciples, but he will know from their actions and speech that they are not believers!

"When Jesus knew in himself that his disciples murmured at it, he said unto them, Doth this offend you?" (6:61). How solemn this is! These men could not deceive Christ. They might have walked with Him for a time (v. 66); they might have posed as His disciples (v. 60); they might have taken their place in the synagogue (v. 59), and listened with seeming attention and reverence while He taught them; but He knew their hearts: those they could not hide from Him. Nor can men do so today. *He* is not misled by all the religiosity of the day. His eyes of fire pierce through every mask of hypocrisy. Learn, then, the consummate folly and utter worthlessness of "a form of godliness" without its power (II Tim. 3:5).

"When Jesus *knew in himself* that his disciples murmured at it, he said unto them, Doth this offend you?" How this evidenced, once more, His deity! At the beginning of our chapter He had been regarded as a "prophet"; but a greater than a prophet was here. Later, an insulting contrast had been drawn between Moses and Christ; but a greater than Moses was before them. Neither Moses nor any of the prophets had been able to read the hearts of men. But here was One who knew *in Himself* when these disciples murmured. He knew, too, *why* they murmured. He knew they were offended. Plainly, then, this must be God Incarnate, for none but the Lord Himself can read the heart.

"What and if ye shall see the Son of man ascend up where he was before?" (6:62). Here we have the third great fact which this chapter brings out concerning Christ. First, He referred to the Divine incarnation: He was the Bread which had "come down from heaven" (v. 41). Second, He was going to die, and die a death of violence: the repeated mention of His "blood," showed that (vv. 52, 55, etc.). Third, He would ascend to heaven, thus returning to that place from whence He had come. His ascension involved, of necessity, His resurrection. Thus does our chapter make clear reference to each of the vital crises in the history of Christ.

"What and if ye shall see the Son of man ascend up where he was before?" Soon would the Son of God return to that sphere of unmingled blessedness and highest glory from whence he came to Bethlehem's manger; and that, in order to go to Calvary's Cross. But He would return there as "the Son of man." This is indeed a marvel. A *man* is now seated upon the throne of the Father—the God-man. And because of His descent and ascent, heaven is the home of every one who, by eating His flesh and drinking His blood, becomes a partaker of His life. And because of this, earth becomes a wilderness, a place of exile, through which we pass, the children of faith, as strangers and pilgrims. Soon, thank God, shall His prayer be answered: "Father, I will that they also, whom thou hast given me, be *with me* where I am" (John 17:24).

"What and if ye shall see the Son of man ascend up where he was before?" This is one of several intimations that during the days of His earthly ministry the Lord Jesus looked beyond the Cross, with all its dread horror, to the joy and rest and glory beyond. As the apostle tells us in Heb. 12:2, "Looking unto Jesus the author and finisher of our faith; who for *the joy that was set before him* endured the cross, despising the shame." It is striking to note how the *ascension* is made typically prominent at the beginning of John 6: see vv. 3 and 15 – "Jesus went up into *a mount*."

It is to be observed that Christ did not positively declare that these murmurers *should* "see" Him as He ascended, but He merely asked them if they would be offended at such a sight. It seems to us He designedly left the door open. There is no room for doubt but that many became real believers for the first time *after* He had risen from the dead. The fact that I Cor. 15:6 tells us He was seen of "above five hundred *brethren*" proves this. It is quite likely that some of these very men who had listened to His blessed teaching in the Capernaum synagogue were among that number. But at the time of which our lesson treats they were unbelievers, so He continued to address them accordingly.

"It is the Spirit that quickeneth" (6:63). The Lord here presses upon His critics what He had first said in v. 44. To believe on Him, to appropriate the saving value of His death, was not an act of the flesh: to do this, they must first be "drawn by the Father," that is, be "quickened by the Spirit." There *must* be life before there can be the activities of life. Believing on Christ is a manifestation of the Divine life already in the one that believes. The writer has no doubt at all that the words, "It is the Spirit that quickeneth," refer to the regenerating power of the Holy Spirit. John 6:63 is complementary to 5:21. In the former, "quickening" is referred to both God the Father, and God the Son; here, to God the Holy Spirit. Thus by linking the two passages together we learn that regeneration is the joint work of the three Persons in the Holy Trinity. So, in like manner, by linking together Eph. 1:20, John 10:18 and Rom. 8:11, we learn that each Person of the Trinity was active in the resurrection of the Lord Jesus.

"It is the Spirit that quickeneth: the flesh profiteth nothing" (6:63). This is indeed a searching word and one that greatly needs emphasizing today. The flesh "profiteth *nothing*." The flesh has *no part* in the works of God. All fleshly activities amount to nothing where the regeneration of dead sinners is concerned. Neither the logical arguments advanced by the mind, hypnotic powers brought to bear upon the will, touching appeals made to the emotions, beautiful music and hearty singing to catch the ear, nor sensuous trappings to draw the eye—none of these are of the slightest avail in stirring *dead* sinners. It is not the choir, nor the preacher, but "the Spirit that quickeneth." This is very distasteful to the natural man, because so humbling; that is why it is completely ignored in the great majority of our modern evangelistic campaigns. What is urgently needed today is not mesmeric experts who have made a study of how to produce a religious "atmosphere," nor religious showmen to make people laugh one minute and weep the next, but faithful preaching of God's Word, with the saints on their faces before God, humbly praying that He may be pleased to send His quickening Spirit into their midst.

"The words that I speak unto you, they are spirit, and they are life" (6:63). This confirms our interpretation of the first part of the verse. Christ is speaking of regeneration, which was the one great need of those who were offended at His teaching. They could not discern spiritual things till they had spiritual life, and for *that* they must be "quickened" by the Spirit of God. First, He told them *who* did .the quickening—"the Spirit"; now He states *what* the Spirit uses to bring about that quickening—the "words" of God. The Spirit is the Divine Agent; the Word is the Divine instrument. God begets "with the word of truth" (James 1:18). We are born again of incorruptible seed, "by the word of God" (I Peter. 1:23). We are made partakers of the Divine nature by God's "exceeding great and precious promises" (II Pet. 1:4). And here in John 6:63 Christ explains how this is: the words of God are "spirit, and they are life." That is, they are spiritual, and employed by the Holy Spirit to impart life. Thus, we say again, The great need of today, as of every age, is the faithful preaching of *God's* Word; "not with enticing words of man's wisdom, but in demonstration of the Spirit and of power" (I Cor. 2:4). What is needed is less anecdotal preaching, less rhetorical embellishment, less reliance upon logic, and more direct, plain, pointed, *simple* declaration and exposition of the Word itself. Sinners will never be saved without this—"the flesh profiteth *nothing*"!

"The words that I speak unto you, they are spirit, and they are life." How Christ here maintained the *balance* of truth! "It is the Spirit that quickeneth" speaks of the *Divine* side. In connection with *it* man has no part. There, the "flesh" is ruled out entirely. Are we, then, to fold our arms and act as though we had no obligations at all? Far from it. Christ guards against this by saying, "The words that I speak *unto you*, they are spirit, and they are life." This was addressed to *human responsibility*. These "words" are given to be *believed;* and we are under direct obligation to set to our seal that God is true. Let then the sinner read God's Word; let him see himself mirrored in it. Let him take its searching message to himself; let him follow the light whithersoever it leads him; and if he be sincere, if he is truly seeking God, if he longs to be saved, the Holy Spirit shall quicken *him* by that same Word of life.

"But there are some of you that believe not" (6:64). This affords further confirmation of what we have said above. Christ was addressing human responsibility. He was pressing upon His hearers their need of *believing* on Him. He was not deceived by outward appearances. They might pose as His disciples, they might seem to be very devoted to Him, but He knew that they *had not* "believed." The remainder of the verse is a parenthetical statement made by John (under the inspiration of God) at the time he wrote the Gospel. "For Jesus knew from the beginning who they were that believed not, and who should betray him." Very striking is this. It is one more of the many evidences furnished by this fourth Gospel, that Christ is none other than the Son of God.

"And he said, Therefore said I unto you, that no man can come unto me, except it were given unto him of my Father" (6:65). Here He repeats what He had said in v. 44. He is still addressing their responsibility. He presses upon them their moral inability. He affirms their need of Divine power working within them. It was very humbling, no doubt. It furnished *proof* that "the flesh profiteth nothing." It shut them up to God. To the

Father they must turn; from Him they must seek that drawing power, without which they would never come to Christ and be saved. Not only "would not" but *could not*. The language of Christ is unequivocal. It is not "no man will," but "no man *can* come unto me, except it were given him of my Father." The will of the natural man has nothing to do with it. John 1:13 expressly declares that the new birth is "*not* of the will of the flesh." Contrary this may be to *our* ideas! distasteful to *our* minds and hearts; but it is *God's* truth, nevertheless, and all the denials of men will never alter it one whit.

"From that time many of his disciples went back, and walked no more with him" (6:66). While the preceding verses contain words of Christ which were addressed to human responsibility, we must not overlook the fact that they also expressed the Divine side of things. The "drawing" of the Father is exercised according to His *sovereign* will. He denies it to none who sincerely seek; but the truth is, that the seeking itself, the desire *for* Christ, is the initial *effect* of this "drawing." That all men do not seek Christ may be explained from two view points. From the human side the reason is that, men are so depraved they love the darkness and hate the light. From the Divine side, that any do seek Christ, is because God in His sovereign grace has put forth a power in them which overcomes the resistance of depravity. But God does not work thus in all. He is under no moral obligation so to do. Why *should* He make an enemy love Him? Why should He "draw" to Christ, one who wants to remain away? That He *does* so with particular individuals is according to His own eternal counsels and sovereign pleasure. And once this is pressed upon the natural man he is offended. It was so here: "From that time many of his disciples went back, and walked no more with him." What a contrast was this from what occurred at the beginning of that day! Then, the many had crossed the Sea and sought Him out; now, the many turned their backs upon Him: so unreliable and so fickle is human nature.

"From that time many of his disciples went back, and walked no more with him." This verse is parallel with what we read of in Luke 4: "But I tell you of a truth, many widows were in

Israel in the days of Elias, when the heaven was shut up three years and six months, when great famine was throughout all the land; but unto *none of them* was Elias sent, *save* unto Sarepta, a city of Sidon, unto a woman which was a widow. And many lepers were in Israel in the time of Eliseus the prophet; and *none of them* was cleansed *saving Naaman* the Syrian" (vv. 25-27). Here Christ, in the synagogue of Nazareth, pressed upon His hearers how in the past God had most evidently acted according to His mere sovereign pleasure. And what was the effect of this on those who heard? The very next verse tells us: "And all they in the synagogue, when they heard *these things,* were filled with *wrath.*" And human nature has not changed. Let the sovereign rights of God be emphasized today, and people will be "filled with wrath"; not only the men of the world will be, but the respectable attenders of the modern synagogue. So it was here in our lesson: "*From that time* many of his disciples went back." From what time? From the time that Christ had declared, "No man can come unto me, except it were given unto him of my Father" (v. 65). *This* was too much for them. They would not remain to hear any more. And mark it carefully, that those who left were "many of *his disciples.*" Then let not the one who faithfully preaches the sovereignty of God today be surprised if he meets with a similar experience.

"Then said Jesus unto the twelve, Will ye also go away?" (6:67). Christ desires no unwilling followers; so, on the departure of the "many disciples," He turns to the twelve and inquires if they also desire to leave Him. His question was a test, a challenge. Did they prefer to be found with the popular crowd, or would they remain with what was, outwardly, a failing cause? Their answer would evidence whether or not a Divine work of grace had been wrought *in them.*

"Will *ye also* go away?" The same testing question is still being put to those who profess to be the followers of Christ. As He sees some being carried along by the different winds of erroneous doctrines, now blowing in every direction; as He beholds others going back into the world, loving pleasure more than they love God; as He marks others offended by the faithful and searching ministry of His servants, He says to you and to me, "Will *ye also* go away?" O that Divine grace may enable us to stand and to withstand. O that we may be so attracted by the loveliness of His person that we shall gladly go forth "unto him, without the camp (the camp of Christianized Judaism) bearing his reproach" (Heb. 13:13).

"Then Simon Peter answered him, Lord, to whom shall we go? Thou hast the words of eternal life" (6:68). A blessed reply was this. The wondrous miracles had attracted the others, but the *teaching* of Christ had repelled them. It was the very opposite with the apostles, for whom, as usual, Peter acted as spokesman. It was not the supernatural works, but the Divine *words* of the Lord Jesus which held them. Peter had, what the "many disciples who went back" had not—the hearing ear. Christ had said, "The *words* that I speak unto you, they are spirit, and they are life" (v. 63), and Peter believed and was assured of this: "Thou *hast* the *words* of eternal life" he confessed. "The words of Christ had sunk deep into his soul. He had felt their power. He was conscious of the blessing they had imparted to him" (C.E.S.). It is ever this which distinguishes a true Christian from the formal professor.

"And we believe and are sure that thou art that Christ, the Son of the living God" (6:69). Notice carefully the *order* here: "We believe and are sure." It is the Divinely appointed and unchanging order in connection with spiritual things. It supplies one out of a thousand illustrations that God's thoughts and ways are *different*, radically different, always different, from ours. Whoever heard of believing in order to be sure? Man wants to make sure first before he is ready to believe. But God always reverses man's order of things. It is impossible, utterly impossible, to be *sure* of Divine truth, or of any part thereof, until we have *believed* it. Other illustrations of this same principle may be adduced from Scripture. For example, the Psalmist said, "I had fainted, unless I had *believed to see* the goodness of the Lord in the land of the living" (27:13). This also is the very opposite of human philosophy. The natural man says, 'Seeing is believing'; but the spiritual man believes in order to see. So, again, in Heb. 11:3 we read, "Through faith we understand."

How many desire to *understand* the mystery of the Trinity or the doctrine of election, *before* they will believe it. They might live to be as old as Methuselah, and they would "understand" neither the one nor the other until they had *faith* in what God had revealed thereon. It is *through* faith that we do understand any part of Divine truth. "We believe *and* are sure." To sum up: assurance, vision, knowledge, are the *fruits* of "believing." God rewards our faith by giving us assurance, discernment and understanding; but the unbelieving are left in the darkness of ignorance so far as spiritual things are concerned.

"And we believe and are sure that thou art that Christ, the Son of the Living God." Certainty that Christ is "the Son of the living God" comes not by listening to the labored arguments of seminary professors, nor by studying books on Christian Evidences, but by *believing* what God has *said* about His Son in the Holy Scriptures. Peter was sure that Christ was the Son of God, because he had believed "the *words* of eternal life" which he had heard from His lips. It is indeed striking to note that in Matthew's Gospel this confession is placed right after the apostles had *seen* Christ walking on the waters and after they had received Him into the ship (14:33); for it is thus that Israel, in a coming day, will be brought to believe on Him (cf. Zech. 12:10). But here in John's Gospel, which treats of the *family* of God, this confession is evoked by the assurance which comes from believing His *words*. How beautifully this illustrates the opening verse of John's Gospel, and how evident it is that God Himself has *placed* everything in these Gospels!

"Jesus answered them, Have not I chosen you twelve, and one of you is a devil? He spake of Judas Iscariot, the son of Simon: for he it was that should betray him, being one of the twelve" (6:70, 71). "Jesus *answered* them." This was in reply to Peter's avowal, "*We* believe and are sure." Christ showed that *He* knew better than His disciple. It was the omniscience of the Lord Jesus displayed once more. He was not deceived by Judas, though it is evident that all the apostles were. Proof of this is found in the fact that when He said, "One of you shall betray me," instead of them answering, Surely you refer to Judas, they asked, "Lord, is it I?" But from the beginning Christ *knew* the character of the one who should sell Him to His enemies. Yet not now will Christ openly identify him. What we read of in v. 71 is the apostle's inspired comment, written years afterwards.

That Judas was *never* saved is clear from many considerations. Here in our text Christ is careful to *except* him from Peter's confession—"We believe." So, too, in John 13. After washing the feet of His disciples, which symbolized the removal of every defilement which hindered communion with Him, He said, "Ye are clean," but then He was careful to add, "but *not all*" (13:10), and then John supplies another explanatory comment —"for he knew who should betray him; *therefore* said he, Ye are not all clean" (v. 11). Again; the fact that Christ here calls him a "devil"—and this was six months before he betrayed Him—proves positively that he *was not* a child of God. Acts 1:25—"Judas by transgression fell"—is sometimes appealed to in proof that he fell from grace. But the first part of the verse makes quite clear *what* it was from which Judas fell: it was "ministry and apostleship." This raises the question, Why was there a Judas in the apostolate? The Divine answer to our question is furnished in John 17:12, where Christ tells us plainly that "the son of perdition" was lost in order that "the Scriptures might be fulfilled." The reference was to Psa. 41:9 and similar passages. When that prophecy was uttered it seemed well-nigh incredible that the Friend of sinners should be betrayed by one intimate with Him. But no word of God can fall to the ground. It had been written that, "Mine own familiar friend, in whom I trusted, which did eat of my bread, hath lifted up his heel against me," and the son of perdition was lost in order that this scripture might be accomplished. But why did God ordain this? Why should there be a Judas in the apostolate? Mysterious as this subject is, yet, a number of things seem clear. The following ends, at least, were accomplished:—

1. *It furnished an opportunity for Christ to display His perfections.* When the Son became incarnate, He declared, "Lo I come to do *thy will,* O God" (Heb. 10:7), and this will of God for Him was written "in the volume of the book." Now in that book it was recorded that a familiar friend should lift up his

heel against him. This was indeed a sore trial, yet was it part of the Divine will for God's Servant. How, then, does He act? John 6:70 answers: He deliberately "chose" one to be His apostle, whom He knew at the time was a "devil"! How this displays the perfections of Christ! It was in *full subjection* to the Divine will, "written in the book," that He thus acted. Even though it meant having Judas in closest association with Him for three years (and what must *that* have been to the Holy One of God!), though it meant that even when He retired from His carping critics to get alone with the twelve, there would then be *a devil* next to Him, He hesitated not. He bowed to God's will and "chose" him!

2. *It provided an impartial witness to the moral excellency of Christ.* His Father, His forerunner, His saved apostles, bore testimony to His perfections; but lest it should be thought that these were *ex parte* witnesses, God saw to it that an *enemy* should also bear testimony. Here was a man that was "a devil"; a man who was in the closest possible touch with the life of Christ, both in public and in private; a man who would have seized eagerly on the slightest flaw, if it had been possible to find one; but it was not: "I have betrayed the *innocent* blood" (Matt. 27:4), was the unsought testimony of an impartial witness!

3. *It gave occasion to uncover the awfulness of sin.* The fulness of redemption must bring to light the fulness of the wickedness of that for which atonement is to be made: only thus could we thoroughly see what is that terrible thing from which we are saved. And how could the heinousness of sin be more fittingly exposed at that time than by allowing a man to company with the Saviour, to be inside the circle of greatest earthly privilege, and to be himself convinced of the innocency of that One who was to be the sacrificial victim; and yet, notwithstanding, for *him* to basely betray that One and sell Him into the hands of His enemies! Never was the vileness of sin more thoroughly uncovered.

4. *It supplies sinners with a solemn warning.* The example of Judas shows us how near a man may come to Christ and yet be lost. It shows us that outward nearness to Christ, external

contact with the things of God, is not sufficient. It reveals the fact that a man may witness the most stupendous marvels, may hear the most spiritual teaching, may company with the most godly characters, and yet himself never be born again.

5. *It tells us we may expect to find hypocrites among the followers of Christ.* A hypocrite Judas certainly was. He was not a deceived soul, but an out and out impostor. He posed as a believer. He forsook the world and followed Christ. He went out as a preacher and heralded the Gospel (Matt. 10:4). He did not manifest any offence at the teaching of Christ, and did not follow those who turned back and walked no more with Him. Instead, he remained by the Saviour's side right up to the last night of all. He even partook of the passover supper, and yet all the time, he was an hypocrite; and his hypocrisy was undetected by the eleven. And history repeats itself. There are still wolves in sheep's clothing.

6. *It shows us that a devil is to be expected among the servants of God.* It was thus when Christ was here on earth; it is so still. Scripture warns us plainly against "false prophets," and "false apostles" who are "the ministers of Satan." And the case of Judas gives point to these warnings. Whoever would have expected to find a "devil" among the twelve! Whoever would have dreamed of finding a Judas among the apostles chosen by Christ Himself! But there was. And this is a solemn warning to us to place confidence in *no man*.

7. *It affords one more illustration of how radically different are God's thoughts and ways from ours.* That God should appoint a "devil" to be one of the closest companions of the Saviour; that He should have selected "the son of perdition" to be one of the favored twelve, seemed incredible. Yet so it was. And as we have sought to show above, God had *good* reasons for this selection; He had *wise* reasons for this appointment. Let this, then, serve to show us that, however mysterious may be God's ways, they are ever dictated by omniscience!

The following questions are to help the student prepare for the next chapter on John 7:1-13:—

1. What relation does v. 1 have to the rest of the lesson?

2. What do you know about the feast of tabernacles? v. 2. Look up Old Testament references.
3. Who are "His brethren" v. 3?
4. Why did His brethren make the request of v. 4?
5. To what was Christ referring in vv. 6 and 8?
6. In view of vv. 1 and 8, why did Christ go to the feast at all? v. 10.
7. What is the meaning of the last clause of v. 10?

CHAPTER TWENTY-FIVE

Christ and the Feast of Tabernacles

John 7:1-13

Below we give a rough Analysis of the passage which is to be before us: –

1. Jesus walked in Galilee: v. 1.
2. Time: immediately before the Feast of Tabernacles: v. 2.
3. The request of Christ's brethren: vv. 3-5.
4. Christ's reply to them: vv. 6-8.
5. Christ still in Galilee: v. 9.
6. Christ goes up to the Feast: v. 10.
7. The attitude of men toward Christ: vv. 11-13.

John 7 begins a new section of this fourth Gospel. Our Lord's ministry in Galilee was now over, though He still remained there, because the Judeans sought to kill Him. The annual Feast of tabernacles was at hand, and His brethren were anxious for Christ to go up to Jerusalem, and there give a public display of His miraculous powers. To this request the Saviour made a reply which at first glance appears enigmatical. He bids His brethren go up to the Feast, but excuses Himself on the ground that *His* time was not yet fully come. After their departure, He abode still in Galilee. But very shortly after, He, too, goes up to the Feast; as it were in secret. The Jews who wished to kill Him, sought but were unable to discover Him. Among the people He formed the principal subject of discussion, some of whom considered Him a good man, others regarding Him as a deceiver. And then, in v. 14 we are told, "Now about the midst of the feast Jesus went up into the temple, and taught." Such is a brief summary of the passage which is to be before us.

That our passage will present a number of real difficulties to the cursory reader is not to be denied, and perhaps the more diligent student may not be able to clear up all of them. The simplest and often the most effective way of studying a portion of God's Word is to draw up a list of questions upon it. This will insure a more definite approach: it will save us from mere generalizations: it will reveal the particular points upon which we need to seek God's help.

Who are meant by "his brethren"? (v. 3) – brethren who did not "believe in him" (v. 5). To what did Christ refer when He said, "My time is not yet come" (v. 6)? Why did Christ refuse to go up to the Feast with His brethren (v. 8)? And why, after saying that His time was not yet come, did He go to the Feast at all (v. 10)? What is meant by "He went not openly, but as it were in secret" (v. 10)? If He went up to the Feast "as it were in secret," why did He, about the midst of the Feast, go into the temple, and teach (v. 14)? These are some of the more pertinent and important questions which will naturally occur to the inquiring mind.

It should be obvious that the central item in our passage is the Feast itself,* and in the scriptural significance of this Feast of tabernacles must be sought the solution of most of our difficulties here. It will be necessary, then, to compare carefully the leading scriptures which treat of this Feast, and then shall we be the better able to understand what is before us. Having made these preliminary remarks we shall now turn to our passage and offer an exposition of it according to the measure of light which God has been pleased to grant us upon it.

"After these things Jesus walked in Galilee" (7:1). The first three words intimate that a new section of the Gospel commences here – cf. 6:1 and our comments thereon. "After *these* things" probably has a double reference. In its more general significance, it points back to the whole of His Galilean ministry, now ended. There is a peculiar and significant arrangement of the contents of the first seven chapters of John: a strange alternating between Judea and Galilee. In John 1 the scene is laid in Judea (see v. 28); but in 2:1-12 Christ is seen in Galilee. In 2:13 we are told that "Jesus went up to Jerusalem," and He

* **Note there is a sevenfold reference to the "Feast" in John 7.**

remained in its vicinity till we reach 4:3, where we are told, "He left Judea, and departed again into Galilee." Then, in 5:1, we read, "Jesus went up to Jerusalem," and He is viewed there to the end of the chapter. But in 6:1 we are told, "After these things Jesus went over the sea of Galilee." And now in John 7 we are to see Him once more in Jerusalem.

But *why* this strange and repeated alternation? In the light of Matt. 4:15—"Galilee *of the Gentiles*"—we would suggest two answers: First, this fourth Gospel, in a special manner, concerns the *family* of God, which is made up of Jew *and* Gentile; hence the emphasis here by our attention being directed, again and again, to *both* Judea and Galilee. But note that Judea always comes before Galilee: "To the Jew first" being the lesson taught. In the second place, if our references above be studied carefully, it will be seen that the passages treating of Galilee and what happened there, come in *parenthetically;* inasmuch as Jerusalem is both the geographical and moral center of the Gospel.

"After *these* things," then, points back to the conclusion of His Galilean ministry: 2:1-11; 4:43-54; 6:1-71. But we also regard these words as having a more restricted and specific reference to what is recorded at the close of chapter 6, particularly v. 66. "After *these* things" would thus point, more directly, to the forsaking of Christ by many of His Galilean disciples, following the miracles they had witnessed and the teaching they had heard.

"After these things Jesus *walked* (literally, "was walking") in Galilee." It appears as though the Lord was reluctant to leave Galilee, for it seems that He never returned there any more. It was useless to work any further miracles, and His teaching has been despised, nevertheless, His *person* He would still keep before them a little longer. Jesus walking in Galilee, rather than dwelling in privacy, suggests the thought of the continued public manifestation of Himself: let the reader compare John 1:36; 6:19; 10:23 and 11:54 for the other references in this Gospel to Jesus "walking", and he will find confirmation of what we have just said. Again, if John 7:1 be linked with 6:66 (as the "after *these* things" suggests) the marvelous grace of the

Saviour will be evidenced. Many of His disciples went back and *walked no more* "with him." Notwithstanding, *He* continued to "walk," and that too, "in *Galilee*"!

"After these things Jesus walked in Galilee: for he would not walk in Jewry, because *the Jews* sought to kill him" (7:1). Let the reader turn back and consult our remarks on 5:15 concerning "the Jews." It is indeed solemn to trace right through this fourth Gospel what is said about them. "The Jews" are not only to be distinguished from the Galileans, as being of Judea, but also from the common people of Judea. Note how in our present passage "the people" are distinguished from "the Jews": see vv. 11, 12, 13. "The Jews" were evidently the leaders, the religious leaders. Notice how in 8:48 it is "the Jews" who say to Christ "Thou art a Samaritan, and hast a demon." It was "the Jews" who cast out of the synagogue the man born blind, whose eyes Christ had opened (9:22, 34). It was "the Jews" who took up stones to stone Christ (10:31). It was "the officers of *the Jews*" who "took Jesus, and bound him" (18:12). And it was through "fear of the Jews" that Joseph of Arimathaea came secretly to Pilate and begged the body of the Saviour (19:38). And so here: it was because of *the Jews,* who sought to kill Him, that Jesus would not walk in Judea, but remained in Galilee. Christ here left us a perfect example. By His actions, He teaches us not to court danger, and unnecessarily expose ourselves before our enemies. This will be the more evident if we link this verse with 11:53, 54: "From that day forth they took counsel together for to put him to death. Jesus *therefore* walked no more openly among the Jews; but went thence unto a country near to the wilderness," etc. It will thus appear that our Lord used prudence and care to avoid persecution and danger till His time was fully come; so it is our duty to endeavor by all wise means and precautions to protect and preserve ourselves, that we may have opportunities for further service.

"Now the Jews's feast of tabernacles was at hand" (7:2). By comparing this verse with 6:4 it will be seen that upwards of six months is spanned by John 6 to 7:1. John 6:4 says the Passover was nigh, and from Lev. 23:5 we learn that this Feast was kept in the first month of the Jewish year; whereas Lev

23:34 tells us that the Feast of tabernacles was celebrated in the seventh month. How evident it is then that John was something more than an historian. Surely it is plain that the Holy Spirit has recorded what He has in this fourth Gospel (as in the others) according to a principle of selection, and in consonance with a definite design.

"Now the Jews' feast of tabernacles was at hand." As already intimated, it will be necessary for us to give careful attention to the leading scriptures of the Old Testament on the Feast of tabernacles, that we may ascertain its historical and typical significance, and thus be the better prepared to understand the details of the passage now before us.

Lev. 23 reveals the fact that there were seven Feasts in Israel's religious calendar, but there were three of these which were singled out as of special importance. This we gather from Deut. 16:16, where it is recorded that Jehovah said to Israel, "Three times in a year shall all thy males appear before the Lord thy God in the place which he shall choose i.e. in the tabernacle, and afterwards the temple; in the feast of unleavened-bread inseparably connected with the passover, and in the feast of weeks i.e. pentecost, and in the feast of tabernacles." We reserve a brief comment on the first two of these, until we have considered the third.

The first time the Feast of tabernacles is mentioned by name is in Lev. 23, namely, in vv. 34-36 and 39-44. As this passage is too long for us to quote here in full, we would request the reader to turn and read it through carefully before going farther. We give now a brief summary of its prominent features. First, the Feast began on the fifteenth day of the seventh month (v. 34). Second, it was a "holy convocation," when Israel was to offer "an offering made by fire unto the Lord" (v. 36). Third, it lasted for eight days (v. 39). Fourth, those who celebrated this Feast were to take "boughs of goodly trees" (v. 40). Fifth, they were to "rejoice before the Lord their God seven days" (v. 40). Sixth, they were to "dwell in booths" (v. 42). Seventh, the purpose of this was to memorialize the fact that "Jehovah made their fathers to dwell in booths, when he brought them out of the land of Egypt" (v. 43). In Num. 29:12-40 we have a detailed record of the ritual or sacrificial requirements connected with this Feast.

Though Lev. 23 is the first time the Feast of tabernacles is mentioned by name, there is one earlier reference to it, namely, in Ex. 23:16, where it is termed the Feast of Ingathering,* "which is the end of the year (i.e. of the sacred calendar of Feasts), when thou hast gathered in thy labours out of the field." The Feast of tabernacles, then, was the grand Harvest Festival, when the Lord of the harvest was praised for all His temporal mercies. This one was the most joyous Feast of the year. It was not observed by Israel till after they had entered and settled in Canaan: their dwelling in booths at this Feast memorialized their wanderings in the wilderness.

The Old Testament records but two occasions when this Feast was ever observed by Israel in the past, and they are most significant. The first of these is found in I Kings 8, see vv. 2, 11, 13, 62-66, and note particularly the "seventh month" in v. 2 and the "eighth day" in v. 66. This was in the days of Solomon at the completion and dedication of the Temple. In like manner, the antitypical Feast of tabernacles, will not be ushered in till the completion of the spiritual "temple," which God is now building (Eph. 2:22; I Pet. 2:5). The second account of Israel's past celebration of this Feast is recorded in Neh. 8:13-18. The occasion was the settlement of the Jewish remnant in Palestine, after they had come up out of captivity.

We cannot offer here anything more than a very brief word on Deut. 16:16. The three great Feasts which God required every male Israelite to observe annually in Jerusalem, were those of unleavened-bread (inseparably connected with the passover), of weeks (or pentecost), and tabernacles. The first has already received its antitypical accomplishment at the Cross. The second began to receive its fulfillment on the day of pentecost (Acts 2), but was interrupted by the failure of the nation to repent (see Acts 3:19-21). The third looks forward to the future.

"Now the Jews' feast of tabernacles was at hand." Someone has pointed out that in John 5, 6, and 7 there is a striking order

* That this is the same Feast appears by a comparison of Deut. 16:16 with Exod. 23:14-17.

followed in the typical suggestiveness of the contents of these chapters. In John 5 Israel may be seen, typically, as being delivered from the bondage *of Egypt*: this was adumbrated in the deliverance of the impotent man from lifelong suffering. In John 6 there is repeated reference made to Israel *in the wilderness*, eating the manna. While here in John 7 Israel is viewed *in the land*, keeping the Feast of tabernacles.

"His brethren therefore said unto him, Depart hence, and go into Judea, that thy disciples also may see the works that thou doest" (7:3). These "brethren" were the brothers of Christ according to the flesh: that is, they were sons of Mary too. That they were completely blind to His Divine glory is evident from the fact they here told *Him* what to do. Blind to His glory, they were therefore devoid of all spiritual discernment, and hence their reasoning was according to the carnal mind. But what did they mean by "Go into Judea, that thy *disciples* also may see the works that thou doest"? The answer is to be found in the "also" and the "therefore" at the beginning of the verse—"His brethren *therefore* said unto him," etc. The "therefore," of course, looks back to something previous. What this is, we find in the closing verses of John 6. In the first part of that chapter we have recorded a wonderful "work" performed by the Lord. But in v. 66 we are told, "From that time many of his *disciples* went back, and walked no more with him." Now, said these brethren according to the flesh, do not waste any further efforts or time here, but go to Judea. They were evidently piqued at the reception which Christ had met with in Galilee. His work there seemed to amount to very little, why not, then, try Jerusalem, the headquarters of Judaism! Moreover, now was an opportune time: the Feast of tabernacles was at hand, and Jerusalem would be full.

"For there is no man that doeth anything in secret, and he himself seeketh to be known openly. If thou do these things, show thyself to the world" (v. 4). Note the "if" here. There was evidently a slightly veiled taunt in these words. We take it that these brethren were really challenging Christ, and that the substance of their challenge was this: 'If these works of yours are genuine miracles, why confine yourself to villages and small country-towns in Galilee, where the illiterate and unsophisticated habituate. Go up to the Capital, where people are better qualified to judge. Go up to the Feast, and there display your powers, and if they will stand the test of the public scrutiny of the leaders, why, your disciples will gather around you, and your claims will be settled once for all.' No doubt, these "brethren" really hoped that He *would* establish His claims, and in that event, as His near kinsmen, *they* would share the honors which would be heaped upon Him. But how insulting to our blessed Lord all this was! What indignities He suffered from those who were blind to His glory!

"If thou do these things, show thyself to the world." How these words betrayed their hearts! They were men of the world: consequently, they adopted its ways, spoke its language, and employed its logic. "Show thyself to the world" meant, Accompany us to Jerusalem, work some startling miracle before the great crowds who will be assembled there; and thus, not only make yourself the center of attraction, but convince everybody you *are* the Messiah. Ah! how ignorant they were of the mind of God and the purpose of His Son's mission! It was "the pride of life" (I John 2:16) displaying itself. And how much of this same "pride of life" we see today, even among those who profess to be followers of that One whom the world crucified! What are the modern methods of evangelistic campaigns and Bible conferences—the devices resorted to to draw the crowds, the parading of the preacher's photo, the self-advertising by the speakers—what are these, but the present-day expressions of "*Show thyself* to the world"!

"If thou do these things, show thyself to *the world*." One other comment, an exegetical one, should be made on this before we pass on to the next verse. Here is a case in point where "the world" does not always signify the whole human race. When these brethren of Christ said, "Go show thyself to *the world*," it is evident that they did not mean, 'Display yourself before all mankind.' No, here, as frequently in this Gospel, "the world" is merely a *general* term, signifying *all classes* of men.

"For neither did his brethren believe in him" (7:5). How this illustrates the desperate hardness and depravity of human nature. Holy and perfect as Christ was, faultless and flawless as were His character and conduct, yet, even those who had been brought up with Him in the same house believed not in Him! It was bad enough that the nation at large believed not on Him, but the case of these "kinsmen" (Mark 3:21, margin) was even more excuseless. How this demonstrates the imperative need of God's almighty regenerating grace! And how this exemplifies Christ's own teaching that "No man can come to me except the Father which hath sent me draw him"! And how striking to note that the unbelief of His "brethren" was the fulfillment of Old Testament prophecy: "I am become a stranger unto my brethren, and an alien unto *my mother's children*" (Psa. 69:8).

"Then Jesus said unto them, My time is not yet come: but your time is alway ready" (7:6). These words of Christ must be interpreted in the light of the immediate context. His brethren had said, "Go *show* thyself to the *world.*" But His time to do this had not then come, nor has it yet arrived. Not then would He vindicate Himself by openly displaying His glory. This was the time of His humiliation. But how plainly His words here imply that *there is* a time coming when He will publicly reveal His majesty and glory. To this He referred when He said, "And they shall *see* the Son of man coming in the clouds of heaven with power and great glory" (Matt. 24:30). And what will be the effect of this on "the world"? Rev. 1:7 tells us: "Behold, he cometh with clouds; and every eye shall *see* him, and they also which pierced him: and all kindreds of the earth shall *wail* because of him." And solemn will be the accompaniments of this showing of Himself to the world. Then shall He say, "But those mine enemies, which would not that I should reign over them, bring hither, and slay them before me" (Luke 19:27); see, too, the last half of Rev. 19. How little, then, did these brethren realize the import of their request! Had He openly manifested Himself then—before the Cross—it would have involved the perdition of the whole human race, for then there had been no atoning-blood under which sinners might shelter! Thankful must we ever be that He did not do what they asked. And how often *we* ask Him for things, which He in His Divine wisdom and grace denies us! How true it is that "we know not what we should pray for as we ought" (Rom. 8:26)!

"Then Jesus said unto them, My time is not yet come: but your time is alway ready." There was *no* "pride of life" in Christ. He demonstrated this in the great Temptation. All the kingdoms of the world and the glory of them could not tempt Him. Instead of seeking to *show Himself* before the world, instead of advertising Himself, instead of endeavoring to attract attention, He frequently drew a veil over His works and sought to hide Himself: see Mark 1:36-38; 7:17; 7:36; 8:26, etc. After He had been transfigured on the holy mount and His glory had appeared before the eyes of the three apostles, He bade them "that they should tell no man what things they had seen" (Mark 9:9). How truly did He make Himself of "no reputation"! But how different with these brethren. "Your time is alway ready," He said. *They* were ever willing and wanting to win the applause of men, and make themselves popular with the world.

"The world cannot hate you; but me it hateth, because I testify of it, that the works thereof are evil" (7:7). How this helps us to fix the meaning of the last clause of the previous verse. "Your time is alway ready" meant, as we have said, Your time to display yourself before the world, in order to court its smiles, is ever to hand. But how solemn is the *reason* Christ here gives for this! It was because they had not cast in their lot with this One who was "despised and rejected of men." Because of this, the world would not hate *them*. And why? Because they were *of* the world. Contrariwise, the world *did* hate Christ. It hated Christ because He testified *of it* (*not* "against" it!), that its works were evil. The holiness of *His* life condemned the worldliness of theirs. And right here is a solemn and searching test for those who profess to be His followers today. Dear reader, if you are *popular* with the world, that is indeed a solemn sign, an evil omen. The world has not changed. It still *hates* those whose lives condemn theirs. Listen to the words of Christ to His apostles, "If ye were of the world, the world would love his own: but because ye are not of the world, but I have chosen you out of the world, therefore the world hateth you" (John 15:19). Here our Lord tells us plainly that the world hates those who are truly His. This, then, is a searching test: does the world "hate" *you?*

"Go ye up unto this feast: I go not up yet unto this feast; for my time is not yet full come. When he had said these words unto them, he abode still in Galilee" (7:8, 9). The meaning of these verses is really very simple. Christ plainly qualified Himself. He did not say that He *would not* go up to the Feast; what He said was, He would not go *then*—His time to go had not "*yet* come." "My time" must not be confounded with "Mine hour" which He used when referring to His approaching death. The simple force, then, of these verses is that Christ declined to go up to the Feast *with His brethren.*

"But when his brethren were gone up, then went he also up unto the feast" (7:10). How tragic is this. How it reveals the hearts of these "brethren." They *left* Christ for the Feast! They preferred a religious festival for fellowship with the Christ of God. And how often we witness the same thing today. What zeal there is for religious performances, for forms and ceremonies, and how little heart for Christ Himself.

"But when his brethren were gone up, then went he also up unto the feast, not openly, but as it were in secret" (7:10). The first part of this verse supplies another reason why He would not accompany His brethren to the Feast, as well as explains the somewhat ambiguous "as it were in secret." The general method of travel in those days, and especially at festival seasons, was to form caravans, and join together in considerable companies (cf. Luke 2:44). And when such a company reached Jerusalem, naturally it became known generally. It was, therefore, to avoid such publicity that our Lord waited till His brethren had gone, and then He went up to the Feast, "not openly, (R.V. "publicly"), but as it were in secret," i.e., in private. "But *when* his brethren were gone up, *then* went he also up unto the feast." The words we have placed in italics are not so much a time-mark as a word of explanation. The "when" has the force of *because* as in 4:1; 6:12; 6:16, etc.

"Then went *he also* up unto the feast." This simple sentence gives us a striking revelation of our Lord's perfections. In order to appreciate what we have here it is necessary to go back to the first verse of the chapter, where we are told, "Jesus walked in Galilee, for he would not walk in Jewry, because the Jews *sought to kill him*." Why is it that the Holy Spirit has begun the chapter thus? The central incident in John 7 is Christ in Jerusalem at the Feast of tabernacles. Why, then, *introduce* the incident in this peculiar way? Ah! the Holy Spirit ever had the glory of Christ in view. Because the Jews "sought to kill him" He "walked in Galilee." And therein, as pointed out, He left us an example not to needlessly expose ourselves to danger. But now in v. 10 we find that He *did* go to Judea, yes to Jerusalem itself. Why was this? We have to turn back to Deut. 16:16 for our answer. There we read, "Three times in a year shall *all thy* males appear before the Lord thy God in the place which he shall choose; in the feast of unleavened bread, and in the feast of weeks, and in the *feast of tabernacles*." According to the flesh Christ was an Israelite, and "made under the law" (Gal. 4:4). Therefore, did He, in perfect submission to the will of His Father, go up to Jerusalem to keep the feast. In the volume of the book it was "written of him," and even though the Jews "sought to kill him," He promptly *obeyed* the written Word! And here, too, He has left us an example. On the one hand, danger should not be courted by us; on the other, when the Word of God plainly bids us follow a certain line of conduct, we are to do so, no matter what the consequences.

"Then the Jews sought him at the feast, and said, Where is he? And there was much murmuring among the people concerning him: for some said, he is a good man: others said, Nay; but he deceiveth the people. Howbeit no man spake openly of him for fear of the Jews" (7:11-13). Mark what a strange variety of opinions there were concerning Christ even at the beginning! In the light of this passage the differences and divergencies of religious beliefs today ought not to surprise us. As said the late Bishop Ryle, "They are but the modern symptoms of an ancient disease." Christ Himself distinctly affirmed, "Think not that I am come to send peace." Whenever God's truth is faithfully proclaimed, opposition will be encountered and strife stirred up. The fault is not in God's truth, but in human nature. As the sun shines on the swamp it will call forth malaria: but the fault is not in the sun, but in the ground. The very same rays call forth fertility from the grainfields. So the truth of God will yield spiritual fruit from a believing heart, but from the carnal mind it will evoke endless cavil and blasphemy. Some thought Christ a good man; others regarded Him as a deceiver: sufficient for the disciple to be as His Master.

"Some said, he is a good man: others said, Nay; but he deceiveth the people" (7:12). "The Lord might bring blessing out of it, but they were *reasoning* and *discussing*. In another place He asks His disciples, 'Whom do men say that I the Son of man am?' They tell Him, 'Some say that thou art John the Baptist; some Elias; and others, one of the prophets.' It was all *discussion*. But when Peter replies, 'Thou art the Christ, the Son of the living God,' He tells him, 'Blessed art thou Simon Barjona: for flesh and blood hath not revealed it unto thee, but my Father which is in heaven'. There was *personal recognition of Himself*, and where there is that, there is no *discussion*. Discussing Him as subject-matter in their minds, they had not submitted to the righteousness of God. Where people's minds are at work discussing the right and the wrong, there is not the mind of the new-born babe; they are not receiving, but judging" (J.N.D.).

"Howbeit no man spake openly of him for fear of the Jews" (7:13). What a solemn warning to us is this! What an awful thing is the fear of man! How often it has silenced faithful witness for Christ! It is written, "The fear of man bringeth a snare" (Prov. 29:25). This is still true. Let us pray then for holy boldness that we may testify faithfully for an absent Saviour before a world that cast Him out.

The following questions on our next portion may help the student: —

1. Wherein is v. 15 being repeated today?

2. Why did Christ speak of His "doctrine" rather than doctrines, v. 16?
3. What is the relation of v. 17 to the context?
4. Wherein does v. 18 help us to carry out I John 4:1?
5. What is the difference between "the law of Moses" (v. 23) and "the law of God" (Rom. 7:22, 25)?
6. To what did the speakers refer in the second half of v. 27—cf. v. 42?
7. What comforting truth is illustrated in v. 30?

CHAPTER TWENTY-SIX

Christ Teaching in the Temple

John 7:14-31

Below is an outline Analysis of the passage which is to be before us: —

1. Christ in the Temple, teaching: v. 14.
2. The Jews marvelling and Christ's answer: vv. 15-19.
3. The people's question and Christ's response: vv. 20-24.
4. The inquiry of those of Jerusalem: vv. 25-27.
5. The response of Christ: vv. 28, 29.
6. The futile attempt to apprehend Christ: v. 30.
7. The attitude of the common people: v. 31.

In the last chapter we discussed the first thirteen verses of John 7, from which we learned that notwithstanding "the Jews" (Judean leaders) sought to kill Him (v. 1), Christ, nevertheless, went up to Jerusalem to the Feast of tabernacles (v. 10). We pointed out how this manifested the perfections of the Lord Jesus, inasmuch as it demonstrated His submission to the will and His obedience to the word of His Father. Our present chapter records an important incident which transpired during the midst of the Feast. The Saviour entered the Temple, and, refusing to be intimidated by those who sought His life, boldly taught those who were there assembled.

"Now about the midst of the feast Jesus went up into the temple, and taught" (7:14). Twice previously has "the temple" been mentioned in this Gospel. In John 2 we behold Christ as the Vindicator of the Father's house, cleansing the Temple. In 5:14 we read how Christ found in the temple the impotent man whom He had healed. But here in John 7, for the first time, we find our Lord *teaching* in the Temple.

The Holy Spirit has not seen well to record the details of *what* it was that our Lord "taught" on this significant occasion, but He intimates that the Saviour must have delivered a discourse of unusual weight. For in the very next verse we learn that even His enemies, "the Jews," *marvelled* at it. In keeping with His usual custom, we doubt not that He took advantage of the occasion to speak at length upon the different aspects and relations of the Feast itself. Most probably He linked together the various Old Testament scriptures which treat of the Feast, and brought out of them things which His hearers had never suspected were in them. And then there would be a searching application of the Word made to the consciences and hearts of those who listened.

"And the Jews marvelled, saying, How knoweth this man letters, having never learned?" (7:15). "These words undoubtedly refer to our Lord's great acquaintance with the Scriptures, and the judicious and masterly manner in which He taught the people out of them, with far greater majesty and nobler eloquence than the scribes could attain by a learned education." (Dr. Philip Doddridge). But how their very speech betrayed these Jews! How this exclamation of theirs exposed the state of their hearts! It was not their consciences which were exercised, but their curiosity that was aroused. It was not the claims of God they were occupied with, but the schools of men. It was not the discourse itself they were pondering, but the manner of its delivery that engaged their attention.

"How knoweth this man letters, having never learned?" How like the spirit which is abroad today! How many there are in the educational and religious world who suppose it is impossible for man to expound the Scriptures gracefully and to the edification of his hearers unless, forsooth, he has first been trained in some college or seminary! Education is an altar which is now thronged by a multitude of idolatrous worshippers. That, no doubt, is one reason why God's curse has fallen on almost all our seats of learning. He is jealous of His glory, and anything which enters into competition with Himself He blights and withers. An unholy valuation of human learning, which supplants humble dependence upon the Holy Spirit is, perhaps, the chief reason why God's presence and blessing have long since departed from the vast majority of our centers of Christian education. And in the judgment of the writer, there is an immediate and grave danger that we may shortly witness the same tragedy in connection with our Bible Schools and Bible Institutes.

If young men are taught, even though indirectly and by way of implication, that they *cannot* and must not expect to become able ministers of God's Word unless they first take a course in one of the Bible Institutes, then the sooner all such institutions are shut down the better both for them and the cause of God. If such views are disseminated, if a course in some Bible School is advocated in preference to personal waiting upon God and the daily searching of the Scriptures *in private,* then God will blast these schools as surely as He did the seminaries and universities. And such an event is not so far beyond the bounds of probability as some may suppose. Already there are not wanting signs to show that "Ichabod" has been written over some of them. One of the principle Bible training schools in England closed down some years ago; and the fact that one of the leading Institutes in this country is constantly sending out urgent appeals for financial help is conclusive evidence that it is now being run in the energy of the flesh.

"Jesus answered them, and said, My doctrine is not mine, but his that sent me" (7:16). Let every young man who reads these lines ponder carefully this sentence from Christ. If he is fully assured that he has received a call from God to devote his life to the Lord's service, and is now exercised as to *how* he may become equipped for such service, let him prayerfully meditate upon these words of the Saviour. Let him remember that Christ is here speaking not from the standpoint of His essential glory, not as a member of the Godhead, but as the Son of God *incarnate,* that is, as the *Servant* of Jehovah. Let him turn to John 8:28 and compare its closing sentence: "As *my Father* hath *taught* me, I speak these things." It was in no human schools He had learned to teach so that men marvelled. This discourse He had delivered originated not in His own mind. His doctrine came from the One who sent Him.

It was the same with the apostle Paul. Hear him as he says to the Galatians, "But I certify you, brethren, that the gospel which was preached of me is not after man. For I neither received it of man, neither was I taught it, but by the revelation of Jesus Christ" (1:11, 12). And these things, dear brethren, are recorded for our learning. No one *has to* take a course in any Bible School in order to gain a knowledge and insight of the Scriptures. The man most used of God last century—Mr. C. H. Spurgeon—was a graduate of no Bible Institute! We do not say that God has not used the Bible schools to help many who have gone there; we do not say there may not be such which He is so using today. But what we *do* say is, that such schools are not an *imperative* necessity. You have the same Bible to hand that they have; and you have the same Holy Spirit to guide you into all truth. God may be pleased to use human instruments in instructing and enlightening you, or He may give you the far greater honor and privilege of teaching you *directly*. That is for *you* to ascertain. Your first duty is to humbly and diligently look to HIM, *wait* on Him for guidance, *seek* His will, and the sure promise is, "The meek will he *guide* in judgment: and the meek will he *teach his way*" (Psa. 25:9).

"My doctrine is not mine, but his that sent me." These words were spoken by Christ to *correct* the Jews, who were unable to account for the wondrous words which fell from His lips. He would assure them that His "doctrine" had been taught Him by no man, nor had He invented it. "My doctrine is not mine, *but his that sent me*." How zealous He was for the Father's honor! How jealously He guarded the Father's glory! Let every servant of God learn from this blessed One who was "meek and lowly in heart." Whenever people praise *you* for some message of help, fail not to disclaim *all* credit, and remind your God-dishonoring admirers that the "doctrine" is not yours, but His that sent you.

"My doctrine is not mine." Observe that Christ does not say "My doctrines are not mine," but "My doctrine." The word "doctrine" means "teaching," and the teaching (truth) of God is one correlated and complete whole. In writing to Timothy, Paul said, "Take heed unto thyself, and unto the *doctrine*" (not doctrines—I Tim. 4:6). And again he wrote, "All Scripture is given by inspiration of God and is profitable for *doctrine*" (II Tim. 3:16). In striking contrast from this, Scripture speaks of "the doctrines of men" (Col. 2:22); "strange doctrines" (Heb. 13:9); and "doctrines of demons" (I Tim. 4:1). Here the word is pluralized because there is no unity or harmony about the teachings of men or the teachings of demons. *They* are diverse and conflicting. But God's truth is indivisible and harmonious.

"If any man will do his will, he shall know of the doctrine, whether it be of God, or whether I speak of myself" (7:17). The wording of this verse in the A.V. leaves something to be desired; we give, therefore, the translation found in Bagster's Interlinear:* "If any one desire his will to practise, he shall know concerning the teaching whether from God it is, or I from myself speak." The Greek word here rendered "desire" signifies no fleeting impression or impulse, but a deeply rooted determination. The connection between this verse and the one preceding is as follows: "What you have just heard from My lips is no invention of Mine, but instead, it proceedeth from Him that sent Me. Now if you really wish to test this and prove it for yourselves you must take care to preserve an honest mind and cultivate a heart that yields itself unquestioningly to God's truth."

"If any man will do his will, he shall know of the doctrine, whether it be of God, or whether I speak of myself." In this declaration our Lord laid down a principle of supreme practical importance. He informs us how *certainty* may be arrived at in connection with the things of God. He tells us how spiritual discernment and assurance are to be obtained. The fundamental condition for obtaining spiritual *knowledge* is a genuine heart-desire to carry out the revealed will of God in our lives. Wherever the heart is right God gives the capacity to apprehend His truth. If the heart be not right, wherein would be the value of knowing God's truth? God will not grant light on His Word unless we are truly anxious to walk according to that light. If

* This is a work we strongly recommend to those who desire to be students of the Word. It gives the original Greek and immediately beneath, a literal, word for word, English translation. Obtainable from the publisher of this book.

the motive of the investigator be pure, then he will obtain an assurance that the teaching of Scripture *is* "of God" that will be far more convincing and conclusive than a hundred logical arguments.

"If any man will do his will, he shall know of the doctrine, whether it be of God, or whether I speak of myself." How this word *rebuked*, again, these worldly-minded Jews; and how it reverses the judgment of many of our moderns! One does not have to enter a seminary or a Bible Institute and take a course in Christian Apologetics in order to obtain assurance that the Bible is inspired, or in order to learn how to interpret it. Spiritual intelligence comes not through the intellect, but via the heart: it is acquired not by force of reasoning, but by the exercise of faith. In Heb. 11:3 we read, "Through faith we *understand*," and faith cometh not by schooling but by *hearing*, and hearing by the Word of God! Thousands of years ago one of Israel's prophets was moved by the Holy Spirit to write, "Then shall we *know*, if we *follow on* to know THE LORD" (Hos. 6:3).

"He that speaketh of himself seeketh his own glory: but he that seeketh his glory that sent him, the same is true, and no unrighteousness is in him" (7:18). Christ here appealed to the manner and purpose of His teaching, to show that He was no impostor. He that speaketh of, or better *from*, himself, means, he whose message originates with himself, rather than God. Such an one seeketh *his own* glory. That is to say, he attracts attention to himself: he aims at his own honor and aggrandizement. On the other hand, the one who seeks the glory of Him that sent him, the same is "true" or genuine (cf. "true" in 6:32 and 15:1), i.e. a genuine servant of God. And of such, Christ added, "and no unrighteousness is in him." Interpreting this in the light of the context (namely, vv. 12 and 15), its evident meaning is, The one who seeks God's glory is no impostor.

"He that speaketh of himself seeketh his own glory: but he that seeketh his glory that sent him, the same is true, and no unrighteousness is in him." What a searching word is this for every servant of God today! How it condemns that spirit of self-exaltation which at times, alas, is found (we fear) in all of us. The

Pharisees sought "the praise of men," and they have had many successors. But how different was it with the apostle Paul, who wrote, "I am the least of the apostles, that am not meet to be called an apostle" (I Cor. 15:9). And again, "Unto me, who am less than the least of all saints" (Eph. 3:8). And what an important word does this eighteenth verse of John 7 contain for those who sit under the ministry of the professed servants of God. Here is one test by which we may discover whether the preacher has been called of God to the ministry, or whether he ran without being sent. Does he magnify himself or his Lord? Does he seek his own glory, or the glory of God? Does he speak about himself or about Christ? Can he truthfully say with the apostle, "We preach not ourselves, but Christ Jesus the Lord" (II Cor. 4:5)? Is the general trend of his ministry, Behold me, or Behold the church, or Behold the Lamb of God?

"Did not Moses give you the law, and yet none of you keepeth the law? Why go ye about to kill me?" (7:19). Here Christ completely turns the tables upon them. They were saying that He was unlettered, and now He charges *them* with having the letter of the Law, but failing to render obedience to it. They professed to be the disciples of Moses, and yet there they were with murder in their hearts, because He had healed a man on the Sabbath. He had just declared there was no unrighteousness in Himself; now He uncovered the unrighteousness which was in *them,* for they stood ready to break the sixth commandment in the Decalogue. His question, "Why go ye about to kill me?" is very solemn. It was a word of more than local application. Where there is no heart *for* the truth, there is always an heart *against* it. And where there is enmity against the truth itself there is hatred of those who faithfully proclaim it. No one who is in anywise acquainted with the history of the last two thousand years can doubt that. And it is due alone to God's grace and restraining power that His servants do not now share the experiences of Stephen, and Paul, and thousands of the saints who were "faithful unto death" during the Middle Ages. Nor will it be long before the Divine restraint, which now holds Satan in leash and which is curbing the passions of God's enemies, shall be removed. Read through the prophecies of the

Revelation and mark the awful sufferings which godly Jews will yet endure. Moreover, who can say how soon what is now transpiring in Russia may not become general and universal!

"The people answered and said, Thou hast a devil: who goeth about to kill thee?" (7:20). "The people" evidently refers to the miscellaneous company of Israelites in the Temple courts. At that season they came from all parts of Palestine up to Jerusalem to observe the Feast. Many of them were ignorant of the fact that the Judean leaders had designs upon the life of Christ; and when He said to the Jews (of v. 15) "Why go ye about to kill me?" (v. 19, and cf. v. 1), these "people" deemed our Lord insane, and said "Thou hast a demon," for insanity is often one of the marks of demoniacal possession. This fearful blasphemy not only exposed their blindness to the glory of Christ, but also demonstrated the desperate evil of their hearts. To what awful indignities and insults did our blessed Lord submit in becoming incarnate! "Thou hast a demon:" is such an aspersion ever cast on thee, fellow-Christian? Then remember that thy Lord before thee was similarly reviled: sufficient for the disciple to be as his Master.

"Jesus answered and said unto them, I have done one work, and ye all marvel" (7:21). Christ ignored the horrible charge of "the people," and continued to address Himself to "the Jews." And herein He has left us a blessed example. It is to be noted that in the passage where we are told, "Christ also suffered for us, leaving us an example, that we should follow his steps," the Holy Spirit has immediately followed this with, "who did no sin, neither was guile found in his mouth: who, when he was reviled, reviled not again" (I Pet. 2:22, 23). What a beautiful illustration John 7 gives of this! When He was reviled, *He* "reviled not again." He made no answer to their blasphemous declamation. O that Divine grace may enable us to "follow his steps." When Christ said to the Jews, "I have done one work, and ye all marvel," He was referring to what is recorded in John 5:1-16.

"Moses therefore gave unto you circumcision; (not because it is of Moses, but of the fathers;) and ye on the sabbath day circumcise a man. If a man on the sabbath day receive circumcision, that the law of Moses should not be broken; are ye angry at me, because I have made a man every whit whole on the sabbath day?" (7:22, 23). Our Lord continued to point out how unreasonable was their criticism of Himself for healing the impotent man on the Sabbath day. He reminds them that circumcision was performed on the Sabbath; why then should they complain because He had made a poor sufferer whole on that day! By this argument Christ teaches us that works of necessity and works of mercy may be legitimately performed on the Sabbath. Circumcision was a work of necessity if the Law of Moses was to be observed, for if the infant reached its eighth day on the Sabbath, it was then he must be circumcised. The healing of the impotent man was a work of mercy. Thus are we permitted to engage in both works of necessity and works of mercy on the holy Sabbath.

It is to be observed that Christ here refers to circumcision as belonging to "the law *of Moses.*" For a right understanding of the teaching of Scripture concerning the Law it is of first importance that we distinguish sharply between "the law of God" and "the law of Moses." The Law of God is found in the ten commandments which Jehovah Himself wrote on the two tables of stone, thereby intimating that they were of lasting duration. This is what has been rightly termed the moral Law, inasmuch as the Decalogue (the ten commandments) enunciates a rule of conduct. The moral Law has no dispensational limitations, but is lastingly binding on every member of the human race. It was given not as a means of salvation, but as expressing the obligations of every human creature to the great Creator. The "law of Moses" consists of the moral, social, and ceremonial laws which God gave to Moses *after* the ten commandments. The Law of Moses *included* the ten commandments as we learn from Deut. 5.

In one sense the Law of Moses is wider than "the law of God," inasmuch as it contains far more than the Ten Commandments. In another sense, it is narrower, inasmuch as "the law of Moses" is binding only upon Israelites and Gentile proselytes; whereas "the law of God" is binding on Jews and Gentiles alike.* Christ clearly observes this distinction by referring to circumcision as belonging not to "the law of God," but as being an essential part of "the law of Moses" which related only to Israel.

"Judge not according to the appearance, but judge righteous judgment" (7:24). The connection between this verse and the preceding ones is clear. Christ had been vindicating His act of healing the impotent man on the Sabbath day. To His superficial critics it might have seemed a breach of the Sabbatic law; but in reality it was not so. Their judgment was hasty and partial. They were looking for something they might condemn, and so seized upon this. But their verdict, as is usually the case when hurried and prejudiced, was altogether erroneous. Therefore, did our Lord bid them; "Judge not according to the appearance, but judge righteous judgment." He exhorted them to be fair; to take into account all the circumstances; to weigh *all* that God's Word revealed about the Sabbath. "In it thou shalt not do *any* work," was not to be taken absolutely: other scriptures plainly modified it. The ministrations of the priests in the temple on the Sabbath, and the circumcising of the child on that day when the Law required it, were cases in point. But the Jews had overlooked or ignored these. They had judged by appearances. They had not considered the incident according to its merits, nor in the light of the general tenor of Scripture. Hence, their judgment was *un*righteous, because unfair and false.

"Judge not according to the appearance, but judge righteous judgment." This is a word which each of us much need to take to heart. Most of us fail at this point; fail in one of two directions. Some are prone to form too good an opinion of people. They are easily deceived by an air of piety. The mere fact that a man professes to be a Christian, does not prove that he is one. That he is sound in his morals and a regular attender of religious services, is no sure index to the state of his heart. Remember that all is not gold that glitters. On the other hand, some are too critical and harsh in their judgment. We must not make a man an offender for a word. In many things we *all* offend. "There

* See the author's booklet "The Law and the Saint" for a fuller discussion of this subject. Obtainable from the publisher of this book. 30 cents.

is not a just man on earth that doeth good and sinneth not" (Ecc. 7:20). The evil nature, inherited from Adam, remains in every Christian to the end of his earthly course. And too, God bestows more grace on one than He does on another. There is real danger to some of us lest, forgetting the frailties and infirmities of our fellows, we regard certain Christians as unbelievers. Even a nugget of gold has been known to be covered with dust. It is highly probable that all of us who reach heaven will receive surprises there. Some whom we expected to meet will be absent, and some we never expected to see will be there. Let us seek grace to heed this timely word of our Lord's: "Judge not according to the appearance, but judge righteous judgment."

"Then said some of them of Jerusalem, Is not this he, whom they seek to kill? But, lo, he speaketh boldly, and they say nothing unto him. Do the rulers know indeed that this is the very Christ?" (7:25, 26). In this chapter one party after another stands exposed. The Light was shining and it revealed the hidden things of darkness. First, the "brethren" of Christ (vv. 3-5) are exhibited as men of the world, unbelievers. Next, "the Jews" (the Judean leaders) display their carnality (v. 15). Then, the miscellaneous crowd, "the people" (v. 20) make manifest their hearts. Now the regular inhabitants of Jerusalem come before us. They, too, make bare their spiritual condition. In sheltering behind "the rulers" they showed what little anxiety they had to discover for themselves whether or not Christ was preaching the truth of God. Verily, "there is no difference, for *all* have sinned, and come short of the glory of God." The common people were no better than the rulers; the Lord's brethren no more believed on Him than did the Jews; the inhabitants of Jerusalem had no more heart for Christ than they of the provinces. How plain it was, then, that *no man* would come to Christ except he had been drawn of the Father! It is so still. One class is just as much opposed to the Gospel as any other. Human nature is the same the world over. It is nothing but the distinguishing grace of God that ever makes one to differ from another.

"Howbeit we know this man whence he is: but when Christ cometh, no man knoweth whence he is" (7:27). What pride of heart these words evidence! These men of Jerusalem deemed themselves wiser than their credulous rulers. The religious leaders might stand in some doubt, but *they* knew whence Christ was. Evidently they were well acquainted with His early life in Nazareth. Supposing that Joseph was His father, they were satisfied that He was merely a man: "We know *this man*" indicates plainly the trend of their thoughts.

"But when Christ cometh, no man knoweth whence he is." This sentence needs to be pondered with v. 42 before us. From Matt. 2:4, 5 it is also plain that it was well known at the time that the Messiah should first appear in Bethlehem. What, then, did these people mean when they said, "When Christ cometh, no man knoweth *whence* he is"? With Dr. Doddridge, we regard this statement as an expression of the Jewish belief that the Messiah would be *supernaturally born,* i.e. of a virgin, as Isa. 7:14 declared.

"Then cried Jesus in the temple as he taught, saying, Ye both know me, and ye know whence I am: and I am not come of myself, but he that sent me is true, whom ye know not" (7:28). It appears to the writer that in the first part of this utterance the Lord was speaking ironically. Some of them who lived in Jerusalem had declared, "We know this man whence he is." Here Christ takes up their words and refutes them. "Ye both know me, and ye know whence I am," such was their idle boast; but, continues the Saviour, "I am not come of myself, but he that sent me is true, whom ye *know not.*" So they did not know whence He was. When Christ here declared of the Father, "He that sent me is true," He looked back, no doubt, to the Old Testament Scriptures. God had been "true" to His promises and predictions, many of which had already been fulfilled, and others were even then in course of fulfillment; yea, *their* very rejection of His Son evidenced the Father's veracity.

"But I know him: for I am from him, and he hath sent me" (7:29). It was because Christ knew the Father, and was from Him, that He could reveal Him; for it is by the Son, and by Him alone, that the Father is made known. "No man knoweth the Son but the Father; neither knoweth any man the Father, save the Son, and he to whomsoever the Son will reveal him" (Matt. 11:27). None cometh unto the Father but by Christ; and none knoweth the Father but by Him.

"Then they sought to take him: but no man laid hands on him, because his hour had not yet come" (7:30). This verse sets forth a truth which should be of great comfort to God's people, and indeed it is so, when received by unquestioning faith. We find here a striking example of the restraining hand of God upon His enemies. *Their* purpose was to apprehend Christ. They *sought* to take Him, yet not a hand was laid upon Him! They thirsted for His blood, and were determined to kill Him; yet by an invisible restraint from above, they were powerless to do so. How blessed, then, to know that everything is under the immediate control of God. Not a hair of our heads can be touched without His permission. The demon-possessed Saul might hurl his javelin at David, but hurling it and killing him were two different things. Daniel might be cast into the den of lions, but as his time to die had not then come, their mouths were mysteriously sealed. The three Hebrews were cast into the fiery furnace, but of what avail were the flames against those protected by Jehovah!

"Then they sought to take him: but no man laid hands on him, because his hour was not yet come." How this evidences the invincibility of God's eternal decrees! "There is no wisdom nor understanding nor counsel against the Lord" (Prov. 21:30). God had decreed that the Saviour should be betrayed by a familiar friend, and sold for thirty pieces of silver. How, then, was it possible for these men to seize Him? They could no more arrest Christ than they could stop the sun from shining. "There are many devices in a man's heart; nevertheless the counsel of the Lord, that shall stand" (Prov. 19:21). What an illustration of this is furnished by the incident before us!

"No man laid hands on him, *because* his hour was not yet come." Not until the sixty-ninth "week" of Dan. 9:24 had run its courses could Messiah the Prince be "cut off." All the hatred of men and all the enmity of Satan and his hosts could not hasten Christ's appointed death. Until God's foreordained hour struck, and the incarnate Son bowed to His Father's good pleasure, He was immortal. And blessed be God, it is our privilege to be assured that the hand of death *cannot* strike *us* down before God's predestined "hour" arrives for us to go hence. The enemy may war against us, and he may be permitted to strike our bodies; but shorten our lives he cannot, anymore than he could Job's. A frightful epidemic of disease may visit the neighborhood in which I live, but I am immune till *God* suffers me to be affected. Unless it is *His* will for *me* to be sick or to die, no matter how the epidemic may rage, nor how many of those around me may fall victims to it, it cannot harm me. "I will say of the Lord, he is *my* refuge and *my* fortress: my God, in him will I trust." His reassuring voice answers me: "Thou shalt not be afraid for the terror by night; nor for the arrow that flieth by day; nor for the pestilence that walketh in darkness; nor for the destruction that wasteth at noonday. A thousand shall fall at thy side, and ten thousand at thy right hand; but *it shall not come nigh thee*" (Psa. 91:2, 6, 7). Should any be inclined to think we have expressed ourselves too strongly, we ask them to ponder the following scriptures: "Is there not an appointed time for man upon earth? are not his days also like the days of an hireling?"—that is, strictly numbered (Job 7:1). "Seeing his days *are determined*, the number of his months are with thee, thou *hast appointed* his bounds that he cannot pass . . . If a man die, shall he live again? all the days of my *appointed time* will I wait, till my change come" (Job 14:5, 14).

"No man laid hands on him, because his hour was not yet come." How this brings out the fact that all of Christ's sufferings were undergone *voluntarily*. He did not go to the Cross because He was unable to escape it; nor did He die because He could not prevent it. Far, far from it. Had He so pleased, He could have smitten down these men with a single word from His mouth. But even that was not necessary. They were prevented from touching Him without so much as a single word being spoken!

"And many of the people believed on him, and said, When Christ cometh, will he do more miracles than these which this man hath done?" (7:31). Whether or not this was a saving faith it is rather difficult to ascertain. Personally, we do not think it was. Rather do we regard this verse as parallel with John 2:23: "Now when he was in Jerusalem at the passover, in the feast day, many believed in his name, when they saw the miracles which he did." But that theirs was *not* a saving faith is evident from what follows: "But Jesus did not commit himself unto *them,* because he knew all." So here, the remainder of v. 31 seems to argue against a saving faith. "When Christ cometh," intimates that they did not really regard the Lord Jesus as the Messiah himself. And their closing words, "Will he do more miracles than these which *this* (fellow) hath done?" shows what a derogatory conception they had of the incarnate Son of God.

The following questions bear upon our next chapter: John 7:32-53:—

1. What is there in v. 34 which unmistakably brings out the Deity of Christ?
2. What does v. 35 go to prove?
3. Does v. 38 describe *your* spiritual experience? If not, why?
4. What solemn warning is conveyed by vv. 41, 42?
5. What do vv. 50, 51 go to show?
6. Were the Pharisees correct in v. 52?
7. What is there in this passage which magnifies Christ as "the Word"?

CHAPTER TWENTY-SEVEN

CHRIST IN THE TEMPLE (Concluded)

John 7:32-53

The following is a general Outline of the passage which is to be before us: —

1. The Pharisees' attempt to apprehend Christ: v. 32.
2. Christ's words to their officers: vv. 33, 34.
3. The mystification of the Jews: vv. 35, 36.
4. Christ's words on the last day of the Feast: vv. 37-39.
5. The divided opinion of the common people: vv. 40-44.
6. The confession of the officers: vv. 45, 46.
7. The conference of the Pharisees broken up by Nicodemus: vv. 47-53.

The passage for our present consideration continues and completes the one that was before us in our last lesson. It views our Lord still in the Temple, and supplies additional evidences of His absolute Deity. It also affords further proofs of the desperate wickedness of the human heart. There is a strange mingling of the lights and the shadows. First, the Pharisees send officers to arrest Christ, and then we find these returning to their masters and confessing that never man spake as He did. On the one hand, we hear of Christ ministering blessing to the thirsty souls who come unto Him and drink; on the other, we learn of there being a division among the people because of Him. The Sanhedrin sit in judgment upon Christ, and yet one of their own number, Nicodemus, is found rebuking them.

Before examining in detail the closing verses of John 7 this will be the best place, perhaps, to call attention (though very briefly) to the significant *order* of truth found in John 5, 6, and

7. This may be seen in two different directions: First, concerning Christ Himself; second, concerning His people. In John 5 Christ is seen disclosing His Divine attributes, His essential perfections. In John 6 He is viewed in His humiliation, as the One come down from heaven, and who was to "give his life" for the world. But here in John 7, He says, "Yet a little while am I with you, and then I *go* unto him that sent me" (v. 33), and speaks of the gift of the Holy Spirit, which was subsequent upon His glorification (v. 39). So, too, there is a similar progressive unfolding of truth in connection with the believer. In John 5 he is viewed as "quickened" (v. 21). In John 6 we see the result of this: he comes to Christ and is saved. Now, in John 7, we hear of "rivers of living water" flowing from him to others!

"The Pharisees heard that the people murmured such things concerning him; and the Pharisees and the chief priests sent officers to take him" (7:32). Things began to move swiftly. An interval of but six months divides between the time contemplated in our lesson and the actual crucifixion of Christ. The shadows commence to fall more thickly and darkly across His path. The opposition of His enemies is more definite and relentless. The religious leaders were incensed: their intelligence had been called into question (v. 26), and they were losing their hold over many of the people (v. 31). When these tidings reached the ears of the Pharisees and chief priests, they sent out officers to arrest the Saviour.

"Then said Jesus unto them, Yet a little while am I with you, and then I go unto him that sent me" (7:33). This was tantamount to saying, My presence here is a source of annoyance to your masters, but not for long will this be continued. But our Lord did not forget to remind these officers that *He* was complete master of the situation. None could remove Him until His work was finished: "Yet a little while *am* I with you." True that little while spanned only six months, but until these had run their course He *would be* with them, and no power on earth could prevent it; no power either human or satanic could shorten that little while by so much as a single day or hour. And when that little while had expired He would "go." He would return to His Father in heaven. Equally powerless would they be to prevent this. Of His own self He would lay down His life, and of His own self would He take it again.

"Then said Jesus unto them, Yet a little while am I with you, and then I go unto him that sent me." How solemnly these words apply to our own age! Christ is now here in the Person of the Holy Spirit. But not forever is the Holy Spirit to remain in the world. When the fulness of the Gentiles be come in, then shall the Holy Spirit return to the One that sent Him. And how many indications there are that this is not far distant! Verily, we are justified in saying to sinners, *"Yet a little while"* will the Holy Spirit be "with you" and then He will "go unto him" that sent Him. Then resist Him no longer: *"Today* if ye will hear his voice, harden not your hearts."

"Ye shall seek me, and shall not find me: and where I am, thither ye cannot come" (7:34). This, no doubt, received its first fulfillment immediately after our Lord had risen from the dead. When "some of the watch" came to Jerusalem and made known to the chief priests that Christ had risen, that the sepulchre was empty, we may be sure that a diligent search was made for Him. But never again did any of them set eyes upon Him—the next time they shall behold Him will be at the Great White Throne. Whither He had gone they could not come, for "Except a man be born again he *cannot* enter the kingdom of God." And how tragically have these words of Christ received a continual verification in connection with Israel all through the centuries. In vain have the Jews sought their Messiah: in vain, because there is a veil over their hearts even as they read their own Scriptures (II Cor. 3:15).

"Ye shall seek me, and shall not find me: and where I am, thither ye cannot come" (7:34). These words also have a solemn message for unsaved Gentiles living today. In applying the previous verse to our own times we pointed out how that the words, "Yet a little while am I with you, and then I go unto him that sent me" find their fulfillment in the presence of the Spirit of Christ in the world today, a presence so soon to be removed. And once He *is* removed, once the Spirit of Christ returns to heaven, He will be sought in vain. "Ye shall seek me, and shall not find me" will receive a most solemn verification in a soon-coming day. This is very clear from Prov. 1:24-28: "Because I have called, and ye refused; I have stretched out my hand, and no man regarded; But ye have set at nought all my counsel and would none of my reproof: I also will laugh at your calamity; I will mock when your fear cometh; When your fear cometh as desolation, and your destruction cometh as a whirlwind; when distress and anguish cometh upon you. Then shall they call upon me, *but I will not answer;* they shall seek me early, *but they shall not find me."* Nor does this solemn passage stand alone: "Strive to enter in at the strait gate, for many, I say unto you, will seek to enter in, *and shall not be able* when once the master of the house is risen up, and hath shut to the door" (Luke 13:24, 25). In view of these solemn warnings let every unsaved reader heed promptly that imperative word in Isa. 55:6: "Seek ye the Lord *while he may be found,* call ye upon him *while he is near."*

"And where I am, thither ye cannot come." How this brings out the Deity of Christ. Mark He does not say, "Where I shall be," or "Where I *then* am, ye cannot come"; but, though still on earth, He declared, "Where *I am,* thither ye cannot come." In the previous verse He had said, "I *go* unto him that sent me." These two statements refer severally, to His distinct natures. "Where I *am"* intimated His perpetual presence in heaven by virtue of His Divine nature; His *going* there was yet a future thing for His human nature!

"Then said the Jews among themselves, Whither will he go, that we shall not find him? Will he go unto the dispersed among the Gentiles, and teach the Gentiles?" (7:35). How true it is that "the natural man receiveth not the things of the Spirit of God: for they are foolishness unto him, neither can he know them, because they are spiritually discerned" (I Cor. 2:14). Devoid of any spiritual perception, these Jews were unable to understand Christ's reference to His return to heaven. When they asked, "Will he go to the dispersed among the Gentiles?" they were referring to those Jews who lived away from Palestine. The Greek word is "diaspora" and signifies the Dispersion. It is found only here and in Jas. 1:1 where it is rendered "The twelve tribes *which are scattered abroad*," literally, "in the dispersion", and in I Pet. 1:1, "sojourners of the dispersion." Further, these Jews asked, "Will he teach the Gentiles?" What an evidence is this that unbelief will think about anything but God? God not being in their thoughts, it never occurred to them that the Lord Jesus might be referring to His Father in heaven; hence their minds turned to the dispersion and the Gentiles. It is thus even with a Christian when he is under the control of unbelief: the last one he will think of is *God*. Solemn and humbling commentary is this on the corruption of our natural heart.

"What manner of saying is this that he said, Ye shall seek me, and shall not find me: and where I am, thither ye cannot come?" (7:36). And mark it, these were not illiterate men who thus mused, but men of education and religious training. But no amount of culture or religious instruction can impart spiritual understanding to the intellect. A man must be Divinely illumined before he can perceive the meaning and value of the things of God. The truth is that the most illiterate babe in Christ has a capacity to understand spiritual things which an unregenerate university graduate does not possess. The plainest and simplest word from God is far above the reach of the natural faculties.

"In the last day, that great day of the feast, Jesus stood and cried, saying, If any man thirst, let him come unto me, and drink" (7:37). Their celebration of this Feast of tabernacles was drawing to a close. The "last" or eighth day had now arrived. It is here termed "the last *great* day of the feast"; in John 19:31 the same word is rendered "*high* day." It was so called because on this closing day there was a general and solemn convocation of the worshippers (see Lev. 23:36). On this eighth day, when the temple courts would be thronged with unusually large crowds, Jesus "stood and cried." What a contrast this pointed between Himself and those who hated Him: they desired to rid the world of Him; He to minister unto needy souls.

"Jesus stood and cried, saying, If any man thirst, let him come unto me, and drink." Here is the Gospel in a single short sentence. Three words in it stand out and call for special emphasis—"thirst," "come," "drink." The first tells of a recognized need. Thirst, like hunger, is something of which we are acutely conscious. It is a craving for that which is not in our actual possession. There is a soul thirst as well as a bodily. The pathetic thing is that so many thirst for that which cannot slake them. Their thirst is for the things of the world: pleasure, money, fame, ease, self-indulgence; and over all these Christ has written in imperishable letters, "Whosoever drinketh of this water shall thirst again."

But in our text Christ is referring to a thirst for something infinitely nobler and grander, even for Himself. He speaks of that intense longing for Himself which only the Spirit of God can create in the soul. If a poor sinner is convicted of his pollution and desires cleansing, if he is weighted down with the awful burden of conscious guilt and desires pardon, if he is fully aware of his weakness and impotency and longs for strength and deliverance, if he is filled with fears and distrust and craves for peace and rest,—then, says Christ, let him "come unto me." Happy the one who *so* thirsts after Christ that he can say, "As the hart panteth after the waterbrooks, so panteth my soul after thee, O God" (Psa. 42:1).

"Let him *come* unto me." "Come" is one of the simplest words in the English language. It signifies our *approach* to an object or person. It expresses action, and implies that the will is operative. To come to Christ means, that you do with your heart and will what you would do with your feet were He standing in bodily form before you and saying, "Come unto me." It is an act of faith. It intimates that you have turned your back upon the world, and have abandoned all confidence in everything about yourself, and now cast yourself empty-handed, at the feet of incarnate Grace and Truth. But make sure that nothing whatever is substituted for *Christ*. It is not, come to the Lord's table, or come to the waters of baptism, or come to the priest or minister, or come and join the church; but come to *Christ Himself*, and to none other.

"And *drink.*" It is here that so many seem to fail. There are numbers who give evidence of an awakened conscience, of heart-exercise, of a conscious need of Christ; and there are numbers who appear to be seeking Him, and yet stop short at that. But Christ not only said, "Come unto me," but He added, "and *drink.*" A river flowing through a country where people were dying of thirst, would avail them nothing unless they drink of it. The blood of the slain lamb availed the Israelite household nothing, unless the head of that household had *applied* it to the door. So Christ saves none who do not receive Him by faith. "Drinking" is here a figurative expression, and signifies *making Christ your own.* In all ages God's saints have been those who saw their deep need, who came to the Lord, and *appropriated* the provision of grace.

"If any man thirst, let him come unto me, and drink." Let us not forget *where* these words were first uttered. The Speaker was not in a penitentiary, but in the Temple. Christ was not addressing a company of profligates, but a religious crowd who were observing a Divinely-instituted Feast! What an example for each of His servants! Brother preacher, take nothing for granted. Do not suppose that because those you address are respectable people and punctual in their religious exercises they are necessarily saved. Heed that word of your Master's, and "preach the gospel to *every* creature," cultured as well as illiterate, the respectable as well as the profligate, the religious man as well as the irreligious.

"He that believeth on me, as the scripture hath said, out of his belly shall flow rivers of living water" (7:38). The language used by our Lord really implies that He had some definite passage in mind. We believe that He referred to Isa. 58:11, "And thou shalt be like a watered garden, and like *a spring of water,* whose waters fail not." Our Lord applies the promise to believers of the present dispensation. The believer should not be like a sponge – taking in but not giving out – but like a spring, ever fresh and giving forth. Twice before had Christ employed "water" as a figure, and it is striking to observe the progressive order. In John 3:5 He had spoken of a man being born "of *water* and of the Spirit": here the "water" comes down *from*

God—cf. 3:3 margin, "born from above." In John 4:14 He says, "The *water* that I shall give him shall be in him a well of *water* springing up into everlasting life." Here the "water" springs up *to God,* reaching out to the Source from whence it came. But in John 7:38 He says, "Out of his belly shall flow rivers of *living water.*" Here the "water" flows forth *for God* in blessing to others.

"He that believeth on me, as the scripture hath said, out of his belly shall flow rivers of living water." This verse describes the normal Christian, and yet, how many of us would say that its contents are receiving a practical exemplification in our daily lives? How many of us would make so bold as to affirm that out of *our* innermost part *are* flowing "rivers of living water"? Few indeed, if we were honest and truthful. What, then, is wrong? Let us examine the verse a little more attentively.

"Out of his belly shall flow." What is the "belly"? It is that part of man which *constantly craves.* It is that part which, in his fallen condition, is the natural man's *god*—"Whose god is their belly" (Phil. 3:19), said the apostle: styled their "god" because it receives the most care and attention. The "belly" is that part of man which is never really *satisfied,* for it is constantly crying for something else to appease its cravings. Now the remarkable thing, yea, the *blessed* thing, is, that not only is the believer himself satisfied, but he *overflows with that* which satisfies—out of his innermost parts "flow (forth) rivers of living water." The thought indeed is a striking one. It is not merely "from him" shall flow, but "*out of his belly* shall flow;" that is, from that very part of our constitution which, in the natural man, is never satisfied, there shall be a constant overflow.

Now *how* is the believer satisfied? The answer is, By "coming" to Christ and *drinking;* which mean *receiving* from Him: by having his emptiness ministered to from His fulness. But does this refer only to *a single act?* Is this something that is done once for all? Such seems to be the common idea. Many appear to imagine that grace is a sort of thing which God puts into the soul like a seed, and that it will grow and develop into more. Not that we deny that the believer grows, but the believer grows *in grace*; it is not the grace in him which grows! O dear Christian reader, we are to *continue* as we began. Where was it that you found rest and peace? It was in Christ. And *how* did you obtain these? It was from a consciousness of your need (thirsting), and your coming to Christ to have this met, and by appropriating from Him. But why stop there? This ought to be a *daily* experience. And it is our failure at this very point which is the reason why John 7:38 does not describe *our* spiritual history.

A vessel will not *overflow* until it is full, and to be full it has to be filled! How simple; and yet how searching! The order of Christ in the scripture before us has never changed. I must first come to Him and "drink" *before* the rivers of living water will flow forth from my satisfied soul. What the Lord most wants from us is *receptiveness,* that is, the capacity to receive, to receive from Him. I *must* receive *from* Him, before I can give out *for* Him. The apostles came to Christ for the bread before they distributed to the hungry multitude. Here is the secret of all *real* service. When my own "belly" has been filled, that is, when my own needy heart has been *satisfied* by Christ, then no effort will be required, but out from me *shall* flow "rivers of living water." O may Divine grace teach us daily to first come *to* Christ before we attempt anything *for* Him.

"But this spake he of the Spirit, which they that believe on him should receive: for the Holy Ghost was not yet given: because that Jesus was not yet glorified" (7:39). This intimates a further reason why we are told in v. 37 that the words there recorded were uttered by Christ on "the *last*" day, that is the eighth day of the Feast. In Scripture eight ever refers to a *new beginning,* and for this reason, like the numeral three, eight is also the number of *resurrection*: Christ arose on the eighth day, "in the end of the Sabbath, as it began to dawn toward the first of the week" (Matt. 28:1). And, doctrinally considered, Christ was here speaking as from resurrection ground. He was referring to that which could not receive its accomplishment till after He had risen from the dead. When he said "the Holy Spirit was not yet," John meant that He was not yet publicly *manifested* on earth. His manifestation was subsequent to the glorification of Christ.

"Many of the people therefore, when they heard this saying, said, Of a truth this is the Prophet" (7:40). The line of thought found in this verse and the twelve that follow it might be termed, The testing of men by the truth, and their failure to receive it. The first class brought before us here is the common people. Many of them were impressed by the gracious words which proceeded out of the mouth of Christ. They said, "Of a truth this is the Prophet." Their language was identical with that of the Galileans, recorded in 6:14. But observe they merely *said,* "This is the Prophet." We are not told that they received Him as such. Words are cheap, and worth little unless followed by action. It is significant, however, that John was the only one of the Evangelists that records these sayings of the people, for they were in harmony with his special theme. As its first verse intimates, the fourth Gospel presents Christ as "the Word," that is, the Speech, the Revealer, of God. A "prophet" is God's spokesman!

"Others said, This is the Christ. But some said, Shall Christ come out of Galilee? Hath not the scripture said, That Christ cometh of the seed of David, and out of the town of Bethlehem, where David was?" (7:41, 42). Here is another illustration of an acquaintance with the letter of the Word which failed to regulate the walk. These people could quote prophecy while they rejected Christ! How vain is an intellectual knowledge of spiritual things when unaccompanied by grace in the heart! These men knew where Christ was to be born. They referred to the Scriptures as though familiar with their contents. And yet the eyes of their understanding were not enlightened. The Messiah Himself stood before them, but they knew Him not. What a solemn warning is there here for us! A knowledge of the letter of Scripture is not to be despised, far from it: would that all the Lord's people today were as familiar with the Word as probably these Jews were. It is a cause for deep thankfulness if we were taught to read and memorize Scripture from our earliest childhood. But while a knowledge of the letter of Scripture is to be prized, it ought not to be over-estimated. It is not sufficient that we are versed in the historical facts of the Bible, nor that we have a clear grasp, intellectually, of the doctrines of Christianity. Unless our hearts are affected and our lives moulded by God's Word, we are no better off than a starving man with a cook book in his hand.

"Others said, This is the Christ. But some said, Shall Christ come out of Galilee? Hath not the Scripture said, that Christ cometh of the seed of David, and out of the town of Bethlehem, where David was?" These words are recorded for our learning. We must not pass them over hurriedly as though they contained no message for us. They should lead us to solemnly and seriously examine ourselves. There are many today who, like these men of old, can quote the Scriptures readily and accurately, and yet who give no evidence that they have been born again. An experiential acquaintance with Christ is the one thing needful. A heart knowledge of God's truth is the vital thing, and it is that which no schooling or seminary training can confer. If you have discovered the plague of your own heart; if you have seen yourself as a lost sinner, and have received as yours the sinner's Saviour; if you have tasted for yourself that the Lord is gracious; if you are now, not only a hearer but a doer of the Word; then, abundant cause have you to thank God for thus enlightening you. You may be altogether ignorant of Hebrew and Greek, but if you know *Him,* whom to know is life eternal, and if you sit daily at *His* feet to be taught of Him, then have you that which is above the price of rubies. But O make quite sure on the point, dear reader. You cannot afford to remain in uncertainty. Rest not, until by Divine grace you can say, "One thing I know, that, whereas I was blind, now I see." And if your eyes have been opened, pray God daily to give you a better *heart-knowledge* of His Word.

"So there was a division among the people because of him" (7:43). How this fulfilled His own predicted word. Near the beginning of His public ministry (cf. Matt. 10:34 , 35) He said, "Suppose ye that I am come to give peace on earth? I tell you, Nay; but rather *division.* For from henceforth there shall be five in one house *divided,* three against two, and two against three," etc. (Luke 12:51, 52). So it proved then, and so it has been ever since. *Why* we do not know. God's ways are ever different from ours. There will be another "*division*" among the people of the earth when the Lord Jesus leaves the Father's throne and descends into the air; yea, a "*division*" also among the people in the graves. Only the "dead in Christ" shall then be raised, and only the living ones who have been saved by Him will be "caught up together to meet the Lord in the air." The rest will be left behind. What a "division" that will be! In which company would *you* be, dear reader, were Christ to come today?

"So there was a division among the people because of him." If this was the case when Christ was upon earth, then we must not be surprised if those who faithfully serve Him occasion a "division" during His absence. Scripture says, "Woe unto you when *all* men speak well of you." Read through the book of Acts and note what "divisions" the preaching of the apostles caused. Mark that solemn but explicit word in I Cor. 11:19, "For there *must be* also *factions* among you, that they that are approved may be made manifest among you" (R.V.). How senseless, then, is all this modern talk about the union of Christendom. Fellow-preacher, if you are faithfully declaring all the counsel of God, be not surprised, nor be dismayed, if there is a "division" because of *you*. Regard it as an ominous sign if it be otherwise.

"And some of them would have taken him; but no man laid hands on him" (7:44). This is similar to what was before us in v. 30. Again and again is this noted in John's Gospel: cf. 5:16, 18; 17:1; 8:20; 10:39, etc. But they were powerless before the decrees of God. "Some of them *would have* taken him." The Greek word means they "desired" to do so. They had a will to, but not the ability. Ah! men may boast of their will-power and of their "free will," but after all, what does it amount to? Pilate said, "Knowest thou not that *I have power* to crucify thee, and have power to release thee" (John 19:10). So he boasted, and so he really believed. But what was our Lord's rejoinder? "Jesus answered, Thou couldest have no power at all against me, *except it were given thee from above*." It was so here: these men *desired* to arrest Christ, but they were not given power from above to do so. Verily, we may say with the prophet of old, "O Lord, I know that the way of man is not in himself: it is not in man that walketh to direct his steps" (Jer. 10:23).

"Then came the officers to the chief priests and Pharisees; and they said unto them, Why have you not brought him?" (7:45). Well might they ask such a question, for they were totally ignorant of the real answer. Well might Pharaoh now ask, Why did I fail in destroying the Hebrews? Or Nero, Why did I not succeed in exterminating all the Christians? Or the king of Spain, Why did my "invincible Armada" fail to reach the English ports and destroy the British navy? Or the Kaiser, Why did my legions not succeed in taking Paris? In each case the answer would be, Because *God* did not allow you to! Like these other infamous characters, the Pharisees had reckoned without God. They sent their officers to arrest Christ: they might as well have ordered them to stop the sun from shining. Not all the hosts of earth and hell could have arrested Him one moment before God's predestined hour had arrived. Ah, dear reader, the God of the Bible is no mere figurehead. He is Supreme in fact as well as in name. When *He* gets ready to act none can hinder; and until He *is* ready, none can speed Him. This is a hateful thought for His enemies, but one full of comfort to His people. If you, my reader, are fighting against Him, be it known that the great God laughs at your consummate folly, and will one day ere long deal with you in His fury. On the other hand, if you are, by sovereign grace, one of His children, then He is *for* you, and if *God be for you*, who can be against you? Who, indeed!

"The officers answered, Never man spake like this man." (7:46). What a testimony was this from unbelievers! Instead of arresting Him, they had been arrested by what they had heard, Mark again how this magnifies Christ as "*the Word*"! It was not His miracles which had so deeply impressed them, but His speech! "Never man *spake* as this man." True indeed was their witness, for the One they had listened to was *more* than "man" – "the Word was God"! No man ever spake like Christ because *His* words were spirit and life (John 6:63). What sayest *thou* of Christ, my reader? Do you own that "never man spake as this man"? Have His words come *to you* with a force that none other's ever did? Have they pierced you through to "the dividing asunder of soul and spirit"? Have they brought life to your soul, joy to your heart, rest to your conscience, peace to your mind? Ah, if *you* have heard *Him* say "Come unto me, all ye that labor and are heavy laden, and I will give you rest," and you have responded to His voice, then can you say indeed, "Never man spake like *this* man."

"Then answered them the Pharisees, Are ye also deceived? Have any of the rulers or of the Pharisees believed on him?" (7:47, 48). The "rulers" were men of official rank; the "Pharisees," the religious formalists of that day. Few "rulers" or men of eminent standing, few "scribes" or men of erudition, few "Pharisees" or men of strict morality, were numbered among the followers of the Lamb. They were too well satisfied with themselves to see any need of a Saviour. The sneering criticism of these Pharisees has been repeated in every age, and the very fact that it *is* made only supplies another evidence of the veracity of God's Word. Said the apostle Paul, "*Not many* wise men after the flesh, *not many* mighty, *not many* noble, are called: but God hath chosen the foolish things of the world to confound the wise; and God hath chosen the weak things of the world to confound the things which are mighty; and base things of the world, and things which are despised, hath God chosen, yea, and things which are not, to bring to naught things which are" (I Cor. 1:26-28). And why?—"that no flesh *should glory* in his presence"!

"But this people who knoweth not the law are cursed" (7:49). "This people" was a term of contempt. It has been rendered by some scholars, "This rabble—this mob—this riff raff." Nothing was more mortifying to these proud Pharisees, and nothing is more humiliating to their modern descendants than to find harlots and publicans entering the kingdom while they are left outside.

"Nicodemus saith unto them, (he that came to Jesus by night, being one of them,) Doth our law judge any man, before it hear him, and know what he doeth?" (7:50, 51). Have *any* of the Pharisees believed on Christ, they asked? Not many had, but at least one had, as Nicodemus gave evidence. Here is the one ray of light which relieves this dark picture. Sovereign grace had singled out one of these very Pharisees, and gave him courage to rebuke his unrighteous fellows. It is true that Nicodemus does not appear to have said much on this occasion, but he said sufficient to break up their conference. Not yet did he come out boldly on the Lord's side; but he was no longer one of His enemies. The work of grace proceeds slowly in some hearts, as in the case of Nicodemus; for eighteen months had elapsed since what is recorded in John 3. With others the work of grace acts more swiftly, as in the case of Saul of Tarsus. Here, as everywhere, God acts according to His own sovereign pleasure. Later, if the Lord will, Nicodemus will come before us again, and then we shall behold the full corn in the ear. John's Gospel depicts three stages in the spiritual career of Nicodemus. In John 3 it is midnight: here in John 7 it is twilight: in John 19 it is daylight in his soul.

"They answered and said unto him, Art thou also of Galilee? Search, and look: for out of Galilee ariseth no prophet" (7:52). But they were wrong. Their own Scriptures refuted them. Jonah was a "prophet," and he arose from *Galilee*: see II Kings 14:25. So, most probably, did one or two other of their prophets. When they asked Nicodemus, "Art thou also of Galilee?" they evidently meant, Art thou also a Galilean, that is, one of His party?

"And every man went unto his own house" (7:53). The reference here is to "every man" mentioned throughout this chapter. The Feast was now over. The temporary "booths" would be taken down: and all would now retire to their regular dwellings. "Every man *went* unto his own house" is very solemn. *Away* from Christ they went. Him they left! They desired His company no longer. And there the curtain falls.

The following questions are designed to prepare the student for the next chapter on John 8:1-11: —

1. Wherein does this passage supply a further proof of the awful condition of Israel?

2. What is the force and significance of "He *sat down*"? v. 2 —contrast "Jesus *stood*" in 7:37.
3. Wherein lay the "temptation"? v. 6.
4. What was the significance of Christ writing with His finger on the ground? v. 6.
5. Why did He "again" write on the ground? v. 8.
6. According to which of the Divine attributes was Christ acting in v. 11?
7. What do the words "go, and sin no more" (v. 11) evidence?

Exposition of the Gospel of JOHN

Three Volumes Complete and Unabridged in One

Arthur W. Pink

VOLUME TWO — *John 8 to 15:6*

CHAPTER TWENTY-EIGHT

Christ and the Adulterous Woman

John 8:1-11

We begin with the customary Analysis: —

1. Jesus retires to the mount of Olives: v. 1.
2. Jesus teaching in the temple: v. 2.
3. The Pharisees confront Him with an adulterous woman: vv. 3-6.
4. Christ turns the light upon them: vv. 6-8.
5. The Pharisees overcome by the light: v. 9.
6. The woman left alone with Christ: v. 10.
7. The woman dismissed with a warning: v. 11.

In this series of expositions of John's Gospel we have sedulously avoided technical matters, preferring to confine ourselves to that which would provide food for the soul. But in the present instance we deem it necessary to make an exception. The passage which is to be before us has long been the subject of controversy. Its authenticity has been questioned even by godly men. John 7:53 to 8:11 inclusive is not found in a number of the most important of the ancient manuscripts. The R.V. places a question mark against this passage. Personally we have not the slightest doubt but that it forms a part of the inspired Word of God, and that for the following reasons:

First, if our passage be a spurious one then we should have to pass straight from 7:52 to 8:12. Let the reader try this, and note the effect; and then let him go back to 7:52 and read straight through to 8:14. Which seems the more natural and reads the more smoothly?

Second, if we omit the first eleven verses of John 8, and start the chapter with v. 12, several questions will rise unavoidably and prove very difficult to answer satisfactorily. For example: "*Then* spake Jesus"—when? What simple and satisfactory answer can be found in the second part of John 7? But give John 8:1-11 its proper place, and the answer is, Immediately after the interruption recorded in v. 3. "Then spake Jesus again *unto them*" (v. 12)—unto whom? Go back to the second half of John 7 and see if it furnishes any decisive answer. But give 8:2 a place, and all is simple and plain. Again in v. 13 we read, "The *Pharisees* therefore said unto him": this was in the temple (v. 20). But how came the Pharisees there? 7:45 shows them elsewhere. But bring in 8:1-11 and this difficulty vanishes, for 8:2 shows that this was the day following.

In the third place, the contents of John 8:1-11 are in full accord with the evident design of this section of the Gospel. The method followed in these chapters is most significant. In each instance we find the Holy Spirit records some striking incident in our Lord's life, which serves to introduce and *illustrate* the teaching which follows it. In chapter 5 Christ quickens the impotent man, and makes that miracle the text of the sermon He preached immediately after it. In John 6 He feeds the hungry multitude, and right after gives the two discourses concerning Himself as the Bread of life. In John 7 Christ's refusal to go up to the Feast publicly and openly manifest His glory, is made the background for that wondrous word of the *future manifestation* of the Holy Spirit through believers—issuing from them as "rivers of living water." *And the same principle may be observed here in John* 8. In 8:12 Christ declares, "I am *the light* of the world," and the first eleven verses supply us with a most striking illustration and solemn demonstration of the *power* of that "light." Thus it may be seen that there is an indissoluble link between the incident recorded in John 8:1-11 and the teaching of our Lord immediately following.

Finally, as we shall examine these eleven verses and study their contents, endeavoring to sound their marvelous depths, it will be evident, we trust, to every spiritual intelligence, that no uninspired pen drew the picture therein described. The internal evidence, then, and the spiritual indications (apprehended and appreciated only by those who enter into God's thoughts) are far more weighty than external considerations. The one who is led and taught by the Spirit of God need not waste valuable time examining ancient manuscripts for the purpose of discovering whether or not this portion of the Bible is really a part of God's own Word.

Our passage emphasizes once more the abject condition of Israel. Again and again does the Holy Spirit call our attention to the fearful state that Israel was in during the days of Christ's earthly ministry. In chapter 1 we see the ignorance of the Jews as to the identity of the Lord's forerunner (1:14), and blind to the Divine Presence in their midst (1:26). In chapter 2 we have illustrated the joyless state of the nation, and are shown their desecration of the Father's House. In chapter 3 we behold a member of the Sanhedrin dead in trespasses and sins, needing to be born again (3:7), and the Jews quibbling with John's disciples about purifying (3:25). In chapter 4 we discover the callous indifference of Israel toward their Gentile neighbors—"the Jews have no dealings with the Samaritans" (4:9). In chapter 5 we have a portrayal of God's covenant people in the great multitude of impotent folk, "blind, halt and withered." In chapter 6 they are represented as hungry, yet having no appetite for the Bread of life. In chapter 7 the leaders of the nation send officers to arrest Christ. And now in chapter 8 Israel is contemplated as Jehovah's unfaithful wife—"adulterous."

"Jesus went unto the mount of Olives" (8:1). This points a contrast from the closing verse of the previous chapter. There we read, "Every man went unto his own house." Here we are told, "Jesus went unto the mount of Olives." We believe that this contrast conveys a double thought, in harmony with the peculiar character of this fourth Gospel. All through John two things concerning Christ are made prominent: His essential glory and His voluntary humiliation. Here, the Holy Spirit presents Him to us as the eternal Son of God, but also as the Son come down from heaven, made flesh. Thus we are given to behold, on the one hand, His uniqueness, His peerless excellency; and on the other, the depths of shame into which He descended. Frequently these are placed almost side by side. Thus in chapter 4, we read of Him, "wearied with his journey"

(v. 6); and then in the verses that follow, His Divine glories shine forth. Other examples will recur to the reader. So here in the passage before us. "Jesus went unto the *mount* of Olives" (following 7:53) suggests the *elevation* of Christ. But no doubt it also tells of the *humiliation* of the Saviour. The foxes had holes, and the birds of the air had nests, but the Son of man had not where to lay His head (Matt. 8:20): therefore, when "every man went unto *his own* house," "Jesus went unto the mount of Olives," for *He* "owned" no "house" down here. He who was rich for our sakes became poor.

"And early in the morning he came again into the temple" (8:2). There is nothing superfluous in Scripture. Each one of these scenes has been drawn by the Heavenly Artist, so we may be fully assured that every line, no matter how small, has a meaning and value. If we keep steadily before us the *subject* of this picture we shall be the better able to appreciate its varied tints. The theme of our chapter is the outshining of the Light of life. How appropriate then is this opening word: the *early* "morning" is the hour which introduces the daylight!

"And early in the morning he came again into the temple." This word also conveys an important practical lesson for us, inasmuch as Christ here leaves an example that we should follow His steps. In the first sermon of our Lord's recorded in the New Testament we find that He said, "Seek ye *first* the kingdom of God, and his righteousness" (Matt. 6:33), and *He* ever practised what he preached. The lesson which our Redeemer here exemplified is, that we need to *begin* the day by seeking the face and blessing of God! The Divine promise is, "They that seek me *early* shall find me" (Prov. 8:17). How different would be our lives if we *really* began each day with God! Thus only can we obtain that fresh supply of grace which will give the needed strength for the duties and conflicts of the hours that follow.

"And all the people came unto him" (8:2). This is another instance where the word "all" must be understood in a modified sense. Again and again is it used relatively rather than absolutely. For example, in 3:26 we read of the disciples of John coming to their master in complaint that Christ was attracting so many to Himself: "*all* come to him," they said. Again, in 6:45 the Lord Jesus declared, "They shall be *all* taught of God." So here, "*all* the people came unto him." These and many other passages which might be cited should prevent us from falling into the errors of Universalism. For example, "I, if I be lifted up from the earth will draw *all* unto me" (John 12:32), does not mean all without exception. It is a very patent fact that everybody *is not* "drawn" to Christ. The "all" in John 12:32 is *all without distinction.* So here "*all* the people came unto him" (8:2) signifies all that were in the temple, that is, all kinds and conditions of men, men of varied age and social standing, men from the different tribes.

"And he sat down, and taught them" (8:2). Jesus *stood;* Jesus *walked;* Jesus *sat.* Each of these expressions in John's Gospel conveys a distinctive moral truth. Jesus "stood" directs attention to the dignity and blessedness of His person, and it is very solemn to note that in no single instance (where this expression occurs) was the glory of His person recognized: cf. 1:26; 7:37 and what follows; 20:14, 19, 26; 21:4. Jesus "walked" refers to the public manifestation of Himself: see our notes on 7:1. Jesus "sat" points to His condescending lowliness, meekness and grace: see 4:6; 6:3; 12:15.

"And the scribes and Pharisees brought unto him a woman taken in adultery; and when they had set her in the midst, They say unto him, Master, this woman was taken in adultery, in the very act. Now Moses in the law commanded us, that such should be stoned: but what sayest thou? This they said, tempting him, that they might have to accuse him" (8:3-6). Following the miscarriage of their plans on the previous day—through the failure of the officers to arrest Christ (7:45)—the enemies of Christ hit upon a new scheme: they sought to impale Him on the horns of a dilemma. The roar of the "lion" had failed; now we are to behold the wiles of the "serpent."

The awful malignity of the Lord's enemies is evident on the surface. They brought this adulterous woman to Christ not because they were shocked at her conduct, still less because they were grieved that God's holy law had been broken. Their object was to use this woman to exploit her sin and further their own evil designs. With coldblooded indelicacy they acted, employing the guilt of their captive to accomplish their evil intentions against Christ. Their motive cannot be misinterpreted. They were anxious to discredit our Lord before the people. They did not wait until they could interrogate Him in private, but, interrupting as He was teaching the people, they rudely challenged Him to solve what must have seemed to them an unsolvable enigma.

The problem by which they sought to defy Infinite Wisdom was this: A woman had been taken in the act of adultery, and the law required that she should be stoned. Of this there is no room for doubt, see Lev. 20:10 and Deut. 22:22.* "What sayest thou?" they asked. An insidious question, indeed. Had He said, "Let her go," they could then accuse Him as being an enemy against the law of God, and His own word "Think not that I am come to destroy the law, or the prophets: I am not come to destroy, but to fulfill" (Matt. 5:17) had been falsified. But if He answered, "Stone her," they would have ridiculed the fact that He was the "friend of publicans and sinners." No doubt they were satisfied that they had Him completely cornered. On the one hand, if He ignored the charge they brought against this guilty woman, they could accuse Him of compromising with sin; on the other hand, if He passed sentence on her, what became of His own word, "For God sent not his Son into the world to condemn the world; but that the world through him might be saved" (John 3:17)? Here, then, was the dilemma: if Christ palliated the wickedness of this woman, where was His respect for the holiness of God and the righteousness of His law; but if He condemned her, what became of His claim that He had come here to "seek and to save that which was lost" (Luke 19:10)? And yet of what avail was their satanic subtlety in the presence of God manifest in flesh!

Ere passing on it may be well to notice how this incident furnishes an illustration of the fact that wicked men can quote the Scriptures when they imagine that it will further their evil designs: "Now Moses in the law commanded us, that such should be stoned." But what cared they for the law? They were

* Where the form of death was not specified, it was by stoning.

seeking to turn the point of the Spirit's "sword" against the One they hated; soon they were to feel its sharp edge of themselves. Let us not be deceived then and conclude that every one who quotes Scripture to us must, necessarily, be a God-fearing man. Those who quote the Scriptures to condemn others are frequently the guiltiest of all. Those who are so solicitous to point to the mote in another's eye, generally have a beam in their own.

But there is far more here than meets the eye at first glance, or second too. The whole incident supplies a most striking portrayal of what is developed at length in the epistle to the Romans. It is not difficult to discern here (skulking behind the scenes) the hideous features of the great Enemy of God and His people. The hatred of these scribes and Pharisees was fanned by the inveterate enmity of the Serpent against the woman's "Seed." The subject is profoundly mysterious, but Scripture supplies more than one plain hint that Satan is permitted to *challenge* the very character of God—the book of Job, the third of Zechariah, and Rev. 12:10 are proofs of that. No doubt one reason why the Lord God suffers this is for the instruction of the unfallen angels—cf. Eph. 3:10.

The problem presented to Christ by His enemies was no mere local one. So far as human reason can perceive it was the profoundest moral problem which ever could or can confront God Himself. That problem was how justice and mercy could be harmonized. The law of righteousness imperatively demands the punishment of its transgressor. To set aside that demand would be to introduce a reign of anarchy. Moreover, God is holy as well as righteous; and holiness burns against evil, and cannot allow that which is defiled to enter His presence. What, then, is to become of the poor sinner? A transgressor of the law he certainly is; and equally manifest is his moral pollution. His only hope lies in mercy; his salvation is possible only by grace. But how can mercy be exercised when the sword of justice bars her way? How can grace flow forth except by slighting holiness? Ah, human wisdom could never have found an answer to such questions. It is evident that these scribes and Pharisees thought of none. And we are fully assured that at the beginning Satan himself could see no solution to this mighty problem. But blessed be His name, God *has* "found a way" whereby His banished ones may be restored (II Sam. 14: 13, 14). What this is we shall see hinted at in the remainder of our passage.

Let us observe how each of the essential elements in this problem of all problems is presented in the passage before us. We may summarize them thus: First, we have there the person of that blessed One who had come to seek and to save that which was lost. Second, we have a sinner, a guilty sinner, one who could by no means clear herself. Third, the law was against her: the law she had broken, and the declared penalty of it was death. Fourth, the guilty sinner was brought before the Saviour Himself, and was *indicted* by His enemies. Such, then, was the problem now presented to Christ. Would grace stand helpless before law? If not, wherein lay the solution? Let us attend carefully to what follows.

"But Jesus stooped down, and with his finger wrote on the ground" (8:6). This was the first thing that He here did. That there was a symbolical significance to His action goes without saying, and what this is we are not left to guess. Scripture is its own interpreter. This was not the first time that the Lord had written "with his finger." In Ex. 31:18 we read, "And he gave unto Moses, when he had made an end of communing with him upon mount Sinai, two tables of testimony, tables of stone, *written with the finger of God*." When, then, our Lord wrote on *the ground* (from the ground must the "tables of *stone*" have been taken), it was as though He had said, You remind Me of the *law!* Why, it was *My* finger which wrote that law! Thus did He show these Pharisees that He had come here, not to destroy the law, but to fulfill it. His writing on the ground, then, was (symbolically) a *ratification* of God's righteous law. But so blind were His would-be accusers they discerned not the significance of His act.

"So when they *continued* asking him" (8:7). It is evident that our Lord's enemies mistook His silence for embarrassment. They no more grasped the force of His action of writing on the ground, than did Belshazzar understand the writing of that same Hand on the walls of his palace. Emboldened by His silence, and satisfied that they had Him cornered, they continued to press their question upon Him. O the persistency of evil-doers! How often they put to shame our *lack* of perseverance and importunity.

"So when they continued asking him, he lifted up himself, and said unto them, He that is without sin among you, let him first cast a stone at her" (8:7). This, too, has a far deeper meaning than what appears on the surface. God's Law was a holy and a righteous one, and here we find the Lawgiver Himself turning its white light upon these men who really had so little respect for it. Christ was here intimating that *they*, His would-be *accusers*, were no fit subjects to demand the enforcement of the law's sentence. None but a holy hand should administer the perfect law. In principle, we may see here the great Adversary and Accuser *reprimanded*. Satan may stand before the angel of the Lord to resist "the high priest" (Zech. 3:1), but, morally, *he* is the *last* one who should insist on the maintenance of righteousness. And how strikingly this reprimanding of the Pharisees by Christ adumbrated what we read of in Zech. 3:2 ("The Lord *rebuke* thee, O Satan") scarcely needs to be pointed out.

"And again he stooped down, and wrote on the ground" (8:8). Profoundly significant was this, and unspeakably blessed. The symbolic meaning of it is plainly hinted at in the word "again": the Lord wrote on the ground *a second time*. And of what did that speak? Once more the Old Testament Scriptures supply the answer. The first "tables of stone" were dashed to the ground by Moses, and broken. A *second* set was therefore written by God. And what became of the second "tables of stone"? *They* were laid up in the ark (Ex. 40:20), and were covered by the blood-sprinkled mercy-seat! Here, then, Christ was giving more than a hint of *how* He would save those who were, by the law, condemned to death. It was not that the law would be set aside: far from it. As His first stooping down and with His finger writing on the ground intimated, the law would be "*established*." But as He stooped down and wrote the *second* time, He signified that the shed blood of an innocent substitute should come between the law and those it condemned!

"And they which heard it, being convicted by their own conscience, went out one by one, beginning at the eldest, even unto the last" (8:9). Thus was "the strong man bound" (Matt. 12:29). Christ's enemies had thought to ensnare Him by the law of Moses; instead, they had its searching light turned upon themselves. Grace had not defied, but had upheld the law! One sentence from the lips of Holiness incarnate and they were all silenced, all convicted, and all departed. At another time, a self-righteous Pharisee might boast of his fastings, his tithes and his prayers; but when God turns the light on a man's heart, his moral and spiritual depravity become apparent even to himself, and shame shuts his lips. So it was here. Not a word had Christ uttered against the law; in nowise had He condoned the woman's sin. Unable to find any ground for accusation against Him, completely baffled in their evil designs, convicted by their consciences, they slunk away: "beginning at the eldest," because he had the most sin to hide and the most reputation to preserve. And in the conduct of these men we have a clear intimation of how the wicked will act in the last great Day. Now, they may proclaim their self-righteousness, and talk about the injustice of eternal punishment. But then, when the light of God flashes upon them, and their guilt and ruin are fully exposed, they shall, like these Pharisees, be speechless.

"And they which heard it, being convicted by their own conscience, went out." There is a solemn warning here for sinners who may be exercised in mind over their condition. Here were men who were "convicted by their own conscience," yet instead of this causing them to cast themselves at the feet of Christ, it resulted in them *leaving* Christ! Nothing short of the Holy Spirit's quickening will ever bring a soul into saving contact with the Lord Jesus.

"And they which heard it, being convicted by their own conscience, went out one by one, beginning at the eldest, even unto the last: and Jesus was left alone, and the woman standing in the midst" (8:9). This is exceedingly striking. These scribes and Pharisees had challenged Christ from the law. He met them on their own ground, and vanquished them by the law. "When Jesus had lifted up himself, and saw none but the woman, he said unto her, Woman, where are those thine accusers? hath *no man* condemned thee? She said, *No man*, Lord. And Jesus said unto her, Neither do *I* condemn thee" (8:10, 11). The law required two witnesses before its sentence could be executed (Deut. 19:15), yet, those witnesses must assist in the carrying out of the sentence (Deut. 17:7). But here not a single witness was left to testify against this woman who had merely been indicted. Thus the law was powerless to touch her. What, then, remained? Why, the way was now clear for Christ to act in "grace *and* truth."

"Neither do I condemn thee: go, and sin no more" (8:11). No doubt the question occurs to many of our readers, Was this woman saved at the time she left Christ? Personally, we believe that she was. We believe so because *she* did not leave Christ when she had opportunity to do so; because she addressed Him as "Lord" (contrast "Master" of the Pharisees in v. 4); and because Christ said to her, "Neither do I condemn thee." But, as another has said, "In looking at these incidents of Scripture, we need not ask if the objects of the grace act in the intelligence of the story. It is enough for us that here was a sinner exposed in the presence of Him who came to meet sin and put it away. Whoever takes the place of this woman meets the word that clears of condemnation, just as the publicans and sinners with whom Christ eats in Luke 15, set forth this, that if one takes the place of the sinner and the outcast, he is at once received. So with the lost sheep and the lost piece of silver. There is no intelligence of their condition, yet they set forth that which, if one take, it is representative. To make it clear, one might ask, 'Are you as sinful as this woman, as badly lost as that sheep or piece of silver?'" (Malachi Taylor)

"And they which heard it, being convicted by their own conscience, went out one by one, beginning at the eldest, even unto the last: and Jesus was left alone, and the woman standing in the midst. When Jesus had lifted up himself, and saw none but the woman, he said unto her, Woman, where are those thine accusers? hath no man condemned thee? She said, No man, Lord. And Jesus said unto her, Neither do I condemn thee: go, and sin no more." How striking and how blessed is this sequel to what has been before us! When Christ wrote on the ground the *second* time (not before), the "accusers" of the guilty departed! And then, after the last accuser had disappeared, the Lord said, "Neither do I condemn thee." How perfect the picture! And to complete it, Christ added, "Go, and sin no more," which is still His word to those who have been saved by grace. And the *ground,* the *righteous* ground, on which He pronounced this verdict "Neither do I condemn thee," was, that in a short time *He* was going to be "condemned" in her stead. Finally, note the *order* of these two words of Christ to this woman who owned Him as "Lord" (I Cor. 12:3). It was not, "Go and sin no more, *and* I will not condemn thee," for that would have been a death-knell rather than good news in her ears. Instead, the Saviour said, "Neither do I condemn thee." And to every one who takes the place this woman was brought into, the word is, "There is therefore now *no condemnation*" (Rom. 8:1). "And sin no more" placed her, as we are placed, under the *constraint* of His love.

This incident then contains far more than that which was of local and ephemeral significance. It, in fact, raises the basic question of, How can mercy and justice be harmonized? How can grace flow forth except by slighting holiness? In the scene here presented to our view we are shown, not by a closely reasoned out statement of doctrine, but in symbolic action, that this problem is *not* insoluable to Divine wisdom. Here was a concrete case of a guilty sinner leaving the presence of Christ *un*-condemned. And it was neither because the law had been slighted nor sin palliated. The requirements of the law were strictly complied with, and her sin was openly condemned—"sin *no more*." Yet, she herself, was not condemned. She was dealt with according to "grace *and* truth." Mercy flowed out to her, yet not at the expense of justice. Such, in brief, is a summary of this marvelous narrative; a narrative which, verily, no man ever invented and no uninspired pen ever recorded.

This blessed incident not only anticipated the epistle to the Romans, but it also outlines, by vivid symbols, the Gospel of the grace of God. The Gospel not only announces a Saviour for sinners, but it also *explains how* God can save them consistently with the requirements of His character. As Rom. 1:17 tells us, in the Gospel is "the *righteousness* of God revealed." And this is precisely what is set forth here in John 8.

The entire incident is a most striking amplification and exemplification of John 1:17: "For the law was given by Moses, but *grace and truth* came by Jesus Christ." The grace of God never conflicts with His law, but, on the contrary, upholds its authority, "As sin hath reigned unto death, even so might grace reign *through righteousness* unto eternal life by Jesus Christ our Lord" (Rom. 5:21). But as to *how* grace might reign "through righteousness" was a problem which God alone could solve, and *Christ's* solution of it here marks Him as none other than "God manifest in flesh." With what blessed propriety, then, is this incident placed in the fourth Gospel, the special design of which is to display the Divine glory of the Lord Jesus!

Perhaps a separate word needs to be said on v. 7, in connection with which some have experienced a difficulty; and that is, Do these words of Christ enunciate a principle which *we* are justified in using? If so, under what circumstances? It is essential to bear in mind that Christ was not here speaking as Judge, but as One in the place of the Servant. The principle involved has been well stated thus, "We have no right to say to an official who in condemning culprits or in prosecuting them is simply discharging a public duty, 'See that your own hands be clean, and your own heart pure before you condemn another'; but we have a perfect right to silence a private individual who is officiously and not officially exposing another's guilt, by bidding him remember that he has a beam in his own eye which he must first be rid of" (Dr. Dods).

The "scribes and Pharisees" who brought the guilty adulteress to Christ must be viewed as *representatives of their nation* (as Nicodemus in John 3 and the impotent man in John 5). What, then, was the spiritual condition of Israel at that time? It was precisely that of this guilty woman: an "evil and adulterous generation" (Matt. 12:37) Christ termed them. But they were blinded by self-righteousness: they discerned not their awful condition, and knew not that they, equally with the Gentiles, were under the curse that had descended upon all from our father, Adam. Moreover; they were under a deeper guilt than the Gentiles—they stood convicted of the additional crime of having broken their covenant with the Lord. They were, in fact, the unfaithful, the adulterous wife of Jehovah (see Ezek. 16; Hosea 2, etc.). What, then, did Jehovah's law call for in such a case? The answer to this question is furnished in Num. 5, which sets forth "the law of jealousy," and describes the Divinely-ordered procedure for establishing the guilt of an unfaithful wife.

We cannot here quote the whole of Num. 5, but would ask the reader to turn to and read vv. 11-31 of that chapter. We quote now vv. 17, 24, 27:—"And the priest shall take holy water in an earthen vessel; and of the dust that is in the floor of the tabernacle the priest shall take, and put it into the water . . . And he shall cause the woman to drink the bitter water that causeth the curse: and the water that causeth the curse shall enter into her, and become bitter . . . And when he hath made her to drink the water, then it shall come to pass, that, if she be defiled, *and have done trespass against her husband*, that the water that causeth the curse shall enter into her, and become bitter, and her belly shall swell, and her thigh shall rot: and the woman shall be a curse among her people!"

What light these verses cast upon our Lord's dealings with the Pharisees (representatives of Israel) here in John 8. "Water" is the well-known emblem of the Word (Eph. 5:26, etc.). This water is here termed *"holy."* It was to be in an *earthen* vessel (cf. II Cor. 4:7). This water was to be mixed with "the dust which is in the floor of the tabernacle." Thus the water becomes *"bitter* water," and the woman was made to drink it. The result would be (in case she was guilty) that her guilt would be *outwardly evidenced* in the swelling of her belly (symbol of pride) and the rotting of her thigh—her strength turned to corruption. Now put these separate items together, and is it not precisely what we find here in John 8? The Son of God is there incarnate, "made flesh," an "earthen vessel." The "holy water" is seen in His holy words—"He that is without sin among you, let him first cast a stone at her." In stooping down and writing on the floor of the temple, He mingled "the dust" with it. As He did this it became "bitter" to the proud Pharisees. In the conviction of their consciences we see *how* "bitter," and in going out, one by one, abashed, we see the withering of their strength! And thus was the guilt of Jehovah's unfaithful wife made fully manifest!

The following questions bear upon the next chapter:—

1. What is meant by "the world" in v. 12? Do not jump to conclusions.
2. What kind of *light* does "the world" enjoy? v. 12
3. What is "the light of life"? v. 12.
4. To *what* "witness of the Father" was Christ referring? v. 18.
5. What does "die in your sins" (v. 21) prove concerning the Atonement?
6. What is the meaning of v. 31?
7. What does the truth make free *from*? v. 32.

CHAPTER TWENTY-NINE

Christ, the Light of the World

John 8:12-32

The following is a Summary of the passage which is to be before us:—

1. Christ the Light of the world: v. 12.
2. The Pharisees' denial: v. 13.
3. Christ enforces His claim to absolute Deity: vv. 14-18.
4. The Pharisees' question and Christ's reply: vv. 19, 20.
5. Christ's solemn warning to the Pharisees: vv. 21-24.
6. The Pharisees' question and Christ's reply: vv. 25-29.
7. The many who "believed" and Christ's warning to them; vv. 30-32.

The first division of John 8 forms a most striking and suitable introduction to the first verse of our present lesson, which, in turn, supplies the key to what follows in the remainder of the chapter. The Holy Spirit records here one of the precious discourses of "The Wonderful Counsellor," a discourse broken by the repeated interruptions of His enemies. Christ announces Himself as "the light of the world", but this is prefaced by an incident which gives wonderful force to that utterance.

As we saw in our last chapter, the first eleven verses of John 8 describe a venomous assault made upon the Saviour by the scribes and Pharisees. A determined effort was made to discredit Him before the people. A woman taken in adultery was brought, the penalty of the Mosaic law was defined, and then the question was put to Christ, "*But* what sayest *thou?*" We are not left to speculate as to their motive: the passage tells us "This they said, tempting him, that they might have *to accuse* him." Think of it! They imagined that they could substantiate an accusation against the Lawgiver Himself! What perversity: what blindness: what depravity! Yet how effectively this serves as a *dark* back-ground on which to display the better, "the light"! Nor is that all that this introduction effected.

In our exposition of these verses we intimated that what was there presented to Christ was the problem—altogether too profound for creature wisdom—how to harmonize justice and mercy. The woman was guilty; of that there could be no doubt. The sentence of the law was plainly defined. What reply, then, could Christ make to the open challenge, "What sayest thou?" There is little need for us to repeat what was said in the previous chapter, though the theme is a most captivating one. By symbolic action our Lord showed that it was not the Divine intention for mercy to be exercised at the expense of justice. He intimated that the law would be enforced. But by writing on the ground the *second* time, He reminded His would-be accusers that a shelter from the exposed law was planned, and that a blood-sprinkled covering would protect the guilty one from its accusing voice. Thus did the Redeemer intimate that God's *righteousness* would be magnified in the Divine method of saving sinners, and that His *holiness* would shine forth with unsullied splendor. And "*light*" is the emblem of holiness and righteousness! Fitting introduction, then, was this for our Lord's announcement of Himself as "the *light* of the world."

But not only did the malice of the Lord's enemies supply a dark background to bring into welcome relief the outshining of the Divine Light; not only did their attack supply Christ with an opportunity for Him to manifest Himself as the Vindicator of God's holiness and righteousness; but we may also discover a further reason for the Holy Spirit describing this incident at the beginning of our chapter. Following His symbolic action of writing on the ground, the Lord uttered one brief sentence, and one only, to His tempters, but that one was quite sufficient to rout them completely. "He that is without sin among you, let him first cast a stone at her" was what He said. The effect was startling: "Being convicted by their conscience" they "went out one by one, beginning at the eldest, even unto the last: and Jesus was left alone, and the woman standing in the midst." It was the holy "light" of God which smote their sin-darkened understandings, and their departure demonstrated the *power* of that light! Observe, too, the words of Christ to the adulterous woman: "Go," He said, *not* "in peace"; but "GO, and *sin no more*." How that evidenced the spotless *purity* of "the light"! Thus we see, once more, the great importance of studying and weighing the *context;* for here, as everywhere, it gives meaning to what follows.

"Then spake Jesus again unto them" (8:12). *"Then"* signifies after the departure of the Pharisees and after the adulterous woman had gone. "Then spake Jesus again *unto them*." This takes us back to the second verse of our chapter where we are told that in the early morning Christ entered the temple, and, as all the people came unto Him, He sat down and taught them. Now, after the rude interruption from certain of the scribes and Pharisees, He resumed His teaching of the people, and spake "again unto them." And herein we may discover, once more, the perfections of the God-man. The disagreeable interruption had in no wise disturbed His composure. Though fully aware of the malignant design of the Pharisees, He possessed His soul in patience. Without exhibiting the slightest perturbation, refusing to be turned aside from the task He was engaged in, He returned at once to the teaching of the people. How differently *we* act under provocation! To us disturbances are only too frequently perturbances. If only we realized that *everything* which enters our life is ordered by God, and we acted in accord with this, then should we maintain our composure and conduct ourselves with unruffled serenity. But only one perfect life has been lived on this earth; and our innumerable imperfections only serve to emphasize the *uniqueness* of that life.

"Then spake Jesus again unto them, saying, I am the light of the world" (8:12). This is the second of the "I am" titles of Christ found in this fourth Gospel. It calls for most careful consideration. We may observe, in the first place, that this announcement by Christ was in full accord with the Old Testament prophecies concerning the Messiah. Through Isaiah God said concerning the Coming One, "I the Lord have called thee in righteousness, and will hold thine hand, and will keep thee, and give thee for a covenant of the people, for a *light* of the Gentiles"

(42:6). And again, "And he said, It is a light thing that thou shouldest be my servant to raise up the tribes of Jacob, and to restore the preserved of Israel: I will also give thee for *a light* to the Gentiles, that thou mayest be my salvation unto the end of the earth" (49:6). And again, He was denominated "the *sun* of righteousness" who should arise "with healing in his wings" or "beams" (Mal. 4:2).

"I am the light of the world." We may notice, in the second place, that "light" is one of the three things which *God* is said to be. In John 4:24 we are told, "God is *spirit.*" In I John 1:5, "God is *light*"; and in I John 4:8, "God is *love.*" These expressions relate to the *nature* of God, what He is in Himself. Hence, when Christ affirmed "I am *the light* of the world," He announced His absolute Deity. Believers are said to be "light *in the Lord*" (Eph. 5:8). But Christ Himself *was* "the light."

But what is meant by "I am the light *of the world*"? Does this mean that Christ is the Light of the whole human race, of every man and woman? If so, does this prove that Universalism is true? Certainly not. The second part of our verse disproves Universalism: it is only the one who "follows" Christ that has "the light of life." The one who does not "follow" Christ remains in darkness. The words of Christ in John 12:46 supply further repudiation of Universalism: "I am come a light into the world, that whosoever *believeth on me* should not abide in darkness." But if "I am the light of the world" does not teach Universalism, what does it mean? We believe that its force will best be ascertained by comparing John 1:4, 5, 9. As we have given an exposition of these verses in the second chapter of Vol. I, we would ask the reader to turn to it. Suffice it now to say we understand that "light" in these passages is not to be restricted to the spiritual illumination enjoyed by believers, but is to be taken in its widest signification. If John 1:4 be linked with the preceding verse (as it should be), it will be seen that the reference is to the relation sustained by the *Creator* to "men." The "light" which lightens every man that cometh into the world is that which constitutes him a responsible being. Every rational creature is morally enlightened. Christ is the Light of the world in the widest possible sense, inasmuch as all creature intelligence and all moral perception proceed from Him.

Perhaps it may be well to ask here, Why is it that "the world" is mentioned so frequently in this fourth Gospel? The "world" occurs only fifteen times in the first three Gospels added together; whereas in John it is found seventy-seven times! Why is this? The answer is not far to seek. In this fourth Gospel we have a presentation of what Christ is *essentially* in His own person, and not what He was in *special* relation to the Jews, as in the other Gospels. John treats of the *Deity* of Christ, and as *God* He is the Creator of all (1:3). and therefore the life and light of His creatures (1:4). It is true that in a number of instances "the world" has a restricted meaning, but these are not difficult to determine: either the context or parallel passages show us when the term is to be understood in its narrower sense. The principle of interpretation is not an arbitrary one. When something is predicated of "the world" which is true only of the redeemed, then we know it is only *the world of believers* which is in view: for instance, Christ giving (not proffering) life—here *eternal* life as the context shows—unto the world (John 6:33). But when there is nothing that is predicated of "the world" which is true *only* of believers, then it is "the world of the ungodly" (II Pet. 2:5) which is in view.

"He that followeth me shall not walk in darkness, but shall have the light of life" (8:12). At first glance this clause will seem, perhaps, to conflict with the definition we have given of "light" in the first part of the verse. "I am the light of the world" we understand to signify (in accord with John 1:4, 5, 9), I am the One who has bestowed intelligence and moral sensibility on all men. But now Christ says (by necessary implication) that unless a man "follows" Him he will "walk in *darkness*." But instead of conflicting with what we have said above, the second part of v. 12 will be found, on careful reflection, to confirm it. "He that followeth me" said our Lord, "shall not walk in darkness [Greek, "the darkness"], but shall," shall what? "enjoy the light"? no, "shall have the light of life." These words point a contrast. In the former sentence He spoke of Himself as the *moral* light of men; in the second He refers to the *spiritual* light which is possessed by believers only. This is clear from the expression used: he "shall have" not merely "light"—which all rational creatures possess; but "he shall have the light *of life*," that is, of spiritual, Divine light, which is something possessed only by those who "follow" Christ.

"He that followeth me shall not walk in darkness, but shall have the light of life." In these words, then, Christ defined the state of the natural man. The unregenerate *have* "light": they are capable of weighing moral issues; they have a conscience which either "accuses or excuses them" (Rom. 2:15); and they have the capacity to recognize the innumerable evidences which testify to the existence and natural attributes of the great Creator (Rom. 1:19); so that "they are without excuse" (Rom. 1:20). But *spiritual* light they do not have. Consequently, though they are endowed with intelligence and moral discernment, spiritually, they are "in the darkness." And it was because of this that the Saviour said, "He that followeth me shall not walk in the darkness, but shall have the light of life." The necessary implication of these words is that the world *is in* spiritual darkness. It was so two thousand years ago. The Greeks with all their wisdom and the Romans with all their laws were spiritually in the dark. And the world is the same today. Notwithstanding all the discoveries of science and all the efforts to educate, Europe and America are in the dark. The great crowds see not the true character of God, the worth of their souls, the reality of the world to come. And *Christ* is the only hope. He has risen like the sun, to diffuse life and light, salvation and peace, in the midst of a dark world.

"He that followeth me shall not walk in darkness, but shall have the light of life." What is it to "follow" Christ? It is to commit ourselves unreservedly to Him as our only Lord and Saviour in doctrine and conduct (see 1:37 and contrast 10:5). A beautiful illustration (borrowed from Bishop Ryle) of this is to be found in the history of Israel in the wilderness as they followed the "cloud." Just as the "cloud" led Israel from Egypt to Canaan, so the Lord Jesus leads the believer from this world to heaven. And to the one who really follows Christ the promise is, he shall not, like those all around him, walk in darkness.

"Light," in Scripture, is sometimes the emblem of true knowledge, true holiness, true happiness; while "darkness" is the figure for ignorance and error, guilt and depravity, privation and misery. Because the believer follows the One who is Light, he does not grope his way in doubt and uncertainty, but he sees where he is going, and not only so, he enjoys the light of God's countenance. But this is his experience only so far as he really "follows" Christ. Just as if it were possible to follow the sun in its complete circuit, we should always be in broad daylight, so the one who is actually following Christ shall not walk in darkness.

"The Pharisees therefore said unto him, Thou bearest record of thyself; thy record is not true" (8:13). Christ had just made the fullest claim to Deity when He said "I am the light of the world" the Pharisees could not understand Him to mean anything less. Jehovah-Elohim was the God of light, as numerous passages in the Old Testament plainly taught. When Jesus made this asseveration the Pharisees *therefore* said, "Thou bearest record of thyself; thy record is not true." The force of their objection seems to be this: That *God* is the Light of the world we fully allow, but when *you* avow this of yourself we cannot accredit it; what you say is false.

"The *Pharisees* therefore said unto him." Evidently these were a different company of Pharisees than those who had brought in the adulteress. Enraged by the discomfiture of their brethren, their fellows insultingly said to the Lord, Thy record is not true. They shrank from the Light. They could not endure the holy purity of its beams. They desired only to extinguish it. How solemnly this illustrated John 1:5—"The light shineth in darkness, and the darkness comprehended it not!"

"Jesus answered and said unto them, Though I bear record of myself, yet my record is true: for I know whence I came, and whither I go; but ye cannot tell whence I come, and whither I go;" (8:14). Here the Lord tersely replies to the unbelieving denial of the Pharisees, and ratifies what He had said just previously. Though My Divine glory is now veiled, though at present I am not exercising My Divine prerogatives, though I stand before you in *servant* form, nevertheless, when I affirmed that

I am the Light of the world I spoke the truth. My record *is* true because "I know whence I came and whither I go," which is a knowledge possessed absolutely by none else. He had come from the Father in heaven, and thither He would return; and therefore, as the Son, He could not give a false witness. But as to His heavenly nature and character they were in complete ignorance, and therefore altogether incompetent to form, and still less to pass, a judgment.

"Though I bear record of myself yet my record is true." Some have experienced a difficulty in harmonizing this with what we read of in 5:31 – "If I bear witness of myself, my witness is not true." But if each of these statements be interpreted in strict accord with the context the difficulty vanishes. In John 5 the Lord was proving that the witness or record He bore was not in *independence* of the Father, but in perfect accord therewith. The Father himself (5:37) and the Scriptures inspired by the Father (5:39) *also* testified to the absolute Deity of Christ. But here in John 8 the Lord Jesus is making *direct* reply to the Pharisees who had said that His witness was false. This He denies, and insists that it was true; and immediately after He appeals again to the confirmatory witness of the Father (see 8:18).

"Ye judge after the flesh; I judge no man" (8:15). We believe that there is a double thought here. When Christ said "Ye judge after (according to) the flesh," He meant, we think, first, You are deciding My claims according to what you see; you are judging according to outward appearances. Because I am in the likeness of sinful flesh you deem it impossible for *Me* to be "the light of the world." But appearances are deceptive. I do not form My judgments thus: I look on the heart, and see things as they actually are. But again; when Christ said: "Ye judge after the flesh," this was to affirm that they were *incapable* of judging Him. They adopted the world's principles, and judged according to carnal reasoning. Because of this they were incapable of discerning the Divine nature of His mission and message.

"I *judge* no man" has been variously interpreted. Many understand it to signify that Christ here reminded His critics that He was not then exercising His judicial prerogatives. It is regarded as being parallel with the last clause of John 12:47. But we think it is more natural, and better suited to the context, to supply an ellipsis, and understand Christ here to mean, *I do not* judge any man *after the flesh;* when I judge, it is according to spiritual and Divine principles. The Greek word signifies "to determine, to form an estimate, to arrive at a decision," and here it has precisely the same force in each clause. When Christ said to these Pharisees, "Ye *judge* after the flesh," He did not refer to a judicial verdict, for He was not then replying to some formal pronouncement of the Sanhedrin. Instead, He meant, You have *formed your estimate* of Me after the flesh, but not so do I form My estimates.

"And yet if I judge, my judgment is true: for I am not alone, but I and the Father that sent me" (8:16). This confirms what we have just said upon the last clause of the previous verse. "If I judge," or better "*when* I judge" *My* judgment is true. *You* may determine according to carnal principles; but I do not. I act on spiritual principles. I judge not according to appearances, but according to reality. My judgment is according to truth, for it is the judgment *of God*—"I am not alone, but I and the Father that sent me." This was a full claim to Deity. It affirmed the absolute oneness of the Son with the Father. This statement of Christ's is parallel with the one He made later: "I and my Father are one" (John 10:30). He speaks here in John 8 of the Divine wisdom which is *common* to the Father and the Son. This being so, how could His judgment be anything but true?

"It is also written in your law, that the testimony of two men is true. I am one that bear witness of myself, and the Father that sent me beareth witness of me" (8:17, 18). Here Christ repeats in another form what He had just affirmed. His testimony was not unsupported. The Mosaic law required two witnesses to establish the truth. The present case was not one where this law was strictly applicable; nevertheless, the circumstances of it were in fullest accord therewith. Christ bore personal witness to His Divine person and mission, and the Father also bore witness thereto. *How* the Father bore witness to the Son was before us in the fifth chapter of this Gospel. He bore witness to Him in the prophecies of the Old Testament, which were now so gloriously fulfilled in His character, teaching, actions, and even in His very rejection by men. The Father had borne witness to the Son through the testimony of His servant, John the Baptist (see John 1). He had borne witness to Him at the Jordan, on the occasion of His baptism. Thus by the principles of their own law these Pharisees were *condemned*. Two witnesses established the truth, but here *were* two Witnesses, the Father and the Son, and yet they rejected the truth! It was not, as several of the commentators have thought, that Christ was here *appealing to* the law in order to *vindicate* Himself. His manifest purpose was to condemn *them*, and that is why He says, "*your* law" rather than "*the* law."

"Then said they unto Him, Where is thy Father? Jesus answered, Ye neither know me, nor my Father: if ye had known me, ye should have known my Father also" (8:19). How the Light revealed the hidden things of darkness! Christ had appealed to the testimony of the Father, but so obtuse were these Pharisees, they asked, "Where is thy Father?" In our Lord's answer to them we are shown once more how that none can know the Father save through and by the Son. As He declared on another occasion, "Neither knoweth any man the Father, save the Son, and he to whomsoever the Son will *reveal him*" (Matt. 11:27).

"These words spake Jesus in the treasury, as he taught in the temple; and no man laid hands on him; for his hour was not yet come" (8:20). "The treasury was in the forecourt of the women, in which were placed thirteen bronze chests, to receive the taxes and free-will offerings of the people. The mention of the treasury here would be quite in keeping with the genuineness of the history of the woman taken in adultery. To the court of the women only could she have been brought to meet the Lord. Of these chests, nine were for legal payment of the worshippers, and four for free-will offerings" (C.E.S. from Barclay's Talmud).

"And no man laid hands on him: for his hour was not yet come." This plainly intimates that the Pharisees were greatly incensed at what Christ had said, and had it been possible they would have at once subjected Him to violence. But it was not possible, and never would have been unless God had withdrawn

His restraining hand. It is indeed striking to note how this feature is repeated again and again in the fourth Gospel, see 7:30; 7:44; 8:59; and 10:39, etc. These passages show that men were unable to work out their evil designs until God permitted them to do so. They demonstrate that God is complete master of all; and they prove that the sufferings Christ did undergo were endured voluntarily.

"Then said Jesus again unto them, I go my way, and ye shall seek me, and shall die in your sins" (8:21). The word "again" looks back to 7:33, 34, where on a previous occasion Christ had made a similar statement. "I go my way" signifies I shall very shortly leave you. It was a solemn word of warning. "And ye shall seek me, and shall die in your sins." Christ here addressed these Pharisees as the representatives of the nation, and looked forward to the sore trials before it. In but a few years, Israel would suffer an affliction far heavier than any they had experienced before; and when that time came, they would seek the delivering help of their promised Messiah, but it would be in vain. Having refused the Light they would continue in the darkness. Having despised the Saviour, they should "die in their sins." Having rejected the Son of God, it would be impossible for them to come whither He had gone.

"Ye shall seek me, and shall die in your sins." It is unspeakably solemn that these words have a present application. How dreadful! that the Saviour may be sought, but *sought in vain.* A man may have religious feelings about Christ, even weep at the thought of His Cross, and yet have no saving acquaintance with Him. Sickness, the fear of death, a serious financial reverse, the drying up of creature-sources of comfort—these frequently draw out much religiousness. Under a little pressure a man will say his prayers, read his Bible, become active in church work, profess to seek Christ, and become quite a different character; but only too often such an one is but reformed, and not transformed. And frequently this is made apparent in this world. Let the pressure be removed, let health return, let there be a change of circumstances, and how often we behold the zealous professor returning to his old ways. Such an one may have "sought" Christ, but because his motive was wrong, because it was not the effect of a deep conviction of being lost and undone, his seeking was in vain.

"Ye shall seek me, and shall die in your sins." Far more solemn is the application of these words to a class of people today which we greatly fear is by no means a small one. How many there are who, under the superficial and temporary influence of the modern evangelistic meetings, come forward to the front seeking Christ. For the moment, many of them, no doubt, are in earnest; and yet the sequel proves that they sought in vain. Why is this? Two answers may be returned. First, with some, it is because they were not in dead earnest. Of old God said, "Ye shall seek me, and *find* me, when ye shall search for me *with all* your heart" (Jer. 29:13). Second, with others, and with by far the greater number, it is because they do not seek *in the right place*. The seeker in the average meeting is exhorted to "lay his all upon the altar," or is told that he must "pray through." But Christ is not to be found by either of these means. "*Search the Scriptures*" was the word of the Saviour Himself, and the reason given was, "they are they which testify of me." In the volume of the book it is written of Christ. It is in the written Word that the incarnate Word is to be found.

"Ye shall seek me, and shall die in your sins." These words will yet have a further application to a coming day, when it will be *too late* to find Christ. Then the "door" will be shut. Then sinners will call upon God but He will not answer; they shall seek the Lord, but they shall not find Him (Prov. 1:28, etc.).

"Whither I go, ye cannot come" (8:21). Not "ye shall not come," but "ye *cannot* come." Cannot because the *holiness* of God makes it impossible: that which is corrupt and vile cannot dwell with Him; there can be no communion between light and darkness. Cannot because the *righteousness* of God makes it impossible. Sin must be punished; the penalty of the broken law must be enforced; and for the reprobate "there remaineth no more sacrifice for sins." Cannot because they have *no character* suited to the place whither Christ has gone. In the very nature of the case every man must go to "his *own* place" (Acts 1:25), the place for which he is fitted. If, by grace, he has the nature of God, then later on he will go and dwell with

Him (John 13:36); but if he passes out of this world "*dead* in sins" then, of necessity, he will yet be cast into the Lake of Fire, "which is the second death" (Rev. 20:14). If a man *dies* "in his sins" he *cannot* enter heaven. How completely this shatters the "Larger Hope"!

"Then said the Jews, Will he kill Himself? because he saith, Whither I go, ye cannot come?" (8:22). The Pharisees replied with profane levity, and with an impious sneer. This is frequently the resort of a defeated opponent: when unable to refute solid argument, he will avail himself of ridicule. With what infinite grace did our Lord forbear with His enemies!

"And he said unto them, Ye are from beneath; I am from above: ye are of this world; I am not of this world" (8:23). There seems to be a double thought conveyed by these words. First, Christ pointed out the reason or cause why they understood not His words and received not His witness. There was an infinite gulf separating Him from them: they were from beneath, He was from above. Second, Christ explained *why* it was that whither He was going they could not come. They belonged to two totally different spheres: they were of the world, He was not of the world. The friendship of the world is enmity against God, how then could they who were not only in the world, but *of it,* enter heaven, which was His home?

"I said therefore unto you, that ye shall die in your sins: for if ye believe not that I am he, ye shall die in your sins" (8:24). How terrible is the end of unbelief! The one who persists in his rejection of the Christ of God will die in his sins, unpardoned, unfit for heaven, unprepared to meet God! How unspeakably solemn is this! How little are we impressed by these fearful words, "die in your sins"—true of the vast majority of our fellows as they pass out of this world into an hopeless eternity. And how sadly mistaken are they who say that it is harsh and uncharitable to speak of the future destiny of unbelievers. The example of Christ should teach us better. *He* did not hesitate to press this awful truth, nor should we. In the light of God's Word it is criminal to remain silent. In the judgment of the writer this is the one truth which above all others needs to be pressed today. Men will not turn to Christ until they recognize their imminent danger of the wrath to come.

"Ye shall die in your sins." This is one of many verses which exposes a modern error concerning the Atonement. There are some who teach that on the Cross Christ bore all the sins of all men. They insist that the entire question of sin was dealt with and settled at Calvary. They declare that the *only* thing which will now send any man to hell, is his rejection of Christ. But such teaching is entirely unscriptural. Christ bore all the sins *of believers,* but for the sins of unbelievers *no* atonement was made. And one of the many proofs of this is furnished by John 8:24: "Ye shall die in your *sins*" could never have been said if the Lord Jesus removed *all* sins from before God.*

"Then said they unto him, Who art thou? And Jesus saith unto them, Even the same that I said unto you from the beginning" (8:25). We believe that this is given much more accurately in the R.V., especially the marginal rendering: "They said therefore unto him, Who art thou? Jesus said unto them, *Altogether that which I also speak unto you.*" This was a remarkable utterance. The Pharisees had objected that Christ's witness of Himself was not true (v. 13). The Lord replied that His witness *was* true, and He proved it by an appeal to the corroborative witness of the Father. Now they ask, "Who art thou?" And the incarnate Son of God answered, I am essentially and absolutely that which I have declared myself to be. I have spoken of "light": *I am* that Light. I have spoken of "truth": *I am* that Truth. I am the very incarnation, personification, exemplification of them. Wondrous declaration is this! None but He could really say, I am Myself that of which I am speaking to you. The child of God may speak the truth and walk in the truth, but he is not the Truth itself. A Christian may let his light "shine," but he is not the Light itself. But Christ was, and therein we perceive His exalted uniqueness. As we read in I John 5:20, "We know that the Son of God is come, and hath given us an understanding, that we may know him that is true," not "him who taught the truth," but "him that is true."

* See the author's booklet, "The Atonement," also his "The Sovereignty of God." Both are obtainable from the publishers of this book.

"I have many things to say and to judge of you: but he that sent me is true; and I speak to the world those things which I have heard of him" (8:26). As nearly as we can gather, the force of this verse is as follows: 'Your incredulity is very reprehensible, and your insulting sneers deserve the severest censure, but I forbear.' If Christ had dealt with these insulting opponents as they thoroughly merited, not only would He have upbraided them, but He would have passed an immediate sentence of condemnation upon them. Instead of doing so, He contented Himself by affirming once more that the witness He bore of Himself was true, because it was in the most perfect accord with what the Father Himself had said. Perfect example for us. Whenever the servant of Christ is criticized and challenged because of the message he brings, let him learn of his Master, who was meek and lowly in heart. Instead of passing sentence of condemnation on your detractors, simply press upon them the eternal veracity of Him in whose name you speak.

"They understood not that he spake to them of the Father" (8:27). O the blinding power of prejudice; the darkness of unbelief! How solemnly this reveals the woeful condition that the natural man is in. Unable to understand even when the Son of God was preaching to them! "Except a man be born again he *cannot* see." And this is the condition of *every man* by nature. Spiritually, the unregenerate American is in precisely the same darkness that the heathen are in, for both are in *the darkness of death!* Men need something more than external light; they need *inward* illumination. One may sit all his life under the soundest Gospel ministry, and at the end, understand no more *with the heart* than those in Africa who have never heard the Gospel. Let these solemn words be duly weighed—"they *understood not*," understood not the words which none other than the Son of God was saying to them! Then let every reader who *knows* that he is saved, praise God fervently because He "hath *given US an understanding,* that we may know him that is true" (I John 5:20).

"Then said Jesus unto them, When ye have lifted up the Son of man, then shall ye know that I am he, and that I do nothing of myself; but as my Father has taught me, I speak these things"

(8:28). His "lifting up" referred to His approaching death and the manner of it, see John 12:32, 33. "Then shall ye know that I am he" intimated that the crucifixion would be accompanied and followed by such manifestations of His Divine glory that He would be fully vindicated, and many would be convinced that He was indeed the Messiah, and that He had done and said only what He had been commissioned by the Father to do and say. How strikingly was this word of Christ verified on the day of Pentecost! Thousands, then, of the very ones who had cried, "Crucify him", were brought to believe on Him as "both Lord and Christ."

"And he that sent me is with me: the Father hath not left me alone; for I do always those things that please him" (8:29). "Whatever opinion men might form of His doctrines or conduct, He knew that in all He said, and in all He did, He was the Father's elect servant upheld and delighted in by Him—His beloved Son, in whom He was well pleased" (Dr. John Brown). Men who were blinded by Satan might regard Him as an impostor, and as a blasphemer, but He knew that the Father approved and would yet vindicate Him fully. How could it be otherwise when He did *always* those things that pleased Him? —a claim none other could truthfully make.

"As he spake these words, many believed on him" (8:30). This does not mean that they believed to the saving of their souls, the verses which follow evidence they had not. Probably nothing more is here signified than that they were momentarily impressed so that their enmity against Him was, temporarily, allayed. Many were evidently struck by what they observed in the demeanor of Christ—bearing the perverseness of His enemies so patiently, speaking of so ignominious a death with such holy composure, and expressing so positively His sense of the Father's approbation. Nevertheless, the impression was but a fleeting one, and their believing on Him amounted to no more than asking, "When Christ cometh, will he do more miracles than these which this man hath done?" (John 7:31).

"Then said Jesus to those Jews which believed on him, If ye continue in my word, then are ye my disciples indeed" (8:31). Our Lord here describes one of the marks of a *genuine* disciple of His. Continuance in His word is not a condition of discipleship, rather is it the *manifestation* of it. It is this, among other things, which distinguishes a true disciple from one who is merely a professor. These words of Christ supply us with a sure test. It is not how a man begins, but how he continues and ends. It is this which distinguishes the stony ground hearer from the goodground hearer—see Matt. 13: 20, 23, and contrast Luke 8:15. To His apostles Christ said "He that endureth to the end shall be saved" (Matt. 10:22). Not, we repeat, that enduring to the end is a *condition* of salvation, it is an evidence or *proof* that we have already passed from death unto life. So writes the apostle John of some who had apostatized from the faith: "They went out from us, but they were not of us; for if they had been of us, they *would* have *continued* with us," etc. (I John 2:19).

"If ye continue in my word, then are ye my disciples indeed." The word "indeed" signifies truly, really, genuinely so. By using this word Christ here intimated that those referred to in the previous verse, who are said to have "believed on him," *were not* "genuine disciples." The one who has been truly saved will not fall away and be lost; the one who does fall away and is lost, was never truly saved. To "continue" in Christ's word is to "keep his word" (Rev. 3:8). It is to hold fast whatever Christ has said; it is to perseveringly follow out the faith we profess to its practical end.

"And ye shall know the truth, and the truth shall make you free" (8:32). "To know the truth is something more definite than to know what is true; it is to understand that revelation with regard to the salvation of men, through the mediation of the incarnate Son, which is so often in the New Testament called, by way of eminence, 'the truth',—the truth of truths,—the most important of all truths,—the truth of which He is full,—the truth that came by Him, as the law came by Moses,—the truth, the reality in opposition to the shadows, the emblems, of the introductory economy,—what Paul termed, 'the word of the truth of the Gospel', Col. 1:5" (Dr. John Brown).

"The truth shall make you free." Note the striking connection between these three things: (1) "continue in my word," v. 31; (2) "ye shall know the truth," v. 32; (3) "the truth shall make you free," v. 32. This order cannot be changed. The truth gives spiritual liberty; it frees from the blinding power of Satan (II Cor. 4:4). It delivers from the darkness of spiritual death (Eph. 4:18). It emancipates from the prison-house of sin (Isa. 61:1). Further enlargement upon the character and scope of spiritual freedom will be given when we come to v. 36. Let the student first work on the following questions:—

1. To what extent is the sinner the "servant" (*bondslave*) of sin? v. 34.
2. What does v. 36 teach about the will of the natural man?
3. What is the difference between Abraham's "children" (v. 39), and his "seed" (v. 33)?
4. What is the meaning of v. 43?
5. What is the force of "of God" in v. 47?
6. What is the meaning of v. 51?
7. To what was Christ referring in v. 56?

CHAPTER THIRTY

CHRIST, THE LIGHT OF THE WORLD
(Concluded)

John 8:33-59

The passage for our present consideration continues and completes the portion studied in our last chapter. It brings before us Christ as the Light revealing the hidden things of darkness, exposing the pretensions of religious professors, and making manifest the awful depths of human depravity. We shall miss that in it which is of most importance and value if we localize it, and see in these verses nothing more than the record of a conversation between the Lord and men long since past and gone. We need to remind ourselves constantly that the Word of God is a *living* Word, depicting things as they *now* are, describing the opposition and activities of the carnal mind as they obtain today, and giving counsel which is strictly pertinent to ourselves. It is from this viewpoint we shall discuss this closing section of John 8. Below we give a Summary of our passage:—

1. Bondage and liberty: vv. 33-36.
2. Abraham's seed and Abraham's children: vv. 37-40.
3. Children of the Devil and children of God: vv. 41-47.
4. Christ dishonored by men, the Father honored by Christ: vv. 48-50.
5. Life and death: vv. 51-55.
6. Abraham and Christ: vv. 56-58.
7. The Saviour leaves the Temple: v. 59.

"They answered him, We be Abraham's seed, and were never in bondage to any man: how sayest thou, Ye shall be made free?" (8:33). This was the reply made by the Jews to the words of the Lord recorded in the previous verses. There we find Him describing the fundamental characteristic of a genuine disciple of His: he is one who continues in Christ's word (v. 31, re-read our comments thereon). The one who continues in the Word shall know the truth, and the truth shall make him *free* (v. 32). But to be told about being *made* free is something the natural man does not like to hear. The plain implication is that *before* he knows the truth he is *in bondage.* And such indeed is the case, little as men realize or recognize the fact. There are four things about themselves which are particularly hateful, because so humbling, to the unregenerate. First, that they are destitute of righteousness (Isa. 64:6) and goodness (Rom. 7:18), and therefore "unclean" (Isa. 64:6) and "vile" (Job 40:4). Second, that they are destitute of wisdom (Rom. 3:11) and therefore full of "vanity" (Psa. 39:5) and "foolishness" (Prov. 22:15). Third, that they are destitute of "strength" (Rom. 5:6) and "power" (Isa. 40:29), and therefore unable to do anything good of or from themselves (John 15:5). Fourth, that they are destitute of freedom (Isa. 61:1), and therefore in a state of bondage (II Pet. 2:19).

The condition of the natural man is far, far worse than he imagines, and far worse than the average preacher and Sunday school teacher supposes. Man is a fallen creature, totally depraved, with no soundness in him from the sole of his foot even unto the head (Isa. 1:6). He is completely under the dominion of sin (John 8:34), a bond-slave to divers lusts (Titus 3:3), so that he "*cannot* cease from sin" (II Pet. 2:14). Moreover, the natural man is thoroughly under the dominion of it. He is taken captive by the Devil at his will (II Tim. 2:26). He walks according to the Prince of the power of the air, the spirit that now *worketh in* the children of disobedience (Eph. 2:2). He fulfills the lusts of his father, the Devil (John 8:44). He is completely dominated by Satan's power (Col. 1:13). And from this thraldom nothing but the truth of God can deliver.

Ye shall be made free (8:33). As already stated, this signifies that the natural man is in bondage. But this is a truth that the natural man cannot tolerate. The very announcement of it stirs up the enmity within him. Tell the sinner that there is *no* good thing in him, and he will not believe you; but tell him that he is completely the slave of sin and the captive of Satan, that he *cannot* think a godly thought of himself (II Cor. 3:5), that he *cannot* receive God's truth (I Cor. 2:14), that he *cannot* believe (John 12:39), that he *cannot* please God (Rom. 8:8), that he *cannot* come to Christ (John 6:44), and he will indignantly deny your assertions. So it was here in the passage before us. When Christ said "the truth shall make you free", the Jews replied "We be Abraham's seed, and were *never in bondage* to any man."

The proud boast of these Jews was utterly unfounded; nothing could have been further from the truth. The very first view which Scripture gives us of Abraham's seed after they became a nation, is in bitter and cruel bondage (Ex. 2). Seven times over in the book of Judges we read of God delivering or selling Israel into the hands of the Canaanites. The seventy-years captivity in Babylon also gave the lie to the words of these Jews, and even at the time they spoke, the Romans were their masters. It was therefore the height of absurdity and a manifest departure from the truth for them to affirm that the seed of Abraham had never been in bondage. Yet no more untenable and erroneous was this than the assertions of present-day errorists who prate so loudly of the freedom of the natural man, and who so hotly deny that his will *is* enslaved by sin. "How sayest thou, Ye shall be made free?": equally ignorant are thousands in the religious world today. Deliverance from the Law, emancipation from bad habits they have heard about, but real spiritual freedom they understand not, and cannot while they remain in ignorance about the universal bondage of sin.

"Jesus answered them, Verily, verily, I say unto you, Whosoever committeth sin is the servant [bond-slave] of sin" (8:34). In saying "*whosoever* . . . is the bondslave" Christ was intimating to these Jews that *they* were no exception to the general rule, even though they belonged to the favored seed of Abraham. Christ was not speaking of a particular class of men more lawless than their fellows, but was affirming that which is true of *every* man in his natural condition. "Whosoever *committeth* sin," refers to the regular practice, the habitual course of a man's life. Here is one thing which distinguishes the Christian from the non-Christian. The Christian sins, and sins daily; but the non-

Christian does nothing but sin. The Christian sins, but he also repents; moreover, he does good works, and brings forth the fruit of the Spirit. But the life of the unregenerate man is one unbroken course of sin. Sin, we say, not crime. Water cannot rise above its own level. Being a sinner by nature, man is a sinner by practise, and cannot be anything else. A corrupt tree *cannot* bring forth good fruit. A poisoned fountain *cannot* send forth sweet waters. Because the sinner has no spiritual nature within him, because he is totally depraved and in complete bondage to sin, because he does nothing for *God's* glory, every action is polluted, every deed unacceptable to the Holy One.

"Whosoever committeth sin is the bond-slave of sin." How different are God's thoughts from ours! The man of the world imagines that to become a Christian means to forego his freedom. He supposes that he would be fettered with a lot of restrictions which nullified his liberty. But these very suppositions only evidence the fact that the god of this world (Satan) has *blinded* his mind (II Cor. 4:4). The very opposite from what he supposes is really the case. It is the one out of Christ, not the one in Christ, who is in bondage—in "the bond of iniquity" (Acts 8:23). He is impelled by the downward trend of his nature, and the very freedom which the sinner supposes he is exercising in the indulgence of his evil propensities is only additional proof that he *is* the "bond-slave of sin." The love of self, the love of the world, the love of money, the love of pleasure—these are the tyrants which rule over all who are out of Christ. Happy the one who is *conscious* of such bondage, for this is the first step toward liberty.

"And the bond-slave abideth not in the house forever: but the Son abideth ever" (8:35). The commentators are far from being in agreement in their interpretation of this verse, though we think there is little room for differences of opinion upon it. The "bond-slave" is the same character referred to in the previous verse—the one who makes a constant practise of sinning. Such an one abideth not in the house forever—the "house" signifies *family*, as in the House of Jacob, the House of Israel, the House of God (Heb. 3:5, 6). We take it that our Lord was simply enunciating a general principle or stating a well-known fact, namely, that a slave has only a *temporary* place in a family. The application of this principle to those He was addressing is obvious. The Jews insisted that they were Abraham's seed (v. 32), that they belonged to the favored family, whose were the covenants and promises. But, says our Lord, the mere fact that you are the natural descendants of Abraham, gives you no title to the blessings which belong to his spiritual children. This was impossible while they remained the bond-slaves of sin. Unless they were "made free" they would soon be cut off even from the temporary place of external privilege.

"But the Son abideth ever." These words point a contrast. The slave's place was uncertain, and at best temporary, but the Son's place in the family is permanent—no doubt the word "abideth" here (as everywhere) suggests the additional thought of *fellowship*. The history of Abraham's family well illustrated this fact, and probably Christ has the case of Ishmael and Isaac in mind when He uttered these words. "The Son abideth ever." Though this statement enunciated a general principle—something that is true of every member of God's family—yet the direct reference was clearly to Christ Himself, as the next verse makes plain, for "the Son" of v. 36 is clearly restricted to the Lord Jesus.

"If the Son therefore shall make you free, ye shall be free indeed" (8:36). The "therefore" here settles the application of the previous verse. "*The* Son" is none other than the Lord Jesus Christ, and He is able to make free the bond-slaves of sin because He *is* the Son. The Son is no bond-slave in the Father's family, but He is one in purpose and power with the Father; He is in perfect fellowship with Him, and *therefore* He is fully competent to liberate those under the tyranny of sin and the dominion of Satan. To make His people "free" was the central object in view in the Divine incarnation. The first ministerial utterance of Christ was to the effect that the Spirit of the Lord had anointed Him to preach "deliverance to the captives . . . to set at liberty them that are bruised" or "bound" (Luke 4:18). And so thoroughly are men under the thraldom of sin, so truly do they love darkness rather than light, they have to be *made* free. (cf. "*maketh* me to lie down" Psa. 23.)

"Ye shall be free indeed." Free *from what?* This brings before us the truth of Christian freedom: a most important subject, but one too wide to discuss here at any length*. To sum up in the fewest possible words, we would say that Christian liberty, spiritual liberty, consists of this: First, deliverance from the condemnation of sin, the penalty of the law, the wrath of God—Isa. 42:7; 60:1; Rom. 8:1. Second, deliverance from the power of Satan—Acts 26:18; Col. 1:13; Heb. 2:14, 15. Third, from the bondage of sin—Rom. 6:14, 18. Fourth, from the authority of man—Gal. 4:8, 9; 5:1; Col. 2:20-22. So much for the negative side; now a word on the positive.

Christians are delivered from the things just mentioned that they may be free to *serve God*. The believer is "the Lord's freeman" (I Cor. 7:22), not Christ's freeman, observe, but "*the Lord's,*" a Divine title which ever emphasizes our submission to His authority. When a sinner is saved he is not free to follow the bent of his old nature, for that would be lawlessness. Spiritual freedom is not license to do as I please, but emancipation from the bondage of sin and Satan that I may do as I ought: "that we being delivered out of the hand of our enemies *might serve him* without fear, in holiness and righteousness before him, all the days of our life" (Luke 1:74, 75). Rom. 6:16-18 and 22 contains a Divine summary of the positive side of this subject: let the reader give it careful and prayerful study.

"I know that ye are Abraham's seed; but ye seek to kill me, because my word hath no place in you" (8:37). Our Lord's object in these words is evident. He was further emphasizing the fact that though these Jews were the seed of Abraham, they certainly were not the children of God. Proof of this was furnished by the awful enmity then at work in their hearts. They sought (earnestly desired) to kill Him who was the Son. Certainly then, they were not *God's* children. Moreover, His word had no place in them—the Greek word translated "no place" signifies no entrance. They received it not (contrast I Thess. 2:13). They were merely *wayside* hearers. It is this which distinguishes, essentially, a saved man from a lost one. The

* See the author's booklet, "Christian Liberty," obtainable from the publishers, 10 cents.

former is one who *receives* with meekness the engrafted Word (James 1:21). He hides that Word in his heart (Psa. 119:11). The believer gives that Word the place of trust, of honor, of rule, of love. The man of the world gives the Word no place because it is too spiritual, too holy, too searching. He is filled with his own concerns, and is too busy and crowded to give the Word of God a real place of attention. Unspeakably solemn are those awful words of Christ to all such: "He that rejecteth me, and receiveth not my words, hath one that judgeth him: the word that I have spoken, *the same* shall judge him in the last day" (John 12:48).

"I speak that which I have seen with my Father: and ye do that which ye have seen with your father" (8:38). Christ further emphasizes the infinite gulf which separated these Jews from Himself. In the previous verse He had furnished proof that these men who were the seed of Abraham certainly were not the children of God. Here He leads up to their real parentage. In the first part of this verse our Lord insists that the doctrine He taught was what He had received from the Father, and its very nature and tendency clearly showed *who* His Father was. Its spirituality evidenced that it proceeded from the thrice Holy One: its unworldliness testified to the fact that it came from Him who is Spirit: its benignity showed it was from Him who is Love. Such was *His* Father.

"Ye do that which ye have seen with your father." "'Your actions tell who your father is, as My doctrine tells who My Father is.' In both cases 'father' here seems to mean spiritual model—the being after whom the character is fashioned—the being, under whose influences the moral and spiritual frame is formed. The thought that lies at the bottom of this representation is, 'Men's sentiments and conduct are things that are formed, and indicate the character of him who forms them. Your actions, which are characterized by falsehood and malignity, distinctly enough prove, that, in a moral and spiritual point of view, neither Abraham, nor the God of Abraham, is your father. The former of your spiritual character is not in heaven, wherever else he may be found'" (Dr. J. Brown).

"They answered and said unto him, Abraham is our father" (8:39). These Jews surely had a suspicion of whither our Lord's remarks in the previous verse were pointing; but they pretended not to observe, and sought to represent Him as a calumniator of Abraham. When they said, "Abraham is our father," it was but the self-righteousness of the natural man exhibiting itself. They were contrasting themselves from the heathen. 'The heathen are in bondage we allow; but You are now talking to those who belong to the covenant people: *we* belong to the Jewish Church,' this was the force of their remarks. It is not difficult to perceive how well this describes what is a matter of common observation today. Let the servant of God preach in the churches of this land on the ruined and lost condition of the natural man; let him faithfully apply his message to those present; and the result will be the same as here. The great mass of religious professors, who have a form of godliness but know nothing and manifest nothing of its power, will hotly resent being classed with those on the outside. They will tell you, *We* belong to the true Church, *we* are Christians, not infidels.

"Jesus saith unto them, If ye were Abraham's children, ye would do the works of Abraham" (8:39). Very simple, yet very searching was this. The "seed" of Abraham Christ acknowledged them to be (v. 37), but the "children" of Abraham they certainly were not. Natural descent from their illustrious progenitor did not bring them into the family of God. Abraham is "the father" only of "them *that believe*" (Rom. 4:11). This distinction is specifically drawn in Rom. 9:7: "Neither, because they are the seed of Abraham, are they all children." "Children" of Abraham refers to a *spiritual* relationship; "seed" of Abraham is only a fleshly tie, and "the flesh profiteth nothing" (John 6:63).

"If ye *were* Abraham's children, ye would *do* the works of Abraham." Here was and still is the decisive test. Natural descent counts for nothing, it is a spiritual relationship with God which is the great desideratum. The profession of our lips amounts to nothing at all if it be not confirmed by the character of our lives. Talk is cheap; it is our works, what we *do*, which evidences what we really *are*. A tree is known by its fruits. The "works of Abraham" were works of faith and obedience—faith in God and submission to His Word. But His Word had "no place *in them*." Idle then was their boast. Equally so is that of multitudes today, who say Lord, Lord, but *do not* the things which He has commanded.

"But now ye seek to kill me, a man that hath told you the truth, which I have heard of God: this did not Abraham" (8:40). "Abraham acted not thus. If ye were Abraham's children in a spiritual sense—if you were conformed to his character—you would imitate his conduct. But your conduct is the very reverse of his. You are desiring and plotting the murder of a man who never injured you, whose only crime is that He has made known to you important and salutary, but unpalatable truth. Abraham never did anything like this. He readily received every communication made from heaven. He never inflicted injury on any man, far less on a Divine messenger, who was merely doing his duty. No, no! If children are like their parents, Abraham is not your father. He whose deeds you do, he is your father" (Dr. J. Brown).

"Ye do the deeds of your father. Then said they to him, We be not born of fornication; we have one Father, even God" (8:41). When the Jews replied, "We be not born of fornication," we take it that they meant, 'We are not bastard Jews, whose blood has been contaminated with idolatrous alliances, as is the case with the Samaritans.' It seems likely that this word was provoked by what our Lord had said in v. 35—"the bondslave abideth not in the house," which was an oblique reference to Ishmael. If so, their words signified, 'We are genuine descendants of Abraham; we are children not of the concubine, but of the wife.'

"We have one Father, even God." How this same claim is being made on every side today! Those in far-distant lands may be heathen; but America is a Christian country. Such is the view which is held by the great majority of church members. The universal Fatherhood of God and the universal brotherhood of man are the favorite dogmas of Christendom: "We have one Father, even God" is the belief and boast of the great religious masses. How this justifies our opening remark, that the passage before us is not to be limited to a conversation which took place nineteen hundred years ago, but also contains a representation of human nature as it exists today, manifesting the same spirit of self-righteousness, appealing to the same false ground of confidence, and displaying the same enmity against the Christ of God.

"Jesus said unto them, If God were your father, ye would love me: for I proceeded forth and came from God; neither came I of myself, but he sent me" (8:42). This was an indirect but plain denial that God *was* their Father. If they were the children of God they would *love* Him, and if they loved Him they would most certainly love His only begotten Son, for "he that loveth him that begat, loveth him that is begotten of him" (I John 5:1). But they did *not* love Christ. Though He was the image of the invisible God, the brightness of His glory, and the express image of His person, they despised and rejected Him. They were the bond-slaves of sin (v. 34); Christ's Word had no place in them (v. 37); they sought to kill Him (v. 40). Their boast therefore was an empty one; their claim utterly unfounded.

"Why do ye not understand my speech? even because ye cannot hear my word" (8:43). Christ was here addressing Himself to their consciences. His question – no doubt there was a pause before He answered it – ought to have exercised their hearts. *Why* do you not understand My speech? You claim to be the children of the Father, why then are My words so obscure and mysterious to you? My language *is that of the Father,* surely then there is something wrong somewhere! The same question comes with equal pertinency to every one who hears the Word of God today. If that Word comes to me as that of an unknown tongue, then this shows I am a *stranger* to God. If I understand not His speech, I cannot be one of His children. That does not mean, of course, that I shall be able to fathom the infinite depths of His wonderful Word. But, speaking characteristically, if I understand not His speech – which is addressed not to the intellect but to the heart – then there is every reason why I should gravely inquire as to the *cause* of this.

"Even because ye cannot hear my word." The word "hear" (an Hebrew idiom) signifies to receive and believe – compare John 9:27; 10:3; 12:47; Acts 3:22, 23, etc. And *why* was it that these Jews "could not hear" His Word? It was because they were children in whom was no faith (Deut. 32:20). It was because they had no ear for God, no heart for His Word, no desire to learn His will. Proof positive was this that they were dead in trespasses and sins, and therefore *not* children of God. Unspeakably solemn is this. Hearing God's Word is an attitude of heart. We speak now not of the Divine side, for true it is that the Lord Himself must prepare the heart (Prov. 16:1) and give the hearing ear (Prov. 20:12). But from the human side, man is fully responsible *to* hear. But he *cannot* hear the still small voice of God while his ears are filled with the siren songs of the world. That he has no *desire to hear* does not excuse him, rather does it the more condemn him. The Lord grant that the daily attitude of writer and reader may be that of little Samuel, "Speak, Lord, for thy servant heareth."

"Ye are of your father the Devil, and the lusts of your father ye will do. He was a murderer from the beginning, and abode not in the truth, because there is no truth in him. When he speaketh a lie, he speaketh of his own; for he is a liar, and the father of it" (8:44). This was the prime point our Lord had been leading up to. First, He had repudiated their claim of being the children of Abraham. Second, He had demonstrated that God was not their Father. Now He tells them in plain language who their father really was, even the Devil. Their characters had been formed not under Divine influence, but under a diabolical influence. The moral likeness of that great Enemy of God was plainly stamped upon them. "Your inveterate opposition to the truth, shows your kinship to him who is the father of the Lie, and your desire to kill Me evidences that you are controlled by that one who was a murderer from the beginning."

"Ye are of your father the Devil" is true of every unregenerate soul. Renouncing their dependency on God, denying His proprietorship, loving darkness rather than light, they fall an easy prey to the Prince of darkness. He blinds their minds; he directs their walk, and works in them both to will and to do of his evil pleasure (Eph. 2:2). Nor can sinners turn round and cast the blame for this upon God. For as Christ here declares, the lusts of their father *they* will do, or they *desire* to do, which is the correct meaning of the word. They were cheerful servants; voluntary slaves.

"And because I tell you the truth, ye believe me not" (8:45). The human race is now reaping what was sown at the beginning. Our first parents rejected God's truth and believed the Devil's lie, and ever since then man has been completely under the power of falsehood and error. He will give credence to the most grotesque absurdities, but will regard with skepticism what comes to him with a thousand fully authenticated credentials. Some will believe that there are no such things as sin and death. Some will believe that instead of being the descendants of fallen Adam, they are the offspring of evolving apes. Some believe that they have no souls and that death ends all. Others imagine that they can purchase heaven with their own works. O the blindness and madness of unbelief! But let the truth be presented; let men hear that God says they are lost, dead in trespasses and sins; that eternal life is a gift, and eternal torment is the portion of all who refuse that gift; and men believe them not. They believe not God's truth because their hearts love that which is false—"They go astray as soon as they be born, speaking lies" (Psa. 58:3); they "delight in lies" (Psa. 62:4); they make lies their "refuge" (Isa. 28:15), therefore it is that they "turn away their ears from the truth" (II Tim. 4:4); and though they are ever learning, yet are they "never able to come to the knowledge of the truth" (II Tim. 3:7). And therefore Christ is still saying to men, "*because* I tell you *the truth*, ye believe me not."

"Which of you convinceth me of sin? And if I say the truth, why do ye not believe me?" (8:46). We take it Christ was here anticipating an objection. The charge He had just made against them was a very severe and piercing one, yet He openly challenges them to refute it. If you deny what I have said and charge Me with falsehood, how will you prove your charge? Which of you can fairly convince Me of that or of any other sin? But, on the other hand, if it be evident that I have told you the truth, then why do ye not believe Me? Such, in brief, we take to be our Lord's meaning here.

"He that is of God heareth God's words: ye therefore hear them not, because ye are not of God" (8:47). The force of this we understand as follows: Every member of God's family is indwelt by the Holy Spirit, and in virtue of this receives with affection, reverence, and obedient regard the words of his heavenly Father, by whomsoever they are brought; hence, the reason why you do not receive My words is because you are not His children. "He that is *of God*" carries a double thought. First, it signifies, he that belongs to God by eternal election. A parallel to this is found in John 10:26, "Ye believe not, because ye are not *of my sheep*." It is this which, in time, distinguished the elect from the non-elect. The former, in due time, hear or receive God's words; the latter do not. Second, "He that is of God" signifies, he that has been born of God, he that is in the family of God. A parallel to this is found in John 18:37: "Every one that is *of the truth* heareth my voice."

"Then answered the Jews, and said unto him, Say we not well that thou art a Samaritan, and hast a demon?" (8:48). This was a plain admission that they were unable to answer the Lord. Completely vanquished in argument, they resort to vulgar and blasphemous declamation. But why should these Jews have called Christ these *particular* names at *this* time? We believe the answer is found in what Christ had just said to them. He had declared that they were not the true children of Abraham (v. 39); and He had affirmed that the Devil was their father (v. 44). In reply, they retorted, "Thou art a Samaritan, and hast a demon." The general meaning of these epithets is clear: by "a Samaritan" they meant one who was an ěnemy to their national faith; by "thou hast a demon" they intimated one obsessed by a proud and lying spirit. What frightful insults did the Lord of glory submit to!

"Jesus answered, I have not a demon; but I honour my Father, and ye do dishonour me" (8:49). To the first of their reproaches He made no reply. He passed it by as unworthy of notice, the irritated outburst of wanton malice. To the second He returns a blank denial, and then adds, "but I honour my Father." One who is controlled by the Devil is a liar, but Christ had told them the truth. One who is prompted by the Devil flatters men, but Christ had depicted fallen human nature in the most humbling terms. One who is moved by the Devil is inflated with pride, seeks honor and fame; but Christ sought only the honor of Another, even the Father. Divinely calm, Divinely dignified. Divinely majestic was such an answer. How the longsufferance of Christ, His patient bearing with these villifiers, His unruffled spirit and calm bearing, evidenced Him to be none other than the Son of God.

"And I seek not mine own glory: there is one that seeketh and judgeth" (8:50). "'If I did, I should not have told you the truth. Had My own aggrandizement been My object, I should have followed another course; and My not obtaining "glory"—a good opinion—from you, no way disheartens Me. There is One who seeketh, that is, who seeketh My glory. There is One who will look after My reputation. There is One who is pledged in holy covenant to make Me His firstborn, higher than the kings of the earth. And He who seeketh My glory, judgeth. He will sit in judgment on your judgment.' These words seem plainly intended to intimate, in a very impressive way, the fearful responsibility they had incurred. He was doing His Father's will: they were treating Him with contumely. The Father was seeking the honour of His faithful Servant, His beloved Son; and dreadful would be the manifestation of His displeasure against those who, so far as lay in their power, had put to shame the God-man, whom He delighted to honor" (Dr. J. Brown).

"Verily, verily, I say unto you, If a man keep my saying, he shall never see death." (8:51). Christ had just pointed out the fearful consequence of rejecting Him and His Word—there was One who would *judge* them. Locally this pointed to the awful visitation from God upon their nation in A.D. 70; but the ultimate reference is to eternal judgment, which is "the second death." Now in sharp and blessed contrast from the doom awaiting those in whom the Word had "no place," Christ now says, "If a man keep my saying, he shall never see death"! Blessed promise was this for His own. But mark how human responsibility is here pressed—the promise is only to the one who *keeps* Christ's Word. To "keep" the Word is to hide it in the heart (Psa. 119:11). It is to retain it in the memory (I Cor.

15:3). It is to be governed by it in our daily lives (Rev. 3:8). "He shall never see (know, experience) death" refers to penal death, the wages of sin, eternal separation from God in the torments of Hell. For the believer physical dissolution is not death (separation), but to be *present* with the Lord (II Cor. 5:8).

"Then said the Jews unto him, Now we know that thou hast a devil. Abraham is dead, and the prophets; and thou sayest, If a man keep my saying, he shall never taste of death. Art thou greater than our father Abraham, which is dead? and the prophets are dead: whom makest thou thyself?" (8:52, 53). What a striking exemplification was this of what our Lord had said in v. 43: they understood not His speech and heard not His words. Devoid of discernment, they had no capacity to perceive the spiritual import of what He said. Such is the awful condition of the natural man: the things of God are foolishness to him (I Cor. 2:14). What is revealed to babes in Christ is completely hidden from those who are wise and prudent in their own estimation and in the judgment of the world (Matt. 11:25). No matter how simply and plainly the truths of Scripture may be expounded, the unregenerate are unable to understand them. Unable because their interests are elsewhere. Unable because they will not humble themselves and cry unto God for light. Unable because their hearts are estranged from Him. Christian reader, what abundant reason have you to thank God for giving *you* an understanding (I John 5:20)!

"Jesus answered, if I honour myself, my honour is nothing; it is my Father that honoureth me; of whom ye say, that he is your God" (8:54). "It is my Father that honoureth me": precious words are these and worthy of prolonged study and meditation. To "honour" is to do or speak that of a person which shall not only manifest our own esteem for him, but shall lead others to esteem him too. The Father's esteem for the Son is evidenced by His love and admiration for Him, as well as His desire to make Him the loved and admired of others. God honoured Him at His birth, by sending the angels to herald Him as Christ the Lord. He honoured Him during the days of His infancy, by directing the wise men from the east to come and worship the young King. He honoured Him at His baptism, by proclaiming Him His beloved Son. He honoured Him in death, by not suffering His body to see corruption. He honoured Him at His ascension, when He exalted Him to His own right hand. He will honour Him in the final judgment, when every knee shall be made to bow before Him and every tongue confess that He is Lord. And throughout eternity He shall be honoured by a redeemed people who shall esteem Him the Fairest among ten thousand to their souls. Infinitely worthy is the Lamb to receive honour and glory. Let then the writer and reader see to it that our daily lives honour Him who has so highly honoured us as to call us "brethren."

"Yet ye have not known him; but I know him: and if I should say, I know him not, I shall be a liar like unto you: but I know him, and keep his saying" (8:55). The One who honoured Him they knew not, despite their profession to be His children. But on the other hand, if He were to deny the knowledge He had of the Father, then He would be as false as they were in pretending to know Him. But He would not deny Him; nay more, He would continue to give evidence of His knowledge of the Father by keeping His Word. For Him that Word meant to finish the work which had been given Him to do, to become obedient unto death, even the death of the Cross. A searching word is this for us. If we really know the Father it will be evidenced by our subjection to His Word!

"Your father Abraham rejoiced to see my day: and he saw it, and was glad" (8:56). More literally the Greek reads, "Abraham, your father, was transported with an exultant desire that he should see My day, and he saw it and rejoiced." The Greek is much more expressive and emphatic than our English translation. It intimates that Abraham looked forward with joy to meet the Object of his desires, and exulted in a sight of it. But to what did our Lord refer when He said, Abraham saw "my day"? In the Greek the "day" is emphasized by putting it before the pronoun—"day, my." We believe that "day" is here to be understood in its dispensational sense, as signifying the entire Dispensation of Christ, which embraces the two advents. Probably what Abraham saw and rejoiced in was, first, the humiliation of

Christ, terminating in His death, which would occasion the patriarch great joy as he knew *that* death would blot out all his sins: second, the vindication and glorification of Christ.

But *how* did Abraham "see" Christ's "day"? We believe that a threefold answer may be returned: First, Abraham saw the day of Christ *by faith* in the promises of God (Heb. 11:13). Heb. 11:10 and 16 intimate plainly that the Spirit of God made discoveries to Abraham which are not recorded on the pages of the Old Testament. Second, Abraham saw the day of Christ *in type*. In offering Isaac on the altar and in receiving him back in figure from the dead, he received a marvelous foreshadowing of the Saviour's death and resurrection. Third, by *special revelation*. The "secret of the Lord" is with them that fear Him, and there is no doubt in our mind but that God was pleased to show the Old Testament saints much more of His covenant than is commonly supposed among us (see Psa. 25:14).

"Your father Abraham rejoiced to see my day: and he saw it, and was glad." The relevancy of this remark of Christ and its relation to what had gone before are easily perceived. More immediately, it was part of His answer to their last question in v. 53—"Whom makest thou thyself?" More remotely, it furnished the final proof that *they* were not the children of Abraham, for they did not his work (v. 39). If these Jews *rejoiced not* at the appearing of Christ before them, then in no sense were they like Abraham.

"Then said the Jews unto him, Thou art not yet fifty years old, and hast thou seen Abraham?" (8:57). How blind they were! How thoroughly incompetent to understand His speech. Christ had not spoken of seeing Abraham, but of Abraham seeing His "day." There was a vast difference between these two things, but they were incapable of perceiving it.

"Jesus said unto them, Verily, verily, I say unto you, Before Abraham was, I am" (8:58). Here was the full disclosure of His glory; the affirmation that He was none other than the Eternal One. That they so understood Him is evident from what follows.

"Then took they up stones to cast at him: but Jesus hid himself, and went out of the temple, going through the midst of them, and so passed by" (8:59). "It is Immanuel: but there is no knee bent to Him, no loving homage tendered. They took up stones to stone Him, and He hiding Himself for the moment from their sacrilegious violence, passes out of the temple" (F. W. Grant).

"Jesus hid himself, and went out of the temple, going through the midst of them, and so passed by." Fearfully solemn is this in its present-day application. The chief design of the whole chapter is to present Christ as the "light" and to show us *what* that Light revealed. Not by observation can we discover the full ruin which sin has wrought. It is only as the Light shines that man is fully exposed. And that which is particularly discovered here is the utter vanity of the religious pretensions of the natural man.

Apart from spiritual discernment, the religious professor presents before us a fair appearance. His evident sincerity, his punctiliousness, his unquestionable zeal, his warm devotion, his fidelity to the cause he has espoused, are frequently a mask which no human eye can penetrate. It is not until such professors are exposed to the searching *light of God* that their *real* characters are laid bare. It is only as *the Word* is faithfully applied to them that their awful depravity is revealed. It was not profligate outcasts, but orthodox Jews who are here seen taking up stones to cast at the Son of God, and they did this not on the public highway, but in the temple; Nor have things changed for the better. Were Christ here today in Servant-form, and were He to enter our churches and tell the great mass of religious professors that *they* were the bondslaves of sin, and that *they* were of their father the Devil and that *his* lusts *they* delighted in doing, they would conduct themselves exactly as their fellows did eighteen centuries ago. Terribly significant then is the final word of our chapter: the Saviour "*hid* himself" from them, and went out of the temple. It is so still. From the self-righteous and self-sufficient but blinded religious formalists, Christ still hides Himself; those who deny that *they* need to be made free from the slavery of sin He still leaves to themselves. But thank God it is written, "I dwell in the high and holy place, with him *also* that is of a *contrite and humble spirit*" (Isa. 57:15).

The following questions are to help the interested student on the next chapter, John 9:1-7:—

1. What is the great doctrinal teaching of this passage?
2. What typical picture does it contain?
3. Why does it open with the word "And"? v. 1.
4. To what was Christ referring in v. 4?
5. Why did Christ *again* say "I am the Light of the world" v. 5.
6. What was the symbolical meaning of vv. 6 and 7?
7. What force has "therefore" in v. 7?

CHAPTER THIRTY-ONE

Christ and the Blind Beggar

John 9:1-7

Below will be found an Analysis of the passage which is to be before us: —

1. Jesus beholds the man born blind: v. 1.
2. The disciples' question: v. 2.
3. Christ's answer: vv. 3-5.
4. Christ anoints the blind man: v. 6.
5. Christ sends the man to the Pool: v. 7.
6. The man's prompt obedience: v. 7.
7. The miracle completed: v. 7.

That there is an intimate connection between John 8 and John 9 is manifest from the first word of the latter, and when the Holy Spirit has thus linked two things together it behooves us to pay close attention to the law of comparison and contrast. The little conjunction at the opening of John 9 is very appropriate, for in the previous verse we read of Jesus *hiding* Himself from those who took up stones to cast at Him; while in 9:1 we behold a man blind from his birth, *unable to see* the passing Saviour. That these two chapters are closely related is further seen by a comparison of 8:12 and 9:5: in both Christ is revealed, specifically, as "the light of the world." As we read carefully the opening verses of the chapter now before us and compare them with the contents of John 8 it will be found that they present to us a series of contrasts. For example, in John 8 we behold Christ as "the light" exposing the darkness, but in John 9 He communicates sight. In John 8 the Light is despised and rejected, in John 9 He is received and worshipped. In John 8 the Jews are seen stooping down — to pick up stones; in John 9 Christ is seen stooping down — to make anointing clay. In John 8

Christ hides Himself from the Jews; in John 9 He reveals Himself to the blind beggar. In John 8 we have a company in whom the Word has no place (v. 37); in John 9 is one who responds promptly to the Word (v. 7). In John 8 Christ, inside the Temple, is called a demoniac (v. 48); in John 9, outside the Temple, He is owned as Lord (v. 36). The central truth of John 8 is the Light testing human responsibility; in John 9 the central truth is God acting in sovereign grace *after* human responsibility has failed. This last and most important contrast we must ponder at length.

In John 8 a saddening and humbling scene was before us. There Christ was manifested as "the light" and woeful were the objects that it shone upon. It reminds us very much of that which is presented right at the beginning of God's Word. Gen. 1:2 introduces us to a ruined earth, with darkness enveloping it. The very first thing God said there was, "Let there be light," and we are told, "There was light." And *upon what* did the light shine? what did its beams *reveal?* It shone upon an earth that had become "without form and void"; its beams revealed a scene of desolation and death. There was no sun shining by day nor moon by night. There was no vegetation, no moving creature, no life. A pall of death hung over the earth. The light only made manifest the awful ruin which sin (here, the sin of Satan) had wrought, and the need for the sovereign goodness and almighty power of God to intervene and produce life and fertility.

So it was in John 8. Christ as the Light *of the world* discovers not only the state of Israel, but too, the common atheism of man. He affirmed His power to make free the bondslaves of sin (8:32): but His auditors denied that they were in bondage. He spoke the words of the Father (8:38): but they neither understood nor believed Him. He told them that their characters were formed under the influence of the Devil and that they desired it to be so (8:44): in reply they blasphemously charged Him with having a demon. He declared that He was the Object who had rejoiced the heart of Abraham (8:56): and they scoffed at Him. He told them He was the great and eternal "I am" (8:58): and they picked up stones to cast at Him. All of this furnishes us with a graphic but accurate picture of the character of the natural man the world over. The mind of the sinner is enmity against God, and he hates the Christ of God. He may be very religious, and left to himself, he may appear to be quite pious. But let the light of God be turned upon him, let the bubble of his self-righteousness be punctured, let his awful depravity be exposed, let the claims of Christ be pressed upon him, and he is not only skeptical, but furious.

What, then, was Christ's response? Did He turn His back on the whole human race? Did He return at once to heaven, thoroughly disgusted at His reception in this world? What wonder if the Father had there and then called His Son back to the glory which He had left. Ah! but God is the God of all grace, and grace needed the dark background of sin so that its bright lustre might shine the more resplendently. Yet grace would be misunderstood and unappreciated were it shown to all alike, for in that case men would deem it a right to which they were entitled, a meet compensation for God allowing the race to fall into sin. O the folly of human reasoning! Grace would be no more grace if fallen men had any claims upon it. God is under *no* obligations to men: every title to His favor was forfeited forever when they, in the person of their representative, rebelled against Him. Therefore does He say, "I will have mercy on whom *I will* have mercy" (Rom. 9:15). It is *this* side of the truth which receives such striking illustration in the passage which is to be before us.

In John 8 we are shown the utter ruin of the natural man—despising God's goodness, hating His Christ. Here in John 9 we behold the Lord dealing in grace, acting according to His sovereign benignity. This, this is the central contrast pointed by these two chapters. In the former it is the Light testing human responsibility; in the latter, the Light acting in sovereign mercy after the failure of human responsibility had been demonstrated. In the one we see the sin of man exposed, in the other we behold the grace of God displayed.

"And as Jesus passed by, he saw a man which was blind from his birth" (9:1). That which is dominant in this passage is intimated in the opening verse. The *sovereignty* of Divine grace is exemplified at once in the actions of our Lord and in the character of the one upon whom His favors were bestowed. The Saviour saw a certain man; the man did not see Him, for he had no capacity to do so, being blind. Nor did the blind man call upon Christ to have mercy upon him. The Lord was the one to take the initiative. It is ever thus when sovereign grace acts. But let us admire separately each detail in the picture here.

"And as Jesus passed by, he *saw* a man." How blessed. The Saviour was not occupied with His own sorrows to the exclusion of those of others. The absence of appreciation and the presence of hatred in almost all around Him, did not check that blessed One in His unwearied service to others, still less did He abandon it. Love "suffereth long," and "beareth all things" (I Cor. 13). And Christ was Love incarnate, therefore did the stream of Divine goodness flow on unhindered by all man's wickedness. How this perfection of Christ rebukes our imperfections, our selfishness!

"He saw a man which was blind from his birth." What a pitiable object! To lose an arm or a leg is a serious handicap, but the loss of sight is far more so. And this man had *never* seen. From how many enjoyments was he cut off! Into what a narrow world did his affliction confine him! And blindness, like all other bodily afflictions, is one of the effects of sin. Not always so directly, but always so remotely. Had Adam never disobeyed his Maker the human family had been free from disease and suffering. Let us learn then to *hate sin* with godly hatred as the cause of all our sorrows; and let the sight of suffering ones serve to remind us of what a horrible thing sin is. But let us also remind ourselves that there is something infinitely more awful than physical blindness and temporal suffering, namely, sickness of soul and a blinded heart.

"He saw a man which was blind from his birth." Accurately did he portray the terrible condition of the natural man. The sinner is blind spiritually. His understanding is darkened and his heart is blinded (Eph. 4:18). Because of this he cannot see the awfulness of his condition: he cannot see his imminent danger: he cannot see his need of a Saviour—"Except a man be born again he *cannot see*" (John 3:3). Such an one needs more than light; he needs the capacity given him to see the light. It is not a matter of mending his glasses (reformation), or of correcting his vision (education and culture), or of eye ointment (religion). None of these reach, or can reach, the root of the trouble. The natural man is *born blind* spiritually, and a faculty missing at birth cannot be supplied by extra cultivation of the others. A "transgressor from the womb" (Isa. 48:8). shapen in iniquity and conceived in sin (Psa. 51:5), man needs a Saviour from the time he draws his very first breath. Such is the condition of God's elect in their unregenerate state—"by nature the children of wrath, even as others" (Eph. 2:3).

"He saw a man which was blind from his birth." The late Bishop Ryle called attention to the significant fact that the Gospels record more cases of blindness healed than that of any other one affliction. There was one deaf and dumb healed, one sick of the palsy, one sick of a fever, two instances of lepers being healed, three dead raised, but five of the blind! How this emphasizes the fact that man is in the dark spiritually. Moreover, the man in our lesson was a beggar (v. 8)—another line in the picture which so accurately portrays our state by nature. A beggar the poor sinner is: possessing nothing of his own, dependent on charity. A blind beggar—what an object of need and helplessness! Blind from his birth—altogether beyond the reach of man!

"And his disciples asked him, saying, Master, who did sin, this man, or his parents, that he was born blind?" (9:2). How little pity these disciples seem to have had for this blind beggar, and how indifferent to the outflow of the Lord's grace. Instead of humbly and trustfully waiting to see what Christ would do, they were philosophizing. The point over which they were reasoning concerned the problem of suffering and the inequalities in the lot of human existence—points which have engaged the minds of men in every clime and age, and which apart from the light of God's Word are still unsolved. There are many who drift along unexercised by much of what goes on around them. That some should be born into this world to enter an environment of comfort and luxury, while others first see the light amid squalor and poverty; that some should start the race of mortality with a healthy body and a goodly reserve of vitality, while others should be severely handicapped with an organism that is feeble or diseased, and still others should be crippled from the womb, are phenomena which affect different people in very different ways. Many are largely unconcerned. If all is well with them, they give very little thought to the troubles of their fellows. But there are others who cannot remain indifferent, and whose minds seek an explanation to these mysteries. Why is it that some are born blind?—a mere accident it cannot be. As a punishment for sin, is the most obvious explanation. But if this be the true answer, a punishment for *whose* sins?

"Master, who did sin, this man, or his parents, that he was born blind?" Three theories were current among the philosophers and theologians of that day. The first obtained in some measure among the Babylonians, and more extensively amongst the Persians and Greeks, and that was the doctrine of re-incarnation. This was the view of the Essenes and Gnostics. They held that the soul of man returned to this earth again and again, and that the law of retribution regulated its varied temporal circumstances. If in his previous earthly life a man had been guilty of grievous sins, special punishment was meted out to him in his next earthly sojourn. In this way philosophers sought to explain the glaring inequalities among men. Those who now lived in conditions of comfort and prosperity were reaping the reward of former merit; those who were born to a life of suffering and poverty were being punished for previous sins. That this theory of re-incarnation obtained in measure even among the Jews is clear from Matt. 16:13, 14. When Christ asked His disciples, "Whom do men say that I the Son of man am?" they said, "Some say that thou art John the Baptist: some, Elijah; and others, Jeremiah, or one of the prophets" which shows that some of them thought the soul of one of the prophets was now re-incarnated in the body of Jesus of Nazareth. Further evidence that this view obtained to some extent among the Jews is supplied by the Apocrypha. In "The Wisdom of Solomon"—8:19, 20—are found these words, "Now I was a goodly child, and a goodly soul fell to my lot. Nay rather, *being good,* I came into a body undefiled"!

But among the rabbins this theory held no place. It was so completely without scriptural support, yea, it so obviously clashed with the teaching of the Old Testament, they rejected it in toto. How then could *they* explain the problem of human suffering? The majority of them did so by the law of heredity. They considered that Ex. 20:5 supplied the key to the whole problem: all suffering was to be attributed to the sins of the parents. But the Old Testament ought to have warned them against such a sweeping application of Ex. 20:5. The case of Job should have at least modified their views. With some it did, and among the Pharisees a third theory, still more untenable, was formulated. Some held that a child could sin even in the womb, and Gen. 25:22 was quoted in support.

It was in view of these prevailing and conflicting theories and philosophies which then obtained that the disciples put their question to the Lord: "Master, who did sin, this man, or his parents, that he was born blind?" Evidently they desired to hear what He would say upon the matter. But what is the present-day application of this verse to us? Surely the reasoning of these disciples in the presence of the blind beggar points a solemn warning. Surely it tells of the danger there is of us theorizing and philosophizing while we remain indifferent to human needs. Let us beware of becoming so occupied with the problems of theology that we fail to preach the Gospel to lost souls!

"Jesus answered, Neither hath this man sinned, nor his parents: but that the works of God should be made manifest in Him" (9:3). The Lord returned a double answer to the disciples' inquiry: negatively, this man was not born blind because of sin. "Neither did this man sin *nor his parents*" must not be understood absolutely, but like many another sentence of Scripture has to be modified by its setting. Our Lord did not mean that this man's parents had never sinned, but that their sin was not the reason *why* their son had been born blind. All suffering is *remotely* due to sin, for if sin had not entered the world there would have been no suffering among humankind. But there is much suffering which is not due immediately to sin. Indirectly the Lord here rebukes a spirit which all of us are prone to indulge. It is so easy to assume the role of judge and pass sentence upon another. This was the sin of Job's friends, recorded for our learning and warning. The same spirit is displayed among some of the "Faith-healing" sects of our day. With them the view largely obtains that sickness is due to some sin in the life, and that where healing is withheld it is because that sin is unconfessed. But this is a very harsh and censorious judgment, and must frequently be erroneous. Moreover, it tends strongly to foster pride. If I am enjoying better health than many of my fellows, the inference would be, it is because I am not so great a sinner as they! The Lord deliver us from such reprehensible Phariseeism.

"But that the works of God should be made manifest in him." Here is the positive side of our Lord's answer, and it throws some light upon the problem of suffering. God has His own wise reasons for permitting sickness and disease; ofttimes it is that *He* may be glorified thereby. It was so in the case of Lazarus (John 11:4). It was so in connection with the death of Peter (John 21:19). It was so in the affliction of the apostle Paul (II Cor. 12:9). It was so with this blind beggar: he was born blind that the power of God might be evidenced in the removal of it, and that Christ might be glorified thereby.

"But that the works of God should be made manifest in him." Let us not miss the present application of this to suffering saints today. Surely this word of the Saviour's contains a message of consolation to afflicted ones among His people now. Not that they may expect to be relieved by a miracle, but that they may comfort themselves with the assurance that God has a wise (if hidden) purpose to be served by their affliction, and that is, that in some way *He* will be glorified thereby. That way may not be manifested at once; perhaps not for long years. At least thirty years (see v. 23) passed before God made it evident *why* this man had been born blind. As to *what* God's purpose is in our affliction, as to *how* His purpose will be attained, and as to *when* it will be accomplished, these things are none of our affair. Our business is to meekly submit to His sovereign pleasure (I Sam. 3:18), and to be duly "exercised thereby" (Heb. 12:11). Of this we may be sure, that whatever is for God's glory *in* us, will ultimately bring blessing *to* us. Then do not question God's love, but seek grace to rest in sincere faith on Rom. 11:36 and 8:28.

"I must work the works of him that sent me" (9:4). And what were these works? To reveal the perfections of God and to minister to the needs of His creatures. Such "works" the Son *must* do because He was *one* both in will and in nature with the Father. But no doubt there is another meaning in these words. The "works of him" that sent Christ were not only works that were *pleasing* to God, but they were works which had been *predestinated* by God. These works *must* be done because God had eternally decreed them—cf. the "must" in 4:4 and 10:16.

"The night cometh, when no man can work. As long as I am in the world, I am the light of the world" (9:4, 5). More specifically this statement had reference to what Christ was about to do—give sight to the blind beggar. This is clear from the opening words of v. 6: "When he had *thus* spoken." The miracle Christ was about to perform gave a striking illustration of the yet greater miracle of the Divine bestowment of spiritual vision upon an elect sinner. Such an one *must* be illumined for the eternal counsels of Deity so determined—compare the "must" in Acts 4:12. The saving of a sinner is not only entirely the "work" of God, but it is, pre-eminently, that in which He delights. This is what these words of Christ here plainly intimate. How blessed to know, then, that the most glorious of all God's works is displayed in the saving of lost and hell-deserving sinners, and that the Persons of the Trinity co-operate in the outflow of grace.

"The night cometh, when no man can work." Christ here teaches us both by word and example the importance of making the most of our present opportunities. His earthly ministry was completed in less than four years, and these were now rapidly drawing to a close. He *must* then be about His Father's business. A Divine constraint was upon Him. May a like sense of urgency impel us to redeem the time, knowing the days are evil (Eph. 5:16). What a solemn word is this for the sinner: "the night cometh, when no man can work"! This is life's day for him; in front lies the blackness of darkness forever (Jude 13).

Unsaved reader, your "night" hastens on. *"Today* if ye will hear his voice harden not your hearts." "Behold *now* is the accepted time; behold, *now* is the day of salvation" (II Cor. 6:2).

"As long as I am in the world, I am the light of the world." Christ seems to be referring to the attempt which had just been made upon His life (8:59). Soon the appointed time would come for Him to leave the world, but until that time had arrived man could not get rid of Him. The light *would* shine despite all man's efforts to put it out. The stones of these Jews could not intimidate or hinder this One from finishing the work which has been given Him to do. "Light of the world" He had just demonstrated Himself to be by exposing their wicked hearts. "Light of the world" He would now exhibit Himself by communicating sight and salvation to this poor blind beggar.

"When he had thus spoken, he spat on the ground, and made clay of the spittle, and he anointed the eyes of the blind man with the clay" (9:6). This was a parable in action and deserves our closest attention. Christ's mode of procedure here though extraordinarily peculiar was, nevertheless, profoundly significant. Peculiar it certainly was, for the surest way to blot out vision would be to plaster the eye with wet clay: and yet this was the only thing Christ did to this blind beggar. Equally sure is it that His mysterious action possessed some deep symbolic significance. What that was we shall now inquire.

"When he had thus spoken, he spat on the ground, and made clay of the spittle, and he anointed the eyes of the blind man with the clay." The first thing we must do is to study this carefully in the light of the context. What is before us in the context? This: the "light of the world" (8:12), the "sent one" (8:18), the "Son" (8:36) was despised and rejected of the Jews. And why was that? Because He appeared before them in such lowly guise. They judged Him "after the flesh" (8:15); they sought to kill Him because He was "a *man* that had told them the truth" (8:40). They had no eyes to discern His Divine glory and were stumbled by the fact that He stood before them in "the likeness of men."

Now what do we have here in John 9? This: once more Christ affirms that He *was* "the light of the world" (9:5); then, immediately following, we read, "When he had *thus* spoken, he spat on the ground, and made clay of the spittle, and he anointed the eyes of the blind man with the clay." Surely the meaning of this is now apparent. "As a figure, it pointed to the *humanity* of Christ in earthly humiliation and lowliness, presented to the eyes of men, but with Divine efficacy of life in Him" (J.N.D.). Christ had presented Himself before the Jews, but devoid of spiritual perception they recognized Him not. And did the blind beggar, who accurately represented the Jews, did *he* see when Christ applied the clay to his eyes? No; he did not. He was still as blind as ever, and even though he had not been blind he could not have seen now. What, then, must he do? He must *obey* Christ. And what did Christ tell him to do? Mark carefully what follows.

"And said unto him, Go, wash in the pool of Siloam, (which is by interpretation, Sent)" (9:7). This, too, was a sermon in action. What the blind beggar needed was *water*. And of what did *that* speak? Clearly of the written Word (see our notes on 3:5, and cf. Eph. 5:26). It was just because the Jews *failed* to use the water of the Word that the eyes of their hearts remained closed. Turn to John 5, and what do we find there? We see the Jews seeking to kill Christ because He made Himself equal with God (v. 18). And what did He bid them do? This: "Search the Scriptures" (5:39). We have the same thing again in John 10: the Jews took up stones again to stone Him (v. 31). And the Lord asked them why they acted thus. Their answer was, "Because that thou, *being a man*, makest thyself God" (v. 33). What reply did Christ make, "Jesus answered them, Is it not *written?*" It was then, this very thing which (symbolically) the Lord commanded the blind beggar to do. He obeyed implicitly, and the result was that he obtained his sight. The difference between the Jews and the beggar was this: they thought they could see already, and so refused the testimony of the written Word; whereas the beggar knew that he was blind and therefore used the water to which Christ referred him. This supplies the key to the 39th verse of this chapter which sums up all that has gone before. "And Jesus said, For judgment I am come into this world, that they which see not might see; and that they which see might be made blind."

We turn now to consider the *doctrinal* significance of what has just been before us. The blind beggar is to be viewed as a representative character, i.e., as standing for each of God's elect. Blind from birth, and therefore beyond the help of man; a beggar and therefore having nothing, he fitly portrays our condition by nature. Sought out by Christ and ministered to without a single cry or appeal from him, we have a beautiful illustration of the activities of sovereign grace reaching out to us in our unregenerate state. Our Lord's method of dealing with him, was also, in principle, the way in which He dealt with us, when Divine mercy came to our rescue.

"He spat on the ground, and made clay of the spittle, and he anointed the eyes of the blind man with the clay." This seems to have a double meaning. *Dispensationally* it symbolized Christ presenting Himself in the flesh before the eyes of Israel. *Doctrinally* it prefigured the Lord pressing upon the sinner his lost condition and need of a Saviour. The placing of clay on his eyes *emphasizes* our *blindness*. "And said unto him, Go, wash in the pool of Siloam." This intimates our need of turning to the Word and *applying* it to ourselves, for it is the entrance of God's words which, alone, give light (Psa. 119:130).

The name of the Pool in which the blind beggar was commanded to wash is not without its significance, as is seen by the fact that the Holy Spirit was careful to interpret it to us. God incarnate is the Object presented to the needy sinner's view: the One who was *"anointed"* by the Holy Spirit (Acts 10:38). *How* is He presented to us? Not as pure spirit, nor in the form of an angel; but as "made flesh." *Where* is He to be thus found? In the written Word. As we turn to that Word we shall learn that the man Christ Jesus is none other than the "sent one" of the Father. It is through the Word alone (as taught by the Holy Spirit) that we can come to know the Christ of God.

"He went his way therefore, and washed, and came seeing" (9:7). The simple obedience of the blind beggar is very beautiful. He did not stop to reason and ask questions, but promptly did what was told him. As the old Puritan, John Trapp (1647), quaintly puts it, "He obeyed Christ blindly. He looked not upon Siloam with Syrian eyes as Naaman did upon Jordan; but, passing by the unlikelihood of a cure by such means, he believeth and doeth as he was bidden, without hesitation." Let the interested student go over the whole chapter carefully and prayerfully, seeking the *personal* application of this passage. Let the following questions be studied:—

1. How do vv. 8 and 9 apply to the history of a newly saved soul?
2. What do vv. 10 and 11 teach us concerning the young convert?
3. How do v. 12 fit in with the application of this passage to a babe in Christ?
4. Study vv. 13-16 from a similar viewpoint.
5. What do the beggar's words in v. 17 intimate? Cf. our remarks on 4:19.
6. What does v. 18 teach the young believer to expect?
7. What do vv. 20-23 teach the babe in Christ be must do?

CHAPTER THIRTY-TWO

Christ and the Blind Beggar (Continued)

John 9:8-23

We begin with our usual Analysis of the passage which is to be before us:—

1. The uncertainty of the neighbors: vv. 8, 9.
2. Their questioning of the beggar: v. 10.
3. The beggar's answers: vv. 11, 12.
4. The Pharisees and the Sabbath: vv. 13, 14.
5. The beggar before the Pharisees: vv. 15-17.
6. The skepticism of the Jews: v. 18.
7. The beggar's parents interrogated: vv. 19-23.

In our last chapter we pointed out how that the opening verses of John 9 supply us with a blessed illustration of the outflow of sovereign grace toward an elect sinner. Every detail in the picture contributes to its beauty and accuracy. Upon the dark background of the Jews' hatred of Christ (chapter 8) we are now shown the Saviour ministering to one who strictly portrays the spiritual condition of each of God's elect when the Lord begins His distinguishing work of mercy upon him. Seven things are told us about the object of the Redeemer's compassion:

First, he was found *outside* the Temple, portraying the fact that, in his natural condition, the elect sinner is alienated from God. Second, he was blind, and therefore unable to see the Saviour when He approached him. Third, he had been blind from birth: so, too, is the sinner—"estranged from the womb" (Psa. 58:3). Fourth, he was therefore quite beyond the aid of man: helpless and hopeless unless *God* intervened. Fifth, he was a beggar (v. 8), unable to purchase any remedy if remedy there was; completely dependent upon charity. Sixth, he made no appeal to the Saviour and uttered no cry for mercy; such is our condition before Divine grace begins to work within us. Seventh, the reasoning of the disciples (v. 2) illustrates the sad fact that no human eye pities the sinner in his spiritual wretchedness.

Our Lord's dealings with this poor fellow shadow forth His gracious work in us today. Note, again, seven things, in connection with Christ and the blind beggar. First, He *looked* in tender pity upon the one who so sorely needed His healing touch. Second, He declared that this man had been *created* to the end that the power and grace of God might be manifested in him (v. 3). Third, He intimated that *necessity* was laid upon Him (v. 4): the eternal counsels of grace "must" be accomplished in the one singled out by Divine favor. Fourth, He announced Himself as the One who had power to *communicate light* to those in darkness (v. 5). Fifth, He *pressed upon* the blind beggar his desperate need by emphasizing his sad condition (v. 6). Sixth, He pointed him to the *means of blessing* and put his faith to the test (v. 7). Seventh, the beggar obeyed, and in his obedience obtained evidence that *a miracle of mercy* had been wrought upon him. Each of these seven things has their counterpart in the realm of grace today.

As we follow the Divine narrative and note the experiences of the blind beggar *after* he had received his sight, we shall find that it continues to mirror forth that which has its analogy in the spiritual history of those who have been apprehended by Christ. What is before us here in John 9 is something more than an incident that happened in the long ago—it accurately depicts what is transpiring in our own day. The more the believer studies this passage in the light of his own spiritual history, the more will he see how perfectly this narrative describes *his own* experiences.

"The neighbours therefore, and they which before had seen him that he was blind, said, Is not this he that sat and begged?" (9:8). When a genuine work of grace has been wrought in a soul it is impossible to conceal it from our neighbors and acquaintances. At first they will talk among themselves and discuss with a good deal of curiosity and speculation what has happened. The unsaved are always skeptical of God's miracles.

When one of their fellows is saved, they cannot deny that a radical change has taken place, though the nature of it they are completely at a loss to explain. They know not that the manifestation of Christ in the outward life of a quickened soul is due to Christ now dwelling within. Yet, even the unbelieving world is compelled to take note and indirectly acknowledge that regeneration is a real thing. Ah! dear reader, if the Lord Jesus has lain His wondrous hand on you, then those with whom you come into daily contact will recognize the fact. "They will see that it is not with thee as it used to be—that a real change has passed upon thee—that the tempers and lusts, habits and influences which once ruled thee with despotic power, now rule thee no longer—that though evil may occasionally break out, it does not habitually bear sway—that though it dwells within it does not reign—though it plagues it does not govern."

"Some said, This is he: others said, He is like him: but he said, I am he" (9:9). How marvellously accurate is this line in the picture! When one who is dead in trespasses and sins has been quickened into newness of life he becomes a new creature in Christ, but the old man still remains. Not yet has he been delivered from this body of death; for that, he must await the return of our Lord. In the one who has been born again there are, then, *two* natures: the old is not destroyed, but a new has been imparted. This is plainly foreshadowed in the verse before us: some recognized the one they had known before his eyes were opened; others saw a different personality. It is this which is so puzzling in connection with regeneration. The individual is still the same, but a new principle and element have come into his life.

"Therefore said they unto him, How were thine eyes opened?" (9:10). How true to life again! The one who has found mercy with the Lord is now put to the proof: his faith, his loyalty, his courage must be tested. It is not long before the quickened soul discovers that he is living in a world that is unfriendly toward him. At first God may not permit that unfriendliness to take on a very aggressive form, for He deals very tenderly with the babes in His family. But as they grow in grace and become strong in the Lord and in the power of His might,

He suffers them to be tested more severely and no longer shields them from the fiercer assaults of their great enemy. Nevertheless, testing they must have from the beginning, for it is thus that faith is developed by casting us upon the Lord and perfecting our weakness in His strength.

"Therefore said they unto him, How were thine eyes opened?" Here was an opportunity afforded this one who had so wondrously received his sight to bear witness to His gracious Benefactor. To *confess* Christ, to tell of what great things the Lord hath done for him, is the first duty of the newly saved soul, and the promise is, "Whosoever shall confess me before men, him shall the Son of man also confess before the angels of God" (Luke 12:8). But this is the last thing which the world appreciates or desires: that blessed Name which is above every name is an offence to them. It is striking to observe how the neighbors of the beggar framed their question: "How were thine eyes opened?" not "*Who* opened thine eyes?" They wished to satisfy their curiosity, but they had no desire to hear about Christ!

"He answered and said, A man that is called Jesus made clay, and anointed mine eyes, and said unto me, Go to the pool of Siloam, and wash: and I went and washed, and I received sight" (9:11). The witness borne by this man was simple and honest. As yet he did not have much light, but he was faithful to the light that he did have; and that is the way to obtain more. He did not speculate nor philosophize, but gave a straightforward account of what the Lord had done to him. Two things in this man's confession should be noted as accurately illustrating the witness of a newly saved soul today. First, it was the *work* of Christ rather than His *person* which had most impressed him; it was what Christ had *done,* rather than *who* He was that was emphasized in his testimony. It is so with us. The first thing we grasp is that it is the Cross-work of the Lord Jesus, His sacrificial death which put away our sins; the infinite value of His person we learn later, as the Spirit unfolds it to us through the Word. Second, in connection with the person of Christ it was His *humanity,* not His Deity that this man spoke of. And was it not so with us? "A man that is called Jesus"—was it not *that* aspect of His blessed person which first filled our vision! "A man that is called Jesus" speaks of His lowliness and humiliation. Later, as we study the Scriptures and grow in the knowledge of the Lord, we discover that the man Christ Jesus is none other than the Son of God.

"He answered and said, A man that is called Jesus made clay, and anointed mine eyes, and said unto me, Go to the pool of Siloam, and wash: and I went and washed, and I received sight." That precious name of "Jesus" was the most hated of all to those Jews; yet did the beggar boldly confess it. "It would manifestly have served the poor man's worldly interest to cushion the truth as to what had been done for him. He might have enjoyed the benefit of the work of Christ, and yet avoided the rough path of testimony for His name in the face of the world's hostility. He might have enjoyed his eyesight, and, at the same time, retained his place within the pale of respectable religious profession. He might have reaped the fruit of Christ's *work* and yet escaped the reproach of confessing His *name.*

"How often is this the case! Alas, how often! Thousands are very well pleased to hear of what Jesus has done; but they do not want to be identified with His outcast and rejected Name. In other words, to use a modern and very popular phrase, 'They want to make the best of both worlds'—a sentiment from which every true-hearted lover of Christ must shrink with abhorrence—an idea of which genuine faith is wholly ignorant. It is obvious that the subject of our narrative knew nothing of any such maxim. He had had his eyes opened, and he could not but speak of it, and tell who did it, and how it was done. He was an honest man. He had no mixed motives. No sinister object, no undercurrent. Happy for him!" (C.H.M.).

"He answered and said, A man that is called Jesus made clay, and anointed mine eyes, and said unto me, Go to the pool of Siloam, and wash." There is one little detail here which strikingly evidences the truthfulness of this narrative, and that is one little *omission* in this man's description of what the Saviour had done to him. It is to be noted that the beggar made no reference to Christ spitting on the ground and making clay of the spittle. Being blind he could not *see* what the Lord *did,* though he could *feel* what He *applied!* It is in just such little undesigned coincidences, such artless touches, as this, that makes the more apparent the genuineness of these Divine narratives.

"Then said they unto him, Where is he? He said, I know not" (9:12). Equally commendable was the modesty of this man here. He acted up to the light that he had, but he did not go beyond it. He pretended not to possess a knowledge not yet his. O that we were all as simple and honest. When the neighbors enquired, "Is not this he that sat and begged?", he answered, "I am he"—though it is most unseemly for a Christian to advertise the sins of his unregenerate days, yet it is equally wrong for him to deny what he then was when plainly asked. Next, they had asked, "How were thine eyes opened?", and he unhesitatingly told them, not forgetting to boldly confess the name of his Benefactor. Now they said, "Where is he?", and he frankly replied, "I know not." The babe in Christ is *guileless* and hesitates not to acknowledge that he is ignorant of much. But it is sad to observe how pride so often comes in and destroys this simplicity and honesty. Christian reader, and especially the babe in Christ, hesitate not to avow your ignorance; when asked a question that you cannot answer, honestly reply, "I know not." Feign not a knowledge you do not possess, and have not recourse to speculation.

"They brought to the Pharisees him that aforetime was blind" (9:13). "Now the former blind beggar was to become an object of special notice by the Pharisees. Very likely many of them had passed him unheeded. A blind beggar! Which of them would bestow a thought on him whose condition they regarded as an evidence that he was born in sin? But the beggar, no longer blind, was quite a different matter. Were they anxious to learn of the favor he had received in order to honor his Benefactor, or to solicit in their turn favors from Him? Quite the contrary. Their efforts were directed to discredit the miracle as being wrought by One sent from God. He who had shortly before affirmed of Himself in the Temple court, that He was God, had now opened that man's eyes. The insult to the Divine Majesty, as the Jews regarded it, in asserting His Deity, was followed by this miracle, of which the beggar in the Temple precincts was the subject. To discredit the Lord was their purpose. He was a Sabbath-breaker they declared; and therefore that miracle must be disowned as being any display of almighty power and benevolence" (C. E. Stuart).

"They brought to the Pharisees him that aforetime was blind." This was a much more severe trial for him than what he had just passed through at the hands of his neighbors. It was a real test of his faith. The opposition of the Pharisees against the Lord, and their desire to get rid of Him were well known; and their determination to excommunicate any one who confessed Him as the Christ was no secret (see v. 22). To face them, then, was indeed an ordeal. Alas that this part of the history is being repeated today. Repeated it certainly is, for the ones who will treat worst the young believer are not open infidels and atheists, but those who are loudest in their religious professions. These Pharisees have many successors: their tribe is far from being extinct, and their descendants will be found occupying the same position of religious leadership as did their fathers of old.

"And it was the Sabbath day when Jesus made the clay, and opened his eyes" (9:14). There are two observations which we would make on this verse. First, our Lord here teaches us that the words of the fourth commandment "In it [the Sabbath] thou shalt not do *any* work," are not to be taken absolutely, that is, without any modification. By His own example He has shown us that works of necessity and also works of mercy are permissible. This 14th verse therefore reflects the glory of Christ. It was the Sabbath day: how was He occupied? First, (and note the order) He had gone to the Temple, there to minister God's Word; second, now He is seen ministering in mercy to one in need. Perfect example has He left us.

In the next place, we would call attention to the fact that our Lord knew full well that His performing of this miracle on the Sabbath would give offence to His enemies. He proceeded to its execution, nevertheless. We have another illustration of the same principle in Mark 7:2: "When they saw some of his disciples eat bread with defiled, that is to say, with unwashen hands, they found fault." Though rendering perfect obedience to all the laws of God, Christ paid no regard to the commandments of men. Here too He has left us a perfect example. Let not the believer be brought into bondage by heeding the mandates of religious legislators, when their rules and regulations have no support from the Holy Scriptures.

"Then again the Pharisees also asked him how he had received his sight. He said unto them, He put clay upon mine eyes, and I washed, and do see" (9:15). This was an honest effort on the part of these Pharisees to investigate the teaching of that blessed One whose voice they had recently heard and whose power had now been so signally displayed. They – or the influential among them at least, for in this Gospel "the Jews" ever refer to the religious leaders or their agents – had already agreed that if any did confess that Jesus was the Christ, he should be put out of the synagogue (see v. 22). Thus had they deliberately closed their eyes against the truth, and therefore it was impossible that they should now discern it, blinded by prejudice as they were. Their object here was twofold: to discredit the miracle, and to intimidate the one who had been the subject of it. Note the form of their question. They, too, asked the beggar *how* he had received his sight, not *who* was the one who had so graciously blest him.

"He said unto them, He put clay upon mine eyes, and I washed, and do see." The enlightened beggar was not to be cowed. He had returned a straightforward answer to the inquiries of his neighbors, he is equally honest and bold now before the open enemies of Christ. His faithful testimony here teaches us an important lesson. Behind his human interrogators it is not difficult to discern the great Enemy of souls. Satan it is who hurls the fiery darts, even though he employs religious professors as his instruments. But they fall powerless upon the shield of faith, and it is this which is illustrated here. One may be the veriest babe in Christ, but so long as he walks according to the measure of light which God has granted, the Devil is powerless to harm him. It is when we quench that light, or when we are unfaithful to Christ, that we become powerless, and fall an easy prey to the Enemy. But the one before us was acting up to the light that he had, therefore the lion roared in vain against him.

"Therefore said some of the Pharisees, This man is not of God, because he keepeth not the Sabbath day" (9:16). A striking contrast is this from what has just been before us. These Pharisees had turned their backs upon the Light, and therefore was their darkness now even more profound. Devoid of spiritual discernment they were altogether incapable of determining what was a right use and lawful employment of the Sabbath and what was not. They understood not that "The sabbath was made for man" (Mark 2:27), that is, for the benefit of his soul and the good of his body. True, the day which God blest at the beginning was to be kept holy, but it was never intended to bar out works of necessity and works of mercy, as they should have known from the Old Testament Scriptures. In thus finding fault with Christ because He had opened the eyes of this blind beggar on the Sabbath day, they did but expose their ignorance and exhibit their spiritual blindness.

"Others said, How can a man that is a sinner do such miracles? And there was a division among them" (9:16). We wonder if one of those who spoke up thus was Nicodemus! The argument used here is strictly parallel with the words of that "Master in Israel" which we find in John 3:1, 2. That we are next told, "And there was a division among them" shows that the second speakers held their ground and refused to side-in with the open enemies of our Lord. On this verse the Puritan Bullinger remarked, "All *divisions* are not necessarily evil, nor all concord and unity necessarily good"!

"They say unto the blind man again, What sayest thou of him, that he hath opened thine eyes?" (9:17). The Devil is powerless in his efforts to gain an advantage over the sheep of Christ. Repulsed for the moment by the unexpected friendliness toward Christ on the part of some of the Pharisees, the Enemy turned his attention once more to the beggar: "They say unto the blind man *again*": note the frequency with which this word is used in this passage—vv. 15, 17, 24, 26. The Devil's perseverance frequently puts our instability to shame.

"What sayest thou of him, that he hath opened thine eyes?" A searching question was this. The faith of the beggar was now openly challenged: he must now either confess or deny his Benefactor. But he did not flinch or dissemble. Boldly he answered, "He is a prophet." Divine grace did not fail him in the hour of need, but enabled him to stand firm and witness a good confession. Blessed be His name, the grace of God is as *sufficient* for the youngest and feeblest as for the most mature and established.

"He said. He is a prophet" (9:17). There is a decided advance here. When answering his neighbors, the beggar simply referred to Christ as, "A man that is called Jesus" (v. 11); but now he owns Him as One whose word is *Divine,* for a "prophet" was a mouthpiece of God. This was most blessed. At first he had been occupied solely with the work of Christ, now he is beginning to discern the glory of His *person;* increased intelligence was his. Nor is God arbitrary in the bestowment of this. When the believer walks faithfully according to the light which he has, more is given to him. It was so here; it is so now. This is the meaning of that verse which has perplexed so many: "Take heed therefore how ye hear: for whosoever hath, to him shall be given; and whosoever hath not, from him shall be taken even that which he seemeth to have" (Luke 8:18): the reference here being to *light* used and unused – note the "therefore" which looks back to v. 16. In Matthew's account it reads, "For whosoever hath, to him shall be given, and he shall have more abundance." A striking illustration of this is furnished in John 9. Light the beggar now had; and that light he let shine forth, consequently *more* was given to him; later, we shall see how a "more abundance" was vouchsafed to him.

"He said, He is a *prophet.*" This is not the first time we have had Christ owned as "prophet" in this Gospel. In 4:19 we read that the woman of Samaria said to the Saviour at the well, "I perceive that thou art a *prophet.*" In 6:14 we are told, "Then those men, when they had seen the miracle that Jesus did, said, This is of a truth that *prophet* that should come into the world." Once more, in 7:40 we read, "Many of the people therefore, when they heard this saying, said, Of a truth this is *the prophet.*"

These references are in striking accord with the character and theme of this fourth Gospel. A prophet was *the mouthpiece* of God, and the great purpose of John's Gospel, as intimated in its opening verse, is to portray the Lord Jesus as "the Word"!

"But the Jews did not believe concerning him, that he had been blind, and received his sight, until they called the parents of him that had received his sight" (9:18). How skeptical are the unregenerate! "Children in whom is *no faith*" (Deut. 32:20) is what the Scriptures term them. A wonderful miracle had been performed, but these Jews were determined not to believe it. The simple but emphatic testimony of the one on whom it had been wrought went for nothing. What a lesson is this for the young convert. Marvelling at what the Saviour has so graciously done for and in him, anxious that others should know Him for themselves, he goes forth testifying of His grace and power. Full of zeal and hope, he expects that it will be a simple matter to convince others of the reality of what the Lord has done for him. Ah! it will not be long before his bright expectations meet with disappointment. He will soon discover something of that dreadful and inveterate unbelief which fills the hearts of his unsaved fellows. He must be shown that *he* has no power to convince them; that nothing but a miracle of mercy, the putting forth of invincible power by God Himself, is sufficient to overcome the enmity of the carnal mind.

"And they asked them, saying, Is this your son, who ye say was born blind? how then doth he now see?" (9:19). This was a desperate move. They had been unable to intimidate the one who had been dealt with so graciously by Christ. They were unable to meet the arguments which had been made by some of the more friendly Pharisees. They now decide to summon the beggar's parents. It was their last hope. If they could succeed in getting them to deny that their son had been born blind, the miracle would be discredited. With this object in view they arraign the parents. And Satan still seeks to discredit the witness of the young Christian by getting his relatives to testify against him! This is an oft-used device of his. Let us daily seek grace from God that we may so act in the home that those nearest to us will have no just ground for condemning our profession.

"His parents answered them and said, We know that this is our son, and that he was born blind: But by what means he now seeth, we know not; or who hath opened his eyes, we know not: he is of age; ask him: he shall speak for himself" (9:20, 21). How this serves to expose the folly of a wish we have often heard expressed. People say, "O that I had lived in Palestine during the days of Christ's public ministry; it had been so much easier to have believed in Him!" They suppose that if only they had witnessed some of the wonderful works of our Lord, unbelief had been impossible. How little such people know about the real nature and seat of unbelief; and how little acquainted must they be with the four Gospels. These plainly record the fact (making no effort at all either to conceal or excuse it) that again and again the Lord Jesus put forth His supernatural power, producing the most amazing effects, and yet the great majority of those who stood by were nothing more than temporarily impressed. It was so here in the passage before us. Even the parents of this man born blind believed not on Christ. They were evidently afraid of their inquisitors; and yet their answer nonplussed the Pharisees.

"These words spake his parents, because they feared the Jews" (9:22). They represented a large class of religious professors who surround us on every side today—in such bondage are men and women, otherwise intelligent, to religious leaders and authorities. How true it is that "the fear of man bringeth a snare." The only ones who are fearless before men are those who truly *fear* God. This is one of our daily needs: to cry earnestly unto the Lord that He will put *His* "fear" upon us.

"These words spake his parents, because they feared the Jews: for the Jews had agreed already, that if any man did confess that he was Christ, he should be put out of the synagogue" (9:22). Mark here the desperate lengths to which prejudice will carry men. They were determined not to believe. They had made up their minds that no evidence should change their opinions, that no testimony should have any weight with them. It reminds us very much of what we read of in Acts 7. At the close of

Stephen's address we read that his enemies *"stopped their ears,* and ran upon him with one accord" (v. 57). This is just what these Pharisees did, and it is what many are doing today. And this is the most dangerous attitude a sinner can assume. So long as a man is honest and open-minded, there is hope for him, no matter how ignorant or vicious he may be. But when a man has deliberately turned his back upon the truth, and refuses to be influenced by any evidence, it is very rare indeed that such an one is ever brought into the light.

"Therefore said his parents, He is of age; ask him" (9:23). Typically, this tells us that the young and tried believer must not look to man for help; his resources must be in God alone. This man might well have expected his parents to be filled with gratitude at their son's eyes being opened, that they would perceive how God had wrought a miracle of mercy upon him, and that they would readily stand by and corroborate his witness before this unfriendly tribunal. But little help did he receive from them. The onus was thrown back upon himself. And this line in the picture is not without its due significance. The young believer might well expect his loved ones to appreciate and rejoice over the blessed change they must see in him; but oftentimes they are quite indifferent if not openly antagonistic. So too with our fellow-Christians. If we look to *them* for help when we get in a tight place, they will generally fail us. And it is perhaps well that it should be so. Anything that really casts us *upon God Himself* is a blessing, even though it be disguised and appear to us a calamity at the time. Let us learn then to "have no confidence in the flesh" (Phil. 3:3), but let our expectation be in the Lord, who will fail us not.

Let the interested student ponder the following questions:

1. What is meant by "Give God the praise" (v. 24)? Cf. Josh. 7:19.
2. Explain the first half of v. 25 so as not to conflict with v. 33.
3. What other verse in John's Gospel does the second half of v. 29 call to mind?
4. What connection is there between v. 31 and what has gone before?

5. Why did Christ wait till the beggar had been "cast out" (v. 34) before He revealed Himself as the Son of God (v. 35)?
6. Why are we told nothing more about the beggar after what is said in v. 38?
7. What is the meaning of v. 39? Contrast 3:17.

CHAPTER THIRTY-THREE

Christ and the Blind Beggar (Concluded)

John 9:24-41

The following is offered as an Analysis of the passage which is to be before us: —

1. The beggar challenged and his reply: vv. 24, 25.
2. The beggar cross-examined and his response: vv. 26, 27.
3. The beggar reviled: vv. 28, 29.
4. The beggar defeats his judges: vv. 30-33.
5. The beggar cast out by the Pharisees, sought out by Christ: vv. 34, 35.
6. The beggar worships Christ as the Son of God: vv. 36-38.
7. Christ's condemnation of the Pharisees: vv. 39-41.

We arrive now at the closing scenes in this inspired narrative of the Lord's dealings with the blind beggar and the consequent hostility of the Pharisees. In it there is much that is reprehensible, but much too that is praiseworthy. The enmity of the carnal mind is again exhibited to our view; while the blessed fruit of Divine grace is presented for our admiration. The wickedness of the Pharisees finds its climax in their excommunication of the beggar; the workings of grace in his heart reaches its culmination by bringing him to the feet of the Saviour as a devoted worshipper.

The passage before us records the persistent efforts of the Pharisees to shake the testimony of this one who had received his sight. Their blindness, their refusal to be influenced by the most convincing evidence, their enmity against the beggar's Benefactor, and their unjust and cruel treatment of him, vividly forecasted the treatment which the Lord Himself was shortly to receive at their hands. On the other hand, the fidelity of the beggar, his refusal to be intimidated by those in authority, his Divinely-given power to non-plus his judges, his being cast out of Judaism, and his place as a worshipper at the feet of the Son of God *on the outside,* anticipated what was to be exemplified again and again in the history of the Lord's disciples following His own apprehension.

"Then again called they the man that was blind, and said unto him, Give God the praise: we know that this man is a sinner" (9:24). The one to whom sight had been so marvellously imparted had been removed from the court of the Sanhedrin while the examination of his parents had been going on. But he is now brought in before his judges again. The examination of his parents had signally failed to either produce any discrepancy between the statements of the parents and that of their son, or to bring out any fact to the discredit of Christ. A final effort was therefore made now to shake the testimony of the man himself.

"Then again called they the man that was blind, and said unto him, Give God the praise: we know that this man is a sinner." These shameless inquisitors pretended that during his absence they had discovered something to the utter discredit of the Lord Jesus. Things had come to light, so they feigned, which proved Him to be more than an ordinary bad character—such is the force of the Greek word here for "sinner," compare its usage in Luke 7:34, 37, 39; 15:2; 19:7. It is evident that the Sanhedrin would lead the beggar to believe that facts regarding his Benefactor had now come to their knowledge which showed He could not be the Divinely-directed author of his healing. Therefore, they now address him in a solemn formula, identical with that used by Joshua when arraigning Achan—see Josh. 7:19. They adjured him by the living God to tell the whole truth. They demanded that he forswear himself, and join with them in some formal statement which was dishonoring to Christ. It was a desperate and blasphemous effort at intimidation.

"He answered and said, Whether he be a sinner or no, I know not: one thing I know, that, whereas I was blind, now I see" (9:25). It is refreshing to turn for a moment from the unbelief and enmity of the Pharisees to mark the simplicity and honesty of this babe in Christ. The Latin Vulgate renders the first clause of this verse, "If he is a sinner I know not." The force of his utterance seems to be this: 'I do not believe that He is a sinner; I will not charge Him with being one; I refuse to unite with you in saying that He is.' Clear it is that the contents of this verse must not be explained in a way so as to clash with what we have in v. 33, where the beggar owned that Christ was "of God." The proper way is to view it in the light of the previous verse. There we find the Pharisees adjuring him to join with them in denouncing Christ as a sinner. This the beggar flatly refused to do, and refused in such a way as to show that he declined to enter into a controversy with his judges about the character of Christ.

"Whether he be a sinner or no, I know not: one thing I know, that, whereas I was blind, now I see." This was tantamount to saying, 'Your charge against the person of Christ is altogether beside the point. You are examining me in connection with what Christ has *done for* me, therefore I refuse to turn aside and discuss His *person.*' The Pharisees were trying to change the issue, but the beggar would not be side-tracked. He held them to the indisputable fact that a miracle of mercy had been wrought upon him. Thereupon he boldly declared again what the Lord had done for him. That his eyes had been opened could not be gainsaid: all the argument and attacks of the Pharisees could not shake him. Let us not only admire his fearlessness and truthfulness, but seek grace to emulate him.

"One thing I know, that, whereas I was blind, now I see." These are words which every born-again person can apply to himself. There are many things of which the young believer has little knowledge: there are many points in theology and prophecy upon which he has no light: but "one thing" he *does* know—he knows that the eyes of his understanding have been opened. He knows this because he has seen himself as a lost sinner, seen his imminent danger, seen the Divinely-appointed refuge from the wrath to come, seen the sufficiency of Christ to save him. Can a man repent and not know it? can he believe on the Lord Jesus Christ to the saving of his soul and not know it? can he pass from death unto life, be delivered from the power of darkness and translated into the kingdom of God's dear Son, and not know it? We do not believe it. The saints of God are a people that "know." They *know* Whom they have believed (II Tim. 1:12). They *know* that their Redeemer liveth (Job 19:26). They *know* they have passed from death unto life (I John 3:14). They *know* that all things work together for their good (Rom. 8:28). They *know* that when the Lord Jesus shall appear they shall be like Him (I John 3:2). Christianity treats not of theories and hypotheses, but of certainties and realities. Rest not, dear reader, till *you* can say, "One thing *I know,* that, whereas I was blind, now I see."

"Then said they to him again, What did he to thee? how opened he thine eyes?" (9:26). Unable to get this man to deny the miracle which had been wrought upon him, unable to bring him to entertain an evil opinion of Christ, his judges inquire once more about the *manner* in which he had been healed. This inquiry of theirs was merely a repetition of their former question – see v. 15. It is evident that their object in repeating this query was the hope that he would vary in his account and thus give them grounds for discrediting his testimony. They were seeking to "shake his evidence": they hoped he would contradict himself.

"Then said they to him again, What did he to thee? how opened he thine eyes?" This illustrates again how that unbelief is occupied with the modus operandi rather than with the result itself. *How* you were brought to Christ – the secondary causes, where you were at the time, the instrument God employed – is of little moment. The one thing that matters is whether or not the Lord *has* opened the sin-blinded eyes of your heart. Whether you were saved in the fields or in a church, whether you were on your knees at a "mourner's bench" or upon your back in bed, is a detail of very little value. Faith is occupied not with the manner in which you held out your hand to receive God's gift, but with Christ Himself! But unbelief is occupied with the "how" rather than with the "whom."

"He answered them, I have told you already, and ye did not hear: wherefore would ye hear it again? will ye also be his disciples?" (9:27). With honest indignation he turns upon his unscrupulous inquisitors and refuses to waste time in repeating what he had already told them so simply and plainly. It is quite useless to discuss the things of God with those whose hearts are manifestly closed against Him. When such people continue pressing their frivolous or blasphemous inquiries, only one course remains open, and that is "Answer a fool according to his folly, lest he be wise in his own conceit" (Prov. 26:5). This Divine admonition has puzzled some, because in the preceding verse we are told, "*Answer not* a fool according to his folly, lest thou also be like unto him." But the seeming contradiction is easily explained. When God says, "Answer not a fool according to his folly, lest thou also be like unto him," the meaning is, I must not answer a fool *in a foolish manner*, for this would make me a sharer of his folly. But when God says, "*Answer* a fool according to his folly, lest he be wise in his own conceit," the meaning is, that I must answer him in a way *to expose his folly*, lest he imagine that he has succeeded in propounding a question which is unanswerable. This is exactly what the beggar did here in the lesson: he answered in such a way as to make evident the folly and unbelief of his judges.

"Then they reviled him, and said, Thou art his disciple; but we are Moses' disciples" (9:28). The word "reviled" is hardly strong enough to express the original. The Greek word signifies that the Pharisees hurled their anathemas against him by pronouncing him an execrable fellow. How true to life! Unable to fairly meet his challenge, unable to justify their course, they resort to villification. To have recourse to invectives is ever the last resort of a defeated opponent. Whenever you find men calling their opponents hard names, it is a sure sign that their own cause has been defeated.

"They reviled him, and said, Thou art *his* disciple." The man of the world has little difficulty in locating a genuine "disciple" of Christ. This man had not formally avowed himself as such, yet the Pharisees had no difficulty in deciding that he *was* one. His whole demeanor was so different from the cringing servility which they were accustomed to receive from their own followers, and the wisdom with which he had replied to all their questions, stamped him plainly as one who had *learned* of the God-man. So it is today. Real Christians need no placards on their backs or buttons on their coat lapels in order to inform their fellows that they belong to the Lord Jesus. If I am walking as a child of light, men will soon exclaim, "Thou art *his* disciple." The Lord enable writer and reader to give as clear and ringing a testimony in our lives as this beggar did.

"But we are Moses' disciples." A lofty boast was this, but as baseless as haughty. The Lord had already told them, "Had ye believed Moses, ye would have believed me; for he wrote of me" (5:46). This too has its present-day application. Multitudes are seeking shelter behind high pretensions and honored names. Many there are who term themselves Calvinists that Calvin would be ashamed to own. Many call themselves Lutherans who neither manifest the faith nor emulate the works of the great Reformer. Many go under the name of Baptists to whom our Lord's forerunner, were he here in the flesh, would say, "Flee from the wrath to come." And countless numbers claim to be Protestants who scarcely know what the term itself signifies. It is one thing to say "We are—disciples," it is quite another to make demonstration of it.

"We know that God spake unto Moses" (9:29). Such knowledge was purely intellectual, something which they venerated as a religious tradition handed down by their forebears; but it neither moved their hearts nor affected their lives. And *that* is the real test of a man's orthodoxy. An orthodox creed, intellectually apprehended, counts for nothing if it fails to mould the life of the one professing it. I may claim to regard the Bible as the inspired and infallible Word of God, yea, and be ready to defend this fundamental article of the faith; I may refuse to heed the infidelistic utterances of the higher critics, and pride myself on my doctrinal soundness—as did these Pharisees. But of what worth is this if I know not what it means to *tremble* at that Word, and if my walk is not regulated by its precepts? None at all! Rather will such intellectual light serve only to increase my condemnation.

"As for this fellow, we know not from whence he is" (9:29). Proofs went for nothing. The testimony of this man and the witness of his parents had been spread before these Pharisees, yet they believed not. Ah! faith does not come that way. Hearing the testimony of God's saints will no more regenerate lost sinners than listening to the description of a dinner I ate will feed some other hungry man. That is one reason why the writer has no patience with "testimony meetings": another is, because he finds no precedent for them in the Word of God. But this beggar *had* faith, and his faith came as the result of being made the personal subject of the mighty operation of God. Nothing short of this avails. Sinners may witness miracles as Pharaoh did; they may listen to the testimony of a believer as these Pharisees; they may be terrified by the convulsions of nature, but none of these things will ever lead a single sinner to believe in Christ. "Faith cometh by hearing, and hearing by the Word of God" (Rom. 10:17)—by the Word applied in the omnipotent power of the Holy Spirit.

"As for this fellow, we know not from whence he is." How inconsistent is unbelief! In the seventh chapter of this Gospel we find the Jews refusing to believe on Christ because they declared they *did* know whence He was. Hear them, "Howbeit we know this man whence he is: but when Christ cometh, no man knoweth whence he is" (7:27). But now these Pharisees object against Christ, "We know not from whence he is." Thus do those who reject the truth of God contradict themselves.

"The man answered and said unto them, Why herein is a marvellous thing, that ye know not from whence he is, and yet he hath opened mine eyes" (9:30). Quick to seize the acknowledgement of the ignorance as to whence Christ came, the beggar turned it against them. Though he spoke in the mildest of terms yet the stinging import of his words is evident. It was as though he had said, "You who profess yourselves fully qualified to guide the people on all points, and yet in the dark on a matter like this!" A poor beggar he might be, and as such cut off from many of the advantages they had enjoyed, nevertheless, *he* knew what they did not—he knew that Christ was "of God" (v. 33)! How true it is that God reveals things to babes in Christ which He hides from the wise and prudent! hides because they *are* "wise"—wise in their own conceits. Nothing shuts out Divine illumination so effectively as prejudice and pride: nothing tends to blind the heart more than egotism. "If any man among you seemeth to be wise in this world, let him become a fool, that he *may be* wise" (I Cor.3:18); "Proud, knowing nothing" (I Tim. 6:4).

"Now we know that God heareth not sinners: but if any man be a worshipper of God, and doeth his will, him he heareth" (9:31). This verse like many another must not be divorced from its setting. Taken absolutely, these words "God heareth not sinners," are not true. God "heard" the cry of Ishmael (Gen. 21:17); He "heard" the groanings of the children of Israel in Egypt, long before He redeemed them (Ex. 2:24); He "heard" and answered the prayer of the wicked Manasseh (II Chron. 33: 10-13). But reading this verse in the light of its context its meaning is apparent. The Pharisees had said of Christ, "We know that this man is a *sinner*" (v. 24). Now says the beggar, "We know that God heareth not *sinners*," which was one of their pet doctrines. Thus, once more, did the one on trial turn the word of his judges against themselves. If Christ were an impostor as they avowed, then how came it that God has assisted Him to work this miracle?

"Since the world began was it not heard that any man opened the eyes of one that was born blind" (9:32). This was his reply to their statement that they were Moses' disciples. He reminds them that not even in Moses' day, not from the beginning of the world had such a miracle been performed as had been wrought on him. It is a significant fact that among all the miracles wrought by Moses, never did he give sight to a blind man, nor did any of the prophets ever open the eyes of one born blind. *That* was something that only Christ did!

"If this man were not of God, he could do nothing." This beggar was now endowed with a wisdom to which these learned Pharisees were strangers. How often is this same principle illustrated in the Scriptures. The Hebrew lad from the dungeon, not the wise men of Egypt, was the one to interpret the dream of Pharaoh. Daniel, not the wise men of Babylon, deciphered the mysterious writing on the walls of Belshazzar's palace. Unlettered fishermen, not the scribes, were taken into the confidences of the Saviour. So here, a mouth and wisdom were given to this babe in Christ which the doctors of the Sanhedrin were unable to resist.

"If this man were not of God, he could do nothing." What a beautiful illustration is this of Prov. 4:18!—"But the path of the just is as the shining light, that shineth *more and more* unto the perfect day." First, this beggar had referred to his Benefactor as "a man that is called Jesus" (v. 11). Second, he had owned Him as "a prophet" (v. 17). And now he declares that Christ was a man "of God." There is also a lesson here pointed for us: as we walk according to the light we have, God gives us more. Here is the reason why so many of God's children are in the dark concerning much of His truth—they are not faithful to the light they *do* have. May God exercise both writer and reader about this so that we may earnestly seek from Him the grace which we so sorely need to make us faithful and true to all we have received of Him.

"They answered and said unto him, Thou wast altogether born in sins, and dost thou teach us?" (9:34). Alas, how tragically does history repeat itself. These men were too arrogant to receive anything from this poor beggar. They were graduates from honored seats of learning, therefore was it far too much beneath their dignity to be instructed by this unsophisticated disciple of Christ. And how many a preacher there is today, who in his fancied superiority, scorns the help which ofttimes a member of his congregation could give him. Glorying in their seminary education, they cannot allow that an ignorant layman has light on the Scriptures which *they* do not possess. Let a Spirit-taught layman seek to show the average preacher "the way of the Lord more perfectly," and he must not be surprised if his pastor says—if not in so many words, plainly by his bearing and actions—"dost *thou* teach us?" How marvellously pertinent is this two-thousand-year-old Book to our own times!

"And they cast him out" (9:34). "Happy man! He had followed the light, in simplicity and sincerity. He had borne an honest testimony to the truth. His eyes had been opened to see and his lips to testify. It was no matter of wrong or wicked lewdness, but simple truth, and for that they cast him out. He had never troubled them in the days of his blindness and beggary. Perhaps some of them may have proudly and ostentatiously tossed him a trifling alms as they walked past, thus getting a name amongst their fellows for benevolence; but now this blind beggar had become a powerful witness. Words of truth now flowed from his lips—truth far too powerful and piercing for them to stand, so they 'thrust him out.' Happy, thrice happy man! again we say, This was the brightest moment in his career. These men, though they knew it not, had done him a real service. They had thrust him out into the most honored position of identification with Christ as the despised and rejected One" (C.H.M.).

"And they cast him out." How cruelly and unjustly will religious professors treat the real people of God! When these Pharisees failed to intimidate this man they excommunicated him from the Jewish church. To an Israelite the dread of excommunication was second only to the fear of death: it cut him off from all the outward privileges of the commonwealth of Israel, and made him an object of scorn and derision. But all through the ages some of the faithful witnesses of Christ have met with similar or even worse treatment. Excommunication, persecution, imprisonment, torture, death, are the favorite weapons of ecclesiastical tyrants. Thus were the Waldenses treated; so Luther, Bunyan, Ridley, the Huguenots; and so, in great probability, will it be again in the near future.

"And they cast him out." Ah! Christian reader, if *you* did as this man you would know something of his experience. If you bore faithful testimony for *Christ* by lip and life; if you refused to walk arm-in-arm with the world, and lived here as a stranger and pilgrim; if you declined to follow the customs of the great religious crowd, and regulated your walk by the Word, *you* would be very *un*popular—perhaps the very thing that you most fear! You would be cut off from your former circle of friends, as not wanted; cut off because your ways condemned theirs. Yea, if true to God's Word you might be turned out of your church as an heretic or stirrer up of strife.

"Jesus heard that they had cast him out; and when he had found him, he said unto him, Dost thou believe on the Son of

God?" (9:35). This is indeed precious. No sooner had the Sanhedrin excommunicated the beggar than the Saviour sought him out. How true it is that those who honor God are honored by Him. Faithfully had this man walked according to his measure of light, now more is to be given him. Great is the compassion of Christ. He knew full well the weight of the trial which had fallen upon this newly-born soul, and He proved Himself "a very presesnt help in trouble." He cheered this man with gracious words. Yea, He revealed Himself more fully to him than to any other individual, save the Samaritan adulteress. He plainly avowed His deity: He presented Himself in His highest glory as "the Son of God."

"Jesus heard that they had cast him out; and when he had found him, he said unto him, Dost thou believe on the Son of God?" The connection between this and the previous verse should be carefully noted: the beggar was "cast out" *before* he knew Christ as the Son of God. The Nation as such denied this truth, and only the despised few on the *outside* of organized Judaism had it revealed to them. There is a message here greatly needed by many of the Lord's people today who are inside man-made systems where much of the truth of God is denied. True, if they are the Lord's, they are saved; but not to them will Christ *reveal Himself*, while they continue in a position which is dishonoring to Him. It is the Holy Spirit's office to take of the things of Christ and to show them unto us. But while we are identified with and lend our support to that which *grieves* Him, He will not delight our souls with revelations of the excellencies of our Saviour. Nowhere in Scripture has God promised to honor those who *dis*honor Him. God is very jealous of the honor of His Son and He withholds many spiritual blessings from those who fellowship that which is an offence to Him. On the outside *with Christ* is infinitely preferable to being on the inside with worldly professors who know Him not. The time is already arrived when many of God's people are compelled to choose between these two alternatives. Far better to be "cast out" because of faithfulness to Christ, or to "come out" (II Cor. 6:17) because of others' unfaithfulness to Christ, than to remain in the Laodicean system which is yet to be "spued out" by Christ

(Rev. 3:16). Whatever loss may be entailed by leaving unscriptural and worldly churches, it will be more than compensated by the Lord. It was so with this beggar.

"He answered and said, Who is he, Lord, that I might believe on him?" (9:36). It is indeed beautiful to mark the spirit of this man in the presence of Christ. Before the Sanhedrin he was bold as a lion, but before the Son of God he is meek and lowly. Here he is seen addressing Him as "Lord." These graces, seemingly so conflicting, are ever found together. Wherever there is uncompromising boldness toward men, there is humility before God: it is the God-fearing man who is fearless before the Lord's enemies.

"And Jesus said unto him, Thou hast both seen him, and it is he that talketh with thee" (9:37). This is one of the four instances in this Gospel where the Lord Jesus expressly declared His Divine Sonship. In 5:25 He foretold that "the dead shall hear the voice of *the Son of God*: and they that hear shall live." Here He says "Dost thou believe on *the Son of God?* . . . it is he that talketh with thee." In 10:36 He asked "Say ye of him, whom the Father hath sanctified, and sent into the world, Thou blasphemest; because I said, I am *the Son of God?*" In 11:4 He told His disciples "This sickness is not unto death, but for the glory of God, that *the Son of God* might be glorified thereby." Nowhere in the other Gospels does He explicitly affirm that He was the Son of God. John's record of each of these four utterances of the Saviour is in beautiful accord with the special theme and design of his Gospel.

"And he said, Lord, I believe. And he worshipped him" (9:38). What a lovely climax is this in the spiritual history of the blind beggar! How it illustrates the fact that when God begins a good work He continues and completes it. All through the sacred narrative here the experiences of this man exemplify the history of each soul that is saved by grace. At first, seen in his wretchedness and helplessness: sought out by the Lord: pointed to that which speaks of the Word: made the subject of the supernatural operation of God, sight imparted. Then given opportunity to testify to his acquaintances of the merciful work which had been wrought upon him. Severely tested by the Lord's enemies, he, nevertheless, witnessed a good confession. Denied the support of his parents, he is cast back the more upon God. Arraigned by the religious authorities, and boldly answering them according to the light he had, more was given him. Confounding his opponents, he is reviled by them. Confessing that Christ was of God, he is cast out of the religious systems of his day. Now sought out by the Saviour, he is taught the excellency of His person which results in him taking his place at the feet of the Son of God as a devoted worshipper. And here, most suitably, the Holy Spirit leaves him, for it is *there* he will be forever—a worshipper *in the presence of* the One who did so much for him. Truly naught but Divine wisdom could have combined with this historical narrative an accurate portrayal of the representative experiences of an elect soul.

"And Jesus said, For judgment I am come into this world, that they which see not might see; and that they which see might be made blind" (9:39). "This is deeply solemn! 'For judgment I am come into this world.' How is this? Did He not come to seek and to save that which was lost? So He Himself tells us (Luke 19:10), why then speak of 'judgment'? The meaning is simply this: the *object* of His mission was salvation; the *moral effect* of His life was judgment. He judged no one, and yet He judged every one.

"It is well to see this effect of the character and life of Christ down here. He was the light of the world, and this light acted in a double way. It convicted and converted, it judged and it saved. Furthermore it dazzled, by its heavenly brightness, all those who thought they saw; while, at the same time, it lightened all those who really felt their moral and spiritual blindness. He came not to judge, but to save; and yet when come, He judged every man, and put every man to the test. He was different from all around Him, as light in the midst of darkness; and yet He saved all who accepted the judgment and took their true place.

"The same thing is observed when we contemplate the cross of our Lord Jesus Christ. 'For the preaching of the cross is to them that perish foolishness; but unto us which are saved it is the power of God . . . But we preach Christ crucified, unto the Jews a stumblingblock, and unto the Greeks foolishness; but unto them which are called, both Jews and Greeks, Christ the power of God, and the wisdom of God' (I Cor. 1:18, 23, 24). Looked at from a human point of view, the cross presented a spectacle of weakness and foolishness. But, looked at from a Divine point of view, it was the exhibition of power and wisdom. 'The Jew', looking at the cross through the hazy medium of traditionary religion stumbled over it; and 'the Greek', looking at it from the fancied heights of philosophy, despised it as a contemptible thing. But the faith of a poor sinner, looking at the cross from the depths of conscious guilt and need, found in it a Divine answer to every question, a Divine supply for every need. The death of Christ, like His life, judged every man, and yet it saves all those who accept the judgment and take their true place before God" (C.H.M.). This was all announced from the beginning: "And Simeon blessed them, and said unto Mary his mother, Behold, this child is set for the fall *and* rising again of many in Israel" (Luke 2:34).

"And some of the Pharisees which were with him heard these words, and said unto him, Are we blind also? Jesus said unto them, If ye were blind, ye should have no sin: but now ye say, We see; therefore your sin remaineth" (9:40, 41). This receives explanation in John 15:22-24: "If I had not come and spoken unto them, they had not had sin: but now they have no cloak (excuse) for their sin. He that hateth Me hateth My Father also. If I had not done among them the works which none other man did, they had not had sin: but now have they both seen and hated both Me and My Father." The simple meaning then of these words of Christ to the Pharisees is this: "If you were sensible of your blindness and really desired light, if you would take this place before Me, salvation would be yours and no condemnation would rest upon you. But because of your pride and self-sufficiency, because you refuse to acknowledge your undone condition, your guilt remaineth." How strikingly this confirms our interpretation of v. 6 and the sequel. The blind man made to see illustrates those who accept God's verdict of man's lost condition; the self-righteous Pharisees who refused to bow to the Lord's decision that they were "condemned already" (3:18), continued in their blindness and sin.

Let the interested student carefully ponder the following questions on John 10:1-10:—

1. What is the "sheepfold" of v. 1?
2. What is "the door" by which the shepherd enters the sheepfold? (v. 2).
3. Who is "the porter" of v. 3?
4. Leadeth the sheep "out of" *what?* (v. 3).
5. What is the meaning of "I am the door of the sheep" (v. 7)?
6. What entirely different line of thought does "I am the door" of v. 9 give us?
7. Who is "the thief" of v. 10?

CHAPTER THIRTY-FOUR

Christ, the Door

John 10:1-10.

Below is an Analysis of the passage which is to be before us:

1. Entrance into the Sheepfold: lawful and unlawful: vv. 1, 2.
2. The Shepherd admitted by the porter: v. 3.
3. The Shepherd leading His sheep out of the fold: vv. 3, 4.
4. The attitude of the sheep toward strangers: v. 5.
5. Christ's proverb not understood: v. 6.
6. The true Shepherd and the false shepherds contrasted: vv. 7-9.
7. Antichrist and Christ contrasted: v. 10.

As a personal aid to the study of this passage the writer drew up a list of questions, of which the following are samples: To whom is our Lord speaking? What was the immediate occasion of His address? Why does He make reference to a "sheepfold?" What is meant by "climbing up some other way" into it? What is signified by "the door"? *What* "sheepfold" is here in view?—note it is one into which thieves and robbers could climb; it was one entered by the shepherd; it was one out of which the shepherd led his sheep. Who does "the porter" bring before us? Such questions enable us to focalize our thoughts and approach this section with some degree of definiteness.

Our passage begins with "Verily, verily, I say unto you." The antecedent of the *you* is found in "the Pharisees" of the previous chapter. The occasion of this word from Christ was the excommunication of the beggar by the Pharisees (9:34). The mention of "the sheepfold" at once views these Pharisees in a pastoral relationship. The reference to "thieves and robbers" climbing up some other way denounced the Pharisees as *false* shepherds, and rebuked them for their unlawful conduct. In the course of this "parable" or "proverb," the Lord contrasts Himself from the Pharisees as the true Shepherd. These things are clear on the surface, and the confusion of some of the commentators can only be attributed to their failure to attend to these simple details.

There are two chief reasons why many have experienced difficulty in apprehending the Lord's teaching in this passage: failure to consider the circumstances under which it was delivered, and failure to distinguish between the *three* "doors" here spoken of —there is the "door into the sheepfold" (v. 1); the "door of the sheep" (v. 7); and the "door" of salvation (v. 9). In the previous chapter we find our Lord had given sight to one born blind. This aroused the jealousy of the Pharisees, so that when the beggar faithfully confessed it was Jesus who had opened his eyes, they cast him out of the synagogue. When Christ heard of this He at once sought him out, and revealed Himself as the Son of God. This drew forth the confession, "Lord, I believe." Thus did he evidence himself to be one of "the sheep," responding to the Shepherd's voice. Following this, our Lord announced, "For judgment I am come into this world, that they which see not might see; and that they which see might be made blind" (9:39). Some of the Pharisees heard Him, and asked, "Are *we* blind also?" To which the Saviour replied, "If ye were blind, ye should have no sin: but now ye say, We see; therefore your sin remaineth." It was the self-confidence and self-complacency of these Pharisees which proved them to be blind, and therefore in their sins. Unto them, under these circumstances, did Christ deliver this memorable and searching proverb of the shepherd and his sheep.

It will probably be of some help to the reader if we describe briefly the character of the "sheepfold" which obtains in Eastern lands. In Palestine, which in the pastoral sections was infested with wild beasts, there was in each village a large sheepfold, which was the common property of the native farmers. This sheepfold was protected by a wall some ten or twelve feet high. When night fell, a number of different shepherds would lead their flocks up to the door of the fold, through which they passed, leaving them in the care of the porter, while they went home or sought lodging. At the door, the porter lay on guard through the night, ready to protect the sheep against thieves and robbers, or against wild animals which might scale the walls. In the morning the different shepherds returned. The porter would allow each one to enter through the door, calling by name the sheep which belonged to his flock. The sheep would respond to his voice, and he would lead them out to pasture. In the lesson before us *this* is what the Lord uses as a figure or proverb.

"Verily, verily, I say unto you, he that entereth not by the door into the sheepfold, but climbeth up some other way, the same is a thief and a robber. But he that entereth in by the door is the shepherd of the sheep" (10:1, 2). The "sheepfold" here is not Heaven, for thieves and robbers do not climb up into it. Nor is it "The Church" as some have strangely supposed, for the Shepherd does not lead His sheep out of that, as He does from this fold (see v. 3). No, the "sheepfold" is manifestly *Judaism*—in which some of God's elect were then to be found—and the contrast pointed in these opening verses between the true Shepherd and the false ones, between Christ and the Pharisees. The "door" here must not be confused with "the Door" of v. 9. Here in v. 1 it is simply contrasted from the "climbing up some *other* way." It signifies, then, the *lawful* "way" of entrance for the Shepherd, to those of His sheep then to be found in Judaism.

"But he that entereth in by the door is the shepherd of the sheep." The simple meaning of this is, that Christ presented Himself to Israel in a lawful manner, that is, in strict accord with the Holy Scriptures. "He submitted Himself to all the conditions established by Him who built the house. Christ answered to all that was written of the Messiah, and took the path of God's will in presenting Himself to the people" (Mr. Darby). He had been born of a virgin, of the covenant people, of the Judaic stock, in the royal city—Bethlehem. He had conformed to everything which God required of an Israelite. He had been "born under the law" (Gal. 4:4). He was circumcised the eighth day (Luke

2:21), and subsequently, at the purification of His mother, He was presented to God in the Temple (Luke 2:22).

"To him the porter openeth" (10:3). The word "porter" signifies door-keeper. The only other time the word occurs in John's Gospel is in 18:16, 17, and how strikingly these two references illustrate, once more, the law of contrast! "But Peter stood at the door without. Then went out that other disciple, which was known unto the high priest, and spake unto her that *kept the door* (the porter), and brought in Peter. Then saith the damsel that kept the door unto Peter, Art not thou also one of this man's disciples? He saith, I am not." In John 10 the "porter" refers, ultimately, to the Holy Spirit, while the door-keeper in John 18 is a woman that evidently had no sympathy with Christ. In John 10 the porter opens the door to give the Shepherd access to the sheep, whereas in John 18 the door is opened that a sheep might gain access to the Shepherd. In John 10 the sheep run to the Shepherd, but in John 18 the sheep is seen in the midst of wolves. In John 10 the sheep follow the Shepherd: in John 18 one of the sheep denies the Shepherd!

"To him the porter openeth." The "porter" was the one who vouched for the shepherd and presented him to the sheep. As to the identity of the "porter" in this proverb there can be no doubt. The direct reference was to John the Baptist who "prepared the *way* of the Lord." He it was who formally introduced the Shepherd to Israel: "that he should be *made manifest* to Israel, therefore am I come baptizing" (1:31), was his own confession. But, in the wider application, the "porter" here represented the Holy Spirit, who officially vouched for the credentials of the Messiah, and who now presents the Saviour to each of God's elect.

"To him the porter openeth; and the sheep hear his voice; and he calleth his own sheep by name, and leadeth them out" (10:3). Three things mark the genuine shepherd: first, he entered the fold by "the door," and climbed not over the walls, as thieves and robbers did. Second, he entered the door by "the porter" opening to him. Third, he proved himself, by "the sheep" recognizing and responding to his voice. Mark, then, how fully and perfectly these three requirements were met by Christ in His relation to Israel, thus evidencing Him to be the true Shepherd.

As we have seen, the "door" was the legitimate and appointed entrance into the fold, and this figure meant that the Messiah came by the road which Old Testament prophecy had marked out beforehand. The "porter" presented the shepherd to the sheep. Not only had the prophets borne witness to Christ, but, in addition, when He appeared, a forerunner heralded Him, introducing Him to the people. Besides this, when the true Shepherd of Israel was manifested, the sheep recognized His voice. The true sheep were known to Him, for He called them by name. The call was to follow Him, and to *follow* Him was to take their place with the despised and rejected One *outside* of Judaism. How beautifully this links up with what was before us in John 9 it is not difficult to perceive.

In John 9 Christ had shown how that He had entered the door into the sheepfold, for He had come working the works of God (9:4), and had thus shown Himself to be in the confidence of the Owner of the fold, and therefore the approved Shepherd of the flock. The Pharisees, on the contrary, were resisting Him and attacking the sheep; therefore they must needs be "thieves and robbers." The blind beggar was a sample of the flock, for refusing to listen to the voice of strangers, he, nevertheless, knew the voice of the Shepherd, and drawn to Him, he found salvation, security, and sustenance.

All of this, strikingly illustrated in John 9, receives interpretation and amplification in chapter 10, where we have a blessed commentary on the condition of the excommunicated one. The Pharisees imagined they had cut him off from the place of safety and blessing, but the Lord had shown him that it was only then he had really entered the true place of blessing. Had he remained inside Judaism he would have been the constant object of the assaults of the "thieves and robbers"; but now he was in the care of the true Shepherd, the good Shepherd, who instead of killing him, would die for him! It is beautiful to compare 10:3 with 9:34. The Pharisees' "casting out" of the poor beggar was, in reality, the Shepherd *leading him out* from the barren wilderness of Judaism to the green pastures of Christianity. Thus are we given to see the Lord Himself *behind* the human instruments—a marvellous example is this of how God ofttimes employs even His enemies to accomplish a good turn for His people.

"To him the porter openeth; and the sheep hear his voice: and he calleth his own sheep by name, and leadeth them out." Mark carefully the qualification here: it is not He calleth the sheep by name, but "he calleth *his own* sheep by name." His "own sheep" were those who had been given to Him by the Father from all eternity; and when He calls, all of these "sheep" *must* come to Him, for it is written, "*All* that the Father giveth me *shall come* to me" (John 6:37). These "sheep," then, were the elect of God among Israel. Not to the Nation at large was Christ's real ministry; rather did He come unto "the lost sheep *of* the house of Israel." That these "lost sheep" were not co-extensive with the whole Nation is clear from the twenty-sixth verse of this chapter, for there we find the Shepherd saying to unbelieving Israelites, "But ye believe not, because *ye* are *not of* my sheep." The sheep, then, whom Christ "called" during the days of His earthly ministry were the elect of God, whom He led out of Judaism. This was strikingly foreshadowed of old. Moses, while estranged from Israel, kept the flock of his father in other pastures, near "the mount of God" (Ex. 3:1).

"And when he putteth forth his own sheep, he goeth before them, and the sheep follow him: for they know his voice" (10:4). Christ began His ministry *inside* the fold of Judaism, for it was there His Jewish sheep were to be found, though mixed with others: from these they needed to be separated when the true Shepherd appeared. Therefore does His voice sound, calling the lost sheep of the House of Israel unto Himself. As they responded, they were put forth outside the fold, to follow Him.

"And the sheep follow him: for they know his voice." Link this up with the third clause in the previous verse. "He calleth his own sheep by name . . . and the sheep follow him: for they know his voice." A number of blessed illustrations of this are found scattered throughout the Gospels. "And as Jesus passed forth from thence, he saw a man, named Matthew, sitting at the receipt of custom: and he saith unto him, Follow me. And he arose, and followed him" (Matt. 9:9). Here was a lone sheep of Christ. The Shepherd called him; he recognized His voice, and promptly *followed* Him.

"And when Jesus came to the place, he looked up, and saw him, and said unto him, Zacchæus, make haste, and come down; for today I must abide at thy house" (Luke 19:5). Here was one of the sheep, called *by name.* The response was prompt, for we are told, "And he made haste, *and came down,* and received him joyfully" (v. 6).

"The day following Jesus would go forth into Galilee, and findeth Philip, and saith unto him, Follow me" (John 1:43). This shows us the Shepherd *seeking* His sheep before He called him.

John 11 supplies us with a still more striking example of the drawing power of the Shepherd's voice as He calleth His own sheep. There we read of Lazarus, in the grave; but when Christ calls His sheep *by name*—"Lazarus, come forth"—the sheep at once responded.

As a touching example of the sheep *knowing* His voice we refer the reader to John 20. Mary Magdalene visited the Saviour's sepulchre in the early morning hour. She finds the stone rolled away, and the body of the Lord gone. Disconsolate, she stands there weeping. Suddenly she sees the Lord Jesus standing by her, and "knew not that it was Jesus." He speaks to her, but she supposed Him to be the gardener. A moment later she identified Him, and says, "Rabboni." What had happened in the interval? What enabled her to identify Him? Just one word from Him—"Mary"! The moment He *called His sheep by name* she "*knew* his voice"!

It has been thus with God's elect all down the ages. It is so today. There is a general "call" which goes forth to all who hear the Gospel, for "many are called," though few are chosen (Matt. 20:16). But to each of Christ's "sheep" there comes a particular, a special call. This call is inward and invincible, and therefore effectual. Proof of this is found in Rom. 8:30 and many other scriptures: there we read, "Whom he called, *them he also* justified." But all are not justified, therefore all are *not* "called." Who then are "the called"? The previous clause of Rom. 8:30 tells us—"Whom he did *predestinate,* them he *also* called." And who were the ones "predestinated"? They were those whom God did "foreknow" (8:29). And who were they? The previous verse makes answer—they who were "the called according to his purpose." Called not because of anything in them, foreseen or actual, but solely by His own sovereign will or purpose.

This effectual *call* from God is heard by each of the "sheep" because they are given "ears to hear": "The hearing ear, and the seeing eye, the Lord hath made even both of them" (Prov. 20:12). This effectual call comes to none but the sheep; the "goats" hear it not—"But ye believe not, *because* ye are not of my sheep" (John 10:26).

There is, no doubt, a secondary application of these verses to the under-shepherds of Christ today, and considered thus they supply us with several important principles which enable us to identify them with certainty. First, a true under-shepherd of Christ is one who gains access to the sheep in the Divinely-appointed way: unlike the Pharisees, he does not intrude himself into this sacred office, but is called to it by God. Second, he is, in the real meaning of the word, a *shepherd* of the sheep: he has their welfare at heart, and ever concerns himself with their interests. Third, to such an one "the porter openeth": the Holy Spirit sets before him an "open door" for ministry and service. Fourth, the sheep hear his voice: the elect of God recognize him as a Divinely appointed pastor. Fifth, he calleth his own sheep by name: that portion of the flock over which God has made him overseer, are known to him individually: with a true pastor's heart he seeks them out in the home and acquaints himself with them personally. Sixth, he "leadeth them out" into the green pastures of God's Word where they may find food and rest. Seventh, "he goeth before them": he sets before them a godly example, asking them to do nothing which he is not doing himself; he seeks to be "an example of the believers, in word, in conversation, in charity, in spirit, in faith, in purity" (I Tim. 4:12). May the Lord in His grace increase the number of such faithful undershepherds. Let the reader, especially the preacher, consult the following passages: Acts 20:28; II Thess. 3:9; I Peter 5:2-4.

"And a stranger will they not follow, but will flee from him: for they know not the voice of strangers" (10:5). This is very important, for it describes a mark found on all of Christ's sheep. A strange shepherd they will not heed. This can hardly mean that they will *never* respond to the call of the false shepherds, but that the redeemed of Christ will not absolutely, unreservedly, completely give themselves over to a false teacher. Instead, speaking characteristically, they will *flee* from such. It is not possible to deceive the elect (Matt. 24:24). Let a man of the world hear two preachers, one giving out the truth and the other error, and he can discern no difference between them. But it is far otherwise with a child of God. He may be but a babe in Christ, unskilled in theological controversies, but instinctively he will detect vital heresy as soon as he hears it. And why is this? Because he is indwelt by the Holy Spirit, and has received an "unction" from the Holy One (I John 2:20). How thankful we should be for this. How gracious of the Lord to have given us this capacity to separate the precious from the vile!

"This parable spake Jesus unto them: but they understood not what things they were which he spake unto them" (10:6). This points a contrast, bringing out as it does the very reverse of what was before us in the previous one. There we learn of the spirit of discernment possessed by all of Christ's sheep; here we see illustrated the solemn fact that those who are not His sheep are quite unable to understand the truth even when it is plainly presented to them. Blind indeed were these Pharisees, and therefore totally incapacitated to perceive our Lord's meaning. Equally blind are all the unsaved today. Well educated they may be, and theologically trained, but unless they are born again the Word of God is a sealed book to them.

"Then said Jesus unto them again, Verily, verily, I say unto you, I am the door of the sheep" (10:7). The "door of the sheep" is to be distinguished from the "door of the sheepfold" in v. 1. The latter was the Divinely-appointed way by which Christ had entered Judaism, in contrast from the false pastors of Israel whose conduct evidenced plainly that they had thrust themselves into office. The "door of the sheep" was Christ Himself, by which the elect of Israel passed out of Judaism. The Lord had not come to restore Judaism, but to lead out His own unto Himself. A striking illustration of this is to be found in Exod. 33. At the time viewed there Judaism was in a state of unbelief and rebellion against God. Accordingly, Moses, the shepherd of Israel, "took the tabernacle, and pitched it *without* the camp, afar off from the camp, and called it the Tabernacle of the congregation. And it came to pass, that every one which sought the Lord *went out unto* the tabernacle of the congregation, which was without the camp" (v. 7). Those who really sought the Lord had to *leave* "the camp," and go forth unto the shepherd on the outside. It is beautiful to note the sequel: "And it came to pass, as Moses entered into the tabernacle, the cloudy pillar descended, and stood at the door of the tabernacle, and the Lord talked with Moses" (v. 9). God was *with* His shepherd on the outside of the camp! So here in John 10, Christ, the antitype of Moses (Deut. 18:18), tabernacles outside Judaism, and those whose hearts sought the Lord went forth unto Him. And history has repeated itself. God is no longer with the great organized systems of Christendom, and those of His people whose hearts cleave to *Him* must go forth "outside the camp" if they would commune with Him! The "door" here then speaks of *exit,* not entrance.

"All that ever came before me are thieves and robbers: but the sheep did not hear them" (10:8). It is abundantly clear that here we have another instance in John's Gospel where the word "all" cannot be taken absolutely. The Lord had been speaking of *shepherds,* the shepherds of Israel; but not *all* of them had been "thieves and robbers." Moses, Joshua, David, the prophets, Nehemiah, and others who might be mentioned, certainly could not be included within this classification. The "all" here, as is usually the case in Scripture, must be restricted. But restricted to whom? Surely to the scribes and Pharisees, who were here being addressed by the Lord. Bishop Ryle has a helpful note on this verse: "Let it be noted," he says, "that these strong epithets show plainly that there are times when it is right to rebuke sharply. Flattering everybody, and complimenting all teachers who are zealous and earnest, without reference to their soundness in the faith, is not according to Scripture. Nothing seems so offensive to Christ as a false teacher of religion, a false prophet, or a false shepherd. Nothing ought to be so much dreaded in the Church, and if needful, be so plainly rebuked, opposed, and exposed. The strong language of our Reformers, when writing against Romish teachers, is often blamed more than it ought to be."

It is a notable fact that the severest denunciations which are to be found in the Scriptures are reserved for false teachers. Listen to these awful words of Christ: "Woe unto you scribes and Pharisees, hypocrites! . . . ye blind guides, which strain at a gnat, and swallow a camel! . . . ye serpents, ye generation of vipers, how can ye escape the damnation of hell?" (Matt. 23:14, 24, 33). So, too, His forerunner: "O generation of vipers, who hath warned you to flee from the wrath to come?" (Matt. 3:7). So, too, the apostle Paul: "For such are false apostles, deceitful workers, transforming themselves into the apostles of Christ" (II Cor. 11:13). So Peter: "These are wells without water, clouds that are carried with the tempest; to whom the mist of darkness is reserved forever" (II Pet. 2:17). So Jude: "clouds they are without water, carried about of winds; trees whose fruit withereth, without fruit, twice dead, plucked up by the roots; Raging waves of the sea, foaming out their own shame; wandering stars, to whom is reserved the blackness of darkness for ever" (vv. 12, 13). Unspeakably solemn are these; would that their alarm might be sounded forth today, as a warning to those who are so careless *whose* ministry they sit under.

But *why* should our Lord term the Pharisees "thieves and robbers"? Wherein lay the propriety of such appellations? We believe that light is thrown on this question by such a scripture as Luke 11:52: "Woe unto you, lawyers! for ye have *taken away* the key of knowledge: ye entered not in yourselves, and them that were entering in ye hindered." With this should be compared the parallel passage in Matt. 23:13. The Pharisees were *thieves* inasmuch as they seized positions which they had no right to occupy, exerted an authority which did not justly belong to them, and unlawfully demanded a submission and subjection to which they could establish no valid claim.

What, may be asked, is the distinction between "thieves" and "robbers"? The word for "thief" is "kleptes" and is always so rendered. It has reference to one who uses stealth. The word for "robbers" is "lestes," and is wrongly translated "thief" in Matt. 21:13; Luke 10:30, 36, etc. It has reference to one who uses violence. The distinction between these two words is closely preserved all through the New Testament with the one exception of v. 10, where it seems as though the Lord uses the word "kleptes" to *combine* the two different thoughts, for there the "thief" is said not only to "steal," but also to "kill and destroy."

"I am the door: by me if any man enter in, he shall be saved" (10:9). Notice carefully the broader terms which Christ uses here. No longer does He say, as in v. 7, "I am the door of the sheep," but "I am the door," and this He follows at once with, "If *any man* enter in, he shall be saved." Why this change of language? Because up to this point the Lord had been referring solely to elect Israelites, which He was leading out of Judaism. But now His heart reaches forth to the elect among the Gentiles, for not only was He "a minister of the circumcision for the truth of God, to confirm the promises made unto the fathers," but He also came "that the Gentiles might glorify God for His mercy" (Rom. 15:8, 9). The "door" in v. 1 was God's appointed way for the shepherd *into* Judaism. The "door" in v. 7 was the Way *out of* Judaism, by Christ leading God's elect in separation unto Himself. Here in v. 9 the "door" has to do with salvation, for elect Jew and Gentile alike.

"I am the door: by me if any man enter in, he shall be saved." This is the "door" into the presence of God. By nature we are separated, yea, "alienated" from God. Sin as a barrier comes in between and bars us out of His holy presence. This is one of the first things a convicted soul is made conscious of. I am defiled and condemned, how can I draw near to God? I am made to realize my guilty distance from Him who is Light, how then can I be reconciled to Him? Then, from God's Word,

I learn heaven's answer to these solemn questions. The Lord Jesus has bridged that awful gulf which separated me from God. He bridged it by taking my place and being made a curse in my stead. And as the exercised soul bows to God's sentence of condemnation, and receives by faith the marvelous provision which His grace has made, I, with all other believers, learn, "But now in Christ Jesus ye who sometimes were afar off *are made nigh* by the blood of Christ" (Eph. 2:13).

"I am the door: by me if any man enter in, he shall be saved." This is one of the precious words of Christ which is well worthy of prolonged meditation. A "door" speaks of easy ingress and is contrasted from the high walls in which it is set. There are no difficult walls which have to be scaled before the anxious sinner can obtain access to God. No, Christ is the "door" into His presence. A "door" may also be contrasted from a long, dreary, circuitous passage—just one step, and those on the outside are now within. The soul that believes God's testimony to the truth of salvation by Christ *alone,* at once enters God's presence. But mark the definite article: "I am *the* door." There was only one door into the ark in which Noah and his family found shelter from the flood. There was only one door into the Tabernacle, which was Jehovah's dwelling-place. So there is only one "door" into the presence of the Father—"Neither is there salvation in any other: for there is *none other* name under heaven, given among men, whereby we must be saved" (Acts 4:12). And again, "I am *the* way," said Christ. "No man cometh unto the Father *but by me*" (John 14:6). Have *you* entered by this "door," dear reader? Remember that a door is not to be looked at and admired, but to be used! Nor do you need to knock: the Door is open, and open for "any man" who will enter. Soon, though, the Door will be shut (see Luke 13:25), for the present Day of salvation (II Cor. 6:2) will be followed by the great Day of wrath (Rev. 6:17). Enter then while there is time.

Such are some of the simplest thoughts suggested by the figure of "the door." What follows is an extract from an unknown writer who signed himself "J.B. Jr":—"The door suggests the thought of the dwelling-place to which it is the means of entrance. Within we find the possession or portion of those who can by right enter by the door. Thus it is as a place set apart for its possessors from all that which is outside. In this way we may say it is a sanctuary. These things are rightly connected with a door, it being the only right way of entrance."

"I am the door: by me if any man enter in, he shall be saved." Notice Christ did not say, "I am the door: if any man enter in, he shall be saved," but, "*by me* if any man enter in." Man cannot enter of himself, for being by nature "dead in trespasses and sins" he is perfectly helpless. It is only by Divine aid, by the impartation to us of supernatural power, that any can enter in and be saved. Without Christ we can do *nothing* (John 15:5). Writing to the Philippians the apostle said, "For unto you *it is given* in the behalf of Christ, not only *to believe on him,* but also to suffer for his sake" (1:29). Not only is it a fact that no one can come to Christ except the Father draw him (John 6:44), but it is also true that none can come to the Father except Christ empowers. This is very clear from the sixteenth verse of our chapter: "And other sheep I have, which are not of this fold: them also I must *bring.*" The "sheep" enter through the Door into God's presence because Christ "brings" them. Beautifully is this portrayed in Luke 15:5, 6: "And when he hath found it (the lost sheep), he *layeth it on his shoulders,* rejoicing. And when he cometh home, he calleth together his friends and neighbours, saying unto them, Rejoice with me."

"I am the door: by me if any man enter in, he shall be saved, and shall go in and out, and find pasture." To go "in and out" is a figurative way to express perfect freedom. This was something vastly different from the experiences of even saved Israelites under the law of Moses. One of the chief designs of the ceremonial law was to hedge Israelites around with ordinances which kept them separate from all other nations. But this was made an end of by Christ, for through His death the "middle wall of partition" was broken down. Thus were His sheep perfectly free to "go in and out." It is indeed striking to discover in Neh. 3 that of the ten gates referred to there, of the *sheep* gate only are *no* "locks and bars" mentioned. This chapter concerns the *remnant* after their captivity, and clearly foreshadows in a wonderful way the truth here taught by Christ. "The fulness of this freedom is intercourse with other saints, and in deliverance from the yoke of the (ceremonial) laws (Acts 15:10), was only by degrees apprehended. That lesson, taught Peter on the housetop at Joppa (Acts 10), was the first real step in the *realization* of that freedom" (Mr. C. E. Stuart).

"And find pasture." This tells of the gracious provision made for the nourishment of the sheep. Our minds at once turn to that matchless Psalm which records the joyous testimony of the saints: "The Lord is my Shepherd; I shall not want. He maketh me to lie down in green pastures: he leadeth me beside the still waters." The "pastures," then, speak not only of food, but of *rest* as well. This too is a part of that wondrous portion which is ours in Christ. A beautiful type of this is found in Num. 10:33: "And they departed from the mount of the Lord three days' journey: and the ark of the covenant of the Lord went before them in the three days' journey, to search out *a resting place* for them." All through the Old Testament the "ark of the covenant" is a lovely figure of the Saviour Himself, and here it is seen seeking out a resting place—the pastures—for Israel of old.

"I am the door: by me if any man enter in, he shall be saved, and shall go in and out, and find pasture." Seven things are enumerated in this precious verse. First, "I am the door": Christ the only Way to God. Second "*By me* if any man enter": Christ the Imparter of power *to* enter. Third, "If *any* man enter": Christ the Saviour for Jew and Gentile alike. Fourth, "If any man *enter in*": Christ *appropriated* by a single act of faith. Fifth, "he shall be saved": Christ the Deliverer from the penalty, power, and presence of sin. Sixth, "he shall go in and out": Christ the Emancipator from all bondage. Seventh, "and find pasture": Christ the Sustainer of His people.

Finally, it is blessed to see how the contents of this precious verse present Christ to us as the Fulfiller of the prophetic prayer of Moses: "And Moses spake unto the Lord, saying, Let the Lord, the God of the spirits of all flesh, set *a man* over the congregation, Which may *go out* before them, and which may *go in* before them, and which may *lead them out*, and which may *bring them in;* that the congregation of the Lord be not as sheep which have no shepherd" (Num. 27:15-17).

"The thief cometh not, but for to steal, and to kill, and to destroy" (10:10). It will be observed that Christ here uses the singular number. In v. 8 He had spoken of "thieves and robbers" when referring to all who had come before Him; but here in v. 10 He has some particular individual in view—"*the* thief." It should also be noted that in speaking of this particular "thief" our Lord *combines* in one the two distinct characters of thieves and robbers. As intimated in our comments on v. 8 the distinctive thought associated with the former is that of *stealth;* that of the latter, is *violence.* Here "*the* thief" cometh to steal, and to kill, and to destroy. Who then is the Lord referring to? Surely it is to the last false shepherd of Israel, the "idol shepherd," the anti-christ, of whom it is written, "For lo, I will raise up a shepherd in the land, which shall not visit those that be cut off, neither shall seek the young one, nor heal that that is broken, nor feed that that standeth still: but he shall eat the flesh of the fat, and tear their claws in pieces. Woe to the idol shepherd that leaveth the flock! the sword shall be upon his arm, and upon his right eye: his arm shall be clean dried up, and his right eye shall be utterly darkened" (Zech. 11:16).

"I am come that they might have life, and that they might have it more abundantly" (10:10). Why say this *after* having already declared that "By me if any man enter in, he shall *be saved*"? Mark this follows His reference to "the thief." Here then our Lord seems to be looking forward to the Day of His second advent, as it relates to Israel. This indeed will be the time when *abundant* life will be theirs. As we read in Rom. 11:15, "If the casting away of them be the reconciling of the world, what shall the receiving of them be, but *life from the dead?*" In striking accord with this it should be noted that the Lord's title "I am the door" (v. 9) is the *third* of His "I am" titles in this Gospel—the number which speaks of *resurrection.* Immediately following we find Christ saying here "I am the good Shepherd" (v. 11). This is the *fourth* of His "I am" titles—the number of *the earth.*

As preparation for the next chapter let the interested student ponder carefully the following points:

1. Study the typical "shepherds" of the Old Testament.
2. Precisely what is the meaning of "for" in v. 11?
3. Did the Shepherd give His life for any besides "the sheep"?
4. What other adjectives besides "good" are applied to Christ as the "Shepherd"?
5. Who is referred to by "a hireling" (v. 12)?
6. Who are the "other sheep" of v. 16?
7. Look up proofs in the Gospels of the first part of v. 18.

CHAPTER THIRTY-FIVE

Christ, the Good Shepherd

John 10:11-21

The following is submitted as an Analysis of the passage which is to be before us: —

1. The good Shepherd dies for His sheep: v. 11.
2. The character and conduct of hirelings: vv. 12, 13.
3. The intimacy between the Shepherd and the sheep: v. 14.
4. The intimacy between the Father and the Son: v. 15.
5. Gentile sheep saved by the Shepherd: v. 16.
6. The relation of the Shepherd to the Father: vv. 17, 18.
7. The division among the Jews: vv. 19-21.

The passage before us completes our Lord's discourse with the Pharisees, following their excommunication of the beggar to whom He had given sight. In this discourse, Christ does two things: first, He graphically depicts their unfaithfulness; second, He contrasts His own fidelity and goodness. They, as the religious leaders of the people, are depicted as "strangers" (v. 5), as "thieves and robbers" (v. 8), as "hirelings" (vv. 12, 13). *He* stands revealed as "the door" (vv. 9, 11), and as "the good Shepherd" (v. 11).

The Pharisees were the shepherds of Israel. In casting out of the synagogue this poor sheep, the man that was born blind, for doing what was right, and for refusing to do what was wrong, they had shown what manner of spirit they were of. And this was but a sample of their accustomed oppression and violence. In them, then, did the prophecy of Ezekiel receive a fulfillment, that prophecy in which He had testified of those shepherds of His people who resembled thieves and robbers. Ezek. 34 (which like all prophecy has a *double* fulfillment) supplies a sad commentary upon the selfish and cruel conduct of the scribes and Pharisees. The whole chapter should be read: we quote but a fragment—"And the word of the Lord came unto me, saying, Son of man, prophesy against the shepherds of Israel, prophesy, and say unto them, Thus saith the Lord God unto the shepherds; Woe be to the shepherds of Israel that do feed themselves! should not the shepherds feed the flocks? Ye eat the fat, and ye clothe you with the wool, ye kill them that are fed: but ye feed not the flock. The diseased have ye not strengthened, neither have ye healed that which was sick, neither have ye bound up that which was broken, neither have ye brought again that which was driven away, neither have ye sought that which was lost; but with force and with cruelty have ye ruled them" (vv. 1-4).

The same prophecy of Ezekiel goes on to present the *true* Shepherd of Israel, the Good Shepherd: "For thus saith the Lord God; Behold, I, even I, will both search my sheep, and seek them out. As a shepherd seeketh out his flock in the day that he is among his sheep that are scattered; so will I seek out my sheep, and will deliver them out of all places where they have been scattered in the cloudy and dark day . . . I will feed my flock, and I will cause them to lie down, saith the Lord God. I will seek that which was lost, and bring again that which was driven away, and will bind up that which was broken, and will strengthen that which was sick . . . And I will set up one shepherd over them, and he shall feed them, even my servant David; he shall feed them, and he shall be their shepherd . . . Thus shall they know that I the Lord their God am with them, and that they, even the house of Israel, are my people, saith the Lord God. And ye my flock, the flock of my pasture, are men, and I am your God, saith the Lord God" (vv. 11, 12, 15, 16, 23, 30, 31).

Ezekiel is not the only prophet of the Old Testament who presents the Saviour under the figure of a "shepherd." Frequently do the Old Testament Scriptures so picture Him. In His dying prediction, Jacob declared, "From thence (the mighty God of Jacob) is *the Shepherd,* the Stone of Israel" (Gen. 49:24). The Psalmist declared, "The Lord is my *Shepherd*"

(23:1). Through Isaiah it was revealed, "The Lord God will come with strong hand, and his arm shall rule for him: behold, his reward is with him, and his work before him. He shall feed his flock like *a shepherd*: he shall gather the lambs with his arm, and carry them in his bosom, and shall gently lead those that are with young" (40:10, 11). In Zechariah occurs that remarkable word "Awake, O sword, against *my shepherd,* and against the man that is my fellow, saith the Lord of hosts: smite *the shepherd,* and the sheep shall be scattered: and I will turn mine hand upon the little ones" (13:7).

In addition to the prophecies, the Old Testament is particularly rich in the *types* which foreshadow Christ in the character of a "shepherd." So far as we have been able to trace, there are five individual shepherds who pointed to Christ, and each of them supplies some distinctive line in the typical picture. First, *Abel,* for in Gen. 4:2 we are told that "Abel was a keeper of sheep." The distinctive aspect of typical truth which he exemplifies is *the death* of the Shepherd—slain by wicked hands, by his brother according to the flesh. The second is *Jacob,* and a prominent thing in connection with him as a shepherd is his *care* for the sheep—see Gen. 30:31; 31:38-40; and note particularly 33:13, 14. The third is *Joseph*: the very first thing recorded in Scripture about this favorite son of Jacob is that he *fed* the flock (Gen. 37:2). The fourth is *Moses.* Three things are told us about him: he *watered, protected* and *guided* the sheep: "Now the priest of Midian had seven daughters: and they came and drew water, and filled the troughs to water their father's flock. And the shepherds came and drove them away: but Moses stood up and helped them, and *watered* their flock . . . Now Moses *kept* the flock of Jethro his father-in-law, the priest of Midian: and he *led* the flock to the backside of the desert, and came to the mountain of God, even to Horeb" (Ex 2:16, 17; 3:1). The fifth is *David,* and he is presented as *jeopardizing his life* for the sheep—"And David said unto Saul, Thy servant kept his father's sheep, and there came a lion, and a bear, and took a lamb out of the flock: And I went out after him, and smote him, and delivered it out of his mouth: and when he arose against me, I caught him by his beard, and smote him, and slew him. Thy servant slew both the lion and the bear" (I Sam. 17:34-36). There is one other individual "shepherd" referred to in the Old Testament and that is "the idol shepherd" (Zech. 11:16, 17), and he is the Antichrist—how significant that *he* is the *sixth!* The only other individual "shepherd" mentioned in Scripture is the Lord Jesus, and He is *the seventh!* Seven is the number of perfection, and we do not reach perfection till we come to Christ, the Good Shepherd!

"I am the *good* shepherd." The word for "good" is a very comprehensive one, and perhaps it is impossible to embrace in a brief definition all that it included within its scope. The Greek word is "kalos" and is translated "good" seventy-six times: it is also rendered "fair," "meet," "worthy," etc. In order to discover the prime elements of the word we must have recourse to the law of first mention. Whenever we are studying any word or expression in Scripture, it is very important to pay special attention to the initial mention of it. The first time this word "good" occurs in the New Testament is in Matt. 3:10, where we read, "Every tree which bringeth not forth *good* fruit is hewn down, and cast into the fire." The word "tree" is there used metaphorically. It is the unregenerate who are in view. No *un*believer is able to bring forth "good fruit." The "good fruit," then, is what is produced in and through a Christian. What *kind* of "fruit" is it which a Christian bears? It is *Divine* fruit, *spiritual* fruit: it is the product of the new nature. It is Divine as contrasted from what is human; spiritual as contrasted from what is fleshly. Thus in the light of this first occurrence of the word "good" we learn that when Christ said, "I am the *good* shepherd" He signified, "I am the *Divine* and *spiritual* Shepherd." All other shepherds were human; He was the Son of God. The "shepherds" from whom He is here contrasting Himself were the Pharisees, and they were carnal; but He was *spiritual.*

It will also repay us to note carefully the *first* occurrence of this word "good" in John's Gospel. It is found in 2:10. When the Lord Jesus had miraculously turned the water into wine, the servants bore it to the governor of the feast, and when he had tasted it, he exclaimed, "Every man at the beginning doth set forth *good* wine; and when men have well drunk, then that which is worse: but thou hast kept the *good* wine until now." Here the meaning of the word "good" signifies *choice,* or *excellent,* yea, that which is pre-eminently excellent, for the "good wine" is here contrasted from the inferior. This usage of "kalos" helps us still further in ascertaining the force of this adjective in John 10:11. When Christ said, "I am the *good* shepherd," He intimated that He was the *pre-eminently excellent* Shepherd, infinitely elevated above all who had gone before Him.

"I am the good *shepherd.*" This was clearly an affirmation of His absolute Deity. He was here addressing Israelites, and Israel's "Shepherd" was none other than Jehovah (Psa. 23:1; 80:1). When then the Saviour said, "I *am* the good shepherd." He thus definitely identified Himself with the Jehovah of the Old Testament.

"I am the good shepherd." This, like every other of our Lord's titles, views Him in a *distinctive relationship.* He was, says Dr. John Gill, "a Shepherd of His Father's appointing, calling, and sending, to whom the care of all His sheep, or chosen ones, was committed; who was set up as a Shepherd over them by Him, and was entrusted with them; and who being called, undertook to feed them." In the Greek it is more emphatic than in the English: literally it reads, "I am the shepherd, the good."

"The good shepherd giveth his life for the sheep" (v. 11). The word for "giveth" is usually translated "layeth down." "*For* the sheep" signifies, on their behalf. The good Shepherd gave His life freely and voluntarily, in the room and stead of His people, as a ransom for them, that they might be delivered from death and have eternal life. The Ethiopic Version reads, "The good Shepherd gives His life for *the redemption of* the sheep."

"The good shepherd giveth his life for the sheep." This is one of the many scriptures which clearly and definitely defines both the nature and extent of the Atonement. The Saviour "gave his life" not as a martyr for the truth, not as a moral example of self-sacrifice, but for *a people.* He died that they might live. By nature His people are dead in trespasses and sins, and had not the Divinely-appointed and Divinely-provided Substitute died for them, there had been no spiritual and eternal life for them.

Equally explicit is this verse concerning those *for whom* Christ laid down His life. It was not laid down for fallen angels, but for sinful men; and not for men in general, but for His own people in particular; for "the sheep," and not for "the goats." Such was the announcement of God through the prophets, "For the transgression of *my people* was he stricken" (Isa. 53:8). As said the angel to Mary, "Thou shalt call his name Jesus: for he shall save *his people* from their sins" (Matt. 1:21); and as said the angel to the shepherds, "Behold I bring you good tidings of great joy, which shall be to all *the people*" (Luke 2:10). The same restriction to be observed in the words of Christ at the Supper: "This is my blood of the new testament which is shed for *many* for the remission of sins" (Matt. 26:28). (Cf. also Acts 20:28; Titus 2:14; Heb. 2:17, etc.)

"But he that is an hireling, and not the shepherd, whose own the sheep are not, seeth the wolf coming, and leaveth the sheep, and fleeth: and the wolf catcheth them, and scattereth the sheep" (10:12). It seems evident that our Lord is here pointing once more to the Pharisees, the unfaithful shepherds of Israel. The hireling shepherd is not the *owner* of the sheep—note "whose own the sheep *are not*"; he has neither a proprietorship over them nor affection for them. The "hireling" is *paid* to guard and watch them, and all such mind their own things, and not the things of the Lord. And yet in view of Luke 10:7—"The laborer is worthy of his *hire*"—and other Scriptures, we must be careful not to interpret the use of this figure here out of harmony with its context. "It is not the bare receiving of hire which demonstrates a man to be a hireling (the Lord hath ordained that they who preach the Gospel should live of the Gospel); but the loving of hire; the loving the hire more than the work; the working for the sake of the hire. He is a hireling who would not work, were it not for the hire" (John Wesley). The "hireling" in a word is a professing servant of God who fills a position simply for the temporal advantages which it affords. A hireling is a mercenary: has no other impulse than the lust of lucre.

"But he that is an hireling, and not the shepherd, whose own the sheep are not, seeth the wolf coming, and leaveth the sheep, and fleeth: and the wolf catcheth them, and scattereth the sheep." We do not think that the "wolf" here has reference, directly, to Satan, for the false shepherds do not flee at his approach; rather does it seem to us that "the wolf" points to any enemy of the "sheep," who approaches to attack them. Note in passing the care of Christ here in the selection of His words: "the wolf catcheth them and *scattereth* the sheep," not *devoureth,* for no "sheep" of Christ can ever perish.

"The hireling fleeth, because he is an hireling, and careth not for the sheep" (10:13). At first glance this saying of Christ's seems very trite, yet a little reflection will show that it enunciates a profound principle—a man does what he does because he is what he is. There is ever a rigid consistency between character and conduct. The drunkard drinks because he is a drunkard. But he is a drunkard *before* he drinks to excess. The liar lies because he is a liar; but he is a liar before he *tells* a lie. The thief steals because he is a thief. When the testing time comes each man reveals what he is by what he does. Conduct conforms to character as the stream does to the fountain. "The hireling fleeth because he is an hireling": this is a philosophical explanation of the fugitive's deed. It was the flight which demonstrated the man.

The same principle holds good on the other side. The Christian acts christianly because he is a Christian; but a man must be a Christian *before* he can live a Christian life. Christian *profession* is no adequate test, nor is an orthodox *creed.* The demons have a creed, and it causes them to tremble, but it will not deliver them from Hell; It is by our *fruit* that we are known: it is *deeds* which make manifest the heart.

"The hireling fleeth, because he is an hireling." Character is revealed by our conduct in the *crises* of life. When is it that the hireling fleeth? It is when he seeth "the wolf coming." Ah! it is the wolf that discovers the hireling! You might never have known what he was had not the wolf come. Very suggestive is this figure. It has passed into our common speech, as when poverty and starvation is represented by "the wolf is at the door." It suggests a crisis of trial or fierce testing. St. Paul made use of this simile when addressing the Ephesian elders: "For I know this, that after my departing shall greivous *wolves* enter in among you, not sparing the flock" (Acts 20:29). This is all very searching. How do *you* act when you see "the wolf" coming! Are you terror stricken? Or, does approaching danger, temptation, or trial, cast you back the more upon the Lord?

"I am the good shepherd, and know my sheep, and am known of mine" (10:14). There seem to be three lines of thought suggested by this figure of the "shepherd" as applied to the Lord Jesus. First, it refers to His *mediatorial* office. The shepherd is not the owner of the flock, but the one to whom the care of the sheep is entrusted. So Christ as Mediator is the One appointed by the Father to act as shepherd, the One to whom He has committed the salvation of His elect – note how in the types, Joseph, Moses, and David tended not their own flock, but those of their *fathers*. Second, the figure speaks of *fellowship*, the Saviour's *presence* with His own. The shepherd never leaves his flock. There is only one exception to this, and that is when he commits them into the care of the "porter" of the sheepfold; and that is at night-fall. How suggestive is this! During the *night* of Christ's absence, the Holy Spirit has charge of God's elect! Finally; the shepherd-character speaks of Christ's care, faithfulness, solicitude for His own.

In two other passages in the New Testament is Christ presented as "the shepherd," and in each with a different descriptive adjective. In Heb. 13:20 we read, "Now the God of peace, that brought again from the dead our Lord Jesus, that *great* shepherd of the sheep, through the blood of the everlasting covenant." Again in I Pet. 5:4, we are told, "When the *chief* shepherd shall appear, ye shall receive a crown of glory which fadeth not away." There is a striking order to be observed in the three "shepherd" titles of our Lord. Here in John 10, the reference is plainly to the Cross, so that He is the "good" Shepherd *in death*, laying down His life for the sheep. In Heb. 13 the reference is to the empty sepulchre, so that He is the "great" Shepherd *in resurrection*. While in I Pet. 5:4 the reference is to His glorious return, so that He will be manifested as the "chief" Shepherd.

"I am the good shepherd, and know *my sheep*." Why does the Lord refer to His people under the figure of "sheep"? The figure is very suggestive and full. We shall not attempt to be exhaustive but merely suggestive. Under the Mosaic economy a sheep was one of the few *clean* animals: as such it suitably represents God's people, each of which has been cleansed from all sin. A sheep is a *harmless* animal: even children will approach them without fear. So God's people are exhorted to be "wise as serpents and *harmless* as doves" (Matt. 10:16). Sheep are *helpless*: nature has endowed them neither with weapons of attack nor defence. Equally helpless is the believer in himself: "without me," says Christ, "ye can do *nothing*." Sheep are *gentle*: what so tame and tractable as a lamb! This is ever a grace which ought to distinguish the followers of Christ: "*gentle*, easy to be entreated, full of mercy and good fruits" (James 3:17). The sheep are entirely *dependent* upon the shepherd This is noticeably the case in the Orient. Not only must the sheep look to the shepherd for protection against wild animals, but *he* must lead them to the pastures. May we be cast back more and more upon God. Sheep are preeminently characterized by *a proneness to wander*. Even when placed in a field with a fence all around it, yet if there be a gap anywhere, they will quickly get out and stray. Alas, that this is so true of us. Urgently do we all need to heed that admonition, "Watch and pray *lest* ye enter into temptation." A sheep is a *useful* animal. Each year it supplies a crop of wool. In this too it prefigures the Christian. The daily attitude of the believer should be, "Lord, what wouldst thou have me to do?"

"I am the good shepherd, and *know* my sheep." Very blessed is this. The Lord Jesus knows each one of those whom the Father has given to Him with a special knowledge of approbation, affection, and intimacy. Though unknown to the world—"the world *knoweth us not*" (I John 3:1)—we are known *to Him*. And Christ only knoweth *all* His sheep. Ofttimes we are deceived. Some whom we regard as "sheep" are really "goats"; and others whom we look upon as outside the flock of Christ, belong thereto notwithstanding. Whoever would have concluded that *Lot* was a "righteous man" had not the New Testament told us so! And who would have imagined that *Judas* was a devil when Christ sent him forth as one of the twelve! "And know my sheep": fearfully solemn is the contrast presented by Matt. 7:23 – "I *never* knew you"!

"And am *known* of mine" (10:14). Christ is known experientially; known personally. Each born-again person can say with Job, "I *have* heard of thee by the hearing of the ear, but *now* mine eye seeth thee" (42:6). The believer knows Christ not merely as the outstanding Figure in history, but as the Saviour of his soul. He has a heart knowledge of Him. He knows Him as the Rest-giver, as the Friend who sticketh closer than a brother, as the good Shepherd who ever ministereth to His own.

"As the Father knoweth me, even so know I the Father" (10:15). The word "knoweth" here, as frequently in Scripture, signifies a knowledge of approbation: it is almost the equivalent of *loveth*. The first part of this verse should be linked on to the last clause of the previous one, where Christ says, I "know my sheep, and am known of mine." The two clauses thus make a complete sentence, and a remarkable one it is. The mutual knowledge of Christ and His sheep, is like unto that which exists between the Father and the Son: it is a knowledge, an affection, so profound, so spiritual, so heavenly, so intimate, so blessed, that no other analogy was possible to do it justice: *as* the Father knoweth the Son, and *as* the Son knoweth the Father, *so* Christ knows His sheep, and *so* the sheep know Him.

"And I lay down my life *for* the sheep" (10:15). The precise significance of the preposition is unequivocally defined for us in Rom. 5:6-8, where the same Greek term ("huper") occurs: "For when we were yet without strength in due time Christ died *for* the ungodly. For scarcely *for* a righteous man will one die: yet peradventure *for* a good man some would even dare to die. But God commendeth his love toward us, in that while we were yet sinners, Christ died *for* us." The word "for" here means not merely on the behalf of, but *in the stead of*: "the Greek expression for "dying for any one," never has any signification other than that of rescuing the life of another at the expense of one's own" (Parkhurst's Lexicon).

"And other sheep I have, which are not of this fold" (10:16). It is clear that the Lord is here contemplating His elect among the Gentiles. Not only for the elect Jews would He "lay down his life," but for "the children of God that were scattered abroad" (John 11:52) as well. But note Christ does not here say, "other sheep I *shall* have," but "other sheep I *have*." They were His even then; His, because given to Him by the Father from all eternity. A parallel passage is found in Acts 18. The apostle Paul had just arrived in Corinth, and the Lord spoke to him in a vision by night, and said unto him, "Be not afraid, but speak, and hold not thy peace; for I am with thee, and no man shall set on thee to hurt thee, *for I have much people* in this city" (vv. 9, 10). How positive, definite, and unequivocal these statements are! How they show that everything is to be traced back to the eternal counsels of the Godhead!

"And other sheep I have, which are not of this fold: them also *I must* bring, and they *shall* hear my voice" (10:16). Equally positive is this. This is no uncertainty, no contingency. There is no "*if* they are *willing* to listen." How miserably man perverts the truth of God, yea, how wickedly he *denies* it! It is not difficult to understand what is the cause of it; it is lack of faith to believe what the Scriptures so plainly teach. These "other sheep" Christ *must bring* because necessity was laid upon Him. He had covenanted with the Father to redeem them. And they *would* be brought, they *would* hear His voice, for there can be *no* failure with Him. The work which the Father gave His Son to do *shall* be perfectly performed and successfully accomplished. Neither man's stubbornness nor the Devil's malice can hinder *Him.* Not a single one of that favored company given to Christ by the Father shall perish. Each of these *shall* hear His voice, because they were predestinated so to do, and it is written, "*As many as* were ordained to eternal life believed" (Acts 13:48). "They *shall* hear my voice" was both a promise and a prophecy.

"And other sheep I have, which are not of this fold: them also I must bring, and they shall hear my voice." Upon this verse the Puritan Trapp has some most suggestive thoughts in his excellent commentary—a commentary which, so far as we are aware, has been out of print for over two hundred years. "Other sheep—the elect Gentiles, whose conversion to Christ was, among other types, not obscurely foretold in Lev. 19:23-25—'And when ye shall come into the land, and shall have planted all manner of trees for food, then ye shall count the fruit thereof as uncircumcised; three years shall it be as uncircumcised unto you: it shall not be eaten of. But in the fourth year all the fruit thereof shall be holy to praise the Lord withal. And in the fifth year shall ye eat of the fruit thereof, that it may yield unto you the increase thereof: I am the Lord your God'. The first three years *in Canaan,* the Israelites were to cast away the fruits of the trees as *un*circumcised. So our Saviour planted the Gospel in that land for the first 'three years' of His public ministry: but the uncircumcision was *cast away;* that is, to the uncircumcised Gentiles, the Gospel was not preached. The fruit of the fourth year was consecrated to God: that is, Christ in the fourth year from His baptism, laid down His life for His sheep, rose again, ascended, and sent His Holy Spirit; whereby His apostles, and others were consecrated as the firstfruits of the Promised Land. But in the fifth year, the fruit of the Gospel planted by Christ began to be common, for the Gospel was no longer shut up within the narrow bounds of Judaism, but began to be preached to all nations for the obedience of faith!"*

"And there shall be one fold, and one shepherd" (10:16). Everywhere else in the New Testament the Greek word for "fold" is translated "flock," as it should be here, and as it is in the R. V. In the first part of this verse the Greek uses an entirely different word which is correctly rendered "fold"—"Other sheep I have which are not of this fold." "*This* fold" referred to Judaism, and the elect Gentiles were *outside* of it, as we read in Eph. 2:11, 12, "Ye being in time past Gentiles in the flesh, who are called uncircumcision by that which is called the circumcision in the flesh made by hands; That at that time ye were without Christ, being *aliens from* the commonwealth of Israel, and *strangers from* the covenants of promise, having no hope, and without God in the world." But now the Lord tells us, "there *shall be* one flock, and one Shepherd." This has been

* Let the reader carefully re-read this paragraph.

already accomplished, though not yet is it fully manifested—"For he is our peace, who hath made both (believing Jews and believing Gentiles) one, and hath *broken down* the middle wall of partition" (Eph. 2:14). The "one flock" comprehends, we believe, the whole *family* of God, made up of believers before the nation of Israel came into existence, of believing Israelites, of believing Gentiles, and of those who shall be saved. The "one flock" will have been gathered from *various* "folds."

"Therefore doth my Father love me, because I lay down my life, that I might take it again" (10:17). Christ is here speaking as the Mediator, as the Word who had become flesh. As one of the Godhead, the Father had loved Him from all eternity. Beautifully is this brought out in Prov. 8:30: "Then I was by him, as one brought up with him, and I was daily his *delight*, rejoicing always before him"—the previous verses make it plain that it is the Son who is in view, personified as "Wisdom." But the Father also loved Christ in His incarnate form. At His baptism, the commencement of His mediatorial work, He declared, "This is my *beloved* son, in whom I am well pleased." Here the Son declares, "Therefore doth my Father love me, because I lay down my life that I might take it again", for the laying down of His life was the supreme example of His devotion to the Father as the next verse clearly shows—it was *in obedience* to the Father that He gave up His spirit.

"No man taketh it from me, but I lay it down of myself" (10:18). When Christ died, He did so of His own voluntary will. This is a point of vital importance. We must never give a place to the dishonoring thought that the Lord Jesus was powerless to prevent His sufferings, that when He endured such indignities and cruel treatment at the hands of His enemies, it was because He was unable to avoid them. Nothing could be farther from the truth. The treachery of Judas, the arrest in the Garden, the arraignment before Caiaphas, the insults from the soldiers, the trial before Pilate, the submission to the unjust sentence, the journey to Calvary, the being nailed to the cruel tree—all of these were *voluntarily* endured. Without His own consent none could have harmed a hair of His head. A beautiful type of this is furnished in Gen. 22:13, where we read that the ram, which was placed on the altar as a substitute for Isaac, was "caught in a thicket by his *horns*." The "horns" speak of strength and power (see Hab. 3:4, etc.). Typically they tell us that the Saviour did not succumb to death through weakness, but that He gave up His life in the full vigor of His strength. It was not the nails, but the strength of His love to the Father and to His elect, which held Him to the Cross.

The pre-eminence of Christ was fully manifested at the Cross. In birth He was unique, in His life unique, and so in His death. Not yet have we read aright the inspired accounts of His death, if we suppose that on the Cross the Saviour was a helpless victim of His enemies. At every point He demonstrated that no man took His life from Him, but rather that He laid it down of Himself. See the very ones sent to arrest Him in the Garden, there prostrate on the ground before Him (John 18:6): how easily could He have walked away unmolested had it so pleased Him! Hear Him before Pilate, as He reminds that Roman officer, "Thou couldest have no power at all against me, except it were given thee from above" (John 19:11). Behold Him on the Cross itself, so superior to His sufferings that He makes intercession for the transgressors, saves the dying robber, and provides a home for His widowed mother. Listen to Him as He cries with a *loud* voice (Matt. 27:46, 50) – no exhausted Sufferer was this! Mark how triumphantly He "*gave up* the ghost" (John 19:30). Verily "no *man*" took His life from Him. So evident was it that He triumphed in the hour of death itself, the Roman soldier was made to exclaim, "Truly *this was* the Son of God" (Matt. 27:54).

"I have power to lay it down, and I have power to take it again" (10:18). Here our Lord ascribes His resurrection to His own power. He had done the same before, when, after cleansing the temple, the Pharisees had demanded from Him a sign: "Destroy this temple, and in three days *I will* raise it up" (John 2:19) was His response. In Rom. 6:4 we are told that Christ was "raised from the dead by the glory of *the Father*." In Rom. 8:11 we read, "But if *the Spirit* of him that raised up Jesus from the dead dwell in you, he that raised up Christ from the dead shall also quicken your mortal bodies by his Spirit that dwelleth in you." These passages are not contradictory, but complementary; they supplement one another; each contributing a separate ray of light on the glorious event of which they speak. Putting them together we learn that the resurrection of the Saviour was an act in which each of the three Persons of the Trinity concurred and co-operated.

"This commandment have I received of my Father." This is parallel with what we read of in Phil. 2:8, "And being found in fashion as a man, he humbled himself, and *became obedient* unto death, even the death of the cross." It was to this our Lord referred in John 6:38, "For I came down from heaven not to do mine own will, but the will of him that sent me."

"There was a division therefore again among the Jews for these sayings" (10:19). This had been foretold of old: "He shall be for a sanctuary; but for a stone *of stumbling* and for a rock *of offence* to both the houses of Israel, for *a gin* and for *a snare* to the inhabitants of Jerusalem" (Isa. 8:14). Similarly, Simeon announced in the temple, when the Saviour was presented to God, "Behold, this child is set (appointed) for *the fall* and rising again of many in Israel" (Luke 2:34). So had the Saviour Himself declared. "Think not that I am come to send peace on earth: I came not to send peace, but a sword" (Matt. 10:34). From the Divine side this is a profound mystery to us. It had been an easy matter for God to have subdued the enmity in men's hearts and brought them all as worshippers to the feet of Christ. But instead of this, He permitted His Son to be despised and rejected by the great majority, and He permitted this because He Himself eternally decreed it (see Acts 2:23; I Pet. 2:8, etc).

"And many of them said, He hath a devil, and is mad; why hear ye him?" (10:20). Terrible indeed was the condition of these men. The Son of God called a demoniac, Truth incarnate deemed insane! "Tigers rage," says a Puritan, "at the fragrancy of sweet spices: so did these monsters at the Saviour's sweet sayings." How humbling to remember that the same corrupt heart indwells each of us! O what grace we daily need to keep down the iniquity which is to be found in every Christian. Not until we reach the glory shall we fully learn how deeply indebted we are to God's wondrous grace.

"Others said, These are not the words of him that hath a devil. Can a devil open the eyes of the blind?" (10:21). Notice it was the "many" who deemed Christ a madman. But there were *some* — "others" — even among the Pharisees who had, even then, a measure of light, and recognized that the Saviour neither spake nor acted like a demoniac. This minority group was made up, no doubt, by such men as Nicodemus and Joseph of Arimathea. It is significant that they were impressed more with His "*words*" than they were with His miraculous works.

As a preparation for our exposition of the remainder of John 10, let the interested reader study the following points: —

1. What is the force of "it was winter" (v. 22) in the light of what follows?
2. Mark the contrasts between 10:23 and Acts 3:11 and 5:12.
3. What verses in John 8 are parallel with 10:26?
4. Enumerate the seven proofs of the believer's *security* found in vv. 27-29.
5. Trace out the seven things said about "the sheep" in John 10.
6. Trace out the seven things said about the "shepherd."
7. What is the meaning of "sanctified" in v. 36?

CHAPTER THIRTY-SIX

Christ, One with the Father

John 10:22-42

It is by no means a simple task either to analyze or to summarize the second half of John 10. The twenty-second verse clearly begins a new section of the chapter, but it is equally clear that what follows is closely related to that which has gone before. The Lord is no longer talking to "the Pharisees," but to "the Jews." Nevertheless, it is in His shepherd character, as related to His own, that He is here viewed. Yet while there is this in common between the first and second halves of John 10, there is a notable difference between them. In the former, Christ is seen in His mediatorship; in the latter, it is His essential glories which are the more prominent.

In the first part of John 10 it is Christ in "the form of a servant" which is before us. He gains entrance to the sheepfold by "the porter opening to him" (v. 3). He is the "door" into God's presence (v. 9), the *Way* unto the Father. There, He is seen as the One who was to "give his life for the sheep" (v. 11). There, we behold Him in the place of obedience, in subjection to the "commandment" of the father (v. 18). But mark the contrast in the second half of John 10. Here, He presents Himself as the One endowed with the sovereign right to "give eternal life" to His own (v. 28); as One possessed of almighty power, so that none can pluck them out of His hand (v. 28); as *one* with the Father (v. 30); as "the Son of God" (v. 36). It seems evident then that the central design of the passage before us is to display the *essential* glories of the person of the God-man. It is not so much the Godhood of Christ which is here in view, as it is the Deity *of the One* who humbled Himself to become man.

What is recorded in the latter half of John 10 provided a most pertinent, though tragic, *conclusion* to the first section of the Gospel. It was *winter-time* (v. 22); the season of ingathering was now over; the "sun of righteousness" had completed His official circuit, and the genial warmth of summer had now given place to the season of chilling frosts. The Jews were celebrating "the feast of the dedication," which commemorated the purification of the temple. But for the true Temple, the One to whom the temple had pointed – God tabernacling in their midst – they had no heart. The Lord Jesus is presented as walking in the temple, but it is to be carefully noted that He was "in Solomon's porch" (v. 23). which means that He was *on the outside* of the sacred enclosure, Israel's "house" was left unto them desolate (cf. Matt. 23:38)! While here in the porch, "the Jews" (the religious leaders) came to Christ with the demand that He tell them openly if He were "the Christ" (v. 24), saying, "How long dost thou make us to doubt?" This was the language of unbelief, and uttered at that late date, showed the hopelessness of their condition. Following this interview of the Jews with Christ, and their unsuccessful attempt to apprehend Him, the Lord retires *beyond Jordan,* "unto the place where John at first baptized" (v. 40). Thus did Israel's Messiah return to the place where He had formally dedicated Himself to His mission. Further details will come before us in the course of the exposition. Below is an attempt to analyze our passage:

1. During the feast of dedication Jesus walks in Solomon's porch: vv. 22, 23.
2. The Jews demand an open proclamation of His Messiahship: v. 24.
3. The Lord explains why a granting of their request was useless: vv. 25, 26.
4. The eternal security of His sheep: vv. 27-30.
5. The Jews attempt to stone Him because of His avowal of Deity: vv. 31:33.
6. Christ's defence of His Deity: vv. 34-38.
7. Christ leaves Jerusalem and goes beyond Jordan, where many believe on Him: 39, 42.

"And it was at Jerusalem the feast of dedication, and it was winter" (10:22). The feast of dedication was observed at Jerusalem in memorial of the purification of the Temple after it had been polluted by the idolatries of Antiochus Epiphanes. Proof of this is to be found in the fact that we are here told the time was "winter." Therefore the "feast" here mentioned could not be in remembrance of the dedication of Solomon's temple, for this temple had been dedicated at harvest-time (I Kings 8:2); nor was it to celebrate the building of Nehemiah's temple, for that had been dedicated in the spring-time (Ezra 6:15, 16). The "feast" here referred to must be that which had been instituted by Judas Maccabaeus, on his having purified the temple after the pollution of it by Antiochus, about 165 B. C. This "feast" was celebrated every year for eight successive days in the month of December (I Macc. 4:52, 59), and is mentioned by Josephus (Antiq. 12:7, etc.). Thus the words, "and it was winter" enable us to identify this feast.

"And it was at Jerusalem the feast of the dedication, and it was winter." Here, as always in Scripture, there is a deeper meaning than the mere historical. The mention of "winter" at this point is most significant and solemn. This tenth chapter of John closes the first main section of the fourth Gospel. From this point onwards the Lord Jesus discourses no more before the religious leaders. His public ministry was almost over. The Jews knew not their "day of visitation," and henceforth the things which "belonged to their peace" were hidden from their eyes (Luke 19:42). So far as they were concerned the words of Jeremiah applied with direct and solemn force: "The harvest is past, *the summer is ended,* and we are not saved" (8:20). For them there was nothing but an interminable "*winter.*" Significant and suitable then is this notice of the season of coldness and barrenness as an introduction to what follows.

What we have just pointed out in connection with the moral force of this reference to "winter" encourages us to look for a deeper significance in this mention here of "the feast of the dedication." Nowhere else in Scripture is this particular feast referred to. This makes it the more difficult to ascertain its significance here. That there *is* some definite reason for the Holy

Spirit noticing it, and that there *is* a pertinent and profound meaning to it when contemplated in its connections, we are fully assured. What, then, is it?

As already pointed out, the last half of John 10 closes the first great section of John's Gospel, a section which has to do with the *public* ministry of Christ. The second section of this Gospel records His *private* ministry, concluding with His death and resurrection. The distinctive character of these two sections correspond exactly with the two chief purposes of our Lord's incarnation, which were to present Himself to Israel as their promised Messiah, and to offer Himself as a sacrifice for sin. What, then, remained? Only the still more important work which was to be accomplished by His death and resurrection. He had presented Himself to Israel; now, shortly, He would offer Himself as a sacrifice to God. It is to this "the *dedication*" here points.

It is in this Gospel, alone of the four, that the Lord Jesus is hailed as "the *lamb* of God," and if the reader will turn back to Ex. 12 he will find that the "lamb" was to be *separated* from the flock some days before it was to be killed (see vv. 3, 5, 6). In keeping with this, note how in this passage (and nowhere else) the Lord Jesus speaks of Himself as the One whom the Father had "sanctified" (v. 36), and mark how at the end of the chapter He is seen *leaving* Jerusalem and going away "beyond Jordan" (v. 40)! That the Holy Spirit has here prefaced this final conversation between the Saviour and the Jews by mentioning "the feast of the *dedication*" is in beautiful and striking accord with the fact that from this point onwards Christ was now dedicated to the Cross, as hitherto He had been engaged in manifesting Himself to Israel.

The interpretation suggested above is confirmed and established by two other passages in the New Testament. The Greek word rendered "dedication" occurs nowhere else in the New Testament, but it is found twice in its verbal form. In Heb. 9:18 we read, "Whereupon neither the first testament was *dedicated* without blood" (Heb. 9:18). In Heb. 10:19, 20 we are told, "Having therefore, brethren, boldness to enter into the holiest by the blood of Jesus, by a new and living way, which he hath consecrated *[dedicated]* for us, through the veil, that is to say, his flesh." In each of these instances "dedication" is connected with *blood-shedding!* And it was to this, the shedding of His precious blood, that the Lord Jesus was now (after His rejection by the Nation) dedicated! An additional item still further confirming our exposition is found in the fact that the historical reference in John 10:22 was to the dedication of the *temple,* and in John 2:19 the Saviour refers to Himself as "this temple"—"destroy this *temple,* and in three days I will raise it up." The anti-typical *dedication of the temple* was the Saviour offering Himself to God! Most fitting then was it that the Holy Spirit should here mention the typical dedication of the temple *immediately after* the Lord had thrice referred to His "laying down" His life (see vv. 15, 17, 18)!

"And Jesus walked in the temple in Solomon's porch" (10:23). Josephus informs us (Antiq. 8:3) that Solomon, when he built the temple, filled up a part of the valley adjacent to mount Zion, and built a portico over it toward the East. This was a magnificent structure, supported by a wall four hundred cubits high, made out of stones of vast bulk. It continued to the time of Agrippa, which was several years after the death of Christ. Twice more is mention made of "Solomon's porch" in the New Testament, and what is found in these passages points a sharp contrast from the one now before us. In Acts 3:11 we are told that, following the healing of the lame beggar by Peter and John, "all the people ran together unto them in the porch that is called Solomon's, greatly wondering." But here in John 10:23, following our Lord's healing of the blind beggar, there is no hint of any wonderment among the people! Again in Acts 5:12 we read, "And they were all *with one accord* in Solomon's porch." This is in evident contrast, designed contrast, from what is before us in our present passage. Here, immediately after the reference to our Lord walking in Solomon's porch, we read, "then came the Jews round about him, and said unto him, How long dost thou make us to doubt?" *They* were manifestly *out of accord* with Him. They were opposed to Him, and like beasts of prey sought only His life. Thus we see once more the importance and value of comparing scripture with scripture. By thus linking together these three passages which make mention of "Solomon's porch" we discern the more clearly how that the design of our passage is to present the God-man as "despised and rejected of men."

"Then came the Jews round about him, and said unto him, How long dost thou make us to doubt? If thou be the Christ, tell us plainly" (10:24). The appropriateness of this incident at the close of John 10, and the force of this request of the Jews—obviously a disingenuous one—should now be apparent to the reader. Coming as it does right at the close of the first main section of this Gospel, a section which is concerned with the *public* ministry of Christ before Israel, this demand of the religious leaders makes it plain how useless it was for the Messiah to make any further advances toward the Nation at large, and how justly He might now abandon them to that darkness which they preferred to the light. By now, it was unmistakably plain that the religious leaders "received him not," and this request of theirs for Him to tell them "plainly" or "openly" if He were the Messiah, was obviously made with no other purpose than to gain evidence that they might apprehend Him as a rebel against the Roman government. But, if such was their evil design, did they not already have the needed evidence to formulate the desired charge against Him? The answer is, No, not evidence sufficiently explicit.

"How long dost thou make us to doubt? if thou be the Christ, tell us plainly." It is a significant thing that the Lord Jesus *had not* declared, plainly and openly in public, that He *was* the Messiah. He had avowed His Messiahship to His disciples (1:41, 49, etc.); to the Samaritans (4:42), and to the blind beggar (9:37); but He had not done so before the multitudes or to the religious leaders. This designed omission accomplished a double purpose: it made it impossible for the authorities to lawfully seize Him before God's appointed time, and it enforced the *responsibility* of the Nation at large. That the Lord Jesus *was* the One that the prophets announced should come, had been abundantly attested by His person, His life, and His works; yet the absence of any formal announcement in public served as an admirable *test* of the people. His miraculous works—ever termed "signs" in John's Gospel—were more than sufficient to prove Him to be the Messiah unto those who were open-minded; but yet they were not such as to make it possible for the prejudiced to refuse their assent. This is ever God's way of dealing with moral agents. There are innumerable tokens for the existence of a Divine Creator, sufficient to render all men "without excuse"; yet are these tokens of such a nature as not to have banished atheism from the earth. There are a thousand evidences that the Holy Scriptures are the inspired Word of God, yet are there multitudes who believe them not. There is a great host of unimpeachable witnesses who testify daily to the Saviourhood of the Lord Jesus, yet the great majority of men continue in their sins.

Before we pass from this verse a word should be said upon the turpitude of these Jews. "How long dost *thou* make us to doubt?" was inexcusable wickedness. They were seeking to transfer to Him the onus of their unbelief. They argued that *He* was responsible for their unreasonable and God-dishonoring doubting. This is ever the way with the unregenerate. When God arraigned Adam, the guilty culprit answered, "The woman whom *thou* gavest to be with me, *she* gave me of the tree, and I did eat" (Gen. 3:12). So it is today. Instead of tracing the cause of unbelief to his own evil heart, the sinner blames God for the insufficiency of convincing evidence.

"Jesus answered them, I told you, and ye believed not: the works that I do in my Father's name, they bear witness of me" (10:25). The Lord had told them that He was "the Son of man," and that as such the Father had "given him authority to execute judgment" (5:27). He had told them that He was the One of whom Moses wrote (5:46). He had told them that He was the "living bread" which had come down from heaven (6:51). He had told them that Abraham had rejoiced to see His day (8:56). All of these were statements which intimated plainly that He was the promised One of the Old Testament Scriptures.

In addition to what He had taught concerning His own person, His "works" bore conclusive witness to His Messianic office. His "works" were an essential part of His credentials, as is clear from Luke 7:19-23: "And John calling unto him two of his disciples sent them to Jesus, saying, Art thou he that should come? or look we for another? . . . Jesus answering said unto them, Go your way, and tell John what things ye have seen and heard; how that the blind see, the lame walk, the lepers are cleansed, the deaf hear, the dead are raised, to the poor the gospel is preached. And blessed is he, whosoever shall not be offended in me." These were the precise verifications as to what was to take place when the Messiah appeared—compare Isa. 35:5, 6.

"But ye believe not, because ye are not of my sheep, as I said unto you" (10:26). Unspeakably solemn was this word. They were reprobates, and now that their characters were fully manifested the Lord did not hesitate to tell them so. The force of this awful statement is definite and clear, though men in their unbelief have done their best to befog it. Almost all the commentators have expounded this verse as though its clauses had been reversed. They simply make Christ to say here to these Jews that they were *un*believers. But the truth is that the Lord said far more than that. The commentators understand "the sheep" to be nothing more than a synonym for born-again and justified persons, whereas in fact it is equivalent to God's elect, as the sixteenth verse of this chapter clearly shows. The Lord did not say "Because ye are not of my sheep ye believe not," but, "Ye believe not, because ye are not of my sheep." Man always turns the things of God upside down. When he comes to something in the Word which is peculiarly distasteful, instead of meekly submitting to it and receiving it in simple faith because *God* says it, he resorts to every imaginable device to make it mean something else. Here Christ is not only charging these Jews with unbelief, but He also explains why faith had not been granted to them—*they* were *not* "of his sheep": they were not among the favored number of God's elect. If further proof be required for the correctness of this interpretation, it is furnished below. A man does not have to believe to become one of Christ's "sheep": he "believes" *because he is* one of His sheep.

"But ye believe not, because ye are not of my sheep, *as I said unto you.*" To what is our Lord referring? When had He previously avowed that these Jews were not of God's elect? When had He formerly classed them among the reprobates? The answer is to be found in chapter eight of this same Gospel. There we find this same company—"the Jews" (see v. 48)—antagonizing Him, and to them He says, "Why do ye not understand my speech? even because ye cannot hear my word" (v. 43). This is strictly parallel with "ye believe not" in 10:26. Then, in John 8, He explains *why* they could not "hear his word"—it was because *they* were "of their father the devil" (v. 44). Again, in the forty-seventh verse of the same chapter He said to the Jews, "He that is of God heareth God's words: ye therefore hear them not, because ye are *not of God.*" Strictly parallel is this with 10:26. They "heard not" *because* they were not *of* God: they "believed not" *because* they were not *of* His sheep. In each instance He gives as the reason why they received Him not the solemn fact that they belonged not to God's elect: they were numbered among the reprobates.

"My sheep hear my voice, and I know them, and they follow me" (10:27). Here the Lord contrasts the elect from the nonelect. God's elect *hear* the voice of the Son: *they* hear the voice of the Shepherd because they belong to His sheep: they "hear" because a sovereign God imparts *to them* the capacity *to hear,* for "The hearing ear and the seeing eye, the Lord hath made even both of them" (Prov. 20:12). Each of the sheep "hear" when the irresistible call comes to them, just as Lazarus in the grave heard when Christ called him.

"And I know them, and they follow me" (10:27). Each of the sheep are known to Christ by a *special* knowledge, a knowledge of approbation. They are valued by Him because entrusted to Him by the Father. As the Father's love gift, He prizes them highly. The vast crowd of the nonelect He "*never* knew" (Matt. 7:23) with a knowledge of approbation; but each of the elect are known affectionately, personally, eternally. "And they follow me." They "follow" the example He has left them; they follow in holy obedience to His commandments; they follow from love, attracted by His excellent person; they follow on to know Him better.

"And I give unto them eternal life; and they shall never perish, neither shall any pluck them out of my hand" (10:28). The connection between this and what has gone before should not be lost sight of. Christ had been speaking about His approaching death, His laying down His life for the sheep (v. 15, etc.). Would this, then, *imperil* the sheep? No, the very reverse. He would lay down His life in order that it might be imparted *to them*. This "life," Divine and eternal, would be *given* to them, not sold or bartered. Eternal life is neither earned as a wage, merited as a prize, nor won as a crown. It is a free gift, sovereignly bestowed. But, says the carping objector, All this may be true, but there are certain *conditions* which must be fulfilled if this valuable gift is to be *retained*, and if these conditions are not complied with the gift will be forfeited, and the one who receives it will be lost. To meet this legalistic skepticism, the Lord added, "and *they* shall never perish." Not only is the life given "eternal," but the ones on whom this precious gift is bestowed shall *never* perish: backslide they may, "perish" they shall not, and cannot, while the Shepherd lives! Hypocrites and false professors make shipwreck of *the* faith (not *their* faith, for they never had any), but no real saint of God did or will. There are numerous cases recorded in Scripture where individuals backslided, but never one of a *real* saint apostatizing. A believer may fall, but he shall not be utterly cast down (Psa. 37:24). Quite impossible is it for a sheep to become a goat, for a man who has been born again to be un*born*.

"Neither shall any man (any one) pluck them out of my hand." Here the Lord anticipates another objection, for the fertile mind of unbelief has rarely evidenced more ingenuity than it has at this point, in opposing the blessed truth of the eternal security of God's children. When the objector has been forced to acknowledge that this passage teaches that the life given to the sheep is "eternal," and that those who receive it shall "never perish," he will next make shift by replying, True, no believer will destroy himself, but what of his many enemies, what of Satan, ever going about as a roaring lion seeking whom he may devour? Suppose a believer falls into the toils of the Devil, what then? This, assures our Lord, is equally impossible. The believer is in the hand of Christ, and none is able to pluck from thence one of His own. Tease and annoy him the Devil may, but seize the believer he cannot. Blessed, comforting, re-assuring truth is this! Weak and helpless in himself, nevertheless, the sheep is secure in the hand of the Shepherd.

"My Father, which gave them me, is greater than all: and none is able to pluck them out of my Father's hand" (10:29). Here the Lord anticipates one more objection. He knew full well that there would be some carping quibblers who would be foolish enough to say, True, the Devil is unable to pluck us from the hand of Christ, but we are still "free agents," and therefore could *jump out* if we chose to do so. Christ now bars out this miserable perversion. He shows us how that it is *impossible* for a sheep to perish even if it desired to—as though one ever did! The "hand of Christ" (v. 28) is beneath us, and the "hand" of the Father is above us. Thus are we secured between the clasped hands of Omnipotence!

No stronger passage in all the Word of God can be found guaranteeing the absolute security of every child of God. Note the *seven* strands in the rope which binds them to God. First, they are Christ's *sheep,* and it is the duty of the shepherd to care for each of his flock! To suggest that any of Christ's sheep may be lost is to blaspheme the Shepherd Himself. Second, it is said "They *follow*" Christ, and no exceptions are made; the Lord does not say they *ought to,* but declares they *do*. If then the sheep "follow" Christ they *must* reach Heaven, for that is where the Shepherd is gone! Third, to the sheep is imparted *"eternal life"*: to speak of eternal life ending is a contradiction in terms. Fourth, this eternal life is "*given*" to them: they did nothing to merit it, consequently they can do nothing to *de*merit it. Fifth, the Lord Himself declares that His sheep "*shall never* perish," consequently the man who declares that *it is* possible for a child of God to go to Hell makes God a liar. Sixth, from the *Shepherd's* "hand" none is able to pluck them, hence the Devil is *unable* to encompass the destruction of a single one of them. Seventh, above them is *the Father's* "hand," hence it is impossible for them to jump out of the hand of Christ even if they tried to. It has been well said that if one soul who trusted in Christ should be missing in Heaven, there would be one vacant seat there, one crown unused, one harp unstrung; and this would grieve all Heaven and proclaim a disappointed God. But such a thing is utterly impossible.

"I and my Father are one" (10:30). The R.V. correctly renders this verse, "I and *the* Father are one." The difference between these two translations is an important one. Wherever the Lord Jesus says, "my Father," He is speaking as *the Mediator*, but whenever He refers to "the Father," He speaks from the standpoint of His *absolute* Deity. Thus, "*my* Father is greater than I" (John 14:28) contemplates Him in the *position* of inferiority. "I and *the* Father are one" affirms Their unity of nature or essence, one in every Divine perfection.

"I and the Father are one." There are those who would limit this oneness between the Father and Son to unity of will and design—the Unitarian interpretation of the passage. Dr. John Brown has refuted the error of this so ably and simply that we transcribe from his exposition: "Harmony of will and design, is not the thing spoken of here; but harmony or union of power and operation. Our Lord first says of Himself, 'I give unto my sheep eternal life, and none shall pluck them out of my hand.' He then says the same thing of the Father—'None is able to pluck them out of my Father's hand.' He plainly, then, ascribes the same thing to Himself that He does to the Father, not the same will, but the same work—the same work of power, therefore the same power. He mentions the reason *why* none can pluck them out of the Father's hands,—because He is the Almighty, and no created power is able to resist Him. The thing spoken of is *power,*—power *irresistible*. And in order to prove that none can pluck them out of HIS hand, He adds, 'I and the Father are one.' One in what? unquestionably in the work of power whereby He protects His sheep and does not suffer them to be plucked out of His hand. What the Father is, that the Son is. What the work of the Father is, that the work of the Son is. As the Father is almighty, so is the Son likewise. As nothing can resist the Father, so nothing can resist the Son.

Whatsoever the Father hath, the Son hath likewise. The Father is in the Son, and the Son in the Father. These two are one – in nature, perfection and glory."

"I and the Father are one." It is most blessed to observe the connection between this declaration and what had preceded it. All the diligent care and tender devotion of the Shepherd for the sheep but expresses the mind and heart of the *Owner* toward the flock. The Shepherd and the Owner are *one,* one in their relation and attitude toward the flock; one both in power and in Their loving care for the sheep. Immutably secure then is the believer. It was the laying hold of these precious truths which caused our fathers to sing,

> How firm a foundation
> Ye saints of the Lord,
> Is laid for your faith,
> In His excellent Word.
> What more can He say,
> Than to you He hath said,
> To you who to Jesus
> For refuge have fled.

"*Then* the Jews took up stones again to stone him" (10:31). This is quite sufficient to settle the meaning of the previous verse. These Jews had no difficulty in perceiving the force of what our Lord had just said to them. They instantly recognized that He had claimed absolute equality with the Father, and to their ears this was blasphemy. Instead of saying anything to correct their error, if error it was, Christ went on to say that which must have confirmed it.

"Then the Jews took up stones again to stone him." Fearful wickedness was this! Who could imagine that any heart would have been so base, or any hand so cruel, as to have armed themselves with instruments of death, against such a Person, while speaking such words! Yet we behold these Jews doing just this thing, and that within the sacred precincts of the Temple! A frightful exhibition of human depravity was this. Christ had done these Jews no wrong. They hated Him *without a cause.* They hated Him because of His holiness; and this, because of their sinfulness. Why did Cain hate Abel? "Because his own works were evil, and his brother's righteous" (I John 3:12).

Why did the Jews hate Christ?—"But me it hateth, because I testify of it that the works thereof are evil" (John 7:7). And in that measure in which believers are like Christ, in the same proportion will they be hated by unbelievers: "If the world hate you, ye know that it hated me before it hated you" (John 15:18).

"Jesus answered them, Many good works have I showed you from my Father; for which of those works do ye stone me?" (10:32). The word "works" is to be understood here in its widest sense. The Lord appeals to the whole course of His public ministry—His perfect life, His gracious deeds in ministering to the needs of others, His wondrous words, wherein He spake as never man had spoken. When He terms these works as "from the Father" He means not only that they met with the Father's full approval, but that they had been done by His authority and command—"I have finished the work *which thou* gavest me to do" (John 17:4).

"The Jews answered him, saying, For a good work we stone thee not; but for blasphemy; and because that thou, being a man, makest thyself God" (10:33). It was most appropriate for this to be recorded in *John's* Gospel, the great design of which is to present the *Deity* of the Saviour. The carnal mind is "enmity against *God,*" and never was this more fully evidenced than when God incarnate appeared in the midst of men. During His infancy, an organized effort was made to slay Him (Matt. 2). In one of the Messianic Psalms there is more than a hint that during the years Christ spent in seclusion at Nazareth, repeated attempts were made upon His life—"I am *afflicted* and ready to die from *my youth up*" (Psa. 88:15. The very first word spoken by Him in the Nazareth synagogue after His public ministry began, was followed by an attempt to murder Him (Luke 4:29). And from that point onwards to the Cross, His steps were dogged by implacable foes who thirsted for His blood. Wonderful beyond comprehension was that grace of God which suffered His Son to sojourn in such a world of rebels. Divine was that infinite forbearance which led Christ to endure "the contradiction of sinners against himself." Deep, fervent, and perpetual should be our praise for that love which saved us at such a cost!

"Jesus answered them, Is it not written in your law, I said, Ye are gods? If he called them gods, unto whom the word of God came, and the scripture cannot be broken; Say ye of him, whom the Father hath sanctified, and sent into the world, Thou blasphemest; because I said, I am the Son of God? If I do not the works of my Father, believe me not. But if I do, though ye believe not me, believe the works: that ye may know, and believe, that the Father is in me and I in him" (10:34-38). Upon these verses we cannot do better than quote from the excellent remarks of Dr. John Brown:

"Our Lord's reply consists of two parts. In the first, He shows that the charge of blasphemy, which they founded on His calling Himself the Son of God, was a rash one, even though nothing more could have been said of Him, than that He had been 'sanctified and sent by the Father'; and secondly, that His miracles were of such a kind, as that they rendered whatever He declared of Himself, as to His intimate connection with the Father, however extraordinary, worthy of credit.

"Our Lord's argument in the first part of this answer is founded on a passage in the eighty-second Psalm, verse six; 'I have said, Ye are gods; and all of you are children of the most high.' These words are plainly addressed to the Jewish magistrates, commissioned by Jehovah to act as His vicegerents in administering justice to His people: who judged for God—in the room of God; whose sentences, when they agreed with the law, were God's sentences; whose judgment, was God's judgment, and rebels against whom, were rebels against God.

"The meaning and force of our Lord's argument is obvious. If, in a book which you admit to be of Divine authority, and all whose expressions are perfectly faultless, men which have received a Divine communication to administer justice to the people of God are called 'gods' and sons of the Highest; is it not absurd to bring against One who has a higher commission than they (One who had been sanctified and sent by the Father), and who presented far more evidence of His commission, a charge of blasphemy, because He calls Himself 'the Son of God'? You dare not charge blasphemy on the Psalmist;—why do you charge it on Me? . . . He reasoned with the Jews on their own principles. Were the Messiah nothing more than you expect Him to be, to charge One who claims Messiahship with blasphemy, because He calls Himself the Son of God, is plainly gross inconsistency. Your magistrates are called God's sons, and may not your Messiah claim the same title?

"The second part of our Lord's reply is contained in the thirty-seventh and thirty-eighth verses. It is equivalent to—I have declared that I and the Father are one—one in power and operation. I do not call on you to believe this merely because of My testimony, but I do call on you to believe on My testimony *supported by* the miracles I have performed, works which nothing but a Divine power could accomplish. These works are the voice of God, and its utterance is distinct: it speaks plainly, it utters no dark saying. You cannot refuse to receive the doctrine that I and the Father are one, that the Father is in Me, and I in Him, without contradicting *His* testimony and calling *Him* a liar."

Let us notice one or two details in these verses before we turn to the conclusion of our chapter. The word "gods" in the eighty-second Psalm, quoted here by Christ, has occasioned difficulty to some. The magistrates of Israel were so called because of their *authority* and *power,* and as representing the Divine majesty in government.

Mark how in v. 35 the Saviour said, "The scripture cannot be broken." What a high honor did He here place upon the written Word! In making use of this verse from the Psalmist against His enemies, the whole point of His argument lay *in a single word*—"gods"—and the fact that it occurred in the book Divinely inspired. The Scriptures were the final court of appeal, and here the Lord insists on their absolute authority and verbal inerrancy.

Observe here *Christ's* use of the word "sanctified" in v. 36 refutes many modern heretics. There are those who teach that to be sanctified is to have the carnal nature eradicated. They insist that sanctification is moral purification. But how thoroughly untenable is such a definition in the light of what the Master says here. He declares that *He* was "sanctified." Certainly that cannot mean that He was cleansed from sin, for He was the Holy One. Here, as everywhere in Scripture, the term sanctified can only mean *set apart*. Observe the order: Christ was first sanctified and then sent into the world. The reference is to the Father's eternal appointment of the Son to be the Mediator.

"Therefore they sought again to take him: but he escaped out of their hand" (10:39). This signifies that these Jews sought to apprehend the Lord Jesus so that they might bring Him before the Sanhedrin, but they were unable to carry out their evil designs. Soon He would deliver Himself into their hands, but until the appointed hour arrived they might as well attempt to harness the wind as lay hands on the Almighty.

"And went away again beyond Jordan into the place where John at first baptized; and there he abode. And many resorted unto him, and said, John did no miracle: but all things which John spake of this man were true. And many believed on him there" (10:40-42). We have already pointed out the significance of this move of Christ. In leaving Jerusalem—to which He did not return until the appointed "hour" for His death had arrived—and in going *beyond* Jordan to where His forerunner had been, the Lord gave plain intimation that His *public* ministry was now over. The Nation at large must be left to suffer the due reward of their iniquities. In what follows we have a beautiful illustration of this present dispensation: "*Outside* the camp" Christ now was, but in this place, as the despised and rejected One, many resorted to Him. God would not allow His beloved Son to be universally unappreciated, even though organized Judaism had turned its back upon Him. Here beyond Jordan He works no public miracle (as He does not today), but many believed on Him because of what John had *spoken*. So it is now. It is the *Word* which is the means God uses in bringing sinners to believe on the Saviour. Happy for these men that they knew the day of *their* visitation, and improved the brief visit of Christ.

Let the interested student study the following questions on the first part of John 11: —

1. Why did not the sisters name the sick one? v. 3.
2. What is the force of the "therefore"? v. 6.
3. Why did not Christ hasten to Bethany at once? v. 6.
4. Why "into Judea" rather than "to Bethany"? v. 7.
5. Why did Christ refer to the "twelve hours in the day"? v. 9.
6. What is meant by the second half of v. 9?
7. What is meant by "walking in the night"? v. 10.

CHAPTER THIRTY-SEVEN

Christ Raising Lazarus

John 11:1-10

Below is an Analysis of the first ten verses of John 11.

1. Lazarus and his sisters, vv. 1, 2.
2. Their appeal to the Lord, v. 3.
3. God's design in Lazarus' sickness, v. 4.
4. The delay of love, vv. 5, 6.
5. Christ testing His disciples, v. 7.
6. The disciples' trepidation, v. 8.
7. The Lord re-assuring the disciples, vv. 9, 10.

Before taking up the details of the passage which is to be before us a few words need to be said concerning the principle design and character of John 11 and 12. In the preceding chapters we have witnessed the increasing enmity of Christ's enemies, an enmity which culminated in His crucifixion. But before God suffered His beloved Son to be put to death, He gave a most blessed and unmistakable witness to His glory. "We have seen, all through John, that no power of Satan could hinder the manifestation of the Person of Christ. He met with incessant opposition and undying hatred, the result, however, being that glory succeeds glory in manifestation, and God was fully revealed in Jesus. That was His *purpose,* and *who* could hinder its accomplishment? 'Why do the heathen rage and the people imagine a vain thing?' Man's rage against Christ, only served as an occasion *for* the manifestation of His glory. Here in John 11 the Son of God is glorified, the glory of God answering to the rejection of the Person of Christ in the preceding chapters" (R. Evans: Notes & Meditations on John's Gospel).

It is indeed a striking fact, and one to which we have not seen attention called, that the previous chapters show us Christ *rejected* in a threefold way, and then God answering by *glorifying* Christ in a threefold way. In 5:16 we read, "Therefore did the Jews persecute Jesus, and *sought to slay him,* because he had done these things on the sabbath day": this was because of His *works.* In John 8:58 we are told, "Jesus said unto them, Verily, verily, I say unto you, Before Abraham was, I am"; and immediately following, it is recorded, "*Then* took they up stones *to cast at him*"; this was because of His *words.* While in 10:30 the Lord affirmed, "I and my Father are one," which is at once followed by, "*Then* the Jews took up stones *again* to stone him": this was on account of the claim which He had made concerning His person.

The threefold witness which God caused to be borne to the glory of Christ in John 11 and 12 corresponds exactly with the threefold rejection above, though they are met in their inverse order. In John 10:31 it was Christ in His absolute Deity, as God the Son, who was rejected. Here in John 11 His *Divine* glory shines forth most manifestly in the raising of Lazarus. In John 8 He was rejected because He declared "Before *Abraham* was, I am." There it was more in His *Messianic* character that He was despised. Corresponding to this, in John 12:12-15 we find Him in full Messianic glory entering Jerusalem as "King of Israel." In John 5 Christ is seen more in His *mediatorial* character, in incarnation as "the Son of man"—note 5:27. Corresponding to this we find in the third section of John 12 the *Gentiles* seeking the Lord Jesus, and to them He answered: "The hour is come, that the *Son of man* should *be glorified*" (12:23)!

Man had fully manifested *himself.* The Light had shone in the darkness, and the darkness comprehended it not. The deep guilt of men had been demonstrated by their refusing the sent One from the Father, and their deadness in trespasses and sins had been evidenced by the absence of the slightest response to the eternal Word then tabernacling in their midst. They had seen and hated both Him and His Father (15:24). The end of Christ's public ministry was, therefore, well-nigh reached. But before He goes to the Cross, God gave a final testimony to the glory of His beloved. Beautiful is it to behold the Father so jealously guarding the honor of His Son in this threefold way ere He left the stage of public action. And solemn was it for Israel to be shown so plainly and so fully WHO it was they had rejected and were about to crucify.

The darker the night, the more manifest the light which illumines it. The more the depravity and enmity of Israel were exhibited, the brighter the testimony which God caused to be borne to the glory of His Son. The end was almost reached, therefore did the Lord now perform His mightiest work of all—save only the laying down of His own life, which was *the* wonder of all wonders. Six miracles (or as John terms them, "signs") had already been wrought by Him, but at Bethany He does that which displayed His Divine power in a superlative way. Previously we have seen Him turning water into wine, healing the nobleman's son, restoring the impotent man, multiplying the loaves and fishes, walking on the sea, giving sight to the blind man; but here he raises the dead, yea, brings back to life one who had lain in the grave four days. Fitting climax was this, and most suitably is it the *seventh* "sign" in this Gospel.

It is true that Christ had raised the dead before, but even here the climax is again to be seen. Mark records the raising of Jairus' daughter, but she had only just died. Luke tells of the raising of the widow's son of Nain, but he had not been buried. But here, in the case of Lazarus, not only had the dead man been placed in the sepulchre, but corruption had already begun to consume the body. Supremely true was it of the just One (Acts 3:14) that His path was as the shining light, which shone "more and more unto the perfect day" (Prov. 4:18).

The same climactic order is to be seen in connection with *the state of the natural man* which John's "signs" typically portray. "They have no wine" (2:3), tells us that the sinner is a total stranger to Divine joy (Judges 9:13). "Sick" (4:46), announces the condition of the sinner's soul, for sin is a disease which has robbed man of his original health. The "impotent man" (5:7), shows us that the poor sinner is "without strength" (Rom. 5:6), completely helpless, unable to do a thing to better his condition. The multitude without any food of their own (6:5), witnesses to the fact that man is destitute of that which imparts strength. The disciples on the storm-tossed sea (6:18), before the Saviour came to them, pictures the dangerous position which the sinner occupies—already on the "broad road" which leadeth to *destruction.* The man blind from his birth (9:1), demonstrates the fact that the sinner is altogether incapable of perceiving either his own wretchedness and danger, or the One who alone can deliver him. But in John 11 we have that which is much more solemn and awful. Here we learn that the natural man is spiritually *dead,* "dead in trespasses and sins." Lower than this we cannot go. Anything more hopeless cannot be portrayed. In the presence of death, the wisest, the richest, the most mighty among men have to confess their utter helplessness. This, this is what is set before us in John 11. Most suitable background for Christ to display Himself as "the resurrection and the life." And most striking is this climax of the "signs" recorded in the fourth Gospel, displaying both the power of Christ and the condition of the natural man.

"Now a certain man was sick, named Lazarus, of Bethany, the town of Mary and her sister Martha" (11:1). The object of our Lord's resurrection-power is first presented to our notice. His name was Lazarus. At once our minds revert back to Luke 16, where another "Lazarus" is seen. But how striking the contrast, a contrast most evidently designed by the Holy Spirit. There are only two mentioned in the New Testament which bear this name. Here again the 'law of comparison and contrast' helps us. The Lazarus of Luke 16 was a beggar, whereas everything goes to show that the Lazarus of John 11 (cf. 12:2, 3) was a man of means. The Lazarus of Luke 16 was uncared for, for we read of how the dogs came and licked his sores; but the one in John 11 enjoyed the loving ministrations of his sisters. The Lazarus of Luke 16 was dependent upon the "crumbs" which fell *from* another's table; whereas in John 12, after his resurrection, the Lazarus of Bethany is seen *at* "the table" where the Lord Jesus was. The one in Luke 16 died and remained in the grave, the one in John 11 was brought-again from the dead.

The Holy Spirit has been careful to identify the Lazarus of John 11 as belonging to *Bethany*—a word that seems to have a double meaning: "House of Figs," and "House of Affliction." It was the "town" (more accurately "village") of Mary and her sister Martha. Though not mentioned previously by John, this is not the first reference to these sisters in the Gospel records. They are brought before us at the close of Luke 10, and what is there recorded about them sheds not a little light upon some of the details of John 11.

Martha was evidently the senior, for we are told "Martha received him into *her* house" (Luke 10:38). This is most blessed. There were very few homes which were opened to the Lord Jesus. He was "despised and rejected of men." Men hid as it were their faces from Him and "esteemed him not." Not only was He unappreciated and unwelcome, but He was "hated." But here was one who had "received him," first into her heart, and then into her home. So far so good. Of her sister, it is said, "And she had a sister called Mary, which also sat at Jesus' feet and heard his word" (Luke 10:39). It is indeed striking to note that each time Mary is mentioned in the Gospel, she is seen *at the feet* of Christ. She had the deeper apprehension of the glory of His person. She was the one who enjoyed the most intimacy with Him. Her's was the keener spiritual discernment. We shall yet see how this is strongly confirmed in John 11 and 12.

Next we are told, "But Martha was cumbered about much serving, and came to him and said, Lord, dost thou not care that my sister hath left me to serve alone? bid her therefore that she help me" (Luke 10:40). The word "cumbered" means "weighted down." She was burdened by her "*much* serving." Alas, how many there are like her among the Lord's people to-day. It is largely due to the over-emphasis which has been placed upon "Christian service"—much of which is, we fear, but the feverish energy of the flesh. It is not that service is wrong, but it becomes a snare and an evil if it be allowed to crowd out worship and the cultivation of one's own spiritual life: note the order in I Tim. 4:16, "Take heed unto thyself, *and* to thy teaching."

"And Jesus answered and said unto her, Martha, Martha, thou art careful and troubled about many things" (Luke 10:41). This is very solemn. The Lord did not commend Martha for her "much serving." Instead, He reproved her. He tells her she was distracted and worried because she had given her attention to "*many* things." She was attempting more than God had called her to do. This is very evident from the previous verse. Martha felt that her load was too heavy to carry alone, hence her "bid her therefore that she help *me.*" Sure sign was this that she had run without being sent. When any Christian feels as Martha here felt, he may know that he has undertaken to do more than the Lord has appointed.

"But one thing is needful: and Mary hath chosen that good part, which shall not be taken away from her" (Luke 10:42). Though the Lord reproved Martha, He commended Mary. The "one thing needful" is "that good part" which Mary had chosen, and that is to *receive* from Christ. Mary sat at His feet "*and* heard his word." She was conscious of her deep need, and came to Him to be ministered unto. Later, we shall see how she ministered unto Christ, and ministered so as to receive His hearty commendation. But the great lesson for us here is, that *we* must first be ministered unto before we are qualified to minister unto others. We must be *receivers,* before we can give out. The vessel must be filled, before it can overflow. The difference then between Martha and Mary is this: the one ministered *unto* Christ, the other received *from* Him, and of the latter He declared, she "hath chosen that good part which shall not be taken away from her." This brief examination of Luke 10, with the information it gives about the characters of the two sisters of Lazarus will enable us to understand the better their respective actions and words in John 11.

"It was that Mary which anointed the Lord with ointment, and wiped his feet with her hair, whose brother Lazarus was sick" (11:2). This explains why Mary is mentioned first in the previous verse—the only time that she is. The commentators have indulged in a variety of conjectures, but the reason is very obvious. John's Gospel was written years after the first three, one evidence of which is supplied in the verses before us. The opening verse of our chapter clearly supposes that the reader is acquainted with the contents of the earlier Gospels. Bethany was "the town (village) of Mary and her sister Martha." This Luke 10:38 had already intimated. But in addition, both Matthew and Mark record how that Mary had "anointed" the Lord with her costly ointment in the house of Simon the leper who also resided in Bethany. It is true her name is not given either by Matthew or Mark,* but it is very clear that her name must have been known, for how else could the Lord's word have been carried out: "Verily I say unto you, Wheresoever this gospel shall be preached throughout the whole world, this also that she hath done shall be spoken of for a memorial of her" (Mark 14:9). It is this which explains why Mary is mentioned first in John 11:1—she was the better known!

It was at Bethany that Lazarus lived with his sisters. Bethany was but a village, yet had it been marked out in the eternal counsels of God as the place which was to witness the greatest and most public miraculous attestation of the Deity of Christ. "Let it be noted that the presence of God's elect children is the one thing which makes towns and countries famous in God's sight. The village of Martha and Mary is noticed, while Memphis and Thebes are not named in the New Testament. A cottage where there is grace, is more pleasant in God's sight than a palace where there is none." (Bishop Ryle). It was at Bethany there was to be given the final and most conclusive proof that He who was on the point of surrendering *Himself* to death and the grave was none other than the resurrection and the life. Bethany was less than two miles from Jerusalem (11:18), the headquarters of Judaism, so that the news of the raising of Lazarus would soon be common knowledge throughout all Judea.

"Therefore his sisters sent unto him, saying, Lord, behold, he whom thou lovest is sick" (11:3). This must not be regarded as a protest; it was not that Martha and Mary were complaining against Christ because He suffered one whom He loved to fall sick. Instead, it was simply an appeal to the heart of One in whom they had implicit confidence. The more closely this brief message from the sisters is scrutinized, the more will their becoming modesty be apparent. Instead of prescribing to Christ what should be done in their brother's case, they simply acquainted Him with his desperate condition. They did not request Him to hasten at once to Bethany, nor did they ask Him to heal

* It is characteristic of John to give us her name, for he presents Christ as God manifest in the flesh, therefore everything comes out into the light: cf. the fact that John alone tells us the name of the priest's servant, whose ear the Saviour healed (John 18:10).

their brother by a word from a distance, as once He had restored to health the nobleman's son (John 4). Instead, they left it for *Him* to decide what should be done.

"Lord, behold, he whom thou lovest is sick." Each word in this touching message of Martha and Mary is worthy of separate consideration. "Lord" was the language of believers, for no unbeliever ever so addressed the despised Nazarene. "Lord" acknowledged His Deity, owned His authority, and expressed their humility. "Lord, behold": this is a word which arrests attention, focalizes interest, and expressed their earnestness. "He whom thou lovest." This is highly commendable. They did not say, "he who loves thee." Christ's fathomless love for us, and not our feeble love for Him, is what we ever need to keep steadily before our hearts. Our love varies; His knows no change. It is indeed striking to note the way in which the sisters refer to Lazarus. They did not blame him! They did not even say, "our brother," or "thy disciple," but simply "he whom thou lovest is sick." They knew that nothing is so quick in discernment as *love;* hence their appeal to the omniscient love of Christ. "He whom thou lovest is *sick.*" There are two principle words in the Greek to express sickness: the one referring to the disease itself, the other pointing to its effects—weakness, exhaustion. It is the latter that was used here. As applied to individual cases in the N.T. the word here used implies deathly-sick—note its force in Acts 9:37 and Phil. 2:26, 27. In John 5:3 and 7 it is rendered "impotent." It is not at all likely that Martha and Mary would have sent to Christ from such a distance had not their brother's life been in danger. The force, then, of their message was, "He whom thou lovest *is sinking.*"

The verse now before us plainly teaches that sickness in a believer is by no means incompatible with the Lord's *love* for such an one. There are some who teach that sickness in a saint is a sure evidence of the Lord's displeasure. The case of Lazarus ought forever to silence such an error. Even the chosen friends of Christ sicken and die. How utterly incompetent then are we to estimate God's love for us by our temporal condition or circumstances! "No man knoweth either love or hatred *by* all that is *before* them" (Ecc. 9:1). What then is the practical lesson for us in this? Surely this: "Therefore judge nothing before the time" (I Cor. 4:5). The Lord loves Christians as truly when they are sick as when they are well.

It is blessed to mark how Martha and Mary acted in the hour of their need. They sought the Lord, and unburdened their hearts to Him. Do we always act thus? It is written, "God is our refuge and strength, a very *present* help in trouble" (Psa. 46:1); yet, to our shame, how little we *know* Him as such. When the people murmured against Moses, we are told that, "he cried unto the Lord" (Ex. 15:25). When Hezekiah received the threatening letter from Rabshakeh, he "spread it before the Lord" (Isa. 37:14). When John the Baptist was beheaded his disciples "went and told Jesus" (Matt. 14:12). What examples for us! We have not an High Priest who cannot be touched with the feeling of our infirmities. No, He is full of compassion, for when on earth He, too, was " acquainted with grief." He sympathizes deeply with His suffering people, and invites them to pour out the anguish of their hearts before Him. What a blessed proof of this we find in John 20. When He met the tearful Mary on the morn of His resurrection, He asked her, "Woman, why weepest thou?" (20:15). Why ask here such a question? Did He not know the cause of her sorrowing? Certainly He did. Was it a reproach? We do not deem it such. Was it not rather because He wanted her to unburden her heart before Him! "Cast thy burden upon the Lord" is ever His word. This is what Martha and Mary were doing. The Lord grant that every tried and troubled reader of these lines may go and do likewise.

The action of these sisters and the wording of their appeal afford us a striking example of *how* we should present our petitions to the Lord. Much of the present-day teaching on the subject of prayer is grossly dishonoring to God. The Most High is not our servant to be brought into subjection to *our* will. Prayer was never designed to place *us* on the Throne, but to bring us to our knees before it. It is not for the creature to dictate to the Creator. It *is* the happy privilege of the Christian to make known His requests with thanksgiving. But, "requests" are not commands. Petitioning is a very different matter from commanding. Yet we have heard men and women talk to God not only as if they were *His* equals, but as though they had the right to order Him about. Coming to the Throne of Grace with "boldness" does not mean with impious impudence. The Greek word signifies "freedom of speech." It means that we may tell out our hearts *as* God's children, never forgetting though, that He is our *Father*.

The sisters of Lazarus acquainted the Lord with the desperate condition of their brother, appealed to His love, and then left the case in His hands, to be dealt with as *He* saw best. They were not so irreverent as to tell Him *what* to do. In this they have left all praying souls a worthy example which we do well to follow. "*Commit* thy way unto the Lord": that is our responsibility. "Trust also *in him*"; that is our happy privilege. "*Trust* also in him," not dictate to Him, and not demand from Him. People talk of "claiming" from God. But *grace* cannot be "claimed," and *all* is of grace. The very "throne" we approach is one of *grace*. How utterly incongruous then to talk of "claiming" anything from the Sitter on *such* a throne. "Commit thy way unto the Lord, trust also in him, and he shall *bring it to pass*." But it must ever be kept in mind that He will "bring it to pass" in His *own* sovereign way and in His *own* appointed time. And oftentimes, usually so in fact, *His* way and time will be different from ours. He brought it *to pass* for Martha and Mary, though not in the time and way they probably expected. The Apostle Paul longed to preach the Gospel in Rome, but how slow he was in realizing his desire and in what an altogether unlooked-for manner went he there!

"When Jesus heard that, he said, This sickness is not unto death, but for the glory of God" (11:4). We take it that this was our Lord's answer to the messenger, rather than a private word to His disciples, though probably it was spoken in their hearing. And what a mysterious answer it was! How strangely worded! How cryptic! What did He mean? One thing was evident on its surface: Martha and Mary were given the assurance that both the sickness of Lazarus and its issue were perfectly known to Christ—how appropriately was the record of this reserved for *John's Gospel;* how perfectly in accord with the whole tenor of it!

"This sickness is not unto death." This declaration is similar in kind to what was before us in 9:3, "Neither hath this man sinned, nor his parents: but that the works of God should be made manifest in him"—compare our comments thereon. The sickness of Lazarus was "not unto death" in the ordinary sense of the word, that is, unto *abiding* death—death would not be the *final end* of this "sickness." But why not have told the exercised sisters plainly that their brother would die, and that He would raise him from the dead? Ah! that is not God's way; He would keep *faith* in exercise, have *patience* developed, and so order things that we are constantly driven to our knees! The Lord said sufficient on this occasion to encourage hope in Martha and Mary, but not enough to make them leave off seeking God's help! Bishop Ryle has pointed out how that we encounter the same principle and difficulty in connection with much of unfulfilled prophecy: "There is sufficient for faith to rest upon and to enkindle hope, but sufficient also to make us cry unto God for light"!

"This sickness is not unto death, *but for the glory of God.*" What a word was this! How far, we wonder, had those two sisters entered into such a thought concerning the sickness of their brother. But now they were to learn that it was Divinely ordained, and from the sequel we are shown that Lazarus' sickness, his death, the absence of Christ from Bethany, and the blessed issue, were all arranged by Him who doeth *all* things well. Let us learn from this that God has a purpose in connection with *every* detail of our lives. Many are the scriptures which show this. The case of the man born blind provides a parallel to the sickness and death of Lazarus. When the disciples asked why he had been born blind, the Saviour answered, "That the works of God should be manifest in him." This should teach us to look behind the outward sorrows and trials of life to the Divine purpose in sending them.

"This sickness is not unto death, but for the glory of God, that the Son of God might be glorified thereby" (11:4).. How this shows that the glory of God is one with the glory of the Son! The two are inseparable. This comes out plainly, again, if we compare John 2:11 with 11:40. In the former we are told,

"This beginning of miracles did Jesus in Cana of Galilee and manifested forth *his* glory." In the latter we find Him saying to Martha, as He was on the point of raising Lazarus, "Said I not unto thee, that, if thou wouldest believe, thou shouldest see the *glory of God*." The same truth is taught once more in 14:13, "Whatsoever ye shall ask in my name, that will I do, that *the Father* may be glorified *in the Son*." What then is the lesson for us? This: "All men should honour the Son, *even as* they honour the Father" (5:23).

"Now Jesus loved Martha, and her sister, and Lazarus" (11:5). Here the order of their names is reversed from what we have in verse 1. Martha is now mentioned first. Various conjectures have been made as to why this is. To us it appears the more natural to mention Mary first at the beginning of the narrative, for she would be the better known to the readers of the Gospel records. In 11:5, and so afterwards, it was suitable to name Martha first, seeing that she was the senior. But in addition to this, may it not be the Holy Spirit's design to show us that each sister was *equally* dear to the Saviour! It is true that Mary chose the better part, whilst Martha struggled with the needless unrest of her well-meaning mind. But though these sisters were of such widely dissimilar types, yet were they one in Christ! Diverse in disposition they might be, yet were they both loved with the same eternal, unchanging love!

"Now Jesus loved Martha, and her sister, and Lazarus." A precious thought will be lost here unless we mark carefully the exact place in the narrative that this statement occupies. It is recorded not at the beginning of the chapter, but immediately before what we read of in v. 6, where we are told that the Lord Jesus "abode two days still in the place where he was." Such a delay, under such circumstances, strikes us as strange. But, as we shall see, the delay only brought out the perfections of Christ—His absolute *submission* to the Father's will. In addition to that, it is beautiful to behold that His delay was also in full keeping with His *love* for Martha and Mary. Among other things, Christ designed to strengthen the faith of these sisters by suffering it to endure the bitterness of death, in order to heighten its subsequent joy. "His love wittingly delays that it may more gloriously console them after their sufferings" (Stier). Let *us* learn from this that when God makes us *wait,* it is the sign that He purposes to *bless,* but in His own way—usually a way so different from what *we* desire and expect. What a word is that in Isa. 30:18, "And therefore will the Lord *wait,* that he may be *gracious* unto you, and therefore will he be exalted, that he may have mercy upon you: for the Lord is a God of judgment: blessed are all they that *wait* for him"!

"When he had heard therefore that he was sick, he abode two days still in the same place where he was" (11:6). The Lord knows best at what time to relieve His suffering people. There was no coldness in His affection for those tried sisters (as the sequel clearly shows), but the right moment for Him to act had not then come. Things were allowed to become more grievous: the sick one died, and still the Master tarried. Things had to get worse at Bethany before He intervened. Ofttimes God brings man to the end of himself before He comes to his relief. There is much truth in the old proverb that "Man's extremity is God's opportunity." Frequently is this the Lord's way; but how trying to flesh and blood! How often we ask, with the disciples, "Master, carest thou not that we perish?" But how awful to question the tender compassion of such a One! And how foolish was the question of these disciples: how could they "perish" with *Christ* on board! What cause we have to hang our heads in shame! "When circumstances look dark, our hearts begin to question the love of the One who permits such to befall us. Oh, let me press upon you this important truth: *the dealings of the Father's hand must ever be looked at in the light of the Father's heart.* Grasp this. Never try to interpret love by its manifestations. How often our Father sends chastisement, sorrow, bereavement, pressure! How well He could take me out of it all—in a moment—He has the power, but He leaves me there. Oh, may He help us to rest patiently in Himself at such times, not trying to read His love by circumstances, but them, whatever they may be, through the love of His heart. This gives wondrous strength—knowing that loving heart, and not questioning the dealings of His hand" (C.H.M.).

But *why* did Christ abide two days still in the same place where He was? To test the faith of the sisters, to develop their patience, to heighten their joy in the happy sequel. All true; but there was a much deeper reason than those. Christ had taken upon Him the form of a servant, and in perfect submission to the Father He awaits His orders from *Him*. Said He, "I came down from heaven, not to do mine *own* will, but the will of him that sent me" (6:38). Most beautifully was this demonstrated here. Not even His love for Martha and Mary would move Him to act before the Father's time had come. Blessedly does this show us the anti-typical fulfillment of one detail in a most wondrous type found in Lev. 2. The meal offering plainly foreshadowed the incarnate Son of God. It displays the perfections of His Divine-human person. Two things were rigidly excluded from this offering: "No meat offering, which ye shall bring unto the Lord, shall be made with leaven: for ye shall burn *no* leaven, *nor any honey,* in any offering of the Lord made by fire" (Lev. 2:11). The leaven is the emblem of evil. "Honey" stands for the sweetness of natural affections, what men term "the milk of human kindness." And how strikingly this comes out here.

How differently Christ acted from what you and I most probably would have done! If we had received a message that a loved one was desperately sick, would we not have hastened to his side without delay? And *why* would we? Because we sought *God's glory?* or because our natural affections impelled us? Ah! in this, as in everything, we behold the uniqueness of the Lord Jesus. The Father's glory was ever dearest to the heart of the Son. Here then is the force of the "therefore." "When *therefore* he heard that he is sick, then *indeed* he remained in which he was place two days" (Bagster's Interlinear—literal translation). The "therefore" and the "indeed" look back to v. 4—"this sickness . . . is for the glory of God." And how what we read of in the intervening verse serves to emphasize this—Christ's love for His own never interfered with His dependence on the Father. His first recorded utterance exhibited the same principle: to Mary and Joseph He said, "Wist ye not that I must be about *my Father's* business?" The Father's claims were ever supreme.

"Then after that saith he to his disciples, Let us go into Judea again" (11:7). Notice the manner in which the Lord expressed Himself. He did not say, Let us go to Lazarus, or to Bethany. Why not? We believe the key to the Lord's thought here lies in the word "again": note the disciples' use of the same word in the following verse. The Lord was *trying* the disciples: "Let *us* go into Judea again." If we refer back to the closing verses of John 10 the force of this will be more evident. In 10:39 we read that His enemies in Judea "sought again to take him." Judea, then, was now the place of opposition and danger. When, then, the Lord said, "Let us go into *Judea* again," it was obviously a word of *testing*. And how this illustrates a common principle in the Lord's way of dealing with us! It is not the smooth and easy-going path which He selects for us. When we are led by Him it is usually into the place of testing and trial, the place which the flesh ever shrinks from.

"His disciples say unto him, Master, the Jews of late sought to stone thee; and goest thou thither again?" (11:8). The Greek is more definite and specific than the A.V. rendering here. What the disciples said was, "Master, the Jews *just now* sought to stone thee; and goest thou thither again?" The attempt of His enemies to stone Christ was still *present* before the eyes of the disciples, though they had now been some little time at Bethabara. The disciples could see neither the need nor the prudence of such a step. How strange the Lord's ways seem to His shortsighted people; how incapable is our natural intelligence to understand them! And how this manifests the folly of believers being guided by what men term "common sense." How much all of us need to heed constantly that word, "Trust in the Lord with all thine heart; and *lean not unto thine own understanding*. In all thy ways acknowledge him, and he shall direct thy paths" (Prov. 3:5, 6). God often leads His own into places which are puzzling and perplexing and where we are quite unable to perceive His purpose and object. How often are the servants of Christ today called upon to fill positions from which they naturally shrink, and which they would never have chosen for themselves. Let us ever remember that the One who is our Lord and Master knows infinitely better than we the best road for us to travel.

"Jesus answered, Are there not twelve hours in the day? If any man walk in the day, he stumbleth not, because he seeth the light of this world" (11:9). This verse has proved a puzzle to many, yet we believe its meaning can be definitely fixed. The first thing to bear in mind is that the Lord Jesus here was answering the timidity and unbelief of the disciples. They were apprehensive: to return to Judea, they supposed, was to invite certain death (cf. 11:16). Christ's immediate design, then, was to rebuke their fears. "Are there not twelve hours in the day?" That is, Has not the "day" a definitely *allotted* time? The span of the day is *measured,* and expires not before the number of hours by which *it is* measured have completed their course. The night comes not until the clock has ticked off each of the hours assigned to the day. The application of this well-known fact to the Lord's situation at that time is obvious.

A work had been given Him to do by the Father (Luke 2:49), and that work He *would* finish (John 17:4), and it was impossible that His enemies should take His life *before* its completion. In John 10:39 we are told that His enemies "sought again to take him," but "he *went forth* out of their hand"—not simply "escaped" as in the A.V. What the Lord here assures His disciples, is, that His death *could not* take place before the time *appointed* by the Father. The Lord had expressly affirmed the same thing on a previous occasion: "The same day there came certain of the Pharisees, saying unto him, Get thee out, and depart hence; for Herod will kill thee." And what was His reply? This, "Go ye, and tell that fox, Behold, I cast out demons, and I do cures today and tomorrow, and the third day I shall be perfected" (Luke 13:32)! "As a traveler has twelve hours for his day's journey, so also to Me there is a space of time appointed for My business" (Hess). What we have here in John 11:9 is parallel to His statement in 9:4—"I *must* work the works of him that sent me, while it is day"—"must" because the Father had decreed that He *should!*

This word of Christ to His disciples had more than a local significance: it enunciated a principle of general application. There is no need for us to enlarge upon it here, for we have already treated of it in our remarks upon 7:30. God has allotted to each man a time to do his life's work, and no calamity, no so-called accident can shorten it. Can man make the sun set one hour earlier? Neither can he shorten by an hour his life's day.

In the second part of the ninth verse the Lord announced another reason why it was impossible for men to shorten His life: "If any man walk in the day, he stumbleth not, because he seeth the light of this world." To walk in the day is to walk in the light of the sun, and such an one stumbleth not, for he is able to see the obstacles in his way and so circumvent them. Spiritually, this means, It is impossible that one should fall who is walking with God. To "walk in the day" signifies to walk in the presence of Him who is Light (I John 1:5), to walk in communion with Him, to walk in obedience to His will. None such *can* stumble, for *His* Word is a lamp unto our feet and a light unto our path. It is beautiful to see the application of this to the Lord Jesus in the present instance. When He got word that Lazarus was sick, He did not start at once for Bethany. Instead, He tarried where He was till *the Father's* time for Him to go had come. He *waited* for the "light" to guide Him – a true Israelite watching for the moving of the Cloud! Christ ever walked in the full light of God's known will. How impossible then for Him to "stumble."

"But if a man walk in the night, he stumbleth, because there is no light in him" (11:10). Very solemn and searching is this in its immediate application to the disciples. It was a *warning* against their refusing to accompany Him. Christ was the true Light, and if they continued not with Him they would be in the dark, and then "stumbling" was inevitable. The thought here is different from what we get at the close of 9:4. There Christ speaks of a "night" in which no man *could* "work"; here of a "night" in which no believer *should* "walk." The great lesson for us in these two verses is this, No fear of danger (or unpleasant consequences) must deter us from doing our duty. If the will of God clearly points in a certain direction our responsibility is to move in that direction unhesitatingly, and we may go with the double assurance that no power of the Enemy can shorten our life till the Divinely appointed task is done, and that such light will be vouchsafed us that no difficulties in the way will make us "stumble." What shall we say to such a blessed assurance? What but the words of the apostle Jude, "Now unto him that is able *to keep you from falling,* and to present you faultless before the presence of his glory with exceeding joy, to the only wise God our Saviour, be glory and majesty, dominion and power, both now and ever. Amen" (vv. 24, 25).

The following questions are designed to help the interested student for our next lesson: —

1. Death is likened to "sleeping," v. 11: what thoughts are suggested by this figure?
2. Why did the disciples misunderstand Christ, v. 13?
3. Why was Christ "glad" for the disciples sake, v. 15?
4. What is signified by the "four days," v. 17?
5. Why are we told of the nearness of Jerusalem to Bethany, v. 18?
6. Why "resurrection" before "life" in v. 25?
7. What is the force of "shall never die," v. 26?

CHAPTER THIRTY-EIGHT

Christ Raising Lazarus (Continued)

John 11:11-27

The following is a suggested Analysis of the passage which is to be before us: –

1. Christ announces Lazarus' death, but the disciples misunderstand Him, vv. 11-13.
2. Christ rejoices for their sake that He had been absent from Bethany, vv. 14, 15.
3. Thomas' melancholy devotion, v. 16.
4. Lazarus in the grave four days already, v. 17.
5. The nearness of Jerusalem to Bethany, v. 18.
6. Many Jews come to comfort the sisters, v. 19.
7. The conversation between Christ and Martha, vv. 20-27.

In the previous lesson we have seen how the Lord Jesus received a touching message that Lazarus was dying; in the passage now before us we behold Him making for Bethany, Lazarus having died and been buried in the interval. The central thing in John 11 is Christ made known as the resurrection and the life, and everything in it only serves to bring out by way of contrast the blessedness of this revelation. Resurrection can be displayed only where death has come in, and what is so much emphasized here is the desolation which death brings and man's helplessness in the presence of it. First, Lazarus himself is dead; then Thomas speaks of the disciples accompanying the Lord to Bethany that they may die with Him (11:16); then Martha comes before us; and though in the presence of Christ, she could think only of the death of her brother (11:21); it was the same with Mary (11:32); finally, the Jews who had come to comfort the bereaved sisters are seen "weeping" (11:33), and even as the Lord stands before the grave, they have no thought that He was about to release the tomb's victim (11:37). What a background was all this for Christ to display His wondrous glory!

It is not difficult for us to discern here behind the dark shadows that which is far more solemn and tragic. Physical death is but the figure, as well as the effect, of another death infinitely more dreadful. The natural man is dead in trespasses and sins. The wages of sin is death, and when the first man sinned he received those fearful wages. In the day that Adam ate of the forbidden fruit he *died,* died spiritually, as a penal infliction. And Adam died spiritually not only as a private individual, but as the head and public representative of his race. Just as the severing of the trunk of a tree from its roots, means (in a short time) the death of each of its boughs, twigs and leaves, so the fall of Adam dragged down with him every member of the human race. It is for this reason that every one born into this world enters it "*alienated* from the life of God" (Eph. 4:18).

Yes, the natural man, the world over, is spiritually *dead.* He is alive worldwards, selfwards, sinwards, but dead Godwards. It is not that there is a spark of life within which by careful cultivation or religious exercises may be fanned into a flame; he is completely devoid of Divine life. He needs to be born again; an altogether new life, than the one he possesses by nature, must be imparted to him, if ever he is to enter the kingdom of God. The sinner's condition is far, far worse than he has any idea of, or than the great majority of the *doctors* of divinity suppose. Of what use is a "remedy" to one who is *dead?* and yet the thoughts of very few rise any higher when they think and talk of the Gospel. Of what use is it to reason and argue with a corpse? and yet that is precisely what the sinner is from the standpoint of God. "Then, why preach the Word to sinners at all, if they are incapable of hearing it?" is the question which will naturally occur to the reader. Sad, sad indeed that such a question is asked at this late day—sad, because of the God-dishonouring ignorance which it displays.

No intelligent servant of God preaches the Word because he imagines that the will and mind of the sinner is capable of responding to it, any more than when God commanded Ezekiel to "Prophesy upon these *bones,* and say unto *them,* O ye dry bones, hear the word of the Lord" (Ezek. 37:4), he supposed the objects of *his* message were capable of responding. "Well, why preach at all?" First, because God has *commanded* us to do so, and who are we to call into question *His* wisdom? Second, because the very words we are commanded to preach, "*they* are spirit, and they are life" (John 6:63). The Word we are to "hold forth" is "the word of *life*" (Phil. 2:16). The new birth is "*not* of blood (by natural descent), *nor* of the will of the flesh (his own volition), *nor* of the will of man (the preacher's persuasion), but OF GOD" (John 1:13), and the seed which God uses to produce the new birth is His own Word (James 1:18).

Now this is what is so strikingly and so perfectly illustrated here in John 11. Lazarus was dead, and that he *had* died was unmistakably evidenced by the fact that his body was already corrupting. In like manner, the spiritual death of the natural man is plainly manifested by the corruptions of his heart and life. In the opening paragraph we have sought to bring out how that which is emphasized here in John 11 is the utter helplessness of man in the presence of death. And this is what the servant of God needs to lay hold of in its spiritual application. If it was only a matter of stupidity in the sinner, *we* might overcome *that* by clearly reasoned statements of the truth. If it was simply a stubborn will that stood in the way of the sinner's salvation, *we* could depend upon *our* powers of persuasion. If it was merely that the sinner's soul was sick, *we* could induce him to accept some "remedy." But in the presence of *death* we are impotent.

"All of this sounds very discouraging," says the reader. So much the better if it results in bringing us upon our faces before God. Nothing is more healthful than to be emptied of self-sufficiency. The sooner we reach this place the better. "For we," said Paul, "have *no confidence* in the flesh" (Phil. 3:3). The quicker we are made to realize our own helplessness, the more likely are we to seek help from God. The sooner we recognize that "the flesh profiteth *nothing*" (John 6:63), the readier shall we be to cry unto God for *His* all-sufficient grace. It is not until we cease to depend upon ourselves that we begin to depend upon God. "With men this *is* impossible; but with God all things are possible" (Matt. 19:26), and this, be it remembered, was said by Christ in answer to the disciples' query, "*Who* then can be saved?"

Here, then, is where light breaks in. Here is where the "glory of God" (John 11:4) shines forth. *Man* may be helpless before death, not so *God*. Lazarus could not raise himself, nor could his beloved sisters and sorrowing friends bring him back from the grave. Ah! but He who is, Himself, "the resurrection and the life" comes on the scene, and all is altered. And *what* does He do? Why, He did that which must have seemed surpassingly strange to all who beheld Him. He cried to the dead man, "Come forth." But what was the use of doing *that*? Had Lazarus the power in himself *to* come forth? Most certainly not—had Mary or Martha, or any of the apostles cried, "Lazarus, come forth" *that* would have been unmistakably evidenced. No man's voice is able to pierce the depths of the tomb. But it was One who was more than man, who now spake, and He said, "Come forth" not because Lazarus was *capable* of doing so, but because it was *life-giving* Voice which spake. The same omnipotent lips which called a world into existence by the mere fiat of His mouth, now commanded the grave to give up its victim. It was the Word of *power* which penetrated the dark portals of that sepulchre. And here, dear reader, is the comforting, inspiring, and satisfying truth for the Christian worker. We are sent forth to preach the Word to lost and dead sinners, because, under the sovereign application of the Holy Spirit, that Word is "the word of *life*." Our duty is to cry unto God daily and mightily that He may be pleased to make it such to some, at least, of those to whom we speak.

Before we come to the actual raising of Lazarus, our chapter records many interesting and instructive details which serve to heighten the beauty of its central feature. The Lord Jesus was in no hurry; with perfect composure He moved along in Divine dignity and yet human compassion to the grief-stricken home at Bethany. At every point two things are prominent: the imperfections of man and the perfections of Christ.

"These things said he: and after that he saith unto them, Our friend Lazarus sleepeth" (11:11). The "these things" are the declaration that the sickness of Lazarus was for the glory of God, that the Son of God might be glorified thereby (11:4); His expressed intention of returning to Judea (11:7); and His avowed assurance that there could be no "stumbling" seeing that He ever walked in the unclouded light of the Father's countenance (11:9). In these three things we learn the great principles which regulated the life of Christ—lowliness, dependence, obedience. He now announced that Lazarus was no longer in the land of the living, referring to his death under the figure of "sleep." The figure is a very beautiful one, and a number of most blessed thoughts are suggested by it. It is a figure frequently employed in the Scriptures, both in the Old and New Testaments: in the former it is applied to saved and unsaved: but in the N.T. it is used only of the Lord's people.* In the N.T. it occurs in such well-known passages as I Cor. 15:20, 51: "Now is Christ risen from the dead, and become the firstfruits of them that *slept*. . . . Behold, I show you a mystery; We shall not all *sleep*, but we shall all be changed"; and I Thess. 4:14, 5:10: "For if we believe that Jesus died and rose again, even so them also which *sleep* in Jesus will God bring with him. . . . Who died for us, that, whether we wake or sleep, we should live together with him." Below we give some of the leading thoughts suggested by this figure:—

First, sleep is perfectly harmless. In sleep there is nothing to fear, but, much to be thankful for. It is a friend and not a foe. So, for the Christian, is it with death. Said David, "Yea, though I walk through the valley of the shadow of death I will fear *no* evil." Such ought to be the triumphant language of every child of God. The "sting" has gone from death (I Cor. 15:56, 57), and has no more power to hurt one of Christ's redeemed, than a hornet has after its sting has been extracted.

Second, sleep comes as a welcome relief after the sorrows and toils of the day. As the wise man declared, "The sleep of a

* The only apparent exception is the case of Jairus' daughter.

labouring man is *sweet*" (Eccl. 5:12). Death, for the believer, is simply the portal through which he passes from this scene of sin and turmoil to the paradise of bliss. As I Cor. 3:22 tells us, "death" is *ours*. Sleep is a merciful provision, not appreciated nearly as much as it should be. The writer learned this lesson some years ago when he witnessed a close friend, who was suffering severely, seeking sleep in vain for over a week. Equally merciful is death for one who is prepared. Try to imagine David still alive on earth after three thousand years! Such a protracted existence in this world of sin and suffering would probably have driven him hopelessly crazy long ago. How thankful we ought to be that we have not the longevity of the antediluvians!

Third, in sleep we lie down to rise again. It is of but brief duration; a few hours snatched from our working time, then to awaken and rise to a new day. In like manner, death is but a sleep and resurrection, an awakening. "And many of them that *sleep* in the dust of the earth shall *awake,* some to everlasting life, and some to shame and everlasting contempt" (Dan. 12:2). On the glorious resurrection morn the dead in Christ shall be awakened, to sleep no more, but live forever throughout the perfect Day of God.

Fourth, sleep is a time of rest. The work of the day is exchanged for sweet repose. This is what death means for the Christian: "Blessed are the dead which die in the Lord from henceforth: Yea, saith the Spirit, that they may *rest* from their labours" (Rev. 14:13). This applies only to the "intermediate state," between death and resurrection. When we receive our glorified bodies there will be new ministries for us to engage in, for it is written, "His servants shall *serve* him" (Rev. 22:3).

Fifth, sleep shuts out the sorrows of life. In sleep we are mercifully unconscious of the things which exercise us throughout the day. The repose of night affords us welcome relief from that which troubles us by day. It is so in death. Not that the believer is unconscious, but that those in paradise know nothing of the tears which are shed on earth. Scripture seems to indicate that there is one exception in their knowledge of what is transpiring down here: the salvation of sinners is heralded on high (Luke 15:7, 10).

Sixth, one reason perhaps why death is likened to a sleep is to emphasize the *ease* with which the Lord will quicken us. To raise the dead (impossible as it appears to the skeptic) will be simpler to Him than arousing a sleeper. It is a singular thing that nothing so quickly awakens one as being addressed by the voice. So we are told "the hour is coming, in the which all that are in the graves shall hear his *voice*" (John 5:28).

Seventh, sleep is a time when the body is fitted for the duties of the morrow. When the awakened sleeper arises he is refreshed and invigorated, and ready for what lies before him. In like manner, the resurrected believer will be endued with a new power. The limitations of his mortal body will no longer exist. That which was sown in weakness shall be raised in power.

But O how vastly different is it for one who dies in his sins. The very reverse of what we have said above will be his portion. Instead of death delivering him from the sorrows of this life, it shall but introduce him to that fearful place whose air is filled with weeping and wailing and gnashing of teeth. It is true that sinners too shall be raised from the dead, but it will be unto "the resurrection of damnation." It will be in order to receive bodies in which they will suffer still more acutely the eternal torments of the lake of fire. To all such, death will be far worse than the most frightful nightmare. And O unsaved reader, there is but a *step* between thee and death. Your life hangs by a slender thread, which may snap at any moment. Be warned then, ere it is too late. Flee, even now, from the wrath to come. Seek ye the Lord while He may be found, for there is *no* hope beyond the grave.

"After that he saith unto them, Our friend Lazarus sleepeth; but I go, that I may awake him out of sleep" (11:11). What marvelous condescension was it for the Lord of glory to call a poor worm of the earth His "friend"! But note He said, "*Our* friend." This, we believe, was a word of rebuke to His fearful and distrustful disciples; Our friend—yours, as well as Mine. He has also shown *you* kindness. You have professed to love him; will you now leave him to languish! His sisters are sorrowing, will you ignore them in their extremity! That is why He here says "I go"—contrast the "us" in vv. 7 and 15. *Our* friend—*I go*. I to whom the danger is greatest. *I* am ready to go. It was both a rebuke and an appeal. He had told them that the sickness of Lazarus was in order that the Son of God might be glorified thereby (11:4), would they be indifferent as to *how* that glory would be displayed!

"I go that I may awaken"—go, even though to His own death. He "pleased not himself." Thoughts of His own personal safety would no more retard Him than He had allowed personal affection to hasten Him. What is before Him was the Father's glory, and no considerations of personal consequences would keep Him from being about His Father's business. The moment had come for the Father's glory to shine forth through the Son: therefore, His "I go," sharply contrasted from the "he abode two days still" of 11:6. He was going to awaken Lazarus: "None can awaken Lazarus out of *this* sleep, but He who made Lazarus. Every mouse or gnat can raise us from that other sleep; none but an omnipotent power from this." (R. Hall).

"Then said his disciples, Lord, if he sleep, he shall do well. Howbeit Jesus spake of his death: but they thought that he had spoken of taking of rest in sleep" (11:12, 13). It is clear from their language that the disciples had not understood the Lord: they supposed He meant that Lazarus was recovering. Yet, the figure He had used was not obscure; it was one which the Old Testament scriptures should have made them thoroughly familiar with. Why then, had they failed to perceive His meaning? The answer is not hard to find. They were still timid and hesitant of returning to Judea. But why should that have clouded their minds? Because they were occupied with temporal circumstances. It was "stoning" they were concerned about, the stoning of their beloved Lord—though if He was stoned, there was not much likelihood that they would escape. And when our thoughts are centered upon temporal things, or when selfish motives control us, our spiritual vision is eclipsed. It is only as our eye is single (to God's glory) that our whole body is full of light.

"Then said Jesus unto them plainly, Lazarus is dead" (11:14). What a proof was this of the omniscience of Christ. He *knew* that Lazarus was already dead, though the disciples supposed he was recovering from his sickness. No second message had come from Bethany to announce the decease of the brother of Martha and Mary. And none was needed. Though in the form of a servant, in the likeness of man, Christ was none other than the Mighty God, and clear proof of this did He here furnish. How blessed to know that our Saviour is none other than Immanuel!

"And I am glad for your sakes that I was not there, to the intent ye may believe; nevertheless let us go unto him" (11:15). But *why* should Christ be glad for the disciples' sake that He was absent from Bethany at the time Lazarus was sinking? Because the disciples would now be able to witness a *higher* manifestation of His glory, than what they otherwise would had He been present while Lazarus was sick. But what difference would His presence there have made? This: it is impossible to escape the inference that had the Lord Jesus been there, Lazarus had not died – impossible not only because His words to the disciples plainly implied it, but also because of what other scriptures teach us on that point. The implication is plain: what the Lord unmistakably signified here was that it was inconsistent with *His presence* that one should die in it. It is a most striking thing that there is no trace of any one having died in the presence of the Prince of Life (Acts 3:15). And furthermore, the Gospel records show that whenever Christ came into the presence of death, death at once fled before Him! As to the non-possibility of any one dying in the presence of Christ, we have an illustration in connection with what took place in Gethsemane. When the officers came to arrest the Saviour, Peter drew his sword and smote the high priest's servant, with the obvious intention of slaying him. But in vain. Instead of cleaving his head asunder he simply severed an ear! More striking still is the case of the two thieves who were crucified with Him: *They* died *after* He had given up *His* spirit! As to death fleeing at the approach of Christ we have a most remarkable example in the case of the widow's son of Nain. Here it was different than in the instances of Jairus' daughter and the brother of Martha and Mary. Each of these had appealed to Him but here it was otherwise. A man was about to be buried, and as the funeral cortege was on the way to the cemetery, the Lord Jesus approached, and *touching the bier* He said to the young man, "Arise," and at once "the dead sat up, and began to speak" (Luke 7:14, 15)!

"And I am glad for your sakes that I was not there, to the intent ye may believe" (11:15). How perfect are the ways of God! If Martha and Mary had had *their* wish granted, not only would *they* (and Lazarus too) have been denied a far greater blessing, but the disciples would have missed that which must have strengthened their faith. And too, Christ would have been deprived of this opportunity which allowed Him to give the mightiest display of His power that He ever made prior to His own death; and the whole Church as well would have been the loser! How this should show us both the wisdom and goodness of God in thwarting *our* wishes, in order that His own infinitely better will may be done.

This verse also teaches a most important lesson as to *how* the Lord develops faith in His own. The hearts of the disciples were instructed and illuminated *gradually*. There was no sudden and violent action made upon them. They did not attain to their measure of grace all at once. Their eyes were slowly opened to perceive who and what Christ was; it was by repeated manifestations of Divine power and human compassion that they came to recognize in Him a Messiah of a far higher order than what they had been taught to expect. John 2:11 illustrates the same principle: "This beginning of miracles did Jesus in Cana of Galilee, and manifested forth his glory; and his *disciples believed* on him." And God deals with us in the same way. There is, in the development of our faith, first the blade, then the ear, then the full corn in the ear. Compare the development of Abraham's faith through the increasingly severe trials through which God caused him to pass.

"Nevertheless let us go unto him" (11:15). Lazarus was *dead*, and yet the Lord speaks of going to *him*. "O love, stronger than death! The grave cannot separate Christ and His friends. Other friends accompany us to the brink of the grave, and then they leave us. 'Neither life nor death can separate from the love of Christ'" (Burkitt). Lazarus could not come to Christ, but Christ would go to him.

"Then said Thomas, which is called Didymus, unto his fellow-disciples, Let us also go, that we may die with him" (11:16). No wonder that he said this to his fellow-disciples rather than to the Lord. Very melancholy was his utterance. Thomas was a man who looked on the dark side of things. Lazarus is dead, Christ is going to die, let *us* go and die too! And this, after the Lord had said, "I go, that I may awaken him out of sleep" (11:11)! How difficult is it for man to enter into the thoughts of God! Christ was going to Bethany to give life. Thomas speaks only of dying. Evident is it that he had quite failed to understand what Christ had said in 11:9. How much of unbelief there is even in a believer! And yet we must not overlook the spirit of devotion which Thomas' words breathed: Thomas had rather die than be separated from the Saviour; Though he was lacking in intelligence, he was deeply attached to the person of the Lord Jesus.

"Let us also go, that we may die with him" (11:16). "This was the language of a despairing and despondent mind, which could see nothing but dark clouds in the picture. The very man who afterwards could not believe that his Master had risen again, and thought the news too good to be true, is just the one of the twelve who thinks that if they go back to Judea they must all die! Things such as these are deeply instructive, and are doubtless recorded for our learning. They show us that the grace of God in conversion does not so re-mold a man as to leave no trace of his natural bent of character. The sanguine do not altogether cease to be sanguine, nor the desponding to be despondent, when they pass from death to life, and become true Christians. This shows us that we must make large allowances for natural temperament in forming our estimate of individual Christians. We must not expect all God's children to be exactly one and the same. Each tree in a forest has its own peculiarities of shape and growth, and yet all at a distance look one mass of leaf and verdure. Each member of Christ's body has his own distinct bias, and yet all in the main are led by one Spirit and love one Lord. The two sisters Martha and Mary, the apostles Peter and John and Thomas, were certainly very unlike one another in many respects. But they all had one point in common: they loved Christ and were His friends" (Bishop Ryle).

"Then when Jesus came, he found that he had lain in the grave four days already" (11:17). Christ did not correct the error of Thomas, but calmly left the truth to do, in due time, its own work. The reference here to the "four days" makes it evident that in John 11 we have something more than a typical picture of the spiritual condition of the nation of Israel. From a doctrinal viewpoint, the condition of Lazarus in the grave accurately portrayed the state of the natural man dead in trespasses and sins, a mass of corruption. It is true that Lazarus was a Jew, but "as in water face answereth to face, *so* the heart of man to man" (Prov. 27:19). The third chapter of Romans shows plainly that the state of Israel was also the state of the Gentiles. The "day" here, as usually in this Gospel, signifies (in its deeper meaning) a thousand years. "Four days," had man been in the place of death—alienation from God—for there were exactly four thousand years from the fall of Adam to the coming of Christ. God allowed the awful state of man to be completely manifested before He sent Christ to this earth.

"Then when Jesus came, he found that he had lain in the grave four days already." Note that this verse does not say "When Jesus came *to Bethany*, he found that *Lazarus* had lain in the grave four days already," but instead, "When Jesus came, he found that he had lain in the grave four days already." The Holy Spirit had a reason for putting it so indefinitely, and that reason we have sought to show above. When "Jesus came" to this earth, "he," fallen man, had been "in the grave"—the place of death—"four days already"—four thousand years. O the minute and marvelous accuracy of Scripture!

"Now Bethany was nigh unto Jerusalem, about fifteen furlongs off" (11:18). There seems to be a double reason why this topographical reference is made here. First, it explains why the "many Jews" had come to Bethany to comfort Martha and Mary (11:19). Second, it shows how very near to Jerusalem the raising of Lazarus occurred. It was less than two miles from the headquarters of Judaism, within walking distance, almost within sight of the Temple. All room for excuse was thereby removed for any ignorance in the leaders of the nation as to the identity of the person of Christ. His last and greatest "sign" was given before many eye-witnesses almost at the very doors of the Sanhedrin. Thus in this seemingly unimportant detail the Holy Spirit has emphasized the deep guilt of those who were most responsible for rejecting Christ.

"And many of the Jews came to Martha and Mary, to comfort them concerning their brother" (11:19). And poor comforters they must have made. They are in view again in 11:37. When they witnessed the tears of the Lord Jesus by the graveside of Lazarus, they said, "Could not this man, which opened the eyes of the blind, have caused that even this man should not have died?" While no doubt they looked upon Christ as a miracle-worker, it is clear they had no apprehension of the glory of His person—"this man" shows that. Furthermore, it never seems to have entered their minds that He was capable of raising the dead. How then could *they* "comfort" the sorrowing sisters? It is impossible for an unbeliever to minister real comfort to a child of God. God alone can bind up the brokenhearted. Only the Divine Comforter can speak peace to the troubled soul, and not knowing Him, an unsaved person is incapable of pointing another to the one Source of consolation and rest.

"And *many* of the Jews came to Martha and Mary, to comfort them concerning their brother." Mark here the over-ruling wisdom of God. By waiting four days before raising Lazarus, a much greater number witnessed his resurrection, and thus the miracle of Christ was more decisively authenticated, for it would be given greater publicity. The Hand which controls all things so shaped events that it was impossible for the Sanhedrin to discredit this last great "sign" of Israel's Messiah. Here then was a further reason for the "therefore" in 11:6. God not only has a good reason for each of His delays, but generally a manifold reason. Many various ends are accomplished by each of *His* actions. Not only wicked but utterly senseless are our criticisms of His ways.

"Then Martha, as soon as she heard that Jesus was coming, went and met him" (11:20). This action was thoroughly characteristic of Martha. Even though the Lord Jesus was not yet come into the village (11:30), she advances to meet Him. The verses that follow show us something of the condition of her mind at this time. "But Mary sat still in the house." "It is impossible not to see the characteristic temperament of each sister coming out here. Martha—active, stirring, busy, demonstrative—cannot wait, but runs impulsively to meet Jesus. Mary—quiet, gentle, pensive, meditative, meek—sits passively at home" (Bishop Ryle). What marks of truth are these minor details! How evident that the same One who inspired Luke 10 moved John to record these little marks of character here!

"Then said Martha unto Jesus, Lord, if thou hadst been here, my brother had not died" (11:21). There are some who think that Martha spoke in a spirit of petulancy, that she was reproaching the Lord for not having responded more promptly to the message sent Him while He was in Bethabara. But we think this is a mistake. Rather do we regard Martha's words as a sorrowful lament, the telling out the grief of her heart. Martha's words show plainly what had been uppermost in the minds of the sisters during those trying four days—note that Mary says almost the same thing when she met Christ (11:32). There was a strange mingling of the natural and the spiritual, of faith and unbelief in this statement of Martha's. She had confidence in Christ, yet she limited His power. She believed that her brother had not died, no matter how low he were, had Christ only been present; yet the thought never seems to have entered her mind that He was able to raise Lazarus now that he was dead. "Lord, I *believe*; help thou mine *unbelief*" would well have suited her condition at that time. And how often it is appropriate for us! Alas, that it should be so. The Christian is a strange paradox; a dual personality indeed.

"Then said Martha unto Jesus, Lord, if thou hadst been here, my brother had not died." That which is reprehensible in this utterance of Martha is that she was making distance a limitation of Christ's power. And have not *we* often been guilty of the same thing? Have not we often envied those who were in Palestine during the time that the Word tabernacled among men? But now, alas, He is absent; and Heaven seems so far away! But it is not: it was not too far distant for Stephen to see right into it! But suppose it were; what then? Do we not have the precious promise of the Saviour, "Lo, I am *with you* alway, even unto the end of the age"! But, says the reader, Christ is *bodily* absent. True, and that was what had exercised Martha. Yet it ought not; had not the Lord healed both the centurion's servant and the nobleman's son *at a distance* by His word! He had; but memory failed Martha in the hour of trial and suffering. Alas, that this is so often the case with us.

"But I know, that even now, whatsoever thou wilt ask of God, God will give it thee" (11:22). It is this additional word which indicates that there was a different meaning in Martha's words of 11:21 from Mary's in 11:32. Surely Martha must have said what she did here without any deliberation. With characteristic impulsiveness she most probably uttered the first thoughts which came into her mind. And yet we can hardly conceive of one making such a statement if she knew Christ as God the Son. The word she used for "*ask* God" indicates that she did not recognize that Christ was the One in whom dwelt all the fulness of the Godhead bodily. In New Testament Greek there are two words for "ask." The first, "aiteo," signifies a familiar asking. The second, "eroteo," means a supplicatory petitioning. The one is suited to express the favor asked of the Creator by the creature, the other for a son's asking of the Father. The former is never used of Christ with the Father except here on the lips of Martha! It was a dragging down of Christ to the level of the prophets. It was the inevitable outcome of having sat so little at His feet listening to His words.

"Jesus said unto her, Thy brother shall rise again" (11:23). These were the first words of the Lord Jesus now that He had arrived at the confines of Bethany. He was about to give "beauty for ashes, the oil of joy for mourning, the garment of praise for the spirit of heaviness" (Isa. 61:3); but not yet did He specifically announce His gracious purpose. Instead, He first gave the broad and general promise, "Thy brother shall rise again," without announcing when or how. It is the Lord's way to draw out by degrees His grace in the hearts of His own. He said enough to encourage hope and strengthen faith, but not sufficient to exclude exercise of heart. Light is given us upon the great mysteries of life gradually. "Here a *little* and there a *little*." Faith has to be disciplined, and knowledge is imparted only as the heart is able to receive it. "I have yet many things to say unto you, but ye cannot bear them *now*" (John 16:12) still holds good. Unto the Corinthians Paul had to say, "And I, brethren, could not speak unto you as unto spiritual, but as unto carnal, even as unto babes in Christ. I have fed you with milk, and not with meat: for hitherto ye *were not able* to bear it, neither yet now are ye able" (I Cor. 3:1, 2). Alas that *we* are so dull and make such slow progress in the things of God.

"Martha saith unto him, I know that he shall rise again in the resurrection at the last day" (11:24). Martha supposed that He was gently setting aside her implied request that He would "ask of God," and that He was pointing her forward to a future and far-distant hope. Poor Martha! As yet she had learned little from the Lord Jesus. She had nothing better than the common hope of Jews — the resurrection of the dead "at the last day." Does not this suggest another reason why the Holy Spirit tells us in 11:18 that "Bethany was *nigh* unto Jerusalem" — less than two miles away. Martha was still under the influence of Judaism! But these words of hers also contain a warning for us. Martha, like the woman at the well, understood not the *nearness* of the benefit. In each case, half despondingly, they put it into the future. To the Samaritan woman Christ said, "The hour cometh, *and now is,* when the true worshippers shall worship the Father in spirit and in truth: for the Father seeketh such to worship him." To this she replied, "I know that Messiah cometh, which is called Christ: *when he is come,* he will tell us all things." To Martha He had said, "Thy brother shall rise again," and she replied: "I know that he shall rise again in the resurrection *at the last day.*" Each had only the vague, inoperative idea of a future and final good; whereas He spoke to each of a *present* blessing. It is easier to believe things which are in the far off (which occasion us no exercise of heart!) than it is to appropriate now that which ministers comfort and strength for the present trial. It makes less demand upon faith to believe that in a future day we shall receive glorified bodies, than to rest now on the heartening assurance that, "They that wait upon the Lord shall renew their strength."

"Jesus saith unto her, I am the resurrection, and the life" (11:25). This was like what the Lord said to the woman at the well. When she had, by her word, *postponed* the blessing, He answered at once, "I am that speaketh unto you"; so now He says to Martha, "I am the resurrection, and the life." Here is something of vital importance for our souls. It is not simply that He corrected the vision of these women by turning them from the distant future to the immediate present, but that He fixes their eyes upon Himself! It is not future *events* but the *Person* of the Lord, ever present with us, that we need most to be occupied with. Strength, blessing, comfort, are imparted just so far as we are taken up with Christ Himself.

"I am the resurrection, and the life." "See how the Lord proceeds to instruct and to elevate her mind; how graciously He bears with her passing fretfulness; how tenderly He touches the still open wounds; how He leads her from grieving over her brother to believe yet more fully in her Saviour; how He raises her from dwelling on Lazarus dead, to repose implicitly in Him who is the Lord of life; how He diverts her from thinking only of a remote and general resurrection to confide in Him who is even at this present, the Resurrection and the Life" (Dr. G. Brown). So too does He remove our ignorance, help our unbelief, and bear with our peevishness. Wondrous condescension, matchless patience, fathomless grace! And how the realization of these should humble us, and cause us to blush for very shame! "Lord, increase our faith" in Thyself.

"I am the resurrection, and the life." This is what He *is*, in His own peerless Person. What He would here press upon Martha was that all power resided in Himself. Soon she would witness a display of this, but in the meantime the Lord would occupy her with what, or rather *who* He was in Himself. Blessed, thrice blessed is it for the soul to lay hold of this sustaining and satisfying truth. Infinitely better is it for us to be occupied with the Giver than His gifts.

But why this order: the resurrection *and* the life? For at least a threefold reason. First, this is the *doctrinal* order. In *spiritual* experience Christ is to us the resurrection *before* He is the life. The sinner is dead in trespasses and sins, in the grave of guilt, separated from God. He has his dwelling "among the tombs" (Mark 5:3). His first need is to be brought out of this awful place, and this occurs at his regeneration. The new birth is a passing from death unto life (John 5:24); it is the being brought on to resurrection ground. The same double thought of leaving the place of death and receiving resurrection life is found again in 5:25: "The hour is coming, and now is, when *the dead* shall hear the voice of the Son of God: and they that hear shall *live*." Lazarus in the grave, raised to life by the word of Christ, gives us a perfect illustration of God's mighty work of grace in the hearts of His elect.

Second, This was the *dispensational* order. The Old Testament saints were all in the grave when He who is "The Life" came down to this earth. Therefore it is in *resurrection* power that *they* will know the Christ of God. But believers in Palestine at the time when the eternal Word tabernacled among men knew Him as the Living One, God manifest in the flesh. And yet it was not until after the Cross that they knew Him as such in the fullest sense of the word. It was not until the day of His own resurrection that He breathed on the disciples and said, "Receive ye the Holy Spirit" (20:22). It is the life of a risen and never-dying Saviour which the believer now has as an inalienable and eternal possession. Christ *is* the resurrection *because* He is the life, and He *is* the Life *because* He is the Resurrection.

Third, This will be the *prophetic* order. When the Lord Jesus leaves His Father's throne and descends into the air, His people will be found in two great companies; by far the greater part will be (as to their bodies) asleep in the grave; the others will be alive on the earth. But "flesh and blood" cannot inherit the kingdom of God. The living saints will need to be "changed," just as much as the sleeping saints will need raising. Therefore to the one Christ will be the resurrection, to the other the life. The two companies of believers are clearly distinguished in I Thess. 4:16, "The dead in Christ shall rise first; then we which are alive and remain shall be caught up together with them in the clouds, to meet the Lord in the air." The "changing" of the living believers is mentioned in I Cor. 15:51. It is to this "change" of believers who have not entered the grave that Rom. 8:11 refers: "But if the Spirit of him that raised up Jesus from the dead dwell in you, he that raised up Christ from the dead shall also quicken (give life to) your *mortal bodies* by his Spirit that dwelleth in you." Marvellously full were these words of Christ, "I am the resurrection and the life."

"He that believeth in me, though he were dead, yet shall he live" (11:25). This was brought in to show that what Christ had just spoken of was elective and not common to all men as such. He was referring to something peculiar to His own: "he that believeth" *limits* the first part of the verse to God's elect. The resurrection of unbelievers, not to "life" but to the second death, where, however they shall *exist* in conscious torment forever and ever, is mentioned in other scriptures such as Dan. 12:2; John 5:29; Rev. 20, etc.

"He that believeth in me, though he were dead, yet shall he live." The Greek here is very explicit and impressive. The verb, "though he *were* dead," is in the past tense, and with it is coupled a *present* participle, "yet shall he *live,*" i.e. continue to live; but this, be it noted, is predicated of one who believes. How this word of Christ tells of the indestructibility of faith—its ever-living, never-dying character! Primarily, this was a message of comfort to Martha; it went beyond what He had said to her in 11:23. First He said, "Thy brother shall rise again"; next He directed attention to Himself as "the resurrection and the life"; now He intimates that though Lazarus had died, yet, because he was a believer, he should live. "Because I live, ye shall live also" (14:19) we regard as a parallel promise.

"And whosoever liveth and believeth in me shall never die" (11:26). At the close of the previous verse Christ had referred to physical resurrection, bodily life; here, He speaks of death in its ultimate sense. Rev. 20:6 repeats the same blessed truth: "Blessed and holy is he that hath part in the first resurrection: on such the second death *hath no power*." At the close of the previous verse the Lord Jesus had spoken of believers who had fallen asleep—they shall live. But here He speaks of living believers—they shall never die. The Lord had made the same assertion on a previous occasion: "If a man keep my saying, he shall *never* see death."

"Believest thou this?" (11:26). Every Divine communication challenges the heart to which it is made. We understand Christ's "this" to include all that He had said in 11:25, 26. "*Believest* thou this?" Have you really laid hold of it? How little we grasp that which has been presented to us. How little we enter into what we believe in a half-*hearted* and general way! The sequel (11:39) clearly shows that Martha had not *really* "believed" what Christ here said to her—a most searching warning for us. Much of what we *thought* we held is found to have made no impression upon us when the hour of testing comes.

"She saith unto him, Yea, Lord: I believe that Thou art the Christ, the Son of God, which should come into the world" (11:27). Most of the commentators are quite astray here. They look upon this utterance of Martha's as an evidence that the mists of doubt had now disappeared and that at last her faith had come out into the full sunlight. But what we read of in 11:39 clearly refutes such a view, and what is before us here must be interpreted in harmony with her final words at the grave itself. How then are we to understand her utterance in 11:27? Pressed as she was by the searching question in the previous verse, it seems to us that she fell back on a general answer, which affirmed her belief that the Lord Jesus was the promised Messiah. Having confessed Him as such, she at once went her way. She felt there was a depth to the Lord's words which she was quite incapable of fathoming. And here we must stop.

Let the interested reader ponder the following questions to prepare him for the next lesson:—

1. Why did Martha leave Christ and seek out her sister, v. 28?
2. What does v. 30 reveal to us about Christ?
3. Why did Jesus weep, v. 35?
4. What is the meaning of the "therefore," v. 38?
5. Why were *they* bidden to remove the stone, v. 39?
6. What is the spiritual significance of v. 44?

CHAPTER THIRTY-NINE

CHRIST RAISING LAZARUS (Concluded)

John 11:28-44

The following is submitted as an Analysis of the passage which is to be before us:—

1. Mary goes to meet Jesus, vv. 28-30, 32.
2. The Jews follow her, v. 31.
3. Jesus groaning and weeping, vv. 33-35.
4. The comments of the Jews, vv. 36-38.
5. Martha's unbelief and Christ's rebuke, vv. 39, 40.
6. Jesus praying and praising, vv. 41, 42.
7. The raising of Lazarus, vv. 43, 44.

The central design of John's Gospel is to present Christ to us as the Eternal Word become flesh, the Lord of glory in the likeness of men. Two things are made prominent throughout: His Divine dignity and His human perfections. Wonderfully perfect is the blending of these in the God-man: everything is there in Him to draw out our hearts in adoring love and reverent worship. Here we are shown His mighty power, and also His blessed tenderness. Here we behold not only His absolute authority, but also His entire dependency. It is not only that we gaze upon one of the Persons of the Holy Trinity, come down from heaven to earth, but also on One who entered fully into the conditions and circumstances of men, sin only excepted. Strikingly do these two lines of truth meet in John 11. The very chapter which chronicles His mightiest "sign" reveals the principles by which He walked—submission, dependence, obedience. Side by side with the record of His omnipotent voice calling the dead to life again, do we read of Him groaning and weeping. Absolutely unique is this wondrous Person.

The blending of Christ's *Divine* glories and *human* perfections meet us at every turn in this fourth Gospel. If John is the only one of the four Evangelists who enters into the pre-incarnate dignities of Christ, showing Him to us as the One who subsisted in the beginning, both being with God, and God Himself: the Creator of all things; if John is the only one who contemplates Him as the great "I am," equal with the Father; he also brings before us details concerning His humanity which are not to be met with in the Synoptists. John is the only one who tells us of Christ being "*wearied* with his journey" (4:6), *groaning* as He beheld the tears of His own, and *thirsting* as He hung upon the Cross. Christ became Man in the fullest sense of the word, and nowhere do we behold His human sympathies and perfections more blessedly displayed than in this very Gospel which portrays Him as God manifest in flesh.

It is in John's Gospel, pre-eminently, that we see the antitype of the veil, which speaks so plainly of the Son of God *incarnate*. "And thou shalt make a veil of blue, and purple, and scarlet, and fine twined linen of cunning work" (Ex. 26:31). This order "blue, purple and scarlet" is repeated over twenty times in Exodus, and is never varied. The blue and scarlet are never placed in juxtaposition in any of the fabrics of the tabernacle. This of itself is sufficient to show that the Holy Spirit intimates there is an important truth here in connection with the person of Christ. The "blue" is the color of heaven, and speaks of Christ as the Son of God. The "scarlet" is both the color of sacrifice and human glory. The "purple" is a color produced by the mixing together of blue and scarlet. Without the purple, the blue and the scarlet would have presented too vivid a contrast to the eye; the purple coming in between them shaded off the one extreme from the other.

Now the antitype of these colors is found in the incarnate Christ. He was both God and man, and yet these two vastly dissimilar natures unite in one perfect Person. The "purple," then, coming in between the "blue" and the "scarlet" tells of the perfect *blending* or union of His two natures. The great marvel (as well as mystery) of His unique person is that in Him were *combined* all the fulness of the Godhead with all the sinless feelings and affections of man. And it is just this which is so beautifully brought out in John's Gospel, and nowhere more strikingly than in John 11. When the sisters sent to Christ telling Him that their brother was sinking, instead of hastening at once to him, He remained two days where He was. Did this show that He was devoid of human feelings? No; His purpose was to manifest the Divine glory. But mark the sequel. When He arrives at Bethany, His heart is profoundly moved as He beholds the sorrowing sisters. And who but the God-man would have shed tears by the grave of Lazarus when He was on the very point of restoring the dead to life! Each of the three colors of the veil are clearly seen. The "blue" in the Divine power which raised the dead; the "scarlet" in the groans and tears. Now behold the "purple." When Lazarus came forth from the sepulchre he was still bound with the grave-clothes. The spectators were so amazed, so awed, so bewildered, *they* made no effort to remove them. "Loose him" were the words which proceeded from *Christ*. And who but the God-man would have been occupied with such a detail? We witness the same thing again at the Cross; "It is finished" exhibits the "blue"; "I thirst," the "scarlet"; and the "purple" is evidenced in His tender thought for His widowed mother, commending her to His beloved John!

In our previous lessons upon the first sections of John 11 we have seen the Lord at Bethabara with His disciples, and then on the confines of Bethany, whither Martha, unbidden, with characteristic impatience rushed to meet Him. We sought to weigh her utterances as she gave expression to the first thoughts that entered her mind. We saw how that the responses made by Christ were quite beyond her depth, and how that in answer to His searching "Believest thou this?" she replied, "Yea, Lord: I believe that thou art the Christ the Son of God, which should come into the world." Immediately following this we read, "And when she had *so* said, she went her way, and called Mary her sister secretly, saying, The Master is come, and calleth for thee" (11:28).

In her impulsive hurry to meet the Lord (11:20) Martha, for the time, forgot all about her sister; but now she goes to call Mary. There is nothing in the narrative to show that Christ had *asked* for Mary—if He had, John would surely have told us so. Was it then a fabrication on Martha's part? We do not so regard it: rather do we think she concluded that the profound words of Christ were more suited to her sister than herself. When Christ said, "I am the resurrection, and the life: he that believeth in me, though he were dead, yet shall he live; and whosoever liveth and believeth in me shall never die," she felt that *Mary* must hear this; *she* will be able to understand.

"And when she had so said, she went her way, and called Mary her sister secretly, saying, The Master is come, and calleth *for thee*" (11:28). The cryptic utterances of Christ Martha considered as a "call" for the more spiritual Mary. What a tribute this was to the discernment of the one whom she had formerly criticized! She called her "secretly" so as not to attract the attention of the many Jews who were with her in the house (11:19). These Jews had come from Jerusalem and Martha knew that most of the people there were antagonistic to the Saviour. "Christianity doth not bid us abate anything of our wariness and honest policy, yea, it requires us to have no less the wisdom of the serpent as the harmlessness of the dove" (R. Hall). And, too, she probably felt that it was more fitting that Mary should enjoy an interview with Christ in undisturbed privacy. Mark that Martha terms Christ "Master" (the Teacher), not "Lord!"

"As soon as she heard that, she arose quickly, and came unto him" (11:29). With characteristic quietness and calm Mary had remained seated in the house, but now she hears that the One at whose feet she had loved to sit, was here at hand, she rises and goes forth to meet Him at once, "quickly." The knowledge that *He* was "calling" her lent wings to her feet. She needed not to tarry and inquire *who* was meant by "the Master"—she had none other, and that one word was sufficient to identify the One who was the Fairest among ten thousand to her soul.

"Now Jesus was not yet come into the town, but was in that place where Martha met him" (11:30). Very striking indeed is this. He was still in the same place where Martha had talked with Him. In the interval she had returned to Bethany, entered the house and spoken to her sister, and Mary had herself traveled the same distance to meet Him in whom her soul delighted. And when she completed the journey—how long a one it was we do not know—she found her Beloved awaiting her. How this brings out the calmness of Christ: there was no undue haste to perform the miracle! And how blessedly it illustrates the fact that He never hides Himself from a seeking soul. He would not disappoint this one who so valued His presence. If she "arose quickly" to go to Him, He waited patiently for her arrival!

"The Jews then which were with her in the house, and comforted her, when they saw Mary, that she rose up hastily and went out followed her, saying, She goeth unto the grave to weep there" (11:31). This too is striking. Man proposes but God disposes. Martha's secrecy came to nothing. God had purposed that the last great "sign" of Israel's Messiah should be given before many eye-witnesses. The Jews followed Mary because they supposed she had gone to the grave to weep *in private,* but He who doeth all things according to the counsel of His own will, drew them there, that the miracle of the raising of Lazarus should be done *in public.* Doubtless their intention was to "comfort" her, and for their kindliness God would not let them be the losers. Has He not said, "whosoever shall give to drink unto one of these little ones a cup of cold water only in the name of a disciple, verily I say unto you, he shall in no wise lose his reward" (Matt. 10:42)? Beautifully was that verified on this occasion.

The Jews who had journeyed from Jerusalem to Bethany had felt for Martha and Mary in their heavy bereavement, and came to offer what comfort they could. By so doing they reaped a rich and unexpected reward. They beheld the greatest miracle which Christ ever wrought, and as the result many believed on Him (11:45). "We need not doubt that these things were written for our learning. To show sympathy and kindness to the sorrowful is good for our souls. To visit the fatherless and widows in their affliction, to weep with them that weep, to try and bear one another's burdens and lighten one another's cares,—all of this will make no atonement for sin and will not take us to Heaven. Yet it is healthy employment for our hearts, and employment which we ought not to despise. Few persons are aware that one secret of being miserable is to live only for ourselves, and one secret of being happy is to try to make others happy. In an age of peculiar selfishness and self-indulgence it would be well that we took this to heart" (Bishop Ryle). It is significant that these Jews did not leave the house when Martha left it!

"Then when Mary was come where Jesus was, and saw him, she fell down at his feet, saying unto him, Lord, if thou hadst been here, my brother had not died" (11:32). This was the language of perplexity and grief. Like Martha, Mary was thinking of what *might* have happened. How often we look back on the past with an "if" in our minds! How often in our sore trials we lash ourselves with an "if." And small comfort does it bring! How often we complain "it might have been" (Mark 14:5). As Whittier says, "Of all sad words of tongue and pen, the saddest are these, 'It might have been.'" Only too often these words express the inveterate sadness of one who is swallowed up with sorrow. Ofttimes it issues from forgetfulness of the Lord: He *permitted* it, so it must be for the best. It may not appear so to our dim vision; but so *it* is. It was so with Martha and Mary, as they were soon to behold.

"Then when Mary was come where Jesus was, and saw him, she fell down at his feet, saying unto him, Lord, if thou hadst been here, my brother had not died." While this was the language of grief and perplexity, it certainly was not a reproachful murmur, as her casting herself at the feet of Christ clearly shows. Nor does Mary here add an apologetic reflection as had her sister (11:22). Her words had quite a different meaning from the very similar language of Martha. We say very similar, for their utterances were not identical, as a reference to the Greek will show. They each used the same words, but the *order* of them varied, and in this may be seen what was uppermost in each of their minds. The A.V. gives a literal rendering of the original language of Martha (11:21); but what Mary said was, "Lord, if thou hadst been here, had not died my brother." That which was uppermost in the thoughts of Martha, was her brother's death; that which was discerned by Mary was that none *could* die in the presence of Christ. *Her* words then were an expression of worship, as the casting of herself at Christ's feet was an act of adoring homage.

"Then when Mary was come where Jesus was, and saw him, she fell down at his feet." This was ever *her* place. It is beautiful to observe that each time the New Testament presents Mary to us, she is seen "at the feet of Jesus"—expressive of her worshipful spirit. But there is no mere repetition. In Luke 10, at Christ's feet she owned Him as *Prophet,* hearing His word (v. 39). Here in John 11 she approaches Christ as *Priest*—that great High Priest that can be "touched with the feeling of our infirmities," who shares our sorrows, and ministers grace in every time of need. In John 12:3 Mary, at His feet acknowledged Him as "King"—this will appear if we compare Matt. 26:7, from which we learn that she *also* anointed "the head" of the rejected King of the Jews!

"When Jesus therefore saw her weeping, and the Jews also weeping which came with her, he groaned in the spirit, and was troubled" (11:33). The Greek word here for "groaned" is expressive of deep feeling, sometimes of sorrow, more often of indignation. In this instance the Holy Spirit has recorded the cause of Christ's groaning—it was the sight of Mary and her comforters weeping. He was here in the midst of a groaning creation, which sighed and travailed over that which *sin* had brought in. And this He felt acutely. The original suggests that He was distressed to the extremest degree: moved to a holy indignation and sorrow at the terrific brood which sin had borne. Agitated by a righteous detestation of what evil had wrought in the world. "And was troubled" is, more literally, "he troubled himself"; He caused Himself to be troubled by what made others weep and wail. And how this "groaning" and "troubling of himself" brings out the perfections of the incarnate Son! He would not raise Lazarus until He had entered in spirit into the solemnity of the awfulnes of death. Mark 8:12 intimates that the miracles which He performed *cost Him something.* Plainer still is the testimony of Matt. 8:17: "himself took our infirmities, and bare our sicknesses"—He felt the *burden* of sickness before He removed it.

"And said, Where have ye laid him? They said unto him, Lord, come and see" (11:34). What a mark of genuineness is this line in the picture! Who that was inventing a fictitious story would have introduced such a detail in a scene like this! But how thoroughly in keeping with everything else which the Gospels record about Christ. There was no ostentation about Him. He never used His Omniscience for the mere sake of display. He wished to be invited to the sepulchre.

"Jesus wept" (11:35). The shortest verse in the Bible, yet what volumes it contains. The Son of God weeping, and weeping on the very eve of raising the dead man! Who can fathom it? Three times in the New Testament we read of the Lord Jesus weeping: here, over Jerusalem, (Luke 19:41), and in Gethsemane (Heb. 5:7). Each time His tears were connected with the effects or consequences of sin. By the graveside of Lazarus these tears expressed the fulness of the grief which His heart felt. They manifested the perfectness of His love and the strength of His sympathy. He was the Man of sorrows and "acquainted with grief." Yet, here too was more than an expression of human sympathy. Here were souls upon which rested the weight of the dark shadow of death, and they were souls which He loved, and He *felt* it.

"Jesus wept": "The consciousness that He carried resurrection-virtue in Him, and was about to fill the house at Bethany with the joy of restored life, did not stay the current of natural affections. 'Jesus wept.' His heart was still alive to the sorrow, as to the degradation of death. His calmness throughout this exquisite scene was not *indifference,* but elevation. His soul was in the sunshine of those deathless regions which lay far away and beyond the tomb of Lazarus, but He could visit that valley of tears, and weep with those that wept" (J. G. Bellett).

"Then said the Jews, Behold how He loved him!" (11:36). How these tears demonstrated "the profound sympathy of the heart of Jesus with us in all the sorrows and trials through which we pass. Had those sisters for a moment questioned the love of Jesus for them and His sympathy with them in their sorrow, how they would be rebuked by these groans and tears! 'Jesus wept.' What tender sympathy and grace! And He is the same today. It is true the surroundings are different, but His heart is the same: 'Jesus Christ, *the same yesterday, and to-day, and forever.*' He 'wept.' How we see the reality of His human nature! Yes; it was a perfect human heart. He wept for the sorrow and desolation which sin has brought into the world; and He entered into it as no other could. Oh! what groans and tears! How they tell out the heart of our precious Lord Jesus! He truly loved these tried ones, and they proved it. So shall we if we rest in the same tender, gracious, sympathizing Lord" (C.H.M.).

"And some of them said, Could not this man, which opened the eyes of the blind, have caused that even this man should not have died?" (11:37). This sounds very much like the language of men determined to believe nothing good of our Lord, insistent on picking a hole or finding a fault, if possible, in any thing that He did. Their words have a sarcastic ring about them. Some have wondered why these carping critics did not mention the raising of Jairus' daughter or the widow's son. But it should be remembered that both of these miracles had been performed in Galilee. Moreover, the healing of the blind man in Jerusalem was much more recent. It is clear that they had no thought of help being available now that Lazarus was dead, and so they openly reproach Christ for allowing him *to* die. And men in their petulance and unbelief, especially at funerals, still ask much the same questions: 'Why should the Almighty have permitted this?' They forget that "He giveth not account of any of his matters" (Job 33:13). "What I do thou knowest not now; but thou shalt know hereafter" (John 13:7) is sufficient for faith.

"Jesus therefore again groaning in himself cometh to the grave. It was a cave, and a stone lay upon it" (11:38). This time, as the "therefore" indicates, the *groaning* was occasioned by the carping unbelief of those mentioned in the previous verse. Here it was a matter of Christ "enduring the contradiction of sinners against himself" (Heb. 12:3). It shows how He *felt* the antagonism of those who knew Him not. It was not as a stoic that He passed through these scenes. Everything that was contrary to His holy nature, moved Him deeply. How blessed it is for us to remember this as we, who have the firstfruits of the Spirit, "groan within ourselves, waiting for the adoption, the redemption of our body" (Rom. 8:23). How comforting to know that our Redeemer felt the same thing which the new nature within us feels; only felt it a thousand times more acutely. Not for nothing was He termed "a man of sorrows" (Isa. 53:3). In us there is ever a conflict; one nature feeding on, the other repelled by, the things of this world. But with the Holy One of God there was nothing to neutralize, nothing to modify, the anguish which His spirit felt from His daily contact with evil and corruption. As Hebrews tells us, "He *suffered* being tempted." It is true there was nothing in Him to which Satan could appeal, and therefore there was no possibility of Him yielding. But nevertheless the temptation was a fearful reality. His holy nature recoiled from the very presence of the Evil One, as His "get thee hence, Satan" plainly intimates. His spotless purity was sickened by the vile solicitations of the tempter. Yes, He *suffered* to a degree we do not and cannot. Suffered not only from the temptation of Satan, but from the evil which surrounded Him on every side. The "groaning" which the Holy Spirit has here recorded gives us a glimpse of what must have gone on constantly in the spirit of that blessed One so deeply "acquainted with grief."

"Jesus said, Take ye away the stone" (11:39). "What majestic *composure* in the midst of this mighty emotion!" (Stier). Though weeping outwardly and groaning inwardly, the Lord Jesus was complete master of Himself. He acts and speaks with quiet dignity. The miracles of God avoid with the supremest propriety all that is superfluous. So often in the mighty works of God we may observe an economy of Divine power. What man *could* do, he is required to do. We have little use for the hackneyed saying that "God helps those who help themselves," for God very often helps those who are *unable* to help themselves. Yet, on the other hand, it remains true that it is not God's general way to do for us what we are responsible and capable of doing for ourselves. God is pleased to bless our use of the means which are at hand. If I am a farmer, I shall harvest no crops unless I plow and sow and care for my fields. Just as in the first miracle of this Gospel Christ ordered men to fill the jars with water, so here He ordered men to roll away the stone.

"Jesus said, Take ye away the stone." There is another lesson for us to learn here. He might have commanded the stone to roll itself away, or He might have bidden Lazarus to come forth through the impediment of the stone. Instead, He bade the bystanders remove it. Christ modestly avoided all pomp and parade and mingled the utmost simplicity with the most amazing displays of power. What an example He thus set *us* to avoid all ostentation!

"Martha, the sister of him that was dead, saith unto him, Lord, by this time he stinketh: for he hath been dead four days" (11:39). What a characteristic word was this from one who was "careful about many things," ever anxious about circumstances. Did Martha suppose that Christ only desired to view the body? It would seem so. And yet how sad is the unbelief which her utterance expressed. Lazarus' own sister would put an obstacle in the way of the manifestation of Christ's glory! She supposed it was useless to remove the stone. How solemnly this warns us that natural affections can never rise to the thoughts of God, and that only too frequently we are opposed to His workings even where it is for *the blessing* of those whom we love most tenderly! How often has a husband, a wife, a parent, sought to resist the Word or providences of God, as they were operating in or on the object of their affection! Let us take to heart this lamentable resistance of Martha.

"Jesus said unto her, Said I not unto thee, that, if thou wouldest believe, thou shouldest see the glory of God?" (11:40). There is considerable difference of opinion as to what our Lord referred to when He declared, "Said I not unto thee?" etc. Many suppose He was reminding her of some word of His spoken just before, when she had met Him alone, and which is not recorded in the context. This is mere supposition, and an unlikely one at that. It seems more natural to regard it as pointing back to the answer Christ had sent her from Bethabara: "This sickness is not unto death, but for the glory of God, that the Son of God may be glorified thereby" (11:4). Others think it was as though He said, "Martha, thou art forgetting the great doctrines of faith which I have ever taught thee. How often you have heard Me say, All things are possible to him that believeth." There may be a measure of truth in this as well.

"Jesus saith unto her, Said I not unto thee, that, if thou wouldest believe, thou shouldest see the glory of God?" Profound word was this. "The glory of God"! That which rejoices the soul when seen and known; that, without which we must forever remain unsatisfied and unblest; that, in comparison with which all sights are as nothing,— is "the glory of God." This was what Moses prayed to see: "I beseech thee, show me thy glory" (Ex. 33:18). The glory of God is the revelation of His excellencies, the visible display of His invisible perfections. It was the glory of God which Christ came here to make manifest, for He is the outshining of God's glory (Heb. 1:3). But the one special point to which our Lord here referred, was His own glory as the Bringer of life out of death. It was this which He came to reveal, both in His own person, by dying and rising again, and in the works of His hands—here in the raising of Lazarus. To remove the wages of death, to undo the work which sin had wrought, to conquer him that had the power of death, to swallow up death in victory—this was indeed a special manifestation of glory.

"God, who commanded the light to shine out of darkness, hath shined in our hearts, to give the light of the knowledge of the glory of God in the face of Jesus Christ" (II Cor. 4:6). Now it is unbelief which hinders our seeing the glory of God. It is not our unworthiness, our ignorance, nor our feebleness, that stand in the way, but our unbelief, for there is far more of unbelief than faith in us, as well as in Martha. Those searching words, "Said I not unto *thee*" apply to writer and reader. He was reminding Martha of a word given her before, but which had not been "mixed with faith." Alas, how often His words to us have fallen on unresponsive hearts. Mark the order of the two verbs here: "Believe" comes before "see," and compare our remarks on 6:69.

"Then they took away the stone from the place where the dead was laid" (11:41). As pointed out previously, two things stand out conspicuously all through this chapter: the glory of

Christ and the failure of men; His perfections and their imperfections confront us at every point. Christ had bidden the bystanders "Take ye away the stone"—doubtless a heavy one (cf. Matt. 27:60) which would require several men to move. But they had not responded. They paused to listen to Martha's objection. It was not until He had replied to her, not until He had spoken of the glory of God being seen, that they obeyed—"*Then* they took away the stone." How slow is man to obey the Word of God! What trifles are allowed to hinder!

"And Jesus lifted up his eyes, and said, Father, I thank thee that thou hast heard me" (11:41). Very beautiful is this. It manifested Christ as the dependent One. Perfectly did He fulfil Prov. 3:5, 6: "Trust in the Lord with all thine heart, and lean not unto thine own understanding. In *all* thy ways *acknowledge him.*" But more: it was the Son giving the Father the honor for the miracle which was about to be performed. He directed attention away from Himself to One in heaven. Well might He say, "learn of me; for I am *meek* and *lowly* in heart" (Matt. 11:29). And too, there is another thing here. In view of His words in the next verse it seems clear that He also lifted up His eyes for the sake of those standing around. His miracles had been blasphemously attributed to Satan and Hell; He would here show the true Source from which they proceeded—"Jesus *lifted up* his eyes." Note also His, "Father, *I thank* thee." He *began* with this. Christ has left us a perfect example, not only of prayerfulness but of thankfulness as well. We are always more ready to ask than thank: but see Phil. 4:6.

"And Jesus lifted up his eyes, and said, Father, I thank thee that thou hast heard me." "We now reach a point of thrilling and breathless interest. The stone had been removed from the mouth of the cave. Our Lord stands before the open grave, and the crowd stands around, awaiting anxiously to see what would happen next. Nothing appears from the tomb. There is no sign of life at present; but while all are eagerly looking and listening, our Lord addresses His Father in Heaven in a most solemn manner, lifting up His eyes, and speaking audibly to Him in the hearing of all the crowd. The reason He explains in the next verse. Now, for the last time, about to work His mightiest miracle, He once more makes a public declaration that He did nothing separate from His Father in heaven, and that in this and all His work there is a mysterious and intimate union between Himself and the Father" (Bishop Ryle).

"And I knew that thou hearest me always" (11:42). What perfect confidence in the Father had this One here in servant form! And what was the ground of His confidence? Has He not Himself told us in John 8:29?—"He that sent me is with me; the Father hath not left me alone; *For* I do *always* those things that *please* him"! The Lord Jesus never had a thought which was out of harmony with the Father's will, and never did a thing which in the slightest degree deviated from His Father's word. He *always* did those things which pleased Him (Psa. 16:8); therefore did the Father always hear Him. What light this throws on our *un*-answered prayers! There is an intimate relation between our conduct and the response which we receive to our supplications: "If I regard iniquity in my heart, the Lord will not hear me" (Psa. 66:18). Equally clear is the New Testament. "And whatsoever we ask, we receive of him, *because* we keep his commandments, and do those things that are *pleasing* in his sight" (I John 3:22). Very searching is this. It is not what men term "legalism" but the Father maintaining the demands of holiness. For God to answer the prayers of one who had no concern for His glory and no respect to His commandments, would be to place a premium upon sin.

"And I knew that thou hearest me always." Very, very blessed is this. Unspeakable comfort does it minister to the heart that rests upon it. Christ did not cease to pray when He left this earth: He still prays, prays for us, His people: "Wherefore he is able also to save them to the uttermost that come unto God by him, seeing he ever liveth to make intercession for them" (Heb. 7:25). How much we *owe to* His intercession eternity will reveal—far, far more than we now realize. Read through John 17 and note the different things He has asked (and possibly, still asks) the Father for us. He asks that His joy may be fulfilled in us (v. 13), that we may be kept from evil in the world (v. 15), that we may be sanctified through the truth (v. 17), that we may be one (21), that we may be made perfect in one (v. 23), that we may be with Him where He is (v. 24), that we may behold His glory (v. 24). None of these things are yet ours in their fulness; but how unspeakably blessed to *know* that the time is coming when *all* of them *will* be! The Father hears Christ "always," therefore these things *must* be made good to us!

"But because of the people which stand by I said it, that they may believe that thou hast sent me" (11:43). How this reminds us of Elijah on mount Carmel! "Elijah the prophet came near and said, Lord God of Abraham, Isaac, and of Israel, let it be known this day that thou art God in Israel, and *that I am thy servant,* and that I have done all these things at thy word. Hear me, O Lord, hear me, that *this people may know* that thou art the Lord God" (I Kings 18:36, 37)! This scripture supplies the key to the meaning of the Lord's words beside the tomb of Lazarus. Like Elijah's, Christ's mission was unto Israel, and like Elijah, He here prayed that God would authenticate His mission. If *the Father* had not sent Him, He would not have heard Him in anything; the Father hearing Him here at the graveside of Lazarus was therefore a clear proof and full evidence of His *Divine* mission.

"And when he had thus spoken, he cried with a loud voice, Lazarus, come forth" (11:43). This "loud voice" was also for the people's sake, that all might hear. Lazarus was addressed personally for, as it has been well remarked, had Christ simply cried "come forth" Hades would have been emptied and every tenant of the grave would have been raised from the dead. We have here, in miniature, what will take place on the resurrection morn. "The Lord himself shall descend from heaven *with a shout* . . . and the dead in Christ shall rise" (I Thess. 4:16, 17). So, too, will it be when the wicked dead shall be resurrected: "Marvel not at this; for the hour is coming, in the which *all* that are in the graves shall *hear his voice*" (John 5:28). It is striking to note that Christ here did nothing except to say, "Lazarus, come forth." It was the last great public witness to Christ as the incarnate *Word*. And, too, it perfectly illustrated the means which God employs in regeneration. Men are raised spiritually, pass from death unto life, by means of the written Word, and by that alone. Providences, personal testimonies, loss of loved ones, deeply as these sometimes may stir the natural man, they *never* "quicken" a soul into newness of life. We are born again, "not of corruptible seed, but of incorruptible by *the word of God,* which liveth and abideth forever" (I Pet. 1:23).

"Lazarus, come forth. And he that was dead came forth" (11:44). At the sound of that Voice the king of terrors at once yielded up his lawful captive, and the insatiable grave gave up its prey. Captivity was led captive and Christ stood forth as the Conqueror of sin, death and Satan. There it was demonstrated that He who was in the form of a Servant, nevertheless, held in His own hand "the keys of death and hades." Here was public proof that the Lord Jesus had absolute power over the material world and over the realm of spirits. At His bidding a soul that had left its earthly tenement was called back from the unseen to dwell once more in the body. What a demonstration was this that He who could work such astounding miracles must be none other than one "who is over all, God blessed for ever" (Rom. 9;5). Thank God for an all-mighty Saviour. How can any sheep of *His* ever perish when held in *such* a hand!

"And he that was dead came forth" (11:44). "This shows us what the energy, the utmost energy, of evil can do over those who are the beloved of the Lord; but it also shows us how the Lord Jesus sets it altogether aside in the energy and in the strength of His own power. We have here the full result of Satan's power, and the perfect triumphing of the Lord over that power. Death is the result of the power of Satan. By bringing in sin, he brought in death: 'the wages of sin'; this is the utmost of Satan's power. He brought in this at the commencement, he brought it in by deceit; for 'he was a murderer from the beginning, and abode not in the truth.' Such has he been ever since; he is called the old Serpent and the Deceiver; and having deceived, he became the murderer of the first Adam, and in one sense, of the last Adam. He was and is a liar; that is his character, as exactly opposed to Christ, who is the truth. In like manner all the variations of his character are set in opposition to that of Christ. He is the destroyer, and Christ is the Giver of life; He is the accuser of the brethren, and Christ the Mediator for them; Christ the Truth of God, and Satan the father of lies. In this character he is first brought before us. By misrepresenting the truth and character of God, he became the murderer of the souls of men, and brought in death—this was his power. Christ came to destroy him that had the power of death, that is, the Devil. The Son of God came to destroy the works of the Devil by bringing souls from the power of Satan to the power of the living God. This is what is so strikingly illustrated here in John 11" (Mr. J. N. Darby).

There are two ways in which the Lord Jesus has become the resurrection and the life of His people: First, in purchasing their redemption from the wages of sin, by paying Himself the full price which Divine justice demanded for their trangressions. This He did by His own voluntary and vicarious sufferings; being made a curse for us. Second, by making us one with Himself who is the very life of all being: "he that is joined unto the Lord is one spirit" (I Cor. 6:17). It was this He prayed for in John 17: "That they all may be *one;* as thou, Father, art in me, and I in thee, that they also may be *one in us*" (v. 21). This is made good by the Holy Spirit: "If any man be in Christ he is a new creation" (II Cor. 5:17). The believer is "in Christ" not only by the eternal choice of the Father (Eph. 1:4), not only by His being constituted our federal Head (I Cor. 15:22), but also by *vital union.* In this double way then is Christ unto us "the resurrection and the life," and thus has He completely triumphed over him (the Devil) who *had* (no longer "has") the power of death. A most striking figure of this was Lazarus. Dead, in the grave, his body already gone to corruption. At the almighty word of Christ "he that was dead came forth." The children of God are the children of the resurrection. Where Christ is made the life of the soul, there is the certainty of a resurrection to life eternal *in Christ's life*: when *His* life is communicated to us, we have that within us over which the power of Satan is unable to prevail. Dimly, but beautifully, was this foreshadowed of old in the case of Job. Afflict him Satan might, destroy his possessions he was permitted to do, but touch his *life* he could not!

The picture presented here in John 11 is Divinely perfect. It was during the bodily absence of Christ from Bethany that death exercised its power over Lazarus. It is so with us now. What we have in John 11 is not merely an individual, but a *family*—a family beloved of the Lord. How clearly this prefigured the family of God now upon earth! While Christ was bodily absent, the power of death was felt, and sorrow and grief came in. But tears gave place to rejoicing. After abiding "two days" where He was, Christ came to that afflicted family, and His very presence manifested the power of life. So, when Christ returns for His people, it will be in this same twofold character: as the Resurrection and the Life. Then will He put away not only the grief of His people, but that which has *caused* it. In the interval, His "tears" (*before* He raised Lazarus) assure us of His deep sympathy!

"And he that was dead came forth, bound hand and foot with graveclothes: and his face was bound about with a napkin" (11:44). This line in the picture in nowise mars its accuracy, rather does it intensify it. Whether we view the raising of Lazarus as a figure of the regeneration of a sinner, or the glorification of the believer, the "graveclothes" here and the *removal* of them, are equally significant. When a sinner is born again, God's work of grace in his soul is not perfected, rather has it just commenced. The old nature still remains and the marks of the grave are still upon him. There is much to impede the movements of the "new man," much from which he needs to be "loosed," and which his spiritual resurrection did not of itself effect. The language of such a soul was expressed by the apostle Paul when he said, "to will is present with me, but how to perform that which is good I find not. . . . For I delight in the law of God after the inward man; but I see another law in my members, warring against the law of my mind, and bringing me into captivity to the law of sin which is in my members" (Rom. 7:18, 22, 23). It was so here with Lazarus when the Lord called him from the tomb; he did not leave the hampering graveclothes behind him, but came forth "bound hand and foot."

"Jesus saith unto them, Loose him, and let him go" (11:44). How this brings out the moral glory of Christ. The fact that

He had to *ask* the bystanders to liberate the risen man shows that the spectators were all overcome with amazement and awe. The Lord alone remained serene and collected. That the Lord invited *them* to "loose him" (rather than, by a miracle, cause the clothes to fall from him) points a beautiful lesson. In gracious condescension the Lord of glory links human instruments with Himself in the work which He is now doing in the world. Again and again is this seen in John's Gospel. He used the servants at the wedding-feast, when He turned the water into wine. He fed the hungry multitude through the hands of His disciples. He bade the spectators of this last public miracle roll the stone away from the grave; and now He asks them to free Lazarus from the graveclothes. And this is still His blessed way. He alone can speak the word which quickens dead sinners; but He permits us to *carry* that word to them. What an inestimable privilege—an honor not given even to the angels! O that we might esteem it more highly. There is no higher privilege this side of Heaven than for us to be used of the Lord in rolling away gravestones and removing graveclothes.

"Jesus saith unto them, Loose him, and let him go." But there is a yet deeper and even more blessed truth taught us here. In its ultimate application the raising of Lazarus points, as we have seen, to the full manifestation of Christ as the resurrection and the life at the time when He returns to His sorrowing "family." Then will God's wondrous work of sovereign grace be perfected. No longer shall we be left in a groaning creation, but removed to His own place on high. No longer shall we be imprisoned in these tabernacles of clay, for we shall be "delivered from the bondage of corruption" and enter into "the glorious *liberty* of the children of God." No more shall our face be "bound about with a napkin," which now causes us to see "through a glass darkly," but in that glad day we shall see "face to face" (I Cor. 13:12). Then shall this corruptible put on incorruption and mortality shall be "swallowed up of life" (II Cor. 5:4). It is of *this* that the "Loose him" speaks. No more shall we wear the habiliments of death, but then shall we rejoice in that One who has forever set us free that we might walk with Him in newness of life. Then, ah, then, shall we obtain joy and gladness, and sorrow and sighing shall flee away.

"Loose him." This was to satisfy the onlookers that they had not been deceived by any optical delusion. With their own hands they were permitted to handle his body. It is very striking to observe that in this final "sign" of Christ, conclusive evidence was offered to three of their senses — nostrils, eyes, and hands: the "stink" must have been apparent when the stone was removed from the cave; they *saw* Lazarus come forth a living man; they were suffered to *touch* and handle him. All possible deception was therefore out of question.

"And let him go." The spectators were not allowed to satisfy an idle curiosity. Lazarus was to retire to the privacy of home. Those who had witnessed the miracle of his resurrection, were not suffered to pry into the secrets of the grave or ask him curious questions. "Let him go" was the authoritative word of Christ, and there the curtain falls. And fitly so. When the Lord Jesus leaves His Father's throne on high and descends into the air, we too shall *go* — go from these scenes of sin and suffering, go to be "forever with the Lord." Glorious prospect! Blessed climax! Blissful goal! May our eyes be steadily fixed upon it, running with perseverance the race set before us, looking off unto Him who "for *the joy that was set before him,* endured the cross, despising the shame, and is set down at the right hand of the throne of God" (Heb. 12:2).

The following questions are to prepare the student for the closing section of John 11: —

1. How explain the different actions of the spectators, vv. 45, 46?
2. What important truth is illustrated in v. 50?
3. What is meant by "this spake he not of himself," v. 51?
4. What do vv. 51, 52 teach about the Atonement?
5. "Gather together" in *one* what, v. 52?
6. Why did Jesus "walk *no more* openly among the Jews," v. 54?
7. What is meant by "to purify themselves," v. 55?

CHAPTER FORTY

Christ Feared By the Sanhedrin

John 11:45-57

The following is submitted as an Analysis of the passage which is to be before us: –

1. The effects of Christ's great miracle, vv. 45, 46.
2. The Council and their predicament, vv. 47, 48.
3. Caiaphas and his counsel, vv. 49, 50.
4. The Holy Spirit's interpretation, vv. 51, 52.
5. The Council's decision and Christ's response, vv. 53, 54.
6. The Feast of the Passover and the purification of the Jews, vv. 55, 56.
7. The commandment of the Council, v. 57.

In the closing section of John 11 we are shown the *effects* of the awe-inspiring miracle recorded in the earlier part of the chapter. And we are at once struck with what is here *omitted.* The Holy Spirit has told us of the varying impressions made upon the "many Jews" who witnessed the raising of Lazarus, but nothing whatever is said of the feelings of either Lazarus or his sisters! Several reasons may be suggested for this. In the first place, the Bible is not written to satisfy an idle curiosity. It would not have suited the ways of God for us to know now what was retained by the memory of Lazarus as he returned from the Unseen to this world. It is not God who moves Spiritualists to pry into that which lies behind the veil. In the second place, there is a beautiful *delicacy* in concealing from us the emotions of Martha and Mary. We are not allowed to obtrude into the privacy of their home after their loved one had been restored to them! In the third place, may we not reverently say, the joy of the sisters was *too great for utterance.* An impostor inventing this story would have made *this* item very prominent, supposing that it would furnish a suitable and appropriate climax to the narrative. But the spiritual mind discerns that its very omission is an evidence of the Divine perfections of this inspired record.

"Then many of the Jews which came to Mary, and had seen the things which Jesus did, believed on him" (11:45). Though John says nothing about the effects which the raising of Lazarus had upon any of the members of the Bethany family, it is striking to observe how the Holy Spirit here adheres to His unity of purpose. All through this Gospel He has shown us the growing enmity of the "Jews," an enmity which was now so swiftly to culminate in the crucifixion of the Lord of glory. So now, without stopping to draw any moral from the great "sign" which the Messiah had just given, without so much as making a single comment upon it He at once tells us how it was regarded by the Jews! They, as ever, were *divided* about the Lord Jesus (cf. 7:43; 9:16; 10:19). A goodly number of those who had witnessed the coming forth of Lazarus from the tomb "believed on him." Without attempting to analyze their faith, this we may safely say: *their* enmity was subdued, *their* hostility was discarded, temporarily at least.

"Then many of the Jews which came to Mary, and had seen the things which Jesus did, believed on him." "It is remarkable that our Evangelist speaks of them as those who had come to *Mary*. Their regard for *her* led them to have regard to *Him* whom she so deeply loved. Perhaps too they had conversed with her about Him, and she had borne testimony unto Him, and impressed them favorably concerning Him, and prepared them for their faith in Him" (Dr. John Brown). The wording of this 45th verse is most significant. It does not say, "Then many of the Jews came to Mary, *who,* seeing the things which Jesus did, believed on him," but "Then many of the Jews which came to Mary, *and* had seen the things which Jesus did, believed on him." The *two* things are linked together—the coming to Mary *and* the seeing the things which He did—as explaining *why* they "believed on him." It reminds us of what we read of in 4:39, 41, 42: "And many of the Samaritans believed on him for *the saying of the woman,* which testified, He told me all that ever I did. . . . *And* many more believed because *of his own word;* And said unto the woman, Now we believe, not because of thy saying; for we have heard him ourselves, and know that this is indeed the Christ, the Saviour of the world."

"But some of them went their ways to the Pharisees, and told them what things Jesus had done" (11:46). "But": ominous word is this. Solemn is the contrast now presented. Some of those who had witnessed the miracle went at once to the Pharisees and told them of what Christ had done. Most probably they were their spies. Their motive in reporting to these inveterate enemies of our Lord cannot be misunderstood; they went not to modify but to inflame their wrath. What an example of incorrigible hardness of heart! Alas, what is man! Even *miracles* were to some "a savor of death unto death"!

"Then gathered the chief priests and the Pharisees a council" (11:47). The "chief priests" were, in all probability, Sadducees; we know that the high priest was, see Acts 5:17. The "Pharisees" were their theological opponents. These two rival sects hated each other most bitterly, yet, in this evil work of persecuting the Lord Jesus, they buried their differences, and eagerly joined together in the common crime. The same thing is witnessed in connection with Herod and Pilate: "And Herod with his men of war set him at nought, and mocked him, and arrayed him in a gorgeous robe, and sent him again to Pilate. And *the same day* Pilate and Herod were made friends together: for *before* they were at enmity between themselves" (Luke 23:11, 12)! Each of these cases was a fulfillment of the prophecy which the Holy Spirit had given through David long before: "The kings of the earth set themselves, and the rulers take counsel *together,* against the Lord, and against His Christ" (Psa. 2:2).

"Then gathered the chief priests and the Pharisees a council, and said, What do we? for this man doeth many miracles" (11:47). The "council" was deeply stirred by the evidence before them. Jesus had clearly demonstrated that he was the Christ, and they ought forthwith to have acknowledged Him. Instead of doing so they chided themselves for their delay at not having apprehended and silenced Him before. "What do we?" they asked. Why are we so dilatory? On a previous occasion, these same men had sent officers to arrest Christ (7:32), but instead of doing so they returned to their masters saying, "Never man spake like this man," and then, in the providence of God, Nicodemus objected, "Doth our law judge any man before it hear him, and know what he doeth?" (7:51), and this broke up their conference. But now things had come to a head. They *did* know what He was doing. "For this man doeth many miracles." This they could not deny. Very solemn was it. They *owned* the genuineness of His miracles, yet were their consciences unmoved. How this exposes the uselessness of much that is being done today. Some think they have accomplished much if they demonstrate to the intellect the *truth* of Christ's miracles. We often wonder if such men really believe in the *total* depravity of human nature. Souls are not brought into the presence of God, or saved, by such means. The *wisdom* of this world is foolishness with God. Nothing but omnipotent and sovereign grace is of any avail for those who are lost. And the *only* thing God uses to quicken the dead is His own Word. One who has really passed from death unto life has *no need* for so-called "Christian Evidences" to buttress his faith: one who is yet dead in trespasses and sins has *no capacity* of heart to appreciate them. Preach the Word, not argue and reason about the miracles of the Bible, is our business!

"If we let him thus alone, all men will believe on him" (11:48). How these words reveal the awful enmity of their hearts: no matter what others did, they were determined not to believe. In our first chapter on John 11 we called attention to the link between this chapter and Luke 16. In each instance there was a "Lazarus." The very *name*, then, of the one whom Christ had just raised at Bethany, should have served to remind them of His warning words at the close of Luke 16. Well did Christ say of them, "If they hear not Moses and the prophets, *neither* will they *be persuaded*, though one rose from the dead" (v. 31). What a proof that witnessing miracles will not bring dead sinners to the feet of Christ! "We must never wonder if we see abounding unbelief in our own times, and around our own homes. It may seem at first inexplicable to us, how men cannot see the truth which seems so clear to ourselves, and do not receive the Gospel which appears so worthy of acceptation. But the plain truth is, that man's unbelief is a far more deeply-seated disease than is generally reckoned. It is proof against the logic of facts, against reasoning, against moral suasion. Nothing can melt it down but the grace of God. If we ourselves believe, we can never be too thankful. But we must never count it a strange thing, if we see many of our fellow men as hardened and unbelieving as the Jews" (Bishop Ryle).

"If we let him thus alone, all men will believe on him; and the Romans shall come and take away both our place and nation" (11:48). It was only to be expected that the resurrection of Lazarus would raise a wave of popular excitement. Any stir among the common people the leaders considered would be dangerous, especially at passover time, then nigh at hand, when Jerusalem would be filled with crowds of Israelites, ready to take fire from any spark which might fall among them (cf. 12:12, 13). The Council therefore deemed it wisest to concert measures at once for repressing the nascent enthusiasm. Something must be done, but *what* they hardly knew. They feared that a disturbance would bring Rome's heavy hand down upon them and lead to the loss of what national life still remained to them. But their fears were not from any concern which they had for God's glory, nor were they even moved by patriotic instinct. It was sordid self-interest. "They will take away *our* place," the temple (Greek "topos" used in Acts 6:13, 14; 21:28, 29, where, plainly, the temple is in view), which was the center and source of all their influence and power. They claimed for themselves what belonged to God. The holy things were, in their eyes, their special property.

Palestine had been annexed as a province to the Roman Empire, and as was customary with that people, they allowed those whom they conquered a considerable measure of self-government. The Jews were permitted to continue the temple services and to hold their ecclesiastical court. It was those who were in position of power who here took the lead against Christ. They imagined that if they continued to leave Him alone, His following would increase, and the people set Him up as their King. It mattered not that He had taught, "My kingdom is *not* of this world"

(18:36); it mattered not that He retired when the people *had* desired to take Him by force and make Him their King (6:15). Enough that they supposed His claims threatened to interfere with their schemes of worldly prosperity and self-aggrandizement.

It is indeed striking to see the utter blindness of these men. They imagined that if they stopped short the career of Christ they would protect themselves from the Romans. But the very things they feared came to pass. They crucified Christ. And what was the sequel? Less than forty years afterward the Roman army *did* come, destroyed Jerusalem, burned the temple and carried away the whole nation into captivity. A thoughtful writer has remarked on this point: "The well-read Christian need hardly be reminded of many like things in the history of Christ's Church. The Roman emperors persecuted the Christians in the first three centuries, and thought it a positive duty not to let them alone. But the more they persecuted them the more they increased. The blood of the martyrs became the seed of the Church. So, too, the English Papists, in the days of Queen Mary persecuted the Protestants and thought that truth was in danger if they left them alone. But the more they burned our forefathers, the more they confirmed men's minds in steadfast attachment to the doctrines of the Reformation. In short, the words of the second Psalm are continually verified in this world. The kings of the earth set themselves and the rulers take counsel against the Lord. But 'He that sitteth in the heavens shall laugh; the Lord shall have them in derision.' God can make the designs of His enemies work together for the good of His people, and cause the wrath of men to praise Him. In days of trouble, and rebuke, and blasphemy, believers may rest patiently in the Lord. The very things that at one time seem likely to hurt them, shall prove in the end to be for their gain."

"And one of them, named Caiaphas, being the high priest that same year, said unto them, Ye know nothing at all, nor consider that it is expedient for us, that one man should die for the people, and that the whole nation perish not" (11:49, 50). The Council was puzzled. They saw in Christ, as they thought, a menace to their interests, but what course to follow they scarcely knew. Up to this point they had simply asked one another questions. Impatient at the vacillations of the priests and Pharisees, the high priest brusquely and contemptuously swept aside their deliberations with, "Ye know nothing at all." "The one point to keep before us is our own interests. Let that be clearly understood. When we once ask, What is expedient for *us*, there can be no doubt about the answer. This Man must die! Never mind about His miracles, or His teachings, or the beauty of His character, His life is a perpetual danger to *our* prerogatives. I vote for death." As 11:53 shows us, the evil motion of Caiaphas was carried. The Council regarded it as a brilliant solution to their difficulty. "If this popular Nazarene be slain not only will suspicion be removed from us, but our loyalty to the Roman Empire will be unmistakably established. The execution of Jesus will not only show that we have no intention of revolting, but rather will the slaying of this Man, who is seeking to establish an independent kingdom, plainly evidence our desire and purpose to remain the faithful subjects of Cæsar. Thus our watchful zeal for the integrity of the Empire will not only establish confidence but win the applause of the jealous power of Rome!" Caiaphas spoke as an unscrupulous politician who sacrifices righteousness and truth for party interests. So too in accepting his policy, the Council persuaded themselves that political prudence required the carrying out of his counsel rather than that the Romans should be provoked.

"*Our* place" was what *they* considered. It was precisely what the Lord had foretold: "But when the husbandmen saw him, they reasoned among themselves, saying, This is the heir: come, let us kill him, that the inheritance may be *ours*" (Luke 20:14). Favor from Cæsar rather than from God, was what their hearts desired. "Unlike Abraham they took riches from the king of Sodom instead of blessings from the hands of Melchizedek. They chose the patronage of Rome rather than know the resurrection-power of the Son of God" (Mr. Bellett). Solemn warning is this for us to be governed by higher principles than "expediency."

"And this spake he not of himself: but being high priest that year, he prophesied that Jesus should die for that nation" (11:51). "There are many devices in a man's heart; nevertheless the counsel of the Lord that shall stand" (Prov. 19:21). Strikingly was this illustrated here. Caiaphas was actuated by political expediency: the Lord Jesus was to be a State victim. Little did he know of the deep meaning of the words that he uttered, "It is expedient that one man die for the people": little did he realize that he had been moved of God to utter a prophecy to the honor of Him whom he despised. What we have in this verse and in the one following is the Holy Spirit's parenthetical explanation and amplification upon this saying of the high priest's. Altogether unconscious of the fact, Caiaphas had "prophesied," and as II Peter 1:20, 21 tells us, "No prophecy of the scripture is of any private interpretation i.e. human origination, for the prophecy came not at any time by the will of man." The instance before us is closely parallel with the case of Balaam in the O.T., who also "prophesied" *against* his will.

The subject is indeed a profound one, and one which human wisdom has stumbled over in every age, nevertheless the teaching of Scripture is very clear upon the point: *all things*, in the final analysis, are of God. Nowhere is this more evident than in connection with the treatment which the Lord Jesus received at the hands of wicked men. Referring to this very decision of the Council (among other things) Acts 4:26-28 tells us, "The kings of the earth stood up, and the rulers were gathered together against the Lord, and against his Christ. For of a truth against thy holy servant Jesus, whom thou hast anointed, both Herod and Pontius Pilate, with the Gentiles, and the people of Israel were gathered together, for to do *whatsoever thy hand and thy counsel determined before to be done.*" It had been decreed in the eternal counsels of the Godhead that Christ should die, and die for Israel, and when Caiaphas advanced his proposal he was but a link in the chain which brought that decree to pass. This was not *his* intention, of course. *His* motive was evil only, and therein was he justly guilty. What we have here is the antitype of that which had been foreshadowed long centuries before. The brethren of Joseph by their cruel counsels thought to defeat the purpose of God, who had made it known that they should yet pay homage to their younger brother. Yet in delivering him up to the Ishmaelites, though their intention was evil only, nevertheless, they did but bring to pass the purpose of God. So Caiaphas fulfilled the very counsel of God concerning Christ, which he meant to bring to nothing, by prophesying that He should die for the people. Well may Christ have said to Caiaphas, as Joseph had said to his brethren, "But as for you, *ye* thought *evil* against me; but *God* meant it unto *good,* to bring to pass, as it is this day, to *save* much people alive" (Gen. 50:20)!

"And this spake he not of himself: but being high priest that year, he prophesied that Jesus should die for that nation" (11:51). What light this throws on the *nature* of Christ's death! It brings out its twofold aspect. From the human side it was a brutal murder for political ends: Caiaphas and the priests slaying Him to avoid an unpopular tumult that might threaten their prerogatives; Pilate consenting to His death to avoid the unpopularity which might follow a refusal. But from the Divine side, the death of Christ was a vicarious sacrifice for sinners. It was God making the wrath of man to praise Him. "The greatest crime ever done in the world is the greatest blessing ever given to the world. Man's sin works out the loftiest Divine purpose, even as the coral insects blindly building up the reef that keeps back the waters or, as the sea in its wild, impotent rage, seeking to overwhelm the land, only throws upon the beach a barrier that confines its waves and curbs its fury" (Dr. MacLaren).

"And not for that nation only, but that also he should gather together in one the children of God that were scattered abroad" (11:52). As the previous verse gives us the Holy Spirit's explanation of the words of Caiaphas, this one contains His amplification: as v. 51 informs us of the *nature* of Christ's death, v. 52 tells us of the *power* and *scope* of it. The great Sacrifice was not offered to God at random. The redemption-price which was paid at the Cross was not offered without definite design. Christ died not simply to make salvation *possible,* but to make it *certain.* Nowhere in Scripture is there a more emphatic and explicit statement concerning the objects for which the Atonement was made. No excuse whatever is there for the vague (we should say, *un*scriptural) views, now so sadly prevalent in Christendom, concerning the ones for whom Christ died. To say that He died for the human race is not only to fly in the face of this plain scripture, but it is grossly dishonoring to the sacrifice of Christ. A large portion of the human race die *un-saved,* and if Christ died for *them,* then was His death largely in vain. This means that the *greatest* of all the works of God is comparatively a failure. How horrible! What a reflection upon the Divine character! Surely men do not stop to examine whither their premises lead them. But how blessed to turn away from man's perversions to the Truth itself. Scripture tells us that Christ "*shall* see of the travail of his soul and be *satisfied.*" No sophistry can evade the fact that these words give positive assurance that every one for whom Christ died will, most certainly, be saved.

Christ died for sinners. But everything turns on the significance of the preposition. What is meant by "Christ died *for* sinners"? To answer that Christ died in order to make it possible for God to righteously receive sinners who come to Him through Christ, is only saying what many a Socinian has affirmed. The testing of a man's orthodoxy on this vital truth of the Atonement requires something far more definite than this. The saving efficacy of the Atonement lies in the *vicarious* nature of Christ's death, in His representing *certain persons,* in His bearing *their* sins, in His being made a curse for *them,* in His *purchasing* them, spirit and soul and body. It will not do to evade this by saying, "There is such a fulness in the satisfaction of Christ, as is *sufficient* for the salvation of the whole world, were the whole world to believe in Him." Scripture always ascribes the salvation of a sinner, not to any *abstract* "sufficiency," but to the *vicarious nature,* the *substitutional* character of the death of Christ. The Atonement, therefore, is in no sense sufficient for a man, unless the Lord Jesus died *for* that man: "For God hath not appointed *us* to wrath, but to obtain salvation by our Lord Jesus Christ, *who died for us*" (I Thess. 5:9, 10). "If the nature of this 'sufficiency' for all men be sifted, it will appear to be nothing more than a *conditional* 'sufficiency,' such as the Arminians attribute to their universal redemption—the condition is: were the whole world *to* believe on Him. The condition, however, is not so easily performed. Many professors speak of faith in Christ as comparatively an easy matter, as though it were within the sinner's power; but the Scriptures teach a different thing. They represent men by nature as spiritually bound with chains, shut up in darkness, in a prison-house. So then all their boasted 'sufficiency' of the Atonement is only an *empty offer* of salvation on certain terms and conditions; and such an Atonement is much too weak to meet the desperate case of a lost sinner" (Wm. Rushton).

Whenever the Holy Scriptures speak of the sufficiency of redemption, they always place it in the *certain efficacy* of redemption. The Atonement of Christ is sufficient because it is absolutely efficacious, and because it effects the salvation of *all for whom* it was made. Its sufficiency lies not in affording man a *possibility* of salvation, but in *accomplishing* their salvation with invincible power. Hence the Word of God never represents the *sufficiency* of the Atonement as wider than the *design* of the Atonement. How different is the salvation of God from the ideas now popularly entertained of it! "As for *thee* also, by the blood of *thy* covenant I have sent forth *thy prisoners* out of the pit wherein is no water" (Zech. 9:11). Christ, by His death paid the ransom, and made sin's captives His own. He has a *legal right* to all of the persons for whom He paid that ransom price, and therefore with God's own right arm they are brought forth.

For whom did Christ die? "For the transgression of *my people* was he stricken" (Isa. 53:8). "Thou shalt call his name JESUS: *for he* shall save *his people* from their sins" (Matt. 1:21). "The Son of man came not to be ministered unto, but to minister, and to give his life a ransom for *many*" (Matt. 20:28). "The good Shepherd giveth his life *for the sheep*" (John 10:11). "Christ also loved *the church* and gave himself *for it*" (Eph. 5:25). "Who gave himself for us, that he might *redeem us* from all iniquity, and purify unto himself *a peculiar people*" (Titus 2:14). "To make propitiation for the sins of *the people*" (Heb. 2:17). Here are seven passages which gave a clear and simple answer to our question, and their testimony, both singly and collectively, declare plainly that the death of Christ was not an atonement for sin abstractedly, nor a mere expression of Divine displeasure against iniquity, nor an indefinite satisfaction of Divine justice, but instead, a ransom-price paid for the eternal redemption of a certain number of sinners, and a plenary satisfaction for *their* particular sins. It is the glory of redemption that it does not merely render God *placable* and man *pardonable*, but that it *has* reconciled sinners to God, put away their sins, and forever perfected His set-apart ones.

"He prophesied that Jesus should die for that nation" (v. 51). The *nature* of Christ's death is here intimated in the word "for": it was *in the stead* of others. Christ died for "*that* nation," (i.e. that "holy nation," I Pet. 2:9). Mark here the striking accuracy of Scripture. Caiaphas did not say that Christ should die for "*this* nation," (namely, the Jewish nation); but for "*that* nation." Isa. 53 will be the confession of that "holy nation," as the beginning of Isa. 54 plainly shows. Then shall it be said, "Thy people also shall be *all* righteous: they shall inherit the land forever, the branch of my planting, the work of my hands, that I may be glorified" (Isa. 60:21).

"And not for that nation only, but that also he should gather together in one the children of God that were scattered abroad" (11:52). Here the Holy Spirit tells us that the *scope* of Christ's death also includes God's elect from among *the Gentiles*. As the Saviour had announced on a former occasion, "I lay down my life for *the* sheep. And *other* sheep I have, which are not of *this* fold: them also I must bring, and they shall hear my voice; and there shall be *one* flock, and one shepherd" (John 10: 15, 16). Here then are the "other sheep," namely, God's elect scattered throughout the world. They are here called "the children of God" because they *were* such in His eternal purpose. Just as Christ said "other sheep I *have*," and just as God said to the Apostle, "I *have* much people in this city" (Acts 18:10), so in the mind of God these were *children*, though "scattered abroad," when Christ died. There is a most striking correspondency between John 11:51, 52 and I John 2:2: the one explains the other. Note carefully the threefold parallelism between them. Christ died with a definite end in view, and the Father had an express purpose before Him in giving up His Son to death. That end and that purpose was that "Israel" should be redeemed, and that "the children of God," scattered abroad, should be gathered together in one—*not* "one body," for the Church is nowhere contemplated (corporeately) in John's writings; but *one* family. It shall yet be fully demonstrated that Christ did not die in vain. The prayer of our great High Priest will be fully answered: "Neither pray I for these alone, but for them also which shall believe on me through their word; that they all may be *one*" (John 17:20,21). Then shall He "see of the travail of his soul and be *satisfied*" (Isa. 53:11).

"Then from that day forth they took counsel together for to put him to death" (11:53). What a fearful climax was this to all that had gone before! Again and again we have noted the incorrigible wickedness of the Jews. Not only was He not "received" by His own, but they cast Him out. Not only was He despised and rejected by men, but they thirsted for His blood. The religious head of the Nation, the high priest, moved for His death, and the Council passed and ratified his motion. Nothing now remained but the actual execution of their awful decision. Their only consideration now was *how* and *when* His death could best be accomplished without creating a tumult among the people. No doubt they concluded that the raising of Lazarus would result in a considerable increase in the number of the Lord's followers, hence they deemed it wise to use caution in carrying out their murderous plan.

"Jesus therefore walked no more openly among the Jews" (11:54). How quietly, with what an entire absence of parade, does the Holy Spirit introduce some of the most striking points in Scripture! How much there is in this word "therefore." It shows plainly that God would have us *meditate* on every jot and tittle of His matchless Word. The force of the "therefore" here is this: the Lord Jesus *knew* of the decision at which the Council had arrived. He *knew* they had decreed that He should die. It is another of the many inconspicuous proofs of His Deity, which are scattered throughout this Gospel. It witnessed to His omniscience. The Holy Spirit has shown us that *He* knew what took place in that Council, for He has recorded the very words that were uttered there. And now Christ shows us by His action here that *He* also knew. We may add that the word for "no more" signifies "not yet," or "no more at present"; "openly" signifies "publicly."

"Jesus therefore walked no more openly among the Jews; but went thence unto a country near to the wilderness, into a city called Ephraim, and there continued with his disciples" (11:54). Though near at hand, His "hour" had not yet come: Christ therefore retired into a place about which nothing is now known, there to enjoy quiet fellowship with His disciples. "Like the former cases of retirement, this place is significant. Ephraim means 'fruitlessness': it is the name given to the tribes in apostasy, in the Prophets, *forecasting* thus what was in God's heart about them, even though they were in rebellion and ruin. Can anything exceed the grace of God, or anything but man's depravity and obduracy bring it into action and display, and be a fitting cause and occasion for all its riches and wonders! Ah they who have been met by God in that grace, are yet to meet Him in the glory of it, to know as all through the history of their sad failures they have been known. Thus we have in chapter ten the Church gathered to the Son of God, here (anticipatively) Israel; but He must die for this" (Malachi Taylor).

"And the Jews' passover was nigh at hand: and many went out of the country up to Jerusalem before the passover, to purify themselves" (11:55). Here was man's religiousness, punctilious about ceremonial ablutions, but with no heart for inward purity. The very ones who were so careful about ordinances, were, in a few days, willing to shed innocent blood! What a commentary upon human nature! According to the Mosaic law no Israelite who was ceremonially defiled could keep the passover at the regular time, though he was allowed to keep it one month later (Num. 9:10, 11). It was to avoid this delay, that many Jews here came up to Jerusalem *before* the passover that they might be "purified," and hence entitled to keep it in the month Nisan.

"Then sought they for Jesus, and spake among themselves, as they stood in the temple, What think ye, that he will not come to the feast?" (11:56). Two things gave rise to this questioning among those who had come up to Jerusalem from all sections of Palestine. Each of the two previous years Christ *had* been present at the Feast. In 2:13 we read, "And the Jews' passover was at hand, and *Jesus went up* to Jerusalem." It was at this season the Lord had manifested Himself as the Vindicator of the honour of His Father's House, and a deep impression had been made on those who had witnessed it. A year later, during the course of the Feast He had fed the hungry multitude on the Mount. This so stirred the people that they wanted, by force, to make Him their king (John 6:14,15). But now the leaders of the nation were incensed against Him. They had decreed that Jesus must die, and their decree was now public knowledge. Hence the one topic of interest among the crowds of Jews in Jerusalem was, would this miracle worker who claimed to be not only the Messiah but the Son of God, enter the danger zone, or would He be afraid to expose Himself?

"Now both the chief priests and the Pharisees had given a commandment, that, if any man know where he were, he should show it that they might take him" (11:57). Behind the edict of the Council we may discover the enmity of the Serpent working against the woman's Seed. This verse supplies the climax to the chapter, showing the full effect of the Divine testimony which had been borne in the raising of Lazarus. The resurrection-power of the Son of God had brought to a head the hatred of him who had the power of death. It is true that Christ had raised the dead on other occasions, but here He had given a public display of His mighty power on the very outskirts of Jerusalem, and *this* was an open affront to Satan and his earthly instruments. The glory of the Lord Jesus shone out so brightly that it seriously threatened the dominion of "the prince of this world," and consequently there was no longer a concealment of the resolution which he had moved the religious world to make—Jesus must die. But how blessed to know that the very enmity of the Devil himself is overruled by God to the outworking of His eternal purpose!

1. In whose house was the "supper" made, v. 2?

Let the student give careful attention to the following questions on our next section, John 12:1-11—

2. What do vv. 2 and 3 hint at about the eternal state?
3. What is intimated by Mary wiping Christ's feet with her "hair," v. 3?
4. What spiritual truth is suggested by the last clause of v. 3?
5. How many contrasts are there here between Mary and Judas?
6. What blessed truth is suggested by "Let her alone," v. 7?
7. Why were the "chief priests" so anxious to get rid of Lazarus, v. 10?

CHAPTER FORTY-ONE

Christ Anointed at Bethany

John 12:1-11

Below is an Analysis of the passage which we are about to study:—

1. Jesus at Bethany again, v. 1.
2. The supper, v. 2.
3. Mary's devotion, v. 3.
4. Judas' criticism, vv. 4-6.
5. Christ's vindication of Mary, vv. 7, 8.
6. The curiosity of the crowd, v. 9.
7. The enmity of the priests, vv. 10, 11.

What is recorded in John 12 occurred during the last week before our Lord's death. In it are gathered up what men would term the "results" of His public ministry. For three years the unvarying and manifold perfections of His blessed Person had been manifested both in public and in private. Two things are here emphasized: there was a deepening appreciation on the part of His own; but a steady hardening of unbelief and increasing hostility in His enemies. Three most striking incidents in the chapter illustrate the former: first, Christ is seen in the midst of a circle of His most intimate friends in whose love He was permanently embalmed; second, we behold how that a striking, if transient, effect, had been made on the popular mind: the multitude hailed Him as "king"; third, a hint is given of the wider influence He was yet to wield, even then at work, beyond the bounds of Judaism: illustrated by the "Greeks" coming and saying, "*We* would see Jesus." But on the other hand, we also behold in this same chapter the workings of that awful enmity which would not be appeased until He had been put to death. The hatred of Christ's enemies had even penetrated the inner circle of His chosen apostles, for one of them was so utterly lacking in appreciation of His person that he openly expressed his resentment against the attribute of love which Mary paid to his Master. And at the close of the first section of this chapter we are told, "But the chief priests consulted that they might put Lazarus also to death." "In this hour there meet a ripeness of love which Jesus has won for Himself in the hearts of men, and a maturity of alienation which forebodes that His end cannot be far distant" (Dr. Dods).

In a most remarkable way and in numerous details John 12 abounds in contrasts. What could be more exquisitely blessed than its opening scene: Love preparing a feast for its Beloved; Martha serving, now in His presence; Lazarus seated with perfect composure and in joyous fellowship with the One who had called him out of the grave; Mary freely pouring out her affection by anointing with costly spikenard Him at whose feet she had learned so much. And yet what can be more solemn than the death-shades which fall across this very scene: the Lord Himself saying, "Against the day *of my burying* hath she kept this," so soon to be followed by those heart-moving words, "Now is my soul troubled" (12:27). His own death was now in full view, present, no doubt, to His heart as He had walked with Mary to the tomb of Lazarus. As we have seen in John 11, He felt deeply the groaning and travailing of that creation which once had come so fair from His own hands. It was sin which had brought in desolation and death, and soon He was to be "made sin" and endure in infinite depths of anguish the judgment of God which was due it. He was about to yield Himself up to death for the glory of God (12:27, 28), for only in the Cross could be laid that foundation for the accomplishment of God's eternal counsels.

Christ had ever been the Object of the Father's complacency. "When he appointed the foundations of the earth: *then* I was by him, as one brought up with him and I was daily his delight" (Prov. 8:29, 30). So too at the beginning of His public ministry, the Father had declared, "This is my beloved Son, in whom I am well pleased" (Matt. 3:17). But now He was about to give the Father *new* ground for delight: "*Therefore* doth my Father love me, *because* I lay down my life, that I might take it again" (John 10:17). Here then was the deepest character of His glory, and the Father saw to it that a fitting testimony should be borne to this very fact. His grace prepared one to enter, in some measure at least, into what was on the eve of transpiring. Mary's heart anticipated what lay deepest in His, even before it found expression in words (13:31). She not only knew that He would die, but she apprehended the infinite preciousness and value of that death. And how more fittingly could she have expressed this than by anointing His body "to the burying" (Mark 14:8)!

The link between John 11 and 12 is very precious. There we have, in figure, one of God's elect passing from death unto life; here we are shown that into which the new birth introduces us: Lazarus sitting at meat with the Lord Jesus. "But now, in Christ Jesus, ye who some times were far off, *are made nigh* by the blood of Christ" (Eph. 2:13). This is the marvel of grace. Redemption brings the sinner into the presence of the Lord, not as a trembling culprit, but as one who is at perfect ease in that Presence, yea, as a joyful worshipper. It is this which Lazarus *sitting* at "the table" with Christ so sweetly speaks of. And yet the opening scene of John 12 looks forward to that which is still more blessed.

The opening verses of John 12 give us *the sequel* to what is central in the preceding chapter. *Here* we are upon resurrection ground. That which is foreshadowed in this happy gathering at Bethany is what awaits believers in the Glory. It is that which shall follow the complete manifestation of Christ as the resurrection and the life. Three aspects of our glorified state and our future activities in Heaven are here made known. First, in Lazarus seated at the table with Christ we learn of both our future position and portion. To be where Christ is, will be the place we shall occupy: "That where *I* am, there *ye* may be also" (John 14:3). To share with Christ His inherited reward will be our portion. And how blessedly this comes out here: "They made *him* a supper . . . Lazarus was one of them that sat *at the table with him*." This will find its realization when Christ shall say, "The glory which thou gavest *me* I have given *them*" (John 17:22)! "And Martha *served*." As to our future occupation in the endless ages yet to come Scripture says very little, yet this we do know, "his servants shall *serve* him" (Rev. 22:4). Finally, in Mary's loving devotion, we behold the unstinted worship which we shall then render unto Him who sought and bought and brought us to Himself.

"Then Jesus six days before the passover came to Bethany, where Lazarus was which had been dead, whom he raised from the dead" (12:1). This verse has long presented a difficulty to the commentators. A few have demurred, but by far the greater number in each age have considered that Matthew (chap. 26) and Mark (chap. 14) record the same incident that is found in John 12. But both Matthew and Mark introduce the anointing at Bethany by a brief mention of that which occurred only "*two* days" before the passover; whereas John tells us it transpired "*six* days" before the passover (see Matt. 26:2; Mark 14:1; John 12:1). But the difficulty is *self* created, and there is no need whatever to imagine, as a few have done, that Christ was anointed *twice* at Bethany, with costly ointment, by a different woman during His last week. The fact is, that, excepting the *order* of events, there is nothing whatever in the Synoptists which in any wise conflicts with what John tells us. How could there be when the Holy Spirit inspired every *word* in each narrative? Both Matthew and Mark begin by telling us of the decision of the Sanhedrin to have Christ put to death, and then follows the account of His anointing at Bethany. But it is to be carefully noted that after recording the decision of the Council "two days" before the passover, Matthew *does not* use his characteristic term and say "*Then* when Jesus was in Bethany, he was anointed"; nor does Mark employ his customary word and say, "And *immediately*" or "*straightway* Jesus was anointed." But how are we to explain Matthew's and Mark's description of the "anointing" *out of its chronological order?*

We believe the answer is as follows: The conspiracy of Israel's leaders to seize the Lord Jesus is followed by a *retrospective* glance at the "anointing" because what happened at Bethany *provided them with an instrument* which thus enabled them to carry out their vile desires. The plot of the priests was successful through the instrumentality of *Judas,* and that which followed Mary's expression of love shows us *what immediately occasioned* the treachery of the betrayer. Judas protested against Mary's extravagance, and the Lord *rebuked* him, and it was immediately afterward that the traitor went and made his awful pact with the priests. Both Matthew and Mark are very definite on this point. The one tells us that immediately following the Lord's reply "*Then* one of the twelve called Judas Iscariot, went unto the chief priests" (26:14); Mark linking together without a break, the rebuke of Christ and the betrayer's act by the word "and" (14:10). John mentions the "supper," at Bethany in its historical order, Matthew and Mark treat of the events *rising out of* the supper, bringing it in to show us that the rebuke of Christ rankled in the mind of Judas and caused him to go at once and bargain with the priests.

But how are we to explain the discrepancies in the different accounts? We answer, There are none. Variations there are, but nothing is inconsistent. The one supplements the other, not contradicts. When John describes any event recorded in the Synoptists, he rarely repeats all the circumstances and details specified by his predecessors, rather does he dwell upon other features not mentioned by them. Much has been made of the fact that both Matthew and Mark tell us that the anointing took place in the house of Simon the leper, whereas John is silent on the point. To this it is sufficient to reply, the fact that the supper was in Simon's house explains why Jesus tells us Lazarus "sat at the table with him": if the supper had been in Lazarus' house, such a notice would have been superfluous. Admire then the silent harmony of the Gospel narratives.*

"Then Jesus six days before the passover came to Bethany" (12:1). The R.V. more correctly renders this, "Jesus *therefore* six days before the passover came to Bethany." But what is the force of the "therefore"? with what in the context is it connected? We believe the answer is found in 11:51: Caiaphas "prophesied that Jesus should *die* for that nation" etc. — "Jesus *therefore* six days before *the passover* came to Bethany." He was the true paschal Lamb that was to be *sacrificed for* His people,

* Other points which have occasioned difficulty to some will be dealt with in the course of this exposition.

therefore did He come to Bethany, which was within easy walking distance of Jerusalem, where He was to be slain. It is very striking to note that the very ones who thirsted so greedily for His blood said, "*Not* on the feast day, lest there be an uproar among the people" (Matt. 26:5—repeated by Mark 14:2). But God's counsels could not be thwarted, and at the very hour the lambs were being slain, the true passover was sacrificed. But why "*six* days before the passover"? Perhaps God designed that in this interval *man* should fully show forth what he was.

"Then Jesus six days before the passover *came to Bethany.*" The memories of Bethany cannot fail to touch a chord in the heart of any one who loves the Lord Jesus. His blood-bought people delight to dwell upon anything which is associated with *His* blessed name. But what makes Bethany so attractive is that He seemed to find in the little company there a resting-place in His toilsome path. It is blessed to know that there was one oasis in the desert, one little spot where He who "endured the contradiction of sinners against himself" could retire from the hatred and antagonism of His enemies. There was one sheltered nook where He could find those who, although they knew but little, were truly attracted to Him. It was to this "Elim" in the wilderness (Ex. 15:27) that the Saviour now turned on His last journey to Jerusalem.

"Where Lazarus was which had been dead, whom he raised from the dead." This is very blessed as an introduction to what follows. The Lord Jesus interpreted the devotion of Mary as "against the day of *my burying* hath she kept this" (12:7). The Father ordered it that His beloved Son should be "anointed" here in this home at Bethany in the presence of Lazarus whom Christ had raised from the dead: it attested the power of *His* own resurrection!

"There they made him a supper" (12:2). This evening meal took place not at the home of Martha, but, as we learn from the other Evangelists, in the house of Simon, who also dwelt at Bethany. He is called "the leper" (as Matthew is still named the "tax-gatherer" *after* Christ had called him) in remembrance of that fearful disease from which the Lord, most probably, had healed him. It is quite likely that he was a relative or an intimate friend of Martha and Mary, for the elder sister is here seen ministering to his guests as her own, superintending the entertainment, doing the honors, for so the original word may here imply—compare the conduct of the mother of Jesus at the marriage in Cana: John 2. It is blessed to observe that this "supper" was made *for Christ,* not in honor of Lazarus!

"There they made him a supper." Note the use of the plural pronoun. Though this supper was held in the house of "Simon the leper" it is evident that Martha and Mary had no small part in the arranging of it. This, together with the whole context, leads us to the conclusion that a feast was here made as an expression of deep gratitude and praise for the raising of Lazarus. Christ was there to share their happiness. In the previous chapter we have seen Him weeping with those who wept, here we behold Him rejoicing with those who rejoice! When He restored to life the daughter of Jairus, He gave the child to her parents and then withdrew. When He raised the widow's son at Nain, He restored him to his mother and then retired. And why? because so far as the record informs us He was a *stranger* to them. But here, after He had raised Lazarus, He *returned* to Bethany and partook of their loving hospitality. It was *His* joy to behold *their* joy, and share in the delight which His restoration of the link which death had severed, had naturally produced. *That* is His "recompense": to rejoice in the joy of His people. Mark another contrast: when He raised Jairus' daughter He said "Give *her to eat";* here after the raising of Lazarus, they *gave Him* to eat!

"There they made him a supper." This points another of the numerous contrasts in which our passage abounds. Almost at the very beginning of His ministry, just before He performed His *first* public "sign," we see the Lord Jesus invited to a marriage-feast; here, almost at the very close of His public ministry, just after His *last* public "sign," a supper is made for Him. But how marked the antithesis! At Cana He turned the water into wine—emblem of the joy of life; here at Bethany He is anointed in view of His own burial!

"And Martha *served.*" This is most blessed. This was *her* characteristic method of showing her affection. On a former occasion the Lord had gently reproved her for being "cumbered with much serving," and because she was anxious and troubled about many things. But she did not peevishly leave off serving altogether. No; she still served: served not the less attentively, but more wisely. Love is unselfish. We are not to feast on our *own* blessings in the midst of a groaning creation, rather are we to be channels of blessing to those around: John 7:38, 39. But mark here that Martha's service is connected *with the Lord*: "They made *him* a supper *and* Martha served." This alone is true service. We must not seek to imitate others, still less, work for the sake of building up a reputation for zeal. It must be done to and for Christ: "Always abounding in the work *of the Lord*" (I Cor. 15:58).

"And Martha served": no longer *outside* the presence of Christ, as on a former occasion – note her "serve alone" in Luke 10:40. "In Martha's 'serving' now we do not find her being 'cumbered', but something that is acceptable, as in the joy of resurrection, the new life, unto Him who has given it. Service is in its true place when we have first *received* all from Him, and the joy of it as begotten by Himself sweetly ministers to Him" (Malachi Taylor).

"But Lazarus was one of them that sat at the table with him" (12:2). This illustrated the true Christian *position.* Lazarus had been dead, but now alive from the dead, he is *seated* in the company of the Saviour. So it is (positionally) with the believer: "when we are dead in sins, hath quickened us together with Christ . . . And hath raised us up together, and made us *sit* together in the heavenlies in Christ Jesus" (Eph. 2:5, 6). We have been "made meet to be partakers of the inheritance of the saints in light" (Col. 1:12). Such is our perfect standing before God, and there can be no lasting peace of heart until it be apprehended by faith.

"But Lazarus was one of them that sat at the table with him." This supplies more than a vague hint of our condition in the resurrected state. In this age of rationalism the vaguest views are entertained on this subject. Many seem to imagine that Christians will be little better than disembodied ghosts throughout eternity. Much is made of the fact that Scripture tells us "flesh and blood shall not inherit the kingdom of God," and the expression "spiritual body" is regarded as little more than a phantasm. While no doubt the Scriptures leave much *un*said on the subject, yet they reveal not a little about the nature of our future bodies. The body of the saint will be "fashioned like unto" the glorious body of the resurrected Christ (Phil. 3:21). It will therefore be a *glorified* body, yet *not* a *non*-material one. There was no blood in Christ's body after He rose from the dead, but He *had* "flesh and bones" (Luke 24:39). True, our bodies will not be subject to their present limitations: sown in weakness, they shall be "raised in *power*." A "spiritual body" we understand (in part) to signify a body *controlled by* the spirit — the highest part of our beings. In our glorified bodies we shall *eat*. The daughter of Jairus needed food after she was restored to life. Lazarus is here seen at the table. The Lord Jesus ate food after He had risen from the dead.

"But Lazarus was one of them that sat at the table with him." "A happy company it must have been. For if Simon was healed by the Lord at some previous time, as has been supposed, full to overflowing must his heart have been for the mercy vouchsafed. And Lazarus, there raised from the dead, what proofs were two of that company of the Lord's power and goodness! God only could heal the leper; God only could raise the dead. A leper healed, a dead man raised, and the Son of God who had healed the one, and had raised the other, here also at the table — never before we may say without fear of contradiction had a supper taken place under such circumstances" (C. E. Stuart).

"Then took Mary a pound of ointment of spikenard, very costly, and anointed the feet of Jesus" (12:3). Mary had often heard the gracious words which proceeded out of His mouth: the Lord of glory had sat at their humble board in Bethany, and she had sat at His feet to be instructed. In the hour of her deep sorrow He had wept with her, and then had He delivered her brother from the dead, crowning them with lovingkindness and tender mercy. And how could she show some token of her love to Him who had first loved her? She had by her a cruse of precious ointment, too costly for her own use, but not too costly for Him. She took and broke it and poured it on Him as a testimony of her deep affection, her unutterable attachment, her worshipful devotion. We learn from 12:5 that the value of her ointment was the equivalent of *a whole year's wages* of a labouring man (cf. Matt. 20:2)! And let it be carefully noted, this devotion of Mary was prompted by no sudden impulse: "against the day of my burying hath she *kept* this" (12:7)—the word means "diligently preserved," used in John 17:12, 15!

"Then took Mary a pound of ointment of spikenard, very costly, and anointed the feet of Jesus." Mary's act occupies the central place in this happy scene. The ointment was "very costly," but not too costly to lavish upon the Son of God. Not only did Mary here express her own love, but she bore witness to the inestimable value of the person of Christ. She entered into what was about to be done to and by Him: she anointed Him for burial. He was despised and rejected of men, and they were about to put Him to a most ignominious death. But before any enemy's hand is laid upon Him, love's hands first anoint Him! Thus another striking and beautiful contrast is here suggested.

"Then took Mary a pound of ointment of spikenard, very costly, and anointed the feet of Jesus." Mark tells us she "broke the box" before she poured it on the Saviour. This, in figure, spoke of the breaking of His body, of which the broken bread in the Lord's Supper is the lasting memorial. Both Matthew and Mark tell us that she anointed the *head* of Christ. This is no discrepancy. Evidently, Mary anointed *both* His head and feet, but most appropriately was John led to notice only the latter, for as the Son of God it was fitting that this disciple should take her place in the dust before Him!

"And wiped his feet with her hair" (12:3). How the Holy Spirit delights in recording that which is done out of love to and for the glory of Christ! How many little details has He preserved for us in connection with Mary's devotion. He has told us of the kind of ointment it was, the box in which it was contained, the weight of it, and its value; and now He tells us something which brings out, most blessedly, Mary's discernment of the glory of Christ. *She* recognized something of what was due Him, therefore after anointing Him she wiped His feet with her "hair" – *her* "glory" (I Cor. 11:15)! Her silent act spread around the savour of Christ as One infinitely precious. Before the *treachery* of Judas, Christ receives the testimony of Mary's *affection*. It was the Father putting this seal of deepest devotion upon the One who was about to be betrayed.

"And the house was filled with the odour of the ointment" (12:3). This is most significant, a detail not supplied in the Synoptics, but most appropriate here. Matthew and Mark tell us how Christ gave orders that "Wheresoever this gospel shall be preached throughout the whole world, this also that she hath done shall be spoken of for a memorial of her" (Mark 14:9). This John omits. In its place he tells us, "And the house was filled with the odour of the ointment." In the other Gospels the "memorial" goes forth: here the fragrance of Christ's person abides in "the *house*." There is much suggested here: not simply the "room" but "the house" was filled with the sweet fragrance of the person of Christ anointed by the spikenard. Sooner or later, all would know what had been done to the Lord. The people on the housetop would perceive that something sweet had been offered below. And do not the angels above know what we below are now rendering unto Christ (cf. I Cor. 11:10, etc.)!

"Mary came not to hear a sermon, although the first of Teachers was there; to sit at His feet and hear His word, was not now her purpose, blessed as that was in its proper place. She came not to make known her requests to Him. Time was when in deepest submission to His will she had fallen at His feet, saying, 'Lord, if thou hadst been here, my brother had not died'; but to pour out her supplications to Him as her only resource was not now her thought, for her brother was seated at the table. She came not to meet the saints, though precious saints were there, for it says 'Jesus loved Martha and Mary and Lazarus.' Fellowship with them was blessed likewise and doubtless of frequent occurrence; but fellowship was not her object now. She came not after the weariness and toil of a week's battling with the world, to be refreshed from Him, though surely she, like every saint, had learned the trials of the wilderness; and none more than she, probably, knew the blessed springs of refreshment that were in Him. But she came, and that too at the moment when the world was expressing its deepest hatred of Him, to pour out what she had long treasured up (12:7), that which was most valuable to her, all she had upon earth, upon the person of the One who had made her heart captive, and absorbed her affections. She thought not of Simon the leper—she passed the disciples by—her brother and her sister in the flesh and in the Lord engaged not her attention then—'Jesus only' filled her soul—her eyes were upon Him. Adoration, homage, worship, blessing, was her one thought, and that in honor of the One who was 'all in all' to her, and surely such worship was most refreshing to Him" (Simple Testimony).

"Then saith one of His disciples, Judas Iscariot, Simon's son, which should betray him, Why was not this ointment sold for three hundred pence, and given to the poor?" (12:4, 5). What a contrast was this from the affectionate homage of Mary! But how could he who had no heart for Christ appreciate her devotion! There is a most striking series of contrasts here between these two characters. She *gave* freely what was worth *three hundred* pence; right afterwards Judas *sold* Christ for *thirty* pieces of silver. She was in a "Simon's" house; He was a "Simon's son." Her "box" (Mark 14:3); his "bag" (John 12:6). She a worshipper; he a thief. Mary drew the attention of all *to* the Lord; Judas would turn away the thoughts of all *from* Christ to "the poor." At the very time Satan was goading on the heart of Judas to do the worst *against* Christ, the Holy Spirit mightily moved the heart of Mary to pour out her love *for* Him. Mary's devotion has given her a place in the hearts of all who have received the Gospel; Judas by his act of perfidy went to "his own place"—the Pit!

Everything is traced to its source in this Gospel. Matthew 26:8 tells us that "When his disciples saw it [Mary's tribute of love], they had indignation, saying, To what purpose is this waste?" But John shows us who was the one that had injected the poison into their minds. *Judas* was the original protester, and his evil example affected the other apostles. What a solemn case is this of evil communications corrupting good manners (I Cor. 15:33)! Everything comes out into the light here. Just as John is the only one who gives us the name of the woman who anointed the Lord, so he alone tells us who it was that started the criticising of Mary.

In 12:3 we have witnessed the devotedness of faith and love never surpassed in a believer. But behind the rosebush lurked the serpent. It reminds us very much of Psa. 23:5: "Thou preparest *a table* before me in *the presence of mine* enemies: thou *anointest* my head *with oil*"! The murmuring of Judas right after the worship of Mary is most solemnly significant. True valuation of Christ always brings out the hatred of those who are of Satan. No sooner was He worshiped as an infant by the wise men from the East, then Herod sought to slay Him. Immediately after the Father proclaimed Him as His "beloved Son," the Devil assailed Him for forty days. The apostles were seized and thrown into prison because the leaders of Israel were incensed that they "taught the people and preached *through Jesus* the resurrection from the dead" (Acts 4:2, 3). So in a coming day many will be beheaded "for the testimony of *Jesus*" (Rev. 20:4).

"Why was not this ointment sold for three hundred pence, and given to the poor?" (12:5). This was the criticism of a covetous soul. How petty his range of vision! How sordid his conception! He argued that the precious ungent which had been lavished upon Christ ought to have been sold. He considered it had been wasted (Mark 14:4). His notion of "waste" was crude and material in the extreme. Love is never "wasted." Generosity is never "wasted." Sacrifice is never "wasted." Love grudges nothing to the Lord of love! Love esteems its costliest nard all inferior to *His* worth. Love cannot give Him too much. And where it is given out of love to Christ we cannot give too much for His servants and His people. How beautifully this is expressed in Phil. 4:18: "having received of Epaphroditus the things which were sent from you, *an odour of a sweet smell,* a sacrifice acceptable, well-pleasing to God."

Judas had no love for Christ, hence it was impossible that he should appreciate what had been done for Him. Very solemn is this: he had been in the closest contact with the redeemed for three years, and yet the love of money still ruled his heart. Cold-heartedness toward Christ and stinginess toward His cause always go together. "To whom little is forgiven, the same loveth little" (Luke 7:47). There are many professing Christians today infested with a Judas-like spirit. They are quite unable to understand true zeal and devotedness to the Lord. They look upon it all as fanaticism. Worst of all, such people seek to cloak their miserliness in giving to Christian objects by a pretended love for the poor: 'charity begins at home' expresses the same spirit. The truth is, and it had been abundantly demonstrated all through these centuries, that those who do the most for the poor are the very ones who are most liberal in supporting the cause of Christ. Let not Christians be moved from a patient continuance in well doing by harsh criticisms from those who understand not. We must not expect professors to do anything *for* Christ when they have no sense of indebtedness *to* Christ.

"Why was not this ointment sold for three hundred pence and given to the poor?" These are the *first* words of Judas recorded in the Gospels; and how they reveal his heart! He sought to conceal his base covetousness under the guise of benevolence. He posed as a friend of the poor, when in reality his soul was dominated by cupidity. It reminds us of his hypocritical "kiss." It is solemn to contrast his *last* words, "I have betrayed innocent blood" (Matt. 27:4).

"This he said, not that he cared for the poor; but because he was a thief, and had the bag, and bare what was put therein" (12:6). It is good to care for the poor, but at that moment the whole mind of God was centered on the Person and work of His Son, evidenced by His moving Mary to anoint the Saviour for His burial. Opportunities for relieving the poor they always had, and it was right to do so. But to put them in comparison with the Lord Jesus at such a time, was to put them out of their place, and to lose sight of Him who was supremely precious to God.

Judas evidently acted as treasurer for the apostolic company (cf. 13:29), having charge of the gifts which the Lord and His disciples received: Luke 8:2, 3. But the Holy Spirit here tells us that he was a "thief." We believe this intimates that the "field" (or "estate") which he purchased (Acts 1:18) "with the reward of iniquity" (or, "price of wrong doing") had been obtained by the money which he pilfered from the same "bag." Usually this "field" is confounded with the "field" that was bought with the thirty pieces of silver which he received for the betrayal of His Master. But *that* money he *returned* to the chief priests and elders (Matt. 27:3, 5), and with it *they* bought "the potter's field to bury strangers in" (Matt. 27:7).

"Then said Jesus, Let her alone" (12:7). How blessed! Christ is ever ready to defend His own! It was the Good Shepherd protecting His sheep from the wolf. Judas condemned Mary, and others of the apostles echoed his criticism. But the Lord approved of her gift. Probably others of the guests misunderstood her action: it would seem an extravagance, and a neglect of duty towards the needy. But Christ knew her motive and commended her deed. So in a coming day He will reward even a cup of water which has been given in His name. "Let her alone": did not this foreshadow His work on high as our Advocate repelling the attacks of the enemy, who accuses the brethren before God day and night (Rev. 12:10)!

"Against the day of my burying hath she kept this" (12:7). This points still another contrast. Other women "brought sweet spices, that they might come and *anoint* him" (Mark 16:1), *after* He was dead; Mary anointed Him "*for* his burial" (Matt. 26:12) six days before He died! Her faith had laid hold of the fact that He *was* going to die—the apostles did not believe this (see Luke 24:21 etc.). She had learned much at His feet! How much we miss through our failure at this point!

Matthew and Mark add a word here which is appropriately omitted by John. "Verily I say unto you, Wheresoever this gospel shall be preached throughout the whole world, this also that she hath done shall be spoken of for a memorial of her" (Mark 14:9). He whose Name is "as ointment poured forth" (S. of S. 1:3), commended her who, all unconsciously, fulfilled the prophecy, "While the king sitteth at his table my spikenard sendeth forth the sweet smell thereof" (S. of S. 1:12). In embalming Him, she embalmed herself: her love being the marble on which her name and deed were sculptured. Note another contrast: Mary gave Christ a momentary embalming; He embalmed her memory forever in the sweet incense of His praise. What a witness is this that Christ will never forget that deed, however small, which is done wholeheartedly in His name and for Himself!

"Hereupon we would further remark that while this can not diminish the sin of Judas, by making his covetousness any thing but covetousness, yet but for his mean remonstrance, we might not have known the prodigality of her love. But for the objection of Judas, we might not have had the commendation of Mary. But for his evil eye, we should have been without the full instruction of her lavish hand. Surely 'The wrath of man shall praise thee'!" (Dr. John Brown).

"For the poor always ye have with you: but me ye have not always" (v.8). There is a little point here in the Greek which is most significant, bringing out, as it does, the minute accuracy of Scripture. In the previous verse "Let alone (aphes) her" is in the singular number, whereas, "The poor always *ye* have (exete) with you" is in the plural number. Let her alone was Christ's rebuke to Judas, who was the first to condemn Mary; here in v. 8 the Lord addresses Himself to the Twelve, a number of whom had been influenced by the traitor's words. Remarkably does this show the entire consistency and supplementary character of the several narratives of this incident. Let us admire the *silent harmonies* of Scripture!

"For the poor always ye have with you: but me ye have not always" (12:8). There is a very searching message for *our* hearts in these words. Mary had *fellowship* with His sufferings, and her *opportunity* for this was brief and soon passed. If Mary had failed to seize her chance to render love's adoring testimony to the preciousness of Christ's person at that time, she could never have recalled it throughout eternity. How exquisitely suited to the moment was her witness to the fragrance of Christ's death before God, when men deemed Him worthy only of a malefactor's cross. She came beforehand to anoint Him "for his burial." But how soon would such an opportunity pass! In like manner we are privileged today to render a testimony to Him in this scene of His rejection. We too are permitted to have *fellowship* with His *sufferings*. But soon this opportunity will pass from us forever! There is a real sense in which these words of Christ to Mary, "me ye have not always" apply to us. Soon shall we enter into the fellowship of His *glory*. O that we may be constrained by His love to deeper devotedness, a more faithful testimony to His infinite worth, and a fuller entering into His sufferings in the present hour of His rejection by the world.

"For the poor always ye have with you: but me ye have not always." One other thought on this verse before we leave it. These words of our Lord's "me ye *have not* always" completely overthrow the Papist figment of transubstantiation. If language means anything, this explicit statement of Christ's positively repudiates the dogma of His "real presence," under the forms of bread and wine at the Lord's Supper. It is impossible to harmonize that blasphemous Romish doctrine with this clear-cut utterance of the Saviour. The "poor *always* ye have with you" in like manner disposes of an idle dream of Socialism.

"Much people of the Jews therefore knew that he was there; and they came not for Jesus' sake only, but that they might see Lazarus also, whom he had raised from the dead" (12:9). "This sentence is a genuine exhibition of human nature. Curiosity is one of the most common and powerful motives in man. The love of seeing something sensational and out of the ordinary is almost universal. When people could see at once both the subject of the miracle and Him that worked the miracle we need not wonder that they resorted in crowds to Bethany" (Bishop Ryle).

"But the chief priests consulted that they might put Lazarus also to death; because that by reason of him many of the Jews went away, and believed on Jesus" (12:10, 11). "Lazarus is mentioned throughout this incident as forming an element in the unfolding of the hatred of the Jews which issued in the Lord's death: notice the climax, from the mere connecting mention in v. 1, then nearer connection in v. 2,—to his being the cause of the Jews flocking to Bethany in v. 9,—and the joint object with Jesus of the enmity of the chief priests in v. 10" (Alford). Mark it was not the Pharisees but the "chief priests," who were Sadducees, (cf. Acts 5:17), that "consulted that they might also put *Lazarus* to death": They would, if possible, kill him, because he was a striking witness *against* them, denying as they did the truth of resurrection. But how fearful the state of their hearts: they had rather commit murder than acknowledge they were wrong.

Let the thoughtful student ponder carefully the following questions:—

1. What does v. 13 teach us about prophecy?
2. Why a "young ass," v. 14?
3. V. 15 (cf. Zech. 9:9); why are some of its words omitted here?
4. In what sense did Christ then "come" as *King,* v. 15?
5. Why did not the disciples "understand," v. 16?
6. Why does v. 17 come in just here?

CHAPTER FORTY-TWO

CHRIST'S ENTRY INTO JERUSALEM

John 12:12-20

The following is an Analysis of the passage which is to be before us: –

1. The crowd going forth to meet Jesus, v. 12.
2. The joyous acclamations of the people, v. 13.
3. The Saviour mounted on an ass, v. 14.
4. The king's presentation of Himself to Israel, v. 15.
5. The dullness of the disciples, v. 16.
6. The cause why the people sought Jesus, vv. 17, 18.
7. The chagrin of the Pharisees, v. 19.

The passage which is to be before us brings to our notice one of the most remarkable events in our Lord's earthly career. The very fact that it is recorded by all the four Evangelists at once indicates something of uncommon moment. The incident here treated of is remarkable because of its *unusual* character. It is quite unlike anything else recorded of the Lord Jesus in the Gospels. Hitherto we have seen Him withdrawing Himself as much as possible from public notice, retiring into the wilderness, avoiding anything that savoured of display. He did not court attraction: He did not "cry nor strive, nor cause his voice to be heard in the streets" (Matt. 12:19). He charged His disciples they should "tell no man that he was Jesus the Christ" (Matt. 16:20). When He raised the daughter of Jairus, He "straitly charged them that no man should know of it" (Mark 5:43). When He came down from the Mount of Transfiguration He gave orders to His disciples that "they should tell no man what things they had seen, till the Son of man was risen from the dead" (Mark 9:9).

We wish to press upon the reader the *uniqueness* of this action of Christ entering Jerusalem in the way that He did, for the more this arrests us the more shall we appreciate the motive which prompted Him. "When Jesus therefore perceived that they (the multitude which He had fed) would come and take him by force, to make him *a king*, he *departed* again into a mount himself alone" (John 6:15). When His brethren urged, "show thyself to the world" (John 7:4), He answered, "My time is not yet come." Here, on the contrary, we see Him making a public entry into Jerusalem, attended by an immense crowd of people, causing even the Pharisees to say, "Behold, the world has gone after him." And let it be carefully noted that Christ Himself *took the initiative* here at every point. It was not the multitude who brought to Him an animal richly caparisoned, nor did the disciples furnish the colt and ask Him to mount it. It was the Lord who *sent* two of the disciples to the entrance of Bethphage to get it, and the Lord *moved* the owner of the ass to give it up (Luke 19:33). And when some of the Pharisees asked Him to rebuke His disciples, He replied, "I tell you, that, if these should hold their peace, the stones would immediately cry out" (Luke 19:40).

How, then, are we to account for this startling change of policy on the part of Christ? What is the true explanation of His conduct? In seeking an answer to this question, men have indulged in the wildest conjectures, most of which have been grossly dishonouring to our Lord. The best of the commentators see in the joyous acclamations of the crowds an evidence of the *power* of Christ. He *moved* them to own Him as their "king," though as to *why* He should here do so they are not at all clear, nor do they explain why His moving their hearts produced such a *transient* effect, for four days later the same crowds shouted "Crucify him." We are therefore obliged to look elsewhere for the key to this incident.

We need hardly say that here, as everywhere, the perfections of the Lord Jesus are blessedly displayed. Two things are incontrovertible: the Lord Jesus ever acted with the Father's *glory* before Him, and ever walked in full accord with His Father's *Word*. "In the volume of the book" it was written of Him, and when He became incarnate He declared "I come to do *thy* will, O God." These important considerations must be kept in mind as we seek a solution to the difficulty before us. Furthermore, we need to remember that the counsel of the Father always had in view *the glory of the Son.* It is by the application of these fundamental principles to the remarkable entry into Jerusalem that light will be shed upon its interpretation.

Why, then, did the Lord Jesus send for the ass, mount it, and ride into the royal city? Why did He suffer the crowds, unrebuked, to hail Him with their "Hosannas"? Why did He permit them to proclaim Him their king, when in less than a week He was to lay down His life as a sacrifice for sin? The answer, in a word, is, because *the Scriptures so required!* Here, as ever, it was submission to His Father's Word that prompted Him. Loving obedience to the One who sent Him was always the spring of His actions. His cleansing of the temple was the fulfilment of Psa. 69:9. The testimony which He bore to Himself was the same as the Old Testament Scriptures announced (John 5:39). When on the cruel Cross He cried, "I thirst," it was not in order for His sufferings to be alleviated, but "that the scripture might be fulfilled" (John 19:28). So here, He entered Jerusalem in the way that He did in order that the Scriptures might be fulfilled.

What scriptures? The answer to this question takes us back, first of all, to the prophecy which dying Jacob made, a prophecy which related what was to befall his descendants in "the last days"—an Old Testament expression referring to the times of the Messiah: begun at His first advent, completed at His second. In the course of His Divine pronouncement, the aged patriarch declared, "the sceptre shall not depart from Judah, nor a lawgiver from between his feet until Shiloh come; and unto him shall the *gathering* of the people be. Binding his foal unto the vine, and his ass's colt unto the choice vine" (Gen. 49:9-11). The word "sceptre" here signifies *tribal rod.* Judah was to preserve the separate independency of his tribe until the Messiah came. The fulfilment of this is seen in the Gospels. Though the ten tribes had long before been carried into captivity, from which they never returned, Judah (the "Jews"), were still in Palestine when the Son of God became incarnate and tabernacled among men. Continuing his prophecy, Jacob announced, "And unto him [Shiloh—the *Peacemaker*—cf. 'thy peace' in Luke 19:42], shall the *gathering* of *the* people be." This received its first fulfilment at Christ's official entry into Jerusalem. But mark the next words, "Binding his foal unto the vine, and his ass's colt unto the choice vine." The "vine" was Israel (Isa. 5, etc); the "choice vine" was Christ Himself (John 15:1). Here, then, was *the fact itself* prophetically announced. But this by no means exhausts the scriptural answer to our question.

We turn next to that remarkable prophecy given through Daniel respecting the "seventy weeks." This prophecy is found in Dan. 9:24-27. We cannot now attempt an exposition of it,* though it is needful to make reference to it. This prophecy was given while Israel were captives in Babylon. In it God made known the length of time which was to elapse from then till the day when Israel's transgressions should be finished, and everlasting righteousness be brought in. "Seventy weeks" were to span this interval. The Hebrew word for "weeks" is "hebdomads," and simply means *septenaries;* "Seventy sevens" gives the true meaning. Each of the "hebdomads" equals seven years. The "seventy sevens," therefore, stood for four hundred and ninety years.

The "seventy sevens" are divided into three unequal parts. Seven "sevens" were to be spent in the rebuilding of Jerusalem: the books of Ezra and Nehemiah record the fulfilment of this. After Jerusalem *had been* restored, sixty-two more "sevens" were to run their course "unto the Messiah the Prince." And then we are told, "After threescore and two sevens (added to the previous seven 'sevens', making sixty-nine in all), shall Messiah be cut off." Here, then, is a definite computation, and a remarkable and most important Messianic prophecy. "Messiah *the Prince*" (cf. Rev. 1:5), was to present Himself to Jerusalem (note "thy holy city" in Dan. 9:24), after the expiration of the sixty-ninth "seven," or more specifically, precisely four hundred

*** This wonderful and important prophecy is carefully, interestingly, and most helpfully dealt with in The Seventy Weeks and the Great Tribulation by Mr. Philip Mauro. New, revised edition now available ($2.50) from the Bible Truth Depot, Swengel, Pa. Don't fail to secure a copy. (I.C.H.)**

and eighty-three years after God gave this prophecy to His beloved servant.

Now, it is *this* prophecy which received its fulfilment and supplies the needed key to what is before us in John 12. The entry of the Lord Jesus into Jerusalem in such an auspicious manner, was the Messiah *formally and officially presenting Himself to Israel as their "Prince."* In his most excellent book "The Coming Prince," the late Sir Robert Anderson marshalled conclusive proofs to show that our Saviour entered Jerusalem *on the very day* which marked the completion of the sixty-ninth "hebdomad" of Dan. 9. We make here a brief quotation from his masterly work.

"No student of the Gospel-narrative can fail to see that the Lord's last visit to Jerusalem was not only in fact, but in the purpose of it, the crisis of His ministry, the goal towards which it had been directed. After the first tokens had been given that the Nation would *reject* His Messianic claims, He had shunned all public recognition of them. But now the two-fold testimony of His words and works had been fully tendered. His entrance into the Holy City was to proclaim His Messiahship, and to receive His doom. Again and again His apostles even had been charged that they *should not* make Him known. But now He accepted the acclamations of 'the whole multitude of the disciples,' and silenced the remonstrance of the Pharisees with indignation.

"The full significance of the words which follow in the Gospel of Luke is concealed by a slight interpolation in the text. As the shouts broke forth from His disciples, 'Hosanna to the Son of David, blessed is the King of Israel that cometh in the name of the Lord,' He looketh off toward the Holy City and exclaimed, 'If *thou* also hadst known, even *on this day,* the things which belong to thy peace! but now they are hid from thine eyes' (Luke 19:42). The time of Jerusalem's visit had come, and she knew it not. Long ere this, the Nation had rejected Him, but this was the predestined day when their choice must be irrevocable."

One other prophecy remains to be considered, in some respects the most wonderful of the three. If God announced through Jacob the simple fact of the gathering of the people unto the Peacemaker, if by Daniel He made known the very year and day when Israel's Messiah should officially present himself as their Prince, through Zechariah He also made known the very *manner* of His entry into Jerusalem. In Zech. 9:9 we read: "Rejoice greatly, O daughter of Zion, shout, O daugther of Jerusalem; behold, thy king cometh unto thee: He is just, and having salvation; lowly and riding upon an ass, and upon a colt, the foal of an ass." As we shall see, several words in this prophecy are not quoted in the Gospels, therefore this prediction (like all prophecy) will receive *another* fulfilment; it will be completely realized when the Lord Jesus returns to this earth.

Before we come to the detailed exposition, let us offer a brief comment upon what has just been before us. At least three prophecies were fulfilled by Christ on His official entry into Jerusalem, prophecies which had been given hundreds of years before, prophecies which entered into such minute details that only one explanation of them is possible, and that is *God Himself* must have given them. This is the most incontrovertible and conclusive of all the proofs for *the Divine inspiration* of the Scriptures. Only He who knows the end from the beginning is capable of making accurate forecasts of what shall happen many generations afterwards. How the recorded accomplishment of these (and many other) prophecies *guarantees* the fulfilment of those which are still future!

"On the next day much people that were to come to the feast, when they heard that Jesus was coming to Jerusalem, took branches of palm trees, and went forth to meet him, and cried: 'Hosanna! Blessed is the King of Israel that cometh in the name of the Lord'" (12:12, 13). It is important to note the opening words of this quotation. What we have here is the sequel to the first verse of our chapter. "Then Jesus six days before the passover came to Bethany." During the week preceding the passover Jerusalem was crowded with Jews, who came in companies from every section of Palestine. They came early in order that they might be ceremonially qualified to partake of the feast (11:55). Already we have learned that the main topic of conversation among those who thronged the temple at this time was whether or not *Jesus* would come up to the feast (11:56). Now, when the tidings reached them that He *was* on the way to Jerusalem, they at once set out to meet Him.

In view of what we read of in 11:57, some have experienced a difficulty here. "Both the chief priests and the Pharisees had given a commandment, that, if any man knew where he were, he should show it, that they might take him." How came it then that we now read of "*much* people . . . took palm branches and went forth to meet him?" The difficulty is quickly removed if only close attention be paid to what the Holy Spirit has said. First, note that in 11:57 the past tense is used, "*had* given commandment": this was before the Lord Jesus retired to Ephraim (11:54). Second, observe that 11:55 tells us "many went *out of the country* up to Jerusalem" (11:55). It is evident therefore that many (if not all) of those who now sallied forth with palm branches to greet the Lord were men of *Galilee*, pilgrims, who had come up to the metropolis from the places where most of His mighty works were done. It was the *Galileans* who on a previous occasion sought to make Him "a king" (John 6:15, cf. 7:1). They were not only far less prejudiced against Him than were those of Judea, but they were also much less under the influence of the chief priests and Pharisees of Jerusalem. Marvelously accurate is Scripture. The more minutely it is examined the more will its flawless perfections be uncovered to us. How this instance shows us, once more, that our 'difficulties' in the Word are due to our negligence in carefully noting exactly what it says, and *all* it says on any given subject!

"Took branches of palm trees, and went forth to meet him" (v. 13). This was a sign of joy, a festival token. In connection with the feast of tabernacles God instructed Moses to tell Israel, "And ye shall take you on the first day the boughs of goodly trees, *branches* of palm trees . . . and ye shall *rejoice* before the Lord your God" (Lev. 23:40). In Rev. 7:9, where we behold the "innumerable multitude before the throne and before the Lamb," they have "*palms* in their hands."

"And cried, Hosanna! Blessed is the King of Israel that cometh in the name of the Lord." The word Hosanna means "Save now!" It is a cry of triumph, not of petition. As to how far these people entered into the meaning of the words which they here uttered, perhaps it is not for us to say. The sequel would indicate they were only said under the excitement of the moment. But looking beyond their intelligent design, to Him whose overruling hand directs everything, we see here the Father causing a public testimony to be borne to the glory of His Son. At His birth He sent the angels to say to the Bethlehem shepherds, "Unto you is born this day in the city of David, a Saviour, which is Christ the Lord," and now He suffered this multitude to hail Him as the Blessed One come in the Name of the Lord. Again; before the public ministry of Christ commenced, the wise men from the East were led to Jerusalem to announce that the *king* of the Jews had been born; and now that His public ministry was over, it is again testified to that He is "the *King* of Israel."

"And Jesus, when he had found a young ass, sat thereon; as it is written" (12:14). This is simply a comprehensive statement, gathering up in a word the results of the details supplied by the other Evangelists, and which John takes for granted we are familiar with. The fullest account of the *obtaining* of the young ass is furnished by Luke, and very striking is it to note what occurred—*see* Luke 19:29-35. There is nothing in his account which conflicts with the shorter statement which John has given us. "And Jesus, when he had found a young ass, sat thereon." *He* "found" it because He directed the disciples *where* to find it! It is another of those incidental allusions to the *Deity* of Christ, for in an unmistakable way it evidenced His omniscience; He knew the precise spot where the ass was tethered!

"Fear not, daughter of Sion; behold, thy King cometh, sitting on an ass's colt" (12:15). Emphasis is here laid on the age of the animal which Christ rode. It was a "young" one; Luke tells us that it was one "whereon yet never man sat" (19:30). This is not without deep significance. Under the Mosaic economy only those beasts which had never been worked were to be used for sacrificial purposes (see Num. 19:2; Deut. 21:3). Very striking is this. Like His birth of a *virgin,* like His burial in a *new* sepulchre, "wherein was never man yet laid" (John 19:41); so here, on the only occasion when He assumed anything like majesty, He selected a colt which had never previously been ridden. How blessedly this points to the dignity, yea, the uniqueness of His person hardly needs to be dwelt upon.

"Sat thereon, *as it is written.*" How this confirms what we said at the beginning. It was in order to fulfil the prophetic Word that the Lord Jesus here acted as He did. That which was "written" was what ever controlled Him. He lived by *every* word which proceeded out of the mouth of the Lord. The incarnate Word and the written Word never conflicted. What ground then had He to say, "I do *always* those things that please him"! O that *we* might have more of *His* spirit!

"Fear not, daughter of Sion: behold, thy King cometh, sitting on an ass's colt." Momentous hour was this. Israel's true king, David's Son and Lord, now officially presented Himself to the nation. Various have been the attempts made to interpret this. In recent years the view which has had most prominence among students of prophetic truth is, that Christ was here *offering* the kingdom to Israel, and that had Israel received Him the millennial reign would have been speedily inaugurated. It is worse than idle to speculate about what would have happened *if* the nation had acted differently from what they did; idle, because "secret things belong unto the Lord." Our duty is to search diligently and study prayerfully "those things which *are* revealed" (Deut. 29:29), knowing that whatever difficulties may be presented, Israel's rejection and crucifixion of the Lord Jesus were according to what God's hand and counsel "*determined before* to be done" (Acts 4:28).

What then was Christ's purpose in presenting Himself to Israel as their King? The immediate answer is, To meet the requirements of God's prophetic Word. But this only takes the inquiry back another step. What was *God's purpose* in requiring Israel's Messiah to so act on this occasion? In seeking an answer to this, careful attention must be paid to the setting.

As we turn to the context we are at once impressed by the fact that one thing there is made unmistakably prominent—the *death* of Christ looms forward with tragic vividness. At the close of John 11 we find the leaders of the nation "took counsel together for to put him to death" and the Council issued a decree that, "If any man knew where he was, he should show it, that they might take him" (11:53, 57). The 12th chapter opens with the solemn intimation that it now lacked but six days to the passover. The all-important "hour" for the slaying of the true Lamb drew on apace. Then we have the anointing of Christ by Mary, and the Saviour interpreted her act by saying, "Against the day of my *burying* hath she kept this."

Here, then, is the key, hanging, as usual, right on the door. The Lord of glory was about to lay down His life, but before doing so the dignity of His person must first be publicly manifested. Moreover, wicked hands were about to be laid on Him, therefore the guilt of Israel must be rendered the more inexcusable by them now learning *who* it was they would shortly crucify. The Lord therefore purposely drew the attention of the great crowds to Himself by placing Himself prominently before the eyes of the nation. What we have here is, Christ pressing Himself upon *the responsibility* of the Jews. None could now complain that they knew not who He was. On a former occasion they had said to Him, "How long dost thou make us to doubt? If thou be the Christ, tell us plainly" (10:24). But now all ground for ignorance was removed; by fulfilling the prophecies of Jacob, of Daniel, and of Zechariah, the Lord Jesus demonstrated that *He* was none other than Israel's true king. It was His last public testimony to the nation! He *was* their "King," and in fulfilment of the plain declarations of their own Scriptures He here presented Himself before them.

The prophecy of Zechariah is not quoted in its entirety by any of the Evangelists, and it is most significant to mark the different words in it which they omit. First of all, none record the opening words, "Rejoice greatly, O daughter of Zion; shout, O daughter of Jerusalem." The reason for this is obvious; Israel could not be called upon to "rejoice" while she was *rejecting* her King! That part of the prophecy awaits its realization in a future day. Not until she has first *"mourned"* as one mourneth for his only son (Zech. 12:10), not until Israel "acknowledge their offence" (Hosea 5:15), not until they "repent" (Acts 3:19), not until they say, "Come, and let us *return* unto the Lord: for he hath torn, and he will heal us; he hath smitten, and he will bind us up" (Hosea 6:1); in short, not until their sins are put away, will the spirit of joy and gladness be given unto them.

In the second place, the words "just and having salvation" are omitted from each of the Gospels. This also is noteworthy, and is a striking proof of the *verbal* inspiration of the Scriptures. It was not in *justice,* but in *grace,* that the Lord Jesus came to Israel the first time. He came "to seek and to save that which was lost." He appeared "to put away sin by the sacrifice of himself." But when He comes the second time, God's word through Jeremiah shall receive its fulfilment—"Behold, the days come, saith the Lord, that I will raise unto David a *righteous* branch, and a king shall reign and prosper, and shall execute *judgment and justice* in the earth." But why the omission of "having salvation?" Because Israel as a nation would not have salvation. Ofttimes would He have gathered her children together, but they "would not."

One other omission remains to be noticed: the smallest, but by no means the least significant. Zechariah foretold that Israel's king should come *"lowly,* and riding upon an ass." Matthew mentions the lowliness of Christ, though in the A. V. it is rendered "meek" (21:5). But this word is *left out by John.* And why? Because it is the central design of the fourth Gospel to emphasize the *glory* of Christ. (See 1:14; 2:11; 11:4, etc.)

"Fear not, daughter of Sion; behold, thy King cometh, sitting on an ass's colt" (12:15). The fact that the Lord Jesus was seated upon "an ass" brings out His mortal glory. As the Son of David according to the flesh, He was "made under the law" (Gal. 4:4), and perfectly did He fulfil it at every point. Now, one thing that marked out Israel as God's peculiar people was the absence of the *horse,* in their midst. The "ox" was used in plowing, and the "ass" for riding upon, or carrying burdens. An express decree was made forbidding the king to multiply horses to himself: "But he *shall not* multipy horses to himself, nor cause the people to return to Egypt, to the end that he should multiply *horses*" (Deut. 17:16). Thus the king of God's separated people was to be sharply distinguished from the monarchs of the Gentiles—note how Pharaoh (Ex. 14:23; 15:1), the kings of Canaan (Josh. 11:4), Naaman (II Kings 5:9), the king of Assyria (Isa. 37:8), are each mentioned as the possessors of many horses and chariots. But the true Israelites could say, "Some trust in chariots, and some in horses: *but we* will remember the name of the Lord our God" (Psa. 20:7). It is remarkable that the first recorded sin of Solomon was concerning this very thing: "And Solomon had forty thousand stalls of horses for his chariots, and twelve thousand horsemen" (I Kings 4:26). It was, therefore, as One *obedient* to the Law, that Christ purposely selected an "ass"!

"Fear not, daughter of Sion: behold, thy King cometh, sitting on an ass's colt." How evident it is that Christ *had* laid aside His glory (John 17:5). He who was in the form of God, and thought it not robbery to be equal with God, made Himself of "no reputation," and took upon Him the form of a *servant*. Not only does this action of our wonderful Saviour mark His perfect subjection to the law of Moses, but it also brings out His gracious lowliness. When He formally presented Himself to Israel as their king, He rode not in a golden chariot, drawn by powerful stallions, but instead He came seated upon the colt of an ass. Neither was the beast harnessed with any goodlier trappings than the garments which His disciples had spread thereon. And even the ass was not His own, but borrowed! Truly the things which are "highly esteemed among men are abomination in the sight of God" (Luke 16:15). "No Roman soldier in the garrison of Jerusalem, who, standing at his post or sitting in his barrock-window, saw our Lord riding on an ass, could report to his centurion that He looked like one who came to wrest the kingdom of Judea out of the hands of the Romans, drive out Pontius Pilate and his legions from the tower of Antonia, and achieve independence for the Jews with the sword" (Bishop Ryle). How evident it was that *His* kingdom was "not of this world!" What an example for us to "Be not conformed to this world" (Rom. 12:2)!

Perhaps some may be inclined to object: But does not Rev. 19:11 *conflict* with what has just been said? In no wise. It is true that there we read, "And I saw heaven open, and behold a white *horse;* and he that *sat upon him* was called Faithful and True." There is no room to doubt that the Rider of this "white horse" is any other than the Lord Jesus Christ. But He will appear thus at His *second* advent. Then everything shall be changed. He who came before in humiliation and shame shall return in power and majesty. He who once had not where to lay His head shall then sit on the throne of His *glory* (Matt. 25:31). He who was nailed to a malefactor's Cross shall, in that day, wield the sceptre of imperial dominion. Just as the "ass" was well suited to the One who had laid aside His glory, so the white "war-horse" of Rev. 19 is in perfect keeping with the fact that He is now "crowned with glory and honour."

"These things understood not his disciples" (12:16). How ingenuous such a confession by one of their number! No impostor would have deprecated himself like this. How confidently may we depend upon the veracity of such honest chroniclers! Like us, the apostles apprehended Divine things but slowly. Like us, they had to "*grow* in grace and in the knowledge of our Lord and Saviour Jesus Christ." But mark, it does not say "these things *believed not* his disciples." It is our privilege, as well as our bounden duty, to believe *all* God has said, whether we "understand" it or not. The more implicitly we believe, the more likely will God be pleased to honour our faith by giving us understanding (Heb. 11:3).

"But when Jesus was glorified, then remembered they that these things were written of him, and that they had done these things unto him" (12:16). From the fact that the plural number is twice used here—"these things"—and from the very similar statement in John 2:22 we believe that the entire incident of our Lord's entry into Jerusalem, with all its various accompaniments, are here included. Probably that which most puzzled the disciples is what Luke has recorded: "And when he was come near, he beheld the city, and *wept over it*" (19:41). In view of this verse it would be more accurate to speak of our Lord's *tearful* entry into Jerusalem, rather than His *triumphant* entry. Christ was not misled by the exalted cries of the people. He knew that the hour of His crucifixion, rather than His coronation, was near at hand. He knew that in only a few days' time the "Hosannas" of the multitudes would give place to their "Away with him!" He knew that the nation would shortly consummate its guilt by giving Him a convict's gibbet instead of David's throne.

But *why* should the disciples have been so puzzled and unable to understand "these things?" It was because they were so reluctant to think that this One who had power to work such mighty miracles should be put to a shameful death. To the very end, they had hoped He would restore the kingdom and establish His throne at Jerusalem. The honours of the kingdom attracted, the shame of the Cross repelled them: It was because of this that on the resurrection-morning He said to the two disciples, "O fools, and slow of heart to believe all that the prophets have spoken; ought not Christ to have suffered these things and to enter into his glory?" (Luke 24:25, 26). Yes, there had to be the sufferings *before* the glory, the Cross before the Crown (cf. I Pet. 1:11). But when Jesus was "glorified," that is, when He had ascended to heaven and the Holy Spirit had been given to guide them into all truth, *then* "remembered they that these things *were* written of him."

"The people therefore that were with him when he called Lazarus out of his grave and raised him from the dead, bare record. For this cause the people also met him, for that they heard that he had done this miracle" (12:17, 18). This line in the picture is supplied only by John, and suitably so, for it was in the raising of Lazarus that the glory of *the Son of God* had been manifested (11:4). They who had witnessed that notable miracle had reported it in Jerusalem, and now it was known that He who had power to restore the dead to life was nearing the Capital, many came forth to meet Him. Doubtless one reason why this is brought in here is to emphasize the deep guilt of the nation for rejecting Him whose credentials were so unimpeachable.

"The Pharisees therefore said among themselves, Perceive ye how ye prevail nothing? behold, the world is gone after him"

(12:19). Here is one of the many evidences of the truthful consistency of the independent accounts which the different Evange lists have given us of this incident. Luke tells us: "And some of the Pharisees from among the multitude said unto him, Master, rebuke thy disciples" (19:39), and the Lord had answered them, "I tell you that, if these should hold their peace, the stones would immediately cry out." Here we are shown their chagrin. They were envious of His popularity; they feared for their own hold over the people.

But here a difficulty confronts us, and one which we have seen no real effort to solve. The majority of the commentators suppose that the joyous greetings which the Lord Jesus received from the crowds on this occasion were the result of a secret putting forth of His Divine power, attracting their hearts to Himself. But how shall we explain the *evanescent* effect which it had upon them? how account for the fact that less than a week later the same crowds cried, "Crucify him"? To affirm that this only illustrates the *fickleness* of human nature is no doubt to say what is sadly too true. But if *both* of their cries were simply expressions of "human nature," where does the influencing of their heart by *Divine* power come in? We believe the difficulty is self-created, made by attributing the first cry to a wrong cause.

Two things are very conspicuous in God's dealings with men: His *constraining* power and His *restraining* power. As illustrations of the former, take the following examples. It was *God* who gave Joseph favour in the sight of the keeper of the prison (Gen. 39:22), who moved Balaam to bless Israel when he was hired to curse them (Num. 23:20), who stirred up the spirit of Cyrus to make a proclamation giving the Jews the right to return to Palestine (Ezra 1:1, 2). As illustrations of the latter, mark the following cases. It was God who "withheld" Abimelech from sinning (Gen. 20:6); the brethren of Joseph "conspired against him to *slay* him" (Gen. 37:18), but God did not allow them to carry out their evil intentions.

Now, these same two things are given a prominent place in the Gospels in connection with the Lord Jesus. At His bidding the leper was cleansed, the blind saw, the dead were raised. At His word the disciples forsook their nets, Matthew left the seat of custom, Zaccheus came down from his leafy perch and received Him into his house. At His command the apostles went forth without bread or money (Luke 9:3); made the hungry multitudes sit down for a meal, when all that was in sight were five small loaves and two little fishes. Yes, a mighty *constraining* power did He wield. But equally mighty, if not so evident, was the *restraining* power that He exerted. At Nazareth His rejectors "led him into the brow of the hill . . . that they might cast him down headlong. But he, *passing through the midst of them,* went his way" (Luke 4:29, 30). In John 10:39 we are told "They sought again to take him, but *he went forth out of their hands.*" When the officers came to arrest Him in the Garden, and He said, "I am," they "went backward and fell to the ground" (18:6)!

But the *restraining* power of Christ was exercised in another way than in the above instances. He also *checked* the fleshly enthusiasm of those who were ready to welcome Him as an Emancipator from the Roman yoke. When they would "come and take him by force, to make him a king, he *departed*" (6:15). All through His ministry He discouraged all public tokens of honour from the people, lest (humanly speaking) the envy of His enemies should bring His preaching to an untimely end. But His public ministry was over, so He now *removes the restraint* and allows the multitudes to hail Him with their glad Hosannas, and this, not that He now craved pomp, but in order that the Scriptures might be fulfilled. These transports of joy from the Galileans were raised because they imagined that He would there and then set up His temporal kingdom. Hence, when *their* hopes were disappointed, their transports were turned into rage and therefore did *they* join in the cry of "crucify him"!

Ponder the following questions as a preparation for our next chapter: —

1. Why did the Greeks seek out Philip, v. 21?
2. Why did Philip first tell Andrew, not Christ, v. 22?

3. What is meant by "glorified" in v. 23?
4. Why did Christ say v. 24 at this time?
5. What is meant by v. 31?
6. What is meant by "draw," v. 32?
7. Why did Jesus "hide" Himself, v. 36?

CHAPTER FORTY-THREE

Christ Sought by Gentiles

John 12:20-36

The following is a suggested Analysis of the passage which is to be before us: —

1. The desire of the Greeks to see Jesus, vv. 20-23.
2. Christ's response, vv. 24-26.
3. Christ's prayer and the Father's answer, vv. 27, 28.
4. The people's dullness, vv. 29, 30.
5. Christ's prediction, vv. 31-33.
6. The people's query, v. 34.
7. Christ's warning, vv. 35, 36.

The end of our Lord's public ministry had almost been reached. Less than a week remained till He should be crucified. But before He lays down His life His varied glories must be witnessed to. In John 11 we have seen a remarkable proof that He was the *Son of God*: evidenced by His raising of Lazarus. Next, we beheld a signal acknowledgment of Him as *the Son of David*: testified to by the jubilant Hosannas of the multitudes as the king of Israel rode into Jerusalem. What is before us now concerns Him more especially as *the Son of man*. As the Son of David He is related only to Israel, but His Son of man title brings in a wider connection. It is as "the Son of man" He comes to the Ancient of days, and as such there is "given him dominion and glory, and a kingdom, that *all* people, nations, and languages, should serve him" (Dan. 7:14). In perfect keeping with this, our present passage shows us Gentiles seeking Him, saying, "We would see," not "the Christ," but "*Jesus*." Thus the Father saw to it that His blessed Son should receive this threefold witness ere He suffered the ignominy of the Cross.

It is both instructive and blessed to trace the *links* which unite passage to passage. There is an intimate connection between this third section of John 12 and what has preceded it. Again and again in the course of these expositions we have called attention to the *progressive unfolding* of truth in this Gospel, and here, too, we would observe, briefly, the striking *order* followed by Christ in His several references to His own death and resurrection. In John 10 the Lord Jesus is before us as the Shepherd, leading God's elect out of Judaism and bringing them into the place of liberty, and in order to do this He *lays down His life* that He may possess these sheep (vv. 11, 15, 17, 18). In John 11 He is seen as the resurrection and the life, as *the Conqueror of death,* with power in Himself to raise His own – a decided advance on the subject of the previous chapter. But in John 12 He speaks of Himself as "the corn of wheat" that falls into the ground and dies, that it may bear "much fruit." This speaks both of *union and communion,* blessedly illustrated in the first section of the chapter, where we have the happy gathering at Bethany *supping* with Him.

If the Lord Jesus is to be to others the "resurrection" and the "life", we now learn what this involved *for Him.* He should be glorified by being the firstborn among many brethren. But how? Through death: "Except a corn of wheat fall into the ground and *die,* it abideth *alone*: but if it die, it bringeth forth much fruit" (12:24). Life could not come to us but through His death; resurrection-life out of death accomplished. *Except* a man be born again he cannot enter the kingdom of God; and *except* Christ had died none could be born again. The new birth is the impartation of a new life, and that life none other than the life of a resurrected Saviour, a life which has passed through death, and, therefore, forever *beyond* the reach of judgment. "The gift of God is eternal life *in* Jesus Christ our Lord" (Rom. 6:23 Greek).

Some have experienced a difficulty here: If the Divine life in the believer is the life of the *risen* Christ, then what of the Old Testament saints? But the difficulty is more fanciful than real. It is equally true that there could be *no salvation* for any one, no putting away of sins, until the great Sacrifice had been offered to God. But surely none will infer from this that no one *was* saved before the Cross. The fact is that both life and salvation flowed *backwards* as well as forwards from the Cross and the empty sepulchre. It is a significant thing, however, that nowhere in the Old Testament are we expressly told of believers then possessing "eternal life," and no doubt the reason for this is stated in II Tim. 1:10, "But is now made manifest by the appearing of our Saviour Jesus Christ, who hath abolished death, and *hath brought* life and immortality *to light* through the gospel."

It is very striking to observe that our Lord did not speak of the union and communion of believers with Himself until the *Gentiles* here sought Him. It is a higher truth altogether than any which He ever addressed to Israel. His Messiahship resulted from a fleshly relationship, the being "Son of David," and it is on *this* ground that He was to sit upon the throne of His father David and "reign over the house of Jacob" (Luke 1:32, 33). But this was not the goal before Him when He came to earth the first time: to bring a people to His own place in the glory was the set purpose of His heart (John 14:2, 3). But a heavenly people must be related to Him by something higher than fleshly ties: they must be joined to Him in spirit, and this is possible only on the resurrection side of death. Hence that word; "Wherefore henceforh know we no man after the flesh: yea, though we have known Christ *after the flesh,* yet now henceforth know we him no more" (II Cor. 5:16). It is the One who has been "lifted up" (*above* this earth) that now draws *all*—elect Gentiles as well as Jews—unto Himself.

"And there were certain Greeks among them that came up to worship at the feast: The same came therefore to Philip, which was of Bethsaida of Galilee, and desired him, saying, Sir, we would see Jesus" (12:20, 21). This is very striking. The rejection of Christ by Israel was soon to be publicly evidenced by them delivering Him up to the Romans. As Daniel had announced centuries before, after sixty-nine weeks "shall Messiah be cut off" (9:26). Following His rejection by the Jews, God would visit the Gentiles "to take out of them a people for his name" (Acts 15:14). This is what was here foreshadowed by "the Greeks" supplicating Him. The *connection* is very striking: in v. 19 we find the envious Pharisees saying, "The *world* is gone after him," here, "*And* . . . certain *Greeks* . . . saying, We would see Jesus." It was a "first-fruit," as it were, of a coming harvest. It was the pledge of the "gathering together into one the children of God that were scattered abroad" (11:52). It was another evidence of the fields being "white already to harvest" (4:35). These "Greeks" pointed in the direction of those other "sheep" which the Good Shepherd must also bring. It is also significant to note that just as Gentiles (the wise men from the East) had sought Him soon after His birth, so now these "Greeks" came to Him shortly before His death.

Exactly who these "Greeks" were we cannot say for certain. But there are two things which incline us to think that very likely they were Syro-Phoenicians. First, in Mark 7:26, we are told that the woman who came to Christ on behalf of her obsessed daughter, was "a *Greek,* a Syro-Phoenician by nation." Second, the fact that these men sought out *Philip,* of whom it is expressly said that he "was of Bethsaida of Galilee"—a city on the borders of Syro-Phoenicia. The fact that Philip sought the counsel of *Andrew,* who also came from Bethsaida in Galilee (see 1:44), and who would therefore be the one most likely to know most about these neighbouring people, provides further confirmation. That these "Greeks" were not idolatrous heathen is evidenced by the fact that they "came up to *worship* at the feast," the verb showing they were in the habit of so doing!

These "Greeks" took a lowly place. They "desired" Philip: the Greek word is variously rendered "asked," "besought," "prayed." They supplicated Philip, making known their wish, and asking if it were possible to have it granted; saying, "Sir, we would see Jesus," or more literally, "Jesus, we desire to see." At the very time the leaders of Israel sought to *kill* Him, the Greeks desired to *see* Him. This was the first voice from the outside world which gave a hint of the awakening consciousness that Jesus was about to be the Saviour of the Gentiles as well as the Jews. Of old it had been said, "And the *Desire* of all nations shall come" (Hag. 2:7). That it was more than an idle curiosity which prompted these Greeks we cannot doubt, for if it were only a physical sight of Him which they desired, that could have been easily obtained as He passed in and out of the temple or along the street of Jerusalem, without them interviewing Philip. It was a *personal* and *intimate* acquaintance with Him that their souls craved. The form in which they stated their request was prophetically significant. It was not "We would *hear* him," or "We desire to witness one of his mighty works," but "We would *see Jesus.*" It is so to-day. He is no longer here in the flesh: He can no longer be handled or heard. But He *can* be *seen,* seen by the eye of faith!

"Philip cometh and telleth Andrew" (12:22). At first sight this may strike us as strange. Why did not Philip go at once and present this request of the Greeks to the Saviour? Is his tardiness to be attributed to a lack of love for souls? We do not think so. The first reference to him in this Gospel pictures a man of true evangelical zeal. No sooner did Philip become a follower of Christ than he "*findeth* Nathanael, and saith unto him, We have found him, of whom Moses in the law, and the prophets did write, Jesus of Nazareth" (1:45). How, then, shall we account for his now seeking out Andrew instead of the Lord? Does not Matt. 10:5 help us? When Christ had sent forth the Twelve on their first preaching tour, He expressly commanded them, "*Go not into* the way of the *Gentiles,* and into any city of the Samaritans enter ye not." Furthermore, the disciples had heard Him say to the Canaanitish woman, "I am not sent but unto the lost sheep of the house of Israel" (Matt. 15:24). Most probably it was because these definite statements were in Philip's mind that he now sought out Andrew and asked his advice.

"And again Andrew and Philip tell Jesus" (12:22). In the light of what has just been before us, how are we to explain this action of the two disciples? Why did they not go to the "Greeks" and politely tell them that it was impossible to grant their request? Why not have said plainly to them, Jesus is the Messiah of Israel, and has no dealings with the Gentiles? We believe that what had happened just before, had made a deep impression upon the apostles. The Saviour mounting the ass, the acclamations of the multitudes which He had accepted without a protest, His auspicious entrance into Jerusalem, His cleansing of the temple immediately afterwards (Matt. 21:12, 13), no doubt raised their hopes to the highest point. Was the hour of His ardently desired exaltation really at hand? *Would* "the *world*" now go after Him (John 12:19) in very truth? Was this request of the "Greeks" a further indication that He was about to take the kingdom and be "a light to lighten the Gentiles" as well as "the glory of his people Israel?" In all probability *these* were the very thoughts which filled the minds of Andrew and Philip as they came and told Jesus.

"And Jesus answered them, saying, The hour is come, that the Son of man should be glorified" (12:23). Now, for the first time, the Lord declared that His "hour" had come. At Cana He had said to His mother, "Mine hour is not yet come" (2:5), and about the midst of His public ministry we read, "No man laid hands on him because his hour was not yet come" (7:30). But here He announced that His hour *had* arrived, the hour when He, as Son of man, would be "glorified." But what is here meant by Him being "glorified?" We believe there is a double reference. In view of the connection here, the occasion when the Lord Jesus uttered these words, their first meaning evidently was: the time has arrived when the Son of man should be glorified by receiving the worshipful homage of the Gentiles. He intimated that the hour was ripe for the blessing of all the families of the earth through Abraham's seed. But, linking this verse with the one that immediately follows, it is equally clear that He referred to His approaching death. To His followers, the Cross must appear as the lowest depths of humiliation, but the Saviour regarded it (also) as His glorification. John 13:30, 31 fully bears this out: "He then having received the sop went immediately out: and it was night. *Therefore,* when he was gone out, Jesus said, *Now* is the Son of man *glorified, and God is glorified in him.*" The two things are intimately related: salvation could not come to the Gentiles except through His death.

"And Jesus answered them, saying, The hour is come, that the Son of man should be glorified" (12:23). It is by no means easy to determine to whom Christ uttered these words. We strongly incline to the view that they were said to the disciples. The record is silent as to whether or not the Lord here granted these "Greeks" an interview; that is, whether He left the temple-enclosure where He then was, and went into the outer court, beyond which Gentiles were not permitted to pass. Personally, we think, everything considered, it is most unlikely that He suffered them to enter His presence. If the wish of these "Greeks" was not granted, it would teach them that salvation was not through His perfect life or His wondrous works, but by faith in Him as the *crucified* One. They must be taught to look upon Him not as the Messiah of Israel, but as "the lamb of God which taketh away the sin of *the world*."

"Verily, verily, I say unto you, Except a corn of wheat fall into the ground and die, it abideth alone: but if it die, it bringeth forth much fruit" (12:24). Very different were the thoughts of Christ from those which, most probably, filled the minds of His disciples on this occasion. He looked, no doubt, to the distant future, but He also contemplated the near future. Death lay in His path, and this engaged His attention at the very time when His disciples were most jubilant and hopeful. There must be the suffering before the glory: the Cross before the Crown. Outwardly all was ready for His earthly glory. The multitudes had proclaimed Him king; the Romans were silent, offering no opposition (a thing most remarkable); the Greeks sought Him. But the Saviour knew that before He could set up His royal kingdom He must first accomplish the work of God. None could be with Him in glory except He died.

"Except a corn of wheat fall into the ground and die, it abideth alone, but if it die, it bringeth forth much fruit." "Nature is summoned here to show the law of increase which is stamped upon her; and that creative law is made an argument for the necessity of the death that is before Him. What an exaltation of the analogies in Nature to exhibit and use them in such a way as this! And what a means of interpreting Nature itself is here given us! How it shows that Christ, ignored by the so-called 'natural' theology, is the true key to the interpretation of Nature, and that the Cross is stamped ineffacably upon it! Nature is thus invested with the robe of a primeval prophet, and that the Word, who is God, the Creator of all things, becomes not merely the announcement of Scripture, but a plainly demonstrated fact before our eyes today.

"The grain of wheat falls into the ground and dies: it has life in it, and carries it with it through death itself. The death which it undergoes is in the interest even of the life, which it sets free from its encasement—from the limitations which hedge it in—to lay hold of and assimilate the surrounding material, by which it expands into the plant which is its resurrection, and thus at last into the many grains which are its resurrection-fruit. How plain it is that this is no accidental likeness which the Lord here seizes for illustration of His point. It is as real a prediction as ever came from the lips of an Old Testament prophet: every seed sown in the ground to produce a harvest is a positive prediction that the Giver of life must die. The union of Christ with men is not in incarnation, though that, of course, was a necessary step towards it. But the blessed man, so come into the world, was a new, a Second Man, who could not unite with the old race, and the life was the light of men; but if that were all, the history would be summed up in the words that follow: 'And the light shineth in darkness and the darkness comprehended it not. He was in the world . . . and the world knew him not.' To the dead, life must be communicated that there may be eyes to see. Men can only be born again into the family of God, of which the Son of God as Man is the beginning.

"Yet the life cannot simply communicate the life. Around Him are the bands of eternal righteousness, which has pronounced condemnation upon the guilty, and only by the satisfaction of righteousness in the penalty incurred can these bands be removed. Death—death as He endured it—alone can set Him free from these limitations: He is '*straitened* till it be accomplished.' In resurrection He is enlarged and becomes the Head of a new creation; and 'if any man be in Christ, it is new creation' (II Cor. 5:17). In those redeemed by His blood the tree of life has come to its precious fruitage" (Numerical Bible).

"He that loveth his life shall lose it; and he that hateth his life in this world shall keep it unto life eternal" (12:25). First of all, this was a word of warning for the beloved disciples. They had just witnessed the palms of victory waving in His path: soon they should see Him numbered with the transgressors. The echoes of the people's "Hosannas" were still sounding in their ears: in four days' time they should hear them cry, "Crucify him." Then they would enter into the followship of His sufferings. But these things must not move them. They must not, any more than He, count their life dear unto them. He warns them against selfishness, against cowardice, against shrinking from a martyr's cross. But the principle here is of wider application.

There is no link of connection between the natural man and God. In the man Christ Jesus there *was* a life in perfect harmony with God, but because of the condition of those He came to save He must lay it down. And He has left us an example that we should follow His steps. If we would save our natural life, we must lay it down: the one who loves his life in this world must necessarily lose it, for it is "*alienated*" from God; but if by the grace of God a man *separates himself in heart* from that which is at enmity with God (James 4:4), and devotes all his energies to God, then shall he have it again in the eternal state.

"If any man serve me, let him follow me; and where I am, there shall also my servant be: if any man serve me, him will my Father honour" (12:26). If the previous verse was a *warning* to the disciples, this was spoken for their *encouragement*. "Each grain of wheat that is found on the parent stem follows of necessity by the law of its own nature the pattern of the grain from which it came. His people, too, must be prepared to follow Him upon the road on which He was going. Here is the rule, here is the reward of service: to be with Christ where He is, is such reward as love itself would seek, crowned with the honour which the Father puts upon such loving service. The way of attainment is by the path which He had trodden, and what that was, in its general character at least, is unmistakably plain" (Mr. F. W. Grant).

"Now is my soul troubled: and what shall I say?" (12:27). That was the beginning of the Saviour's travail ere the new creation could be born. He was seized by an affrighting apprehension of that dying of which He had just spoken. His holy soul was moved to its very depths by the horror of that coming "hour." It was the prelude to Gethsemane. It reveals to us something of His inward sufferings. His anguish was extreme; His heart was suffering torture—horror, grief, dejection, are all included in the word "troubled." And what occasioned this? The insults and sufferings which He was to receive at the hands of men? The wounding of His heel by the Serpent? No, indeed. It was the prospect of being "made a *curse* for us," of suffering the righteous wrath of a sin-hating God. "What shall I say?" He asks, *not* "What shall I *choose?*" There was no wavering in purpose, no indecision of will. Though His holy nature shrank from being "made sin," it only marked His perfections to ask that *such* a cup might pass from Him. Nevertheless, He bowed, unhesitatingly, to the Father's will, saying, "But for this cause came I unto this hour." The bitter cup was accepted.

"Father, glorify thy name" (12:28). Christ had just looked death, in all its awfulness as the wages of sin, fully in the face, and He had bowed to it, and that, that the Father might be glorified. This it was which was ever before Him. Prompt was the Father's response. "*Then* came there a voice from heaven, saying, I have both glorified, and will glorify again" (12:28). The Son of God had been glorified at the grave of Lazarus as Quickener of the dead, and now He is glorified as Son of man by this voice from heaven. But there is more than this here: the Father uses the future tense—"I *will* glorify again." This He would do in bringing again from the dead our Lord Jesus, that great Shepherd of the sheep: "raised up from the dead by *the glory* of the Father" (Rom. 6:4).

"The people therefore, that stood by, and heard, said that it thundered: others said, An angel spake to him" (12:29). What a proof was this that the natural man is incapable of entering into Divine things. A similar instance is furnished in the Lord speaking from heaven to Saul of Tarsus at the time of his conversion. In Acts 9:4 we read that a voice spoke unto him, saying, "Saul, Saul, why persecutest thou me?" In 22:9 we are told by Paul, "They that were with me saw indeed the light, and were afraid; but they heard not the voice of him that spake to me." They perceived not what He said. As the Saviour had declared on a former occasion, "Why do ye not understand my speech? Even because ye cannot hear my word" (John 8:43). How the failure of these Jews to recognize the Father's voice emphasized the absolute necessity of the Cross!

"Jesus answered and said, This voice came not because of me, but for your sakes" (12:30). Three times the Father spoke audibly unto the Son: at the beginning, in the middle, and at the end of His Messianic career, and in each case it was in view of His *death.* At the Jordan Christ went down, symbolically, into the place of death; on the Holy Mount Moses and Elijah had talked with Him "of his decease" (Luke 9:31); and here, Christ had just announced that His "hour" was at hand. It is also to be observed that the first time the Father's voice was heard was at Christ's consecration to His *prophetic* office; the second time it was in connection with His forthcoming decease, His *priestly* work, the offering Himself as a Sacrifice for sin; here, it followed right on His being hailed as *king,* and who was about to be invested (though in mockery) with all the insignia of royalty, and wear His title, "The *king* of the Jews," even upon the Cross itself. Mark also the *increasing publicity* of these three audible speakings of the Father. The first was heard, we believe, only by John the Baptist; the second by three of His disciples; but the third by those who thronged the temple. "For your sakes": to strengthen the faith to the disciples; to remove all excuse from unbelievers.

"Now is the judgment of this world" (12:31). How this brings out the importance and the value of the great work which He was about to do! In this and the following verse, three consequences of His death are stated. First, the world was "judged": its crisis had come: its probation was over: its doom was sealed by the casting forth of the Son of God. Henceforth, God would save His people *from* the world. Second, the world's Prince here received his sentence, though its complete execution is yet future. Third, God's elect would be drawn by irresistible power to the One whom the world rejected.

"Now shall the prince of this world be cast out" (12:31). The tense of the verb here denotes that the "casting out" of Satan would be as *gradual* as the "drawing" in the next verse (Alford). The Lord here anticipates His victory, and points out the way in which it should be accomplished: a way that would have never entered into the heart of men to conceive, for it should be by shame and pain and death; a way that *seemed* an actual triumph for the enemy. Not only was life to come out of death, but victory out of apparent defeat. The Saviour crucified is, *in fact*, the Saviour glorified!

"Now shall the prince of this world be *cast out*." As pointed out above, the casting out of Satan was to be a gradual process. In the light of this verse, and other passages (e.g., Heb. 2:14, 15), we believe that Satan's hold over this world was broken at the Cross. The apostle tells us that Christ "spoiled principalities and powers, having made a show of them openly; triumphing over them" (Col. 2:15), and this statement, be it noted, is linked with His Cross! We believe, then, the first stage in the "casting out" of Satan occurred at the Cross, the next will be when he is "*cast out*" of heaven into the earth (Rev. 12:10); the next, when he is "*cast into* the bottomless pit" (Rev. 20:3); the final when he is "*cast into* the lake of fire and brimstone" (Rev. 20:10).

"And I, if I be lifted up from the earth, will draw all unto me. This he said, signifying what death he should die" (12:32, 33). A truly wonderful and precious word is this. It is Christ's own declaration concerning His death and resurrection. "I, if I be lifted up from the earth" referred to His crucifixion; but "*will* draw all unto me" looked to the resurrection-side of the Cross, for a *dead* Saviour could "draw" nobody. Yet the two things are most intimately connected. It is not simply that Christ is the magnet; it is the crucified Christ. "It is crucifixion which has imparted to Him His attractive power; just as it is death which has given Him His life-giving power. It is not Christ without the Cross; nor is it the Cross without Christ; it is both of them together" (H. Bonar). And wherein lies the attraction? "*Because of the love which it embodies.* Herein is love—the love that passeth knowledge! What so magnetic as love? *Because of the righteousness which it exhibits.* It is the Cross of righteousness. It is righteousness combining with love taking the sinner's side against law and judgment. How attractive is righteousness like this! *Because of the truth which it proclaims.* All God's truth is connected with the Cross. Divine wisdom is concentrated there. How can it but be magnetic? *Because of the reconciliation which it publishes.* It proclaims peace to the sinner, for it has made peace. Here is the meeting-place between men and God" (Ibid).

But what is meant by "I will draw"? Ah, notice the sentence does not end there! "I will draw all *unto me.*" The word "men" is not in the original. The "all" plainly refers to all of *God's elect.* The scope of the word "all" here is precisely the same as in 6:45—"And they shall be *all* taught of God." It is the same "all" as that which the Father has given to Christ (6:37). "The promise, 'I will draw all unto me' must, I think, mean that our Lord after His crucifixion would draw men of all nations and kindreds and tongues to Himself, to believe in Him and be His disciples. Once crucified, He would become a great centre of attraction, and draw to Himself; releasing from the Devil's usurped power, vast multitudes of all peoples and countries, to be His servants and followers. Up to this time all the world had blindly hastened after Satan and followed him. After Christ's crucifixion great numbers would turn away from the power of Satan and become Christians" (Bishop Ryle). Christ's design was to show that His grace would not be confined to Israel.

The Greek word here used for "draw" is a very striking one. Its first occurrence is in John 6:44, "No man can come to me, except the Father which hath sent me *draw* him." Here it is the power of God overcoming the enmity of the carnal mind. It occurs again in 18:10, "Then Simon Peter having a sword *drew* it, and smote the high priest's servant." Here the term signifies that Peter *laid firm hold of* his sword and *pulled it out* of its sheath. It is found again in 21:6, 11, "Simon Peter went up and *drew* the net to land full of great fishes." Here it signifies the putting forth of strength so as to *drag* an inanimate and heavy object. It is used (in a slightly different form) in James 2:6, "Do not rich men oppress you and *draw* you before the judgment seats?" Here it has reference to the *impelling of unwilling* subjects. From its usage in the New Testament we are therefore obliged to understand Christ here intimated that, following His crucifixion, He would put forth an invincible power so as to effectually draw unto Himself all of God's elect, which His omniscient foresight then saw scattered among the Gentiles. A very striking example of the Divine drawing-power is found in Judges, 4:7, "And *I will draw* unto thee to the river Kishon, Sisera, the captain of Jabin's army, with his chariots and his multitude; and I will deliver him into thine hands." In like manner Christ draws us unto Himself.

"Thus it is His heart relieves itself. The glory of God, the overthrow of evil, the redemption and reconciliation of men is to be accomplished by that, the cost of which is to be for Him so much. He weighs the gain against the purchase-price for him, and is content" (Mr. Grant).

"The people answered him, We have heard out of the law that Christ abideth for ever: and how sayest thou, The Son of man must be lifted up? who is this Son of man?" (12:34). It seems exceedingly strange that men acquainted with the Old Testament should have been stumbled when their Messiah announced that He must die. Isaiah 53, Daniel's prophecy that He should be "cut off" (9:26), and that solemn word through Zechariah, "Awake, O sword, against my shepherd, and against the man that is my fellow, saith the Lord of hosts: smite the shepherd" (13:7), should have shown them that His exaltation could be only after His sufferings.

"Then Jesus said unto them, Yet a little while is the light with you. Walk while ye have the light, lest darkness come upon you: for he that walketh in darkness knoweth not whither he goeth" (12:35). His questioners, most probably, in their malignant self-conceit, flattered themselves that they had completely puzzled Him. But He next spoke as though He had not heard their cavil. They were not seeking the truth, and He knew it. Instead of answering directly, He therefore gave them a solemn warning, reminding them that only for a short space longer would they enjoy the great privilege then theirs, and stating what would be the inevitable consequence if they continued to despise it.

"While ye have light, believe in the light, that ye may be the children of light. These things spake Jesus, and departed, and did hide himself from them" (12:36). "Christ had spoken. Introduced at the commencement of the Gospel as the Light of men (1:4), He had proclaimed Himself to be the Light of the world, that whosoever should follow Him should not walk in darkness, but have the light of life (8:12). He had also said that, as long as He was in the world, He was the light of it (9:5). Soon would the Light be withdrawn, His death being near at hand. Is there not, then, something awfully solemn in these few words of our chapter (12:35, 36)? He had preached among them. He had wrought miracles among them. He had kept, too, in His ministry to the land which God had promised to Abraham. He had never ministered outside of it. The people in it had enjoyed opportunities granted to none others. What, now, was the result, as His public ministry was thus terminating? 'He departed, and did hide himself from them.' Who of them all mourned over His departure? or sought where to find Him?" (Mr. C. E. Stuart).

Study the following questions on our next lesson: —

1. What is the central design of this passage, 12:37-50?
2. Why is Isa. 53 quoted here, v. 38?
3. Why was it "they could not believe" v. 39?
4. Whose "glory" is referred to in v. 41?
5. Had those mentioned in v. 42 *saving* faith?
6. When and where did Jesus say what is found in vv. 44-50?
7. What is the "commandment" of vv. 49, 50?

CHAPTER FORTY-FOUR

Christ's Ministry Reviewed

John 12:37-50

The following is an Analysis of the closing section of John 12: –

1. The nation's response to Christ's ministry, v. 37.
2. The forecast of Israel's unbelief by Isaiah, vv. 38-41.
3. The condition of those who had been impressed by Christ, vv. 42, 43.
4. Christ's teaching about His relation to the Father, vv. 44, 45.
5. Christ's teaching concerning the design of His ministry, vv. 46, 47.
6. Christ's teaching concerning the doom of all who despised Him, vv. 48, 49.
7. Christ's teaching concerning the way of life, v. 50.

The passage before us is by no means an easy one to understand. The previous section closes as follows: "These things spake Jesus, and *departed,* and did *hide* himself from them" (12:36). Many have thought, and we believe rightly so, that this statement brings the *public* ministry of Christ to a close in this Gospel. When we enter the thirteenth chapter it is very evident that a new section there begins, for from the beginning of 13 to the end of 17 the Lord is *alone* with His apostles; while in the 18th He is arrested and led to judgment. But if 12:36 marks the ending of Christ's public ministry, how are we to understand the verses which follow to the end of the chapter? especially in view of what is said in v. 44: "Jesus cried and said," etc.

Now, we believe the answer to this question has been well stated by Dr. John Brown: "The paragraph itself (12:37-50) is of a peculiar, I had almost said unique, structure and character. The history of our Lord's public ministry is closed. It terminates in the verse immediately preceding. The account of His private interview with His friends, previous to His passion, is about to commence. It begins with the first verse of the following chapter. One scene in the eventful history is closed; another is about to open. The curtain is, as it were, falling upon the theatre in which the public acts of Jesus were performed, and the Evangelist is about to conduct us into the sacred circle of His disciples, and communicate to us the sublime and consoling conversations which the Redeemer, full of love, had with them before His final departure. But before He does this he makes a pause in the narrative, and, as it were, looks back and around; and, in the paragraph before us, presents us in a few sentences with a brief but comprehensive view of all the Lord had taught and done during the course of His public ministry, and of the effects which His discourses and miracles had produced on the great body of His countrymen."

John here gives us a resume of Christ's public ministry, mentioning His miracles and recapitulating His teaching. The closing section of John 12 forms an epilogue to that chapter of our Lord's life which had just been brought to a close in 12:36. Four vital truths which had occupied a prominent place in Christ's oral ministry are here singled out: His appeal to the Father which sent Him (12:44, 45, 49); Himself the Light of the world (12:46); the danger of unbelief (12:47-49); the end of faith (12:50). The Holy Spirit's design in moving John to pen this section was, we believe, at least two-fold: to explain the seeming failure of Christ's public ministry, and to show that the guilt of unbelief rested inexcusably upon Israel.

"The rejection of Jesus Christ by the great body of His fellow-countrymen, the Jews, is a fact which, at first view, may seem to throw suspicion on the greatness of His claims to a Divine mission, as indicating the evidence adduced in their support did not serve its purpose with those to whom it was originally presented, and who, in some points of view, were placed in circumstances peculiarly favorable for forming a correct estimate of its validity. It may be supposed that had the proofs of His Divine mission and Messiahship been as strong and striking as the friends of Christianity represent them, the prejudices of the Jews, powerful as they unquestionably were, must have given way before them; and the believers of His doctrine must have been as numerous as the witnesses of His miracles. Such a supposition, though plausible, argues on the part of its supporters, imperfect and incorrect views of the human constitution, intellectually and morally" (Ibid). In other words, it ignores the *total depravity* of man!

Now, in the closing section of John 12 the Holy Spirit has most effectively disposed of the above objection. He has done so by directing our attention to Old Testament predictions which accurately forecast the very reception which the Messiah met with from the Jews. First, Isa. 53 is referred to, for in this chapter it was plainly foretold that He should be "despised and rejected of men." And then Isa. 6 is quoted, a passage which tells of God judicially blinding His people because of their inveterate unbelief. Thus the very objection made against Christianity is turned into a most conclusive argument in its favour. The very fact that the Lord Jesus was put to death by His countrymen demonstrates that He *is* their Messiah! Thus has God, once more, made "the wrath of man to praise him."

"But though he had done so many miracles before them, yet they believed not on him" (12:37). Fearful proof was this of the depravity of the human heart. The miracles of Christ were neither few in number nor unimpressive in nature. The Lord Jesus performed prodigies of power of almost every conceivable kind. He healed the sick, expelled demons, controlled the winds, walked on the sea, turned water into wine, revealed to men their secret thoughts, raised the dead. His miracles were wrought openly, in the light of day, before numerous witnesses. Nevertheless "they"—the nation at large—"believed not on him." Altogether inexcusable was their hardness of heart. All who heard His teaching and witnessed His works, ought, without doubt, to have received Him as their Divinely-accredited Messiah and Saviour. But the great majority of His countrymen refused to acknowledge His claims.

"The prevalence of unbelief and indifference in the present day ought not to surprise us. It is just one of the evidences of that mighty foundation-doctrine, the total corruption and fall of man. How feebly we grasp and realize that doctrine is proved by our surprise at human incredulity. We only half believe the heart's deceitfulness. Let us read our Bibles more attentively, and search their contents more carefully. Even when Christ wrought miracles and preached sermons there were numbers of His hearers who remained utterly unmoved. What right have we to wonder if the hearers of modern sermons in countless instances remain unbelieving? 'The disciple is not greater than his Master.' If even the hearers of Christ did not believe, how much more should we expect to find unbelief among the hearers of His ministers? Let the truth be spoken and confessed: man's obstinate unbelief is one among many of the indirect proofs that the Bible is true" (Bishop Ryle).

"That the saying of Isaiah the prophet might be fulfilled which he spake, Lord, who hath believed our report? and to whom hath the arm of the Lord been revealed?" (12:38). This does not mean that the Jews continued in unbelief with the conscious design of fulfilling Old Testament prophecy. Nor does the Holy Spirit here teach that God exercised a secret influence upon the hearts of the Jews, which prevented them from believing, in order that the prophecy of Isaiah might not fail of accomplishment. The Jews *did* fulfil the predictions of Isaiah, but it was ignorantly and unwittingly, As one able expositor has well said, "The true interpretation here depends on the fact, that the participle rendered *that,* in the sense of *in order that,* sometimes signifies *so that,* pointing out, not the connection of cause and effect, but that of antecedent and consequence, prediction and accomplishment. For example, in the question of the disciples, 'Who did sin, this man or his parents, *that* he was born blind?' the meaning plainly is, 'Is this man's blindness *the consequence* of his parents' sin, or of his own in some preexistent state?'" We believe it had been better to render it thus: "They believed not, *consequently* the saying of Isaiah was fulfilled." God does not have to put forth any power to cause any sinner *not* to believe: if He leaves him to himself, he never will believe.

It is highly significant that Isa. 53 opens in the way it does. That remarkable chapter tells of the treatment which the Saviour met with from Israel when He was here the first time. As is well known, the Jews will not own it as a prophecy concerning the Messiah: some of them have attempted to apply it to Jeremiah, others to the nation. How striking then that the Triune-God has opened it with the question, "Who hath *believed* our report?" Most suitably does John apply it to the unbelieving nation in his day. "And to whom is the arm of the Lord revealed?" The "arm of the Lord" signifies the *power* of God as it had been manifested by the Messiah. There are therefore two things here: "Who hath believed our *report?*" points to Christ's *oral* ministry; "to whom is the *arm* of the Lord revealed?" to His *miracles*.

"Therefore they could not believe, because that Isaiah said again" (12:39). This is exceedingly solemn. It is explained in the next verse. In consequence of their rejection of Christ, the nation as a whole was judicially blinded of God, that is, they were *left* to the darkness and hardness of their own evil hearts. But it is most important to mark the *order* of these two statements: in 12:37 they *did not* believe; here in 12:39, they *could not* believe. The most attractive appeals had been made: the most indubitable evidence had been presented: yet they despised and rejected the Redeemer. They *would not* believe; in consequence, God gave them up, and now they *could not* believe. The harvest was past, the summer was ended, and they were not saved. But the fault was entirely theirs, and now they must suffer the just consequences of their wickedness.

"He hath blinded their eyes, and hardened their heart; that they should not see with their eyes, nor understand with their heart, and be converted, and I should heal them" (12:40). This was God's response to the wicked treatment which Israel had meted out to His beloved Son. They had refused the light, now darkness shall be their dreadful portion. They had rejected the truth, now a heart which loved error should be the terrible harvest. Blinded eyes and a hardened heart have belonged to Israel ever since; only thus can we account for their continued unbelief all through these nineteen centuries; only thus can we explain Israel's attitude toward Christ to-day.

"All through His Divine ministry in this Gospel, the Lord had been acting in grace, as the 'son of the Father' and as 'the light of the world.' His presence was *day-time* in the land of Israel. He had been shining there, if haply the darkness might comprehend Him, and here, at the close of His ministry (12:35, 36) we see Him still as the light casting forth His last beams upon the land and the people. He can but shine, whether they will comprehend Him or not. While His presence is there it is still day-time. The night cannot come till He is gone. 'As long as I am in the world, I am the light of the world'! But here, He '*departed* and did *hide* himself from them' (12:36); and then God, by His prophet, brings the *night* upon the land: 12:40" (Mr. J. G. Bellett).

Fearfully solemn is it to remember that what God did here unto Israel He will shortly do with the whole of unbelieving Christendom: "And for this cause *God shall send them* strong delusion, that they should believe a lie: that they all might be damned who believe not the truth, but had pleasure in unrighteousness" (II Thess. 2:11, 12). Just as in the days of Nimrod God "gave up" the entire Gentile world because they despised and rejected the revelation which He had given them (Rom. 1); just as He abandoned Israel to their unbelief, through the rejection of His Son; so in a soon-coming day He will cause unfaithful Christendom to receive the Antichrist because "they received not the love of the truth, that they might be saved" (II Thess. 2:10). Oh, dear reader, be warned by this. It is an unspeakably solemn thing to trifle with the overtures of God's grace. It is written, "How shall *we escape* if we neglect so great salvation?" (Heb. 2:3). Then "Seek ye the Lord *while he may be found*, call ye upon him *while he is near*" (Isa. 55:6).

"These things said Isaiah, when he saw his glory, and spake of him" (12:41). A striking testimony is this to the absolute Deity of Christ. The prediction quoted in the previous verse is found in Isa. 6. At the beginning of that chapter the prophet sees "Jehovah sitting upon a throne, high and lifted up, and his train filled the temple." Above the throne stood the seraphim, with veiled face, crying, "Holy, holy, holy, is the Lord of hosts." The sight was too much for Isaiah, and he cried, "Woe is me! for I am undone." Then a live coal was taken from off the altar and laid upon his mouth, and thus cleansed, he is commissioned to go forth as God's messenger. And here the Holy Spirit tells us in John 12, "These things said Isaiah, when he saw *his* glory, and spake of him"—the context makes it unmistakably plain that the reference is to the Lord Jesus. One of the sublimest descriptions of the manifested Deity found in all the Old Testament is here applied to Christ. That One born in Bethlehem's manger was none other than the Throne-Sitter before whom the seraphim worship.

"Nevertheless among the chief rulers also many believed on him; but because of the Pharisees they did not confess him, lest they should be put out of the synagogue" (12:42). Here is a statement which affords help on such verses as John 2:23; 7:31; 8:30; 10:42; 11:45; 12:11. In each of these passages we read of *many* "believing" on the Lord Jesus, concerning whom there is nothing to show that they had saving faith. In the light of the verse now before us it would seem that John, all through his Gospel, divides the unbelieving into *two* classes: the hardened mass who were altogether unmoved by the wondrous works of Christ; and a company, evidently by no means small, upon whom a temporary impression was made, but yet who failed to yield their hearts captive to the Saviour—the fear of man, and loving the praise of man, holding them back. And do we not find the same two classes in Christendom to-day? By far the greater number of those who come under the sound of the Gospel remain unmoved, heeding neither its imperative authority nor being touched by its winsome tidings. They are impervious to every appeal. But there is another class, and its representatives are to be found, perhaps, in every congregation; a class who *are* affected in some measure by the Word of the Cross. They do not despise its contents, yet, neither are their *hearts* won by it. On the one hand, they are not openly antagonistic; on the other, they are not out and out Christians.

"Nevertheless among the chief rulers also many believed on him; but because of the Pharisees they did not confess him, lest they should be put out of the synagogue." This points a most solemn warning to the class we have just mentioned above. A faith which does not *confess* Christ is not a *saving* faith. The New Testament is very explicit on this. Said the Lord Jesus, "Whosoever shall *confess me* before men, him shall the Son of man also confess before the angels of God: But he that *denieth me* before men shall be denied before the angels of God" (Luke 12:8, 9). And in the Epistle to the Romans we are told, "If thou shalt *confess* with thy mouth the Lord Jesus, and shalt believe in thine heart that God hath raised him from the dead, thou shalt be saved" (10:9). These Jews referred to in our text were satisfied that Christ was neither an impostor nor a fanatic, yet were they not prepared to forsake all and follow Him. They feared the consequences of such a course, for the Jews had agreed already "that if any man did *confess* that he was Christ, he should be put out of the synagogue" (9:22). These men then deemed it wisest to conceal their convictions and wait until the Messiah should place Himself in such a position that it would be safe and advantageous for them to avow themselves His disciples. They were governed by *self-interest*, and they have had many successors. If any should read these lines who are attempting to be *secret* disciples of the Lord Jesus, fearing to come out into the open and acknowledge by lip and life that He is their Lord and Saviour, let them beware. Remember that the *first* of the eight classes mentioned in Rev. 21:8 who are cast into the lake of fire are the *"fearful"*!

"For they loved the praise of men more than the praise of God" (12:43). These men, whose minds were convinced but whose hearts remained unmoved, not only *feared* the religious authorities, but they also *desired* the approbation of their fellows. They were determined to retain their good opinion, even though at the expense of an uneasy conscience. They preferred the good will of other sinners above the approval of God. O the shortsighted folly of these wretched men! O the madness of their miserable choice! Of what avail would the good opinion of the Pharisees be when the hour of death overtook them? In what stead will it stand them when they appear before the judgment-throne of God? "What shall it profit a man if he shall gain the whole world, and lose his own soul?" How we are reminded of our Saviour's words, "How can ye believe which receive honour *one of another*, and seek not the honour that cometh from God only?" (John 5:44). Let us remember that we cannot have both the good-will of sinners and the good-will of God: "Know ye not that the friendship of the world is enmity with God? whosoever therefore will be a friend of the world is the enemy of God" (James 4:4).

"Jesus cried and said, He that believeth on me, believeth not on me, but on him that sent me" (12:44). Notice that nothing whatever is said about either the time or the place where the Saviour made this utterance. We believe that John still continues his epilogue, giving us in 12:44-50 a summary of Christ's teaching. The substance of what he here says plainly indicates this. "How strange that this supposed discourse of Jesus should to an extent of which there is no previous example, consist of *repetitions* alone, and, moreover, of only such words as are already found in John's Gospel. Did the Lord ever *recapitulate* in this style, uttering connectedly so long a discourse without any new thoughts and distinct sayings? but, when for once St. John recapitulates, seeming (though only seeming) to put *his* words into the Lord's lips, what an instructive example he gives us, not venturing to add anything of his own! Yea, verily, all this the Lord *had said*, each saying in its season; but St John unites them all retrospectively together" (Stier). The tense of the verbs here, "Jesus *cried* and *said*," signify, as Stier and Alford have pointed out, that Christ was *wont* to, that it was His customary course of repeated action.

"And he that seeth me seeth him that sent me" (12:45). That John *is* giving us in these verses a summary of the teachings of Christ is evidenced by a comparison of them with earlier statements in this Gospel. For example: compare "He that believeth *on me*, believeth not on me, *but on him that sent me*" (12:44) with 5:24 – "He that heareth *my word and believeth on him that sent me*." So here: "He that seeth me seeth him that sent me." Compare with this 8:19, "If ye had known *me*, ye should have known *my Father also*;" and 10:38, "That ye may know and believe that the Father is in me, and *I in him*." This was one of the vital truths which occupied a prominent place in our Lord's teachings. No man had seen God at any time, but the only begotten Son had come here to "declare" *Him* (1:18). What we have here in 12:45 is a reference to the frequent mention made by Christ to that mysterious and Divine union which existed between Himself and the Father.

"I am come a light into the world, that whosoever believeth on me should not abide in darkness" (12:46). Clearly this is parallel with 8:12 and 9:5: "I am the light of the world: he that followeth me shall not walk in darkness . . . As long as I am in the world, I am the light of the world." "I am come a light into the world": upon this verse Dr. John Brown has the following helpful comments: "This proves, first, that Christ existed *before* His incarnation, even as the sun exists before it appears above the eastern hills; second, it is implied that He is the *one* Saviour of the world, as there is but *one* sun; third, that He came, not for one nation only, but for *all;* even as the sun's going forth is from the end of the heaven, and his circuit unto the ends of it; and there is nothing hid from the heat therof." This verse continues John's reference to the general teaching of Christ concerning the character and tendency of His mission. He had come here into this world as a *light*—revealing God and exposing man—and this, in order that all who believed on Him should be delivered from the *darkness,* that is, from the power of Satan (Col. 1:13) and the ruin of sin (Eph. 4:18).

"And if any man hear my words, and believe not, I judge him not: for I came not to judge the world but to save the world" (12:47). Here the Evangelist calls attention to another truth which had held a prominent place in our Lord's teachings. It respected His repeated announcement concerning the character and design of His mission and ministry. It tells of the lowly place which He had taken, and of the patient grace which marked Him during the time that He tabernacled among men. It brings into sharp contrast the purpose and nature of His two advents. When He returns to this earth it will be in another character and with a different object from what was true of Him when He was here the first time. Before, He was here as a lowly servant; then, He shall appear as the exalted Sovereign.

Before, He came to woo and win men; then, He shall rule over them with a rod of iron.

"And if any man hear my words, and believe not, I judge him not." With this compare 5:45, "Do not think that *I* will accuse you to the Father. For I came not to judge the world, but to save the world," compare with this John 3:17, "For God sent not his Son into the world to condemn the world; but that the world through him might be saved," and note our original comments upon John 3:17.

"He that rejecteth me, and receiveth not my words, hath one that judgeth him: the word that I have spoken, the same shall judge him in the last day" (12:48). This solemn utterance of Christ corrects an erroneous conclusion which has been drawn by some Calvinists, who deny the responsibility of unregenerate souls in connection with the Gospel. They argue that because the natural man is devoid of spiritual life, he cannot believe; a *dead* man, they say, *cannot* receive Christ. To this it might be replied, A *dead* man cannot *reject* Christ. But many do! It is true that a dead man cannot believe, yet he *ought* to. His inability lies not in the absence of necessary faculties, but in the wilful perversion of his faculties. When Adam died spiritually, nothing in him was annihilated; instead, he became "*alienated* from the life of God" (Eph. 4:18). Every man who hears the Gospel *ought* to believe in Christ, and those who do not will yet be punished for this unbelief, see II Thess. 1:7. As Christ here teaches, the rejector of Him will be judged for his sin. Let any unsaved one who reads these lines thoughtfully ponder this solemn word of the Lord Jesus.

"He that rejecteth me, and receiveth not my words, hath one that judgeth him." The first part of this verse is almost identical with what we read of in 3:18: "But he that believeth not is condemned already, because he hath not believed in the name of the only begotten Son of God." "The words that I have spoken, the same shall judge him in the last day." This takes us back to Deut. 18:19, where, of the great Prophet God promised to raise up unto Israel He declared, "And it shall come to pass, that whosoever will not hearken unto my words which he shall speak in my name, I will *require it of him*."

"The word that I have spoken, the same shall judge him in the last day." Very solemn indeed is this, for its application is to *all* who have heard the Gospel. It tells us three things.

First, there is to be a "last day." This world will not remain forever. The bounds of its history, the length of its existence are Divinely determined, and when the appointed limit is reached, "The day of the Lord will come as a thief in the night; in the which the heavens shall pass away with a great noise, and the elements shall melt with fervent heat, the earth also and the works that are therein shall be burned up" (II Peter 3:10).

Second, this last day will be one of *judgment*: "Because he hath appointed a day, in the which he will judge the world in righteousness by that man whom he hath ordained" (Acts 17:31). Then shall hidden things be brought to light: the righteous vindicated, and the unrighteous sentenced. Then shall God's broken law be magnified, and His holy justice honored. Then shall all His enemies be subjugated and God shall demonstrate that He *is* GOD. Then shall every proud rebel be made to bow in subjection before that Name which is above every name, and confess that Jesus is Lord to the glory of God the Father.

Third, *Christ's Word* will judge sinners in that Day. His Word was a *true* Word, a *Divine* Word, a Word *suited* to men. Yet men have slighted it, attacked it, denied it, made its holy contents the subject of blasphemous jesting. But in the last great Day it shall *judge* them. First and foremost among the "books" which shall be opened and out of which sinners shall be "judged" (Rev. 20:12) will be, we believe, the written Word of God—"In the day when God shall judge the secrets of men by Jesus Christ *according to my gospel*" (Rom. 2:16).

"For I have not spoken of myself; but the Father which sent me, he gave me a commandment, what I should say, and what I should speak" (12:49). This was something which Christ had affirmed repeatedly, see John 5:30; 7:16; 8:26-28, etc. It expressed that intimate and mysterious union which existed between the Father and Himself. His purpose was to impress upon the Jews the awfulness of their sin in refusing *His* words: in so doing, they affronted *the Father Himself*, for *His* were the very words which the Son had spoken to them. In like manner, to-day, "he that believeth not God hath made him a liar; because he believeth not the record that God gave *of his Son*" (I John 5:10). How terrible then is the sin of despising the testimony of Christ!

"And I know that his commandment is life everlasting: whatsoever I speak therefore, even as the Father said unto me, so I speak" (12:50). This is an abstract of what we read of in 3:11; 5:32; 8:55. It brings out once more the perfections of the incarnate Son. He acted not in independency, but in perfect oneness of heart, mind, and will, with the Father. Whether the Jews believed them or not, the messages which Christ had delivered were Divinely true, and therefore were they words of life to all who receive them by simple faith. This closing sentence in John's summary of Christ's teachings is very comprehensive: "*whatsoever*" He had spoken, was that which He had received of the Father. Therefore in refusing to heed the teaching of Christ, the Jews had despised the God of their fathers, the God of Abraham, the God of Isaac, and the God of Jacob.

"And I know that his commandment is life everlasting: whatsoever I speak therefore, even as the Father said unto me, so I speak" (12:50). Once more we have a declaration which is not confined to its local application. This verse speaks in clarion tones to all who come under the sound of the Gospel to-day. God has given not an "invitation" for men to act on at *their* pleasure, but a "*commandment*" which they disobey at their imminent peril. That commandment is "that we should believe on the name of his Son Jesus Christ" (I John 3:23), hence at the beginning of the Epistle to the Romans, where Paul refers to the Gospel of God, he says, "By whom we have received grace and apostleship, for faith-*obedience* among all nations" (1:5). This commandment is "life everlasting" to all who receive it by the obedience of faith. Adam brought death upon him by disobeying God's commandment: we receive life by obeying God' commandment. Then "see that ye *refuse not* him that speaketh. For if they escaped not who refused him that spake on earth, much more shall not we escape, if we turn away from him that speaketh from heaven" (Heb. 12:25).

Study the following questions in view of our next lesson: —

1. What is meant by the last clause of v. 1?
2. What "supper" is referred to in v. 2?
3. What is the symbolic significance of Christ's actions in v. 4?
4. What is signified by the washing of the disciples' feet, v. 5?
5. Why is Peter so prominent in vv. 6-9?
6. What is meant by "no part with Me" v. 8?
7. What is the meaning of v. 10?

CHAPTER FORTY-FIVE

Christ Washing His Disciples' Feet

John 13:1-11

Below is an Analysis of the passage which is to be before us: –

1. Christ's unchanging love, v. 1.
2. Judas's inveterate hatred, v. 2.
3. Christ's return to the Father, v. 3.
4. Christ performing a slave's work, vv. 4, 5.
5. Peter's blundering ignorance, vv. 6-9.
6. Bathing and cleansing, v. 10.
7. The traitor excepted, v. 11.

We are now to enter upon what many believers in each age have regarded as the most precious portion of this Gospel, yea, as one of the most blessed passages in all the Word of God. John 13 begins a new section, a section clearly distinguished and separated from what has gone before. At the beginning of the Gospel two things were stated in connection with the *outcome* of Christ's mission and ministry: the nation, as such, "received him *not*": this has been fully demonstrated, especially in chapters 5 to 12; second, those who *did* "receive him" were to be brought into the place of children of God. In chapters 13 to 17 we see Christ alone with His own, separated from the world, telling them of their peculiar portion and privileges.

At the close of Christ's public ministry, we are told "He departed and did *hide* himself from them"; that is, from the nation (12:36). In 13 to 17 we find the Saviour, in most intimate fellowship with His disciples, *revealing* to them the wondrous place which they had in His love, and how that love would be continually exercised on their behalf now that He was about to leave them and go to the Father. He had told them that, "the

Son of man came not to be ministered unto, but *to minister*, and to give his life a ransom for many" (Matt. 20:28). All through His career Christ *had* "ministered" to His own, but now, His public ministry was over and He was on the eve of giving His life a ransom for them, to be followed by Him taking His place on high. It would, therefore, be natural for the disciples to conclude that His "ministry" unto them was *also ended*. But not so. It would continue, and *that* is what *this* blessed section of John's Gospel is primarily designed to show us. He loved these disciples (and us) not only unto the Cross, but "unto *the end*." His return to the Father would neither terminate nor diminish the activities of His love for His own: in Heaven He is still occupied with the interest of His people.

The central design of the "Paschal Discourse" of Christ was to lead His own into a spiritual understanding of their *new* place before the Father, and their *new* position in the world, as distinguished from the portion and place which they had had in Judaism. What we have in John 13 to 17 takes the place of the long Olivet discourse recorded by each of the Synoptists. Here, instead of taking His seat upon the Mount, He brings the disciples, in spirit, into Heaven, and reveals the glories, blessedness, and holiness of the Sanctuary there. Instead of treating of the horrors of the Tribulation, He discloses to the family of God the activities of their great High Priest, as well as their own sorrows and joys during the time of their journey through this wilderness.

While there is a marked contrast between what we have at the close of John 12 and the beginning of 13, there is also a close link of connection between them, a link which further develops the progressive unfolding of truth in this wondrous Gospel. In chapter 12 Christ had spoken of Himself as "the corn of wheat" which had to die in order that it might bring forth "much fruit." As we have seen, this speaks of *union and communion*—blessedly illustrated in the opening scene, the "supper" in Bethany. But here in chapter 13 and onwards, He makes known His own most gracious work for *maintaining* believers in fellowship with Himself. Two things, each most blessed and evidencing His perfections, are to be noted. First, His eye is on the heavenly sanctuary (13:1); second, His eye is upon His own (13:4). He *guards* the holy requirements of God, and He *cares* for and *ministers* to His people. We are left here in this world, and its dust is defiling, unfitting us for entrance into the Holiest. Here in John 13 we see Christ fitting us *for* that place. It is important for us to recognize, though, that it is *God's* interests which He has at heart in washing our feet! Christ is here seen as the *Laver* which stood between the brazen altar and the sanctuary, and which was approached only after the brazen altar had done its work.

There is a further link between John 12 and 13 which brings out a most blessed contrast—let the student be constantly on the lookout for these. At the beginning of John 12 we behold the *feet* of the Lord; in John 13 we see the *feet* of the disciples. The "feet" of Christ were *anointed,* those of the disciples were *washed.* As the Saviour passed through this sinful world He contracted no defilement. He left it as He came: "holy, harmless, and undefiled." The "feet" speak of the *walk,* and the fact that Christ's feet were *anointed* with the fragrant spikenard tells of the sweet savor which ever ascended from Him to the Father, perfectly glorifying Him as He did in every step of His path. But in sharp contrast from Him, the walk of the disciples *was* defiled, and the grime of the way must be removed. Note, also, that the anointing of the Saviour's feet is given *before* the washing of the disciples' feet—in all things *He* must have "the preeminence" (Col. 1:18)!

That which opens this section and introduces the "Paschal Discourse" is the Lord washing the feet of His disciples. The first thing to observe, particularly, is that it was *water* and not blood which was used for their cleansing. It is deeply important to note this, for many of the Lord's own people seem to be entirely ignorant about the distinction. Their speaking of a *re*-application of the blood, of coming anew to "the fountain" which has been opened for sin and uncleanness when they have transgressed, proves that this is only too sadly true. The New Testament knows nothing whatever of a *re*-application of the blood, or of sinning Christians needing to be washed in it again. To speak of such things is to grossly *dishonor* the all-efficacious sacrifice of the Cross. The blood of Jesus Christ God's Son cleanseth us from *all* sin (I John 1:7). By "one offering he hath *perfected forever* them that are set apart" (Heb. 10:14). This being so, what provision, we may ask, has been made for the removal of the defilements which the Christian contracts by the way? The answer is "water."

A careful study will show that in the Old and New Testaments alike the "blood" is *Godward,* the "water" is *saintward,* to remove impurity in practice: the one affects our standing, the other our state; the former is for *judicial* cleansing, the latter is for *practical* purification. In the types, Lev. 16 makes known God's requirements for the making of atonement; Num. 19 tells of God's provision for the defilements of the way, as Israel journeyed through the wilderness. The latter was met not by blood, but by "the *water* of purification." Judicial cleansing from the guilt of *all sin* is the inalienable portion of every believer in the Lord Jesus Christ. Moral cleansing, the practical purification of the heart and ways from all that defiles and hinders our communion with God is by *water,* that is, *the Word,* applied to us in power by the Holy Spirit.

"Now before the feast of the passover, when Jesus knew that his hour was come that he should depart out of this world unto the Father, having loved his own which were in the world, he loved them unto the end" (13:1). This opening verse supplies us with the first key to what follows. What we have here *anticipates* that which was in view in Christ's *return* to the Father. He graciously affords us a symbolic representation of His *present* service for us in Heaven. He is seated at the right hand of the Majesty on High, but He is there in *our interests,* ever living to make intercession for us, ever there as our Advocate with the Father, ever maintaining and succouring us by the way.

"Now before the feast of the passover," immediately before, for on the morrow Christ was to die as the true Lamb. The "passover" itself was eaten at the close of the *fourteenth* day of Nisan (Ex. 12:6, 8); but "the feast," which lasted seven days, began on the *fifteenth* (Num. 28:17). What we have here, then, transpired on the eve before our Lord's death.

"When Jesus knew that his hour was come." Christ is the only One who has ever trod this earth that was never taken by surprise. All was known and felt in the Father's presence. "That he should depart out of this world": note "*this* world," not "the world." It is striking to see how frequently this term occurs at the close of His life: "And Jesus said, For judgment I am come into *this world*" (9:39); "He that hateth his life in *this world* shall keep it unto life eternal" (12:25); "Now is the judgment of *this world*: now shall the Prince of *this world* be cast out" (12:31). "*This world*" was evidently a terrible place in the Lord's mind! He could not stay here. *He* had made *the* world (1:10), but *sin* has made *this* world what it is. Note "that he should depart out of this world *unto the Father*," not unto *heaven!* How blessed! It was *the Father's* presence His heart desired!

"Having loved his own which were in the world, he loved them unto the end." "*His own*"! After all the previous conflicts with an unbelieving world, after all His unavailing appeals to Israel, Christ now comforts His heart by lavishing His love upon the few who despised Him not. What a blessed expression—"his own"! "Ye are *not your own*" (I Cor. 6:19); we belong to Christ. We all know the delight which comes from being able to call something *our own*. It is not so much the value of what is possessed which constitutes this satisfaction, as it is the simple consciousness that it is *mine*. It is the Holy Spirit here declaring the heart of the Saviour in the terms of love. It is not with our poor estimate of Him, still less with our wretched selves, that He would occupy us. He would have us taken up with *Christ's* thoughts about us! We belong to the Lord Jesus in a threefold way. First, by *the Father's eternal election*. We are the Father's love-gift to the Son: "chosen in Christ before the foundation of the world." Second, we are His by *His own redemptive rights*. He paid the purchase price. He bought us for Himself: "Christ also loved the church, and gave himself *for* it." Third, we are His by *the effectual call of the Holy Spirit*. If any one be in Christ, he is a new creation, and we are created anew by the Third Person of the Holy Trinity: "born of the Spirit."

"He loved them unto the end." Here is the care of the Good Shepherd for the sheep. Unto "the end" *of what?* Who can define it? First, unto the end of our earthly pilgrimage. We *need* the assurance of His love as we pass through this wilderness. We shall *not* need it when we see Him face to face and know as we are known. But we *do* need the full *assurance* of it now. And what a resting-place for the poor heart amid all the buffetings of this life—the bosom of the Saviour! It is here that John turned (13:23), and it is blessedly accessible to us, in spirit. Yea, it is to maintain us in the unending enjoyment of our place there, that the Lord Jesus is here seen washing the disciples' feet *before* He begins the long discourse which follows to the end of chapter 16. The love of Christ must be *occupied about its objects,* and this is what we see here. God is "light" (I John 1:5), and God is "love" (I John 4:16). In the first twelve chapters of this Gospel Christ is seen as *light,* revealing the Father, exposing men (1:7; 3:19; 8:12; 9:5). But now we behold Him (with "his *own*") as *love* (cf. 13:34; 14:12; 15:9; 17:26, etc.). But mark it, it is a *holy* love. Divine love cannot allow that which is unclean. Therefore does the holy love of Christ *begin* by removing defilement from the feet of His disciples! Most blessed is this. We delight to contemplate the love which caused Him to lay down His life for us, but let us never lose sight of the *present* activities of it.

"He loved them unto the end!" Not only unto the last, but to the *farthest extent* of their need and of His grace. He knew that Philip would misunderstand Him, that three of them would sleep while He prayed and agonized, that Peter would deny Him, that Thomas would doubt Him, that *all* would "forsake him"—yet He "loved *them* unto the end"! And so it is with us, dear Christian reader. "His own" are the *objects* of His love; "unto the end" is the *extent* of His love. He loves us unto "the end" of our miserable failures, unto the "end" of our wanderings and backslidings, unto the "end" of our unworthiness, unto the "end" of our deep need.

His love *no* end or measure knows,
No change can turn its course;
Eternally the same it flows
From one eternal Source.

The first part of our verse intimates two things about the Lord Jesus at this time: the Cross was before Him with all its horrors; the joy of returning to the Father was before Him with all its bliss; yet neither the fearful prospect of woe nor the hope of unspeakable rest and gladness shook His love for His own. He is the *same* yesterday, and to-day, and forever, therefore His love never varies. *He is eternal,* therefore has He loved us with an *everlasting* love. He is *Divine,* therefore is His love different from all others, passing human knowledge.

"And supper being ended, the devil having now put into the heart of Judas Iscariot, Simon's son, to betray him" (13:2). What a fearful contrast! From love to hate; from the Saviour to Satan; from "his own" to the traitor! The mention of Judas here seems to be for the purpose of enhancing the beauty of what follows. The Devil had full mastery over the heart of the betrayer: thus *in figure* the Cross was passed—Satan had accomplished his design.

"Jesus knowing that the Father had given all things into his hands, and that he was come from God, and went to God" (13:3) "These statements of Christ's Divine origin, authority, and coming glory, are made so as to emphasize the amazing condescension of the service to which He humbled Himself to do the office of a bondslave" (Companion Bible).

"Jesus knowing that the Father had given all things into his hands, and that he was come from God, and went to God; he riseth from supper, and laid aside his garments; and took a towel, and girded himself" (13:3, 4). "It was not in forgetfulness of His Divine origin, but in full consciousness of it, He discharged this menial function. As He had divested Himself of the 'form of God' at the first, stripping Himself of the outward glory attendant on recognized Deity; and had taken upon Himself 'the form of a servant,' so now He laid aside His garment and girded Himself; assuming the guise of a household slave. For a fisherman to pour water over a fisherman's feet was no great condescension; but that He, in whose hands are all human affairs and whose nearest relation is the Father, should thus condescend, is of unparalleled significance. It is this kind of action that is *suitable* to One whose consciousness is Divine. Not only does the dignity of Jesus vastly augment the beauty of the action, but it also sheds new light on the Divine character" (Dr. Dods).

Three things are to be carefully noted here as *reasons* why He washed His disciples' feet on this occasion. First, He knew that His hour was come when He should depart out of this world (13:1); second, He loved His own unto the end (13:1); third, because all things had been given into His hands, and He that had come from God was returning to God—for these reasons He arose from the table and girded Himself with a towel. As we shall see, all of this finds its explanation in the Lord's words to Peter, "If I wash thee not, thou hast *no part with me*" (13:8). For three years the disciples *had* had "a part" with Him. But now He was about to leave them; but before doing so He would assure them (and us) that His wondrous love continues undiminished and unchanged after His return to the Father. Christ began a service in the Glory which, in another manner, He will continue forever. The service in which He is now engaged is to *maintain* our "part" with Him.

There has been much controversy as to *what* "supper" is referred to here in John 13. Most assuredly it was *not* the "Lord's Supper," for in 13:26 we find Christ giving the "sop" to Judas, and the Synoptists make it unmistakably plain that this was at the *paschal* supper. The Lord's Supper receives no mention in the fourth Gospel. On this fact Bishop Ryle strikingly says, "I think it was specially intended to be a witness forever against the growing tendency of Christians to make an idol out of the sacraments. Even from the beginning there seems to have been a disposition in the Church to make a religion of forms and ceremonies rather than of heart, and to exalt outward ordinances to a place which God never meant them to fill. Against this teaching St. John was raised up to testify. The mere fact that in his Gospel he leaves out the Lord's Supper altogether, and does not even name it, is strong proof that the Lord's Supper cannot be, as many tell us, the first, chief, and principle thing in Christianity. His perfect silence about it can never be reconciled with this favorite theory. It is a most conspicuous silence,

I can only see one answer: it is because it is not a primary, but a secondary thing in Christ's religion."

"He riseth from supper." In the order of events this comes right after what we read of in 13:1: the time-mark there being connected with Christ's action here. Evidently it was just before the beginning of the meal that the Lord Jesus rose from the table—the meal being the paschal one. It is important to note that John's narrative carries everything on in strict connection from this point to 14:31, and then on to 18:1: therefore this "supper" and Christ's discourse to His disciples was at once followed by the going forth to Gethsemane. The question of Peter in 13:24 is inexplicable if the paschal supper had already taken place (as quite a number have insisted), for the Synoptists are explicit that our Lord named the betrayer during this meal. Most of the difficulty has been created by the first clause of 13:2, which should be rendered, "when the supper arrived," i.e., was ready. Mark how that 13:12 shows us Christ *resuming His* place at the table.

"He riseth from supper, and laid aside his garments: and took a towel, and girded himself" (13:4). Everything here, we doubt not, has a deep symbolical meaning. The "supper" was the paschal one, and clearly spoke of Christ's death. The *rising* from supper and the *laying aside* of His garments (cf. 20:6) pictured our Lord on the resurrection-side of the grave. The girding Himself speaks of *service*, the *heavenly* service in which He is now engaged on behalf of His people. It is a wonderful thing that the Lord never relinquished His *servant* character. Even which the modern advocates of the so-called sacramental system can never get over, or explain away. If the sacrament of the Lord's Supper really is the first and chief thing in Christianity, why does St. John tell us nothing about it? To that question after His return to the Glory He still ministers to us. Beautifully was this typified of old in connection with the Hebrew servant in Exodus 21. "If thou buy an Hebrew servant, six years he shall serve: and in the seventh he shall go out free. . . .If the servant shall plainly say I love my master, my wife, and my children; I will *not* go out free, then his master shall bring him unto the judges; he shall also bring him to the door, and unto the door-post; and his master shall bore his ear through with an aul; and he shall serve him forever" (vv. 2-5, 6). This has been expounded at length in our "Gleanings in Exodus." Suffice it now to say that it affords us a most blessed foreshadowment of the perfect Servant. *Christ* will "serve forever." To-day He is serving us, applying the Word (by His Spirit) to our practical state, dealing with what unfits us for fellowship with Himself on high. Luke 12:37 gives us a precious word upon His *future* service: "Blessed are those servants, whom the Lord when he cometh shall find watching: verily I say unto you, that he shall *gird* himself, and make them to sit down to meat, and will come forth and *serve* them." And *how* will He "serve" us then? By ministering to our happiness and enjoyment as "His guests"!

"After that he poureth water into a basin," etc. (13:5). Everything here is Divinely perfect. *Seven* distinct actions are attributed to the Saviour: "He (1) riseth from supper, and (2) laid aside his garments, and (3) took a towel, and (4) girded himself. After that he (5) poureth water into a basin, and (6) began to wash the disciples' feet, and (7) to wipe them with the towel wherewith he was girded." It was their *feet* which He here proceeded to wash. Their *persons* were already cleansed. They had been brought out of Judaism, and a heavenly portion was now theirs—a place in the Father's House. But their conduct must be suited to that House. Their *walk* must be in accord with their heavenly calling. They must be kept clean in their ways.

The water with which the Saviour here cleansed the soiled feet of His disciples was an emblem of the Word: "Wherewithal shall a young man *cleanse* his *way*? by taking heed thereto according to thy *word*" (Psa. 119:9). Fully and blessedly is this brought out in Eph. 5:25, 26: "Christ also loved the church, and gave himself for it; that he might sanctify and cleanse it with the washing of water by the word." "Every clause of this passage is found here in John 13. He 'loved' them, the Church. He 'gave himself' for them, the 'supper' setting forth that: that He might 'sanctify,' separate to Himself, thus they were 'his own'; and 'cleanse' it with the washing of water by the Word. It is complete; His constant, perfect provision for our being kept clean" (Mr. Malachi Taylor). It is to be particularly observed that the Lord did not leave this work unfinished or half done: like a perfect servant, our Lord not only "washed" their feet, but He "wiped" them as well!

"Then cometh he to Simon Peter: and Peter saith unto him, Lord, dost thou wash my feet?" (13:6). Simon was ever blundering, and his sad faults and failings are recorded for our learning. "In Divine things the wisdom of the believer is subjection to Christ and confidence in Him. What He does we are called on to accept with thankfulness of heart, and as Mary said to the servants at the marriage-feast, 'Whatsoever he saith unto you, do it.' This Simon Peter did not, for when the Lord approached him in the form of a servant or bond-man, he demurred. Was there not faith 'working by love' in Peter's heart? Both, undoubtedly, yet not then in action, but buried under superabundant feeling of a human order, else he had not allowed his mind to question what the Lord saw fit to do. He had rather bowed to Christ's love and sought to learn, as He might teach, what deep need must be in him and his fellows to draw forth such a lowly yet requisite service from his Master. . . . Too self-confident and indeed ignorant not only of himself and the defiling scene around, but of the depths and constancy of Christ's love, Peter says to Him, 'Lord, dost thou wash my feet?' Granting that he could not know what was not yet revealed, but was it comely of him, was it reverent, to question what the Lord was doing? He may have thought it humility in himself, and honour to the Lord, to decline a service so menial at His hands. But Peter should never have forgotten that as Jesus never said a word, so He never did an act save worthy of God and demonstrative of the Father; and now more than ever were His words and ways an exhibition of Divine grace, as human evil set on by Satan, not only in those outside, but within the innermost circle of His own, called for increased distinctness and intensity.

"The truth is we need to learn from God *how* to honour Him, and learn to love *according to His mind*. And if any man think that he knoweth anything, he knoweth nothing yet as he ought to know; this, too, was Peter's mistake. He should have suspected his thoughts, and waited in all submissiveness on Him who, as many confessed that knew far less than he did, 'hath done all things well,' and was absolutely what He was saying, truth and love in the same blessed Person. The thoughts of God are never as ours, and saints slip into those of man, unless they are taught of God, by faith, in detail, too, as well as in the main; for we cannot, ought not, to trust ourselves in anything. God the Father will have the Son honoured; and He is honoured most when believed in and followed in His humiliation. Peter therefore was equally astray when he once ventured to rebuke the Lord for speaking of His suffering and death, as now when he asks, 'Dost thou wash my feet?'" (Bible Treasury).

"Jesus answered and said unto him, What I do thou knowest not now; but thou shalt know hereafter" (13:7). We take it that the force of this is, briefly, as follows: Peter, this gives a picture, a sample, of the work which I shall perform for My people when I return to the Father. You do not see the significance of it now, but you *will* later, when the Holy Spirit has come. This was really a rebuke; but given tenderly. Peter ought to have known that in his Lord's mysterious action there must be a purpose and a meaning in it worthy of His subjection to the Father and expressive of His love for His own. But like us, Peter was dull of discernment, slow to learn. Instead of gladly submitting to the most high Sovereign now performing the service of a slave, he plunges still further into worse error: "Peter saith unto him, Thou shalt never wash my feet." It was ignorance, yea, affection, which prompted him; but that did not excuse him. But how blessed that he had, and that we have, to do with One who bears with us in our dullness, and whose grace corrects our faults!

"Peter saith unto him, Thou shalt never wash my feet" (13:8). We are all ready to censure Peter for not complying immediately with the Lord's will when he knew it. But let us beware lest *we* be guilty of something more inexcusable than what we condemn in the apostle. Peter said he would not submit, yet he *did*, and that very quickly. Is it not sadly true of us, that we often *say* we will submit, and yet remain obstinately disobedient? As another has said, "We do not *use* Peter's words, but we *act* them, which he durst not do. What, then, is the difference between us and him? Is it not just the difference between the two sons in the parable—the one of whom said, 'I go, and went not,' the other of whom said, 'I will not go, and afterwards repented and went?' Which of these did the will of the father? Whether do you think Peter's refractory expression, or our disobedient conduct, most deserving of censure?"

"Jesus answered him, If I wash thee not, thou hast no part with me" (13:8). "If *I* wash thee not": we cannot wash our own feet; we are totally incompetent, not only for the saving of our souls, but also for the cleansing of our defiled walk. Nor has even the Word *apart from His living presence* any efficacy. Our feet must be in *His* hands, that is to say, we must completely *yield* to Him. It is not simply that we are to judge our ways according to *our* apprehension of the Word, and its requirements, but *He* must interpret and apply it, and for this we *must* be in His presence.

But what is meant by "no part with me?" Ah, here is the key that unlocks the chamber that conducts us to the very center of this incident. The word "part" has reference to *fellowship*. This is seen from our Lord's words concerning the sister of Martha: "Mary hath chosen *that good part*" (Luke 10:42). The meaning of this word "part" is clearly defined again in II Cor. 6:15, "What concord hath Christ with Belial? or what *part* hath he that believeth with an infidel?"

What is the "washing"? "If I *wash* thee not, thou hast no part with me." It is something which is needed by *all* believers. We say "believers," for though all such have a portion *in* Christ, how often they fail to enjoy their "part" *with* Him. This "washing" is something more than confession of sin and the consequent forgiveness. It is the searching out of the Word, in the *presence* of God, of that which led me into evil; it is judging the *root*, of which sins are the fruit. Yet this "washing" must not be *limited* to God's remedy for our declension and failure, rather should we view it as His gracious provision for our daily need, as a *preservative* and *preventative* against outward failures. We need to get alone with our Lord each day, opening our hearts to the light as the flower does its petals to the sun. Alas! that we have so little consciousness of our deep need for this, and that there is so little retirement and examination of our ways before God. To really place our feet for washing in the blessed hands of Christ is to come before Him in the attitude of the Psalmist: "Search me, *O God,* and *know* my heart: *try* me, and know my thoughts: And see if there be any wicked way in me, and lead me in the way everlasting" (139:23, 24). This is imperatively necessary if, while in such a defiling place as this world, we *are* to have a "part" *with Him.*

"Simon Peter saith unto him, Lord, not my feet only, but also my hands and my head" (13:9). Here, with characteristic impulsiveness, Peter rushes to the opposite extreme. As he hears that he could have no part with Christ *except* the Lord wash him, he is ready now to be washed all over. It was the passionate outburst of a warm-hearted if dull-minded disciple. Nevertheless, his ignorance voiced another error. He needed not now to be washed all over. The sinner does, but the saint does not. It is only our *walk* which needs cleansing.

"Jesus saith to him, He that is washed needeth not save to wash his feet, but is clean every whit" (13:10). The distinction which our Lord here drew is of vital importance. "He that is washed," better, "He who has been *bathed,*" that is, his whole person cleansed: "needeth not save to wash his *feet,*" then is he completely fit for communion with the Lord. There is a washing which believers have in Christ that needs not to be ever repeated. In Him there is to be found a cleansing which is never lost. "By one offering he hath *perfected forever* them that are set apart" (Heb. 10:14). The believer has been purged from *all* sin, and *made meet* to be a partaker of the inheritance of the saints in light (Col. 1:12). *This* purging needs no repetition. It is of first moment that the Christian should be clear upon this basic truth. The benefits which Christ confers upon the believer are never recalled; the efficacy of His precious blood abides upon him eternally. The moment a sinner, drawn by the Holy Spirit, comes to Christ, he is completely and finally cleansed. It is the apprehension of this which gives a firm rock for my feet to rest upon. It assures me that my hope is a stable one; that my standing before God is immutable. It banishes doubt and uncertainty. It gives the heart and mind abiding peace to know that the benefits I have found in Christ are never to be recalled. I am brought out from under condemnation and placed in a state of everlasting acceptance. All this, and more, is included in the "bathing" which Christ has declared needs not to be repeated. I stand resplendent in the sight of God in all the Saviour's beauty and perfections. God looks upon believers not merely as forgiven, but as *righteous*: as truly as Christ was "made sin" for us, so have we been "made the righteousness of God in him."

But side by side with this blessed truth of a *bathing* in Christ which needs not, and cannot be, repeated, stands another truth of great practical importance: "He that is bathed needeth not save to *wash his feet*, but is clean every whit." There is a *partial cleansing* which the believer still needs, a daily washing to counteract the defiling effects of this world. Our daily contact with the evil all around causes the dust of defilement to settle upon us so that the mirror of our conscience is dimmed and the spiritual affections of our heart are dulled. We need to come afresh into the presence of Christ in order to learn what things really are, surrendering ourselves to His judgment in everything, and submitting to His purging Word. And who is there that, even for a single day, lives *without* sin? Who is there that does not need to daily pray, "Forgive us our trespasses"? Only One has ever walked here and been unsoiled by the dust of earth. He went as He came, unstained, uncontaminated. But who is there among His people that does not find much in his daily walk that makes him blush for shame! How much unfaithfulness we all have to deplore! Let me but compare my walk with *Christ's*, and, unless I am blinded by conceit or deceived by Satan, I shall at once see that I come infinitely short of Him, and though "following his steps" (not "*in* his steps" as it is so often misquoted), it is but "afar off." So often my acts are *un*-Christlike in character, so often my disposition and ways have "the flesh" stamped upon them. Even when evil does not break out in open forms, we are conscious of much *hidden* wrong, of sins of thought, of vile desires. How real, then, how deep, is our daily need of putting our feet in the hands of Christ for cleansing, that everything which hinders communion with Him may be removed, and that He can say of us, "Ye are *clean*"!

Is it not most significant that nothing is said in this chapter about the washing of the disciples' *hands?* Does it not point a leading contrast between the Mosaic and the Christian dispensations? Under the law, where there was so much of doing, the priests were required to wash both their hands and their feet (Ex. 30:19); but under grace all has been done for us, and if the *walk* be right, the *work* will be acceptable!

"And ye are clean, but not all. For he knew who should betray him; therefore said he, Ye are not *all* clean" (13:10,11). Christ here referred to Judas, though He did not name the Traitor. Judas must have known what He meant, but his conscience was seared as with a red-hot iron, and his heart was harder than the nether mill-stone. Even this touching exhibition of the condescending love and grace of Christ toward His disciples made no impression upon him. In less than one hour he went forth to sell his Master. In his case it was not a matter of *losing* spiritual life, but of *manifesting* the fact that he never had it. It was not a sheep of Christ becoming unclean, but of a dog returning to his vomit. Unspeakably solemn warning is this for those who, for a time, maintain an *outward* form of godliness, but are strangers to its inward power.

The following questions are to help the student prepare for the next lesson:—

1. What is the typical teaching of v. 12?
2. What is the important lesson on reverence in v. 13?
3. How are *we* to obey, vv. 14, 15?
4. What is the thought suggested by v. 16 coming right after vv. 14, 15?
5. What lessons are to be learned from v. 17?
6. What is the meaning of v. 19?
7. What blessed truth is expressed in v. 20?

CHAPTER FORTY-SIX

CHRIST'S EXAMPLE FOR US

John 13:12-20

The following is given as an Analysis of the second section of John 13:—

1. Christ's searching question, v. 12.
2. Christ's dignity and authority, v. 13.
3. Christ's example for us to follow, vv. 14, 15.
4. Christ's warning against pride, v. 16.
5. Christ's approval of practical godliness, v. 17.
6. Christ's word about the Traitor, vv. 18, 19.
7. Christ's encouragement to His servants, v. 20.

The opening portion of John 13 makes known the provision which Divine love has made for failure in our walk as we journey through this world-wilderness, and the means which are used to maintain us in fellowship with Christ. Its central design is stated by the Lord when He said to Peter, "If I wash thee not, thou hast no part with me." The washing of our feet is imperative if we are to enjoy fellowship with the Holy One of God. "Grace" has given us a place *in Christ,* now "truth" operates to maintain our place *with Christ.* The effect of this ministry is stated in v. 10: "He that is bathed needeth not save to wash his feet, but is clean *every whit.*"

There is a *double* washing for the believer: the one of his entire person, the other of his feet; the former is once for all, the latter needs repeating daily. In both instances the "washing" is by *the Word.* Of the former we read, "Nor thieves, nor covetous, nor drunkards, nor revilers, nor extortioners, shall inherit the kingdom of God. And such were some of you: but ye are *washed,* but ye are sanctified, but ye are justified in the name of the Lord Jesus, and by the Spirit of our God" (I Cor 6:10, 11). And again, "Not by works of righteousness which we have done, but according to his mercy he saved us, by *the washing* of regeneration, and renewing of the holy Spirit" (Titus 3:5). The "washing of regeneration" is not by blood, though it is inseparable from redemption by blood; and neither the one nor the other is ever repeated. Of the latter we read, "Christ also loved the church, and gave himself for it: That he might sanctify and cleanse it *with the washing of water* BY THE WORD. That he might present it to himself a glorious church, not having spot, or wrinkle, or any such thing; but that it should be holy and without blemish" (Eph. 5:25-27). This same distinction was plainly marked in the Old Testament. When Aaron and his sons were consecrated, they were bathed all over (Exodus 29:4; Lev. 8:6): but at the "laver" it was only their hands and feet which were daily cleansed (Exodus 30:19, 21).

In our last chapter we pointed out how that the "blood" is *Godward,* the "water" *saintwards.* The one is for legal expiation, the other for moral purification. Now, while both the "bathing" (Titus 3:5) and the "washing" of the saints' feet is by the "water of the word," there *is* a "cleansing" by blood—"the blood of Jesus Christ his Son cleanseth us from all sin" (I John 1:7). But *this* "cleansing" is *judicial,* not experiential. The precious blood has *not* been applied to my *heart,* but it *has* cancelled my *guilt.* It has *washed out* the heavy and black account which was once against me on high. A "book of remembrance" is written before God (Mal. 3:16), but in it there is not left on record a single sin against any believer. Just as a damp sponge passed over a slate removes every chalk mark upon it, so the blood of Christ has *blotted out* every transgression which once was marked up against me. How deeply significant, then, to read that when the Roman soldier pierced the side of the dead Saviour that "*forthwith* came there out blood *and* water" (John 19:34)! The blood for penal expiation, the water for moral purification. But mark the *order*: first, the "blood" to satisfy the demands of a holy *God,* then the "water" to meet the needs of His defiled *people!*

The distinction between the bathing of the entire body and the washing of the feet was aptly illustrated by the ancient custom of bathers. A person returning from the public baths, was, of course, clean, and needed not to be re-bathed. But wearing only sandals, which covered but part of the feet, he quickly needed the foot-bath to cleanse himself from the dust of travel encountered on his way from the baths to his home. Even to-day bathers in the sea are often seen going to their dressing-room with a pail of water to cleanse their soiled feet. This may be regarded as a parable of the spiritual life. Believers were bathed, completely cleansed, at the new birth. The "dressing-room" is Heaven, where we shall be robed in white raiment and garments of glory. But the pail of water is needed for our present use in connection with the daily walk.

In the second section of John 13 the Lord Jesus makes a practical application to the disciples of what He had just done for them. He intimates very plainly that there was a spiritual meaning in His washing of their feet: "Know ye not what I have done to you?" He tells them expressly that *they* ought to wash one another's feet. If they shrank from such lowly service, He reminds them that none other than He, their Master and Lord, had done so much for them. He warns them that a theoretical knowledge of these things was of no value, unless it resulted in an actual carrying out of them: "If ye know these things, happy are ye *if* ye *do* them." Then He recurs again to the fact that one of their number must be excepted. The presence of the traitor seems to have cast a shadow upon Him, but He tells them beforehand that the Scriptures had predicted his defection, so that when the betrayer delivered up their Master into the hands of His enemies the faith of the other disciples might not falter. Finally, He encourages them with the assurance that whosoever received His servants received Himself, yea, received the One who had sent Him. What dignity that gave to their calling!

"So after he had washed their feet, and had taken his garments, and was set down again, he said unto them, Know ye what I have done to you?" (13:12). It is important to note that it was from the "supper" that the Lord arose when He girded

Himself for the washing of His disciples' feet; to it He now returns. Typically, it was Christ's "leaving the place of communion, as if this were interrupted, until His necessary work for them should renew it once more. He rises, therefore, from supper, and girded Himself for a fresh service. His sacrificial work is over, the shedding of blood is no more needed, but only the washing of water; and here also not the 'bath of regeneration' (Titus 3:5 Gk.), but simply as He pointed out to Peter, the washing of the feet. It is defilement contracted in the walk that is in question; and He puts Himself at their feet to wash them. As of old, Jehovah could say to Israel, 'Thou hast made me to *serve* with thy sins' (Isa. 43:24), so may He still say to us; but His unchanging love is equal to all possible demands upon it. Notice here that *all* the disciples need it, and that thus He invites us all to-day to put *our* feet into His hands continually, that they may be cleansed according to *His* thought of what is cleanness, who alone is capable of judging according to the perfect standard of the Sanctuary of which He is indeed Himself the Light" (Numerical Bible).

"So after he had washed their feet, and had taken his garments, and was set down again, he said unto them, Know ye what I have done to you?" This is the sequel to what we read of in 13:4. There He had *lain aside* His outer garments, here He *resumes* them. We believe that the former act had a *double* symbolical meaning. First, we are told, "he riseth from supper": *what* supper is not here specified. Now, "supping" speaks of *communion*, therefore when we are told "he riseth *from* supper *and* laid aside his garments and took a towel and girded himself," the first and deepest meaning would be, He left His place on high, where from all eternity He had been the Father's delight, and with whom He had enjoyed perfect communion as the Son, but now divested Himself of His outward glory and took upon Him the *form* of a servant. But the "supper" is also the memorial of His death, hence the *rising* from it and the laying aside of His garments would suggest the additional thought of His resurrection. Now, we believe that the Lord's action here in 13:12 connects with and is the sequel to the *first* thing pointed out above. The *putting on* of His garments and the *sitting down again* would typify His return to the Father's presence, the resumption of His original glory (John 17:5), and His resting on high.

The Lord was about to explain (in part) and enforce what He had done unto the disciples. Before pondering what He had to say, let us first admire the calmness and deliberation which marked His actions. He quietly resumed His garments (there is no hint of the apostles offering to assist Him!) ere He seated Himself upon the couch or cushion, in His character of Teacher and Lord, thus giving His disciples time to recover from their surprise, collect their thoughts, and prepare themselves for what He was about to say. This gives additional meaning to His posture. Note that ere He began the "Sermon on the Mount" He first *seated* Himself (Matt. 5:1); so it was while *seated* in a ship (Matt. 13:2) He delivered the seven parables of the kingdom; so while He "*sat* upon the mount of Olives" (Matt. 24:3), He gave His longest prophetic announcement; so here He *seated* Himself before giving the great Paschal Discourse. The force of these notices is seen by comparing them with Luke 5:3: "He *sat down* and *taught* the people." Study the passages in John's Gospel where Jesus "stood," and then where He "walked"—see 7:1 and our remarks.

"So after he had washed their feet," that is, the feet of each of the twelve. "We may learn an important lesson here as to dealing with offenders in the assembly. The Lord knew all about Judas, and all he was doing, but treated him as one of the apostles, till he displayed himself. There may be suspicion about some individual, that all is not right with him; but mere suspicion will not suffice to act on. The matter must come clearly out, ere it can be rightly dealt with. Were this remembered, cases of discipline, instead of causing trouble in the assembly through lack of common judgment, would be clear to all unprejudiced persons, and the judgments of the assembly be accepted as correct. Has it not at times been the reverse?" (Mr. C. E. Stuart).

"He said unto them, Know ye what I have done to you?" Very searching was this. In washing the feet of His disciples He had not only displayed a marvellous humility, which He would have them take to heart, but He had cared for them in holy love. Not only had He saved them, but He was concerned about their fellowship with Himself, and for this, strict attention must be paid to the walk. For when the feet are soiled, the dust of this world must be removed. In His question the Lord illustrates how that it is His way to teach us *afterwards* the good which He has *already* done for us; as we grow up in Him in the truth, we are enabled to enter into and appreciate more deeply what at first we understood but slightly. The same grace which brought salvation *teaches* us, that "denying ungodliness and worldly lusts, we should live soberly, righteously, and godly, in this present world; looking for that blessed hope" (Titus 2:11, 12). Deeply humbling is it to discover how little we understood the love and the grace which *had been* acting on our behalf.

"Know ye what I have done to you?" "This is a question which we should often put to ourselves respecting what our Lord says, and what He does to us. None of His works are 'the unfruitful works of darkness.' They are all full of meaning. They are all intended to serve a purpose, and a good one; and it is of importance, in most cases, that we should be aware of it. If we look at His work in the light of His Word, and seek the guidance of His good Spirit, we shall generally be able to discern His wise and benign purpose, even in dispensations at first sight very strange and mysterious. He only can explain His intentions, and He will not suffer His humble, enquiring disciples to remain ignorant of them, if it be for their real benefit to know them" (Dr. John Brown).

"Ye call me Master and Lord: and ye say well; for so I am" (13:13). Beautifully does this bring out the fact that the Lord Jesus *is* "full of grace *and* truth." Though He had just fulfilled for His disciples the most menial office of a slave, yet He had not abandoned the place of authority and supremacy. He reminds them that He is still their "Master and Lord," and that, by their own confession, for the word "call" here signifies *address* —"Ye address Me as Master and Lord." In *thus* owning the incarnate Son of God they "did well." Alas! that so many of His professing followers now treat Him with so much *less* respect than that which He here commended in the Twelve. Alas! that so many who owe their all for time and eternity to that peerless One who was "*God* manifest in flesh," speak of Him simply as "Jesus." Jesus is the Lord of glory, and surely it is due the dignity and majesty of His person that this should be *recognized* and *owned,* even in our very references to Him. We do not expect that those who despise and reject Him should speak of Him in any more exalting terms than "The Nazarene," or "Jesus"; but those who have been, by amazing grace, given "an understanding, that we may know him that is true" (I John 5:20) ought gladly to confess Him as "*The Lord* Jesus Christ"!

"Ye call me Master and Lord: and ye say well; for so I am." Surely this is sufficient for any humble-minded Christian. If our blessed Redeemer says we "*say well*" when we address Him as "Master and Lord," how can we afford to speak of Him in terms upon which His approval is *not* stamped? Never once do we find the apostles addressing Him as "Jesus" while He was with them on earth. When He exhorted them to make request of Him for an increase of laborers He bade them, "Pray ye therefore *the Lord* of the harvest" (Matt. 9:38). When He sent forth the disciples to secure the ass on which He was to ride into Jerusalem, He ordered them to say, "*The Lord* hath need of him" (Luke 19:31). When He required the use of the upper room, it was "*The Lord* saith, My time is at hand; I will therefore keep the passover at thy house" (Matt. 26:18).

Above, we have said that the apostles never once addressed our Lord simply as "Jesus." Mark, now, *how they did* refer to the Blessed One. "And Peter answered him and said, LORD, if it be thou, bid me come unto thee on the water" (Matt. 14:28). "And when his disciples James and John, saw this, they said, *Lord,* wilt thou that we command fire to come down from heaven, and consume them?" (Luke 9:54). "And they were exceeding sorrowful, and began every one of them to say unto him, *Lord,* is it I?" (Matt. 26:22). "And they rose up the same hour, and returned to Jerusalem, and found the eleven gathered together, and them that were with them, saying, *The Lord* is risen indeed" (Luke 24:33, 34). "Thomas saith unto him, *Lord,* we know not whither thou goest" (John 14:5). "That disciple whom Jesus loved saith unto Peter, It is *the Lord*" (John 21:7).

It may be objected that the Gospel narratives commonly refer to the Lord as "Jesus." It was *Jesus* who was led of the Spirit into the wilderness to be tempted of the Devil. It was *Jesus* who was moved with compassion as He beheld the sufferings and sorrows of humanity. It was *Jesus* who taught the people, etc. This is true, and the explanation is not far to seek. It was the *Holy Spirit of God* who, through the pens of the Evangelists, *thus* referred to Him, and this makes all the difference. What would be thought of one of the subjects of king George referring to the reigning monarch of Great Britian and saying, "I saw *George* pass through the city this morning"? If, then, it would be utterly incongruous for one of *his* subjects to speak thus of the king of England, how much more so is it to refer to the *King of kings* simply as Jesus! But now, king George's *wife* might refer to and speak of her husband as "George" with perfect propriety. Thus it is that the *Holy Spirit* refers to our Lord by His personal name in the Gospel narratives.

Our modern hymns are largely responsible for the dishonour that is now so generally cast upon that "worthy name" (James 2:7), and we cannot but raise our voice in indignant protest against much of the trash (for such it is) that masquerades under the name of "hymns" and religious "songs." It is sad and shocking to hear Christians sing "There's not a friend like the lowly Jesus." There is *no* "lowly Jesus" to-day. The One who once passed through unparalleled humiliation has been "made both Lord and Christ" (Acts 2:36), and is now seated at the right hand of the Majesty on high. If the earnest student will turn to the four Gospels and note *how* different ones addressed the Son of God he will be well repaid. The *enemies* of Christ constantly referred to Him as *Jesus* (Matt. 26:71, etc.), and so did the *demons* (Mark 1:23, 24). Let us pray God to deliver us from this flippant, careless, and irreverent manner of speaking of His Blessed Son. Let us gladly own our Saviour as "Lord" during the time of His rejection by the world. Let us remember His own words: "All should honour the Son, *even as* they honour the Father. He that honoureth not the Son honoureth not the Father which hath sent him" (John 5:23). This is no trivial or trifling matter, for it stands written, "By thy *words* thou shalt be *justified*, and by thy *words* thou shalt be *condemned*" (Matt. 12:37).

"If I then, your Lord and Master, have washed your feet" (v. 14). "Master" means *teacher*. The "teacher" is *believed;* the "Lord" is *obeyed*. Here Christ proceeded to enforce and apply what He had just done unto them. The connection is obvious, not only with what precedes, but also with that which follows. If the Greatest could minister to the least, how much more should the lesser minister to his equal! If the Superior waited upon His admitted inferiors, much less should that inferior wait upon his fellows. And mark the premise from which He draws this conclusion. He did not say, "I *am* your teacher and Lord," but "*Ye call* me teacher and Lord." It was from the confession of their own lips that He now proceeds to instruct them. The order in which these titles occur is significant. First, these disciples had heard Christ as "teacher," and later they had come to know Him as their "Lord." But now Christ *reverses* the order: "If I then, your Lord and teacher." Why is this? Because *this* is the experimental order now. We must surrender to Him as "Lord," bowing to His authority, submitting to His yoke, *before* He will *teach us!*

"Ye also ought to wash one another's feet" (13:14). So they ought, and why had they not already done so? The supper-room here was already supplied with water, pail, and towel. Why had not *they used* them? Luke 22:24 tells us, "And there was also a strife among them, which of them should be accounted *the greatest*." This occurred, be it noted, at this very time. It was then that the Saviour shamed them by saying, "For whether is greater, he that sitteth at meat, or he that serveth? is not he that sitteth at meat? but *I* am among you as He that *serveth*" (Luke 22:27).

"Ye also ought to wash one another's feet." Let us consider the application of these words to ourselves: "In discovering any stain that may be resting on the feet of our brethren, we are not to blind ourselves to its presence, or to hide from ourselves its character by calling evil good. If we are to be honest and faithful in respect of ourselves, we shall be equally honest and truthful in respect of others. On the other hand, we have to beware of looking on the sins and failures of our brethren with Pharisaic complacency and cold indifference. What condition is more awful than that one who finds his joy in searching out iniquities, and exulting in exposing and magnifying them when discovered? Such, indeed, have reason to remember that with whatsoever judgment they judge, they shall be judged; and that the measure they mete out to others shall be meted out to themselves again. How continually should we remind ourselves that the love of the same gracious Lord that is toward us is toward our brethren likewise, and that one of our chief privileges is the title to appeal to it and intercede on their behalf, asking that sins, even of deepest dye, may be removed; and that the deserved results of chastisement and sorrow might be averted. So we should not be as those who 'bite and devour one another,' but be as those who 'wash one another's feet'" (Mr. B. W. Newton).

Yes, a most needful word is this for us all, ever ready as we are to lift up the skirts of a brother and say, "See how soiled his feet are"! But much exercise of soul, much judging of ourselves, is needed for such lowly work as this. I have to *get down* to my brother's feet if I am to wash them! That means that "the flesh" in me must be subdued. Let us not forget that searching word in Gal. 6:1, 2: "Brethren, if a man be overtaken in a fault, ye which are spiritual restore such an one in the *spirit of meekness;* considering thyself, lest thou also be tempted. Bear ye one another's burdens, and *so* fulfil the law of Christ." I must be emptied of *all* sense of self-superiority before I can restore one who is "out of the way." It is the *love of Christ* which must constrain me as I seek to be of help to one of those for whom He died. It is as "*dear children*" (Eph. 5:1) that we are called upon to be "imitators of God"! Very wonderful and blessed is what is here before us: when the Lord appoints on earth a witness of *His* ways in Heaven, He tells us to wash one another's feet, and to love one another (13:34). There must be a patient forbearing with our brother's faults, a faithful but tender applying of the Word to his particular case, and an earnest and daily intercession for him: these are the main things included in this figure of "washing." But let us not stop short at the "washing": there must be the "drying," too! The service when done must be regarded as a service *of the past.* The failure which called for it, is now removed, and therefore is to be buried in the depths of oblivion. It ought never to be cast against the individual in the future.

"For I have given you an example, that ye should do as I have done to you" (13:15). It is well known that not a few have regarded this as a command from Christ for His followers now to practice *literal* foot-washing, yea, some have exalted it into a "Church ordinance." While we cannot but respect and admire their desire to *obey* Christ, especially in a day when laxity and self-pleasing is so rife, yet we are fully satisfied that they have mistaken our Lord's meaning here. Surely to insist upon literal foot-washing from this verse is to miss the meaning as well as the spirit of the whole passage. It is *not* with literal water (any more than the "water" is literal in John 3:5; 4:14; 7:38) that the Lord would have us wash one another. It is the Word (of which "water" is the emblem) He would have us apply to our fellow-disciples' walk. This should not need arguing, but for the benefit of those who think that the Lord here instituted an ordinance which He would have practised today, we would ask them to please weigh carefully the following points:

That that which the Lord Jesus here did to His disciples looked beyond the literal act to its deep symbolic significance is clear from these facts: First, the Lord's word to Peter, "What I do thou *knowest not* now" (13:7): certainly Peter knew that his feet had been literally washed! Second, the further words of Christ to Peter, "If I wash thee not, thou hast *no part* with me" (13:8): certainly there are multitudes of believers that *have* a part with Christ who have never practised foot-washing as a religious ordinance. Third, His words, "Ye are clean, but not all" (13:10): Judas could never have been *thus* excepted if only literal foot-washing was here in view. Fourth, His question, "Know ye what I have done to you?" clearly intimates that the Lord's act in washing the feet of the disciples had a profound *spiritual* meaning. Fifth, note that here in 13:15 the Lord *does not* say "Ye should do *what* I have done unto you," but "*as*

I have done to you!" Add to these considerations the fact that this incident is found in *John's* Gospel, which is, pre-eminently, the one which treats of *spiritual* relationships under various *figures*—bread, water, Shepherd and sheep, vine and the branches, etc., and surely all difficulty disappears.

"For I have given you an example, that ye should do as I have done to you." We take it that the force of these words of Christ is this: I have just shown you how spiritual love *operates*: it ever seeks the good of its objects, and esteems no service too lowly to secure that good. It reminds us very much of the Lord's words following His matchless picture of the Good Samaritan who had compassion on the wounded traveller, dismounting, binding up his wounds, pouring in oil and wine, setting him on *His own* beast, bringing him to the inn and taking care of him—"Go, and do thou likewise" (Luke 10:33-37). When real love is in exercise it will perform with readiness difficult, despised, and even loathsome offices. There are some services which are even more menial and repulsive than the washing of feet, yet, on occasion, the service of *love* may call for them. It should hardly be necessary to add, that Christians living in Oriental lands, where sandals are worn, *should* be ready to wash *literally* the feet of a weary brother, not simply as an act of courtesy, but as a service of love.

"For I have given you an example, that ye should do *as* I have done to you." We believe that one thing included in this comparative "as" is that it looks back to a detail in 13:4 which is usually overlooked: it was *as girded with a towel* that Christ washed the feet of His disciples, and that which was *signified* by the "towel" *applies to us*. The "towel" was that with which Christ was *girded*: it bespoke the servant's attitude. Then the Lord *used* that with which He was girded upon their feet: emblematically, this was *applying to them the humility* which marked Him. Mr. Darby tells us that it was a *linen* towel which was employed, and in the New Testament "linen" signifies "the *righteousness* of saints" (Rev. 19:8, R.V.). It was His own spotless love which fitted Him to approach His disciples and apply the Word to them. How searching is all of this for us! If we would imitate Him in this labour of love we must ourselves be clothed with humility, we must employ nothing but the Word, and we must have on the linen towel of practical righteousness to dry with.

"Verily, verily, I say unto you, The servant is not greater than his lord; neither he that is sent greater than he that sent him" (13:16). The Lord acts as His own interpreter. He here gives plain intimation of the meaning of His symbolic action. He draws an important lesson from what He had just done, the more needful because He was about to withdraw from them. It would fare ill with His people if their leaders were found disputing among themselves, devouring one another. Surrounded as they were by Judaism and Paganism, lambs in the midst of wolves, much depended upon their humility and mutual helpfulness. Much needed by every Christian, and especially by those engaged in Christian service, is that word of Christ's, "Take my yoke upon you, and learn of me; for I am meek and lowly in heart."

"Verily, verily, I say unto you, The servant is not greater than his lord, neither he that is sent greater than he that sent him." That this is of more than ordinary importance is evidenced by the solemn and emphatic "Verily, verily" with which the Lord prefaced it. Moreover, the fact that at a later point in this same discourse the Lord said to His apostles, "*Remember* the word that I said unto you, The servant is not greater than his lord" (15:20), shows that it is one which is specially needed by his ambassadors. How many a dark page of "Church History" had never been written if the ministers of Christ had heeded this admonition! How vain the pretensions of those who have lorded it over God's heritage in the light of this searching word! Sad indeed have been the manifestations of Nicolaitanism in every age. Even before the last of the apostles left this world he had to say, "I wrote unto the church: but Diotrephes, who loveth to have the pre-eminence among them, receiveth us not" (III John 9); and the same spirit is far from being dead today.

"If ye know these things, happy are ye if ye do them" (13:17). If ye know *what* "things"? First, the vital need of placing *our* feet in the hands of Christ for cleansing (13:8).

Second, the owning of Christ as "Master and Lord" (13:13). Third, the need of washing one another's feet (13:14). Fourth, the performing of this ministry *as* Christ performed it—in lowly love (13:15). Now, said our Saviour, If ye *know* "these things," happy or blessed are ye if ye *do* them. A mere speculative knowledge of such things is of no value. An intellectual apprehension, without the embodiment of them in our daily lives, is worse than useless. It is both significant and solemn to note that the one Christ termed a wise man that built his house upon the rock is, "Whoso heareth these sayings of mine and *doeth* them" (Matt. 7:24). No one *knows* more truth than the Devil, and yet none works more evil!

"If ye know these things, happy are ye if ye do them." "It has been well remarked that our Lord does not say, 'Happy are ye if these things be *done to* you,' but 'Happy are ye if *ye* do them.' We are apt to suppose that we should be happy if men loved *us*, and were ready on every occasion to serve *us*. But, in the judgment of Christ, it would more conduce to our happiness that our hearts were like His, full of love to all our brethren, and our hands like His, ever ready to perform to them even the humblest offices of kindness. We often make ourselves unhappy by thinking that we are not treated with the deference and kindness to which we consider ourselves entitled. If we would be really happy, we must think more of others and less of ourselves. True happiness dwells within; and one of its leading elements is the disinterested self-sacrificing love which made the bosom of Jesus its constant dwelling-place" (Dr. John Brown).

"I speak not of you all: I know whom I have chosen" (13:18). The immediate reference is to what the Lord had said in the previous verse. Just as in 13:10 He had said to the twelve, "Ye are clean," and then added, "but not all," so after saying, "Happy are ye if ye do them," He at once says, "I speak not of you all." Faithfulness required Him to make an exception. There was no happiness for Judas; before him lay "the blackness of darkness for ever." When Christ said, "I know whom I have chosen" it is evident that He was not speaking of election to salvation, but to the apostolate. Where *eternal election* is in view the Scriptures uniformally ascribe it to God the Father. But where it is a question of ministry or service, in the New Testament, the choice and the call usually proceed from the Lord Jesus—see Matt. 9:30; 20:1; 28:18-20; Acts 1:24; 26:16; Eph. 4:11, etc. His words here in 13:18 are parallel with those in 6:70: "Have not I chosen you twelve? and one of you is a devil?"

"But that the scripture may be fulfilled, He that eateth bread with me, hath lifted up his heel against me" (13:18). As to *why* the Lord Jesus chose Judas to be one of the twelve, see our remarks on 6:70, 71. Very remarkable is this statement here in the light of the context. Christ had washed the feet of the very one whose heel was raised against Himself! Into what depths of humiliation did the Son of God deign to descend! He now foretells the defection of Judas, and announces that this was but the fulfilment of the prophetic Word. The reference is to the 41st Psalm, which exposes the awful character of the betrayer; the 109th Psalm makes known the outcome of his treachery. Christ then had suffered the traitor to remain with Him that the Scriptures might be fulfilled; but as soon as the "sop" had been given to Him, Christ would say, "That thou doest, do quickly" (13:27). "How wondrous the patience which, knowing all from the beginning, bore all to the end, without a frown or sign of shrinking from the traitor! But so much the more withering must be the sentence of judgment when it comes from His lips, the Lord of glory, the hated and despised of men" (Mr. W. Kelly).

"He that eateth bread with me, hath lifted up his heel against me." The local reference in Psa. 41 is to what David suffered at the hands of Ahithophel, but that was but a foreshadowment and type of what the Saviour suffered from Judas. In now quoting from this prophetic Psalm the Lord Jesus evidenced His Divine knowledge of what lay before Him, and testified to the inestimable value of the Scriptures. Nothing proves more conclusively their Divine origin than the accurate and literal fulfilment of their prophecies. Predictions were made of events which were not to transpire till hundreds, and in some cases thousands, of years afterwards, minute details are furnished, and the specific accomplishment of them can only be accounted for on the one ground that He who knows the end from the beginning was their Author.

The wording of this prophecy about Judas is very striking. "*His* heel! the most contemptible rejection possible: was it not such to sell the Lord of glory for the price of a slave? It was as if *he* would inflict upon Christ the Serpent's predicted wound (Gen. 3:15)!" (F. W. Grant.)

"Now I tell you before it come, that, when it is come to pass, ye may believe that I am" (13:19). What care did He evince for His own! What blessed proof was this of His loving them "unto the end"! Christ would here assure the disciples that *everything* which befell Him, even that which was most staggering to faith, was but the strict fulfilment of what had long ago been recorded. He was the great One typified and prophesied throughout the Old Testament, and He now assures the apostles of Judas' perfidy *before* he went forth to bargain with the priests, that they might know *He had not* trusted in him, nor had He been deceived by him, as had David by Ahithophel! Thus, instead of the apostles being stumbled by the apostasy of one of their number, it should strengthen their faith in every written word of God to know that that very Word had long before announced what they were on the eve of witnessing. Moreover, their faith in Christ should be strengthened, too. By calling their attention to the fulfilment of Psalm 41 He showed them that *He* was the Person there marked out; that *He* was a true Prophet, announcing the certain accomplishment of David's prediction before it came to pass; and that *He* was the great "I am" who "searcheth the hearts and trieth the reins of the children of men," being fully acquainted with their secret thoughts and most carefully concealed designs.

"Verily, verily, I say unto you, He that receiveth whomsoever I send receiveth me; and he that receiveth me receiveth him that sent me" (13:20). At first sight there appears to be no connection between this verse and the ones preceding, yet a little thought will soon discover the link between them. The Lord had been exhorting His disciples to follow the example which He had given, assuring them they would be happy if they did so.

Then He announced the apostasy of Judas. Now He informs them that *their* vocation was by no means affected by the defection of the betrayer. "The whole circle of the apostles seemed to be disorganized by the treachery of Judas; and therefore the Lord *confirms* the faithful in their election, and that very fittingly by a repetition of that earlier promise (Matt. 10:42) on which all depended" (Stier). It was the Lord *comforting* His own and most graciously *establishing* their hearts by turning their attention away from the traitor to their Master, who abides forever the same, as does the Father.

Judas had been one of the twelve whom the Lord had sent forth to preach the Gospel and to work miraculous signs in His name (Matt. 10). Would then all that *he* had done as an apostle be discredited, when his real character became known? This important question here receives answer from our Lord: "He that receiveth *whomsoever* I send receiveth me." The Lord knew how apt His people are to despise the work done if the worker proves to be unworthy; therefore does He teach us to look beyond the instrument to the One who sent him. The Lord has the right to appoint whom He pleases. If, then, the *message* is from God's Word, reject it not because the messenger proves a fraud. What matters it to me whether the postman be black or white, pleasant or unpleasant, so long as he hands me the right letter?

"He that receiveth whomsoever I send receiveth me; and he that receiveth me receiveth him that sent me." There is another important principle here. The apostles were the *ambassadors* of the Lord, and in the person of an ambassador the sovereign himself is received or set at naught. As *His* ambassadors, how circumspectly ought each of His servants to walk! And as *His* ambassadors, how dutiful and respectful in its reception should the Church be of them! As *He* was sent from the *Father,* so *they* were sent from *Him.* By this gracious analogy He arms them with authority and inspires them with courage. Thus the Lord fully *identifies* them with Himself.

The following questions need studying to prepare for our next lesson: –

1. What three things are clearly implied in v. 22?
2. Why did not Peter ask the Lord directly, v. 24?
3. Why did Jesus say to Judas, v. 27?
4. In how many respects was the Son of man glorified at the Cross, v. 31?
5. What attributes of God were glorified at the Cross, v. 31?
6. In what sense was it a "new commandment," v. 34?
7. What is the meaning of v. 36?

CHAPTER FORTY-SEVEN

Christ's Warnings

John 13:21-38

Below is an Analysis of the passage which is to be before us:—

1. The betrayer and his identification, vv. 21-26.
2. The departure of Judas and the thoughts of the Eleven, vv. 27-30.
3. A threefold glorification, vv. 31-32.
4. The new commandment, v. 34.
5. The badge of Christian discipleship, v. 35.
6. Peter's questions, vv. 36-37.
7. Christ's warning prediction, v. 38.

We have entitled this chapter Christ's Warnings: it scarcely covers everything in the passage, yet it emphasizes that which is most prominent in it. At the beginning of our present section Christ warns Judas; at the close, He warns Peter. In between, there are some gracious and tender instructions for the beloved disciples, and these too partake very largely of the nature of *warnings*. He warns them against misinterpreting the nature of His death, 13:31-32. He warns them of His approaching departure, 13:33. He warns them of their need of a *commandment* that they should "love one another", 13:34. He warns them that only by the exercise of *love* toward each other would it be made manifest that they were *His* disciples, 13:35.

Our passage opens with a solemn word identifying the Saviour's betrayer. This betrayer had been plainly announced in Old Testament prophecy: "He that eateth bread with me hath lifted up his heel against me" (Psa. 41:9). "A man's *foes*," said the Lord, "are they of his own household" (Matt. 10:36), and fearfully was this verified in His own case. A "familiar friend" became a *familiar fiend*. How this exposes the error of those who suppose that all that fallen man needs is *example* and *instruction*. Judas enjoyed both, yet was not his evil heart moved. For three years had he been not only in the closest possible contact, but in the nearest intimacy with the Saviour. His had been a favoured place in the innermost circle of the Twelve. Not only had he listened to the daily preaching of Christ as He taught the people, not only had he witnessed most, at least, of His wondrous miracles, but he had also gazed upon the perfections of Christ in His private life. And yet, after all this, Judas was unmoved and unchanged. Nothing could more forcefully demonstrate our Lord's utterance, "Except a man *be born again* he *cannot* see the kingdom of God"! So near to Christ, yet unsaved! What a challenge for every heart!

The case of Peter points a most solemn warning of quite another character. Outwardly Judas *posed* as a disciple of Christ; inwardly Simon *was* a believer in Him. The one exhibits the sin and madness of hypocrisy; the other the danger and sad results of self-confidence. It was to Peter that the Lord said, "The spirit (the new nature) indeed is willing, but the flesh (the natural man) is weak." But this utterance was never intended as an *excuse*, behind which we might take refuge when we fail and fall; but was given as a lasting warning to have "*no* confidence in the flesh" (Phil. 3:3). The Holy Spirit has faithfully recorded the sad defection of one who was especially dear to the heart of the Saviour, that all Christians who follow Him might seek grace from God to avoid the snare into which he fell.

From a human view, Peter failed at his *strongest* point. By nature he was bold and courageous. Probably there was not a stouter heart among the apostles. He quailed not before the marvellous scene on the Mount of Transfiguration. He it was who stepped out of the ship and started to walk across the waves to Christ. And he it was who drew his sword in the Garden, and smote the high priest's servant as the officers arrested his beloved Master. No coward was Peter. And yet *he* trembled in the presence of a maid, and when taxed with being a disciple of Christ, denied it with an oath! How is this to be explained?

Only on the ground that in order to teach him and us the all-important lesson, that if left to ourselves, the strongest is as weak as water. It is in conscious weakness that our *strength* lies (II Cor. 12:10). Peter was fully assured that though *all* should be offended yet would not *he* (Mark 14:29). And, without a doubt, he fully meant what he said. But he did not *know himself*; he had not learned, experientially, the exceeding deceitfulness of the human heart; he knew not as yet that without the upholding power and sustaining grace of the Lord he could do *nothing* (John 15:5). O that we might learn from him.

"We fancy sometimes, like Peter, that there are some things *we* could not possibly do. We look pityingly upon others who fall, and plume ourselves in the thought that at any rate *we* should not have done so. We know nothing at all. The seeds of *every* sin are latent in our hearts, even when renewed, and they only need occasion, or carelessness, or the withdrawal of God's grace for a season, to put forth an abundant crop. Like Peter, we think we can do wonders for Christ, and like Peter, we learn by bitter experience that *we* have no might and power at all. A humble sense of our own innate weakness, a constant dependency on the Strong for strength, a daily prayer to be held up, because we cannot hold up ourselves—these are the true secrets of safety" (Bishop Ryle). Surely the outstanding lesson for us in connection with the fall of Peter is this: "Let him that thinketh he standeth take heed lest he fall" (I Cor. 10:12).

"When Jesus had thus said, he was troubled in spirit, and testified, and said, Verily, verily, I say unto you, that one of you shall betray me" (13:21). The Lord had been ministering to His disciples, teaching and comforting them. He had spoken of their future, but in the midst of these anticipations a dark shadow falls upon Him, troubling Him. Already had He hinted at it, now He proceeds to testify more plainly to the traitor who was among the Twelve. The Lord was "troubled in spirit." It is remarkable that this is mentioned most frequently by the very Evangelist whose special design it was to portray the Lord Jesus as God manifest in flesh—cf. 11:33, 38; 12:27. These statements prove the reality of His humanity, showing that He had a real human soul as well as body. They also prove that it is no infirmity or imperfection to be *troubled* by the presence of evil. Christ was no stoic: He felt keenly all that was contrary to God. Really, none was so truly and so completely sensitive as He. He was the Man of sorrows, and it is just because He has Himself passed through this scene, suffering within at every step of the way, that He is able to be touched with "the feeling of *our* infirmities."

"When Jesus had thus said, he was troubled in spirit, and testified, and said, Verily, verily, I say unto you, that one of you shall betray me." It is well to remind ourselves that what the Lord Jesus endured upon the Cross was but the climax and completion of His sufferings. Throughout His life He suffered at the hands of Satan, His enemies, and His friends. He felt acutely the unbelief and hostility of the scribes and Pharisees. His tearful lament over Jerusalem evidences the depths of His anguish over Israel's rejection. Here it was the bitter sorrow of seeing one of the apostles deliberately becoming an apostate. Nothing wounds more deeply than ingratitude; and that one, who had been a constant companion with Him for three years, should now raise his heel against Him, was a sore trial. If Judas was unmoved, the Lord was not. Seeing no beauty in Christ after all he had heard and witnessed during years of closest contact with Him, unaffected by His marvellous grace to sinners, caring only for paltry gain, dominated by self, and the rebuke he had received in Simon's house rankling within, he turned against his Master and arranged to sell Him to His enemies. No wonder the Lord was "troubled" as He thought of such deceit, treachery, and cupidity. He had said "Ye are clean, but *not* all," and still Judas retained his place, and gave no sign of retiring.

"Verily, verily, I say unto you, that one of you shall betray me." There is a melancholy emphasis on the pronoun here: one of *you* at the table with Me; one of *you* whose feet I have just washed; one of *you* who have had the high honour of being My first ambassadors, shall take advantage of your intimacy with Me and knowledge of My ways, to guide the enemy to My place of retirement, and deliver Me into the hands of those who seek

My life. He was "troubled" by the enormity of the crime, and no doubt, too, over the awful doom which lay before Judas.

How deeply "troubled" the Saviour was we may learn from His words in Psa. 55: "Wickedness is in the midst thereof: deceit and guile depart not from her streets. For it was not an enemy that reproached me; then I could have borne it: neither was it he that hated me that did magnify himself against me; then I would have hid myself from him: But it was thou, a man mine equal, my guide, and mine acquaintance. We took sweet counsel together and walked unto the house of God in company" (vv. 11-14). How vividly this brings out before us the *grief* with which the Man of sorrows was "acquainted"! How deeply His holy soul was stirred, we may learn from the solemn but righteous imprecations which He called down upon the base ingrate in Psa. 109: "Let his days be few; and let another take his office; let his children be fatherless, and his wife a widow" (vv. 8, 9), etc.

"Then the disciples looked one on another, doubting of whom he spake" (13:22). Three things are made very evident by this verse: one thing about the disciples, one about Judas, and one about the Lord Himself. First, it is plain that what Christ had said in 13:18 had made no impression upon the Eleven. And this was the most natural. No doubt their minds were so occupied with what the Saviour had just done for them that they had scarcely recovered from their surprise. They were so impressed by His amazing condescension that His statement "He that eateth bread with me hath lifted up his heel against me" fell upon ears that heeded Him not. But now He speaks more plainly and directly, and they exchanged puzzled glances with each other, wondering which of them it was to whom He had referred.

Second, the fact that "The disciples looked one on another, doubting of whom he spake" is proof positive that Judas had succeeded in concealing his turpitude from his fellows. His outward conduct had given the other apostles no occasion to suspect him. To what lengths cannot hypocrisy go! Matthew tells us that when Christ announced to the Twelve that one of them should betray Him, "They were exceedingly sorrowful, and began every one of them to say, Lord, is it I?" (26:22), upon which Matthew Henry says: "They are to be commended for their charity, in that they are more jealous of themselves than of each other. It is the law of charity to hope the best, because we assuredly know, therefore we may justly expect, more evil of ourselves than of our brethren. They are also to be commended for their acquiescence in what Christ said. They trusted, as we would do well to do, more to His words, than to their own hearts, and therefore do not say, 'It is not—it cannot be—I'; but 'Lord, is it I'? See if there be such a way of wickedness, such a root of bitterness in me, and discover it to me, that I may pluck up the root, and stop up that way." Boldly playing his role of duplicity to the last, Judas dares to ask, "*Master,* is it I?" (Matt. 26:25)—a clear proof, though, that *he* was unsaved, for no man can say *Lord* Jesus but by the Holy Spirit (I Cor. 12:3).

Third, the fact that the apostles were perplexed, wondering to whom the Lord had referred, brings out most blessedly the infinite patience with which Christ had borne with the son of perdition. Throughout His ministerial life He must have treated Judas with the same condescending grace, gentleness, kindness, as the Eleven. He could not have exhibited any aversion against him, or the others would have noticed it, and known now of whom He spake. How this tells of the perfections of our Saviour! His kindness ill-requited, His favours unappreciated, His holy soul loathing such a sink of iniquity so near to Him—yet He bowed to the sovereign will and authoritative word of the Father, and patiently bore this trial.

"Now there was leaning on Jesus' bosom one of his disciples, whom Jesus loved" (13:23). Here is one of those striking contrasts in which this Gospel abounds, and a most blessed one it is. Our attention is diverted for a moment from the base treachery and horrible hatred of Judas to one whom Christ had attracted, whose heart had been won by His beauty, and who now affectionately reposed on the Saviour's breast. It is blessed, and an evident mark of the Holy Spirit's guidance to see how John here refers to himself. It was not "one who loved Jesus," though truly he did; but "one of his disciples whom

Jesus loved." Nor does he mention his own name—love never advertises itself.

"Simon Peter therefore beckoned to him, that he should ask who it should be of whom he spake" (13:24). This is one of many statements in the New Testament which effectually disposes of the Roman Catholic figment that Peter was the pope of the apostolate. As one of the older Protestant writers well said, "So far from Peter having any primacy among the apostles, he here uses the intercession of John." There was no doubt a moral reason why Peter put his question through John, instead of asking it direct. Is it not clear from 13:6, 8, 37 that Peter's state of soul was not altogether right before God? And, does not his fearful fall, that very evening, supply still further proof? Matthew tells us that after the arrest of the Saviour, Peter "followed him *afar off* unto the high priests' palace" (26:38), and a sense of *distance* began to make itself felt in Peter's soul even here—there was a measure of reserve between himself and the Lord.

"He then lying on Jesus' breast saith unto him, Lord, who is it?" (13:25). The contrast here between John and Peter is very noticeable. John was close to the Lord: affection had drawn him there. He was so near to Christ and his spirit so unclouded, he could look up into the face of the Saviour and ask Him any question. This is the blessed portion and privilege of every Christian. Alas! that so many are like Peter on this occasion—ready to turn to a *brother,* rather than to the Lord Himself. Why is it that when the average Christian meets with some difficulty in his reading of the Word, or some problem in his spiritual life, he says, "I will ask or write brother so-and-so?" Why not enjoy the blessed privilege of referring *directly* to the Lord Jesus? It is a question of intimacy with Him, and that is very searching. While there is any self-confidence, as in Peter's case, or any known hindrance in my spiritual life, that at once places me at a moral distance from Christ. But is it not blessed to see that, at the end, Peter came to the same place which John is seen occupying here? "And he said unto him, Lord, thou knowest all things; thou knowest that I love thee" (21:17). He threw open his heart. What was it but saying, Lord, there was a time when I would not ask You questions, but now I can invite

You to look into my heart! Let us then come before Him now, asking Him to search our hearts and put His finger on anything that hinders us from having direct access to Him in everything. Let us ever be on the watch that we do not enjoy a greater intimacy with some brother than with the Lord Himself.

"Jesus answered, He it is, to whom I shall give a sop, when I have dipped it" (13:26). It seems clear from what follows that these words of Christ must have been whispered to John or spoken in such a low tone that the other disciples were unable to catch them. At last the Lord Jesus identified the betrayer. The mask of hypocrisy which he had worn had thoroughly deceived the apostles, but He with whom "all things are naked and open" cannot be imposed upon. While man looked on the outward appearance, He looks upon the heart; so He now unmasks the false disciple, and shows him to be – what *He* always knew, though none else suspected that he was – a traitor.

"And when he had dipped the sop, he gave it to Judas Iscariot, the son of Simon" (13:26). The sign given by Christ to identify the betrayer was suggestive and solemn. "It was a mark of honour for the host to give a portion to one of the guests. The Lord had appealed to the *conscience* of Judas in 13:21, now He appeals to his *heart*" (Companion Bible). The "sop" was, most probably, a piece of unleavened bread, now dipped in the sauce prepared for the eating of the paschal lamb. That Judas accepted it shows the unthinkable lengths to which he carried his hypocrisy. Determined as he was to perpetrate the foulest treachery, yet he hereby renews his pledge of friendship. It' makes us think of the "Hail Master" and the "kiss" when he was in the act of delivering Him to His enemies. But how wonderful, how blessed, the meekness of our Lord; surely none but He *could* have acted thus. In complete command of Himself, no sign of ill-will toward the one who had already taken counsel with the chief priests, He gives him the sop. Closely did this correspond with the prophetic declaration already referred to, "He that *eateth* with me hath lifted up his heel against me."

"And after the sop Satan entered into him" (13:27). The receiving of the sop, expressive of friendship, ought to have broken him down in an agony of repentance; but it did not. He was like those mentioned in Heb. 6:8: ground on which the rain came oft, but which instead of bringing forth herbs, bore only thorns and briars, whose end is to be burned. It is remarkable to note that not until now are we told of Satan's entrance into him. Equally striking is it to observe that as soon as he *had* received the "sop" the Enemy took full possession of his only too willing victim.

"Then said Jesus unto him, That thou doest, do quickly" (13:27). Fearful words were these. Space for repentance had now passed forever. His doom was sealed. But what else lay behind these words of Christ? We believe it was the formal announcement of the Saviour surrendering Himself to the Father's will. It was as though He said, *I am ready* to be led as a lamb to the slaughter; go, Judas, and do that which you are so anxious to do; *I* will not withstand thee! But again; may we not regard this word of Christ as in one sense parallel with the one He had addressed to the Devil at the close of the great temptation. There was a needs-be for Him to be tempted of the Devil for forty days; but when that needs-be was fully met, He said, "Get thee *hence,* Satan" (Matt. 4:10). So, in order that Scripture might be fulfilled, it was necessary for there to be a Judas in the apostolate, so that he could eat with Christ. But now that prophecy had been accomplished, now that the traitor's heel had been lifted against his Master, Christ says, "Depart"! Moreover, was not this the formal dismissal of Judas from the Lord's service? Christ had *called* him to a place in the apostolate: for three years He had used him: now He announces his discharge; later, another shall "take *his bishoprick.*" Finally, we believe it can be established from the other Gospels that it was right after this that the Lord instituted His own "supper" as a lasting memorial of Himself; but before doing so He first banishes the traitor, for *that* "supper" is for His own only.

"Now no man at the table knew for what intent he spake this unto him" (13:28). At this point John, at least, and most probably Peter also, knew who it was who should betray their beloved Master, yet in the light of this verse it is evident that none of them suspected that the act of treachery was so soon to be perpetrated. None of them perceived the awfulness of the issues then pending.

"For some of them thought, because Judas had the bag, that Jesus had said unto him, Buy those things that we have need of against the feast; or, that he should give something to the poor" (13:29). "These thoughts of the disciples were mistaken ones, but they do them no discredit. They are excusable and even praiseworthy. They indicate the operation of the charity which thinketh no evil, but is ever disposed to put on words and actions the most favorable construction they will reasonably admit. The mistakes of charity are wiser and better than the surmises of censoriousness, even when they turn out to be according to the truth. Judas had all along been a bad man; but hitherto he had given no such evidence of his unprincipled character as would have warned his fellow-disciples to entertain suspicions of him. Knowing that he was the treasurer and steward of this little society, they supposed that the words of the Master might refer to his speedily obtaining something which would be requisite for the feast of the passover, which lasted for a week; that he should immediately give some alms to the poor.

"It is plain from these words that our Lord and His disciples were in the habit of giving, especially at the time of the great festivals, out of their scanty pittance, something to those more destitute than themselves. Their 'deep poverty abounded unto the riches of their liberality': and by His example He has taught us not merely that it is the duty of those who may have but little to spare to give of that little to those who have still less, but that religious observances are gracefully connected with deeds of mercy and alms-giving. He joined humility with piety in His practice as well as in His doctrine; and in this He hath left us an example that we should follow His steps" (Dr. John Brown). To these remarks we may add that the fact the disciples had supposed Judas had gone to *purchase* things for "the feast" is clear proof that the Lord did not work miracles in order to procure the food needed by Himself and His apostles. It also shows that they did not *beg*, but managed their temporal affairs with prudence and economy (cf. 4:8).

But far different were the base designs of Judas from what the apostles had charitably supposed. "It was not to buy things needful, but to *sell* the Lord and Master; it was no preparation for the feast, but that to which it, not they, had ever looked onward—the fulfilment of God's mind and purpose in it, though it were the Jews crucifying their own Messiah, by the hands of lawless men; it was not that *Judas* should *give* to the poor, but that *He should* who was rich yet for our sakes became poor, that we through His poverty might be made rich" (Bible Treasury).

"He then having received the sop went immediately out: and it was night" (13:30). There is something more here, something deeper, than a mere reference to the time of the day. As Judas went forth on his dastardly errand, there then began that "hour" of the Power of *darkness* (Luke 22:53), when God suffered His enemies to put out the Light of life. So, too, it was "night" in the soul of Judas, for he had turned his back on "the *light*." Like Cain he went out from the "presence of the Lord"; like Baalim he loved "the wages of unrighteousness"; like Ahithophel he went to betray his "familiar friend." It was *night*: "Men love darkness rather than light, because their deeds are *evil*": fitting time was it, then, for the son of perdition to perpetrate his dark deed! "*Immediately*" he went: *his* feet were "swift to shed blood"!

"Therefore, when he was gone out, Jesus said, Now is the Son of man glorified" (13:31). A most remarkable word was this. The Lord Jesus spoke of His *death*, but He regarded it neither as a martyrdom nor as a disgrace. There is nothing quite like this in the other Gospels. Here, as ever, John gives us the highest, the *Divine* viewpoint of things. The Saviour contemplates His death on the shameful tree as His *glorification*. "It seems very strange that, in these circumstances, Jesus should say, 'Now—now is the Son of man glorified.' It would not have been wonderful if, on the banks of Jordan after His baptism, with the mystic dove descending and abiding on Him, and the voice of the Eternal pealing from the open heaven, 'This is my beloved Son, in whom I am well pleased'; or, on the summit of the Mount of Transfiguration, when 'His face did shine as the sun, and His garments became white as the light,' and Moses and Elijah appeared with Him in glory, and a voice came forth from the cloud of glory. 'This is my beloved Son, hear him,' our Lord had said, in holy exaltation, '*Now* is the Son of man glorified'! But, when these words were spoken, what was before the Redeemer but the deepest abasement, and the severest sufferings—heavy accusations—a condemnatory sentence—insults—infamy—the fellowship of thieves—the agonies of death—the lonely sepulchre! How does He, in these circumstances, say, 'Now is the Son of man glorified'" (Dr. John Brown).

But *wherein was* Christ's death on the Cross His *glorification?* Notice, first, that He said, "Now is the *Son of man* glorified." It was the Son of God *as incarnate* who was "glorified" on the Cross. But how? Wherein? First, in that He there performed the greatest work which the whole history of the entire universe ever witnessed, or ever will witness. For it the centuries waited; to it the centuries look back. Second, because there He reversed the conduct of the first man. The first Adam was *disobedient* unto death, the last Adam was *obedient* unto death, even the death of the Cross. The glory of man is to glorify God; and never was God more glorified than when His own incarnate Son laid down His life in submission to His command (10:18); and never was human nature so glorified as when the Son of man thus glorified God. Third, because through death He destroyed him who had the power of death, that is the devil (Heb. 2:14). What a notable achievement was this, that One made in the likeness of sin's flesh should accomplish the utter defeat of the arch-enemy of God and man! Fourth, because at the Cross was paid the ransom-price which purchased for Himself all the elect of God. What glory for the Son of man was this, that He should do what none other in all the realm of creation could do (through immeasurable suffering and shame)—"bring many sons unto glory." The manner in which He wrought this work also glorified Him: He was a willing sufferer; the price was cheerfully paid; He was led, not driven, as a lamb to the slaughter; He endured the Cross, despising the shame; and not until offended justice and a broken law were fully satisfied did He cry, "It is finished." Finally, by virtue of His Cross-work, a glory was acquired by the Mediator: there is now a glorified

Man at God's right hand (John 17:22). "*Wherefore* God also hath highly exalted him, and given him a name which is above every name" (Phil. 2:10).

"And God is glorified in him" (13:31). What a theme! One which no human pen can begin to do justice to. The Cross-work of Christ was not only the basis of our salvation, and the glorification of the Son of man Himself, but it was also the brightest manifestation of the glory *of God*. Every attribute of Deity was superlatively magnified at Calvary.

The *power* of God was exceedingly glorified at the Cross. There the kings of the earth and the rulers took counsel together against God and against His Christ; there the terrible enmity of the carnal mind and the desperate wickedness of the human heart did their worst; there the fiendish malignity of Satan was put forth to its fullest extent. But God had laid help upon One that is *mighty* (Psa. 89:19). None was able to take His life from the Saviour (John 10:18). After man and Satan had done their worst, the Lord Jesus remained complete master of Himself, and not until *He* saw fit did He *lay down* His life of Himself: never was the power of God more illustriously displayed. Christ was crucified "through weakness" (II Cor.(13:4), offering no resistance to His enemies: but it is written, "The weakness of God is *stronger* than men" (I Cor. 1:25), and gloriously was that demonstrated at the Cross, when the power of God sustained the humanity of Christ as He endured His outpoured wrath.

The *justice* of God was exceedingly glorified at the Cross. Of old He declared that He "will by no means clear the guilty" (Exodus 34:7), and when the Lord laid on our blessed Substitute "the iniquities of us all" He hung there as *the* Guilty One. And God is so strictly and immutably just that He would not spare His own Son when He had made Him to be sin for us. He would not abate the least mite of that debt which righteousness demanded. The penalty of the broken law must be enforced, even though it meant the slaying of His well Beloved. Therefore did the cry go forth, "Awake, O sword, against my Shepherd, and against the man that is my fellow, saith the Lord of hosts: *smite* the Shepherd" (Zech. 13:7). The justice of

God was more illustriously glorified by the propitiation which was made by the Lord Jesus than if every member of the human race were to suffer in Hell forever.

The *holiness* of God was exceedingly glorified at the Cross. He is "of purer eyes than to behold evil, and canst not look on iniquity" (Hab. 1:13), and when Christ was "made a curse for us" (Gal. 3:13) the thrice Holy One turned away from Him. It was this which caused the agonizing Saviour to cry, "My God, My God, why hast thou *forsaken* me?" Never did God so manifest His hatred of sin as in the sufferings and death of His Only-begotten. There He showed it was impossible for Him to be at peace with that which had raised its defiant head against Him. All the honour due to the holiness of God by all the holy angels, and all the cheerful obedience and patient suffering of all the holy men who have ever existed, or ever will exist, are nothing in comparison with the offering of Christ Himself in order that every demand of God's holiness, which sin had outraged, might be fully met.

The *faithfulness* of God was exceedingly glorified at the Cross. God had sworn, "The soul that sinneth it shall die," and when the Sinless One offered to receive the full and fearful wages of sin, God showed to all heaven and earth that He had rather that the blood of His Fellow be spilt than that one tittle of the Word should fail. In the Scriptures He had made it known that His Son should be led as a lamb to the slaughter, that His hands and His feet should be pierced, that He should be numbered with transgressors, that He should be wounded for our transgressions and bruised for our iniquities. These and many other predictions received their exact fulfilment at Calvary, and their accomplishment there supplied the greatest proof of all that God cannot lie.

The *love* of God was exceedingly glorified at the Cross. "God so loved the world that he gave his only begotten Son" (John 3:16). "Herein is love, not that we loved God, but that he loved us, and sent his Son to be the propitiation for our sins" (I John 4:10). "The light of the sun is always the same, but it shines brightest at noon. The Cross of Christ was the noontide of everlasting love—the meridian-splendour of eternal mercy. There were many bright manifestations of the same love before; but they were like the light of the morning that shines more and more unto the perfect day; and that perfect day was when Christ was on the Cross, and darkness covered all the land" (McLaurin).

O when we view God's grand design,
To save rebellious worms,
How vengeance and compassion join
In their sublimest forms!

Our thoughts are lost in rev'rent awe—
We love and we adore;
The first archangel never saw
So much of God before!

Here each Divine perfection joins,
And thought can never trace,
Which of the glories brightest shines—
The justice or the grace.

"If God be glorified in him, God shall also glorify him in himself, and shall straightway glorify him" (13:32). "This verse may be paraphrased as follows: 'If God the Father be specially glorified in all His attributes by My death, He shall proceed at once to place special glory on Me, for My personal work, and shall do it without delay, by raising Me from the dead, and placing Me at His right hand.' It is the same idea that we have in the seventeenth chapter more fully. 'I have glorified thee on the earth; now, O Father, glorify thou me with thine own self'" (Bishop Ryle).

"Little children, yet a little while I am with you. Ye shall seek me: and as I said unto the Jews, Whither I go, ye cannot come; so now I say to you" (13:33). Here for the first time the Lord Jesus addressed His disciples by this special term of endearment, "little children." It is striking to observe that the Lord waited until *after* Judas had gone out before using it: teaching us that *un*believers must not be addressed as *God's* "children"! "Ye shall seek Me" tells of their love for Him, as the "little children" had expressed His love for them. "Whither I go, ye cannot come" seems to have a different force from what it signified when addressed to the unbelieving Jews in 7:33. He declared to them, "I go unto him that sent me . . . and where I am, thither ye cannot come." The reference is the same in 8:21. But here the Saviour was not speaking of His return to the Father, but of His going to the Cross—*thither* "they" could not come. In His great work of redemption He was alone. Just as in the type, "There shall be *no man* in the tabernacle of the congregation when he (the high priest) goeth in to make an atonement" (Lev. 16:17), so in the antitype.

"A new commandment I give unto you, That ye love one another; as I have loved you, that ye also love one another" (13:34). "The immense importance of Christian love cannot possibly be shown more strikingly than the way that it is urged on the disciples in this place. Here is our Lord leaving the world, speaking for the last time, and giving His last charge to the disciples. The very *first* subject He takes up and presses on them is the great duty of loving one another, and that with no common love; but after the same patient, tender, unwearied manner that He had loved them. Love must needs be a very rare and important grace to be so spoken of! The want of it must needs be plain proof that a man is no true disciple of Christ. How vast the extent of Christian love ought to be" (Bishop Ryle).

"A new commandment I give unto you, That ye love one another; as I have loved you, that ye also love one another." The nation now disappears. It is no question of loving one's neighbour, but of Christ's disciples, and their mutual love according to His love. Nor is it here activity of zeal in quest of sinners, blessed as that is; but the unselfish seeking of the good of saints, as such, in lowliness of mind. The Law required love of one's neighbour, which was a *fleshly* relationship; Christ enjoins love *to our brethren,* which is a *spiritual* relationship. Here, then, is the first sense in which this "commandment" was a *new* one. But there is a further sense brought out by John in his Epistle: "A new commandment I write unto you, which thing is true *in him* and in you" (I John 2:8). *Love* had now been manifested, yea, personified, as never before. Christ had displayed a love superior to the faults of its objects, a love which never varied, a love which deemed no sacrifice too great.

Scott has well observed on this new commandment, "Love was now to be explained with new clearness, enforced by new motives and obligations, illustrated by a new example, and obeyed in a new manner."

"By this shall all know that ye are my disciples, if ye have love one to another" (13:35). Love is the *badge* of Christian discipleship. It is not knowledge, nor orthodoxy, nor fleshly activities, but (supremely) *love* which identifies a follower of the Lord Jesus. As the disciples of the Pharisees were known by their phylacteries, as the disciples of John were known by their baptism, and every school by its particular shibboleth, so the mark of a true Christian is *love;* and that, a genuine, active love, not in words but in deeds. I Cor. 13 gives a full exposition of this verse.

"Simon Peter said unto him, Lord, whither goest thou? Jesus answered him, Whither I go, thou canst not follow me now; but thou shalt follow me afterwards" (13:36). How evident it is that even the Eleven had not grasped the fact that their beloved Master was going to be taken from them! Often as He had spoken to them of His death, it seems to have made no lasting impression upon them. This illustrates the fact that men may receive much religious instruction, and yet take in very little of it, the more so when it clashes with their preconceptions. The Christian teacher needs much patience, and the less he expects from his work, the less will he be disappointed. Christ's words here, "Whither I go" had a different meaning than in 13:33. There He had spoken of taking His place alone in death: here He refers to His return to the Father, therefore is He careful to add, "thou *shalt* follow me afterwards."

"Peter said unto him, Lord, why cannot I follow thee now? I will lay down my life for thy sake" (13:37). Peter knew and really loved the Lord, but how little he as yet knew himself! It was right to feel the Lord's absence; but he should have heeded better the mild, but grave, admonition that where Christ was going he was not able to follow Him now; he should have valued the comforting assurance that he should follow Him later. Alas! how much we lose now, how much we suffer afterwards, through *not* laying to heart the deep truth of Christ's words! We soon see the bitter consequences in Peter's history; but we know, from the future words of our Lord in the close of this Gospel, how grace would ensure in the end the favour, compromised by that self-confidence at the beginning, which He here warned against.

"But we are apt to think most highly of ourselves, of our love, wisdom, moral courage, and every other good quality, when we least know and judge ourselves in God's presence, as here we see in Peter; who, impatient of the hint already given, breaks forth into the self-confident question, 'Lord, why cannot I follow thee now? I will lay down my life for thy sake.' Peter therefore must learn, as we also, by painful experience, what he might have understood even better by subjection of heart, in faith, to the Lord's words. When He warns, it is rash and wrong for us to question; and rashness of spirit is but the precursor of a fall in fact, whereby we must be taught, if we refuse otherwise" (Bible Treasury).

"Jesus answered him, Wilt thou lay down thy life for my sake? Verily, verily, I say unto thee, The cock shall not crow, till thou hast denied me thrice" (13:38). Once more the Lord manifests His omniscience, this time by foretelling the fall of one of His own. Utterly unlikely did it seem that a real believer would deny his Lord, and not only so, but at once follow it up with further denials. Little likelihood did there appear that one who was so devoted to Christ, who had enjoyed such unspeakable privileges, and who was expressly warned that he should "watch and pray *lest* ye enter into temptation," should prove so unworthy. Yet incredible as it might appear to the Eleven the Lord foresaw it all, and here definitely announces the fearful sin of Peter. He knew that so far from Peter laying down his life for His sake, he would that very night try to save his own life, by a cowardly denial that he was His disciple. And yet the Lord did not cast him off. He loved even Peter "unto the end," and after His resurrection sought him out and restored him to fellowship again. Truly such love passeth knowledge. O that we were so fully absorbed with it that, for very shame, we might be withheld from doing anything that would grieve it.

The following questions are to help the student to prepare for the lesson on the first section of John 14:—

1. What is meant by "*believe* also in me," v. 1?
2. What is meant by the "Father's House," v. 2?
3. How is Christ "preparing a place for us," v. 3?
4. What is meant by "the way," v. 4?
5. What did Philip mean, v. 8?
6. How did the disciples see the Father in Christ, v. 9?
7. What "works' sake" did Christ refer to in v. 11?

CHAPTER FORTY-EIGHT

Christ Comforting His Disciples

John 14:1-11

Below is an Analysis of the passage which is to be before us: —

1. Christ's call to faith in Himself, v. 1.
2. Christ's teaching about Heaven, v. 2.
3. Christ's precious promises, vv. 3, 4.
4. Thomas' question, v. 5.
5. Christ perfectly suited to us, vv. 6, 7.
6. Philip's ignorance, v. 8.
7. Christ's reproof, vv. 9-11.

It is in the fourteenth chapter of John that the Lord Jesus really begins the Paschal Discourse, a discourse which for tenderness, depth, and comprehensiveness is unsurpassed in all the Scriptures. The circumstances under which it was delivered need to be steadily borne in mind. This heart-melting Address of Christ was given to the Eleven on the last night before He died, affording a manifestation of Him which has been strikingly likened to the "glorious radiance of the setting sun, surrounded with dark clouds, and about to plunge into darker, which, fraught with lightning, thunder, and tempest, wait on the horizon to receive him." Most blessedly do His words here bring out the perfections of the God-man. Any other man, even a man of superior strength of mind and kindliness of heart, placed, so far as he could be placed in our Lord's circumstances, would have had his mind thrown into such a state of uncontrollable agitation, and most certainly would have been too entirely occupied with his own sufferings and anxieties to have any power or disposition to enter into and soothe the sorrows of others. But though completely aware of all that awaited Him, though feeling the weight of the awful load laid upon Him, though tasting the bitter cup which He must drain, He not only retained full self-possession, but took as deep an interest in the fears and sorrows of the apostles as if He Himself had not been a sufferer. Instead of being occupied with what lay before Himself, He spent the time in comforting His disciples: He "loved them unto the end."

During His public ministry and in His private intercourse with them, the apostles had heard repeated statements from His lips concerning His approaching sufferings and death, statements which appear to us simple and plain, but which perplexed and amazed them. It is most charitable, and perhaps most reasonable, to conclude that His disciples regarded His references to His coming passion as *parables,* which were not to be understood literally; and that, at any rate, He could not mean anything inconsistent with His immediately restoring the kingdom to Israel. They were fully convinced that *He* was the Messiah, and their only idea in connection with the Messiah was that of an illustrious Conqueror, a prosperous king; therefore, whatever was obscure in their Master's sayings, must be understood in the light of these principles. And it is probable that their hopes had never risen higher than when they had seen Him ride into Jerusalem amid the joyous acclamations of the multitudes hailing Him as the Son of David.

But right after His entry into Jerusalem they had heard Him speak of Himself as the "corn of wheat" which must fall into the ground and die, and this, at least, must have awakened dark forebodings. And, too, His conduct and sayings during the passover-supper, and what followed, must have deeply perplexed and distressed them. "Now is my soul troubled, and what shall I say? Father, save me from this hour?" must have filled them with painful misgivings. He had said, "Yet a *little* while I am with you. Ye shall seek me: and as I said unto the Jews, Whither I go, *ye* cannot come; so now I say to you." This was, indeed, sufficient to fill them with anxiety and sorrow. They dearly loved Him. The thought of Him dying, and of their parting with Him, was unbearable. Moreover, they must have asked themselves, How can *this* be reconciled with His Messiahship? Are we, after all, to give up our hope that this is He who would redeem Israel? And what is to become of us! We have forsaken all to follow Him, will He now forsake us, leaving us amid enemies, as sheep in the midst of wolves, to suffer the fierce malignity of His triumphant foes!

"Our Lord, who knew what was in man, was well aware of what was passing in the minds of His disciples. He knew how they were troubled, and what anxious, desponding, and despairing thoughts were arising in their hearts, and He could not but be touched with the feeling of their infirmities. There lay on His own mind a weight of anguish which no being in the universe could bear along with Him. *He* could not have the alleviation of sympathy. He must tread the winepress alone. They could not enter into *His* feelings; but He, the magnanimous One, could enter into theirs. There was room in His large heart for *their* sorrows, as well as His own. He feels their griefs, as if they were His own; and kindly comforts those whom He knew were soon to desert Him in the hour of *His* deepest sorrows! 'In all their afflictions, He was afflicted;' and He shows in the address which He made to them that 'the Lord who anointed Him to comfort those who mourn,' and to bind up the broken-hearted, had indeed 'given to Him the tongue of the learned that He might speak a word in season to them who were weary' (Isa. 61:1; 50:4)". (Dr. John Brown).

"Let not your heart be troubled" (14:1). It was the sorrows of their hearts which now occupied the great heart of love. "Troubled" they were; deeply so. They were troubled at hearing that one of their number should betray Him (13:21). They were troubled at seeing their Master "troubled in spirit" (13:21); troubled because He would remain with them only a "little while" (13:33); troubled over the warning He had given to Peter, that he would deny His Lord thrice. Thus this little company of believers were disquieted and cast down. Wherefore the Saviour proceeded to comfort them.

"Ye believe in God, believe also in me" (14:1). Commentators have differed widely as to the precise meaning of these words. The difficulty arises from the Greek. Both verbs are exactly the same, and may be translated (with equal accuracy) either in the imperative or the indicative mood. Either will make good sense, and possibly each is to be kept in mind. The R.V. reads: "Believe in God, believe also in me." Thus translated, it is a *double exhortation*. The force of it would then be: Your perturbation of spirit arises from *not* believing what God has spoken by His prophets concerning My sufferings and the glory which is to follow. God has announced in plain terms that I *was to be* despised and rejected of men, that I am to be wounded for your transgressions and bruised for your iniquities. These are the words of Jehovah Himself; then doubt them not. "Believe also in me." I too have warned you what to expect. I have told you that I am to suffer many things at the hands of the chief priests and scribes and be killed. These things *must* be. Then hold fast the beginning of your confidence steadfast unto the end: be not "offended" in Me, even though I go to a criminal's cross.

But it should be remembered that the Lord was speaking not only to the Eleven, but to *us* as well. Even so, the above interpretation supplies an exhortation which we constantly need. "Believe in God," O Christian. Let not your heart be troubled, *for* thy Father is possessed of infinite power, wisdom, and goodness. He knows what is best for thee, and He makes all things work together for thy good. *He* is on the Throne, ruling amid the army of heaven and among the inhabitants of the earth, so that none can stay His hand. Why, then, art thou cast down, O my soul? God is our refuge and strength, a very present help in trouble; therefore will we not fear, though the earth be removed, and though the mountains be carried into the midst of the sea; though the waters thereof roar and be troubled, though the mountains shake with the swellings thereof. What though trials come thick and fast, what though I am misunderstood and unappreciated, what though Satan roar and rage against me? "If God be for us who can be against us?" *Believe in God*. Believe in His absolute sovereignty, His infinite wisdom, His unchanging faithfulness, His wondrous love. "Believe also in me." I am the One who died for thy sins and rose again for thy justification; I am the One who ever liveth to make intercession for thee. I am the *same,* yesterday, and to-day, and forever. I am the One who shall come again to receive you unto Myself, and ye shall be forever with Me. Yes, *"believe also in me!"*

While the above interpretation is fully justified by the Greek, while the double exhortation was truly needed both by the Eleven and by us to-day, and while many able expositors have advanced it, yet we cannot but think that the A.V. gives the truer force of our Lord's words here, rendering the first verb in the indicative and the second in the imperative. "Believe also in me." What, then, did Christ mean? The apostles *had* already, by Divine illumination, recognized Him as the Christ, the Son of the living God. It is clear, then, that He was not here challenging their faith. We take it that what the Lord had in view was this: the apostles already believed in Him as the Messiah, and as the Saviour, but their confidence reposed in One who dwelt in their midst, who went in and out among them in the sensible relationship of daily companionship. But He was about to be *removed* from them, and He whom they had seen with their eyes and had handled with their hands (I John 1:1) was to be *invisible* to the outward eye. Now, says He, "Ye believe in God," *who is invisible;* you believe in His love, though you have never seen His form; you are conscious of His care, though you have never touched the Hand that guides and protects you. "Believe, also, in *me*"; that is to say, In like manner you must have full confidence in My existence, love, and care, even though I am no longer present to sight. *This* comfort remains for *us;* this is the faith in which we are now to live: "Whom having not seen, ye love; in whom, though now ye see him not, yet believing, ye rejoice with joy unspeakable and full of glory" (I Peter 1:8).

"Believe also in me." The "also" here brings out the absolute Deity of Christ in a most unmistakable manner. "Here thou seest plainly that Christ Himself testifies that He is equal with God Almighty; because we must believe in Him even as we believe in God. If He were not true God with the Father, this faith would be false and idolatrous" (Dr. Martin Luther).

"In my Father's house are many mansions" (14:2). The Father's "house" is His dwelling-place. It is noteworthy that the Lord Jesus is the only one who ever referred to the "Father's house," and He did so on three occasions. First, He had said of the temple in Jerusalem, "Make not my Father's *house* a house of merchandise" (John 2:16). Then He had mentioned it in connection with the "prodigal son" and his elder brother: "As he came and drew nigh to the *house* (the 'father's') he heard music and dancing"; here it is presented as the place of joy and gladness. In John 14 Christ mentions it as the final abode of the saints.

The glories and blessedness of Heaven are brought before us in the New Testament under a variety of representations. Heaven is called a "country" (Luke 19:12; Heb. 11:16); this tells of its vastness. It is called a "city" (Heb. 11: 10; Rev. 21; this intimates the large number of its inhabitants. It is called a "kingdom" (II Peter 1:11); this suggests its orderliness. It is called "paradise" (Luke 23:43; Rev. 2:7); this emphasizes its delights. It is called the "Father's house," which bespeaks its permanency.

The temple at Jerusalem had been called the Father's "house" because it was there that the symbol of His presence abode, because it was there He was worshipped, and because it was there His people communed with Him. But before the Lord Jesus closed His public ministry He disowned the temple, saying, "Behold *your* house is left unto you desolate" (Matt. 23:38). Therefore does the Saviour now transfer this term to the Father's dwelling-place on High, where He will grant to His redeemed a more glorious revelation of Himself, and where they shall worship Him, uninterruptedly, in the beauty of holiness.

The "Father's house" has been the favourite term for Heaven with most Christians. It speaks of *Home,* the Home of God and His people. Sad it is that in this present evil age one of the most precious words in the English language has lost much of its fragrance. Our fathers used to sing, "There is no place like home." To-day the average "home" is little more than a boarding-house—a place to eat and sleep in. But "home" used to mean.

and still means to a few, the place where we are loved for our own sakes; the place where we are always welcome; the place whither we can retire from the strife of the world and enjoy rest and peace, the place where loved ones are together. Such will Heaven be. Believers are now in a strange country, yea, in an enemy's land; in the life to come, they will be at *Home!*

"In my Father's house are *many mansions*." The many rooms in the temple prefigured these (see I Kings 6:5, 6; Jer. 35:1-4, etc.). The word for "mansions" signifies "abiding-places" – a most comforting term, assuring us of the *permanency* of our future home in contrast from the "tents" of our present pilgrimage. Blessed, too, is the word "many"; there will be ample room for the redeemed of the past, present, and future ages; and for the unfallen angels as well.

"If it were not so, I would have told you" (14:2). Had there been no room for believers in the many mansions of the Father's House, Christ would have said so. He had never deceived them; truth was His only object – "To this end was I born, and for this cause came I into the world, that I should bear witness unto the truth" (John 18:37). It was because full provision had been made for their complete and eternal happiness that He encouraged them to entertain such high hopes. He would never have brought them into such an intimacy with Himself if that was now to end forever.

"I go to prepare a place for you" (14:2). "He does not explain how the place in the Father's House should be prepared for them; nor were they yet, perhaps, able to understand. The Epistle to the Hebrews will show us, if we turn to it, that the heavenly places had to be purified by the better sacrifices which He was to offer, in which all the sacrifices of the law would find their fulfilment. Ephesians speaks similarly of the 'redemption of the purchased possession'; and Colossians of the 'reconciliation of things in heaven' (Heb. 9:23; Eph. 1:14; Col. 1:20). Such thoughts are even now strange to many Christians; for we are slow to realize the extent of the injury that sin has inflicted, and equally, therefore, the breadth of the application of the work of Christ. This is not the place to enlarge upon it; but it is not difficult to understand that wherever sin has raised question of God—and it has done so, as we know, in Heaven itself—the work of Christ as bringing out in full His whole character in love and righteousness regarding that which had raised the question, has enabled Him to come in and restore, consistently with all that He is, what had been defiled with evil. Thus our High Priest, to use as the apostle does, the figure of Israel's day of atonement, has entered into the Sanctuary to reconcile with the virtues of His sacrifice the holy places themselves, and make them accessible to us" (Numerical Bible).

"I go to prepare a place for you." We also understand this to mean that the Lord Jesus has procured *the right*—by His death on the Cross—for every believing sinner to enter Heaven. He has "prepared" for us a place there by entering Heaven as our Representative and taking possession of it on behalf of His people. As our Forerunner He marched in, leading captivity captive, and there planted His banner in the land of glory. He has "prepared" for us a place there by entering the "holy of holies" on High as our great High Priest, carrying our names in with Him. Christ would do all that was necessary to secure for His people a welcome and a permanent place in Heaven. Beyond this we cannot go with any degree of certainty. The fact that Christ has promised to "prepare *a place*" for us—which repudiates the vague and visionary ideas of those who would reduce Heaven to an intangible nebula—guarantee that it will far surpass anything down here.

"I go to prepare a place for you." God never has, and never will, take His people into a place *un*-prepared for them. In Eden God first "planted a garden," and then placed Adam in it. It was the same with Israel when they entered Canaan: "And it shall be, when the Lord thy God shall have brought thee into the land which he swear unto thy father, to Abraham, to Isaac, and Jacob, to give them great and goodly cities, which *thou* buildest not, and houses full of all good things, which *thou* filledst not, and wells digged which *thou* diggedst not, vineyards and olive trees which *thou* plantedst not" (Deut. 6:10, 11). And what can we say of the grace manifested by the Lord of glory going to prepare a place for us? He will not entrust such a task to the angels. Proof, indeed, is this that He loves us "unto the end."

"And if I go and prepare a place for you" (14:3). "A special people taken from the earth in a risen Christ must have a special place. A new thing was to take place, *men brought into Heaven!* Man was not made for Heaven, but for the earth, and so placed here to till the earth and live upon it. By sinning he lost the earth and the earth shared his ruin. But by sinning he brought down the Son of God from Heaven, who by His descent opened Heaven as the normal place for those believing on Christ, and so in Him" (Mr. Malachi Taylor).

"I will come again." The Lord will not *send* for us, but come in person to conduct us into the Father's House. How precious we must be to Him! "The Lord *himself* shall descend from Heaven with a shout, with the voice of the arch-angel, and with the trump of God; and the dead in Christ shall rise first: Then we which are alive and remain shall be caught up together with them in the clouds, to meet the Lord in the air" (I Thess. 4:16, 17).

"And receive you unto myself." Notice, not "take" but *receive.* The Holy Spirit has charge of us during the time of our absence from the Saviour; but when the mystical body of Christ is complete then is *His* work done here, and He hands us over to the One who died to save us. "And receive you *unto myself.*" To have us with Himself is His heart's desire. To the dying thief He said, "Today shalt thou be *with me* in paradise." To the Church it is promised that we shall "ever be *with the Lord*" (I Thess. 4:17).

"That where I am, there ye may be also" (14:3). The place which was due the *Son* is the place which grace has given to the *sons.* This is the blessed sequel to what was before us in John 13. There Christ said, "If I wash thee not, thou hast no part with me." There, it is the Saviour maintaining His own on earth in communion with Himself. Here, in due time, we shall be with Him, to enjoy unbroken fellowship forever. This had been *promised* before: "If any man serve me, let him follow me; and *where I am* there shall *also* my servant be"

(John 12:26). Here it is formally *declared.* In John 17:24 it is *prayed for*: "Father I will that they also, whom thou hast given me, be *with me* where I am."

Here then, is the Divine specific for heart-trouble; here, indeed, is precious consolation for one groaning in a world of sin. First, faith in the Lord Jesus Christ. Second, the assurance that the Father's House on high will be our eternal Home. Third, the realization that the Saviour has done and is doing everything necessary to secure us a welcome there and fit that Home for our reception. Fourth, the blessed hope that He is coming in person to receive us unto Himself. Finally, the precious promise that we are to be with Him forever. But, and mark it well, it is only in proportion as *we* are "troubled" by our absence from Him, that we shall be comforted and cheered by these precious words! Here is solid ground for consolation, conclusive arguments against despondency and disquietude in the present path of service and suffering, the Saviour lives and loves and cares for us! He is active, promoting our interests, and when God's time arrives He shall come and receive us unto Himself.

"And whither I go ye know, and the way ye know" (14:4). To understand this verse it is necessary to keep in mind the connection. Only a very short time before, Peter had asked, "Lord *whither* goest thou?" (13:36), and when He replied, "Whither I go, thou canst not follow me now; but thou shalt follow me afterwards," he rejoined, "Why cannot I follow thee now?" Both of these questions of Peter, and they probably expressed the thoughts of all the apostles, were answered by our Lord in the verses which have just been before us. "It is as if He had said, You are troubled in spirit because you know not whither I go; and because I have said, ye cannot follow Me now. I am going to My Father; to His House of many mansions; let not, therefore, these fears about Me distress you; and as to your following Me—as to the reason why you cannot follow Me now—and as to the way in which you are to follow Me hereafter, know that arrangements must be made for your coming to where I am going. I go to make these arrangements, and when they are completed I will come and take you to Myself, that where I am, there ye may be also. That is whither I am going—that is the reason why you do not go with Me, or follow Me now—that is the way in which you *are* afterwards to come where I am going: and, i.e. *thus* 'ye know', for I have plainly told you 'whither I go' and the 'way' in which you are to come whither I shall have gone" (Dr. John Brown). The "whither" was *unto the Father;* the "way" was the *process* by which *they* would arrive there. It was not simply the *goal,* but the *path* to it; not simply the *whither* but the *how* which Christ had just revealed to them.

"Thomas saith unto him, Lord, we know not whither thou goest; and how can we know the way?" (14:5). Our Lord had spoken very simply and plainly, yet was He misunderstood. The Father, His House, its many mansions, Christ going there to prepare a place and His promise to come and receive His people unto Himself and share His place with us—these things were dim and unreal to the materialistic and rationalistic Thomas. His mind was on earthly things. Did the "father's house" mean some palace situated outside Palestine, and did Christ's "going away" signify His removing to that palace? He was not sure, and tells the Lord so. Well, if we brought *our* difficulties unto Him. But let us not forget that the Spirit of truth had not yet been given to the disciples to *show* them "things to come" (John 16:13). He *has* been given to us, therefore is our ignorance the more excuseless.

"Jesus saith unto him, I am the way, the truth, and the life" (14:6). Before sin entered the world Adam enjoyed a threefold privilege in relation to God; he was in communion with his Maker; he knew Him, and he possessed spiritual life. But when he disobeyed and fell, this threefold relationship was severed. He became alienated from God, as the hiding of himself painfully demonstrated; having believed the Devil's lie, he was no longer capable of perceiving the truth, as the making of fig-leaf aprons clearly evidenced; and he no longer had spiritual life, for God's threat *"In the day* thou eatest thereof thou shalt *surely die"* was strictly enforced. In this same awful condition has each of Adam's descendants entered this world, for "that which is born of the flesh is flesh"—a fallen parent can beget nought but a fallen child. Every sinner, therefore, has a threefold need—reconciliation, illumination, regeneration. This threefold need is perfectly met by the Saviour. He is the Way to the Father; He is the Truth incarnate; He is the Life to all who believe in Him. Let us briefly consider each of these separately.

"I am the way." Christ spans the distance between God and the sinner. Man would fain manufacture a ladder of his own, and by means of his resolutions and reformations, his prayers and his tears, climb up to God. But that is impossible. *That* is the way which *seemeth right* unto a man, but the end thereof are the ways of death (Prov. 14:12). *It is Satan* who would keep the exercised sinner on his self-imposed journey to God. What faith needs to lay hold of is the glorious truth that Christ has come all the way down to sinners. The sinner could not come in to God, but God in the person of His Son has come out to sinners. He is *the Way*, the Way to the Father, the Way to Heaven, the Way to eternal blessedness.

"I am the truth." Christ is the full and final revelation of God. Adam believed the Devil's lie, and ever since then man has been groping amid ignorance and error. "The way of the wicked is as *darkness;* they know not at what they stumble" (Prov. 4:19). "Having the understanding darkened, being alienated from the life of God through the *ignorance* that is in them, because of the *blindness* of their heart" (Eph. 4:18). A thousand systems has the mind devised. "God hath made man upright; but they have sought out *many* inventions" (Eccl. 7:29). "There is none that understandeth" (Rom. 3:11). Pilate voiced the perplexity of multitudes when he asked, "*What is* truth?" (John 18:38). Truth is not to be found in a system of philosophy, but in a Person—Christ is "the truth": He reveals God and exposes man. In Him are hid "all the treasures of wisdom and knowledge" (Col. 2:3). What tremendous folly to ignore Him! What will it avail you in Hell, dear reader, even though you have mastered all the sciences of men, were acquainted with all the events of history, were versed in all the languages of mankind, were thoroughly acquainted with the politics of your day? O, how you will wish then that you had read your newspapers less and your Bible more; that with all your getting you had got understanding; that with all your learning you had bowed before Him who is *the Truth!*

"I am the life." Christ is the Emancipator from death. The whole Bible bears solemn witness to the fact that the natural man is spiritually lifeless. He walks according to the course of this world; he has no love for the things of God. The fear of God is not upon him, nor has he any concern for His glory. *Self* is the centre and circumference of his existence. He is alive to the things of the world, but is *dead* to heavenly things. The one who is out of Christ exists, but he has no spiritual life. When the prodigal son returned from the *far* country the father said, "This, my son, was *dead,* and is alive again; he was lost, and is found" (Luke 15:24). The one who believes in Christ has passed out of death into life (John 5:24). "He that believeth on the Son hath everlasting life" (John 3:36). Then turn to Him who is *the Life.*

"I am the way." Without Christ men are Cains—*wanderers.* "They are all gone out of the way" (Rom. 3:12). Christ is not merely a Guide who came to show men the path in which they ought to walk: He is Himself *the Way* to the Father. "I am the truth." Without Christ men are *under the power of the Devil,* the father of lies. Christ is not merely a Teacher who came to reveal to men a doctrine regarding God: He is Himself *the Truth* about God. "He that hath seen me hath seen the Father." "I am the life." Without Christ men are *dead* in trespasses and sins. Christ is not merely a Physician who came to invigorate the old nature, to refine its grossness, or repair its defects. "I am come," said He, "that they might have *life,* and that they might have it more abundantly" (John 10:10).

"No man cometh unto the Father but by me" (v. 6). Christ is the *only* way to God. It is utterly impossible to win God's favour by any efforts of our own. "Other foundation can no man lay than that is laid, which is Jesus Christ" (I Cor. 3:11). "Neither is there salvation in any other; for there is none other name under heaven given among men, whereby we must be saved" (Acts 4:12). "There is one God, and one mediator between God and men, the man Christ Jesus" (I Tim.

2:6). Let every Christian reader praise God for His unspeakable Gift, and "Having therefore, brethren, boldness to enter into the holiest by the blood of Jesus, by a new and living *way*, which he hath newly-made for us, through the veil, that is to say, his flesh; and having an high priest over the house of God; let us draw near with a true heart in full assurance of faith" (Heb. 10:19-22).

"If ye had known me, ye should have known my Father also: and from henceforth ye know him, and have seen him" (v. 7). This is intimately connected with the whole of the immediate context. The reason why the apostles found it so hard to understand the Lord's references to the Father, the Father's House, and His and their way there, was because their views respecting Himself were so defective and deficient. The true knowledge of the Father cannot be obtained but by the true knowledge of the Son; and if the Son be really known, the Father is known also. The Father is known just so far as the Son is known; no farther. Christ was more than a manifestation *of* God; He *was* "God manifest in flesh." He was the Only-begotten, who fully declared Him.

"From henceforth ye know him, and have seen him." "These words of our Lord are a prediction, which, like many predictions, is uttered in the present tense—the event not only being as certain as if it had already taken place, but appearing as accomplished to the mind of the prophet, rapt into the future by the inspiring impulse. It is equivalent to, 'yet a very little while and ye shall know Him—know Him so clearly that it may be said you *see* Him!' The prediction was accomplished on the day of Pentecost. From the time these words were uttered, a series of events took place, in close succession, in which through the atoning sufferings, and death, and glorious resurrection of our Lord Jesus, the character of God the Father, was gloriously illustrated. But, till after the resurrection, the disciples saw only the dark side of the cloud in which Jehovah was; and even till 'the Spirit was poured out from on High,' they but indistinctly discerned the true meaning of these events. Then, indeed, 'the darkness was passed, and the true light shone.' The Holy Spirit took of the things of Christ and showed them unto them" (Dr. John Brown).

"Philip saith unto him, Lord, show us the Father, and it sufficeth us" (14:8). What the Lord had just said to Thomas, Philip was unable to thoroughly grasp. With that strange faculty of the human mind to pass over the most prominent and important points of a subject and to seize only on that on which our own mind had been running, this disciple can think only of "seeing" the Father, not *how* He is *to be* seen. Possibly Philip's mind *reverted* to the experience of Moses on the Mount, when, in answer to earnest prayer, he was placed in a cleft of the rock and permitted to see the retiring glory of Jehovah as He passed by; or, he may have remembered what Moses, Aaron, Nadab and Abihu and the seventy elders of Israel were permitted to witness when "they saw the God of Israel, and under his feet, as it were, a paved work of a sapphire stone, and, as it were the body of heaven in his clearness" (Exodus 24:10). He may have recalled that prophecy, "The glory of the Lord shall be revealed, and all flesh shall *see it* together" (Isa. 40:5).

"Jesus saith unto him, Have I been so long time with you, and yet hast thou not known me, Philip? He that hath seen me hath seen the Father; and how sayest thou then, Show us the Father?" (14:9). This was a rebuke, the more forceful by being addressed to Philip individually. He had said, "Show *us* the Father." Christ replied, "Hast *thou* not known me, Philip?" The force of this was: Have you never yet apprehended *who* I am? The corporeal representation of God, such as Philip desired, was unnecessary; unnecessary because a far more glorious revelation of Deity was there right before him. The Word, made flesh, was tabernacling among men, and *His* glory was "the glory of the only-begotten of the Father." He was the visible Image of the invisible God. He was the "brightness of his glory, and the express image of his person." In Him dwelt all the fulness of the Godhead bodily.

"Believest thou not that I am in the Father, and the Father in me? The words that I speak unto you I speak not of myself: but the Father that dwelleth in me he doeth the works" (14:10). Christ was in the Father and the Father was in Him. There was the most perfect and intimate union between Them. Both His words and His works were a perfect revelation of Deity. It is very striking to note here that the Son refers to *His* "words" as *the Father's* "works." *His* words were works, for they were words of power. "He *spake* and it was *done;* he commanded, and it stood fast"! He *said* "Lazarus, come forth"; and he that was dead came forth.

"Believe me that I am in the Father, and the Father in me: or else believe me for the very works' sake" (14:11). This is solemn. The Lord has to descend to the level that He took when speaking to His enemies—"Though ye believe not me *believe the works* that ye may know, and believe that the Father is in me and I in him" (John 10:38). So now He says to Philip, If ye will not, on My bare word, believe that I am One with the Father, at least acknowledge the proof of it in My works. How thankful we should be that the Holy Spirit has been given to us, to make clear what was so dark to the disciples. Let us praise God that "we know that the Son of God is come, and hath given us an understanding, that we may know him that is true" (I John 5:20).

Let the interested student carefully ponder the following questions:—

1. For whom are the promises in v. 12 intended?
2. Who has ever done anything "greater" than Christ did, v. 12?
3. What does it mean to ask "in the name of" Christ, v. 13?
4. How is v. 14 to be qualified?
5. Is obeying God's commandments "legalism," v. 15?
6. Why cannot "the world" receive the Holy Spirit, v. 17?
7. What is the meaning of v. 20?

CHAPTER FORTY-NINE

CHRIST COMFORTING HIS DISCIPLES
(Continued)

John 14:12-20

Below is an Analysis of the passage which is to be before us: —

1. Christ's cause furthered by His return to the Father, v. 12.
2. Praying in the name of Christ, vv. 13, 14.
3. Love evidenced by obedience, v. 15.
4. The coming of the Comforter, vv. 16, 17.
5. Christians not left orphans, v. 18.
6. Our life secured by Christ's, v. 19.
7. Knowledge of Divine life in believers, v. 20.

At first reading there does not appear to be much direct connection between the several verses of our present passage. This second section of John 14 seems to lack a central unity. Yet, as we read it more attentively, we notice that both 14:13 and 14:16 open with the word "And," which at once makes us suspect that our first hasty impression needs correcting. The fact is that the more closely this Paschal Discourse of Christ be studied, the more shall we perceive the close connection which one part of it sustains to another, and many important lessons will be learned by noting the *relation* which verse has to verse.

The first verse of our passage opens with the remarkable promise that the apostles of Christ should do even greater works than their Master had done. Then, in the next two verses reference is made to *prayer,* and the fact that these are prefaced with the word "And" at once indicates that there is an intimate relation between the doing of these works and the supplicating of God. This is the more striking if we recall the central thing in the former section. The opening verse of John 14 is a call to faith in Christ, and the closing verse (11) repeats it. Following the word upon prayer, the Lord next said, "If ye love me, keep my commandments" (14:15). Here we seem to lose the thread again, for apparently a new subject is most abruptly introduced. But only *seemingly* so, for, in truth, it is just here that we discover the *progress* of thought. The *faith* and the *praying* (the two essential pre-requisites for the doing of the "greater works") have their root in an already existing *love,* which is now to be evidenced by pleasing its Object. What comes next? The promise of "another Comforter." Surely this is most suggestive. It was only by the coming of the Holy Spirit that the apostles' faith in Christ was established, that power was communicated for the performing of mighty works, and that their love was purified and deepened. Thus we have a most striking example of the importance and value of studying closely the connection of a passage and noting the relation of one verse to another.

Having remarked upon the relation between the verses of our present passage, let a brief word be said upon the connection which exists between it *as a whole* and the first section of John 14. The Lord began by saying, "Let not your heart be troubled." All that followed was the assigning of various reasons *why* the apostles should not be so excessively perturbed at the prospect of His approaching departure. He began, by setting before them three chief grounds of comfort: *He* was going to the Father's House of many mansions. He was going there to prepare a place *for them.* When His preparations were complete, He would *come for them* in person to conduct them to Heaven, so that His place might be theirs forever. Then He had been interrupted by the question of Thomas and the request of Philip, and in response He had stated with great plainness the truth concerning both His person and His mission. Now, in the section before us, the Lord brings forward *further* reasons why the sorrowing disciples should not let their hearts be troubled. These additional grounds of consolation will come before us in the course of our exposition.

Though the Lord continues in this second section of His Discourse what He began in the first, yet there is a striking *advance* to be noted. At the beginning of John 14, Christ had referred to what the apostles *should* have known, namely, that the Son on earth had perfectly declared the Father, and this ought to have been the means of their apprehending *whither* He was going. This they knew (14:4), however dull they might be in perceiving the consequences. But now the Lord discloses to them that which they *could not* understand till the Holy Spirit was given. It was by the descent of the Comforter that they would be guided into *all* truth. It was by the Holy Spirit that Christ would come to them (14:18). And it was by the Spirit they would know that Christ was in the Father, and they in Him and He in them. The Lord did not say that they ought to have understood, even then, these things: the apprehension of them would not be until the day of Pentecost.

"Verily, verily, I say unto you, He that believeth on me, the works that I do shall he do also" (14:12). The "works" of which Christ here spake were His *miraculous* works, the same as those mentioned in the two preceding verses, works to which He appealed as proofs of His Divine person and mission. The one to whom Christ promised this was "He that believeth on me." Some have understood this to refer to *all* the genuine followers of Christ. But this is manifestly wrong, for there is *no* Christian on earth today who can do the miracles which Christ did—cleanse the leper, give sight to the blind, raise the dead. To meet this difficulty it has been replied, This is due to a deficiency in the Christian's faith. But, this is simply a begging of the question. Our Lord did not say, "He that believeth on me *may* do the works that I do, but *shall* do!" But of whom, then, was Christ speaking?

We submit that "He that believeth on me," like the expression "them that believe" in Mark 16:17, of whom it was said certain miraculous signs should follow them, refers to a *particular* class of persons, and that these expressions must be modified by their reference and setting. In each case the promise was limited to those whom our Lord was addressing. "The only safe way of interpreting the whole of this Discourse, and many other passages in the Gospels, is to remember that it was addressed to *the apostles*—that everything in it has a direct reference to them—that much that is said of them, and to them, may be said of, and to, all Christian ministers, all Christian men—but that much that is said of them and to them, cannot be truly said either of the one or the other of these classes, and that the propriety of applying what is applicable to them, must be grounded on some other foundation than its being found in this Discourse.

"It is plain from the New Testament that there was a faith which was specially connected with miraculous powers. This faith was that Christ is possessed of omnipotence, and that He intends, through my instrumentality, to manifest His omnipotence in the performance of a miracle. But, this faith, like all faith, *must rest on a Divine revelation made to the individual;* where this is not the case, there can be no faith—there may be fancy, there may be presumption, but there can be no faith. Such a revelation Christ made to the apostles and to the seventy disciples, when He said 'Behold, I give unto *you* power to tread on serpents and scorpions, and over all the power of the enemy; and nothing shall by any means hurt *you*' (Luke 10:19). No man, to whom such a revelation *has not* been made, can work such miracles, and it would seem that even in the case of those to whom such a revelation *was* made, a firm belief of the revelation and reliance on the power and faithfulness of Him who made it, was necessary to the miracles being effectively produced in any particular instance.

"Keeping these undoubted facts in view, there is little difficulty in interpreting Christ's words here. The disciples had derived great advantage of various kinds from the exercise of their Master's power to work miracles. They were quite aware that if He should *leave them,* not only would they be deprived of the advantage of His superior powers, but that their own, which were entirely dependent on Him, would be withdrawn also. Now our Lord assures them in the most emphatic manner, by a repetition of the formula of affirmation, 'Verily, verily, I say unto you,' that His miraculous power was to *continue* to be exercised through them as a medium, and that, to its being exercised henceforth, as hitherto, faith in Him, on their part, would be at once necessary and effectual. Such a statement was obviously calculated to reassure their shaken minds, and comfort their sorrowing hearts. And we find the declaration was filled to the letter. They, believing on Him, *did* the works which He did. We find them, like Him, instantaneously healing the sick, casting out demons, and raising the dead" (Dr. John Brown). Hebrews 2:4 records the fulfilment of Christ's promise: "God also bearing them witness, both with signs and wonders, and with divers miracles, and gifts of the Holy Spirit."

"And greater than these shall he do" (14:12). It is important to note that the word "works" in the second clause is *not* found in the original. We do not think Christ was now referring to miracles in the technical sense of that term, but to something else which, in magnitude and importance, would exceed the miracle done by Himself and the apostles. "Greater *things*" would be better. What these greater things were it is not difficult to determine. The preaching of a risen and exalted Saviour, the proclaiming of the Gospel to "every creature," the turning of souls from darkness to light, and from the power of Satan to the service of the living God, the causing of heathen to demolish with their own hands the temples of idolatry, the building of that temple of living stones of which Christ is both the foundation and the chief-corner, and which far surpassed the temple at Jerusalem—these things were far greater than any interferences with the course of nature's laws. Thus did the Father honour His Son, owning the perfect work which He had done, by the greater wonders which the Holy Spirit effected through the disciples.

"Because I go unto my Father" (14:12). It is important to note how that in this "because" the Lord Jesus has Himself given us a partial explanation here of how His promise would be made good, though it is largely lost by placing a full stop at the end of 14:12. If we read straight on through 14:13 the Saviour's explanation is the more apparent: "Greater things than these shall he do, *because* I go unto my Father, *And* whatsoever ye shall ask in my name, that will I do." Christ would henceforth give to their prayers power from on high, so that what *they* did, *He* would do in and through them. Thus, in His "seed" was the pleasure of the Lord to prosper (Isa. 53:10). If the full stop be insisted on and its force rigidly pressed, 14:12 would then teach that, the disciples must now continue to work in the place of their Lord the still greater things, *because He Himself was no longer there.* But this is obviously wrong. He left them, it is true; but He also returned to indwell them (14:18), and in this way came the *harvest* of His own seed-sowing. "And herein is that saying true, One soweth, and another reapeth. I sent you to reap that whereon ye bestowed no labour" (4:37, 38). Link 14:13 with 14:12 and all is plain and simple: thus connected we are taught that the greater things done by the apostles were, in reality, done by Christ Himself! As Mark 16:20 tells us, "And they went forth, and preached everywhere, *the Lord* working with them." But what He did was *in answer to* their believing prayers!

"And whatsoever ye shall ask in my name, that will I do, that the Father may be glorified in the Son" (14:13). The connection of this with the whole context is very precious. Let it be kept steadily in mind that Christ was here *comforting* His *disciples,* who were troubled at the prospect of His leaving them, and that He was calling them to an *increased confidence* in Himself. In the previous verse He had just assured them that His cause would not suffer by His return to the Father, for even greater things should be done through and by them as a testimony of His glory. Now He reminds them that His corporeal absence would only unite these apostles to Him more intimately and more effectually in a spiritual way. True, He would be in Heaven, and they on earth, but *prayer* could remove all sense of distance, prayer could bring them into His very presence at any time, yea, prayer was all-essential if they were to do these "greater" things. And had he not already given them a perfect example? Had He not *shown* them that there was an intimate connection between the great works which He had done and the prayers which He had offered to the Father? Had they not heard Him repeatedly "ask" the Father (see 6:11; 11:41; 12:28, etc.)? Then let them do likewise. He was *interpreting* His own words at the beginning of this Discourse: "Believe also in me." Faith *in His person* was now to be manifested by prayer *in His name!*

"If ye shall ask any thing in my name, I will do it" (14:14). Very blessed is this. The disciples were invited to count upon a power that could not fail, if sought aright. Christ was no mere man whose departure must necessarily bring to an end what He was wont to do upon earth. Though absent, He would manifest His Deity by granting their petitions: whatsoever they asked *He* would do. All power in Heaven is His. The Father hath committed *all* judgment unto the Son (5:22) and in the exercise of this power He gives His own whatsoever they need.

"If ye shall ask any thing in my name, I will do it." What is meant by asking *in the name of Christ?* Certainly it is much more than the mere putting of His name at the end of our prayers, or simply *saying,* "Hear me for Jesus' sake." First, it means that we pray *in His person,* that is, as standing in His place, as fully *identified* with Him, asking by virtue of our very union with Himself. When we truly ask in the name of Christ, *He* is the real petitioner. Second, it means, therefore, that we plead before God the merits of His blessed Son. When men use another's name as the authority of their approach or the ground of their appeal, the one of whom the request is made looks beyond him who presented the petition to the one for whose sake he grants the request. So, in all reverence we may say, when we truly ask in the name of Christ, the Father looks past us, and sees the Son as the real suppliant. Third, it means that we pray only for that which is according to *His* perfections and what will be for *His* glory. When we do anything in another's name, it is *for* him we do it. When we take possession of a property in the name of some society, it is not for any private advantage, but for the society's good. When an officer collects taxes in the name of the government, it is not in order to fill his own pockets. Yet how constantly do we overlook this principle as an obvious condition of acceptable prayer! To pray in Christ's name is to seek what He seeks, to promote what He has at heart!

"If ye shall ask any thing in my name, I will do it." From what has been said above it will be seen that Christ was very far from handing His disciples a 'blank check' (as some have expressed it), leaving *them to* fill it in and assuring them that God would honor it because it bore His Son's signature. Equally so is it a carnal delusion to suppose that a Christian has only to work himself up to an expectation to suppose that God *will* hear his prayer, in order to obtain what he asks for. To apply to God for any thing in the name of Christ, the petition must be *in keeping with* what Christ is. We can only rightly ask God for that which will magnify His Son. To ask in the name of Christ is, therefore, to set aside our own will, and bow to the perfect will of God. If only we realized this more, what a *check* it would be on our ofttimes rash and illconsidered requests! How many of our prayers would never be offered did we but pause to inquire, Can I present *this* in *that* Name which is above every name?

> Not what I wish, but what I want,
> O let Thy grace supply;
> The good unasked, in mercy grant,
> The ill, though asked, deny.
> —Cowper.

"If ye love me, keep my commandments" (14:15). There seems to be a most abrupt change of subject here, and many have been puzzled in finding the connection. Let us first go back to the opening verse of our chapter. The apostles were troubled at heart at the prospect of their Master's departure, and this evidenced, unmistakably, their deep affection for Him. Here, with tender faithfulness, He *directs* their affection. Your love for Me is to be manifested not by inconsolable regrets, but by a glad and prompt compliance with My commandments. So much is clear; but what of the link with the more immediate context? In seeking the answer to this, let us ask, "*What is the leading subject* of the context?" This, as we have seen, is a call to *faith* in an ascended Christ: in the previous verse, a faith evidenced by praying in His name. Now He says, "If ye love me, keep my commandments." Surely then the answer is plain: *love* is the *spring* of true *faith* and the *goal* of real *prayer*. "If ye shall ask any thing in my name, I will do it" He had just said, and this that the Father might be glorified in the Son. *For what*, then, shall we ask? is the natural inquiry which is now suggested? Here then is our Lord's response: an increase of *love* (in myself and in all who are Christ's) which will evidence itself by *doing* His will. Unless this be the first and foremost desire of our hearts, all other petitions will remain unanswered. "And whatsoever we ask, we receive of him, *because* we keep his commandments, and do those things that are pleasing in his sight" (I John 3:22).

"All sentimental talking and singing about love are vain. Unless, by grace, we show a truthful obedience, the profession of affection is worse than affectation. There is more hypocrisy than we suppose. Love is practical, or it is not love at all" (Mr. P. W. Heward).

"If ye love me, keep my commandments." How this verse rebukes the increasing Antinomianism of our day! In some circles one cannot use the word "commandments" without being frowned upon as a "legalist." Multitudes are now being taught that Law is the enemy of Grace, and that the God of Sinai is a stern and forbidding Deity, laying upon His creatures a yoke grievous to be borne. Terrible travesty of the truth is this. The One who wrote upon the tables of stone is none other than the One who died on Calvary's Cross; and He who here says "If ye *love me,* KEEP MY COMMANDMENTS" also said at Sinai that He would show mercy unto thousands of them "that *love me* and KEEP MY COMMANDMENTS"! It is indeed striking to note that this tender Saviour, who was here comforting His sorrowing disciples, also maintained His Divine majesty and insisted upon the recognition of His Divine authority. Mark how His Deity appears here: "Keep *my* commandments": we never read of Moses or any of the prophets speaking of *their* commandments!

"If ye love me, keep my commandments." What are Christ's commandments? We will let another answer: "The whole revelation of the Divine will, respecting what I am to believe and feel and do and suffer, contained in the Holy Scriptures is the law of Christ. Both volumes of Christ are the work of the Spirit of Christ. His first and great commandment is: 'Thou shalt love the Lord thy God with all thy heart, and soul, and strength'; and the second great commandment is like unto the first: 'Thou shalt love thy neighbour as thyself.' The commandments of Christ include whatever is good and whatever God hath required of us" (Dr. John Brown). That the One who brought Israel out of

Egypt, led them across the wilderness, and gave them the Law, was Christ Himself, is clear from I Cor. 10:9: "Neither let us tempt *Christ,* as some of them *also* tempted, and were destroyed by serpents" (cf. I Cor. 10:4).

"Obedience to the commandments of Christ is the test of love to Him, and there will be no difficulty in applying the test, if there be only an honest desire to have the question fairly settled; for there are certain qualities of obedience, which are to be found in every lover of Christ, and which are never found in any one else, and it is to these we must attend, if we would know what is our character. Every lover of Christ keeps His commandments *implicitly*: that is, he does what he does because Christ bids him. The doing what Christ commands may be agreeable to my inclinations or conducive to my interest; and if it is on *these* grounds I do it, I serve myself, not the Lord Jesus Christ. What Christ commands may be commanded by those whose authority I acknowledge and whose favour I wish to secure; if I do it on these grounds, I keep man's commandments, not *Christ's.* I keep Christ's commandments only when I do what He bids me *because* He bids me. If I love Christ, I shall keep His commandments *impartially.* If I do anything *because* Christ commands me to do it, I shall do *whatever* He commands. I shall not 'pick and choose.' If I love Christ, I shall keep His commandments *cheerfully.* I shall esteem it a privilege to obey *His* law. The thought that they are the commandments of Him whom I love, because of His excellency and kindness, makes me love His law, for *it* must be excellent because it is His, and it must be fitted to promote my happiness for the same reason. If I love Christ I shall keep His commandments *perseveringly.* If I really love Him I can never cease to love Him, and if I never cease to love Him, I shall never cease to obey Him" (Condensed from Dr. John Brown).

"And I will pray the Father, and he shall give you another Comforter, that he may abide with you forever" (14:16). Note that this verse begins with "And." In the previous one the Lord had been speaking of the disciples' love for Him, marked by an obedient walk. Here He reveals His love for them, evidenced by His asking for One who should shed abroad the love of God in their hearts (Rom. 5:5) and thus empower them to keep His commandments! Until now Christ had been their Comforter, but He was going to leave them; therefore does He ask the Father that another Comforter should be given to them. Here, again, we behold the Saviour loving them "unto the end"! There is also a blessed link of connection between this verse and vv. 13, 14. There the Lord had taught *them* to "ask in His name," and in Luke 11:13, He had told them that the Father would give the Holy Spirit if they "asked for him." But here Christ is before them: *His* prayer precedes theirs—He would "ask" the Father for the Comforter to be sent unto them.

There has been a great deal of learned jargon written on the precise meaning of the Greek word here rendered "Comforter." Personally, we believe that no better term can be found, providing the original meaning of our English word be kept in mind. Comforter means more than Consoler. It is derived from two Latin words, *com* "along side of" and *fortis* "strong." A comforter is one who stands alongside of one in need, to strengthen. The reference here is, of course, to the Holy Spirit, and the fact that He is termed "*another* Comforter" signifies that He was to fill the place of Christ, doing for His disciples all that He had done for them while He was with them on earth, only that the Holy Spirit would minister from within as Christ had from without. The Holy Spirit would comfort, or strengthen in a variety of respects: consolation when they were cast down, grace when they were weak or timid, guidance when they were perplexed, etc. The fact that the Lord here called the Holy Spirit "*another* Comforter" also proves Him to be a *person,* and a *Divine* person. It is striking to observe that in this verse we have mentioned each of the three Persons of the blessed Trinity: "*I* will pray *the Father,* and he shall give you *another* Comforter"! One other thought suggested by the "*another* Comforter." The believer has *two* Comforters, Helpers or Strengtheners: the Holy Spirit on earth, and Christ in Heaven, for the same Greek word here rendered "Comforter" is translated "Advocate" in I John 2:1,—an "advocate" is one who aids, pleads the cause of his client. Christ "maketh intercession" for us on High (Heb. 7:25), the Holy Spirit within us (Rom. 8:26)! And this other "Comforter," be it noted, was to abide with them not just so long as they grieved Him not, but "for ever." Thus is the eternal preservation of every believer Divinely assured.

"Even the Spirit of truth; whom the world cannot receive, because it seeth him not, neither knoweth him" (14:17). The Lord had just promised the apostles "another Comforter," that is, One like unto Himself and in addition to Himself. Here He warns them against expecting a *visible* Person. The One who should come is "the Spirit." Two thoughts are suggested by the title here given Him: "the Spirit of truth," or more literally, "the Spirit of *the* truth." The "truth" is used both of the incarnate and the written Word. Christ had said to the disciples, "*I am* the way, the *truth,* and the life"; a little later He would say to the Father, in their hearing, "*Thy Word* is truth" (17:17). The Spirit, then, is the Spirit *of Christ,* because sent by Him (16:7), and because He is here to glorify Christ (16:14). The Spirit is also the Spirit of *the written Word,* because He moved men to write it (II Peter 1:21), and because He now interprets it (16:13). Hitherto Christ had been their Teacher; henceforth the Holy Spirit should take His place (14:26). The Holy Spirit works not independently of the written Word, but through and by means of it.

"Whom the world cannot receive." Very solemn is this. It is not "will not," but *cannot* receive. Unable to receive the Spirit "the world" demonstrates its real character—opposed to the Father (I John 2:16). The whole world lieth in the wicked one (I John 5:19), and he is a liar from the beginning: how then could the world receive "the Spirit *of truth*"? Our Lord adds another reason, "because it seeth him not, neither knoweth him." But what did the Lord mean? How can the invisible Spirit be seen? I Cor. 2:14 tells us: "The natural man receiveth not the things of the Spirit of God: for they are foolishness unto him; neither can he know them, because they are *spiritually* discerned." It is *spiritual* "seeing" which is in view, as in 6:40. And *why* cannot those who are of the "world" *see* Him? Because they have never been born again: "Except a man be born again, he *cannot see* the kingdom of God." And *why* should the Lord have made this statement *here*?

Surely for the *comfort* of the disciples. "Another Comforter" had been promised them; One who should abide with them for ever; even the Spirit of Truth. What glorious conquests might they now expect to make for Christ! Ah! the Lord warns them of what would really take place: "the world" would not, could not, receive Him.

"But ye know him: for he dwelleth with you, and shall be in you" (14:17). "But" points a contrast: indicating at once that the work of the Spirit would be to separate the people of Christ from the world. "He dwelleth *with* you": He did, even then, for Christ was full of the Spirit (Luke 4:1; John 3:34). "And shall be *in* you" was future. The Lord Jesus here promised that the Third Person of the Holy Trinity should take up His abode within believers, making their bodies His temple. Marvellous grace was this. But, on *what ground* does the Holy Spirit enter and indwell the Christian? Not because of any personal fitness which He discovers there, for the old evil nature still remains in the believer. How, then, is it possible for the *Holy* Spirit to dwell where sin is still present? It is of the first moment that we obtain the correct answer to this, for multitudes are confused thereon: yet there is no excuse for this; the teaching of Scripture is abundantly clear. Jehovah of old, dwelt in the midst of Israel, even when they were stiff-necked and uncircumcised in heart. He did so *on the ground of atoning blood* (see Lev. 16:16). In like manner, the Holy Spirit indwells the believer now, as the witness to the excellency and sufficiency of that one offering of Christ's which has "perfected for ever them that are set apart" (Heb. 10:14). Strikingly was this foreshadowed in the types. The "oil" (emblem of the Holy Spirit) was placed upon the blood—see Lev. 8:24, 30; 14:14, 17, etc.

"I will not leave you comfortless, I will come to you" (14:18). The marginal rendering here is to be preferred: "I will not leave you *orphans*." It looks back to 13:33 where the Lord had addressed them as "little children". They were not to be like sheep without a shepherd, helpless believers in a hostile world, without a defender, forsaken orphans incapable of providing for themselves, left to the mercy of strangers. "I will come to you": how precious is this! Before we go to His place to be with

Him (14:2, 3), He comes to be with us! But what is meant by "*I* will come to you"? We believe that these words are to be understood in their widest latitude. He came to them *corporeally*, immediately after His resurrection. He came to them *in spirit* after His ascension. He will come to them *in glory* at His second advent. The present application of this promise to believers finds its fulfilment in the gift of the Holy Spirit—indwelling us individually, present in the midst of the assembly collectively. And yet we must not limit the coming of Christ to His children to the presence of the Holy Spirit. The mystery of the Holy Trinity is altogether beyond the grasp of our finite minds. Yet the New Testament makes it clear that in the unity of the Godhead, the advent of the Holy Spirit was also Christ coming, invisibly, to be really present with His own. "Lo, *I* am with you alway, even unto the end of the age" (Matt. 28:20). "*Christ* liveth in me," said the apostle Paul (Gal. 2:20). "*Christ* among you, the hope of glory" (Col. 1:27). How unspeakably blessed is this! Friends, relatives, yea, professing Christians may turn against us, but He has promised, "*I will never* leave thee nor forsake thee" (Heb. 13:5).

"Yet a little while, and the world seeth me no more" (14:19). The last time "the world" saw the Lord of glory was as He hung upon the Cross of shame. After His resurrection He appeared unto none but His own. "The world seeth me no more" is not an accurate translation, nor is it true. "The world" *shall* see Him again. "Yet a little while and the world me *no longer* sees" is what the original says, "*Every* eye shall see him" (Rev. 1:7). When? When He is seated upon the Great White Throne to judge the wicked. Then shall they be punished with "everlasting destruction from the presence of the Lord, and from the glory of his power" (II Thess. 1:9).

"But ye see me" (14:19). They saw Him then, while He was speaking to them. They saw Him, again and again, after He had risen from the dead. They saw Him, as He went up to Heaven, till a cloud received Him out of their sight. They saw Him, by faith, after He had taken His seat at the right hand of God, for it is written, "We *see* Jesus, who was made a little lower than the angels for the suffering of death, crowned with glory and honor" (Heb. 2:9). They see Him now, for they are *present with the Lord.* They shall see Him at His second coming: "When he shall appear, we shall be like him; for we shall *see* him as he is" (I John 3:2). They shall see Him for ever and ever throughout the *Perfect Day*: for it is written, "And they shall *see* his face; and his name shall be in their foreheads" (Rev. 22:4).

"Because I live, ye shall live also" (14:19). "Your spiritual life now, and your eternal life hereafter, are both secured by *My* life. I live, have life in Myself, can never die, can never have My life destroyed by My enemies, and shall live on to all eternity. Therefore: ye shall live also—your life is secured forever, and can never be destroyed; you have everlasting life now, and shall have everlasting glory hereafter" (Bishop Ryle). The blessed truth here expressed by Christ is developed at length in the Epistles: there the Holy Spirit shows us, believers are so absolutely one with Christ that they partake with Him of that holy happy life into which, in the complete enjoyment of it, Christ entered, when He rose again and sat down on the Father's Throne.

"At that day ye shall know that I am in my Father, and ye in me, and I in you" (14:20). The first reference in "that day" is to Pentecost, when Christ came, spiritually, to His disciples; came not merely to visit, but to *abide* with and in them. Then were they brought into the consciousness of their oneness of life with Him. The ultimate reference, no doubt, is to the Day of His glorious manifestation: then shall we know even as we are known.

The following questions are on the closing section of John 14:—

1. How does Christ "manifest" Himself to us, v. 21?
2. What is the difference between "commandments" in v. 21 and "words" in v. 23?
3. What is the double "peace" of v. 27?
4. How is the Father "greater" than Christ, v. 28?
5. "Believe" what, v. 29?
6. What is the meaning of v. 30?
7. What is the spiritual significance of the last clause in v. 31?

CHAPTER FIFTY

Christ Comforting His Disciples (Concluded)

John 14:21-31

The following is an Analysis of the closing section of John 14:

1. Christ manifested to the believer, v. 21.
2. The quandary of Judas, v. 22.
3. Christ's explanation, vv. 23-25.
4. The ministry of the Spirit, v. 26.
5. The gift of Christ's peace, v. 27.
6. The failure in the disciples' love, vv. 28-29.
7. The coming conflict, vv. 30-31.

That the central design of Christ in the first main section of this Paschal Discourse was to *comfort* His sorrowing disciples, and that this section does not close until we reach the end of John 14 is clear from v. 27: "Let not your heart be troubled." The Lord here repeats what He had said in the first verse, and then adds, "neither let it be afraid." That the first section of the Discourse *does* terminate at the close of the chapter, is obvious from its final words: "Arise, let us go hence."

Many and varied were the grounds of comfort which the Lord had laid before the apostles. First, He assured them that He was going to the Father's House. Second, that He would make provision for their coming there. Third, that when the necessary preparations were completed, He would come and conduct them thither. Fourth, that He had opened the way for them, had made them acquainted with the way, and would give them the energy necessary to go along that way. Fifth, that He would not withdraw from them the miraculous powers which He had conferred upon them, but would enable them to do still greater things. Sixth, that whatever they needed for the discharge of the work to which He had called them, on asking in His name, they should assuredly obtain. Seventh, that a Divine Person should be sent to supply His place, acting as their instructor, guide, protector and consoler. Eighth, that they should not be "left orphans," but He would return to them in possession of an endless life, of which they should be partakers. Ninth, that in a soon-coming day they should apprehend the oneness of life, shared by the Father and the Son and the sons.

In the passage which is to be before us we find the Lord adding to these grounds of comfort. Tenth, He would manifest Himself to those who kept His commandments. Eleventh, those who kept His Word should be loved by the Father. Twelfth, the Holy Spirit would bring back to their remembrance all things Christ had said unto them. Thirteenth, Peace He left with them. Fourteenth, His own peace He bequeathed unto them. No wonder that He said, "*Let not* your heart be troubled, neither let it be afraid"!

"He that hath my commandments, and keepeth them, he it is that loveth me: and he that loveth me shall be loved of my Father, and I will love him, and will manifest myself to him" (14:21). In this instance we shall depart from our customary method of expounding the different clauses of a verse in the order in which they occur; instead, we shall treat this verse more or less topically. That in it which is of such vital importance is the final clause, where the Saviour promised to manifest Himself to the obedient believer. Now there is nothing the real Christian desires so much as a personal manifestation of the Lord Jesus. In comparison with this all other blessings are quite secondary. In order to simplify, let us ask and attempt to answer three questions: *How* does the Saviour now "manifest" Himself? What are the *effects* of such manifestation? What are the *conditions* which I have to meet?

In what way does the Lord Jesus now manifest Himself? It is hardly necessary to say, not *corporeally*. No longer is the Word, made flesh, tabernacling among men. No more does He say, as He said to Thomas, "Reach hither thy finger, and behold my hands, and reach hither thy hand, and thrust it into my side"

(John 20:27). No longer may He be seen by our physical eyes (I John 1:1). Nor is the promise of Christ which we are now considering made good through *visions*. We recall the vision which Jacob had at Bethel, when a ladder was set upon earth, whose top reached unto heaven, upon which the angels of God ascended and descended. We think of that wondrous vision given to Isaiah, when he saw the Lord sitting upon a throne, before which the seraphim cried, "holy, holy, holy." No, it is not in visions or in dreams that the Lord promises to come to His people. What then? It is a *spiritual* revelation of Himself to the soul! It is a vivid realization of the Saviour's being and nearness, in a deep and abiding sense of His favour and love. "By the power of the Spirit, He makes His Word so luminous, that as we read it, He Himself seems to draw near. The whole biography of Jesus becomes in this way a precious reality. We see His form. We hear *His* words." It is through the written Word that the incarnate Word "manifests" Himself to the heart!

And what are the *effects* upon the soul of such a manifestation of Christ. First and foremost, He Himself is made a blessed and glorious reality to us. The one who has been granted such an experience can say with Job, "I *have* heard of thee by the hearing of the ear, *but now* mine eye (the eye of the heart) *seeth thee*" (42:5). Such a one now discerns the surpassing beauty and glory of His person and exclaims, "*Thou* art fairer than the children of men." Again: such a manifestation of Christ to the soul *assures* us of His *favour*. Now we hear Him saying (through the Scriptures) "As the Father hath loved me, so I have loved *you*." And now I can respond, "My beloved *is* mine, and I *am* his." Another consequence of this manifestation of Christ is "*comfort and support* in trials, especially in those trials, which, on account of their personal nature, are beyond the reach of human sympathy and love – the trials of desertion and loneliness, from which Jesus Himself suffered so keenly; heart trials, domestic trials, secret griefs, too sacred to be breathed in the ears of men – all these trials in which nothing can sustain us but the sympathy which His own presence gives." Just as the Son of God appeared to the three faithful Hebrews in the fiery furnace, so does He now come to those in the place of trial and anguish. So too in the last great trial, should we be called upon to pass through it ere the Saviour comes. Then to earthly friends we can turn no longer. But we may say with the Psalmist, "Though I walk through the valley of the shadow of death, I will fear *no* evil, for *thou* art with me."

Now, let us inquire, What are the *terms* on which the Saviour thus draws near? Surely every Christian reader is most anxious to secure the key to an experience so elevating, so blessed. Listen now to the Saviour's words, "He that hath my commandments, and keepeth them, he it is that loveth me: and he that loveth me shall be loved of my Father, and I will love him, and will manifest myself to him." The faith by which we are saved does not destroy the necessity for an obedient walk. "Faith is the root of which obedience is the beautiful flower and fruit. And it is only when faith has issued in obedience, in an obedience which stumbles not at sacrifices, and halts not when the way is rough and dark; in an obedience that cheerfully bears the cross and shame—it is only then that this highest promise of the Gospel is fulfilled . . . When love for the Saviour shall lead us to keep His holy Word—lead us to an immediate, unreserved, unhesitating obedience—lead us to say, in the spirit of entire self-surrender and sacrifice, 'Thy will, not mine, be done,' then, farewell to doubt and darkness, to loneliness and sorrow! Then shall we mourn no more an *absent* Lord. Then shall we walk as seeing Him who is invisible, triumphant over every fear, victorious over every foe."*

This manifestation of Christ is made only to the one who really loves Him, and the proof of love to Him is not by emotional displays but by submission to His will. There is a vast difference between sentiment and practical reality. The Lord will give no direct and special revelation of Himself to those who are in the path of *disobedience*. "He that *hath* my commandments," means, hath them at heart. "And *keepeth* them," that is the real test. We *hear*, but do *we heed?* We *know*, but are we *doing* His will? "My little children, let us not love in

* The above quotations are from an article by the late Mr. Inglis, in "Waymarks in the Wilderness."

word, neither in tongue; but in *deed* and in *truth*" (I John 3:18)!

"And he that loveth me shall be loved of my Father." There are three different senses in which Christians may be considered as objects of the loving favour of the Father and of the Son: as persons *elected* in sovereign grace to eternal life; as persons actually *united* to Christ by believing: and as persons *transformed* by the sanctifying work of the Spirit. It is in this last sense that Christ here speaks. Just as the Father is said to love the Son because of His obedience (John 10:17, 18), so is He said to love the believer for the same reason. It is the love of complacency, as distinguished from the love of compassion. The Father was well pleased with His incarnate Son, and He is well pleased with us when we honour and glorify His Son by obeying His commandments.

"Judas saith unto him, not Iscariot, Lord, how is it that thou wilt manifest thyself unto us, and not unto the world?" (14:22). This question had in view the Lord's words when He had just said, "The world seeth me no more" (14:19), and that He would "manifest" Himself to him who kept His commandments. This conflicted sharply with the Jewish ideas of the Messiah and His kingdom. As yet Judas had failed to perceive that the *truth* of God must *sever* between those who receive it and those who reject it, and that therefore *His* kingdom was "*not* of this world" (18:36). And why was it that Judas understood this not? I Cor. 2:10, 11 tells us – the Spirit had not yet been given.

"Judas saith unto him, not Iscariot." "There is something very affecting in this brief parenthesis; the short, sad sentence which our Evangelist throws in – 'Judas, not Iscariot.' The one is not for a moment to be confounded with the other; the true apostle with the traitor. How widely different may men be who yet bear the same name! How many have but the name in common!" (Dr. John Brown.) The Judas who asked this question was the brother of James, the son of Alphæus, see Luke 6:16.

"Lord, how is it that thou wilt manifest thyself unto us, and not unto the world?" How many there are to-day who, by means of legislation and social amelioration, wish to press on the world those teachings of Christ which are only for His own! Judas did not go quite so far as the unbelieving brethren of Christ according to the flesh—"Go show thyself to the world" (7:4); but he was sorely puzzled at this breach between the world and them. Dull indeed was Judas, for the Lord had just said, "Even the Spirit of truth, whom the world *cannot* receive, because it seeth him not, neither knoweth him" (14:17). But equally dull, most of the time, are all of us.

"Jesus answered and said unto him, If a man love me, he will keep my words: and my Father will love him, and we will come unto him, and make our abode with him" (14:23). "If Judas had known what the world is, and what every human heart is by nature, instead of being puzzled at the Lord's withdrawal from the world, he would have wondered how Jesus could reveal Himself to any man" (Stier). The Lord here repeats that God has fellowship only with those whose hearts *welcome* Him, who love Him, and whose love is manifested by submission to His Word. *Then* He loves in return. The Old Testament taught precisely the same thing. "I love them that love me" (Prov. 8:17). "If a man love me *he will keep* my word." Let not renewed souls torture themselves by attempting to define too nicely the extent of their "keeping." Let those who are tempted to do so meditate upon John 17:6—"I have manifested thy name unto the men which thou gavest me out of the world: thine they were, and thou gavest them me; and they *have kept* thy Word." Mark it well that this was said by the Saviour in full view of all the infirmities and failures of the disciples, and said prior to the day of Pentecost!

To "keep" God's commandments is to obey them, and the primary, the fundamental thing in obedience, is the *desire* of the *heart*, and it is on the heart that God ever looks. Two things are true of every Christian: deep down in his heart there is an intense, steady longing and yearning to please God, to do His will, to walk in full accord with His Word. This yearning *may be* stronger in some than in others, and in each of us *it is* stronger at some times than at others; nevertheless, it is there! But in the second place, no real Christian *fully realizes* this desire. Every genuine Christian has to say with the apostle Paul,

"*Not* as though I had already attained, either were already perfect: but *I follow after*, if that I may lay hold of that for which I am laid hold of by Christ Jesus" (Phil. 3:12).

Now we believe that it is this *heart*-obedience, this *inward* longing to be fully conformed to His will, this burning desire of the renewed soul, of which Christ here speaks. "If a man love me, he *will* keep my word." Every true believer loves Christ; therefore every true believer "keeps" His Word, keeps it in the sense thus defined. Let it be repeated, God looks at the heart; whereas we are constantly occupied with the *outward* appearance. As we scrutinize our *deeds,* if we are honest, we have to acknowledge that we have "kept his word" very imperfectly; yea, it seems to us, that we are not entitled to say that we *have* "kept" it at all. But the Lord looks *behind* the deeds, and knows the longings within us. The case of Peter in John 21 is a pertinent illustration. When Christ asked him a third time, "Lovest thou me?" His disciple answered, "Lord, thou knowest *all things;* THOU knowest that I love thee" (21:17). My disgraceful *actions* contradicted my love; my fellow-disciples have good reason to doubt it, but Thou who searchest the heart knowest better. In one sense it is an intensely solemn and searching thing to remember that *nothing* can be hidden from Him before whom all things are open and naked; but in another sense it is most blessed and comforting to realize that *He* can see in my heart what I cannot often discover in my ways, and what my fellow-believers cannot—a real love for Him, a genuine longing to please and glorify Him.

Let not the conclusion be drawn that we are here lapsing into Antinomian laxity, or making it a matter of no moment what our outward lives are like. To borrow words which treat of another subject, "As there was a readiness to *will* so there should be a *performance also*" (II Cor. 8:11). Though the apostle acknowledged that he had not "already attained," yet he continued to "follow after." Where there is love for Christ, there cannot but be bitter sorrow (as with Peter) when we know that we have grieved Him. And more; there will be a sincere confession of our sins, and confession will be followed by earnest supplication for grace to enable us to do what He has bidden.

Nevertheless, it is blessed to know that He who is the Truth declares, positively and without qualification, "If a man love me, he *will* keep my word;" and in the light of John 17:6, this must mean: first and absolutely, in the desire of his heart; secondly and relatively, in his walk.

It is to be noted that the Lord here makes a change of terms from what He had said in 14:21; a slight change, but an important one. There He had said, "He that hath my *commandments*, keepeth them;" here, "If a man love me, he will keep my *word*" – in the Greek the singular number is used. "This is a beautiful difference, and of great practical value, being bound up with the measure of our attentiveness of heart. Where obedience lies comparatively on the surface, and self-will or worldliness is not judged, a 'commandment' is always necessary to enforce it. People ask, '*Must* I do this? Is there any harm in that?' To such the Lord's will is solely a question of commandment. Now there are commandments, the expression of His authority, and they are not grievous. But, besides, where the heart loves Him deeply, His 'word' will give enough expression of His will. Even in nature a parent's *look* will do it. As we well know, an obedient child catches the mother's desire before the mother has uttered a word. So, whatever might be the word of Jesus, it would be heeded, and thus the heart and life be formed in obedience" (Mr. W. Kelly).

"True also it is that something of both characters of love, as Christ affirms them, will be found in all true Christians – overborne by so much contrary influence that, like Peter in the high priest's palace, only He who knoweth all things can detect the true disciple beneath the false. There is the false within us all, as well as the true, Alas, in many, so often uppermost. The results cannot fail to follow: the blessing of which the Lord speaks attaches to that with which He here connects it. We find it in proportion as we answer to the character.

"Looked at in this way, there is no difficulty in seeing the deeper nature of a love that keeps Christ's 'word', as compared with that which keeps 'commandments' only. Not to keep a positive command is simple, rank rebellion, nothing less. His 'word' is wider, while it addresses itself with less positiveness of authority to the one whose heart and conscience is less prompt to the appeal of love" (Numerical Bible). I do not "command" a *friend*: my mind is made known to *him* by my *words*, and he acts accordingly. One word has greater weight with him than a hundred commands have on one at a distance! A *servant* receives my commands and obeys them, but he knows not my heart; but my *friend* walks with me in the intelligence of my deepest thoughts. Ah! is this so with us? Are we really walking with Him who calls us not servants, but *friends*—see John 15:15!

"And my Father will love him, and we will come unto him, and make our abode with him." Just as there is a marked advance from His "commandments" in 14:21 to His "word" in 14:23, so there is in the blessings respectively attached to the keeping of the one and the other. In the former He promises to *manifest* Himself to the heart, in the latter He speaks of both the Father and Himself coming to make Their *abode* with such a soul. "Abiding" speaks of *fellowship* all through John's writings. Not only is *our* fellowship with the Father and His Son (I John 1:3), but to the one who truly heeds the Word, *They* will come and have fellowship with him. This is the reward of loving obedience. The "result will be to manifest the competency of Scripture for the 'man of God' to whom alone it is pledged as competent,—'able to furnish throughly unto all good works.' Who is the man of God, but he who is out and out for God, and who else can expect to be furnished in this way, but he who is honestly intentioned to use his knowledge as before Him who gave it? The very passage which we are quoting here reminds us of where the profit is to be found: 'All Scripture is profitable for doctrine, for reproof, for correction, for instruction in righteousness.' If we do not mean to accept the reproof and the correction, where is the use of talking about the rest?" (Numerical Bible).

"He that loveth me not keepeth not my sayings" (14:24). Here was the final word to Judas: the line between "the world" and "his own" is clearly drawn by the "whoso *loveth* me, whoso loveth me *not*." Not to love the Loveliest is because of *hatred*.

There is no other alternative. Of old Jehovah had declared that He would visit the iniquities of the fathers upon the children unto the third and fourth generation of them that *hated* Him, but that He would show mercy unto thousands of them that *loved* Him and kept His commandments (Exodus 20: 6). What seems to be *indifference* is really *enmity*. All who are not *with* Christ are *against* Him (Luke 11:23).

"He that loveth me not keepeth not my sayings." Observe the change. In the previous verse the one who loves Christ keeps His *Word;* here the one who loves Him not, His *sayings* or words. Why this variation? Because unbelief does not combine *in their unity* the individual sayings, but dismisses them as they are isolated. The true believer hears in all God's words one Word —Him, the unbeliever heeds not! An unbeliever may observe *some* of Christ's words as a matter of policy and prudence, because they commend themselves to his reason; but others, which to him are distasteful, which appear impracticable or severe, he esteems not. If he loved Christ he would value His Word as a whole; but he does not; therefore he keeps not His words.

"And the word which ye hear is not mine, but the Father's which sent me" (14:24). Thus the Lord concludes this point by magnifying the *Word*. Here, we say again, was the final answer to the question, "How is it that thou wilt manifest thyself unto us, and *not* unto *the world?*" Does the world believe on Me? Does it love Me? Does it keep My commandments? How, then, can I manifest Myself to it? "Thus did the Lord dispose of the three main stumbling blocks which hindered these disciples: the offence of Thomas, who would know all with his natural understanding; the offence of Philip, who was eager for visible manifestations to the outward senses; the offence of Judas, who would too readily receive the whole world into the kingdom of God" (Lange).

"These things have I spoken unto you, being yet present with you" (14:25). In the light of the verse which immediately follows we understand this to mean: I said what I have in view of My near departure. Because I am yet with you, these things make little impression upon your hearts, but when the Holy

Spirit has come you will be able to enter the better into their meaning and blessedness.

"But the comforter, which is the Holy Spirit, whom the Father will send in my name, he shall teach you all things" (14:26). This is one of many verses which contains clear proof of the Divine personality of the Holy Spirit. A mere abstract influence could not *teach*. Moreover, "*he* shall teach you," being a masculine pronoun, could not be applied to any but a real *person*. The Comforter would be sent by the Father, but *in the name of Christ*. The significance of this can best be ascertained by a reference to John 5:43: just as the Saviour had come in the *Father's name*, so the Holy Spirit would be sent in the Son's name: that is to say, in His stead, for His interests, with His authority. Just as the Son had made *known the* Father, so the Spirit would take of the things of Christ and show them to His people. Just as the Son had *glorified* the Father, so the Spirit would glorify Christ. Just as, hitherto, the Saviour had supplied all the needs of His own, henceforth the Comforter should fully provide for them.

"He shall teach you all things." Here is another instance where the words of Scripture are *not* to be taken in their absolute sense. If the apostles were to be taught all things without any qualification, they would be omniscient. Nor did Christ mean that the Holy Spirit would teach them all that it was *possible* for finite creatures to know: He would not make known to them the secrets of futurity, or the occult workings of nature. Rather would He teach them all that it was necessary for them to know for their spiritual well-being, and this, particularly, in connection with what Christ had taught them, either fully or in germ form. He would make clear to them that which, as yet, was mysterious in their Master's sayings.

"He shall teach you all things, and bring all things to your remembrance, whatsoever I have said unto you" (14:26). Two striking examples of that are recorded in this very Gospel. In 2:22 we are told, "When therefore he was risen from the dead, his disciples *remembered* that he had said this unto them." Again, in 12:16 we read, "These things understood not his disciples at the first; but when Jesus was glorified, then *remembered* they that these things were written of him." No doubt this promise of Christ applies in a general way to all real Christians. Hundreds of times has the writer prayed to God, just before entering the pulpit, that He would be pleased to strengthen his memory and enable him to recall the exact words of Scripture as he quoted them; and graciously has He answered us. We would confidently urge our fellow-believers to plead this verse before God on sleepless nights, or when on a bed of sickness, as well as before going to teach a Sunday School class, asking Him to bring back to your remembrance the comforting promises of His Word; or, when tempted, that His precepts might flash upon you.

"Peace I leave with you, my peace I give unto you" (14:27). Without being dogmatic, we believe that there is a *double* "peace" spoken of here: a peace *left* and a peace *given*. In the New Testament "peace" is spoken of in a twofold sense: as signifying reconciliation, contrasted from alienation: and a state of tranquillity as contrasted from a state of tumult. The one is objective, the other subjective. The former is referred to in Rom. 5:1: "Being justified by faith we have peace *with* God." His holy wrath against us and our vile opposition against Him are ended forever. The latter is mentioned in Phil. 4:7: "The peace *of* God, which passeth all understanding shall keep your hearts and minds through Christ Jesus." The one who fully unbosoms himself before the throne of grace enjoys rest within. The one then is judicial, the other, experiential. "Peace I leave with you" would be the result of the Atonement. "My peace I give unto you," would be enjoyed through the indwelling Spirit. The one was for the conscience; the other for the heart.

"My peace I give unto you." This was the personal peace which He had enjoyed here on earth. He was never ruffled by circumstances, and never resisted the will of the Father. He was ever in a state of most perfect amity with God. The peace He here promised His disciples was the peace which filled His own heart, as the result of His unbroken communion with the Father. "For us it is restlessness of will which disturbs this—the strife with His will which this means, and the dissatisfaction of soul which follows every gain that may seem to make in that direction. Doing only *His* will, there can be no proper doubt as to the issue" (Numerical Bible).

"Not as the world giveth, give I unto you" (14:27). The peace which the worldling has is shallow, unstable, unsatisfying, false. It *talks* much about peace, but *knows* little of the thing itself. We have peace-societies, peace-programmes, a peace-palace, and a League of Nations to promote peace; yet all the great powers are armed to the teeth! "When they shall *say,* Peace and safety; then sudden destruction cometh upon them" (I Thess. 5:3). The world's peace is a chimera: it fails under trial. When the world gives, it is to the ungodly, not to the godly, whom they hate. When the world gives, it gives away, and has no longer. But Christ gives by bringing us into what is eternally His own. When Christ gives He gives forever, and never takes away.

"Let not your heart be troubled, neither let it be afraid" (14:27). Here the Lord concludes that section of His discourse which had been devoted to the comforting of His sorrowing disciples. Abundant had been the consolation He had proffered them. Their hearts ought now to have been at perfect peace, their minds being stayed upon God. And yet while this verse terminated the first section of the address, it is closely connected with the verses which follow where the Lord proceeded to make application of what He had been saying.

"Ye have heard how I said unto you, I go away, and come unto you. If ye love me, ye would rejoice, because I said, I go unto the Father: for my Father is greater than I" (14:28). Connecting this verse with the one immediately preceding, the force of our Lord's words is this: If you only believed what I have been saying to you, your cares and fears would vanish, and joy would take the place of sorrow. But what did the Lord mean by "*If* ye loved me?" Was He not *instructing* and *directing* their love, in order to purify it? He knew that they loved Him, and what He had said in 14:15, 21, 23, assumed it. But their love was not yet sufficiently *dis-interested*: they were occupied too much with the thought of their own bereavement, instead of the heavenly joy into which the Redeemer was about to enter. If they had loved Him with a pure love, they would have been happy at His exaltation and forgotten themselves.

"My Father is greater than I." This is the favourite verse with Unitarians, who deny the absolute Deity of Christ and His perfect equality with the Father—a truth which is clearly taught in many scriptures. Those who use these words of our Lord in support of their blasphemous heresy, wrest them from their context, ignoring altogether the connection in which they are found. The Saviour had just told the apostles that they ought to rejoice because He was going to the Father, and then advances this reason, "*For* my Father is greater than I." Let this be kept definitely before us and all difficulty vanishes. The Father's being greater than Christ was the reason assigned *why* the disciples should rejoice at their Master's going to the Father. This at once fixes the meaning of the disputed "greater," and shows us the sense in which it was here used. The contrast which the Saviour drew between the Father and Himself was *not* concerning *nature*, but official character and position.

Christ was not speaking of Himself in His essential Being. The One who thought it not robbery to be "*equal* with God" had taken the servant form, and not only so, had been made in the likeness of men. In both these senses, namely, in His official status (as Mediator) and in His assumption of human nature, He was inferior to the Father. Throughout this discourse and in the Prayer which follows in chapter 17, the Lord Jesus is represented as the Father's Servant, from whom He had received a commission, and to whom He was to render an account; for whose glory He acted, and under whose authority He spake. But there is another sense, more pertinent, in which the Son was inferior to the Father. In becoming incarnate and tabernacling among men, He had greatly humiliated Himself, by choosing to descend into shame and suffering in their acutest forms. He was now the Son of man that had not where to lay His head. He who was rich had for our sakes become poor. He was the Man of sorrows, and acquainted with grief. In view of this, Christ was now contrasting His *situation* with that of the Father in the heavenly Sanctuary. The Father was seated upon the throne of highest majesty; the brightness of His glory was uneclipsed; He was surrounded by hosts of holy beings, who worshipped Him with uninterrupted praise. Far different was it with His incarnate Son—despised and rejected of men, surrounded by implacable enemies, soon to be nailed to a criminal's cross. In *this* sense, too, He was inferior to the Father. Now in going to the Father, the Son would enjoy a vast improvement of situation. It would be a gain unspeakable. The contrast then was between His present state of humiliation and His coming state of exaltation to the Father! Therefore, those who really loved Him should have rejoiced at the tidings that He *would* go to the Father, because the Father was greater than He—greater both in official status and in surrounding circumstances. It was Christ *owning* His place as Servant, and ***magnifying*** the One who had sent Him.

"And now I have told you before it come to pass, that, when it is come to pass, ye might believe" (14:29). "The question naturally occurs, Believe what? That question is answered by referring to the parallel statement in reference to the treachery of Judas: 'Now I tell you, that when it is come to pass, ye might believe that I am' (13:19)—that I am the Messiah, the Divinely appointed, qualified, promised, accredited Saviour: and of course, that *all* that I have taught you is indubitably true; and all I have promised is absolutely certain. The disciples did believe this, but their faith was feeble; it required confirmation. It was to be exposed to severe trials, and needed support: and the declaration by Him of these events before they took place was of all things the best fitted for giving their faith that required confirmation and support" (Dr. John Brown).

"Hereafter I will not talk much with you" (14:30). In a very short time He would be cut off from them, while He undertook His greatest work of all. In reminding them that it would be impossible for Him to say much more to them, He hinted at the deep importance of them pondering over and over what He had just said, and what He was on the point *of saying* to them. This was to be His last address in His humbled state, and during the next few hours they would sorely need the sustaining and comforting power of these precious promises if they were not to faint.

"For the prince of this world cometh, and hath nothing in me" (14:30). The awful enmity of the Serpent was now to be fully vented upon the woman's Seed: he was to be allowed to bruise the Saviour's heel. All that this meant we are incapable of entering into. It would seem that Satan began his assault in the Garden, and ceased not till he had moved Pilate to seal the sepulchre and place a guard about it. The words "and hath nothing in me" refer to His inherent holiness. As the sinless One there was nothing within to which the Devil could appeal. How completely different is it with us! Throw a lighted match into a barrel of gunpowder, and there is a fearful explosion; cast it into a barrel of water and it is quenched!

"For the prince of this world cometh, and hath nothing in me." This too was said for the consolation of the apostles: the Saviour would assure them beforehand that the issue of the approaching conflict was not left in any doubt. There was *no* weak point in Him for Satan to find; therefore He must come forth more than Conqueror. Satan *could* find something in Noah, Abraham, David, Peter, but Christ was the Lamb "*without* blemish."

"But that the world may know that I love the Father; and as the Father gave me commandment, even so I do. Arise, let us go hence" (14:31). Most blessed is this. The last words of this sentence look back to the end of the previous verse. The prince of this world cometh—but, nevertheless, *I* suffer him *to* come against Me, and I go to meet Him. Christ's love to the Father was thus evidenced by His willingness to allow the dragon to lay hold upon Him. He went forth to meet Satan because He had received "commandment" from the Father to do so. It is remarkable that this is the *only* time that Christ ever *spoke* of His love to the Father; it was now that He was to give the supreme proof of it. How this rebukes those who are ever talking and singing of *their* love for the Lord! In the words "Arise, let us go hence," the Lord must have got up from the supper-table, and apparently was followed by His apostles into the outer room, where they remained until they left for Gethsemane, cf. 18:1.

The following questions are to help the student on the first section of John 15: –

1. What is meant by "the true vine," v. 1?
2. In what sense is the Father the husbandman, v. 1?
3. What is meant by "He taketh away," v. 2?
4. What is meant by "purgeth," v. 2?
5. What is meant by "abide in Me," v. 4?
6. What is meant by the last clause of v. 5?
7. Who is in view in v. 6?

CHAPTER FIFTY-ONE

Christ the True Vine

John 15:1-6

The following is an Analysis of the passage which is to be before us: —

1. The vine and the husbandman, v. 1.
2. The fruitless branch cared for, v. 2.
3. The purging of fruitless branches, v. 2.
4. Clean through the Word, v. 3.
5. Conditions of fruit-bearing, v. 4.
6. The absolute dependency of Christians, v. 5.
7. The consequences of severed fellowship, v. 6.

The passage which is to engage our attention is one that is, most probably, familiar to all of our readers. It is read as frequently, perhaps, as any chapter in the New Testament. Yet how far do we really understand its teachings? Why does Christ here liken Himself to a "vine"? What are the leading thoughts suggested by the figure? What does He mean when He says, "Every branch in me that beareth not fruit he taketh away"? What is the "fruit" here referred to? And what is the force of "If a man abide not in me, he is cast forth as a branch and is withered; and men gather them, and cast into the fire, and they are burned"? Now as we approach any portion of Scripture for the purpose of studying it, it is essential to keep in mind several elementary but important principles: *Who* are the persons addressed? In *what* connection are they addressed? What is the *central* topic of address? We are not ready to take up the details of any passage until we have first settled these preparatory questions.

The persons addressed in John 15 were the eleven apostles. It was not to unsaved people, not to a mixed audience that

Christ was speaking; but to believers only. The remote context takes us back to 13:1. In chapters 13 and 14 we are taught what *Christ* is doing for us while He is away—maintaining us in communion with Himself, preparing a place for us, manifesting Himself to us, supplying our every need through the Holy Spirit. In John 15, it is the other side of the truth which is before us. Here we learn what *we* are to be and do for Him during the interval of His absence. In 13 and 14 it is the freeness and fulness of Divine grace; in 15 it is our responsibility to bear fruit.

The immediate context is the closing sentence of chapter 14: "Arise, let us go hence." Christ had just said, "Peace I leave with you, my peace I give unto you." He had said this while seated at the supper-table, where the emblems of His death—the *basis* of our peace—were spread. Now He gets up from the table, which prefigured His resurrection from the dead. Right afterwards He says, "I am the true vine." Christ's symbolic action at the close of 14, views Him on resurrection-ground, and what we have here in 15 is in perfect accord with this. There must be resurrection-life before there can be resurrection-fruit. The central theme then is *not* salvation, how it is to be obtained or the danger of losing it. Instead, the great theme here is fruit-bearing, and the conditions of fertility. The word "fruit" occurs *eight* times in the chapter, and in Scripture eight is the *resurrection*-number. It is associated with *a new beginning*. It is the number of *the new creation*. If these facts be kept in mind, there should be little difficulty in arriving at the general meaning of our passage.

The figure used by our Saviour on this occasion was one with which the apostles must have been quite familiar. Israel had been likened unto a "vine" again and again in the Old Testament. The chief value of the vine lies in its fruit. It really serves no other purpose. The vine is a thing of the earth, and in John 15, it is used to set forth the relation which exists between Christ and His people *while they are on earth*. A vine whose branches bear fruit is a *living* thing, therefore the Saviour here had in view those who had a living connection with Himself. The vine and its branches in John 15 *does not* represent what men term "the visible Church," nor does it embrace the whole sphere of Christian profession, as so many have contended. Only *true* believers are contemplated, those who have passed from death unto *life*. What we have in 15:2 and 6 in nowise conflicts with this statement, as we shall seek to show in the course of our exposition.

The word which occurs most frequently in John 15 is "abide," being found no less than fifteen times in the first ten verses. Now "abiding" always has reference to fellowship, and only those who have been born again are capable of having fellowship with the Father and His Son. The vine and its branches express *oneness*, a common life, shared by all, with the complete dependency of the branches upon the vine, resulting in fruit-bearing. The relationship portrayed is that of which *this world* is the sphere and *this life* the period. It is here and now that we are to glorify the Father by bearing much fruit. Our salvation, our essential oneness with Christ, our standing before God, our heavenly calling, are neither brought into view nor called into question by anything that is said here. It is by *dragging in* these truths that some expositors have created their own difficulties in the passage.

A few words should now be said concerning the place which our present section occupies in this Paschal Discourse of our Lord. In the previous chapter we have seen the apostles troubled at the prospect of their Master's departure. In ministering to their fearful and sorrowing hearts, He had assured them that His cause in this world would not suffer by His going away: He had promised that, ultimately, He would return for them; in the meantime, He would manifest Himself to them, and He and the Father would abide in them. Now He further assures them that their *connection* with Him and their connection with each other, should not be dissolved. The *outward* bond which had united them *was* to be severed; the Shepherd was to be smitten, and the sheep scattered (Zech. 13:7). But there was a deeper, a more intimate bond, between them and Him, and between themselves, a *spiritual* bond, and while this remained, increasing fruitfulness would be the result.

The link of connection between the first two main sections of the discourse, where Christ is first comforting and then instructing and warning His disciples, is found in the closing verses of chapter 14. There He had said, "Hereafter, I will not talk much with you; for the prince of this world cometh, and hath nothing in me. But that the world may know that I love the Father; and as the Father gave me commandment, even so I do." In the light of this, chapter 15 intimates: Let My Father now (when the prince of this world cometh, but only as an instrument in the hands of His government) do with Me as He will. It will only issue in the bringing forth of that which will glorify the Father, if the corn of wheat died it would bring forth "much fruit" (12:24). Fruit was the end in view of the Father's "commandment" and the Son's obedience. Thus the *transition* is natural and logical.

"I am the true vine" (15:1). This word "true" is found in several other designations and descriptions of the Lord Jesus. He is the "*true* Light" (1:9). He is the "*true* bread" (6:32). He is "a minister of the sanctuary, and of the *true* tabernacle" (Heb. 8:2). The usage of this adjective in the verses just quoted help to determine its force. It is not true in opposition to that which is false; but Christ was the perfect, essential, and enduring reality, of which other lights were but faint reflections, and of which other bread and another tabernacle were but the types and shadows. More specifically, Christ was "the *true* light" in contrast from His forerunner, John, who was but a "lamp" (John 5:35 R.V.), or light-bearer. Christ was "the *true* bread" as contrasted from the "manna", which the fathers did eat in the wilderness and died. He was a minister of "the *true* tabernacle" in contrast from the one Moses made, which was "the example and shadow of heavenly things" (Heb. 8:5).

But in addition to these instituted types of the Old Testament, there are types in nature. When our Lord used this figure of the "vine," He did not arbitrarily select it out of the multitude of objects from which an ordinary teacher might have drawn illustrations for his subject. Rather was the vine created and constituted as it is, that it might be a fit representation of Christ and His people bringing forth fruit to God. "There is a double type here, just as we find a double type in the 'bread,' a reference to the manna in the wilderness, and behind that, a reference to bread in general, as the staff of human life. The vine itself is indeed constituted to be an earthly type of a spiritual truth, but we find a previous appropriation of it to that which is itself a type of the perfect reality which the Lord at length presents to us. We refer to the passages in Psalms and prophets where Israel is thus spoken of" (Waymarks in the Wilderness).

In Psalm 80:8-9 we read, "Thou hast brought a *vine* out of Egypt: Thou hast cast out the heathen, and planted it. Thou preparedst room before it, and didst cause it to take deep root, and it filled the land." Again, in Isaiah we are told "Now will I sing to my well-beloved, a song of my beloved touching his *vineyard*. My well-beloved hath a vineyard in a very fruitful hill: And he fenced it, and gathered out the stones thereof, and planted it with the choicest *vine*, and built a tower in the midst of it, and also made a winepress therein: and he looked that it should bring forth grapes and it brought forth wild grapes. . . . For the vineyard of the Lord of hosts is *the house of Israel*, and the men of Judah his pleasant plant" (5:1, 2, 7). These passages in the Old Testament throw further light on the declaration of Christ that *He* was "the *true* vine." Israel, as the type, had proved to be a failure. "I had planted thee a *noble vine*, wholly a right seed: how then art thou turned into the degenerate plant of a *strange vine* unto me?" (Jer. 2:21): "Israel is an empty vine, he bringeth forth fruit unto himself" (Hosea 10:1). In contrast from this failure and degeneracy of the typical people, Christ says "I am the *true* vine"—the antitype which fulfills all the expectations of the Heavenly Husbandman. Many are the thoughts suggested by this figure: to barely mention them must suffice. The beauty of the vine; its exuberant fertility; its dependency—clinging for support to that on which and around which it grows; its spreading branches; its lovely fruit; the juice from which maketh glad the heart of God and man (Judges 9:13; Psa. 104:15), were each perfectly exemplified in the incarnate Son of God.

"And my Father is the husbandman" (15:1). In the Old Testament the Father is represented as the *Proprietor* of the vine, but here He is called the Husbandman, that is the *Cultivator*, the One who cares for it. The figure speaks of His love for

Christ and His people: Christ as the One who was made in the form of a servant and took the place of *dependency*. How jealously did He watch over Him who "grew up before him as *a tender plant*, and as a root out of a dry ground" (Isa. 53:2)! Before His birth, the Father prevented Joseph from putting away his wife (Matt. 1:18-20). Soon after His birth the Father bade Joseph to flee into Egypt, for Herod would seek the young Child to destroy Him (Matt. 2:13). What proofs were these of the Husbandman's *care* for the true Vine!

"And my Father is the husbandman." The Father has the same loving solicitude for "*the branches*" of the vine. Three principal thoughts are suggested. His *protecting care*: His eye is upon and His hand tends to the weakest tendril and tenderest shoot. Then it suggests His *watchfulness*. Nothing escapes His eye. Just as the gardener notices daily the condition of each branch of the vine, watering, training, pruning as occasion arises; so the Divine Husbandman is constantly occupied with the need and welfare of those who are joined to Christ. It also denoted His *faithfulness*. No branch is allowed to run to waste. He spares neither the spray nor the pruning knife. When a branch is fruitless He tends to it; if it is bearing fruit, He purgeth it, that it may bring forth more fruit. "*My Father* is the husbandman." This is very blessed. He does not allot to others the task of caring for the vine and its branches, and this assures us of the widest, most tender, and most faithful care of it. But though this verse has a comforting and assuring voice, it also has a searching one, as has just been pointed out.

"Every branch in me that beareth not fruit he taketh away" (15:2). This has been appealed to by Arminians in proof of their view that it is possible for a true Christian to perish, for they argue that the words "taketh away" signify eternal destruction. But this is manifestly erroneous, for such an interpretation would flatly contradict such explicit and positive declarations as are to be found in John 4:14; 10:28; 18:9; Rom. 5:9-10; 8:35-39, etc. Let us repeat what we said in the opening paragraph: Christ was not here addressing a mixed audience, in which were true believers and those who were merely professors. Nor was He speaking to the twelve—Judas had already gone out! Had Judas been present when Christ spoke these words there might be reason to suppose that He had him in mind. But what the Lord here said was addressed to the eleven, that is, to *believers* only! *This* is the first key to its significance.

Very frequently the true interpretation of a message is discovered by attending to the character of those addressed. A striking example of this is found in Luke 15 – where a case the very opposite of what we have here is in view. There the Lord speaks of the lost sheep and the lost coin being found, and the wayward son coming to the Father. Many have supposed that the Lord was speaking (in a parable) of the restoration of *a backslidden believer*. But the Lord was *not* addressing His disciples and warning them of the danger of getting out of communion with God. Instead He was speaking to His *enemies* (Luke 15:2) who criticised Him because He received *sinners*. Therefore, in what follows He proceeded to describe *how* a sinner is saved, first from the Divine side and then from the human. Here the case is otherwise. The Lord was not speaking to professors, and warning them that God requires truth in the inward parts; but He is talking to genuine believers, instructing, admonishing and warning them.

"Every branch in me that beareth not fruit he taketh away." Many Calvinists have swung to the other extreme, erring in the opposite direction. We greatly fear that their principal aim was to overthrow the reasoning of their theological opponents, rather than to study carefully this verse in the light of its setting. They have argued that Christ was *not* speaking of a real believer at all. They insist that the words "beareth not fruit" described one who is within the "visible Church" but who has not vital union with Christ. But we are quite satisfied that this too is a mistake. The fact is, that we are so accustomed to concentrate everything on our own salvation and so little accustomed to dwell upon *God's glory* in the saved, that there is a lamentable tendency in all of us to apply many of the most pointed rebukes and warnings found in the Scriptures (which are declared to be "profitable for *reproof* and *correction*," as well as "for instruction in righteousness") to those who are *not saved*, thus losing their salutary effects on ourselves.

The words of our Lord leave us no choice in our *application* of this passage—as a whole and in its details—no matter what the conclusions be to which it leads us. Surely none will deny that they are *believers* to whom He says "*Ye* are the branches" (15:5). Very well then; observe that Christ employs the *same* term in this needed word in 15:2: "Every *branch* in me, that beareth not fruit." To make it doubly clear as to whom He was referring, He added, "Every branch *in me* that beareth not fruit." Now if there is one form of expression, which, by *invariable* and unexceptional use, indicates a *believer* more emphatically and explicitly than another, it is this:—"in me," "in him," "in Christ." Never are these expressions used loosely; never are they applied to anv but the children of God: "If *any one* be in Christ (he is) a new creation" (II Cor. 5:17).

"Every branch in me that beareth not fruit he taketh away." If then, it is a real believer who is in view here, and if the "taketh away" does not refer to perishing, then what is the force and meaning of our Lord's words? First of all, notice the tense of the first verb: "Every branch in me not *bearing* fruit he taketh away" is the literal translation. It is not of a branch which *never* bore fruit that the Lord is here speaking, but of one who is *no longer* "bearing fruit." Now there are three things which cause the branches of the natural vine *to become* fruitless: either through running to leaf, or through disease (a blight), or through old age, when they wither and die. The same holds good in the spiritual application. In II Peter 1:8, we read: "For if these things be in you, and *abound*, they make you that ye shall neither be barren nor unfruitful in the knowledge of our Lord Jesus Christ." The unescapable inference from this is that, if the "these things" (mentioned in II Peter 1:5-7) do not abound in us, we *shall be* "barren and unfruitful"—compare Titus 3:14. In such a case we bring forth nothing but leaves—the works of the flesh. Unspeakably solemn is this: one who has been bought at such infinite cost, saved by such wondrous grace, may yet, in this world, fall into a barren and unprofitable state, and thus fail to glorify God.

"*He* taketh away." Who does? The "husbandman," the *Father*. This is conclusive proof that an unregenerate sinner is not in view. "*The Father* judgeth no man, but hath committed *all* judgment unto the Son" (John 5:22). It is *Christ* who will say, "Depart from me" (Matt. 25). It is *Christ* who shall sit upon the Great White Throne to judge the wicked (Rev. 20). Therefore it cannot be a mere professor who is here in view—taken away unto judgment. Again a difficulty has been needlessly created here by the English rendering of the Greek verb. "Airo" is frequently translated in the A.V. "lifted up." For example: "And they lifted up their voices" (Luke 17:13, so also in Acts 4:24). "And Jesus lifted up his eyes" (John 11:41). "Lifted up his hand" (Rev. 10:5), etc. In none of these places could the verb be rendered "taken away." Therefore, we are satisfied that it would be more accurate and more in accord with "the analogy of faith" to translate, "Every branch in me that beareth not fruit he *lifteth up*"—from trailing on the ground. Compare with this Dan. 7:4: "I beheld till the wings thereof were plucked, and it was *lifted* up from the earth, and made to stand upon the feet like a man."

"And every branch that beareth fruit he purgeth it, that it may bring forth more fruit" (15:2). The words "branch in me," though clearly understood, *are not expressed* in the Greek. Literally, it is "And every one that fruit bears," that is, every one of the class of persons mentioned in the previous clause. How this confirms the conclusion that if *believers* are intended in the one case, they must be in the other also! The care and method used by the Husbandman are told out in the words: "He purgeth it." The majority of people imagine that "purgeth" here is the equivalent of "pruning," and understand the reference is to affliction, chastisement, and painful discipline. But the word "purgeth" here does not mean "pruning," it would be better rendered, "cleanseth," as it is in the very next verse. It may strike some of us as rather incongruous to speak of *cleansing* a branch of a vine. It would not be so if we were familiar with the Palestinian vineyards. The reference is to the washing off of the deposits of insects, of moss, and other parasites which infest the plant. Now the "water" which the Husbandman uses in cleansing the branches is *the Word,* as 15:3 tells us. The thought, then, is the removal by the Word of what would obstruct the flow of the life and fatness of the vine through the branches. Let it be clearly understood that this "purging" *is not* to fit the believer for Heaven (that was accomplished, once for all, the first moment that faith rested upon the atoning sacrifice of the Lord Jesus Christ), but is designed to make us more fruitful, while we are here in this world.

"And every branch that beareth fruit, he purgeth it, that it may bring forth more fruit." "It is that action of the Father by which He brings the believer more fully under the operation of the 'quick and powerful' Word. The Word is that by which the believer is born, with that new birth to which no uncleanness attaches (I Peter 1:23). But while by second birth he is 'clean,' and in relation to his former condition is 'cleansed,' he is ever viewed as exposed to defilement, and consequently as needing ***to** be* 'cleansed.' And as the Word was, through the energy of the Spirit, effectual in the complete cleansing, so in regard to defilement by the way and in regard to the husbandman's purging to obtain more fruit, the purging is ever to be traced up to the operation of the Word (Psa. 119:9; II Cor. 7:1). Whatever other means may be employed, and there are many, they must be viewed as subordinate to the action of the 'truth,' or as making room for its purging process. Thus when affliction as a part of the process is brought into view, it is only as a means to the end of the soul's subjection and obedience to the Word. So the Psalmist said, 'Before I was afflicted, I went astray: but now have I kept thy word . . . It is good for me that I have been afflicted; that I might learn thy statutes' (119:67, 71). It will, we think, be apparent, that all means which Divine wisdom employs to bring to real subjection to the Word, must be regarded as belonging to the process of 'purging' that we may bring forth more fruit.

"It would be interesting to pursue our inquiry into the course of our purging but our present limits forbid this. We may just remark that much that may be learned on this point from such passages as those of which, without any extended remark, we cite one or two. Here is one which suggests a loving rebuke of all *impatience* under the operations of the Husbandman's hand: 'For a season *if need be,* ye are in heaviness through manifold trials' (I Peter 1:7). Then we have a text in James, which calls for *joy* under the Father's faithful purging: 'My brethren, count it all joy when ye fall into divers trials; knowing this, that the trying of your faith worketh patience. But let patience have her perfect work, that ye may be perfect and entire, wanting nothing,' (1:2-4). Once more, we take the words of Christian exultation which declare our fellowship with God in the whole process and fruit of our purging: 'And not only so, but we *glory* in tribulations also: knowing that tribulation worketh patience; and patience, experience; and experience, hope. And hope maketh not ashamed; because the love of God is shed abroad in our hearts by the Holy Spirit which is given unto us' (Rom. 5:3-5). O that we might learn from these revelations of the Father's work, upon us and in us, quietly and joyfully to endure; and rightly to interpret all that befalls us, only desiring that He may fulfill in us all the good pleasure of His will, that we may be fruitful in every good work" (Mr. C. Campbell).

"Now (better, 'already') ye are clean through the word which I have spoken unto you," (15:3). The purging or cleansing of the previous verse refers to the believer's *state;* the cleanness here describes his *standing* before God. The one is progressive, the other absolute. The two things are carefully distinguished all through. We *have* purified our souls in obeying the truth through the Spirit (I Peter 1:22), yet we need *to be purifying* ourselves, even as Christ is pure (I John 3:3). We "*are* washed" (I Cor. 6:11), yet there is constant need that He who washed us from our sins at first should daily wash our feet (John 13:10). The Lord, having had occasion to speak here of a purging which is constantly in process, graciously stopped to assure the disciples that they were *already* clean. Note He makes *no* exception—"ye": the branches spoken of in the previous verses. If the Lord had had in mind two entirely different classes in 15:2 (as almost all of the best commentators argue), namely, formal professors in the former part of the verse and genuine believers in the latter, He would necessarily have qualified His statement here. This is the more conclusive if we contrast His words in 13:10: "Ye are clean, but *not all*"! Let the reader refer back to our remarks upon John 13:10 for a fuller treatment of this cleanness.

"Abide in me" (15:4). The force of this cannot be appreciated till faith has laid firm hold of the previous verse: "Already ye *are clean.*" "Brethren in Christ, what a testimony is this: He who speaks what he knows and testifies what He has seen, declares us 'clean every whit.' Yea, and He *thus* testifies in the very same moment as when He asserts that we had need to have our feet washed; in the very same breath in which He reveals our need of cleansing in order to further fruit-bearing. He would thus assure us that the defilement which we contract in our walk as pilgrims, and the impurity which we contract as branches do in nowise, nor in the least degree, affect the absolute spotless purity which is ours in Him.

"Now in all study of the Word this should be a starting-point, the acknowledgement of our real oneness with Christ, and our cleanness in Him by His Word. It may be observed that He cannot 'wash our feet' till we *know* that we are *cleansed* 'every whit'; and we cannot go on to learn of Him what is needful fruit-bearing unless we first drink in the Word, 'Ye are already clean.' We can only receive His further instruction when we have well learned and are holding fast the first lesson of His love —our completeness in Him" (Mr. C. Campbell).

"Clean every whit," Thou saidst it, Lord!
Shall one suspicion lurk?
Thine surely is a faithful Word,
And Thine a finished Work.

"Abide in me," "To be" *in Christ* and "*to abide*" in Him are two different things which must not be confounded. One must first be "*in* him" before he can "abide in him." The former respects a union effected by the creating-power of God, and which can neither be dissolved nor suspended. Believers are never exhorted *to be* "in Christ"—*they are in Him* by new creation (II Cor. 5:17; Eph. 2:10). But Christians are frequently exhorted to *abide* in Christ, because this privilege and experience *may be* interrupted. "To 'abide,' 'continue,' 'dwell,' 'remain' in Christ—by all these terms is this one word translated —has always reference to the maintenance of fellowship with God in Christ. The word 'abide' calls us to vigilance, lest at any time the *experimental* realization of our union with Christ should be interrupted. To abide in Him, then, is to have sustained conscious communion with Him" (Mr. Campbell). To abide in Christ signifies the constant occupation of the heart with Him—a daily active faith in Him which, so to speak, maintains the dependency of the branch upon the vine, and the circulation of life and fatness of the vine in the branch. What we have here is parallel with that other figurative expression used by our Lord in John 6:56: "He that eateth my flesh, and drinketh my blood, dwelleth (*abideth*) in me, and I in him." This is but another way of insisting upon the continuous exercise of faith in a crucified and living Saviour, deriving life and the sustenance of life from Him. As the initial act of believing in Him is described as "coming" to Him, ("He that *cometh* to me shall never hunger; and he that *believeth* on me shall never thirst": 6:35), so the *continued* activity of faith is described as "*abiding* in him."

"Abide in me, and *I in you*" (15:4). The two things are quite distinct, though closely connected. Just as it is one thing to be "*in* Christ," and another to "*abide* in him," so there is a real difference between His being *in us*, and His *abiding* in us. The one is a matter of His grace; the other of our responsibility. The one is perpetual, the other may be interrupted. By our *abiding* in Him is meant the happy conscious fellowship of our union with Him, in the discernment of what He is for us; so by His abiding in us is meant the happy conscious recognition of His presence, the assurance of His goodness, grace and power—*Himself the recourse of our soul* in everything.

"As the branch cannot bear fruit of itself, except it abides in the vine; no more can ye, except ye abide in me" (15:4). "Thus our Lord enforces the necessity of maintaining fellowship. He is not only the source of all fruit, but He also puts forth His power while there is personal appropriation of what He is for us, and in us. And this, if we receive it, will lead us to a right judgment of ourselves and our service. In the eyes of our own brethren, and in our own esteem, we may maintain a goodly appearance as fruitbearing branches. But whatever our own judgment or that of others, unless the *apparent* springs from 'innermost fellowship and communion' the true Vine will never own it as *His* fruit.

"Moreover, all this may, by His blessing, bring us to see *the cause* of our imperfect or sparse fruit bearing. Thousands of Christians are complaining of barrenness; but they fail to trace their barrenness to its right source—the meagerness of their communion with Christ. Consequently, they seek fruitfulness in activities, often right in themselves, but which, while He is unrecognized, can never yield any fruit. In such condition, they ought rather to cry, 'Our leanness! Our leanness'; and they ought to know that leanness can only be remedied by that *abiding* in Christ, and He in them, which 'fills the soul with marrow and its fatness.' 'Those that be planted in the house of the Lord (an Old Testament form for "abiding in Him") shall flourish in the courts of our God. They shall bring forth fruit in old age; they shall be fat and flourishing' (Psa. 92:13, 14). We are surely warranted to say, Take heed to the fellowship, and the fruit *will* spring forth" (Mr. C. Campbell).

"I am the vine, ye are the branches: he that abideth in me, and I in him, the same bringeth forth much fruit" (15:5). This is very blessed, coming in just here. It is a word of assurance. As we contemplate the failure of Israel as God's vine of old, and as we review *our own* past resolutions and attempts, we are discouraged and despondent. This is met by the announcement, "*I am the vine,* ye are the branches." It is not a question of *your* sufficiency; yea, let your insufficiency be admitted, as settled once for all. In your self you are no better than a branch *severed* from the vine—dry, dead. But "he that abideth in me, and I in him, the same bringeth forth much fruit." "No figure could more forcibly express the complete dependence of the believer on Christ for all fruit-bearing than this. A branch cannot bear fruit of itself, except it abide in the vine. In itself it has *no* resources though in union with vine it is provided with life. This is precisely the believer's condition: 'Christ liveth in me.' The branch *bears* the clusters, but it does not *produce* them. It bears what *the vine* produces; and so the result is expressed by the Apostle, 'to me to live *is Christ.*' It is important that in this respect, as well as with reference to righteousness before God, we should be brought to *the end of self* with all its vain efforts and strivings. And then there comes to us the assurance of unfailing resources in Another" ("Waymarks in the Wilderness").

"For without me (better '*severed from* me') ye can do nothing" (15:5). Clearly this refers not to the vital union existing between Christ and the believer, which shall never be broken, either by his own volition or the will of God, through all eternity (Rom. 8:38-39); but to the interruption of fellowship and dependency upon Him, mentioned in the immediate context. This searching word is introduced here to *enforce* our need of heeding what had just been said in the previous verse and repeated at the beginning of this.

"Severed from me ye can do nothing." There are many who believe this in a general way, but who fail to apply it in detail. They know that they cannot do the important things without Christ's aid, but how many of the *little* things we attempt in *our own* strength! No wonder we fail so often. "Without me ye can do *nothing*". "Nothing that is spiritually good; no, not any thing at all, be it little or great, easy or difficult to be performed; cannot think a good thought, speak a good word, or do a good action; can neither begin one, nor when it is begun, perfect it" (Dr. John Gill). But mark it well, the Lord did not say, "Without you *I* can do nothing." In gathering out His elect, and in building up His Church, He employs human instrumentality; but that is not a matter of necessity, but of choice, with Him; *He could* "do" without them, just as well as with them.

"Severed from me ye can do nothing." Urgently do we need this warning. Not only will the allowance of any known sin break our fellowship with Him, but concentration on any thing but *Himself* will also surely do it. Satan is very subtle. If only he can get us occupied with ourselves, our fruit-bearing, or our fruit, his purpose is accomplished. Faith is nothing apart from its *object*, and is no longer in operation when it becomes occupied with itself. Love, too, is in exercise only while it is occupied with its beloved. "There is a disastrous delusion in this matter when, under the plea of witnessing for Christ and relating their experience, men are tempted to parade their own attainments: their love, joy and peace, their zeal in service, their victory in conflict. And Satan has no more effectual method of severing the soul from Christ, and arresting the bringing forth of fruit to the glory of God, than when he can persuade Christians to feast upon their own fruit, instead of eating the flesh and drinking the blood of the Son of man. But shall we not bear witness for Christ? Yes, verily, but let your testimony be *of Him*, not of yourself" ("Waymarks in the Wilderness").

"If a man abide not in me, he is cast forth as a branch, and is withered; and men gather them, and cast into the fire, and they are burned" (15:6). This is another verse which has been much misunderstood, and it is really surprising to discover how many able commentators have entirely missed its meaning. With scarcely an exception, Calvinistic expositors suppose that Christ here referred to a different class from what had been before Him in the three previous verses. Attention is called to the fact that Christ did not say, "If a *branch* abide not in me he is cast forth," but "If a *man* abide not in me." But really this is inexcusable in those who are able, in any measure, to consult the Greek. The word "man" is not found in the original at all! Literally rendered it is, "unless any one abide in me he is cast out as the branch" (Bagster's Interlinear). The simple and obvious meaning of these words of Christ is this: If any one of the *branches,* any believer, continues out of fellowship with Me, he is "cast forth." It could not be said of any one who had *never* "come" to Christ that He does not *abide* in Him. This is made the more apparent by the limitation in this very verse: "he is cast forth *as* a branch." Let it be remembered that the central figure here employed by the Lord has reference to our sojourn *in this world,* and the bringing forth of fruit to the glory of the Father. The "casting forth" is done by the Husbandman, and evidently had in view the stripping of the believer of the gifts and opportunities which he failed to improve. It is similar to the *salt* "losing its savour" (Matt. 5:13). It is parallel with Luke 8:18: "And whosoever hath not, *from him* shall be taken even that which he seemeth to have."* It is analogous to that admonition in II John 8: "Look to yourselves, that we *lose not*

* See our comments on this verse under John 9:17.

those things which we have wrought, but that we receive a full reward."

But what is meant by, "Men gather them, and cast into the fire, and they are burned"? Observe, first, the plural pronouns. It is not "men gather *him* and cast into the fire, and *he* is burned," as it would most certainly have been had an unbeliever, a mere professor, been in view. The change of number here is very striking, and evidences, once more, the minute accuracy of Scripture. "Unless any *one* abide in me, he is cast forth as a branch, and men gather *them* and cast into the fire and *they* are burned." The "them" and the "they" are what *issues from* the one who has been cast forth "*as* a branch." And *what* is it that issues from such a one—what but *dead works*: "wood, hay, stubble"! and what is to become of his "dead works." I Cor. 3:15 tells us: "If any man's work shall be *burned* (the very word used in John 15:6!), he shall suffer loss: but he himself shall be saved; yet so as by *fire*." *Lot* is a pertinent example: he was out of fellowship with the Lord, he ceased to bear fruit to His glory, and his dead works were all burned up in Sodom; yet he himself was saved!

One other detail should be noticed. In the original it is *not* "men gather them," but "*they* gather them." Light is thrown on this by Matt. 13:41, 42: "The Son of man shall send forth his *angels* and *they* shall *gather* out of his kingdom all things that offend, and them which do iniquity: And shall cast them into a furnace of fire: There shall be wailing and gnashing of teeth." Note the two distinct items here: the angels gather "all *things* that *offend*" and "*them* which *do iniquity*." In the light of John 15:6 the first of these actions will be fulfilled at the session of the judgment-seat of Christ (II Cor. 5:10), the second when He returns to the earth.

Here then is a most solemn warning and heart-searching prospect for every Christian. Either your life and my life is, as the result of continuous fellowship with Christ, bringing forth fruit to the glory of the Father, fruit which will remain; or, because of neglect of communion with Him, we are in immense danger of being set aside as His witnesses on earth, to bring forth only that which the fire will consume in a coming Day. May the Holy Spirit apply the words of the Lord Jesus to each conscience and heart.

Studying the following questions will prepare for our next lesson:

1. What is the connection between v. 7 and the context?
2. How is "ye shall ask what ye will" in v. 7 to be qualified?
3. What is meant by "so shall ye be my disciples," v. 8?
4. What is the relation between vv. 9-12 and the subject of fruit-bearing?
5. What constituted Christ's "joy," v. 11?
6. What is suggested by "friends," vv. 13-15?
7. Why does Christ bring in election in v. 16?

Exposition of the Gospel of JOHN

Three Volumes Complete and Unabridged in One

Arthur W. Pink

VOLUME THREE—*John 15:7 to end*

CHAPTER FIFTY-TWO

CHRIST THE TRUE VINE (Concluded)

John 15:7-16

Below is an Analysis of the second section of John 15:—

1. Fellowship and prayer, v. 7.
2. The Father glorified by much fruit, v. 8.
3. Fruit found in love, vv. 9-10.
4. Fruit found in joy, v. 11.
5. Fruit found in peace, v. 12.
6. The proofs of Christ's love, vv. 13-15.
7. The purpose of Christ's choice, v. 16.

That the theme of this second section of John 15 is the same as was before us in its opening portion is clear from vv. 8 and 16: in both of these verses the word "fruit" is found, and as we shall see, all that lies between is intimately connected with them. Before taking up the study of our present passage let us summarize what was before us in our last lesson.

The vine and its branches, unlike the "body" and its head, does not set forth the vital and indissoluble union between Christ and His people—though *that* is manifestly presupposed; instead, it treats of that relationship which exists between Him and them while they are upon earth, a relationship which may be interrupted. The prominent thing is fruit-bearing and the conditions of fertility. Three conditions have already been before us. First, to be a fruit-bearing branch of the vine, one must be *in Christ*. Second, to be a fruit-bearing branch of the vine, the Father must *purge* him by the cleansing action of the Word. Third, to be a fruit-bearing branch of the vine, he must *abide* in Christ. The first two are solely of God's grace: they are Divine actions. But the third is a matter of Christian responsibility, and this is what is enforced throughout John 15.

As pointed out in the introduction to our last chapter, the broad distinction between John 14 and 15 is that in the former we have the *grace* of God unfolded; in the latter Christian *responsibility* is pressed. Further evidence of this will be found in the frequent repetition of two pronouns. In John 14 the emphasis is upon the "me"; in John 15 upon the "ye." In John 14 it is: "believe also in *me*" (v. 1); "no man cometh unto the Father but by *me*" (v. 6); "If ye had known *me*, ye should have known my Father also" (v. 7); "Have I been so long time with you, and yet hast thou not known *me*, Philip?" (v. 9); and so on. Whereas in John 15 it is "*ye* are clean" (v. 3); "Herein is my Father glorified that *ye* bear much fruit" (v. 8); "continue *ye* in my love" (v. 9); "*Ye* are my friends, if" etc. (v. 14). The word "ye" occurs no less than twenty-two times in John 15!

That which is of such deep importance for the Christian is the *third* condition noted above; hence our Lord's repeated emphasis upon it. Mark how in 15:4 the word "abide" occurs no less than three times. Note how the same truth is reiterated in 15:5. Observe how 15:6 is devoted to a solemn statement of the consequences of *failure to* "abide" in Christ. Observe also how this same word "abide" is found again in 15:7, 9, 10, 11, and 16. Just as necessary and imperative as Christ's command "Come unto me" is to the sinner, so absolutely essential is His "Abide in me" to the saint. As then this subject of *abiding in Christ* is of such moment, we will now supplement our previous remarks upon it.

First, to abide in Christ is to continue in the joyful recognition of the value of His perfect sacrifice and the efficacy of His precious blood. There can be *no* fellowship with the Lord Jesus, in the full sense of the word, while we harbor doubts of our personal salvation and acceptance with God. Should some soul troubled on this very point be reading these lines, we would earnestly press upon him or her the fact that the *only* way to be rid of torturing uncertainty is to turn the eye away from self, *unto the Saviour*. Here are His own blessed words: "He that eateth my flesh, and drinketh my blood, dwelleth (*abideth*) in me, and I in him" (John 6:56). That means that I feed upon, am satisfied with, that Sacrifice of sweet savour which has fully satisfied God.

Second, to abide in Christ is to maintain a spirit and an attitude of entire *dependency* on Him. It is the consciousness of my helplessness; it is the realization that "severed from him, I can do nothing." The figure which the Lord here employed strongly emphasizes this. What are the branches of a vine but helpless, creeping, clinging, things? They cannot stand alone; they need to be supported, held up. Now there can be no abiding in Christ while we entertain a spirit of self-sufficiency. To have *no* confidence in the flesh, to renounce our own might, to lean not unto our own understanding, precedes our turning unto Christ: there must be a recognition of my own emptiness before I shall turn to and draw from His fulness. "As the branch *cannot* bear fruit *of itself,* except it abide in the vine; *no more can ye,* except ye abide in me." In itself a branch has absolutely no resources: in union with the vine it is pervaded with life.

Third, to abide in Christ is to *draw from His fulness.* It is not enough that I turn *from* myself in disgust, I must turn *to* Christ with delight. I must *seek* His presence; I must be occupied with His excellency; I must commune with Him. It is no longer a question of my sufficiency, my strength, or my anything. It is solely a matter of *His* sufficiency. The branch is simply a conduit through which flows the fruit-producing juices, which result in the lovely clusters of grapes. Remember that the branch *does not produce,* but simply *bears* them! It is the *vine* which produces, but produces through the branch, by the branch being in the vine. It is not that the believer finds in Christ a place of rest and support, whither he may go in order to produce *his own* fruit. This is the sad mistake made by those who are ever speaking of their own self-complacency, self-glorifying experiences, which shows that *their* souls are occupied with themselves rather than with Christ. It is of the greatest practical importance to know that *Christ* is "all and in all"—not only as our standing before God and our ultimate perfection, but also as to our *present life* to the glory of the Father.

"If ye abide in me, and my words abide in you, ye shall ask what ye will, and it shall be done unto you" (15:7). The connection between this verse and the ones preceding it is as follows. In 15:4 and 5 the Lord had exhorted His disciples to abide in Him. In 15:6 He had warned them what would be the consequences if they did not. Now He turns, or rather returns, to the consolatory and blessed effects which would follow their compliance with his admonition. Three results are here stated. First, the answer to whatever prayers they presented to God; the glorification of the Father; the clear witness to themselves and to others that *they were* His disciples. Thus would Christ most graciously encourage us.

"If ye abide in me, and my words abide in you, ye shall ask what ye will, and it shall be done unto you." What erroneous conclusions have been drawn from these words! How often they have been appealed to in order to justify the most unworthy views of prayer! The popular interpretation of them is that if the Christian will only work himself up to an importunate pleading of this promise before the throne of grace, he may then ask God for what he pleases, and the Almighty will not—some go so far as to say He *cannot*—deny him. We are told that Christ has here given us a blank check, signed it, and left us to fill it in for what *we* will. But I John 5:14 plainly repudiates such a carnal conception—"And this is the confidence that we have in him, that, *if* we ask any thing *according to his will,* he heareth us." Therefore, what we ask shall not be done unto us unless *our* will is subordinated to and is in accord with the will of *God.*

What then is the meaning of our Lord's promise? Certainly it does not give praying souls *carte blanche.* For God to gratify us in everything we requested, would not only be dishonouring to Himself, but, ofttimes, highly injurious to ourselves. Moreover, the experience of many of those who frequent the throne of grace dissipates such a delusion. All of us *have* asked for many things which have not been "done unto" us. Some have asked in great earnestness, with full expectation, and they have been very importunate; and yet their petitions have been denied them. Does this falsify our Lord's promise? A thousand times no! Every word *He* uttered was God's infallible truth. What then? Shall we fall back upon the hope that *God's time* to answer has not yet come; but that shortly He *will* give us the desire of our hearts? Such a hope may be realized, or it may not. It all depends upon whether the *conditions* governing the promise in John 15:7 are being met. If they are not, it will be said of us "Ye ask, and have not, because *ye ask amiss*" (James 4:3).

Two conditions here qualify the promise: "*If* ye abide in me." *Abiding* in Christ signifies the *maintaining* of heart communion with Christ. "*And* my words abide in you": not only must the heart be occupied with Christ, but the life must be regulated by the Scriptures. Note it is not here "my word," but "my words." It is not the Word as a whole, but the Word, as it were, broken up. It is the precepts and promises of Scripture personally appropriated, fed upon by faith, hidden in the heart. It is the practical heeding of that injunction, "Man shall not *live* (his daily life) by bread alone, but by every word that proceedeth out of the mouth of God." And mark that it is Christ's words *abiding* in us. It is no fitful, spasmodic, occasional exercise and experience, but constant and habitual communion with God through the Word, until its contents become the substance of our innermost beings.

"Ye shall ask what ye will." But for what *would* such a one ask? If he continues in fellowship with *Christ*, if *His* "words" remain in him, then his *thoughts* will be *regulated* and his *desires formed* by that Word. Such an one will be raised above the lusts of the flesh. Such an one will "bring into captivity every thought to the obedience of Christ" (II Cor. 10:5), proving "what is that good, and acceptable, and perfect will of God" (Rom. 12:2). Consequently, such an one will ask *only* for that *which is* "according to *his* will" (I John 5:14); and *thereby* will he verify the Lord's promise "it *shall* be done unto you."

Such a view of prayer is glorifying to God and satisfying to the soul. For one who communes with the Saviour, and in whom His Word dwells "richly," supplication is simply the pulsation of a heart that has been won to God. While the believer is in fellowship with the Lord and is governed from within by His Word, he will *not* ask for things "amiss." Instead of praying in the energy of the flesh (which, alas, all of us so often do), he will pray "in the Spirit" (Jude 20). "Why is there so little power of prayer like this in our own times? Simply because there is so little close communion with Christ, and so little strict conformity to His words. Men do not 'abide in Christ,' and therefore pray in vain. Christ's words do not abide in them, as their standard of practice, and therefore their prayers are not answered. Let this lesson sink down into our hearts. He that would have answers to his prayers, must carefully remember Christ's directions. We must keep up intimate friendship with the great advocate in Heaven, if our petitions are to be granted" (Bishop Ryle).

"Herein is my Father glorified, that ye bear much fruit" (15:8). This is an appeal to our hearts. The "glory" of the Father was that which Christ ever kept before Him, and here He presses it upon us. He would have us concerned as to whether our lives honour and magnify the Father, or whether they are a reproach to Him. An unfruitful branch is a *dishonour* to God. What an inducement is this to "abide in Christ"!

It is time that we now inquire as to the *nature* or *character* of the "fruit" of which Christ here speaks. *What is* the "fruit," the much fruit, by which the Father is glorified? Fruit is not something which is attached to the branch and fastened on from without, but is the organic product and evidence of the inner life. Too often attention is directed to the *outward* services and actions, or to the *results* of these services, as the "fruit" here intended. We do not deny that this fruit *is* frequently manifested externally, and that it also finds expression *in* outward works is clear from 15:6: "Severed from me ye can *do* nothing." But there is a twofold evil in *confining* our attention to these. First, it often becomes a *source of deception* in those who may do many things in the will and energy of the flesh, but these are dead works, often found on corrupt trees. Second, it becomes a *source of discouragement* to children of God who, by reason of sickness, old age, or unfavourable circumstances, cannot engage in such activities, and hence are made to believe that *they* are barren and useless.

"We may say, in brief, that the fruit borne by the branches is precisely that which is produced by the Vine; and what *that* is, may be best understood by looking at what *He* was as God's witness in the world. The fruit is *Christlike* affections, dispositions, graces, as well as the works in which they are displayed. We cannot undervalue the work of faith and labour of love; but we would remember that 'the fruit of the Spirit is love, joy, peace, longsuffering, gentleness, goodness, faith, meekness, temperance'; and those who are prevented from engaging in the activities of Christian service, may often be in circumstances most favourable to the production of the fruit of the Spirit" ("Waymarks in the Wilderness").

It is deeply important for us to recognize that the "fruit" is the outflow of our union with Christ; only thus will it be traced to its true origin and source. Then will it be seen that our fruit is produced not merely by Christ's power acting upon us, but, as it truly is, as the fruit of the vine. Thus, in every branch, is *His* word literally verified: "From *me* is thy fruit found" (Hosea 14:8), and therefore should every branch say, "Not I, but the grace of God." This is all one as to say that *our* fruit is *Christ's* fruit; for God's operations of grace are only wrought in and by Christ Jesus. Thus saints are "filled with the fruits of righteousness which are *by Jesus Christ* to the praise and glory of God" (Phil. 1:11). If there be any love, it is "the *love of Christ*" (II Cor. 5:14); if there be any joy, it is *Christ's* joy (John 15:11); if there be any peace, it is *His* peace, given unto us (John 14:27); if there be any meekness and gentleness it is "the meekness and gentleness of *Christ*" (II Cor. 10:1). How thoroughly this was realized by the apostle, to whom it was given to be the most signal example of the vine sending forth fruit by His branches, may be gathered from such expressions: "I will not dare to speak of any of those things which *Christ* hath not wrought by me" (Rom. 15:18). "*Christ* speaking in me" (II Cor. 13:3); "*He* that wrought effectually *in* Peter . . . was mighty *in* me" (Gal. 2:8); "*Christ* liveth in me" (Gal. 2:20): "I can do all things through *Christ* who strengtheneth me" (Phil. 4:13). Thus, and thus only as this is recognized, all dependency upon and all glorying in self is excluded, and Christ becomes all in all.

"Herein is my Father glorified, that ye bear much fruit" (15:8). There are four relationships which need to be distinguished. Life *in* Christ is salvation. Life *with* Christ is fellowship. Life *by* Christ is fruit-bearing. Life *for* Christ is service. The "fruit" is Christ manifested through us. But note the gradation: in 15:2 it is first "fruit," then "*more* fruit," here "*much* fruit." This reminds us of the "some thirty-fold, some sixty, and some an hundred" (Mark 4:20).

"So shall ye be my disciples" (15:8). With this should be compared 8:31: "*If ye continue* in my Word, then are ye my disciples *indeed*." Continuance in the Word is not a *condition* of discipleship, but an *evidence* of it. So here, to bear much fruit will make it *manifest* that we *are* His disciples. Just as good fruit on a tree does not *make* the tree a good one, but marks it out as such, so we prove ourselves to be Christ's disciples by displaying Christlike qualities.

"As the Father hath loved me, so I have loved you" (15:9). There is no change of theme, only another aspect of it. In the two previous verses the Lord had described three of the *consequences* of abiding in Him in order to fruitfulness; here, and in the three verses that follow, He names three of the *varieties* of the fruit borne; and it is very striking to note that they are identical with the first three and are given in the same order as those enumerated in Gal. 5:22, where the "fruit of the Spirit" is defined. Here in 15:9, it is *love;* in 15:11, it is *joy;* while in 15:12 it is *peace*—the happy issue of brethren loving one another.

"As the Father hath loved me, so have I loved you." "As the Father loved Him from everlasting, so did He love them; as His Father loved Him with a love of complacency and delight, so did He love them; as the Father loved Him with a special and peculiar affection, with an unchanging, invariable, constant love, which would last forever, in like manner does Christ love His people; and with this He enforces the exhortation which follows" (Dr. John Gill).

"As the Father hath loved me, so have I loved you; continue ye in my love." (15:9). Christ's love to us is unaffected by our changeableness, but our *enjoyment* of His love depends upon our *continuance* in it. By this continuance in His love, or abiding in it, as it should be (the Greek word is the same), is meant our actual assurance of it, our reposing in it. No matter how mysterious His dispensations be, no matter how severe the trials through which He causes us to pass, we must never doubt His immeasurable love for us and to us. The *measure* of His love for us was told out at the Cross, and as He is *the same* to-day as yesterday, therefore He loves us just as dearly now, every moment, as when He laid down His life for us. To "abide" in His love, then, is to be occupied with it, to count upon it, to be persuaded that nothing shall ever be able to separate us from it. Dwelling upon *our* poor, fluctuating love for Him, will make us miserable; but having the heart fixed upon *His* wondrous love, that love which "passeth knowledge," will fill us with praise and thanksgiving. Very blessed but very searching is this. To "abide" in Christ is to abide in His love. Our growth proceeds from love to love.

"If ye keep my commandments, ye shall abide in my love." (15:10). Even still more searching is this. There can be no fruit for the Father, no abiding in Christ's love, unless there be real subjection of will. It is only in the path of obedience that He will have fellowship with us. Alas, how many err on this point. We are living in an age wherein lawlessness abounds. Insubordination is rife on every hand. In many a place even professing Christians will no longer tolerate the word "commandments." Those who would urge the duty of obedience to the Lord, are regarded as enemies of the faith, seeking to bring Christians into bondage. Satan is very subtle, but we are not ignorant of his devices. He seeks to persuade sinners that they *must* keep God's commandments in order to be saved. He tries to make saints believe that they *must not* keep God's commandment, otherwise they will be putting themselves "under law," beneath a yoke grievous to be borne. But let these specious lies of the Devil be tested by Scripture, and their falsity will soon appear. I Cor. 9:21 tells us that *we are* "under the law to Christ." Romans 13:10 assures us that "love is the fulfilling of the law": the *fulfilling* mark, not the abrogating of it, nor a substitution for it. The apostle Paul declared that he "*de-*

lighted in the law of God after the inward man," and that he "*served* the law of God" (Rom. 7:22-25). And here in John 15 the Lord Himself said to His disciples, "If ye *keep my commandments,* ye shall abide in my love." O fellow Christians, let no sophistry of man (no matter how able a Bible teacher you may deem him), and no deceptive art of Satan, rob you of this word of the Saviour's; a word which we all need, never more than now, when all authority, Divine and human, is more and more flouted. Note that this was not the only time that Christ made mention of His commandments and *pressed* upon His people their obligations to keep them. See John 13:34; 14:15; 15:10; Matt. 28:20, etc.

"Even as I have kept my Father's commandments, and abide in his love" (15:10). Here is the final word against those who decry godly obedience as "legalism." The incarnate Son walked according to His Father's commandments. He "pleased not himself" (Rom. 15:3). *His* meat was to do the will of the One who had sent Him. And He has left us an example that we should follow His steps. "He that saith he abideth in him ought himself also so to walk even as he walked" (I John 2:6). The one who disregards God's "commandments" *is not* walking as Christ walked; instead, he is walking as the world walks. Let no one heed the idle quibble that the "commandments" of *Christ* are opposed to or even different from the commandments of *the Father*. Christ and the Father are *one*—one in nature, one in character, one in authority. "The commandments of Christ include the whole of the preceptive part of the inspired volume, with the exception of those ritual and political statutes which refer to the introductory dispensations which have passed away" (Dr. John Brown). And let it be said again, that no Christian can abide in Christ's love unless he is *keeping* Christ's commandments!

"Even as I have kept my Father's commandments, and abide in his love." The "even as" refers to the *character* of Christ's obedience to the Father. "His obedience was the obedience of *love,* and so must ours be. His obedience was but the expression of His love. External obedience to Christ's commandments, if not the expression of *love,* is, in His estimation, of less than no value, for He sees it to be what it is—vile hypocrisy or mere selfishness. No man will continue in His love by such obedience. His obedience was, in consequence of its being the result of love, *cheerful* obedience. He delighted to do the will of His Father. It was His meat to do the Father's will, and so must be *our* obedience to Him. We must run in the way of His commandments with enlarged hearts. We are to keep them, not so much because we *must* keep them as because we choose to keep them, or, if a necessity is felt to be laid upon us, it should be the sweet necessity resulting from perfect approbation of the law, and supreme love to the Law-giver. Christ's obedience to the Father was *universal* – it extended to every requisition of the law. There was no omission, no violation; and in our obedience to the Saviour, there must be no reserves – we must count His commandments to be in all things, what they are – right; and we must abhor every wicked way. Christ's obedience to the Father was *persevering*. He was faithful unto death; and so must *we* be. This is His promise: 'To him that overcometh will I give to sit with me on my throne, even as I have overcome, and am set down with my Father on his throne' (Rev. 3:21). It is thus, then – only thus – by keeping the commandments of our Lord as He kept the commandments of His Father, that we shall continue in His love, as He continued in His Father's love" (Dr. John Brown).

"These things have I spoken unto you, that my joy might remain in you" (15:11). The "these things" covers the whole of the ten preceding verses. The fruit of the Spirit (Gal. 5:22) is "love, joy, peace." Having mentioned love in the previous verse, Christ now goes on to speak of joy. Just as in 14:27 there is a double "peace," so here there is a twofold joy. First, there is the joy of Christ Himself, that joy which had been His during His sojourn on earth. He mentions this in His prayer in John 17: "These things I speak in the world, that they might have *my joy* fulfilled in themselves" (v. 13). How this reveals to us the inner life of the Saviour! Abiding in His Father's love, He had a joy which certainly not His enemies and perhaps His friends would have credited the "Man of sorrows." His joy was in pleasing the Father, in doing His will and glorifying His name. Then, too, He rejoiced in the prospect before Him: "Looking unto Jesus the author and finisher of faith; who for *the joy* that was *set before him* endured the cross" (Heb. 12:2). This double joy of the incarnate Son, is mentioned in Psalm 16, where the Spirit of prophecy recorded the Saviour's words long beforehand: "I have set the Lord always before me: because he is at my right hand, I shall not be moved. Therefore my heart is *glad,* and my glory *rejoiceth*" (vv. 8, 9). This was the joy of communion and obedience. "Thou wilt show me the path of life: in thy presence is fulness of joy; at thy right hand there are pleasures forevermore" (v. 11): this was the joy "set before him."

"These things have I spoken unto you, that my joy might remain in you." The "these things" refers, more specifically, to the maintaining of communion with Christ, and the conditions upon which they may be realized. When fellowship with the Lord Jesus is broken, joy disappears. This was illustrated in the experience of the Psalmist. David had sinned; sinned grievously against the Lord, and in consequence, he no longer enjoyed a comforting sense of His presence. David was wretched in soul, and after making earnest confession of his sin, he cried, "Restore unto me *the joy* of thy salvation" (51:12): salvation he had not lost, but the joy of it he had. It was the same with Peter: he "went out and *wept bitterly*" (Luke 22:62). A child of God can only be miserable when he is away from Christ. It is important for us to recognize and realize that we need Christ just as much for *our everyday life,* as we do for eternity; just as really for the fruit which the Father expects from us, as for our title to Heaven.

"And that your joy might be full" (15:11). The grounds of the Christian's joy are not in himself, but in Christ: "Rejoice in the Lord" (Phil. 4:4). But the measure in which we enter into this is determined by our daily communion with the Lord. "Our fellowship is with the Father, and with his Son Jesus Christ, *and* these things write we unto you that your *joy* may be full" (I John 1:3, 4). Our joy ought to be steady and constant, not fitful and occasional: "Rejoice in the Lord *alway*: and again I say, Rejoice" (Phil. 4:4). Joy is not "happiness" as the world uses the term; it is much deeper. The worldling finds his happiness in circumstances and surroundings; but the Christian is quite independent of these. Paul and Silas, in the Philippian dungeon, with backs bleeding, "sang praises unto God" (Acts 16:25). What a blessed triumphing *over* circumstances was that! Prison-walls could not cut them off *from Christ!* But how this puts us to shame! The reason why we are so often dull and despondent, the cause of our restlessness and discontent, is because we walk so little in the light of the Lord's countenance. May we earnestly seek grace to heed the things which He has "spoken unto us" that our joy *may be* "full."

"This is my commandment, That ye love one another, as I have loved you" (15:12). "Love is benignant affection, and the appropriate display of it. In this most general meaning of the term, 'love is the fulfilling of the law.' The exercise of this principle in supremacy, in a well-informed intelligent being, secures the performance of all duty. It cannot co-exist with selfishness and malignity, the great causes of sin. In the degree it prevails, they are destroyed. 'Love does'—love can do—'no evil' (Rom. 13:10). Love does—love must do—all practical good. If evil is done—if good is not done—it is just because love is not there in sufficient force" (Dr. John Brown).

It is important that we distinguish between love and benevolence. The benevolence of Christ knows no limits to any of His people. Just as the Father maketh His sun to rise on the evil and on the good, and sendeth the rain on the just and on the unjust, so Christ ever ministers to and supplies the every need of each of His people, whether they are abiding in Him or no. But just as He *abides* only in the one who is abiding in Him, just as he finds complacency only in him who keeps His commandments (14:21), so the Christian is to regulate his actions and *manifest* his love. "As a Christian I am to cherish and exercise love toward every one who gives evidence that he is a brother in Christ. It is only in *this* character that he has any claim upon my brotherly affection, and the degree not of my good will, for that should in every case be boundless; yet my esteem of, and complacency in a Christian brother, should be proportioned to the *manifestation* which he makes of the various excellencies of the Christian character. The better he is, and shows himself to be, I should love him the better. *My* love should be regulated on the same principle as Christ's, whose *benevolence* knows *no limit* in reference to any of His people, but whose *esteem* and *complacency* are always *proportioned to* holy principles and conduct on the part of His people" (Dr. John Brown).

"Greater love hath no man than this, that a man lay down his life for his friends" (15:13). It is to be observed that these words follow right on after Christ saying, "love one another *as I have loved you*." In view of this, we believe that 15:13 to 16 set forth a number of proofs of Christ's love, each of which manifested some distinctive feature of it, and that these are here advanced in order to teach us *how* we should love one another. The Lord places first the *highest* evidence of His love: *He* laid down His life for His people. It is to be observed that in the Greek the word "man" is not found in this verse. Literally rendered it reads, "Greater than this love no one has, that one his life lay down for friends his." Christ emphasizes once more the great fact that His death, imminent at the time He spoke, was purely *voluntary*. He "laid down" His life; none took His life from Him. This life was laid down for His friends, and in thus dying on their behalf, in their stead, He furnished the supreme demonstration of His love to and for them. Romans 5:6-10 emphasizes the same truth, only from a different standpoint. There, the objects of Christ's atoning sacrifice are described as Divine *justice* saw them, they are viewed as they were *in themselves*, by nature and practice—ungodly, sinners, enemies. But here in John 15 the Saviour speaks of them in the terms of Divine *love*, and as they were by election and regeneration—His "friends."

"Greater love hath no man than this, that a man lay down his life for his friends." Now in this verse the Lord not only speaks of His own unselfish, sacrificial, illimitable love, but He does so for the express purpose of supplying both a motive and an example for us. He has given us a commandment that we "love one another," and that we love our brethren as *He* loved them.

There is to be no limitation in our love: if occasion requires it we are to be ready to lay down our life one for another. The same truth is found in John's first Epistle: "Hereby perceive we the love of God, because he laid down his life for us; and we ought to lay down our lives for the brethren" (3:16). "Herein is love, not that we loved God, but that he loved us, and sent his Son to be the propitiation for our sins. Beloved, if God so loved us, we ought also to love one another." How these scriptures rebuke us! What is it worth if we hold the theory that we *are* ready, in obedience to God's Word, to lay down our lives for our brethren, when we fail so sadly in ministering to the common and daily needs and sufferings of God's children? "My little children, let us not love in word, neither in tongue; but in *deed* and in *truth*" (I John 3:18)!

"Ye are my friends, if ye do whatsoever I command you" (15:14). Here is the second proof of Christ's love for His own. He had treated them with unreserved intimacy. He had brought them into close fellowship with Himself. He had dealt with them not as strangers, nor had He acted as men do toward casual acquaintances. Instead, He had, in infinite condescension, given them the unspeakable privilege of being His friends. And such they would continue, so long as they did whatsoever He had commanded them, for the Lord will not be on intimate terms with any who are out of the path of obedience. This was something far higher than the attitude which the Rabbis maintained toward their disciples, and higher still than the feeling which a master entertained for his servants. The Lord of glory deigned to treat his disciples and servants as *friends!*

"Ye are my friends, if ye do whatsoever I command you." It is to be carefully noted that Christ did not here say, "*I* am your friend!" "Just now there is a great deal in the more popular hymnbooks about Jesus as *our* friend. How few seem to appreciate the desire of our Lord to make us *His* friends! The difference is very real. When a man who has attained the highest position in the nation notices a man of the laboring class and calls him his friend, it is a condescension, for he hereby exalts that unknown man to his own level. But for the insignificant man to say of the famous one, 'He's my friend,' by no means exalts that one; indeed, it might be considered a presumption, a piece of impudence. This familiarity, this calling Jesus *our Friend*, is dimming in people's hearts the consciousness that He is something more than that: He is our Saviour! He is our

Lord! He is really, in His own essential nature, our God" (Mr. C. H. Bright). The same rebuke is called for by those who term the incarnate Son of God their elder Brother! It is true that He, in marvellous grace, is "not ashamed to call *us* brethren," but it ill requites that grace for us to term Him *our* "Elder Brother." Let us ever remember His own word "Ye call me *Master* and *Lord*: and ye say *well*; for so I am" (13:13).

"Henceforth I call you not servants: for the servant knoweth not what his Lord doeth: but I have called you friends: for all things that I have heard of my Father I have made known unto you" (15:15). Here is the third proof of the love of Christ for His own. He not only *treated* the disciples as friends, but He *owned* them as such, and took them fully into His confidence. Our thoughts at once revert to Abraham, who is expressly called "the *friend* of God" (James 2:23). The reference no doubt is to what we read of in Gen. 18:17. God was about to destroy Sodom. Lot knew nothing of this, for he was at too great a moral distance from God. But the Lord said, "Shall I hide from Abraham that thing which I do?" In Abraham God found delight, and therefore did He make him the confidant of His counsels. It is striking that Abraham is the *only* Old Testament saint directly termed the *friend* of God (see Isa. 41:8). But Abraham is "the father of all them that believe," and here the Lord calls his believing children His "friends." The term speaks both of confidence and intimacy—not our confidence in and intimacy with Him, but He in and with us. He would no longer call them "servants," though they were such; but He makes them His companions. He reveals to them the Father's thoughts, bringing them into that holy nearness and freedom which He had with the Father. What a place to put them into! If they were not fit to receive these intimacies, He would be betraying the confidence of the Father! It is the *new nature* which gives us the needed fitness.

"I have called you friends." This is not to be restricted to the Eleven, but applies equally to all His blood-bought people. The King of kings and Lord of lords not only pities and saves all them that believe in Him, but actually calls them His *friends!* In view of such language, we need not wonder that the apostle said, "The love of Christ passeth knowledge." What *encouragement* this should give us to pour out our hearts to Him in prayer! Why should we hesitate to unbosom ourselves to One who calls us His "friends"! What *comfort* this should give us in trouble. Will He not minister of His own mercy and grace to His "friends"! And what *assurance* is here for the one who doubts the final issue. Weak and unworthy, we all are in ourselves, but Christ will never forsake His "friends"!

"For all things that I have heard of my Father I have made known unto you" (15:15). The "all things" here were those which pertained to His Mediatorship. Mark 4 supplies us with a striking illustration of how the Lord made His disciples His special confidants: "And he said unto them, *Unto you* it is given to know the mystery of the kingdom of God: but unto them that are without, all these things are done in parables. . . . Without a parable spake he not unto them (the multitudes): and when they were alone, he expounded all things *to his disciples*" (vv. 11, 34). And again in the Gospel records we find the Saviour distinguishing His disciples by similar marks of His love. To them only did He confide His approaching betrayal into the hands of wicked men. To them only did He declare that His place in the Father's House should be theirs. To them only did He announce the coming of the Comforter.

In like manner Christ has revealed many things to us in His Word which the wise of this world know nothing about. "For yourselves know perfectly that the day of the Lord so cometh as a thief in the night. For when they shall say Peace and safety: then sudden destruction cometh upon them as travail upon a woman with child; and they shall not escape. But *ye*, brethren, *are not in darkness*, that that day should overtake you as a thief" (I Thess. 5:2-4). How highly we should value such confidences. How much *would* He reveal to us, now hidden, if only we gave more diligent heed to His commandments! Ever remember that "the secret of the Lord is with *them that fear him*"! Ere passing to the next verse let it be pointed out again that the Lord was not only here referring to the evidences of *His own* love for us, but was also making known how our love should be manifested one toward another. "He that hath friends will *show himself friendly*" (Prov. 18:24). Then let us abstain from encroaching on a brother's spiritual liberty; let us not usurp dominion over a brother's faith; let us treat our brother not as a servant, still less as a stranger, but as a *friend!*

"Ye have not chosen me, but I have chosen you, and ordained you, that ye should go and bring forth fruit, and that your fruit should remain; that whatsoever ye shall ask of the Father in my name, he may give it you" (15:16). "This love was at the *foundation* of all for them: and to it they owed, and we owe, that choice was on His side, not ours. 'Ye have not chosen me,' He says, 'but I have chosen you.' Thus in conscious weakness the power of God is with us: and as He sought us when lost, when there was nothing but our misery to awaken His compassion—so we may count assuredly upon Him, whatever our helplessness, to perfect the work He has begun. What comfort lies for us in the royal work, 'I have chosen you'!

"But grace enables us to fulfill the conditions necessarily imposed by the holiness of the Divine nature, and cannot set these aside: therefore the closing words. They are in the same line with others that we have lately heard: which they emphasize only in a somewhat different way. Fruit that *abides* is that which alone satisfies God. How much that looks well has not that quality in it which ensures permanence. How much that seems truly of God reveals its character by its decay! This 'abiding' connects itself, in the Gospel of John, with the Divine side of things which is seen all through" (Numerical Bible).

The following questions are to help the student prepare for our next lesson:

1. What is the link between vv. 17 to 27 with the context?
2. What is our Lord's central design in this passage?
3. Wherein is the depravity of man exhibited?
4. Why does Christ repeat v. 12 in v. 17?
5. What is the meaning of v. 19?
6. What is the force of "had not had sin," vv. 22, 24?
7. Of what does the testimony of vv. 26, 27 consist?

CHAPTER FIFTY-THREE

Christ Fortifying His Disciples

John 15:17-27

The following is an Analysis of the closing section of John 15: —

1. Christians commanded to love one another, v. 17.
2. Christians warned of the world's hatred, v. 18.
3. Causes of the world's hatred, vv. 19-21.
4. The greatness of the world's guilt, vv. 22-24.
5. The fulfilment of God's Word, v. 25.
6. The witness of the Spirit, v. 26.
7. The witness of Christians, v. 27.

The principal subject in the passage which is to be before us is the world's hostility against Christ and His people. Its *hatred* is mentioned seven times—solemn witness to its awful entirety and inveteracy. The transition from the preceding section is quite natural and easy. The Lord had been speaking to and of *"his own;"* now He contemplates *"the world."* He had just declared that His disciples are His *friends;* now He turns to describe His and their *enemies.* He had set before the apostles the proofs of His *love* for them; now He warns them of the world's *hatred.* The connection between the last verse of the previous section and the opening one of our present portion is most significant. "These things I command you, that ye love one another." Various *motives* had been presented for them loving one another, chief among them being the example of His own wondrous love. Now an entirely new and different reason is advanced: Christians need to be united together by the bonds of brotherly affection *because* the world, their common enemy, hated them.

A loving heart would feign discover or induce love everywhere. To be ungratified in that desire and more than that, to be hated, is a hard and bitter lot, the bitterest ingredient in all affliction. Therefore does the Lord here faithfully prepare His disciples for such an experience, that they might not marvel at the world's hostility nor be stumbled by it—"Marvel not, my brethren, if the world hate you" (I John 3:13). Graciously did the Saviour proceed to fortify His disciples against the storm of persecution which He knew full well would burst upon them shortly after His departure. Charged with such a mission, proclaiming such a message, invested with miraculous powers of benevolence, the apostles might fondly imagine that the world would soon be won to Christ. But they must be prepared for disappointment. Therefore, did Christ arm them beforehand, that their spirits might not be overwhelmed by the bitter malice and opposition which they would surely encounter.

There is little or nothing in the Gospel records to intimate that the apostles had been subjected to persecution while their Master was with them. After the seventy were sent forth, we read that they "returned again with joy, saying, Lord, even the demons are subject unto us through thy name" (Luke 10:17). When the scribes and Pharisees were offended because the disciples transgressed the tradition of the elders, eating with unwashen hands, instead of assailing them directly, the complaint was laid before the Lord Jesus (Matt. 15:2). When the Saviour was arrested in the Garden, He said to the officers, "Let these (the apostles) go their way" (John 18:8). Even after His crucifixion, they were allowed to go, unmolested, back to their fishing (John 21:23). But after His return to the Father, they too would experience the world's malignity. Therefore did the Lord forewarn them of the treatment which they must expect and would certainly receive at the hands of the ungodly.

The warning which the Lord Jesus here gave the apostles is much needed by young believers to-day. The inexperienced Christian supposes that the hatred of the world against him is a reproach. He thinks that he is to blame for it. He imagines that if only he were kinder, more gentle, more humble, more Christlike, the enmity of unbelievers would be overcome. This is a great mistake. The truth is, the more Christlike we are the more shall we be antagonized and shunned. The most conclusive proof of this is found in the treatment which our blessed Saviour received when He was in the world. *He* was "despised and rejected of men." If then the purest love which was ever manifested on earth, if goodness incarnate was hated by men in general, if the brighter His love shone, the fiercer was the enmity which it met with in response, then how can *we* expect to be admired and esteemed by the world? Surely none will entertain the horrible thought that any of us can surpass the prudence of the Son of God!

And how all of this rebukes the *popularity* which so many professing Christians, yea, and many of the professed servants of the Christ now enjoy! Have we forgotten that severe rebuke, "Ye adulterers and adulteresses, know ye not that the *friendship* of the world is enmity with God? Whosoever therefore will be a *friend* of the world is the *enemy* of God" (James 4:4)! Solemn indeed are the terms used here. Adulterers and adulteresses are they who seek and enjoy *illicit* love. In like manner, for a professing Christian – one who claims to love Christ – to seek his delight in the world, to company with the ungodly, is to be guilty of *spiritual adultery*. "*Love not* the world, neither the things that are in the world. If any man love the world, the love of the Father is not in him" (I John 2:15). "*Be not conformed* to this world: but be ye transformed by the renewing of your mind" (Rom. 12:2).

"These things I command you, that ye love one another" (15:17). There is something peculiarly searching and heart-rebuking in this. How humbling to find that Christ had to *command* us to love one another! How humbling to hear Him *repeating* this command, for He has already given this same commandment to His disciples in 13:34! And how humbling to find Him here repeating it *again*, for He had only just said, "This is my commandment, That ye love one another, as I have loved you" (15:12)! Was it because He foreknew *how little* Christian love *would* be exercised among His people? Was it because He knew how much there is in each of us that is so *unlovely?* Was it because He foresaw that the Devil would stir up bitterness and strife among His followers, seeking to make them bite and devour one another? Whatever may or may not have been before Him, one thing cannot be denied—Christ has expressly commanded His people to love one another.

"These things I command you, that ye love one another." Not only does the insistent emphasis of our Lord upon this world indicate that here is something which every Christian needs to take seriously to heart, but the large place given to it in the Epistles adds strong confirmation. The following commandments of the Holy Spirit through the apostles are but repetitions and expansions of the precept now before us: "Be kindly affectioned one to another" (Rom. 12:10). "Forbearing one another in love" (Eph. 4:2). "Endeavoring to keep the unity of the Spirit in the bond of peace" (Eph. 4:3). "Be ye kind one to another, tenderhearted, forgiving one another" (Eph. 4:32). "If any man have a quarrel against any: even as Christ forgave you, so also do ye" (Col. 3:13). "See that ye love one another with a pure heart fervently" (I Peter 1:22). "Love the brotherhood" (I Peter 2:17). "And above all things have fervent charity among yourselves" (I Peter 4:8). "Finally, be ye all of one mind, having compassion one of another, love as brethren, be pitiful, be courteous" (I Peter 3:8). Envy, malice, ill-feeling, evil-speaking among brethren are a sure proof of the *lack* of this brotherly love!

"If the world hate you, ye know that it hated me before it hated you" (15:18). Here the Lord introduces the subject of the world's enmity, and He begins by pointing out to His apostles that what *they* would suffer was only what He had suffered before them; they must not be surprised then at finding themselves in the midst of a hostile people. For their part they must be meek and gentle, living peaceably with all men so far as they would allow them to. They must do nothing maliciously to provoke or warrant the hatred of the world; but if they were faithful to the Lord, they must be prepared for the same evil treatment which *He* met with.

"Ye know that it hated me before it hated you." The word "before" here refers not so much to time as it does to experience.

Christ was assuring them that He trode the very same path which they would be called on to follow. He had preceded them in it: "When he putteth forth his own sheep he goeth before them" (John 10:4). How this should comfort us! It was Christ identifying the disciples with Himself. If we belong to the Lord Jesus that is sufficient to arouse the world's rancour. But it is blessed to know that it hates us because of Him, not because of ourselves! It is the repulsion of human nature for what is of God. And nowhere is the awful depravity of fallen man more evidenced than in his hatred of that which is pure, lovely, good, holy.

"If ye were of the world, the world would love his own; but because ye are not of the world, but I have chosen you out of the world, therefore the world hateth you" (15:19). Here the Lord proceeds to state the various *causes* of the world's hatred. Two are given in this verse: first, His people are no longer "of the world;" second, Christ had "chosen them out of the world." The two are really resolvable into one: it is because Christ has chosen us out of the world that we no more belong to it. We no longer share its spirit, are no more actuated by its aims, are not now governed by its principles. Note the Lord's emphatic emphasis here: five times in this one verse does the Lord mention "the world"! Do you, He seems to ask, desire the smiles of men, are you anxious to stand high in their favour? That would be tragic indeed; that would prove you also belonged to the world. In 8:23, Christ had declared of Himself, "Ye are from beneath; I am from above; ye are of this world; I am not of this world." Now, for the first time, He predicates the same thing of His disciples. It is striking to note that this was not until *after* 14:31, and Christ had (figuratively) taken His place—identifying the disciples with Himself in that place—on *resurrection* ground. It is only as united to a risen Christ that we are taken (positionally) *out of* "the world."

"I have chosen you out of the world, therefore the world hateth you." It is remarkable that the *first* reason Christ here gives as to *why* the world hates believers, is because of their *election*. "The world cannot endure the thought of God's sovereignty and electing love" (Mr. F. W. Grant). The world is enraged at the very idea of Christians being the singled-out favourites of God. Strikingly was this demonstrated almost at the beginning of our Lord's public ministry. After announcing that the prophecy of Isa. 61:1, 2 found its fulfilment in His mission, He went on to say how that while the heaven was shut up for three years and a half, during the subsequent famine, though there were many widows in Israel, God, in His sovereign grace, sent Elijah unto *none* but the widow of Zarephath; and though there were *many* lepers in Israel in the time of Elisha, none of them were cleansed, though God in His sovereign mercy healed Naaman, the Syrian. The response to our Lord's words was very shocking. "And all they in the synagogue, when they heard *these things,* were filled with wrath, and rose up and thrust him out of the city, and led him unto the brow of the hill whereon their city was built, that they might cast him down headlong" (Luke 4:28, 29).

It is just the same to-day. Nothing so stirs up the enmity of the carnal mind as to hear of God's absolute sovereignty: choosing some, passing by others. Then how much *worldliness* there must now be in many professing Christians! It should be noted in the example cited above that it was the *religious world* which was so enraged against Christ: it was the synagogue-worshippers that sought to murder the Saviour, because He pressed upon them the fact that God had compassion on whom He pleases. Nor have things changed for the better. Let any servant of God to-day expound the truths of Divine election and foreordination, and he will be assailed the most fiercely by those who claim to be the people of God. So, too, with believers in general. Let their lives attest their calling, let their walk make it manifest that they *are not* "of the world," because "chosen out of it," and the bitter enmity of the ungodly will indeed be excited. But let us not be cast down at this, rather let us see in the hostility of unbelievers a precious evidence that we are one with Him whom the world cast out.

"Therefore the world hateth *you.*" It will not hate mere professors. The man who is conformed to this world, who takes part in its politics, who shares its pleasures, who acts according to its principles, even though he bears the name of Christ, will not be ostracised or persecuted. The woman who is conformed to this world, who follows its fashions, who enjoys its society, who works for its reformation, will not be shunned by it. The world loves its own. But those who walk in separation from the world (and they are *few* in number), those who follow a rejected Christ, will know something of what it means to enter into "the fellowship of his sufferings" (Phil. 3:10). God has said, "Yea, and *all* that will live godly in Christ Jesus *shall* suffer persecution" (II Timothy 3:12). But let such recall and be cheered by those words of our Saviour, "*Blessed are they* which are persecuted for righteousness' sake: for theirs is the kingdom of heaven. *Blessed are ye,* when men shall revile you, and persecute you and shall say all manner of evil against you falsely, for my sake. Rejoice, and be exceeding glad, for great is your reward in heaven: for so persecuted they the prophets which were before you" (Matt. 5:10, 12).

"Remember the word that I said unto you, The servant is not greater than his lord" (15:20). How touching is this! Christ would have us forget no words spoken by Him! He here reminds the apostles of what He had said to them a little previously, though in another connection—showing how full His utterances are, designed for various applications. His purpose here is to press upon us that it is a mark of genuine discipleship if we share the experiences of our Master, encountering the hatred of the world. "If they have persecuted me, they will also persecute you; if they have kept my saying, they will keep yours also" (15:20). The "if" looks back to the same word at the beginning of 15:18 and 19. If you are *My* followers, *My* friends, then must you have fellowship in My sufferings. They have persecuted the Lord, and just so far as they live and act accordingly, they will also persecute His servants. The world may boast of its liberal principles; it may for a time tolerate a lukewarm Christianity; but, let the people of God be out and out for Him, and the secret hatred of the heart will soon manifest itself. When the "I have chosen you out of the world" becomes a *practical* reality, then the world's rage and ban will be displayed. But after all, what is the world's hatred in comparison with Christ's love! And yet, as has been said, "If there is anything that true Christians seem incessantly forgetting, and seem to need incessantly reminding of, it is the real feeling of unconverted people towards them, and the treatment they must expect to meet with" (Bishop Ryle).

"If they have persecuted me, they will also persecute you; if they have kept my saying, they will keep yours also." There seems to be a note of irony here. The Lord had spoken nought but the unadulterated truth of God, yet the world had not kept His sayings. And why? Because His sayings *condemned* them. "For every one that doeth evil hateth the light, neither cometh to the light, lest his deeds should be reproved" (7:20). "The world cannot hate you (His unbelieving brethren); but me it hateth, *because* I testify of it, that the works thereof are evil" (7:7). And just so far as we proclaim the truth of God, so will men (in general) reject our message! "They are of the world: therefore speak they of the world, and the world heareth them. We are of God: he that knoweth God heareth us; he that is not of God heareth not us" (I John 4:5, 6).

"But all these things will they do unto you for my name's sake, because they know not him that sent me" (15:21). Here the Lord gives the deepest reason why His disciples would be hated by the world. "For my name's sake" means, of course, on account of it. It was because they would represent Him, acting as His ambassadors, that men would persecute them. Christ would grant His people the high privilege of sharing His sufferings: "If ye be reproached for the name of Christ, happy are ye; for the spirit of glory and of God resteth upon you" (I Peter 4:14). It is the confession of *Christ's name* which arouses the enmity of depraved hearts. May we, like Moses, "esteem the *reproach* of Christ greater riches than the treasures of Egypt"—the world (Heb. 11:26). "Because they know not him that sent me": far from this ignorance affording an excuse, it was inexcusable, because wilful.

"If I had not come and spoken unto them, they had not had sin: but now they have no cloak for their sin" (15:22). Here is an example of where the words of Scripture cannot be taken in their absolute sense. When our Lord declared of the Jews that if He had not become incarnate and spoken unto them "they had not had sin," He does not mean that they would have been without sin in every sense. The chief design of the first three chapters of Romans is to establish the fact that all the world, Jew and Gentile alike, were "guilty before God." Christ was speaking in a *comparative* sense. Compared with their immeasurable guilt of rejecting the Lord of glory, their personal sins were as nothing. Similar instances where things are represented absolutely, though intended in a comparative sense, are frequent in Scripture. For example: "All nations before him are as *nothing;* and they are counted to him less than nothing" (Isa. 40:17). "So then neither is he that planteth *any thing,* neither he that watereth; but God that giveth the increase" (I Cor. 3:7).

There had been sin all along, and the governmental dealings of God with men clearly evidenced that He took account of it. But evil as man had shown himself all through his history, the coming of Christ to the earth brought sin to such a head, that all that had gone before was relatively speaking, a trifling thing when compared with the monstrous evil that was done against incarnate Love. It is a question of the *standard of measurement.* There are a number of passages which clearly teach that there will be *degrees of punishment* meted out to those who are lost: Matt. 11:22; Heb. 10:28, 29, etc. The degree of punishment will be determined by the *heinousness* of the sins committed, and that will be decided by the *degree of light* sinned against. When One who was more than man came into the world, the Divine dignity of His person, the love and light which He manifested, brought in a *new standard* of measurement. Christ was here speaking according to the glory of His person. It will be more tolerable for Sodom and Gomorrah in the Day of judgment than for Capernaum. And why? Because the latter turned its back upon the King of kings and Lord of lords.

The principle here enunciated by the Saviour is very solemn in its application, and one which we all do well to take to heart. Spiritual privileges carry with them heavy responsibilities: "For unto whomsoever much is given, of him shall be much required." (Luke 12:48)! To dwell in a land of open Bibles and preached

Gospel, places men on a very different footing before God than the heathen who have never heard of Christ. Judgment will be according to the light enjoyed! The mere fact that men *knew* the way of truth, and walked not therein, will only increase their condemnation. To receive Divine instruction and not improve it, is, as Christ here plainly declares, to leave men *without* any cloak (or "excuse") for their sin.

"He that hateth me hateth my Father also" (15:23). The Lord here furnished proof that the sin of despising Him involved guilt of unparalleled magnitude. Christ's words were not only His own words, but the Father's also. He and the Father were one. The idea of some that they can acceptably worship the Father while rejecting His Son is a deceit of man's depraved heart and a lie of the Devil. "The Jews professed that they loved God, and that on the ground of that love they hated Christ; the God however, whom they loved was not the true God, but a phantom which they named God. The fact that they rejected Christ, in spite of all His words of spirit and truth, showed them to be the enemies of the Father" (Hengstenberg).

"He that hateth me hateth my Father also." Very solemn is this. In the previous verses the Lord had shown that the principal reason why the world would hate His disciples was because of their oneness with Himself. Now He shows that the reason why the world hated Him was because of *His* oneness with *the Father*. Christ revealed the Father. He was the express image of His person. In Him dwelt all the fullness of the Godhead bodily. He that saw Him, saw the Father also. His doctrine was the truth of God. His life revealed the perfections of God. His laws expressed the will of God. To dislike *Him*, then, was proof positive that they hated *God*. It is a most fearful fact, but one most clearly revealed in Scripture, that men in their natural state are "haters of God" (Rom. 1:30); their minds being "enmity against God" (Rom. 8:7). It is this hatred of God which causes people to reject Christ and dislike Christians. Conversely their rejection of Christ *demonstrates* their hatred of God. *Christ* is the test of the state of every human heart! "What think ye of Christ?" honestly answered, reveals whether we are His friends or His enemies. There is no God in the universe except the God and Father of our Lord Jesus Christ, and if men do not believe in, love, worship and serve the Son, they *hate* the Father. Just as faith begets love, so unbelief begets hatred.

"If I had not done among them the works which none other man did, they had not had sin: but now have they both seen and hated both me and my Father" (15:24). How decidedly does the Lord Jesus place Himself *above* all the other messengers of God that had preceded Him! The words "they had not had sin" have the same force here as in 15:22. If Israel had not enjoyed such *privileges,* they had not contracted *such guilt.* If they had not heard Him who spake as never man spake, and if they had not witnessed works such as never man performed, their criminality in the sight of God would have been so much less that, in comparison with their culpability now that they *had* heard and seen and believed not, had been as nothing. It is to be noted that Christ *first* mentioned what He had *spoken* unto them (15:22), and they referred to the works which He had *done* among them.

"If I had not done among them the works which none other man did, they had not had sin, but now have they both seen and hated both me and my Father." "The presence and testimony of the Son of God had the gravest possible results. It was not only an infinite blessing in itself and for God's glory, but it left men, and Israel especially, reprobate. Law had proved man's weakness and sin, as it put under the curse all who took their stand on the legal principle. There was none righteous, none that sought after God, none that did good, no, not one. The heathen were manifestly wicked, the Jews proved so by the incontestable sentence of the law. Thus every mouth was stopped, and all the world obnoxious to God's judgment. But the presence of Christ brought out, not merely failure to meet obligations as under law, but *hatred of Divine goodness* come down to men in perfect grace . . . Sin before or otherwise was swallowed up in the surpassing sin of rejecting the Son of God come in love and speaking not merely as man never spoke, but as God had never spoken."

"But this cometh to pass, that the word might be fulfilled that is written in their law, They hated me without a cause" (15:25).

Terrible indictment of Israel was this. "There was nothing in Christ to provoke hatred in any but morally disordered, depraved minds. Nothing in His character, it was faultless; nothing in His doctrines, they were all true; nothing in His laws, they were holy, just and good. He never had done the world any harm: He had spent His life in bestowing favors on men. Why, then, did they hate Him, why did they persecute Him, why did they put Him to death? They hated Him because they hated His Father" (Dr. John Brown.)

"But this cometh to pass, that the word might be fulfilled that is written in their law, They hated me without a cause." Here the Lord was tracing the world's enmity back to its true source. *He* had given no cause for it; it must therefore be attributed to their desperately wicked hearts. The Lord was further fortifying His disciples. They must not be surprised nor offended at the bitterness and malice of the ungodly. *His* conduct had been mild and benevolent; yet they hated Him. Let us see to it that *we* give men no "cause" to hate us. Let their enmity against us be provoked only by fellowship with Christ: "It is enough for the disciple that he be as his Master, and the servant as his Lord. If they have called the Master of the house Beelzebub, how much more shall they call them of his household!" (Matt. 10:25).

"But this cometh to pass, that the word might be fulfilled that is written in their law, They hated me without a cause." No doubt Christ was also anticipating an objection here. How is such hatred possible? Why does God permit it? The Lord answers by saying, This hatred of the world is but the fulfillment of God's Word, and therefore of His inscrutable counsels. So little do the wicked affect by their malice, they only fulfil the Scriptures—while they draw down upon themselves the judgments which other passages therein announce. In quoting here from "their law," Christ showed that the written Word testified *against* Israel!

"But when the Comforter is come, whom I will send unto you from the Father, even the Spirit of truth, which proceedeth from the Father, he shall testify of me" (15:26). The connection here is apparent. The Lord had been warning the disciples of the opposition they would meet with from that kingdom over which Satan is "the Prince." But that only distresses the more their already saddened hearts, therefore did their tender Master revert again to His original promise—the one promise repeated most frequently in this Paschal Discourse—that the Divine Comforter would come to their relief. It was presupposed in 15:20, 21 that His disciples would be hated, like Himself, on account of their *word*. He predicted their fate to them as His *witnesses*. It was obvious that they should think, But how shall we poor, weak men persist in our testimony, yea, even bear it in the face of such predicted hatred? He therefore confirms to them their vocation, and predicts to them with equal clearness that they *shall* bear Him testimony in the future (15:27). "Not of themselves, however, and in their own human persons: the Paraclete (the Comforter) will conduct the cause. He then, however, returns to the former again, and consoles them by the emphatic assurance that they might not stumble at this: I have now (more clearly than ever before) *foretold to you* both the coming of the Spirit as a Witness against the hatred of the world, and at the same time the continuance of that hatred in spite of His testimony" (Stier).

"But when the Comforter is come, whom I will send unto you from the Father, even the Spirit of truth, which proceedeth from the Father, he shall testify of me." That the Spirit is here said to "proceed from the Father" (a statement which has split the Greek from the Roman "Church," into whose differences we shall not here enter) is *supplementary* to what the Lord had said in 14:26. There the Comforter was to be sent in Christ's name: here He proceeds from the Father. The two statements placed side by side, bring out the *unity* of the Godhead. This additional word also shows that the Spirit was not exclusively subordinate to Christ, as some have argued from 14:26. "He shall testify of me," amplifies His former word in 14:16, "*another* Comforter." The Spirit would further Christ's interests, and be unto the disciples (only in another way) all that Christ would have been unto them had He remained on earth.

"But when the Comforter is come, whom *I* will send unto you from the Father, even the Spirit of truth, which proceedeth from the Father, he shall testify of me." "Here the Comforter is viewed as *sent* by the ascended Christ from the Father, and consequently as witness of His *heavenly* glory. This is an advance on what we saw in the previous chapter where Christ *asks* and the Father gives the Paraclete to be with them forever, sending Him in His Son's name. Here the Son Himself *sends*, though of course, from the Father. The Spirit of truth is thus the suited Witness of Christ as He is above" (The Bible Treasury). "Whom *I* will send" brings out the glory of the exalted Saviour in a most striking way.

"And ye also shall bear witness, because ye have been with me from the beginning" (15:27). Here the Lord explains to the disciples *how* the Spirit would testify and of *what* it would consist. He would not make any corporeal manifestation of Himself as had the Son, but He would bear witness in and through the disciples. He would testify that which they had already seen in Him, and that which they had already heard from Him—nothing besides, essentially different or new. Thus it will be seen that the two "testimonies" of 15:26 and 27 are not separate and independent, but natural and harmonious.

"And ye also shall bear witness." Marvellous grace was this. Neither hostility nor hatred had quenched the compassion of Christ. The world might cast Him out, yet still would His mercy linger over it. Before *judgment* ultimately descended on the world, a further witness to *Himself* should be given it, a witness which has already continued for over eighteen centuries! May Divine power enable every real Christian to witness faithfully and constantly for our absent Lord. May we by lip and life bear testimony, in season and out of season, to His excellency, and to Him as our sufficiency.

The following questions are to aid the student on the opening portion of John 16:—

1. What is the central theme of vv. 1-11?
2. What is the meaning of v. 1?
3. What does the last clause of v. 2 go to prove?
4. What blessings would "remembrance" bring the apostles, v. 4?
5. Why did the apostles ask "Whither goest Thou?" v. 5?
6. Why "expedient" for Christ to go, v. 7?
7. In what way does the Spirit "reprove the world," v. 8?

CHAPTER FIFTY-FOUR

Christ Vindicated by the Spirit

John 16:1-11

The following is an Analysis of the passage which is to be before us: —

1. Reason why Christ warned His disciples, v. 1.
2. Details of what they would suffer, v. 2.
3. Cause of the world's hostility, v. 3.
4. Christ's tender solicitude, v. 4.
5. The disciple's self-occupation, vv. 5, 6.
6. The promise of the Spirit, v. 7.
7. The Spirit vindicating Christ, vv. 8, 11.

The chapter division between John 15 and 16 is scarcely a happy one, though perhaps it is not an easy matter to indicate a better: 16:12 would probably have been a more suitable point for the break, for v. 12 obviously begins a new sub-section. In the passage which is to be before us we find the Lord continuing the subject which had engaged Him at the close of chapter 15. There He had been speaking of the *hatred* of the world—against the Father, against Himself, and against His disciples. Then He had assured them that He would send the Holy Spirit to conduct His cause. The *character* in which Christ mentioned the Third Person of the Godhead—"the Comforter"—should have quieted the fears and sorrows of the apostles. Now Christ returns to the world's hatred, entering more into detail. Previously, He had spoken in general terms of the world's enmity; now He proceeds to speak more particularly, sketching as He does the future fortunes of Christianity, describing the first chapter of its history.

Most faithfully did the Saviour proceed to warn His disciples of the treatment which would be meted out to them by their enemies. Strikingly has Mr. John Brown commented upon our Lord's conduct on this occasion. "The founders of false religions have always endeavoured to make it appear to be the *present* interest of those whom they addressed to acquiesce in their pretentions and submit to their guidance. To his countrymen the Arabian impostor held out the lure of present sensual indulgence; and when he at their head, made war in support of his imposture, the terms proffered to the conquered were proselytism, with a full share in the advantages of their victors, or continued unbelief with slavery or death. It has indeed been the policy of all deceivers, of whatever kind, to conceal from the dupes of their artifice, whatever might *prejudice* against their schemes, and skillfully to work on their hopes and fears by placing in a prominent point of view all the advantages which might result from them embracing their *schemes,* and all the *disadvantages* which might result from their rejecting them. An exaggerated view is given both of the probabilities of success, and of the value of the benefits to be secured by it, while great care is taken to throw into the shade the privations that must be submitted to, the labour that must be sustained, the sacrifices that must be made, the sufferings that must be endured, and the ruin that may be incurred, in joining in the proposed enterprise.

"How different the conduct of Jesus Christ! He had no doubt promised His followers a happiness, ample and varied as their capacities of enjoyment, and as enduring as their immortal souls; but He distinctly intimated that this happiness was *spiritual* in its nature, and to be fully enjoyed only in a *future* world! He assured them that, following Him, they should all become inheritors of a kingdom; but He with equal plainness stated that that kingdom was not of this world, and that he who would enter into it must 'forsake all,' and 'take up his cross.' Himself poor and despised, 'a Man of Sorrows and acquainted with grief.' He plainly intimated that His followers must be 'in the world, *as* He was in the world.'"

The disciples of Christ were to be hated by the world! But it is highly important that we do not form too narrow a view of what is meant by "the world." Satan has tried hard to obliterate the line which separates between those who are "*of* the world" and those who are "not of the world." And to a large extent he has succeeded. The professing "Church" has boasted that it would convert the world. To accomplish this aim, it has sought to popularize "religion." Innumerable devices have been employed – many of which even a sense of propriety should have suppressed – to attract the ungodly. The result has been the world has converted the "professing Church." But notwithstanding this it still remains true that "the world" *hates* the true followers of the Lamb. And nowhere is this more plainly evident than in those who belong to what we may term the *religious* world. This will come before us in the course of our exposition.

The closing verses of our present portion announce the relationship of the *Holy Spirit* to "the world" and it is this which *distinguishes* the first division of John 16 from the closing section of John 15. In the concluding verses of John 15 the Lord had spoken of the world's hatred, and this still engages Him in the first few verses of chapter 16. But in v. 7 He refers once more to the Holy Spirit, and in vv. 8:11 presents Him as His Vindicator. It is this which has guided us in selecting the title of our present chapter: its suitability must be determined by the interpretation which follows.

"These things have I spoken unto you, that ye should not be offended" (16:1). Before the Lord describes in detail the forms in which the world's hostility would be manifested, He paused to acquaint the disciples with His *reasons* for announcing these things. First, it was in order that they should not be "offended" or "stumbled" or "scandalized" as the word means. To be forewarned is to be forearmed. Christ would prepare His people beforehand by telling them plainly what they might expect. Instead of contending among themselves which should be the greatest, He bids them prepare to drink of the cup He drank of and to be baptised with the baptism wherewith He was to be baptised. It was not that He would discourage them, far from it; He would fortify them against what lay ahead. And how this evidenced the tender concern of their Master! How it demonstrates once more that He "loved them unto the end"! And how gracious of the Lord to thus warn us! Should we not often have *stumbled* had He not told us beforehand what to expect?

"These things have I spoken unto you, that ye should not be offended." That there was *need* for this warning is very evident. Already the question had been asked, "Behold, we have forsaken all, and followed thee; *what shall we have* therefore?" (Matt. 19:27). Moreover, that very night all *would be* "offended" because of Him: "Then saith Jesus unto them, All ye shall be offended because of me this night; for it is written, I will smite the shepherd, and the sheep of the flock shall be scattered abroad" (Matt. 26:31). But, it may be asked, *Why* should Christ here forewarn the disciples when He knew positively that they *would be* offended? Ah! why tell Peter to "watch and pray *lest* he enter into temptation" (Mark 14:38), when the Lord had already foretold that he *would* deny Him thrice! Why command that the Gospel should be preached to every creature when He foreknows that the great majority *will not* believe it! The answer to each of these questions is: to *enforce* human responsibility.

"They shall put you out of the synagogues: yea, the time cometh, that whosoever killeth you will think that he doeth God service" (16:2). Out of the catalogue of sufferings to which the disciples should be subjected, the Lord selects for mention two samples of all the rest: an extreme torture of the mind and the final infliction upon the body. It is indeed solemn to observe that this persecution of Christ's people comes from the *religious* world. The first fulfilment of this prophecy was from the Jews, who professed to be the people of God. But Christ indentifies them with *the world*. Their sharing in and display of its spirit showed plainly where they belonged. And the same is true to-day. Where profession is not real, even those who bear the name of Christ are part of "the world," and they are the first to persecute those who *do* follow Christ. When the walk of the Christian condemns that of the worldly professor, when faithfulness to his Lord prevents him from doing many things which the world does, and when obedience to the Word obliges him to do many things which the world dislikes, then enmity is at once aroused and persecution follows—persecution just as bitter and real to-day, though its *forms* be changed.

"To be 'put out of the synagogue' was more than simply to be excluded from the place of public worship. It cut a man off from the privileges of his own people, and from the society of his former associates. It was a sort of moral outlawry, and the physical disabilities followed the sufferer even after death. To be under this ban was almost more than flesh and blood could bear. All men shunned him on whom such a mark was set. He was literally an outcast; in lasting disgrace and perpetual danger. Those familiar with the history of the dark ages, or who are acquainted with the effects of losing *caste* among the Hindoos, will be able to realize the terrors of such a system" (Mr. Geo. Brown).

Sometimes the degradation of excommunication was the prelude to death. Cases of this are recorded in the book of Acts. We find there mention made of a class called "zealots." They were a desperate and fanatical faction who thirsted for the blood of Christians. "And when it was day, certain of the Jews banded together, and bound themselves under a curse, saying that they would neither eat nor drink, till they had *killed* Paul. And they were more than forty which had made this conspiracy" (Acts 23:12, 13). That such men were not restricted to the lower classes is evident from the case of Saul of Tarsus, who tells us that in his unregenerate days, "I verily thought with myself, that I ought to do many things contrary to the name of Jesus of Nazareth. Which thing I also did in Jerusalem: and many of the saints did I shut up in prison, having received authority from the chief priests; and when they were put to death, I gave my voice against them" (Acts 26:9, 10).

How fearfully do such things manifest the awful depravity of the human heart! It has been the same in every age: godliness has always met with hatred and hostility. "Cain, who was of the wicked one, and slew his brother. And wherefore slew he him? Because his own works were evil, and his brother's righteous" (I John 3:12). "He that is upright in the way is abomination to the wicked" (Prov. 29:27). "They *hate* him that rebuketh in the gate, and they abhor him that speaketh uprightly"

(Amos 5:10). It is the same now. Faithfulness to Christ will stir up religious rancour. In spite of the boasted liberalism of the day, men are still intolerant, and manifest their enmity just so far as they dare.

"And these things will they do unto you, because they have not known the Father, nor me" (16:3). Here the Lord traces, once more, the world's undying ill-will to its true source: it is because they are not acquainted with the Father and the Son. Hatred and persecution of God's children are both the consequence and the proof of the spiritual ignorance of their enemies. Had the Jews really known the Father in whom they vainly boasted, they would have acknowledged the One whom He had sent unto them, and acknowledging Him, they would not have mistreated His followers. Thus it is to-day! "Whosoever believeth that Jesus is the Christ is born of God. And every one that loveth *Him* that begat loveth *him also* that is begotten of Him" (I John 5:1).

"But these things have I told you, that when the time shall come, ye may remember that I told you of them" (16:4). The Lord had already given one reason (16:1), *why* He had spoken these things to the disciples, now He gives them another: He made these revelations that their *faith* in Him might be increased when the events should confirm His prophecy. The fulfilment of this prediction would deepen their assurance in Him as the omniscient God, and this would encourage them to depend upon the *veracity* of His *promises*. If the evil things which He foretold came to pass, then the good things of which He had assured them must be equally dependable.

"And these things I said not unto you at the beginning, because I was with you" (16:4). "The Lord also tells them why He had not told them *at the first*. The full revelation was more than their weak hearts could bear. They would be staggered at the prospect. They must be gradually trained to this. Not all at once, but by little and little, as they were able to bear it, He unfolds the scheme of His cross, and of their duties and dangers. The Lord has milk for His babes, and meat for His strong men. And there was as yet no need for this. For He Himself was with them, and by the less could prepare for the greater. He was with them, as a nurse with her children; to lead them on from strength to strength, from one degree of grace and Christian virtue to another. But now that He was about to depart from them, and leave them, as it were, to themselves; to see how they will acquit themselves in that contest for which He has been training them all the while; it is necessary that all the more plainly and fully He should lay before them their future—at first this was not needed. 'Sufficient unto the day is the evil thereof.' And He was yet with them and could gradually unfold it to them. And there was yet time. But as time goes on, we see Him and hear Him opening page after page of the volume of His secret Providence to their opening minds; till finally, as here, He tells them plainly and fully even of the extremest trials that are coming upon them" (Mr. Geo. Brown).

"And these things I *said not* unto you at the beginning, because I was with you." But how are we to reconcile this with such passages as Matt. 5:10, 12; 10:21, 28, etc.? In addition to the solution offered above, namely, that Christ *gradually* unfolded these things to the apostles, we may point out: First, He had not previously said that *the world* would do these things unto them; that is, He had not hitherto intimated that they would be hated by *all* men. Second, previously He had not declared that the reason for this hatred was because of men's *ignorance* of the Father and the Son. Third, He had not previously predicted that such persecution would proceed from the delusion that the perpetrators would imagine that they were doing God a service!

"But now I go my way to him that sent me" (16:5). There are some who would connect this first clause of the verse with the end of 16:4, thus: "And these things I said not unto you at the beginning, because I was with you; but now I go my way to him that sent me." And then after a brief pause, the Lord asked, "And does no one of you ask whither I go; but because I have thus spoken to you, your heart is filled with sorrow." This is quite likely, and seems a natural and beautiful connection.

"And none of you asketh me, Whither goest thou?" (16:5). In 13:36, we find Peter asking Christ, "Whither goest thou?" But this was an unintelligent forwardness, for he evidently thought that the Lord was going on an earthly journey (cf. 7:5). In 14:5: Thomas said, "We know not whither thou goest," but this was more by way of objection. What the Lord wanted was an intelligent, sympathetic, affectionate response to what He had been saying. But the apostles were so absorbed in grief that they looked not beyond the cloud which seemed to overshadow them. they were so occupied with the present calamity as not to think of the blessing, which would issue from it. They were depressed at the prospect of their Master's departure. Had they only asked themselves *whither* He was going, they would have felt glad for Him; for though it was their loss, it was certainly His gain—the joy of being with His Father, the rest of sitting down on high, the blessedness of entering again into the glory which He had before the foundation of the world. It was therefore a rebuke for their self-occupation, and how tenderly given!

"But because I have said these things unto you, sorrow hath filled your heart" (16:6). How often it is thus with us! We magnify our afflictions, and fail to dwell upon the blessings which they bear. We mourn and are in heaviness in the "cloudy and dark day," when the heavens are black with clouds and the wind brings a heavy rain, forgetting the beneficial effects upon the parched earth, which only thus can bring forth its fruits for our enjoyment. We wish it to be always spring, and consider not that without winter first, spring cannot be. It was so with the disciples. Instead of making the most of the little time left them with their Master, in asking Him more about His place and work in Heaven, they could think of nothing but His departure. What a warning is this against being swallowed up by over-much sorrow! We need to seek grace to enable us to keep it under control.

"But because I have said these things unto you, sorrow hath filled your heart." It is blessed to learn that the disciples did not continue for long in this disconsolate mood. A very different spirit was theirs after the Saviour's resurrection. Strikingly is this brought out in the concluding verses of Luke's Gospel: "And he led them out as far as to Bethany, and he lifted up his hands, and blessed them. And it came to pass, while he blessed them, he was parted from them, and carried up into heaven. And they worshipped him, and returned to Jerusalem *with great joy*: And were continually in the temple, praising and blessing God." Forty days of fellowship with Him after He had come forth victor of the grave, had removed their doubts, dispelled their fears, and filled their souls with joy unspeakable.

"Nevertheless I tell you the truth; it is expedient for you that I go away: for if I go not away, the Comforter will not come unto you" (16:7). Blessed contrast! The disciples, at the moment, had no thought for Him, but He was thinking of them and assured them that though they lost Him for a while, it would be their gain. Though they had failed to ask, their compassionate Master did not fail to answer. Ever more ready to hear than we are to pray, and want to give more than we desire; ready to make allowance for them in their present distress, and thinking always more of the sufferings of others than His own; thinking more now of those He is leaving behind, than of the agony He is going forth to meet – before they call He answers, answers what should have been their request, declaring unto them the expediency of His departure.

"Nevertheless" is adversative: I know you are saddened at the prospect of My departure, *but* My going is needful for you. "*I* tell you the truth": the personal pronoun is emphatic in the Greek – I who love you, I who am about to lay down My life for you: therefore you must believe what I am saying. I tell you *the truth*. Your misgivings of heart have beclouded your understandings, you misapprehend things. You think that if I remain with you, all the evils which I have mentioned would be prevented. Alas, you know not what is best for you. "It is expedient for you that I go away": It is for your profit, your advantage. It is striking to note the *contrast* between our Lord's use here of "expedient" from the same words on the lips of Caiaphas in 11:50!

But what did the Lord mean? *How* was His going away their *gain?* We believe that there is a double answer to this question according as we understand Christ's declaration here to have a double reference. Notice that He did not say "It is expedient for you that I go my way *to him* that sent me?" as He *had* said in 16:4. He simply said, "it is expedient for you that I *go away*."

We believe that Christ designedly left it abstract. *Whither was* He "going" when He spake these words? Ultimately, to the Father, but *before* that He must go to the *Cross*. Was not His first reference then to His impending death? And was it not highly *expedient* for the disciples and for us, that the Lord Jesus *should* go to and through the sufferings of Calvary?

"For if I go not away, the Comforter will not come unto you." "The atoning death of Christ was necessary to make it consistent with the Divine government to bestow on men these spiritual blessings which are necessarily connected with the saving influence of the Holy Spirit. All such blessings from the beginning had been bestowed with a reference to that atonement; and it was fitting that these blessings, in their richest abundance, should not be bestowed till that atonement was made" (Mr. John Brown). "'Unless I go away,' that is, unless I die, nothing will be done—you will continue as you are and everything will remain in its old state: the Jews under the law of Moses, the heathen in their blindness—all under sin and death. No scripture would then be fulfilled, and I should have come in vain" (Mr. Martin Luther).

But while we understand our Lord's first reference in His words "If I go not away" to be to His death, we would by no means limit them to this. Doubtless He also looked forward to His return to the Father. This also was expedient for His disciples. "So fond had they grown of His fleshly presence, they could not endure that He should be out of their sight. Nothing but His corporeal presence could quiet them. We know who said, If Thou hadst been here, Lord, as if absent, He had not been able to do it by His Spirit, as present by His body. And a tabernacle they would needs build Him to keep Him on earth still; and ever and anon they were still dreaming of an earthly kingdom, and of the chief seats there, as if their consummation should have been in the flesh. The corporeal presence therefore is to be removed, that the spiritual might take place" (Bishop Andrews).

In other ways, too, was it "expedient" for His disciples that the Saviour should take His place on High. It is of a *glorified* Christ that the Spirit testifies, and for *that* the Saviour had to "go away." Moreover, had Christ remained on earth He had been *localized,* His bodily presence confined to one place: whereas by the Spirit He is now omnipresent—where two or three disciples are gathered together in His name, *there* is *He* in the midst. Again; had the Lord Jesus remained on earth there had been far less room and opportunity for His people to exercise faith. Furthermore, this cannot be gainsaid: after Christ had ascended and the Spirit descended, the apostles were new men. They did far more for an absent Lord, than they ever did while He was with them in the flesh.

"But if I depart, I will send him unto you" (16:7). "Every rendering of this verse ought to keep the distinction between 'apeltho' and 'poreutho,' which is not sufficiently done in the English Version, by 'going away' and 'depart.' 'Depart' and 'go' would be better! The first expressing merely the leaving *them,* the second, the *going up* to the Father" (Dean Alford). We believe our Lord's fine discrimination here confirms our interpretation above of the double reference in His "if I go not away," though we know of no commentator who takes this view.

"And when he is come, he will reprove the world of sin, and of righteousness, and of judgment" (16:8). There is hardly a sentence in this Gospel which has been more generally misunderstood than the one just quoted. With rare exceptions this verse is understood to refer to the benign activities of the Holy Spirit among those who hear the Gospel. It is supposed to define His work in the conscience prior to conversion. It is regarded as a description of His gracious operations in bringing the sinner to see his need of a Saviour. So firmly has this idea taken root in the minds even of the Lord's people, it is difficult to induce them to study this verse for themselves—study it in the light of what precedes, study it in the light of the amplification which follows, study the terms employed, comparing their usage in other passages. If this be done carefully and dispassionately, we feel confident that many will discover how untenable is the popular view of it.

It should be very evident that something must be wrong if this verse be interpreted so as to clash with Christ's explicit statement in John 14:17, "The Spirit of truth, whom the world *cannot* receive." What then is the *character* of the "reproof" that is here spoken of? Is it an evangelical conviction wrought in the heart, or is it something that is altogether external? Almost all the older commentators regarded it as the former. We, with an increasing number of later writers, believe it is the latter. One of the leading lexicons of the twentieth century gives as the meaning of *elencho,* "to bring in guilty; to put to shame by proving one to be wrong; to convict with a view to condemnation and judgment, but not necessarily to convince; to bring in guilty without any confession or feeling of guilt by the guilty one."

The general use of the word in the New Testament decidedly confirms this definition. It occurs in John 3:20: "For every one that doeth evil hateth the light, neither cometh to the light, lest his deeds should be reproved," which obviously means: lest the evil nature of his deeds should be so manifested by the light that excuse of extenuation would be impossible. It is found again in John 8:46, "Which of you convinceth me of sin?": most certainly Christ did not mean, Which of you is able to *convince* Me, or make Me *realize* I have sinned. Rather, Which of you can substantiate a charge? which of you can *furnish proof of* sin against Me? It is rendered "reproved" in Luke 3:19, meaning "charged," not made to feel guilty. So too in Eph. 5:11; II Tim. 4:2.

Thus, in each of the above passages "elencho" refers to an objective condemnation, and *not* to a subjective *realization* of condemnation. In I Tim. 5:20 it is rendered, "rebuke". So also in Titus 1:13; 2:15; Heb. 12:5; Rev. 3:19. Clearer still, if possible, is its force in James 2:9, "But if ye have respect of persons, ye commit sin, and are *convicted* of the law as transgressors." Rightly did Bishop Ryle say in his comments on John 16:8, "Inward conviction is certainly not the meaning of the word rendered 'reprove.' It is rather refutation by proofs, convicting by unanswerable arguments as an advocate, that is meant."

The next point to be considered is, *How* does the Holy Spirit "reprove the world of sin," etc.? In order to answer this question aright it needs to be pointed out that our Lord was not, in these verses, describing the *mission* of the Holy Spirit, that is, the specific work which He would perform when He came to earth. We grant that at first sight the words "*He will* reprove" *appear* to describe His actual operations, but if everything in the passage is attentively studied, it should be seen that this is not the case. We believe our present verse is similar in its scope and character to Matt. 10:34, "I came not to send peace, but a sword." To send a "sword" was not the nature of Christ's mission, but, because of the perversity of fallen human nature, it was the *effect* of His being here. Again, in Luke 12:49 He said, "I am come to send fire on the earth." It is the very presence of the Spirit on earth which, though quite unknown to them, reproves or condemns the world.

The Holy Spirit ought not to be here at all. That is a startling statement to make, yet we say it thoughtfully. From the standpoint of the world, Christ is the One who *ought* to be here. The Father sent Him into the world, Why, then, is He not here? The world would not have Him. The world hated Him. The world cast Him out. But Christ would not leave His own "orphans" (John 14:18, margin). He graciously sent the Holy Spirit to them, and, to the angels and His saints, the very *presence* of the Holy Spirit on earth "reproves," or brings in guilty, the "world." The Holy Spirit is here to take the place (unto His disciples) of an *absent* Christ, and thus the *guilt* of the world is demonstrated.

Confirmatory of what has been pointed out, observe particularly the *character* in which the third person of the Godhead is here contemplated: "and *he* shall reprove." *Who* shall do so? The previous verse tells us, "The Comforter." The Greek word is "paracletos" and is rightly rendered "Advocate" in I John 2:1. Now an "advocate" produces a "conviction" not by bringing a wrong-doer to realize or feel his crime, but by producing proofs before a court that the wrong-doer *is* guilty. In other words, he "reproves" objectively, *not* subjectively. Such is the thought of our present passage: it is the actual presence of the Holy Spirit on earth which *objectively* reproves, rebukes, convicts "the world."

"Here the Holy Spirit is not spoken of as dealing with individuals when He regenerates them and they believe, but as bringing conviction to the world because of sin. The Holy Ghost being here, convicts the world, i.e., what is outside where He is. Were there faith, He would be in their midst: but the world doth not believe. Hence Christ is, as everywhere in John, the standard for judging the condition of men" (Mr. W. Kelly).

But some may object, If this passage be not treating of a subjective work of evangelical conviction, why *does* the Holy Spirit "reprove" the world at all? what is gained if the world knows it not? But such a question proceeds on an entire mis-conception. We say again, these verses are not treating of what the Spirit *does*, but mention the *consequence* of His being here. John 9:39 gives us almost a parallel thought, "And Jesus said, For judgment I am come into this world, that they which see not might see; and that they which see might be made blind." In John 3:17 we are told, "For God sent not his Son into the world to condemn the world." How then are these two passages to be harmonized? John 3:17 give us the *mission* on which God sent His Son; John 9:39 names one of the *consequences* which resulted from His coming here. His very presence judged everything that was contrary to God. So the presence of the Spirit on earth judges the world, condemns it for Christ's being absent.

"Of sin, because they believe not on me" (16:9). The presence of the Divine Paraclete on earth establishes three indictments against "the world." First "of sin." "He was in the world, and the world was made by him, and the world knew him not" (1:10). The word "knew" here means far more than to be cognizant of or to be acquainted with. It means that the world *loved* Him not, as the word "know" is used in John 10:4, 5, 14, 15, etc. In like manner, unbelief is far more than an error of judgment, or nonconsent of the mind: it is aversion of *heart*. And "the world" is unchanged. It has no more love for Christ now than it had when its princes (I Cor. 2:8) crucified Him. Hence the present tense here: "because they believe not on me."

"Of righteousness, because I go to my Father, and ye see me no more" (16:10). The personal "I" links up with 16:7, the last clause of which should be carefully noted: "*I* will send him unto you." The Paraclete is here as *Christ's* "Advocate." Now the office and duty of an "advocate" is to vindicate his client when his cause permits of it: to do so by adducing evidence which shall silence his adversary. It is in *this* character that the Holy Spirit is related to "the world." He is here not to improve it, and make it a better place to live in, but to establish its consummate sin, to furnish proof of its guilt, and *thus* does He *vindicate* that blessed One whom the world cast out.

If it were the subjective work of the Holy Spirit in individual souls which was here in view, it had necessarily read, "He will convict the world . . . of *un*righteousness," because it is destitute of it. But this is not the thought here at all. It is the Spirit's presence on earth which establishes Christ's "righteousness," and the evidence is that He has gone to the Father. Had Christ been an impostor, as the religious world insisted when they cast Him out, the Father had not received Him. But the fact that the Father *did* exalt Him to His own right hand demonstrates that He was completely innocent of the charges laid against Him; and the proof that the Father *has* received Him, is the presence now of the Holy Spirit on earth, for Christ has "sent" Him from the Father. The world was unrighteous in casting Him out; the Father righteous in glorifying Him, and this is what the Spirit's presence here established.

"Of judgment, because the prince of this world is judged" (16:11). Had our passage been describing the work of the Spirit in producing conversion *this order* had been reversed, the "judgment" would have preceded the (un) "righteousness." Let this detail be carefully pondered. If the Spirit's reproof of "sin" means His bringing the sinner to realize his lost condition, and His reproving of "righteousness" means making him feel his need of Christ's righteousness, then *wherein* would be the need of still further convincing of "judgment"? It does not seem possible to furnish any satisfactory answer! But understanding the whole passage to treat of the *objective* consequences of the

Spirit's presence on earth, then 16:11 furnished a fitting conclusion.

"Of judgment, because the prince of this world is judged." This is the logical climax. The world stands guilty of refusing to believe in Christ: its condemnation is attested by the righteousness of Christ, exhibited in His going to the Father: therefore nothing awaits it but judgment. The Spirit's presence here is the evidence that the Prince of this world has been judged—when He departs sentence is *executed,* both on the world and on Satan. "This, therefore, is the testimony of the Holy Spirit to the world. It is heaven's reversal of the world's treatment of Christ. It is the answer of the righteous Father to what the world has done to His Son, and must not be interpreted of Gospel conviction" ("Things to Come," Vol. 5, p. 142).

The following questions are to aid the student for our next lesson:

1. What did Christ mean by "ye cannot bear them now," v. 12?
2. Have the "many things" been said, v. 12?
3. What is implied by the word "guide," v. 13? Meditate on it.
4. What is meant by "he shall not speak of himself," v. 13?
5. Where has the Spirit shown us "things to come," v 13?
6. To whom was Christ referring in v. 16?
7. Find the verse which records the disciples "rejoicing," v. 22.

CHAPTER FIFTY-FIVE

Christ Glorified by the Spirit

John 16:12-22

Below is an Analysis of the passage which is to be before us: —

1. The need for the Spirit's coming, v. 12.
2. The purpose of the Spirit's coming, v. 13.
3. The end accomplished by the Spirit's coming, v. 14.
4. The subordination of the Spirit, v. 15.
5. The effect of the Spirit's coming, v. 16.
6. The disciples' mystification, vv. 17-19.
7. The Lord's profound prediction, vv. 20-22.

That which is central in this second section of John 16 is the Holy Spirit glorifying the Lord Jesus. The more closely our present passage be studied, the more will it be found that *this* is the keynote of it. At first sight there does not seem to be any *unity* about this portion of Scripture. In 16:12, the Lord declares that He had yet many things to say unto the apostles, but they were unable to bear them. In 16:13-15, Christ made direct reference to the Holy Spirit, and what He would do for and in believers. In 16:16 the Saviour uttered an allegorical proverb (see 16:25), which mystified the disciples, causing them to ask one another what He meant by it. While in the last three verses He made mention of their sorrow and of the joy which would follow His departure. Yet, varied as these subjects appear to be, closer study will show that they are intimately connected and logically grow out of what is found in the opening verses.

Nowhere else did our Lord give so full a word concerning the blessed person and work of the Holy Spirit. *Seven* things are here postulated of Him. He would act as "the Spirit of truth," He would guide believers into all truth, He would not speak of Himself, He would speak what He heard; He would show believers things to come; He would glorify Christ; He would take of the things of Christ and show them unto His people. Why, then, it may be asked, have we not entitled this chapter, The Work of the Spirit with and in Christians? Because what is here predicated of Him is in special and direct relation to Christ. It is the Holy Spirit *glorifying* the Lord Jesus, glorifying Him by *magnifying* Him before believers. Not only is this expressly affirmed in 16:14, but the *character* in which He acts throughout affords further proof.

In 16:7 the Saviour declared, "But I *the truth* say to you, It is profitable for you that I should go away: for if I go not away the Paraclete will not come" (Bagster's Interlinear). Now in 16:13, He says, "But when he, the Spirit of the truth, [the Greek has the article] has come, he will guide you into all the truth." It is, then, as the Spirit *of Christ* that He is here viewed. This is further emphasized in 16:14: "He shall glorify me, for he shall receive of *mine*, and shall show it unto you"—words which are repeated in 16:15. It is therefore plain that the central and distinguishing subject of our present section is *Christ glorified by the Spirit.* How this applies to the closing verses will be indicated in the course of our exposition.

"It has been repeatedly shown, and in this chapter most expressly, that the presence of the Spirit depended on the departure of Christ to heaven consequently fitting the saints for the new truths, work, character, and hopes of Christianity. The disciples were not ignorant of the promises that the Spirit should be given to inaugurate the reign of the Messiah. They knew the judgment under which the chosen people abide, 'until the Spirit be poured upon us from on high, and the wilderness be a fruitful field, and the fruitful field be counted for a forest,' so vast outwardly, no less than inwardly, the change when God puts forth His power for the Kingdom of His Son. They know that He will pour out His Spirit upon all flesh; not only the sons and daughters, the old and young of Israel enjoying a blessing far beyond all temporal favours, but the servants and the handmaidens, in short, all flesh, and not the Jews alone sharing it.

But here it is the sound heard when the great High Priest goes in into the sanctuary before Jehovah (Ex. 28:35), and not only when He comes out for the deliverance and joy of repentant Israel in the last days. It is the Spirit given when the Lord Jesus went on high, and by Him thus gone. For this they were wholly unprepared, as indeed it is one of the most essential characteristics, of God's testimony between the rejection and the reception of the Jews; and the Spirit, when given, was to supply what the then state of the disciples could not bear" (Bible Treasury.)

Never can we be sufficiently thankful for the gift of the Holy Spirit. Though our blessed Saviour is in heaven, we have a *Divine Person* with us on earth: a person who quickens us (John 5:21), who indwells us (I Cor. 6:19), who loves us (Rom. 15:7), who leads us (Rom. 8:14), who gives us assurance of our sonship (Rom. 8:16), who helpeth our infirmities by making intercession for us (Rom. 8:26), and who has sealed us unto the day of redemption (Eph. 4:30). O that we may not grieve Him. O that we may recognize His indwelling presence and act accordingly. O that we may avail ourselves of His Divine fullness and power.

"I have yet many things to say unto you, but ye cannot bear them now" (16:12). The contents of 16:8 to 11 are parenthetical in their character, in that in 16:1 to 7 Christ has been speaking of and to His disciples, digressing for a moment to complete what He said previously about "the world." Now He turns to consider His own again, and they in connection with the sending of the Holy Spirit to them. The Lord had yet many things to say unto those who had followed Him in the day of His rejection, things which it was deeply important for them to know, but things which they were then in no condition to receive—"ye cannot bear them now." The Greek word here for "bear" is used in a double sense in the New Testament, literally and figuratively. In John 10:31 it is rendered, "Then the Jews *took up* stones again to stone Him": they *laid hold of* these stones. In Luke 10:4 it is translated, "*Carry* neither purse nor scrip." In Matt. 20:12, the word is employed figuratively: "Thou hast made them equal with us which have *borne* the burden and heat of the day." So in Rev. 2:2: "I know thy works, and thy labour, and thy patience, and how thou canst not bear them which are evil." From these references it would appear that our Lord signified that the apostles were then incapable of laying hold of or retaining what He, otherwise, would have said to them; incapable because they could not endure such revelations.

"I have yet many things to say unto you, but ye cannot bear them now." The fact that the Eleven were in no condition to receive, unable to endure these further revelations from the Saviour, demonstrated their *need* for the Holy Spirit to come and guide them into all the truth: suitable introduction, then, was that for this new section! Moreover, it hints strongly of the *nature* of the "many things" which Christ then had in mind. The apostles were prejudiced. Their hearts were set on the establishment of the Messianic kingdom. They could not tolerate the thought of Christ leaving them and returning to the Father. But the Lord Jesus could not at that time ascend the throne of David. Israel had *rejected Him,* and bitter would be the results for them, though most merciful would be the consequences for the Gentiles. Hence, we take it, that what our Lord here had in view was God's rejection of Israel, and His turning unto the Gentiles: the abolishing of the old covenant, and the introduction of the new: the abrogation of the ceremonial law and the bringing in of another order of priesthood: instructions for the government of His churches: prophecies concerning the future.

"I have yet many things to say unto you, but ye cannot bear them now." This is both blessed and searching. Blessed, because it shows our Lord's tender considerateness: He would not press upon them what they were in no condition to receive. Few things are more irritating than to hear without understanding. What an example for teachers now to follow! Much discernment and wisdom is needed if we are to minister the Word "in season," a word suited to the spiritual condition of our hearers, and such wisdom can only be obtained by earnest waiting upon God. But there is also a searching and solemn force to this utterance of Christ's. How many a communication would He not make to *us,* could we "bear" it! Paul had to have a thorn in the flesh sent him, lest he be exalted above measure through "the abundance of the revelations" which he received when he was caught up into Paradise; and in view of this, we are strongly inclined to believe that the "many things" which Christ had in mind also included revelations about Paradise and Heaven, the more so in view of 16:5: "But now I go my way to him that sent me; and *none* of you *asketh* me, Whither goest thou?" But "sorrow" had filled their hearts (16:6), and this *unfitted* them for fuller disclosures about the Higher World.

"Howbeit when he, the Spirit of truth is come, he will guide you into all truth" (16:13). Here is the answer to a question which must have occurred to many in meditating upon the previous verse: Did these apostles ever after bewail a lost opportunity? No; graciously did the Lord provide against that. "Howbeit," even so, though they could not bear these things *then,* when the Paraclete had come, He *should* guide them into *all* the truth! The One who would thus undertake for them is called "The Spirit of the truth." In addition to affirming that He was the Spirit *of* "the truth" (of Christ), this title also emphasized His suitability for such a task, His competency as the Saviour's Witness. The Spirit was fully qualified *because He is* "the Spirit of *the truth*": because of His perfect knowledge of the Truth, because of His infinite love for the Truth, and because of His absolute incapacity for falsehood. Scripture speaks of "the spirit of *error*" (I John 4:6). There is a lying spirit who controls the blind, that *leads* the blind, and in consequence they "both fall into the ditch."

Another thing suggested by this title of the third person of the Godhead is His relation to and connection with the *written* Word, which, like the incarnate Word is also called "the truth": "Sanctify them through thy truth: thy word *is truth*" (John 17:17). The inspiration of the Holy Scriptures is in an unique sense the work of the Holy Spirit: "holy [separated] men of God spake moved *by* the Holy Spirit" (II Peter 1:21). So too the interpretation of Scripture is the special work of the Spirit: "Eye hath not seen, nor ear heard, neither have entered into the heart of man, the things which God hath prepared for them that love him. But God *hath* revealed unto us *by his Spirit*: for the Spirit searcheth *all* things, yea, the deep things of God. For what man knoweth the things of a man, save [by] the spirit of man which is in him? Even so the things of God knoweth no man, but [by] *the Spirit of God*" (I Cor. 2:9-11). Before he can see, man must have both sight and light. Eyes cannot see in the darkness, and light shows nothing to the blind. So with regard to the Truth: there must be the seeing eye *and* illuminating light. For an interpreter we need a trustworthy guide, an infallible teacher; and he is to be found not in the "Church," the "voice of tradition," the "intuitive faculty," or in reason, but in the Spirit of God. He it is who quickens, illumines, interprets, and the *only* instrument which He uses is the *written* Word. Therefore is He called "the Spirit of *the truth.*"

"He will *guide* you." There are three classes of people who need to be "guided": those who are blind, those who are too weak to walk alone, or those journeying through an unknown country. In each of these senses does the Holy Spirit guide God's elect. By nature, we are spiritually blind, and He guided us into the way of "truth" (II Peter 2:2). Then as "babes" in Christ, He has to teach us how to walk (Rom. 8:14). Then as travellers through this wilderness scene, as we journey to the Heavenly Country, He points out the "narrow way which leadeth unto life." Note carefully, "He will *guide* you into all the truth," *not* "bring you into": there must be a *yieldedness* on our part, a corresponding *obedience!* If the Spirit "guides" our steps, the necessary implication is that we are walking *with Him,* that we are closely *following* His directions. This term also suggests an orderly, gradual and progressive advancing: we *grow* in "knowledge" as well as in "grace" (II Peter 3:18).

"He will guide you into all the truth," not all *truths,* but "all the truth." God's truth is one connected, harmonious, indivisible whole (compare our remarks on 7:16). "All the truth" here means all *revealed* truth, which is recorded in the written Word. That we *have* in our hands "*all* the truth" is clearly implied by one of the closing verses in the last book of the Bible: "If any man shall *add* unto these things, God shall add unto him the plagues that are written in this Book" (Rev. 22:18).

"For he shall not speak of himself." This does not mean, as some suppose, that He should not speak *about* Himself. He has told us much about Himself in every section of the Scriptures. But He would not speak *from* Himself, *independently* of the Father and the Son. As the Son came not to act independently of the Father, but to serve His Father, so the Spirit is here to serve the Son. The reference is to His administrative position.

"I can of mine own self do nothing: as I hear, I judge: and my judgment is just: because I seek not mine own will, but the will of the Father which hath sent me" (5:30). "I have many things to say and to judge of you: but he that sent me is true; and I speak to the world these things which I have heard of him" (8:26). "These declarations respecting both the Son and Spirit must appear inconsistent with Their supreme Divinity, to every one who does not know the doctrine of the economical subordination of the Son and Spirit in the great plan of human redemption. *Essentially* the Spirit and the Son are equal to, for they are one with, the Father. *Economically*, the Father is greater than the Son and the Spirit, for He *sends* Them; the Son is greater than the Spirit, for He sends Him. Without apprehending this distinction, we cannot interpret the sacred Scriptures, nor form any clear notion of the way of salvation. The Spirit like the Son, would be faithful to Him who appointed Him. In speaking to the apostles, in conveying information to their minds, He would communicate just what He was sent to communicate, without excess, without defect, without variation" (Mr. Brown).

"But whatsoever he shall hear, that shall he speak" (16:13). This is parallel with 15:15, "For all things that I have *heard* of my Father, I have made known unto you." What a searching word is this for every teacher! "If the Spirit may not speak of Himself, if He speaks only what He has heard of the Father and the Son—O, preacher! how canst thou draw thy preaching out of thyself, out of thy head, or even thy heart?" (Gossner).

"And he will show you things to come" (16:13). Mark the progressive order in these several statements concerning the work of the Spirit. In 14:26 the Lord declared that the Spirit would recall to the apostles *the past*: "But the Comforter, the Holy Spirit, whom the Father will send in my name, he shall teach you all things and *bring all things to your remembrance*, whatsoever I *have said* unto you." In 15:26, we learn that the Spirit would testify of the *present* glory of Christ. But here, in 16:13, it is promised that He would show them things concerning the *future!* There are many prophecies scattered throughout the Epistles—far more than most people imagine—which the Spirit has given. But the main reference, no doubt, in this word of Christ, was to the book of the Revelation, the opening sentence of which reads, "The Revelation of Jesus Christ, which God gave unto him, to show unto his servants things which must shortly *come to pass.*" It is the Revelation *of Jesus Christ,* for He is its chief subject and object; yet it was *given* by the Holy Spirit, hence the seven times repeated, "He that hath an ear to hear, let him hear what *the Spirit saith* unto the churches!" Thus whether it be things past, things present, or things to come, Christ is the grand Center of the Spirit's testimony!

"He shall glorify me: for he shall receive of mine, and shall show it unto you" (16:14). This is the prime object before the Spirit: whether it be revealing the truth, speaking what He hears, or showing things to come, the *glorification of Christ* is the grand end in view. The light of the knowledge of the glory of God in the face of Jesus Christ (II Cor. 4:6) is both the center and capstone of Divine truth. *This* is the vital test for every lying spirit which would obtrude itself into the place of the Spirit: rationalism, ritualism, fanaticism, philosophy, science falsely so-called, all *dishonour* Christ, but the Spirit always *magnifies* Him. It is a notable fact that (so far as the writer is aware) nowhere in the Epistles has the Holy Spirit told us anything about *the Father* which had not previously been revealed in and by the Lord Jesus; but He *has* told us many things about *the Son,* which Jesus uttered not in the days of His humiliation.

"He shall glorify me: for he shall receive of mine, and shall show it unto you." The blessed work of the Spirit in revealing to believers the precious things of God is strikingly brought out in I Cor. 2: "Eye hath not seen, nor ear heard, neither have entered into the heart of man the things which God hath prepared for them that love him" (2:9). This is a reference to Isaiah 64, and most Christians when quoting it stop at this point, but the very next verse goes on to say, "But God *hath revealed* them unto us *by his Spirit*: for the Spirit searcheth all things, yea, the deep things of God."

"All things that the Father hath are mine" (16:15). Very blessed is this: the Lord Jesus would not speak of His own glory apart from that of the *Father*. It is very similar to His words in 17:10: "And all mine are thine, and thine are mine." "Thus there is opened for us a glimpse into the living blessed bond of love in receiving and giving in the eternal ground of the triune essence of the Godhead. The Father hath from eternity given to the Son to have life and all things in Himself, yet always He is the Son who revealeth the Father, only as the Fatherhood remains with the Father. But all things the Son bringeth and giveth to the Father again, honoreth and glorifieth Him in His being glorified in His people. And this through *the Spirit,* who with equal rights in this unity taketh from the sole fullness of the Father and the Son, all that He livingly offers in His announcement" (Stier). "Take of mine" should be "*receive* of mine" as in the previous verse, otherwise the force of "therefore" here would be lost – in the Greek the word is the same in both verses.

"A little while, and ye shall not see me: and again, a little while and ye shall see me, because I go to the Father" (16:16). In the previous verses Christ had touched upon lofty things, now He comes down to the level of His apostles' needs. He condescends to stoop to their weakness, by addressing Himself to their anguished hearts. From the awful heights of the three persons of the Godhead, He descends to the sorrows and joys of His disciples. "A little while, and ye shall not see me: and again, a little while, and ye shall see me." But what did the Saviour mean? This cryptic utterance of His sorely puzzled those to whom it was first addressed, as is clear from the verses which follow. Christ Himself termed it a *proverbial* form of speech

(16:25), and this must be kept in mind as we seek its interpretation. Before inquiring into the meaning of our Lord's words here, let us first ask as to His purpose in thus speaking so enigmatically.

The Lord had previously said to the disciples, "Now is the Son of man glorified, and God is glorified in him. Little children, yet *a little while* I am with you. Ye shall seek me: and as I said unto the Jews, Whither I go, ye cannot come; so now I say unto you" (13:31, 33). But it is plain that they understood Him not: "Simon Peter said unto him, Lord, *whither* goest thou?" (13:36). He had said, "I go to prepare a place for you . . . and whither I go ye know, and the way ye know" (14:2, 4). But Thomas had responded, "Lord, we *know not whither thou goest; and how* can we know the way?" (14:5). He had said, "Yet a little while, and the world seeth me no more." (14:19). But they were unresponsive: "Now I go my way to him that sent me; and none of you asketh me, *Whither* goest thou?" (16:4). Now the Lord repeats in parabolic form what He had previously announced, in order to *arouse* them from their stupor of sorrow and to make a deeper impression upon their minds. That His end was gained is evident from the next verse. But we believe that He had a still deeper reason: He was also supplying them with material for comfort in future days of trial. Later, when they recalled these words, they would recognize that the *first* part of them had received fulfilment—a "little while" after He had spoken and they saw Him not; and this would cheer them with the sure hope that in another "little while" they *would* see Him again.

"A little while, and ye shall not see me: and again, a little while, and ye shall see me." In less than two hours, most likely, He was arrested in the Garden, and there the apostles lost sight of their Master—even Peter and John saw Him but for a very little while longer. But He not only disappeared from their bodily vision, but *spiritually* too they lost sight of Him. Their faith was eclipsed. The words of the two disciples on the way to Emmaus no doubt expressed the common sentiment among His followers at that time: "But we trusted that it *had* been he which should have redeemed Israel" (Luke 24:21). The fact that they believed not (Mark 16:11, 13) when they first heard of His resurrection, revealed their state of heart. They were in the darkness of doubt, and therefore could not see *Christ* with the eye of faith. But their seeing Him not, physically and spiritually, was of short continuance. After "a little while"—only three days—He reappeared to them, and then He disappeared again for another "little while" from their bodily vision, though never more would they spiritually lose sight of their Lord and their God.

Now while the above is probably the primary reference in our Lord's words, we have no doubt but that they contain a much deeper meaning, and an application to the whole company of Christians. "There is, as for Christ Himself, the breaking through death into life, so for the disciples a deeply penetrating, fundamental *change from sorrow to joy*. By no means merely their sorrow at His death, and their joy on His living again, after the analogy of the sorrow and joy of the children of men in their changing experience; but as the mediating expression of an essential internal process which the Holy Spirit completed in their case, but which is still going on to the end of all. Thus as *the way of the disciples through sorrow to joy* between the crucifixion and resurrection of our Lord was already for them something preparatory and typical, it becomes to us a *type* of the way which *all His future disciples* have also to pass through that godly sorrow which distinguishes them fully from the world into the joy of faith and life in Christ Jesus" (Stier).

"A little while, and ye shall not see me: and again a little while, and ye shall see me." We believe that it is misleading to place a comma after the word "again," because there are two distinct periods here in view, two "little while's": "a little while and ye shall not see me" referred, first, to the interval between His death and resurrection; "*and* again a little while and ye shall see me," which first found its fulfilment after His resurrection, but in its deeper meaning signifies ye shall see Me in a more intimate and *spiritual* sense. Only ten days after His ascension, by the aid of the Spirit, they *saw* Him in a new, a deeper, a fuller way than ever before. But there is still a further meaning, with a wider application: "And again a little while": compare with this Heb. 10:37: "For yet a little while, and he that shall come will come, and will not tarry"! After this present interval of Christ's session at God's right hand, believers will "*see* him as he is" and be forever with Him.

"Because I go to the Father." This is assigned as the reason why the disciples should "see" Him after a "little while." It must be remembered that He was going to the Father in a *special* character; namely, as the One who had gloriously finished the work which had been given Him to do. He was therefore going to the Father as One entitled to a rich reward. This reward would be bestowed upon Him personally, but also upon the people whom He had purchased for Himself. Hence, His going to the Father thus guaranteed the sending of the Holy Spirit to that people (Acts 2:33) and it was by the Spirit they were enabled to "see" Him (Heb. 2:9). Thus it was His glorification which afforded the means for Him to now reveal Himself unto us *spiritually*. Moreover, *because* He has gone to the Father in this character, He will yet come again and receive us unto Himself (John 14:23) when we shall see Him, no longer through a glass darkly. *His* going to the Father thus manifested His title and fitness to introduce *us* to the Father's House!

"Then said some of his disciples among themselves, What is this that he saith unto us, A little while, and ye shall not see me: and again, a little while, and ye shall see me: and, Because I go to the Father?" (16:17). The Lord's words sounded strangely in the ears of the disciples, and some of them began to discuss the seeming paradox. That they should see Him, and that they should not see Him!—it sounded like a contradiction in terms. And even His expression of going to the Father was by no means plain to them. They thought that the Messiah would *remain* on the earth (12:34). There was no place in their theology for His leaving them and returning to the Father. And yet there *ought* to have been: see Psalms 68:18: 110:1. They erred through not knowing the Scriptures; hence their bewilderment here. How forcibly this illustrates the fact that the *difficulties* we find in the words of Scripture are *self*-created—due to our preconceptions and prejudices.

"They said therefore, What is this that he saith, A little while? We cannot tell what he saith" (16:18). This refers, apparently, to the answer which others among the Eleven made to those of their number (mentioned in the previous verse) who were quietly discussing what the Lord had just said. The first group were completely bewildered; the second puzzled mainly by the "little while." They "desired" to ask Christ, as is clear from 16:19; yet they refrained from doing so. And how slow, oftentimes, are *we* to *seek* for light! "Ye have not, because ye *ask* not" (James 4:2)! God has designedly put many things in His Word in such a way that their meaning cannot be obtained by a rapid and careless reading. He has done so in order to exercise us, and to drive us to our knees; to make us cry, "Open thou mine eyes, that I may behold wondrous things out of thy law" (Psa. 119:18); and to pray, "That which I see not, teach thou me" (Job 34:32).

"Now Jesus knew that they were desirous to ask him, and said unto them, Do ye inquire among yourselves of that I said, A little while, and ye shall not see me: and again a little while, and ye shall see me?" (16:19). "It may seem strange that the desire did not at once find expression in direct inquiry; for surely they had been long enough with Him, and had known Him sufficiently well to induce the conviction that He was 'meek and lowly in heart,' and always more ready to give, than they were to receive, instruction. The truth seems to be, that on this occasion they were both ashamed and afraid to seek the information which they were anxious to obtain—ashamed to acknowledge their ignorance on a subject on which their Master had so often addressed them; and afraid, it may be equally, that they should draw down on themselves a faithful, though kindly rebuke. What is said of a former declaration, seems to have been true of that which now perplexed them, 'they understood not the saying, and they were *afraid* to ask him'; Mark 9:32" (Mr. John Brown).

"It is to be noted that the Lord did not reply directly to their intended question. He does not give them further information on the subject concerning which they were curious. The point which perplexed them was His promised speedy return. They had half made up their minds to lose Him. They had a kind of vague, undefined suspicion that their worst fears regarding Him were about to be realized: but if so, what could He mean by speaking of this quick return? If He must die, how can it be only for 'a little while?' As yet they knew not the Scriptures what the rising from the dead should mean. Their minds were confused, and their hearts filled with sorrow. So the Lord dwells upon this point of time, though He does not directly answer the desired question. He prefers now rather to give them some general prospect of brighter days to come: their sorrow shall give place to *joy*: that should be short, this should be lasting; *that* for a time only, *this* forever." (Mr. George Brown).

The Lord knows what things we have need of before we ask: all things are open before Him, even our hearts! He would not leave His disciples in uncertainty: "Before they call I will answer; and while they are yet speaking, I will hear" (Isa. 65:24). There is something very impressive in the way in which the Lord Jesus here *repeats* what He had said just before: evidently with the intention of fixing these words in their minds. *Seven* times in these four verses occurs this expression "a little while." How the Spirit would impress upon us the *brevity* of our earthly pilgrimage! How the Lord here emphasizes the blessed truth that we should be daily, hourly, *expecting* His return!

"Verily, verily, I say unto you, That ye shall weep and lament, but the world shall rejoice: and ye shall be sorrowful, but your sorrow shall be turned into joy" (16:20). There is no change of subject here as some have strangely thought. Instead, the Lord mentions the *effects* of not seeing Him *and* seeing Him again. The *double* meaning of His words in 16:16 must be borne in mind—their immediate reference to the apostles, and their wider application to all Christians. As they concerned the Eleven, Christ made it known that they would first mourn for Him as one dead, and not only would the decease of their unfailing Comforter result in deep lamentation, but the rejoicing of the world over its seeming victory and His defeat would intensify their sorrows. But after a short season their grief would be turned into rejoicing.

Strikingly was this prediction fulfilled. When Mary Magdalene came to the apostles to announce the Saviour's triumph over the grave, she found them mourning and weeping (Mark 16:10). When Christ approached the two disciples walking to Emmaus, He asked "What manner of communications are these that ye have one to another? as ye walk and *are sad*" (Luke 24:17). How often during those three days must they have remembered His words "Ye shall weep and lament." And while the beloved disciples were sunk in sorrow, their enemies were rejoicing. Solemnly does this come out in the prophetic plaint of the Messiah: "Let not them that are mine enemies wrongfully rejoice over me: neither let them wink with the eye that hate me without a cause" (Psa. 35:19). But these words of Christ also have a direct application to *all* His people on earth: "Sorrow" is their portion too—how could it be otherwise as *identified with* the Man of sorrows during the time of His rejection! The awful enmity of men against God; the way in which the world still treats His beloved Son; the many false prophets who dishonour the Lord; the absence of the Saviour Himself; and the sight of our fellow-creatures rushing heedlessly to destruction, these are enough to make Christians "weep and lament." Add to these our own sad failures, and the failures of our brethren—often more apparent to us than our own—and we can at once perceive the force of the apostle's words, "Even we ourselves *groan* within ourselves waiting for the adoption, the redemption of our body" (Rom. 8:23).

"But your sorrow shall be turned into joy" (16:20). The woman who saw the risen Saviour as they returned from the sepulchre "with fear *and great joy*" (Matt. 28:8) ran to announce the glad tidings to the disciples. When He Himself appeared to them we read, "Then were the disciples *glad*, when they saw the Lord" (John 20:20). And when He ascended on high "they worshipped Him and returned to Jerusalem with *great joy*" (Luke 24:52). But mark here the minute discrimination of our Lord's language. It was not only that their sorrow should *give place* to joy, but be "turned into joy." Their sorrowing became joy! The very *cause* of their sorrow—the death of Christ—now became the *ground* and *subject* of their joy! Grief would not only be replaced by joy, but be transmuted into joy, even as the water was turned into wine! The Cross of Christ is glorified into an eternal consolation. And *what* was it, or rather *Who* was it that brought this about? None other than the Holy Spirit. He has so interpreted for us the death of the Saviour that we now cry, "God forbid that I should glory save in the cross of our Lord Jesus Christ" (Gal. 6:14). So our title for this chapter still holds good here: it is *Christ glorified by the Spirit.*

The final meaning of this profound and full word of Christ's, "your sorrow shall be turned into joy," will find its ultimate realization in all His people when He comes to receive us unto Himself. Weeping may endure for a night, but joy cometh in the morning. And even here the exactitude of our Lord's language is to be seen: *our* "sorrow" shall be "*turned into* joy": our present groanings are but creating within us a larger capacity for joy in the grand hereafter: "Our light affliction, which is but for a moment, *worketh for us* a far more exceeding and eternal weight of glory" (II Cor. 4:17). But how fearful the contrast in the case of unbelievers: "Woe unto you that *laugh* now: for ye *shall* mourn and weep" (Luke 6:25)!

"A woman when she is in travail hath sorrow, because her hour is come: but as soon as she is delivered of the child, she remembereth no more the anguish, for joy that a man is born into the world" (16:21). Plain and simple though this verse appears to be, yet we believe, there is a depth and fulness in it which has never been fully apprehended. First of all it is evident that we have a double parallelism: "a little while and ye shall not see me" (16:16), "ye shall weep and lament, but the world shall rejoice, and ye shall be sorrowful" (16:20), "a woman when she is in travail hath sorrow, because her hour is come" (16:21), all refer to the same thing—the same period of time, the same experience. So too "again a little while and ye shall see me" (16:16), "your sorrow shall be turned into joy" (16:20), and "as soon as she is delivered of the child, she remembereth no more the anguish, for joy that a man is born into the world" (16:21), also correspond. What we have here in verse 21 *repeats*, but in *figurative* language, what Christ had said in the previous verses. The Lord now *illustrates* by a reference to the most familiar of all examples of joy issuing from sorrow. The force of the figure used to portray our sufferings intimates the necessity of them, their severity, their brief duration, and the fact that they are antecedent to and productive of joy. So much is clear on the surface. But in its deeper meaning the figure which the Saviour here employed went *beyond* His literal language in the previous verse.

The symbolical domain of nature has much to teach us if we have eyes to see and hearts to receive. God has wisely and graciously ordered it that the pangs of the mother are compensated in her joy over the fruit of her anguish. And this is a symbolical prophecy, written in nature by the Creator's finger, of the birth of the new man. That, too, is preceded by travail, both on the part of the Spirit and of the one He brings forth: but here travail gives place to joy. The same process is also repeated in the Christian life. The travail-pangs of "mortification" are the precursors of resurrection-joys. There must be, for us too, the *cross* before the crown. There must be *fellowship* with the sufferings of Christ, before we share His glory (Rom. 8:17). Plain intimation of this is given in His words here: "her *hour* is come"—the same expression used by Him so often in conjunction with *His own* "travail" The Holy Spirit has also used this same figure of a travailing woman to set forth the relation in which this present life stands to the future life: see Rom. 8:12, 19, 22, 23.

Marvellously full is this word of Christ's. Fulfilled not only in the experience of the apostles, fulfilled in our regeneration, it is still further fulfilled in our Christian life.

"And ye now therefore have sorrow: but I will see you again, and your heart shall rejoice, and your joy no man taketh from you" (16:22). There is little need for us to enter into a lengthy exposition of this verse. In it the Lord gathers up into a brief summary all that He had said from 16:15 onwards. There is the same fulness of reference as before. Directly, it applied, to the case of the apostles. For a short season they sorrowed over their Master's death and absence. This gave place to rejoicing at His resurrection and ascension. But the *permanency* of their joy—"none taketh from you"—was secured by the coming of the Spirit. But our Lord's words were also addressed to the entire body of His people, therefore, as has been said, "The way of the first disciples between the Passion and Pentecost is a type of the whole interval of the Lord's Church between His departure to the Father and His final return" (Stier).

The following questions are to aid the student on the closing portion of John 16: —

1. In what "day," v. 23?
2. What is meant by "ask me nothing," v. 23?
3. What is the meaning of the first part of v. 24?
4. When did Christ show them "plainly," v. 25?
5. What is the meaning of v. 26?
6. Did the disciples really understand Christ now, v. 29?
7. In what sense did Christ "overcome the world," v. 33?

CHAPTER FIFTY-SIX

Christ's Concluding Consolations

John 16:23-33

The following is an Analysis of the closing section of John 16:—

1. Asking the Father in the name of Christ, vv. 23, 24.
2. Christ's promise to show the Father plainly, v. 25.
3. The Father's love made known, vv. 26, 28.
4. The confession of the apostles, vv. 29, 30.
5. Christ's challenge of their faith, v. 31.
6. Christ's solemn prediction, v. 32.
7. Christ's comforting assurance, v. 33.

Our present section contains the closing words of our Lord's Paschal Discourse. We trust that many readers have shared the writer's sense of wonderment as we have passed from chapter to chapter and verse to verse. A truly wondrous one was this address of Christ. It stands quite by itself, for there is nothing else like it in the four Gospels. Here the Saviour is alone with His own, and most blessedly does He reveal His tender affections for them. Here He speaks no longer to those whose hopes were to be realized in Judaism. Here He anticipates what is treated of in fuller detail in the Epistles, speaking as He does of the *Christian's* position, portion, privileges and responsibilities. There is a fulness in His words which it is impossible for us to exhaust, a depth we can never completely fathom in this life. Every verse will richly repay the most diligent and prolonged study.

In the closing verses of John 16 the Lord Jesus proceeds to set forth even more fully the blessings and privileges which were to issue from His going to heaven, declaring, too, the Father's love for those whom He had given to the Son. First, He assures believers of the readiness of the Father to grant unto them whatsoever they asked Him in the Son's worthy name. Next, He tells them that in thus asking, their joy should be made full. Then He announces that the time would come when He should no more speak in dark sayings, but He would show plainly of the Father. This is followed by the declaration that the Father loveth them because they loved the Son. Then He reminds them again that, having come forth from the Father into the world, He would leave the world and return to the Father. After this there is a break made by the disciples affirming their faith in Him. This is met by the solemn warning that, nevertheless, they would forsake Him. Then He closes by His never-to-be-forgotten words, "Be of good cheer, I have overcome the world." May the Spirit of the Truth grant us His sorely needed guidance as we ponder this passage together.

"In that day ye shall ask me nothing" (16:23). This short sentence has proven a sore puzzle to many of the commentators. There is wide difference of opinion, both as to *what* "day" is in view here, and as to what is signified by "ye shall *ask* me *nothing*." That Christ was here looking forward needs not to be argued; but *how far* forward is what many have not found it easy to decide. Did He mean that day, after the brief interval of separation when they should meet again, of His resurrection? Did He mean the day of pentecost, when the Spirit was to descend upon them, enduing them with power? Did He mean the whole period of Christianity, the "day of salvation?" Or, did He employ this term in the sense that it has in so many Old Testament prophecies(see Isa. 2:11; 5:30; 11:10, etc.), the day of His public manifestations? Or, did He look beyond the bounds of earth's history to the unending perfect "day", the Day of glory? Each of these meanings has been severally contended for by able expositors, and in view of the profound fulness of our Lord's words, we would hesitate to limit them to any one of these possible alternatives: probably several of them are to be combined.

"And in that day ye shall ask me nothing." This is not the first time that this expression was used by Christ. In 14:20 we find that He said, "At [in] that day ye shall know that I am in my Father and ye in me, and I in you." But even there this expression can hardly be limited to one specific reference. If the reader will turn back to our comments on that verse he will find that we have explained it to signify: first, the day when the Holy Spirit was given to guide believers into all the truth; second, and ultimately, to the day of glory, when we shall know even as we are known. It is thus that we understand "In that day" here in 16:23; having both a narrower and wider meaning, a nearer and a remoter application.

"When in immediate connection with what has just been said, we find the greatest promise connected with the strikingly prominent 'in that day' it becomes needful to mark carefully the meaning of this formula. It is obvious that it cannot mean any individual *day;* and we cannot avoid seeing that the *time* signified by it *begins with the day* of the resurrection, if we rightly understood the great turning point of the future, which our Lord since 14:3 has had always before His eyes, has its commencement in the resurrection-morning after the night of suffering and death. But as certain as we have seen embraced in 16:20-22, a comprehensive glance at all the future of the Church, must we in this *connected* but heightened conclusion of all, give the words their furtherest reach of signification. The Lord, as we think at least, intends this 'in that day' to include first of all, the whole period of the dispensation of the Spirit, which already typically commenced in His first return and seeing them again:—and then, pre-eminently, the *end* of this time, the *consummation of the fulness of the Spirit* in His own when He shall have unfolded and imparted all that is Christ's to His people. This is plain from the greatness of the promise connected with it, which can never have its full realization till that goal is reached. 'And in that day *ye shall ask me nothing.* Great and unfathomable word.'" (Stier.)

But what is meant by "ye shall *ask* me nothing?" Strangely and deplorably has this been perverted by some. There have been a few who have argued from this verse that we are here *forbidden* to address *Christ,* directly, in prayer. But Acts 1:24;

7:59, to say nothing of many passages in the Epistles, clearly refutes such an error.

"Ye shall ask me nothing." The first key to this is found in the particular term our Lord here employed. In the Greek another word is used in the latter part of this same verse where He says, "Whatsoever ye shall *ask* the Father in my name, he will give it you." While it is true that these two words are used, in some passages, almost interchangeably, yet that they *have a distinct* meaning is clear from several considerations. If the usage of each word be carefully traced through the New Testament it will be found that the former (erotao) is expressive of *familiar entreaty*, whereas the second (aiteo) signifies a *lowly petition*. Hence, whilst the Lord Jesus is found employing the former in *His* asking the Father on behalf of His disciples, never once does He use the latter term. Even more significant is it to find that *Martha*—who had not sat at His feet and learned of Him as had her more spiritual sister—used the *latter* word when she said, "I know that even now, whatsoever thou wilt *ask* of God, God will give it thee" (John 11:22); failing to discern the Divine glory of His person, she supposed that He would have to appeal to God as a suppliant.

According to its classical usage, "erotao" signifies "to ask questions, to make inquiry in order to obtain information." It is employed in this sense in a number of passages: to seek no further, we find it bearing this meaning in 16:19. "Now Jesus knew that they were desirous to *ask* him, and said unto them, Do you *inquire* among yourselves?" But like the words "in that day," so "ye shall ask me nothing" seem to have a *double* significance here—a relative and an absolute, an immediate and remote, a primary and an ultimate.

"Verily, verily, I say unto you, Whatsoever ye shall ask the Father in my name, he will give it you" (16:23). Here is the second key to the first part of this verse, so far as its primary meaning and immediate application is concerned: asking the Father everything, is contrasted from asking the Son nothing. "In that day" refers primarily to the time when the Holy Spirit was given to them, in which "day" *we* are now living. But when the Holy Spirit came, Christ would be absent; then, instead of asking the Saviour questions (as they did constantly while He was with them), they would petition the Father. "The Lord is really signifying the great change from recourse to Him as their Messiah on earth for every difficulty, not for questions only, but for all they might want day by day, to that access to the Father into which He would introduce them as the accepted Man and glorified Saviour on high" (Mr. W. Kelly). This accounts for the "Verily, verily" with which Christ introduced this second statement: it emphasized the certainty and sufficiency of the new *recourse* of the disciples which He now made known unto them. And how this emphasized His "it is *expedient for you* that I go away" (16:7)! Petitions in Christ's all-prevailing name the apostles would be permitted to present to *the Father,* which was something no saint before the Cross had ever been instructed to urge. As the *God* of Israel He had been known: but now believers were to approach Him in the conscious relationship of children addressing their *Father!*

But if we look forward to the ultimate fulfilment of Christ's words "in that day ye shall ask me nothing," they signify that *in the Glory* we shall know even as we are known, and there will no longer be any need to interrogate Him about any of the problems which now so sorely perplex us. Then we shall—to speak in the language of the context—understand the meaning of our present "sorrows" and "rejoice" forever, for the wise Love that appointed them. Having thus pointed us forward to the final goal, the Lord provides encouragement for us as we journey toward it—"Whatsoever ye shall ask the Father in my name he will give it you." The "whatsoever" must be qualified by whatever is for the Father's glory, will promote His Son's interests, and is for our good.

"Hitherto have ye asked nothing in my name" (16:24). The Lord was not reproving His disciples for a failure in their prayer-life, but was announcing one of the consequences of the great change then at hand. If the reader will note carefully what we said on 14:13, 14, he will see how impossible it was for saints to pray in the name of the Lord Jesus before His ascension. In the previous verses we have learned what the results of the coming of the Spirit would be *saintwards,* here we are shown the effects

Godwards. Consequent on Christ's exaltation, the Spirit in and with believers would draw out their hearts in prayer, teaching them to present their petitions to the Father in the all-prevailing name of the Son.

"Ask, and ye shall receive, that your joy may be full" (16:24). "I enjoin you thus to pray, that not only may you be delivered from all despondency and heart-trouble, but that in the enjoyment of all heavenly and spiritual blessings, and in the possession of all that is necessary and sufficient to secure the success of the great enterprise on which you are about to enter, you may be filled with holy happiness, heavenly joy—joy in the Holy Spirit. There is a close connection between the two advices given by an apostle under the influence of the Spirit of His Master: 'Rejoice evermore: pray without ceasing' (I Thess. 5:16, 17). The second is the means of securing the first. If we cease to pray, we are likely to cease to rejoice—we must 'pray without ceasing' that we may 'rejoice evermore': and were we, instead of being anxious, careful, and troubled about many things, to 'be anxious about nothing, but in everything by prayer and supplication, make our requests known unto God, with thanksgiving' (Phil. 4:6), assuredly the 'peace of God, *would* keep our hearts and minds through Christ Jesus'; and, amid external troubles, our joy would be full" (Mr. John Brown).

"These things have I spoken unto you in proverbs: but the time cometh when I shall no more speak unto you in proverbs, but I shall show you plainly of the Father" (16:25). It will be noted that the margin gives "parables" as an alternative for "proverbs." In this word of Christ there is, again, a fullness of meaning which no brief definition can comprehend. In the Greek there are two words used (for the one Hebrew word "mashal")—"parabole" and "paroimia": the former is never used in John's Gospel: the latter occurs in 10:6 and here. Possibly it had been better to render it "dark saying" in the present instance, as the Lord sets it in antithesis from "showing *plainly* of the Father." And yet the thoughts connected with "proverbs" is not to be excluded. The wisdom of Solomon is recorded in *his* "Proverbs." So the Lord here intimates that He, the Truth, the "greater than Solomon," would not do otherwise than speak in sentences with a fulness of meaning which no mere mental acumen can penetrate. But again, the Greek word here may properly be rendered "parables," and the distinctive idea connected with this term is probably to be included as well.

"Parables are truths given and yet concealed from those who cannot or will not receive them; but to the ready heart that can take them in, they can be made known, as we see in Matt. 13:13-16. The parables there were not understood by His enemies and would not have been by the disciples, but He opened them. A parable is not a story to illustrate a truth; it is the truth itself. As though He would say, 'It will not be received, but I will speak it nevertheless.' It is like a nut, needing to be cracked open, but the kernel is there; and rich too. Now He had spoken to them in that way. Many of the incidents that occur have truth in them that would be open only to the ear and eye of the new man, enlightened and exercised by the Holy Spirit.

"He had said these things, whether they understood them or not; but the hour was coming when He would no more speak unto them in parables, but would show them plainly of the Father. That is now by the Holy Spirit. There is no book in the Scripture that is more full of teaching that requires fellowship with the subject, and the mind of the writer—the Spirit—than the Gospel of John. Wherein we fail, it is that we are so little in fellowship with Him. The deeper the fellowship, the more thoroughly we would understand all that has been told. That is, then, the reason for speaking in parables, but not doing it when the Holy Spirit comes (there are *no* parables in the Epistles, and note II Cor. 3:12: A.W.P.). The Holy Spirit's business is to take of the things of Christ and tell them out and make them actually ours." (Mr. Malachi Taylor).

The Lord went on to say that the time (hour) was at hand when He would speak no more obscurely to the disciples, but would plainly "show them of the Father." This promise began to be accomplished even before Pentecost. On the very day of His resurrection, "beginning at Moses and all the prophets, he expounded" to the two disciples on the way to Emmaus, "the things concerning himself" (Luke 24:27). To Mary Magdalene He made known that *His* Father was His *brethren's* Father (John 20:17). So in Luke 24:45 we are also told, "Then opened he their understanding, that they might understand the Scriptures." But the complete fulfilment was given in the coming of the Spirit to guide them into all the Truth: then the veil was completely taken off their hearts, and with open face they contemplated the glory of God in the face of Jesus Christ. In 16:14 the Lord had said *the Spirit* would "show," here He says "*I* will show"; there He had spoken of the Spirit showing the things "of *mine,*" here "I will show of *the Father.*" This interchange strikingly attests the *unity* of the three Persons in the Godhead.

"At that day ye shall ask in my name" (16:26). In the day of the Spirit believers would ask the Father in the name of Christ, not only plead His name as a motive, but come to God in the value of His person. What an incentive is this for each Christian reader to engage in this holy exercise! "The benefit of prayer is so great that it cannot be expressed. Prayer is the dove which, when sent out, returns again, bringing with it the olive-leaf, namely, peace of heart. Prayer is the golden chain which God holds fast, and lets not go until He blesses. Prayer is the Moses' rod which brings forth the water of consolation out of the Rock of Salvation. Prayer is Samson's jawbone, which smites down our enemies. Prayer is David's harp, before which the evil spirit flies. Prayer is the key to heaven's treasures" (John Gerhard.)

"And I say not unto you, that I will pray the Father for you." The first design of Christ in these words was to repel a false notion which many have entertained, namely that the Father must be besought by Christ before He will notice us. It is not that Christ here denies that He would intercede for us, but He would assure us that such intercession on His part is not needed to induce the Father *to* love us—the next verse makes it very clear. It was Christ assuring His disciples that, following His exaltation ("in that day"), the way would be open for them to come into the Father's presence. "I say not unto you, that I will pray the Father for you." "This no more denies Christ's intercession for us, than 16:23 forbids the servant praying to his Lord about His work or His house. It is not an absolute statement, but it is simply an ellipse, which the words following explain." (Mr. W. Kelly.)

"For the Father himself loveth you, because ye have loved me, and have believed that I came out from God." (16:27). This at once indicates the line of thought in the Saviour's mind at the close of the previous verse. It was not that He had to coerce the Father either to hear our prayers or to love us. The favours which we receive from the Father are not extorted from Him by the importunate pleading of the Saviour. So far from the Father having no regard for our happiness He *loves us,* loves us with a special love of approbation because we love His Son: therefore is He ever ready to minister to our welfare, watching over us with paternal affection and care. The Father does not love us because Christ intercedes for us; but Christ intercedes for us because we are the objects of the Father's special love. What a blessed word is this! Spoken for our assurance and comfort as we journey homewards. "Whatsoever they ask in Christ's name shall be given them, is secured by the love of the Father, no less than by the intercession of Christ; nay, even more so, inasmuch as the only fountain is more than the only channel, though both are equally necessary in their own places." (Mr. John Brown.)

"For the Father himself loveth you, because ye have loved me, and have believed that I came out from God." It is to be noted that "love" is here placed before "believing." One reason for this was because Christ had just been speaking of love in the previous verse; now He proceeds to speak of faith so as to prepare the way for that profession of faith which the disciples at once made. But no doubt the word "believe" here is used as in 14:1. It was not the initial act of faith in the Lord Jesus, but the *confiding* in and on Him *after* His return to the Father.

"I came forth from the Father, and am come into the world; again, I leave the world, and go to the Father." (16:28). "Having been led to mention His coming forth from God, our Lord concludes His explicatory remarks by stating in the fewest words the truths which, above all others, it was of importance that the disciples should hold fast in the hour of temptation, which was just coming on them to try them." (Mr. John Brown.) These are the vital facts for faith to lay hold of. First, Christ came forth from the Father. He is the heavenly One come down to earth; not only "sent" officially, but "come" by voluntary consent. Second, He came into the world; and why? That He might be the Saviour of sinners. Third, He has gone back to the Father. How? Through death and resurrection. With what intent? To diffuse from on high the benefits of His redeeming work. Christ's design here was to show the apostles how fully warranted was their confidence in Himself.

"His disciples said unto him, Lo, now speakest thou plainly, and speakest no proverb. Now are we sure that thou knowest all things, and needest not that any man should ask thee: by this we believe that thou camest forth from God." (16:29, 30). This confession of the apostles looks back to what Christ had just said in 16:27, 28. The assurance that the Father Himself loved them had comforted their hearts: the declaration from their Master's own lips that *they* "loved and believed" in Him gave them new confidence. As Calvin beautifully puts it: "The disciples did not fully understand the meaning of Christ's discourse; but though they were not capable of this, the mere odor of it refreshed them." All was no longer dark to them; their faith was confirmed. When they declared, "now speakest thou plainly, and speakest no proverb" (obscure saying), they were looking back to what He had said in 16:25. It seems clear that the apostles imagined the "day" the Lord mentioned had already arrived, and that their Master was now making good His promise to them. This is the more evident from their statement, "Now are we sure that thou knowest all things, and needest not that any man should *ask* thee," which looks back to 16:23: "And in that day ye shall ask *me* nothing."

"Now are we sure that thou knowest all things, and needest not that any man should ask thee: by this we believe that thou camest forth from God." The disciples perceived that the Lord had accurately discerned their thoughts, and, unasked, had solved their difficulties. Yet it is clear that they failed to take in the fulness of what He had just said. They believed that He had come forth from "God" (16:27). So far, so good. But *He* had spoken of coming forth from "the Father" and of returning to Him (16:28). Upon this they were silent, and for a very good reason: at that time they neither believed nor understood that deeper point of view. The "Father" is God truly. But *God* speaks of the one Divine Being who is over all—Creator, Governor, Sustainer, Judge. *Father* speaks of *relationship,* the relationship of God to His *children.* Of this the disciples, as yet, understood little, perhaps nothing.

"We believe that thou camest forth *from God.*" Really this went no further than a confession that He was the promised *Messiah.* Nicodemus said, "Rabbi, we know thou art a teacher come *from God*" (John 3:2). The woman of Samaria exclaimed, "Come see a man who told me all things that ever I did: is not this *the Christ?*" (4:29). Those who witnessed the miracle of the loaves avowed, "This is of a truth that prophet that should come into the world" (6:14). Peter testified, "We believe, and are sure that thou art *that Christ,* the Son of the living *God*"—not "Father"! (6:69). Martha said, "Yea, Lord, I believe that thou art *the Christ*, the Son of *God,* which should come into the world." (11:27). The word of the apostles here in 16:30 went no farther than these other confessions. "We believe that thou camest forth *from God.*" In truth they had apprehended nothing that raised them above the effect of Christ's *rejection;* only the realization that He came forth from *the Father* and was returning to Him, could give this.

"They had no conception of the mighty change from all that they had gathered of the Kingdom as revealed in the Old Testament, to the new state of things that would follow His absence with the Father on high and the presence of the Holy Spirit here below. It sounded plain to their ears; but even up to the ascension they feebly, if at all, caught a glimpse of it. They to the last clung to the hopes of Israel, and these surely remain to be fulfilled another day. But they understood not *this* 'Day,' during which, if the Jews are treated as reprobate, even as He was rejected of them, those born of God should in virtue of Christ and His work be placed in immediate relationship with *the Father*. His return to the Father was a parable still, though the Lord does not correct their error, as indeed it was useless: they would soon enough learn how little they knew. But at least even then, they had the inward consciousness that He knew all, and, as He penetrated their thoughts had no need that any should ask Him. 'Herein we believe that thou camest out from God.' Undoubtedly—yet how far below the truth He had uttered (in 16:28), is that which they were thus confessing! The Spirit of His Son sent into their hearts would give them in due time to know the Father; as redemption accomplished and accepted could alone provide the needful ground for this" (The Bible Treasury). No wonder the Lord had just previously announced to the apostles: "I have yet many things to say unto you, but ye cannot bear them *now*"!

"Jesus answered them, Do ye now believe?" (16:31). It seems to us that the Lord was here *challenging* their faith. In a real sense they *did* believe that He was the promised Messiah—"come out from God." But their faith was on the eve of being severely tested, and under that testing it would be shaken to its very foundations; though fail it would not. He with His own omniscient foresight, knew what lay ahead of them. The indignity, the sufferings, the crucifixion of their Master would indeed cause them to be "offended." Their faith was genuine; but it was not strong *as they* supposed. This explains, we think, the "now"—"Jesus answered them, Do ye *now* believe?"; ye believe Me while I am with you and things are going according to *your* minds, but what will you do when I shall be taken from you, delivered into the hands of the Gentiles, die, and be buried! The Lord then was *warning* them against their self-confidence.

"We need not doubt that the profession of the Eleven was real and sincere. They honestly meant what they said. But they did not know themselves. They did not know what they were capable of doing under the pressure of the fear of men and strong temptation. They had not rightly estimated the weakness of the flesh, the power of the Devil, the feebleness of their own resolutions, the shallowness of their own faith. All this they had yet to learn by painful experience. Like young recruits, they had yet to learn that it is one thing to know the soldier's drill and wear the uniform, and quite another to be steadfast in the day of battle. Let us mark these things and learn wisdom. The true secret of spiritual strength is self-distrust and deep humility. 'When I am weak, then am I strong' (II Cor. 12:10). None of us, perhaps, have the least idea how much we might fall if placed suddenly under the influence of strong temptation. Happy is he who never forgets the words, 'Let him that thinketh he standeth take heed lest he fall,' and, remembering our Lord's disciples, pray daily, 'Hold thou me up and then I shall be safe.'" (Bishop Ryle).

"Behold, the hour cometh, yea, is now come, that ye shall be scattered, every man to his own, and shall leave me alone" (16:32). This was spoken for the disciples' sakes, that His prediction of the heavy hour of pressure might prepare them for it. It was said to humble them, to destroy their present self-confidence. Note the opening, "Behold" to arrest their attention! "Ye shall be scattered!" Without the Shepherd, they would be dispersed abroad. "Every man to his own"—his own shelter or hiding-place. Each of them would provide for *his own* safety. When the storm burst there was shelter for all *but Christ*. He performed His Work of Atonement *alone,* because He *alone* was qualified to do it.

"And yet I am not alone, because the Father is with me" (16:32). How gracious of the Saviour to address this word for the comfort of *their* hearts! Moreover, the consciousness of the Father's presence was the stay of His own heart. This is clear from Isa. 50:7, "For the Lord God will help me; therefore shall I not be confounded; therefore have I set my face like a flint, and I know that I shall not be ashamed." "Let us here, in transition to the following verse mark how all this is a type for the entire future of the Church. Often is this scattering of the disciples from His presence repeated, in various degrees and with various manifestations, but He is not alone. And even if in this day all men were to leave Him, He abides what He is, and the Father is with Him. His holy cause can never be forsaken or lost" (Stier). Similarly Calvin remarks: "Whosoever well ponders this will hold firm his faith though the world shake, nor will the defection of all others overturn his confidence; we do not render God full honour unless He alone is felt to be sufficient to us."

"These things I have spoken unto you, that in me ye might have peace" (16:33). Having made a final reference to the awful "hour" then at hand, the Lord winds up His matchless discourse with a parting word of *encouragement* and *victory*. He here condenses into a single sentence the instruction which He had given them in the upper room. The "peace" of His own was what His tender heart was concerned about. "Ever thinking more of others than of Himself, even in this near prospect of the bitter Cross, He forgets His own grief in the grief of His disciples. He is occupied in comforting those who ought to have been *His* comforters" (Mr. G. Brown). The "peace" of which He spake can be enjoyed only by communion with Himself. In the previous verse He had mentioned *their* forsaking Him; but *He* had not forsaken them. Three days later He would return with His "peace be unto you" (20:19), then did they learn, once for all, that *in Him alone* was peace to be found. But He does not hide from them the fact that "in the world" they should have "tribulation," but He *first* assures them that, notwithstanding this, there *was* peace for them in Him.

"In the world ye shall have tribulation" (16:33). This is not to be restricted to the *violent* enmity of the ungodly. It is a *general* term for distress of any kind. The Latin word from which our "tribulation" is taken, was used of the *flail* which separated the wheat from the chaff. There are temptations, trials, troubles in the world as well as *from* it. "In the world" is to be in the place of testing. While the Christian is left down here he suffers from the weakness and weariness of the body, from temporal losses and disappointments, from the severing of cherished ties, as well as from the sneers and taunts, the hatred and persecution of the world. But though "in the world" is *tribulation,* "in Christ" there is "*peace.*" The world cannot rob us of that, nor can its evil "prince" destroy it. But let us never forget that this "peace" is *only* enjoyed by *faith.* It is only as we abide in conscious communion with the Saviour that we can anticipate the unclouded and unending joys of the future. The peace which is for us in Christ is appropriated just so far as faith lays hold of our perfect acceptance, our eternal security, and our wondrous portion in Him.

"But be of good cheer; I have overcome the world" (16:33). The influence and power of "the world" is powerful, but not all-powerful. It has been fought and overcome. One greater than it, mightier than its "prince," has been here, and vanquished it. The world did its utmost in the battle, but the Son of God prevailed. Noah *condemned* the world (Heb. 11:7), but Christ *conquered* it. It has no longer any power left but what He permits. It was in the way of temptation, suffering and obedience that He fought and won. Therefore let us "Be of good cheer." The world is a conquered world; it has been conquered for us by Christ. Then let us take courage. The storms of trial and persecution may sometimes beat fiercely upon us; but let them only drive us closer to Christ.

"But be of good cheer; I have overcome the world." What a glorious close for this Discourse! The foundation of peace is our Saviour's personal victory, here anticipated by Him *before* the conflict! How this should stimulate us. The world is still essentially the same; *but so is Christ!* And our Lord is still saying, "Be of good cheer; I have overcome the world." There must be no surrender, no compromise, no fellowship with the world. Here is our Lord's war-cry: "To him that overcometh will I grant to sit with me in my throne, even as I also overcame, and am set down with my Father in his throne" (Rev. 3:21). Ere long the conflict will cease by the victory gained, for "Whatsoever is born of God overcometh the world; and this is the victory that overcometh the world, even our faith" (I John 5:4). The day is nigh at hand when Christ shall come to reward His servants. Then shall the victor be crowned. "And oh, the delight of casting these crowns at His feet, and ascribing forever and ever, glory, and honour, and dominion and blessing to the Great Overcomer, to Him who conquered for us, who conquered in us, who made us more than conquerors! It is sweet to anticipate this glorious result of all our tribulations and struggles; and in the enjoyment of *peace in Him* amidst these struggles and tribulations, to raise, though in broken accents, and with a tremulous voice, the song which, like the sound of great waters, shall unceasingly, everlastingly, echo through heaven, 'Worthy is the Lamb that was slain'" (Mr. John Brown).

Let the student work on the following questions as preparation for our next lesson:—

1. What does the "lifting up of His eyes" teach us, v. 1?
2. What did Christ refer to in "glorify thy Son," v. 1?
3. How is v. 2 related to Christ's petition?
4. Does v. 3 give a *definition* of "eternal life" or—?
5. Why did Christ refer to the Father as "the only true God," v. 3?
6. What was Christ's "glory" before the world, v. 5?
7. By how many different pleas (in vv. 1, 4) does Christ support His petition in v. 5?

CHAPTER FIFTY-SEVEN

Christ Interceding

John 17:1-5

The following is an Analysis of the first section of John 17:

1. The Son praying, v. 1.
2. His desire for the Father's glory, v. 1.
3. His own glory subsidiary, v. 1.
4. The consequences of His glorification, v. 2.
5. The way to and means of eternal life, v. 3.
6. The Son rendering an account of His stewardship, v. 4.
7. His reward, v. 5.

The seventeenth of John contains the longest recorded prayer which our Lord offered during His public ministry on earth, and has been justly designated *His High Priestly Prayer*. It was offered in the presence of His apostles, after the institution and celebration of the Lord's Supper, and immediately following the Paschal discourse recorded in 14 to 16. It has been appropriately said, "The most remarkable prayer followed the most full and consoling discourse ever uttered on earth" (Matt. Henry). It differs from the prayer which Christ "taught his diciples," for in that there are petitions which the Saviour could not offer for Himself, while in this there are petitions which none else but Christ could present. In this wonderful prayer there is a solemnity and elevation of thought, a condensed power of expression, and a comprehensiveness of meaning, which have affected the minds and drawn out the hearts of the most devoted of God's children to a degree that few portions of Scripture have done.

In John 17 the veil is drawn aside, and we are admitted with our great High Priest into "the holiest of all." Here we approach the secret place of the tabernacle of the Most High, therefore it behoves us to put off our shoes from off our feet, listening with humble, reverent and prepared hearts, for the place whereon we now stand is indeed holy ground. We give below a few brief impressions of other writers.

"This is truly, beyond measure, a warm and hearty prayer. He opens the depths of His heart, both in reference to us and to His Father, and He pours them all out. It sounds so honest, so simple; it is so deep, so rich, so wide, no one can fathom it" (Martin Luther).

Melanchthon, another of the Reformers, when giving his last lecture before his death, said on John 17: "There is no voice which has ever been heard, either in heaven or in earth, more exalted, more holy, more fruitful, more sublime, than the prayer offered up by the Son to God Himself."

The eminent Scottish Reformer, John Knox, had this chapter read to him every day during his last illness, and in the closing scene, the verses that were read from it consoled and animated him in the final conflict.

"The seventeenth chapter of the Gospel by John, is, without doubt, the most remarkable portion of the most remarkable book in the world. The Scripture of truth, given by inspiration of God, contains many wonderful passages, but none more wonderful than this—none so wonderful. It is the utterance of the mind and heart of the Godman, in the very crisis of His great undertaking, in the immediate prospect of completing, by the sacrifice of Himself, the work which had been given Him to do, and for the accomplishment of which He had become incarnate. It is the utterance of these to the Father who had sent Him. What a concentration of thought and affection is there in these few sentences! How 'full of grace,' how 'full of truth.' How condensed, and yet how clear the thoughts,—how deep, yet how calm, the feelings which are here, so far as the capabilities of human language permit, worthily expressed! All is natural and simple in thought and expression—nothing intricate or elaborate, but there is a width in the conceptions which the human understanding cannot measure—a depth which it cannot fathom. There is no bringing out of these plain words all that is seen and felt to be in them" (Mr. John Brown).

"The chapter we have now begun is the most remarkable in the Bible. It stands alone, and there is nothing like it" (Bishop Ryle).

Even Mr. W. Kelly with his caution and conservatism writes, "Next follows a chapter which one may perhaps characterise truly as unequalled for depth and scope in all the Scriptures."

This prayer of our Lord is wonderful as a specimen of the communications which constantly passed between the Son and His Father while He was here on earth. Vocal prayer seems to have been habitual with our Saviour. While being baptised He was engaged in prayer (Luke 3:21). Immediately on the commencement of His public ministry we find that, after a short repose, following a day of unremitting labour, "He rose up a great while before day, and went out, and departed into a solitary place, and there prayed" (Mark 1:35). On the eve of selecting the twelve apostles He "went out into a mountain to pray, and continued all night in prayer to God" (Luke 6:12). It was while engaged in the act of prayer that He was transfigured (Luke 9:29). And it was while praying that He ceased to breathe (Luke 23:46). Only the briefest mention is made as to the substance of these prayers—in most instances none at all. But here in John 17, the Holy Spirit has been pleased to record at length His prayer in the upper room. How thankful we should be for this!

Perhaps the most interesting way to view this prayer is as a *model* of His high priestly intercession for us, which He continually makes in the immediate presence of God, on the ground of His completed and accepted sacrifice. The first intimation of this is found in the fact that the Lord Jesus here prayed audibly in the presence of His disciples. He prayed that their interests might be secured, but He prayed audibly that they should be aware of this, that they might know what a wondrous place they had in His affections, that they might be assured that all His influence with the Father would be employed for their advantage. More plainly still is this intimated in 17:13: "And now come I to thee and these things I speak in the world, *that* they might have my joy fulfilled in themselves"—*q.d.* "These are intercessions which in heaven I will never cease to make before God; but I make them now in the world, in your hearing, that you may more distinctly understand how I am there to be employed in promoting your welfare, so that you may be made, in large measure, partakers of *My* happiness." "The petitions for Himself are much briefer than those which He presents for His people—the former being only two, or, rather, but one, variously expressed; while the latter are quite a number, earnestly urged, with a variety of pleas. This arrangement and division of the matter of the prayer justifies the view which has not unfrequently been taken of it: that it was throughout *intercessory* and the substance and model of that intercession which He constantly makes in heaven as our great High Priest" (Mr. T. Houston).

It is in His *mediatorial* character that the Saviour here prays: as the eternal Son, now in the form of a Servant. The office of a mediator or day's-man is "to lay his hand upon both" (Job 9:33); to treat with each party. In the previous chapters we have beheld Christ dealing with believers in the name of the Father, opening His counsels to them; now we find Him dealing with the Father on behalf of believers, presenting their cause to Him, just as Moses, the typical mediator, spoke to God (Exodus 19:19) and from God (Exodus 20:19), so did our blessed Saviour speak from God and to God. And He is still performing the same office and work: speaking to us in the Word, speaking for us in His intercession on High.

The prayer that we are now about to meditate upon is a standing monument of Christ's affection for the Church. In it we are permitted to hear the desires of His heart as He spreads them before the Father, seeking the temporal, spiritual and eternal welfare of those who are His own. This prayer did not pass away as soon as its words were uttered, or when Christ ascended to heaven, but retains a perpetual efficacy. "Just as the words of creation hath retained their vigor these six thousand years: 'Increase and multiply: Let the earth bring forth after its kind,' so this prayer of Christ's retains its force, as if but newly spoken" (Mr. T. Manton). Let us remember our Lord's words, "Father, I thank thee that thou hast heard me. And I knew that thou hearest *me always*" (John 11:41, 42) as we ponder this prayer together.

"These words spake Jesus, and lifted up his eyes to heaven" (17.1). The first four words look backwards and their meaning is fixed by the opening clause in 16:33. They refer to the whole consolatory discourse recorded in the three preceding chapters. Having completed His address to the disciples, He now lifted up His eyes and heart to the Father. The connection is emphasized by the Spirit: "These words spake Jesus, *and* lifted up his eyes to heaven, and said." What an example for all of His servants! He had said everything to the apostles which a wise kindness could dictate in order to sustain them in the supremely trying circumstances in which they were about to be placed, and as the hour was at hand when they were to be separated from Him, He employs the few moments now remaining in commending them to the care of the Father—His Father and their Father. From *preaching* He passed to *prayer!* Thereby He teaches us that after we have done all we can to promote the holiness and comfort of those with whom we are connected, we should in prayer and supplication beseech Him, who is the author of all good, to bless the objects of our care and the means which we have employed for their welfare. "Doctrine has no power, unless efficacy is imparted to it from above. Christ holds out an example to teach them, not to employ themselves only in sowing the Word, but by mingling prayers with it, to implore the assistance of God, that His blessing may render their labours fruitful" (John Calvin).

"And lifted up his eyes to heaven." While delivering the discourse recorded in the previous chapters His eyes, no doubt, had been fixed with tender solicitude upon His disciples. But now as a token that He was about to engage in prayer, He lifts up His eyes toward heaven. "This shows that bodily gestures in prayer and worship of God are not altogether to be overlooked as unmeaning" (Bishop Ryle). The gesture naturally expresses withdrawal of the thoughts and the affections from earthly things, deep veneration, and holy confidence. It denoted *the elevation of His heart* to God. Said David, "Unto thee O Lord, do I *lift up* my soul" (Psa. 25:1). In true prayer the affections go out to God. Our Lord's action also teaches us the *spiritual reverence* which is due God: the heaven of heavens is His dwelling-place, and the turning of the eyes toward His Throne expresses a recognition of God's majesty and excellence. "Unto thee *lift I up* mine eyes, O thou that dwellest in the heavens" (Psa. 123:1). Again, such a posture signifies *confidence in God*. There can be no real prayer until there is a turning away from all creature dependencies: "I will *lift up* mine eyes unto the hills. From whence cometh my help? My help cometh from the Lord, which made heaven and earth" (Psa. 121:1, 2). The believer looks around, and finds no ground for help; his relief must come from God above.

"And said, Father." The Mediator here addresses God as *Father*. He was His "Father" in a threefold sense. First, by virtue of His human nature, miraculously produced. His body was "prepared" for Him by God (Heb. 10:5). Just as in the human realm the begetter of the child is its father, so the One who made the body of Christ, became the Father of His human nature: "And the angel answered and said unto her [Mary], the Holy Spirit shall come upon thee, and the power of the Highest shall overshadow thee: therefore also that holy thing which shall be born of thee shall be called *the Son of God*" (Luke 1:35). The *man* Christ Jesus is thus in a peculiar sense, the Son of God. In like manner, Adam, who was created by God in His own image and likeness, is called "the son of God" (Luke 3:38). Second, God stands in the relation of "Father" to our Lord as the *Head* and *Representative* of the holy family redeemed from among men. He is thus "The first born among many brethren" (Rom. 8:29). To this the apostle seems to refer when he applies to the Lord Jesus that Old Testament word "I will be to him a *Father*, and he shall be to me a Son" (Heb. 1:5). Third, the appellation "Father" given to the first person of the Trinity by our Saviour, primarily, and usually refers to that *essential* relation which subsisted between the first and second persons of the God head from all eternity. *Identity of nature* is the chief idea suggested by the term. In Rom. 8:32, Christ is spoken of as God's "*own* Son," intimating that He is a Son in a sense absolutely peculiar to Himself.

"And said, Father." Two things were expressed. First, *relationship*: the relationship of sonship. This was His claim to be heard. It was as though He had said, "O thou with whom I have existed in unity of essence, perfection, and enjoyment from the unbegun eternity, and by whose will and operation I have been clothed miraculously with human nature and constituted the Head of all appointed unto salvation—I now come to thy throne of grace." Second, it indicated *affection*. It expressed love, veneration, confidence, submission. In whom should a son trust if not in his father? It was as though He had said, "I trust Thy power, Thy wisdom, Thy benignity, Thy faithfulness. Into Thy hands I commend Myself. I know that Thou wilt hear My prayer for Thou art My Father!" Previously Christ had commanded prayer: here, by His own blessed example He *commends* to us this holy exercise.

"The hour is come." This is the seventh and last time that the Lord Jesus refers to this most momentous "hour"—see our remarks on 2:4. This was the greatest "hour" of all—because most critical and pregnant with eternal issues—since hours began to be numbered. It was the hour when the Son of God was to terminate the labours of His important life by a death still more important and illustrious. It was the hour when the Lord of glory was to be made sin for His people, and bear the holy wrath of a sin-hating God. It was the hour for fulfilling and accomplishing many prophecies, types and symbols which for hundreds and thousands of years had pointed forward to it. It was the hour when events took place which the history of the entire universe can supply no parallel: when the Serpent was permitted to bruise the heel of the woman's Seed; when the sword of Divine justice smote Jehovah's Fellow; when the sun refused to shine; when the earth rocked on its axis; but when the elect company were redeemed, when Heaven was gladdened, and which brought, and shall bring to all eternity, "glory to God in the highest."

But why did the Saviour begin His prayer by referring to this "hour"? As a *plea* to support the petitions that He was about to present. "In our Lord's prayer for Himself there is pleading as well as petition. Prayer is the expression of desire for benefit by one who needs it, to one who, in his estimation, is able and disposed to confer it. Request or petition is therefore its leading element; but in the expression of desire by one intelligent being to another, it is natural that the reasons *why* the desire is cherished, and the request presented, should be stated, and the grounds unfolded, on which the hope is founded, that the desire should be granted. Petitions and pleading are thus connected in prayer from man to man; and they are so, likewise, in prayer from men to God. Whoever reads carefully the prayers uttered by holy men, influenced and guided by the Spirit of God, recorded in Scripture, will be struck with the union of petition and pleading, by which they are distinguished. When they are brought 'near to God'—when they, as Job says, 'find him and come even to his seat,' how do 'they *order their cause* before him, and fill their mouths with arguments' (Job 23:3-4)? They '*plead*' with Him, as Jeremiah expresses it" (12:1). (Mr. John Brown).

Christ's first plea was the intimate and endearing relation in which He stood to the object of worship: "*Father* . . . glorify thy *Son*." There is a powerful plea in each of these words. His second plea was "the hour is come"—the time *appointed* for granting this petition had arrived. Like so many of His words in these closing chapters, "the hour" here seems to have a *double* significance: referring not only to His sufferings, but also looking forward to the resurrection-side of the Cross—compare our remarks on 13:31. "This is the appointed period for the remarkable glorification of the Son by the Father in His sufferings, by His sufferings, for His sufferings—under them, after them. 'The time, yea, the set time, is come,' and if the time be come shall not the event take place? It is a matter of Divine purpose, and when was a Divine purpose falsified! It is a matter of Divine promise, and when was a Divine promise frustrated!" (Mr. John Brown).

"Glorify thy Son, that thy Son also may glorify thee" (17:1). This is so closely connected with what follows in the next two verses that it is difficult to treat of it separately. In 17:2 and 3 Christ describes the particular mode of glorifying the Father on which His heart was set, and the *aspect* of the glorification of Himself which He here prays for, namely, to have power over all flesh and to give eternal life to as many as the Father had given Him. There was a *double* object of desire, a *double* subject of prayer; the glorification of the Father in the bestowal of eternal life upon the elect, and the glorification of the Son as subsidiary to this as the necessary and effectual means of accomplishing it. Thus we see the perfect *disinterestedness* of Christ. He prayed to be "glorified" not for His *own* sake, but that *the Father* might be glorified in *our* salvation! Here again we see Him loving us "unto the end!"

"Glorify thy Son." This was the Saviour requesting the Father to support Him on the Cross, afterwards to bring Him out of the grave and set Him at His own right hand, so as to bring to a triumphant completion the work given Him to do; and this in order that the glorious attributes of the Father—His justice, holiness, mercy and faithfulness—might be exhibited and magnified, for God is most "glorified" when the excellencies of His character are manifested to and acknowledged by His creatures. The glorification of the Son, in accord with the double meaning of the "hour" here, would mean Glorify Me *in* My sufferings, and glorify Me *after* My sufferings. In both of these aspects was His prayer answered. The angel sent to strengthen Him in the Garden, the testimony of Pilate—"I find no fault in him,"—the drawing of the dying thief to the Saviour while He hung upon the Cross, the rending of the temple veil, the confession of the centurion, "Truly, this was the Son of God," were all so many responses of the Father to this petition. His resurrection and exaltation to the highest seat in Heaven, was His glorification following His sufferings.

There is much for us to learn here. First, mark the connection: "the hour is come, glorify thy Son." "The true remedy of tribulation is to look to the succeeding glory, and to counterbalance future dangers with present hopes. *This* was comfort against *that* sad hour. So it must be our course: not to look at things which are seen, but to things which are not seen (II Cor. 4:17); to defeat sense by faith. When the mind is in heaven it is fortified against the pains which the body feeleth on earth" (Mr. Thos. Manton—Puritan). Second, observe *what* Christ sought: to be "glorified" by the Father—not to be enriched by men, not to be honoured by the world. This should be our desire too. Christ rebuked those who received honour one from another instead of *seeking* the honour that cometh from God (John 5:44), and because they loved the praise of men, more than the *praise* of God (12:43). We should not only seek for grace, but glory. Third, note that Christ asked for *what* He knew *would be* given Him. The Father had said "I have both glorified, and will glorify again" (12:28). Neither promises nor providence render prayer meaningless or useless. Fourth, Christ prayed for this glory in order that *He* might glorify *the Father*. Here too, He has left us an example. Whatsoever we do is to be done to the glory of God, and nothing should be asked from Him save for *His* glory.

"As thou hast given him power over all flesh, that he should give eternal life to as many as thou hast given him" (17:2). "The Father is first of all to be glorified in the humanity of the God-man, who presents Himself to that end; then, through Him in His disciples, so that in this first word concerning the mutual glorification, that is already involved and included which follows in 17:10. In 17:2 we have a more specific development and explanation of the sense in which this glorification of the Father to and in fallen humanity is meant" (Stier). We regard the connecting "as" or "according as" as having a double force, supplying a *reason for* and describing *the manner of* the Father's glorification of Christ. Let us examine the verse in this order of thought.

Verse 2 contains the third plea which the Saviour presented to the Father: to glorify the Son was in accord with the place which the Father had destined Him to fill, and the work which He had appointed Him to perform: the glorification of the Son was necessary to His filling that place and executing that work. The place which God had destined Him to occupy was that of rightful authority over the whole human race, with complete control of all events in connection with them (see John 5:22; Eph. 1:19-21, etc.). The work appointed Him was to give eternal life to all the elect. But in order to the *accomplishment* of this purpose the Son must be glorified in and by and for His sufferings. He must be glorified by expiating sin upon the Cross, by being raised from the dead, and by being set at God's right hand so as to be put into actual possession of this authority and power. How cogent then was His plea! Unless the Father glorified Him, He could not accomplish the ends of His mediatorial office.

The Father, in His eternal counsels, had appointed the Son to save a portion of the human race; to conduct to glory many sons, who, like their brethren in the flesh, were going to destruction. These had been given Christ to save. By nature they were "dead in trespasses and sins": guilty, depraved, destitute of spiritual life, incapable of thinking, feeling, choosing, acting, or enjoying; communion with the all-holy, ever-blessed One. If ever they were to be saved they must have eternal life bestowed upon them by the Saviour, and for Him to impart this inestimable boon, He must be exalted to the place of supreme dominion. This, then, was the Saviour's "argument" or plea here: the Father's glory being the *end* in view.

Verse 2 also describes *the manner* of the Father's glorification in and by the Son: let Thy Son glorify Thee by saving souls "according as" Thou hast appointed Him so to do. "As thou *hast* given" obviously means promised to give—see such scriptures as Psa. 89:27; Dan. 7:14, etc. The fact that this "power" or authority over all flesh is *given* to Christ, at once shows the *character* in which He here appears, namely, as Mediator. That Christ *receives* this "gift" shows us that free grace is no dishonourable tenure. Why should haughty sinners disdain Divine charity, when the God-man was willing to accept a gift from the Father! "Power over all flesh" means, first, dominion over the whole human race. But it also means, most probably, authority over all creatures, for Christ "is gone into heaven, and is on the right hand of God; *angels* and authorities and powers being *made subject unto him*" (I Peter 3:22). "All power in heaven and earth" has been given to Him (Matt. 28:18). Not only is He the "head of every man" (I Cor. 11:3), but the "head of all principality and power" (Col. 2:10).

"As thou hast given him power over *all flesh*, that he should give eternal life to *as many as* thou hast given him." We must distinguish between Christ's universal authority and His narrower charge. Authority has been given Him over all; but out of this "all" is an elect company, committed to Him as a charge. This was typified by Joseph of old; authority over *all* Egypt was conveyed to him by the king, but his *brethren* had a special claim upon his affections. "The keys of heaven are in the hands of Christ; the salvation of every human soul is at His disposal" (Bishop Ryle). How blessed to rest upon this double truth—the universal dominion of Christ, His affection for His own. All has been put into the hands of our Saviour, therefore the Devil himself cannot move except so far as Christ allows. This universal dominion has been bestowed upon Christ "that" (in order that) He may *give* eternal life to God's elect. The elect were given to Christ by way of *reward* (Isa. 53:10-12), and by way of *charge* (John 6:37; 18:9).

"And this is life eternal that they might know thee the only true God, and Jesus Christ, whom thou hast sent" (17:3). There has been considerable difference of opinion as to what is meant by "this is eternal life." We shall not canvass the various interpretations that have been given, rather shall we seek to indicate what we believe was our Lord's meaning here. "This is life eternal," more literally, "this is the eternal life—that," etc. A parallel form of speech is found in 3:19: "And this is the condemnation—that," etc. In the words that follow in 3:19 the *ground* and *way* of condemnation are stated—"light is come into the world, and men loved darkness rather than light, because their deeds were evil." This helps us to arrive at the first meaning here: "This is the eternal life—that they might know thee," etc.—*this* is the way to it. Again, in 12:50 we read, "His commandment is—life everlasting" that is, the outward *means* of it. Once more, in I John 5:20, we read, "*This is* the true God and eternal life"—Christ is the *Author* of it. Taken by themselves the words of this verse might be understood as speaking of the characteristics and manifestations of "eternal life," but the context would forbid this. Christ is here *amplifying* the *plea* of the previous verse. Thus: unless I am glorified, I cannot bestow eternal life; without My ascension the Holy Spirit will not come, and without Him there can be *no knowledge* of the Father and His Son, and so bv consequence, no eternal life, for "knowing God" and "eternal life" are inseparable. Therefore "this is eternal life—that they might know thee" etc., obviously signifies, This is the *way to,* the *means of* eternal life, namely, by the knowledge of God imparted by Jesus Christ.

"This is the eternal life, that they know thee" (literal rendering). The knowledge spoken of here is not speculative but practical, not theoretical but experimental, not intellectual but spiritual, not inactive but saving. That it is a saving knowledge, which is here in view is clear from the *double* object—God and Christ. He that knoweth God in Christ knoweth Him as His reconciled Father, and so resteth on and in Him. "And they that know thy name will put their trust in thee" (Psa. 9:10). The knowledge here spoken of presupposes a walk in harmony with it, produced by it: "Hereby we do know *that* we *know* him, if we *keep* his commandments" (I John 2:3). How this strengthened the plea of the Saviour here scarcely needs pointing out. What would bring more "glory" to the Father than that He should be known (trusted, loved, served) by those to whom the Son gave eternal life! "Eternal life" contains the essence of *all* blessing: "This is *the* promise that he hath promised us—eternal life" (I John 2:25). Spiritual or eternal life consists in knowing, living on, having communion with, and enjoying endless satisfaction in the Triune God through the one Mediator.

"Know thee, the *only* true God." Appeal is made to this by Unitarians in their horrible efforts to disprove the Godhead of the second and third persons of the Trinity. That Christ cannot be here denying the Deity of Himself and of the Spirit we well know from many other passages, but what did He mean by affirming that the Father is "the only true God"? We believe the answer is twofold:—

First, Christ was here *excluding the idols* of the Gentiles—false gods, cf., I Thess. 1:9:—to denote that that Godhead is only true that is in the Father. The Son and the Spirit are not excluded because they are of the same essence with the Father. The Son and the Spirit are "true God," not without, but in the

Father. "I and the Father are one" (10:30); "the Father is in me, and I in him" (10:38): not divided in essence, but distinguished in personality. In I John 5:20 the Son Himself is called "the only true God!" Which no more excludes the Father than 17:3 excludes the Son. Many such exclusive statements are to be found in Scripture, that must be expounded by the analogy of faith. For example: "No one knoweth the Father, but the Son, and none knoweth the Son, but the Father" (Matt. 11:27); but this excludes not the Spirit, for He "searcheth the depths of God" (I Cor. 2:10). One person of the Trinity does not exclude the others. When Scripture insists there is no God but one, it simply denies that all others who are "*called* gods" *are* such.

Second, Christ was here speaking in view of the *order* and *economy* of salvation, for He had just mentioned the giving of "eternal life." In the economy of salvation the Father is ever represented as *Supreme*, the One in whom the sovereign majesty of Deity resideth. The Son sustains the office of *Mediator*, and in *this* character He could rightly say, "My Father is greater than I" (14:28) In like manner, during the present dispensation, the Holy Spirit is the *Servant* of the Godhead (see Luke 4:17-23 and cf. John 16:13 and our remarks thereon). In the order of redemption the Father is the principal party representing the whole Godhead, because He is the Originator and Fountain of it.

"And Jesus Christ whom thou hast sent." The connecting "*and*" gives plain warning that the Father, "the only true God" cannot be "known" *apart from* "Jesus Christ"! Just as the "only true God" is opposed to the vanities of the Gentiles, so is "Jesus Christ whom thou hast sent" to the blindness of the Jews! "Sent" has a threefold intimation and signification. It points to His Deity: "We believe that thou *camest forth from God*" (16:30). It refers to His incarnation: "When the fullness of the time was come, God *sent forth* His Son made of a woman" (Gal. 4:4). It also signified His office of Mediator and Redeemer. For this reason He is called "The apostle and high priest of our profession" (Heb. 3:1), and "apostle" means the *sent* one. Jesus Christ is the great Ambassador to treat with us from God.

It is worthy of note that this is the *only* place in the New Testament where our Lord called Himself "Jesus Christ." In so doing He affirmed that He, *Jesus* the Son of man, and Son of God was the only true *Christ* (Messiah): thereby He repudiated every false notion of the Messiah, as in the previous clause He had excluded every false god. It is very striking to observe how that in I John 5:1 we are told, "Whosoever believeth that *Jesus* is *the Christ* is born of God," while in 5:5 we read, "Who is he that overcometh the world, but he that believeth that *Jesus* is *the Son of God?*" Do you, dear reader, *know* the Father and the Son – the Father as revealed in and by Jesus Christ! If you do not, you have not eternal life.

"I have glorified thee on the earth" (17:4). Here is the next plea of the Saviour: I have glorified Thee, do Thou now glorify Me. God has been glorified in creation (Psa. 19:1) and by His providences (Ex. 15:6-7, etc.); but to a superlative degree, in an altogether unique way, He had been glorified by the Son. Christ has glorified the Father in His person (Heb. 1:3). He glorified Him by His miracles (Matt. 9:8, etc.). He glorified Him by His words, constantly ascribing all praise to Him (Matt. 11:25, etc.). But above all He had glorified Him by His holy life. The Saviour was sent into the world as the Representative of His people, to render obedience to that law which they had violated (Gal. 4:4); and perfectly had He in thought and word and deed discharged this duty. In Him – full of grace and truth – the disciples had beheld a moral glory possessed by none save Him who abode in the bosom of the Father. "I have glorified thee *on the earth*" – in the place where He had been so grievously dishonored.

In view of having glorified the Father on earth, the Son said "glorify thou me." "The more we examine the Gospel of John, the more we shall see One who speaks and acts as a Divine Person – one with the Father – alone could do, but yet always as One who has taken the place of a servant, and *takes* nothing to Himself but *receives* all from His Father. 'I have glorified thee': 'now glorify me.' What language of equality of nature and love! But He does not say, 'And now I will glorify myself.' He has taken the place of man to receive all, though it be a glory He had with the Father before the world was. This is of exquisite beauty. I add, it was out of this the enemy sought to seduce Him, in vain, in the wilderness" (Mr. Darby).

"I have finished the work which thou gavest me to do" (17:4). Here is the *final plea* of the Saviour for His glorification. When He entered this world, He affirmed, "Lo, I come *to do* thy will, O God" (Heb. 10:7). At the age of twelve, He said, "Wist ye not that I must be about my Father's *business?*" (Luke 2:49). In John 4:34 He declared, "My meat is to do the will of him that sent me, and to *finish his work.*" Now He says, *"I have finished* the work which thou gavest me to do." He anticipated by a few hours His cry from the Cross, "It is finished" (19:30). The Saviour referred to His work on earth as though He had been already exalted to heaven. How evident it is all through His prayer that His *heavenly mediation* is in view—"Now I am no more in the world" (17:11)!

"I have finished the work which thou gavest me to do." As the eternal Son He had, in the character of the faithful Servant, done what none other could do. He had performed the Father's will: He had delivered His message: He had not only taught but perfectly exemplified the truth. He had "finished transgression and brought in everlasting righteousness" (Dan. 9:24). He had put away sin by the sacrifice of Himself. He had "restored that which He took not away" (Psa. 69:4). Thus had He glorified the Father upon earth and finished the work given Him to do. There was every reason then *why* He should be "glorified." Every moral attribute of Deity required it. Having endured the Cross, He was fully entitled to enter "the joy set before Him." Having poured out His soul unto death, it was but meet that the Father should "divide him a portion with the great" (Isa. 53:12). Having glorified Him on earth, it was fitting that the Saviour should be glorified in heaven.

"And now, O Father, glorify thou me with thine own self, with the glory which I had with thee before the world was" (17:5). Having presented the various pleas suited to His glorification, the Son now returns to His petition. The verse before us conducts us to a height which we have no means of scaling. All that we can do is to humbly ponder its words in the light of the context and parallel scriptures. When the Saviour says, "glorify thou me" He speaks as *the Mediator,* as "Jesus Christ" (17:3). *As* Jesus Christ He had been humiliated; now, *as* Jesus Christ, He was to be glorified. The Father's answer to *this* is seen in Acts 2: "*This Jesus* hath God raised up . . . let all the house of Israel know assuredly, that God hath made *that same Jesus,* whom ye have crucified, both Lord and Christ" (vv. 32, 36) — compare also Phil. 2:9-11. But the glorification here must not be confined to His *humanity,* as the remainder of the verse shows. As the *eternal Son* He has humbled Himself (Phil. 2:6), and as *the Son* He has been exalted and magnified see Psa. 21:1-6; 110:1; Eph. 1:17-23; Rev. 5:11-14.

That Christ *asked to be* "glorified," demonstrated His perfections: not even as risen did He glorify Himself. In addition to the fact that His glorification had been promised and earned by Him, three reasons may be given *why* He asked for it. First, for the *comfort* of His apostles who were troubled over His humiliation. Second, for our instruction: to teach us that suffering for God is the highway to glory. Third, for the *benefit* of His Church: Christ must be glorified before it could prosper. The example of the Saviour here teaches that we should pray that the Father may be pleased to honour us by fitting and using us to lead men to a knowledge of the only true God through Jesus Christ, and to enable us, in our creature measure, to glorify Him on earth and to finish the work which He has given us to do.

The following questions are to help the student on the next section: —

1. How many pleas does Christ here present on behalf of His own, vv. 6,12?
2. Of whom is Christ speaking in v. 6?
3. In what senses were the elect "given" to Christ, v. 6?
4. What important truth is pointed in the "ands" of v. 8?
5. How harmonize v. 9 with Luke 23:34?
6. Why "Holy" Father, v. 11?
7. What is the unity of v. 12?

CHAPTER FIFTY-EIGHT

Christ Interceding (Continued)

John 17:6-12

The following is an Analysis of the second section of John 17: —

1. What Christ had done for God's elect, v. 6.
2. The response of the elect, vv. 6, 7.
3. The consequent assurance of the elect, v. 8.
4. The elect alone prayed for by the Mediator, v. 9.
5. Reasons why Christ prayed for the elect, vv. 9-11.
6. Christ praying for their preservation and unity, v. 11.
7. Christ's accompanying plea, v. 12.

John 17 is the sequel to chapter 13. In each the actions of our great High Priest are in view. But the services are different, both together giving us a full representation of our Advocate on high. "In the 13th chapter He had, as it were, laid one hand on the defiled feet of His saints; here He lays the other hand on the throne of the Father, forming thus a chain of marvellous workmanship reaching from God to sinners. In the 13th chapter His body was girt, and He was stooping down towards our feet; here, His eyes are lifted up (17:1), and He is looking in the face of the Father. What that is asked for us, by One who fills up the whole distance between the bright throne of God and our defiled feet, can be denied? All must be granted—such an One is heard always. Thus we get the sufficiency and acceptability of the Advocate" (Mr. J. G. Bellett).

That *order* in which the Saviour here presents His petitions, and the *pleas* by which He urges them, are deserving of the closest notice. The prayer has three main divisions: in 17:1 to 5

He prays for *Himself;* in 17:6 to 19 He prays for ***the disciples*** then alive: in 17:20 to 26 He prays for those ***who should believe.*** In praying for Himself, His own glorification, the great end in view is *the Father's* glory. In 17:1 He says: "glorify thy Son, *that* thy Son also may glorify thee," and in 17:5 He adds: "glorify thou me *with thine own self.*" This, be it noted, is ***before*** He asks a single thing for His people. Just as in The disciples' prayer, "Our Father which art in heaven, hallowed be thy name" was the *opening* petition, so here in "The Lord's Prayer" the Father's interests come first. Inseparably connected are the two things: the Father's glory and the Son's glory. In praying for Himself before His people He shows us that in *all* things He has the pre-eminence (Col. 1:18).

In studying the different pleas for His own glorification, we find that they were seven in number, and this supplies us with the first of a most striking series of sevens which runs through this prayer. The various pleas were as follows: First, because of His filial relationship with God—"Father," 17:1. Second, because the appointed time for it had arrived—"The hour is come," 17:1. Third, because authority over all flesh had been given Him by Divine appointment and promise, 17:2. Fourth, because His bestowal of eternal life on God's elect had also been promised Him, 17:2. Fifth, because in bestowing eternal life on the elect He would be bringing them to a knowledge of the Father, 17:3. Sixth, because He had glorified the Father on the earth, 17:4. Seventh, because He had finished the work which had been given Him to do, 17:4. For these reasons He asks that His request be granted.

Ere passing from the first section of this prayer, attention should be called to the lovely manner in which the Son there kept before Him the glory of the Father. First, He had said: "Father . . . glorify *thy* Son" (17:1), not "*the* Son": He desired no glory for Himself apart from the Father! Second, "that thy Son *also* may glorify thee" (17:1): not separately, but in perfect union. Third, "As *thou* hast given him power over all flesh" (17:2): blessed is it to see the place which He gives the Father. Fourth, "that he should give eternal life to as many as"—He redeems with His blood? No; but—"to as many as ***thou*** hast given him" (17:3)! Thus, again, does He refer all to the Father. Fifth, "And this is life eternal that they might know *me*"? No; but—"that they might know *thee*, and Jesus Christ, whom *thou* hast sent" (17:3). Sixth, "I have finished the work which *thou* hast given me to do" (17:4): nothing was done for self. He ascribes honour to the Father for originating and appointing that work! Finally, when He prays to be glorified, it is touching to see how He puts it: "glorify thou me with thine own self, with the glory which I had before the world was", No, no; but instead—"with the glory which I had *with thee* before the world was": not for a moment would He dissociate His own glory from His Father! Truly is this altogether Lovely One "fairer than the children of men."

We have now completed the first main section of John 17, vv. 1-5, where Christ is seen praying for Himself. In the second section, vv. 6-19, He prays for the *living disciples*. This second section is also subdivided into two parts, though it is not easy to classify them. In vv. 6 to 12 the fundamental reason is brought out as to *why* the Saviour prays for His disciples and not for the world—because of their *relation* to Himself. Out of this grows the petition for their *preservation*—the essence of all intercession. In vv. 13 to 19 the Lord prays for His disciples as left here in the world, presenting their several needs as growing out of this. We shall confine ourselves now to the first subdivision.

While this prayer resolves itself into three divisions there is a most striking apparent *unity* about it. The substance of Christ's prayer for Himself is: Place Me in circumstances in which I may glorify Thee in the salvation of men. The substance of His prayer for the disciples is: Fit them for glorifying Thee in promoting the salvation of men, through prosecuting the work to which I have called them as My instrumental agents. The substance of His prayer for the whole company of the redeemed (17:20-26) is: Bring them to entire conformity to Thyself in mind, will and enjoyment, that Thou mayest be glorified to the uttermost by their being saved to the uttermost. Thus the glory of the Father is the paramount consideration from the beginning to the end. A close study of the details will fully bear this out. But though everything is subordinated by Christ to the

Divine glory, yet the blessings asked for the apostles and the whole company of the redeemed are viewed not only in reference to the glory of the Father directly, but to the glory of the Son, in whom and by whom the Father was to be glorified. The plea for blessing them is that "I am glorified in them" (17:10), and the ultimate design is "that they may behold my glory" (17:24).

"The prayer of our Lord for His apostles, like the prayer for Himself, comprehends both petition and pleading. He asks blessings for them, and He states the grounds on which He asks these blessings for them. The transition at the beginning of the sixth verse is similar to that at the twentieth verse, though not so distinctly defined. There He says, 'I pray not for them alone,' i.e., the apostles (rather the entire company of disciples at that time, A.W.P.), 'but for them also which shall believe in me through their word.' Here He in effect says, 'I pray not for myself alone, but for the men to whom I have manifested thy name.'

"The great blessing which our Lord asks for the apostles is that they may be *one,* as the Father and the Son are; that is, that they may be united with Them as to mind and will, and aim and operation in the great work of glorifying God in the salvation of men. *That* is the ultimate object of His desire in reference to them; the other petitions are for what is necessary in order to this. The blessings necessary to the obtaining of this blessing are two: First, *Conservation*—'Keep them through, or in, or in reference to, thine own name'; 'Keep them from the evil one or the evil thing that is in the world, that they may be one, as we are.' Then, second, *Consecration*—'Sanctify them through, or in reference to, thine own name'; all the rest is occupied with pleadings—most powerful and appropriate pleadings" (Mr. John Brown).

While it is true that in 17:6 to 19 the Lord is praying directly and immediately for His *apostles,* it is clear to us that they are here viewed, as in the preceding chapters, in a *representative* character. Were this not the case, there would be *no place* at all in this prayer for all the others of His believing disciples at that time, for 17:20 speaks only of those who were to believe at a later date. The careful student will note that Christ was most particular to *describe* the ones He here intercedes for in terms which are common to *all* believers. It is with this understanding that we shall now proceed with our exposition.

"I have manifested thy name unto the men which thou gavest me out of the world: thine they were, and thou gavest them me, and they have kept thy word" (17:6). Four things are to be carefully noted in this and the following verses: the *persons* for whom Christ intercedes; the *characters* in which they are presented; the *petitions* offered on their behalf; and the *particular pleas* by which each separate petition is urged. It is to be noted that the Lord did not begin by asking for the blessing of His disciples; rather did He first *describe* the ones he was about to pray for: in 17:6 to 10 it is *presentation,* in 17:11 and 12 it is *supplication.* It is beautiful to see that as the Saviour here comes before the Father as intercessor, He presents "His own" *along with Himself.* It reminds us of His word, spoken long before by the spirit of prophecy, "Behold I *and* the children whom the Lord hath given me" (Isa. 8:18, quoted in Heb. 2:13). It was the fulfilment of what had been so strikingly foreshadowed by the high priest of Israel: "And Aaron shall bear the names of the *children of Israel* in the breastplate of judgment upon his heart when *he goeth in* unto the holy place, for a memorial before the Lord continually" (Ex. 28:29). So here, when *our* great High Priest entered the presence of the Father, *He* bore our names on His heart before Him! That which made this possible was His own glorification, consequent upon His "finished work" (17:4, 5).

"I have manifested thy name unto *the men* which thou gavest me out of the world." Here is the first proof that the Lord had *more* than the eleven apostles in view. He designedly employed language that was strictly applicable to *all* His believing people at that time. During His earthly life He had made known the Father's name to far more than the Eleven. I Cor. 15:6 speaks of the risen Saviour being seen by "over five hundred brethren at once." So, too, far more than the apostles had been *given to Christ* out of the world; and again, a larger company than the apostles had "kept his word." Three things were here mentioned by Christ to recommend to the Father these objects of His petition: they were acquainted with the Father's name; they were the subjects of His distinguishing grace; they were obedient to His will. Thus the Lord Jesus spoke of what *He* had done, what *the Father* had done, and what *the disciples* had done.

"I have *manifested thy name* unto the men which thou gavest me out of the world." Herein Christ fulfilled that prophecy, "I will *declare thy name* unto my brethren: in the midst of the congregation will I praise thee" (Psa. 22:22). To make known the Father's name was to reveal Him, manifest His character, display His perfections. As we are told at the beginning of this Gospel, "No man hath seen God at any time; the only begotten Son, which is in the bosom of the Father, *he hath declared* him." The Son alone was competent for this. Christ had manifested the Father's perfections in His perfect life, wondrous miracles and sublime teaching. But only those who had been given Him by the Father were able to receive this manifestation. Christ has made known the Father to *all* the elect: "I write unto you, *little children,* because *ye* have known the Father" (I John 2:13). So perfectly did Christ discharge this office that He could say, "He that hath seen *me* hath seen the *Father*" (John 12:9).

"Thine they were, and thou gavest them me." All creatures belong to the Father by creation (Heb. 12:9), but this is not what is here in view. Christ is speaking of a *special* company which had been given to Him. The reference, then, is to the sovereign election of God, whereby He chose a definite number to be His "peculiar people"—His in a peculiar or special way. These were *eternally* His: "chosen in Christ before the foundation of the world" (Eph. 1:4); and by the immutability of His purpose of grace (Rom. 11:29), they are *always* His. This plea was made by Christ to the Father not only for the urging of the petition which followed, but for the *comfort* of the disciples. Despised by Israel they might be, hated by men in general, the special objects of Satan's enmity; yet were they the peculiar favourites of God. Again, this plea of Christ's affords us *instruction* in prayer. The more we discern the Father's interests in us, the greater our confidence when we come to Him in prayer. What assurance would be ours if, when we approached the throne of grace, we realized that the Father's heart had been set upon us from the beginning of all things!

"And thou gavest them me." Thine by foreordination; Mine by special donation. "The acts of the three persons of the Trinity are commensurate; of the same sphere and latitude; those whom the Father chooseth, the Son redeemeth and the Spirit quickeneth. The Father loveth none but those which are given to Christ, and Christ taketh charge of none but those that are loved by the Father. Your election will be known by your interest in Christ, and your interest in Christ by the regeneration of the Spirit. All God's flock are put into Christ's hands, and He leaveth them in the care of the Spirit: 'Elect according to the foreknowledge of God the Father, through sanctification of the Spirit, unto obedience and sprinkling of the blood of Jesus Christ' (I Peter 1:2). There is a chain of salvation; the beginning is from the Father, the dispensation through the Son, the application by the Spirit; all cometh from the Father, and is conveyed to us through Christ by the Spirit" (Mr. Thos. Manton).

"Thou gavest them me." The elect are given to Christ, first by way of *reward*: "When thou shalt make his soul an offering for sin, he shall see his seed . . . He shall see of the travail of his soul, and be satisfied: by his knowledge shall my righteous servant justify many; for he shall bear their iniquities. *Therefore* will I divide him a portion with the great, and he shall divide the spoil with the strong" (Isa. 53:10-12. "*Ask of me,* and I shall give thee the heathen for thine *inheritance,* and the uttermost parts of the earth for thy possession" (Psa. 2:8). The elect were given to Christ, secondly, by the way of *charge*. "All that the Father giveth me shall come to me, and him that cometh to me I will in no wise *cast out* [reject] . . . And this is the Father's will which hath sent me, that of all which he hath given me I should *lose nothing,* but should raise it up again at the last day" (John 6:37, 39). The elect were intrusted to Christ to take care of. Thus the *faithfulness* of Christ to the Father is engaged on our behalf. If a single one of God's elect were to perish, the glory of the perfect Servant would be tarnished for all eternity. How absolute, then, is our security!

"And they have kept thy word." The last reference, no doubt, is to God's *call*, which went forth through Christ. When these disciples heard that word of command, they rose up, left all, and followed Him. Moreover, they had *continued* with Him. When many "went back and walked no more with him," the Saviour said unto the Twelve, "Will ye also go away?" Their answer, through Peter, was prompt and unwavering: 'To whom shall we go? Thou hast the words of eternal life" (John 6:66-68); contrast 5:38. The Lord spoke here absolutely from the standpoint of their faith, no notice being taken of their failures to apprehend that Word. How beautiful, how blessed, to see our great High Priest, notwithstanding the feebleness of their faith and their frequent unbelief, presenting the disciples before the Father according to the perfections of *His own love*—that love which "imputeth no evil" (1 Cor. 13:5). They had kept the Father's word, but O how imperfectly. But love notices not their defects, dwelling only upon their faith, submission and obedience! Satan is an accuser, and even speaks evil of believers; but Christ, our Advocate, takes our part, and ever speaks well of us. This is the highest commendation Christ could give His people: "They have kept thy word."

"Now they have known that all things whatsoever thou hast given me are of thee" (17:7). The Lord continues to speak in commendatory terms of His disciples. "These are wonderful words when we consider the character of the eleven men to whom they were applied. How weak was their faith! How slender their knowledge! How shallow their spiritual attainments! How faint their hearts in the hour of danger! Yet a very little while after Jesus spoke these words they all forsook Him and fled, and one of them denied Him with an oath. No one, in short, can read the four Gospels with attention and fail to see that never had a great Master such weak servants as Jesus had in the eleven apostles. Yet these very servants were the men of whom the gracious Head of the church speaks here in high and honourable terms. The lesson before us is full of comfort and instruction. It is evident that the Lord sees far more in His believing people than they see in themselves, or than others see in them. The least degree of faith is very precious in His sight. Though it be no larger than a grain of mustard seed, it is a plant of heavenly growth, and makes a boundless difference between the possessors of it and the men of the world. The eleven apostles were weak and unstable as water; but they believed and loved their Master when millions refused to own Him. And the language of Him who declared that a cup of cold water given in the name of a disciple should not lose its reward, shows plainly that their constancy was not forgotten" (Bishop Ryle).

It is blessed to note the *characters* in which Christ here presents the disciples to His Father. "It is most comforting to find that all these glorious desires for the saints our Lord grounds simply on this: that they have received the Son's testimony about the Father, and had believed surely in the Father's love. How full of blessing it is to see that we are presented before God simply as believing that love! How surely does it tell us that the pleasure of our God is this: that we should know Him in love, know Him as the Father, know Him according to the words of Him who has come out from His bosom. This is joy and liberty. And it is indeed only as having seen God in love, seen the Father and heard the Father in Jesus, that makes us the family. It is not the graces that adorn us, or the services that we render, but simply that we *know the Father*. It is this which distinguishes the saint from the world, and gives him his standing, as here, in the presence of the Father" (Mr. J. G. Bellett).

"For I have given unto them the words which thou gavest me; and they have received them, and have known surely that I came out from thee, and they have believed that thou didst send me" (17:8). The "for" which here introduces what follows explains the *all things* in the previous verse. The disciples had entered, by grace, into that of which the world was completely ignorant, namely, that the Father was the source of all that was given to the Son. Some "wondered" at His words and works; others, in their enmity, blasphemously attributed them to Satan. Not only had the disciples learnt that He came out from the Father, but they had perceived that the *means* (the "words") of bringing them into such blessing were also of the Father.

The Saviour had treated them as "friends," committing to them those intimate communications of grace which the Father gave to Him, and this that they might know the Divine relationship into which His wondrous love had brought them. Nor had this been in vain. Slow of heart they truly were (as, alas! are we), yet they *received* the truth, and receiving it they knew that He was the Son of the Father's love. Thus does the Saviour explain *how* souls are brought into such nearness to the Father.

It is instructive to note the *order* here: "For I have given unto them the words which thou gavest me; *and* they have received them, *and* have known surely that I came out from thee, *and* they have believed that thou didst send me." How this makes manifest the fact that "faith cometh by hearing, and hearing by the word of God" (Rom. 10:17). How plain is the lesson here taught us! If our faith is to be strengthened, deepened and increased, it can only be by our diligent attention to, prayerful meditation upon, and personal appropriation of the words of God! So, too, *knowledge,* spiritual knowledge—discernment and understanding—is the fruit of "receiving" God's words. It is to be noted that the initial "receiving" has preceded it. The "believing" comes last here, though the Lord Jesus admits no other faith than that which is based upon an intelligent acquaintance with His person—cf. Rom. 10:13.

"I pray for them: I pray not for the world; but for them which thou hast given me; for they are thine" (17:9). The world here is a general name for mankind in their fallen state. There is a "fashion of this world" (I Cor. 7:31), a common mould, according to which the characters of men are formed. There is "a course of this world" (Eph. 2:2), in which all walk, except those who are on the "narrow way" which leadeth unto life. All who have not been "transformed by the renewing of their minds" (Rom. 12:2) are, as a matter of course, "conformed to this world." For the unbelieving, Christ prayed not: "For whom He is the Propitiation, He is an Advocate; and for whom He died, He makes intercession, and for no others in a spiritual saving way." (Mr. John Gill).

"I pray not for the world." But how is this to be harmonized with the fact that while He was on the Cross the Saviour did pray for His enemies—"Father, forgive them, for they know not what they do"? It is important that we should distinguish between the prayers of Christ as the perfect *Man* and the prayers of Christ as *Mediator*. There are several of the Psalms which plainly intimate that the Lord Jesus prayed for His foes, but this was to show us that as a perfect Man, subject to that holy law which required each one to love his neighbor as himself, He harboured no revenge. He prayed for the ungodly in answer to His human duty, but not officially as the Mediator. So He taught His disciples, "Love your enemies, bless them which curse you, do good to them that hate you, and pray for them which despitefully use you, and persecute you" (Matt. 5:44). But here in John 17 Christ is seen as the great High Priest, therefore He prays only for "His own."

"But for them which thou hast given me." How this should bow our hearts in adoring worship! What thanksgivings it calls for! Oh what an inestimable privilege to be one of the objects of *Christ's* intercession. Millions passed by unprayed for by Him; but those who belong to the "*little* flock" (Luke 12:32) are held up by Him before the throne of grace. One of the disciples asked Him, "Lord, how is it that thou wilt manifest thyself unto us, and not unto the world?" (John 14:22). So may we ask, "How is it that Thou wilt *pray for us*, and not for the world?" Others more accomplished, with more pleasing dispositions, who daily put us to shame in many ways, *left out*, and we taken in! The finite mind, yea the renewed mind, can discover no answer. All that we can say is, it was the *sovereign grace* of the sovereign God who singled us out to be the objects of His distinguishing favors. Let the world call it *selfishness* in us if they will, but let us express in praise to God our profoundest gratitude, and seek to live as becometh His elect ones. Let us also follow the example of Christ here and manifest *our* greatest love for those who have been chosen out of the world. "As we have therefore opportunity, let us do good unto all, *especially* unto them who are of the household of faith" (Gal. 6:10). But do Christ's words in John 17:9 forbid us to pray for the wicked? No, indeed. Christ's mediatorial acts as our great High Priest are not our standard of conduct; but in His walk as the perfect

Man He *has* left us "an example." On the Cross *He* prayed for His *enemies*. So we are commanded to pray for our enemies; and it is our duty to pray for all men. See Rom. 10:1; I Tim. 2:1.

"For they are thine." In the previous verses the Saviour had *described the characters* of those for whom He was about to intercede, now He *presents the reasons why* He prayed for them. The first is, "*for* they are thine." Though given to the Mediator by grant—both as a reward and as a charge—they are still the Father's; that is, He has not relinquished His right and property over them. As a father who giveth his daughter in marriage to another does not lose his fatherly propriety, so those given to Christ are still the Father's "for *they* (in sharp contrast from 'the world') are thine" fixes the meaning of "thine they were" in 17:6—"thine" not by creation, but by *election*. "The world" *also* belongs to the Father by creation! What a powerful plea was this; the ones for whom Christ was about to pray were *the Father's*, therefore, for His own glory and because of His affection for that which belonged to Him, He would keep them.

"And all mine are thine, and thine are mine" (17:10). Here is the second motive for His request: the interests of the Father and the Son could not be separated; what belonged to the one belonged to the other. Indubitable proof of His absolute Deity; it is because the Saviour is one with the Father that They have rights and interests no less boundless than common. The Holy Spirit is not here mentioned, though He is certainly not to be excluded. As Mr. Manton well said, "They are the Father's children, Christ's members, and the Spirit's temples."

"And I am glorified in them" (17:10). This was His third plea. Since the Son was the supreme Object of the Father's affections, then this was another reason for Him preserving those in whom the Saviour was glorified. What a place for us! To be the subjects of this mutual affection of the Father and the Son! The world knew Him not, Israel received Him not; but these disciples by their faith, love, and obedience, glorified Him; therefore did He make special intercession for them. And how intensely practical is this for us! The more we glorify Christ, the more confidence shall we have of His intercession for us

—"Whosoever therefore shall confess me before men, him will I confess also before my Father which is in heaven" (Matt. 10:32).

"And now I am no more in the world, but these are in the world, and I come to thee. Holy Father, keep through thine own name those whom thou hast given me, that they may be one, as we" (17:11). What a touching plea is this! The Saviour reminds the Father that the disciples would be deprived of His personal care as present with them, and this would expose them the more to the world. He had been their Guide, their Guardian, their ever-present and all-sufficient Friend. And how He had borne with their infirmities, upheld them in weakness, protected them from evil! But now He was leaving them, going to the Father, and into *His* hands He now commits His own charge.

"But these are in the world." God could take each saint to Heaven the very day he believed (as He did the dying thief) did He so please; but for reasons of His own He leaves them here for a shorter or longer season. He does so for His own wise purposes: "I pray not that thou shouldest take them *out of* the world, but that thou shouldest keep them from the evil" (17:15). He gets more glory by leaving us here. As a quaint old writer said, "It is more wonderful to maintain a candle in a bucket of water than in a lantern." God's power is made perfect in our weakness (II Cor. 12:9). God sent Jacob and his family into Egypt that He might there exhibit before his descendants His mighty power on Pharaoh. We are left here that we might be tried: "Be not slothful, but followers of them who through *faith and patience* inherit the promises" (Heb. 6:12). There is a measure of sufferings appointed (I Thess. 3:3), and each of us must receive his share. Another reason why we are left in the world is to make us appreciate the more the coming glory. The roughness of our pilgrim path makes us yearn for rest; our present strangership deepens our desire to be at Home.

"Holy Father, keep through thine own name those whom thou hast given me." The term "holy" is here descriptive of character. The root meaning of the word is *separation*, and as applied to

God it signifies that He is far removed from evil. But this is simply negative. God is not only elevated high above all impurity, but He is absolutely, essentially pure in Himself. That God is *holy* signifies that He is lifted high above all finite creatures. "Who shall not fear thee O Lord, and glorify thy name? For thou only art holy" (Rev. 15:4).

The titles of God in Scripture are suited to the requests made of Him: "Now the Lord of *peace* himself give you *peace*" (II Thess. 3:16); "Now the God of *patience* and *consolation* grant you to be likeminded one toward another" (Rom. 15:5), where the apostle prays for brotherly forbearance among the saints. The *connection* in which the Saviour here addresses "the holy Father" is striking. He was asking for the preservation and unification of His disciples, and He requests the Father to do this for them in strict accord with His holy nature. The Lord would have us know with whom we have to do; He would have us pray for an ever-deepening abhorrence of sin—"Ye that love the Lord, hate evil" (Psa. 97:10).

"Keep through thine own name those whom thou hast given me." How this brings out the *value* Christ sets upon us and the deep *interest* He has in us! About to return to the Father on high, He asks the Father that He will preserve those so dear to His heart, those for whom He bled and died. He hands them over to the care of the very One who had first given them to Him. It was as though He said: I know *the Father's* heart! *He* will take good care of them! And why was it, why is it, that we *are* so highly esteemed by Christ? Clearly not for any excellency which there is, intrinsically, in us. The answer must be, Because we are *the Father's love gift to the Son.* It is striking to observe that just *seven* times in this chapter Christ speaks of those whom the Father had "given" Him—see vv. 2, 6 (twice) 9, 11, 12, 24. In John 3:16 we learn of the Father's love *to us;* here in John 17 we behold the Father's love to *Christ.* God so loved the world as to give His only begotten Son; and He so loved His Son as to give Him a people who, conformed to His image, shall through all eternity, show forth His praises. Marvellous fact! We are the Father's love gift to His Son. Who then can estimate the value which Christ puts upon us! The *worth* of a gift depends upon the one who made it; its intrinsic value may be paltry, but when made by a loved one it is highly prized for *his* sake. So we, utterly unworthy in ourselves, are ever regarded by Christ in all the inestimable worth of that love of the Father which gave us to Him! Thus does the eye of our great High Priest ever look upon us with affection and delight. How this ought to endear Him to our hearts!

Little wonder then, in view of what has just been before us, that the *first* thing the Saviour asked for on behalf of those given to Him by the Father was their *preservation*. He was leaving them in a hostile world: "He asks that they may be kept from evil, from being overcome by temptation, from being crushed by persecution, from every device and assault of the Devil" (Bishop Ryle). But some find a difficulty here, *why* should Christ pray for their continuance in grace? Was not such a request meaningless, useless? Had He not affirmed that no sheep of His *should* ever perish! Ah, how futile for the finite mind to *reason* about spiritual and Divine things! But does Scripture throw any light on this apparently needless petition of Christ? Yes; it shows us, throughout, that God's *decrees* do not render void the use of *means;* yea, many of God's decrees are accomplished through the employment of instrumental agencies; and one of these chief means is *prayer!* It is the old nature, still in the Christian, which makes needful the intercession of Christ!

"That they may be *one,* as we." This refers not to a manifestation of ecclesiastical oneness; rather is it a oneness of personal knowledge of and fellowship with the Father and the Son, and therefore oneness in spirit, affection, and aim. It is a oneness which is the outcome not of human agreement or effort, but of Divine power, through making each and all "partakers of the divine *nature*." Has this request of the Saviour been granted? It has. In Acts 4:32 we read, "And the multitude of them that believed were of *one* heart and of *one* soul." And is it not still true that among the *real* people of God, despite all their minor differences, there is still a real, a fundamental, and a blessed, underlying unity—they all believe God's Word is inspired, inerrant, of final authority; they *all* believe in the glorious person and rest upon the all-sufficient sacrifice of the Lord Jesus Christ; they *all* aim at the glory of God; they *all* pant for the time when they shall be forever with the Lord. "One *as we*" shows that the union here prayed for is a Divine, spiritual, intimate, invisible, unbreakable one!

"While I was with them in the world, I kept them in thy name; those that thou gavest me I have kept, and none of them is lost, but the son of perdition; that the scripture might be fulfilled" (17:12). "The Lord, then, in committing His own to the Father, whom in that name He was keeping whilst here, speaks of having kept them safe, save that one who was doomed to destruction. Awful lesson! that even the constant presence of Jesus fails to win where the Spirit brings not the truth home to the conscience. Does this enfeeble Scripture? On the contrary, the Scripture was thereby fulfilled. Chapter 13 referred to Judas that none should be stumbled by such an end of his ministry. Here it is rather that none should therefore doubt the Lord's care. He was not one of those given to Christ by the Father, though called to be an apostle; of those so given He had lost none. Judas was an apparent, not a real, exception, as he was not a child of God but the son of perdition. To see the awful end of so heartless a course would only give more force to His works of grace who, if He left the world for the Father, was bringing them into His own associations before the Father" (Bible Treasury).

"While I was with them in the world, I kept them in thy name; those that thou gavest me I have kept." None but a Divine person *could* "keep" them. He had preserved them from the machinations of the world, the flesh, and the devil. None had apostatized; all had "*continued*" with Him in the day *of His* humiliation (Luke 22:28).

"And none of them is lost, but the son of perdition." Note carefully, He did not say, "*except* the son of perdition," rather, "*but* the son of perdition." He belonged *not* to "them," that is, to those who had been given Him by the Father. The disjunctive participle is used here, as frequently in Scripture, to *contrast* those belonging to two *different* classes. *Compare* Matt.

12:4; Acts 27:22; Rev. 21:27. Not one of them given to Christ can or will be lost. "Father, *I will* that they also, whom thou hast given me, be with me where I am."

"That the scripture might be fulfilled." The reference is to Psalms 41 and 109. The presence of the traitor among the apostles was one of the many proofs that the Lord Jesus *was* the promised Messiah. Four reasons may be suggested for Christ referring to Judas here. To show there was no failure in discharging the trust which the Father had committed to Him; to assure the disciples of this, so that their faith might not be staggered; to demonstrate that Christ had not been deceived by Judas; to declare God's hand and counsel in it—"that the scripture might be fulfilled."

The following questions are to prepare the student for our next lesson:—

1. What is meant by "my joy fulfilled in themselves," v. 13?
2. What is meant by "they are not of the world," v. 14?
3. Why are believers left here in the world, v. 15?
4. Why the repetition of v. 14 in v. 16?
5. What is the "sanctification" of v. 17?
6. What is the meaning of v. 18?
7. How did Christ "sanctify himself," v. 19?

CHAPTER FIFTY-NINE

Christ Interceding (Continued)

John 17:13-19

The following is an Analysis of the passage which is to be before us: —

1. Christ's desire for His disciples' joy, v. 13.
2. The disciples hated by the world, v. 14.
3. Christ's prayer for their preservation, v. 15.
4. The disciples identified with Christ in separation from the world, v. 16.
5. Christ's prayer for their sanctification, v. 17.
6. The disciples sent into the world as Christ was, v. 18.
7. Christ's provision for their sanctification, v. 19.

One chief reason why the Lord Jesus uttered audibly the wonderful prayer recorded in John 17 in the hearing of His apostles was that they might be *instructed* and *comforted* thereby, and not the apostles only, but all His people since then. This is clear from v. 13: "And now come I to thee; and these things I speak in the world that (in order that) they might have my joy fulfilled in themselves." "He addresses His Father as taking His own place in departing, and giving His disciples theirs (that is, His own), with regard to the Father and to the world, after He had gone away to be glorified with the Father. The whole chapter is essentially putting the disciples in His own place, after laying the ground for it in His own glorifying and work. It is, save the last verses, His place on earth. As He was divinely in heaven, and showed a divine, heavenly character on earth, so (He being glorified as man in heaven) they, united with Him, were in turn to display the same. Hence we have first the place He personally takes, and the Work which entitled them to it" (Mr. J. N. Darby).

The above quotation (rather clumsily worded) will repay careful thought. It is to be noted that the final ground on which the Saviour asked to be glorified was not His own personal perfections, not His essential oneness with the Father, but, instead, that *Work* which He completed here below. In this He presented a valid and sure title *for us* to join Him in the same heavenly blessedness, and also laid the foundation for *us* taking *His* place here below. Mark how this is emphasized all through: First, "I have given *them* the words which thou gavest *me*" (17:8). Second, "that *they* might have *my* joy fulfilled in themselves" (17:13). Third, "*they* are not of the world, *even as I* am not of the world" (17:16). Fourth, "As thou hast *sent me* into the world, even so have I *sent them* into the world" (17:18). Fifth, "I sanctify *myself* that *they also* might be *sanctified*" (17:19). Sixth, "the glory which thou gavest *me*, I have given *them*" (17:22). Seventh, "that the love wherewith thou hast loved *me* may be *in them*" (17:26). What a place! What a privilege! What an honor! Amazing the grace and the love which bestowed it.

Wondrous is the position we occupy, the place which is ours — the same place of blessing which *Christ* enjoyed *when* He was here. It is true that we are blest through Christ, but that is not all the truth, nor by any means the most striking part of it: we are also blest *with* Him. The love wherewith the Father had loved the Son, should be in the disciples. They should enter into the consciousness of it, and thus would *His* joy be fulfilled in them. It is *this* that we are called to, the enjoyment in this world of the love which Christ knew here below: His Father's love. What was *His* delight? Was it from the world? Surely not. He was *in* the world, but never *of* it; His joy was from and in the Father. And He has communicated to us the *means* which ministers to this joy: "I have given unto them the words which thou gavest me" (17:8).

The above aspect of truth is further developed in John 17 in the *sevenfold* way in which the Lord Jesus has *identified* us with Himself. First there is identity in *fellowship*: "As thou hast given him power over all flesh that he should give eternal life (Himself, see I John 1:1) to as many as thou hast given him" (17:2). Second, identity of *spirit* and *aim*: "that they may be one as we" (17:11). Third, identity in *separation*: "they are not of the world *even as* I am not of the world" (17:14). Fourth, identity of *mission*, "*as* thou hast sent me into the world, *even so* have I sent them into the world" (17:18). Fifth, identity in *fellowship*: "*As* thou Father art in me, and I in thee, that *they also* may be one in us" (17:21). Sixth, identity of imparted *glory*: "The glory which thou gavest me I have given them" (17:22). Seventh, identity in *love*: "that the world may know that thou hast sent me, and hast loved them, *as* thou hast loved me" (17:23).

Another thing which it is blessed to behold is that, in this Prayer the Lord Jesus *renders an account* of His work to the Father, and this in *seven* particulars: First, He had glorified the Father on earth (17:4). Second, He had finished the work which had been given Him to do (17:4). Third, He had manifested the Father's name unto His own (17:6). Fourth, He had given them the Father's words (17:8, 14). Fifth, He had kept them as a shepherd keeps his sheep (17:12). Sixth, He had sent them forth into the world (17:18). Seventh, He had given them the glory which the Father had bestowed upon Him (17:22)—mark the "I have" in each verse. How striking it is to note that in His work among the saints everything was in connection with *the Father*: it was the Father He had glorified; it was the Father's name He had manifested, etc.

The portion which is now to engage our attention is the second division of the second section of this Prayer. In the first section, 17:1-5, the Saviour prays for Himself. In the second section, 17:6-19, He prays for His disciples. From 17:6 to v. 12, He is principally engaged in presenting to the Father the persons of those for whom He was about to intercede, interspersing two petitions for their preservation and unification. In 17:13-19, He continues His supplications on their behalf, v. 13 being the transitional point between the two sub-divisions.

"And now I come to thee; and these things I speak in the world, that they may have my joy fulfilled in themselves" (17:13). Though it be by no means easy to trace the connection between this verse and those which precede and follow, yet the meaning of its contents is clear and blessed. The Saviour would not only have His people safe in eternity, but He desires them to be happy here and now: He would have them enter into His joy. It was for this reason He had uttered this Prayer while He was here upon earth. How this reveals the affections of our great High Priest! He might have offered this Prayer in silence to the Father, so that we had known nothing of its gracious and comforting details. But that would not have satisfied the heart of the Lord Jesus. He spoke audibly so that the apostles might hear Him, and He has caused it to be written down too, so that we also might know of His deep interest in us. How it behoves us, then, to prayerfully read and re-read and meditate frequently upon what is here recorded for our peace, our edification, our happiness!

"And now come I to Thee." The commentators are divided as to whether these words signify, And now *I address* Thee in prayer, or, And now I am leaving the earth and *returning* to Thee. Probably both senses are to be combined. The whole of this Prayer was in view of His almost immediate departure from the world and His ascension on high. But it is more than this. As pointed out in the introductory remarks of our first chapter on John 17, what we have here is also a *pattern*, a *sample* we might almost say, of the intercession which the Mediator is now making at God's right hand. This Prayer was first uttered on earth, therefore the "now come I to thee" would signify, I supplicate before Thy throne of grace. This Prayer is now being repeated in Heaven (whether audibly or not we cannot say), and for that, Christ had to return to the Father, hence "now come I to thee" would have this additional force.

In the verse before us there is both declaration and supplication. The Saviour is pressing His suit on behalf of those whom the Father had given Him. In view of His own departure, and their condition in the world, He justifies His earnestness in prayer for them. I am leaving them, therefore I must make provision for them. I approach Thee on their behalf; I am speaking aloud for their benefit; I have let them know that I am to be restored to that glory which I had with Thee before the world was; I have given them the assurance that they are the objects of Thy distinguished favour, and that they are Thy love gift to Me; I have let them see how deeply concerned I am about their preservation and unification—and all of this that "they might have my joy fulfilled in themselves."

"These things I speak in the world, that they might have my joy fulfilled in themselves." In the immediate application to the apostles, we understand our Lord's reference to be: In view of their deep dejection, I have sought to turn their sorrow into joy, by permitting them to hear Me commending them and their cause, with such cheerful confidence, to My Father and their Father. But this by no means exhausts the scope of His words here. There was a more specific reference in His mind, something which was designed for the instruction and consolation of *all* His people.

"That they might have *my joy* fulfilled in themselves." *What* joy? The joy that He had at that very time, the joy which had been the portion of His heart all through those thirty-three years while He tabernacled among men. It was the joy of *fellowship with the Father*. It was *this* which He had before Him when, speaking by the Spirit of prophecy long before, He said: "The Lord is the portion of mine inheritance and of my cup: thou maintainest my lot. The lines are fallen unto me in pleasant places; yea, I have a goodly heritage. I will bless the Lord, who hath given me counsel; my reins also instruct me in the night seasons. I have set the Lord always before me: because he is at my right hand, I shall not be moved. Therefore my heart is *glad*, and my glory *rejoiceth*" (Psa. 16:5-9). Though a Man of sorrows and acquainted with grief, yet "the joy of the Lord" was His "strength" (Neh. 8:10). It was to this He referred when He said to the disciples "I have meat to eat (*a satisfying portion*) that ye know not of" (John 4:32).

"That they might have my joy fulfilled in themselves." *This* was what the heart of the Saviour craved for His people, and for this He had made full provision. In this Prayer, Christ makes it known that *we* have been brought into the same position before the Father that *He* had held, and just in proportion as we consciously enter into it, *His* joy *is* fulfilled in us. As the result of His finished work every barrier has been removed, the veil has been rent, a "new and living way" has been opened for us, and therefore have we access into "the holiest of all," and are invited to "draw near with a true heart in full assurance of faith" (Heb. 10:19-22). *His* Father is *our* Father; His *relation* to God—that of Son—is now ours; for "because ye are sons, God hath sent forth the Spirit of his Son into your hearts, crying, Abba, Father" (Gal. 4:6). Therefore does the Holy Spirit tell us, "Truly *our fellowship* is with the Father, and with his Son Jesus Christ. And these things write we unto you, THAT *your joy may be full*" (I John 1:3-4).

It is blessed to mark how solicitous the Saviour was over the happiness of His people. When He departed He sent the Holy Spirit to be their Comforter. In His Paschal Discourse He said, "These things have I spoken unto you, that my joy might remain in you, and *your joy* might be full" (15:11). In His instructions He bade them: "Ask and ye shall receive, that *your joy* may be full" (16:24). A miserable Christian is therefore a self-contradiction. A joyless Christian is one who is out of communion with the Father: other objects have engaged his heart, and in consequence he walks not in the light of His countenance. What is the remedy? To confess our sins to God; to put away everything which hinders our communion with Him; to make regular use of the means which He has graciously provided for the maintenance of our joy—the Word, prayer, meditation, the daily occupation of the heart with Christ, dwelling constantly on the glorious future that awaits us, proclaiming to others the unsearchable riches of Christ.

"I have given them thy word; and the world hath hated them" (17:14). The connection of this with the previous verse is easy to perceive. In 17:8, the Lord had said, "I have given unto them the *words* which thou gavest me": this means more than that He had expounded to them the Old Testament Scriptures. The reference, we believe, is to what we read of in Isaiah 50:4. "The Lord God hath given me the tongue of the learned, that I should know how to speak a word in season to him that is weary: he wakeneth morning by morning. He wakeneth mine ear to hear, as the learned." Each morning had the perfect Servant waited upon the Father for *His* message or messages for each day, and those messages had been faithfully delivered. But here He says, "I have given them thy *word.*" It was the testimony of what the Father was—*that* was the source of *His* joy, and now would be of *theirs.* "*And* the world hath hated them": "In proportion as they had their joy in God, would it be realized how far the world was away from Him, and it would hate them as not of it. The light would bring its shadows, and they would be identified with Him in sorrow and joy alike" (Numerical Bible).

"And the world hath hated them, because they are not of the world" (17:14). The inhabitants of this world are fully under the dominion of its "prince," and led by him are wholly taken up with the things of time and sense, namely, all that is "not of the Father" (I John 2:16). Therefore do the men of the world bear an implacable hatred to Christ and His people, *because* "they are not of the world." Once Christians *were* "of the world," they followed its "course," and were fully "conformed" to its policy, its principles, its aims, But grace has delivered them from this "present evil world" (Gal. 1:4), so that they now have new affections, new interests, a new Master. They have been separated from the world, and in proportion as they follow Christ their lives *condemn* the world (Heb. 11:7). Therefore does the world hate them: it secretly plots against them, it inwardly curses them, it says all manner of evil against them, it opposes them, it rejoices when any evil befalls them.

"Even as I am not of the world." "The first man is of the earth, earthy: the second man is the Lord from heaven" (I Cor. 15:47). Christ never was of the world. He was "holy, harmless, undefiled, *separate* from sinners" (Heb. 7:26). So He declared to the Jews: "Ye are from beneath; I am from above; ye are of this world; I am not of this world" (John 8:23). But *how* is it also true of His people that *they* are "not of the world?" Because, "If any man be in Christ he is a new creation" (II Cor. 5:17). In consequence of this, he is a "partaker of the heavenly calling" (Heb. 3:1), his "citizenship is in heaven" (Phil. 3:20), he has been begotten unto an heavenly inheritance (I Peter 1:3-5). In view of this, he is but a "stranger and pilgrim" here, journeying to his Home on High.

"I have given them thy word; and the world hath hated them, because they are not of the world, even as I am not of the world." This is another argument or plea—their *danger*—by which the Saviour urges His petition for their preservation. They were being left by Him in the midst of an hostile world, therefore were they in sore need of protection. They no longer had anything in common. They could have no fellowship with the world: they could not take part in its worship: they could not further its plans. Therefore would they be despised, boycotted, persecuted. "They also that render evil for good are mine adversaries; *because* I follow the thing that is good" (Psa. 38:20). "For Herod feared John, knowing that he was a *just* man and an *holy*" (Mark 6:20). "Marvel not, my brethren, if the world hate you" (I John 3:13). The Saviour knowing that the world would not change, therefore besought the Father on behalf of those whom He left here.

"I pray not that thou shouldest take them out of the world, but that thou shouldest keep them from the evil" (17:15). "This also He speaks, most assuredly, for the instruction of the hearers of His prayer. He thus admits that it might be reasonable *to* ask this: on the one hand, it must appear to the disciples a good and desirable thing, while on the other hand, by declining such a prayer intimates that it would be the reverse . . . So, also, contrary to the deep desire which all future disciples would feel: a desire which is not to be compared, however, with that of Elijah, oppressed by despondency (I Kings 19:4), nor to be regarded as the desire of lethargy, but such as the apostle expressed in Phil. 1:23. In their first conversion and joy almost all more or less feel a desire to be at once with Him above. And often we think concerning others, Well for them now to die, for they would be safe in Heaven! But the Lord knows better, and we should learn a better lesson from His words on this occasion. *He* asked not for this, then ask it not *thyself,* either for thyself or for others! Reply to thine own desires to depart, nevertheless, it is *better,* for it is more *needful,* to remain in the flesh and in the world. Content thyself with praying for thy *preservation,* until thou hast fulfilled all thy work" (Stier). Bishop Ryle has pointed out that, "Three of the only prayers *not* granted to saints, recorded in Scripture, are the prayers, of Moses, Elijah, Jonah *to be* 'taken out of the world.'" How very striking!

"I pray not that Thou shouldest take them out of the world, but that thou shouldest keep them from the evil." In 17:11 Christ had said, "Holy Father, keep through thine own name those whom thou hast given me," here He amplifies for the benefit of His disciples—"keep them *from the evil.*" The Greek word for "evil" may be translated either "evil one" or "evil thing": probably both are included. "Keep them from the author of evil, and from evil itself; from sin, from the power and snares of the Devil, from destruction, until their course is run. Satan is the author; the world is the bait; sin is the hook. Keep them from the Devil that they may not come under his power; from the world, that they may not be deceived by its allurements" (Mr. Manton). A spiritual victory over it is therefore better than a total exemption from it. Thus the Lord again teaches us here how to pray: not to be delivered from the world, but from its evil. That Christ asked the Father to "keep us" shows that it is not within our power to keep ourselves: "kept by *the power of God* through faith unto salvation ready to be revealed in the last time" (I Peter 1:5).

God has many ways of keeping us, but they may be reduced to two: by His Spirit or His providence. The one is inward, the other is outward. By the power of the Holy Spirit the evil within us is restrained: "I also *withheld* thee from sinning against me" (Gen. 20:6). By the Spirit grace is imparted to us: "I will put my fear in their hearts that they shall not depart from me" (Jer. 32:40). By His providences He removes occasions to and objects of sin: "For the rod of the wicked shall not rest upon the lot of the righteous; *lest* the righteous put forth their hands unto iniquity" (Psa. 125:3). "God is faithful, who will not suffer you to be tempted above that ye are able; but will with the temptation also make a way to escape, that ye may be able to bear it" (I Cor. 10:13).

The fact that we are unable to keep ourselves should work in us the spirit of dependency. Our daily confession should be, "O our God, wilt thou not judge them? For *we* have *no* might against this great company that cometh against us; neither know we what to do: but our eyes are upon thee" (II Chron. 20:12); our daily prayer should be, "*Lead us not* into temptation, but *deliver* us from evil." The fact that God is able and willing to keep us should inspire confidence, deepen assurance, and fill us with praise: "I know whom I have believed, *and am persuaded* that he is able to keep that which I have committed unto him against that day." Just as the diver, encased in his watertight suit is surrounded by water, but preserved from it, so the believer, living in this evil world is kept by the mighty power of God, His arm encircling us.

"They are not of the world, even as I am not of the world" (17:16). The same words are found in 17:14, but in a different connection: there He was stating the chief reason why the world hated them; here He is advancing a reason *why* He asked the Father to keep them from evil—because "they are not of the world." The truth of this verse applies in a sevenfold way: First, Christians have a different *standing* from those who belong to the world: their standing is in Adam, ours in Christ; they are under condemnation, we "accepted in the beloved." Second, we possess a different *nature*: theirs is born of the flesh, ours "of the Spirit"; theirs is evil and corrupt, ours holy and Divine. Third, we serve a different *Master*: they are of their father the Devil, and the desires of their father they do; we serve the Lord Christ. Fourth, we have a different *aim*: theirs is to please self, ours to glorify God. Fifth, we have a different *citizenship*: theirs is on earth; ours in heaven. Sixth, we live a different *life*: far below the standard set before us it is true: nevertheless, no Christian (in the general tenor of his conduct) goes to the same excess of sin as does the worldling. Seventh, we have a different *destiny*: theirs is the Lake of Fire, ours is the Father's House on High. The "world" is a system built up away from God, and from it we have been taken, delivered, separated. The Lord grant needed grace to us all that we may *manifest* this in our daily walk.

"They are not of the world, even as I am not of the world." "It is a fact and not an obligation, though the firmest ground of obligation. They *are* not of the world, not merely they ought not to be; whilst if they are not, it is grievous inconsistency to seem to be of the world. It is false to our relationship for we are the Father's and given to the rejected Son who has done with the world; and if it be said that this is to bring in everlasting and heavenly relationships now be it so: this is exactly what Christianity means in principle and practice. It is faith possessing Christ who gives the believer His own place of relationship and acceptance on high, as well as of testimony apart from His rejection by the world below; which He has to make good in words and ways, in spirit and conversation, whilst waiting for the Lord . . . That the world improves for Christ or His own is as false as that the flesh can ameliorate. It is the light become darkness! It is the natural man knowing enough to forego what is shameless, and invested with a religious veil; it is the world essentially occupying itself with the things of God in profession, but in reality of the world where common sense suffices for its services and its worship, and the mind of Christ would be altogether inapplicable. What a triumph to the enemy! It is just what we see in Christendom; and nothing irritates so much as the refusal so to walk, worship or serve.

"It does not matter how loudly you denounce or protest: if you join the world, they will not mind your words, and you are faithless to Christ. Nor does it matter how much grace and patience you show: if you keep apart as not of the world, you incur enmity and hatred, and contempt. A disciple is not above his Master, but every one that is perfected shall be as his Master. To act as not of the world is felt to be its strongest condemnation! And no meekness or love can make it palatable. Nor does God intend that it should, for He means it as part of the testimony to His Son. And as the world neither receives nor understands the Father's Word, so it hates those who have and act on that Word" (Bible Treasury).

"Sanctify them through thy truth: thy word is truth" (17:17). On no detail in this Prayer, perhaps, has there been wider difference of opinion than on this verse. Those who regard 17:6-19 as containing our Lord's intercession for the apostles only (among whom is Mr. John Brown as well as several other eminent expositors), understand this to mean: Consecrate them (as were Israel's priests of old) to the important mission that lies before them, i.e., by anointing them with the Holy Spirit. But against this view there are, in our judgment, insuperable objections. Not only is it, we think, abundantly clear, that the Saviour was here praying for *all* His people, but the preposition used in this verse precludes such a thought: it is "Sanctify them *through* [*by*] thy truth." Had it been a matter of setting apart unto ministerial duties it would have been "Sanctify them *for* (unto) thy truth."

The subject of *sanctification* is a deeply important one; one on which much ignorance prevails, and we are tempted to turn aside and discuss it at some length; but this would be beside the scope of our present work; suffice it now if we offer a bare outline. First of all, the word "*sanctify*" (so "holy") has one uniform meaning throughout Scripture, namely, *to set apart;* usually but not always, some one or some thing set apart unto God for His use. The word never has reference to inward cleansing, still less to the eradication of the carnal nature. Take its usage in 17:19: "For their sake I *sanctify myself.*" This can *only* mean, For their sakes *I set Myself apart.*

In Jude 1, we read of those who are "sanctified by God *the Father.*" The reference there is to His eternal predestination of the elect when He set them apart in Christ from our doomed race. In Heb. 10:10 (cf. Heb. 13:12), we read of being sanctified "through the offering of the body *of Jesus Christ,* once for all." The reference there is to our being set apart by ransom from those who are the captives of Satan. In II Thess. 2:13 and I Peter 1:2, we read of "sanctification of *the Spirit.*" The reference there is to the new birth, when He sets us apart from those who are dead in trespasses and sins. Here in John 17:17 sanctification is "by *the truth,*" that is, by the written Word of God. The sanctification of the Father, of Jesus Christ, and of the Spirit, each have to do with that which is *positional* and *absolute,* admitting of no degrees, concerned not with a gradual process, but with what is complete and final. But "sanctification by the truth" is *practical* and *progressive.* Just so far as I walk according to God's Word shall I be *separated* from evil. Thus we discover a most intimate connection between these two petitions of Christ for His own: "keep them from the evil" (17:15), "Sanctify them by thy truth" (17:17): the former is secured by the latter. So also we may perceive the close relation of 17:17 to v. 16: "They are not of the world, even as I am not of the world"—now "sanctify them by thy truth": because they *are not* of the world, cause them to walk in separation from it.

"Thy word is truth." The written Word *is* (not "contains") unadulterated truth, because its Author cannot lie. In it there is no error. Because the Word is God's truth it is of final authority. By it every thing is to be tested. By it our thoughts are to be formed and our conduct is to be regulated. Just because God's Word is *truth* it *sanctifies* those who obey it: "according to the faith of God's elect, and the acknowledging of the truth *which is after godliness*" (Titus 1:1). If then the Word is truth what a high value we should put upon it. If it is by the truth we are sanctified, how dearly we should prize it. How solemn too is the converse: if truth *separates* from evil, error *conducts into* evil. It was so at the beginning: it was believing the Devil's lie which plunged our race into sin and death! Then beware of error: as poison is to the body, so is error to the soul. Shun those who *deny* any part of God's truth as you would a deadly plague: "Take heed *what* ye hear" (Mark 4:24).

"As thou hast sent me into the world, even so have I also sent them into the world" (17:18). Wonderful statement is this, anticipatory of what He says in 20:21: "as my Father hath sent me, so send I you." How evident that Christ *has* given us *His* place—*His* place of acceptance on high, His place of witness here below! But those who witness here below have a special character: it is as those belonging *to Heaven* that we are called upon to bear testimony in the world. Christ did not belong to the world, He was the Heavenly One come down to earth; so we, as identified with Him, as partakers of the heavenly calling, are now commissioned to represent Him here below. What a proof that we *are not* "of the world!" It is only as first "chosen out of the world," that we can be "sent into the world!" That this is not limited to the apostles is clear from I John 4:17, which is speaking of *all* believers—"as *he* is, *so* are we in this world."

"As thou hast sent me into the world, even so have I sent them into the world." Christ was sent here to reveal the Father, to show forth His glory, so we are sent into the world to show forth Christ's glory, which is to the glory of the Father. Christ was sent here on an errand of mercy, to seek and to save that which was lost; so we are here as His agents, His instruments, to preach His gospel, to tell a world dead in sin of One who is mighty to save. Christ was here "full of grace and truth"; so we are to commend our Master by gracious and faithful lives. Christ was here as the Holy One in the midst of a scene of corruption; so we are to be the "salt of the earth." Christ was here as the Light; so we are to shine as lights in this dark place. Christ was furnished with the Spirit, who anointed, filled, and led Him; so we have received the Spirit, to anoint, fill and guide us. Christ was ever about His Father's business, pleasing not Himself, but ever making the most of His brief sojourn here below; so we are to redeem the time, to be instant in season and out of season, always abounding in the work of the Lord. It is thus that Christ is "glorified" *in* us (17:10). What a dignity this gives to our calling!

"As thou hast sent me into the world, even so have I also sent them into the world." The connection of this verse with the previous one is most significant. There the Saviour had prayed the Father to sanctify by the truth those that He was leaving behind; here He adds, I have sent them into the world. This is a plea to support His petition. It was as though He had said: "Father, Those for whom I am interceding are to be *My* representatives here below, as I have been *Thy* Representative; therefore separate them from the pollutions of this evil world, fill them with the spirit of devotedness, that they may be examples of holy living." It is to be noted that when Christ first sent forth the Twelve, He instructed them: "Go not into the way of the Gentiles, and into any city of the Samaritans enter ye not. But go rather to the lost sheep of the house of Israel" (Matt. 10:5-6). But now He sends them into the "world," to preach the Gospel to every creature. The chosen nation does not occupy the place of distinctive blessing during this dispensation; Christianity bears a witness to Jew and Gentile alike.

"And for their sakes I sanctify myself, that they also might be sanctified through the truth" (17:19). "This is the second plea advanced by Christ in support of His petition in 17:17. He had urged their commission, now His own merit. Justice might interpose and say, 'They are unworthy'; but Christ saith, 'I sanctify myself for them.' He dealeth with the Father not only by way of entreaty, but merit; and applieth Himself not only to the goodwill of the Father, as His beloved One, but to His justice, as One that was ready to lay down His life as a satisfaction" (Mr. Manton).

"And for their sakes I sanctify myself." Just as there is a *double* meaning to the "hour" (17:1), and "I come to thee" (17:13) etc., so is there to "I sanctify myself." Its first and most obvious reference is to *the Cross.* I, the great High Priest, set apart Myself for My people—I devote Myself as the Lamb of God to be slain for them, see Heb. 10:14. In saying He did this that *they* might be "sanctified by the truth," He affirmed that His own official sanctification was the *meritorious cause* of their being sanctified practically. In declaring that He sanctified Himself, the Lord Jesus called attention to how *freely* and *voluntarily* He entered upon His sacrificial service. There was no necessity or compulsion: He laid down His life of Himself (John 10:18). This He did for "*their* sakes," namely, the whole company of God's elect—another sure proof that *all* His people are in view throughout this Prayer! "Christ also loved *the church,* and gave himself for it; that he might *sanctify* and cleanse it" (Eph. 5:25, 26)! "Wherefore Jesus also, that he might sanctify *the people* with his own blood, suffered without the gate" (Heb. 13:12)!

"And for their sakes I sanctify myself, that they also might be sanctified through the truth." The deeper and ultimate reference of Christ in these words was to His being set apart on High as the glorified Man, the object of His people's affections, contemplation, and worship. "He set Himself apart as a heavenly man above the heavens, a glorified man in the glory, in order that all truth might shine forth in Him, in His Person, raised up from the dead by the glory of the Father—all that the Father is, being thus displayed in Him; the testimony of divine righteousness, of divine love, of divine power; the perfect model of that which man was according to the counsels of God, and as the expression of His power morally and in glory—the image of the invisible God, the Son, and in glory. Jesus set Himself apart, in this place, in order that the disciples might be sanctified by the communication to them of what He was; for this communication was the truth, and created them in the image of that which it revealed. So that it was the Father's glory revealed by Him on earth, and the glory into which He had ascended as man; for this is the complete result—the illustration in glory of the way in which He had set Himself apart for God, but on behalf of His own. Thus there is not only the forming and governing of the thoughts by the Word, setting us apart morally to God, but the blessed affections flowing from our having this truth in the Person of Christ, our hearts connected with Him in grace" (Mr. J. N. Darby).

The following questions are to prepare the reader for our closing study on John 17:—

1. How many series of sevens can you find in John 17?
2. What is the unity prayed for in v. 21?
3. What is the "glory" of v. 22?
4. What is the unity of v. 23?
5. What is the connection of v. 24?
6. Why "righteous" Father, v. 25?
7. What is the meaning of v. 26?

CHAPTER SIXTY

CHRIST INTERCEDING (CONCLUDED)

John 17:20-26

The following is an Analysis of the closing section of John 17: —

1. Christ's heart embracing all the redeemed, v. 20.
2. Christ's prayer for their unity, v. 21.
3. Christ's imparting to them His glory, v. 22.
4. Christ and His saints manifested in glory, v. 23.
5. Christ yearning for us to be with Himself, v. 24.
6. Christ contrasting the world from His own, v. 25.
7. Christ assuring us of the Father's love, v. 26.

We have now arrived at the closing section of this wonderful Prayer, a section which supplies a glorious climax to all that has gone before. In it our Lord gives the gracious assurance that He was here praying not for the apostles only, nor simply for the entire company of those who had followed Him while He was here on earth, but for *all* His people: "Neither pray I for these alone, but for *them also which shall believe* in me through their word" (17:20). It is not that the Saviour now begins to present *separate* petitions for *another* company than those prayed for in the preceding verses, but that those who were to believe, all through the generations that should follow, are here *linked with* the first Christians.

Seven things Christ asked the Father for the whole company of His redeemed. First, He prayed for their *preservation*: "Holy Father, *keep* through thine own name those whom thou hast given me" (17:11). Second, for their *jubilation*: "that they might have my *joy* fulfilled in themselves" (17:13). Third, for their *emancipation* from evil: "that thou shouldst keep them *from the evil*" (17:15). Fourth, for their *sanctification*: "*sanctify* them by thy truth" (17:17). Fifth, for their *unification*: "that they all may be *one*" (17:21). Sixth, for their *association* with Himself: "that they also, whom thou hast given me, *be with me* where I am" (17:24). Seventh, for their gratification: "that they may *behold my glory*" (17:24).

A careful analysis of this Prayer reveals the fact that just as the Lord urged the one petition which He made for Himself by *seven* pleas, so He supported the *seven* petitions for His people by *seven* pleas. First, He asked the Father to preserve, sanctify and glorify His people, because they were the Father's love-gift to the Son; see 17:9: this was an appeal to the Father's love for *Him*. Second, because of the Father's personal interest in them, see 17:9, 10. What a mighty plea was this: "they are thine"—Thine elect, Thy children; therefore undertake for them! Third, because His own glory was connected with them, 17:10: Mine honour and glory are infinitely dear to Thee, and what glory have I in the world save what comes from My redeemed! These are they who show forth My praises here below! were they to perish, were they to apostatize, where would My honour be? Note how the Saviour presses this again at the end of 17:21 and in v. 23. Fourth, because He was leaving them: He pleads their desolation, and asks the Father to make it up to them in another way. Fifth, because He was leaving them "in the world," see 17:11, 15: consider, O Father, *where* I am leaving them: it is a wicked, polluting place—then protect them for My sake. Sixth, the world hated them, see 17:14: they are surrounded by bitter enemies, and urgently need Thy protection. Seventh, because He set Himself apart (died) for their sakes, see v. 19: therefore, let not My costly sacrifice be in vain!

It is also to be observed that in this Prayer believers are contemplated in a *sevenfold* relation to the world. First, they are given to Christ out of the world, 17:6. Second, they are left in the world, 17:11. Third, they are not of the world, 17:14. Fourth, they are hated by the world, 17:14. Fifth, they are kept from the evil in the world, 17:15. Sixth, they are sent into the world, 17:18. Seventh, they will yet be manifested in glorified unity before the world, 17:23.

There are *seven* "gifts" referred to in this chapter: four of which are bestowed upon the Mediator, and three upon His people. First, Christ has been given universal "power" or dominion (17:2). Second, He was given a "work" to do (17:4). Third, He was given a "people" to save (17:6). Fourth, He has been given a richly-merited "glory" (17:22). Fifth, we have been given "eternal life" (17:2). Sixth, we have been given the Father's "word" (17:8). Seventh, we have been given the "glory" which the Father gave to the Son (17:22).

Though vv. 20-26 form a clearly-defined separate section of John 17, yet are they so closely connected with the previous sections that the perfect unity of the whole is apparent. That which is *distinctive* about these closing verses is the *glorification* of Christ's people. The Lord looks forward to the blessed consummation, while tracing the several steps or stages which lead up to it. Just as it was with the Head Himself, so is it with His members: in His own case, His impending *sufferings* merged into His *glorification* (17:1, 4), so after speaking of the afflictions which His people would suffer while in the world (17:14-19), He turns now to *their* glorification (17:22, 24). Thus did He fill out His "I am glorified in them" (17:10)—nothing more being said of them entering the kingdom of God through much tribulation.

The position which 17:20-26 occupy in this Prayer is the key to their interpretation. They are found at the *end* of it. This of itself is sufficient to indicate the scope of its contents. In the previous sections the Lord Jesus had prayed for His people according to their needs while they were here *in the world*. But now He looks forward to the time when they shall no more be in the world; when, instead, they shall be where He now is. Therefore does He pray that they may be unified, glorified, and satisfied. This will come before us in detail in the course of our exposition.

"Neither pray I for these alone, but for them also which shall believe on me through their word" (17:20). Up to this point the Lord had referred specifically only to the body of disciples alive at that time, but now He lets us know that He was here praying for *all* Christians. The "neither *pray* I for these alone" takes in *all* the petitions and pleas contained in 17:6 to 19; "but for them *also*" intimates that not only does He hereby appropriate to all future disciples what He had just said of and asked for the living disciples of that day, but also that *they*, as well as we, were included in all that follows. What honour did the Lord here put upon individual believers: *their* names are in Christ's will or testament; *they* are bound up in the same bundle of life with the apostles. Just as David, when about to die, prayed not only for Solomon his successor, but also for all the people, so Christ not only prayed for the apostles, to whom was committed the government of the church after His departure, but for all believers unto the end of the age.

"Neither pray I for these alone." How this reveals Christ's love for *us!* He thought of us before we had our being: He provided for us before we were born! As parents provide for their children's children yet unborn, so did the Lord Jesus remember *future* believers, as well as those of the first generation. Christ foresaw that the Gospel would prevail, notwithstanding the world's hatred, and that numbers would yield themselves to the obedience of faith; therefore, to show that *they* had a place in His heart, He names them in this His testament. It was Esau's complaint, "Hast thou but one blessing, O my father?" when he came too late, and Jacob had already carried away the blessing. But *we* were not born too late to receive the blessing of Christ's prayers. He had regard to us even then; therefore, each born-again-soul can say, "He prayed for *me*"! "Who can reckon up the numbers which have been saved? Who can say how many more will be brought to swell the dimensions of the one flock, ere Christian testimony shall have attained its predestined consummation? Till then the full tale of those for whom the Lord prayed will not be disclosed" (Mr. C. E. Stuart). As this wondrous Prayer stretches forward into eternity, only in eternity will it be fully understood.

"But for them also which shall believe on me through their word." Note three things: the persons prayed for; the mark by which they are identified—faith in Christ; the ground and warrant of their faith—the Word. Once again (cf. 17:9) the Lord makes it known that believers, and believers only, have an interest in His mediatorial intercessions. Christ still confines Himself to the elect! He does not pray for all men, whether they believe or no. "His prayers on earth do but explain the virtue and extent of His sacrifice. He sueth out what He purchased, and His intercession in heaven is but a representation of His merit; both are acts of the same office. Partly because it is not for the honour of Christ that *His* prayers should fall to the ground: 'I know that thou hearest me always' (John 11:42). Shall the Son of God's love plead in vain; and urge His merit and not succeed? Then farewell the sureness and firmness of our comfort. Christ's prayers *would* fall to the ground if He should pray for them that shall never believe" (Mr. Manton).

The *description* here given of those who *do* have an interest in Christ's intercession is their *faith* in Him. *This* is the fundamental mark of their identification. He mentions not their love, their obedience, their steadfastness (though these *are* necessary in their place), but their faith. Wherever our participation of the benefits of Christ's death and resurrection are spoken of, the one thing named is *faith*. Why? Because this is a grace which compels us to look *outside* of ourselves *to Him!* Faith is the great essential, for faith is the mother of obedience and the other graces. But mark it is no vague and undefined faith: "which shall believe *on me*." To believe in Christ is to have confidence in and to rely upon Him; it is to trust Him, to rest upon Him.

The *ground* and *warrant* of our faith is "their word," that is, the word of the apostles. "Before the apostles fell asleep, they, under the guidance of the Holy Spirit, embodied in the books of the New Testament their doctrine and its evidence, gave an account of what they had taught, and of the miraculous works which had proved that they *were* taught of God. In these writings they *still* continue to testify the Son. The apostles alone are *'God's ambassadors'* in the strict sense of that word. They alone stand 'in Christ's stead' (II Cor. 5:20). They had 'the mind of Christ' in a sense peculiar to themselves; and that mind is in *their writings*. 'Their sound is gone out into all the earth, and their words unto the ends of the world.' Rom. 10:18." (Mr. J. Brown). It is only through the Word that we believe in Christ (Rom. 10:14, 17).

"Neither pray I for these alone, but for them also which *shall* believe in me through their word." This is the more blessed if we bear in mind the circumstances under which these words were uttered. The public ministry of Christ was now over, and those who believed on Him, in comparison with those who believed not, were few indeed. And now He was to be put to a criminal's death, and the faith of His disciples, already severely tried, would be made to tremble in the balance. How blessed then to listen to these words of His; He was not discouraged; He knew that the corn of wheat, which was to fall into the ground and die, *would* bring forth much fruit; like Abraham of old, He "staggered not at the promise of God (that He should have a 'Seed' that would satisfy him) through unbelief, but was strong in faith, giving glory to God." He looked to the future, from things seen to things unseen, and beheld them who were yet to swell the numbers of His "little flock." "This was the 'joy set before him' (Heb. 12:2), and 'these things he spake in the world,' in the presence of His apostles, 'that they might have his joy fulfilled in themselves' (17:13). How well fitted was His cheerful confidence to re-assure their failing spirits —to revive their all-but-expiring hopes! And how must the recollection of this Prayer have delighted them amid their painful yet joyous labors, when He successfully employed them to 'gather to Him His saints, those with whom He had made covenant by sacrifice,' Psa. 50:5!" (Mr. J. Brown).

"That they all may be one; as thou, Father, art in me, and I in thee, that they also may be one in us: that the world may believe that thou hast sent me" (17:21). Upon this verse we write with some reserve, not being at all sure of the *nature* of the *unity* here prayed for by Christ. In 17:11 He had asked for the oneness of all His people who were on earth at that time, here He adds to them those who were afterwards to believe— "that they *all* may be one." In 17:11 His request was that His people "may be one *as* we," here that "they all may be one as thou, Father, art *in* me, and I *in* thee, that they also may be one *in* us." It seems that a *mystical* union is in view here. But who is competent to *define* the *manner* in which the Father is *in* the Son and the Son *in* the Father! No doubt one reason why the Saviour mentioned the *unity* of His people so frequently in this Prayer (17:11, 21, 22, 23) was to intimate that the middle wall of partition which had for so long divided Jews from the Gentiles was on the point of being broken down, and that now He would "make in himself of twain *one new man*" (Eph. 2:15).

"That the world may believe that thou hast sent me." This is what presents a real difficulty to the writer. The previous part of the verse seems to speak of the *mystical* union which binds believers together; but the last clause shows that it is one that shall powerfully affect the world. It is clear then the unity here prayed for by the Lord is yet to be *manifested* upon the earth. But it is equally clear that this manifestation is still *future*, for Christ is here speaking of those which *were* to believe on Him (17:20), and now asks, "that *they all* may be one."

"That the world may believe that thou hast sent me." It is to be carefully noted Christ *did not* here pray that the result of the manifested unity of His people should be that "the world may *believe in me*," but "that the world may believe that thou hast *sent me*." These two things are widely different. By the "world" is here meant, the world of the ungodly. But unregenerate men are never brought to believe in Christ by any *external displays* of Divine power and goodness—the benevolent miracles wrought by Him clearly prove this. Nothing but the *Word applied by the Spirit* ever quickened sinners into newness of life.

"And the glory which thou gavest me I have given them" (17:22). Christ here speaks of a "glory" which the Father had given to Him. Clearly, this is not His *essential* glory, which He possessed as the eternal Son, as co-equal with the Father; which glory He never relinquished. Nor is it the visible and external glory which He laid aside when He took the Servant form (Phil. 2:6, 7), when He "who was rich," for our sakes became "poor," which glory He had asked to be restored to

Him again (17:5). Rather is it that "glory" which He *acquired* as the incarnate One, as the reward for His perfect work here on earth. It is to this that Isaiah referred when he said, "Therefore will I divide him a portion with the great, and he shall divide the spoil with the strong, because he hath poured out his soul unto death" (53:12). An inheritance has been given Him (Heb. 1:2), and this He will share with His own, for, by wondrous grace, we are "joint-heirs" with Christ (Rom. 8:17).

But what is meant by "the glory which thou gavest me I *have* given them"? The Lord is speaking from the standpoint of the Divine decrees, and thus "calleth those things which be not as though they were" (Rom. 4:17). It is parallel with Rom. 8:30: "Whom he justified, them he also glorified"—not "will glorify." So absolutely certain *is* our future glorification that it is spoken of as a thing already accomplished. But though the actual bestowment of the glory be yet future, it is presented for faith to lay hold of and enjoy even now, for "faith is the substance of things *hoped for,* the evidence of things not seen" (Heb. 11:1).

"That they may be one, even as we are one" (v. 22). V. 22 opens with the word "And," and what follows explains what the Lord had said in the previous verse. The union referred to is *the consequence* of "glory given" to us—"the glory which thou gavest me I have given them; *that* (in order that) they may be one, even as we are one"! Our spiritual union is begun now, but it only attains its full fruition in the life to come. That this oneness *results from* Christ's bestowal on us of His acquired glory proves that it is no man-made unity about which we hear so much talk and see so little evidence these days!

"I in them, and thou in me, that they may be made perfect in one; and that the world may know that thou hast sent me, and hast loved them, as thou hast loved me" (17:23). Here is further evidence that the unity for which our Lord prayed in 17:21 is one that is to be manifested in *the future,* for 17:22 and 23 follow without any break. The being "made perfect in one" is to have its realization at the return of Christ for His saints: "Till we all come in *the unity of the faith,* and of the knowledge of the Son of God, unto a *perfect* man, unto the measure of the stature of the fulness of Christ" (Eph. 4:13). "God having provided some better thing for us (New Testament saints), that they (Old Testament saints) without us should not *be made perfect*" (Heb. 11:40). It is then that Christ will "present it to himself a glorious church . . . holy and without blemish" (Eph. 5:27). Then will there be perfect oneness in faith, knowledge, love, holiness, glory.

"That the world may know that thou hast sent me, and hast loved them, as thou hast loved me." When God's elect have all been gathered together in one (John 11:52), when the glory which Christ received from the Father has been imparted to them, when they shall have been made perfect in one, then shall the world have such a clear demonstration of God's power, grace and love toward His people, they shall *know* that the One who died to make this glorious union possible was the sent One of the Father, and that they had been loved by the Father as had the Son, for "When Christ, who is our life, shall appear, then shall ye also appear with him *in glory*" (Col. 3:4); then "he shall come to be glorified in his saints and admired in all them that believe . . . in that day" (II Thess. 1:10).

"And hast loved them, *as* thou hast loved me." As one has rightly said, "This expression is stupendous—God loveth the saints as He loveth Christ." Mr. Manton points out that "The 'as' is a note of casuality as well as similitude. He loveth us *because* He loved Christ, therefore it is said, 'He hath made us accepted in the Beloved' (Eph. 1:6). The ground of all that love God beareth to us is for Christ's sake. We are chosen in Him as the Head of the elect (Eph. 1:4), pardoned, sanctified, glorified, in and through Him. All these benefits and fruits of God's love are procured by Christ's merit. Three chief ends are accomplished thereby. First, it makes the more for them the *freeness of His grace* that the reason why He loveth us is to be found outside of ourselves. Second, it makes for *His own glory*: God could not love us with honour to Himself if His wisdom had not found out this way of loving us in Christ: there was a double prejudice against us—our corrupt nature was loathed by His holiness, our transgressions provoked a quarrel with His justice. Third, it makes for *our comfort,* for if God should love us for our own sakes it would be a very imperfect love, our graces being so weak, and our services so stained."

The particle "as" also signifies a similitude and likeness. First, there is likeness in the *grounds* of it. The Father loveth Christ as His *Son,* so He loveth us as His *sons* (I John 3:1). Again; the Father loveth Christ as His *Image,* He being "the brightness of his glory and the express image of his person" (Heb. 1:3); so He loveth the saints, who are by grace renewed after His image (Col. 3:10). Second, there is a likeness in the *properties* of it. He loves Christ *tenderly;* so us—"as *dear* children" (Eph. 5:1): He loves Christ *eternally*: so us—"I have loved thee with an *everlasting* love" (Jer. 31:3). He loves Christ *unchangeably*: so us—see Mal. 3:6. Third, there is a likeness in the *fruits* of it. In the intimacies of communion: John 5:30, cf. 15:15. In the bestowal of spiritual gifts: John 3:35, cf. I Cor. 3:22, 23. In reward: Psa. 2:7, 8, cf. Rev. 2:26. What a stay for our poor hearts is this! What comfort when hated by the world, to know that the Father loved us *as* the Son! What a glorious theme for our daily meditation! What cause for adoring worship!

"Father, I will that they also, whom thou hast given me, be with me where I am; that they may behold my glory, which thou hast given me" (17:24). As we have meditated upon the different verses of this profound chapter the words of the Psalmist have occurred to us again and again: "Such knowledge is too wonderful for me; it is high, I cannot attain unto it" (Psa. 139:6). How pertinently do they apply to the lofty point which we have now reached! This 24th verse may well be regarded as the *climax* of this wonderful Prayer. Once more, the Redeemer says, "Father," for He is suing for a child's portion for each of His people; it is not simply wages, such as a servant receives from his master, but an inheritance such as children receive from their parents—the inheritance being the Father's House, where the Saviour now is. Here for the first time in this prayer Christ says "I will." It was a word of authority, becoming Him who was God as well as man. He speaks of this as His right, on account of His *purchase* and of the *covenant* transactions between the Father and the Son concerning those given to Him. "I will" comported with the *authority* (17:2) which the Father has given Him over all flesh and the *glory* into which He has entered (17:5, 22). Or again, this "I will," uttered just before His death, may be regarded as His "testament"—this was the legacy which He bequeathed to us: Heaven is ours, an inheritance left us by Christ!

"Father, I will that they also, whom thou hast given me, be with me where I am." What *comfort* is here! What sweeter words for *meditation* than these of Christ? What *assurance* they breathe: not one of the elect shall fail to enter Heaven! What *joy* is here: "In thy presence is fulness of joy; at thy right hand there are pleasures forevermore" (Psa. 16:11). The queen of Sheba said, "Happy are thy men, happy are these thy servants, which stand continually before thee, and that hear thy wisdom" (I Kings 10:8). They that shall stand before the Lord and see *His* glory are much more happy. How this reveals to us the heart of the Saviour: He will not be satisfied till He has all His blood-bought ones in His presence—"for ever with the Lord." For this He is coming personally to take us to be with Himself: "I will come again, and receive you unto myself; that where I am, there ye may be also" (John 14:3).

"That they may behold my glory, which thou hast given me." "It is not on the one hand that which is personal from everlasting to everlasting, beyond creature ken, that in the Son which I presume none really knows nor can, save the Father who is not said to reveal Him. Neither is it on the other hand the glory given to the blessed Lord which is to be manifested even to the world in that day, in which glory we are to be manifested along with Him. Here it is proper to Himself on high, yet given Him by the Father, as we are in His perfect favour to behold it: a far higher thing than any glory shared along with us, and which the Lord, reckoning on unselfish affections Divinely formed in us, looks for our valuing accordingly as more blessed in beholding Him thus than in aught conferred in ourselves. It is a joy for us alone, wholly outside and above the world, and given because the Father loved Him before its foundation. None but the Eternal could be thus glorified, but it is the secret glory which none but His own are permitted to contemplate—'blest answer to reproach and shame'—not the public glory in which every eye shall see Him. Nothing less than that meets His desire for us. How truly even now our hearts can say that He is worthy!" (Bible Treasury).

"For thou lovest me before the foundation of the world" (17:24). This is mentioned as the reason why the Father had given Him this glory. And how it supplies us with a standard for measurement—the glory which has been conferred upon our blessed Saviour is commensurate with the everlasting love which the Father had for Him! What a glory must it be! And O the privilege, the honour, the bliss of beholding it. How this should make us yearn for the time when we shall gaze upon His resplendent glory!

"O righteous Father, the world hath not known thee; but I have known thee" (17:25). It is not easy to determine the precise relation which the last two verses of John 17 bear to the preceding ones. If their words be attentively considered, they will be seen to express no desire and to ask for no blessing, nor do they contain any plea to enforce the previous petitions. With Mr. Manton we are inclined to say, "It is a part of Christ's supplication; He had made His will and testament, and now allegeth the equity of it." Thus we understand the "O *righteous* Father" here to have a double force. First, God is not only merciful, but just, in glorifying the elect; His grace reigns through righteousness (Rom. 5:21). It expressed the Saviour's confidence in the *justice* of the Father that He would do all things well. "He was asking for what *He* was entitled to according to the stipulation of the eternal covenant. *Justice* required that His requests should be granted." (Mr. John Brown).

The words "O righteous Father" are also to be connected with what follows—"the world hath not known thee." This is very solemn. Christ not only left the world without His intercession, but He turned it over to the justice of the Father. Not only did Divine *righteousness* bestow heavenly glory on the elect, but Divine *righteousness* refuses to bestow it on the unbelieving world. "The world hath not known thee." therein lies their guilt—"Because that which *may be* known of God is manifest to them; for God hath showed it unto them. For the invisible things of him from the creation of the world are clearly seen, being understood by the things that are made, even his eternal power and Godhead; so that they are *without excuse*" (Rom. 1:19, 20).

"O righteous Father, the world hath not known thee; but I have known thee, and these have known that thou hast sent me." "The Lord draws the line definitely between the world and His own, and makes it turn not on rejecting Himself but on ignoring His Father. Here, therefore, it is a question of judgment in result, however grace may tarry and entreat; and therefore He says, 'Righteous Father,' not 'Holy Father,' as in 17:11 where He asks Him to keep those in His name, as He had done whilst with them. Now He sets forth not the lawlessness of the world, not its murderous hatred of Himself or of His disciples, nor yet of the grace and truth revealed in the Gospel, nor of the corruptions of Christianity and the church, which we are sure lay naked and open before His all-seeing eyes, but that on the one side the world knew not the Father, and on the other that the Son did, as the disciples that the Father sent the Son: words simply and briefly said, but how solemn in Lord here linking us with Himself—"I have known . . . these character and issues!" (Bible Treasury). How blessed to see the have known!"

"And I have declared unto them thy name, and will declare it: that the love wherewith thou hast loved me may be in them, and I in them" (17:26). Here the Lord briefly sums up what He had done and would still do for His disciples—make known the Father unto them. He returns at the end to what He had said at the first, see v. 6. The I "*will* declare it" is not to be limited; true, Christ is now, by the Spirit, revealing the Father, but He will continue so to do throughout eternity. Then He states *why* He is the Declarer of the Father's name "*that* [in order that] the love wherewith thou hast loved me may be in them, and I in them." "Where Christ is known as the Father's sent One, the deepest blessing and the highest privileges are even now given, and not merely what awaits the saints at Christ's coming. If ever there was one capable of estimating another, it was the Son in respect of the Father; and His name, the expression of what He was, with equal competency He made known to us. He had done it on earth to the disciples; He would do so from heaven whither He was going; and this that He might give them and us, the consciousness of the same love of the Father which rested ever on Himself here below. As if to cut off the not unnatural hesitation of the disciples He added the blessed guarantee of His own being in them, their life. For they could understand that, if they lived of His life, and could be somehow as He before the Father, the Father might love them as Him. This is just what He does give and secure by identification with them, or rather as He puts it, 'and I in them.' Christ is all and in all." (Bible Treasury).

"And I have declared unto them thy name, and will declare it; that the love wherewith thou hast loved me may be in them, and I in them." How striking to note that *love,* not eternal life, or faith, or even glory, is the last word here: "And now abideth faith, hope, love, these three, but *the greatest* of these is *love*" (I Cor. 13:13). But let it be particularly observed that the love of the Father dwelleth in us only through the mediation of the Son, hence the final words, "and I in them," cf. 17:23. Again, how blessed the conjunction here: Christ in us, the love of the Father in us, by the power of the *Holy Spirit,* "the love of God is shed abroad in our hearts *by the Holy Spirit*" (Rom. 5:5)! Suitable close was this. The section began with, "having loved his own which were in the world, he *loved* them unto the end" (13:1), and it closes with "that *the love* wherewith thou hast loved me may be in them, and I in them!" In the genial warmth and glorious radiance of that love shall we bask throughout eternity.

The following questions are to prepare the student for our next lesson:

1. What type was fulfilled in v. 1?
2. What is suggested by the "garden," v. 1?
3. Why is there no reference here to His agony?
4. What made them fall to the ground, v. 6?
5. Why did Christ repeat His question, v. 7?
6. In what character did Christ speak at the end of v. 8?
7. What important practical truth is exemplified in v. 11?

CHAPTER SIXTY-ONE

Christ in the Garden

John 18:1-11

Below is an Analysis of the passage which is to be before us:—

1. Jesus and His disciples cross the Cedron, v. 1.
2. Judas' knowledge of this place of retirement, v. 2.
3. Judas conducting the Lord's enemies there, v. 3.
4. Christ's challenge and their response, vv. 4, 5.
5. Christ's power and their lack of discernment evidenced, vv. 6, 7.
6. Christ protecting His own, vv. 8, 9.
7. Peter's rashness and Christ's rebuke, vv. 10, 11.

The eighteenth chapter begins a new section of our Gospel. Chapter 1 is introductory in its character; 2 to 12 record our Lord's ministry in the world; 13 to 17 show Him alone with His disciples, preparing them for His departure; 18 to 21 is the closing division, giving us that which attended His death and resurrection. Here, too, everything is in perfect accord with the distinctive character of John's delineation of Christ. The note struck here is in quite a different key from the one heard at the end of the Synoptics. That which is prominent in the closing scenes of the fourth Gospel is not the *sufferings* of the Saviour, but the lofty *dignity* and Divine *glory* of the God-man.

"As the last section (13 to 17) involved His death, it must take place. He has given in His record to Him who sent Him, whose counsels had determined before what was to be done, and whose prophets showed before that Christ should suffer (Acts 2:23; 3:18; 4:28); and now that must be which makes all these assertions true. Without these two chapters (18, 19), therefore, none of the precious things which have thrilled the heart in the previous chapters could be possible; nay more, none of His own assertions as to what He would be and do, of giving eternal life, of having any of the world, of coming again for them, of sending the Holy Spirit, of preparing a place for them, of having them in the glory with Him, or of having that glory at all; there would be no assembly of God, no restoration of Israel, no gathering of the nations, no millennium, no new heavens and new earth, no adjustment in righteousness of the 'creation of God' of which He is the beginning, no display of grace, no salvation, no revelation of the Father—all these and much more were contingent on His death and resurrection. Without these all things in this book drop out and leave a blank, the blackness of darkness" (Mr. M. Taylor).

John 18 opens with an account of the Saviour and His disciples entering the Garden, but in recording what took place there nowhere is the presiding hand of the Holy Spirit more evident. Nothing is said of His taking Peter and James and John into its deeper recesses, that they might "watch with him." Nothing is said of His there praying to the Father. Nothing is said of His falling upon His face, of His awful agony, of the bloody sweat, of the angel appearing to strengthen Him. Perfectly in place in the other Gospels, they are passed over here as unsuited to the picture which John was inspired to paint. In their place other details are supplied—most appropriate and striking—which are not found in the Synoptics.

"Into that Garden, hallowed by so many associations, the Lord entered, with the Eleven; and there took place the Agony related in the Synoptics, but wholly passed over by John. Yet *he* was very near the Lord, being one of the three taken apart from the rest by Christ, and asked to watch with Him. The rest were told to sit down a little way off from the Master. If any of the Evangelists then could have written with authority of that solemn time *John* was the one best fitted to do it. Yet he is the one who omits all reference to it! It might be thought that what the others had written was sufficient. Why, then, did he describe so minutely circumstances connected with the Lord's apprehension! The special line of his Gospel, presenting the Lord as a Divine Person, will alone explain this. As Son of God incarnate he presents Him, and not as the suffering Son of man. We shall learn, then, from him that which none of the others mention, though Matthew was present with Him, how the Lord's personal presence at first over-awed Judas and the company with that traitor" (Mr. C. E. Stuart).

In each of the Synoptics, as the end of His path drew near, we find the Saviour speaking, again and again, of what He was to suffer at the hands of men; how that He would be scourged and spat upon, be shamefully treated by Jew and Gentile alike, ending with His crucifixion, burial and resurrection. But here in John, that which is seen engaging His thoughts in the closing hours was His *return to the Father* (see 13:1; 14:2; 16:5; 17:5). And everything is in perfect accord with this. Here in the Garden, instead of Christ falling to the ground before the Father, we behold those who came to arrest the Saviour falling to the ground before Him! Nowhere does the perfect supremacy of the Lord Jesus shine forth more gloriously: even to the band of soldiers He utters a *command,* and the disciples are allowed to go unmolested.

"When Jesus had spoken these words, he went forth with his disciples over the brook Cedron" (18:1). The "these words" refer to the paschal Discourse and the High Priestly prayer which have engaged our attention in the previous chapters. Having delivered His *prophetic message,* He now prepares to go forth to His *priestly work.* The "Garden" is the same one mentioned in the other Gospels, though here the Holy Spirit significantly omits its name—Gethsemane. In its place, He mentions the "brook Cedron," identical with "Kidron," its Hebrew name, which means "dark waters"—emblematic of that black stream through which He was about to pass. The Cedron was on the east side of the city, dividing Jerusalem from the Mount of Olives (Josephus). It was on the west side of the city that He was crucified: thus did the Son of Righteousness complete His atoning circuit!

What, we may ask, was our Lord's design and purpose in entering the "Garden" at this time? First, in accord with the typical teaching of the Day of Atonement. The victim for the *sin*-offering (unlike the burnt offering) was destroyed "*without* (outside) the camp" (see Lev. 4:12, 21; 16:27); so the Lord Jesus offered Himself as a sacrifice for sin *outside* of Jerusalem: "Wherefore Jesus also that he might sanctify the people with his own blood, suffered *without* the gate" (Heb. 13:12). Therefore, as His atoning sufferings began here, He sought the Garden, rather than remain in Jerusalem.

Second, in crossing the brook Cedron, accompanied by His disciples, another Old Testament type was most strikingly fulfilled. In II Samuel 15 (note particularly vv. 23, 30, 31) we read of David, at the time of his shameful betrayal by his familiar friend Ahithophel, crossing the same brook; crossing it in tears, accompanied by his faithful followers. So David's Son and Lord, crossed the Cedron while Judas was betraying Him to His foes.

Third, His object was to afford His enemies the more free scope to take Him. The leaders of Israel had designed to lay hands on Him for some time past, but they feared the common people; therefore, that this impediment might be removed, the Saviour chose to go out of the city to the Garden, where they might have full opportunity to apprehend Him, and carry Him away in the night, quietly and secretly. In addition to these reasons, we may add, His arrest in the solitude of the Garden made it the easier for His disciples to escape.

The entrance of Christ into the Garden at once reminds us of Eden. The contrasts between them are indeed most striking. In Eden, all was delightful; in Gethsemane, all was terrible. In Eden, Adam and Eve parleyed with Satan; in Gethsemane, the last Adam sought the face of His Father. In Eden, Adam sinned; in Gethsemane, the Saviour suffered. In Eden, Adam fell; in Gethsemane, the Redeemer conquered. The conflict in Eden took place by day; the conflict in Gethsemane was waged at night. In the one Adam fell before Satan; in the other, the soldiers fell before Christ. In Eden the race was lost; in Gethsemane Christ announced, "Of them which thou gavest me have I lost none" (John 18:9). In Eden, Adam took the fruit from Eve's hand; in Gethsemane, Christ received the cup from His Father's hand. In Eden, Adam hid himself; in Gethsemane, Christ boldly showed Himself. In Eden, God sought Adam; in

Gethsemane, the last Adam sought God! From Eden Adam was "driven"; from Gethsemane Christ was "led." In Eden the "sword" was drawn (Gen. 3:24); in Gethsemane the "sword" was sheathed (John 18:11).

"Where was a garden, into which he entered and his disciples" (18:1). Christ did not dismiss the apostles as they left the upper-room in Jerusalem, but took them along with Him to Gethsemane. He would have them witness the fact that He was not seized there as a helpless victim, but that He voluntarily delivered Himself up into the hands of His foes. He would thereby teach them, from His example, that it is a Christian duty to offer no resistance to our enemies, but meekly bow to the will of God. He would also show them His power to protect His own under circumstances of greatest danger.

"And Judas also, which betrayed him, knew the place" (18:2). "Our Lord and Saviour knew that He should be taken by Judas, and that this was the place appointed by His Father wherein He should be taken; for the 4th verse tells us 'Jesus therefore, knowing all things that should come upon him,' etc. He knew that Judas would be there that night, and, therefore, like a valiant champion, He cometh into the field first, afore His enemy. He goeth thither to choose, and singles out this place on purpose" (Mr. Thomas Goodwin).

"For Jesus ofttimes resorted thither with his disciples" (18:2). This was the Saviour's place of prayer during the last week—a quiet spot to which He frequently retired with His apostles. In Luke 21:37 we read, "And in the daytime he was teaching in the temple; and at night he went out, and abode in the mount that is called the mount of olives." In Luke 22:39 we read, "And he came out, and went, *as he was wont* to the mount of olives; and his disciples *also* followed him." This was Christ's place of devotion, and the place, no doubt, where many precious communications had passed between Him and the disciples; it is mentioned here to show the obduracy of the traitor's heart—it also aggravated his sin.

The Saviour knew full well that the treacherous apostate was well acquainted with this spot of holy associations, yet did He, nevertheless go there. On previous occasions He had *avoided* His enemies. "Then took they up stones to cast at him; but Jesus *hid* himself, and went out of the temple" (8:59). "These things spake Jesus, and departed, and did *hide* himself from them" (12:36). But now "the hour" was come; therefore did He make for that very place to which He knew Judas would lead His enemies.

"Judas then, having received a band of men and officers from the chief priests and Pharisees, cometh thither with lanterns and torches and weapons" (18:3). The "band" which Judas "received" evidently signifies a detachment of Roman soldiers, which Pilate had granted for the occasion; the Greek word means the tenth part of a legion, and therefore consisted of four or five hundred men. Some have questioned this, but the words of Matt. 26:47, "a great multitude with him"—strongly confirms it. The "officers from the chief priests and Pharisees" refer to the servants of Israel's leaders. Luke 22:52 shows that the heads of the Nation themselves also swelled the mob—"Then Jesus said unto the chief priests, and captains of the temple, and the elders, which were come to him, Be ye come out, as against a thief, with swords and staves?" As Christ was to die for sinners both of the Jews and Gentiles, so God ordered it that *Gentiles* (Roman soldiers) and *Jews* should have a hand alike in His arrest and in His crucifixion!

"Cometh thither with lanterns and torches and weapons" (18:3). What an anomaly! Seeking out the Light of the world with torches and lanterns! Approaching the Good Shepherd with "weapons!" As though *He* would seek to hide Himself; as though *He* could be taken with swords and staves! Little did they know of His readiness to be led as a lamb to the slaughter. Significant too is the general principle here symbolically illustrated: attacks upon the Truth were made by artificial lights and carnal weapons! It has been thus ever since. The "light of reason" is what men depend upon; and where that has failed, resort has been had to brute force, of which the "weapons" speak. How vain these are, when employed against the Son of God, He plainly demonstrated in the sequel.

"Jesus therefore, *knowing all things* that should come upon him" (18:4). With this should be compared 13:3, which presents a most striking comparison and contrast: "Jesus *knowing* that the Father had given *all things* into his hands"; the comparison is between our Lord's omniscience in either reference; the contrast between the subjects of His knowledge there and here. In 13:3 Christ spoke of "all things" being *given* into His hands; here in 18:4 He anticipates the moment when "all things" were to be *taken from* Him, when He was to be "cut off" and "have *nothing*" (Dan. 9:26). His foreknowledge was perfect: for Him there were no surprises. The *receiving* of "all things" from the Father's hands was not more present to His spirit than the *loss* of "all things" by His being cut off. In John 13 He contemplates the *glory;* here the *sufferings,* and He passed from the one to the other in the unchanging blessedness of absolute perfection.

"Jesus therefore, knowing all things that should come upon him." These were the "all things" decreed by God, agreed upon by the Son in the eternal covenant of grace, predicted in the Old Testament Scriptures, and foretold, again and again, by Himself; namely, all the attendant circumstances of His sufferings and death.

"Jesus therefore, knowing all things that should come upon him, *went forth*"—not out of the Garden as 18:26 plainly shows, but from its inner recesses, where He had prayed alone. "Went forth," first to awaken the sleeping three (Matt. 26:46), then to rejoin the eight whom He had left on the outskirts of the Garden (Matt. 26:36), and now to meet Judas and his company. This "went forth" shows the perfect harmony between John and the Synoptics.

"And said unto them, Whom seek ye?" (18:4). Our Lord was the first to speak: He did not wait to be challenged. His reason for asking this question is indicated in the "therefore" of the previous clause—"Jesus *therefore,* knowing all things that should come upon him, *went forth,* and said unto them, Whom seek ye?" That which the Holy Spirit has here emphasized is the *willingness* of Christ to suffer, His *readiness* to go forth to the Cross. He knew full well for what fell purpose these men were there, but He asks the question so that He might solemnly and formally surrender Himself to them. Once, when they wanted to take Him by force and make Him a king, He departed from them (6:15); but now that He was to be scourged and crucified, He boldly advanced to meet them. This was in sharp contrast from the first Adam in Eden, who, after his sin, *hid* himself among the trees of the garden. So, too, Christ's act and question here bore witness to the futility and folly of their "lanterns and torches and weapons."

"They answered him, Jesus of Nazareth. Jesus said unto them, I am" (18:5). Why did they not answer, "Thee!"? Jesus of Nazareth stood before them, yet they did not say, "Thou art the one we have come to arrest." It is plain from this circumstance that they did not recognize Him, nor did Judas, who is here expressly said to have "stood with them." Despite their "lanterns and torches" their eyes were holden! Does not this go far to confirm our thought on the closing words of 18:3—the Holy Spirit designedly intimated that something more than the light which nature supplies is needed to discover and discern the person of the God-man! And how this is emphasized by the presence of Judas, who had been in closest contact with the Saviour for three years! How solemn the lesson! How forcibly this illustrates II Cor. 4:3, 4: "But if our gospel be hid, it is hid to them that are lost: in whom the god of this world hath *blinded* the minds of them which believe not." Even the traitor failed now to recognize the Lord: he too was stricken with dimness of vision. The natural man is spiritually blind: the Light shone in the darkness, and the darkness comprehended it not (1:5)! It is only as the light of God shines in our hearts that knowledge is given us to behold the glory of God in the face of Jesus Christ (II Cor. 4:6)!

"And Judas, also, which betrayed him, stood with them" (18:5). Only a few hours previous he had been seated with Christ and the Eleven, now he is found with the Lord's enemies, acting as their guide. Some have argued that there is a discrepancy here between John's account and what we read of in the Synoptics. In the latter we are told Judas had arranged with the soldiers that he would give them a sign, identifying the

One they should arrest by kissing Him. This he did, and they laid hands on Him. But here in John 18 he is viewed as failing to recognize the Saviour, yet there is no discrepancy at all. John does not relate what Matthew and the others give us, but instead, supplies details which they were guided to omit. John tells us what took place in the Garden *before* the traitor gave his vile sign. If the reader will compare Luke's account he will see that the kiss was given by Judas at a point between what we read of in John 18, vv. 9, 10.

"As soon then as he had said unto them, I am, they went backward, and fell to the ground" (18:6). Another reason why notice is taken of Judas at the close of the preceding verse is to inform us that he, too, fell to the ground. Observe the words "they went *backward*." They were there to arrest Him, but instead of advancing to lay hands on Him, they retreated! Among them were five hundred Roman soldiers, yet they retired before His single "I am." They fell back in consternation, not forward in worship! All He said was "I am"; but it was fully sufficient to overawe and overpower them. It was the enunciation of the ineffable Name of God, by which He was revealed to Moses at the burning bush (Ex. 3:14). It was a display of His Divine majesty. It was a quiet exhibition of His Divine power. It was a signal demonstration that *He* was "the word" (1:1)! He did not strike them with His hand—there was no need to; He simply spoke two monosyllables and they were completely overcome.

But why, we may ask, should our Lord have acted in such a manner on this occasion? First, that it might be clearly shown He was *more* than "Jesus of Nazareth": He was "*God* manifest in flesh," and never was this more unmistakably evidenced. Second, that it might appear with absolute clearness that He *voluntarily* delivered Himself up into their hands—that it was not they who apprehended Him, but He who submitted to them. He was not captured, for He was not to (passively) *suffer* merely, but to (actively) *offer* Himself as a sacrifice to God. Here is the ultimate reason why it is recorded that "Judas also, which betrayed him, stood with them": the traitor's perfidy was needless and the captor's weapons useless against One who is *giving up* Himself *unto* death and was soon to give Himself *in* death. If none had power to take His life from Him (10:18, 19), none had power to arrest Him. He here showed them, and us, that *they* were completely at *His* mercy—helpless on the ground—and not He at theirs. How easy for Him then to have walked quietly away, unmolested! First, they failed to recognize Him; now they were prostrate before Him. What was to hinder Him from leaving them thus? Nothing but His Father's will, and to it He submissively bowed. Thus did the Saviour give proof of His willingness to offer Himself as a sacrifice for sin. In the third place, it left these men *without excuse*. Every detail in connection with our Lord's passion had been determined by the Divine counsels, yet God did not treat those who had a hand in it as mere machines, but as responsible moral agents. Before Pilate sentenced Christ to death, God first gave him a plain intimation that it was an *innocent* Man who stood before him, by warning his wife in a dream (Matt. 27:19). So here with these Roman soldiers, who may never have seen Christ before. They cannot plead in the Day of judgment that they were ignorant of the glory of His person: they cannot say that they never witnessed His miraculous power, and had no opportunity given them to believe on Him. This exhibition of His majesty, and their laying hands on Him afterwards, makes their condemnation *just!*

It is very striking to observe that the Lord Jesus had uttered the same words on previous occasions, but with very different effects. To the woman at the well He had said "I am" (4:26), and she at once recognized Him as the Christ (4:29). To the disciples on the storm-lashed sea He had said, "I am" (6:20—see Greek), and we are told "they willingly received him into the ship." But here there was no conviction wrought of His Messiahship, and no willing reception of Him. Instead, they were terrified, and fell to the ground. What a marvelous demonstration that the *same* Word is to some "a savour of life unto life," while to others it is "a savour of death unto death"! Observe, too, that His Divine "I am" to the disciples in the ship was accompanied by "Be not afraid" (6:20); how solemn to mark its omission here!

Vividly does this forewarn sinners of how utterly helpless they will be before the Christ of God in a coming Day! "What shall He do when He comes to judge, who did this when about to be judged? What shall be His might when He comes to reign, who had this might when He was at the point to die?" (Augustine.) What, indeed, will be the effect of that Voice when He speaks in judgment upon the wicked!

"As soon then as he had said unto them, I am, they went backward, and fell to the ground." This was a remarkable fulfilment of an Old Testament prophecy given a thousand years before. It is recorded in the 27th Psalm, the whole of which, most probably, was silently uttered by the Saviour as He journeyed from the upper-room in Jerusalem, across the brook Cedron, into the Garden. "The Lord is my light and my salvation; whom shall I fear? The Lord is the strength of my life; of whom shall I be afraid? When the wicked, even my enemies and my foes, came upon me to eat up my flesh, *they stumbled and fell*" (vv. 1, 2). Let the reader pause and ponder the remainder of this Psalm: it is blessed to learn *what* comforted and strengthened the Saviour's heart in that trying hour. Psalm 27 gives us the musings of Christ's heart at this time, *Godwards*. Psalm 35 recorded His prayers against His enemies, *manwards*: "Let them be confounded and put to shame that seek after my soul: let them be *turned back* and *brought to confusion* that devise my hurt" (v. 4). Still another Psalm should be read in this connection, the 40th. That this Psalm is a Messianic one we know positively from vv. 7, 8. Verses 11-17 were, we believe, a part of His prayer in Gethsemane, and in it He asked, "Let them be ashamed and confounded together that seek after my soul to destroy it; let them be *driven backward* and *put to shame* that wish me evil" (v.14). Thus was both Messianic prophecy fulfilled and prayer answered in this overwhelming of His enemies.

"Then asked he them again, Whom seek ye?" (18:7). "This second question carries a mighty conviction, a mighty triumph with it over their conscience as if He had said, I have told you I am; and I have told it you to purpose, have I not? Have you not learned by this *who* I am, when your hearts are so terrified that you all fell down before Me! They had been taught by woeful experience who He was, when He blew them over, flung them down with His breath; and it might have turned to a blessed experience had God struck their hearts, as He did their outward man" (Mr. Thomas Goodwin).

"And they said, Jesus of Nazareth" (18:7). They would not own Him as *the Christ*, but continued to speak of Him according to the name of His humiliation—"Jesus of Nazareth." How striking and how solemn is this after what has been before us in 18:6—such an exhibition of Divine majesty and power, yet their hard hearts unmoved! No outward means will soften those who are resolved on wickedness. No miracles, however awesome, will melt men's enmity: *nothing* will suffice except God works *directly* by His Word and Spirit. Another signal proof of the desperate hardness of men's hearts in the case of those who were appointed to guard the Saviour's sepulchre. While keeping their watch, God sent an earthquake, and then an angel to roll away the stone from the grave's mouth, and so awful were these things to the keepers that they "became as dead men." And yet, when they reported to their masters and were offered a bribe to say His disciples stole the body of Christ while they slept, they were willing parties to such a lie. O the hardness of the human heart: how "desperately wicked"! Even Divine judgments do not subdue it. In a coming day God will pour out on this earth the vials of His wrath, and what will be the response of men? This: "They gnawed their tongues for pain, and *blasphemed* the God of heaven because of their pains and their sores, and *repented not* of their deeds" (Rev. 16:10, 11). Nothing but a miracle of sovereign grace, the putting forth of omnipotent power, can bring a blaspheming rebel out of darkness into God's marvelous light. Many a soul has been terrified, as were these men in the Garden, and yet continued in their course of alienation from God.

"Jesus answered, I have told you that I am" (18:8). The dignity and calmness of our Lord are very noticeable here. Knowing full well all the insults and indignities He was about to suffer, He repeats His former declaration, "I am"; then He added, "if therefore ye seek me, let these go their way." "Christ was about to suffer for them, and therefore it was not just that they should suffer too; nor was it proper that they should suffer *with* Him, lest their sufferings should be thought to be a part of the price of redemption. These words then may be considered as an emblem and pledge of the acquittal and discharge of God's elect, through the surety-engagements and performances of Christ who drew near to God on their behalf, substituting Himself in their room, and undertaking for them in the counsel and covenant of peace, and laid Himself under obligation to pay their debts. Now, as there was a discharge of them from eternity, a non-imputation of sin to them, and a *secret* letting of them go upon the surety-engagements of Christ; so there was now an *open* discharge of them all upon the apprehension, sufferings, death and resurrection of Him" (Mr. John Gill).

"If therefore ye seek me, let these go their way" (18:8). In 13:1 we are told of Christ that "having loved his own which were in the world, he loved them unto *the end*." How blessedly this is seen here. Christ's first thought is not of Himself and what He was about to suffer, but of His disciples. It was the Shepherd protecting His sheep. "The tender sympathy and consideration of our great High Priest for His people came out very beautifully in this place, and would doubtless be remembered by the Eleven long afterwards. They would remember that the very last thought of their Master, before He was made a prisoner, was for them and their safety" (Bishop Ryle). And how the Saviour's majesty here shines forth again! He was about to be taken prisoner, but He acts as no helpless captive, but rather like a king. "Let these go their way" was a command. Here am I, take Me; but I charge you not to meddle with them —touch not Mine anointed! He speaks as Conqueror, and such He was; for He had thrown them to the ground by a word from His lips. They were about to tie His hands, but before doing so He first tied theirs!

"If therefore ye seek me, let these go their way." There is much for us to learn here. First, it supplied another proof of how easily He could have saved Himself had He so pleased: He that saved others could have saved Himself; He who had authority to command them to let these go, had authority to command them to let Himself go. Second, Christ only was to suffer: in the great work before Him none could follow—"And there shall be *no man* in the tabernacle of the congregation when he goeth in to make an atonement" (Lev. 16:17). He was to tread the winepress alone. Third, Christ had other work for them yet to do, and until that work was done their enemies should and must leave them alone. So long as God has something for His servants to do the Devil himself cannot seize them. "Go," said Christ, when warned that Herod would kill Him, "and tell that fox, Behold, I cast out demons, and I do cures today *and* tomorrow" (Luke 13:32). I will do those things in spite of him; he cannot prevent Me. Fourth, here we see *grace*, as in the previous verse Divine *power*, exercised by this One who so perfectly "declared the Father" (v. 18). Fifth, Christ would thus show His disciples how fully competent He was to preserve them amid the greatest dangers. We have no doubt but that these Roman soldiers and Jewish officers intended to seize the apostles as well—Mark 14:51, 52, strongly indicates this—but the Word of power went forth, "let these go their way," and they were safe. We doubt not that the coming day will make it manifest that this same word of power went forth many times, though we knew it not, when *we* were in the place of danger.

"That the saying might be fulfilled, which he spake, Of them which thou gavest me have I lost none" (18:9). This "saying" refers not to an Old Testament prophecy but to that part of His prayer recorded in 17:12—"While I was with them in the world, I kept them in thy name: those that thou gavest me I have kept, and none of them is lost." Though this has a peculiar respect unto the apostles, it is true of all God's elect, who are given to Christ, and none of them shall be lost, neither their souls nor their bodies; for Christ's charge of them reaches to both: both were given to Him, both are redeemed by Him, and both shall be saved by Him with an everlasting salvation; He saves their souls from eternal death, and will raise their bodies from corporeal death; therefore, that His care of His disciples, with respect to their temporal lives as well as eternal happiness, might be seen, He made this agreement with those who came to take Him, or rather laid this injunction upon them, to dismiss them and which it is very remarkable they did, for they laid hands on none of them, even though Peter drew his sword and struck off the ear of one of them. Thus did Christ give another signal proof of His power over the spirits of men to restrain them; and thus did He again make manifest His Deity.

"Then Simon Peter having a sword drew it, and smote the high priest's servant and cut off his right ear. The servant's name was Malchus" (18:10). Peter exercised a zeal which was not regulated by knowledge: it was the self-confident energy of the flesh acting in unconsidered haste. It was the inevitable outcome of his failure to heed Christ's word, "Watch and pray, lest ye enter into temptation"—it is failure to pray which so often brings us into temptation! Had Peter observed the ways of his Master and heeded His words, he would have learned that carnal weapons had no place in the fight to which He has called him and us. Had he marked the wonderful *grace* which He had just displayed in providing for the safety of His own, he would have seen that this was no time for smiting with the sword. What a fearful warning is this to every Christian for the need of walking in the Spirit, that we fulfil not the lusts of the flesh! The flesh is still in the believer, and a lasting object-lesson of this is the humbling history of Peter—rash yet courageous when he should have been still; a few hours later, cowardly and base when he ought to have witnessed a good confession for Christ. But though Peter failed to act according to grace, the grace of God was signally manifested towards him. No doubt Peter struck with the intention of slaying Malchus—probably the first to lay hands on the Saviour—but an unseen Power deflected the blow, and instead of the priest's servant being beheaded he lost only an ear, and that was permitted so that a further opportunity might be afforded the Lord Jesus of manifesting both His tender mercy and all-mighty power. We may add that the *life* of Malchus was safe while Christ was there, for none ever died in His presence!

"Then Simon Peter having a sword drew it, and smote the high priest's servant, and cut off his right ear." The sequel to this is supplied by Luke: "and he touched his ear, and healed him" (22:51)! Very striking indeed is this; it rendered the more excuseless the act of those who arrested Him, aggravating their sin and deepening their guilt. Christ manifested both His power and His grace *before* they laid hands on Him. This act of healing Malchus' ear was the last miracle of the Saviour before He laid down His life. First, He appealed to their consciences, now to their hearts; but once they had seized their prey He left them to their own evil lusts.

"Then said Jesus unto Peter, Put up thy sword into the sheath" (18:11). This was a rebuke, though mildly administered. Peter had done his best to nullify his Master's orders, "Let these go their way." He had given great provocation to this company armed with swords and staves: he had acted wrongly in resisting authority, in having recourse to force, in imagining that the Son of God needed any assistance from him. "Put up thy sword into the sheath": the *only* "sword" which the Christian is ever justified in using is the Sword of the Spirit, the Word of God.

"The cup which my Father hath given me, shall I not drink it?" (18:11). How blessedly this entire incident brings out the varied glories of Christ: perfect supremacy and perfect subjection. He declared Himself the great "I am," and His enemies fall to the ground; He gives the word of command, and His disciples depart unmolested. Now He bows before the will of the Father, and receives the awful cup of suffering and woe from His hand without a murmur. Never did such perfections meet in any other; Sovereign, yet Servant; the Lion-Lamb!

God's dispensations are frequently expressed as a cup poured out and given to men to drink. There are three "cups" spoken of in Scripture. First, there is the *cup of salvation*: "I will take the cup of salvation, and call upon the name of the Lord" (Psa. 116:13). Second, there is the *cup of consolation*: "Neither shall men tear themselves for them in mourning, to comfort them for the dead; neither shall men give them the cup of consolation to drink for their father or for their mother" (Jer. 16:7). To this the Psalmist referred: "My cup runneth over" (23:5). Our Lord Himself used the same figure, previously when He said, "Father, if it be possible let this cup pass from me" (Matt. 26:39). It was a dreadful cup which He was to drink of. This third one is the cup of tribulation: "Upon the wicked he shall rain snares, fire and brimstone, and an horrible tempest; this shall be the portion of their cup" (Psa. 11:6). So the prophet Jeremiah is bidden, "Take the wine cup of this fury at my hand, and cause all the nations, to whom I send thee, to drink it" (25:15; cf. Psa. 75.8).

"The cup which my Father hath given me, shall I not drink it?" "He doth not say, A necessity is laid upon Me to drink this cup. He doth not simply say, My Father hath commanded Me to drink it, but, 'shall I not drink it?' It is a speech that implies His spirit knew not how to do otherwise than obey His Father, such an instinct that He could not but choose to do it. Even just as Joseph said, 'how then can I do this great wickedness, and sin against God?' (Gen. 39:9), so Christ here, 'shall I not drink it?' It implies the highest willingness that can be" (Mr. Thomas Goodwin).

"The cup which *My Father* hath given me, shall I not drink it?" What a lesson Christ here teaches us. The Serpent was about to bruise His heel; the Gentiles were about to mock and scourge Him; the Jews cry, Away with Him. But the Saviour looks beyond all secondary causes direct to Him of whom and through whom and to whom were all things (Rom. 11:36). Peter's eyes were upon the human adversaries; but no, He saith to Peter, there is a higher Hand in it. Moreover, He did not say, "which the *Judge* of all the earth giveth me," but "my Father"—the One who dearly loveth Me! How this would sweeten *our* bitter cups if we would but receive them from the *Father's* hand! It is not until we see *His* hand in all things that the heart is made to rest in perfect peace.

The following questions are to help the student prepare for our next lesson: —

1. What types and doctrinal truths are suggested by "bound," v. 12?
2. Why is v. 14 inserted here?
3. Why has the Holy Spirit given Peter so prominent a place?
4. Why of "His disciples and doctrine," v. 19?
5. Why did Christ say nothing about His disciples, v. 20-
6. Why did Christ say v. 21?
7. What is the meaning of v. 24?

CHAPTER SIXTY-TWO

Christ Before Annas

John 18:12-27

Below is an Analysis of the second section of John 18:—
1. Christ bound and led to Annas, vv. 12-14.
2. Peter follows and is admitted to the palace, vv. 15, 16.
3. Peter's first denial of Christ, vv. 17, 18.
4. Annas questions Christ, and His reply, vv. 19-21.
5. Christ smitten and His remonstrance, vv. 22, 23.
6. Annas sends Christ to Caiaphas, v. 24.
7. Peter's second and third denials, vv. 25-27.

In the passage before us John again supplies details which are not given by the other Evangelists. The Synoptics describe our Lord's appearing before Caiaphas: in the fourth Gospel this is passed over, and in its place we have His arraignment before Annas. As in the Garden, so in the high priest's palace, two of the Saviour's perfections are prominently displayed: His lowliness and dignity: His immeasurable superiority over all who surrounded Him, friends or foes, and His complete submission before those in the seat of human authority. As the Son of God we see Him exposing the wickedness of all with whom He comes into contact; as the Son of man He carried Himself meekly before those who acted more like fiends than humans.

The structure of our present passage is quite complex. From Christ being led away to Annas, the Holy Spirit pauses to notice Peter following and then entering the high priest's house. After recording Peter's first denial, he is left warming himself at the fire, and then a brief account is given of what passed between Annas and Christ. Following the announcement that Annas sent Jesus bound to Caiaphas, the Spirit returns again to Peter and describes the second and third denials. The central thing is plainly Christ's appearing before Annas and afterwards before Pilate, but the narrative is *interrupted* again and yet again to tell of the apostle's awful fall. Most vividly does this point a solemn lesson. God is not the author of confusion: it is sin which produces *disorder* and *hinders* the Spirit from taking the things of *Christ* and showing them unto us! It is *this* which is written large across John 18 if attention be paid to its structure and order of narrative.

But why is it that the Holy Spirit has made so prominent the sin of Simon in this portion of Scripture? Why has He broken into His account of what befell the Saviour, by mentioning the threefold denial? Why, especially, after having previously recorded the same in each of the Synoptics? Ah, is it not to emphasize the *need* of Christ's atoning death, by showing us the *character* of those for whom He died! Was it not His design to show how fearfully sin *had* "abounded" before He portrayed the super-abounding of *grace!* Was it not suitable that He should first paint a *dark* background, so that the *perfections* of the Holy One might be brought into sharper relief! What comes out so plainly all through John—never more so than in these closing incidents—is Christ glorifying the Father in a scene where the ruin of sin was *complete* and *universal.*

"Then the band and the captain and the officers of the Jews took Jesus, and bound him" (18:12). Behold here the amazing hardness of unconverted men. The company of those who arrested the Saviour was made up of men of marked differences; it was composed of Gentiles and Jews, soldiers and servants of the priests and Pharisees, heathen and those who belonged to the covenant people of Jehovah. But in one respect they were all alike—they were *blind* to the glories of Him whom they apprehended. Both parties had witnessed a signal exhibition of His power, when by a word from His lips He had thrown them all to the ground. Both parties had witnessed His tender mercy, when they saw Him heal the torn ear of the first to lay rough hands on Him. Yet, both remained insensible and unmoved, and now proceeded to coolly carry out their odious business of binding the incarnate Son of God. Terrible indeed is the state of the natural man. Let us not wonder, then, at the unbelief and hardness of heart which we see on every side to-day; these things were manifested in the presence of the Saviour, and will continue until He returns in judgment.

"Behold also the amazing *condescension* of our Lord Jesus Christ. We see the Son of God taken prisoner and led away bound like a malefactor—arraigned before wicked and unjust judges—insulted and treated with contempt. And yet, this unresisting Prisoner had only to will His deliverance, and He would at once have been free. He had only to command the confusion of His enemies, and they would at once have been confounded. Above all, He was One who knew full well that Annas and Caiaphas, and all their companions, would one day stand before His judgment-seat and receive an eternal sentence. He knew all these things and yet condescended to be treated as a malefactor without resisting. One thing at any rate is very clear: the love of Christ to sinners is 'a love that passeth knowledge.' To suffer for those who are in some sense worthy of our affection, is suffering that we can understand. To submit to ill-treatment quietly, when we have no power to resist, is submission that is both graceful and wise. But to suffer voluntarily, when we have the power to prevent it, and to suffer for a world of unbelieving and ungodly sinners, unasked and unthanked—this is a line of conduct which passes man's understanding. Never let us forget that *this* is the peculiar beauty of Christ's sufferings when we read the wonderful story of His cross and passion. He was led away captive, and dragged before the high priest's bar, not because He could not help Himself, but because He had set His heart on saving sinners—by bearing their sins, by being treated as a sinner, and by being punished in their stead" (Bishop Ryle).

"Then the band and the captain and the officers of the Jews took Jesus, and bound him." The first word ought to be translated "Therefore," not "Then:" the words of the previous verse explaining its force: "Then said Jesus unto Peter, Put up thy sword into the sheath: the cup which my Father hath given me, shall I not drink it?" Having rebuked Peter for offering resistance, He bowed to the Father's will. "*Therefore*" they "took Jesus and bound him"—like savage beasts they sprang upon their prey. We believe it was to this the Saviour referred when, speaking by the Spirit of prophecy, He declared, "Many bulls have compassed me: strong bulls of Bashan have beset me round. They gaped upon me with their mouths, as a ravening and a roaring lion . . . dogs have compassed me, the assembly of the wicked have enclosed me." We doubt not that they bound Him with heavy chains, for of him who furnishes, perhaps, the fullest type of Christ it is written, "Joseph was sold for a servant: whose feet they hurt with fetters: he was laid in iron" (Psa. 105:17, 18). Is not the antitype of this more than hinted at in Isa. 53:5, where we are told not only that He was "wounded for our transgressions" but "*bruised* for our iniquities"!—was it not when they "bound" His wrists and ankles with handcuffs and fetters!

Why did they "bind" Him? Four *historical* reasons we may give: because Judas had bidden them hold Him fast (Matt. 26:48), this because he remembered what is recorded in Luke 4:29, 30; John 8:59, etc.; because they would heap shame upon Him, treating Him as a lawless character; because they deemed Him worthy of death, thereby prejudicing His sentence. But behind these we may see a *typical* reason: God overruling for the fulfillment of it. *All* that befell Christ was to fulfil the types and prophecies that went before of Him. The most eminent type of Christ in His sufferings was Isaac, and the *first* thing that Abraham did to him, when about to offer him up as a sacrifice, was to *take* and *bind* him (Gen. 22:9)! So it was with the animals which were offered: "*bind* the sacrifice with cords, unto the horns of the altar" (Psa. 118:27). But deeper still, there was a *mystical* significance to this binding of the Saviour: we were sin's captives, therefore was He theirs! Our sins were the *cause* of His binding, therefore did He, as our Substitute, cry, "innumerable evils have *taken hold upon me;* mine iniquities (ours, made His) *have compassed me about*" (Psa. 40:12)! *He* was bound that *we* might be set free. "It is a certain rule that what should have been done to us, something correspondent was done to Christ; and the virtue of His person was such, though it was done to His body, it brought us freedom from the like due to our souls; and by Him being thus bound and led, He Himself afterward, when He ascended, *led captivity captive*" (Mr. Thomas Goodwin). How ready, then, should we be to be bound for Christ (in Heb. 13:3 afflictions for His sake are called "bonds"!); and how little ought we to be moved by the vileness of those who persecute us, when we remember Him!

"And led him away to Annas first" (18:13). The Saviour was neither "driven" nor "dragged," but *led*: thereby the Holy Spirit informs us, once more, of His *willing submission*. He offered no resistance. With infinitely greater ease than Samson of old, could He have burst His bonds "as a thread when it toucheth the fire"; but as prophecy had announced, "he was *led* as a *lamb* to the slaughter"—gentle and tractable. Here also He fulfilled not only prophecy but type: each animal that was to be offered in sacrifice was first led to *the priest* (Lev. 17:5), so Christ was first brought to Annas. The road followed from the Garden to the house of the high priest was also significant. Gethsemane was at the foot of Olivet, on the east side of Jerusalem, beyond the brook Cedron. In journeying from there to the city, the gate through which they would pass was "the *sheep* gate" (Neh. 3:1, 32; 12:39; John 5:2, and see our notes on the last). The "sheep gate" was nigh unto the temple, and through it the sacrificial animals passed (first having been fed in the meadows adjoining the Cedron); so also went the true Lamb on this occasion! Note a striking contrast here: Adam was *driven* out of the Garden (Gen. 3:24); Christ was *led!*

"And led him away to Annas first; for he was father-in-law to Caiaphas, which was the high priest that same year" (18:13). John is the only one who tells of the Saviour being brought before Annas; the Synoptics describe His appearance before Caiaphas. Both Annas and Caiaphas are called "high priests." The fact that there were *two* high priests shows the confusion which prevailed at that time. Much has been written on the subject that provides neither information nor edification. So far as our own limited light goes, we take it that the Roman rule over Palestine supplies the key. In view of 11:49 it seems that the Romans elected a high priest for Israel each year (compare Acts

4:6, which mentions no less than four, all living, who *had* filled that office), but in the light of Luke 3:1 it is clear that sometimes they were re-elected. According to the Law of God the high priest retained his office till death (Ex. 40:15; Num. 35:25, etc.), therefore in the eyes of the *Jews,* Annas, not Caiaphas, was the real high priest: Caiaphas was formally acknowledged in a civic way, but Annas took precedence over him in ecclesiastical matters. This, we believe, explains why the Saviour was brought *first* before Annas.

"Now Caiaphas was he, which gave counsel to the Jews, that it was expedient that one man should die for the people" (18:14). The reference here is to what is recorded in 11:49-52. Caiaphas apparently, was the first man to make the motion that Christ be put to death. The reason he advanced being a political one, with the evident intention of currying favour with the Romans. The callous selfishness of the man comes out plainly in his "consider that it is expedient *for us* that one man should die for the people" (11:50). He was addressing the Sanhedrin, the Supreme Court of Judaism, and in saying "for us," rather than "for *them*" he shows that he cared more for his office than for his nation.

"Now Caiaphas was he, which gave counsel to the Jews, that it was expedient that one man should die for the people." Why is this mentioned here? To show on *what* ground (from the human side) our Saviour was crucified: it was out of political considerations, and those imaginary at best—lest perchance "the Romans take away our place and nation." The Holy Spirit has premised all the other sufferings of Christ thus, in order to show us that *no equity* is to be expected from all their proceedings against Him. They had resolved, *before* they took Him, to put Him to death, and that for State considerations, therefore they would be sure to keep to their resolutions whether He were innocent or no, whether they could convict Him or not. The judge had given his verdict and determined the sentence *before* the trial took place! Here then is one of the Spirit's reasons for introducing this reference to the words of Caiaphas—to show us that in what follows we must not expect to find any favour shown to the Lord Jesus, nor must we be surprised if His trial was simply a farce, a glaring travesty of justice. In addition to this, we believe that God saw to it that there should be a plain testimony from the *legal head* of the nation as to the purpose and character of His Son's death: He was dying "FOR *the people*"!

"And Simon Peter followed Jesus" (18:15). Matthew tells us that he "followed afar off" (26:58). In following Christ at all on this occasion Peter was clearly acting in the energy of the flesh, for Christ's will as to His disciples had been plainly expressed in the "let these *go* their way" (18:8). "Lovingly anxious to see what was done to Him, yet not bold enough to keep near Him like a disciple. Anyone can see that the unhappy Peter was under the influence of very mixed feelings—love made him ashamed to run away and hide himself; cowardice made him ashamed to show his colours, and stick by his Lord's side. Hence he chose a middle course, the worst, as it happened, that he could have followed" (Bishop Ryle).

"And Simon Peter followed Jesus, and so did another disciple: that disciple was known unto the high priest, and went in with Jesus into the palace of the high priest" (18:15). There has been much discussion and speculation as to who this "other disciple" was. A few of the old commentators and most of the modern believe that he was the writer of this Gospel; but whoever he may have been, it is almost certain that he was *not* John. In the first place, John was a poor fisherman of Galilee—far removed from Jerusalem—therefore it is most unlikely that *he* was on sufficiently intimate terms with the high priest as to enter his house, and have authority over the door-keeper so as to order her to admit Peter. In the second place, John, being a Galilean, would have been recognized and challenged as was Peter (Matt. 26:69, 73). In the third place, whenever John refers to himself in this Gospel it is always as "the disciple *whom Jesus loved*" (13:23; 19:26; 20:2; 21:7, 20). Finally, Acts 4:13 makes it very plain that the high priest was *not* personally acquainted with either Peter or John! Who, then, was this "other disciple"? The answer is, We do not know. It may have been Nicodemus or Joseph of Arimathaea, but we cannot be sure.

"But Peter stood at the door without" (18:16). How significant and suggestive is this little detail—the door was shut! Was it not by *God's providence* that the door was now closed? Happy for Peter had he remained on the outside. The Lord had plainly warned him to "watch and pray lest he *enter* into temptation." But Peter disregards His admonition, and knocks for admission—why else should the other disciple have gone out? There is a practical lesson for *us* right here: God in His mercy put an impediment in Peter's way, *stopping him* from going on to that which should be the occasion of his sin; so does He, ofttimes, with us. Therefore, when we find God, in His providence, placing some barrier in our path, it behooves us to pause, and examine well our grounds for going further along the same path we are in. If our way is warranted *by the Word* and our conscience is clear as to a certain line of duty, then obstacles are to be regarded only as *testings* of faith and patience; but otherwise they are *warnings* from God.

"Then went out that other disciple, which was known unto the high priest, and spoke unto her that kept the door, and brought in Peter" (18:16). Ah! says the reader, does not *this* conflict with what has just been said on the first part of the verse? Would not the coming forth of the other disciple, his speaking to the door-keeper (unasked by Peter), and his bringing him in, indicate that God's providences were working *in favor of* Peter's entering the palace? Did it not look as though *God* were calling Peter to enter? The difficulty seems real, yet it is capable of a simple solution. Peter had *disregarded* the warning of God—the shut door; he had *persisted* in having his *own* way—knocking for entrance; now God *removes* His providential barrier. How solemnly this speaks to us; may the Lord grant to each the hearing ear. When we *disregard* both the Word and warning providence of God, we must not be surprised if He then sets a snare for us. When we *insist on* having our *own* way, we must be prepared if God gives us up to our own heart's lust (Psa. 81:12). Jonah chafed against God's *word,* therefore when he fled from going to Nineveh and set his heart on Tarshish, he found a ship all ready for him to sail in! Here, then, is another most important practical lesson pointed out for us: the outward providences of God must not be taken for our guide when we have *refused* His Word and His warnings!

"Then saith the damsel that kept the door unto Peter, Art not thou also one of this man's disciples? He saith, I am not" (18:17). That the door-keeper was a maid rather than a man was obviously overruled by the providence of God: He would humble the pride of Peter in this way, that his weakness might stand out as a lasting warning against self-confidence. It was neither by one of the Roman soldiers nor one of the Jewish officers that the apostle was first challenged, but by a young woman! *Why* she should ask him the question she did, we are not told; whether she was moved by idle curiosity, or detected that he was a Galilean, or whether his countenance bore marks of agitation and fear, or whether—as is more likely—she concluded from Peter being a friend of the "other disciple" that he "*also*" was a follower of Christ, we cannot be sure. Note how *mildly* she framed her question: not, Are you a follower of this Insurrectionist, this Enemy of Judaism, this Blasphemer against God, but simply, "this man"! Yet, notwithstanding the sex of his questioner, and the mild form of her question, Peter told a downright lie. He said, "I am not." "The betrayal by Judas, though more dreadful, is almost less startling than the denial by Peter. We are less prepared for the cowardice of the one, than for the covetousness of the other. That the one should turn timid seems less natural, so to say—was less to be expected—than that the other should prove a traitor. 'Wherefore let him that thinketh he standeth take heed lest he fall'" (Mr. Geo. Brown).

"And the servants and officers stood there, who had made a fire of coal, for it was cold: and they warmed themselves: and Peter stood with them, and warmed himself" (18:18). What we have here is introductory to the second and third denials, recorded in 18:25-27. Peter was cold. How profoundly and solemnly significant! The Christian who follows Christ "afar off" will soon be chilled and grow cold spiritually; then will recourse be had to fleshly stimulants for warmth and comfort. And the enemies of Christ—the world, the flesh, and the Devil—will provide their "fire"—their places and means of cheer!

"And Peter stood with them." Ominous words are these. Of the traitor it was said "And Judas also, which betrayed him, *stood with them*"; now we find Simon in the same evil company! "The apostle stood among the crowd of his Master's enemies, and warmed himself like one of them, as if he had nothing to think of but his bodily comfort; while his beloved Master stood in a distant part of the hall, cold, and a prisoner. Who can doubt that Peter, in his miserable cowardice, wished to appear one of the party who hated Christ, and sought to conceal his real character by doing as they did? And who can doubt that while he warmed his hands he felt cold, wretched, and comfortless in his own soul?" (Bishop Ryle). How true it is that "The backslider in heart shall be filled *with his own* ways" (Prov. 14:14)! Some have pointed out that the Holy Spirit has here told us "it was cold" in order to impress us the more with the bloody *sweat* of Christ only a short while before!

"The high priest then *asked* Jesus of his disciples, and of his doctrine" (18:19). The gross injustice of such a mode of procedure is glaringly apparent. Instead of preferring a charge against the Saviour, and then summoning witnesses to *prove* it, Annas acted after the manner of the Inquisition, asking questions so as to ensnare the One before him. And this was the religious *head* of Israel, acting altogether against and without law, no indictment having been drawn up, no evidence brought forward to support it; nothing but a cowardly attempt to overawe the Prisoner by browbeating Him, so that he could obtain something which might be used against him.

"The high priest then asked Jesus of his disciples, and of his doctrine." The fact that Annas referred here to our Lord's "disciples" at once indicates the malevolent character of his questioning: it was an ironical reference to those who had forsaken Him and fled! The high priest "asked Jesus of his disciples"—With what design did you gather them round you? Where are they? How many have you in reality now? He asked *of* them; he did not call *for* them: none were allowed to testify on His behalf! "And of his doctrine"—not for edification, but to see if it were a new teaching of His own, so that they might have wherewith to accuse Him. It is plain that at this stage they were at a loss for a charge. "The *disciples* are mentioned as His dependents, His followers, His party, His sworn confidents; the *doctrine* is inquired into as novelty, heresy, dangerous misleading error; both together pointing to the two charges which afterwards were urged—Insurrection against the Roman power, error or blasphemy against the Jewish" (Stier).

"Jesus answered him, I spake openly to the world" (18:20). Not *before*, but *to*, "the world." Why did He not say "to the multitudes"? why "to *the world*"? It was the first hint of the *universality* of His message—note how the "Jews" are referred to *separately*, later in the verse! "I spake *openly* to the world": truth is bold and fears not the light. It is the emissaries of Satan who *hide* the leaven in the meal (Matt. 13:33); it is the servants of the Prince of darkness who haunt the "*secret* chambers" (Matt. 24:26). In saying that He spake *openly* to the world the Lord was indirectly *rebuking* Annas and his co-conspirators for their injustice of refusing Him a trial in open court.

"I ever taught in the synagogue, and in the temple, whither the Jews always resort" (18:20)—there is no article before "synagogue." In affirming that He taught in the established places of public worship, the Lord gave proof that *He* was no lawless separatist, clandestinely proselytising, but honoring the institutions of God and acting as became His Prophet. "Whither the Jews always resort." "He describes His cause and doctrine as properly *national*, for all the Jews. There is in the background of both question and answer, though the Lord put it directly not in words, the meaning that the main point in His teaching was the testimony to Himself as the *Messiah*:—thus where all the Jews as Jews are assembled in their national religion to worship God, there have I testified that which applies to *all* the Jews, that they all *should be* 'My disciples' and *ought to* acknowledge and join themselves to Me!" (Stier).

"And in secret have I said nothing" (18:20). This does not mean that He had never instructed His disciples in private.

The Lord was giving a general description of His public ministry. Moreover, His confidential communications to His own were but explanations or amplifications of what he had taught in the open. He had not two doctrines, one exoteric for the multitudes, and another esoteric for His intimate friends. In secret He had said nothing. In like manner, the badge by which *His* messengers may always be identified is described in II Cor. 4:2: "not walking in craftiness, nor handling the word of God deceitfully; but by *manifestation* of the truth commending ourselves to every man's conscience in the sight of God." In saying "in secret have I said nothing" the Saviour unhesitatingly appropriated to Himself the identical declaration of Jehovah of old—"*I have not spoken in secret,* in a dark place of the earth: I said not unto the seed of Jacob, Seek ye me in vain: I the Lord speak righteousness, I declare things that are right" (Isa. 45:19). It is also blessed to observe that while Christ here gave a full, if brief, answer to Annas concerning His "doctrine," not a word did He say about His "disciples." As the Shepherd He *protected* His sheep! He alone was to suffer, therefore He alone assumed all responsibility!

"Why askest thou me?" (18:21). Mark the quiet dignity of Christ. So far from being cowed, He turned and challenges the judge: "Why," or better, "*Wherefore* askest thou me?" It was one of those questions of the Lord which never failed to pierce the heart. Why, do you, the high priest, pretend to be ignorant of what is common knowledge among the people! You have had many opportunities to hear Me yourself! You have expelled from the synagogue those who believe in Me; what meanest thou, then, by this questioning! It was the Light exposing the "hidden things of dishonesty." It was the Holy One condemning the high priest for attempting to make a prisoner incriminate himself and supply evidence to be used against him.

"Ask them which heard me what I have said unto them: behold, they know what I said" (18:21). By thus appealing to those who had heard Him, the Lord still further rebuked the malicious secrecy which had induced them, through fear of the people, to take Him by night. The direction in which Christ pointed Annas is very striking. He did not say, Summon the deaf, the lame, the blind, the lepers I have healed. He did not say, Send for Lazarus of Bethany and question him! But, "Ask them which *heard* me." It was "the *Word*" challenging them! "Survey the dignity, the clearness, the gentleness, the supremely measured rightness and wisdom of this answer! In the full and perfect consciousness that He was no founder of a sect, deserving inquisition, He began with *I openly*, continued with *I*, and closed with profound feeling *who* He was, yet not expressing it with 'what I have said.' But, with the most proper discretion of one arrested and charged, more righteous than Annas and his foolish questioning:—I may not and will not now, My life and doctrine lying before you, testify *for Myself*, or defend Myself—let all be investigated! Let the testimony of all bear witness!" (Stier).

"And when he had thus spoken, one of the officers which stood by, struck Jesus with the palm of his hand (margin 'with a rod'), saying, Answerest thou the high priest so?" (18:22). How fearfully does this exhibit the enmity of the natural man against God, here manifest in the flesh! Meekly and mildly had our Lord replied to questions which deserved no answer, and all that He received in return was a cruel and cowardly blow. There is no hint of any remonstrance from Annas, nor have we any reason to suppose that he made any. And what shall be thought of a *judge* who allowed a bound prisoner to be treated in this fashion! Unable to meet the convicting and condemning truth, resource was had to force. It was might attempting to crush the right. This was the first blow which the sacred body of our Saviour received from the *hands* of sinners, and this came not from one of the Roman soldiers, but from a Jew! The Greek word signifies "gave a blow on the face," whether with his hand or with a stick is not determined; personally, we believe it was with the latter, and thus fulfilled Micah 5:1—"They shall smite the judge of Israel with a rod upon the cheek."

"Jesus answered him, If I have spoken evil, bear witness of of the evil: but if well, why smitest thou me?" (18:23). There was no hot surging of the flesh here, no angry retort, no spirit of resentment. Under all circumstances the Lord Jesus manifested His perfections. But He only was "without sin": contrast the apostle Paul in Acts 23. When the high priest Ananias commanded them that stood by him to strike their prisoner in the mouth, Paul said, "God shall smite thee thou whited wall." Yet it is beautiful to see how grace in him triumphed over the flesh: as soon as they asked him, "Revilest thou God's high priest?" he answered, "I wist not, brethren, that he was the high priest, for it is written, Thou shalt not speak evil of the ruler of thy people" (23:2-5). But He who is fairer than the children of men never had to retract a single word! O that we may learn of Him who was meek and lowly in heart.

"But if well, why smitest thou me?" The Saviour still acted as became the Son of God: He questioned His questioner! He judged the one who had so unrighteously condemned Him. If the smiter had any sense of justice he must have felt keenly our Lord's calm rebuke.

"Now Annas had sent him bound unto Caiaphas, the high priest" (18:24). The word "had" here is misleading and is not warranted by the Greek. It was *following* what we read of in 18:19-23 that Christ was turned over to Caiaphas. Annas had heard sufficient. He saw that to prolong the uneven contest would damage himself rather than his Prisoner; so, ignoring Christ's piercing question, the blow of the officer and our Lord's rebuke, he sends Him *bound* to his son-in-law, that the specious judgment might proceed as prudently as possible, but with the "If I have *spoken* (not 'done'!) evil, *bear witness* of the evil" ringing in his ears.

"And Simon Peter stood and warmed himself. They said therefore unto him, Art not thou also one of his disciples? He denied it, and said, I am not" (18:25). The first clause here is repeated from 18:18 so as to connect the history. The "therefore" informs us *why it was* that these men should challenge Peter. He was standing "*with* them" (18:18), as one of them, and no doubt it was the flames from their "fire" which lit up his face and caused them to recognize him. He was warming himself—more concerned about his body than his soul. He was listening to their blasphemous talk about his Master, too timid to speak up and witness for Him. And it is written "Be not deceived, evil communications corrupt good manners" (I Cor. 15:33). So it proved here, for when these men asked the apostle if he were one of Christ's disciples, he denied it. This gives additional force to the "therefore": Peter's being in the company of these enemies of the Lord was the occasion of his being challenged, and that became the occasion of his greater sinning! What a solemn warning for us to avoid the company of the ungodly! How urgently we need to heed the command! "Be ye not unequally yoked together with unbelievers"! But note it carefully that Peter did *not* deny that Jesus was the Christ, the Son of God, or the Saviour of sinners—which, we think, none indwelt by the Holy Spirit ever did—but only that *he* was one of His "disciples"!

"One of the servants of the high priest, being his kinsman whose ear Peter cut off, saith Did not I see thee in the garden with him?" (18:26). What a rebuke was this! Peter was standing "with *them*" (18:18), and now one reminds him that, only a little while before, he had stood "with *him*." How this should have searched his conscience; how it ought to have opened his eyes to the place he now occupied. But poor Peter had boasted, "Although all shall be offended yet will not I. . . . I will not deny thee in any wise" (Mark 14:29, 31); and so God left him to stand alone, to show him and us that except omnipotent grace upholds us we are certain to fall. Alas, what is man. What is our boasted strength but weakness, and when we are left to ourselves how our most solemn resolutions melt like snow before the sun!

"Peter then denied again: and immediately the cock crew" (18:27). "If any of his companions had been asked at what point of Peter's character the vulnerable spot would be found, not one of them would have said, He will fall through cowardice. Besides, Peter had a few hours before been so emphatically warned against denying Christ that he might have been expected to stand firm this night at least. Perhaps it was this very warning which betrayed Peter. When he struck the blow in the garden, he may have thought he had falsified his Lord's prediction, and when he found himself the only one who had courage to follow to the palace, his besetting self-confidence returned and led him into circumstances for which he was too weak. He was equal to the test of his courage which he was *expecting,* but when another kind of test was applied in circumstances and from a quarter he had *not* anticipated his courage failed him utterly.

"Peter probably thought he might be brought bound with his Master before the high priest, and had he done so he would probably have stood faithful. But the Devil who was sifting him had a much finer sieve than that to run him through. He brought him to no formal trial, where he could gird himself for a special effort. The whole trial was over before he knew he was being tried. So do most of our real trials come; in a business transaction that turns up with others in the day's work, in the few minutes' talk or the evening's intercourse with friends, it is discovered whether we are so truly Christ's friends that we cannot forget Him or disguise the fact that we are His. In these battles which we must all encounter, we receive no formal challenge that gives us time to choose our ground and our weapons; but a sudden blow is dealt us, from which we can be saved only by habitually wearing a coat of mail sufficient to turn it, and which we can carry into all companies" (Mr. M. Dods).

Many are the lessons which we ought to learn from this sad fall of Peter. First, in himself the believer is as weak as water. Only two hours before, Peter had partaken of the Lord's Supper, had heard the most touching Address and Prayer that ever fell on mortal ears, and had received the plainest possible warning —yet he fell!! Second, it shows us the danger of self-confidence. "It is a beacon mercifully set up in Scripture, to prevent others making shipwreck." Third, it warns us of the consequences of prayerlessness: had Peter watched and prayed when the Lord bade him, he would have found grace to help in time of need. Fourth, it reveals to us the perils of companioning with the wicked. Fifth, it shows us the distastrous influence of the fear of man—"the fear of man bringeth a snare" (Prov. 29:25), making us more afraid of the face of those we can see than the eye of God whom we cannot see. Sixth, it should prepare us against surprise when *our* familiar friends fail us in the crucial hour—God often permits this to cast us back the more on Himself! Seventh, did not God permit Peter to sin more grievously than any of the Eleven because He foreknew the extravagant regard which should afterwards be paid to *him* and his self-styled "successors"!

"After all let us leave the passage with the comfortable reflection that we have a merciful and faithful High Priest, who can be touched with the feeling of our infirmities, and will not break the bruised reed. Peter no doubt fell shamefully, and only rose again after heartfelt repentance and bitter tears. But he *did* rise again; he was not cast off forevermore. The same pitiful Hand that saved him from drowning, when his faith failed him on the waters, was once more stretched out to raise him when he fell in the high priest's hall. Can we doubt that he rose a wiser and better man? If Peter's fall has made Christians see more clearly their own great weakness and Christ's great compassion, then Peter's fall has not been recorded in vain" (Bishop Ryle).

The following questions are to help the student on the closing section of John 18:—

1. Compare the Synoptics for what happened ere Christ appeared before Pilate.
2. What does v. 30 prove?
3. What does the second half of v. 31 go to show?
4. What did Christ mean by v. 36?
5. What is the force of the last clause of v. 37?
6. Why did God cause Pilate to say v. 39?
7. What is the deeper significance of v. 40?

CHAPTER SIXTY-THREE

Christ Before Pilate

John 18:28-40

The following is an Analysis of the closing section of John 18:—

1. Christ brought to Pilate's court, v. 28.
2. Pilate demanding a formal charge, vv. 29, 30.
3. Pilate seeking to shelve his responsibility, vv. 31, 32.
4. Pilate examining Christ, vv. 33-37.
5. Pilate affirms Christ's innocence, v. 38.
6. Pilate's attempt at compromise, v. 39.
7. Pilate's attempt fails, v. 39.

In our last chapter we contemplated the Lord Jesus in the presence of Annas, the *real* high priest of Israel: in the portion of Scripture which is for our present consideration we behold the Saviour arraigned before Pilate. Much that occurred between these two things is omitted by John. In 18:24 we read, "Now Annas sent him bound unto Caiaphas the high priest," and following the account of Peter's second and third denials we are told, "Then led they Jesus from Caiaphas unto the hall of judgment" (18:28). This fourth Gospel tells us nothing about what transpired when our Lord appeared before Caiaphas, the *legal* high priest (by Roman appointment), of Israel. For this we have to compare Matt. 26:57-68; 27:1, 2; Mark 14:53 to 15:2; Luke 22:54 to 23:1. Let us briefly summarize the contents of these passages.

As was pointed out in our last, sentence of death had been passed upon Christ *before* He was brought to trial at all (18:14); the examination before Caiaphas was, therefore, nothing more than a horrible farce. The Saviour was tried before what ought to have been the holiest judicature on earth, but was condemned by the most fearful perversion of justice and abuse of its forms that is recorded anywhere in history. The amazing contrasts presented are intensely affecting. The Friend of sinners was shackled by handcuffs and leg-irons. The Judge of all the earth was arraigned before a fallen son of Adam. The Lord of glory was treated with the foulest scorn. The Holy One was condemned as a blasphemer. Liars bore witness against the Truth. He who is the Resurrection and the Life was doomed to die.

With Caiaphas were assembled the "scribes and elders" (Matt. 26:57): in addition to these were the "chief priests and all the council" (Matt. 26:59). At this decisive crisis, when Israel's rejection of their Messiah took its final and official form, all the leaders of the nation were solemnly convened. Their first act was to summon witnesses *against* the Lord, and the unprincipled character of the Sanhedrin, their utter unrighteousness, is glaringly apparent in that they "SOUGHT *false* witnesses against Jesus" (Matt. 26:59). The Sanhedrin had not the power to execute the death-penalty, therefore, some charge must be preferred against Him when they brought Him before Pilate—hence the seeking of the false witnesses. There were thousands who could have testified to the genuineness of His *miracles;* their own agents had acknowledged that never did man *speak* as He did; but such testimony as this was not what they wanted. Something must be devised which would give a semblance of justice in clamoring for His execution.

For a time their iniquitous quest was fruitless: "though many false witnesses came, yet found they none"—none who could supply what they wanted. But "at the last came two false witnesses"—the minimum number required by the Mosaic law, just as Jezebel obtained two false witnesses to testify against Naboth (I Kings 21:18). They affirmed that Christ had said, "I am able to destroy the temple of God, and to build it in three days." In obedient submission to His Father's Word, the Saviour had stood by in silence while these children of the father of lies had perjured themselves. Evidently dissatisfied at the flimsiness of such a charge, and uneasy at Christ's calm dignity, the high priest arose "and said unto him, Answerest thou nothing? What is it which these witness against thee?" But Jesus held His peace. Alarmed, most probably at the dignified demeanor of his Prisoner, and fearful perhaps that His bearing might move the hearts of some in the Council, Caiaphas said, "I adjure thee by the living God, that thou tell us whether thou be the Christ, the Son of God" (Matt. 26:63). "This was the method among the Israelites of proffering and accepting the oath; the appeal to God (and the formula of curse as the penalty of lying—which, however, was not ventured on now) was made on the one side, and the answer made thereupon was received, without any repetition of the oath being regarded as necessary on the part of the respondent. I adjure Thee by the *living* God (in whose office I stand, under whose power we all are, before whom Thou also standest, who knowest the truth, and judgeth between us and Thee) that Thou tell us, this holy Sanhedrin now here as before God, the truth. Thus does he avow, bearing testimony against himself in this most awful abuse of the name of God, that he *knows* this God as a *living* God who will not be mocked! He testifies of His truth, even while he is aiming to get the victory by a lie; of His power and majesty, while he is pushing his opposition to the uttermost!" (Stier).

Now, for the first time, Christ spoke before Caiaphas. He penetrates the meaning of His questioner, recognizes all the consequences of His affirmation, but hesitates not to answer. As an obedient Israelite, it was His duty to respond to the adjuration of the ruling power (Lev. 5:1; I Kings 22:16). Made "under the law" (Gal. 4:4), He was submissive to the last, even when it was perverted against Him. The Saviour not only replied to His judge, but, maintaining His dignity to the last, added, "Hereafter shall ye see the Son of man sitting on the right hand of power, and coming in the clouds of heaven" (Matt. 26:64):—"Sitting" in contrast from Me now standing before you, while you sit in judgment upon Me; "power" in contrast from His then weakness (i.e., refusing to exercise His might); "*Coming* in the clouds of heaven" in contrast from *going* to the Cross! Caiaphas' response was to rend his official robes—instead of putting them off before the majesty of the great High Priest. In this act Caiaphas did, unknown to himself, but intimate that *God* had rent asunder the Aaronic priesthood! — a garment is only torn to pieces by its owner when he has no more use for it.

Following the rending of his robes, Caiaphas said, "What further need have we of witnesses? Behold, now we have heard His blasphemy. What think ye?" *He* was the blasphemer. "What further need have we of witnesses?" betrayed his uneasy conscience; "Behold, now ye have heard him" was the signal that the mock trial was over. The answer he wanted was promptly given: "He is guilty of death." Elated at their fancied triumph, "*then* did they spit in his face, and buffeted him; and others smote with the palms of their hands, saying, Prophesy unto us thou Christ, who is he that smote thee?" Thus did Israel condemn their Messiah, rebellious man his God.

"When the morning was come, all the chief priests and elders of the people took counsel against Jesus to put him to death: And when they had bound him, they led him away, and delivered him to Pontius Pilate the governor" (Matt. 27:1, 2), thus fulfilling our Lord's prediction, "The Son of man shall be delivered unto the chief priests, and unto the scribes; and they shall condemn him to death, and shall deliver him to the Gentiles: And they shall mock him, and shall scourge him, and shall spit upon him" (Mark 10:33, 34). This brings us to the first point touched upon by John, whose narrative we shall now follow.

"Then led they Jesus from Caiaphas unto the hall of judgment: and it was early" (18:28). "Then," following the decision of the Council, recorded in Matt. 27:1; "led they"; still unresisting, He went as a lamb to the slaughter. Mark tells us (15:1) they "bound" Him; "unto the hall of judgment," Pilate's court-room. "And it was early": the disciples could not watch *with* Him one hour; His enemies had acted *against* Him all through that night! Alas, man has more zeal and energy, because more heart, for that which is evil than for that which is good. The same people who will listen, untired, half a day to a political discussion, or sit three hours through an opera, complain that the preacher is long-winded if he spends the whole hour in expounding the Word of God! "It was early": their one object now was to obtain from Pilate, as swiftly as possible, his confirmation of the death-sentence.

"And they themselves went not into the judgment-hall, lest they should be defiled; but that they might eat the passover" (18:28). The judgment-hall was *Gentile* property and to have entered it the Jews would be ceremonially defiled, and from that there was not time to be cleansed ere the passover feast arrived. Anxious to partake of the passover, they therefore went no further than the entrance to the praetorium. They would not enter Pilate's hall, though they were ready to use him to further their own wickedness! What a proof was this of the worthlessness of religion where it has failed to influence the heart. Fully did they merit those awful words of Christ: "Woe unto you, scribes and Pharisees, hypocrites! for ye are like unto whited sepulchres, which indeed appear beautiful outward, but are within full of dead men's bones, and of all uncleanness. Even so ye also outwardly appear righteous unto men, but within ye are full of hypocrisy and iniquity" (Matt. 23:27, 28).

These very men were here engaged in the vilest act ever perpetrated on earth, and yet they spoke of being "defiled"! They hesitated not to deliver their Messiah to the Gentiles, yet were scrupulous lest they be disqualified from eating the passover. So to-day there are some who are more concerned about the right form of baptism than they are of a scriptural walk; more punctilious about observing the Lord's supper than to bring forth fruit to the glory of the Father. Let us beware lest we also "strain at a gnat and swallow a camel." "These 'rulers of the Jews' and the multitude that followed them were thorough *Ritualists*. It was their ritualism that urged them on to crucify the Son of God. Christ and ritualism are opposed to each other as light is to darkness. The true Cross in which Paul gloried and the cross in which modern ceremonialists glory, have no resemblance to each other. The Cross and the crucifix cannot agree. Either ritualism will banish Christ or Christ will banish ritualism." (Mr. H. Bonar.)

"Pilate then went out unto them" (18:29). That the whole Sanhedrin (Mark 15:1, 2), accompanied by a large crowd (Luke 23:1), should visit him at such a time (the passover feast), was sufficient to convince Pilate that some important matter required his attention; therefore, early morning though it were, he went out to them. That he was not taken by surprise we know, for only the previous night they had secured a cohort of Roman soldiers, which could not have been obtained without his permission. It was clear to him, then, that here was some culprit whom the Jews wished executed before the Feast began.

"And said, What accusation bring ye against this man?" (18:29). Pilate's question here confirms what we have just said above. He did not ask them what was the object of their visit, but simply inquired what charge they preferred against their prisoner. This was in accord with the Roman law which required three things: the making of a specific indictment, the bringing of the accusers before the accused, and the liberty granted to the latter to answer for himself (Acts 25:16). Pilate therefore acted honorably in demanding to know the nature of the crime charged against the Lord Jesus. God saw to it that out of their own mouths they should be condemned.

"They answered and said unto him, If he were not a malefactor, we would not have delivered him up unto thee" (18:30). The Jews were piqued at Pilate's question. They were not anxious to prefer a charge, knowing full well that they had no evidence by which they could establish it. It is clear that they hoped that Pilate would take *their* word for it—especially as they had obtained the soldiers from him so easily—and condemn their Prisoner unheard. With characteristic hypocrisy they now assumed an injured air: they posed as righteous men; they would have Pilate believe that *they* would never have arrested an *innocent* man. Their "if he were not a malefactor, we would not have delivered him up unto thee" was tantamount to saying: "See who is before you—we are none other than the sacred Sanhedrin: we have already tried the case, and our judgment is beyond question: we only ask you now to give the necessary Roman sanction that He may be put to death." Their hands were forced by Pilate, for Luke tells us "they began to accuse him, saying, We found this fellow perverting the nation, and forbidding to give tribute to Caesar, saying that he himself is Christ a king" (23:2).

"Then said Pilate unto them, Take ye him, and judge him, according to your law" (18:31). The whole responsibility now rested on Pilate. He was too well acquainted with the Jews' expectations to suppose that the Sanhedrin would hate and persecute one who would free them from the Roman yoke. Their simulation of good citizenship was too shallow to deceive him. But he did not relish the task before him, and sought to evade it. The real character of the man comes out plainly here—timid, vacillating, temporizing, unprincipled. Pilate wished to have nothing to do with the case; he was anxious for the Jews to shoulder the full onus of Christ's death. What cared he for justice, so long as he could get out of an unpleasant situation! He was anxious not to displease the Jews, therefore did he say, "judge him (sentence Him to death) according to your law."

"The Jews therefore said unto him, It is not lawful for *us* to put any man to death" (18:31). This reply completely thwarted the wretched Pilate's attempt to avoid the necessity of judging our Lord. They pressed upon the Roman governor that the legal power of passing the death sentence was no longer in their hands, therefore it was impossible for them to do as he desired. They here warned Pilate that nothing but the execution of Christ would satisfy them. But a Higher Power was overruling: "Of a truth against thy Holy servant Jesus, whom thou hast anointed, both Herod and Pontius Pilate with the Gentiles, and the people of Israel, were gathered together, for to do whatsoever *thy* hand and *thy* counsel determined before to be done" (Acts 4:27, 28).

"The Jews therefore said unto him, It is not lawful for us to put any man to death." Though they were unaware of it, this was a remarkable confession. It was *their own* acknowledgment that Gen. 49:10 was now fulfilled—"The sceptre shall not depart from Judah, nor a lawgiver from between his feet, until Shiloh come." The heads of Israel here owned that *they* were no longer the rulers of their own nation, but were under the dominion of a foreign power. He that has the right to condemn a prisoner to death is the governor of a country. "It is not lawful" they said; you, the Roman governor, alone can do it. By their consent they no longer had a law-administrator of their own stock.

therefore the *"sceptre"* had departed, and this was proof positive that Shiloh (the Messiah) *had come!* How unaware wicked men are when they fulfil prophecy!

"That the saying of Jesus might be fulfilled, which he spake, signifying what death he should die" (18:32). Here again prediction was being fulfilled, all unconsciously by themselves. The refusal of Israel to take matters into their own hands, when Pilate put it there, only worked for the accomplishment of Christ's own words: "and shall deliver him to the *Gentiles* to mock, and to scourge, and to crucify" (Matt. 20:19). Moreover, had the Jews still possessed the power of inflicting capital punishment for such crimes as they alleged against the Lord Jesus, the mode of execution would have been by stoning. By delivering Him to Pilate this ensured the Roman form of punishment, crucifixion, and thus did the saying of Christ come to pass: "As Moses lifted up the serpent in the wilderness, even so must the Son of man be *lifted up*" (John 3:14); and again, "I, if I be lifted up from the earth, will draw all unto me. This He said, signifying *what* death he should die" (12:32, 33).

"Then Pilate entered into the judgment hall again, and called Jesus, and said unto him, Art thou the King of the Jews?" (18:33). Here we have another glaring example of the gross injustice which was meted out to the Saviour. First Annas, then Caiaphas, now Pilate, displayed the fearful enmity of the carnal mind against God—here manifest in flesh. Roman law required that the accused and the accusers should be brought face to face, and that the former should have an opportunity of replying to the charge laid against him (Acts 23:28), but this Pilate denied Christ. But what was far worse, Pilate examined Christ as the enemy of *Caesar* and the *Jews* were His only accusers! If the Lord Jesus were really opposing the authority and rights of the Emperor, why had not the Roman power taken the initiative? Where were the Gentile witnesses against Him? Were all the Roman officers indifferent to their master's interests! Pilate knew that it was for *envy* (Matt. 27:18) the Sanhedrin had delivered Him up. He knew full well that the Saviour was no malefactor: he could not have been ignorant of His public life—

His deeds of mercy, His words of grace and truth; yet did he refuse Him a fair trial. The fact that Pilate's objection (18:31) was so easily silenced, revealed the pitiable weakness of his character. Sent to be the Governor of these Jews, they, nevertheless, compelled him to be their slave, the executioner of their wrath.

"Then Pilate entered into the judgment hall again, and called Jesus, and said unto him, Art thou the king of the Jews?" What lay behind this question? what was the state of Pilate's mind when he asked it? With Bishop Ryle we are inclined to say, "On the whole, the question seems a mixture of curiosity and contempt." The humble attire and lowly appearance of our Lord cannot fail to have struck the Governor. The entire absence of any signs which the world associates with One possessing a kingdom must have puzzled him. Yet tidings of His "triumphal entrance" into Jerusalem only a few days before had doubtless reached his ears. Who, then, was this strange character who attracted the multitudes, but was hated by their leaders? who had power to heal the sick, yet had not where to lay His head? who was able to raise the dead, yet here stood bound before him?

"Jesus answered him, Sayest thou this thing of thyself, or did others tell it thee of me?" (18:34). Our Lord was addressing Himself to Pilate's conscience. Do you really desire to act justly? Is it information you are in quest of? or are you going to be the tool of those who delivered Me to thee? He would point out to him the injustice of any suspicions he might entertain. If you have reason to think *I am* a "king" in the sense in which you employ the term, then where are the Roman witnesses? If you are influenced only by what you have heard from the Sanhedrin, beware of heeding the word of those who are plainly My enemies. Christ was pressing upon him his individual responsibility of coming to some definite conviction concerning Himself. But why not have answered with a plain Yes or No? Because that, under the circumstances, was impossible? Pilate used the word "king" as a *rival* of Caesar, as a *rebel* against Rome. To have replied Yes, would have misled Pilate; to have said No, without qualification, would have been to deny "the hope of Israel." The Lord therefore presses Pilate for a definition of this ambiguous term. Admire His consummate wisdom.

"Sayest thou this of thyself, or did others tell it thee of me?" "Our Lord, by this, would learn whether His claims to be king of the Jews was challenged by Pilate as protector of the Emperor's rights in Judea, or merely upon a charge of the Jews. Upon this hung, I may say, everything in the present juncture; and the wisdom and purpose of the Lord in giving the inquiry this direction are manifest. Should Pilate say that he had become apprehensive of the Roman interests, the Lord could at once have referred him to the whole course of His life and ministry, to prove that, touching the king, innocency had been found in Him. He had taught the rendering to Caesar the things that are Caesar's. He had withdrawn Himself, departing into a mountain alone, when He perceived that the multitude would have taken Him by force to make Him a king (6:15). His controversy was not with Rome . . . and Pilate would have had His answer according to all this had the challenge proceeded from himself as representative of the Roman power. But it did not" (Mr. J. G. Bellett).

"Pilate answered, Am I a Jew? Thine own nation and the chief priests have delivered thee unto me: what hast thou done?" (18:35). Here Pilate betrayed his insincerity. He evaded Christ's penetrating question. He denied any personal interest in the matter. *I* am no Jew—*I* am not concerned about points of *religious* controversy. "What hast thou *done?*"—let us deal with *practical* matters. We doubt not that Pilate uttered his first question sneeringly—Am I a *Jew!* You forget that I, a noble Roman, can have no patience with visions and dreams. It was the haughty and contemptuous language of a prominent man of affairs. "Thine own nation and the chief priests" are the ones who are interested in ceremonial rites and recondite prophecies, and *they* have "delivered thee to me"! What is it that they have against you? Here he speaks as the judge: let us come to the business in hand.

"Pilate answered, Am I a Jew? Thine own nation and the chief priests have delivered thee unto me: what hast thou done?"

"This answer of Pilate conveyed the full proof of the *guilt of Israel*. In the mouth of him who represented the power of the world at that time, the thing was established, that Israel had disclaimed their King and sold themselves into the hand of another. This, for the present, was everything with Jesus—this at once carried Him beyond the earth, and out of the world. Israel had rejected Him, and His kingdom was, therefore, not from hence: for Zion is the appointed place for the King of the whole earth to sit and rule; and the unbelief of the daughter of Zion must keep the king of the earth away. The Lord, then, as the rejected King, listening to this testimony from the lips of the Roman, could only recognize the present loss of His throne" (Mr. Bellett). Hence Christ's next words.

"My kingdom is not of this world" (18:36). First, observe that He did not say "My kingdom is not *in* this world," but "My kingdom is not *of* this world." Believers are not "of" this world (17:16), yet they *are* "in" it! Second, observe His own qualifying and yet amplifying words at the close of the verse: "but now is my kingdom not from hence." The "now" is explained by Pilate's declaration in the previous verse—re-read Mr. Bellett's comments thereon. This was not said by Christ until after His final and official *rejection by Israel!* Third, observe His explanatory "If my kingdom *were* of this world, *then* would my servants fight"—to deliver their king. Our Lord was graciously explaining to Pilate the *character* of that kingdom over which He will yet preside. Unlike all the kingdoms which have preceded it, *My* kingdom will not originate with man, but be received from God (Dan. 7:13, 14; Luke 19:12); unlike the kingdoms of man, which have been dependent upon the powers of the world, *Mine* will be an absolute theocracy; unlike theirs, which have been propagated by the world's arms, *Mine* will be regulated by heavenly principles; unlike theirs, which have been characterized by injustice and tyranny, Mine will be marked by righteousness and peace.

In answering Pilate as He did we cannot but admire the wondrous grace and patience of our blessed Lord. The contemptuous "Am I a Jew?" of Pilate annulled his right to any further notice; his "what hast thou done?" gave the One before him the full right to maintain silence. But ignoring the insult, Christ continued to address Himself to his conscience. "My kingdom is not of *this* world" warned Pilate that there was *another* world, to which He belonged! "My *kingdom*," which will not be brought in by "fighting," was to assure him there was a Power *superior* to the boasted might of Rome, which then dominated the earth. "Now is my kingdom not *from hence*" intimated that His kingdom would be far otherwise than those in which violence and injustice had ever held sway, and where, after all, there was nothing obtained but the semblance of right and truth. Thus instead of furnishing a positive reply to Pilate's "What hast thou done?" He gave a negative answer which, however, plainly showed that *He* was guilty of no political evil and had done nothing against Caesar.

Some have wondered why Christ did not appeal to His wondrous and benevolent works of mercy when Pilate asked Him, "What hast thou done?" But those were a part of His Messianic credentials (Matt. 11:3-5, etc.), and therefore *only* for Israel. Others have wondered why Pilate did not refer to the smiting of Malchus in the garden, when the Lord affirmed "then would my servants fight." Why had not the Sanhedrin informed Pilate of Peter's temerity? Malchus was a servant of the high priest and nothing was more natural than that he should clamor for redress. The seeming difficulty is at once removed by a reference to Luke 22:51, where we are told that the Saviour "touched his ear and *healed* him." "The miracle satisfactorily explains the suppression of the charge — to have advanced it would have naturally led to an investigation that would have more than frustrated the malicious purpose it was meant to serve. It would have proved too much. It would have manifested His own compassionate nature, His submission to the law, and His extraordinary powers" (Mr. J. Blount).

"Pilate therefore said unto him, Art thou a king then?" (18:37). The Governor was puzzled. The quiet and dignified bearing of the One before him, the threefold reference to His kingdom, the declaration that it was not of this world, the calm assertion that though in bonds *He* was possessed of "servants," plus a strong hint that His dominion would yet be firmly established, though not by the sword, was more than Pilate could grasp. Pilate's change from "Art thou the king *of the Jews?*" in 18:33 to "Art thou a king then?" intimated he was satisfied there was nothing to fear politically, yet that Christ had made a claim which was incomprehensible to his mind. We believe that he had dropped his scornful tone and asked this last question half earnestly, half curiously. That He *was* "king" our Lord would not deny, but boldly acknowledged "to this end was I born," knowing full well what would be the cost of His affirmation. It is to this the Holy Spirit refers, "who before Pontius Pilate witnessed a good confession" (I Tim. 6:13). Though Israel received Him not, yet He *was* their king (Matt. 2:2). Though the husbandmen were casting Him out, yet He *was* the heir of the vineyard. Though His citizens were saying they would not have Him to reign over them, yet He *had been* anointed to the throne in Zion.

"To this end was I born, *and* for this cause came I into the world, that I should bear witness unto the truth" (18:37). Note how the Saviour here linked together His kingdom and His bearing witness unto the truth. Truth is authoritative, imperial, majestic. This was a further word for Pilate's conscience, if only his heart were open to receive it. Christ informs him that He possessed a higher glory than His title to David's throne, even that of Deity, for it was as the Only-begotten of the Father that He was "full of grace and truth," and His "*came* I into the world"—distinguished from His being "born" in the previous clause—was a direct hint that *He* was from *Heaven!* Moreover, the Lord would have it known that there had been no failure in His mission. The great design before Him at His first advent was not to wield the royal sceptre, but to bear witness unto the truth; *that* He had faithfully done, yea, was doing, at that very moment. *This* was His answer, to Pilate's "What hast thou done?" (18:35)—I have witnessed unto, not simply "truth" but, *the* truth; it was as "the *word*" He again spoke!

"Every one that is of the truth heareth my voice" (18:37). He that is "of the truth" means, first, he that is true, honest and sincere; in its deeper meaning, he who is of God: compare 8:47. It is only the one who has a heart for the truth who really hears Christ's voice, for the Author of the truth is also the Teacher, the Interpreter of it. What a word was *this* for Pilate's conscience. If you are really seeking the Truth, which I came into the world to bear witness unto, you will listen unto Me! "Would any one ask how he can know that *he* is 'of the truth'? The Sacred Word supplies a direct answer, leaving none in doubt. 'Let us not love in word, neither in tongue; but in deed and in truth. And *hereby* we know that we *are* of the truth' (I John 3:18, 19). Whoever shows himself to be a partaker of the Divine nature, evidenced by loving in deed and in truth, is of the truth, hears Christ's voice, and will be found in His train among the armies of heaven, when He comes forth to deal with the apostate power on earth" (Mr. C. E. Stuart).

"Pilate saith unto him, What is truth? And when he had said this, he went out" (18:38). There has been wide difference of opinion as to the spirit in which he asked this question. Clearly it was not that of an earnest inquirer, as his at once leaving Christ without waiting for an answer shows—only an awakened conscience is really desirous of knowing *what* is Truth. Many have thought it was more a wail of despair: *What is* truth?: "I have investigated many a system, examined various philosophers, but have found no satisfaction in them." But apart from the fact that everything revealed about his character conflicts with an earnest, persevering quest after light, would he not rather have said, "Truth! there *is* no truth!" had that been his state of mind? Personally, we regard Pilate's words here as an expression of scorn, ending them not with a question mark but an exclamation, the emphasis on the final word—"What is *truth!*" It was the Light now manifesting the darkness. This expressed the settled conviction of a conscienceless politician. "Truth"!—is it for *that* you are sacrificing your life? We think his words in 18:39 bear this out.

"And when he had said this, he went out again unto the Jews, and said unto them, I find in him no fault" (18:38). Pilate was uneasy. The words of Christ had impressed him more deeply than he would care to admit. That He was innocent was clear; that Pilate was now guilty of the grossest injustice is equally patent. If the Roman governor found "no fault" in

Christ he ought to have promptly released Him. But instead of yielding to the voice of conscience he proceeded to confer with those who thirsted for the Saviour's blood. Much is omitted by John at this point which is found in the Synoptics—the chief priest's remonstrance (Mark 15:3-12); Pilate sending Him to Herod; and the brutal treatment which He received at the hands of his soldiers, followed by Herod sending Him back to Pilate (Luke 23:5-18).

"But ye have a custom, that I should release unto you one at the passover: will ye therefore that I release unto you the king of the Jews?" (18:39). The nature of such a proposal at once reveals the unscrupulous character of him who made it. Pilate feared to offend the Jews (feared because an uprising at that time would have brought him into disfavour with Caesar, who had his hands full elsewhere) and so sought an expedient which he hoped would please them, and yet enable him to discharge the Lord Jesus. Remembering the custom which obtained at the passover of releasing a prisoner—a most striking custom it was, *grace, deliverance,* connected with the *passover!*—he suggests that Christ be the one to go free. It was as though he said, Let us suppose that Jesus is guilty; I am willing to declare Him a criminal worthy of death, providing He be freed. Luke tells us that he went so far as to offer to "chastise" Christ before he released Him (23:16). Little did he recognize the type of men he was dealing with, still less the One above who was directing all things.

"Then cried they all again, saying, Not this man, but Barabbas. Now Barabbas was a robber" (18:40). The Jews revealed themselves as worse than Pilate and demanded what he least expected. Thirsting for the blood of their victim, impatient for him to yield up to them their prey, they *all* "cried (the Greek signifies 'shouted') not this man, but Barabbas." Pilate's compromise not only showed plainly that *he* was *not* "of the truth" but only drew out the extent of their enmity. "Barabbas was a robber," better "bandit"—one who used force; Luke says he was a murderer. How very striking: the Jews *chose* Barabbas, and plunders and blood-shedders have ruled over them ever since!! In this their history is without a parallel.

"We have noticed elsewhere how strangely yet significantly this name Barabbas, 'son of the father,' comes in here. It was the Son of the Father – just as that – whom they were refusing now; but of *what* father was this lawless one the son? A shadow it is, surely, of the awful apostasy to come, when they will receive him who comes in his own name (the Antichrist, A.W.P.), true child of the rebel and 'murderer from the beginning.' Yet there is a Gospel side to this also. How good to see that here it is the question, *Shall the Saviour or the sinner suffer?* and to remember that under the law, the unclean animal might be redeemed with a Lamb (Ex. 13), but the lamb could not be redeemed. Impossible for the Saviour to be released in this way. But the sinner may" (Mr. F. W. Grant).

The following questions are to aid the student on John 19:1-11: –

1. Why did God allow Christ to wear "a crown of thorns," v. 2?
2. Why "a purple robe," v. 2?
3. How many times in the four Gospels "I find no fault," v. 4?
4. What was Pilate's aim in "Behold the man"! v. 5?
5. What is the meaning of v. 6 in the light of 18:31?
6. What made Pilate "the more afraid," v. 8?
7. Why did Jesus make no anwser, v. 9?

CHAPTER SIXTY-FOUR

CHRIST BEFORE PILATE (CONCLUDED)

John 19:1-11

Below is an Analysis of the passage which is to be before us:—

1. Christ scourged and mocked, vv. 1-3.
2. Pilate re-affirms His innocency, v. 4.
3. Pilate appeals to the Jews' sympathies, v. 5.
4. The Jews' response, vv. 6, 7.
5. Pilate's fear, vv. 8, 9.
6. Pilate's boast, v. 10.
7. Christ's reprimand, v. 11.

Nowhere in Scripture, perhaps, is there a more striking and vivid demonstration of the sovereignty of God than Pilate's treatment of the Lord Jesus. First, Pilate was *assured* of His *innocency*, acknowledging, no less than seven times, "I find *no* fault in him." Second, Pilate *desired* to release Him: "Pilate therefore *willing* to release Jesus" (Luke 23:20); "I will let him go" (Luke 23:22); "Pilate *sought* to release him" (John 19:12); "Pilate was *determined* to let him go" (Acts 3:13), all prove that unmistakably. Third, Pilate was *urged*, most earnestly by none other than his own wife, *not to sentence* Him (Matt. 27:19). Fourth, he actually *endeavored* to bring about His acquittal: he bade the Jews themselves judge Christ (18:31); he sent Him to Herod, only for Christ to be returned (Luke 23:7); he sought to induce the Jews to have him convict Barabbas in His stead (18:39,40). Yet in spite of all, Pilate *did* give sentence that Christ should be crucified!

What does man's will amount to when it runs counter to the will of God? Absolutely nothing. Here was Pilate, the Roman governor of Judea, *determined* to release the Saviour, yet prevented from doing so. From all eternity God had decreed that Pilate *should* sentence His Son to death, and all earth and hell combined could not thwart the purpose of the Almighty—He would not be *all*-mighty if they could! Christ was "delivered up (Greek) by the determinate counsel and foreknowledge of God" (Acts 2:23). As God's servant fearlessly announced, "Both Herod and Pontius Pilate, with the Gentiles, and the people of Israel, were gathered together for to do *whatsoever* thy hand and thy counsel *determined before* to be done" (Acts 4:27, 28). This is not simply "Calvinism," it is the explicit declaration of Holy Writ, and, woe be unto the one who dares to deny it. Christ *had to be* sentenced by Pilate because the eternal counsels of Deity had foreordained it. Moreover, Christ was dying for sinners *both* of the Jews and of the Gentiles, therefore Divine wisdom deemed it fitting that *both* Jews and Gentiles should have a direct hand in His death.

But, it will at once be objected, *This* reduces Pilate to a mere machine! Our first answer is, What of that?—better far to reduce him to a non-entity than to deny the Word of the living God! Away with the deductions of reason; our initial and never-ceasing duty is to bow in absolute submission to the teaching of the Holy Scriptures. Our second answer is, The deduction drawn by the objector is manifestly erroneous. An honest mind is forced to acknowledge that the Gospel records present Pilate to us as a *responsible agent*. Christ addressed Himself to Pilate's conscience: "Everyone that is of the truth heareth my voice" (18:37); God faithfully warned him that Christ was a *just* Man and to have nothing to do with Him (Matt. 27:19). Should it be asked, How could God *consistently* warn him when He had decreed that he should sentence Christ to death? Our reply is, His decree was a part of His own sovereign counsels; whereas the warning was addressed to Pilate's responsibility, and he will be justly held accountable for disregarding it. Christ announced that Peter *would* deny Him, yet a few minutes later said to him, "Watch and pray, that *ye enter not* into temptation"! Finally, the Saviour Himself told Pilate that he was *sinning* in holding Him: "he that delivered me unto thee hath the *greater* sin" (19:11)—therefore it follows that Pilate's failure to release Him was a *great sin!*

"Then Pilate therefore took Jesus, and scourged him" (19:1). We believe that the real explanation of this awful act of the Roman governor is intimated in v. 4—"Pilate *therefore* went forth again, and saith unto them, Behold, I bring him forth to you, that ye may know that I find no fault in him." It was a desperate move, made against his better judgment, and, also made, we fully believe, *against* the strivings of his conscience. It was his third and last effort at a compromise. First, he had asked the Jews to judge Christ for themselves (18:31). Second, he had pitted against Him a notable outlaw, Barabbas, and made them take their choice. That having failed, he made a final effort to escape from that which he feared to do. He hesitated to speak the irrevocable word, and so scourged the Lord Jesus instead, and suffered the soldiers to brutally mistreat Him. We believe Pilate hoped that when he should present to the gaze of the Jews their suffering and bleeding king, their rage would be appeased. Luke 23:16 bears this out: "I will chastise him *and* release him." How entirely this wretched device failed we shall see by and by.

"Then Pilate therefore took Jesus, and scourged him." "The cruel injury inflicted on our Lord's body, in this verse, was probably far more severe than an English reader might suppose. It was a punishment which among the Romans generally preceded crucifixion, and was sometimes so painful that the sufferer died under it. It was often a scourging with rods, and not always with cords, as painters and sculptors represent. Josephus, the Jewish historian, in his 'Antiquities,' particularly mentions that malefactors were scourged and tormented in every way before they were put to death. Smith's Dictionary of the Bible says that under the Roman mode of scourging, 'The culprit was stripped, stretched with cords or thongs on a frame, and beaten with rods'" (Bishop Ryle).

"And the soldiers plaited a crown of thorns, and put it on his head, and they put on him a purple robe, and said, Hail, king of the Jews! and they smote him with their hands" (19:2, 3). "One question springs from the heart on reading this—How could it be! Where is the lauded Roman justice in this scourging of a bound prisoner of whom the judge says, 'I find no fault in him!' Why is an uncondemned one given into the rude hands of Roman soldiers for them to mock and smite at their pleasure? Where is the cool judgment of Pilate, that a little while ago refused to take action lest injustice be done? Why is Jesus treated in a way wholly unparalleled so far as we know? What is the secret of it all?" (Mr. M. Taylor). Difficult as it would be, impossible perhaps, for unaided reason to answer these questions, the light which Scripture throws on them removes all difficulty.

First, *who* was this One so brutally, so unrighteously treated? He was Immanuel, "God manifest in flesh," and fallen man *hates* God. "The heart is deceitful above all things, and desperately wicked" (Jer. 17:9). "The carnal mind is enmity against God" (Rom. 8:7). "Their throat is an open sepulchre; with their tongues they have used deceit; the poison of asps is under their lips: Whose mouth is full of cursing and bitterness: Their feet are swift to shed blood: destruction and misery are in their ways" (Rom. 3:13-16). Never before or since did these awful facts receive such exemplification. Never were the desperate wickedness of the human heart, the fearful enmity of the carnal mind, and the unspeakable vileness of sin's ways, so unmistakably evidenced as when the Son of God was "*delivered into the hands of men*" (Mark 9:31). All Divine restraint was withdrawn, and human depravity was allowed to show itself in all its naked hideousness.

Second, this was *Satan's hour*. Said the Saviour to those who came to arrest Him in the Garden, "*This* is your hour, *and* the power of darkness" (Luke 22:53). On the day when sin entered the world, Jehovah announced that He would put enmity between the serpent and the woman, and between his seed and her seed (Gen. 3:15). That enmity was manifested when Christ became incarnate, for we are told, "And the dragon stood before the woman which was ready to be delivered, for to *devour* her child as soon as it was born" (Rev. 12:4), and he it was who moved Herod to slay all the young children in Bethlehem. But God interposed and the dragon was foiled. But now God hindered no longer. The hour had arrived when the serpent was to bruise the Saviour's heel, and fully did he now avail himself of his opportunity. Jews and Gentiles alike were "of their father, the devil." and his lusts (desires) they now carried out with a will.

Third, Christ was on the point of making atonement *for sin,* therefore sin must be revealed in all its enormity. Sin is *lawlessness,* therefore did Pilate scourge the innocent One. Sin is *transgression,* therefore did Pilate set aside all the principles and statutes of Roman jurisprudence. Sin is *iniquity* (injustice), therefore did these soldiers smite that One who had never harmed a living creature. Sin is *rebellion against God,* therefore did Jew and Gentile alike maltreat the Son of God. Sin is an *offence,* therefore did they outrage every dictate of conscience and propriety. Sin is *coming short of the glory of God,* therefore did they heap ignominy upon His Son. Sin is *defilement,* uncleanness, therefore did they cover His face with vile spittle.

Fourth, Christ was to die *in the stead* of sinners, therefore must it be shown what was righteously due them. The Law required "an eye for an eye and a tooth for a tooth," a *quid pro quo.* All sin is a revolt against God, a treating of Him with contumacy, a virtual smiting of Him; therefore was Christ *scourged by* sinners. Again, when man became a sinner the righteous curse of the thrice holy God fell upon him, hence Christ will yet say to the wicked. "Depart from me ye *cursed"!* Unto Adam God declared, "cursed is the ground for thy sake . . . *thorns also* and thistles shall it bring forth to thee" (Gen. 3:17, 18); therefore the last Adam, as the Head of those He came to deliver from the curse, was *crowned* with *thorns!* Again, by nature and practice we are defiled: our iniquities cover us from head to foot—sins which are "scarlet" and "crimson" (Isa. 1:18); therefore was the Saviour enveloped in "a *purple robe"*—Matthew actually terms it "a *scarlet* robe" (27:28), and Mark says "they clothed him with *purple*" (15:17). Finally, they mocked Him as "*king* of the Jews," for "sin hath *reigned* unto death" (Rom. 5:21). Here then is the Gospel of our salvation: the Saviour was scourged, that we might go free; He was crowned with thorns, that we might be crowned with blessing and glory; He was clothed with a robe of contempt, that we might receive the robe of righteousness; He was rejected as king, that we might be made kings and priests unto God.

"Pilate therefore went forth again, and saith unto them, Behold, I bring him forth to you that ye may know that I find no fault in him" (19:4). The private interview which Pilate had had with Christ at least convinced him that He had done nothing worthy of death; he therefore returned to the Jews and re-affirmed His innocence. The "therefore" points back to what is recorded in 19:1-3: he had gone as far as he meant to. "I bring him forth to *you*": there is nothing more that *I* intend to do. "I find no fault in him": how striking that the very one who shortly after sentenced Him to death, should give this repeated witness that the Lamb *was* "without blemish!" More striking still is it to observe that at the very time the Lord Jesus was apprehended and crucified as a criminal, God raised up one after another to testify of His guiltlessness. Of old the prophet had asked, "And *who shall declare* his generation? for he was cut off out of the land of the living" (Isa. 53:8). A *sevenfold* answer is supplied in the Gospels. First, Judas declared "I have sinned in that I have betrayed *the innocent* blood" (Matt. 27:4). Second, Pilate declared, "I find *no fault* in him" (John 19:4). Third, of Herod Pilate said, "No, nor yet Herod: for I sent you to him; and, lo, *nothing* worthy of death is done unto him" (Luke 23:15). Fourth, Pilate's wife entreated, "Have thou nothing to do with that *just* man: for I have suffered many things this day in a dream *because of him*." (Matt. 27:19). Fifth, the dying thief affirmed, "We receive the due reward of our deeds: but this man *hath done nothing amiss*" (Luke 23:41). Sixth, the Roman centurion who glorified God, said, "Certainly this was a *righteous* man" (Luke 23:47). Seventh, those who stood with the centurion acknowledged, "Truly this was *the son of God*" (Matt. 27:54)!

"Then came Jesus forth, wearing the crown of thorns, and the purple robe" (19:5). "That our blessed Lord, the eternal Word, should have meekly submitted to be led out after this fashion, as a gazing-stock and an object of scorn, with an old purple robe on His shoulders, a crown of thorns on His head, His back bleeding from scourging, and His head from thorns, to feast the eyes of a taunting, howling, blood-thirsty crowd, is indeed a wondrous thought! Truly such love 'passeth knowledge'" (Bishop Ryle).

"And Pilate saith unto them, 'Behold the man!'" (19:5). We fully believe that Pilate was here appealing to the Jews' pity. See, saith he, what He has already suffered! He had no need to say more. The shame, the bleeding wounds, were tongues sufficiently moving if only they had ears to hear. Pilate hoped that their wrath would now be appeased. Is He not already punished enough! It is surely striking that the Governor said not, "Behold *this* man," but, "Behold *the* man." It was the ungrudging testimony of an unprejudiced witness. Never before had any other who had stood before his bar carried himself as this One. Never before had Pilate seen such quiet dignity, intrepid courage, noble majesty. He was deeply impressed, and avowed the Lord's uniqueness.

"When the chief priests therefore and officers saw him, they cried out, saying, Crucify, crucify" (19:6). Pilate's scheming failed here as completely as had his previous attempts to avoid condemning our Lord; nothing short of His death would satisfy the Jews. The pitiful sight of the bleeding Saviour softened them not a whit. Like beasts of prey that have tasted blood, they thirsted for more. The humiliating figure of their Messiah crowned with thorns by these heathen, instead of humbling, only infuriated them. They were "past feeling." Solemn it is to observe that the *chief priests* were to the fore in demanding His crucifixion—the "officers" were the personal followers and servants of the priests, and would naturally take up the cry of their masters; the word for "cried out" signifies a boisterous shout. It is a painful fact that all through this dispensation the most cruel, relentless, and blood-thirsty persecutors of God's saints have been the religious leaders—in a hundred different instances the "bishops" (?) and "cardinals" of Rome. Nor is it otherwise to-day. The form of persecution may have changed, yet is the opposition which comes from those who profess to be the servants of Christ the most relentless and cruel which God's children have to endure. It is to be noted that the cry was not "Crucify him," but "Crucify, crucify"—*refusing* Him the "*the* man" of Pilate! It was Israel, all through, who hounded Him to His death: how wondrous then that God shall yet have mercy upon them.

"Pilate saith unto them, Take ye him, and crucify: for I find no fault in him" (19:6). Pilate was disgusted at their lawless clamor, indignant at their challenging his decision, angry at their insistence. "Take *ye* him," if you want; "and crucify" if you dare. They had had the effrontery to appeal against the findings of *his* court, now he mocks them in regard to the impotency of their court, for according to their own admission, they were powerless (18:31). The Jews were insisting that Pilate should commit a judicial murder, now he challenges them to defy the Roman law. His "*For I* find no fault in him" was his challenge for them to continue opposing Caesar's authority.

"The Jews answered him, We have a law, and by our law he ought to die, because he made himself the Son of God" (19:7). Their words here show plainly that they discerned the satire in Pilate's offer: had he really given them permission to crucify Christ, they would have acted promptly. They knew that he had not spoken seriously; they felt his biting irony, and stung by his sarcasm they now attempted some defence of their outrageous conduct. "We *have* a law" they insisted, much as you scorn us for wanting to act lawlessly. *We* have a law as well as *you!* "By our law he ought to die, because he made himself the Son of God"—their reference was to Lev. 24:16. Instead of retreating before Pilate's outburst of indignation, they continued to press their demands upon him. We charge your prisoner with having broken our law, the punishment for which is death. Their aim was to make out Christ to be a dangerous impostor as well as a seditious person, opposed both to Jewish religion and Roman law. Pilate had challenged them; now they challenge him. You have dared us to defy the Roman law; we now dare you to refuse to maintain the Jewish law.

"We have a law, and by our law he ought to die, because he made himself the Son of God." It is indeed remarkable that as soon as Pilate said "Behold the *man,*" they proceeded to charge Him with "making himself the Son of *God*"! *Their* motive was an evil one, but how evident that a higher power was overruling!

Finding the charge of sedition had broken down, and that Pilate could not be induced to sentence Him to death on that score, they now accused Christ of blasphemy. But how their hypocrisy was manifested: they appealed to their own "law," yet had no respect for it, for *their* law called for *stoning* not crucifixion, as the penalty for blasphemy! A careful comparison of the Gospel records reveals the fact that the Jews preferred just seven indictments against Christ. First, they charged Him with threatening to destroy the temple (Matt. 26:61); second, with being a "malefactor" (John 18:30); third, with "perverting the nation" (Luke 23:2); fourth, with "forbidding to give tribute to Caesar" (Luke 23:2); fifth, with stirring up all the people (Luke 23:5); sixth, with being "a king" (Luke 23:2); seventh, with making Himself the Son of God (John 19:7). This sevenfold indictment witnessed to the *completeness* of their rejection of Him!

"When Pilate therefore heard that saying, he was the more afraid" (19:8). The meaning of this is evident, yet, strange to say, many of the commentators have missed it. Some have supposed that fear of the Jews is what is intended; others, that Pilate was fearful lest it should now prove impossible to save Christ; others, lest he should take a false step. But the "therefore" is sufficient to show the error of these views: it was the declaration that Christ "made himself the Son of God" which alarmed the Roman Governor. Moreover, the "he was *the more* afraid" shows it was not an emotion which he now felt for the first time. The *person* of the Lord Jesus was what occasioned his fear. We believe that from the beginning there was a conscious uneasiness in his soul, deepened by an *awe* which the bearing and words of Christ had inspired. He had seen many malefactors, some guilty, some innocent, but never one like this. His "Ecce Homo" (19:5) witnesses to his estimate of Christ. The warning which he had received from his wife must also have impressed him deeply; and now that he is reminded his Prisoner called Himself the Son of God, he was the more afraid.

"And went again into the judgment hall, and saith unto Jesus, Whence art thou? But Jesus gave him no answer" (19:9). This was the sixth question Pilate asked Christ, and it is deeply interesting to follow his changing moods as he put them. First, he had asked "Art thou the king of the Jews?" (18:33) – asked, most probably, in the spirit of sarcasm. Second, "Am I a Jew?" (18:35) – asked in the spirit of haughty contempt. Third, "What hast thou done?" (18:35) – a pompous display of his authority. Fourth, "Art thou a king then?" (18:37) – indicating his growing perplexity. Fifth, "What is truth?" (18:38) – asked out of contemptuous pity. Sixth, "Whence art thou?" In what spirit did he ask *this* question? Much turns upon the right answer, for otherwise we shall be at a loss to understand our Lord's refusal to reply.

"Whence art thou?" Not "Whom art thou?" nor, "Art thou the Son of God then?" but "*Whence* art thou?" Yet it is clear that Pilate was not asking about His human origin, for he had already sent Christ as a "Galilean" to Herod (Luke 23:6). Was it then simply a question of idle curiosity? No, the "more afraid" of the previous verse shows otherwise. Was it that Pilate was now deeply exercised and anxiously seeking for light? No, for his outburst of scornful pride in the verse that follows conflicts with such a view. What, then? First, we think that Pilate was genuinely puzzled and perplexed. A man altogether unique he clearly perceived Christ to be. But was He *more* than man? The deepening fear of his conscience made him uneasy. Suppose that after all, this One were from Heaven! That such a thought crossed his mind at this stage we fully believe, and this leads to the second motive which prompted his question: – Pilate hoped that *here* was a way out of his difficulty. If Christ were really from Heaven, then obviously he could not think of crucifying Him. He therefore has Christ led back again into the judgment hall, and says, Tell me privately your real origin and history so that I may know what line to take up with thine enemies. "We may well believe that Pilate caught at this secret hope that Jesus might tell him something about Himself which would enable him to make a firm stand and deliver Him from the Jews. In this hope, again, the Roman Governor was destined to be disappointed" (Bishop Ryle).

"But Jesus gave him no answer." Ominous "but"; perplexing silence. Hitherto He had replied to Pilate's questions; now He declined to speak. At first our Lord's silence surprises and puzzles us, but reflection shows that He could not have acted otherwise. First, the fact that in 19:11 we *do* find Christ speaking to Pilate, shows that His silence here in 19:9 was no arbitrary determination to say no more. "With *us,* when we would patiently suffer in silence, there may be some such arbitrary purpose of our own; or, to put a better construction upon it, *we cannot* actually speak and at the same time suffer in patience, for we have inwardly too much to do with our own spirits, in order to *maintain* our proper posture of mind. But Christ is in His profoundest humanity elevated above this human imperfection; in *His* lips (as we shall hear from the Cross) the Word of God is never bound" (Stier). Second, Christ's silence here makes evident the spirit in which Pilate had put his question: it was not the cry of an earnest soul, honestly seeking light, for our Lord never closed the door against any such! Third, Pilate was *not entitled* to a reply. He had acted in grossest injustice when he refused to release One whom he declared was innocent; he had despised God's warning through his wife; he had declined to wait for an answer to his "What is truth"; he had, against his own conscience, scourged the Saviour and suffered his soldiers to mock and maltreat Him. Why then should Christ reveal to *him* the mystery of His person!

"Pilate had forfeited his right to any further revelation about his Prisoner. He had been told plainly the nature of our Lord's kingdom, and the purpose of our Lord's coming into the world, and been obliged to confess publicly His innocence. And yet, with all this light and knowledge, he had treated our Lord with flagrant injustice, scourged Him, allowed Him to be treated with the vilest indignities by his soldiers, knowing in his own mind all the time that He was a guiltless person. He had, in short, sinned away his opportunities, forsaken his own mercies, and turned a deaf ear to the cries of his own conscience.

"'He gave him no answer.' Most men, like Pilate, have a day of grace, and an open door put before them. If they refuse to enter in, and choose their own sinful way, the door is often shut, and never opened again. There is such a thing as a 'day of visitation,' when Christ speaks to men. If they will not hear His voice, and open the door of their hearts, they are often let alone, given over to a reprobate mind, and left to reap the fruit of their own sins. It was so with Pharaoh, and Saul, and Ahab; and Pilate's case was like theirs. He had his opportunity, and did not choose to use it, but preferred to please the Jews at the expense of his conscience, and to do what he knew was wrong. We see the consequence—'Jesus gave him no answer'" (Bishop Ryle).

In addition to what has been pointed out above, may we not say, that as it had been Divinely appointed Christ *should* suffer for the sins of His people, He declined to say anything which was calculated to *hinder* it! True, Pilate was morally incapable of receiving the truth: to make him a definite answer would simply have been casting pearls before swine, and this the Saviour refused to do. Moreover, *had* He affirmed His Deity, it would have afforded Pilate the very handle he sought for releasing Him. Thus we may say with Bishop Ryle "Our Lord's silence was just and well merited, but it was also part of *God's counsels* about man's salvation." Finally, let *us* learn from Christ's example here that there is "a time to be silent," as well as "a time to speak" (Ecc. 3:7)!

"Then saith Pilate unto him, Speakest thou not unto me? knowest thou not that I have power to crucify thee, and have power to release thee?" (19:10). Here the haughty, fierce, and imperious spirit of the Roman was manifested; the authoritative I asserting itself. We doubt not that all the emphasis was thrown upon the personal pronouns—Thou mayest keep silence before the Jews, the soldiers and before Herod; but *me* also? What lack of respect is this! It was the proud authority of an official politician displaying itself. Knowest Thou not in whose presence Thou standest! You are no longer before Annas and Caiaphas—mere figure-heads. I am the Governor of Judea, the representative of Caesar Augustus. "Speakest thou not unto me?" It was his seventh and last question to our Lord, asked in the spirit of sarcasm and resentment combined. Accustomed to seeing prisoners cringing before him, willing to do anything to obtain his favor, he could not understand our Lord's silence. He was both perplexed and angered: his official pride was mortified.

"Knowest thou not that I have power to crucify thee, and have power to release thee!" How he condemned himself. How he revealed his true character. Here was one on the bench talking about his power to commit a judicial murder! Here was one who had, over and over again, affirmed the innocency of his Prisoner, now owning his power to release Him, and yet shortly after condemned Him to death. And this from a man holding high office, who belonged to the nation which prided itself in its impartial justice! Mark also his consummate folly. Here was a worm of the earth so puffed up with a sense of his own importance, so obsessed with the idea of his own absolute freewill that he has the effrontery to say that the Son of the Highest was entirely at *his* disposal! Mark too his utter inconsistency. He was boasting of his legal authority: but if the Lord were innocent he had *no* judicial power to "crucify" Him; if He were guilty, he had *no* judicial power to "release" Him! Out of his own mouth he stands condemned. Carefully analyzed his words can only mean—*I* am above the law: innocent or guilty, I can do with you as I please.

"This high-handed claim to absolute power is one which ungodly great men are fond of making. It is written of Nebuchadnezzar, 'Whom *he* would he slew; and whom *he* would he kept alive; and whom *he* would he set up; and whom *he* would he put down' (Dan. 5:19). Yet even when such men boast of power, they are often, like Pilate, mere slaves, and afraid of resisting popular opinion. Pilate talked of 'power to release,' but he knew in his own mind that he was afraid, and so unable to exercise it" (Bishop Ryle).

"Jesus answered, Thou couldest have no power at all against me, except it were given thee from above" (19:11). For His Father's honor and as a rebuke to Pilate, the Lord once more spake, giving His last official testimony before He was crucified. Blessed it is to mark carefully the words of grace and truth which now proceeded from His lips. How easy for Him to have given the lie to Pilate's boast by paralyzing the tongue which had just uttered such blasphemy! How easy for Him to have made a display of *His* power before this haughty heathen similar to what He had done in the Garden! But, instead, He returns a calm and measured answer, equally expressive of His glory, though in another way. A careful study of His words here will reveal both His voluntary lowliness and His Divine majesty —how wonderful that *both* should be combined in one brief sentence!

"Jesus answered, Thou couldest have no power at all against me except it were given thee from above." The Lord acknowledged that Pilate *did* have "power" but of quite a different kind, from quite a different source, and under different restrictions from what he supposed. Pilate had boasted of an arbitrary discretion, of a sovereign choice of his own, of a lawless right to do as he pleased. Christ referred him to a power which came from above, delegated to men, limited according to the pleasure of the One who bestowed it. Thus Christ, first, *denied* that Pilate had the "power" to do with Him as he pleased. Second, He maintained His Father's honor by insisting that He alone is absolute Sovereign. Even so temperate a writer as Bishop Ryle says on this verse: "Thou talkest of power: thou dost not know that both thou and the Jews are *only tools* in the hands of a higher Being: you are both, unconsciously, *mere instruments* in the hands of God"!

"Jesus answered, Thou couldest have no power at all against me, except it were given thee from above: therefore he that delivereth me unto thee hath the greater sin." Our Lord conceded that Pilate *did* have power: He acknowledged the authority of the human courts. To the very last Christ respected the law, nor did He dispute the power of the Romans over the Jews. But He insisted that Pilate's power came from above, for, "There is no power but of God: the powers that be are ordained of God" (Rom. 13:1) and *compare Prov.* 8:15, 16. Christ acknowledged that Pilate's power, extended over *Himself*—"no power against *me* except," etc.—so thoroughly had He made Himself of no reputation. But it was because Pilate's "power," both personal and official, *was* "from above," that the Saviour bowed to it. In His "he that delivered me unto thee hath the greater sin," the Lord, as in Luke 22:22, shows us that God's counsels do not abolish the *guilt* of the men who execute them. And mark here, for it is most striking, that the same One who meekly bows to

Pilate's (God-given) authority, manifests Himself as the *Judge* of men, apportioning the comparative guilt of Pilate and the Jews. Thus did He maintain His Divine dignity to the end. *This,* then, was our Lord's reply to Pilate's "Knowest thou not?" *I* know, first, that all the power you have is from above; second, *I* know the precise measure both of your guilt and of him who delivered Me to thee! This, we take it, is the force of the rather difficult "therefore." Mark how, out of respect for Pilate's official personage, the Lord did not actually say "he that delivered me unto thee hath greater sin *than thee*"!—though plainly that was implied. Here, as in Luke 12:47, 48 Christ teaches *degrees* of sin and guilt, and therefore degrees of future punishment. The "*he* who delivered me up" refers not to Judas (*his* was the "*greatest* sin") but Caiaphas, acting as the representative of the nation. Finally observe that the *last* word which Pilate heard from the lips of Christ was "*sin*"!—the next, in all probability, will be the sentence of his eternal doom.

Below are the questions for our next study:—

1. Why did the "chief priests" take the lead, v. 15?
2. Why was Christ "delivered to them," v. 16?
3. Why "in the Hebrew," v. 17?
4. Why were two others crucified with Him, v. 18?
5. Why the inscription, v. 19?
6. Why in three languages, v. 20?
7. What is the meaning of v. 23?

CHAPTER SIXTY-FIVE

Christ Condemned to Death

John 19:12-24

The following is an Analysis of the passage which is to be before us: –

1. Pilate's effort foiled, v. 12.
2. Pilate on the Bench, v. 12.
3. The Jews' rejection of their Messiah, v. 15.
4. Christ delivered to the Jews, v. 16.
5. Christ crucified, vv. 17-18.
6. The inscription of the Cross, vv. 19-22.
7. The soldiers and Christ's garments, vv. 23-24.

The death of Christ may be viewed from five main viewpoints. From the standpoint of *God* the Cross was a *propitiation* (Rom. 3:25-26), where full satisfaction was made to His holiness and justice. From the standpoint of *the Saviour,* it was a *sacrifice* (Eph. 5:2), an *offering* (Heb. 9:14), an act of *obedience* (Phil. 2:8). From the standpoint of *believers,* it was a *substitution,* the Just suffering for the unjust (I Peter 3:18). From the standpoint of *Satan* it was a *triumph* and a *defeat*: a triumph, in that he bruised the heel of the woman's Seed (Gen. 3:15); a defeat, in that through His death Christ destroyed him that had the power of death, that is, the Devil (Heb. 2:14). From the standpoint of *the world* it was a brutal *murder* (Acts 3:15). It is with this last-mentioned aspect of the death of Christ that our present passage principally treats.

The ones who (from the human side) took the *initiative* in the slaying of the Lamb of God, were the Jews; the one who was *judicially* responsible was Pilate. In the introduction to our last chapter we pointed out two things: first, that God had ordained Pilate *should* pass sentence upon His Son; second, that Pilate was, nevertheless, morally guilty in so doing. We shall not review the ground already covered, but would supplement our previous remarks by a few words upon Pilate's final actions.

From the very first move made by the Jews for Pilate to sentence their Messiah, it is evident that he had no relish for the part which they wished and urged him to play; and the more he saw of Christ for himself, the more his reluctance increased. This is apparent from his restless journeying back and forth from the judgment-hall; evidenced by his repeated protestations of Christ's innocence; evidenced by the compromises he offered them; evidenced by the appeals he made to them. If, then, he was *un*willing to pass the death-sentence, how comes it that he, the Roman governor, was finally prevailed upon to do so? In seeking to answer this question we shall now confine ourselves to the *human* side of things.

In the first place, the Jews had charged Christ with perverting the nation, stirring up the people, teaching them to refuse to pay tribute, and claiming Himself to be the king of the Jews (Luke 23:2-5). These were charges which Pilate could not afford to ignore. It is true the preferring of such charges was one thing, and the proving of them quite another; but the Governor was too much of a politician not to know how easy it was to manufacture evidence and to hire false witnesses. In the second place, Pilate had himself incurred the hatred of the Jews by mingling the blood of certain Galileans with their sacrifices (Luke 13:1)—a thing not only morally wrong, but legally reprehensible. In the third place, when Pilate showed signs of weakening, the Jews told him that if he *did* let Jesus go, *he* was no friend of Caesar (John 19:12). Pilate was quick to perceive that if he released his Prisoner, complaint would at once be made to the Emperor, and under a charge of conspiracy and treason, he was likely not only to lose the governorship, but his head as well.

Here, then, was the issue which Pilate had to pass on: on the one hand he knew that Christ was innocent, that He was a unique Man, possibly more than man; on the other hand, he was threatened by the Sanhedrin with exposure before Caesar. In its final analysis, Pilate had to choose between *Christ and the world.* When the issue was clearly defined, he did not hesitate; he decided to please the people and win their applause, rather than intensify their already fierce hatred against him and condemn him to Caesar. "Here is the anticipative result of Pilate's vacillation. When a man begins to temporize with his conscience, to trifle with sin—be it the love of applause, the fear of man, or whatsoever thing is contrary to sound doctrine and plain morality—it is easy to predict what is sure to follow. Sin is at the first like a tiny spark. Tread it out at once—that is your duty. But indulge, foster, toy with it, and it will kindle and spread, and lay waste in a fearful conflagration the very temple of the soul. So here with this unhappy Pilate, trying to join together what God hath forever put asunder—his carnal inclination and his duty; hoping all in vain to harmonize equity and injustice; to comply with the voice of wicked men without, and yet not offend the voice of God within him; thinking to serve two masters—God and mammon. Miserable, impossible compromise" (Mr. Geo. Brown).

"And from thenceforth Pilate sought to release him" (19:12). The time-mark here is significant. Following the Jews' accusation that Christ had "made himself the Son of God" (19:7), Pilate, thoroughly uneasy, had retired within the judgment-hall, and asked the Saviour, "Whence art thou?" (19:9). But the Lord returned him no answer. Thereupon Pilate said, "Speakest thou not unto me? knowest thou not that I have power to crucify thee, and have power to release thee?" To this Christ made reply, "Thou couldest have no power against me, except it were given thee from above: therefore he that delivered me unto thee hath the greater sin." That Pilate was deeply impressed, both by his Prisoner's demeanor and words, we cannot doubt. Previously unwilling to condemn an innocent Man, he now resolves to make a real effort to save Him. Leaving Christ behind in the judgment-hall, Pilate returned once more to the Jews. What he now said to them John has not told us: all we know is that he must have made an earnest appeal to the Saviour's enemies, which they as decisively rejected.

"But the Jews cried out, saying, If thou let this man go, thou art not Caesar's friend: whosoever maketh himself a king speaketh against Caesar" (19:12). The Jews knew their man, for hypocrites are usually the quickest to detect hypocrisy in others. They had reserved their strongest card for the last: with diabolic cunning they insinuated that no matter what the Governor's personal feelings might be, no matter how unwilling he was to please them, he could not afford to displease the Emperor. For him this was a clinching argument. From this moment his hopes of escaping from his unhappy situation were dashed to the ground. It is hard to decide which was the more despicable: the duplicity of the Jews in feigning to care for Caesar's interests, or the cowardice and wickedness of Pilate in conniving at a foul murder. On the one hand we see the descendents of Abraham, the most favoured of all people, professing to be eagerly awaiting the appearing of the promised Messiah, now clamouring for His crucifixion. On the other hand, we behold a judge of one of the high courts of Rome, defying conscience and trampling upon justice. Never did human nature make such a contemptible exhibition. Never was sin more heinously displayed.

"When Pilate, therefore, heard that saying, he brought Jesus forth, and sat down in the judgment seat in a place that is called the Pavement, but in the Hebrew, Gabbatha" (19:13). "'Pilate's playing with the situation,' observes Lange, 'is now passed; now the situation plays with him!' First he said, not *asked,* What is *truth!* Now his frightened heart, to which the Emperor's favor is the supreme law of life, says, What is *justice!* He takes his place on the judgment-seat, therefore, and with what seems something between a taunt and a faint, final plea, says to the Jews, 'Behold your King!'" (Numerical Bible.) Pilate dared no longer oppose the bloody demands of the Jews. There remained nothing now but for him to take his seat publicly on the bench and pronounce sentence. It is striking to note that the trial of Christ before Pilate was in *seven* stages. This is seen by noting carefully the following scriptures, which speak of the Governor passing in and out of the judgment-hall. The first stage was on the outside: 18:28-32. The second on the inside: 18:33-37. Third, on the outside: 18:38-40. Fourth, inside: 19:1-3. Fifth, outside: 19:4-7. Sixth, inside: 19:8-11. Seventh, outside: 19:12-16.

"When Pilate, therefore, heard that saying, he brought Jesus forth, and sat down in the judgment seat in a place that is called the Pavement, but in the Hebrew, Gabbatha." Here, as everywhere in Scripture, if only we have eyes to see, there is a deep significance to the proper noun. The word for "Pavement" is found nowhere else in the New Testament, but its Hebrew equivalent occurs just once in the Old Testament, and it is evident that the Holy Spirit would have us link the two passages together. In II Kings 16:17 we read, "King Ahaz cut off the borders of the bases, and removed the laver from off them; and took down the sea from off the brazen oxen that were under it, and put it upon a *pavement* of stones." In Ahaz's case, his act was the conclusive token of his surrender to abject apostasy. So here of Pilate coming down to the level of the apostate Jews. In the former case it was a Jewish ruler dominated by a Gentile idolator; in the latter, a Gentile idolator dominated by Jews who had rejected their Messiah!

"And it was the preparation of the passover" (19:14). There has been an almost endless controversy concerning this. The Lord and His disciples had eaten the passover together on the previous night (Luke 22:15), and yet we read here of the "*preparation of the passover.*" Sir R. Anderson wrote much that was illuminating on the point. We can only give a brief selection: "These writers one and all confound the Passover-supper with the feast which followed it, and to which it lent its name. The supper was a memorial of the redemption of the firstborn of Israel on the night *before* the Exodus; the feast was the anniversary of their actual deliverance from the house of bondage. The supper was not a part of the feast; it was morally the basis on which the feast was founded, just as the Feast of Tabernacles was based on the great sin-offering of the Day of Expiation which preceded it. But in the same way that the Feast of Weeks can now be commonly designated Pentecost, so the Feast of Unleavened Bread was popularly called the Passover (Luke 22:1). *That* title was common to the supper *and* the feast, including both; but the intelligent Jew never confounded the two. No words can possibly express more clearly this distinction than those afforded by the Pentateuch in the final promulgation of the Law: 'In the fourteenth day of the first month is the passover of the Lord, and in the fifteenth day of this same month is the Feast' (Num. 28:16-17)."

But to what does "the *preparation* of the passover" refer? "Among the Jews 'the preparation' was the common name for the day before *the sabbath,* and it is so used by all the Evangelists. Bearing this in mind, let the reader compare with John 19:14, vv. 31-42, and he will have no difficulty in rendering the words in question, 'it was *Passover Friday.*'" (Sir Robert Anderson.) Let the reader also compare Mark 15:42, which is even more conclusive.

"And about the sixth hour" (19:14). This expression has also occasioned much difficulty to many. It is supposed to conflict with Mark 15:25. "and it was the *third* hour, and they crucified Him." But there is no discrepancy here whatsoever. Mark gives the hour when our Lord was crucified; John is speaking of the Passover Friday, i.e., the day when preparations were made for the sabbath (which began at Friday sunset) preparing food, etc., so that none would have to be cooked on the sabbath. It was about the sixth hour after *this* "preparation" had commenced. This is the view which was taken by Augustine and Dr. Lightfoot. We believe the Holy Spirit has recorded this detail for the purpose of pointing a comparison and a contrast. For six hours the Jews had been working in preparation for the approaching sabbath; during the *next* "six hours" (compare Mark 15:25, 33-37), Christ finished His great work, which brings His people into that eternal rest of which the sabbath was the emblem! "And he said unto the Jews, Behold your king!" (19:14). This was evidently spoken in irony and contempt.

"But they cried out, Away with him, away with him, crucify him" (19:15). As on the previous occasions of Pilate's private appeals, so now this final and public appeal of his had no effect upon the Jews. Once more they raised their fierce, relentless cry, demanding the Prisoner's death by crucifixion. Nothing but His blood would satisfy them. He *must* die: so had God decreed; so they demanded. The decree of the One was from love; the insistence of the other, was from hatred. The design of the One, was mercy unto poor sinners; the aim of the others, barbarous cruelty to Him who was sinless. This rejection of their Messiah by Israel fulfilled two prophecies: "We *hid* as it were our faces *from* him; he was despised, and we esteemed him not" (Isa. 53:3); "Thus saith the Lord, the Redeemer of Israel, and his Holy One, to him whom man despiseth, to him whom *the nation* abhorreth" (Isa. 49:7).

"Pilate saith unto them, Shall I crucify your king?" (19:15). As one has said, "Pilate speaks here with a mixture of compassionate feeling and mockery." For the last time the Roman governor put the decisive question to the Jews, giving them a final chance to relent, throwing the emphasis, we believe, on the word 'crucify.' It was a frightful mode of execution, reserved for slaves and the most abandoned criminals.

"The chief priests answered, We have no king but Caesar" (19:15). "They are entirely infidel, throwing off all allegiance to any but Caesar, and cry that they had no other king. It is purely of the Jews, the whole transaction, for *they* consign to the most cruel death Him whom the Roman governor would have let go. This is *man's religion,* and it will, in the end, enthrone 'the Wilful One' and bow to his image" (Rev. 13). (Mr. M. Taylor).

"The chief priests answered, We have no king but Caesar." God took them at their word: they have been under their own verdict ever since. History repeated itself, though with a tragic addition. In the days of Samuel, Israel said, "Make us a king to judge us like all nations" (I Sam. 8:5), and Jehovah's response was, "Hearken unto the voice of the people in all that they say unto thee: for they have not rejected thee, but they have *rejected me,* that *I* should not *reign* over them." So it was here with their rebellious descendants, when they rejected Christ the king. In consequence of their fatal decision, Israel has abode "many days *without a king,* and without a prince, and without a sacrifice" (Hosea 3:4). Bitter indeed have been the consequences. Jotham's parable has received its tragic fulfilment: "And the bramble said unto the trees, If in truth ye anoint me king over you, then come put your trust in my shadow; and if not, let fire come out of the bramble and *devour the cedars of Lebanon*" (Judges 9:15, and *see* vv. 7-16).

"The chief priests answered, We have no king but Caesar." "It was not the verdict of the Jews alone, and they have not suffered alone. The whole world has been lying under the yoke which they have preferred to the easy yoke of Christ. They have got very tired of Caesar—true; and, as we see by their fitful movements every now and then, would feign be rid of him. They are always crying, 'Give us better government'; but all they can do is, with doubtful betterment, to divide him up into many little Caesars; better as they think, because weaker, and with divided interests, so that the balance of power may secure the even weights of justice. That is still an experiment some think; but this chronic war is never peace, nor can be; and the reason is, men have refused the Prince of Peace. Modify it, rename it, disguise it as you please, the reign of Caesar is the only alternative" (Numerical Bible).

"Then delivered he him therefore unto them to be crucified" (19:16). Between 19:15 and 16 comes in what is recorded in Matthew 27:24-25. Seeing that the Jews would not be turned from their purpose, and afraid to defy them, he took water and washed his hands before them (cf. Deut. 21:1-6; Psa. 26:6), saying, "I am innocent of the blood of this just person: see ye to it." Thus did this cowardly, world-loving Roman betray his trust. Never was a name more justly handed down to the world's scorn than Pilate's. By his act he sought to cast the entire onus upon the Jews. Their terrible response was, "His blood be on us, and on our children." Then, we are told, "Pilate gave sentence that it should be as *they* required . . . He delivered Jesus to *their* will" (Luke 23:24-25). Thus the Lord's execution was now in Jewish hands (Acts 2:23), the centurion and his quaternion of soldiers merely carrying out the decision of the chief priests.

"Then *delivered* he him therefore unto them to be crucified." Our Lord's own estimate of Pilate's act is recorded by the Spirit of prophecy through the Psalmist: "Shall the *throne of iniquity* have fellowship with that which frameth mischief by a law? They gather themselves together against the soul of the righteous, and condemn the innocent blood" (Psa. 94:20, 21)! Let us not forget, however, that behind the governor of Judea, who *delivered* the Lord Jesus unto the Jews, was the Governor of the Universe, who "spared not his own Son, but *delivered him up* for us all" (Rom. 8:32). And why? Because He was "*delivered* for our offences" (Rom. 4:25). Christ was delivered to death, that we might be delivered from death.

"And they took Jesus and led him away" (19:16). Observe the word "led" again. How often has the Holy Spirit repeated it! Christ was neither driven nor dragged, for He made no resistance. As prophecy had foretold long before, "He was *led* as a lamb to the slaughter" (Isa. 53:7).

"And he, bearing his cross, went forth unto a place called the place of a skull, which is called in the Hebrew, Golgotha" (19:17). The Jews lost no time: Christ was taken straight from Gabbatha to Golgotha; from judgment to execution. The Saviour "bearing his cross," had been marvelously foreshadowed of old when "Abraham took the *wood* of the burnt offering, and *laid it upon* Isaac his son" (Gen. 22:6). "He, bearing his cross, *went forth.*" That is, *out of Jerusalem,* or as Heb. 13:12 puts it, "Jesus also, that he might sanctify the people with his own blood, suffered *without* [outside] the gate." This, too, fulfilled an Old Testament type—every detail of thc Passion fulfilled some prophecy or type. In Lev. 16:27 we read, "And the bullock for the sin-offering, and the goat for the sin-offering; whose blood was brought in to make atonement in the holy place shall one carry forth *without the camp.*" "Little did the blinded Jews imagine that when they madly hounded on the Romans to crucify Jesus *outside* the gates, that they were unconsciously perfecting the mightiest sin-offering of all!" (Bishop Ryle).

At this point the other Gospels supply a detail which John, for some reason, was guided to omit. In Matt. 27:32 we are told. "As they came out, they found a man of Cyrene, Simon by name; him they compelled to bear his cross." Almost all of the commentators, both ancient and modern, draw the conclusion that Simon was compelled to bear the Saviour's cross *because* He was staggering and sinking beneath its weight. But there is not a word in the New Testament to support such a conjecture, and everything recorded about Christ after He was nailed to the tree decidedly conflicts with it. That Simon was "*compelled*" to bear His cross, shows there was not one in all that crowd with sufficient compassion and courage to volunteer to carry it for Him!

"Went forth into a place called the place of a skull, which is called in the Hebrew, Golgotha." "The place of a skull—the place of the kingdom of *death*. This is plainly what *the world is*, because of sin—death being the stamp of the government of God upon it. For this the Lord sought it; here His love to men brought Him; only He could lift this burden from them, and for this He must come under it" (Numerical Bible).

"Which is called *in the Hebrew*, Golgotha." This expression—used twice in connection with the Saviour's crucifixion (19:13, 17)—is found elsewhere only in John 5:2: "Now there is at Jerusalem by the sheep-gate a pool, which is called *in the Hebrew tongue* Bethesda." What a contrast; there at Bethesda, we see *His* mercy; here at Golgotha, *their brutality!* Luke gives us the Gentile name, "Calvary" (23:33); John the Hebrew, "Golgotha," of the place where our Saviour was crucified. Compare the same *double* name of the place of Pilate's judgment-seat (19:13). "May it be that in these instances of double meaning that *God* is giving His in the words which He used with His people, and man is giving his in the language of the world? Moreover, this Death was for both Jews and Gentiles! There is a reason for every word which the Holy Spirit records" (Mr. M. Taylor).

"Where they crucified him, and two others with him, on either side one, and Jesus in the midst" (19:18). This one verse records the fulfilment of at least three Old Testament prophecies. First, the *manner* in which the Saviour was to die had been clearly foretold. A thousand years before this He had cried, by the Spirit of prophecy, "they *pierced* my hands and my feet" (Psa. 22:16); this is indeed most striking. The Jewish form of capital punishment was *stoning*. But no word of God can fall to the ground, therefore did Pilate give orders that Christ should be *crucified*, which was the Roman form of execution, reserved only for the vilest criminals. Second, Isaiah had declared, "He was *numbered with* the transgressors" (53:12). The Jews' object was to add a final indignity and insult to the Lord; it was a public declaration that He was counted no better than the scum of the earth. Little did they realize that this expression of their malice was but a means for the carrying out of Messianic prediction! Third, it had been written that He should be "*with the wicked* at his death" (Isa. 53:9 – literal translation). But why did God permit His Beloved to be so outrageously treated? To *show us* the place which His Son had taken. It was the place which was *due us* because of our sins – the place of shame, condemnation, punishment. Moreover, the Lord crucified between the two malefactors, gave Him the opportunity to work one more miracle ere He laid down His life – a miracle of sovereign grace. Let the reader at this point carefully ponder Luke 23:39-43, and there he will find that the One on the central cross clearly demonstrated that He *was* the Redeemer by snatching a brand from the burning, and translating from the brink of the Pit into Paradise, one of these very thieves as the first trophy of His all-sufficient sacrifice.

"And Pilate wrote a title, and put it on the cross. And the writing was, *Jesus of Nazareth, the king of the Jews*" (19:19). "He comes thus into death as King – 'King of the Jews,' indeed, but which in its full rendering implies so much. It faces the Jew, the Greek, the Roman, affirming to each in his own language, with a positiveness which His enemies vainly strive to set aside, a meaning for each one. Here is indeed God's King – King in death as in life – here in a peculiar way affirmed; His Cross henceforth to be the very sign of His power, the scepter under which they bow, in adoring homage" (Numerical Bible). Pilate's reason for placing such a description of our Lord over His cross is not easy to determine; probably it was so worded in anger, and with the aim of annoying and insulting the Jews. Whatever his motive, it was clearly overruled by God. It is well known that the words of the four Evangelists vary in their several descriptions of this title. Enemies of the truth have pointed to this as a "contradiction." But all difficulty is removed if we bear in mind that we are told Pilate wrote the inscription in three different languages – most probably not wording them alike. The Holy Spirit moved Matthew to translate one (most likely the Hebrew) and Luke another (most likely the Greek); Mark only quoting a part of what John had given us—most likely from the Latin. There is, therefore, no discrepancy at all, and nothing for an impartial reader to stumble over.

"This title then read many of the Jews; for the place where Jesus was crucified was nigh to the city" (v. 20). No one could fail to see *who* it was that hung upon the central Cross. Even in death God saw to the guarding of His Son's glory. Before He was born, the angel announced to Mary His "kingdom" (Luke 1:32, 33). In His infancy, wise men from the east heralded Him as "king" (Matt. 2:2). At the beginning of the Passion week, the multitudes had cried, "Blessed is the king of Israel" (John 12:13). Before Pilate, He Himself bore witness to His "kingdom" (18:36-37). And now His royal title was affixed to His very gibbet.

"And it was written in Hebrew, and Greek, and Latin" (19:20). Note that the Holy Spirit has placed "Hebrew" first! Hebrew was the language of the Jews; Greek of the educated world; Latin of the Romans; hence all who were gathered around the cross could read the title in his own language. Remember that the *confusion of tongues* was the sign of Babel's curse (Gen. 11). Significantly are we reminded of this here, when Christ was being made a curse for us! Hebrew was the language of *religion;* Greek of *science, culture* and *philosophy;* Latin of *law.* In each of these realms Christ is "king." In the religious, He is the final revelation of the true God (Heb. 1:2; John 14:9). In science, He is the Force behind all things. "By him all things consist" (Col. 1:17). "Upholding all things by the word of his power" (Heb. 1:3); so, too, in Him are hid "all the treasures of wisdom and knowledge" (Col. 2:3). In jurisprudence, He is supreme; the Law-giver and Law-administrator (I Cor. 9:21).

"Then said the chief priests of the Jews to Pilate, Write not, The king of the Jews; but that He said, I am king of the Jews" (19:21). It is noteworthy that this is the first and only time that they are termed "the chief priests *of the Jews,*" the Holy Spirit thereby intimating that *God* no longer owned them as *His* priests; having rejected their Messiah, Judaism was set aside, and therefore its official leaders are regarded as serving the Jews, but not Jehovah. The words of the priests here show that they resented Pilate's insult. It was most humbling to their pride that this crucified criminal should be publicly designated *their* "king." They desired the Governor to alter the wording of the inscription so that it might appear Christ was nothing more than an empty-boasting imposter.

"Pilate answered, What I have written, I have written" (19:22). Pilate could be firm when it suited him. The haughty, imperious character of the Roman comes out plainly here. His decisive reply evidences his contempt for the Jews: Trouble me no further; what *I* have written must stand; I shall not alter it to please you. "It, therefore, stands written forever. Caiaphas, as representative of the Jews proclaimed the Lord as Saviour of the world; Pilate fastens upon the Jews the hated name of the Nazarene as their King" (Companion Bible). The truth is that God would not allow Pilate to change what he had written. Unknown to himself he was the amanuensis of Heaven. This was part of the Word of God—the Scriptures, the Writings, and not a jot of it shall ever pass away. And wondrously was it manifested that very day that what Pilate had written *was* the Word of God. This was the text used by the Spirit of Truth to bring about the regeneration and conversion of the repentant thief. His "Lord remember me when thou comest into thy *kingdom*," shows that his faith rested on that which the Roman governor had written and placed on the cross, and which his Spirit-opened eyes read and believed!

"Then the soldiers, when they had crucified Jesus, took his garments and made four parts, to every soldier a part" (19:23). "The soldiers having now finished their bloody work, having nailed our Lord to the cross, put the title over His head, and reared the cross on end, proceeded to do what they probably always did—to divide the clothes of the criminal among themselves. In most countries the clothes of a person put to death by the law are the perquisite of the executioner. So it was with our Lord's clothes. They had most likely stripped our Lord naked before nailing His hands and feet to the cross, and had laid His clothes on one side till after they had finished their work. They now turned to the clothes, and, as they had done many a time on such occasions, proceeded to divide them" (Bishop Ryle). There were four soldiers; some think this emblemizes the four quarters of the Gentiles' world. It seems clear that they ripped His several garments to pieces, so as to divide them in equal parts. How this, once more, makes manifest the depths of humiliation into which the Son of God descended!

"And also his coat; now the coat was without seam, woven from the top throughout. They said therefore among themselves, Let us not rend it, but cast lots for it, whose it shall be" (19:23, 24). The deeper significance of this is not difficult to perceive. Garments in Scripture, speak of *conduct,* as a display of *character*—cf. Psa. 109:18; I Peter 5:5, etc. Now, the Saviour's "coat," His outer garment, was of one piece—intimating the unity, the unbroken perfection of His ways. Unlike *our* "garments," which are, at best, so much patchwork, *His* robe was "*without* seam." Moreover, it was "*woven from the top* throughout"—the mind of Him above controlled His *every* action! This "coat" or "robe" was a *costly* one, so owned even by the soldiers, for they declined to tear *it* to pieces. It spoke of the righteousness of Christ, the "*robe of righteousness*" (Isa. 61:10), the "best robe" (Luke 15) with which the Father clothes each prodigal son. For this "robe" the soldiers *cast lots,* and we are told in Prov. 16:33 that "The lot is cast into the lap, but the whole *disposing* thereof *is of the Lord.*" Thus the action of these soldiers declares that the "best robe" is *not* left to the caprice of man's will, but the Lord Himself has determined *whose* it shall be! Note another contrast; the sinful first Adam was clothed by God; the sinless last Adam was unclothed by wicked men.

"That the scripture might be fulfilled, which saith, They parted my raiment among them, and for my vesture they did cast lots. These things *therefore* the soldiers did" (19:24). Three things come out plainly: First, that God Himself was master of this whole situation, directing every detail of it to the outworking of His eternal counsels. Second, that no word of God's can fail. A thousand years before hand it had been predicted that these soldiers *should* both divide the Saviour's raiment among them, and also cast lots for His vesture or coat. Literally was this fulfilled to the very letter. Third, that the One who hung there on the Tree was, beyond a shadow of doubt, the *Messiah of Israel,* the One of whom all the prophets had written.

Below are the questions on the closing section of John 19:—

1. Why "woman," v. 26?
2. What perfections of Christ are seen in v. 28?
3. What was "fiinished," v. 30?
4. Why "bowed His head," v. 30?
5. What is the spiritual meaning of "blood and water," v. 34?
6. What prophecy was accomplished in v. 38?
7. What type was fulfilled in vv. 41, 42?

CHAPTER SIXTY-SIX

Christ Laying Down His Life

John 19:25-42

Below is an Analysis of John 19:25-42:

1. The mother of Jesus and the beloved disciple, vv. 25-27.
2. The Saviour's thirst, vv. 28, 29.
3. The Saviour's victorious death, v. 30.
4. God guarding the Saviour's body, vv. 31-33.
5. The piercing of the Saviour's side, vv. 34-37.
6. The boldness of Joseph and Nicodemus, vv. 38, 39.
7. The Saviour's burial, vv. 40-42.

Each of the Evangelists treats of our Lord's death with more or less fulness of detail. The birth, the baptism, and the temptation of Christ are described in only two of the Gospels; several of His miracles and discourses are found only in one; but the Saviour's Passion is recorded in all four, which at once denotes its supreme importance. But though each Evangelist devotes not a little space to the events of the last hours of Christ, there is a striking variation about their several narratives. Nowhere is the hand of the Spirit more evident than in what He guided each Gospel writer to insert and omit. Each of them was manifestly moved by Him to bring in only that which was strictly pertinent to the distinctive design before him.

The four Gospels are *not* four biographies of Christ, nor do the four together supply one. A harmony of the four Gospels reveals great blanks, altogether incompatible with the theory that they supply us with a "life of Christ." Only the briefest mention is made of His birth and infancy, and then *nothing* more is told us about Him till He had reached the age of twelve. After the few words relating to His boyhood, we see Christ no more till He was about thirty. Even His public ministry is not given us with anything approaching completeness: a journey, a miracle, a discourse, here and there, and that is about all. What, then, *are* the four Gospels, and what was the *principle of selection* which determined what *should* have a place in each of them?

The four Gospels give us delineations of the Lord Jesus in four distinct characters: the principle of selection is, that only that which serves to illustrate and exemplify each of these characters was included. Matthew presents Christ as the Son of David, the king of Israel, and everything in his Gospel contributes to this theme. Mark portrays Him as God's Workman, and everything in his Gospel bears directly upon the Servant and His service. Luke depicts Him as the Son of man, hence it is His human perfections, sympathies, and relations which he dwells upon. John reveals Him as the Son of God incarnate, the Word become flesh, tabernacling among men; hence it is His *Divine* glories, the dignity and majesty of His person, which are most prominent here. Strikingly is this evidenced in what he has related and what he has omitted concerning the Redeemer's sufferings.

John says nothing about the Saviour's agony in Gethsemane, but he and he only does mention the falling backward to the ground of those who came to arrest Him. John omits all details of what took place when our Lord appeared before Caiaphas, but he describes the trial before Annas. The fourth Gospel, and it alone, records our Lord's words to Pilate about His kingdom (18:36), of His coming into this world to bear witness unto the truth (18:37), of his having no power to crucify Him except what God gave (19:11). John alone makes mention of His seamless robe (19:23), His legs not being broken (19:33), and the blood and water which came from His pierced side. John omits altogether the awful cry, "Why hast thou forsaken me?" and in its place gives His triumphant "It is finished." John says nothing of His being numbered with the transgressors, but does tell us of Him being with the rich in His death. John alone mentions the costly spices which Nicodemus brought for the anointing of the Saviour's dead body. Clearer proofs of the *verbal* inspiration of the Scriptures we could not ask for.

Seven times the Saviour *spoke* while He was upon the cross, thus exhibiting His *perfections* as the *Word*, in death, as in life. The first, the word of *forgiveness*, for His enemies (Luke 23:34). The second, the word of *salvation*, to the dying thief (Luke 23:42, 43). The third, the word of *affection*, to and for His mother (John 19:25, 26). The fourth, the word of *anguish*, to God (Matt. 27:46). The fifth, the word of *suffering*, to the spectators (John 19:28). The sixth, the word of *victory*, to His people (John 19:30). The seventh, the word of *contentment*, to the Father (Luke 23:46). The third, fifth and sixth of these cross-utterances are recorded by John, and will come before us in our present study.

"Now there stood by the cross of Jesus his mother, and his mother's sister, Mary the wife of Cleophas, and Mary Magdalene" (19:25). The Jews were present at the crucifixion to satisfy their fiendish craving for His death; the Roman soldiers were there from duty; but here is a group noticed by the Spirit who had been drawn there by affectionate devotion for the central Sufferer. They were not looking on from a distance, nor mingling with the morbid crowds in attendance. They stood "by the cross." A pitiably small company, five in all; yet a deeply significant number, for five is the number of *grace*, and in contrast from the crowds which evidenced man's depravity and enmity, these were the trophies of Divine favour. This little company comprised four women and one man. The first was Mary, the Saviour's mother, who now realized the full force of that prophetic word spoken by the aged Simeon more than thirty years before: "Yet, a sword shall pierce through thine own soul also" (Luke 2:35). The second was Mary the wife of Cleophas, of whom we read but little, yet in that little what a wealth of love! — here at the cross, in Matt. 28:1 at the sepulchre; called here "his mother's sister" — evidently her sister-in-law, sister of Joseph, for it is most unlikely that she was a full-blood sister with the *same* name as herself. The third was Mary of Magdala, out of whom Christ had cast seven demons, and to whom He appeared first when He was risen from the dead. How significant that each of them was named "Mary," which means *bitterness!* What anguish of spirit was theirs as they beheld the dying Lamb! Equally significant is the *absence* of another Mary—the sister of Lazarus! A fourth woman was there—Matt. 27:56—the mother of John, though she is not mentioned here. The fifth one was "the disciple whom Jesus loved"—so far as we know, the only one of the eleven apostles who was present.

"Now there stood by the cross of Jesus his mother." "Neither her own danger, nor the sadness of the spectacle, nor the insults of the crowd, could restrain her from performing the last office of duty and tenderness to her Divine Son on the Cross" (Mr. Doddridge). After the days of His infancy and childhood, we see and hear little of Mary. During His public ministry her life was lived in the background. But now, when strikes the supreme hour of her Son's agony, when the world has cast out the Child of her womb, she stands there by the cross! Baffled, perhaps, at the unprecedented scene, paralyzed at His sufferings, yet bound by the golden chain of love to the dying One, there she stands. His disciples may desert Him, His friends may forsake Him, His nation may despise Him; but His mother is there, where all might see her—near Him in death as in birth. Who can fully appreciate the *mother*-heart!

Marvelous fortitude was Mary's. Hers was no hysterical or demonstrative sorrow. There was no show of feminine weakness; no wild outcry of uncontrollable anguish; no falling to the ground in a swoon. Not a word that fell from her lips on this occasion has been recorded by any of the four Evangelists: apparently she suffered in unbroken silence. The crowds were mocking, the thieves taunting, the soldiers callously occupied with His garments, the Saviour was bleeding—and there was His mother beholding it all! What wonder if she had turned away from such a spectacle! What wonder if she had fled from such a scene! But no! She did not crouch away nor fall in a faint. She *stood* by the cross. What tremendous courage! What love! What reverence for the Saviour!

"When Jesus therefore saw his mother, and the disciple standing by, whom he loved, he saith unto his mother, Woman, behold thy son!" (19:26). Occupied with the most stupendous work ever done, not only on earth but in the entire universe; under a burden which no mere creature could possibly have sustained; the Object of Satan's fiercest malignity! about to drain the awful cup which meant separation from God Himself for three hours; nevertheless, even at such a time, the Lord Jesus did not deem natural ties as unworthy of recognition. To the very end He showed Himself both perfect Son of God and perfect Son of man. In boyhood He had "honored" His parents (Luke 2:52), so does He now on the cross. About to leave this world, He first provides a home for His widowed mother. First He had prayed for His enemies; then He had spoken the words of salvation and assurance to the repentant thief; now He addresses His mother.

"He saith unto his mother, Woman, behold thy son!" Twice do we find our Lord addressing Mary as "Woman": at the Cana marriage-feast (2:4), and here. It is noteworthy that both of these references are found in *John's* Gospel, the Gospel which treats specifically of His *Deity*. The Synoptics present Him in *human* relationships, but John portrays Him as the Son of God—*above* all; hence the perfect propriety of Christ here addressing His mother as "Woman." That this term is neither harsh nor discourteous is clear from a comparison with 20:13. But there was another reason why He would no longer call her "mother"—as, doubtless, He *had* addressed her many a time. The death on the cross made an end of all His *natural* ties: "Henceforth know we no man after the flesh: yet, though we have known Christ after the flesh, yet *now* henceforth know we no more" (II Cor. 5:16)! From now on, believers would be linked to Christ by a closer bond, by a *spiritual* relationship, and *this* is what the Saviour would now teach both His mother and His beloved apostle. "Behold thy *son!*" *I* am *thy* "Son" no longer. It is a striking confirmation of this that Mary is not mentioned at all in connection with Christ's resurrection: the only other time she is referred to in the New Testament is in Acts 1:14, where we see her taking her place among (not *over*) believers at a prayer-meeting.

"Here it is that our Lord lays aside His human affections. He sees His mother and His beloved disciple near the Cross, but it is only to commend them the one to the other, and thus to *separate Himself* from the place which He had once filled among them. Sweet, indeed, it is, to see how faithfully He owned the affection up to the last moment that He could listen to it; no sorrow of His own could make Him forget it! But He was not always to know it. The 'children of the resurrection' neither marry, nor are given in marriage. He must now form their knowledge of Him by other thoughts, for they are henceforth to be joined to Him as 'one spirit'; for such are His blessed ways. If He takes His distance from us, as not knowing us in 'the flesh,' it is only that we may be united to Him in nearer affections and closer interests" (Mr. J. G. Bellett).

"Then saith he to the disciple" (19:27) – the one standing by "whom he loved." In Matt. 26:56 we read concerning the Eleven, "They *all* forsook Him and fled." This was the accomplishment of His own sad prediction, "all ye shall be *offended* because of me this night" (Matt. 26:31) – the Greek signifying "scandalized." They were ashamed to be found in His company. But it is blessed to know that one returned to His side ere He died. And which one was it? *Who* of the little band shall manifest the superiority of *his* love? Even though the Sacred Narrative had concealed his identity, it would not have been difficult for us to name him. But the fact that Scripture informs us that it was the writer of this fourth Gospel supplies one of the many silent but indubitable proofs of the Divine inspiration of the Bible.

"Woman behold thy son! Then said he to the disciple, Behold thy mother!" (19:27). First, to His mother, Behold now this one who cares for you, who has taken his place by your side, who would not allow you to stand here alone. Second, to John, Behold thy mother! – regard her henceforth with the tenderest affection; she is My living legacy to you! Thus did the Redeemer give to the apostle who had leaned on His breast, the one on whose breast He had once rested! Thus did He give to John the place which *He* had filled – a higher place than that which He gave to Peter! The order is indeed striking: Christ bade Mary look to John, *before* He commanded him to care for her—John was to be the stay of Mary, *not* Mary of John!

"And from that hour that disciple took her unto his own home" (19:27). First, the Saviour's act has forever set an example for children to honor their parents—to the end, not only while they are minors. Second, it marked His tender compassion: He would graciously spare His mother the worst, and therefore made arrangements that she would not witness the awful darkness, hear His cry of agony, or be present when He died. Third, it showed Him Son of God, the *Protector* and *Provider* of His people; it was the pledge of His equal care for *all* He leaves behind on earth—while we are here in the world He *will* supply our "every need." Fourth, He here confirmed the law of love, under the shadow of the cross. He *united* together those who loved Him and whom He loved. There was no command, for love needs none; love will respond to a gesture, a glance. The beloved disciple at once understood his Lord's mind. Fifth, He intimated that in providing *for* His people, He would do so *by means of* His people; it was *John* who was to provide hospitality for Mary. Christ is still saying to us: "Behold thy son! . . . Behold thy mother!"—compare Matt. 25:40. How marvelously are the Divine and human perfections of Christ blended here: as Man, honoring His mother; as God, the Head of the family, making arrangements for the children!

"From that hour that disciple took her unto his own home." Of old it had been predicted that the Lord Jesus should act discreetly: "Behold, my Servant shall deal *prudently*" (Isa. 52:13). In commending His mother to the care of His beloved apostle, the Saviour evidenced His wisdom by the choice of her future guardian. Perhaps there was none who understood Him so well as His mother, and it is almost certain that none had apprehended His love so deeply as had John. We see, therefore, how they would be most suited companions for each other, the intimate bond of spiritual love uniting them together and to Christ. None so well fitted to take care of Mary; none whose company she would find so congenial; none whose fellowship either would more appreciate.

"From that hour that disciple took her unto his own home." Here, as ever, the Roman Catholics err—"not knowing the Scriptures, nor the power of God." From this verse they argue that Mary could have had *no other* children, otherwise Christ had never committed her, a widow, to John. But the Word of God plainly declares that she *did* have other children—"Is not his mother called Mary? and his brethren, James and Joses, and Simon, and Judas? and his sisters, are they not all with us?" (Matt. 13:55, 56). The same Word of God also shows us that *they* were, at that time, ill-fitted to be Mary's companions and guardians—"I am become a *stranger* unto my brethren, and an *alien* unto my mother's children" (Psa. 69:8), were the Saviour's own words. How, then, could *they* take the Saviour's place, and be unto Mary what He had been! "We surely need no stronger proof than we have here, that Mary, the mother of Jesus, was never meant to be honored as Divine, or to be prayed to, worshipped and trusted in, as the friend and patroness of sinners. Common sense points out that she who needed the care and protection of another, was never likely to help men and women to heaven, or to be in any sense a mediator between God and man!" (Bishop Ryle). How this incident also illustrates, once more, that spiritual bonds have the preference over natural ties! Moreover, what a heart-piercing rebuke to His unbelieving "brethren" (John 7:5) were His words here to Mary and John.

"After this, Jesus knowing that all things were now accomplished, that the Scriptures might be fulfilled, saith, I thirst" (19:28). What a sight is this—the Maker of heaven and earth with parched lips! the Lord of glory in need of a drink! the Beloved of the Father crying, "I thirst!" First, it evidenced His *humanity*. The Lord Jesus was not a Divine man, nor a humanized God; He was the God-man. Forever God, and now forever man. When the eternal Word became incarnate, He did not cease to be God, nor did He lay aside any of His Divine attributes; but He did become flesh; being made in all things like unto His brethren. He "increased in wisdom and stature" (Luke 2:52); He "wearied" in body (John 4:6); He was "an hungered" (Matt. 4:2); He "slept" (Mark 4:38); He "marvelled" (Mark 6:6); He "wept" (John 11:35); He "prayed" (Mark 1:35); He "rejoiced" (Luke 10:21); He "groaned" (John 11:33); and here, He "thirsted." *God* does not thirst; there is no hint (so far as we are aware) that the *angels* ever do; *we* shall not in the Glory (Rev. 7:16). But *Christ* did, as man, in the depths of His humiliation.

This fifth Cross-utterance of the Saviour, "I thirst," followed right after the three hours of darkness, during which the light of God's countenance had been withdrawn from the Sin-Bearer. It was then that the blessed Saviour endured the fierceness of the outpoured wrath of a holy God. It was this which made Him exclaim, "My moisture is turned into *the drought* of summer" (Psa. 32:4). This cry, then, tells of the *intensity* of what He had suffered, the awful *severity* of the conflict through which He had just passed. "He hath made Me desolate and faint," He cried (Lam. 1:13).

But unparalleled as had been His sufferings, great as was His thirst, it was not desire for the relief of His body that now opened His lips. Far different, far higher, was the motive which prompted Him. This comes out clearly in the first part of 19:28. Carefully has the Holy Spirit guarded the Saviour's glory, with delight has He brought before us His unique perfections. First, the very fact that He *did* now "thirst" evidences His perfect submission. He that had caused water to flow from the smitten rock for the refreshment of Israel in the wilderness, had the same infinite resources at His disposal now that He was on the cross. He who turned the water into wine by a word from His lips, could have spoken the same word of power here, and instantly met His own need. Why, then, did He hang there with parched lips? Because, in the volume of that Book which expressed the will of God, it was written that *He should* thirst! He came here to *do* God's will, and ever did He perfectly perform it.

In death, as in life, Scripture was for the Lord Jesus the authoritative Word of the living God. In the temptation He had refused to minister to His own need apart from that Word by which He lived; so now He makes known His need, *not* that it might be relieved, but that "the Scriptures might be fulfilled"!

Observe that He did not Himself seek to fulfill it—God can be trusted to take care of that; but He gives utterance to His distress so as to provide occasion for the fulfilment. "The terrible thirst of crucifixion is upon Him, but that is not enough to force those parched lips to speak; but it is written, 'In my thirst they gave me vinegar to drink'—this opens them" (Mr. F. W. Grant). Here, then, as ever, He shows Himself in active obedience to the will of God, which He came to accomplish. He simply says, "I thirst," the vinegar is tendered and the prophecy is fulfilled. What perfect absorption in the Father's will!

But mark how His *Divine* perfections come out here: "Jesus *knowing* that all things were now accomplished." How completely self-possessed the Saviour was! He had hung on that cross for six hours, and had passed through suffering unparalleled: nevertheless His mind was perfectly clear and His memory entirely unimpaired. He had before Him, with perfect distinctness, the whole truth of God. He reviewed in a moment the entire scope of Messianic prediction. He remembered there was one prophetic scripture yet unaccomplished. He overlooked nothing. What a proof was this that He was Divinely superior to all circumstances! Finally, mark the wondrous grace here: *He* thirsted on the cross, that *we* might drink the water of life and thirst no more forever!

"Now there was set a vessel full of vinegar; and they filled a sponge with vinegar, and put it upon hyssop, and put it to his mouth" (19:29). The act recorded here must be carefully distinguished from that mentioned in Matthew 27:34, being the same as that found in Matt. 27:48. The first drink of vinegar and gall, commonly given to criminals to deaden their pains, the Lord refused; the drink of vinegar or sour wine, He here accepted—in obedience to His Father's will. The ones who tendered the sponge were, most probably, the Roman soldiers, who carried out the details of the crucifixion. Little did they think that they were executing the counsels of God! In view of the context in Matt. 27 we believe that these Romans had been deeply impressed by the Saviour's words from the cross, and especially by that mysterious darkness for three hours, and that they now acted either out of compassion or reverence.

"When Jesus therefore had received the vinegar, he said, It is finished" (19:30). "It is finished"—a single word in the original. It was the briefest and yet the fullest of His seven cross-utterances. Eternity will be needed to make manifest all that it contains. All things had been done which the law of God required; all things established which prophecy predicted; all things brought to pass which the types foreshadowed; all things accomplished which the Father had given Him to do; all things performed which were needed for our redemption. Nothing was left wanting. The costly ransom was given, the great conflict had been endured, sin's wages had been paid, Divine justice satisfied. True, there was the committal of His spirit into the hands of the Father, which immediately followed His word here; there was His resurrection, ascension, and session on high, but these are the fruit and reward of that work which He completed. Nothing more remained for Him to do; nothing more awaited its fulfilment; His work on earth was consummated.

"It is finished." This was not the despairing cry of a helpless martyr. It was not an expression of satisfaction that the end of His sufferings was now reached. It was not the last gasp of a worn-out life. No, it was the declaration on the part of the Divine Redeemer that all for which He came from heaven to earth to do, was now done; that all which was needful to reveal the glorious character of God had now been accomplished; that everything necessary for the putting away of the sins of His people, providing for them a perfect standing before God, securing for them an eternal inheritance and fitting them for it, had all been done.

"It is finished." The root Greek word here, "teleo," is variously translated in the New Testament. A reference to some of its alternative renditions in other passages will enable us the better to discern the fullness and finality of the term here used by the Saviour. In Matt. 11:1 "teleo" is translated as follows, "When Jesus had *made an end* of commanding His twelve disciples." In Matt. 17:24 it is rendered, "They that received tribute money came to Peter, and said, Doth not your Master *pay* tribute." In Luke 2:39 it is translated, "And when they had *performed* all things according to the law of the Lord." In Luke 18:31 it is rendered, "All things that are written by the prophets concerning the Son of man shall be *accomplished*." Putting these together we learn the scope of Christ's sixth cross-utterance. "It is finished." He cried—it is "made an end of," it is "paid," it is "performed," it is "accomplished." *What* was "made an end of"?—our sins, our guilt! *What* was "paid"?—the price of our redemption! *What* was "performed"?—the utmost requirements of God's law. *What* was "accomplished"?—the work which the Father had given Him to do! *What* was "finished"?—the making of atonement!

"And he bowed his head, and gave up the spirit" (19:30). The *order* of these two actions strikingly evidences the Saviour's uniqueness: with us the spirit departs, and then the head is bowed; with Him it was the opposite! So, too, each of these actions manifested His Deity. First, He "bowed his head"; the plain intimation is that, up to this point, His head had been *held erect*. It was no impotent sufferer who hung there in a swoon. Had *that* been the case, His head had lolled helplessly on His chest, and He would have had no occasion to "bow" it. Weigh well the verb here: it is not that His head "fell forward," but He consciously, calmly, reverently, *bowed* His head. How sublime was His carriage even on the "tree!" What superb composure did He evidence! Was it not His *majestic bearing* on the cross that, among other things, caused the centurion to cry, "Truly this was the Son of God" (Matt. 27:54)!

"And gave up (delivered up) the spirit." None else ever did this or died thus. How remarkably do these words exemplify His own declaration in 10:17, 18: "I lay down my life, that I might take it again. No man taketh it from me, but I lay it down *of myself*. I have power to lay it down, and I have power to take it again"! The uniqueness of Christ's action here may also be seen by comparing His words with those of Stephen's. As the first Christian martyr was dying, he prayed, "Lord Jesus *receive* my spirit" (Acts 7:59). In sharp contrast from Stephen, Christ "*gave up* the spirit"; Stephen's was ***taken from*** him, not so the Saviour's.

"The Jews therefore, because it was the preparation, that the bodies should not remain upon the cross on the Sabbath day (for that sabbath day was an high day), besought Pilate that their legs might be broken, and that they might be taken away" (19:31). The day on which the Saviour was crucified was "an high day": it was on the eve of the regular weekly sabbath and *also* of the first day of the feast of unleavened bread, from which the Jews reckoned the seven weeks to pentecost; the same day was also the one appointed for the presentation and offering of the sheaf of new corn, so that it possessed a treble solemnity. Hence the Jews' urgency here – the breaking of the legs would serve the double purpose of hastening and ensuring death. Behind this motive and act of "the Jews," zealous for the Law (Deut. 21:22, 23), we may behold, again, the over-ruling hand of God. Seemingly, Pilate would have allowed the body of Christ to remain on the cross, perhaps for several days, after He was dead. But the Lord Jesus had declared He *would* be "buried" and that He would be in the grave *three* days. For the fulfilment of this He *must* be buried the same day that He died; therefore did God see to it that no word of His failed! Once again were the Lord's enemies unconsciously executing the Divine counsels.

"Then came the soldiers, and break the legs of the first, and of the other which was crucified with him" (19:32). Why did the soldiers first give their attention to the two thieves? We cannot be certain, but most likely because they perceived that Christ was dead already. The Greek word for "break" here signifies to "shiver to pieces." A heavy mallet or iron bar was used for this. On this verse Bishop Ryle says, "It is noteworthy that the penitent thief, even after his conversion, had more suffering to go through before he entered into Paradise. The grace of God and the pardon of sin did not deliver him from the agony of having his legs broken. When Christ undertakes to save our souls, He does not undertake to deliver from bodily pains and conflict with the last enemy. Penitence, as well as impenitence, must taste death (unless the Saviour returns first, A.W.P.)" Yet it is blessed to know that these Roman soldiers were also the unwitting agents for fulfilling Christ's promise "*Today* shalt thou be with me in paradise"!

"But when they came to Jesus, and saw that he was dead already, they break not his legs" (19:33). This affords further evidence of the *uniqueness* of Christ's death. The Lord Jesus and the two thieves had been crucified together. They had been on their respective crosses the same length of time. But now, at the close of the day, the two thieves were still alive; for, as it is well known, execution by crucifixion, though exceedingly painful, was usually a slow death. No vital member of the body was directly affected, and often the sufferer lingered on for two or three days, before being finally overcome with exhaustion. It was not natural, therefore, that Christ should be dead after but six hours on the cross—observe how that "Pilate *marvelled* if he were *already* dead" (Mark 15:44). The request of the Jews to Pilate shows that they were not expecting the three to die unless death were hastened. In the fact that the Saviour was "dead already" when the soldiers came to Him, though the two thieves still lived, we have a further demonstration that His life *was not* "taken from him," but that He "laid it down of himself"!

"But when they came to Jesus, and saw that he was dead already, they break not his legs." This was the first proof that the Son of God *had* really died. Trained executioners as these Roman soldiers were, it is quite unthinkable that they would make any mistake in a matter like this. Pilate had *given orders* for the legs of the three to be broken, and they would not dare to disobey unless they were absolutely sure that Christ *were* "dead already." Infidels expose themselves to the charge of utter absurdity if they claim that Christ never died, and was only in a swoon. The Roman soldiers are witnesses against them!

"But one of the soldiers with a spear pierced his side, and forthwith came there out blood and water" (19:34). "That *blood* should flow from one now dead, that blood *and* water should issue together, yet separated, was clearly a miracle. The water and the blood came forth to bear witness, that God has given to us eternal life, and that this life is in His Son (I John 5:8-12). We have not here the centurion's confession, 'truly this was the Son of God'; we have not Pilate's wife, nor the convicted lips of Judas, bearing Him witness; Jesus does not here receive witness from men, but from God. The water and the blood are *God's* witnesses to His Son, and to the life that sinners may find in Him. It was *sin* that pierced Him. The action of the soldier was a sample of man's *enmity*. It was the sullen shot of the defeated foe after the battle; the more loudly telling out the deep-seated hatred that there is in man's heart to God and His Christ. But it only sets off the riches of that *grace* which met it, and abounded over it; for it was answered by the love of God. The point of the soldier's spear was touched by *the blood!* The crimson flow came forth to roll away the crimson sin" (Mr. Bellett).

"But one of the soldiers with a spear pierced his side, and forthwith came there out blood and water." Here was the second proof that our Lord *really* died. One of the soldiers determined to make sure work and leave nothing uncertain—in all probability directing his spear at the Saviour's heart. *He* was singled out from the others even while dead between the dying thieves. "*He* has a place even here that belonged to Him alone!" (Mr. W. Kelly). "Behold now the sleeping last Adam, and out of His side formed the evangelical Eve. Behold the Rock which was smitten, and the waters of life gushed forth. Behold the Fountain that is opened for sin and uncleanness" (Augustine). "The blood *and* water signified the two great benefits which all believers partake of through Christ—justification and sanctification. Blood stands for remission, water for regeneration; blood for atonement, water for purification. The two must always go together." (Matthew Henry).

"And he that saw it bear record, and his record is true: and he knoweth that he saith true, that ye might believe" (19:35). The reference is to what is recorded in the previous verse: John vouches as an eye-witness for the flowing of the blood and water from the Saviour's pierced side. It is evident that he had returned to the cross after conducting Mary to his own home, and it is equally evident that he must have remained there to the end. John's solemn asseveration here plainly intimates that what is recorded in the previous verse is a notable miracle. We believe that the "record" of John includes *both* what he has written here and that which he says in his first Epistle: "This is he that came by [i.e., was manifest by means of] water and blood" (I John 5:6). In the Gospel the blood is mentioned first, as satisfying God; then comes the "water" as applied to us. In the Epistle the order is the *experimental* one: we have to be regenerated *before* we have faith in the blood!

"For these things were done, that the scripture should be fulfilled, A bone of him shall not be broken" (19:36). The Holy Spirit here quotes Psa. 34:20: "*He* keepeth all his bones: not one of them is broken." Marvelously had this been fulfilled. God *had* kept all the bones of His incarnate Son. Notwithstanding Pilate's order, the soldiers broke not *His* legs. All the legions of Caesar could not have broken a single bone: they, too, had "*no* power" except what was given them from above! The preservation of Christ's bones was the fulfilment of an ancient type; "Neither shall ye break a bone thereof" (Ex. 12:46), i.e., of the paschal lamb. For fifteen hundred years Israel had punctiliously observed this item in the passover observance, and none of them (so far as we know) had any idea of its meaning. Now the Holy Spirit explains it.

"And again another scripture saith, They shall look on him whom they pierced" (19:37). In a most striking way the piercing of the Saviour's side demonstrated the *sovereignty* of God—His absolute control over all His creatures and their every act. The soldier *had* received instructions to break the legs of Christ, but this he *did not*: had he done so, Scripture had been broken! The soldier *had not* received orders to pierce the Saviour's side, yet this he *did*: had he not, prophecy had failed of its accomplishment! The quotation is from Zech. 12:10 and the reference is to a coming day, when Israel shall look upon Him whom they pierced—*they* pierced Him, though the act was performed by a Roman. Observe here the minute accuracy of Scripture: in 19:36 the word "fulfilled" is suitably used; but here in 19:37 it is significantly absent. And why? Because the *complete* "fulfilment" of Zech. 12:10 is yet future, hence the "another scripture *saith*."

"After this Joseph of Arimathaea, being a disciple of Jesus, but secretly for fear of the Jews, besought Pilate that he might take away the body of Jesus: and Pilate gave him leave. He came therefore and took the body of Jesus" (19:38). This, too, was in fulfilment of prophecy: "Men appointed his grave with the wicked, but he was with the rich in his death" (Isa. 53:9, corrected translation). It is blessed to see the Holy Spirit here bringing Joseph to light in connection with the last offices of love to the precious body of the Lord; he was allowed a privileged part in the accomplishment of Isaiah's prediction. How true it is that man proposes, but God disposes! Wicked men had prepared three graves for the occupants of the three crosses, but one of them was destined to remain unoccupied that day. Just as God would not suffer Christ's bones to be broken, so He would not allow His body to be placed in a malefactor's tomb; but instead, in a sepulchre prepared by one who loved Him. Hitherto, Joseph had, through fear of the Jews, been a secret disciple; but though afraid to own the Saviour while He lived, now that He was dead, he went in "*boldly*" (Mark 15:43) and craved His body. What a witness was this to the *power* of the Redeemer's death!

"And there came also Nicodemus, which at the first came to Jesus by night, and brought a mixture of myrrh and aloes, about a hundred pound weight" (19:39). This also witnessed to the power of Christ's death. Like Joseph, Nicodemus came out into the light but slowly. Timid by nature, yet grace overcoming, here is Nicodemus the only one, apparently, who dared to help Joseph in the holy work of burying the Lord. How great the contrast between his conduct in John 3, when he crept into the Lord's place of lodging under cover of night, and here, where he is not ashamed to openly show himself as one who loved the crucified Saviour! The value of his gift testifies to the greatness of his love. "Joseph and Nicodemus had done what they could. That service done for Christ has never been forgotten. The names of these two are embalmed in the volume of inspiration, and the amount in weight of the spices that Nicodemus brought is likewise recorded. Service done to Christ, or in His name, is never by God forgotten" (Mr. C. E. Stuart).

"Then took they the body of Jesus, and wound it in linen clothes with the spices, as the manner of the Jews is to bury"

(19:40). "They wrapped that incorruptible body in spices, for it is to be fragrant for evermore to all His people as the death like which there is no other" (Mr. F. W. Grant). Here, too, a beautiful type was fulfilled. In II Chron. 16:14 we read, "And they buried him in his own sepulchre, which he had made for himself in the city of David, and laid him in the bed which was filled with *sweet odours* and divers kinds of *spices*."

"Now in the place where he was crucified there was a garden; and in the garden a new sepulchre, wherein was never man yet laid" (19:41). Beautifully suggestive is the reference to the "garden." It was in a "garden" that the first Adam sowed the seed which issued in death; so here, in a "garden" was sown the Seed which was to bear much fruit in immortal life. In the "new" sepulchre "wherein was never yet man laid" we have the fulfilment of still another type: "And a man that is clean shall gather up the ashes of the heifer (previously slain) and lay them up without the camp in a *clean* place" (Num. 19:9).

"There laid they Jesus therefore because of the Jews' preparation; for the sepulchre was nigh at hand" (19:42). Here was the third conclusive proof that the Lord Jesus actually died—He was *buried*. He who had been born of a virgin mother, was laid in a virgin grave; there to remain for three days when He came forth as the mighty Victor.

The following questions are to prepare for our next study:—

1. Why was the "stone" removed, v. 1?
2. What is shown by Mary's words, v. 2?
3. Why seek the two she did, v. 2?
4. Why went not John in, v. 5?
5. What is the significance of v. 7?
6. What was it he "saw" that made him "believe," v. 8?
7. Why did they go "home," v. 10?

CHAPTER SIXTY-SEVEN

Christ Risen from the Dead

John 20:1-10

Below is an Analysis of the first section of John 20:—

1. The stone removed from the sepulchre, v. 1.
2. Mary Magdalene's appeal to the two disciples, v. 2.
3. Love's race to the sepulchre, vv. 3, 4.
4. John's hesitation and Peter's boldness, vv. 5, 6.
5. The grave-clothes and John's conclusion, vv. 7, 8.
6. The disciples' slowness of heart, v. 9.
7. Their return home, v. 10.

The resurrection of Christ was more than hinted at in the first Divine promise and prophecy (Gen. 3:15): if Christ was to bruise the serpent's head *after* His own heel had been bruised by the enemy, then must He rise from the dead. The passing of the ark through the waters of judgment on to the cleansed earth, foreshadowed this same great event (I Peter 3:21). The deliverance of Isaac from the altar, after he had been given up to death three days before (see Gen. 22:4), is interpreted by the Holy Spirit as a receiving of him back, in figure, from the dead (Heb. 11:19). The crossing of the Red Sea by Israel on dry ground, three days after the slaying of the paschal lamb, was a type of Christians being raised together with Christ. The emergence of Jonah after three days and nights in the whale's belly forecast the Saviour's deliverance from the tomb on the third day. Prophecy was equally explicit: "Therefore my heart is glad, and my glory rejoiceth: my flesh also shall rest in hope. For thou wilt not leave my soul in hades; neither wilt thou suffer thine Holy One to see corruption. Thou wilt show me the path of life" (Psa. 16:9-11).

We cannot make too much of the death of Christ, but we can make too little of His resurrection. Our hearts and minds cannot meditate too frequently upon the cross, but in pondering the sufferings of the Saviour, let us not forget the glories which followed. Calvary does not exhaust the Gospel message. The Christian evangel is not only that Christ died for our sins, but also that He rose again the third day according to the Scriptures (I Cor. 15:1-4). He was delivered for our offences and raised again for our justification (Rom. 4:25). Had Christ remained in the sepulchre it had been the grave of all our hopes; "If Christ be not raised," said the apostle, "then is our preaching vain, and your faith is also vain" (I Cor. 15:14). To be a witness of His resurrection was a fundamental qualification for an apostle (Acts 1:22). That God raised up the One whom the Jews had crucified, was the central truth pressed by Peter in his pentecostal sermon (Acts 2:24-36). The same fact was urged again by the apostles in Solomon's porch (Acts 3:15), and before the Sanhedrin (Acts 4:10; 5:30). This foundation-truth was proclaimed also to the Gentiles (Acts 10:40; 13:34). Its prominence in the Epistles is too well-known to require quotations.

The 20th chapter of John records the appearances which the Saviour made to some of His own after He was risen from the dead—we say "after," for none of them witnessed the actual resurrection itself. "As no eye beheld what was deepest in the Cross, so only God looked on the Lord rising from among the dead. This was as it should be. Darkness veiled Him giving Himself for us in atonement. Man saw not that infinite work in His death; yet was it not only to glorify God thereby, but that our sins might be borne away righteously. We have seen the action of the world, and especially of the Jews, in crucifying Him; high and low, religious and profane, all played their part; even an apostle denied Him, as another betrayed Him to the murderous priests and elders. But *Jehovah* laid on Him the iniquities of us all; *Jehovah* bruised and put Him to grief; *Jehovah* made His soul an offering for sin; and as this was *Godward*, so was it invisible to *human* eyes, and God alone could rightly bear witness, by whom He would, of the eternal redemption there obtained, which left Divine love free to act even in a lost and ungodly world.

"So with the resurrection of Christ. He was raised up from the dead by the glory of the Father; God raised up Jesus whom the Jews slew and hanged on a tree; He had laid down His life that He might take it again, in three days raising the temple of His body which they destroyed. But if no man was given to see the act of His rising from the dead, it was to be testified in all the world, as well as His atoning death. Assuredly he who withholds His resurrection maims the glad tidings of its triumphant proof and character, and compromises the believers' liberty and introduction into the new creation, as he immensely clouds the Lord's glory; even as the denial of resurrection virtually charges God's witnesses with falsehood and makes faith vain." (Bible Treasury).

The resurrection of Christ was brought about by the joint action of the three Persons of the Trinity. Just as they co-operated in connection with His incarnation (Heb. 10:5 for the Father; Phil. 2:7 for the Son; Luke 1:35 for the Spirit), just as they had each been active in connection with the atonement (Isa. 53:6, 10 for the Father; Eph. 5:2 for the Son; Heb. 9:14 for the Spirit), so the whole Godhead was engaged on the resurrection-morning. "Christ was raised up from the dead *by* the glory of the *Father*" (Rom. 6:4): "I lay down my life, that *I* might take it again" (John 10:17): "But if *the Spirit* of him that raised up Jesus from the dead dwell in you" etc. (Rom. 8:11).

"The first of the week" (20:1). All the ways of God express His perfect wisdom, and everything recorded of them in Scripture is written for our learning. Most fitting was it that the Lord Jesus, as head of the *new* creation, should rise from the dead on the *first* day of the week—intimating that a new beginning had been inaugurated. The full requirements of the moral law had been met; the shadows of the ceremonial law had all been fulfilled; the old system, connected with man in the flesh, was ended; a new and spiritual dispensation had begun. It was this "first of the week" which the Spirit of prophecy had in mind when He moved the Psalmist to write, "The stone which the builders refused is become the head of the corner. This is the Lord's doing; it is marvelous in our eyes. *This is* *the day* which the Lord hath made (appointed); we will rejoice and be glad in it" (Psa. 118:22-24). Here is the reason why the Lord's people are under obligations to keep Sunday as their day of rest and worship.* During Old Testament times the Sabbath was the memorial of God's finished work in the old creation (Gen. 2:3; Ex. 20:11); in New Testament times the Sabbath is the memorial of Christ's finished work from which issues the new creation.

"The first of the week cometh Mary Magdalene early, when it was yet dark, unto the sepulchre" (20:1). Mark tells us that Mary Magdalene was accompanied to the grave by Mary the mother of James, and Salome (16:1, 2); but John mentions them not. It is characteristic of this fourth Gospel to present *individual* souls to our notice; Nicodemus alone with Christ, the woman at the well, the blind beggar in chapter 9 being well-known examples. Another thing which is prominent in John is the heart's *affection,* the soul finding a satisfying Object: the two disciples who abode with the Lord, on their very first meeting with Him (1:39); the bringing of others to the Saviour, that they also might bask in His presence (1:41, 45); the words of Peter (6:68), the appeal of the sisters (11:3), and the devotion of Mary (12:3), are so many illustrations. It is *this* which Mary of Magdala so vividly exemplifies. To whom much is forgiven, the same loveth much (Luke 7:47), and abundant cause had this woman to love the Saviour, for out of her He had cast seven demons (Luke 8:2).

It was "very early in the morning" (Mark 16:2) that Mary came to the sepulchre; as John tells us "when it was yet dark." But though she had reason for expecting to find the Roman soldiers on guard there (Matt. 27:66), though there had just been "a great earthquake" (Matt. 28:2), though there were no male disciples accompanying her, though this was the midst of the Feast, when thousands of strangers were most probably sleeping under any slight shelter near the walls of Jerusalem, *love* drew Mary to the place where the Saviour's body had been laid. How this devotion of hers puts to shame many of us, who perhaps have greater intelligence in spiritual things, but who manifest far less love for Christ! Few were as deeply at-

* See author's "The Christian Sabbath." (30 cents).

tached to the Redeemer as was this woman. Few had received as much at His gracious hands, and her gratitude knew no bounds. How this explains the listlessness and half-heartedness among us! Where there is little sense of our indebtedness to Christ, there will be little affection for Him. Where light views of our sinfulness, our depravity, our utter unworthiness, are entertained, there will be little expression of gratitude and praise. It is those who have had the clearest sight of their deservingness of hell, whose hearts are most moved at the amazing grace which snatched them as brands from the burning, that are the most devoted among Christ's people. Let us pray daily, then, that it may please God to grant us a deeper realization of our sinfulness and a deeper apprehension of the surpassing worthiness of His Son, so that we may serve and glorify Him with increasing zeal and faithfulness.

"And seeth the stone taken away from the sepulchre" (20:1). Matthew tells us that, "Behold, there was a great earthquake: for the angel of the Lord descended from heaven, and came and rolled back the stone from the door, and sat upon it" (28:2): Upon this Mr. John Gill has said, "This stone was removed by an angel, for though Christ Himself could easily have done it, it was proper that it should be done by a messenger from Heaven, by the order of Divine justice, which had lain Him a prisoner there." The stone was rolled away from Lazarus' sepulchre by human hands (11:41), the stone from Christ's tomb by angelic – in *all* things *He* has the pre-eminence! We believe that God's principal design in sending His angel to remove the stone was that these believers might see for themselves that the sepulchre was now tenantless. The angel seated on the stone (later, inside the sepulchre) would demonstrate that God Himself had intervened. Apparently Mary was the first to perceive that the entrance to the grave was now open.

"Then she runneth, and cometh to Simon Peter, and to the other disciple whom Jesus loved, and saith unto them, They have taken away the Lord out of the sepulchre, and we know not where they have laid him" (20:2). There is no difficulty in reconciling this statement with the record of Matthew if the following points be kept in mind: First, either Mary was in front of the other women as they journeyed to the sepulchre, or else her vision was keener than theirs; at any rate, she appears to have been the first to perceive that the stone had been removed. Second, she was so excited over this that, instead of going right up to the sepulchre with her companions, she at once rushed off to acquaint the apostles—hence she missed seeing the angel. Third, after Mary's hurried departure, the rest of the little party drew near the grave, hardly knowing what to conclude or what to expect. Fourth, Mary was, most probably, a long way on the road to John's dwelling before the other women left the tomb.

Various reasons have been advanced as to why Mary sought out Peter and John. These two seem to have been nearer the Saviour than the other apostles. They were among the highly favoured three who witnessed the transfiguration, and whom He also took with Him further into the Garden than the others (Matt. 26:37). These two had also stuck more closely to Him after His arrest, following to and entering the high priest's residence. Moreover, as another has said, "John alone of all the apostles, had witnessed Peter's sad fall and observed his bitter weeping afterwards. Can we not understand that from Friday night to Sunday morning John would be lovingly employed in binding up the broken heart of his brother, and telling him of our Lord's last words? Can we doubt that they were absorbed and occupied in converse about their Master on this very morning, when Mary Magdalene suddenly ran in with her wonderful news." Mary, then, sought Peter and John because she knew that among the disciples *they* would be most likely to respond (at that early hour) to the anxious inquiry that filled her own soul. It is indeed beautiful to see these two disciples now together: "The love and tender nature of John's character come out most blessedly in his affection for Peter, even after his denial of Christ . . . John clings to him, and has him under his own roof, wherever that was. When Judas fell, he had no friend to raise and cheer him. When Peter fell, there was 'a brother born for adversity' who did not despise him!" (Bishop Ryle).

"And saith unto them, They have taken away the Lord out of the sepulchre and we know not where they have laid him."

How this shows us that *love* needs to be regulated by *faith*. Mary's affection for the Saviour cannot be doubted, and most blessed it was; but her faith certainly was not in exercise. She had judged by the sight of her eyes. The stone had been removed, and she at once jumped to the conclusion that some one had been there and "taken away" the Saviour's body. The thought that He was now alive had evidently not entered her mind. She supposed that He was yet under the power of death. His own repeated declaration that He *would* rise again on the third day had made no impression. "Alas, how little of Christ's teaching the best of us take in! How much we let fall!" What a strange mingling of spiritual intelligence and spiritual ignorance we behold here. "*They* have taken away *the Lord*"! How often we see the same confusion in ourselves and in others! Observe her "*we* know not where they have laid him"—agreeing with Matthew's account that other women had accompanied her on the journey to the sepulchre.

"Peter therefore went forth, and that other disciple, and came to the sepulchre" (20:3). The announcement which Mary had made to them was so startling that the two disciples arose at once, setting forth to ascertain what this removal of the stone from the sepulchre really meant. It is most likely that they would first ask Mary, Are you sure the body is gone? But all she could tell them was that the stone was no longer in its place. Finding that Mary had not actually looked in the sepulchre, they deemed it best to go and inspect it for themselves. Strikingly may we behold here the over-ruling providence of God. According to the Mosaic law a woman was not eligible to bear witness (note no mention of *them* is made in I Cor. 15!), and the truth could not be established by less than *two* men. Here then we *have* the needed two in Peter and John, as eye-witnesses of the empty grave and the orderliness of the clothes which the Saviour had left behind!

"So they ran both together: and the other disciple did outrun Peter, and came first to the sepulchre" (20:4). Their *running* evidences that they were both excited and anxious. "We can well suppose that Mary's sudden announcement completely overwhelmed them, so that they knew not what to think. Who can tell what thoughts did not come into their minds, as they ran, about our Lord's oft-repeated predictions of His resurrection? Could it really be true? Could it possibly prove that all their deep sorrow was going to turn to joy? These are all conjectures, no doubt. Yet a vast amount of thoughts may run through a mind, at a great crisis, in a very few minutes" (Bishop Ryle).

As to the *physical* reason of John's out-distancing Peter we cannot be certain, but the popular idea that John was the younger of the two is most likely correct, for he lived at least sixty years afterwards. As to the *spiritual* reason, we think they err who attribute to Peter a guilty conscience, which made him fearful of a possible meeting with the Saviour. Had this been the case, he had hardly set out for the sepulchre at all, still less would he have gone there on the run! Moreover, the promptness with which he entered the tomb argues against the common view. Yet we cannot doubt that there is a *moral* significance to this detail which the Spirit has recorded for our learning. Peter had not yet been restored to fellowship with the Saviour. John, too, was the one of all the Eleven who was on most intimate terms with the Lord. This is sufficient to account for *his* winning love's race to the sepulchre.

"And he stooping down, saw the linen clothes lying; yet went he not in" (20:5). Here again we are left to conjecture. The simple fact is recorded; *why* John entered not in we are not told. Some say, to prevent himself being ceremonially defiled; but that seems very far-fetched. Others think it was out of reverence for the place where the Saviour had lain; this, while being more plausible, seems negatived by the fact that only a short while after he *did* enter the sepulchre (20:8). It appears to us more likely that, after looking in and seeing the sepulchre *was* empty, he waited for Peter to come up and take the lead—John being the younger of the two, this would be the most gracious thing for him to do. Whatever the motive which guided him, certainly we can see, again, the over-ruling hand of God—*two* must be present to witness the condition of the grave so as to establish the truth!

"And he stooping down, saw the linen clothes lying." What is the moral significance of John's act here? Surely it is this: John would never see the risen Christ while he was "stooping down" and looking within the sepulchre! How many there are to-day who conduct themselves as John did! They wish to ascertain whether or not they are real Christians. And what is the method they pursue? How do they prosecute their inquiry? By self-examination, by introspection, by looking within! They attempt to find in their own hearts that which will give them confidence towards God. But this is like seeking to make fast a ship by casting the anchor within its own hold. The anchor must be thrown *outside* of the ship, so that, lost to sight beneath the waves, it pierces through the mud or sand of the ocean's bed, and grips the rock itself. The surest way to discover whether or not I am trusting in Christ is not to peer within to see if I have faith, but to *exercise* faith, by looking away to its Object—faith is the eye of the soul, and the eye does not look at itself. If I look within, most likely I shall see only what John saw—the tokens of *death!* "Looking off *unto Jesus*" is what the Word says.

"Then cometh Simon Peter following him, and went into the sepulchre" (20:6). "How this illustrates that there are widely different temperaments among believers! Both ran to the sepulchre. John, of the two, the more gentle, quiet, reserved, deep-feeling, stooped down, but went no further. Peter, more hot and zealous, impulsive, fervent and forward, cannot be content without going into the sepulchre, and actually seeing with his own eyes. Both, we may be sure, were deeply attached to our Lord. The hearts of both, at this critical juncture, were full of hopes and fears, anxieties and expectations, all tangled together. Yet each acts in his own characteristic fashion! Let us learn from this to make allowance for wide varieties in the individual character of believers. To do so will save us much trouble in the journey of life, and prevent many an uncharitable thought. Let us not judge brethren harshly, and set them down in a low place, because they do not see or feel things as we see and feel. The flowers in the Lord's garden are not all of one color and one scent, though they are all planted by the One Spirit. The subjects of Christ's kingdom are not all exactly of one tone or temperament, though they all love the same Saviour, and are written in the same book of life. The Church has some in its ranks who are like Peter, and some who are like John, but a place for all, and a work for all to do. Let us love all who love Christ in sincerity, and thank God that they love Him at all" (Bishop Ryle).

"And seeth the linen clothes lie, and the napkin, that was about His head, not lying with the linen clothes, but wrapped together in a place by itself" (20:6, 7). In the Greek the word for "seeth" is different from that for "saw" in the preceding verse: the word used in connection with John signifies to take a glance; the one used of Peter means that he beheld intently, scrutinized. The design of the Holy Spirit in this verse is obvious: He informs us that Peter found in the empty tomb the clearest evidences of a deliberate and composed transaction. There were no signs of haste or fear. What had taken place had been done "decently and in order," not by a thief, and scarcely by a friend. "There they beheld, not their Object, but the trophies of His victory over the power of death. There they see the gates of brass and the bars of iron cut in sunder. The linen clothes and the napkin which had been wrapped around the Lord's head, as though He were death's prisoner, were seen strewing the ground like the spoils of the vanquished, as under the hand of death's Conqueror. The very armor of the strong man was made a show of in his own house; this telling loudly that He, who is the plague of death, and hell's destruction, had been in that place doing His glorious work." (Mr. J. G. Bellett).

"Then went in also that other disciple, which came first to the sepulchre, and he saw, and believed" (20:8). There is wide difference of opinion as to the meaning of this verse. *What* was it that John "saw and believed"? Many say that John saw the grave was *tenantless* and believed what *Mary* had said,—"they have taken away the Lord." But John had *already* looked into the grave and seen the linen clothes (20:5); what is said here in 20:8 is clearly something different. But what alternative is left us? Only this, that John now believed that Christ had risen from the dead. But if this be the reference here, how are we to understand the next verse—"For as yet they knew not the Scripture, that He *must* rise again from the dead?" Does not this bar out the thought that John *now* believed that Christ was alive? We do not think so; the contrast pointed between 20:8 and 9 is not between believing and not believing, but between the *grounds* on which faith rested!

We believe that the key to the meaning of this verse lies in the word "saw." In the Greek it is a different one from that which is used either in 20:5 or v. 6; the word here in v. 8 has the force of "perceived with the understanding." But *what was it* that John now "saw"? In v. 5, when he looked into the sepulchre from the outside, he saw (by a glance) "the linen clothes lying"; but now, on the inside, he saw *also* "the napkin that was about His head not lying with the linen clothes, but wrapped together in a place by itself" (20:7). On this the late Mr. Pierson wrote: "'Wrapped together,' fails to convey the true significance. The original means *rolled up*, and suggests that these clothes were lying in their *original convolutions*, as they had been tightly rolled up around our Lord's dead body. In 19:40 it is recorded how they tightly wound—bound about—that body in the linen clothes; how tightly and rigidly may be inferred from the necessity of *loosing* Lazarus, even after miraculous power had raised up the dead body and given it life (11:44). This explains 20:8: 'And he (John) *saw* and *believed*.' There was nothing in the mere fact of an empty tomb to compel belief in a miraculous resurrection; but, when John saw, on the floor of the sepulchre, the long linen wrappings that had been so tightly wound about the body and the head, lying there undisturbed, in their original convolutions, he knew that nothing but a *miracle* could have made it possible."

John "saw *and* believed" or understood: it was a logical conclusion, an irresistible one, drawn from the evidence before him. The body was gone from the sepulchre; the clothes were left behind, and the condition of them indicated that Christ had passed out of them without their being *un*-wrapped. If *friends* had removed the body, would they not have taken the clothes with it, still covering the honored corpse? If *foes* had removed the body, first stripping it, would they have been so careful to dispose of the clothes and napkin in the orderly manner in which John now beheld them? Everything pointed to deliberation and design, and the apostle could draw only one conclusion—Christ had risen. Our blessed Lord had left the grave-clothes just as they had rested upon Him. He had simply risen out of them by His Divine power. We believe that this shows there is a deeper significance than is generally perceived in the angel's word to the women, "Come *see* the place where the Lord lay" (Matt. 28:6). The *clothes* themselves marked His resting-place, somewhat as one would leave the impression of his form upon the bed on which he had been lying—body, arms, head. Here then we have the first proof that the mighty Victor had risen from the sleep of death.

In leaving behind His grave-clothes an Old Testament type was strikingly fulfilled. *Joseph,* through no fault of his own, was cast into prison—the place of condemnation. While in prison he was numbered with transgressors—two, as Christ was crucified between the two thieves; to the one he was the means of blessing, to the other he was the pronouncer of judgment. All of this is so clear it needs no comment. But Joseph did not remain forever in the prison, any more than Christ continued in the tomb. Joseph's place of shame and suffering was exchanged for one of dignity and glory. But before he left the dungeon "he shaved himself, and *changed his raiment*" (Gen. 41:14). So the Saviour left behind Him the habiliments of death, coming forth clothed in immortality and glory. This was the pledge that at Christ's second coming His people will also be rid forever of everything connected with the old creation—"Who shall change *our* vile body, that it may be fashioned like unto *his* glorious body" (Phil. 3:21).

"For as yet they knew not the scripture, that he must rise again from the dead" (20:9). Very searching and humbling is this. For three years these two leading apostles had heard our Lord speak of His resurrection, yet had they not understood Him. Again and again had He told them that He *would* rise again on the third day, yet had they never taken in His meaning. His *enemies had* remembered what He said (see Matt. 27:63), but His friends had forgotten! What a piercing rebuke was that of the angel's—"He is risen, *as he said*" (Matt. 28:6)! And again, "Why seek ye the living among the dead? He is not here, but is risen: *remember* how he spake unto you when He was yet in Galilee, saying, The Son of man must be delivered into the hands of sinful men, and be crucified, and the third day rise again" (Luke 24:5-7)! But these words of Christ had fallen on unheeding ears. Moreover, the apostles had had the Old Testament Scriptures in their hands from the beginning, and such passages as Psa. 16:9-11, etc., ought to have prepared them for His resurrection. But wrong teaching in childhood, traditions imbibed in their youth (John 12:34), had prejudiced them and made void the Word of God. This statement of John's here brings out, once more, his *trustworthiness* as a witness. "Hereby it appears that they were not only *honest* men, who would not deceive others, but *cautious* men, who would not themselves be imposed upon" (Matthew Henry).

"For as yet they knew not the scripture that he must rise again from the dead." The Holy Spirit here contrasts a faith which rests on the Word of God, with an intellectual assurance which proceeds from mere external evidence. Much has been made by Christian apologists of the value of "evidences," but it has been greatly overrated. Creation demonstrates a Creator, but the outward proofs of His hand do not move the *heart*, nor bring the soul into communion with Him—the written Word, applied by the Spirit, alone does that! "Facts are of high interest and real importance; and as the Israelite could point to them as the basis of his religion, to the call of Abram by God, and the deliverance of the chosen people from Egypt and through the desert and into Canaan, so can the Christian to the incomparably deeper and more enduring ones of the incarnation, death, resurrection, and ascension of the Son of God, with the consequent presence of the Holy Spirit sent down from Heaven. But *faith* to have *moral value*, to deal with the conscience, to purify the heart, is not the pure and simple acceptance of facts on reasonable grounds, but the heart's welcoming God's testimony in His Word. This tests the soul beyond all else, as spiritual intelligence consists in the growing up to Christ in an increasing perception and enjoyment of all that God's Word has revealed, which separates the saint practically to Himself and His will in judgment of self and the world.

"To 'see and believe' therefore is wholly short of what the operation of God gives us; as traditional faith or evidence answers to it now in Christendom. It is human, and leaves the conscience unpurged and the heart without communion. It may be found in him who is in no way born of God (John 2:23-25), but also in the believer as here; if so, it is not what the Spirit seals and in no way delivers from present things. And this it seems to be the Divine object to let us know in the account before us. Faith, to be of value and have power, rests not on sight or inference, but on Scripture. And as the disciples show the most treacherous memory as to the words of the Lord till He was raised up from the dead (2:22), so were they insensible to the force and application of the written Word: after that they believed both, they entered into abiding and enlarging blessing from above. This, as Peter tells us in his first Epistle (1:8), is characteristically the faith of a Christian, who, having not seen Christ, loves Him; and on whom, though not now seeing Him but believing he exults with joy unspeakable and full of glory. The faith that is founded on evidences may strengthen against Deism, Pantheism, or Atheism, but it never gave remission of sins, never led one to cry Abba Father, never filled the heart with His grace and glory who is the Object of God's everlasting satisfaction and delight" (The Bible Treasury).

"Then the disciples went away again unto their own home" (20:10). "Here also we have the further and marked testimony of its powerlessness (John's 'believing' A.W.P.). The fact was known on grounds indisputable to their minds but not yet appreciated in God's sight as revealed in His Word, and hence they return to their own unbroken association" (Bible Treasury). Doubtless this is one reason why the Holy Spirit recorded this detail, but are we not meant to link it up with 19:27 as well—"From that hour that disciple took her unto *his own home.*" Did not Peter and John now hasten to tell the Saviour's mother that He was risen from the dead!

The following questions are to aid the student for our next lesson: —

1. What is the typical picture in vv. 11-23?
2. Why did not Mary recognize Him in v. 15?
3. Why did she recognize Him in v. 16?
4. Why "touch Me not," v. 17?
5. Why refer to the ascension here, v. 17?
6. What do the last words of v. 19 prove?
7. Why the repetition in v. 21 from v. 19?

CHAPTER SIXTY-EIGHT

Christ Appearing to His Own

John 20:11-23

Below is an Analysis of our present passage: —

1. Mary at the sepulchre, vv. 11-13.
2. Christ revealing Himself to Mary, vv. 14-16.
3. Christ commissioning Mary, vv. 17-18.
4. The apostles in the upper room, v. 19.
5. Christ revealing Himself to the apostles, v. 20.
6. Christ commissioning the apostles, v. 21.
7. Christ enduing the apostles, vv. 22, 23.

Our Lord had triumphed o'er the grave, "as he said." Before the sun of this world had risen upon the third day since the crucifixion, the Son of righteousness had already risen; the Bridegroom had gone forth from His chamber (Psa. 19:4). The One whose heel was bruised by the serpent had, through death, become the destroyer of him who had the power of death. The eye of no earthly watcher had beheld the actual resurrection of the body, the rising, and the going forth. That He *had* risen was evident by the stone rolled away, the empty sepulchre, and the condition of the grave-clothes which He had left behind; corroborated, too, by the witness of the angels. But now He was to appear in person unto His own: the manner in which He did so is very striking. "Although the impulse of His love urged Him at once to the company of His own upon earth, who are still in the sorrow of death; yet He does not overwhelm them with sudden surprise at His glorious reappearance, but restrains Himself, yields Himself to their view by degrees, regulated by the highest wisdom of love. Their minds are gradually prepared, each one according to its temperament and need" (Stier).

So far as our present light reveals, the Saviour made *eleven* appearances between His resurrection and ascension. First, to Mary Magdalene alone (John 20:14). Second, to certain women returning from the sepulchre (Matt. 28:9, 10). Third, to Simon Peter (Luke 24:34). Fourth, to the two disciples going to Emmaus (Luke 24:13). Fifth, to the ten apostles in the upper-room (John 20:19). Sixth, to the eleven apostles in the upper-room (John 20:26-29). Seventh, to seven disciples fishing at the sea of Tiberias (John 21). Eighth, to the eleven apostles and possibly other disciples with them (Matt. 28:16). Ninth, to above five hundred brethren at once (I Cor. 15:7). Tenth, to James (I Cor. 15:7). Eleventh, to the eleven apostles, and possibly other disciples on the mount of Olives at His ascension (Acts 1). His twelfth appearance, after His ascension, was to Stephen (Acts 7). His thirteenth, to Saul on the way to Damascus (Acts 9). His fourteenth, to John on Patmos (Rev. 1). And this was the last—how profoundly significant. The *final* appearing was His *fourteenth!* The factors of fourteen are seven and two, seven being the number of *perfection,* and two of *witness.* Thus we have His own *perfect witness* to His triumph over the tomb!! His next appearing will be unto His blood-bought saints all together, when He shall descend into the air with a shout, and catch us up to be with Himself for evermore (I Thess. 4:16). *This* will be His *fifteenth* appearance. The factors of fifteen are three and five, three being the number of *full manifestation,* and five of *grace.* Thus, at His coming for us, His grace, His wondrous grace, will be *fully manifested!!*

It is with the first and the fifth of these appearings of the risen Saviour that our present lesson is concerned. And here, too, the significance of these numerals holds good. One is the number of *God* in the *unity* of His essence. It speaks of His absolute sovereignty. The sovereignty of God comes out here most vividly and blessedly in *the character of the one selected* to have the high honor of being the first to gaze upon the triumphant Redeemer. It was not to the Eleven, not even to John, that Christ *first* showed Himself; it was to a woman, and she the one out of whom He had cast seven demons—one who had been the complete slave of Satan. And to her He revealed Himself as *God the*

Son (see v. 17). And to whom was His *fifth* appearance made? To His mother? No. To Joseph of Arimathaea and Nicodemus? No. It was to the *unbelieving apostles,* to those who had regarded as idle tales the testimony of the women who had seen Him. His *fifth* appearance was made to those who had *least* reason to expect Him, whose faith was the weakest. Wondrous *grace* indeed was this!

"But Mary stood without at the sepulchre weeping" (20:11). This is the sequel to what was before us in the last lesson. At the beginning of the 20th chapter, we read, "The first of the week cometh Mary Magdalene early, when it was yet dark, unto the sepulchre, and seeth the stone taken away from the sepulchre. Then she runneth, and cometh to Simon Peter, and to the other disciple whom Jesus loved, and saith unto them, They have taken away the Lord out of the sepulchre, and we know not where they have laid him." In the interval, the two apostles had been to the sepulchre, inspected the clothes within, and then returned to their home, to acquaint the Saviour's mother that He was risen from the dead. Meanwhile Mary, not knowing of this, had returned to the sepulchre, desolate and sorrowful. But soon her grief was to be turned into gladness: in but a little while the One who had taken captive her heart and who now occupied her every thought would be manifested to her. Strikingly does this illustrate Proverbs 8:17: "I love them that love me; and those that *seek me early* shall find me." Mary, and the other women, were the *first* to *seek* the sepulchre on the resurrection morning, and *they* were the first to whom the Victor of death showed Himself (Matt. 28:9). Alas that so many put off the seeking of Christ till the last hour of life, and then never find Him!

"But Mary stood without at the sepulchre weeping." Here, once more, the Holy Spirit shows us that *love* needs to be regulated by *faith*. It was love for Christ that caused her to weep: she was weeping because the sepulchre was empty, yet in fact *that* was the very thing which should have made her rejoice. Had the Lord's body been still there, she might have wept indeed, for then His promise had failed, His work on the cross had been in vain, and she (and all others) yet in her sins.

The weeping manifested her affection, but it also showed her unbelief. "How often are the fears and sorrows of saints quite needless! Mary stood at the sepulchre weeping, and wept as if nothing could comfort her. She wept when the angels spoke to her: 'Woman,' they said, 'why weepest thou'? She was weeping still when our Lord spoke to her: 'Woman,' He said, 'why weepest thou?' And the burden of her complaint was always the same: 'They have taken away my Lord, and I know not where they have laid Him'! Yet all this time her risen Master was close to her! Her tears were needless. Like Hagar in the wilderness (Gen. 21:19), she had a well of water by her side, but she had not eyes to see it!

"What thoughtful Christian can fail to see that we have here a faithful picture of many a believer's experience? How often we mourn over the absence of things which in reality are within our grasp, and even at our right hand! Two-thirds of the things we fear in life never happen at all, and two-thirds of the tears we shed are thrown away, and shed in vain. Let us pray for more faith and patience, and allow more time for the development of God's purposes: let us believe that things are often working together for our peace and joy, which seem at one time to contain nothing but bitterness and sorrow. Old Jacob said at one time in his life 'all these things are against me' (Gen. 42:36), yet he lived to see Joseph again, rich and prosperous, and to thank God for all that had happened" (Bishop Ryle).

"And as she wept, she stooped down, and looked into the sepulchre" (20:11). Such is ever the effect of uncontrolled grief. When we sorrow, even as others who have no hope, when we walk by sight instead of faith, when we are moved by the flesh instead of the spirit, we stoop down, and are occupied with things below. "Unto thee lift I mine eyes, O thou that dwellest in the heavens" (Psa. 123:1) should ever be the believer's attitude. Mary points a timely warning for us. We are living in days when "men's hearts are failing them for fear, and for looking after those things which are coming on the earth" (Luke 21:26), and the more *we* are occupied with the evil around us, the more will our hearts fail. Heed then the Saviour's admonition, "When these things begin to come to pass, then *look up* and *lift up* your heads; for your redemption draweth nigh" (Luke 21:28). Let us, instead of looking down like Mary, say with the Psalmist, "I will *lift up mine eyes* unto the hills. From whence cometh my help? My help cometh from the Lord, which made heaven and earth" (Psa. 121:1, 2).

"And seeth two angels in white sitting, the one at the head and the other at the feet, where the body of Jesus had lain" (20:12). How long-suffering is our God! How patiently He deals with our dulness! Where the *heart* is really engaged with Christ, even though faith be weak and intelligence small, God will bear with us. Here were two messengers from Heaven ready to re-assure Mary! Their *presence* in the sepulchre was proof positive that God had not suffered it to be rifled by wicked hands. Their very *posture* signified that all was well. Their *number* indicated a testimony from on High, if only this sorrowing woman had eyes to see and ears to hear.

"And seeth two angels in white sitting." The sepulchre was not so deserted as it seemed. Luke tells us of two angels appearing to the other women a little earlier, and it is instructive to note the several points of difference. "And it came to pass, as they were much perplexed thereabout, behold, two men stood by them in shining garments" (24:4). Luke calls them "two men"—from their appearance, we suppose. John is more explicit: "two angels." When these other women saw the two angels, they were on the outside of the sepulchre; but when Mary looked down they were now within. In Luke 24 the angels were "standing," here in John 20 they are "seated"! Nowhere are we told the names of the two angels, but some have thought that they were Michael and Gabriel, arguing that the supreme importance of our Lord's resurrection would call for the presence of the *highest* angels. Probably the same two appeared to the disciples at Christ's ascension (Acts 1:10).

"And seeth two angels in white sitting, the one at the head, and the other at the feet." This is the only place in Scripture where we see angels *sitting*. The fact that they *were* sitting in the place where "the body of Jesus had lain" was God's witness unto the *rest* which was secured by and proceeds from the finished work of the Lord Jesus. It is in striking accord with the character of this fourth Gospel that it was reserved for John to mention this beautiful incident. Who can doubt that the Holy Spirit would have us link up this verse with Exodus 25:17-19—"And thou shalt make a mercy-seat of pure gold . . . and thou shalt make *two* cherubims of gold, of beaten work shalt thou make them, *in the two ends* of the mercy-seat." More remarkable still is the final word which Jehovah spake unto Moses concerning the mercy-seat: "And *there* I will *meet with thee*, and I will commune with thee from above the mercy-seat from between the two cherubims" (Ex. 25:22). Here, then, in *John's* Gospel, do we learn once more that Christ is the true *meeting-place* between God and man!

The question has often been asked, Why did not Peter and John see these two angels when they entered the sepulchre? It seems clear that they must have been there, though invisible. In view of Psalm 91:11 we are satisfied that they had been about that sepulchre from the first moment that the sacred body was deposited there: "For he shall give his angels *charge over thee*, to keep thee in *all* thy ways"—this was God's promise to *Christ*. From the general teaching of the Scripture we learn that the angels of God are visible and invisible, appear and disappear, instantaneously and supernaturally, according as God commissions them. Most probably they are near to each believer every moment of his existence (Heb. 1:14), though we are unaware of their presence. Yet, while they are of a higher order of beings than humans, not the smallest particle of worship is to be given them; for, like ourselves, they are but the *creatures* of God.

That the angels were "in white" denotes purity and freedom from defilement, which is the character of all the inhabitants of heaven. White was the color of our Lord's raiment in the transfiguration; it is the color in which the angels ever appeared; it will be the color of our garments in glory (Rev. 3:4). The late Bishop Andrews drew a timely moral from the positions occupied by the two angels in the sepulchre. "We learn that between the angels there was no striving for places. He that sat at the feet was as well content with his place as he that sat at the head. We should learn from their example. With us, both angels would have been at the *head,* and never one at the *feet!* With us, none would be at the feet; *we* must be *head*-angels all!"

"And they say unto her, Woman, why weepest thou"? (20:13). We have no reason for supposing that the angels were ignorant of the occasion of Mary's lamentation, therefore, we understand their words here as a gentle inquiry, made for the purpose of stirring her mind. *Why* weepest thou? Have you any just cause for those tears? Search your heart! Does not the fact that Christ is *not* here afford ground for rejoicing! It is to be noted that the angels used precisely the same language as the Saviour does in 20:15, thereby intimating that *their* words are ever spoken by the command of God. Observe that their words to the disciples at the ascension of Christ also began with a "Why?" No doubt our unbelief, our fears, our repinings, our lack of obedience and zeal, afford much ground of surprise to these unfallen beings.

"She saith unto them, Because they have taken away my Lord, and I know not where they have laid him" (20:13). Before the angels had time to add the comforting assurance, "He is not here; he is risen, as he said," Mary interrupts by explaining *why* she was so heart-broken – How can I do anything else *but* weep, when *He* is not here, and I know not where they have taken His body! A strange mingling of faith and unbelief, of intelligence and ignorance, of affection and fear, was hers. "Lord," she owned Jesus of Nazareth to be, and yet imagined that some one had taken Him away! It is indeed striking that she replied so promptly and naturally to the angels: instead of being awe-struck at their presence, she answered as though they were nothing more than men. She was so swallowed up with her grief, so occupied with her thoughts about Christ, that she paused not to gaze upon these Heavenly visitors. Mark the change of her language here: to Peter and John she had appropriately said, "They have taken away *the Lord*"; but to the angels she (now alone) says *"my Lord,"* thus expressing the depths of her affections. And how blessed that each individual believer may speak of Him as *"my Lord."* "The Lord is *my* Shepherd" said David (Psa. 23:1). *"My* beloved is mine, and I am his" (Song of S. 2:16). "Who loved *me,* and gave himself for *me*" (Gal. 2:20) said the apostle Paul.

"And when she had thus said she turned herself back" (20:14). Very, very, striking is this. Christ meant so much to her that she turned her back on the angels to seek His body! *He* was the One her affections were set upon, and therefore, even these angels held no attraction for her! How searching is this: if Christ really occupied the throne of our hearts, the poor things of this world would make no appeal to us. It is because we are so little absorbed with Him, and therefore so little acquainted with His soul-satisfying perfection, that the things of time and sense are so highly esteemed. O that writer and reader may be able to say with the Psalmist, and say with ever-increasing fervor and reality, "Whom have I in heaven but *thee?* and there is none upon earth that I desire beside *thee.*"

"And when she had thus said she turned herself back and saw Jesus standing" (20:14). Such devotion as Mary's could not pass unrewarded: to her who loved Him so deeply does the Saviour first appear. "Those who love Christ most diligently and perseveringly, are those who receive most privileges at His hands. It is a touching fact, and one to be carefully noted, that Mary would not leave the sepulchre, even when Peter and John had gone to their own home. Love to her gracious Master would not let her leave the place where He had lain. Where He was now she did not know, but love made her linger about the empty tomb; love made her honor the last place where His precious body had been seen by mortal eyes. And here love reaped a rich reward. *She* saw the angels whom Peter and John had not observed. *She* heard them speak. *She* was the first to see our Lord after He had risen from the dead, the first to hear His voice. Can any one doubt that this was written for our learning? Wherever the Gospel is preached throughout the world, this little incident testifies that those who honor Christ will be honored by Christ" (Bishop Ryle). "And saw Jesus standing." Very blessed is this. *Why* was the Saviour standing there, beside His own sepulchre? Ah, was it not the *response* of His heart to one who loved Him! He was there for the purpose of meeting and comforting this sorely-wounded soul!

"And saw Jesus standing, and knew not that it was Jesus" (20:14). It is strange how many of the commentators have erred on this point. The popular idea is that Mary failed to recognize Christ because her eyes were dimmed with tears. But how comes it, we ask, that when she looked into the sepulchre she *saw* the two angels and the respective positions which they occupied? No; we believe there is far more reason for us to conclude that her eyes were "holden" supernaturally, like the two disciples walking to Emmaus, so that she did not distinguish the figure before her to be that of our Lord. The condition of His resurrection body was very different from that of His body before the crucifixion. Moreover, He was to be known no more "after the flesh" (II Cor. 5:16), but, as the head of the new creation. Yet, as others have pointed out, this incident was a striking emblem of the spiritual experience of many Christians. "I will never leave thee nor forsake thee" is His promise; yet how often are we *un*conscious of His presence with us!

"Jesus saith unto her, Woman, why weepest thou? whom seekest thou?" (20:15). These were the first words of our risen Saviour, and how like Him! He came here to bind up the brokenhearted (Isa. 61:1), and in the end He will wipe away tears from off the faces of all His people (Isa. 25:8; Rev. 21:4). This was His evident design here: He would arouse Mary from the stupefying effects of her sorrow. His first question was a gentle reproof: Ought you not to be rejoicing, instead of repining? His second question was still more searching; *Who* is it you are seeking among the dead? Hast thou forgotten that the crucified One is the Lord of life, the resurrection and the life, the One who laid down His life that He might take it again! Devoted and affectionate as she was, had she not forgotten those words of His which had so often been spoken in her hearing! "*Whom* seekest thou?"—it was only in really finding *Him* that the ever-flowing fountain of her grief could be stayed.

"She, supposing him to be the gardener, saith unto him, Sir, if thou have borne him hence, tell me where thou hast laid him, and I will take him away" (20:15). Notice, first, her artless simplicity. Three times over in these few words did Mary speak of "him" without stopping to define or mention His name. She was so wholly absorbed with Christ that she supposed every one would know *whom* she sought—like the Shulamite crying to the watchman, "Saw ye him whom my soul loveth?" (Song of S. 3:3). Note also her, "*I* will take him away." He was all *her own;* what depth of affection! What a sense of her *title* to Him! But mark how there may be much ignorance even in a devoted believer—she supposed Him to be the "gardener"! And yet, as one has said, "Devout Mary, thou art not much mistaken. As it was the trade of the first Adam to dress the Garden of Eden, so is it the trade of the last Adam to tend the Garden of His Church: He digs up the soil by reasonable affliction; He sows in it the seeds of grace; He waters it with His Word" (Bishop Hall).

"Jesus saith unto her, Mary" (20:16). This was the second utterance of the risen Christ to this devoted soul, and it is important to note that it *was* the second. *Before* He addressed her by name, He first called her "woman"! In addressing her as "woman" He spoke as *God* to His creature; in calling her "Mary" He spoke as *Saviour* to one of His redeemed. The former gave her to know that He was exalted high above every human relationship; the latter intimated His love for one of His own. "I know thee by name, and thou hast found grace in my sight" (Ex. 33:12), said Jehovah in the Mount. So here, Jehovah, now incarnate, knows this woman by name, for she, too, had "found grace" in His sight. In Christ addressing Mary by name we have a beautiful illustration of His own words in John 10:3, "And he calleth his own sheep *by name.*" It was the *seal of redemption*: "But now thus saith the Lord that created thee, O Jacob, and he that formed thee, O Israel, Fear not: for I have *redeemed* thee, I have called thee *by thy name;* thou art *mine*" (Isa. 43:1)!

"She turned herself, and saith unto him, Rabboni; which is to say, Master" (20:16). This shows that Mary now recognized Him. "The sheep follow him, for they *know his voice*" (John 10:4), and here was one of the sheep responding to the call of the Good Shepherd. One word only did He utter, "Mary"! But that was sufficient to transform the weeper into a worshipper. It shows us, once more, the power of *the Word!* "Rabboni," she exclaimed, as she fell at His feet—a Hebrew term signifying "*my* Master." Here was the rich reward for her devotion, her faithfulness, her perseverance. The One who had before cast the demons from her, now addressed Himself to her heart. She knew now that the fairest among ten thousand to her soul had triumphed over the tomb: her sorrow was ended, her cup of joy overflowing. There is one little detail in the picture here, most lovely, which is usually overlooked. As soon as Christ addressed her by name, she "*turned herself,*" and saith unto Him, "Rabboni." After His first word, when she supposed Him to be the gardener, she had turned *away from* Him, her attitude still toward the tomb; but now that He called her by name, she turns her back on the tomb and falls at His feet—it is only as *He* is *known* that we are delivered, experimentally, from the power of death!

"Jesus said unto her, Touch me not; for I am not yet ascended to my Father" (20:17). We believe that these words have a *double* significance and application. First, the "Touch me not," in its *direct* force, is clearly explained by Christ Himself—"*for* I am not yet ascended." Mary had, we think, fallen at His feet, and was on the point of embracing them—remembering, perhaps, the words of the Shulamite, "I found him whom my soul loveth: I *held* him, and would not let him go" (Song of S. 3:4). But the Lord instantly checked her: "Touch me not, for I am not yet ascended." "On this very day, the morrow after the Sabbath, the high priest waved the sheaf of the first fruits before the Lord while He, the First-fruits from the dead (I Cor. 15:23), would be fulfilling the type by presenting Himself before the Father" (Companion Bible). This we are satisfied supplies the key to the *primary* meaning of our Lord's words to Mary, for He who was so jealous of the types would not neglect this one in Lev. 23:10, 11. Yet, we do not think that this exhausts the scope of what Christ said here. Everywhere in this Gospel there is a fulness about the Lord's utterances which it is impossible for us to fathom; and beyond their force to those immediately addressed is ever a wider application. So here.

"Touch me not." These words are not found in the Synoptics and therein lies the key to their deeper meaning and wider application. In Matt. 28:9 we read, "As they went to tell his disciples, behold, Jesus met them, saying, All hail. And they came and *held him by the feet.*" How sharp the contrast here, yet how perfectly in keeping with the particular scope of each Gospel! Matthew presents Christ as the Son of David, in Jewish relationships. But John portrays Him as the Son of God, connected with the sons, as head of the new creation, the members of which know Him *not* "after the flesh" (II Cor. 5:16). Therefore in His "Touch me not" to Mary, the Lord was giving plain intimation that the Christian would know Him only *in spirit*, as the One with the Father on high; hence His "*for* I am not yet *ascended*"! It was the first hint—abundantly amplified in the sequel of the *new* relationship into which the resurrection of Christ has brought us, linking us with Himself as the Son of God in the Father's House! How significant that this was His *third* word to Mary—the number which speaks of *resurrection!*

"But go to my brethren, and say unto them, I ascend [the proper present "*I am ascending*"] unto my Father, and your Father; and to my God, and your God" (20:17). Mary was to be the *first* witness of Christ's resurrection. This illustrates a truth of great practical importance. A *woman*—more devoted, perhaps, than any of the Twelve—had anointed Him for His burial (John 12), and now a *woman* is the first to whom Christ revealed Himself in resurrection glory. How this tells us that the *heart* leads the mind in the apprehension of God's truth. The men were quicker to grasp, *intellectually*, the meaning of the empty tomb, but Mary was the more devoted, and this Christ rewarded. Mary exemplifies the case of those whose hearts seek Christ, but whose minds are ill-informed. It is the *heart* God ever looks at. We may know much truth intellectually, but unless the heart is absorbed with Christ, He will not reveal Himself to such an one in the intimacies of love and communion.

"Go to my brethren, and say unto them, I ascend." This is the *first* time that the Lord Jesus addressed the disciples as "brethren." How blessed! It is on resurrection-ground that we are *thus* related to Christ. "Except the corn of wheat fell into the ground and died, it had abode alone" (12:24), but now that He has emerged from the grave, He is "the firstborn among many brethren" (Rom. 8:29). Of old had the Spirit of prophecy expressed the language of the Messiah thus: "I will declare thy name unto *my brethren*" (Psa. 22:22). Like Joseph after he was delivered from the prison and raised to a position of dignity and honor (Gen. 45:16), so Christ "is not ashamed to call us brethren" (Heb. 2:11). The blessedness of this comes out in the closing words of 20:17: "I ascend unto my Father, *and* your Father; and to my God, *and* your God." Believers are, by amazing grace, brought into the *same* position with Himself before God His Father. It was in view of *this* that the Lord said to Mary, "*Touch* [Greek 'cling to'] *me not*"—we are *detached* from Him by all earthly contact, and instead commune with Him by faith, in spirit, on High.

"Go to my brethren and say unto them, I ascend unto my Father, and your Father; and my God and your God." The terms of this message to His brethren deserve the closest notice. He did not bid Mary say to them "I have *risen*," but "*I ascend*." True, the one necessarily presupposed the other, but it is clear He would have them understand that His resurrection was only a step toward His return unto the Father. That which the Saviour would impress upon His beloved disciples was the fact that He had not left the grave simply to *remain* with them here on earth, but in order to enter Heaven as their Representative and Forerunner. In saying, "I ascend unto *my* Father and *your* Father, and *my* God, and *your God*," He was conveying a message of real comfort. He is *your* Father and God, as well as Mine; all that He is to Me, the Head, He is also to you, the members. But mark His precision: He did not say "*Our* Father, and *our God*." He still maintains His pre-eminency, His uniqueness, for God is *His* Father and God in a singular and incommunicable manner. Finally, note the contrast between Mary's commission here and the one given to the other women in Matt. 28:10: there the message was for the disciples to meet Him in *Galilee*, and accordingly they did so; here, He names no place on earth, but simply tells them that He is going to Heaven, there in spirit to meet them before the Father.

"Mary Magdalene came and told the disciples that she had seen the Lord and that he had spoken these things unto her" (20:18). "As by a woman came the first message of death, so by a woman came also the first notice of the resurrection from the dead. And the place also fits well, for in a garden they came, both" (Bishop Andrews). Observe that Mary told the disciples that she had "seen *the Lord,*" not simply "Jesus"! Mark records the immediate effect of her message: "She went and told them that had been with him, as they mourned and wept. And they, when they had heard that he was alive, and had been seen of her, believed not" (16:10,11). What a tragic forecast of the general reception which the Christian evangelist meets with! How few he finds that promptly receive the glad tidings of which he is the bearer! Often the ones he deems most likely to welcome the good news, are the very ones whose unbelief will be the most outspoken.

"Then the same day at evening, being the first of the week, when the doors were shut where the disciples were assembled for fear of the Jews, came Jesus and stood in the midst" (20:19). Observe in the first place how the Holy Spirit here emphasizes the fact that what follows is a *first*-day scene. On this first Christian Sabbath the "disciples were *assembled*" in separation from the world, and from this point on to the end of the New Testament the first day of the week is stamped with this characteristic: Sunday, not Saturday, was henceforth to be the day set apart for rest from the work and concerns of the world, and for occupation with the things of God. Note in the next place, that from the beginning non-Christians have manifested their opposition to and hatred of these holy exercises. Observe that those gathered together are here called "disciples," not "apostles." It is striking that never once are they termed "apostles" in John's Gospel. The reason for this is not far distant: the word "apostle" means "one sent forth"; but here, where it is the family which is in view, they are always seen *with* Christ!

"Then the same day at evening, being the first of the week, when the doors were shut where the disciples were assembled for fear of the Jews, came Jesus and stood in the midst and saith unto them, Peace be unto you" (20:19). Very striking is this. John is the only one who mentions the doors being "shut" (Greek signifies "*barred*"). But no closed doors could keep out the Conqueror of death. There was no need for Him to knock for admission, nor for an angel to open to Him as for Peter (Acts 12:10); nor do we consider what a miracle was wrought, in the ordinary meaning of that term. Our resurrection-body will not be subject to the limitations of the mortal body: sown in weakness it will be raised in *power* (I Cor. 15:43).

Most blessed is it to ponder our Lord's greeting to the Ten—Thomas was absent. Very touching and humbling was the Lord's gracious salutation. Peter had denied Him, and the others had forsaken Him. How, then, does He approach them? Does He demand an explanation of their conduct? Does He tell them that all is now over, that henceforth He will have no more to do with such unfaithful followers? No, indeed. Well might He have said, "*Shame* upon you!" But, instead He says, "*Peace* be unto you." He would remove from their hearts all fear which His sudden and unannounced appearance might have occasioned. He would quiet each uneasy conscience. Having put away their sins He could now remove their fears. Be not afraid: I come not as judge, to reckon with your perfidy and unbelief; nor do I enter as One who has been injured by you, to utter reproaches. No; I bring from My sepulchre something very different from upbraidings: "Peace be unto *you*" was the blessed greeting of the Prince of peace, and none but He *can* speak peace to any. "Peace" was the subject of the angel's carol in the night of the Lord's nativity; so "Peace" is the first word He pronounced in the ears of His disciples now that He is risen from the dead. So will it be when *we* meet Him face to face—we, with all our miserable failures, both individual and corporate; we with all our sins of omission and commission; we, with all our bitter controversies, and deplorable divisions. Not "Shame! shame!" but "Peace! peace!" will be His greeting. How do we *know* this? Because He is "The *same* yesterday and to-day and forever." Almost His last words to the disciples on the "yesterday" were "these things have I spoken unto you, that in me ye might have *peace*" (John 16:33); so here His first word to them in the "to-day" was *peace;* and *this* is the pledge that "Peace" will be His word *to us* at the beginning of the great "forever."

"And when he had so said, he showed unto them his hands and his side" (20:20). This was, first, to assure the astonished disciples that it was really their Saviour who stood before them. He bade them see with their own eyes that He had a real material body, that it was no ghost now appearing to them. He would have them recognize that He was indeed the *same* person whom they had known before the crucifixion, that He had risen in His incorruptible humanity. Significant is the omission here: Luke tells us that He said, "Behold my hands and my feet, that it is I myself: *handle me,* and see" (24:39). It was most appropriate that *this* word should be recorded in the third Gospel, which portrays Him as the Son of man; and it was most suitable to omit this detail in the Gospel which speaks of His Divine dignity and glory. Observe here, "He showed unto them his hands and his *side.*" Luke says "his hands and his *feet.*" This variation is also significant. Here His word in John would presuppose His "feet," for they, in common with His hands, bore the imprint of the nails. But there was a special reason for mentioning His "side" here—see 19:34: through His pierced side a way was opened to His *heart,* the seat of the affections! In John we see Him as the Son of *God,* and God is *love.*

"And when he had so said, he showed unto them his hands and his side." The "so" indicates there is a close connection between this *act* of Christ's and His *words* at the end of the preceding verse. The marks in His hands and side were shown to the disciples not only to establish His identity, not only as the trophies of His victorious fight, but principally to teach them, and us, that the *basis* of the "peace" He has made, and which He gives, is His death upon the cross. In saying "Peace be unto you" He announced that enmity had been removed, God placated, reconciliation effected; in pointing to the signs of His crucifixion, He showed what had accomplished these. These marks are *still* upon His holy body—Rev. 5:6. These marks our great High Priest shows to God as He intercedes. In a coming day the sight of them will bring Israel to repentance—Zech. 12:10. In the Day of Judgment they will confront and condemn His enemies.

"Then were the disciples glad, when they saw the Lord" (20:20). What must have been their feelings! Their fears all gone; their hopes fulfilled; their hearts satisfied. Now indeed had the Lord made good His promise: "And ye now therefore have sorrow: but I will see you again, and your hearts shall *rejoice*" (16:22). But observe an important distinction here: First, Christ said, "*Peace* be unto you, and when he had *so* said, he *showed* unto them his hands and his side." Second: "Then were the disciples *glad* when they saw *the Lord*." Peace comes through His perfect *work;* joy is the result of being occupied with His blessed *person*. This is a precious secret for our hearts. There are many Christians who suppose that they *cannot* rejoice while they remain in *circumstances of sorrow*. What a mistake! Observe here that Christ did not *change* the circumstances of these disciples; they were still "shut in for fear of the Jews," but He drew out their hearts unto Himself, and thus raised them *above* their circumstances! We see the same principle exemplified in I Peter 1. There we read of saints of God enduring a great fight of afflictions: they were persecuted, scattered abroad, homeless. But what of their spiritual condition? This—"Wherein ye greatly *rejoice,* though now for a season if need be, ye are in heaviness through manifold temptations." And then, having mentioned the person of the Saviour, he at once adds, "Whom having not seen, ye love; in whom, though now ye see him not, yet believing, ye *rejoice* with joy unspeakable" (v. 8). Their circumstances had not been changed, but their hearts were lifted above them. This then is the great secret of *joy*—occupation and fellowship with Christ.

"Then said Jesus to them again, Peace be unto you: as my Father hath sent me, even so send I you" (20:21). This was no mere repetition. Just as the first "Peace be unto you" is interpreted by the Lord's act which at once followed, so this second "Peace" is explained by the next words. The first peace was for the *conscience;* the second for the *heart*. The first had to do with their *position* before God; the second with their *condition* in the world. The first was "peace *with* God" (Rom. 5:1); the second was "the peace *of* God" (Phil. 4:7). The first is the consequence of the atonement: the second is that which issues from communion. These disciples were not going to Heaven with Christ, but were to remain behind in a hostile world, in a world which provides no peace. He therefore communicates to them the secret of *His* peace, which was that of communion with the Father in separation from the world.

"As my Father hath sent me, even so send I you." He now does formally what He contemplated in that wondrous address to the Father: "As thou hast sent me into the world, even so have I also sent them into the world" (17:18). Let it be remembered that it was in immediate connection with this that He said "Neither pray I for these alone, but for them also which *shall believe* on me through their word" (17:20). The mission He announced there was not peculiar to the company He then addressed: it defined the mission of *all* His people in that world which has rejected Him. And what a marvellous mission it is—to *represent* our Lord here below, as He represented the Father. What a wondrous dignity to show in our life and by our words how *He* would speak and walk. *This* is the standard of practical holiness—nothing lower, "He that saith he abideth in Him ought himself also so to walk, *even as he walked*" (I John 2:6). But how unspeakably blessed to observe that the Lord *first* said "Peace be unto you" *before* "I send you." We are constantly disposed to look for peace as the earned reward of service: what a travesty! and how worthless! Such "Peace" is but a transient self-complacency which cannot deceive any one but the self-deluded hypocrite. The truth is that peace is the *preparation* for service: "the joy of the Lord is your strength" (Neh. 8:10). The order in John 20:21 is most significant: "Peace . . . send I you." "The *sons* of peace are not to retain it for themselves; its possession makes them also *messengers* of peace" (Stier). Note the *Son* is a "Sender" in equal authority with the Father. "As my Father hath sent me, *even so* send I you." Christ was sent to manifest the Father, and with a message of grace to this sinful world; we are sent to manifest the Son, and with a similar message. Yet observe how carefully He guarded His glory; two *different* words are here used for "send"—Christ was God, we men; He came to atone, we to proclaim His atonement: He did his work perfectly, we very imperfectly!

"And when he had said this, he breathed on them, *and* saith unto them, Receive ye the Holy Spirit" (20:22). The first key to the Receive ye the Holy Spirit, lies in the "*And* when he had said *this*"—"even so send I you." Christ had entered upon His ministry as One anointed by the Holy Spirit, so should His beloved apostles. *This* was the final analogy pointed by the "as . . . so." The second key is found in the "He *breathed* on them *and* saith, Receive ye the Holy Spirit": the Greek word here used is employed nowhere else in the New Testament, but is the very one used by the Septuagint translators of Gen. 2:7: "And the Lord God formed man of the dust of the ground, and *breathed* into his nostrils the breath of life; and man became a living soul." There, man's original creation was completed by this act of God; who, then, can fail to see that here in John 20, on the day of the Saviour's resurrection, the *new creation* had begun, begun by the Head of the new creation, the last Adam acting as "a quickening spirit" (I Cor. 15:45)! The impartation of the Holy Spirit to the disciples was the "first-fruits" of the resurrection, as well as a proof that the Spirit proceeds from the Son as well as the Father—wonderful demonstration of the Saviour's Godhead! In Gen. 2:7 we have Jehovah "breathing" into Adam; in John 20:22 the Saviour "breathing" upon the apostles; in Ezek. 37:9 the Spirit "breathing" upon Israel. Finally, it is solemn to contrast Isa. 11:4: "With the *breath of His lips* shall he slay the wicked."

"Receive ye the Holy Spirit." This was supplementary to "Go tell my brethren." They were, before this, born from above; but the heir, as long as he is a child, differeth nothing from a servant, though he be lord of all. But the time appointed by the Father had now come. He who came to redeem them that were under the law, that they might receive the adoption of sons, had accomplished His undertaking. They were no more servants but sons; yet it was only by the Spirit of adoption that they could be made conscious of it or enter into the joy of it. From this moment the Spirit *dwelt* within them. We have been accustomed to look upon the change which is so apparent in apostles as dating from the day of pentecost, but the great change had occurred *before* then. Read the closing chapter of each Gospel and the first of Acts, and the proofs of this are conclusive. Their irresolution, their unbelief, their misapprehensions, were all gone. When the cloud finally received the Saviour from their sight, instead of being dispersed in consternation "they worshipped him" and "returned to Jerusalem with great joy" (Luke 24:52) – this was "joy in the Holy Spirit" (Rom. 14:17): Moreover, they continued "with one accord in prayer and supplication" (Acts 1:14) – this was "the unity of the Spirit in the bond of peace" (Eph. 4:3). Peter has a clear understanding of Old Testament prophecy (Acts 1:20) – this was the Spirit guiding into the truth (John 16:13). And these things were *before pentecost*. What happened at pentecost was the baptism of *power*, not the coming of the Spirit to indwell them!

"Whose soever sins ye remit, they are remitted unto them; and whose soever sins ye retain, they are retained" (20:23). Upon this controverted verse we cannot do better than quote from the excellent remarks of the late Bishop Ryle: "In this verse our Lord continues and concludes the commission for the office of ministers, which He now gives to the Apostles after rising from the dead. His work as a public teacher was ended: the Apostles henceforth were to carry it on. The words which formed this commission are very peculiar and demand close attention. The meaning of these words, I believe, may be paraphrased thus: 'I confer on you the power of *declaring* and *pronouncing* authoritatively whose sins are forgiven, and whose sins are not forgiven. I bestow on you the office of pronouncing who are pardoned, and who are not, just as the Jewish high priest pronounced who were clean and who were unclean in cases of leprosy. I believe that nothing more than this *authority to declare* can be got out of the words, and I entirely repudiate and reject the strange notion maintained by some that our Lord meant to depute to the Apostles, or any others, the power of *absolutely* pardoning or not pardoning, absolving, or not absolving, any one's soul.'

"(a) The power of forgiving sins, in Scripture, is always spoken of as the special prerogative of God. The Jews themselves admitted this when they said, 'Who can forgive sins but God only?' (Mark 2:7). It is monstrous to suppose that our Lord meant to overthrow and alter this great principle when He commissioned His disciples.

"(b) The language of the Old Testament shows conclusively that the Prophets were said to *do* certain things when they *declared* them to be done. Thus Jeremiah's commission runs in these words, 'I have this day set thee over the nation and over the kingdom, to root out, and to pull down, and to destroy, and to throw down, to build, and to plant' (1:10). This can only mean to *declare* the rooting out and pulling down, etc. So also Ezekiel says 'I came to destroy the city' (43:3).

"(c) There is not a single instance in the Acts or Epistles of an Apostle taking on himself to absolve, or pardon, any one. When Peter said to Cornelius. 'Whosoever believeth in him shall receive remission of sins' (Acts 10:43), and when Paul said, 'Through this man is preached unto you the forgiveness of sins' (Acts 13:38), they pointed to Christ *alone* as the Remitter."

So Calvin: "When Christ enjoins the apostles to forgive sins, He does not convey to them what is peculiar to Himself. It belongs to *Him* to forgive sins—He only enjoins them, in His name, to *proclaim* the forgiveness of sins."

Add to these the fact that Peter and John were sent down to Samaria to inspect and authorize the work done through Philip (Acts 8:14), that Peter said to Simon Magus, "I *perceive* that thou art in the gall of bitterness, and the bond of iniquity" (Acts 8:23), and that Paul wrote "To whom ye forgive anything, I also: for if I forgave anything, to whom I forgave it, for your sakes forgave I it *in the person of Christ*" (II Cor. 2:10), we have clear evidence of the *unique* authority and power of the apostles.

The question has been asked, Was this ministerial office and commission conferred on the apostles by Christ transferred by them to others? Again we quote Bishop Ryle, "I answer, without hesitation, that in the strictest sense the commission of the apostles *was not* transmitted, but was confined to them and St. Paul. I challenge any one to deny that the Apostles possessed certain ministerial qualifications which were quite peculiar to them, and which they could not, and did not, transmit to others. (1) They had the gift of declaring the Gospel without error, and with infallible accuracy, to an extent that no one after them did. (2) They confirmed their teachings by miracles. (3) They had the power of discerning spirits. In the strictest sense there is no such thing as apostolic succession."

In closing let us admire together the lovely typical picture which our passage contains. Here we have a wondrous portrayal of the essential features of *Christianity*: 1. Christ is known in a *new way*, no longer "after the flesh," but in spirit, on High. "Touch me not . . . ascended" (20:17). 2. Believers are given a *new title*—"brethren" (20:17). 3. Believers are told of a *new position*—Christ's position before the Father (20:17). 4. Believers occupy a *new place*—apart from the world (20:19). 5. Believers are assured of a *new blessing*—"peace" made and imparted (20:19, 21). 6. Believers are given a *new privilege*—the Lord Jesus in their midst (20:19). 7. Believers have a *new joy*—through a vision of the risen Lord (20:20). 8. Believers receive a *new commission*—sent into the world by the Son *as* He was sent by the Father (20:21). 9. Believers are a *new creation*—indicated by the "breathing" (20:22). 10. Believers have a *new Indweller*—even the Holy Spirit (20:22). How Divinely meet that all this was on the "*first* of the week"—indication of a *new beginning*, i.e., Christianity supplanting Judaism!!

The following questions are to aid the student on the closing section of John 20:—

1. What does the absence of Thomas teach us, v. 24?
2. What do his words in v. 25 prove?
3. What is the difference between the "Peace" of v. 26 and vv. 19, 21?
4. Why the great similarity between vv. 19 and 26?
5. What practical lesson does v. 28 teach?
6. What is the meaning of v. 29?

CHAPTER SIXTY-NINE

Christ and Thomas

John 20:24-31

Below is an Analysis of our present passage:—

1. The absence of Thomas, v. 24.
2. The scepticism of Thomas, v. 25.
3. Christ appears to Thomas, vv. 26, 27.
4. The confession of Thomas, v. 28.
5. Christ's last beatitude, v. 29.
6. The signs of Jesus, v. 30.
7. The purpose of this Gospel, v. 31.

In our last chapter we were occupied with the appearing of the Lord unto the apostles as they were assembled together in some room, probably the "upper-room" in which the Lord's Supper was instituted. But on this occasion one of the Eleven, Thomas, was absent. We are not expressly told *why* he was not present with his brethren, but from what we learn of him in other passages, from his words to the Ten when they told him of their having seen the Lord, and from Christ's own words to Thomas when He appeared unto the Eleven, it is almost impossible to avoid the conclusion that *unbelief* was the cause of his absence. In three different passages Thomas is mentioned in this Gospel, and on each occasion he evidenced a gloomy disposition. He was a man who looked on the darker side of things: he took despondent views both of the present and the future. Yet he was not lacking in courage, nor in loyalty and devotion to the Saviour.

The first time Thomas comes before us is in chapter 11. At the close of 10 we read how the enemies of Christ "sought again to take him; but he escaped out of their hand, and went away again beyond Jordan." While there, the sisters of Lazarus sent unto Him, acquainting Him with the sickness of their brother. After waiting two days, the Saviour said unto His disciples, "Let us go into Judea." The disciples at once reminded Him that it was there the Jews had, only lately, sought to stone Him; so they ask, "Goest thou thither again?" At the end of His colloquy with them, He said, "Let us go." And then we are told, "Thomas, which is called Didymus, said unto his fellow-disciples, Let us also go, that we may die with him" (11:16). These words throw not a little light on the character of him who uttered them. First, they reveal Thomas as a man of morbid feeling—*death* was the object which filled his vision. Second, they indicate he had an energetic disposition, "Let us *go*." Third, they exhibit his courage—he was ready *to go* even to death. Fourth, they manifest his affection for Christ—"Let us *also* go, that we may die *with him*."

The next time Thomas is brought to our notice is in chapter 14. The Lord had announced to the apostles that in a little while He would leave them, and whither He was going, they could not come. In consequence, they were filled with sadness. In view of their grief, the Lord said, "Let not your heart be troubled," supporting this with the comforting assurances that He was going to the Father's House, going there to prepare a place for them, and from which He would come and receive them unto Himself: ending with "Whither I go ye know, and the way ye know." Thomas was the first to reply, and his doleful response was, "Lord, we know not whither thou goest; and how can we know the way?" (14:5). Ignoring the precious promises of the Saviour, Thomas saw in His departure only the extinction of hope. Thus we behold, once more, his gloomy nature, and, in addition, his sceptical turn of mind. He reminds us very much of John Bunyan's "Fearing," "Despondency," and "Much Afraid," in his Pilgrim's Progress—types of a large class of Christians who are successors of doubting Thomas.

The third and last time that Thomas occupies any prominence in this Gospel is in the 20th chapter. Here the first thing noted about him is that he was not with the other disciples when the Lord appeared unto them. In view of what has been before us above, this is scarcely to be wondered at. "If the bare possibility of his Lord's death had plunged this loving yet gloomy heart into despondency, what dark despair must have preyed on it when that death was actually accomplished! How the figure of his dead Master had burnt itself into his soul, is seen from the manner in which his mind dwells on the prints of the nails, the wound in His side. It is by these only, and not by well-known features or peculiarity of form, he will recognize and identify his Lord. His heart was with the lifeless body on the cross, and he could not bear to see the friends of Jesus or speak with those who had shared his hopes, but buries his disappointment and desolation in solitude and silence. Thus it was that, like many melancholy persons, he missed the opportunity of seeing what would effectually have scattered his doubts!" (Mr. Dods).

"But Thomas, one of the twelve, called Didymus, was not with them when Jesus came" (20:24). The "But" is ominous and at once exposes the folly of the inventions which have been made to excuse Thomas. The disciples convened in the evening of that first day of the week under most unusual circumstances. John, at least, was satisfied that the Saviour had risen; of the others, some were sceptical, for they believed not the report of the women who had seen Him that very morning. No doubt the apostles assembled with mingled feeling of suspense and excitement. That Thomas was absent can only be accounted for, we believe, by what the other passages reveal of his gloomy and sceptical disposition. Note how the Holy Spirit has here added "Thomas called Didymus," which is evidently designed as a connecting link—cf. 11:16. On the resurrection day *he* least of all believed the tidings of the women, isolating himself in the sorrow of death in wilful unbelief—the wilfulness of it is seen in the next verse.

The state of Thomas' soul coincided with his absence on that memorable evening. He resisted the blessedness of the resurrection, and therefore did not join his brethren, and thus share the joy of the Master's presence in their midst. Slow of heart to believe, he remained for a whole week in darkness and gloom. One important lesson we may learn from this is, how much we lose by our failure to cultivate the fellowship of Christian brethren. "*Not* forsaking the assembling of ourselves together, as the manner of some is" (Heb. 10:25), is the word of Scripture. Two warnings against disobeying this were furnished in connection with Christ's resurrection. In Luke 24:13 we read, "And *behold*, two of them went that same day to a village called Emmaus, which was *from Jerusalem* about three score furlongs": mark the words in italics. These two disciples had turned their backs on their brethren in Jerusalem. Little wonder, then, that when the Lord Himself drew near to them "their eyes were holden that they should not know Him" (Luke 24:16). Yet even to them the Lord manifested His long-suffering grace by making Himself known (v. 31)! And what was the effect upon them? This: "They rose up the same hour, and *returned to Jerusalem* and found the eleven" (v. 33)! When Christians are in fellowship with Christ, they desire and seek the fellowship of His people; conversely, when they are out of fellowship with the Lord they have little or no desire for communion with believers. It was thus with Thomas. Out of fellowship with Christ, through unbelief, he forsook the assembly. And how much he lost! God's blessing, Christ's presence, the Holy Spirit's power, joy of heart, and in addition, a whole week spent in despondency. What a warning for us!

"The other disciples therefore said unto him, We have seen the Lord" (20:25). This is most blessed. The Ten were not callously indifferent to the welfare of their erring brother. They did not say, "O, well, there is no need for us to be troubled; *he* is the loser; if he had been in his proper place, he, too, would have seen the Saviour, heard His blessing of 'Peace be unto you,' and received the Holy Spirit; but he was *not* here, and it only serves him right that he should suffer for his negligence; let us leave him alone." O, no. The selfish world may reason and act thus; but not so those who are truly constrained by the love of Christ. The more we love Him, the more shall we love His people. So it was here. As soon as the Ten had been favoured with this gracious visit from the risen Redeemer, they *sought out Thomas* and communicated to him the glad tidings. How this rebukes some of us! If we were more in fellowship with Christ, we should have more heart for His wayward and wandering sheep. It is those who are "spiritual" that are exhorted to restore the one "overtaken in a fault" (Gal. 6:1)!

"But he said unto them, Except I shall see in his hands the print of the nails, and put my finger into the print of the nails, and thrust my hand into his side, I will not believe" (20:26). This illustrates the same principle so sadly exemplified in 20:18. Those who know Christ will bear testimony of Him to others, but they must be prepared for the unbelief of those whom they address. The Ten spoke to Thomas, but he believed them not. This also shows how that the best of men are subject to unbelief. Thomas had witnessed the resurrection of Lazarus, he had heard the Lord's promises that He *would* rise again on the third day, yet believed not now that He *was* risen. What point this gives to the admonition in Heb. 12:1, where we are exhorted to lay aside "*the* sin (unbelief) which doth so easily beset us!" Thomas refused to accredit the testimony of ten competent witnesses who had seen Christ with their own eyes, men who were his friends and brethren, and who could have no object in deceiving him. But he obstinately declares that he *will not* believe, unless he himself sees and touches the Lord's body. He presumes to prescribe the conditions which must be met before he is ready to receive the glad tidings. Thomas was still sceptical. Perhaps he asked his brethren. Why did not Christ remain with you? Where is He now? Why did He not show Himself to *me?* He implied, though he did not say it directly, that they were labouring under a delusion. And were *they* altogether blameless? They told Thomas "We have *seen* the Lord," but apparently they said nothing of the gracious and wondrous *words* which they had *heard* from His lips! Is there not a lesson, a warning, here for us? It is not *our experiences* which we are to proclaim, but *His words!*

"Except I shall see in his hands the print of the nails, and put my finger into the print of the nails and thrust my hand into his side, I will not believe." This is the only place in the New Testament where the "nails" which pierced the Saviour's hands and feet are actually mentioned. The Romans did not always use nails when crucifying criminals. Sometimes they bound the victims hands and feet to the cross by strong cords.

The fact that "nails" *were* used in connection with the Saviour, and the express mention of them here by Thomas, witnesses to the actual and literal fulfilment of Psa. 22:16: "they *pierced* my hands and my feet."

"And after eight days again, his disciples were within, and Thomas with them: then came Jesus, the doors being shut, and stood in the midst, and said, Peace be unto you" (20:26). "After eight days" signifies, according to the Jewish manner of reckoning time (who counted any part of a day as a whole one), after a week. It was, therefore, on the second Christian sabbath that the Eleven assembled together, this time Thomas being present. Observe that the Holy Spirit mentions the fact that again the doors were shut, for He would emphasize once more the supernatural character of the resurrection-body. The close similarity between this and 20:19 makes it plain that *this* visit of the Saviour was for the special benefit of Thomas. But mark a significant omission here: nothing is *now* said of their "fear of the Jews!" His "Peace be unto you" (20:19) had calmed their hearts and taken away their fear of men. It is one more witness to the power of the Word.

"And Thomas was with them: then came Jesus, the doors being shut, and stood in the midst and said, Peace be unto you." Marvelous grace was this. As we have said, this second manifestation of Christ unto the apostles was expressly made for the special benefit of Thomas. The Saviour made the same mysterious entrance through the closed doors and came with the same comforting salutation. There is much for us to learn from this. How patient and tender is the Lord with *dull* and *slow* believers! Forcefully does this come out here. Christ did not excommunicate His unbelieving disciple, but addressed to him the same word of "Peace" as He had previously saluted the Ten. O, how graciously does He bear with the waywardness and infirmities of His people. Timely are the admonitions of Bishop Ryle: "Let us take care that we drink into our Lord's spirit and copy His example. Let us never set down men in a low place, as graceless and godless, because their faith is feeble and their love is cold. Let us remember the case of Thomas, and be very pitiful and of tender mercy. Our Lord has many weak children in His family, many dull pupils in His school, many raw soldiers in His army, many lame sheep in His flock. Yet He bears with them all, and casts none away. Happy is that Christian who has learned to deal likewise with his brethren. There are many in the Family, who, like Thomas, are dull and slow, but for all that, like Thomas, are real and true believers."

"And said, Peace be unto you." This is the third time that we find the precious word on the lips of the Saviour in this chapter, and on each occasion it was used with a *different* design. The first (20:19), tells of the glorious *consequences of His atoning work*: peace has been made with God, peace is now imparted to those whose sins have been put away. The second (20:21), is His *provision for service,* using that word in its largest scope. It is this which supplies power for our walk, and it is only to the extent that the peace of God *is* ruling our hearts that we are able to rise above the hindrances of our path and the opposition of the flesh. But the third "Peace" is the *means of recovery.* This comes out most strikingly in the next verse. "*Then* saith he to Thomas, Reach hither thy finger, and *behold my hands*"—compare the "*when* he had *so* said ('Peace be unto you' 20:19) he showed unto them his hands and his side" (20:20).

"Then saith he to Thomas, Reach hither thy finger, and behold my hands; and reach hither thy hand, and thrust it into my side, and be not faithless but believing" (20:27). Thus the Lord did for Thomas what He had done for the Ten—He pointed out that which memorialized the *ground* on which true "peace" rests. The Lord went back to first principles with this erring disciple. Thomas needed to be re-established in the truths taught by the pierced hands and side of the Saviour, and therefore he got just what was required to restore his wandering soul. What a lesson for us! When we have gone astray, what is it that recalls us? Not occupation with the intricacies of prophecy or the finer points of doctrine (important and valuable as these are in their place) but the great foundation truth of the Atonement. It was the sight of the Saviour's *wounds* which scattered all Thomas' doubts, overcame his self-will, and brought him to the feet of Christ as an adoring worshipper. So it is with us. Have we grown cold and worldly; are we out of communion with the Lord Jesus—He recalls us to Himself by the same precious truth which first won our hearts. This is what breaks us down:—

"And yet to find Thee still the same—
'Tis this that humbles us with shame."

Was it not for this reason the Lord appointed the loaf and the cup for the Feast of remembrance! It is the emblems of His broken-body and poured-out blood which move the heart, quicken the spirit, thrill the soul, and rekindle the joy which we tasted when we first looked by faith upon His hands and side. This, then, we believe, is the force of the *connection* between 20:27 and what immediately precedes. What a lesson for us; the most effective way of dealing with backsliders is to tenderly remind them of the dying love of the Lord Jesus!

"Then saith he to Thomas, Reach hither thy finger, and behold my hands; and reach hither thy hand and thrust it into my side: and be not faithless but believing." While the link between this and the verse before is unspeakably blessed, yet the actual contents of it are most searching and solemn. The language which the Saviour here employed affords positive proof that He had heard the petulant and sceptical words of Thomas to his fellow-apostles—cf. 20:25. No one had seen the Lord as visibly present when Thomas gave utterance to his unbelief. None had reported his words to Christ. Yet was He fully acquainted with them! He had listened to the outburst of His disciple, and now makes Thomas aware of it. Wondrous proof was this of His omniscience! Searching warning is it for us! The One who died on Calvary's cross was "*God* manifest in flesh," and being God, He not only sees every deed we perform, but also hears every word that we utter. O that we might be more conscious, hour by hour, that the eye of Divine holiness is ever upon us, that the ear of the omnipresent One is ever open to all that we say, that He still stands in the midst of the seven golden candlesticks! To realize *this* is to walk "in the fear of God."

"Reach hither thy hand and thrust it into my side." What solemn light this casts upon what we read in 19:34. It must have been a *large wound* for the Lord to tell Thomas to thrust in his *hand!* What indignities the Saviour suffered for our sakes! Again, do not these wounds of Christ throw light upon the character of the resurrection body? Do they not argue strongly that our personal identity will survive the great transformation? It needs to be borne in mind that the bodies of those who sleep in the dust of the earth are not going to be re-created, but resurrected! And grand and glorious as will be the change from our present mortal bodies, yet it seems clear from several scriptures that our personal identity will be so preserved that recognition will not only be possible but certain.

"Be not faithless, but believing." "This is a rebuke and an exhortation at the same time. It is not merely a reproof to Thomas for his scepticism on this particular occasion, but an urgent counsel to be of a more believing turn of mind for the time to come. 'Shake off this habit of doubting, questioning, and discrediting every one. Give up thine unbelieving disposition. Become more willing to believe and trust.' No doubt the primary object of the sentence was to correct and chastise Thomas for his sceptical declaration to his brethren. But I believe our Lord had in view the further object of correcting Thomas' whole character, and directing his attention to his besetting sin. How many there are among us who ought to take to themselves our Lord's words! How faithless *we* often are, and how slow to believe!" (Bishop Ryle).

"And Thomas answered and said unto him, My Lord and my God" (20:28). How blessed! In a moment the doubter was transformed into a worshipper. Like Paul (Acts 26:19), Thomas "was not disobedient to the heavenly vision." There was no room for scepticism now, no occasion for him to put his finger "into the print of the nails," and thrust his hand "into his side" (20:25). The language of Christ in the next verse—"Because thou hast *seen* me, thou hast believed"—makes it clear that Thomas *did not do* as he had boasted. There was no need for him to handle Christ now: his *intellectual* doubts had vanished because his *heart* was satisfied! The words of Thomas on this occasion gave evidence of his faith *in* Christ, his subjection *to* Him, and his affection *for* Him.

"And Thomas answered and said unto him, My Lord and my God." This is the only time in the Gospels that anyone owned Christ as "*God.*" And what was it that evoked this blessed testimony? The context tells us. The fact that Christ knew the very words which he had used, satisfied Thomas that Immanuel stood before him; hence his worshipful confession. And when *we* meet Him in the air, see the glory streaming through His pierced hands and side ("He had bright beams out of His *side!*" Hab. 3:4), when we hear His "Peace be unto you," when we perceive that He knows all about us, *we* too shall cry "My Lord and my God."

How marvelous are the ways of Divine grace. Doubting Thomas was the one who gave the strongest and most conclusive testimony to the absolute Deity of the Saviour which ever came from the lips of a man! Just as the railing thief became the one to own Christ's Lordship from the cross, just as timid Joseph and Nicodemus were the ones who honoured the dead body of the Saviour, just as the women were the boldest at the sepulchre, just as unfaithful Peter was the one whom Christ bade "Feed my sheep," just as the prime persecutor of the early church became the apostle to the Gentiles, so the sceptical and materialistic Thomas was the one to say "My Lord and my God." Where sin abounded, grace *did* much more abound!

"And Thomas answered and said unto him, My Lord and my God." Mark the word "said unto him." It was no mere ejaculation. Thomas was not here speaking to the Father nor of the Father, but to and of the Son. The fact that Thomas addressed Him as "my *Lord*" evidences that he too had now "received the Holy Spirit" (cf. 20:22), for "no man can say that Jesus is the Lord, but by the Holy Spirit" (I Cor. 12:3). It is very striking to contrast what we read of in I Kings 18:39. When Elijah met the prophets of Baal on Mount Carmel, and in response to his faith and prayer, Jehovah was pleased to manifest Himself by sending fire from heaven to consume the sacrifice and lick up the water; the people exclaimed, "The Lord, he is the God, the Lord, he is the God." But Thomas here did far more than this: he not only acknowledged that Jesus of Nazareth was Lord and God, but he confessed Him as "*my* Lord and *my* God." And how striking that *this* is recorded in connection with the *third* notice of Thomas, and the third appearance of the resurrected Christ in this Gospel – it is only as risen from the dead the Lord Jesus could be *our* Lord and God!

"And Thomas answered and said unto him, My Lord and my God." "This noble confession of Thomas admits of only one meaning: it was a blessed testimony to our Lord's Deity. It was a clear, unmistakable declaration that Thomas believed Him, when he saw Him that day, to be not only man, but God. And, above all, it was a testimony which our Lord received and did not prohibit and a declaration which He did not say one word to rebuke. When Cornelius fell down at the feet of Peter and would have worshipped him, the apostle refused such honour at once: 'Stand up; I myself am a man' (Acts 10:26). When the people of Lystra would have done sacrifice to Paul and Barnabas, 'they rent their clothes and ran in among the people, saying, Sirs, why do ye these things? We are men of like passions with you,' Acts 14:15. (When John fell down to worship before the feet of the angel, he said unto him, 'See thou do it not': Rev. 22:8, 9. – A.W.P.). But when Thomas said to Jesus, 'My Lord and my God,' the words do not elicit a syllable of reproof from our holy and truth-loving Master. Can we doubt that these things were written for our learning?

"Let us settle it firmly in our minds that the Deity of Christ is one of the grand foundation truths of Christianity, and let us be willing to go to the stake rather than deny it. Unless our Lord Jesus is very God of very God, there is an end of His mediation, His atonement, His priesthood, His whole work of redemption. These doctrines are useless blasphemies unless Christ is God. Forever let us bless God that the Deity of our Lord is taught everywhere in the Scriptures, and stands on evidence that can never be overthrown. Above all, let us daily repose our sinful selves on Christ with undoubting confidence, as one that is perfect God as well as perfect man. He is man, and therefore can be touched with the feeling of our infirmities. He is God, and therefore 'is able to save unto the uttermost them that come unto God by him.' That Christian has no cause to fear who can look to Jesus by faith and say with Thomas, 'My Lord and my God.'" (Bishop Ryle).

"Jesus saith unto him, Thomas, because thou hast seen me, thou hast believed: blessed are they that have not seen, and yet have believed" (20:29). Christ accepted Thomas' confession, but reminded him that it was occasioned by outward signs, the appeal to his sight. What a warning against the modern craving for "signs"—a tendency upon which Satan is now trading in many directions. And how it condemns those materialists who say they will not believe in anything which they cannot examine with their physical senses! Thomas had insisted upon *seeing* the risen Christ, and the Lord graciously granted his request. The result was he believed. But the Lord pointed out to His disciple that there is a greater blessedness resting on those who have never seen Him in the flesh, yet who have believed—an expression which looked back to the Old Testament saints as well as forward to us! This was the last of our Lord's beatitudes.

"Blessed are they that have not seen, and yet have believed." What a precious word is this for *our* hearts. *We* have never seen Him in the flesh. Here, then, is a promise for us. Should it be asked: How do you *know* that the rejected One is now in the glory? the answer would be, Because of His own word that when He went there He would send down to His people the Holy Spirit. Therefore, every joy in God which we now have, every longing for Christ, manifests His Spirit's presence in our souls, and this is a precious testimony to the fact that Christ is now on High. These manifestations of the Spirit *here* are the proofs that Christ is *there*. They are the antitype of the "bells" on the robe of the high priest when he went unto the holy of holies on the Day of Atonement (see Ex. 28:33-35). As the people listened on the outside, they *heard* the unseen movements of their representative within; so we are conscious of the presence of *our* High Priest in the Holiest by the *tongues* of the "bells"—the sweet testimony now borne to us by the Holy Spirit. And *why* is there a greater blessedness pronounced on us than upon those who saw Christ during the days when He tabernacled among men? Because *we* own Him during the day of His rejection, and therefore *He* is more honoured by such faith! It is *faith* in Himself, faith which rests alone on the Word, which Christ pronounces "blessed."

"And many other signs truly did Jesus in the presence of his disciples, which are not written in this book" (20:30). This and the following verse comes in parenthetically. The whole of chapter 20 is occupied with a recountal of the appearance of the risen Christ unto His own, and this is continued in chapter 21 as the very first verse shows. We take it that the "many other signs" refer not to what the Lord had done through the whole course of His public ministry, but to the proofs which the risen Christ had furnished His apostles. This is confirmed by the words "Many other signs truly did Jesus *in the presence of his disciples,*" whereas, most of His ministerial signs were performed before the general public. There *were* other signs which the Saviour gave to the Eleven which proved that He had risen from the dead, but the Holy Spirit did not move *John* to record them. Some of them are described in the Synoptics. For example, His appearing to the two disciples on the way to Emmaus (Luke 24:15), His eating in the presence of the Eleven (Luke 24:43), His opening their understandings to understand the Scriptures (Luke 24:45), His appearing to them in Galilee (Matt. 28:16), His declaration that all power was given unto Him in heaven and earth (Matt. 28:18), His commissioning them to make disciples of all nations, baptising them in the name of the triune God (Matt. 28:19, 20). Others of these "signs" are recorded in Acts 1, I Cor. 15, etc. When John says that these "other signs" which Jesus did are not written in *this* book [the fourth Gospel], he implies that they *are* in some other book or books. On this, one has quaintly said, "St. John generously recognizes the existence of other books beside his own, and disclaims the idea of his Gospel being the only one which Christians ought to read. Happy is that author which can humbly say 'My book does not contain everything about the subject it handles. There are other books about it. Read them.'"

"But these are written, that ye might believe that Jesus is the Christ, the Son of God; and that believing ye might have life through his name" (20:31). Here the Holy Spirit tells why the resurrection-signs of Christ mentioned by John *are* recorded in this Gospel. They are written not merely to furnish us with historical information about the Lord Jesus, but that we might *believe* on Him! They are written that we might believe on Him *as* "the Christ," the Messiah, the anointed One – Him to whom the Old Testament prophets pointed. They are written that we might believe on Jesus *as* "the Son of God," the second Person of the Godhead incarnate, the One whose Divine glories are unfolded more particularly in the New Testament. And they are written that we might believe on Him thus in order that we might have "life through his name." It is *faith* in the *written* revelation which God has given of His Son which brings "life" and all that is included in that word – salvation, immortality, eternal glory. Reader, hast *thou* "believed"? Not *about* Christ, but *in* Him? Have you received Him as your Lord and *Saviour?* If so, the blessing of Heaven rests upon you. If not, you are, even now, "under condemnation," and if you remain in your wicked unbelief there awaits you nought but "the blackness of darkness forever."

The following questions are to help the student on John 21:1-14.

1. Why did not the disciples recognize Christ, v. 4?
2. Why did Christ ask the question in v. 5?
3. What does Peter's act denote, v. 7?
4. Why mention the "fire of coals," v. 9?
5. Why was not the net broken, v. 11?
6. What is the spiritual significance of vv. 12, 13?

CHAPTER SEVENTY

Christ by the Sea of Tiberias

John 21:1-14

The following is an Analysis of our present passage:—

1. Christ's third appearing to the apostles, vv. 1, 14.
2. The seven on the sea, vv. 2, 3.
3. Their dulness and emptiness, vv. 4, 5.
4. The miracle of the fishes, v. 6.
5. John's recognition and Peter's response, v. 7.
6. The landing of the six, vv. 8, 9.
7. Christ's welcome, vv. 10-13.

The opening verses of this Gospel are in the nature of a Prologue, so the closing chapter is more or less an Epilogue. In the former, the Holy Spirit has set forth what Christ was *before* He came forth from the Father; in the latter He has shown, in mystical guise, how He now rules the world *after* His return to the Father. "The prologue is intended to exhibit the external life of Christ as it preceded His manifestation in the world; the epilogue appears to have for its scope, to exhibit His spiritual sway in the world as it would continue after He had left it" (Lange). All here has a profound significance. The disciples are on the sea; the Lord, no longer with them, directs from the shore, manifesting His power by working with them in their seemingly lonesome toil, and exhibiting His love in providing food for them. Then the charge is left to "feed his sheep." His final word was a reference to His coming again.

The varied details of chapter 21 supply a most instructive and marvelously complete lesson on *service*. In the previous chapter we have seen the Saviour establishing the hearts of the apostles by His word of "Peace," endowing them with the Holy Spirit, and then commissioning them to proclaim remission of sins.

Here we have, in symbolic form, the apostles engaged in active ministry. The *order* is most suggestive. What we receive from the Lord Jesus is to be used for the good of others. Freely we have received, freely we are now to give. The key to the practical significance of the scene here portrayed lies in the almost identical circumstances when the apostles received their first ministerial call—Luke 5.

The chapter as a whole falls into *seven* parts as we analyze it from the viewpoint of its teaching on *service*. First, we see men serving in the energy of the flesh (21:2, 3). Peter says, "I go a fishing." He had received no call from God to do so. His action illustrates self-will, and the response of the other six men acting under human leadership. Second, we are shown the barrenness of such efforts (21:3-5). They toiled all night, but caught nothing, and when the Lord asked if they had any meat, they had to answer, No. Third, the Lord now directs their energies, telling them where to work (21:6): the result was that the net was filled with fishes. Fourth, we learn of the Lord's gracious provision for His servants (21:12, 13): He had provided for them, and invites them to eat. Fifth, we are taught what is the only acceptable motive for service—love to Christ (21:15, 17). Sixth, the Lord makes known how that *He* appoints the time and manner of the death of those of His servants who die (21:18, 19). Seventh, the Lord concludes by leaving with them the prospect of His return; not *for* death, but *for* Himself they should look (21:20:24).

The miracle in John 21 stands alone: it is the only recorded one which Christ wrought after His resurrection, and most fittingly is it the last narrated in this Gospel. Its striking resemblance to the first miracle which some of these disciples had witnessed (Luke 5:1-11) must have brought to their remembrance the very similar circumstances under which they had been called by Christ to leave their occupation as fishermen and become fishers of men. Thus they would be led to interpret this present "sign" by the past one, and see in it a ***renewed summons*** to their work of catching men, and a renewed assurance that their labour in the Lord would not be in vain. Suitably was it the *last* miracle which they witnessed at the hands of their

Master, for it supplied a symbol which would continually animate them to and in their service for Him. It was designed to assure them that just as He had prospered their efforts while He was with them in the flesh, so they could count on His guidance, power, and blessing when He was absent from them.

This *final* miracle of the Saviour was performed in Galilee, so also was His *first* (i.e., the turning of the water into wine), and it seems clear that the Holy Spirit would have us use the law of comparison and contrast again. The author of "The Companion Bible" has called attention to quite a number of striking correspondences between the two miracles: we mention a few, leaving the interested reader to work out the others for himself. In both miracles there is a striking background: in the one we have the confession of Nathanael (1:49); in the other, the confession of Thomas (20:28). The first miracle was on "the third day" (2:1); the latter was "the third time" the Lord showed Himself to the apostles (21:14). The one was occasioned by them having "no wine" (2:3); the other, by them having no fish (21:3, 5). In both the Lord uttered a command: "Fill the waterpots" (2:7); "Cast the net" (21:6). In both Christ furnished a bountiful supply: the water pots were "filled to the brim" (2:7); "the net *full* of great fishes" (21:11). In both a number is mentioned: "six waterpots" (2:6); "one hundred and fifty and three fishes" (21:11). In both Christ manifested His Deity (2:11; 21:12, 14). How much we lose by not carefully *comparing* scripture with scripture!

"After these things Jesus showed himself again to the disciples at the sea of Tiberias; and on this wise showed he" (21:1). "After these things" always marks off a distinct section in John's writings. The earlier appearances of the risen Saviour were in view of the then condition and need of the apostles to establish their faith and assure their hearts. But here, what the Lord did and said, had a prophetic significance, anticipating and picturing His future relations to them.

"Jesus showed himself," not presenting Himself, but *manifested* His presence, power, and glory. It was not simply that the disciples *saw* him, but that he *revealed* Himself. "His body after the resurrection was only visible by a distinct act of His will. From that time the disciples did not, as before, *see* Jesus, but He *appeared* unto them. It is not for nothing that the language is changed. Henceforth, He was to be recognized not by the flesh, but by the spirit; not by human faculties, but by Divine perceptions: His disciples were to walk by faith, and not by sight" (Chrysostom). When we are told in Acts 1:3 that the Lord Jesus was "seen of them forty days," it does not mean that the Lord was corporeally present with them throughout this period, nor that He was seen by them each day. He was visible and invisible, appeared in one form or another, according to His own pleasure.

"At the sea of Tiberias." In 6:1 we read, "The sea of Galilee, which is the sea of Tiberias," the latter being its Roman name. In Matt. 28:10 we learn that the risen Saviour had said to the women at the sepulchre, "Go tell my brethren that they go into Galilee, and *there* shall they see me." This, then, explains the presence of the seven disciples here in Galilee. Where the other four were, and why they had not yet arrived, we do not know. But it seems clear that these seven had no business there at the sea, for Matt. 28:16 distinctly says, "The eleven disciples went away into Galilee, into a *mountain* where Jesus had *appointed* them." It looks very much as though Peter was restless, and while waiting the coming of the other apostles he said, "I go a fishing" – to the last we see his energetic nature at work. Others have suggested that the reason they went a fishing was in order that they might obtain food for a meal, and possibly this did supply an additional motive – cf. 21:12.

"There were together Simon Peter, and Thomas called Didymus, and Nathanael of Cana in Galilee, and the sons of Zebedee, and two other of his disciples" (21:2). Peter being mentioned first intimates that the enumeration here is the order of *grace*. "Thomas" occupying the second place in the list is a further indication of this. The removal of his doubts had restored the Eleven to unity of faith, and prepared them for mutual fellowship again. "There were *together* Simon Peter *and* Thomas," which is a beautiful contrast from 20:24 – "But

Thomas was *not with* them!" Thomas is named next to Peter, as if he now kept closer to the meetings of the apostles than ever. "It is well if losses by our neglect make us more careful afterwards not to let opportunities slip" (Matthew Henry). Of "Nathanael" we read elsewhere only in 1:45-51: probably he is the "Bartholomew" of Matt. 10:3. Next come the "sons of Zebedee," emphasizing their *fishermen*-character. This is the only place where John *does not* refer to himself as "the disciple whom Jesus loved": the absence of this expression here being in full accord with the fact that it is the order of *grace* which is before us. Who the other two disciples were we are not told.

"Simon Peter saith unto them, I go a fishing. They say unto him, We also go with thee. They went forth and entered into a ship immediately; and that night they caught nothing" (21:3). That Peter is here seen taking the lead is in full accord with what we read elsewhere of his impulsive and impetuous nature. Most of the commentators consider that the disciples were fully justified in acting as they did on this occasion. But the Lord had not given them orders to fish for any but *men*. It seems to us, therefore, that they were acting according to the promptings of nature. The fact that it was *night-time* also suggests that they were not walking as children of light. Nor did the Lord appear to them during that night: they were left to themselves! The further fact that they "caught nothing" is at least a warning hint that servants of the Lord cannot count on His blessing when *they* choose the time and place of their labours, and when they run, unsent. These beloved disciples had to be taught in their own experience, as we all have to be, the truth which the Lord had enunciated just before His death—"Without me, ye can do nothing" (15:5); not, a little, but *nothing!* The further fact that we are told, "*They* went forth, and entered into a ship *immediately*" as soon as Peter had said, "I go a fishing," instead of first looking to God for guidance, or weighing what Peter had said, supplies further evidence that the whole company was acting in the energy of the flesh—a solemn warning for each of God's servants to wait on the Lord for their instructions instead of taking them from a human leader!

"But when the morning was now come, Jesus stood on the shore; but the disciples knew not that it was Jesus" (21:4). The "But" here adds further confirmation to what we have said above on 21:3. That these disciples now failed to recognize the Saviour indicates that their *spiritual* faculties were not then in exercise. It seems evident that they were not expecting Him. And how often He draws near to us and we know it not! And how often our acting in the energy of the flesh and following the example of human leaders is the cause of this! In the Greek, the closing words of this verse are identical with those found at the end of 20:14: "and [Mary] knew not that it was Jesus." She was immersed in sorrow, occupied with death, and she recognized not the Saviour. These men had returned to their worldly calling, and were occupied with their bodily needs and recognized Him not. Surely these things are written for *our* learning!

"Then Jesus saith unto them, Children, have ye any meat? They answered him, No" (21:5). Our Lord's form of address here is also searchingly suggestive. He did not use the term of endearment employed in 13:33, "Little children," but employed the more general form of salutation, which the margin renders "Sirs." He spoke not according to the intimacies of love, but as from a distance—a further hint from the Spirit as to how we are to interpret 21:2, 3. But why did He ask: "Have ye any meat?" He knew, of course, that they had none; what, then, was the purpose of His enquiry? Was it not designed to draw from them a confession of their failure, ere He met their need? And is not this ever His way with His own? Before He furnishes the abundant supply, we must first be made conscious of our emptiness. Before He gives strength, we must be made to feel our weakness. Slow, painfully slow, are we to learn this lesson; and slower still to *own* our nothingness and take the place of helplessness before the Mighty One. The disciples on the sea picture *us*, here in this world; the Saviour on the shore (whither we are bound) Christ in Heaven. How blessed, then, to behold Him occupied with us below, and *speaking* to us from "the shore!" It was not the disciples who addressed the Lord, but He who spoke to them!

"And He said unto them, Cast the net on the right side of the ship, and ye shall find" (21:6). How this evidences the Deity of the One here speaking to these disciples! *He* knew on which side of the ship the net should be cast. But more, did it not show them, and us, that He is sovereign of the sea? These men had fished all their lives, yet had they toiled throughout that night and taken nothing. But here was the Lord telling them to cast their net but once, and assuring them they *should* find. Was it not He, by His invisible power, that *drew* the fishes into their net! And what a striking line is this picture of Christian *service*. How He tells the servants that success in their ministry is due not to their eloquence, their power of persuasion, or *their* any thing, but due alone to *His* sovereign drawing-power. A most blessed foreshadowment did the Saviour here give the apostles of the Divine blessing which should rest upon their labours for Him. In full and striking accord with this was the fact that the Lord bade them "Cast the net on the *right* side of the ship"—cf. Matthew 25:34: "Then shall the king say unto them on his *right* hand, Come, ye blessed of my Father, inherit the kingdom prepared for you *from the foundation of the world!*"

"They cast, therefore, and now they were not able to draw it for the multitude of fishes" (21:6). This is very striking. The Lord was a hundred yards away from them (21:8), yet they heard plainly what He said. Again: He was, so far as their recognition of Him at the moment, an entire stranger to them. Moreover, notwithstanding the fact that they had fished all night and caught nothing, and had already drawn up the net into the boat, as being useless to prolong their efforts; nevertheless, they now promptly cast it into the sea again. How strikingly this demonstrated once more the power of *the Word*—in making them hear His voice, in overcoming whatever scruples they may have had, in moving their hearts to prompt obedience. Verily, "all power in heaven and in earth" *is* His. In the abundant intake the disciples were taught that in "keeping his commandments there is great reward" (Psa. 19:11). And what a lesson for those who seek to serve: *His* it is to issue orders, *ours* to obey—unmurmuringly, unquestioningly, promptly.

"Therefore that disciple whom Jesus loved saith unto Peter, It is the Lord" (21:7). This is in perfect keeping with what we read elsewhere about John—the most devoted of the apostles, *he* possessed the most spiritual discernment. He was the one who leaned on the Master's breast at the supper, and to whom the Lord communicated the secret of the betrayer's identity (13:23-26). He was the one that was nearest to the cross, and to whose care the Saviour committed His mother (19:26, 27). He it was who was the first of the Eleven to perceive that the Lord had risen from the dead (20:8). So here, he was the first of the seven to identify the One on the shore. How perfectly harmonious are the Scriptures! "The tenderest love has the first and surest instincts of the object beloved" (Stier). And what a lesson is here again for the Lord's servants: when He grants success to our labours, when the Gospel-net in our hands gathers fishes, let us not forget to own "It is the *Lord!*" To how much more may and should this principle be applied. As we admire the beauties of nature, as we observe the orderliness of her laws, as we receive countless mercies and blessings every day, let *us* say "It is the *Lord!*" So, too, when our plans go awry, when disappointment, affliction, persecution comes our way, still let us own "It is the *Lord!*" It is not blind chance which rules our lives, but the One who died for us on the cross.

"Now when Simon Peter heard that it was the Lord, he girt his fisher's coat unto him (for he was naked) and did cast himself into the sea" (21:7). This was in full keeping with Peter's character: if John was the first to recognize Christ, Peter was the first to act! Nor do we believe that it was mere impulsiveness which prompted him—his collectedness in first girding himself with the outer garment makes decisively against such a superficial conclusion. Peter, too, was devoted to Christ, deeply so, and it was *love* which here made him impatient to reach Christ. Peter's action makes us recall that night on the stormy sea when the Saviour walked on the waves toward the ship in which the disciples were. Peter it was, then, who said unto the Lord, "Bid me come unto thee on the water" (Matt. 14:28), for he could not wait for his Beloved to reach him. Beautiful it is now to observe that there was ***no reserve*** about

Peter. In the interval between Matt. 14 and John 21, he had basely denied his Master; but in the interval, too, and after the denial, he had heard His "Peace be unto you," and, plainly, this reassuring word had been treasured up in his heart. Observe that Peter left the net full of fishes for Christ, like the Samaritan woman who left her waterpot. The "girding" of himself evidences the deep reverence in which he held the Saviour!

"And the other disciples came in a little ship (for they were not far from the land, but as it were two hundred cubits) dragging the net with fishes" (21:8). Love does not act uniformly; it expresses itself differently, through various temperaments. John did not jump out of the ship, though he was equally devoted as Peter, nor did the other five. The six remained in the skiff or punt which usually accompanied the large fishing vessels, so as to draw the net full of fishes safely to land; illustrating the fact that faithful evangelists will not desert those who have been saved under their preaching, but will labour with them, care for them, and do all in their power to ensure their safely reaching the shore. The parenthetical remark seems to be brought in here to emphasize the miraculous character of this catch of fish, and to teach us that sometimes converts to Christ will be found in the most *unlikely* places— the net was cast *close in* to the shore!

"As soon then as they were come to land, they saw a fire of coals there, and fish laid thereon, and bread" (21:9). This is most blessed. It illustrates once more the precious truth that Jesus Christ is "the same yesterday, and to-day and forever." Even in His resurrection-glory He was not unmindful of their physical needs. Ever thoughtful, ever compassionate for His own, the Saviour here showed His toiling disciples that He cared for their bodies as well as their souls: "For he knoweth our frame; he *remembereth* that we are dust" (Psa. 103:14). We doubt not that this provision of His was miraculously produced: the fire, the fish on it, and the bread by its side, were the creations of Him who has but to will a thing and it is done. It is surely significant that the food which Christ here provided for the disciples was of the same variety as that with which He had fed the hungry multitude close by the same sea. The *fish* and the *bread* would doubtless recall the earlier miracle to the minds of the apostles.

"They saw a fire of coals there, and fish laid thereon, and bread." What is the deeper significance of this? First, it tells us of the Lord's care for His servants, and is the concrete pledge that He *will* supply all their need. Second, the Lord has left us an example to follow: if the Son of God condescended to spread this table for His children after their night of toil, let us not think it beneath us to take loving forethought whenever we have the opportunity of ministering to the physical comfort of His servants: even a cup of water given in His name will yet be rewarded. Third, it signifies that in the midst of labouring for others, *our own* souls need warming and feeding—a lesson which many a servant of God has failed to heed. Fourth, the fact that there were fish already on the fire *before* the disciples drew their full net to land, intimates that the Lord is not *restricted* to the labours of His servants, but that He can and does save souls altogether apart from human instrumentality—another thing we need to take to heart these days when *man* is so much magnified. Finally, does not this gracious provision of Christ forecast the refreshment and satisfaction which will be ours when our toiling on the troublous sea of this world shall be ended, and we are safely landed on the Heavenly shore!

"Jesus saith unto them, Bring of the fish which ye have now caught" (21:10). "In this verse our Lord calls on the disciples to bring proof that, in casting the net at His command, they had not laboured in vain. It was the second word that He spake to them, we must remember, on this occasion. The first saying was, 'Cast the net on the right side of the ship, and ye shall find.' The second saying was, 'Bring of the fish which ye have now caught,' with a strong emphasis on the word 'now.' I believe our Lord's object was to show the disciples that the secret of success was to work at His command, and to act with implicit obedience to His word. It is as though He had said, 'Draw up the net, and see for yourselves how profitable it is to do what I tell you.' Fish for food they did not want now, for it was provided for them. Proof of the power of Christ's blessing, and the importance of working under Him was the lesson to be taught, and as they drew up the net they would learn it" (Bishop Ryle). This also is in full accord with the fact that the *practical* teaching of this chapter is instruction upon *service*.

"Bring of the fish which ye have now caught." Is there not also a *spiritual* hint in this verse? The "fish" symbolize the souls which the Lord enables His servants to gather in. In bidding them bring of the fish *to Him*, He intimated they would have fellowship together, not only in labouring, but also in enjoying the fruits of it! It reminds us of His words in 4:36: "He that reapeth receiveth wages, and gathereth fruit unto life eternal: that both he that soweth and he that reapeth may *rejoice together*." The Lord delights in *sharing* His joy with us. Beautifully is this brought out again in Luke 15:6: "When he cometh home, he calleth together his friends and neighbours, saying unto them, Rejoice *with me*; for I have found my sheep which was lost." How marvelous the grace which here said to the disciples: "Bring of the fish which *ye* have now caught!"

"Simon Peter went up and drew the net to land full of great fishes, an hundred and fifty and three; and for all there were so many, yet was not the net broken" (21:11). Peter drew the net to land: how remarkable is this in view of what is said in 21:6: "*They* were not able to draw it for the multitude of fishes." Surely this points another important lesson in connection with *service*. What six men had been unable to do in their own strength, one man now did when he went to his work from the feet of Christ! Peter was weaker than gossamer thread when he followed his Lord afar off; but in His presence, a sevenfold power came upon him! A similar example is found in Judges 6:14: "The Lord looked upon him [Gideon] and said, Go *in this* thy might." The place of strength is still at the feet of the Saviour, and strength will be imparted exactly in proportion as we are in conscious fellowship with Him and drawing from His infinite fullness. "*He* giveth power to the faint; and to them that have no might he increaseth strength. Even the youths shall faint and be weary, and the young men shall utterly fail;

but they that wait upon the Lord shall renew their strength; they shall mount up with wings as eagles; they shall run, and not be weary; and they shall walk, and not faint" (Isa. 40:29-31). How much each of us need to heed that word, "Wait on the Lord, be of good courage, and he shall strengthen thine heart; wait, I say, on the Lord" (Psa. 27:14). How lamentable, and how humbling, that we are so slow to avail ourselves of the unfailing strength which is to be found in Him; found for the feeblest who will wait on Him in simple faith and earnest entreaty.

"Simon Peter went up, and drew the net to land full of great fishes, an hundred and fifty and three; and for all there were so many, yet was not the net broken." There are two details here upon which the ingenuity of many have been freely exercised: the number of the fish, and the not breaking of the net. There is little room to doubt that Peter would recall the miraculous draught of fishes on a former occasion, when the net *did* break (Luke 5). On that occasion the miracle was followed by the Lord saying unto Simon, "From henceforth thou shalt catch *men*." There it is the work of the *evangelist* which is in view, and therefore there is *no* numbering, for it is impossible for him to count up those who are saved under his Gospel message. Following this second miraculous draught, the Lord said unto Simon, "Feed my *sheep*." Here it is the work of the *pastor* or *teacher* which is in view, and hence there *is* numbering, for he ought to be able to determine which are sheep and which are goats. In the former the net breaks, for though many profess to believe the Gospel, yet few really do so to the saving of their souls. In the latter, the net breaks not, for none of the *elect* (the "right" side of the ship) shall perish. As for the *spiritual* meaning of the numbering of the fish here, observe that they were not counted *till the end*, not in 21:6, but in 21:11; not while in the ship, but *after* "the land" is reached! Not till we come to Heaven shall we know the number of God's elect!

"Jesus saith unto them, Come and dine" (21:12). How beautifully this evidenced the fact that He was still the same loving, gracious, condescending One as in the days of His humiliation! The disciples were not kept at a distance. They were invited to draw near, and partake of the provision which His own compassion had supplied. So He still says to the one who responds to His knocking, "I will come in to him and sup with him, and he with me" (Rev. 3:20). Here for the last time we hear His blessed and familiar "Come." "Come" not "Go." He did not send them away, but invited them to Himself.

"And none of the disciples durst ask him, Who art thou? knowing that it was the Lord" (21:12). "This statement is by no means to be understood as implying any doubt, but on the contrary a full persuasion that it was Christ Himself. Yet may we infer from it the change which had passed upon *Him,* and the awe which possessed *them,* after His resurrection. He was the same, and yet not the same. There was so much of His former appearance as to preclude doubtfulness; there was so much of change as to prevent all curious and carnal questioning. They sat down to the meal in silence, wondering at, while at the same time they well knew, Him Who was thus their Host" (Mr. G. Brown). It was reverence for Him which suppressed their inquiries.

"Jesus then cometh, and taketh bread, and giveth them, and fish likewise" (21:13). As Master of the feast, as Head of the family he now dispensed His mercies. But we may observe that no longer does the Lord give thanks before meat with His guests, as formerly He did (6:11). Then, it was as the perfect Man, the Servant ministering, that He gave thanks to God, with and for and before them all, for what God had given them: but now, as God, He Himself gives, and requires them to recognize Him as the Lord. There, it was His humanity which was the more prominent; here, His Deity. Yet how unspeakably blessed to observe that this One who is now "crowned with glory and honour" was still *their* Minister, caring for them! Not only was this the emblem of that spiritual fellowship which it is our unspeakable privilege to enjoy with Christ even now, but also the pledge of the future relations which will exist. Even in a coming day "He will 'gird' Himself, and make them to sit down to meat, and will come forth and *serve them*" (Luke 12:37). He will yet give us to "eat of the tree of life" (Rev. 2:7), and of the "hidden manna" (Rev. 2:17).

"This is now the third time that Jesus showed himself to his disciples, after that he was risen from the dead" (21:14). This does not mean that the Lord made but three appearances in all, but the third that John was led to record: the other two he mentions, are found in chapter 20. It should be remembered that during the "forty days" of Acts 1, which intervened between His resurrection and ascension, Christ did not consort with His disciples as before, but only showed Himself to them occasionally.

It is deeply interesting to compare the record found in Luke 5 of the earlier miraculous draught of fishes; there are a number of comparisons and contrasts. Both took place at the sea of Galilee; both were preceded by a night of fruitless toil; both evidenced the supernatural power of Christ; both were followed by a commission to Peter. But in the former, the Lord was in the ship; here, on the shore: in the one the net broke, in the other it did not: the one was at the beginning of Christ's public ministry; the latter, after His resurrection: in the former, Peter's commission was to fish for "men"; in the latter, to feed Christ's "sheep"; in the one the number of fishes is not given; in the latter it is.

The following questions are to aid the student on our final section:—

1. Why after "they had dined" did Christ speak, v. 15?
2. Why did Christ ask Peter v. 15?
3. What is the difference between Peter's three commissions, vv. 15, 16, 17?
4. What is meant by "grieved," v. 17?
5. Why did Peter turn around, v. 20?
6. What should Christ's rebuke teach us, v. 22?
7. What is the force of v. 25?

CHAPTER SEVENTY-ONE

Christ and Peter

John 21:15-25

The following is an Analysis of our final section: —

1. The threefold question, vss. 15, 17.
2. The threefold reply, vv. 15, 17.
3. The threefold commission, vv. 15, 17.
4. Christ's prophecy concerning Peter's death, vv. 18, 19.
5. Peter's question concerning John, vv. 20, 21.
6. Christ's reply, vv. 22, 23.
7. John's final testimony, vv. 24, 25.

The final section of this truly wondrous and most blessed Gospel contains teaching greatly needed by our fickle and feeble hearts. The central figures are the Lord and Simon Peter, and what we have here is the sequel to what was before us in chapter thirteen, the Lord washing the feet of His disciples. There, too, Peter was to the fore, and that because he occupies the position of a representative believer; that is, his fall and the cause of it, his restoration and the means employed for it, illustrate the experiences of the Christian and the provisions which Divine grace has made for him. Before we take this up in detail let us add that, just as in the first part of John 21 we have, in symbol, the confirmation of the calling of the Apostles to be fishers of men, so in this second section we have the final establishment of the one to whom the keys of the kingdom were entrusted.

The first thing recorded in connection with Peter's fall is our Lord's words to him before it took place: "Simon, Simon, behold, Satan hath desired to have you, that he may sift you as wheat. But I have prayed for thee, that thy faith fail not: and when thou art converted, strengthen thy brethren" (Luke 22:31, 32). This is very solemn and very blessed. Solemn is it to observe that the Lord prayed not to keep Peter from falling. In suffering His apostle *to* fall, the Lord's mercy comes out most signally, for that fall was necessary in order to reveal to Peter the condition of his heart, to show him the worthlessness of self-confidence, and to humble his proud spirit. The need for Satan's "sifting" was at once made manifest by the Apostle's reply, "And he said unto him, Lord, I am ready to go with thee, both into prison, and to death" (Luke 22:33). "This is a condition which not only exposes one to a fall, but from which the fall itself may be the only remedy. We have to learn that when we are weak only are we strong; and that Christ's strength is made perfect in our weakness. Peter's case is a typical one; and thus it is so valuable for us.

"The Lord Himself, in such a case as this, cannot pray ("cannot" *morally* do so – A.W.P.) that Peter may not fall, but that he may be 'converted' by it, turned from that dangerous self-confidence to consciousness of his inability to trust himself, even for a moment. Here Satan is foiled and made to serve the purpose of that grace which he hates and resists. He can overpower this self-sufficient Peter; but only to fling him for relief upon his omnipotent Lord. Just as the 'messenger of Satan to buffet' Paul (II Cor. 12), only works for what he in nowise desires, to repress the pride so ready to spring up in us, and which the lifting up to the third heaven might tend to foster. Here there had been no fall, and all was over-ruled for fullest blessing; in Peter's case, on the other hand, Satan's effort would be to assail the fallen disciple with suggestions of a sin too great to be forgiven – or, at least, for restoration to that eminent place from which it would be torture to remember he had fallen. What he needed to meet this with was *faith;* and this, therefore, the Lord prays, might not fail him.

"How careful is He to revive and strengthen in the humbled man the practical confidence so needful! The knowledge of it all given him *beforehand* – of the prayer made for him – of the exhortation addressed to him when restored, to 'strengthen his brethren' – all this would be balm indeed for his wounded soul;

but even this was not enough for his compassionate Lord. The first message of His resurrection had to be addressed specially 'to Peter' (Mark 16:7), and to 'Cephas' himself He appears, before the Twelve (I Cor. 15:5). Thus He will not shrink back when they are all seen together. When we find him at the sea of Tiberias, it is easy to realize that all this has done its work. Told that it is the Lord who is there on the shore, he girds on his outer garment, and casts himself into the sea, impatient to meet his Lord. But now he is ready, and only now, for that so necessary dealing with his conscience, when his heart is fully assured" (Numerical Bible).

When the Saviour washed the feet of Peter, he said, "What I do thou knowest not now, but thou shalt know hereafter" (13:7). This cleansing, as we saw, has to do with the *maintenance* of a "part *with*" Christ (13:8). It tells of the Lord's gracious work in restoring a soul which has become defiled and out of communion with Him; the "water" figuring the means which He uses, the Word. Now, at that time Peter had not fallen, and therefore he perceived not the significance of the Saviour's (anticipatory) act. But now he is to learn in his conscience the holy requirements of Christ, and experience the purifying power of the Word and the recovering grace of our great High Priest.

In 21:9 we learn that the first thing which confronted the Apostle when he joined the Lord on the shore was "a *fire* of coals," an expression found again in John's Gospel only in 18:18. There we read of "a *fire* of coals" in the priest's palace, and that Peter stood by its side with Christ's enemies "warming himself." It was *there* that he had denied his Master. How this "fire of coals" by the sea of Tiberias would prick his conscience: a silent preacher, but a powerful one, nevertheless! Christ did not point to it, nor say anything about it; that was unnecessary. Next we read of the seven disciples partaking of the food which the Saviour had provided, showing that the Lord's attitude toward Peter had not changed. The meal being over, He now turned and addressed Simon. It was there by the side of this "fire of coals" that the Lord entered into this colloquy with him, the purpose of which was to bring the Apostle to *judge* himself, for "fire" ever speaks of judgment.

"So when they had dined, Jesus saith to Simon Peter, Simon, son of Jonas, lovest thou me more than these?" (21:15). Mark carefully how the Lord began: not with a reproach, still less a word of condemnation, nor even with a "*Why* did you deny Me?" but "*Lovest* thou me more than these?" Yet, observe that the Lord did not now address him as "Peter," but "Simon son of Jonas." This is not without its significance. "Simon" was his original name, and stands in contrast from the new name which the Lord had given him: "And when Jesus beheld him, he said, thou art Simon the son of Jonas: that shalt be called Cephas (Peter), which is by interpretation, A stone" (1:42). The way in which the Lord now addressed His disciple intentionally called into question the "Peter." Mark how that in Luke 22:31 the Lord said, "*Simon, Simon,* behold Satan hath desired to have you, that he may sift you as wheat." Christ would here remind him of his entire past as a *natural man,* and especially that his fall had originated in "Simon" and not "Peter!" On only one other occasion did the Lord address him as "Simon son of Jonah," and that was in Matt. 16:17, "Jesus answered and said unto him, Blessed art thou, Simon son of Jonah: for flesh and blood hath not revealed it unto thee, but my Father which is in heaven." But note that the Lord is quick to add, "And I say *also* unto thee, that *thou art Peter,* and upon this rock I will build my church: and the gates of hell shall not prevail against it. And I will give unto *thee* the keys of the kingdom." Thus this first word of the Lord to His disciple in John 21:15 was designed to pointedly remind him of his glorious *confession,* which would serve to make him the more sensitive of his late and awful *denial.*

"Lovest thou me more than these?" This was still more searching than the name by which Christ had addressed His Apostle. He would not heal Peter's wound slightly, but would work a perfect cure; therefore, does He as it were, open it afresh. The Saviour would not have him lose the lesson of his fall, nor in the forgiveness forget his sin. Consequently He now delicately retraces for him the sad history of his denial, or rather by His awakening question brings it before his conscience. Peter had boasted, "Though *all* shall be offended, yet will not *I*": he not only trusted in his own loyalty, but congratulated himself that *his* love to Christ surpassed that of the other Apostles. Therefore did the Lord now ask, "Lovest thou me *more* than these?" i.e., more than these apostles love Me?

"He said unto him, Yea Lord; thou knowest that I love thee" (21:15). An opportunity had graciously been given Peter to retract his former boast, and gladly did he now avail himself of it. First, he began with a frank and heartfelt confession—"*thou* knowest." He leaves it to the Searcher of hearts to determine. He could not appeal to his ways, for they had reflected upon his love; he would not trust his own heart any longer; so he appeals to Christ Himself to decide. Yet observe, he did not say "thou knowest *if* (or *whether*) I love thee," but "thou knowest *that* I love thee"—he rested on the Lord's knowledge *of* his love; thus there was both humility and confidence united. "It was as though he said, 'Thou hast known me from the beginning as son of Jonah; drawn me to Thee, hast kindled love in my soul, hast called me Peter; Thou didst warn of my blindness, and pray for my faith, and hast since forgiven me; Thou hast looked, both before and since Thy death, into my heart, with eyes of grace, so *Thou* knowest all! What *I* feel concerning my love is this, that I am far from loving Thee as I ought and as Thou art worthy of being loved; but Thou, O Lord, knowest that in spite of my awful failure, and notwithstanding my present weakness and deficiency, I *do* love Thee'" (Stier).

"He saith unto him, Feed my lambs" (21:15). What marvelous grace was this! Not only does the Lord accept Peter's appeal to His omniscience, but He gives here a blessed commission. Christ was so well satifised with Peter's reply that He does not even confirm it with, "Verily, I *do* know it." Instead, He responds by honouring and rewarding his love. Christ was about to leave this world, so He now appoints others to minister to His people. "Feed my lambs." The change of figure here from fishing to shepherding is striking: the one suggests the evangelist, the other the pastor and teacher. The order is most instructive. Those who have been saved need shepherding—caring for, feeding, defending. And those whom Christ first commends to Peter were not the "sheep" but the "lambs"—the weak and feeble of the flock; and these are the ones who have the first claim on us! Note Christ calls them "*my* lambs," denoting His authority to appoint the under-shepherds.

"He saith to him again the second time, Simon, son of Jonas, lovest thou me?" (21:16). The Lord now drops the comparative "more than these" and confines Himself to love itself. This question is one which He is still asking of each of those who profess to believe in Him. "'Lovest thou me?' is, in reality, a very searching question. We may know much, and do much, and talk much, and give much, and go through much, and make much show in our religion, and yet be dead before God for want of love, and at last go down to the Pit. Do we *love* Christ? That is the great question. Without this there is no vitality about our Christianity. We are no better than painted wax-figures: there is no life where there is no love" (Bishop Ryle).

"He saith unto him, Yea, Lord; Thou knowest that I love thee" (21:16). In this passage there are two distinct words in the Greek which are translated by the one English word "love," and it is most instructive to follow their occurrences here. The one is a much stronger term than the other. To preserve the distinction the one might be rendered "love" and the other "affection" or "attachment." When the Lord asked Peter, "*Lovest* thou me?" He used, both in 21:15 and 16, the stronger word. But when Peter answered, what he really said, each time, was "thou knowest that I *have affection for* thee." So far was he now from boasting of the superiority of his love, he would not own it as the deepest kind of love at all! Once more the response of Divine grace is what Peter receives: "He saith unto him, Feed my sheep" (21:16). The word for "feed" here is more comprehensive than the one which the Lord had used in the previous verse, referring primarily to rule and discipline. Observe the Lord again calls them "*my* sheep," not "*thy* sheep"—thus anticipating and refuting the pretensions of the Pope!

"He saith unto him the third time, Simon, son of Jonas, lovest thou me?" (21:17). Here the Lord Himself uses the weaker term—"Hast thou *affection* for me?" "Grace reigns *through righteousness*" (Rom. 5:21). Three times had Peter *denied* his Master; three times, then, did the Lord *challenge* his love. This was according to "righteousness." But in thus challenging Peter, the Lord gave him the opportunity of now thrice *confessing* Him. This was according to "grace." In His first question the Lord challenged the *superiority* of Peter's love. In His second question the Lord challenged whether Peter had *any love* at all. Here, in His third question the Lord now challenges even his *affection!* Most searching was this! But it had the desired effect. The Lord wounds only that He may heal.

"Peter was grieved because he said unto him the third time, Lovest thou me?" (21:17). Here we are shown once more the power of *the Word.* This was indeed the sequel to John 13. That Peter was "grieved" does not mean that he was offended at the Lord because He repeated His question, but it signifies that he was touched to the quick, was deeply sorrowful, as he recalled his *threefold* denial. It is parallel with his "weeping *bitterly*" in Luke 22:62. This being "grieved" evidenced his perfect *contrition!* But if it was grievous for the disciple to be thus probed and have called to remembrance his sad fall, how much more grievous must it have been to the Master Himself to be denied?

"And he said unto him, Lord, thou knowest all things; thou knowest that I love thee" (21:17). Beautiful is it to behold here the transforming effects of Divine grace. He would not now boast that *his love* was superior to that of others; he would not even allow that he had *any love;* nay more, he is at last brought to the place where he now declines to avow even his affection. He therefore casts himself on Christ's omniscience. "Lord," he says, "*thou* knowest *all* things." *Men* could see no signs of any love or affection when I denied Thee; but *Thou* canst read my very heart; I appeal therefore to Thine all-seeing eye. That Christ knew *all* things comforted this disciple, as it should us. Peter realized that the Lord knew the *depths* as well as the *surfaces* of things, and therefore, that He saw what was in his poor servant's *heart,* though his *lips* had so transgressed. Thus did he once more own the absolute Deity of the Saviour.

Thus, too, did he rebuke those who would now talk and sing of *their* love for Christ! "His self-judgment is complete. Searched out under the Divine eye, he is found and owns himself, not better but worse than others; so self-emptied that he cannot claim *quality* for his love at all. The needed point is reached: the strong man converted to weakness is now fit to strengthen his brethren; and, as Peter descends step by step the ladder of humiliation, step by step the Lord follows him with assurance of the work for which he is destined" (Numerical Bible).

"Jesus saith unto him, Feed my sheep" (21:17). Does this, after all, warrant, or even favour, the pretensions of the Pope? No, indeed. "The Evangelist relates in what manner Peter was restored to that rank of honour from which he had fallen. The treacherous denial, which had been formerly described, had undoubtedly rendered him unworthy of the Apostleship; for how could he be capable of instructing others in the faith, who had basely revolted from it? He had been made an Apostle, but from the time that he had acted the part of a coward, he had been deprived of the honour of Apostleship. Now, therefore, the liberty, as well as the authority of teaching, is restored to him, both of which he had lost through his own fault. That the disgrace of his apostasy might not stand in the way, Christ blots it out and fully restores the erring one. Such a restoration was needed both for Peter and his hearers; for Peter, that he might the more boldly exercise himself, being assured of the calling with which Christ had again invested him; for his hearers, that the stain which attached to him might not be the occasion of despising the Gospel" (John Calvin). We may add that this searching conversation between Christ and Peter took place in the presence of six of the other Apostles: his sin was a public one, so also must be his repudiation of it! Note that in Acts 20:28 *all* the "elders" are exhorted to feed the flock!

"Jesus saith unto him, Feed my sheep." If you love Me, *here* is the way to manifest it. It is only those who truly *love* Christ that are fitted to minister to His flock! The work is so laborious, the appreciation is often so small, the response so discouraging, the criticisms so harsh, the attacks of Satan so fierce, that only the "love of Christ"—His for us and ours for Him—can "constrain" to such work. "Hirelings" will feed the *goats*, but only those who love Christ can feed His *sheep*. Unto this work the Lord now calls Peter. Not only had Christ restored the disciple's *soul* (Psa. 23:3), but also his official *ministry*; another was not to take *his* bishopric—contrast Judas (Acts 1:20)!

"Jesus saith unto him, Feed my sheep." Marvelous grace was this. Not only is Peter freely forgiven, not only is he fully restored to his apostleship, but the Lord commends to him (though not to him alone) that which was dearest to Him on earth—*His sheep!* There is nothing in all this world nearer the heart of Christ than those for whom He shed His precious blood, and therefore He could not give to Peter a more affecting proof of His confidence than by committing to his care the dearest objects of His wondrous love! It is to be noted that the Lord here returns to the same word for "feed" which He had used in 21:15. Whatever may be necessary in the way of rule and discipline (the force of "feed" in 21:16), yet, the first (21:15) and the last (21:17) duty of the under-shepherd is to *feed* the flock—nothing else can take the place of ministering spiritual nourishment to Christ's people!

It is striking to observe that in connection with Peter's restoration he received a threefold commission which exactly corresponds with our Lord's threefold "Peace be unto you" with which He saluted the disciples in the previous chapter. "Feed my lambs" (21:15) answers to the first benediction in 20:19: it is Gospel-exposition needed by the young believer to establish him in the foundation truth of redemption. "Shepherd" or "discipline" My sheep (21:16) answers to the second "Peace be unto you" in 20:21, which relates to service and walk. "Feed my sheep" (21:17) answers to the third "Peace be unto you" in 20:26, spoken for the special benefit of Thomas, and has to do with the work of restoring those who have gone astray. Compare also the threefold written ministry of the Apostle John. unto the "fathers," "young men," and "little children" (I John 2:13).

"Verily, verily I say unto thee, When thou wast young, thou girdest thyself, and walkest whither thou wouldest: but when thou shalt be old thou shalt stretch forth thy hands, and another shall gird thee, and carry thee whither thou wouldest not" (21:18). Here, too, the grace of Christ shines forth most blessedly. Not only had Peter been forgiven, restored, commissioned, but now the Lord takes him back to the fervent declaration which he had made in the energy of the flesh: "Lord, I am ready to go with thee, both into prison, and to death" (Luke 22:33), and assures him that this highest honour of all *shall* be granted him. "Peter might still feel the sorrow of having missed such an opportunity of confessing Christ at the critical moment. Jesus assures him now that if he had failed in doing that of his own will, he should be allowed to do it by the will of God: it should be given him to die for the Lord, as he had formerly declared himself ready to do in his own strength" (Mr. J. N. Darby).

"Verily, verily, I say unto thee, When thou wast young, thou girdest thyself and walkest whither thou wouldest: but when thou shalt be old, thou shalt stretch forth thy hands and another shall gird thee, and carry thee whither thou wouldest not" (21:18). The connection between this verse and those preceding is as follows: the Lord here warns Peter that his love to Him would be sorely tested, that caring for His sheep would ultimately involve a martyr's death—for thus do we understand His words here. A more direct link is found in that Peter had just said, "Lord, thou knowest *all* things": Christ now gave proof that He *did* indeed, for He speaks positively and in minute detail of that which was yet future, and could be known only to God. The beloved disciple again would be placed in such a position that he would have to choose between denying and confessing Christ. As the reward for his good confession here, and to supply an encouragement for the future, the Lord assures him that he *shall* confess Him even to death.

"This spake he, signifying by what death he should glorify God" (21:19). This is a parenthetic remark by John, made for the purpose of supplying a key to the meaning of the Lord's words in the previous verse. When Christ said, "When thou wast young, thou girdest thyself, and walkest whither thou wouldest," He signified that during his earlier days Peter had enjoyed his natural freedom. When he said, "But when thou shalt be old thou shalt stretch forth thy hands," He meant that Peter would do this at the command of another. When He added, "And another shall gird thee," He meant that Peter should be bound as a prisoner with cords—cf. Acts 21:11 where Agabus took Paul's girdle and bound his own hands and feet, to symbolize the fact that the Apostle would be "delivered into the hands of the Gentiles." In His final words, "and carry thee whither thou wouldest not," the Lord did not mean that Peter would resist or murmur ("what death he should *glorify* God" proves that), but that the death he should die would be contrary to nature, disagreeable to the flesh. Peter was to die a death of violence, by crucifixion. In the "thou wouldest not" the Lord further intimated that He does not expect His people to *enjoy* bodily pains, though we are to endure them without murmuring. "But the Pope (to whom Peter says in vain, Follow me, as I follow Christ!) is the reverse: the older he grows the more arbitrarily will he gird and lead others whither *he* will" (Stier).

"This spake he, signifying by what death he should glorify God." It is not only by acting, but chiefly by suffering, that the saints glorify God. Note how the Lord says to Ananias concerning Saul, "I will show him how great things he shall *suffer* [not "do"] for my name's sake" (Acts 9:16)! Note how that when the Apostle would strengthen the wavering Hebrews, instead of reminding them of their works, He said, "Call to remembrance the former days, in which, after ye were illumined, ye *endured* a great fight of afflictions" (Heb. 10:32). But what sweet consolation to realize that our whole future has been forearranged by Christ—by Him who is too wise to err and too loving to be unkind.

"This spake he, signifying by what death he should glorify God." What a lesson is there here for us. True, it is the Lord's return, not death, for which we are to look and wait. Nevertheless, all who have gone before us have died, and we may do so before the Saviour comes. Let us remember, then, that should this be the case, we may "glorify" God in *death* as well as in life. We may be patient sufferers as well as active workers. Like Samson, we may do more for God in our death than we did in our lives. The death of the martyrs had more effect on men than the lives they had lived. "We may glorify God in death by being ready for it when it comes . . . by patiently enduring its pains . . . by testifying to others of the comfort and support which we find in the grace of Christ" (Bishop Ryle). It is a blessed thing when a mortal man can say with David, "Yea, though I walk through the valley of the shadow of death, I will fear no evil: for thou art with me" (Psa. 23:4).

"And when he had spoken this, he saith unto him, Follow me" (v. 19). Here was the final word of grace to the fallen, and now recovered disciple. Now that Peter had discovered his weakness, now that he had judged the root from which his failure had proceeded, now that he had been fully restored in heart, conscience, and commission, the Lord says, "Follow me." This was what he had pretended to do (18:15), when the Lord had told him he could not (Luke 22:33, 34). But now Christ says, You may, you can, you shall. To "follow" Christ means to "deny self" and "take up the cross." In other words, it means to be "conformed to his death." This, *in spirit*; with Peter, in bodily experience, too. This word of Christ supplies one more link with what is found in chapter 13. There the Saviour said to Peter, "Whither I go, thou canst not follow me now; but thou shalt follow me afterwards" (13:36). This is the sequel: "It was a call on him to follow the Lord, through death, up to the Father's House. And upon saying these words to him, the Lord rises from the place where they had been eating, and Peter, thus bidden, rises to follow Him" (Mr. Bellett). The Lord evidently accompanied this final word with a symbolic movement of going on before.

"Then Peter, turning about, seeth the disciple whom Jesus loved following, which also leaned on his breast at supper, and said, Lord, which is he that betrayeth thee?" (21:20). What a line in the picture is this, and how true to life! How humbling! Here was a believer, fully restored to communion, there in the presence of Christ, bidden to follow Him; yet here we find him taking his eye off Christ, and turning round to look at John! There is only one explanation possible—*the flesh* still remains in the believer, and *ever* lusts against the spirit! Though fully restored, the old Simon still remained. Christ had told him to "follow," not look around. Stier suggests that there was here "a side-glance once more of comparison with others," hardly that we think, rather the old tendency of taking his eye off Christ was manifested. In beautiful contrast from the fleshly turning of Peter, is the spiritual "following" of John. Christ had not commanded him to do so, nor had He even directly addressed him; but true love was ever occupied with its object, and here the Apostle of love could do no other than follow Christ. Blessed is it to mark how the Holy Spirit now refers to him, not only as "the disciple whom Jesus loved," but also as the one who "leaned on his breast at the supper." At the beginning of this Gospel (1:18) *Christ* is seen in the bosom of the Father, here at the end, a redeemed sinner is referred to as one who leaned on the bosom of the Saviour!

"Peter seeing him saith to Jesus, Lord, and what shall this man do?" (21:21). This too, evidenced the flesh in Peter. Christ had announced what awaited him, now the apostle is anxious to know how John—the one with whom he was most intimate and between whom there was a very close bond—should fare. The same curiosity which made him beckon to John that he should "*ask* who it should be" that would betray Christ (13:24), now causes him to say, "what [of] this man?" "Peter seems more concerned for another than for himself. So apt are we to be busy in other men's matters, but negligent in the concerns of our own souls—quick-sighted abroad, but dim-sighted at home—judging others and prognosticating what they will do, when we have enough to mind our own business. Peter seems more concerned about events than duties" (Matthew Henry).

"Jesus saith unto him, if I will that he tarry till I come, what is that to thee? follow thou me" (21:22). The Lord rebukes Peter's curiosity about John, and presses upon him his own duty. There is an old saying, Charity begins at home, and there is not a little truth in it. We are naturally creatures of extremes, and it is a hard matter to preserve the balance. On the one side is uncharitable selfishness, which makes us indifferent to the interests of others; on the other side is altruism carried to such an extent that we neglect the cultivation of our own souls. Both are wrong. Let us not be weary in well doing to others, but let us also heed that word of Paul's to Timothy, "Take heed *unto thyself*" (I Tim. 4:16). Unhappily there are not a few who have reason to say, "They made me the keeper of the vineyards; *mine own* vineyard have I not kept" (Song of Sol. 1:6). It was to correct this tendency in Peter that the Lord spoke. His business was to attend to his own duty, fulfil his own course, and leave the future of others in the hands of God—cf. Luke 13:23, 24. What good would it do Peter to know whether John was to live a long life or a short one, to die a violent death or a natural one?—cf. Dan. 12:8, 9. A warning is this to us not to be curious about the decrees of God concerning others—cf. Deut. 29:29. "Follow me" is also His word *to us*: we are to follow Him as Leader of His people, as Shepherd of His flock, as Exemplar for His saints, as Lord of all.

"Then went this saying abroad among the brethren, that that disciple should not die: yet Jesus said not unto him, He shall not die; but, If I will that he tarry till I come, what is that to thee?" (21:23). What plain proof does this afford that the Lord's coming does not refer to the decease of His people. How strange that any should have supposed that it did! Death is the believer going to be with Christ, the Lord's return is His coming to be with us. Yet how curious, that even from the beginning, the Lord's word "I come again" in connection with John, was misunderstood and wrested. Another thing which these words of Christ made evident was that His return is an *impending* event, that is, one which *may* occur at any time, and one which we should be constantly expecting. Note the "If *I* will": a majestic declaration was this that *Christ* is now the Disposer of men's lives: He did not say, if God, or if the Father, wills, but if *I* will. Mark how this verse furnishes *us* with a warning against following *human traditions*, even though they came from "the brethren": how blessed to have the unerring standard of God's written Word!

"If I will that he tarry till I come." What was the deeper meaning in this word of Christ's? First, are we not intended to see in Peter and John *representatives* of the Church in the early and latter days of this dispensation? Peter, who died a death of violence, points to the first centuries, when martyrdom was almost the common experience of believers. John, who is given the hope that he may (though not the promise that he *shall*) live on till the Lord's return, points to this last century, when the truth of the Lord's coming has been so widely made known among His people! But this is not all. The *ministry* of John actually goes on to the end, for in the Revelation he treats at length of those things which are to usher in the Lord's return to the earth, aye, and beyond to the new heaven and the new earth!

It is most blessed to observe that there is no account given in this Gospel of the Lord's *ascension,* and this is in most perfect keeping with the Spirit's design here. The departure of Christ left the disciples behind on earth. But here it is the family, in which—now in spirit, soon in the body—there are to be *no* separations. The last sight we have of the Saviour in John's Gospel, the sons are *with* Him! So shall we be "forever with the Lord."

"This is the disciple which testifieth of these things, and wrote these things: and we know that his testimony is true. And there are also many other things which Jesus did, the which, if they should be written every one, I suppose that even the world itself could not contain the books that should be written. Amen" (21:24, 25). These verses call for little comment. The Gospel closes with the personal seal and attestation of its writer. John, without mentioning his name, vouches for the veracity of what he had recorded, and then adds an hyperbole (cf. Matt. 11:23; Heb. 11:12; for others) to emphasize the fact that it was not possible for him to fully tell out the infinite glories of that One who is the central figure of his Gospel. The final "Amen"—found at the end of each Gospel—is the Holy Spirit's imprimatur.

"The Apostle closes his Gospel with another reminder of the inadequacy of all human words to tell out His glory, of whom he has been speaking. If it were attempted to tell out all, the world would be unable to contain the books that would be written. It would be an impracticable load to lift, rather than a help to clearer apprehension. How thankful we may be for the moderation that has compressed what would be really blessing to us into such a moderate compass! which yet, as we all must know, develops into whatever largeness we may have capacity for. Our Bibles are thus the same, and quite manageable by any. On the other hand, are we burning to know more? We may go on without any limit, except that which our little faith or heart may impose. May God awaken our hearts to test for themselves the expansive power of Scripture, and whether we can find a limit anywhere! Like the inconceivable immensity of the heavens, ever increasing as the power of vision is lengthened, we go on to find that the further we go only the more does the thought of infinity rise upon us; but this infinity is filled with an Infinite Presence; in every leaf-blade, in every atom, yet transcending all His works; and 'to us there is but one God, the Father, of whom are all things, and we for Him; and one Lord, Jesus Christ, by whom are all things, and we by Him'" (Numerical Bible).

CHAPTER SEVENTY-TWO

Conclusion

Our happy task is finished, and it is with a real sense of regret that we take up our pen to add an appendix. Before he commenced this commentary the author devoted ten years of special study to John's Gospel, having gone through it three times in the course of as many pastorates, and since then he has taught it in different Bible classes. For six years more we have laboured hard in preparing a chapter each month. Over forty commentaries and expositions have been read through and their interpretations of each verse carefully weighed, and the endeavour has been made to supplement our own searchings by culling from them what struck us as being most helpful.

Amid many labours and calls upon our time, our gracious God has enabled us to continue and complete this Exposition of John's Gospel, and it is with fervent thanksgiving to Him that we begin these concluding paragraphs. The instruction, the help and blessing which we have received personally, while preparing each chapter, has been a rich compensation for the time, prayer, and work we have put into them. Our own faith in the inerrancy and perfection of the Scriptures has been strengthened, and the conviction we had at the outset, that every verse contains a mine of spiritual wealth, has been confirmed again and again. That our production is very far from being perfect we are fully aware; but such as it is, we lay it before the Lord, and humbly entreat Him to use, own, and bless it to many of His dear people.

One of our aims in prosecuting this work has been to stimulate others to the personal *study* of the Word. The Bible is not only a book to be read devotionally, but it is also a mine of spiritual riches to be worked (Prov. 2:1-5), and the more diligently we seek after its hidden treasures, the greater will be our reward. God does not place a premium on laziness. His call is, "*Study* to show thyself approved unto God, a *workman* that needeth not to be ashamed, rightly dividing the Word of Truth" (II Tim. 2:15). Alas! most of His people have never been taught *how* to study. In this work we have sought to suggest one method which we have personally found to be very beneficial—the *interrogative* method: asking the Bible questions, drawing up a list on each passage as a preliminary to its careful examination.

The point at which so many readers of the Bible fail the worst is that of *concentration*. Their energies are scattered too much. Suppose a man inherited a thousand acres of arable land, and that he found it impossible to hire labourers. It would be useless for him attempting to farm the whole piece. But if he fenced off, say, five acres, devoted himself to this small section, and went in for *intensive* farming, he would be far more likely to succeed. It is thus with the Bible. While every Christian ought to read three or four chapters daily, and thus go through it once each year; it is impossible to really *study* the whole of it within the brief span of a life-time. In addition to extensive reading, there should be *intensive study*. Pray for guidance in your selection and then concentrate on a single book or chapter. If the Christian reader would spend fifteen minutes each day for a whole year on a single chapter—say, Exodus 12, Matt. 13, John 17, Romans 8, or Eph. 1—he would, most probably, be surprised at the fruitful results. The necessity and the importance of *concentration* and its invaluable returns are realized by but few.

If sixty-six Spirit-taught Bible expositors would each of them concentrate on one book in the Bible, devoting the whole of their special studies to it for ten years, at the end of that time (should the Lord not return before) the people of God at large would be enriched immeasurably. No one man is competent to write on *all* the books of Scripture; that is why the condensed commentaries on the Bible as a whole are so disappointing and comparatively worthless. Do not be too ambitious, dear friend. Aim at quality rather than quantity. One chapter thoroughly *studied* will yield more to your soul than a hundred chapters which are read but not studied.

Again, other students of Scripture fail through their lack of *perseverance*. Because a passage does not open up to them at the first or second examination of it, they become discouraged. God often tests our earnestness. It is not the dilatory, but the *diligent* soul that is made fat (Prov. 13:4). "Rest in the Lord, and *wait patiently* for him" (Psa. 37:7) applies as much to Bible-study as it does to prayer. Regular, persistent stick-to-itiveness (to use a word of Spurgeon's) is what counts. Note how one of the marks of the good-ground hearers is that they "bring forth fruit *with patience*" (Luke 8:15). If at first you don't succeed, try, try again.

When Jehovah gave food to His people Israel in the wilderness, He did not furnish them with loaves ready made. Instead, He sent them manna as "a *small* round thing" (Ex. 16:14). Much time and labour were required to gather a sufficient quantity for a day's supply. After the gathering, it had to be "ground" and then "baked." This was a parable in action. It has a voice for us to-day. The way in which most of us learn is "precept upon precept, precept upon precept; line upon line, line upon line; here a *little,* and there a *little*" (Isa. 28:10). Be not disheartened, then, if you appear to get small returns from your Scriptural labours. No time spent in the prayerful study of the Word is ever really lost. To familiarize yourself with the letter of it counts for something, and later (if you keep at it) you *will* reap the benefit.

Oftentimes Christians are almost discouraged when the Spirit of God enables a well-instructed scribe to bring out of his treasures things new and old. They say, "*I* have read that passage again and again, but never saw such beauties in it as *he* has pointed out, or such wonders as he has brought forth." Ah! you may not realize that, probably, he has given that passage special study for years past, that he has prayed over it scores of times, that he examined it again and again and saw no more in it than you did till, ultimately, God rewarded his patience, and now he rejoices as one that "findeth great spoil" (Psa. 119:162).

But something more is needed than concentration and perseverance. We may focalize our attention, be very diligent and patient, but unless the Holy Spirit illumines our understanding, the wonders and beauties of the Word will remain hidden from us. The Bible is addressed not so much to the intellect as it is to the heart. *Prayer* is an essential prerequisite. Before we open the Bible we need, every time, to get down on our knees and humbly beseech God, for Christ's sake, to "open thou mine eyes that I may behold wondrous things out of thy law" (Psa. 119:18). Mysteries of grace which are hidden from the wise and prudent are revealed to "babes," i.e., the simple, humble, dependent ones. It is written, "The meek will he guide in judgment: and the *meek* will he teach His way" (Psa. 25:9). Have no confidence in your own powers: remember that "a man can receive nothing, except it be given him from heaven" (John 3:27). Yet God is ever ready *to* give to those who ask in faith.

When the chapter for your *study* has been selected, begin by asking, What is there here *for my own soul?*—what warnings, what encouragements, what exhortations, what promises? Examine it first of all from the *practical standpoint*, with a view to your own personal needs. Ask God to make the passage speak unto your own soul, and to grant you the hearing ear. Next, and closely related to the former, in fact seeking God's answer to your first question, ask, What is there here *about Christ?* What is there that I can learn about Him, what example has He here left me, what perfections of His are portrayed, what typical picture of Him can I discover? From this, pass on to its *evangelical* message, its gospel bearing. Ask, What does this chapter teach me about sin, about the depravity of man, about the grace of God, about the way of salvation, about the blessedness of the redeemed? Every chapter in the Bible leads, ultimately, to Calvary. Then you may ponder its *doctrinal* bearings, its theological instruction. This will require you to look up marginal references from parallel passages. Ask, What is there here about the sovereignty of God, or the responsibility of man? What of the important truths of justification, sanctification, propitiation, preservation, glorification? This will require you to note the setting of the chapter which you are studying—its relation to those which precede and which follow; its bearing on the other chapters in the Epistle.

These are but hints, yet if heeded, Bible-study will cease to be an irksome duty and become a profitable delight. It is from these angles that the writer has endeavoured to examine each chapter in the Gospel of John, and these are the methods which, under God, he has found yield the best results. In addition to the general principles of study named above, we have also sought to give attention to some of the laws which regulate the interpretation of the Scriptures. God is a God of order, and the God of creation and the God of written revelation are one and the same. Just as we may discern "laws of Nature," so are there "laws of the Bible." Some of these have been pointed out during the course of our exposition: the laws of first mention, of progressive unfolding, of comparison and contrast, of parallelism, of numerics, etc.

In connection with the spiritual arithmetic of the Bible we have been deeply impressed with the constantly recurring *seven* in the Gospel of John, and it is surely not without significance that there are twenty-one chapters or 3x7, in it. It is true that the chapter divisions are of human origin, and that man does nothing perfectly, yet we believe that in the providence of Him who has "magnified his word above all his name" (Psa. 138:1, 2), He has not only superintended the placing of the different books in the Canon of Scripture, but has also guided, or at least overruled, many or most of its chapter divisions. Obviously is this so, we are fully assured, in connection with the Gospels.

Matthew has twenty-eight chapters, 7x4. Now, four is the number of the earth and seven of perfection. How appropriate that the Gospel which most directly concerns God's earthly people and the earthly kingdom of Christ, *should be* thus divided; for no perfection on earth will be witnessed until the Son of Man returns and sets up His throne upon it. Mark has sixteen chapters, 2x8. Two is the number of witness and eight of a new beginning. Most suitably are those numbers here, for in this second Gospel Christ is portrayed as the faithful and true Witness, the perfect Servant of God, laying the foundations of the new creation. Luke has twenty-four chapters, 6x4, or

2x12. Whichever way we divide the twenty-four, the result is in striking accord with the subject of this third Gospel. In Luke Christ is presented as the Son of man, the last Adam. Thus 6x4 would speak of *man* connected with the *earth;* or, 12x2 would tell of that *perfect government* which awaits the return to this earth of the "second Man" (I Cor. 15:47). John has twenty-one chapters, 7x3. How striking this is! For seven speaks of *perfection* and three is the number of *Deity*. Thus, the very number of chapters in this fourth Gospel intimates that here we have revealed *the perfections of God!* These are what have occupied us as we have gone through it chapter by chapter.

Everything in Scripture, down to the minutest detail, has a profound significance. Of course it has, for its Author is Divine. The same God who has expended so much care over the formation and adaptation of every member of our physical bodies—e.g., the eye or the hand—has not devoted less to that Word which is to endure forever. In the Bible God has written a Book *worthy of Himself*. If this fact be firmly grasped, the devout student will *expect* to find in every passage depths, wonders, beauties, such as only the Allwise could produce. But let it not be forgotten that the Inspirer of Holy Writ alone can interpret it to us.

To the reader who has, under God, been helped and blest by this Exposition, we would say, Do everything in your power to make this work known to others. You owe it to your fellow-Christians so to do. Why should not many of them be instructed and gladdened, too? These books are not published as a commercial venture. The demand for this class of literature is tragically small. It takes from five to ten years to sell sufficient for the publisher to get back the bare costs of printing and binding. Nor is advertising of much avail. It is the *personal* word that counts. If you can do so conscientiously, earnestly recommend these volumes both by word of mouth and by letters, to your Christian friends, to your Pastor, to Sunday school teachers and other Christian workers. Bear them in mind when making a present to a friend. Another good way of interesting others is to *loan* your own copies, thus others may be induced to purchase for themselves.

And now, dear reader, my work in composing this commentary and yours in going through it (the first time, at least) is now finished; but there remains *the improvement* which ought to be made of it, and *the account* which must yet be given to God, for He "requireth that which is past" (Ecc. 3:15). It is by attending to the former that we shall be prepared for the latter. I have not written for the sake of providing mere religious entertainment, and we trust that you have read with some higher motive than simply to fill in a few spare hours. Unless each of our hearts has been drawn out in warmer love, deeper devotion, and purer worship unto Him whose manifold glories give lustre to every page of Holy Writ; unless the result of our studies of John's Gospel leads both writer and reader to clearer visions of and more whole-hearted obedience unto the Word made flesh, our labours have been in vain.